UNIVERSITY CASEBOOK SERIES®

STUDIES IN CONTRACT LAW

NINTH EDITION

IAN AYRES
William K. Townsend Professor of Law
Yale Law School

GREGORY KLASS
Agnes N. Williams Research Professor and Professor of Law
Georgetown University School of Law

Authors on previous editions:

EDWARD J. MURPHY
Late John N. Matthews Professor of Law
Notre Dame Law School

RICHARD E. SPEIDEL
Late Beatrice Kuhn Professor of Law
Northwestern University School of Law

FOUNDATION
PRESS

University Casebook Series is a trademark registered in the U.S. Patent and Trademark Office.

© 1970, 1977, 1984, 1991, 1997, 2003 FOUNDATION PRESS
© 2008, 2012 THOMSON REUTERS/FOUNDATION PRESS
© 2017 LEG, Inc. d/b/a West Academic
      444 Cedar Street, Suite 700
      St. Paul, MN 55101
      1-877-888-1330

Printed in the United States of America

ISBN: 978-1-63460-325-6

To Jennifer and Sanjukta

PREFACE

"Contract law has deep roots in the past, and much of its present structure is shaped by historical precedents. But as is true in all vital fields of law, familiar concepts are being reexamined and new patterns are emerging."

Thus began the preface to the first edition of Studies in Contract Law (1970) authored by our departed colleagues Ed Murphy and Dick Speidel. Over the intervening decades, and through eight editions, this book has evolved to chronicle the developments in both doctrine and theory to help teachers and students explore the wonderful world of contract law.

As we update the book to take account of changes in doctrine and new theoretical perspectives, to provide materials on the recent financial crisis, and to say more about the theory of default and altering rules, our goal has been to preserve what was great in the past editions and our hope has been to match our coauthors' substantial accomplishments.

IAN AYRES
GREGORY KLASS

May 2017

ACKNOWLEDGMENTS

The authors acknowledge, with gratitude, the kind permission to reprint copyrighted materials of the following authors and publishers: American Law Institute; American Sociology Law Review; Professor Deborah A. Ballam; Professor Randy Barnett; Professor Jennifer Gerada Brown; Cambridge Law Review; Columbia Law Review; Cornell Law Review; Dow Jones & Company, Inc.; Professor Melvin A. Eisenberg; Professor Daniel Fischel; Professor Michael C. Franczak; Professor Eric Green; Iowa Law Review; Harvard Law Review; Journal of Law and Commerce; Journal of Legal Education; Professor Lewis Kornhauser; Professor Charles L. Knapp; Professor Lewis Kornhauser; Professor Andrew Kull; Law Book Co. of Australia Pty. Ltd.; Michigan Law Review; Minnesota Law Review; Fred B. Rothman & Co.; New York University Law Review; Northwestern University Law Review; Professor Michelle Oberman; Ohio State Journal of Dispute Resolution; Sir David Hughes Parry; Professor Walter F. Pratt, Jr.; Professor Todd D. Rakoff; Professor Robert E. Scott; Professor William K. Sjonstrom, Jr.; Professor Richard E. Speidel; Professor Robert S. Summers; Texas Law Review; Professor G.H. Treitel; United Features Syndicate; Universal Press Syndicate; University of Chicago Law Review; University of Colorado Law Review; University of Southern California Law Review; South Carolina Law Review; Stanford Law Review; Professor Lea S. VanderVelde; Wall Street Journal; West Publishing Company; Professor James J. White; William & Mary Law Review; Professor Glanville Williams; The Honourable Sir Victor Windeyer; Wisconsin Law Review; Yale Law Journal; Professor Eval Zamir.

The Authors also wish to thank the American Law Institute for permission to reproduce passages from the Restatement of the Law, Consumer Contracts, Council Draft No. 3 (December 20, 2016) copyright © 2016 by The American Law Institute (ALI). This Draft was submitted to the meeting of the Council of ALI on January 19–20, 2017. As of the date this draft was printed, it had not been considered by the Council or membership of ALI, and therefore does not represent the position of the ALI on any of the issues with which it deals.

The authors are especially indebted to Ian Engdahl, Brian O'Connor, Kaitlin Puccio, Victoria Stilwell, JeanAnn Tabba and Ryan Yeh, who provided excellent and extensive research assistance on the Ninth Edition.

SUMMARY OF CONTENTS

TABLE OF CONTENTS

TABLE OF CASES

The principal cases are in bold type.

TABLE OF UNIFORM COMMERCIAL CODE CITATIONS

STUDIES IN CONTRACT LAW

NINTH EDITION

CHAPTER ONE

INTRODUCTION TO CONTRACT LAW

1. INTRODUCTION

(A) CONTRACT AS LEGALLY BINDING AGREEMENT

What is a Contract? We all know that the law imposes duties on us. It says that we must or must not do this or that. We have legal duties not to murder, not to steal, not to drive drunk. We have legal duties to take reasonable care to avoid harming others and to pay our taxes. A parent has a legal duty to support his or her minor children, a doctor to provide professionally competent care. None of these legal duties are chosen. People do not get to decide whether or not to be subject to criminal, tort, or tax law. And while a person can decide whether or not to become a parent or physician, she does not get to decide what legal duties attach to those roles.

Contract law is different. The obligations imposed by the law of contract are *chosen obligations*. They are the products of agreements, promises, or other voluntary undertakings. In order to have a contractual *duty* to x, one must first *agree* to x. Lon Fuller, one of the great American contract theorists, compared the power to contract to the power to pass laws: "When a court enforces a promise it is merely arming with legal sanction a rule or *lex* [law] previously established by the party himself. This power of the individual to effect changes in his legal relations with others is comparable to the power of a legislature."[1] The analogy is not perfect. Whereas a legislature typically makes laws for the public at large, the parties to a contract make laws only for themselves. And the formation of a contract can be much more informal than the legislative process ever is. Still, this legislative aspect of contracting gives contract law a different structure from other, purely duty-imposing bodies of law. For a basic understanding of tort or criminal law, for example, you have to answer only two questions: (1) What is the legal duty? (E.g., which acts count as first-degree murder?) (2) What are the legal consequences of its violation? (E.g., what is the punishment for first-degree murder?) In contract cases, another question always comes first: Did the parties undertake legally enforceable duties to one another? That is, was there a contract between the parties?

---

[1]   Lon L. Fuller, *Consideration and Form*, 41 Colum. L. Rev. 799, 806–07 (1941). For more on contract law's legislative aspect, see Gregory Klass, *Three Pictures of Contract: Duty, Power, and Compound Rule*, 83 N.Y.U. L. Rev. 1726 (2008).

Another way of putting this point is that contract cases always involve a story about how the legal duty came into existence. Parties start out having no contractual obligations to one another. Then at some point in time they do something that creates a legal obligation. They enter into an agreement, make a promise under seal, invite some reliance or undertake some other act that creates for one or both parties a legal obligation. Only after a court has established that a contract has been formed does it ask whether a contractual duty was breached and, if so, what the right remedy is. To understand contract, you have to know how contracts are formed. You have to know what the conditions of contractual validity are. Once you've figured that out, you can then ask about the scope of the contractual obligation and the available legal remedies for its breach.

A standard answer to the formation question is that it is necessary (though not sufficient!) that one or both parties *promise* some performance. The promise both creates the obligation and determines its scope. Thus a canonical source for U.S. contract law, the Restatement (Second) of Contracts, defines "contract" as "a promise or a set of promises for the breach of which the law gives a remedy, or the performance of which the law in some way recognizes as a duty." Restatement (Second) § 1.

This definition is fine as far as it goes, so long as one does not read too much into the word "promise."[2] In everyday conversation, we distinguish between agreeing to do something ("I'll do the dishes") and promising to do it ("Really, I promise to do the dishes"). And different promises can be more or less binding. We know from the playground the difference between "I promise" and "I promise, cross my heart and hope to die." There have been times and places where the law required such formal promissory acts of parties who wanted to enter into a legally enforceable agreement.[3] In ancient Rome, a creditor could request a legally binding obligation using the word "*spondesne,*" to which the debtor had to reply "*spondeo.*" Sales agreements in the Middle Ages were sometimes formalized by the buyer giving the seller a "God's penny," a small coin that marked the agreement. Or the parties might consummate the deal with a drink. Medieval Germans would sometimes put their palms together as they held them over their heads. In many African societies, a buyer and seller communicate their agreement by "waving their right hands up and down and then touching each other's palms with

---

[2]   For some theoretical discussion of the ways that contracts are different from promises, see Gregory Klass, *Promise Etc.*, 45 Suffolk U. L. Rev. 695 (2012); Michael Pratt, *Contract: Not Promise*, 35 Fl. St. L. Rev. 801, 802 (2008); Dori Kimel, From Promise to Contract: Towards a Liberal Theory of Contract (2003).

[3]   All of the examples in this paragraph come from Bernard J. Hibbitts's wonderful article, *"Coming to Our Senses": Communication and Legal Expression in Performance Cultures*, 41 Emory L.J. 873 (1992). See also Peter Meijes Tiersma, *Rites of Passage: Legal Ritual in Roman Law and Anthropological Analogues*, 9 J. Legal Hist. 3 (1988).

the fingers stretched away."[4] And of course today parties often "seal the deal" with a handshake.

Although we still sometimes use formalities to indicate a binding commitment, the U.S. law of contract no longer requires any special acts, words or other expressions of intent to undertake a moral or legal commitment. Indeed, it often does not require an express promise. In many cases, all that is necessary is that the parties agree to some performance, even if only implicitly. And as David Hume observed, "Two men, who pull the oars of a boat, do it by agreement or convention, tho' they have never given promises to each other."[5] Consider the following example of what is known as an implied-in-fact promise: "A telephones to his grocer, 'Send me a ten-pound bag of flour.' The grocer sends it." Restatement (Second) § 4, ill. 1. Has A promised to pay for the flour? Not in the playground sense of the word. But by ordering the flour, A has implicitly agreed to pay for it. That is all that the law requires.

Another way of putting this is that contracts are promises only under a very capacious understanding of the word "promise." A promise in the legal sense is more than a prediction or an expression of intent. But it need not involve *saying* that one means to undertake a legal or moral obligation. All that is necessary is some "manifestation of intention to act or refrain from acting in a specified way, so made as to justify the recipient of the promise (the "promisee") in understanding that a commitment has been made." Restatement (Second) § 2(1).[6] As you confront the materials in this book, you should try to develop the legal skill of "hearing" the implicit commitments that often attend our verbal and non-verbal acts, and when these implied commitments constitute an agreement sufficient for the purposes of contract law.

Although it is helpful to think of contracts on the model of agreements rather than promises, we employ the language of promising throughout this book. Courts and commentators regularly talk of "promises" when doing or describing the law of contract. So long as the reader keeps the above caveats in mind, it works well enough. In fact, the language of promising has a distinct advantage. With respect to any given contractual obligation, we can use the terms "promisor" to identify the party under the duty and "promisee" for the party to whom the duty is owed.

One final comment about the meaning of words. In everyday conversation, people often use the word "contract" to refer to a written document—for example, the papers you sign when you apply for a credit

---

[4]   Leonard W. Doob, Communication in Africa: A Search for Boundaries 70 (1961).

[5]   David Hume, *Of Morals*, A Treatise of Human Nature (L. A. Selby-Bigge and P. H. Nidditch, eds.) 490, 1739–1740 (1978).

[6]   The Uniform Commercial Code (UCC) analogously defines "contract": "[a] contract for sale of goods may be made in any manner sufficient to show agreement, including conduct by both parties which recognizes the existence of such a contract." UCC § 2–204(1). For a good discussion of different definitional approaches, see Corbin § 3 (1952).

card, rent an apartment, or take a job. In this book, we will almost always be using the word in a more abstract sense, to refer to the totality of the legal rights and duties that arise from an agreement between two or more parties. Thus a writing between two parties—even one that is very formal and detailed—might not represent the entire contract between them. The writing is a physical thing; the contract is that physical thing's legal effect.

Who Contracts? With a few exceptions, U.S. law of contract does not provide different rules for different sorts of parties. (An important exception is the Uniform Commercial Code's special rules for merchants, discussed later in this Chapter.) In particular, the rules of the common law of contract do not ask whether a party is a *natural person* (a human being) or a *firm* (a corporation or other legal entity). Alan Schwartz and Robert E. Scott have recently argued, however, that in fact contemporary contract law applies primarily to agreements between firms:

> Parties to transactions can be partitioned into individuals and firms. This yields four transactional categories: (1) A firm sells to another firm, (2) an individual sells to another individual, (3) a firm sells to an individual, and (4) an individual sells to a firm. Category 2 contracts, between individuals, are primarily regulated by family law (antenuptial agreements and divorce settlements) and real property law (home sales and some leases). Few litigated contracts between individuals are regulated by the rules of contract law. Category 3 contracts, between a firm as seller and an individual as buyer, are primarily regulated by consumer protection law, real property law (most leases), and the securities laws. Category 4 contracts, between an individual as seller and a firm as buyer, commonly involve the sale of a person's labor, and are regulated by laws governing the employment relation. That leaves Category 1 contracts (those between firms) as the main subject of what is commonly called contract law—namely, the rules in Article 2 of the Uniform Commercial Code (UCC) and the provisions of the Restatement (Second) of Contracts. Such provisions are primarily invoked to resolve disputes arising under Category 1 contracts.[7]

Schwartz and Scott argue that these distinctions are important because, unlike individuals, firms are less likely to be prey to cognitive error, firms are more often legally sophisticated, firms are subject to other forms of legal regulation, and firms are designed with a single goal in mind: maximizing the profits for their shareholders.[8] A law that is designed for Category 2, 3, or 4 contracts might not be suitable for Category 1 contracts.

---

[7] Alan Schwartz and Robert E. Scott, *Contract Theory and the Limits of Contract Law*, 113 Yale L.J. 541, 544 (2003).

[8] Id. at 544–46.

Schwartz and Scott are certainly correct that most of the major litigation in the contracts arena concerns Category 1 transactions. It is not so obvious—and Schwartz and Scott do not argue—that the contract law we have is designed with this fact in mind. Nor would everyone agree with Schwartz and Scott's thesis that the rules of contract law should aim to assist firms in their profit-maximizing goals—that "the state should let the preferences of firms control because firms can better pursue the objective [increased social welfare] that both the state and firms share."[9] Finally, the above categories are not exhaustive. They ignore, for example, contracts that involve governmental bodies, which often raise other important issues.

Still, Schwartz and Scott's basic classification provides a helpful starting point. It illustrates the ways in which some sorts of agreements get pulled out of the arena of contract law and put into other areas of the law—family law, consumer protection law, real property law, etc. And Schwartz and Scott are certainly correct that when thinking about the rules of contract law, we should keep in mind the differences between different sorts of parties, including the differences between individuals and firms. That is another question to think about as you work your way through this book: For whom is contract law designed, and for whom should it be designed?

The Structure of This Book. As we said above, agreement is a necessary condition of contractual validity, but not a sufficient one. While all contracts involve an agreement, not all agreements produce an enforceable contract. Chapters Two through Four of this book explore the conditions of contractual validity and enforcement. Some of those conditions are elements that the plaintiff must establish as part of her affirmative case. The two most important are *consideration* (most of Chapter Two) and *agreement* (Chapter Three). Others are defenses that a defendant can use to avoid liability under what would otherwise be an enforceable contract (Chapter Four). Examples here include absence of a writing, fraud, unconscionability and illegality.

Chapter Five discusses the scope of contractual duties—what contracts require of parties. Because contracts are agreements, determining the scope of the parties' contractual obligations requires interpreting the agreement between them. The study of contractual duties is partly a study of rules of interpretation. We will also see, however, that the legal effects of entering into a contract can outrun the parties' agreement or intentions. Mandatory and gap-filling (or "default") rules of construction, covering matters like the duty of good faith, implied warranties and constructive conditions of exchange, can create or discharge legal obligations in ways that the parties did not intend or even expect. Although contract is the product of agreement, a contract is not simply what the parties have agreed to.

---

[9] Id. at 549.

Once we know the scope of contractual duties, we can look at the consequences of their breach. This is the topic of Chapter Six. As we will see, the most common legal remedy for breach is money damages paid to the injured party to compensate her for her losses. While this definition is relatively easy to state in the abstract, it raises a host of difficulties in application. And there are other possible remedies, such as enforced performance or punitive damages, that must also be considered.

Chapters Seven discusses the rights and obligations of those who are not parties to a contract. The first question here is when a party to a contract can assign the right to performance or delegate the duty to perform to a third party. The second is when a contract might give a nonparty the right to demand performance.

Although the law of contract can be dissected into these different parts, the living limbs comprise a single organism. Each piece of contract law is designed with the others in mind. The rest of this Chapter, therefore, introduces a few important rules that govern the formation of contracts, their interpretation, and the remedies for their breach. It also introduces some of the basic analytic tools that we will need to study the law of contract. As you begin to study the multiple problems of contract law and to draw on both legal materials and your own experience and training, you should keep several recurring questions firmly in mind.

keep in mind

1.   Which promises will be enforced?

2.   When enforceable, what is the scope and content of a promissory obligation?

3.   How will these promises be enforced?

4.   Which of the foregoing answers can the parties contract around (and how)?

(B) SOURCES OF CONTRACT LAW

The Common Law of Contract. Most contracts in the United States are governed by state law. Strictly speaking, therefore, there is no single U.S. law of contract. We have fifty laws of contract spread among the fifty states, plus separate laws of contract that govern the District of Columbia, Puerto Rico, other U.S. jurisdictions, as well as a federal contract law for contracts with the federal government and the like. These separate laws of contract differ from one another in important ways, some of which will be discussed in this book. But almost all of these bodies of law spring from a single source: the English common law. (The most important exception is Louisiana, whose contract law derives from the French Civil Code.) And as these laws of contract have grown and changed over the years, courts and legislatures have looked to one another for guidance and to a small number of national authorities. As a result, though it is important to keep local differences in mind, one can say that there is a distinctive U.S. law of contract. That law is the subject of this book.

Except where displaced by statute, the general law of contract in the United States is a product of judicial decisions in individual cases. This form of lawmaking is one of our most important inheritances from England. The English law of contract emerged largely from the decisions of the common law courts, together with those of the competing Chancery Court (discussed below).[10] Although the judges of these courts proceeded modestly on a case-by-case basis, adjudicating individual controversies brought before them, they did not act without guidance. Important sources for the common law of contract included Roman Law (most significantly, Justinian's *Corpus Juris Civilis*), Canon Law (the law of the Church), and the Law Merchant (customary law developed by merchants in their dealings with one another). Most important, however, was the principle of *stare decisis*, which required that courts follow the holdings of earlier judicial decisions. Judicial adherence to this principle meant that over the course of centuries, there emerged a judicially created, well-defined body of legal rules. The core of U.S. contract law remains largely a creature of the common law. Contract law lives in the records of judicial decisions.

The fact that the law of contract is located in the decisions of courts can make it difficult to find. As a result, treatises and other secondary sources have had a significant influence on the development and harmonization of the law of contract in the United States. The two most important treatises have been and remain Samuel Williston's *The Law of Contracts* (1920) and Arthur Linton Corbin's *Corbin on Contracts* (1950). Williston's work is generally regarded as taking a more formalist approach, emphasizing fixed rules and principles. Corbin's is considered more realist, focusing on practical realities and tensions within the law. But one must be careful not to oversimplify. Both works combine detailed discussions of the case law with theoretical reflection on underlying principles. Over the years, both have also had multiple new editions and new editors, and each has expanded into many volumes. Although Williston's and Corbin's treatises are not law, they enjoy a considerable degree of persuasive authority with courts.

Even more important than these individually authored treatises have been the Restatements of the Law. The American Law Institute (ALI) is a group of lawyers, judges and legal scholars founded in 1923 "to promote the clarification and simplification of the law and its better adaptation to social needs, to secure the better administration of justice, and to encourage and carry on scholarly and scientific legal work."[11] Among the ALI's major early accomplishments was the preparation of the Restatement of Contracts. As the title implies, the work attempted to systematically restate the prevailing law of contract in the United States. Drafting of the Contracts Restatement (along with those covering Torts,

---

[10] See A.W.B. Simpson's monumental work, A.W.B. Simpson, A History of the Common Law of Contract: The Rise of the Action of Assumpsit (1975).

[11] Restatement Contracts viii (1932).

Conflict of Laws and Agency) began in 1923, with Samuel Williston serving as the Reporter on the contracts volume and Arthur Corbin as one of Williston's most important advisors. The final draft was approved in May 1932. Williston reported that "the endeavor in the Restatement is to restate the law as it is, not as new law."[12] The end product, however, had strongly normative aspects as well. Many provisions had only marginal support in the case law and were clearly advanced as improvements upon prevailing doctrine. The Restatement of Contracts, today often referred to as the "First Restatement," was enormously influential and has been cited in thousands of judicial opinions.[13]

In the early 1960s, the ALI began work on the Second Restatement of Contracts with Robert Braucher as the Reporter. Braucher served in that capacity until 1971, when he was appointed to the Supreme Judicial Court of Massachusetts and was succeeded by E. Allan Farnsworth. Sixteen tentative drafts were produced, culminating in a final version adopted by the ALI in 1979 and published in 1981. Like the First Restatement, the Second Restatement's primary purpose is to restate the law as it is, not as it should be. Nevertheless, it too contains some outright innovations, the most significant of which is the increased recognition of reliance as a basis of liability.[14]

At the writing of this edition, the ALI is working on a draft Restatement (Third) of Consumer Contracts, which will supplement the Second Restatement for the special category of contracts between businesses and consumers.

For all their persuasive authority and importance for the development of the common law, it must be remembered that the Restatements are not the law. They represent the collective judgments of a highly respected body of legal experts about what the law is or, in a few instances, what it should be. That said, individual Restatement provisions and the comments to them often provide especially clear and carefully drafted statements of legal rules. For this reason, we will refer extensively to both the First and Second Restatements of Contracts throughout this book.

Legislative Codification. At the end of the nineteenth century, the English Parliament began to codify large segments of commercial law. One of the early statutes was the English Sale of Goods Act, drafted by Mackenzie D. Chalmers and enacted in 1893. Lord Chalmers's mandate from Parliament was to "reproduce exactly as possible the existing law," thereby preserving continuity with case precedent.

In the United States, the National Conference of Commissioners on Uniform State Laws (NCCUSL), composed of Commissioners appointed

---

[12]   3 ALI Proceedings 159 (1925).

[13]   Herbert F. Goodrich and Paul A. Wolkin, The Story of the American Law Institute 39 (1961).

[14]   See E. Allan Farnsworth, Ingredients in the Redaction of the Restatement (Second) of Contracts, 81 Colum. L. Rev. 1 (1981).

by the governors, was created in 1892 to promote efforts to codify and homogenize state laws. In 1902, the NCCUSL entrusted to Samuel Williston the task of drafting a model statute for the sale of goods.[15] The result was the Uniform Sales Act, approved by the Commissioners and recommended to the state legislatures in 1906. In the end, over thirty states adopted the Uniform Sales Act. The Act largely follows the English statute, often copying Chalmers's language verbatim. Because, as in England, an effort was made to preserve a continuity with the common law, the Uniform Sales Act did little to change the basic structure of contract law.

The next major effort at codification, the Uniform Commercial Code (UCC), took a very different approach. Like the Uniform Sales Act, the UCC is a model statute that becomes law only if enacted by a legislature. Whereas the Uniform Sales Act dealt only with the sale of goods, the UCC covers a wide range of commercial transactions, including the sale of goods. Work on the Code began in the early 1940s, under joint sponsorship of the NCCUSL and the ALI. The first edition was approved in 1952. After the New York legislature rejected the 1952 version, revisions were made and a new edition, known as the 1958 Official Text with Comments, was published. New York enacted this revised version, after which many states followed. Today, forty-nine states, plus the District of Columbia and the Virgin Islands, have enacted the UCC. Louisiana has adopted Articles 1, 3, 4 and 5. The focus of this book will be Article 2, which governs the sale of goods.

The primary architect of the Code was Karl Llewellyn,[16] a leading member of the American legal realist movement. Unlike Chalmers and Williston, Llewellyn and his colleagues did not feel a special need or obligation to follow previously charted courses. As a result, the UCC often departs from the common law. Although UCC statutes govern only commercial transactions of specified types, some of their new rules have influenced the subsequent development of the common law of contract.

The UCC has been amended numerous times over the years. Once the NCCUSL has approved a set of amendments, state legislatures usually amend the state statutes to conform. The NCCUSL website keeps an updated list of all uniform rules that the organization has promulgated, as well as of the most recent amendments and which states have enacted them. In 2003, after a fifteen-year revision process, the NCCUSL approved major amendments to Article 2. The proposed changes were quite controversial, and no state adopted the 2003 amendments.[17] Taking note of the lack of enthusiasm on the part of the states, the NCCUSL withdrew the 2003 amendments in the summer of

---

[15] For a history of earlier and largely unsuccessful efforts to codify American law, see John Honnold, The Life of the Law 100–145 (1964).

[16] For a study of Llewellyn, his life, times, ideas and role in UCC drafting, see William Twining, Karl Llewellyn and the Realist Movement (1973).

[17] For some background, see William H. Henning, *Amended Article 2: What Went Wrong?*, 11 Duq. Bus. L.J. 131 (2009).

2011. Although the 2003 amendments are no longer part of the UCC, much less state law, we occasionally discuss them as possible alternatives to or clarifications of existing law.

International Developments. Two important developments in international commerce will be referred to throughout the book.

As of August 2011, the United Nations Convention on Contracts for the International Sale of Goods (CISG) had been ratified by 77 countries, including the NAFTA trading partners: Canada, Mexico and the United States. Brazil and the United Kingdom have not ratified the Convention. The CISG applies to contracts for the sale of goods between parties who do business in different countries when both countries have ratified the Convention. CISG Art. 1(1)(a). When applicable, it preempts the domestic law of sales which, in the United States, is Article 2 of the UCC.[18]

In 1994, the International Institute for the Unification of Private Law (UNIDROIT) finalized the UNIDROIT Principles of International Commercial Contracts. It is trite but accurate to call the document a restatement of international contract principles. The UNIDROIT principles are not law, but they purport to respond to international needs and practices and could be adopted by the parties as the "law" of the contract.[19] The Principles were revised and updated in 2004.[20] In May 2011, the Governing Counsel formally adopted the third edition, UNIDROIT Principles 2010.[21]

Comment: Law and Equity in Contract

As noted above, contract law in the United States comes mainly from the English law of contract as a holdover from our pre-revolutionary status as English colonies. An important part of this inheritance is the distinction between law and equity. Until 1873 in England, jurisdiction over what we would today classify as contract disputes was shared between two separate court systems. From the 13th century on, the courts of *law* existed to enforce the King's law through a system of highly formal writs, or causes of action. Each writ was governed by generally applicable rules laid down by earlier judicial decisions. Alongside the courts of law was the Court of Chancery, which was a court of *equity*. The Court of Chancery was empowered to dispense justice where the relief available in courts of law was inadequate. Whereas the courts of law were governed by strict rules, this court of equity had discretion to consider

---

[18] Materials on CISG can be accessed through a website maintained by Pace University School of Law. http://www.cisg.law.pace.edu. A leading treatise is John Honnold, Uniform Law for International Sales under the 1980 U.N. Convention (4th ed. 2009).

[19] For an overview, see Joseph M. Perillo, *UNIDROIT Principles of International Commercial Contracts: The Black Letter Text and a Review*, 63 Fordham L. Rev. 281 (1994).

[20] See Michael J. Bonell, *From UNIDROIT Principles 1994 to UNIDROIT Principles 2004: A Further Step Towards a Global Contract Law*, 37 UCC L.J. 49 (2004).

[21] Art. 1.6(2) UNIDROIT Principles 2010.

principles of justice and fairness in resolving disputes. The two court systems also had different powers. Whereas courts of law could award only monetary *damages*, courts of equity were able to award *injunctive relief*—i.e., order the parties to undertake actions other than the payment of money.

At the time of the founding, many U.S. states had both courts of law and courts of equity. Most states and the federal government have since merged the powers of law and equity into a single court system. As the U.S. Supreme Court has explained: "Actions are no longer brought as actions at law or suits in equity. Under the [Federal Rules of Civil Procedure] there is only one action—a 'civil action'—in which all claims may be joined and all remedies are available." Ross v. Bernhard, 396 U.S. 531, 539 (1970). Some states, however, retain the dual system, most notably Delaware, whose Court of Chancery hears many contract disputes.

Despite the general merger of law and equity, the distinction between them continues to be important in the law of contract. In applying the contemporary rules of contract law, courts attend to whether the rules derived from law or from equity. When the rule comes from equity, trial courts have greater discretion to take into account the considerations of morality, fairness, and justice, which are not part of the law as such. By the same token, appellate courts often (though not always) adopt a more deferential standard of review of equitable decisions on the theory that equitable rules give a trial court greater freedom to reach what it views as the just decision.

Although the distinction between law and equity is in some sense an accident of history, it arguably reflects a fundamental tension in adjudication generally. Consider the following passage from Aristotle's *Nicomachean Ethics*, written in the fourth century BCE:

> [A]ll laws are universal in statement but about some things it is not possible for a universal statement to be right. So in certain cases, in which a universal statement is necessary but no universal statement can be [completely] right, the law accepts what is mostly or in the majority of cases right without being ignorant that there is error in so doing. . . . So when the law makes a universal statement about a subject but an instance of that subject is not rightly covered by that statement, then it is right to correct the omission made by the legislator when he left some error in his unqualified [i.e., universal] statement; for the legislator himself would have made that correction had he been present, or he would have legislated accordingly had he known.[22]

More recently, Henry Smith has argued that equity provides a "safety valve to deal with the opportunism arising from the simple structures of

---

[22] Aristotle, *The Nicomachean Ethics* 1137, b14–24 (Hippocrates G. Apostle trans. 1975).

the common law."[23] The problem, according to Smith, is that "announcing a bright line invites people to dance around that line."[24] The flexible and fact-sensitive doctrines of equity are designed to seek out and punish such opportunism. Others are more skeptical. Jody Kraus and Robert Scott, for example, argue that an equitable focus on the parties' contractual ends more often than not runs contrary to sophisticated parties' preference for more rule-like adjudication.[25]

2. INTRODUCING SOME BASIC ISSUES

Howard E. Bailey v. Richard E. West

Supreme Court of Rhode Island, 1969.
105 R.I. 61.

■ PAOLINO, JUSTICE. This is a civil action wherein the plaintiff alleges that the defendant is indebted to him for the reasonable value of his services rendered in connection with the feeding, care and maintenance of a certain race horse named "Bascom's Folly" from May 3, 1962 through July 3, 1966. The case was tried before a justice of the superior court sitting without a jury, and resulted in a decision for the plaintiff for his cost of boarding the horse for the five months immediately subsequent to May 3, 1962, and for certain expenses incurred by him in trimming its hoofs. The cause is now before us on the plaintiff's appeal and defendant's cross appeal from the judgment entered pursuant to such decision.

The facts material to a resolution of the precise issues raised herein are as follows. In late April 1962, defendant, accompanied by his horse trainer, went to Belmont Park in New York to buy race horses. On April 27, 1962, defendant purchased "Bascom's Folly" from a Dr. Strauss and arranged to have the horse shipped to Suffolk Downs in East Boston, Massachusetts. Upon its arrival defendant's trainer discovered that the horse was lame, and so notified defendant, who ordered him to reship the horse by van to the seller at Belmont Park. The seller refused to accept delivery at Belmont on May 3, 1962, and thereupon, the van driver, one Kelly, called defendant's trainer and asked for further instructions. Although the trial testimony is in conflict as to what the trainer told him, it is not disputed that on the same day Kelly brought "Bascom's Folly" to plaintiff's farm where the horse remained until July 3, 1966, when it was sold by plaintiff to a third party.

While "Bascom's Folly" was residing at his horse farm, plaintiff sent bills for its feed and board to defendant at regular intervals. According to testimony elicited from defendant at the trial, the first such bill was

---

[23] Henry E. Smith, *The Equitable Dimensions of Contract*, 45 Suffolk U. L. Rev. (2012) (forthcoming).

[24] Id.

[25] Jody S. Kraus and Robert E. Scott, *Contract Design and the Structure of Contractual Intent*, 84 N.Y.U. L. Rev. 1023 (2009).

received by him some two or three months after "Bascom's Folly" was placed on plaintiff's farm. He also stated that he immediately returned the bill to plaintiff with the notation that he was not the owner of the horse nor was it sent to plaintiff's farm at his request. The plaintiff testified that he sent bills monthly to defendant and that the first notice he received from him disclaiming ownership was " * * * maybe after a month or two or so" subsequent to the time when the horse was left in plaintiff's care.

In his decision the trial judge found that defendant's trainer had informed Kelly during their telephone conversation of May 3, 1962, that " * * * he would have to do whatever he wanted to do with the horse, that he wouldn't be on any farm at the defendant's expense * * *." He also found, however, that when "Bascom's Folly" was brought to his farm, plaintiff was not aware of the telephone conversation between Kelly and defendant's trainer, and hence, even though he knew there was a controversy surrounding the ownership of the horse, he was entitled to assume that " * * * there is an implication here that, 'I am to take care of this horse.' " Continuing his decision, the trial justice stated that in view of the result reached by this court in a recent opinion[26] wherein we held that the instant defendant was liable to the original seller, Dr. Strauss, for the purchase price of this horse, there was a contract "implied in fact" between the plaintiff and defendant to board "Bascom's Folly" and that this contract continued until plaintiff received notification from defendant that he would not be responsible for the horse's board. The trial justice further stated that " * * * I think there was notice given at least at the end of the four months, and I think we must add another month on there for a reasonable disposition of his property."

In view of the conclusion we reach with respect to defendant's first two contentions, we shall confine ourselves solely to a discussion and resolution of the issues necessarily implicit therein, and shall not examine other subsidiary arguments advanced by plaintiff and defendant.

I

The defendant alleges in his brief and oral argument that the trial judge erred in finding a contract "implied in fact" between the parties. We agree.

The following quotation from 17 C.J.S. Contracts § 4 at pp. 557–560, illustrates the elements necessary to the establishment of a contract "implied in fact":

> " * * * A 'contract implied in fact,' * * * or an implied contract in
> the proper sense, arises where the intention of the parties is not
> expressed, but an agreement in fact, creating an obligation, is

---

[26] [In *Strauss v. West*, 100 R.I. 388 (1966), the court held that Bascom's Folly was "sound" at the time delivery was tendered by Strauss, that title had passed to West, and that West was liable to Strauss for the purchase price of $1,800.—Eds.]

implied or presumed from their acts, or, as it has been otherwise stated, where there are circumstances which, according to the ordinary course of dealing and the common understanding of men, show a mutual intent to contract.

"It has been said that a contract implied in fact must contain all the elements of an express contract. So, such a contract is dependent on mutual agreement or consent, and on the intention of the parties; and a meeting of the minds is required. A contract implied in fact is to every intent and purpose an agreement between the parties, and it cannot be found to exist unless a contract status is shown. Such a contract does not arise out of an implied legal duty or obligation, but out of facts from which consent may be inferred; there must be a manifestation of assent arising wholly or in part from acts other than words, and a contract cannot be implied in fact where the facts are inconsistent with its existence."

Therefore, essential elements of contracts "implied in fact" are mutual agreement, and intent to promise, but the agreement and the promise have not been made in words and are implied from the facts.

* * *

The source of the obligation in a contract "implied in fact," as in express contracts, is in the intention of the parties. We hold that there was no mutual agreement and "intent to promise" between the plaintiff and defendant so as to establish a contract "implied in fact" for defendant to pay plaintiff for the maintenance of this horse. From the time Kelly delivered the horse to him plaintiff knew there was a dispute as to its ownership, and his subsequent actions indicated he did not know with whom, if anyone, he had a contract. After he had accepted the horse, he made inquiries as to its ownership and, initially, and for some time thereafter, sent his bills to both defendant and Dr. Strauss, the original seller.

There is also uncontroverted testimony in the record that prior to the assertion of the claim which is the subject of this suit neither defendant nor his trainer had ever had any business transactions with plaintiff, and had never used his farm to board horses. Additionally, there is uncontradicted evidence that this horse, when found to be lame, was shipped by defendant's trainer not to plaintiff's farm, but back to the seller at Belmont Park. What is most important, the trial justice expressly stated that he believed the testimony of defendant's trainer that he had instructed Kelly that defendant would not be responsible for boarding the horse on any farm.

From our examination of the record we are constrained to conclude that the trial justice overlooked and misconceived material evidence which establishes beyond question that there never existed between the parties an element essential to the formulation of any true contract, namely, an "intent to contract." Compare Morrissey v. Piette, 103 R.I. 751, 753.

II

The defendant's second contention is that, even assuming the trial justice was in essence predicating defendant's liability upon a quasi-contractual theory, his decision is still unsupported by competent evidence and is clearly erroneous.

The following discussion of quasi-contracts appears in 12 Am.Jur., Contracts, § 6 (1938) at pp. 503 to 504:

"* * * A quasi contract has no reference to the intentions or expressions of the parties. The obligation is imposed despite, and frequently in frustration of, their intention. For a quasi contract neither promise nor privity, real or imagined, is necessary. In quasi contracts the obligation arises, not from consent of the parties, as in the case of contracts, express or implied in fact, but from the law of natural immutable justice and equity. The act, or acts, from which the law implies the contract must, however, be voluntary. Where a case shows that it is the duty of the defendant to pay, the law imputes to him a promise to fulfil that obligation. The duty, which thus forms the foundation of a quasi-contractual obligation, is frequently based on the doctrine of unjust enrichment. * * *

"* * * The law will not imply a promise against the express declaration of the party to be charged, made at the time of the supposed undertaking, unless such party is under legal obligation paramount to his will to perform some duty, and he is not under such legal obligation unless there is a demand in equity and good conscience that he should perform the duty."

Therefore, the essential elements of a quasi-contract are a benefit conferred upon defendant by plaintiff, appreciation by defendant of such benefit, and acceptance and retention by defendant of such benefit under such circumstances that it would be inequitable to retain the benefit without payment of the value thereof. * * *

The key question raised by this appeal with respect to the establishment of a quasi-contract is whether or not plaintiff was acting as a "volunteer" at the time he accepted the horse for boarding at his farm. There is a long line of authority which has clearly enunciated the general rule that "* * * if a performance is rendered by one person without any request by another, it is very unlikely that this person will be under a legal duty to pay compensation." 1 A Corbin, Contracts § 234.

The Restatement of Restitution, § 2 (1937) provides: "A person who officiously confers a benefit upon another is not entitled to restitution therefor." Comment *a* in the above-mentioned section states in part as follows:

" * * * Policy ordinarily requires that a person who has conferred a benefit * * * by way of giving another services * * * should not be permitted to require the other to pay therefor, unless the one conferring the benefit had a valid reason for so doing. A person is not required to deal with another unless he so desires and, ordinarily, a person should not be required to become an obligor unless he so desires."

Applying those principles to the facts in the case at bar it is clear that plaintiff cannot recover. The plaintiff's testimony on cross-examination is the only evidence in the record relating to what transpired between Kelly and him at the time the horse was accepted for boarding. The defendant's attorney asked plaintiff if he had any conversation with Kelly at that time, and plaintiff answered in substance that he had noticed that the horse was very lame and that Kelly had told him: "That's why they wouldn't accept him at Belmont Track." The plaintiff also testified that he had inquired of Kelly as to the ownership of "Bascom's Folly," and had been told that "Dr. Strauss made a deal and that's all I know." It further appears from the record that plaintiff acknowledged receipt of the horse by signing a uniform livestock bill of lading, which clearly indicated on its face that the horse in question had been consigned by defendant's trainer not to plaintiff, but to Dr. Strauss's trainer at Belmont Park. Knowing at the time he accepted the horse for boarding that a controversy surrounded its ownership, plaintiff could not reasonably expect remuneration from defendant, nor can it be said that defendant acquiesced in the conferment of a benefit upon him. The undisputed testimony was that defendant, upon receipt of plaintiff's first bill, immediately notified him that he was not the owner of "Bascom's Folly" and would not be responsible for its keep.

It is our judgment that the plaintiff was a mere volunteer who boarded and maintained "Bascom's Folly" at his own risk and with full knowledge that he might not be reimbursed for expenses he incurred incident thereto.

The plaintiff's appeal is denied and dismissed, the defendant's cross appeal is sustained, and the cause is remanded to the superior court for entry of judgment for the defendant.

NOTES

(1) What were Howard Bailey's two theories of recovery? How did they differ? On what grounds did the court reject each?

(2) Suppose Richard West personally delivered Bascom's Folly to Bailey's farm, but nothing was said specifically about Bailey's caring for the horse or West's paying for that care. Would West be liable? If so, on what theory?

One court has described implied-in-fact promises as follows:

> An implied-in-fact contract has the same legal effect as an express contract. The only difference between them is the means by which the parties manifest their agreement. In an express contract, the parties manifest their agreement by their words, whether written or spoken. In an implied-in-fact contract, the parties' agreement is inferred, in whole or in part, from their conduct. * * * [Nevertheless] an implied contract must still have discernable terms * * * For such a situation to exist, the parties must exhibit mutual expressions of assent.

Novak v. Seiko Corp., 37 Fed.Appx. 239, 243 (9th Cir. 2002) (unpublished) (citations and internal quotation marks omitted).

If an implied-in-fact contract existed in *Bailey*, what would be the terms? For additional discussion of implied-in-fact contracts, see Chapter Three, Section 1.B.

(3) What if Bailey found Bascom's Folly collapsed alongside the highway, took him in and cared for him, and thereafter sought out West. Would West be responsible to Bailey for the care given to the horse? If so, on what theory?

> One who, without intent to act gratuitously, confers a measurable benefit upon another, is entitled to restitution, if he affords the other an opportunity to decline the benefit or else has a reasonable excuse for failing to do so. If the other refuses to receive the benefit, he is not required to make restitution unless the actor justifiably performs for the other a duty imposed upon him by law.

John Wade, *Restitution for Benefits Conferred Without Request,* 19 Vand. L. Rev. 1183, 1212 (1966). For more on restitution and unjust enrichment, see Chapter Three, Section 3.

Comment: Contract Law and Morality

Perhaps the most famous piece of American jurisprudence is Oliver Wendell Holmes's 1897 address to students and faculty at the Boston University Law School, published in the Harvard Law Review as *The Path of the Law*.[27] In the address, Holmes sets out, among other things, to "dispel a confusion between morality and law."[28] And, Holmes writes, "[n]owhere is the confusion between legal and moral ideas more manifest than in the law of contract."[29] He gives the following advice to his audience:

> If you want to know the law and nothing else, you must look at it as a bad man, who cares only for the material consequences which such knowledge enables him to predict, not as a good one,

---

[27] Oliver Wendell Holmes, *The Path of the Law*, 10 Harv. L. Rev. 457 (1897), reprinted in 110 Harv. L. Rev. 991 (1997).

[28] Id. at 992.

[29] Id. at 995.

who finds his reasons for conduct, whether inside the law or outside of it, in the vaguer sanctions of conscience.[30]

Holmes's "bad man" approach to the law has endured more than its share of criticism over the years. But as advice to law students who "want to know the law," it hits the mark, at least when it comes to learning the law of contract.

Consider again the facts in *Bailey v. West*. Bailey took in Bascom's Folly, a horse that apparently no one else wanted, and for several years fed and cared for it. West was the horse's owner and should have felt some responsibility for the animal's wellbeing. But West all but abandoned the beast. According to his trainer, as far as West was concerned, Kelly could "do whatever he wanted to do with the horse." West did not care. Yet in the absence of an agreement between West and Bailey, or a justified expectation of payment on Bailey's part, the law would not force West to pay for Bascom's Folly's food and board. Was this the morally right outcome? The point is that if all you care about is what the law is, it doesn't matter. More to the point, moral intuitions in cases like this are likely to lead one astray when the question is what the law is, as distinguished from what it should be.

Holmes gives two other examples of the divergence between contract law and morality. Whereas morality says *pacta sunt servanda* (agreements are to be kept), the legal remedy for most breaches does not require performance, but only grants payment of money damages. From the perspective of the bad man, then, "[t]he duty to keep a contract at common law means a prediction that you must pay damages if you do not keep it,—and nothing else."[31] And whereas morality holds a promisor only to agreements she has assented to, the legal need for certainty and predictability means that contract law focuses on parties' outward manifestations, rather than their actual intent. Thus "parties may be bound by a contract to things which neither of them intended, and when one does not know of the other's assent."[32]

None of this is to say that contract law is entirely divorced from the moral obligation to keep one's agreements, or that we should not subject the law of contract to moral criticism. Holmes also argues in *The Path of the Law* that "[t]he law is the witness and external deposit of our moral life."[33] Perhaps contract law is designed to enforce, at least to some extent, a promisor's moral obligation to perform.[34] Or perhaps contract damages are meant to ensure justice between the parties after one has

---

[30] Id. at 993.

[31] Id. at 995.

[32] Id. at 996.

[33] Id. at 992.

[34] See, e.g., Stephen A. Smith, Contract Theory (2004); Charles Fried, Contract as Promise (1981).

morally wronged the other.[35] And certainly it would be a cause of concern if the practical effect of the rules of contract law was the dulling of people's moral sensibilities or the erosion of our moral culture.[36] But in order to know whether or not contract law is moral, just, fair, or whatever, we must first know what contract law is.[37] For that purpose, the bad man's perspective is extremely useful.

PROBLEM: FIVE EASY CASES (AND ONE MORE DIFFICULT)

(1)   A sits down at a restaurant. When B, the waiter, arrives, A says: "I want the veggie burger with fries and an iced tea." Fifteen minutes later, B brings A a veggie burger, fries, and an iced tea. Does A have an obligation to pay for the food? If so, on what grounds?

(2)   B wants to transfer $10,000 to C, but makes an error filling in the online form, and the money ends up in A's account. Does A have an obligation to return the money to B? If so, on what grounds?

(3)   Every morning, A stops by B's newsstand for a morning paper. One morning, there is a long line. A grabs a paper from the pile and holds it up for B to see. B winks at A, and A walks away with the paper. Does A have an obligation to pay for the paper? If so, on what grounds?

(4)   Same as in (3), except A simply grabs a paper and walks away with it. Does A have an obligation to pay for the paper? If so, on what grounds?

(5)   A is injured in a car accident and taken unconscious to hospital B. B treats A and sends A a bill for B's services. Does A have an obligation to pay the bill? If so, on what grounds?

(6)   A's 15 year-old daughter C injures her ankle playing basketball. A looks at the ankle and decides that it is merely a sprain. Three days later, when C is visiting a friend, the friend's father D notices that the area around the ankle has turned purple. D immediately takes C to see B, who is a physician. B X-rays C's ankle and finds a hairline fracture. B sends both A and D a bill for B's services. Does either A or D have an obligation to pay the bill? If so, on what grounds?

Bolin Farms v. American Cotton Shippers Association

U.S. District Court, Western District of Louisiana, 1974.
370 F.Supp. 1353.

■ EDWIN F. HUNTER, JR., CHIEF JUDGE. This litigation arises out of the attempts by eleven (11) cotton farmers to test the contracts by which they concededly obligated themselves to sell and deliver their cotton. In essence, defendants agreed to purchase whatever was planted by these

---

[35] See, e.g., Gregory Klass, *Promise Etc.*, 45 Suffolk U. L. Rev. 695 (2012); Curtis Bridgeman, *Reconciling Strict Liability with Corrective Justice in Contract Law*, 75 Fordham L. Rev. 3013 (2007); P.S. Atiyah, Promises, Morals, and Law (1981).

[36] See Seana Valentine Shiffrin, *The Divergence of Contract and Promise*, 120 Harv. L. Rev. 708 (2007).

[37] For a longer defense of this point, see Robin West, Normative Jurisprudence: An Introduction 60–106 (2011).

farmers on specific acreage at a price agreed upon between January and March of 1973, irrespective of what the price might be at harvest time. Meanwhile, the price of cotton unexpectedly skyrocketed to at least double the price agreed upon. The complaints seek a declaration that the contracts are null and void, so that plaintiffs may achieve a better price than they bargained for. The fundamental question in each action involves the enforceability *vel non* of contracts for the advance or forward sale of cotton grown for the 1973 crop.

* * *

The record is a morass of pleadings which can best be unraveled by proceeding to the very core of the case—that is, the validity and enforceability of a contract for the purchase and sale of cotton, entered into between a willing buyer and a willing seller, both adult (experienced cotton farmers on the one hand and experienced cotton buyers on the other hand) on an open and competitive market. The case on summary judgment presents two facets:

(1) The prayer of plaintiffs for a declaratory judgment annulling the cotton sales contracts, and

(2) The prayer of defendants that the contracts be adjudged lawful and valid.

* * *

It is a matter of public record and public knowledge that as a result of the sudden and spectacular rise in the price of cotton in the latter part of 1973, literally scores of suits have been filed, either to enforce or rescind these advance or forward contracts. Defendants have cited thirteen (13) cases that arose between September 18 and November 9, 1973. In each, the validity of the contracts has been upheld by either summary judgment, declaratory judgment, preliminary injunction, and/or permanent injunction.

* * *

The contracts are in evidence. They speak for themselves. No useful purpose would be served by detailing each provision. They were entered into between January 9, 1973 and March 29, 1973. In each, plaintiffs obligated themselves to sell and deliver to the defendant cotton buyers all of the cotton raised and harvested on designated acreage. The price ranged from 29 to 41 cents per pound. The actual cotton produced was physically to be delivered to the buyers, to be by them physically received and paid for on delivery. These contracts were negotiated prior to planting. We call them "forward" sales contracts. Each plaintiff cotton farmer was experienced, having been a cotton producer for several years, and each was familiar with the forward sale contract procedure.

The depositions reveal that during the period of time from January 9th through March 29, 1973, the competitive open market range ran from 28 to 32 cents per pound. On the basis of the record it would be difficult to quarrel with the proposition that the sales were for a fair market price at the time they were made, and as a matter of law we conclude that the price and circumstances prevailing at the time are determinative.

From April through September, the cotton market rose spectacularly. The price of 29 or 30 cents a pound, which looked so good to the farmers in February, no longer looked so good against 80 cents in September.

These farmers certainly have every right to contest the validity of their contracts. Likewise, the buyer has every right to assert the validity of their bargain. To quote the Honorable Wilbur D. Owens, Jr., U.S. District Judge, Middle District of Georgia (see Mitchell-Huntley Cotton Co. v. Fulton Benson, Civil Action 2902):

> "Ladies and Gentlemen, this case illustrates about as well as any case that will ever be in a court room that life is a two way street, that when we make bargains that turn out to be good for us that we keep them and then when we make bargains that turn out to be bad for us that we also keep them. That seems to be the essence of what this case is about.
>
> "The defendants, naturally, don't want to sell cotton because the price has gone up and if I were one of those defendants I would feel the same way. I would be sick as an old hound dog who ate a rotten skunk, but unfortunately—well, not unfortunately—fortunately we all abide by contracts and that (is) the foundation of which all of the business that you have heard about here today is done."

What caused the upward price spiral of April to September? There were many causes. We are unable to pin down any one. Be that as it may, the cause has no relevance to the validity of the contracts. Some of the deponents point to such factors as large export shipments to China, high water and flood conditions in the cotton belt; late plantings forced by heavy rains, and the devaluation of the dollar. These elements and others are reasonable causes, but whatever causes the market to go up and down after the date of a contract has no relevancy to its validity. One facet of plaintiffs' attack is that the cotton buyers had inside information at the time they contracted with plaintiffs, and that these factors would coincide and drive the price of cotton to the level that it had never before reached. The record does not reveal this to be true. The record will reveal that Dallas Thomason sold his cotton at 30 cents; Frank Jones, Jr., Executive Vice-President of Cook Industries, Inc., sold his cotton at 30 cents; Conner Morscheimer, cotton buyer for W. K. Kennedy Co., Inc., sold his cotton at 29 and ½ cents.

Plaintiffs emphasize that the cotton farmer has always been at the mercy of the weather and the boll weevil. This may be true, but by firm forward selling, the farmer shifts many of his risks to the buyer. The farmer guarantees neither quality nor quantity. He obligates himself to sell and the buyer obligates himself to buy all the cotton the farmer harvests from identifiable acreage. He sells it at a price at which he figures at the time of the contract he can make a profit in relation to his expectable costs. Against that firm contract he can arrange his crop financing. The depositions reveal the system used, and there can be no argument that it does give the grower a very real limitation of risk.

* * *

Moving quickly to validity, we appreciate that the 13 cases cited are not controlling, but we do find it extremely persuasive that in 13 recent cases attacking the validity, in federal and state courts, all upheld the contracts.

* * *

Plaintiffs' request in each of these five (5) cases for declaratory judgment annulling the cotton sale is denied; defendants' request that the contracts be adjudged lawful and valid is granted. * * *

NOTES

(1)   Why might the parties to the contracts at issue in *Bolin Farms* have wanted to lock in a price months before harvest? What does the court mean when it says, "by forward selling, the farmer shifts many of his risks to the buyer"? What risks? Does the buyer shift any risks to the seller?

(2)   *Excuse by Reason of Changed Circumstances.* When, if ever, should a promisor be excused because of unexpected events that make performance more costly? Even if it is still possible for the promisor to perform, should a frustration of a party's purpose or objective in entering into the contract be grounds for excusing non-performance? What, for example, of dramatic market price increases or decreases brought on by external events (e.g., war, rationing, or embargoes)?

In the early cases, common law judges had an emphatic answer: no excuse. Absent an explicit qualification of duty in the contract itself, the promisor was obligated to perform regardless of intervening events. *Pacta sunt servanda*! As a seventeenth-century English case stated, "when the party by his own contract creates a duty or charge upon himself, he is bound to make it good, if he may, notwithstanding any accident by inevitable necessity, because he might have provided against it by his contract." Paradine v. Jane, Aleyn 26, 27, 82 Eng. Rep. 897 (K.B.1647). Later cases began to relax this strict rule, and UCC § 2–615 recognizes excuse by failure of presupposed conditions: "Except so far as a seller may have assumed a greater obligation. . .(a) Delay in delivery or non-delivery in whole or in part by a seller. . . is not a breach of his duty under a contract for sale if performance as agreed has been made impracticable by the occurrence of a contingency the non-occurrence of which was a basic assumption on which the contract was made or by compliance in good faith with any applicable foreign or domestic governmental regulation or order whether or not it later proves to be invalid." This subject is treated at length in Chapter Five, Section 5.

Ora Lee Williams v. Walker-Thomas Furniture Co.

United States Court of Appeals, District of Columbia Circuit, 1965.
121 U.S.App.D.C. 315.

■ J. SKELLY WRIGHT, CIRCUIT JUDGE. Appellee, Walker-Thomas Furniture Company, operates a retail furniture store in the District of Columbia. During the period from 1957 to 1962 each appellant in these cases purchased a number of household items from Walker-Thomas, for which payment was to be made in installments. The terms of each purchase were contained in a printed form contract which set forth the value of the purchased item and purported to lease the item to appellant for a stipulated monthly rent payment. The contract then provided, in substance, that title would remain in Walker-Thomas until the total of all the monthly payments made equaled the stated value of the item, at which time appellants could take title. In the event of a default in the payment of any monthly installment, Walker-Thomas could repossess the item.

The contract further provided that "the amount of each periodical installment payment to be made by [purchaser] to the Company under this present lease shall be inclusive of and not in addition to the amount of each installment payment to be made by [purchaser] under such prior leases, bills or accounts; *and all payments now and hereafter made by [purchaser] shall be credited pro rata on all outstanding leases, bills and accounts* due the Company by [purchaser] at the time each such payment is made." [Emphasis added.—Eds.] The effect of this rather obscure provision was to keep a balance due on every item purchased until the balance due on all items, whenever purchased, was liquidated. As a result, the debt incurred at the time of purchase of each item was secured by the right to repossess all the items previously purchased by the same purchaser, and each new item purchased automatically became subject to a security interest arising out of the previous dealings.

On May 12, 1962, appellant Thorne purchased an item described as a Daveno, three tables, and two lamps, having total stated value of $391.10. Shortly thereafter, he defaulted on his monthly payments and appellee sought to replevy all the items purchased since the first transaction in 1958. Similarly, on April 17, 1962, appellant Williams bought a stereo set of stated value of $514.95.[1] She too defaulted shortly thereafter, and appellee sought to replevy all the items purchased since December, 1957. The Court of General Sessions granted judgment for appellee. The District of Columbia Court of Appeals affirmed, and we granted appellants' motion for leave to appeal to this court.

---

[1] At the time of this purchase her account showed a balance of $164 still owing from her prior purchases. The total of all the purchases made over the years in question came to $1,800. The total payments amounted to $1,400.

Appellants' principal contention, rejected by both the trial and the appellate courts below, is that these contracts, or at least some of them, are unconscionable and, hence, not enforceable.

* * *

In other jurisdictions, it has been held as a matter of common law that unconscionable contracts are not enforceable. While no decision of this court so holding has been found, the notion that an unconscionable bargain should not be given full enforcement is by no means novel. In *Scott v. United States*, 79 U.S. (12 Wall.) 443, 445 (1870), the Supreme Court stated:

> " * * * If a contract be unreasonable and unconscionable, but not void for fraud, a court of law will give to the party who sues for its breach damages, not according to its letter, but only such as he is equitably entitled to. * * * "

Since we have never adopted or rejected such a rule, the question here presented is actually one of first impression.

Congress has recently enacted the Uniform Commercial Code, which specifically provides that the court may refuse to enforce a contract which it finds to be unconscionable at the time it was made. 28 D.C.Code § 2–302 (Supp. IV 1965). The enactment of this section, which occurred subsequent to the contracts here in suit, does not mean that the common law of the District of Columbia was otherwise at the time of enactment, nor does it preclude the court from adopting a similar rule in the exercise of its powers to develop the common law for the District of Columbia. In fact, in view of the absence of prior authority on the point, we consider the congressional adoption of § 2–302 persuasive authority for following the rationale of the cases from which the section is explicitly derived. Accordingly, we hold that where the element of unconscionability is present at the time a contract is made, the contract should not be enforced.

Unconscionability has generally been recognized to include an absence of meaningful choice on the part of one of the parties together with contract terms which are unreasonably favorable to the other party. Whether a meaningful choice is present in a particular case can only be determined by consideration of all the circumstances surrounding the transaction. In many cases the meaningfulness of the choice is negated by a gross inequality of bargaining power. The manner in which the contract was entered is also relevant to this consideration. Did each party to the contract, considering his obvious education or lack of it, have a reasonable opportunity to understand the terms of the contract, or were the important terms hidden in a maze of fine print and minimized by deceptive sales practices? Ordinarily, one who signs an agreement without full knowledge of its terms might be held to assume the risk that he has entered a one-sided bargain. But when a party of little bargaining power, and hence little real choice, signs a commercially unreasonable contract with little or no knowledge of its terms, it is hardly likely that his consent, or even an objective manifestation of his consent, was ever given to all the terms. In such a case the usual rule that the terms of the agreement are not to be questioned should be abandoned and the court should consider whether the terms of the contract are so unfair that enforcement should be withheld.

In determining reasonableness or fairness, the primary concern must be with the terms of the contract considered in light of the circumstances existing when the contract was made. The test is not simple, nor can it be mechanically applied. The terms are to be considered "in the light of the general commercial background and the commercial needs of the particular trade or case." Corbin suggests the test as being whether the terms are "so extreme as to appear unconscionable according to the mores and business practices of the time and place." . . . We think this formulation correctly states the test to be applied in those cases where no meaningful choice was exercised upon entering the contract.

Because the trial court and the appellate court did not feel that enforcement could be refused, no findings were made on the possible unconscionability of the contracts in these cases. Since the record is not sufficient for our deciding the issue as a matter of law, the cases must be remanded to the trial court for further proceedings.

So ordered.

■ DANAHER, CIRCUIT JUDGE (dissenting). The District of Columbia Court of Appeals obviously was as unhappy about the situation here presented as any of us can possibly be. Its opinion in the *Williams* case, quoted in the majority text, concludes: "We think Congress should consider corrective legislation to protect the public from such exploitive contracts as were utilized in the case at bar."

My view is thus summed up by an able court which made no finding that there had actually been sharp practice. Rather the appellant seems to have known precisely where she stood.

There are many aspects of public policy here involved. What is a luxury to some may seem an outright necessity to others. Is public oversight to be required of the expenditures of relief funds? A washing machine, e.g., in the hands of a relief client might become a fruitful source of income. Many relief clients may well need credit, and certain business establishments will take long chances on the sale of items, expecting their pricing policies will afford a degree of protection commensurate with the risk. Perhaps a remedy when necessary will be found within the provisions of the "Loan Shark" law, D.C.Code §§ 26–601 et seq. (1961).

I mention such matters only to emphasize the desirability of a cautious approach to any such problem, particularly since the law for so long has allowed parties such great latitude in making their own contracts. I dare say there must annually be thousands upon thousands of installment credit transactions in this jurisdiction, and one can only speculate as to the effect that these cases will have.

* * *

The Walker-Thomas Furniture Company

NOTES

(1)   What is the test for unconscionability according to Judge Wright? Where exactly does it appear in the opinion? Does Judge Danaher, writing in dissent, believe that this is the wrong test, or that there should be no unconscionability defense?

(2)   In an important 1967 article, Arthur Leff distinguished between procedural   unconscionability   and   substantive   unconscionability. *Unconscionability and the Code—The Emperor's New Clause*, 115 U. Pa. L. Rev. 485, 487 (1967). "Procedural unconscionability" refers to defects in the bargaining process, though they may not be significant enough to support an independent defense of fraud, duress, mistake or the like. "Substantive unconscionability" denotes unfairness in the outcome of that process, i.e., in the terms of the agreement. In almost all cases finding a contract unconscionable, the court finds both procedural and substantive unconscionability. The New York Court of Appeals, however, has recognized the possibility of "exceptional cases where a provision of the contract is so outrageous as to warrant holding it unenforceable on the grounds of

substantive unconscionability alone." Gillman v. Chase Manhattan Bank, 534 N.E.2d 824, 829 (N.Y. 1988). Should substantive unconscionability alone ever be enough?

(3)   Richard Epstein writes:

> Properly understood, [the principle of freedom of contract] does not require a court to enforce every contract brought before it. It does, however, demand that the reasons invoked for not enforcing the contract be of one of two sorts. Either there must be proof of some defect in the *process* of contract formation (be it duress, fraud or undue influence); or there must be, but only within narrow limits, some incompetence of the party against whom the agreement is to be enforced. The doctrine of unconscionability is important in both these respects because it can, if wisely applied, allow the courts to police these two types of problems, and thereby improve the general administration of the contract law. Yet when the doctrine of unconscionability is used in its *substantive* dimension, be it in a commercial or consumer context, it serves only to undercut a private right of contract in a manner that is apt to do more social harm than good. The result of the analysis is the same even if we view the question of unconscionability from the lofty perspective of public policy. "[I]f there is one thing which more than another public policy requires, it is that men of full age and competent understanding shall have the utmost liberty of contracting, and that their contracts when entered into freely and voluntarily shall be held sacred and shall be enforced by Courts of justice." Printing and Numerical Registering Co. v. Sampson, L.R. 19 Eq. 462, 465 (1875).

Unconscionability: A Critical Reappraisal, 18 J.L. & Econ. 293, 315 (1975).

(4)   Does it or should it matter whether the plaintiffs in *Williams v. Walker-Thomas Furniture* read the cross-collateralization clause? The traditional rule is that parties have a so-called "duty to read." In the words of one court, "a person is presumed to understand the documents which he signs and cannot be released from the terms of a contract due to his failure to read it." Clanton v. United Skates of America, 686 N.E.2d 896, 899–900 (Ind. Ct. App. 1997).

(5)   Should it matter if the contract was written by one party and presented to the other on a take-it-or-leave-it basis? Doesn't this describe most contracts that most of us enter into?

Comment: The *Ex Ante* and *Ex Post* Perspectives

Breach of contract is often a wrong that harms the nonbreaching party. In many cases, there is a strong intuition that the breaching party should compensate the nonbreaching party for her losses—that the breaching party should be made to pay for the breach. One purpose of awarding damages is to enforce such post-breach obligations. This aspect of contract law is backward looking, or takes an "*ex post*" (after the event) perspective on the transaction.

At the same time, one of the great benefits of having a law of contract is the assurance it gives parties entering into agreements. When you enter into a contract, you know that the other side has a new reason to perform: the threat of legal liability for breach. And you know that you are at least partly insured against breach, most likely in the form of money damages awarded to you as the nonbreaching party. These legal protections make possible value-creating transactions (exchanges in which both sides gain) between parties who otherwise might not trust one another. A second function of contract law is to provide such assurances by giving parties the right incentives. This is a forward looking, or "*ex ante*" (before the event), aspect of contract law.

Contract is hardly the only area of the law that has both *ex ante* and *ex post* functions. A criminal law, for example, can serve both deterrent and retributive functions. Criminalizing theft deters people *ex ante* from stealing by attaching new costs (possible imprisonment) to the act. It also serves to express society's disapproval of the bad act *ex post* by punishing the individual who has committed it.

That said, the distinction between the *ex ante* and *ex post* perspectives is especially important in contract law, and can create significant tensions within the law. When, for example, should the law require that a contract be in writing? From the *ex ante* perspective, requiring a writing is a good idea because it gives parties a new reason to put their agreements on paper. Enforcing oral agreements is more expensive for the courts and less reliable for the parties. Yet we know that no matter what the rule, some parties will enter into agreements based on no more than a handshake. When there is clear proof that the parties entered into an oral agreement, should we let the breaching party get off scot-free simply because it was not reduced to writing? What is the best rule from the *ex post* perspective?

Another area where we will see the two perspectives at work is in the interpretation of contracts, and especially in the difference between formalist and contextualist approaches. Simplifying a bit, formalists tend to emphasize the plain meaning of writings, whereas contextualists are willing to admit more evidence of the circumstances that gave rise to the writing. From the *ex ante* perspective, one advantage of formalism is that case outcomes are more predictable. If an insurance contract says that the insured is protected "against all loss, damage, expense and liability resulting from injury to property," the parties know that it protects against *all* such losses. That is what the written contract says. From the *ex post* perspective, however, a focus on the text can lead to injustice. Perhaps both parties to the contract unquestionably intended to insure only against losses to third parties, not against losses to the insured. True, they did a poor job expressing that agreement in writing. But where there is clear evidence that the parties intended a different meaning, wouldn't it be unjust to ignore that evidence? And yet to allow the evidence is to muddy the waters for future parties, who will be less certain about how a court will interpret their written contract.

One way to explore the *ex ante* perspective is to ask, "Who are the future parties rooting for?" Litigating contractors often just want to win the lawsuit. They view the transaction from the *ex post* perspective. Future parties, who have not yet contracted and so are in the *ex ante* perspective, are often in a better position to evaluate what the law should be. Consider, for example, whom the future parties are rooting for in *Williams v. Walker-Thomas Furniture*. It is unsurprising that consumer groups representing future consumers would oppose the kind of advantage-taking in *Walker-Thomas*. But it is possible that an industry group representing future furniture sellers would also oppose the *Walker-Thomas* practices. Can you see why? Then again, if the new rule drives Walker-Thomas out of business, will anyone be left to sell home furnishings to poor people? While the effect of the decision on future parties is far from certain, considering this effect provides a very different perspective on the decision in the case.

Sullivan v. O'Connor

Supreme Judicial Court of Massachusetts, 1973.
363 Mass. 579.

■ KAPLAN, JUSTICE. The plaintiff patient secured a jury verdict of $13,500 against the defendant surgeon for breach of contract in respect to an operation upon the plaintiff's nose. The substituted consolidated bill of exceptions presents questions about the correctness of the judge's instructions on the issue of damages.

The declaration was in two counts. In the first count, the plaintiff alleged that she, as patient, entered into a contract with the defendant, a surgeon, wherein the defendant promised to perform plastic surgery on her nose and thereby to enhance her beauty and improve her appearance; that he performed the surgery but failed to achieve the promised result; rather the result of the surgery was to disfigure and deform her nose, to cause her pain in body and mind, and to subject her to other damage and expense. The second count, based on the same transaction, was in the conventional form for malpractice, charging that the defendant had been guilty of negligence in performing the surgery. Answering, the defendant entered a general denial.

On the plaintiff's demand, the case was tried by jury. At the close of the evidence, the judge put to the jury, as special questions, the issues of liability under the two counts, and instructed them accordingly. The jury returned a verdict for the plaintiff on the contract count, and for the defendant on the negligence count. The judge then instructed the jury on the issue of damages.

As background to the instructions and the parties' exceptions, we mention certain facts as the jury could find them. The plaintiff was a professional entertainer, and this was known to the defendant. The agreement was as alleged in the declaration. More particularly, judging from exhibits, the plaintiff's nose had been straight, but long and prominent; the defendant undertook by two operations to reduce its prominence and somewhat to shorten it, thus making it more pleasing in relation to the plaintiff's other features. Actually the plaintiff was obliged to undergo three operations, and her appearance was worsened. Her nose now had a concave line to about the midpoint, at which it became bulbous; viewed frontally, the nose from bridge to midpoint was flattened and broadened, and the two sides of the tip had lost symmetry. This configuration evidently could not be improved by further surgery. The plaintiff did not demonstrate, however, that her change of appearance had resulted in loss of employment. Payments by the plaintiff covering the defendant's fee and hospital expenses were stipulated at $622.65.

The judge instructed the jury, first, that the plaintiff was entitled to recover her out-of-pocket expenses incident to the operations. Second, she could recover the damages flowing directly, naturally, proximately and foreseeably from the defendant's breach of promise. These would comprehend damages for any disfigurement of the plaintiff's nose—that is, any change of appearance for the worse—including the effects of the consciousness of such disfigurement on the plaintiff's mind, and in this connection the jury should consider the nature of the plaintiff's profession. Also consequent upon the defendant's breach, and compensable, were the pain and suffering involved in the third operation, but not in the first two. As there was no proof that any loss of earnings by the plaintiff resulted from the breach, that element should not enter into the calculation of damages.

By his exceptions the defendant contends that the judge erred in allowing the jury to take into account anything but the plaintiff's out-of-pocket expenses (presumably at the stipulated amount). The defendant excepted to the judge's refusal of his request for a general charge to that effect, and, more specifically, to the judge's refusal of a charge that the plaintiff could not recover for pain and suffering connected with the third operation or for impairment of the plaintiff's appearance and associated mental distress.

The plaintiff on her part excepted to the judge's refusal of a request to charge that the plaintiff could recover the difference in value between the nose as promised and the nose as it appeared after the operations. However, the plaintiff in her brief expressly waives this exception and others made by her in case this court overrides the defendant's exceptions; thus she would be content to hold the jury's verdict in her favor.

We conclude that the defendant's exceptions should be overruled.

It has been suggested on occasion that agreements between patients and physicians by which the physician undertakes to effect a cure or to bring about a given result should be declared unenforceable on grounds of public policy. . . . But there are many decisions recognizing and enforcing such contracts, see annotation, 43 A.L.R.3d 1221, 1225, 1229–1233, and the law of Massachusetts has treated them as valid, although we have had no decision meeting head on the contention that they should be denied legal sanction. . . . These causes of action are, however, considered a little suspect, and thus we find courts straining sometimes to read the pleadings as sounding only in tort for negligence, and not in contract for breach of promise, despite sedulous efforts by the pleaders to pursue the latter theory. . . .

It is not hard to see why the courts should be unenthusiastic or skeptical about the contract theory. Considering the uncertainties of medical science and the variations in the physical and psychological conditions of individual patients, doctors can seldom in good faith promise specific results. Therefore it is unlikely that physicians of even average integrity will in fact make such promises. Statements of opinion by the physician with some optimistic coloring are a different thing, and may indeed have therapeutic value. But patients may transform such statements into firm promises in their own minds, especially when they have been disappointed in the event, and testify in that sense to sympathetic juries.[2] If actions for breach of promise can be readily maintained, doctors, so it is said, will be frightened into practicing "defensive medicine." On the other hand, if these actions were outlawed, leaving only the possibility of suits for malpractice, there is fear that the public might be exposed to the enticements of charlatans, and confidence in the profession might ultimately be shaken. See Miller, *The Contractual Liability of Physicians and Surgeons*, 1953 Wash. L. Q. 413, 416–423. The law has taken the middle of the road position of allowing actions based on alleged contract, but insisting on clear proof. Instructions to the jury may well stress this requirement and point to tests of truth, such as the complexity or difficulty of an operation as bearing on the probability that a given result was promised. . . .

If an action on the basis of contract is allowed, we have next the question of the measure of damages to be applied where liability is found. Some cases have taken the simple view that the promise by the physician is to be treated like an ordinary commercial promise, and accordingly that the successful plaintiff is entitled to a standard measure of recovery for breach of contract—"compensatory" ("expectancy") damages, an amount intended to put the plaintiff in the position he would be in if the contract had been performed, or, presumably, at the plaintiff's election, "restitution" damages, an amount corresponding to any benefit conferred by the plaintiff upon the defendant in the performance of the contract disrupted by the defendant's breach. See Restatement § 329 and

---

[2] Judicial skepticism about whether a promise was in fact made derives also from the possibility that the truth has been tortured to give the plaintiff the advantage of the longer period of limitations sometimes available for actions on contract as distinguished from those in tort or for malpractice. See Lillich, *The Malpractice Statute of Limitations in New York and Other Jurisdictions*, 47 Cornell L. Q. 339; annotation, 80 A.L.R.2d 368.

comment a, §§ 347, 384(1). Thus in *Hawkins v. McGee*, 84 N.H. 114, the defendant doctor was taken to have promised the plaintiff to convert his damaged hand by means of an operation into a good or perfect hand, but the doctor so operated as to damage the hand still further. The court, following the usual expectancy formula, would have asked the jury to estimate and award to the plaintiff the difference between the value of a good or perfect hand, as promised, and the value of the hand after the operation. (The same formula would apply, although the dollar result would be less, if the operation had neither worsened nor improved the condition of the hand.) If the plaintiff had not yet paid the doctor his fee, that amount would be deducted from the recovery. There could be no recovery for the pain and suffering of the operation, since that detriment would have been incurred even if the operation had been successful; one can say that this detriment was not "caused" by the breach. But where the plaintiff by reason of the operation was put to more pain than he would have had to endure, had the doctor performed as promised, he should be compensated for that difference as a proper part of his expectancy recovery. It may be noted that on an alternative count for malpractice the plaintiff in the *Hawkins* case had been nonsuited; but on ordinary principles this could not affect the contract claim, for it is hardly a defense to a breach of contract that the promisor acted innocently and without negligence. The New Hampshire court further refined the *Hawkins* analysis in *McQuaid v. Michou*, 85 N.H. 299, all in the direction of treating the patient-physician cases on the ordinary footing of expectancy. See McGee v. United States Fid. & Guar. Co., 53 F.2d 953 (1st Cir.) (later development in the *Hawkins* case) * * *

Other cases, including a number in New York, without distinctly repudiating the *Hawkins* type of analysis, have indicated that a different and generally more lenient measure of damages is to be applied in patient-physician actions based on breach of alleged special agreements to effect a cure, attain a stated result, or employ a given medical method. This measure is expressed in somewhat variant ways, but the substance is that the plaintiff is to recover any expenditures made by him and for other detriment (usually not specifically described in the opinions) following proximately and foreseeably upon the defendant's failure to carry out his promise. . . . This, be it noted, is not a "restitution" measure, for it is not limited to restoration of the benefit conferred on the defendant (the fee paid) but includes other expenditures, for example, amounts paid for medicine and nurses; so also it would seem according to its logic to take in damages for any worsening of the plaintiff's condition due to the breach. Nor is it an "expectancy" measure, for it does not appear to contemplate recovery of the whole difference in value between the condition as promised and the condition actually resulting from the treatment. Rather the tendency of the formulation is to put the plaintiff back in the position he occupied just before the parties entered upon the agreement, to compensate him for the detriments he suffered in reliance upon the agreement. This kind of intermediate pattern of recovery for breach of contract is discussed in the suggestive article by Fuller and Perdue, *The Reliance Interest in Contract Damages*, 46 Yale L.J. 52, 373, where the authors show that, although not attaining the currency of the standard measures, a "reliance" measure has for special reasons been applied by the courts in a variety of settings, including noncommercial settings. See 46 Yale L.J. at 396–401.[4]

For breach of the patient-physician agreements under consideration, a recovery limited to restitution seems plainly too meager, if the agreements are to be enforced at all. On the other hand, an expectancy recovery may well be excessive. The factors, already mentioned, which have made the cause of action somewhat suspect, also suggest moderation as to the breadth of the recovery that should be permitted. Where, as in the case at bar and in a number of the reported cases, the doctor has been absolved of negligence by the trier, an expectancy measure may be thought harsh. We should recall here that the fee paid by the patient to the doctor for the alleged promise would usually be quite disproportionate to the putative expectancy recovery. To attempt, moreover, to put a value on the condition that would or might have resulted, had the treatment succeeded as promised, may sometimes put an exceptional strain on the imagination of the fact finder. As a general consideration, Fuller and Perdue argue that the reasons for granting damages for broken promises to the extent of the expectancy are at their strongest when the promises are made in a business context, when they have to do with the production or distribution of goods or the allocation of functions in the market place; they become weaker as the context shifts from a commercial to a noncommercial field. 46 Yale L.J. at 60–63.

There is much to be said, then, for applying a reliance measure to the present facts, and we have only to add that our cases are not unreceptive to the use of that formula in special situations. We have, however, had no previous occasion to apply it to patient-physician cases.[5]

---

[4]   Some of the exceptional situations mentioned where reliance may be preferred to expectancy are those in which the latter measure would be hard to apply or would impose too great a burden; performance was interfered with by external circumstances; the contract was indefinite. See 46 Yale L.J. at 373–386; 394–396.

[5]   In *Mt. Pleasant Stable Co. v. Steinberg*, 238 Mass. 567, the plaintiff company agreed to supply teams of horses at agreed rates as required from day to day by the defendant for his business. To prepare itself to fulfill the contract and in reliance on it, the plaintiff bought two "Cliest" horses at a certain price. When the defendant repudiated the contract, the plaintiff sold the horses at a loss and in its action for breach claimed the loss as an element of damages. The court properly held that the plaintiff was not entitled to this item as it was also claiming (and recovering) its lost profits (expectancy) on the contract as a whole. Cf. *Noble v. Ames Mfg. Co.*, 112 Mass. 492. (The loss on sale of the horses is analogous to the pain and suffering for which the patient would be disallowed a recovery in *Hawkins v. McGee* because he was claiming and recovering expectancy damages.) The court in the *Mt. Pleasant* case referred, however, to *Pond v. Harris*, 113 Mass. 114, as a contrasting situation where the expectancy could not be fairly determined. There the defendant had wrongfully revoked an agreement to arbitrate a dispute with the plaintiff (this was before such agreements were made specifically enforceable). In an action for the breach, the plaintiff was held entitled to recover for his preparations for the arbitration which had been rendered useless and a waste, including the plaintiff's time and trouble and his expenditures for counsel and witnesses. The context apparently was commercial but reliance elements were held compensable when there was no fair way of estimating an

The question of recovery on a reliance basis for pain and suffering or mental distress requires further attention. We find expressions in the decisions that pain and suffering (or the like) are simply not compensable in actions for breach of contract. The defendant seemingly espouses this proposition in the present case. True, if the buyer under a contract for the purchase of a lot of merchandise, in suing for the seller's breach, should claim damages for mental anguish caused by his disappointment in the transaction, he would not succeed; he would be told, perhaps, that the asserted psychological injury was not fairly foreseeable by the defendant as a probable consequence of the breach of such a business contract. See Restatement: Contracts, § 341, and comment a. But there is no general rule barring such items of damage in actions for breach of contract. It is all a question of the subject matter and background of the contract, and when the contract calls for an operation on the person of the plaintiff, psychological as well as physical injury may be expected to figure somewhere in the recovery, depending on the particular circumstances. The point is explained in *Stewart v. Rudner*, 349 Mich. 459, 469. . . . Again, it is said in a few of the New York cases, concerned with the classification of actions for statute of limitations purposes, that the absence of allegations demanding recovery for pain and suffering is characteristic of a contract claim by a patient against a physician, that such allegations rather belong in a claim for malpractice. . . . These remarks seem unduly sweeping.

Suffering or distress resulting from the breach going beyond that which was envisaged by the treatment as agreed, should be compensable on the same ground as the worsening of the patient's condition because of the breach. Indeed it can be argued that the very suffering or distress "contracted for"—that which would have been incurred if the treatment achieved the promised result—should also be compensable on the theory underlying the New York cases. For that suffering is "wasted" if the treatment fails. Otherwise stated, compensation for this waste is arguably required in order to complete the restoration of the *status quo ante*.[6]

---

expectancy. See, generally, annotation, 17 A.L.R.2d 1300. A noncommercial example is *Smith v. Sherman*, 4 Cush. 408, 413–414, suggesting that a conventional recovery for breach of promise of marriage included a recompense for various efforts and expenditures by the plaintiff preparatory to the promised wedding. . . .

[6] Recovery on a reliance basis for breach of the physician's promise tends to equate with the usual recovery for malpractice, since the latter also looks in general to restoration of the condition before the injury. But this is not paradoxical, especially when it is noted that the origins of contract lie in tort. See Farnsworth, *The Past of Promise: An Historical Introduction to Contract*, 69 Col. L. Rev. 576, 594–596; Breitel, J. in Stella Flour & Feed Corp. v. National City Bank, 285 App.Div. 182, 189, 136 N.Y.S.2d 139 (dissenting opinion). A few cases have considered possible recovery for breach by a physician of a promise to sterilize a patient, resulting in birth of a child to the patient and spouse. If such an action is held maintainable, the reliance and expectancy measures would, we think, tend to equate, because the promised condition was preservation of the family status quo. . . .

It would, however, be a mistake to think in terms of strict "formulas." For example, a jurisdiction which would apply a reliance measure to the present facts might impose a more severe damage

In the light of the foregoing discussion, all the defendant's exceptions fail; the plaintiff was not confined to the recovery of her out-of-pocket expenditures; she was entitled to recover also for the worsening of her condition,[7] and for the pain and suffering and mental distress involved in the third operation. These items were compensable on either an expectancy or a reliance view. We might have been required to elect between the two views if the pain and suffering connected with the first two operations contemplated by the agreement, or the whole difference in value between the present and the promised conditions, were being claimed as elements of damage. But the plaintiff waives her possible claim to the former element, and to so much of the latter as represents the difference in value between the promised condition and the condition before the operations.

Plaintiff's exceptions waived.

Defendant's exceptions overruled.

NOTES

(1) In the absence of an enforceable promise to achieve a particular result, to what standard is the doctor held in performing the surgery? In general, the law does not require perfect results, but rather the exercise of that skill and judgment which can reasonably be expected from similarly situated professionals. See Note, *Contorts: Patrolling the Borderland of Contract and Tort in Legal Malpractice Actions*, 22 B.C. L. Rev. 545 (1981). How is it that the plaintiff in *Sullivan* lost her malpractice claim but won on breach of contract?

(2) As the court indicates, promises to achieve particular results by doctors and other providers of professional services are rare. But are the promises themselves against public policy? Why might one worry about the legal enforcement of such promises? How does the court in *Sullivan* address those worries?

(3) *Burden of Proof?* Six years after *Sullivan* was decided, the Massachusetts Supreme Court clarified the "clear proof" standard:

"Clear proof" does not require proof of special consideration for the promise nor does it heighten the burden of proof. What it does require is that the trier of fact give attention to particular factors in deciding whether the physician made a statement which, in the context of the relationship, could have been reasonably interpreted by the patient as a promise that a given result or cure would be achieved. The factors relevant in such an appraisal and their respective values or weights will vary with the circumstances of given cases. Some of the possible factors are noted in the Sullivan

---

sanction for the wilful use by the physician of a method of operation that he undertook not to employ.

[7] That condition involves a mental element and appraisal of it properly called for consideration of the fact that the plaintiff was an entertainer. Cf. McQuaid v. Michou, 85 N.H. 299, 303–304 (discussion of continuing condition resulting from physician's breach).

case. It should be regarded as a negative factor, although one not in itself determinative, that the physician and patient did not focus on the question whether the physician was undertaking to achieve a given result. The trier of fact should not adopt a relaxed attitude that might subject a physician to liability for making statements reasonably calculated only to reassure a patient or, as in this case, for stating the significant consequences that could be expected to follow upon a successful surgical procedure.

Clevenger v. Haling, 379 Mass. 154, 158–59 (1979) (footnote omitted). Does this clarify matters?

(4) *Protected Interests of the Promisee.* Comment (a) to First Restatement § 329 states simply: "In awarding compensatory damages, the effort is made to put the injured party in as good a position as that in which he would have been put by full performance of the contract, at the least cost to the defendant and without charging him with harms that he had no sufficient reason to foresee when he made the contract."

Restatement (Second) § 344 describes the "purposes" of contract remedies as follows:

Judicial remedies under the rules stated in this Restatement serve to protect one or more of the following interests of a promisee:

(a) his "expectation interest," which is his interest in having the benefit of his bargain by being put in as good a position as he would have been in had the contract been performed,

(b) his "reliance interest," which is his interest in being reimbursed for loss caused by reliance on the contract by being put in as good a position as he would have been in had the contract not been made, or

(c) his "restitution interest," which is his interest in having restored to him any benefit that he has conferred on the other party.

The court in *Sullivan* identified these three interests of the promisee that might be protected upon breach by the promisor: expectation, reliance, and restitution. Why did the court suggest that Ms. Sullivan's expectation interest might not be protected? Which expenditures of Ms. Sullivan fit into her restitution interest? Her reliance interest? How would you classify a claim for pain and suffering or mental anguish caused by the breach?

(5) *Why Protect the Expectation Interest?* Why should contract remedies protect the expectation interest? Why not limit recovery to reliance or restitution?

One set of reasons involves the perceived need to support efficient exchange in competitive markets. Protecting expectations (1) rewards risk-taking in market transactions and, therefore, contributes to allocative efficiency, and (2) deters inefficient breach, i.e., a breach where the value derived when the breaching party re-deploys resources committed to the contract is equaled or exceeded by the loss to the promisee. Put affirmatively, when contract law clearly protects the expectation interest, the parties can plan more effectively at the time of contracting, and the breaching party has a reason to assess at the time of breach whether the gains from breach will exceed the costs to the aggrieved party. See Charles Goetz and Robert E. Scott, *Enforcing Promises: An Examination of the Basis of Contract,* 89 Yale L.J. 1261 (1980). The assumption here is that the efficient breach is a good thing, so long as the expectation interest of the aggrieved party is fully protected. There are, of course, skeptics. See, e.g., Seana Valentine Shiffrin, *The Divergence of Contract and Promise*, 120 Harv. L. Rev. 708 (2007); David Friedmann, *The Efficient Breach Fallacy,* 18 J. Legal Stud. 1 (1989); Ian R. Macneil, *Efficient Breach of Contract: Circles in the Sky,* 68 Va. L. Rev. 947 (1982).

Another set of reasons involves the asserted need to protect the reliance interest. The argument is that proof of reliance, whether by action or forbearance, is often costly and uncertain. There is a real risk that reliance which is hidden in opportunities foregone by the promisee will not be compensated. The solution is to award expectation damages, when provable with reasonable certainty, as a surrogate for accurate measurement of reliance. Thus, expectation recovery is viewed as an outer limit of recovery for actual but unprovable costs incurred and opportunities foregone in reliance on the promise. See Melvin A. Eisenberg, *The Bargain Principle and Its Limits,* 95 Harv. L. Rev. 741, 785–98 (1982); L.L. Fuller and William R. Perdue, Jr., *The Reliance Interest in Contract Damages: 1,* 46 Yale L.J. 52, 60–61 (1936).

Are these reasons persuasive? Can you think of other reasons why the law might want to protect the expectation interest?

(6) *Two Meanings of "Restitution."* Courts and commentators use the term "restitution" in two distinct senses. Sometimes, as in *Sullivan v. O'Connor*, the word is used to describe a measure of damages, namely, the value of a benefit conferred. Restitution in this sense is distinguished from both the reliance and the expectation measures. At other times, as in *Bailey v. West*, "restitution" is used to denote a distinct cause of action, also termed "quasi-contract" or "unjust enrichment." If a plaintiff does not have a suit in contract, she might nonetheless succeed in an action for restitution.

(7) *Restitution vs. Disgorgement.* Restitution requires that the party in breach return of any benefit it received from the nonbreaching party. But what about other profits it might earn from breach?

Suppose A runs an iron smelting plant and contracts to sell B its entire output for the month of January at a price of $55 per ton, delivery on February 5. A produces 10,000 tons of iron in January, but on February 5, rather than delivering it to B, A sells the iron to C for $65 per ton. B needs the iron for its manufacturing processes, and so contracts with another supplier to purchase 10,000 tons for $60 per ton. The expectation measure would require that A pay B $50,000 plus any incidental expenses, the amount necessary to compensate B for the extra $5 per ton B had to pay for the iron. But by selling to C, A has earned $100,000 more than it would have under its contract with B. *Disgorgement* would require A to turn all of those profits over to B.

If the reliance measure aims to return the nonbreaching party to the position she would have occupied had the contract never been made, and the expectation measure aims to return the nonbreaching party to the position she would have occupied had the contract been performed, what might be the aim of disgorgement?

PROBLEM: THE OVEN CASES—AN INTRODUCTION TO ARTICLE TWO REMEDIES

Smirgo, Inc., a manufacturer of bakery equipment, specializes in custom ovens. Bisko, Inc. operates a medium-sized bakery in a highly competitive market and sells primarily to restaurants, hotels, and other institutional buyers.

On May 15, Bisko's researchers informed the president that a new kind of bread had been developed for the institutional trade. It was described as "revolutionary" and "likely to sell like hotcakes." The board of directors decided to purchase two new custom ovens and make a concerted effort to expand the business. At this time, Bisko policymakers knew that Caraway Co., a competitor, was working on the development of a similar kind of bread but had no idea what progress had been made.

On June 1, Smirgo and Bisko entered a written contract for the manufacture and sale of two ovens custom-made to bake the new bread. The basic design was supplied by Bisko engineers. The agreed price was $30,000, to be paid in full 90 days after Smirgo had delivered both ovens to Bisko on the promised delivery date, November 1. "Although Smirgo and Bisko had done business before, this was their first contract for custom ovens. At the time the contract was signed, the president of Smirgo was informed that the "ovens will be used in a business expansion," "prompt delivery is critical," and "we have a new product coming out." After the contract was signed, Bisko spent $7,500 in readying its plant for the new ovens.

(1) On November 1, Smirgo loaded the two ovens onto a company truck and drove to Bisko's bakery. After Smirgo arrived, Bisko informed Smirgo that it would not accept the ovens. The bread market was depressed, and Bisko no longer wanted to expand the business. Smirgo comes to you for advice. Can Smirgo recover the contract price from Bisko under Article 2 of the UCC? If not, what other remedies are available? Study the remedy options in UCC § 2–703, and explore the possibilities in §§ 2–704 through 2–710. What formulas would a court calculate damages for Bisko's breach under §§ 2–706(1), 2–708(1) and 2–709(1)? What must the seller prove and/or do to recover under each? Do the damage measures described in these sections protect Smirgo's restitution, reliance or expectation interests?

(2) Suppose, instead, that on November 1, the time agreed for delivery, Smirgo informed Bisko that while the new ovens were completed, they would not be delivered unless Bisko paid $30,000 cash. There was no justification for this demand; it was clearly a breach of contract since a 90-day credit term had been agreed upon. On November 2, Bisko discovered that there were three custom oven manufacturers within a hundred-mile radius that would manufacture the custom-made ovens at an average price of $29,500. The

estimated time of delivery was in six months, however, and no business concern had the type of oven Bisko needed in stock. On November 3, Caraway Co. announced that it was marketing a new bread almost identical to that developed by Bisko. The next day, the Bisko sales manager informed the president that unless the ovens were obtained within ten days, Bisko would lose an estimated $20,000 in profits on six long-term contracts already made and an estimated $100,000 in profits on contracts under negotiation but not yet signed. During the past five years, Bisko's net profits have averaged $100,000 per year.

On the afternoon of November 4, the president of Bisko came to you for legal advice. Assume that Smirgo is in breach of contract and that the Uniform Commercial Code governs this case. Based upon an analysis of UCC Article 2, Part 7, §§ 2–711 through 2–717 and the business situation described, what would you advise Bisko to do? Go as far as you can with the relevant statutory provisions. What formulas would a court calculate damages for Bisko's breach under §§ 2–712(2) and 2–713(1)? Again, do the UCC damage measures described protect the nonbreaching party's restitution, reliance or expectation interests?

Comment: The Uniform Commercial Code and the Sale of Goods

Article 2 of the Uniform Commercial Code is designed to govern (when enacted by a state legislature) all contracts for the sale of goods. UCC § 2–102. Section 2–105(1) defines "goods" as follows:

> "Goods" means all things (including specially manufactured goods) which are movable at the time of identification to the contract for sale other than the money in which the price is to be paid, investment securities (Article 8) and things in action. "Goods" also includes the unborn young of animals and growing crops and other identified things attached to realty as described in the section on goods to be severed from realty (§ 2–107).

Section 2–107 describes when the sale of minerals, crops or other products attached to realty qualifies as a sale of goods. Section 2–106(1) provides that "[a] 'sale' consists in the passing of title from the seller to the buyer for a price."

Some contracts involve both the sale of goods and the provision of non-goods. A contractor renovating a house, for example, might agree to provide many goods (materials, fixtures, appliances, etc.) as well as services (construction work). Courts have held that when a contract involves both goods and services, goods and real property or some other mixture, the UCC applies only if the goods are the "predominant factor." The Eighth Circuit describes the test as follows:

> The test for inclusion or exclusion is not whether they are mixed, but, granting that they are mixed, whether their predominant factor, their thrust, their purpose, reasonably stated, is the rendition of service, with goods incidentally involved (e.g.,

contract with artist for painting) or is a transaction of sale, with labor incidentally involved (e.g., installation of a water heater in a bathroom).

Bonebrake v. Cox, 499 F.2d 951, 960 (8th Cir. 1974).

The Uniform Commercial Code is not designed to replace all of the common law of contract in its areas of application. Thus section 1–103(b) provides that the common law of contract shall supplement the provisions of the UCC where the common law's rules are not "displaced by the particular provisions of [the Code]." The section mentions as examples of non-displaced common law rules the rules governing "capacity to contract, principal and agent, estoppel, fraud, misrepresentation, duress, coercion, mistake, bankruptcy, and other validating or invalidating cause."

As we discussed in Section 1.B of this Chapter, the primary drafter of the UCC was Karl Llewellyn, a member of the legal realist school. Llewellyn and the other drafters did not feel beholden to the existing law, and the UCC departs from the common law in many significant respects. Individual differences are noted throughout this book. The UCC also includes some systematic innovations, both in substance and style. Three bear special mention.

First, whereas the common law of contract does not generally apply different rules to different types of parties, many sections of the Code provide separate rules for merchants and for non-merchants.[38] Section 2–201's rule for when a contract must be in writing, for example, makes it easier to enforce an oral contract against a merchant than against a non-merchant. Section 2–205 provides that a merchant's written firm offer is enforceable without consideration, with no similar rule for non-merchants. And section 2–207 allows terms to enter a contract between merchants even when one side has not expressly agreed to them, whereas consumer contracts require assent to such terms. The definition of "merchant" can be found in section 2–104(1):

> "Merchant" means a person who deals in goods of the kind or otherwise by his occupation holds himself out as having knowledge or skill peculiar to the practices or goods involved in the transaction or to whom such knowledge or skill may be attributed by his employment of an agent or broker or other intermediary who by his occupation holds himself out as having such knowledge or skill.

For the student of the UCC, what all this means is that it is important to pay attention to whether any given UCC rule applies to all transactions, to only transactions between merchants or to only transactions involving a non-merchant.

---

[38] See generally Ingrid M. Hillinger, *The Article 2 Merchant Rules: Karl Llewellyn's Attempt to Achieve the Good, the True, the Beautiful in Commercial Law*, 73 Geo. L.J. 1141 (1985).

Second, there is the Code's attempt to integrate contemporary business practices or customs into the law. As Llewellyn explained in a comment to an early draft of Article 2, "the intention of this Act is to use the standards not of past decisions but of current commerce."[39] Section 2–103(1)(b), for example, defines "good faith" in transactions between merchants to mean "honesty in fact and the observance of reasonable commercial standards of fair dealing in the trade." And section 2–202(b) provides that the terms of a written agreement "may be explained or supplemented by . . . usage of trade," which is "any practice or method of dealing having such regularity of observance in a place, vocation, or trade as to justify an expectation that it will be observed." UCC § 1–303(c). Some scholars have criticized this approach, arguing that business custom is too indeterminate and difficult to verify to serve as an effective legal standard.[40]

Finally, unlike most statutes, the UCC is designed to invite judges to take something like a common law approach when applying it. Richard Danzig describes the approach as follows:

> Article II is rife with such open-ended words (none of them referred to in the definitional section) as "reasonable time," "reasonable medium," "reasonable grounds," even "reasonable price," "reasonable value," "fair and reasonable cause," and "material alter[ation]," as well as the notorious "unconscionability." The use of generalized guides to decision (for example, custom and usage) and open-ended terms (reasonableness, good faith, unconscionability), the injection of "official commentary" declaring the intent of the drafters, and, above all, the scarcity of provisions explicit enough to be applied without a consideration of circumstance, compel a court that would use the Code to move beyond the literalism of "mechanical jurisprudence."[41]

As a result, even if a case is governed by a UCC provision, it is often necessary to look to past judicial decisions to determine exactly what the rule is.

Joseph and Jonah Hadley v. Joseph Baxendale

Court of Exchequer, 1854.
9 Exch. 341.

* * * [T]he plaintiffs carried on an extensive business as millers at Gloucester and. . .on the 11th of May, their mill was stopped by a breakage of the crank shaft by which the mill was worked. The steam-

---

[39] Uniform Revised Sales Act § 99(2), Comment (Proposed Final Draft No. 1, 1944). See generally Richard Danzig, *A Comment on the Jurisprudence of the Uniform Commercial Code*, 27 Stan. L. Rev. 621 (1975).

[40] See, e.g., Lisa Bernstein, *Merchant Law in a Merchant Court: Rethinking the Code's Search for Immanent Business Norms*, 144 U. Pa. L. Rev. 1765 (1996).

[41] Danzig, *A Comment*, supra p. 41, n. 39 at 634 (footnotes omitted).

engine was manufactured by Messrs. Joyce & Co., the engineers, at Greenwich, and it became necessary to send the shaft as a pattern for a new one to Greenwich. The fracture was discovered on the 12th, and on the 13th the plaintiffs sent one of their servants to the office of the defendants, who are the well-known carriers trading under the name of Pickford & Co., for the purpose of having the shaft carried to Greenwich. The plaintiffs' servant told. . .the clerk that the mill was stopped, and that the shaft must be sent immediately; and in answer to the inquiry when the shaft would be taken, the answer was, that if it was sent up by twelve o'clock any day, it would be delivered at Greenwich on the following day. On the following day the shaft was taken by the defendants, before noon, for the purpose of being conveyed to Greenwich, and the sum of £2, 4s. was paid for its carriage for the whole distance; at the same time the defendants' clerk was told that a special entry, if required, should be made to hasten its delivery. The delivery of the shaft at Greenwich was delayed by some neglect; and the consequence was, that the plaintiffs did not receive the new shaft for several days after they would otherwise have done, and the working of their mill was thereby delayed, and they thereby lost the profits they would otherwise have received.

On the part of the defendants, it was objected that these damages were too remote, and that the defendants were not liable with respect to them. The learned Judge left the case generally to the jury, who found a verdict with £25 damages beyond the amount paid into Court.

Whateley, in last Michaelmas Term, obtained a rule *nisi* for a new trial on the ground of misdirection.

* * *

■ ALDERSON, B. We think that there ought to be a new trial in this case; but, in so doing, we deem it to be expedient and necessary to state explicitly the rule which the Judge, at the next trial, ought, in our opinion, to direct the jury to be governed by when they estimate the damages.

It is, indeed, of the last importance that we should do this; for, if the jury are left without any definite rule to guide them, it will in such cases as these, manifestly lead to the greatest injustice.

* * *

Now we think the proper rule in such [a case] as the present is this:— Where two parties have made a contract which one of them has broken, the damages which the other party ought to receive in respect of such breach of contract should be such as may fairly and reasonably be considered either arising naturally, i.e., according to the usual course of things, from such breach of contract itself, or such as may reasonably be supposed to have been in the contemplation of both parties, at the time they made the contract, as the probable result of the breach of it. Now, if the special circumstances under which the contract was actually made were communicated by the plaintiffs to the defendants, and thus known to both parties, the damages resulting from the breach of such a contract, which they would reasonably contemplate, would be the amount of injury which would ordinarily follow from a breach of contract under these special circumstances so known and communicated. But, on the other hand, if these special circumstances were wholly unknown to the party breaking the contract, he, at the most, could only be supposed to have had in his contemplation the amount of injury which would arise generally, and in the great multitude of cases not affected by any special circumstances, from such a breach of contract. For, had the special circumstances been known, the parties might have specially provided for the breach of contract by special terms as to the damages in that case; and of this advantage it would be very unjust to deprive them. Now the above principles are those by which we think the jury ought to be guided in estimating the damages arising out of any breach of contract. It is said, that other cases such as breaches of contract in the non-payment of money, or in the not making a good title to land, are to be treated as exceptions from this, and as governed by a conventional rule. But as, in such cases, both parties must be supposed to be cognizant of that well-known rule, these cases may, we think, be more properly classed under the rule above enunciated as to cases under known special circumstances, because there both parties may reasonably be presumed to contemplate the estimation of the amount of damages according to the conventional rule.

Now, in the present case, if we are to apply the principles above laid down, we find that the only circumstances here communicated by the plaintiffs to the defendants at the time the contract was made, were, that the article to be carried was the broken shaft of a mill, and that the plaintiffs were the millers of that mill. But how do these circumstances shew reasonably that the profits of the mill must be stopped by an unreasonable delay in the delivery of the broken shaft by the carrier to the third person? Suppose the plaintiffs had another shaft in their possession put up or putting up at the time, and that they only wished to send back the broken shaft to the engineer who made it; it is clear that this would be quite consistent with the above circumstances, and yet the unreasonable delay in the delivery would have no effect upon the intermediate profits of the mill. Or, again, suppose that, at the time of the delivery to the carrier, the machinery of the mill had been in other respects defective, then, also the same results would follow. Here it is true that the shaft was actually sent back to serve as a model for a new one, and that the want of a new one was the only cause of the stoppage of the mill, and that the loss of profits really arose from not sending down the new shaft in proper time, and that this arose from the delay in delivering the broken one to serve as a model. But it is obvious that, in the great multitude of cases of millers sending off broken shafts to third persons by a carrier under ordinary circumstances, such consequences would not, in all probability, have occurred; and these special circumstances were here never communicated by the plaintiffs to the defendants. It follows, therefore, that the loss of profits here cannot reasonably be considered such a consequence of the breach of contract as could have been fairly and reasonably contemplated by both the parties when they made this contract. For such loss would neither have flowed naturally from the breach of this contract in the great multitude of such cases occurring under ordinary circumstances, nor were the special circumstances, which, perhaps, would have made it a reasonable and natural consequence of such breach of contract, communicated to or known by the defendants. The Judge ought, therefore, to have told the jury, that, upon the facts then before them, they ought not to take the loss of profits into consideration at all in estimating the damages. There must therefore be a new trial in this case.

Rule absolute.

A modern photograph of the Hadley City Flour Mills

NOTES

(1) The losses claimed in *Hadley v. Baxendale* are termed "consequential" because they were the downstream effects of the defendant's failure to perform, i.e., its failure to ship the mill shaft on the day promised. Why did the court deny recovery for these consequential losses? Suppose that the losses could be proved with reasonable certainty, that the breach unquestionably caused them, and that the plaintiff made every reasonable effort to mitigate the losses by finding a spare shaft. Same result?

(2) *The* Hadley *Rule in the United States.* Courts in the United States generally follow the rule set forth in *Hadley v. Baxendale.* Thus Restatement (Second) § 351 provides in pertinent part:

(1) Damages are not recoverable for loss that the party in breach did not have reason to foresee as a probable result of the breach when the contract was made.

(2) Loss may be foreseeable as a probable result of a breach because it follows from the breach (a) in the ordinary course of events, or (b) as a result of special circumstances, beyond the ordinary course of events, that the party in breach had reason to know.

Cf. UCC 2–715(2) (allowing buyer consequential damages for losses about which seller "had reason to know and could not reasonably be prevented by cover or otherwise"). Some U.S. jurisdictions have experimented with other rules. In *Globe Refining Co. v. Landa Cotton Oil Co.*, Justice Holmes wrote that "mere notice to a seller of some interest or probable action of the buyer is not enough necessarily and as matter of law to charge the seller with special damage on that account if he fails to deliver the goods." 190 U.S. 540, 545 (1903). In addition, Holmes held, the defendant must at least have tacitly agreed to be liable for the loss at issue. Id. Most U.S. courts and commentators today reject the *Globe Refining* test. It is enough that the defendant foresaw or had reason to foresee the losses at issue.

(3) The plaintiff in *Hadley v. Baxendale* would have preferred to be able to recover its lost profits for the time the factory was closed down. Is this the rule that most customers of Pickford & Co., the shipper, would want? Before you answer, think about what effect the anti-*Hadley* rule would likely have on Pickford & Co.'s prices.

The FedEx form contract in effect at the time of this book's publication provides: "With respect to U.S. express package services, unless a higher value is declared and paid for, our liability for each package is limited to US$100. For each package exceeding US$100 in declared value, an additional amount will be charged." What is the benefit to consumers?

(4) *Who Told What to Whom?* Careful readers might wonder why the reporter's headnote states that "[t]he plaintiff's servant told the clerk that the mill was stopped," whereas Baron Alderson concluded "the only circumstances here communicated by the plaintiffs to the defendants . . . were, that the article to be carried was the broken shaft of a mill, and that the plaintiffs were the millers of that mill." James Oldham, based on his extensive knowledge of judicial procedure during that period, argues that the reporter probably did not misreport the facts. Sir Charles Crompton, the trial judge, "was reputedly a meticulous judge who took painstaking care with the facts of his case," and would have sent to the appellate court a detailed report of those facts. That report would have been read out in court and perhaps even given to the court reporter. James Oldham, *Detecting Non-Fiction: Sleuthing among Manuscript Case Reports for What was Really Said, in* Law Reporting in England 133, 139–40 (C. Stebbings, ed. 1995).

So was Baron Alderson just making things up when he suggested that the plaintiff did not tell the defendant that the mill was in fact stopped? Richard Danzig argues that the incongruity can be explained by "an uncertainty in the rudimentary law of agency as it existed at the time." In short, in 1854 it was unclear whether telling the clerk was the equivalent of telling the company.

> This uncertainty may explain Baron Alderson's surprising assertion that the Hadleys failed to serve notice that the mill operations were dependent on the quick return of the shaft. It may be that as a factual matter the Hadleys never served notice on the PIckfords' clerk of their extreme dependence on the shaft, and the Court reporter simply erred in asserting that notice had been served to this effect. But it is also possible that Baron Alderson saw the case as the Pickford's counsel urged: ". . . a mere notice . . . was here given . . . [but it] could not make the defendants liable . . . [and therefore it was to] be rejected from the consideration of the question."

Richard Danzig, Hadley v. Baxendale: *A Study in the Industrialization of the Law*, 4 J. Legal Stud. 249, 262–63 (1975).

PROBLEM: THE CASE OF THE CLATTERING CANDIDATE

Bloat Novelties, in business since 1944, makes magic tricks, gags and other novelty products. Slothrop Computing manufactures and sells programmable microchips. In the fall of 2011, Bloat's design team came up with a new product: the Clattering Candidate, a set of wind-up chattering plastic teeth with a microchip that could be programmed to play a political candidate's voice as the teeth chattered. Based on market tests, Bloat decided to produce a run of 10,000 teeth to sell during the 2012 election cycle.

In April 2012, Bloat and Slothrop entered into a contract under which Slothrop was to supply Bloat with 10,000 custom programmable microchips for use in the Clattering Candidate. Delivery of the microchips was to be on or before July 1, with the contract specifying that time was of the essence. The contract price was $5,000 with 40% to be paid within two weeks of the contract execution and 60% due 30 days after delivery. The parties signed the contract on April 2. On April 9, Bloat made the agreed-upon $2,000 payment to Slothrop.

On June 20, Slothrop informed Bloat that due to a fire at its factory and warehouse, Slothrop would not be able to deliver the microchips. Bloat contacted ten other chip manufactures. None were able to provide microchips before October—too late to get the Clattering Candidate to market before the November election.

Bloat sued Slothrop for breach of contract. The evidence at trial showed that between April and June 2012, Bloat invested $15,000 promoting the Clattering Candidate and $7,000 reconfiguring its factory to produce the product. By July 1, Bloat had received non-binding pre-orders for 5,000 Clattering Candidates. Bloat showed based on past sales that, with so many pre-orders, it would easily have sold the entire run of Clattering Candidates. Taking into account the costs of materials, manufacturing and overhead, Bloat expected to earn $1.50 in profit on each Clattering Candidate it sold.

Suppose Bloat wins its suit against Slothrop. Ignoring for the moment the UCC's more detailed remedial provisions, what would Bloat recover under the restitution, reliance and expectation measures? Based on your reading of *Hadley v. Baxendale*, are there any defenses that Slothrop might explore?

Comment: Default Rules, Altering Rules and Mandatory Rules

The effect of many of the rules that you will study in this course can be altered by agreement of the parties. Such rules that the parties can contract around are often called "default" or "gap-filling" rules. Just as word processing software establishes default margins that the user can alter by changing the settings, so contract law provides default rules about what is sufficient to reach an agreement,[42] about the parties' legal obligations under an agreement,[43] and about the legal consequences of a breach of those obligations.[44] Default rules govern when the parties have remained silent—i.e. in the absence of agreements to the contrary.

When a rule is merely a default, it is important to understand the necessary and sufficient requirements for opting out of it, or what are known as "altering" rules. UCC § 2–206(1)(a), for example, establishes the default that an offer invites acceptance "in any manner and by any medium reasonable in the circumstances." The same section provides that the default will obtain "unless otherwise *unambiguously* indicated" by the offeror. The "reasonable medium" rule is the default, and the "unambiguously indicated" requirement provides the altering rule.

Not every contract rule can be contracted around. Those that cannot be changed are termed "mandatory" or "immutable." This distinction between default and mandatory rules is emphasized in the general provisions of Article 1 of the UCC. Section 1–302(a) provides: "Except as otherwise provided [in the UCC], the effect of provisions of [the UCC] may be varied by agreement." Immediately following this, however, section 1–302(b) stipulates that "[t]he obligations of good faith, diligence, reasonableness, and care . . . may not be disclaimed by agreement."

In learning the rules of contract, it is therefore essential to identify (i) *whether* particular rules can be contracted around and (ii) if so, *how* private parties might opt for an alternative to the legal default. Indeed, a worthwhile exercise after reading each case is to consider what contractual provisions would be sufficient to reverse the court's decision. If there is no language that could reverse the decision (i.e., if there are no

---

[42] UCC § 2–206(1), for example, provides that "[u]nless otherwise unambiguously indicated by the language or circumstances" an offer to buy goods invites acceptance by either a prompt promise to ship or by shipment itself. The offeror, as master of the offer, can alter this rule by "unambiguously indicating" that only a particular type of acceptance will be effective.

[43] If an agreement for the sale of goods fails to specify a price, for example, the UCC fills this gap by establishing the buyer's obligation to pay "a reasonable price." UCC § 2–305(1).

[44] The UCC remedies for breach by the seller, for example, provide that the buyer can typically recover for consequential losses. UCC §§ 2–712(2), 2–713(1), and 2–714(3). Section 2–719(3) also stipulates, however, that "[c]onsequential damages may be limited or excluded unless the limitation or exclusion is unconscionable."

altering rules for displacing the default obligation), then the court is applying a mandatory rule.

It is also important to think about the policy considerations that are relevant to setting legal defaults and altering rules. How should a court or legislature decide what the parties' obligations are absent an agreement to the contrary, or what they need to do to opt out of that default? One factor is what terms the majority of parties would want. If most parties would prefer the *Hadley* rule, setting it as the interpretive default means that fewer parties will have to take the trouble to contract around it, and courts will more often give parties the terms they want. But these are not the only relevant considerations. Sometimes it might be useful to establish defaults that penalize one or both parties in a way that encourages the parties to provide information by contracting around the default. The *Hadley* rule is arguably also an "information-forcing" default of this type. It gives a party with hidden information about its likely losses in the case of breach a new reason to share that information with the other side. Only by revealing that you are likely to suffer unusual losses in the case of breach will you be able to recover for them.[45]

Mandatory rules are established by both courts and legislatures. Many (though not all!) of the rules of formation that you will study in Chapters Two through Four are mandatory rules. The common law has also established immutable limits, for example, on the maximum amount of damages that parties can contract for (restrictions on so-called liquidated damages) and limits on the maximum length of "covenants not to compete." The duty of good faith is a mandatory part of any agreement, although standards of good faith can within reason be altered by agreement. In the last 60 years, legislative (and administrative) bodies have promulgated a host of immutable rules that restrict freedom of contract. Some types of transactions, such as those concerning insurance and employment, have to a large extent been removed from the general law of contract and subject instead to a host of specific mandatory rules. Since 1964, for example, employers have had an immutable duty not to discriminate on the basis of race or gender when making employment decisions. Many other commercial activities are subject to more limited mandatory rules covering issues such as antitrust, consumer protection, and anti-terrorism.[46] Even the relatively simple construction of a private home is awash with immutable regulatory duties.

---

[45] See Ian Ayres and Robert Gertner, *Filling Gaps in Incomplete Contracts: An Economic Theory of Default Rules*, 99 Yale L.J. 87 (1989) (arguing that "penalty defaults" by inducing explicit contracting might produce valuable information for parties to the agreement or third parties—such as courts). See also Ayres and Gertner, *Majoritarian v. Minoritarian Defaults*, 51 Stan. L. Rev. 1591 (1999).

[46] Some commentators have suggested that the preemption of common-law rules by market-specific statutes and/or by the encroachment of tort has rendered contract law "dead" or transformed it into a residual category. See Grant Gilmore, The Death of Contract (1974); Lawrence M. Friedman, Contract Law in America (1965); Malcom P. Sharp, *The Relevance of Contract Theory: A Symposium*, 1967 Wis. L. Rev. 803 (1967). Others focusing on the default nature of law have characterized contract law as an imperialistic theory swallowing large

In thinking about default and mandatory rules from an economic point of view, Ian Ayres and Robert Gertner have observed:

> a surprising consensus among academics at an abstract level on two normative bases for immutability. Put most simply immutable rules are justifiable if society wants to protect (1) parties within the contract, or (2) parties outside the contract. The former justification turns on parentalism; the latter on externalities. Immutable rules displace freedom of contract. Immutability is justified only if unregulated contracting would be socially deleterious because parties internal or external to the contract cannot adequately protect themselves.[47]

Comment: Enforcement of Money Judgments and Secured Transactions

The successful plaintiff in a breach of contract action will typically obtain a money judgment against the defendant. That judgment establishes a right to compensatory damages for breach of contract, sometimes plus interest and costs. Except where a confession of judgment is authorized or the defendant fails to answer the complaint, judgment will be entered after litigation resolves the dispute.

In most U.S. jurisdictions, the judgment does not order the defendant to pay a particular sum. Rather, it orders that the plaintiff shall recover "of the defendant" the stated sum and have "execution" therefor. If the defendant pays, the matter is settled. If the defendant does not pay, the plaintiff must proceed by the process of execution to obtain satisfaction from the defendant's real and personal property.

Execution involves a number of steps and procedures, the details of which vary from state to state. The basic objectives are to impose by attachment, levy, garnishment or docketing of the judgment, i.e., by operation of law, a lien upon the defendant's non-exempt property and eventually, through the sheriff or other public official, to conduct a public sale, the proceeds of which are used to satisfy the judgment. If the proceeds are sufficient, the judgment is discharged and any excess paid to the defendant. But there can be many a slip between the docketing and satisfaction of a judgment. The defendant may not have any property in the jurisdiction. The sheriff may not be able to find it. Other creditors may have liens with priority. The proceeds from the public sale may be insufficient. Or bankruptcy may intervene. Consumer protection concerns have produced further pressure to limit the traditional rights enjoyed by some creditors. Nevertheless, unless the claim reduced to

---

segments of the legal landscape. See, e.g., John Langbein, *The Contractarian Basis of the Law of Trusts*, 105 Yale L.J. 625, 630 (1995) ("Contract has become the dominant doctrinal current in modern American law. In fields ranging from corporations and partnership to landlord and tenant to servitudes to the law of marriage, scholars have come to understand our legal rules as resting mainly on imputed bargains that are susceptible to alteration by actual bargains.").

[47] Ayres and Gertner, *Filling Gaps*, supra note 45 at 48.

judgment is discharged in bankruptcy, the plaintiff normally has a 20-year renewable period to obtain satisfaction.

These various risks in execution may help explain some of the doctrines of contract law and the practices of business people. For example, one way to avoid the need for enforcement is to demand payment before the goods are delivered. Constructive "concurrent" conditions of exchange implement this non-credit transaction in the absence of agreement to the contrary. Similarly, many business people will extend unsecured credit only if convinced that the buyer is willing and able to pay on time. If substantial doubts exist, credit is not extended, or security is demanded.

Another protection is to obtain a secured interest in performance. Under Article 9 of the UCC, sellers of goods on credit or other lenders can easily create by agreement with the buyer or borrower a security interest in personal property and "perfect" it by filing a financing statement in the appropriate public office. A security interest is an "interest in personal property. . .which secures payment or performance of an obligation." UCC § 1–201(b)(35). The written agreement creating the security interest (called a security agreement) is often accompanied by a negotiable promissory note that evidences the debtor's obligation to pay. See UCC § 3–104. Upon default by the debtor on the note or as defined in the security agreement, the secured party—without suing, obtaining judgment or hiring a sheriff—may privately take possession of the property subject to the security interest, so long as such "repossession" can be done without breach of the peace. (That said, "[a] repo man spends his life getting into tense situations." Repo Man (1984).) The ability to privately take possession without delay or legal expense is the key benefit of a secured interest.

Subject to a limited right of redemption and the possible claims of other lien or secured creditors, the secured creditor will usually sell the repossessed property at a public or private sale. The proceeds of the sale will then be used to reimburse the secured creditor for expenses incurred in repossessing, to satisfy the underlying obligation and to satisfy the security interests of those subordinate to the repossessing creditor. If a surplus exists, it is paid to the debtor. If an inadequate sum is produced, the secured party is entitled to seek a deficiency judgment for the balance due and, in effect, becomes unsecured. The entire process, which can occur without the need for direct intervention by a court or sheriff, is closely regulated by Article 9. For example, any public or private sale must be accomplished in a commercially reasonable manner; basic debtor rights cannot be eroded by agreement with the creditor; and the debtor is given extensive private remedies if the creditor fails to comply with Article 9. Even so, many feel that this protection is inadequate for the consumer. Efforts for reform can be found in the 1997 revision of Article 9 (which has been adopted by every state) and legislation such as the Uniform Consumer Credit Code (which has not been widely adopted). A more extensive treatment of financing patterns and problems where personal property or real estate is involved (whether by mortgage or installment sales contract) must be reserved for another course.

3. STUDIES IN CONTRACT LAW

Positive vs. Normative Jurisprudence. Writing in 1776, Jeremy Bentham—the great legal and moral philosopher whose remains reside in a glass-fronted box at University College London—distinguished two ways of studying the law. "To the province of the Expositor, it belongs to explain to us what, as he supposes, the Law is: to that of the Censor, to observe to us what he thinks it ought to be."[48] The expositor's approach asks what the law is and today is often called "positive jurisprudence." A client typically wants her attorney to act as an expositor. The client has a question like: Is our oral agreement a contract? Does this defective product breach a warranty? What happens if I do not perform? What the client needs is concrete, informed answers about what the law is and how it applies to the client's situation. But it would be a huge mistake to neglect the perspective of the Censor, or what is today termed "normative jurisprudence." The attorney, as an expert in the law, should know not only what the law is, but why it is that way and, if there are problems, how it can be made better. The law is a sprawling mechanism built in part by the lawyers who practice it. The job of a lawyer is not only to use the machine, but also to maintain and improve it.

The judicial decisions in this book include a mix of positive and normative jurisprudence. As we have already emphasized, much of U.S. contract law is common law. It is judge made. When a court—especially an appellate court—decides a contract case, it not only applies the law that already exists. It also further determines what the law is going forward. When a legal question is not yet decided, or when it becomes clear that an old rule no longer serves its purpose, the court's job includes making or remaking the law. Thus in *Sullivan v. O'Connor*, supra, the Massachusetts Supreme Court had to decide whether it made sense to enforce a doctor's promise of a certain result. In *Hadley v. Baxendale*, also supra, the Court of the Exchequer had to decide whether it was best to allow contract plaintiffs to recover for losses the defendant could not have foreseen. The answers to those questions could not be found in the positive law. The issues in these cases concerned not only what the law *was*, but also what it *should be*.

How do we know what contract law should be? What is the metric for determining whether a rule of contract law is good or bad? The answer is contestable and contested. Contract law is part of the warp, and contracts the weft, of the social fabric. Political disagreements about how society should be organized therefore include disagreements about what

---

[48] Jeremy Bentham, *A Fragment on Government* (London 1776), A Comment on the Commentaries and A Fragment on Government (J.H. Burns and H.L.A. Hart, eds.) 393, 397 (1977).

contract law should look like. While some contract rules are relatively uncontested (Should an acceptance be effective when it is dropped in a mailbox or when the offeror receives it?), others are highly charged (Should courts ever look to the fairness of an agreement when deciding whether to enforce it?).

The fact that contract cases can involve fundamental questions about how society should work does not mean that there are not better and worse answers to normative questions about contract law. There is a long and still vibrant tradition of contract jurisprudence that asks what contract law should be. The remainder of this Chapter introduces a few major strands. We begin with some answers to the most fundamental question: Why have contract law at all? We then describe three contemporary approaches to the study of contract law.

(A) WHY CONTRACT LAW?

Why does the law enforce agreements between private parties? Consider the following classic statement in Lon Fuller's 1941 article, *Consideration and Form*, a bit of which we quoted in Section 1.A:

> *Private Autonomy.*—Among the basic conceptions of contract law the most pervasive and indispensable is the principle of private autonomy. This principle simply means that the law views private individuals as possessing a power to effect, within certain limits, changes in their legal relations. The man who conveys property to another is exercising this power; so is the man who enters a contract. When a court enforces a promise it is merely arming with legal sanction a rule or *lex* previously established by the party himself. This power of the individual to effect changes in his legal relations with others is comparable to the power of a legislature. It is, in fact, only a kind of political prejudice which causes us to use the word "law" in one case and not in the other, a prejudice which did not deter the Romans from applying the word *lex* to the norms established by private agreement.

* * *

> The principle of private autonomy, properly understood, is in no way inconsistent with an "objective" interpretation of contracts. Indeed, we may go farther and say that the so-called objective theory of interpretation in its more extreme applications becomes understandable only in terms of the principle of private autonomy. It has been suggested that in some cases the courts might properly give an interpretation to a written contract inconsistent with the actual understanding of either party. What justification can there be for such a view? We answer, it rests upon the need for promoting the security of transactions. Yet security of transactions presupposes

"transactions," in other words, acts of private parties which have a law-making and right-altering function. When we get outside the field of acts having this kind of function as their *raison d'être,* for example, in the field of tort law, any such uncompromisingly "objective" method of interpreting an act would be incomprehensible.

* * *

Reliance.—A second substantive basis of contract liability lies in a recognition that the breach of a promise may work an injury to one who has changed his position in reliance on the expectation that the promise would be fulfilled. Reliance as a basis of contract liability must not be identified with reliance as a measure of the promisee's recovery. Where the object of the court is to reimburse detrimental reliance, it may measure the loss occasioned through reliance either *directly* (by looking to see what the promisee actually expended in reliance on the promise), or *contractually* (by looking to the value of the promised performance out of which the promisee presumably expected to recoup his losses through reliance). If the court's sole object is to reimburse the losses resulting from reliance, it may be expected to prefer the direct measure where that measure may be applied conveniently. But there are various reasons, too complicated for discussion here, why a court may find that measure unworkable and hence prefer the contractual measure, even though its sole object remains that of reimbursing reliance.

What is the relation between reliance and the principle of private autonomy? Occasionally reliance may appear as a distinct basis of liability, excluding the necessity for any resort to the notion of private autonomy. An illustration may be found in some of the cases coming under section 90 of the Restatement of Contracts. In these cases we are not "upholding transactions" but healing losses caused through broken faith. In another class of cases the principle of reimbursing reliance comes into conflict with the principle of private autonomy. These are the cases where a promisee has seriously and, according to ordinary standards of conduct, justifiably relied on a promise which the promisor expressly stipulated should impose no legal liability on him. * * *

Unjust Enrichment.—In return for *B*'s promise to give him a bicycle, *A* pays *B* five dollars; *B* breaks his promise. We may regard this as a case where the injustice resulting from breach of a promise relied on by the promisee is aggravated. The injustice is aggravated because not only has *A* lost five dollars but *B* has gained five dollars unjustly. If, following Aristotle, we conceive of justice as being concerned with maintaining a proper proportion of goods among members of society, we may reduce the relations involved to mathematical terms. Suppose A and B have each initially ten units of goods. The relation between them is then one of equivalence, 10:10. A loses five of his units in reliance on a promise by B which B breaks. The resulting relation is 5:10. If, however, A paid these five units over to B, the resulting relation would be 5:15. This comparison shows why unjust enrichment resulting from breach of contract presents a more urgent case for judicial intervention than does mere loss through reliance not resulting in unjust enrichment.

Since unjust enrichment is simply an aggravated case of loss through reliance, all of what was said in the last section is applicable here. When the problem is the quantum of recovery, unjust enrichment may be measured either *directly* (by the value of what the promisor received), or *contractually,* (by the value of the promised equivalent). So too, the prevention of unjust enrichment may sometimes appear openly as a distinct ground of liability (as in suits for restitution for breach of an oral promise "unenforceable" under the Statute of Frauds), and at other times may appear as a basis of liability supplementing and reinforcing the principle of private autonomy (as where the notion of waiver is applied "to prevent forfeiture," and in cases where the inference of a tacit promise of compensation is explained by the court's desire to prevent unjust enrichment).

Substantive Deterrents to Legal Intervention to Enforce Promises.—I have spoken of "the substantive bases of contract liability." It should be noted that the enforcement of promises entails certain costs which constitute substantive objections to the imposition of contract liability. The first of these costs is the obvious one involved in the social effort expended in the legal procedure necessary to enforcement. Enforcement involves, however, another less tangible and more important cost. There is a real need for a field of human intercourse freed from legal restraints, for a field where men may without liability withdraw assurances they have once given. Every time a new type of promise is made enforceable, we reduce the area of this field. The need for a domain of "free-remaining" relations is not merely spiritual. Business deals can often emerge only from a converging series of negotiations, in which each step contains enough assurance to make worthwhile a further exchange of views and yet remains flexible enough to permit a radical readjustment to new situations. To surround with rigid legal sanctions even the first exploratory expressions of intention would not only introduce an unpleasant atmosphere into business negotiations, but would actually hamper commerce. The needs of commerce in this respect are suggested by the fact that in Germany, where the code makes offers binding without consideration, it has become routine to stipulate for a power of revocation.[49]

In addition to the three reasons Fuller identifies—autonomy, reliance and unjust enrichment—we should also keep in mind the role of contract law in our economic system as a whole. As Adam Smith famously observed:

> It is not from the benevolence of the butcher, the brewer, or the baker that we expect our dinner, but from their regard to their own interest. We address ourselves, not to their humanity but to their self love, and never talk to them of our own necessities but of their advantages.[50]

Although it would be a mistake to think of people only as self-interested, rational utility maximizers, the magic of exchange is that it harnesses the self-interest of each party for the benefit of both. To take Fuller's example, *A* has five dollars, but would prefer a bicycle. *B* has a bicycle, but would prefer five dollars. By exchanging the one for the other, both come out ahead—both end up better off than they were before. Exchange increases social welfare.

Contract law enables non-simultaneous exchanges that might otherwise fail for a lack of trust. In Fuller's example, *A* gives *B* five dollars not for *B*'s bicycle, but for *B*'s *promise* to give *A* the bicycle. Why does *A* trust that *B* will perform that promise? If *A* and *B* are friends, perhaps *A* knows she can trust in *B*'s goodwill toward *A*, or in *B*'s moral sense, or that *B* will worry about what *C*, *D* and *E* will think if *B* breaks his promise. But if *A* and *B* are strangers, or if *B* has broken promises in the past, *A* might rely instead on legal enforcement. As Dori Kimel observes, the payment of damages from the breaching to the nonbreaching party both deters breach and insures against it:

> Typically enforceable as they are, contracts provide parties with a special source of reassurance that obligations owed them will be discharged. The availability of remedies need not be thought of merely as a safety net for those who were harmed (or are about to be harmed) as a consequence of breach: by dramatically decreasing the likelihood that a defaulting party would benefit through harming the other party, it functions (or, at any rate, *should* function) as a deterrent to conduct that amounts to causing such harm.[51]

By providing the assurances necessary to support non-simultaneous exchanges, contract law functions not only to increase individual

---

[49] Lon L. Fuller, *Consideration and Form*, 41 Colum. L. Rev. 799, 806–13 (1941).

[50] Adam Smith, An Inquiry Into the Nature and Causes of the Wealth of Nations (C.J. Bullock, ed.) 19 (1776).

[51] Dori Kimel, From Promise to Contract: Towards a Liberal Theory of Contract 57 (2003) (footnotes omitted).

autonomy and do justice between the parties, but also to increase the welfare of society as a whole.

(B) PERSPECTIVES ON CONTRACT LAW

The above discussion only begins to scratch the surface of a deep body of work on contract theory. But it is enough to orient us to some of the several functions of contract law and the different pulls on it. We now describe some major approaches to the normative jurisprudence of contract law.

Formalism and Realism in American Legal Thought. The term "formalism" has several different meanings. Later in this book, we will use it to denote an approach to interpreting contracts that emphasizes the dictionary meanings of written words and tends to discount evidence of surrounding context. Here we use the term to describe a way of understanding the law that was prevalent in the United States in the late nineteenth and early twentieth centuries. Formalism of this second type is often referred to as "Langdellian" formalism, after Christopher Columbus Langdell. Oversimplifying a bit, the core idea of Langdellian formalism is that the rules of any given area of law, such as the law of contract, can be deduced from a small number of basic principles. Langdell, who was the Dean of Harvard Law School from 1870 to 1895, is widely credited with inventing the casebook method of teaching law. Here is his description of the method:

> Law, considered as a science, consists of certain principles or doctrines. To have such a mastery of these as to be able to apply them with constant facility and certainty to the ever-tangled skein of human affairs, is what constitutes a true lawyer; and hence to acquire that mastery should be the business of every earnest student of law. Each of these doctrines has arrived at its present state by slow degree; in other words, it is a growth, extending in many cases through centuries. This growth is to be traced in the main through a series of cases; and much the shortest and best, if not the only way of mastering the doctrine effectually is by studying the cases in which it is embodied.[52]

Morton Horwitz has suggested that the rise of Langdellian formalism is linked to the rise of the legal treatise:

> The legal treatise was regarded by its admirers as above all demonstrating the "scientific" nature of the law. Through classification of subjects, it sought to show that law proceeds not from will but from reason. Through its "black letter" presentation of supposed "general principles" of law it sought to suppress all controversy over policy while promoting the

---

[52] Christopher Columbus Langdell, A selection of cases on the law of contracts: with a summary of the topics covered by the cases: prepared for use as a text-book in Harvard Law, 2d ed. viii (1879) (Preface to the First Edition).

comforting ideal of a logical, symmetrical and, most importantly, inexorable system of law. Finally, its decided focus upon the technicalities of private law illustrates an increasingly well organized and self-conscious profession's yearning for an objective, apolitical conception of law.[53]

Recently, some scholars have questioned just how formalist Langdell and his contemporaries really were.[54] Whether or not those critics are right, subsequent legal thought in the United States has been largely defined by a rejection of formalist approaches to the law (which today are more readily found in Great Britain, Commonwealth countries and in Continental Europe). The first wave of legal scholars to mount a systematic critique of Langdellian formalism called themselves "legal realists."

Oliver Wendell Holmes, who dubbed Langdell "perhaps, the greatest living legal theologian," was the grandfather of American legal realism.[55] Writing in 1880, Holmes argued that "[t]he life of the law has not been logic; it has been experience."[56] In the 1920s and 30s, the legal realists took up Holmes's attack on Langdellian formalism. Karl Llewellyn, who went on to be the primary drafter of the Uniform Commercial Code, listed the realists' "common points of departure":

(1) The conception of law in flux, of moving law, and of judicial creation of law.

(2) The conception of law as a means to social ends and not as an end in itself; so that any part needs constantly to be examined for its purpose, and for its effect, and to be judged in the light of both and of their relation to each other.

(3) The conception of society in flux, and in flux typically faster than the law, so that the probability is always given that any portion of law needs reexamination to determine how far it fits the society it purports to serve.

(4) The *temporary* divorce of Is and Ought for purposes of study. By this I mean that whereas value judgments must always be appealed to in order to set objectives for inquiry, yet during the inquiry itself into what Is, the observation, the description, and the establishment of relations between the things described are to remain *as largely as possible*

---

[53] Morton J. Horwitz, *The Rise of Legal Formalism*, 19 Am. J. Legal Hist. 251, 255–56 (1975).

[54] See, e.g., Bruce A. Kimball, *The Langdell Problem: Historicizing the Century of Historiography,* 1906–2000s, 22 Law & Hist. Rev. 277 (2004); Marcia Speziale, *Langdell's Concept of Law as Science: The Beginning of Anti-Formalism in American Legal Theory,* 5 Vt. L. Rev. 1 (1980).

[55] Oliver Wendell Holmes, *Book Notice of William Anson, Principles of the English Law of Contracts and Christopher Columbus Langdell,* Selection of Cases on the Law of Contracts (2nd ed.), 14 Am. L. Rev. 233, 234 (1880).

[56] Id.

uncontaminated by the desires of the observer or by what he wishes might be or thinks ought (ethically) to be. * * *

(5) Distrust of traditional legal rules and concepts insofar as they purport to *describe* what either courts or people are actually doing. Hence the constant emphasis on rules as "generalized predictions of what courts will do." * * *

(6) Hand in hand with this distrust of traditional rules (on the descriptive side) goes a distrust of the theory that traditional prescriptive rule-formulations are *the* heavily operative factor in producing court decisions. This involves the tentative adoption of the theory of rationalization for the study of opinions. It will be noted that "distrust" in this and the preceding point is not at all equivalent to "negation in any given instance."

(7) The belief in the worthwhileness of grouping cases and legal situations into narrower categories than has been the practice in the past. This is connected with the distrust of verbally simple rules—which so often cover dissimilar and non-simple fact situations (dissimilarity being tested partly by the way cases come out, and partly by the observer's judgment as to how they ought to come out; but a realist tries to indicate explicitly which criterion he is applying).

(8) An insistence on evaluation of any part of law in terms of its effects, and an insistence on the worthwhileness of trying to find these effects.

(9) Insistence on *sustained and programmatic attack* on the problems of law along any of these lines. * * *[57]

Llewellyn's nine "points of departure" describe how many of the most influential judges, legislators and scholars today think about contract law. The answer to what contract law should be lies in an examination of the social policies it serves and its probable effects in the world. When studying contract law, we ask not just what the general principles of contract law are (though those are important for organizing the subject). We also ask about the social purposes of contract law and its practical consequences for individual people and for the economy as a whole.

This basic realist tendency of contract jurisprudence in the United States finds expression in many different ways. Here we describe in broad strokes three contemporary approaches to the normative jurisprudence of contract, all of which can be described as broadly realist.

Law and Economics. For the past thirty years or so, much contract scholarship in the United States has employed economic methods. The economic approach focuses on the incentives legal rules create and their

---

[57] Karl Llewellyn, *Some Realism About Realism—Responding to Dean Pound*, 44 Harv. L. Rev. 1222, 1236–37 (1931).

likely effects on human behavior. What, for example, is the probable effect of the unconscionability doctrine on the prices that poor people will pay for goods? How might different damages measures influence parties' decisions about whether or not to perform? How will the *Hadley* rule affect the flow of information at the time of contracting? When answering such questions, law and economics scholars have traditionally assumed that parties are rational, self-interested utility maximizers. They have assumed that, when deciding how to act, (1) people rationally weigh all costs and benefits of their various options, and (2) each is indifferent as to the costs or benefits that her actions might impose or confer on others.

The economic approach described above is basically predictive. It aims to tell us what effects one or another legal rule will have on people's behavior. Many law and economics scholars combine this predictive method with a normative premise: that the goal of the law should be to maximize social welfare, or overall preference satisfaction. In the second edition of his enormously influential book, *Economic Analysis of Law*, Richard Posner (now a judge on the Seventh Circuit Court of Appeals) identified three functions of contract law. First, it furnishes "incentives for value-maximizing conduct in the future," i.e., conduct that exploits economic resources in such a way that human satisfaction as measured by aggregate consumer willingness to pay for goods and services is maximized. Second, it reduces the "complexity and hence cost of transactions by supplying a set of normal terms that, in the absence of a law of contracts, the parties would have to negotiate expressly." Third, it furnishes "prospective transacting parties with information concerning the many contingencies that may defeat an exchange, and hence. . .assist[s] them in planning their exchange sensibly."[58]

Recently, some economically-minded scholars have begun to explore alternatives to the rational actor model.[59] Results from experimental psychology suggest that people are often systematically non-rational or other-regarding in their decision-making. These "behavioral economists" argue that the lawmakers can and should take into account these biases, heuristics and preferences in designing the law. In the area of contracts, this has produced new arguments for mildly paternalistic rules, such as pro-employee defaults in employment contracts, and for the penalty rule, which prevents parties from contracting for punitive damages for breach.[60]

Relational Contract Theory. In 1963, Stuart Macaulay published in the American Sociological Review his important article, *Non-Contractual*

---

[58] Richard Posner, Economic Analysis of Law 68–69 (2d ed. 1977).

[59] See, e.g., Christine Jolls, Cass R. Sunstein and Richard Thaler, *A Behavioral Approach to Law and Economics,* 50 Stan. L. Rev. 1471 (1998); Donald C. Langevoort, *Behavioral Theories of Judgment and Decision Making in Legal Scholarship: A Literature Review,* 51 Vand. L. Rev. 1499 (1998).

[60] See, e.g., Cass R. Sunstein, *Switching the Default Rule*, 77 N.Y.U. L. Rev. 106 (2002); Melvin Aron Eisenberg, *The Limits of Cognition and the Limits of Contract*, 47 Stan. L. Rev. 213 (1995).

Relations in Business: A Preliminary Study. Macaulay used interviews with business people and lawyers to attempt to answer the questions "What good is contract law? who uses it? when and how?"[61] He concluded that among business people, "contract and contract law are often thought unnecessary because there are many effective non-legal sanctions."[62] Those non-legal sanctions included, for example, refusal to deal with a party in the future and the reputational costs of breach. Macaulay also argued that personal relationships and trust often provided all the assurance that was necessary. In fact, business people reported that too much law and lawyering got in the way of successful transactions:

> Not only are contract and contract law not needed in many situations, their use may have, or may be thought to have, undesirable consequences. Detailed negotiated contracts can get in the way of creating good exchange relationships between business units. If one side insists on a detailed plan, there will be delay while letters are exchanged as the parties try to agree on what should happen if a remote and unlikely contingency occurs. In some cases they may not be able to agree at all on such matters and as a result a sale may be lost to the seller and the buyer may have to search elsewhere for an acceptable supplier. Many businessmen would react by thinking that had no one raised the series of remote and unlikely contingencies all this wasted effort could have been avoided.

> Even where agreement can be reached at the negotiation stage, carefully planned arrangements may create undesirable exchange relationships between business units. Some businessmen object that in such a carefully worked out relationship one gets performance only to the letter of the contract. Such planning indicates a lack of trust and blunts the demands of friendship, turning a cooperative venture into an antagonistic horse trade. Yet the greater danger perceived by some businessmen is that one would have to perform his side of the bargain to its letter and thus lose what is called "flexibility." Businessmen may welcome a measure of vagueness in the obligations they assume so that they may negotiate matters in light of the actual circumstances.

> Adjustment of exchange relationships and dispute settlement by litigation or the threat of it also has many costs. The gain anticipated from using this form of coercion often fails to outweigh these costs, which are both monetary and non-monetary. Threatening to turn matters over to an attorney may cost no more money than postage or a telephone call; yet few are so skilled in making such a threat that it will not cost some

---

[61] Stewart Macaulay, *Non-Contractual Relations in Business: A Preliminary Study,* 28 Am. Soc. Rev. 55, 55 (1963).

[62] Id. at 63.

deterioration of the relationship between the firms. One businessman said that customers had better not rely on legal rights or threaten to bring a breach of contract law suit against him since he "would not be treated like a criminal" and would fight back with every means available.[63]

Since the publication of *Non-Contractual Relations in Business,* many other scholars have studied how parties use non-legal norms, practices and sanctions, as well as the advantages and disadvantages of those mechanisms as compared to legal enforcement and how the law can interfere with and support those non-legal forms of assurance. Different scholars draw different conclusions from the data. For some, the lesson is that contract law should be more attuned to the customs and practices surrounding the parties' agreement and to the fact that contractual arrangements change and grow over time, and that courts should seek enforcement mechanisms that tend to support the extralegal relationship between the parties.[64] Others have argued that more formal and less flexible interpretations are better for parties who want to "allocate aspects of their relationship between the legal and extralegal realms in ways that seek to maximize the value of their transaction."[65]

Critical Approaches. It will be recalled that Llewellyn's sixth realist point of departure was a "distrust of the theory that traditional prescriptive rule-formulations are *the* heavily operative factor in producing court decisions." Courts in the United States give reasons for their decisions. Legal realists commonly argue that the reasons a court gives for a case outcome or rule is often not the whole story. Judicial (and legislative) decisions are influenced by many factors. These can range from the quality of legal representation to the sympathies of the judge or jury to a court's hidden agenda to raw political power. In a case like *Bolin Farms,* for example, we might also ask questions like: Who probably had the better lawyers, the farmers or the cotton wholesaler? Whom was the judge more likely to meet at the club? Might race have played a factor in Louisiana in 1974? And even if none of these factors influenced the outcome of this case, does the rule in the case work to support existing allocations of wealth or power?

Critical contracts scholarship has taken many forms. Morton Horwitz, in his monumental *The Transformation of American Law,* for example, argued that developments in nineteenth century contract law functioned to protect commercial interests and the mercantile class:

> The emergence of the objective theory, then, is another measure of the influence of commercial interests in the shaping of

---

[63] Id. at 64.

[64] See, e.g., Richard E. Speidel, *Article 2 and Relational Sales Contracts,* 26 Loy. L.A. L. Rev. 789 (1993); Ian R. Macneil, *The Many Futures of Contracts,* 47 S. Cal. L. Rev. 691 (1974).

[65] Lisa Bernstein, *Merchant Law In a Merchant Court: Rethinking the Code's Search for Immanent Business Norms,* 144 U. Pa. L. Rev. 1765, 1788 (1996). See also Robert E. Scott, *The Case for Formalism in Relational Contracts,* 94 Nw. U. L. Rev. 847 (2000).

American law. No longer finding it necessary to enter into battle against eighteenth century just price doctrines, they could devote their energies to establishing in the second half of the nineteenth century a system of objective rules necessary to assure legal certainty and predictability. And having destroyed most substantive grounds for evaluating the justice of exchange, they could elaborate a legal ideology of formalism, of which Williston was a leading exemplar, that could not only disguise gross disparities of bargaining power under a façade of neutral formal rules of contract law but could also enforce commercial customs under the comforting technical rubric of "contract interpretation."[66]

Other historically-minded authors have argued that courts in the Reconstruction South used facially neutral contract rules to enforce the continued subjugation of formerly enslaved black people,[67] that in the late nineteenth century negative injunctions were used primarily against female performers to effectively bind them to their male managers,[68] and that judicial hostility toward the enforcement of agreements between spouses has historically systematically disadvantaged women.[69]

Such critical studies show the importance of sometimes taking a skeptical attitude toward the law. Contract law is a tool. Like other tools, it can be put to many different uses. It can serve those uses well or poorly, depending on its design. And the uses themselves can be more or less praiseworthy. The careful study of contract law requires an inquiry into the nature of the tool, the usefulness of its design, and the value of the ends it serves.

DRAFTING EXERCISE: SELLING AN EGG CLEANER

The following exercise draws extensively from William K. Sjostrom, Jr., *An Introduction to Contract Drafting* (2012), which is an excellent resource for identifying basic contractual components and learning how agreements are structured.

(A) Read the contract below and try to identify the following types of provisions: title, preamble, recitals, words of agreement, performance provisions, consideration, representations and warranties, and concluding provisions. In other words, try to identify the function and legal effect of each provision.

---

[66]   Morton J. Horwitz, The Transformation of American Law, 1780–1860 201 (1977).

[67] Jennifer Roback, *Southern Labor Law in the Jim Crow Era: Exploitative or Competitive?,* 51 U. Chi. L. Rev. 1161 (1984).

[68] Lea S. VanderVelde, *The Gendered Origins of the Lumley Doctrine: Binding Men's Consciences and Women's Fidelity,* 101 Yale L. J. 775 (1992).

[69] Jill Elaine Hasday, *Intimacy and Economic Exchange,* 119 Harv. L. Rev. 491 (2005); Reva B. Siegel, *The Modernization of Marital Status Law: Adjudicating Wives' Rights to Earnings,* 1860–1930, 82 Geo. L.J. 2127 (1994).

(B) If you represented the buyer, Yoko E. White, what changes might you request to the proposed contract?

MECHANICAL EGG CLEANER SALE AGREEMENT

Mechanical Egg Cleaner Agreement, dated _____ 2016, between Eggscellent Products Co., a Nevada corporation ("Seller"), and Yoko E. White, an individual residing at _____ ("Buyer").

This Agreement provides for the sale of a Mechanical Egg Cleaner by Seller to Buyer.

Accordingly, the parties agree as follows:

1. Definitions. Terms that were defined in the preamble have their assigned meanings, and the following terms have the meanings assigned to them.

    a. "Agreement" means this Mechanical Egg Cleaner Sale, as amended from time to time.

    b. "Closing" means the consummation of the transactions contemplated in this Agreement.

    c. "Closing Date" has the meaning that Section 4 assigns to it.

    d. "Purchase Price" has the meaning that Section 3 assigns to it.

    e. "Mechanical Egg Cleaner" means the 2014 Sternberg Mechanical Egg Cleaner Egg-Matic 3500

2. Purchase and Sale. Seller shall sell the Mechanical Egg Cleaner to the Buyer, and the Buyer shall purchase the Mechanical Egg Cleaner from the Seller, at the Closing.

3. Purchase Price. At Closing the Buyer shall pay Seller $4,250 (the "Purchase Price") by certified check.

4. Time and Place of the Closing. The Closing shall take place on _____, 2016, or such other date the parties agree upon (the "Closing Date") at Seller's offices at 12:00 PM EST.

5. Seller's Closing Deliveries.

    a. Documents. Seller shall execute and deliver to Buyer at the Closing a bill of sale for the Mechanical Egg Cleaner. Seller shall execute and deliver to Buyer, either at or after the Closing and upon Buyer's reasonable request, any other instrument necessary to vest Buyer with good title in the Mechanical Egg Cleaner.

    b. Mechanical Egg Cleaner and Manuals. Seller shall deliver to the Buyer the Mechanical Egg Cleaner and owner's manuals for operation of the Mechanical Egg Cleaner at the Closing.

6. Seller's Representations and Warranties. Seller represents and warrants to Buyer the following:

a. Ownership. Seller owns the Mechanical Egg Cleaner, and the Mechanical Egg Cleaner is not subject to any liens, claims, or encumbrances.

b. Maintenance. Seller has maintained the Mechanical Egg Cleaner in accordance with the Mechanical Egg Cleaner's owner's manual, and the Mechanical Egg Cleaner is in good operating condition.

7. Buyer's Representations and Warranties. Buyer represents and warrants to Seller the following:

a. Financial Information. The financial information Buyer has furnished to Seller is accurate and complete and fairly presents the financial position of Buyer as of the date of the information.

b. Funding. Buyer has sufficient funds to pay the Purchase Price to Seller at Closing

8. Seller's Covenants. Seller covenants the following from the date of this Agreement to the Closing:

a. Maintenance. Seller shall maintain the Mechanical Egg Cleaner until the Closing in accordance with the owner's manual for the Mechanical Egg Cleaner, and in good operating condition.

9. DISCLAIMER OF WARRANTIES. EXCEPT AS EXPRESSLY PROVIDED IN SECTION 6 OF THIS AGREEMENT, SELLER MAKES NO REPRESENTATION OR WARRANTY, EXPRESS OR IMPLIED, WITH RESPECT TO THE MECHANICAL EGG CLEANER, INCLUDING, BUT NOT LIMITED TO, IMPLIED CONDITIONS OF FITNESS FOR A PARTICULAR PURPOSE, MERCHANTIBILITY, WARRANTIES ARISING FROM COURSE OF DEALING OR USAGE OF TRADE OR ANY OTHER MATTER. NO AGENT, EMPLOYEE OR REPRESENTATIVE OF SELLER HAS ANY AUTHORITY TO BIND SELLER TO ANY AFFIRMATION, REPRESTANTION OR WARRANTY EXCEPT AS STATED IN THIS AGREEMENT.

10. Conditions to Buyer's Obligations. Buyer's obligation to close the transaction this Agreement contemplates is subject to the satisfaction of the conditions below:

a. Representations and Warranties. Seller's representations and warranties must be true on the Closing Date.

b. Covenants. Seller must have performed all of the covenants required of it on or before the Closing Date.

11. Condition to Seller's Obligations. Seller's obligation to close the transaction this Agreement contemplates is subject to the satisfaction of the condition that Buyer's representations and warranties must be true on the Closing Date.

12. Miscellaneous

    a.   Entire Agreement. This Agreement is the final, complete and exclusive statement of the agreement of the parties on the matters this Agreement and supersedes all prior understandings, communications and agreements between the parties on those matters.

    b.   Modification and Waiver. No purported amendment, modification or waiver of any provision of this Agreement shall be binding unless set forth in a writing that has been signed by both parties, or, in the case of waivers, by the party to be charged. Any waiver shall be limited to the circumstance or event specifically referenced in the written waiver document and shall not be deemed a waiver of any other term of the Agreement, or of the same circumstance or event, should it recur.

    c.   Governing Law. This Agreement shall be governed by and construed in accordance with the laws of the State of Illinois without regard to the rules of conflict of laws of Illinois or any other jurisdiction.

    d.   Confidentiality. Buyer agrees to keep the terms of this Agreement confidential.

To evidence their agreement to the provisions of this Agreement, the parties have executed and delivered this agreement on the date set forth in the preamble.

Eggscellent Products Co.

By:

Its:

_____

Yoko E. White

CHAPTER TWO

THE BASES OF CONTRACT LIABILITY

Contract liability is distinguished from both tort and criminal liability by the fact that contractual obligations are willingly undertaken. The obligations of tort and criminal law do not presuppose a prior choice by the potential tortfeasor or criminal. The obligations of contract do. Contractual obligations originate in voluntary undertakings: agreements, promises, assurances and the like.

But not all agreements or statements of commitment result in a contract. A bare promise to x is not enough to create a contractual duty to x. There must be something more. The most important "something more" in U.S. contract law is consideration. A commitment to x is supported by consideration if it is part of an exchange, or *quid pro quo* (a this for a that). Section 1 of this Chapter examines the consideration requirement in detail. The Chapter also discusses three other paths to enforcement: the production of a sealed instrument (discussed in Section 1.C), foreseeable detrimental reliance on the commitment, under the doctrine of promissory estoppel (Section 2), and the existence of an antecedent but legally inoperative obligation, including a moral duty (Section 3).

1. THE CONSIDERATION REQUIREMENT

Imagine contract law as a large city, Contractopolis, with the different neighborhoods representing different rules or doctrines. The geography of Contractopolis is the product of many builders working over multiple generations. The consideration doctrine is a neighborhood located in the heart of the city—an old district with narrow, twisting streets, some of which run into blind alleys. The buildings are a mix of architectural styles, often with modern structures built on much older foundations. Think of Charles Dickens's London, or Diagon Alley. The point is, no matter how rationally laid out the streets, subways and sewers in the rest of Contractopolis, they must connect with those in the consideration district. In this way, the consideration rule influences the shape of the city as a whole.

The goal of this Section is to map out the consideration doctrine and to show how it connects to a few other parts of contract law, such as the rule for one-sided modifications and for agreements that give one or both parties discretion in performance. We will also see how courts and legislatures have reshaped and made exceptions to the doctrine in order to meet parties' practical needs.

(A) HISTORICAL AND DEFINITIONAL NOTE

The New York Court of Appeals provides a helpful summary of the early history of the consideration requirement:

> During the early phases of the development of English common law, an action on an obligation other than one embodied in a sealed instrument was maintainable only through a writ to recover on a debt. The availability of such writs, however, was limited to those narrow situations in which one of the parties withheld payment of a fixed, bargained for sum of money after the other party had performed his part of the bargain by making a loan or delivering goods or services. The underlying theory of the action was that the parties had made a bargain or had agreed upon a *quid pro quo* exchange and the promisor or debtor was now wrongfully withholding the property of the promisee by refusing to make payment after receiving that which he had bargained for. It was from this concept of a bargained for *quid pro quo* that the notion of consideration as a benefit flowing to the promisor was derived (see 1 Corbin, Contracts, § 121; Morgan, Introduction to the Study of Law [2d ed.], pp. 92–93; 1 Williston, Contracts [Jaeger 3d ed.], § 99; Holmes, *Early English Equity*, 1 L.Q. Rev. 162, 171).

> The action on a debt, however, proved unsatisfactory for a variety of reasons, not the least of which was its limited scope. Litigants, as a consequence, turned with increasing frequency to the vehicle of assumpsit, which was originally a simple variant of trespass on the case, the forerunner of our modern tort cause of action (see Ames, *History of Assumpsit*, 2 Harv. L. Rev. 1). Although assumpsit ultimately evolved into a separate and distinct form of action, its earliest uses were confined to claims based upon malfeasance or faulty performance of an assumed duty (see Williston, at p. 384). Consistent with its origins in trespass on the case, the gist of the action in assumpsit remained the injury to the promisee resulting from the promisor's misconduct in improperly performing his obligation. It was apparently not until 1588 that assumpsit was definitively expanded to encompass actions for nonfeasance or simple failure to perform a contractual duty. In that year, it was held that "a promise against a promise will maintain an action upon the case (in assumpsit), as in consideration that you do give me £10 on such a day, I promise to give you £10 such a day after" (Strangborough and Warner's Case, 4 Leon 3, 74 Eng.Rep. 686 [QB]). With this expansion in the availability of assumpsit, the original requirement of an injury resulting from misfeasance was broadened, and an action in assumpsit could thereafter be maintained upon a showing of any detriment, loss

or disadvantage to the promisee arising from the bargain (see, generally, Holdsworth, *Debt, Assumpsit and Consideration*, 11 Mich. L. Rev. 347).

The final critical development in the law of assumpsit occurred in 1602 with the decision in Slade's Case (4 Coke 91a, 92b, 76 Eng.Rep. 1072, 1074 [KB]). That decision paved the way for litigants to sue in assumpsit on claims for fixed sums of money previously maintainable only in the older form of an action based on a *quid pro quo* to recover a debt (see Moses v. Macferlan, 2 Burr. 1005, 1008, 97 Eng.Rep. 676 [KB]). As a result of this development, assumpsit became the primary vehicle for litigation on contractual obligations, and the notion of "consideration" became a term of art encompassing both a benefit to the promisor, the equivalent of the former *quid pro quo*, and a detriment to the promisee, the equivalent of the former requirement of injury in actions sounding in assumpsit (see Williston, at pp. 368–369).

This dual notion of consideration as either a benefit to the promisor *or* a detriment to the promisee has persisted to the present day and has become an integral part of our modern approach to the enforceability of contracts. [Emphasis added.— Eds.] Thus, it has repeatedly been stated that "[a] valuable consideration may consist of some right, interest, profit or benefit accruing to one party, or some forbearance, detriment, loss or responsibility given, suffered or undertaken by the other" (Rector of St. Mark's Church v. Teed, 120 N.Y. 583, 586. . .). Indeed, we have expressly held that a promisee who has incurred a specific, bargained for legal detriment may enforce a promise against the promisor, notwithstanding the fact that the latter may have realized no concrete benefit as a result of the bargain. . . .

Holt v. Feigenbaum, 419 N.E.2d 332 (N.Y. 1981).

The early conception of consideration as either a benefit to the promisor or a detriment to the promisee has today been largely supplanted by what is known as the "bargain" conception of consideration. The bargain conception can be seen in section 71 of the Second Restatement of Contracts:

(1) To constitute consideration, a performance or a return promise must be bargained for.

(2) A performance or return promise is bargained for if it is sought by the promisor in exchange for his promise and is given by the promisee in exchange for that promise.

(3) The performance may consist of: (a) an act other than a promise, or (b) a forbearance, or (c) the creation, modification, or destruction of a legal relation.

(4)   The performance or return promise may be given to the promisor or to some other person. It may be given by the promisee or by some other person.

In contrast to the benefit-detriment conception of consideration, which focuses on the welfare of the parties, the bargain conception focuses on the parties' reasons for entering into the transaction. Although the benefit-detriment framework still exerts considerable influence in England and Commonwealth countries, the bargain theory has largely won the day in the United States. That said, because contract law is the product of judicial decisions, it has many authors and old rules die hard. Although the bargain theory is the dominant approach to consideration, we will see that benefit and detriment still figure into courts' thinking.

How is it that the bargain conception came to replace the benefit-detriment test? In his 1974 book, *The Death of Contract*, Grant Gilmore argued that it arose from the pages of Oliver Wendell Holmes' great work, *The Common Law*. Between the merger of debt and assumpsit at the beginning of the 17th century and 1880, the year *The Common Law* was published, consideration for a promise was defined as either a detriment to the plaintiff or a benefit to the defendant. Holmes argued otherwise. "The root of the whole matter is the relation of reciprocal conventional inducement, each for the other, between consideration and promise." O.W. Holmes, *The Common Law* 230 (M. Howe ed. 1963). Gilmore argued that Holmes's innovation had little or no support in precedent. But it caught on. This "revolutionary doctrine" was then elaborated by Williston and others as the exclusive basis for enforcing promises and began to infect the entire life history of contracts. Even categories of promise on the periphery of the realm of contract—options, requirements contracts, modifications and discharges—felt the influence of the bargain conception and its attendant slogans, such as "mutuality of obligation." Thus, according to Gilmore, the miraculous birth and widespread promotion of the new theory as the exclusive basis for promissory liability narrowed the scope of contract, unrealistically sharpened the differences between contract and tort and left in limbo the question of liability for un-bargained-for benefits voluntarily conferred (moral obligation) and for induced but not bargained-for reliance (promissory estoppel). See G. Gilmore, *The Death of Contract* 5–53 (1974).

Gilmore was a partisan in the debate over why the law should enforce some agreements and not others, and his historical account should be read with more than a grain of salt. But whether or not Gilmore's story is entirely accurate, it captures the enormous influence that the bargain theory has had on contract law in the United States. As we will see in this Chapter and the next, the consideration requirement has affected how courts think about one-sided modifications, discretion in performance, and firm offers. Richard Speidel describes the influence of the bargain theory as follows:

The bargain idea has enjoyed a striking persistence in American contract law. This is partially explained, no doubt, by its strong congruence with basic human behavior. * * * [I]n retrospect, the bargain theory appears to be a very natural adaptation of prevailing economic attitudes to serve important legal needs. As an operating principle, the "bargain" theory of consideration (1) provided a natural formality to channel human conduct and insure deliberation; (2) protected and structured the important market transaction; (3) expanded legal protection by [(a)] supporting the executory exchange—a promise for a promise—and [(b)] shielding the creative or idiosyncratic bargainer from later claims that the agreed exchange was disproportionate; and (4) permitted a fuller development of remedies that protected the plaintiff's expectation interest, that is, the value to the plaintiff of the agreed exchange.

Richard E. Speidel, *An Essay on the Reported Death and Continued Vitality of Contract*, 27 Stan. L. Rev. 1161, 1168–1170 (1975).

(B) WHEN IS AN ACT OR PROMISE BARGAINED FOR AND GIVEN IN EXCHANGE?

Isaac Kirksey v. Angelico Kirksey
Supreme Court of Alabama, 1845.
8 Ala. 131.

Error to the Circuit Court of Talladega.

Assumpsit by the defendant, against the plaintiff in error. The question is presented in this Court, upon a case agreed, which shows the following facts:

The plaintiff was the wife of defendant's brother, but had for some time been a widow, and had several children. In 1840, the plaintiff resided on public land, under a contract of lease, she had held over, and was comfortably settled, and would have attempted to secure the land she lived on. The defendant resided in Talladega county, some sixty, or seventy miles off. On the 10th of October, 1840, he wrote to her the following letter:

"Dear sister Antillico—Much to my mortification, I heard, that brother Henry was dead, and one of his children. I know that your situation is one of grief, and difficulty. You had a bad chance before, but a great deal worse now. I should like to come and see you, but cannot with convenience at present. * * * I do not know whether you have a preference on the place you live on, or not. If you had, I would advise you to obtain your preference, and sell the land and quit the country, as I understand it is very unhealthy, and I know society is very bad. If you will come down and see me, I will let you have a place to raise your family, and I have more open land than I can tend; and on the account of your situation, and that of your family, I feel like I want you and the children to do well."

Within a month or two after the receipt of this letter, the plaintiff abandoned her possession, without disposing of it, and removed with her family, to the residence of the defendant, who put her in comfortable houses, and gave her land to cultivate for two years, at the end of which time he notified her to remove, and put her in a house, not comfortable, in the woods, which he afterwards required her to leave.

A verdict being found for the plaintiff, for two hundred dollars, the above facts were agreed, and if they will sustain the action, the judgment is to be affirmed, otherwise it is to be reversed.

■ ORMOND, J. The inclination of my mind, is, that the loss and inconvenience, which the plaintiff sustained in breaking up and moving to the defendant's, a distance of sixty miles, is a sufficient consideration to support the promise, to furnish her with a house, and land to cultivate, until she could raise her family. My brothers, however, think that the promise on the part of the defendant, was a mere gratuity, and that an action will not lie for its breach. The judgment of the Court below must therefore be reversed, pursuant to the agreement of the parties.

NOTES

(1)   Does it appear from *Kirksey* that a promise, simply because it is a promise, is presumptively enforceable?

(2)   Assuming that the defendant's promise in *Kirksey* was, as characterized by the court, "a mere gratuity," should that, of itself, preclude relief for the plaintiff? Is it a policy of the law to discourage gratuities? Why might a court hesitate, however, to enforce a *Kirksey*-like promise? Does the answer depend in part on what the remedy for breach of contract is?

(3)   Section 17 of the Second Restatement of Contracts provides that, with a few exceptions, "the formation of a contract requires a bargain in which there is a manifestation of mutual assent to the exchange and a consideration." Of these requirements, what was missing in *Kirksey v. Kirksey*?

(4)   *Conditional Promises vs. Promises for Consideration.* The letter in *Kirksey v. Kirksey* stated that the defendant would provide the plaintiff with a place to live "[i]f you will come down and see me." That is, the defendant's promise was conditional: he promised that if the plaintiff came to see him, he would provide her a place to raise her family. Why isn't that condition consideration?

Consider the following three scenarios:

(a)   A tells B, "If it rains tomorrow, I will give you a ride to work."

(b)   A tells B, "If you can be ready by 8 am, I will give you a ride to work."

(c)   A tells B, "If you can pay for the gas, I can give you a ride to work."

In each scenario, A's statement has the form of a conditional promise. In which scenario(s) does the promise appear to be supported by consideration? Would your answer change if you knew that A had an interest in making sure that B didn't oversleep? What if A was broke and couldn't pay for gas herself? For more on these issues, see *Pennsy Supply v. American Ash*, later in this section.

(5)   *Additional Facts.* Generations of law students have wondered about the story of "Sister Antillico." Why did her brother-in-law, Isaac Kirksey, invite her to come stay with him? Was the promise purely gratuitous, or did he expect to get something out from her move? And why did he change his mind two years later about where she could stay, and then eventually eject her from his property entirely?

A 2006 article by William Casto and Val Ricks casts some new light. The details are complicated, but under federal law at the time, squatters on federal lands in Alabama and elsewhere were often able to obtain a "preference" on those lands. A preference allowed the occupant to purchase the land at a below-market price. This fact explains the letter's mention that Angelico might have a "preference on the place you live on." Casto and Ricks argue that it also explains Isaac's reason for promising to allow Angelico to have the place to raise her family. Federal law at the time permitted only one preference per person. If Isaac had already exercised a preference on other lands, the only way he could get more was by having someone else occupy and cultivate land in his possession. That person could gain and exercise a preference on that land, and then transfer it back to Isaac. Why did Isaac evict Angelico after two years? Casto and Ricks find records indicating that Isaac in fact gave joint possession of the property to his son, who turned 21 around the time Angelico was ejected. Once he turned 21, Isaac's son was able to exercise the preference himself, making Angelico's continued occupancy unnecessary. William R. Casto and Val D. Ricks, *"Dear Sister Antillico. . .": The Story of* Kirksey v. Kirksey, 94 Geo. L.J. 321, 335–53 (2006).

If this is the true explanation of the facts in *Kirksey v. Kirksey*, was Isaac's promise in fact supported by consideration? If so, why didn't Angelico's attorney bring these facts to the attention of the court? Casto and Ricks argue that the use of preferences was common enough that the court probably understood the true nature of the transaction anyway. If the rules regarding preference mean that there was in fact consideration, why might the court choose to deny enforcement anyway?

Louisa Hamer v. Franklin Sidway

Court of Appeals of New York, 1891.

124 N.Y. 538.

Appeal from an order of the general term of the supreme court in the fourth judicial department, reversing a judgment entered on the decision of the court at special term in the county clerk's office of Chemung county on the 1st day of October, 1889. The plaintiff presented a claim to the executor of William E. Story, Sr., for $5,000 and interest from the 6th day of February, 1875. She acquired it through several mesne assignments from William E. Story, 2d. The claim being rejected by the executor, this action was brought. It appears that William E. Story, Sr., was the uncle of William E. Story, 2d; that at the celebration of the golden wedding of Samuel Story and wife, father and mother of William E. Story, Sr., on the 20th day of March, 1869, in the presence of the family and invited guests, he promised his nephew that if he would refrain from drinking, using tobacco, swearing, and playing cards or billiards for money until he became 21 years of age, he would pay him the sum of $5,000. The nephew assented thereto, and fully performed the conditions inducing the promise. When the nephew arrived at the age of 21 years, and on the 31st day of January, 1875, he wrote to his uncle, informing him that he had performed his part of the agreement, and had thereby become entitled to the sum of $5,000. The uncle received the letter, and a few days later, on the 6th day of February, he wrote and mailed to his nephew the following letter:

"Buffalo, Feb. 6, 1875. W.E. Story, Jr.—Dear Nephew: Your letter of the 31st ult. came to hand all right, saying that you had lived up to the promise made to me several years ago. I have no doubt but you have, for which you shall have five thousand dollars, as I promised you. I had the money in the bank the day you was twenty-one years old that I intend for you, and you shall have the money certain. Now, Willie, I do not intend to interfere with this money in any way till I think you are capable of taking care of it, and the sooner that time comes the better it will please me. I would hate very much to have you start out in some adventure that you thought all right and lose this money in one year. The first five thousand dollars that I got together cost me a heap of hard work. You would hardly believe me when I tell you that to obtain this I shoved a jack-plane many a day, butchered three or four years, then came to this city, and, after three months' perseverance, I obtained a situation in a grocery store. I opened this store early, closed late, slept in the fourth story of a building in a room 30 by 40 feet, and not a human being in the building but myself. All this I done to live as cheap as I could to save something. I don't want you to take up with this kind of fare. I was here in the cholera season of '49 and '52, and the deaths averaged 80 to 125 daily, and plenty of small-pox. I wanted to go home, but Mr. Fisk, the gentleman I was working for, told me, if I left them, after it got healthy he probably would not want me. I stayed. All the money I have saved I know just how I got it. It did not come to me in any mysterious way, and the reason I speak of this is that money got in this way stops longer with a fellow that gets it with hard knocks than it does when he finds it. Willie, you are twenty-one, and you have many a thing to learn yet. This money you have earned much easier than I did, besides acquiring good habits at the same time, and you are quite welcome to the money. Hope you will make good use of it. I was ten long years getting this together after I was your age. Now, hoping this will be satisfactory, I stop. * * *

"Truly yours, W.E. Story.

"P.S. You can consider this money on interest."

The nephew received the letter, and thereafter consented that the money should remain with his uncle in accordance with the terms and conditions of the letter. The uncle died on the 29th day of January, 1887, without having paid over to his nephew any portion of the said $5,000 and interest.

■ PARKER, J. The question which provoked the most discussion by counsel on this appeal, and which lies at the foundation of plaintiff's asserted right of recovery, is whether by virtue of a contract defendant's testator, William E. Story, became indebted to his nephew, William E. Story, 2d, on his twenty-first birthday in the sum of $5,000. The trial court found as a fact that "on the 20th day of March, 1869, * * * William E. Story agreed to and with William E. Story, 2d, that if he would refrain from drinking liquor, using tobacco, swearing, and playing cards or billiards for money until he should become twenty-one years of age, then he, the said William E. Story, would at that time pay him, the said William E. Story, 2d, the sum of $5,000 for such refraining, to which the said William E. Story, 2d, agreed," and that he "in all things fully performed his part of said agreement." The defendant contends that the contract was without consideration to support it, and therefore invalid. He asserts that the promisee, by refraining from the use of liquor and tobacco, was not harmed, but benefitted; that which he did was best for him to do, independently of his uncle's promise,—and insists that it follows that, unless the promisor was benefitted, the contract was without consideration,—a contention which, if well founded, would seem to leave open for controversy in many cases whether that which the promisee did or omitted to do was in fact of such benefit to him as to leave no consideration to support the enforcement of the promisor's agreement. Such a rule could not be tolerated, and is without foundation in the law. The exchequer chamber in 1875 defined "consideration" as follows: "A valuable consideration, in the sense of the law, may consist either in some right, interest, profit, or benefit accruing to the one party, or some forbearance, detriment, loss, or responsibility given, suffered, or undertaken by the other." Courts "will not ask whether the thing which forms the consideration does in fact benefit the promisee or a third party, or is of any substantial value to any one. It is enough that something is promised, done, forborne, or suffered by the party to whom the promise is made as consideration for the promise made to him." Anson, Cont. 63. "In general a waiver of any legal right at the request of another party is a sufficient consideration for a promise." Pars. Cont. *444. "Any damage, or suspension, or forbearance of a right will be sufficient to sustain a promise." 2 Kent, Comm. (12th Ed.) *465. Pollock in his work on Contracts, (page 166) after citing the definition given by the exchequer chamber, already quoted, says: "The second branch of this judicial description is really the most important one. 'Consideration' means not so much that one party is profiting as that the other abandons some legal right in the present, or limits his legal freedom of action in the future, as an inducement for the promise of the first." Now, applying this rule to the facts before us, the promisee used tobacco, occasionally drank liquor, and he had a legal right to do so. That right he abandoned for a period of years upon the strength of the promise of the testator that for such forbearance he would give him $5,000. We need not speculate on the effort which may have been required to give up the use of those stimulants. It is sufficient that he restricted his lawful freedom of action within certain prescribed limits upon the faith of his uncle's agreement, and now, having fully performed the conditions imposed, it is of no moment whether such performance actually proved a benefit to the promisor, and the court will not inquire into it; but, were it a proper subject of inquiry, we see nothing in this record that would permit a determination that the uncle was not benefitted in a legal sense. Few cases have been found which may be said to be precisely in point, but such as have been, support the position we have taken. In *Shadwell v. Shadwell*, 9 C.B. (N.S.) 159, an uncle wrote to his nephew as follows:

> "My dear Lancey: I am so glad to hear of your intended marriage with Ellen Nicholl, and, as I promised to assist you at starting, I am happy to tell you that I will pay you 150 pounds yearly during my life and until your annual income derived from your profession of a chancery barrister shall amount to 600 guineas, of which your own admission will be the only evidence that I shall receive or require. Your affectionate uncle, Charles Shadwell."

It was held that the promise was binding, and made upon good consideration. * * *

In *Talbott v. Stemmons*, 12 S.W.Rep. 297, (a Kentucky case, not yet officially reported,) the step-grandmother of the plaintiff made with him the following agreement: "I do promise and bind myself to give my grandson Albert R. Talbott $500 at my death if he will never take another chew of tobacco or smoke another cigar during my life, from this date up to my death; and if he breaks this pledge he is to refund double the amount to his mother." The executor of Mrs. Stemmons demurred to the complaint on the ground that the agreement was not based on a sufficient consideration. The demurrer was sustained, and an appeal taken therefrom to the court of appeals, where the decision of the court below was reversed. In the opinion of the court it is said that "the right to use and enjoy the use of tobacco was a right that belonged to the plaintiff, and not forbidden by law. The abandonment of its use may have saved him money, or contributed to his health; nevertheless, the surrender of that right caused the promise, and, having the right to contract with reference to the subject-matter, the abandonment of the use was a sufficient consideration to uphold the promise." * * *

* * * The order appealed from should be reversed, and the judgment of the special term affirmed, with costs payable out of the estate. All concur.

NOTES

(1) Was there equivalency of exchange in *Hamer*? Did the promisor gain a pecuniary advantage? Did he derive any "benefit" from the transaction at all, or is enforcement predicated solely upon "detriment" to the promisee? In what way was the plaintiff's forbearance detrimental?

(2) Section 79(a) of the Second Restatement states: "If the requirement of consideration is met, there is no additional requirement of . . . a gain, advantage, or benefit to the promisor or a loss, disadvantage, or detriment to the promisee." Comment b to the same section observes that some courts say "a 'legal detriment' is sufficient even though there is no economic detriment or other actual loss," but suggests that "[i]t is more realistic to say simply that there is no requirement of detriment." Are there any reasons why a benefit or detriment might still be relevant to showing consideration, even if merely as indirect evidence?

(3) The uncle in *Hamer v. Sidway* made two separate promises: one on March 20, 1869 at a wedding anniversary and a second in a letter on February 6, 1875. The court's analysis of the case focuses entirely on whether the first was supported by consideration. But isn't the suit premised on the second promise? Why might the argument for consideration here be different? See *Browning v. Johnson*, reprinted later in this Chapter, and Restatement (Second) § 74.

(4) Why isn't the title of this case "*Story v. Story*"? Sidway is the executor of uncle William E. Story, Sr.'s estate. William E. Story, Jr. assigned his right to performance to Hamer.

William F. Langer v. Superior Steel Corp.

Superior Court of Pennsylvania, 1932.
105 Pa.Super. 579.

■ BALDRIGE, J. This is an action of assumpsit to recover damages for breach of a contract. The court below sustained questions of law raised by defendant, and entered judgment in its favor.

The plaintiff alleges that he is entitled to recover certain monthly payments provided for in the following letter:

"August 31, 1927.

"Mr. Wm. F. Langer,

"Dear Sir:

"As you are retiring from active duty with this company, as superintendent of the annealing department, on August 31st, we hope that it will give you some pleasure to receive this official letter of commendation for your long and faithful service with the Superior Steel Corporation.

"The Directors have decided that you will receive a pension of $100 per month as long as you live and preserve your present attitude of loyalty to the company and its officers and are not employed in any competitive occupation. We sincerely hope that you will live long to enjoy it and that this and the other evidences of the esteem in which you are held by your fellow employees and which you will today receive with this letter, will please you as much as it does us to bestow them.

> "Cordially yours,
> "(Signed) Frank R. Frost,
> "President."

The defendant paid the sum of $100 a month for approximately four years when the plaintiff was notified that the company no longer intended to continue the payments.

The issue raised by the affidavit of defense is whether the letter created a gratuitous promise or an enforceable contract. It is frequently a matter of great difficulty to differentiate between promises creating legal obligations and mere gratuitous agreements. Each case depends to a degree upon its peculiar facts and circumstances. Was this promise supported by a sufficient consideration, or was it but a condition attached to a gift? If a contract was created, it was based on a consideration, and must have been the result of an agreement bargained for in exchange for a promise. . . . It was held in *Presbyterian Board of Foreign Missions v. Smith*, 209 Pa. 361, 363, that "a test of good consideration is whether the promisee, at the instance of the promisor, has done, forborne or undertaken to do anything real, or whether he has suffered any detriment or whether in return for the promise he has done something that he was not bound to do or has promised to do some act or has abstained from doing something." Mr. Justice Sadler pointed out in *York Metal & Alloys Co. v. Cyclops S. Co.*, 280 Pa. 585, that a good consideration exists if one refrains from doing anything that he has a right to do, "whether there is any actual loss or detriment to him or actual benefit to the promisor or not."

* * *

The plaintiff, in his statement, which must be admitted as true in considering the statutory demurrer filed by defendant, alleges that he refrained from seeking employment with any competitive company, and that he complied with the terms of the agreement. By so doing, has he sustained any detriment? Was his forbearance sufficient to support a good consideration? Professor Williston, in his treatise on Contracts, § 112, states: "It is often difficult to determine whether words of condition in a promise indicate a request for consideration or state a mere condition in a gratuitous promise. An aid, though not a conclusive test in determining which construction of the promise is more reasonable is an inquiry whether the happening of the condition will be a benefit to the promisor. If so, it is a fair inference that the happening was requested as a consideration. * * * In case of doubt where the promisee has incurred a detriment on the faith of the promise, courts will naturally be loath to regard the promise as a mere gratuity, and the detriment incurred as merely a condition."

It is reasonable to conclude that it is to the advantage of the defendant if the plaintiff, who had been employed for a long period of time as its superintendent in the annealing department, and who, undoubtedly, had knowledge of the methods used by the employer, is not employed by a competitive company; otherwise, such a stipulation would have been unnecessary. That must have been the inducing reason for inserting that provision. There is nothing appearing of record, except the condition imposed by the defendant, that would have prevented this man of skill and experience from seeking employment elsewhere. By receiving the monthly payments, he impliedly accepted the conditions imposed and was thus restrained from doing that which he had a right to do. This was a sufficient consideration to support a contract.

The appellee refers to *Kirksey v. Kirksey*, 8 Ala. 131, which is also cited by Professor Williston in his work on Contracts, § 112, note 51, as a leading case on this subject under discussion. The defendant wrote his sister-in-law, the plaintiff: "If you will come down and see me, I will let you have a place to raise your family and I have more open land than I can tend; and on the account of your situation and that of your family, I feel like I want you and the children to do well." The plaintiff left her home and moved her family a distance of 67 miles to the residence of the defendant, who gave her the house and land, and after a period of two years, requested her to leave. The court held that the promise was a mere gratuity. In that case, as well as in *Richards' Ex'r. v. Richards*, 46 Pa. 78, there was no benefit to be derived by the promisor, as in the case at bar, and therefore a good consideration was lacking.

In this view, this contract is enforceable also on the theory of promissory estoppel. This principle has been stated by the American Law Institute in section 90 of the Restatement of the Law of Contracts, as follows: "A promise which the promisor should reasonably expect to induce action or forbearance of a definite and substantial character on the part of the promisee and which does induce such action or forbearance is binding if injustice can be avoided only by enforcement of the promise." As we have already observed, the plaintiff was induced by the promises made to refrain from seeking other employment. A promissory estoppel differs from the equitable estoppel, as it rests upon a promise to do something in the future, while the latter rests upon a statement of a present fact. We have an example of the former in *Ricketts v. Scothorn*, 57 Neb. 51, where a grandfather handed his granddaughter a note for $2,000 saying, "I have fixed out something that you have not got to work any more. * * * None of my grandchildren work and you don't have to." The grandfather did not ask his granddaughter to give up her employment, but merely promised that she would not have to work unless she wanted to. She stopped working, relying upon getting $2,000. The court admitted that there was no consideration, but enforced the promise because it had misled the promisee in such a way that it would be unfair to her to do otherwise; thereby invoking the principle of promissory estoppel. We do not mean to state that in all cases where a gratuitous promise is made, and one relies upon it, the promisee can recover, but, if a detriment of a definite and substantial character has been incurred by the promisee, then the court may enforce the promise.

Judgment is reversed, and the defendant is hereby given permission to file an affidavit of defense to the merits of the plaintiff's claim.[1]

NOTES

(1)   How does the court in *Langer* purport to distinguish *Kirksey?* If the *Langer* court had decided *Kirksey*, would the result likely have been the same?

(2)   The First Restatement defined consideration in § 75(1):

Consideration for a promise is (a) an act other than a promise, or (b) a forbearance, or (c) the creation, modification or destruction of a legal relation, or (d) a return promise, bargained for and given in exchange for the promise.

How does this compare with the definition in Restatement (Second) § 71?

(3)   For a general perspective, see E. Allan Farnsworth, *The Past of Promise: An Historical Introduction to Contract*, 69 Colum. L. Rev. 576 (1969). In this article, the author quotes the following excerpt from Adam Smith's *The Wealth of Nations*:

[M]an has almost constant occasion for the help of his brethren, and it is vain for him to expect it from their benevolences only. He will be more likely to prevail if he can interest their self-love in his favour, and shew them that it is for their own advantage to do for him what he requires of them. Whoever offers to another a bargain of any kind, proposes to do this. Give me that which I want, and you shall have this which you want, is the meaning of every such

---

[1]   [Upon remand, the plaintiff obtained a jury verdict. But plaintiff's judgment was reversed on appeal. Langer v. Superior Steel Corp., 318 Pa. 490 (1935). Reversal was not based on lack of consideration, however, but resulted from a finding that the president lacked authority to bind the corporation.—Eds.]

offer; and it is in this manner that we obtain from one another the far greater part of those good offices which we stand in need of. We address ourselves, not to their humanity but to their self-love, and never talk to them of our own necessities but of their advantages. Nobody but a beggar chooses to depend chiefly upon the benevolence of his fellow citizens.

69 Colum. L. Rev. at 576–77.

(4) The *Langer* court also held that the promise to pay could also be enforced under the doctrine of promissory estoppel. Promissory estoppel is discussed in Section 2 of this Chapter.

Pennsy Supply, Inc. v. American Ash Recycling Corp.

Superior Court of Pennsylvania, 2006.
895 A.2d 595.

[Pennsy was a paving subcontractor in a construction project. The contract required Pennsy to use certain base aggregates, but permitted the use of an alternate material called AggRite which was supplied at no cost by American Ash. Although American Ash was not a party to any of the contracts, the project specifications noticed to bidders the availability from American Ash of a stipulated quantity of AggRite at no cost on a "first come, first served" basis. Pennsy contacted American Ash and obtained 11,000 tons of AggRite for the paving work. When the paving developed extensive cracking, Pennsy remedied the defects at a cost of $251,940, and spent $133,777 to dispose of the AggRite, which was classified as a hazardous waste.]

[Pennsy sued American Ash for breach of contract and breach of express and implied warranties. Pennsy argued that American Ash promoted the use of AggRite, a hazardous material, and benefitted from Pennsy's use by avoiding the substantial cost of disposal. On American Ash's demurrer the trial court held that any agreement between the parties was unenforceable because of a lack of consideration. According to the trial court, "the facts pleaded do not support an inference that disposal costs were part of any bargaining process or that American Ash offered the AggRite with an intent to avoid disposal costs." At best, American Ash had made a conditional gift. Pennsy appealed the dismissal.]

■ MELVIN, J. * * * It is axiomatic that consideration is "an essential element of an enforceable contract." Stelmack v. Glen Alden Coal Co., 339 Pa. 410, 414–415 (1940). See also Weavertown Transport Leasing, Inc. v. Moran, 834 A.2d 1169, 1172 (Pa.Super. 2003). . . . "Consideration consists of a benefit to the promisor or a detriment to the promisee." Weavertown, 834 A.2d at 1172 (citing Stelmack). "Consideration must actually be bargained for as the exchange for the promise." Stelmack, 339 Pa. at 414.

It is not enough, however, that the promisee has suffered a legal detriment at the request of the promisor. The detriment incurred must be the *"quid pro quo,"* or the "price" of the promise, and the inducement for which it was made. . . . If the promisor merely intends to make a gift to the promisee upon the performance of a condition, the promise is gratuitous and the satisfaction of the condition is not consideration for a contract. The distinction between such a conditional gift and a contract is well illustrated in Williston on Contracts, Rev.Ed., Vol. 1, Section 112, where it is said: "If a benevolent man says to a tramp,—'If you go around the corner to the clothing shop there, you may purchase an overcoat on my credit,' no reasonable person would understand that the short walk was requested as the consideration for the promise, but that in the event of the tramp going to the shop the promisor would make him a gift."

Weavertown, 834 A.2d at 1172 (quoting Stelmack, 339 Pa. at 414). Whether a contract is supported by consideration presents a question of law. Davis & Warde, Inc. v. Tripodi, 420 Pa.Super. 450 (1992).

* * *

Upon review, we disagree with the trial court that the allegations of the Complaint show only that American Ash made a conditional gift of the AggRite to Pennsy. In paragraphs 8 and 9 of the Complaint, Pennsy alleged:

American Ash actively promotes the use of AggRite as a building material to be used in base course of paved structures, and provides the material free of charge, in an effort to have others dispose of the material and thereby avoid incurring the disposal costs itself . . . American Ash provided the AggRite to Pennsy for use on the Project, which saved American Ash thousands of dollars in disposal costs it otherwise would have incurred.

Accepting these allegations as true and using the Holmesian formula for consideration, it is a fair interpretation of the Complaint that American Ash's promise to supply AggRite free of charge induced Pennsy to assume the detriment of collecting and taking title to the material, and critically, that it was this very detriment, whether assumed by Pennsy or some other successful bidder to the paving subcontract, which induced American Ash to make the promise to provide free AggRite for the project. Paragraphs 8–9 of the Complaint simply belie the notion that American Ash offered AggRite as a conditional gift to the successful bidder on the paving subcontract for which American Ash desired and expected nothing in return.

We turn now to whether consideration is lacking because Pennsy did not allege that American Ash's avoidance of disposal costs was part of any bargaining process between the parties. The Complaint does not allege that the parties discussed or even that Pennsy understood at the time it requested or accepted the AggRite that Pennsy's use of the AggRite would allow American Ash to avoid disposal costs. However, we do not believe such is necessary.

> The bargain theory of consideration does not actually require that the parties bargain over the terms of the agreement. . . . According to Holmes, an influential advocate of the bargain theory, what is required [for consideration to exist] is that the promise and the consideration be in "the relation of reciprocal conventional inducement, each for the other."

E. Allen Farnsworth, Farnsworth on Contracts § 2.6 (1990) (citing O. Holmes, The Common Law 293–94 (1881)); see also Restatement (Second) of Contracts § 71 (defining "bargained for" in terms of the Holmesian formula). Here, as explained above, the Complaint alleges facts which, if proven, would show the promise induced the detriment and the detriment induced the promise. This would be consideration. Accordingly, we reverse the dismissal of [the breach of contract claim].

* * *

NOTES

(1)   Must the consideration for the promise be actually bargained for or may the bargain be inferred from facts establishing a "reciprocal conventional inducement"? How do courts tell the difference between bargains and conditional gratuitous promises?

(2)   Creative Commons is a nonprofit organization that provides free licenses to owners of intellectual property, such as music or video. See creativecommons.org. The licenses are designed to allow artists and others to distribute their works freely while imposing conditions on what users may do with the work. The Attribution-NoDerivs 3.0 license, for example, allows recipients of the work to redistribute the work for commercial or noncommercial purposes, so long as it is passed along unchanged and in whole and with credit to the licensor. Are the Creative Commons licenses supported by consideration? Suppose a friend gave you a fishing pole on the condition that you not use it on Mondays. Have you entered into a contract?

(3)   *The Case of the Injured Mechanic.* Ray Dehn, a skilled mechanic and traveling representative of Transit Bus Sales Co. of St. Louis, was sent to Knoxville to repair a bus which Ross Palmer had purchased from the company. Dehn inspected the bus and told Palmer a belt was too loose. Palmer's driver went away and got the belt tightened. When the driver returned with the tightened belt, the three of them discussed the matter at length. While Dehn was attempting to show Palmer how tight the belt should be, the driver started the motor, cutting off two of Dehn's fingers. Dehn had thought that the driver was out of the bus and that no one was inside who could start the motor. Palmer immediately rushed Dehn to a local hospital. On the way, Palmer said: "I am awful sorry this happened, but don't worry a minute. I will see you are compensated for loss of your finger, take care of your expenses for the loss of your finger, and all." On these facts, what

theories of liability would you expect Dehn to advance? Was there consideration for Palmer's promise? See Palmer v. Dehn, 29 Tenn.App. 597 (1946).

(4)   *The Case of the Proud Grandfather.* A baby boy was born to Mr. and Mrs. Lanfier on December 17. Two days later, they named the boy "August Dwayne." He was named "August" after his maternal grandfather, August Schultz. A week later, the grandfather promised the parents that if they named the baby "August," he would give them a certain painting, valued at $5,000. They agreed. Was there a binding contract? Cf. Lanfier v. Lanfier, 227 Iowa 258 (1939). Would all doubt concerning enforceability have been removed if, in addition, Schultz had prescribed and received a $1 payment from the Lanfiers? See materials which follow.

PROBLEM: THE CASE OF THE LESSEE'S WELL

Stone leased land to Oil Company for ten years. Oil Company was to operate a service station and had an option to purchase the land at any time for $20,000. The lease provided that Stone was to supply water to Oil Company from an existing well but "in case Lessor's well fails to supply ample water, they are not responsible, and the Lessee will be required to make their own arrangements for securing water." The well failed after 18 months and the parties, after negotiations, agreed to have a new well drilled and to split the cost. A written agreement was prepared and signed by both parties. Shortly after drilling commenced, Stone visited the site and talked with a company representative, Mr. Brinson. Stone asked "What happens to my investment in the well if you exercise the option and buy the land?" and Brinson promptly answered (in front of witnesses) "Don't worry about that, you'll get your money." The well was completed at a cost of $4,000 and the parties each paid the well driller $2,000. Six months later, Oil Company exercised the option but at the closing refused to reimburse Stone for his well drilling expenses. Oil Company argued that Brinson's oral promise, if made, was unenforceable because there was no consideration. Is this argument correct? See Stonestreet v. Southern Oil Co., 226 N.C. 261 (1946).

Comment: Why Consideration?

Why do we have a consideration requirement? Many different answers have been proposed, including that the rule is a historical accident. Here are three other possible explanations.

Value-Creating Exchange and the Economic Functions of Contract Law. Law seeks, among other things, to promote the general welfare. How do lawmakers know which allocations of resources and legal rules will be welfare enhancing? One way is to look to individual choice. As we observed in Chapter One, the magic of voluntary exchange is that it enhances the welfare of both parties to it and, so long as it does not harm third parties, increases overall social welfare. *A* agrees to part with a dollar for a loaf of bread only because *A* values the bread more than the dollar. *B* agrees to part with the loaf of bread for a dollar only because *B* values the dollar more. Both *A* and *B* come out ahead. And so long as the exchange does no harm to *C*, society comes out ahead as well.

Perhaps, then, the reason for the consideration doctrine is our special interest in supporting welfare-enhancing exchange transactions. A promise that is not supported by consideration—that does not occur in the context of an exchange—is not presumptively welfare enhancing. We do not know that the promisee values the promised act more than it costs the promisor to perform it. (Think about why people use wedding registries.) Thus, Richard Posner argued in an early edition of his influential book, *Economic Analysis of Law*, that the doctrine of consideration serves to "deny liability for breach of a promise . . . where there is no exchange and where, therefore, enforcement of the promise would not advance the economic purpose of the law of contracts which is to facilitate exchange. A truly gratuitous, nonreciprocal promise to confer a benefit is not a part of the process by which resources are moved, through a series of exchanges, into successively more valuable uses." Richard Posner, Economic Analysis of Law 68–71 (2d ed. 1977).

Costs of Enforcing Gratuitous Promises. While Posner focuses on the advantages of enforcing exchange agreements, others emphasize the costs of enforcing agreements absent consideration. A promise that is not supported by consideration is a "gratuitous promise." The commitment is given as a gratuity rather than in exchange for some return promise or performance. Why don't courts enforce gratuitous promises? Consider the following explanation:

> Should the law then recognize some new formality to play the role once played by the seal? An obvious candidate is nominal consideration—that is, the form of a bargain—because it can be safely assumed that parties who falsely cast a nonbargain promise as a bargain do so for the express purpose of making the promise legally enforceable. A rule that promises in this form were enforceable would have obvious substantive advantages, but would also involve serious difficulties of administration. As a practical matter, such a form would be primarily employed to render donative promises enforceable. Both morally and legally, however, an obligation created by a donative promise should normally be excused either by acts of the promisee amounting to ingratitude, or by personal circumstances of the promisor that render it improvident to keep the promise. If Uncle promises to give Nephew $20,000 in two years, and Nephew later wrecks Uncle's living room in an angry rage, Uncle should not remain obliged. The same result should ordinarily follow if Uncle suffers a serious financial setback and is barely able to take care of the needs of his immediate family, or if Uncle's wealth remains constant but his

personal obligations significantly increase in an unexpected manner, as through illness or the birth of children.

Form alone cannot meet these problems. Thus the French and German Civil Codes, while providing special forms that enable a donative promise to be rendered legally enforceable, also provide extensive treatment of improvidence and ingratitude as defenses. For example, under article 519(1) of the German Civil Code, a promisor may refuse to keep a donative promise "insofar as, having regard to his other obligations, he is not in a position to fulfill the promise without endangering his own reasonable maintenance or the fulfillment of obligations imposed upon him by law to furnish maintenance to others." Under article 530(1), a donative promise may be revoked "if the donee, by any serious misconduct towards the donor or a close relative of the donor shows himself guilty of gross ingratitude." Similarly, under articles 960–966 of the French Civil Code, a donative promise made by a person with no living descendants is normally revoked by operation of law upon the birth of a child. Under articles 953 and 955, a donative promise can be revoked on the ground of ingratitude that involves serious cruelty, wrongs, or injuries.

As these rules suggest, the common law could not appropriately make donative promises enforceable solely on the basis of a form unless our courts were also prepared to develop and administer a body of rules dealing with the problems of improvidence and ingratitude. Certainly such an enterprise is possible. It may be questioned, however, whether the game would be worth the candle. An inquiry into improvidence involves the measurement of wealth, lifestyle, dependents' needs, and even personal utilities. An inquiry into ingratitude involves the measurement of a maelstrom, because many or most donative promises arise in an intimate context in which emotions, motives, and cues are invariably complex and highly interrelated. Perhaps the civil-law style of adjudication is suited to wrestling with these kinds of inquiries, but they have held little appeal for common-law courts, which traditionally have been oriented toward inquiry into acts rather than into personal characteristics. The question is whether the social and economic benefits of a facility for making donative promises enforceable would be worth its social and economic costs. The answer is that benefits and costs are in rough balance, so that nonrecognition of such a facility is at least as supportable as recognition would be.

Melvin A. Eisenberg, *The Principles of Consideration*, 67 Cornell L. Rev. 640, 659–62 (1982). The above argument turns on considerations of institutional competence and administrative cost. Eisenberg's core claim is that common law courts would simply do a bad job of deciding when a gratuitous promise should be enforced and when it should not be. In a later work, Eisenberg suggests another explanation: widespread enforcement might erode the value of gratuitous promises:

> One of these reasons [for not enforcing gratuitous promises] concerns the impact that enforceability would have on the moral value of gifting. The world of contract is a market world, largely driven by relatively impersonal considerations, and focused on commodities and prices. In contrast, much of the world of gift is driven by affective considerations like love, affection, friendship, gratitude, and comradeship. That world would be morally impoverished if it were to be collapsed into the world of contract. Making simple affective donative promises enforceable would have the effect of commodifying the gift relationship. Legal enforcement of such promises would move the gifted commodity, rather than the affective relationship, to the forefront and would submerge the affective relationship that a gift is intended to totemize. Simple donative promises would be degraded into bills of exchange, and the gifts made to perform such promises would be degraded into redemptions of the bills. It would never be clear to the promisee, or even the promisor, whether a donative promise that was made in an affective spirit of love, friendship, affection, gratitude, or comradeship, was also performed for those reasons, or instead was performed to discharge a legal obligation or avoid a lawsuit. Affective moral values . . . would be undermined if the enforcement of simple affective donative promises was mandated by law.

Melvin A. Eisenberg, *The Theory of Contracts*, The Theory of Contract Law: New Essays (Peter Benson, ed.) 206, 229–30 (2001). See also Aditi Bagchi, *Separating Contract and Promise*, 38 Fla. St. U. L. Rev. 707 (arguing that legal enforcement tends to degrade the value of private promises).

Exchange and Intent to Contract. In his 1941 article, *Consideration and Form*, Lon Fuller argued that the consideration doctrine provides a "natural formality," in that it separates out for legal enforcement those agreements in which "a legal transaction was intended." Lon L. Fuller, *Consideration and Form*, 41 Colum. L. Rev. 799, 815, 801 (1941). The idea here is that people are more likely to expect and want their exchange agreements to be legally enforced, whereas they are less likely to expect or want enforcement of their gratuitous promises. Randy Barnett, who argues that the enforcement of contracts is justified only when parties have consented to legal liability for breach, expands on Fuller's idea:

> The fact that a person has received something of value in return for a "promise" may indeed indicate that this promise was an expression of intention to transfer rights. Moreover, in some circumstances where gratuitous transfers are unusual, the

receipt of a benefit in return for a promise should serve as objective notice to the promisor that the promise has been interpreted by the other party to be legally binding.

Randy E. Barnett, *A Consent Theory of Contract*, 86 Colum. L. Rev. 269, 313 (1986). Or more briefly: we insist on consideration because "the existence of a bargain so frequently corresponds to the existence of a manifested intention to be legally bound." Randy E. Barnett, *Some Problems with Contract as Promise*, 77 Cornell L. Rev. 1022, 1029 (1992).

(C) INTENT TO CONTRACT AND THE SEAL

As noted in the previous Comment, one explanation for the consideration requirement is that parties to exchange agreements are more likely to expect and want legal enforcement. There is a difference between a party's intent to agree to a transaction and the same party's intent to be legally bound to that commitment, that is, his or her "intent to contract." If Clyde promises to cook dinner for Bonny, he intends to commit himself to doing just that. But he probably does not intend to give Bonny the power to sue him if he breaks his promise. Consideration, the argument goes, functions to separate out for enforcement those agreements in which the parties intend not only to commit themselves, but to be legally bound to that commitment.

But if the law really cares about whether the parties intended to contract, why the focus on consideration? What about parties who want to make a legally enforceable promise that is not supported by consideration? Should we allow them to enter into such commitments? If so, how? Coming from the other side, what about parties to exchange agreements who do not want to be legally bound? Should we allow them to opt-out of legal liability? If so, how? And are there some sorts of exchange agreements that should be presumptively unenforceable?

As we will see in this section, the black-letter rule in U.S. law is that an intent to contract is neither necessary nor sufficient for contractual liability to attach. There are, however, exceptions. Some of the exceptions, such as reporters' confidentiality promises, are discussed in this section. Others, such as the rules for missing terms and preliminary agreements, you will encounter later in the book.

In re Edwin Farnham Greene

United States District Court, Southern District of New York, 1930.
45 F.2d 428.

■ WOOLSEY, DISTRICT JUDGE. The petition for review is granted, and the order of the referee is reversed.

I.   The claimant, a woman, filed proof of claim in the sum of $375,700, based on an alleged contract, against this bankrupt's estate. The trustee in bankruptcy objected to the claim.

A hearing was held before the referee in bankruptcy and testimony taken.

The referee held the claim valid and dismissed the objections. The correctness of this ruling is raised by the trustee's petition to review and the referee's certificate.

II. For several years prior to April 28, 1926, the bankrupt, a married man, had apparently lived in adultery with the claimant. He gave her substantial sums of money. He also paid $70,000 for a house on Long Island acquired by her, which she still owns.

Throughout their relations the bankrupt was a married man, and the claimant knew it. The claimant was well over thirty years of age when the connection began. She testified that the bankrupt had promised to marry her as soon as his wife should get a divorce from him; this the bankrupt denied.

The relations of intimacy between them were discontinued in April, 1926, and they then executed a written instrument under seal which is alleged to be a binding contract and which is the foundation of the claim under consideration.

In this instrument, which was made in New York, the bankrupt undertook (1) to pay to the claimant $1,000 a month during their joint lives; (2) to assign to her a $100,000 life insurance policy on his life and to keep up the premiums on it for life, the bankrupt to pay $100,000 to the claimant in case the policy should lapse for nonpayment of premiums; and (3) to pay the rent for four years on an apartment which she had leased.

It was declared in the instrument that the bankrupt had no interest in the Long Island house or in its contents, and that he should no longer be liable for mortgage interest, taxes, and other charges on this property.

The claimant on her part released the bankrupt from all claims which she had against him.

The preamble to the instrument recites as consideration the payment of $1 by the claimant to the bankrupt, "and other good and valuable consideration."

The bankrupt kept up the several payments called for by the instrument until August, 1928, but failed to make payments thereafter.

III. * * * In view of my conclusion that the entire claim is void, however, the matter of damages is of no present importance.

IV. * * * The problem in the present case . . . is one of consideration, not of illegality, and it is clear that the past illicit intercourse is not consideration.

* * *

V. The question, therefore, is whether there was any consideration for the bankrupt's promises, apart from the past cohabitation. It seems plain that no such consideration can be found, but I will review the following points emphasized by the claimant as showing consideration:

(1) The $1 consideration recited in the paper is nominal. It cannot seriously be urged that $1, recited but not even shown to have been paid, will support an executory promise to pay hundreds of thousands of dollars.

(2) "Other good and valuable consideration[s]" are generalities that sound plausible, but the words cannot serve as consideration where the facts show that nothing good or valuable was actually given at the time the contract was made.

(3) It is said that the release of claims furnishes the necessary consideration. So it would if the claimant had had any claims to release. But the evidence shows no vestige of any lawful claim. Release from imaginary claims is not valuable consideration for a promise. In this connection, apparently, the claimant testified that the bankrupt had promised to marry her as soon as he was divorced. Assuming that he did—though he denies it—the illegality of any such promise, made while the bankrupt was still married, is so obvious that no claim could possibly arise from it, and the release of such claim could not possibly be lawful consideration.

(4) The claimant also urges that by the agreement the bankrupt obtained immunity from liability for taxes and other charges on the Long Island house. The fact is that he was never chargeable for these expenses. He doubtless had been in the habit of paying them, just as he had paid many other expenses for the claimant; but such payments were either gratuitous or were the contemporaneous price of the continuance of his illicit intercourse with the claimant.

It is absurd to suppose that, when a donor gives a valuable house to a donee, the fact that the donor need pay no taxes or upkeep thereafter on the property converts the gift into a contract upon consideration. The present case is even stronger, for the bankrupt had never owned the house and had never been liable for the taxes. He furnished the purchase price, but the conveyance was from the seller direct to the claimant.

(5) Finally, it is said that the parties intended to make a valid agreement. It is a non sequitur to say that therefore the agreement is valid.

A man may promise to make a gift to another, and may put the promise in the most solemn and formal document possible; but, barring exceptional cases, such, perhaps, as charitable subscriptions, the promise will not be enforced. The parties may shout consideration to the housetops, yet unless consideration is actually present, there is not a legally enforceable contract.

What the bankrupt obviously intended in this case was an agreement to make financial contribution to the claimant because of his past cohabitation with her, and, as already pointed out, such an agreement lacks consideration.

VI. The presence of the seal would have been decisive in the claimant's favor a hundred years ago. Then an instrument under seal required no consideration, or, to keep to the language of the cases, the seal was conclusive evidence of consideration. In New York, however, a seal is now only presumptive evidence of consideration on an executory instrument. Civil Practice Act, § 342; Harris v. Shorall, 230 N.Y. 343, 348; Alexander v. Equitable Life Assurance Society, 233 N.Y. 300, 307. This presumption was amply rebutted in this case, for the proof clearly shows, I think, that there was not in fact any consideration for the bankrupt's promise contained in the executory instrument signed by him and the claimant.

An order in accordance with this opinion may be submitted for settlement on two days' notice.

NOTES

(1) The parties to the agreement at issue in *In re Greene* apparently wanted the agreement to be legally enforceable. What are the various ways that they tried to get enforcement? Why does the court reject each? Based on the holding in *In re Greene*, would you say that an intent to contract is sufficient to create a contract?

(2) As we will see in subsequent sections, courts distinguish between the *sufficiency* of consideration and the *adequacy* of consideration. A court will not inquire into whether the exchange was a fair one—that is, whether the consideration given was adequate. When discussing minimal consideration, a "peppercorn" is often used as a paradigmatic example as smallest thing one could give in return for someone else's promise. Some contracts have used a literal peppercorn as the promised consideration. For example, the Masonic Lodge of St. Georges in Bermuda rents a lodge from the Governor of Bermuda using an annual sum of a single peppercorn.

Many do, however, insist that merely "nominal consideration" is not sufficient to constitute consideration. Thus, the comments to Restatement (Second) § 71 provide: "[A] mere pretense of bargain does not suffice, as where there is a false recital of consideration or where the purported consideration is merely nominal. In such cases there is no consideration." As usual, there are exceptions. See, for example, the rule for firm offers in Restatement (Second) § 87, discussed later in this Chapter.

(3) Can you think of any other reasons the court might have been especially reluctant to enforce the agreement at issue in *In re Greene*? Of course there is the fact that it was between paramours, one of whom was married. Thus the court relies on public policy considerations to conclude that the bankrupt's promise to marry the claimant after divorcing his wife was unenforceable. We will return to the topic of unenforceability on the basis of public policy in Chapter Four. But what else? Notice that this is a proceeding in bankruptcy. Who is arguing that the agreement should not be

enforced? Do you have any guesses about why the bankrupt and the claimant might have entered into this agreement in the spring of 1926?

(4) In 1930 in New York State, the presence of a seal creates a presumption of consideration. In 1962 the New York legislature passed a statute providing that "the presence or absence of a seal upon a written instrument executed after August thirty-first, nineteen hundred and forty-one shall be without legal effect." N.Y. Gen. Constr. Law § 44–a (McKinney). In New York, therefore, a seal no longer creates a presumption of consideration. Other states retain a presumption rule. See, e.g., Mich. Comp. Laws Ann. § 600.2139 (2016).

Comment: Nominal Consideration, The Seal and The Model Written Obligation Act

In re Greene stands for the proposition that an intent to undertake a legally enforceable commitment is not enough to get you one. In the absence of an authorized formality (such as a seal), a gift promise, even though written, signed and expressly stating an intent to assume a legal obligation, is not enforceable.

Nominal Consideration. It is well established that courts will not inquire into the adequacy of consideration, which is to say the fairness of the bargain that the parties struck. Under a strict reading of this rule, payment of a very small sum—such as one dollar, or a peppercorn—should be enough to satisfy the consideration requirement. And in fact this is the approach advocated by the First Restatement, illustrated as follows:

> A wishes to make a binding promise to his son B to convey to B Blackacre, which is worth $5000. Being advised that a gratuitous promise is not binding, A writes to B an offer to sell Blackacre for $1. B accepts. B's promise to pay $1 is sufficient consideration.

Restatement § 84 ill. 1. It is unclear whether this illustration was supported by the contemporary case law. Many cases permitting nominal consideration involved special sorts of transactions—guarantees, options, and the like—or transactions in which there was also detrimental reliance. See Joseph Siprut, Comment, *The Peppercorn Reconsidered: Why a Promise to Sell Blackacre for Nominal Consideration Is Not Binding, but Should Be*, 97 Nw. U. L. Rev. 1809, 1817–21 (2003).

In any case, *In re Greene* represents the more widely accepted approach today, which rejects mere nominal consideration. Contemporary courts are likely to dismiss as mere "pretense of bargain" parties' attempts to dress up a gift promise with false recitals of consideration or the exchange of a nominal sum. Restatement (Second) § 71 cmt. b. See also id. §§ 79 cmt. d ("Disparity in value, with or without other circumstances, sometimes indicates that the purported consideration was not in fact bargained for but was a mere formality or pretense. Such a sham or "nominal" consideration does not satisfy the requirement of § 71."), 218 ill. 3 (Blackacre example with sham consideration resulting in no contract).

The Seal. Nominal consideration can be viewed as a sort of formality. It is a sign of the parties' intent to achieve a certain legal result. Contracting parties have historically used many different formalities to seal their deals, sometimes as matters of custom and sometimes to comply with official requirements. We find in the Bible Abraham establishing a covenant with God by the scorching of "a three-year-old heifer, a three-year-old she-goat, and a three-year-old ram, and a turtle-dove, and a pigeon." Genesis 15:7–10, 17–18. Both Homer and Herodotus describe a ceremonial libation which accompanied solemn agreements. Merchants in the Middle Ages often confirmed that an agreement was binding by the exchange of a "God's penny." And of course contracting parties today often end a deal with a handshake. All of these conventions reflect the traditional employment of formalities to signal seriousness or enforceability.

An important example of a *legal* formality was the Roman *stipulatio*, or stipulation. Under the Justinian Code, some agreements would be enforced only if the one side requested performance, prefaced by "Spondes-ne . . . ," and the other side responded using the word "Spondeo." See W.W. Buckland, A Manual of Roman Private Law 262–65 (2d ed. 1939). This formality has both ancient and modern counterparts. Today in many civil law countries, the promise in a notarial deed, executed before a notary (a governmental official) is binding precisely because of the method employed in making it.

At common law, the form *par excellence* was the seal. In early days, the seal was a wax substance attached to the document. Later, a paper wafer was often used, or simply the written words "under seal" or "L.S." (*locus sigilli*, place of the seal). The writ of covenant, which was used to enforce certain agreements, conditioned enforcement on the existence of a writing under seal. A.W.B. Simpson, A History of the Common Law of Contract: The Rise of the Action of Assumpsit 22–25 (1987). The legal effect did not derive from the substance of the agreement—e.g., whether it was a bargained-for exchange—but from the formal mode in which the promise was cast. Section 95(1) of the Second Restatement provides the common law rule for when an agreement under seal is binding: "In the absence of statute a promise is binding without consideration if (a) it is in writing and sealed; and (b) the document containing the promise is delivered; and (c) the promisor and promisee are named in the document or so described as to be capable of identification when it is delivered."

Can law rescue Peanuts?

© 1964 United Feature Syndicate, Inc.

During the early twentieth century, many U.S. States passed statutes that radically reduced the legal effect of a sealed writing. Some abolished the seal entirely. This approach is reflected in UCC § 2–203, which "makes it clear that every effect of the seal which relates to 'sealed instruments' as such is wiped out insofar as contracts for sale are concerned." UCC § 2–203 cmt. 1. Other state legislatures retained the seal, but provided that lack of consideration should remain a defense to sealed instruments. See *In re Greene*, supra. Other states have adopted other modifications, such as providing a longer statute of limitations for contracts under seal. For more detail, see the statutory note preceding Restatement (Second) § 95. For the practitioner, this means that it is crucial to know the effect of the seal in the jurisdiction in which you are working.

Model Written Obligations Act. The broad abolition of the seal had its costs. Many regarded the seal as a useful legal device, if for no other reason than it provided a convenient method for making legally binding gratuitous promises. See E. Allan Farnsworth, Changing Your Mind: The Law of Regretted Decisions 82–89 (1998) (arguing that gift promises should be enforceable if the promisor has expressed an intention to assume a legal obligation). It was inevitable that attention would be given to filling the vacuum, and it was most natural to turn to that most common of contemporary "forms," the signed writing. In 1925, largely at the instigation of Samuel Williston, the National Conference of Commissioners on Uniform State Laws approved the draft of the Uniform Written Obligations Act. The recommended statute was a model of brevity:

> A written release or promise made and signed by the person releasing or promising shall not be invalid or unenforceable for lack of consideration, if the writing also contains an additional express statement in any form of language that the signer intends to be legally bound.

The proposal met with a singular lack of success. Only Pennsylvania has adopted and retained the Act. (Query: Could parties in other jurisdictions contract around the consideration requirement by adding a choice of law provision designating that the gratuitous agreement is to be governed by Pennsylvania law?) In 1943, the NCCUSL renamed it the "Model Written Obligations Act." For a discussion, see Reeve, *Uniform Written Obligations Act,* 76 U. Pa. L. Rev. 580 (1928).

In addition, there are a few statutes that accord some extraordinary legal effect to a signed writing. But with the exception of New York, the practical significance of this legislation seems to have been minimal. See New York General Obligations Law §§ 5–1101 through 5–1115.

Uniform Commercial Code. The decline of the seal has not meant the complete abandonment of formal rules. The Uniform Commercial Code provides several examples in which a signed writing can serve as a substitute for consideration. Section 1–306, which covers "Waiver or Renunciation of Claim or Right After Breach," provides that any claim or right arising out of an alleged breach can be discharged without consideration by a written waiver or renunciation signed and delivered by the aggrieved party. Section 2–205 provides:

> An offer by a merchant to buy or sell goods in a signed writing which by its terms gives assurance that it will be held open is not revocable, for lack of consideration, during the time stated or if no time is stated for a reasonable time, but in no event may such period of irrevocability exceed three months; but any such

term of assurance on a form supplied by the offeree must be separately signed by the offeror.

Also relevant here is UCC § 2–201's Statute of Frauds writing requirement, which conditions the enforcement of certain contracts on the existence of a writing and UCC § 2–209, which allows an agreement modifying a contract to binding without consideration so long as it is in good faith and conforms to the statute of frauds.

Dan Cohen v. Cowles Media Co.

Supreme Court of Minnesota, 1990.
457 N.W.2d 199, reversed, 501 U.S. 663 (1991), opinion on remand,
479 N.W.2d 387 (1992).

■ SIMONETT, JUSTICE. This case asks whether a newspaper's breach of its reporter's promise of anonymity to a news source is legally enforceable. We conclude the promise is not enforceable, neither as a breach of contract claim nor, in this case, under promissory estoppel. We affirm the court of appeals' dismissal of plaintiff's claim based on fraudulent misrepresentation, and reverse the court of appeals' allowance of the breach of contract claim.

Claiming a reporter's promise to keep his name out of a news story was broken, plaintiff Dan Cohen sued defendants Northwest Publications, Inc., publisher of the St. Paul Pioneer Press Dispatch (Pioneer Press), and Cowles Media Company, publisher of the Minneapolis Star and Tribune (Star Tribune). The trial court ruled that the First Amendment did not bar Cohen's contract and misrepresentation claims. The jury then found liability on both claims and awarded plaintiff $200,000 compensatory damages jointly and severally against the defendants. In addition, the jury awarded punitive damages of $250,000 against each defendant.

* * *

On October 27, 1982, in the closing days of the state gubernatorial election campaign, Dan Cohen separately approached Lori Sturdevant, the Star Tribune reporter, and Bill Salisbury, the Pioneer Press reporter, and to each stated in so many words:

> I have some documents which may or may not relate to a candidate in the upcoming election, and if you will give me a promise of confidentiality, that is that I will be treated as an anonymous source, that my name will not appear in any material in connection with this, and you will also agree that you're not going to pursue with me a question of who my source is, then I'll furnish you with the documents.

Sturdevant and Salisbury were experienced reporters covering the gubernatorial election and knew Cohen as an active Republican associated with the Wheelock Whitney campaign. Cohen told Sturdevant that he would also be offering the documents to other news organizations.

Neither reporter informed Cohen that their promises of confidentiality were subject to approval or revocation by their editors. Both reporters promised to keep Cohen's identity anonymous, and both intended to keep that promise. At trial Cohen testified he insisted on anonymity because he feared retaliation from the news media and politicians. Cohen turned over to each reporter copies of two public court records concerning Marlene Johnson, the DFL candidate for lieutenant governor. The first was a record of a 1969 case against Johnson for three counts of unlawful assembly, subsequently dismissed; the second document was a 1970 record of conviction for petit theft, which was vacated about a year later.

Both newspapers, on the same day, then interviewed Marlene Johnson for her explanation and reaction. The Star Tribune also assigned a reporter to find the original court records in the dead-storage vaults. The reporter discovered that Gary Flakne, known to be a Wheelock Whitney supporter, had checked out the records a day earlier; no one, before Flakne, had looked at the records for years. The reporter called Flakne and asked why he had checked out the records. Flakne replied, "I did it for Dan Cohen." The Star Tribune editors thereafter conferred and decided to publish the story the next day including Dan Cohen's identity. Acting independently, the Pioneer Press Dispatch editors also decided to break their reporter's promise and to publish the story with Cohen named as the source.

The decision to identify Cohen in the stories was the subject of vigorous debate within the editorial staffs of the two newspapers. Some staff members argued that the reporter's promise of confidentiality should be honored at all costs. Some contended that the Johnson incidents were not newsworthy and did not warrant publishing, and, in any case, if the story was published, it would be enough to identify the source as a source close to the Whitney campaign. Other editors argued that not only was the Johnson story newsworthy but so was identification of Cohen as the source; that to attribute the story to a veiled source would be misleading and cast suspicion on others; and that the Johnson story was already spreading throughout the news media community and was discoverable from other sources not bound by confidentiality. Then, too, the Star Tribune had editorially endorsed the Perpich-Johnson ticket; some of its editors feared if the newspaper did not print the Johnson story, other news media would, leaving the Star Tribune vulnerable to a charge it was protecting the ticket it favored. Salisbury and Sturdevant both objected strongly to the editorial decisions to identify Cohen as the source of the court records. Indeed, Sturdevant refused to attach her name to the story.

Promising to keep a news source anonymous is a common, well-established journalistic practice. So is the keeping of those promises. None of the editors or reporters who testified could recall any other instance when a reporter's promise of confidentiality to a source had been overruled by the editor. Cohen, who had many years' experience in politics and public relations, said this was the first time in his experience that an editor or a reporter did not honor a promise to a source.

The next day, October 28, 1982, both newspapers published stories about Johnson's arrests and conviction. Both articles published Cohen's name, along with denials by the regular Whitney campaign officials of any connection with the published stories. Under the headline, *Marlene Johnson arrests disclosed by Whitney ally*, the Star Tribune also gave Johnson's explanation of the arrests and identified Cohen as a "political associate of IR gubernatorial candidate Wheelock Whitney" and named the advertising firm where Cohen was employed. The Pioneer Press Dispatch quoted Johnson as saying the release of the information was "a last-minute smear campaign."

The same day as the two newspaper articles were published, Cohen was fired by his employer. The next day, October 29, a columnist for the Star Tribune attacked Cohen and his "sleazy" tactics, with, ironically, no reference to the newspaper's own ethics in dishonoring its promise. A day later the Star Tribune published a cartoon on its editorial page depicting Dan Cohen with a garbage can labeled "last minute campaign smears."

Cohen could not sue for defamation because the information disclosed was true. He couched his complaint, therefore, in terms of fraudulent misrepresentation and breach of contract. We now consider whether these two claims apply here.

I.

First of all, we agree with the court of appeals that the trial court erred in not granting defendants' post-trial motions for judgment notwithstanding the verdict on the misrepresentation claim.

For fraud there must be a misrepresentation of a past or present fact. A representation as to future acts does not support an action for fraud merely because the represented act did not happen, unless the promisor did not intend to perform at the time the promise was made. . . . Cohen admits that the reporters intended to keep their promises, as, indeed, they testified and as their conduct confirmed. Moreover, the record shows that the editors had no intention to reveal Cohen's identity until later when more information was received and the matter was discussed with other editors. These facts do not support a fraud claim. For this reason and for the other reasons cited by the court of appeals, we affirm the court of appeals' ruling. Because the punitive damages award hinges on the tort claim of misrepresentation, it, too, must be set aside as the court of appeals ruled.

II.

A contract, it is said, consists of an offer, an acceptance, and consideration. Here, we seemingly have all three, plus a breach. We think, however, the matter is not this simple.

Unquestionably, the promises given in this case were intended by the promisors to be kept. The record is replete with the unanimous testimony of reporters, editors, and journalism experts that protecting a confidential source of a news story is a sacred trust, a matter of "honor," of "morality," and required by professional ethics. Only in dire circumstances might a promise of confidentiality possibly be ethically broken, and instances were cited where a reporter has gone to jail rather than reveal a source. The keeping of promises is professionally important for at least two reasons. First, to break a promise of confidentiality which has induced a source to give information is dishonorable. Secondly, if it is known that promises will not be kept, sources may dry up. The media depend on confidential sources for much of their news; significantly, at least up to now, it appears that journalistic ethics have adequately protected confidential sources.

The question before us, however, is not whether keeping a confidential promise is ethically required but whether it is legally enforceable; whether, in other words, the law should superimpose a legal obligation on a moral and ethical obligation. The two obligations are not always coextensive.

The newspapers argue that the reporter's promise should not be contractually binding because these promises are usually given clandestinely and orally, hence they are often vague, subject to misunderstanding, and a fertile breeding ground for lawsuits. . . . Perhaps so, and this may be a factor to weigh in the balance; but this objection goes only to problems of proof, rather than to the merits of having such a cause of action at all. Moreover, in this case at least, we have a clear-cut promise.

The law, however, does not create a contract where the parties intended none. . . . Nor does the law consider binding every exchange of promises. See, e.g., Minn.Stat. ch. 553 (1988) (abolishing breaches of contract to marry); see also Restatement (Second) of Contracts §§ 189–91 (1981) (promises impairing family relations are unenforceable). We are not persuaded that in the special milieu of media newsgathering a source and a reporter ordinarily believe they are engaged in making a legally binding contract. They are not thinking in terms of offers and acceptances in any commercial or business sense. * * *

* * *

In other words, contract law seems here an ill fit for a promise of news source confidentiality. To impose a contract theory on this arrangement puts an unwarranted legal rigidity on a special ethical relationship, precluding necessary consideration of factors underlying that ethical relationship. We conclude that a contract cause of action is inappropriate for these particular circumstances.

[The court went on to hold that Cohen might claim promissory estoppel under state law, but that the First Amendment barred such a claim, a decision which the U.S. Supreme Court later overruled.]

NOTES

(1)   The court recognizes that there was, seemingly, an offer, an acceptance, and consideration. Why, then, was there not a contract?

(2)   Reporters' promises of confidentiality are not often litigated. The few other courts that have considered similar cases have generally followed *Cohen*'s holding, if not always its reasoning. See Ruzicka v. Conde Nast Publ'ns, Inc., 939 F.2d 578, 582 (8th Cir. 1991) (applying Minnesota law); Pierce v. The Clarion Ledger, 452 F. Supp. 2d 661, 663–64 (S.D. Miss. 2006); Steele v. Isikoff, 130 F. Supp. 2d 23, 31–32 (D.D.C. 2000). In *Ventura v. The Cincinnati Enquirer*, 396 F.3d 784, 791–93 (6th Cir. 2005), the court held that a reporter's confidentiality promise related to information concerning criminal activity was unenforceable on grounds of public policy. In *Doe v. Univision Television Group, Inc.*, 717 So.2d 63, 65 (Fla. App. 1998), on the contrary, the court held that a source should have been allowed to sue for both breach of contract and promissory estoppel.

Comment: Intent to Contract

If the lesson of *In re Greene* is that an intent to be legally bound is not sufficient to create a contract, the lesson of *Cohen* would seem to be that it is sometimes necessary. It is unclear, however, whether *Cohen* should be read broadly, as applying to cases other than those of reporters' promises of confidentiality. Perhaps the Minnesota Supreme Court's reasons for limiting enforcement in *Cohen* had not so much to do with its interest in the parties' intent, but with its concerns that liability in contract might interfere with the newspaper's First Amendment interests—as indicated by its separate holding that the First Amendment barred any promissory estoppel claim.

In fact, section 21 of the Second Restatement suggests nearly the opposite rule from that in *Cohen*: "Neither real nor apparent intention that a promise be legally binding is essential to the formation of a contract. . . ." The comments illustrate the Restatement rule as follows:

> A orally promises to sell B a book in return for B's promise to pay $5. A and B both think such promises are not binding unless in writing. Nevertheless there is a contract, unless one of them intends not to be legally bound and the other knows or has reason to know of that intention.

Id. § 21 cmt. a, ill. 2. Corbin provides a different example:

> There seems to be no serious doubt that a mutual agreement to trade a horse for a cow would be an enforceable contract, even though it is made by two ignorant persons who never heard of a

legal relation and who do not know that society offers any kind of a remedy for the enforcement of such an agreement.

Arthur Linton Corbin, 1 Corbin on Contracts § 34, 135 (1st ed. 1950). According to the Restatement rule, not only is an intent to contract not sufficient for legal liability, but neither is it necessary.

But this is not all there is to it. Section 21 of the Second Restatement goes on to provide that "a manifestation of intention that a promise shall not affect legal relations may prevent the formation of a contract." This accurately restates the judicial practice of generally (though not always!) enforcing TINALEA clauses, which use words like "This is not a legally enforceable agreement." The first half of section 21 says that a manifest intent *to* contract is not necessary for legal liability, while the second half says that a manifest intent *not to* contract is sufficient to defeat legal liability. One can therefore read section 21 as establishing a default: Unless parties to an agreement with consideration manifest a contrary intention, their agreement is enforceable in contract.

But this too oversimplifies matters. As *Cohen* illustrates, in some circumstances courts flip the default and hold that a bargained-for exchange is not enforceable unless the parties specifically said they meant it to be. Thus, comment b to section 21 provides:

> In some situations the normal understanding is that no legal obligation arises, and some unusual manifestation of intention is necessary to create a contract. Traditional examples are social engagements and agreements within a family group. . . . Where the family relation is not close, valuable services rendered in the home may make binding an express or implied promise to pay for the services; but even in such cases it would often be understood that there is no legal obligation while the agreement is entirely executory on both sides.

When should the default be that a bargained-for agreement is not legally enforceable?

The black-letter rules with respect to intent to contract are very different in other countries. The Principles of European Contract Law provide something like a Restatement of the various European laws of contract and say: "In order to be bound by a contract a party must have an intention to be legally bound." *The Commission of European Contract Law*, Principles of European Contract Law (Ole Lando and Hugh Beale, eds.) art. 2:101 cmt. B (2000). Similarly, Article 14(1) of the CISG reads: "A proposal for concluding a contract addressed to one or more specific persons constitutes an offer if it . . . indicates the intention of the offeror to be bound in case of acceptance." And in Great Britain "it has been held that an agreement, though supported by consideration, was not binding as a contract because it was made without any intention of creating legal relations." 1 Chitty on Contracts (H.G. Beale, ed.) 198 (29th ed. 2004); see also Balfour v. Balfour [1919] 2 K.B. 571 (establishing the rule).

It is not obvious, however, that these rules make a difference in practice. Stephen Hedley, after studying the cases, concluded that English courts in fact rarely insist on separate evidence of the parties' intent to be legally bound. "Where the parties are dealing at arms' length, the rule is simple: there is no requirement of intention to create legal relations." Stephen Hedley, *Keeping Contract in Its Place*—Balfour v. Balfour *and the Enforceability of Informal Agreements*, 5 Oxford J. Legal Stud. 391, 412 (1985). Instead, according to Hedley, the rule is invoked to prevent the enforcement of agreements that are disfavored for other reasons. "If liability were thought appropriate on certain facts, it could plausibly be made out as 'intended'; if not, it would be easy to deny the existence of the requisite intention." Id. at 403. Is this what's going on in *Cohen*? For more on these topics, see Gregory Klass, *Intent to Contract*, 95 Va. L. Rev. 1437 (2009).

Should the law care whether the parties intended legal liability? The answer depends, at least in part, on how one thinks about contract law.

> Theorists commonly adopt one of two pictures of contract law. On the first picture, entering into a contract is an act of self-legislation in which the parties create new legal obligations for themselves. * * * On this picture, contract law is what H.L.A. Hart calls a "power-conferring" rule. It enables persons to create and modify their legal obligations to one another. The other picture depicts contract law as concerned with extralegal wrongs, such as breaking a promise, causing reliance harms, or unjustly enriching oneself at the expense of another. * * * On this picture, contract law is what Hart calls a "duty-imposing" rule: It is designed to require promisors to perform or to compensate promisees for the harms caused when they fail to do so.

Gregory Klass, *Three Pictures of Contract: Duty, Power, and Compound Rule*, 83 N.Y.U. L. Rev. 1726, 1727 (2008). If you think of contract law as a sort of private legislative power, it is natural to assume we want legal liability only when the parties intended it. Legislators typically intend their legislative acts to be legally effective. If, on the contrary, you think of contract law as responding to the moral wrong of failing to perform one's agreements, the parties' intent to contract seems less important. From this perspective, contract law is more like tort law: it imposes legal liability based on wrongs, no matter whether the wrongdoer has agreed to it or not.

PROBLEM: THE CASE OF THE NO-HASSLE HOUSE

In 2002, Husband moved out of the house he had occupied with Wife. In an angry email shortly after he left, Husband wrote to Wife, "I don't want to go to court over all this. As far as I'm concerned, you can keep the damn house so long as you leave me the hell alone." Husband and Wife did not divorce, and Husband retained title to the house. For ten years the two had no further contact, and Husband continued to pay the mortgage on the house. In 2012, Husband sold the house, which was still in his name, to Husband's brother. Husband's brother immediately brought an action for the eviction of Wife, and Wife sued Husband for breach of contract. What result? Compare Ferris v. Weaven, [1952] 2 All E.R. 233.

(D) MORAL OBLIGATION

Is it ever the case that events or circumstances occurring *before* the promise is made are sufficient reason for legal enforcement of the promise? The answer is: Maybe. Sometimes where there already exists an obligation that is not legally enforceable, a promise to perform it is enough to create a legal obligation, even in the absence of (additional) consideration. Cases of this sort fall into two broad categories: (1) prior legally enforceable obligations that, at the time of promising, are no longer enforceable due to a statute of limitations or bankruptcy and (2) preexisting moral obligations. The rules with respect to prior obligations of the first sort are fairly clear. There is less agreement about what the proper rule is for prior moral obligations.

First Hawaiian Bank v. Jack Zukerkorn

Intermediate Court of Appeals of Hawaii, 1981.
2 Haw.App. 383.

■ BURNS, JUDGE. Defendant-Appellant Jack Zukerkorn appeals the summary judgment entered against him in favor of Plaintiff-Appellee First Hawaiian Bank (hereinafter "Bank"). The general question is whether this case involves any genuine issues of material fact. The specific question is whether, as a matter of law, Zukerkorn revived two stale debts which otherwise were uncollectible because the applicable period of limitations had run. We hold that the revival question is a genuine issue of material fact.

Zukerkorn executed in favor of the Bank a $6,394.21 demand note dated November 22, 1965, and a $2,500.00 two-year note dated September 23, 1966. He made no payments on either note.

On August 6, 1973, Zukerkorn obtained an automobile purchase loan from the Bank, and he paid it off on April 6, 1976.

On or about December 11, 1975, Zukerkorn applied to the Bank for a master charge credit card. He admits that the Bank told him that he owed "a small amount of money on an old account"; that issuance of the card was conditioned on his agreement to pay $100.00 per month on the old account; that he agreed to the condition; and that he received a credit card. He denies the Bank's assertion that the November 22, 1965, and the September 23, 1966, notes were specifically identified and that his agreement specifically related to them.

Zukerkorn also denies the Bank's assertion that he paid $200.00 in cash at or about the time he made the agreement. Both parties agree that after the agreement, Zukerkorn made payments on the automobile loan, on the master charge account, and that pursuant to his agreement (the terms of which are in dispute), he paid $200.00 on May 12, 1976; $100.00 on June 8, 1976; $100.00 on July 12, 1976; and $100.00 on August 23, 1976.

On March 3, 1978, the Bank sued Zukerkorn on the November 22, 1965, note; the September 23, 1966, note; and on the balance due on the master charge account.

On November 27, 1978, the lower court entered summary judgment in favor of the Bank on all three of its claims.

Pursuant to Hawaii Rules of Civil Procedure, Rule 56(e), we affirm that portion of the summary judgment which relates to the $4,594.60 owed on the master charge account. The Bank's affidavits concerning this account were sufficient and they were not contradicted by Zukerkorn.

We turn, then, to the portion of the summary judgment which relates to the November 22, 1965, and the September 23, 1966, notes. Collection of these notes was barred by the applicable six-year statute of limitations unless something occurred which started it running anew.

After reading the authorities, we state the applicable law to be as follows: A new promise by the debtor to pay his debt, whether then barred by the applicable statute of limitations or not, binds the debtor for a new limitations period. The promise may be express or implied. If it is express, it may be unconditional or conditional, but if conditional, it is not effective until the condition is performed. The promise may be implied from an express acknowledgment of the debt or from part payment thereof. However, an express acknowledgment of the debt or part payment thereof is only *prima facie* evidence of a new promise which may be rebutted by other evidence and by the circumstances under which it is made.

Therefore, we may sustain the summary judgment issued in favor of the Bank only if we conclude that viewed most favorably to Zukerkorn the facts show, as a matter of law, that within six years prior to March 3, 1978, Zukerkorn promised to pay the two stale debts.

Zukerkorn could have promised (1) by an express promise to pay the two stale debts or (2) by an express acknowledgment of the two stale debts or (3) by part payment of the two stale debts. Zukerkorn, however, denies doing any of the three. His evidence is that he agreed to pay and in fact paid "a small amount on an old account"; he denies that he acknowledged the existence of the two stale debts or that he agreed to pay them or that he paid on them.

Further, even if it were admitted that Zukerkorn expressly acknowledged the two debts or that he made part payment on them, such action on his part is only *prima facie* evidence of a new promise which may be rebutted by other evidence and by the circumstances under which it is made. The court below cannot imply a promise from the mere fact of acknowledgment or part payment as an inference of law. It must be left to the trier of fact.

Consequently, we hold that Zukerkorn has raised genuine issues of material fact with respect to his obligation to pay the notes of November 22, 1965, and September 23, 1966, and that the lower court erred in entering summary judgment with respect to them.

The summary judgment is partially affirmed and partially reversed, and this case is remanded for further proceedings consistent with this opinion.

NOTES

(1)   What do you think are the reasons for having a statute of limitations? Is the rule in *First Hawaiian v. Zukerkorn* consistent with some or all of those purposes?

(2)   Restatement (Second) § 82(1) provides:

> A promise to pay all or part of an antecedent contractual or quasi-contractual indebtedness owed by the promisor is binding if the indebtedness is still enforceable or would be except for the effect of a statute of limitations.

What counts as "a promise to pay all or part" of the prior obligation? Section 82(2) provides a broad test:

> The following facts operate as such a promise unless other facts indicate a different intention:
>
> (a)   A voluntary acknowledgment to the obligee, admitting the present existence of the antecedent indebtedness; or
>
> (b)   A voluntary transfer of money, a negotiable instrument, or other thing by the obligor to the obligee, made as interest on or part payment of or collateral security for the antecedent indebtedness; or
>
> (c)   A statement to the obligee that the statute of limitations will not be pleaded as a defense.

Is this broad definition of "a promise to pay" good policy? What incentives does it create for debtors who know the rule? What about for creditors? See the next Comment.

(3)   The Restatement rule for the revival of debts that have been discharged in bankruptcy is somewhat narrower: "An express promise to pay all or part of an indebtedness of the promisor, discharged or dischargeable in bankruptcy proceedings begun before the promise is made, is binding." Restatement (Second) § 83. Why require an express promise to revive debts that have been discharged in bankruptcy? What's the difference between these debts and those that cannot be enforced because the statute of limitations has run? Note, however, that changes to federal bankruptcy law in 1978 and 2005 significantly curtailed a bankrupt person's ability to revive a debt. See, e.g., In re Getzoff, 180 B.R. 572, 574 (B.A.P. 9th Cir. 1995) ("Pursuant to [11 U.S.C. §§] 524(c) and (d), there are five requirements that

must be fulfilled in order to properly reaffirm a previously discharged debt: (1) the agreement must be made prior to discharge; (2) the agreement must advise the debtor that the reaffirmation may be rescinded up to sixty days after it is filed; (3) the agreement must be filed with the court; (4) the debtor cannot already have rescinded the agreement within the proper time frame; and (5) the agreement must be in the best interest of the debtor.").

Comment: Statute of Limitations, Obsolete Debt and Partial Payment Revival

Statutes of limitations vary by state and by the type of contract claim. For credit card debt ("open-ended accounts"), the time to sue ranges from 3 years (for example, in Arizona) to 10 years (in Rhode Island). Most states have established longer statute of limitations periods for promissory notes (such as mortgages) and other written contracts—often at least 6 years. In most states, either an affirmation of indebtedness or a partial payment will be sufficient to "revive" the statute of limitations. Under Section 605(a) of the Fair Credit Reporting Act, 15 U.S.C. § 1681(c), a creditor can maintain a negative comment on a debtor's credit report until the debt becomes "obsolete," which occurs 7 years after default. Thus, under this federal statute, it is possible to have debt which is not obsolete (and thus on your credit report), but for which the statute has run (and thus is not subject to suit).

Debt collectors who are unable to collect on consumer credit accounts in default sometimes sell to "debt buyers" accounts that are not susceptible to suit either because the statute of limitations has run or because the original debtor is deceased (in the industry called "dead debt"). The debt buyers then use a number of techniques to induce the debtors to pay on these accounts. They might try to convince debtors or relatives of debtors that they have a moral duty to pay back the debts. They might try to convince debtors to pay even a small amount on the debt, and then use the payment as evidence to "revive" the debt. Or they might use the threat of posting negative comments to the debtor's credit report on non-obsolete debt.

Is it a deceptive trade practice to "trick" a debtor into paying a small amount after the statute has run and then sue for the remaining balance? Would it be oppressive to contact a grieving child of a recently deceased debtor and argue that the loved one would have wanted her debts paid? The recent financial crisis has made these debt buyer practices more prominent.

On January 30, 2012, the Federal Trade Commission entered into a consent decree with the nation's largest debt buyer, Asset Acceptance, concerning certain allegations regarding attempts to collect on debts after the statute of limitations had run. Under the decree, the defendant agreed *inter alia* to make the following disclosure to debtors after the statute of limitations had run, but who still had non-obsolete debt: "The law limits how long you can be sued on a debt. Because of the age of your debt, we will not sue you for it. If you do not pay the debt, we [Asset Acceptance, LLC] may [continue to] report it to the credit reporting agencies [as unpaid]." Will this disclosure substantially reduce debtor payments? Should it?

Daniel Mills v. Seth Wyman

Supreme Judicial Court of Massachusetts, 1825.
20 Mass. (3 Pick.) 207.

This was an action of assumpsit brought to recover a compensation for the board, nursing, & c., of Levi Wyman, son of the defendant, from the 5th to the 20th of February, 1821. The plaintiff then lived at Hartford, in Connecticut; the defendant, at Shrewsbury, in this county. Levi Wyman, at the time when the services were rendered, was about 25 years of age, and had long ceased to be a member of his father's family. He was on his return from a voyage at sea, and being suddenly taken sick at Hartford, and being poor and in distress, was relieved by the plaintiff in the manner and to the extent above stated. On the 24th of February, after all the expenses had been incurred, the defendant wrote a letter to the plaintiff, promising to pay him such expenses. There was no consideration for this promise, except what grew out of the relation which subsisted between Levi Wyman and the defendant, and Howe, J., before whom the cause was tried in the Court of Common Pleas, thinking this not sufficient to support the action, directed a nonsuit. To this direction the plaintiff filed exceptions.

■ PARKER, C.J. General rules of law established for the protection and security of honest and fair-minded men, who may inconsiderately make promises without any equivalent, will sometimes screen men of a different character from engagements which they are bound in *foro conscientiae* to perform. This is a defect inherent in all human systems of legislation. The rule that a mere verbal promise, without any consideration, cannot be enforced by action, is universal in its application, and cannot be departed from to suit particular cases in which a refusal to perform such a promise may be disgraceful.

The promise declared on in this case appears to have been made without any legal consideration. The kindness and services towards the sick son of the defendant were not bestowed at his request. The son was in no respect under the care of the defendant. He was twenty-five years old, and had long left his father's family. On his return from a foreign country, he fell sick among strangers, and the plaintiff acted the part of the good Samaritan, giving him shelter and comfort until he died. The defendant, his father, on being informed of this event, influenced by a transient feeling of gratitude, promises in writing to pay the plaintiff for the expenses he had incurred. But he has determined to break this promise, and is willing to have his case appear on record as a strong example of particular injustice sometimes necessarily resulting from the operation of general rules.

It is said a moral obligation is a sufficient consideration to support an express promise; and some authorities lay down the rule thus broadly; but upon examination of the cases we are satisfied that the universality of the rule cannot be supported, and that there must have been some preexisting obligation, which has become inoperative by positive law, to form a basis for an effective promise. The cases of debts barred by the statute of limitations, of debts incurred by infants, of debts of bankrupts, are generally put for illustration of the rule. Express promises founded on such preexisting equitable obligations may be enforced; there is a good consideration for them; they merely remove an impediment created by law to the recovery of debts honestly due, but which public policy protects the debtors from being compelled to pay. In all these cases there was originally a *quid pro quo*; and according to the principles of natural justice the party receiving ought to pay; but the legislature has said he shall not be coerced; then comes the promise to pay the debt that is barred, the promise of the man to pay the debt of the infant, of the discharged bankrupt to restore to his creditor what by the law he had lost. In all these cases there is a moral obligation founded upon an antecedent valuable consideration. These promises therefore have a sound legal basis. They are not promises to pay something for nothing; not naked pacts; but the voluntary revival or creation of obligation which before existed in natural law, but which had been dispensed with, not for the benefit of the party obliged solely, but principally for the public convenience. If moral obligation, in its fullest sense, is a good substratum for an express promise, it is not easy to perceive why it is not equally good to support an implied promise. What a man ought to do, generally he ought to be made to do, whether he promise or refuse. But the law of society has left most of such obligations to the *interior* forum, as the tribunal of conscience has been aptly called. Is there not a moral obligation upon every son who has become affluent by means of the education and advantages bestowed upon him by his father, to relieve that father from pecuniary embarrassment, to promote his comfort and happiness, and even to share with him his riches, if thereby he will be made happy? And yet such a son may, with impunity, leave such a father in any degree of penury above that which will expose the community in which he dwells, to the danger of being obliged to preserve him from absolute want. Is not a wealthy father under strong moral obligation to advance the interest of an obedient, well disposed son, to furnish him with the means of acquiring and maintaining a becoming rank in life, to rescue him from the horrors of debt incurred by misfortune? Yet the law will uphold him in any degree of parsimony, short of that which would reduce his son to the necessity of seeking public charity.

Without doubt there are great interests of society which justify withholding the coercive arm of the law from these duties of imperfect obligation, as they are called; imperfect, not because they are less binding upon the conscience than those which are called perfect, but because the wisdom of the social law does not impose sanctions upon them.

A deliberate promise, in writing, made freely and without any mistake, one which may lead the party to whom it is made into contracts and expenses, cannot be broken without a violation of moral duty. But if there was nothing paid or promised for it, the law, perhaps wisely, leaves the execution of it to the conscience of him who makes it. It is only when the party making the promise gains something, or he to whom it is made loses something, that the law gives the promise validity. * * *

* * *

For the foregoing reasons we are all of opinion that the nonsuit directed by the Court of Common Pleas was right, and that judgment be entered thereon for costs for the defendant.

NOTES

(1)   Under what circumstances, if any, should a promise not supported by consideration but motivated by a past benefit conferred be enforceable as a contract? Restatement (Second) § 86 provides: "(1) A promise made in recognition of a benefit previously received by the promisor from the promisee is binding to the extent necessary to prevent injustice. (2) A promise is not binding under Subsection (1), (a) if the promisee conferred the benefit as a gift or for other reasons the promisor has not been unjustly enriched; or (b) to the extent that its value is disproportionate to the benefit." Would *Mills* be decided differently under this section? Suppose it is clear that Mills did not intend to confer a gift on Wyman's son. Why does the law treat someone who originally confers a benefit as a gift (Mother Teresa?) less well than someone who confers the gift non-gratuitously?

(2)   Are you persuaded by Judge Parker's distinction between legal and moral obligations in the making of promises? If, as Posner argues, the doctrine of consideration supports economic efficiency in exchange, what arguments can be made for enforcing promises where there is no bargain and exchange? What might be the efficiency gains from enforcing promises made in recognition of a preexisting moral obligation?

(3)   Geoffrey Watson has argued that the facts stated in *Mills v. Wyman* were "falsely rendered" and that the opinion was "misguided." His research shows that Levi Wyman did not die (as the court stated) from his illness, but recovered and lived for many years. Also, the letter from Seth Wyman to Mills (who expected to be paid) appeared to promise to pay for continued care of Levi, not just for completed services. The jury, however, found that only past services were involved, and this finding was not overturned. Geoffrey R. Watson, *In the Tribunal of Conscience:* Mills v. Wyman *Reconsidered*, 71 Tul. L. Rev. 1749 (1997).

Comment: Lord Mansfield, Consideration and Moral Obligation

In his *Lectures on Legal History*, William John Victor Windeyer describes Lord Mansfield's largely failed attempt to reform the consideration doctrine in England:

By his readiness to enlarge the scope of assumpsit and indebitatus assumpsit, Mansfield greatly assisted the development of the law of contract, which is the basis of all commercial law. But he failed to gain acceptance for a theory of consideration which, if it had been adopted, would have entirely altered the English law of contract. The established principle of English law today is that a merely gratuitous promise is not legally binding, except it be under seal. To make an enforceable agreement, otherwise than by deed, it is necessary that the promise should be given for some valuable consideration. It is not necessary that the consideration should be adequate, but it must be certain and of some value in the eye of the law. "A valuable consideration in the sense of the law, may consist either in some right, interest, profit or benefit accruing to one party, or some forbearance, detriment, loss or responsibility given, suffered or undertaken by the other." The origin of the doctrine of consideration is not free from doubt. . . . Probably it owes something to the notion of *quid pro quo*, an element in the old action of debt which, as we have seen, was superseded by indebitatus assumpsit. Certainly it was chiefly developed as the result of the technicalities of the action of assumpsit in which the plaintiff was required to allege the consideration for the defendant's promise. The canon law too may have made an indirect contribution, for it had, by a singular adaptation of Roman law principles, reached the conclusion that promises were enforceable when supported by *causa*. The meaning of *causa* was not indisputedly defined. "The general meaning on which all were agreed was the necessity of a purpose to be attained. There was *causa*, if the promisor had in view a definite result, either some definite legal act or something more comprehensive, such as peace." The Court of Chancery in the sixteenth century was working out a theory of contract with, as its basis, the canonists' theory of *causa*, which it translated as "consideration". Promises were enforceable if made for a sufficient consideration. A material consideration was not necessary; a good motive, a moral obligation or natural love and affection towards the promisee was enough.

The common law courts never accepted the Chancery Court's doctrine of consideration. The Chancery theory ultimately perished. It was the common law theory of contract and the common law doctrine of valuable consideration which became the accepted principles of English law. Some criterion of the enforceability of agreements was considered necessary as the action of assumpsit developed. The breach of every promise was not to be permitted to give rise to an action of assumpsit. How then could the agreements in respect of which assumpsit would lie be determined? The common lawyers adopted the

Roman principle that *ex nudo pacto non oritur actio*. But they understood this maxim in a sense different from that which it bore in Roman law. Roman law had no generalized theory of consideration. For the common law, a *nudum pactum* was a promise not supported by consideration. A mere naked promise could have no assistance from the common law; but if clothed with a consideration, however scanty, it was received with little less respect than the covenant in its sealed vestment.

By the eighteenth century it seemed clearly established that consideration was an essential condition of an action of assumpsit. But the scope of the doctrine was still unsettled. Mansfield cared little for procedural rules, but much for good faith and honest dealing. He was eager to break down some of the barriers between law and equity and to apply equitable principles in the administration of the common law. He confidently asserted that any moral obligation arising from the dictates of good conscience was a sufficient consideration to make a promise actionable. He went even further and denied that consideration was essential to the validity of a contract. In his view consideration had only an evidentiary value. If a promise was supported by consideration, it showed that the parties had intended their engagement to be legally binding. But this might be evidenced in other ways, for example an agreement which was reduced to writing in obedience to the Statute of Frauds or as the result of commercial custom was, in Mansfield's opinion, binding without consideration. "A *nudum pactum*," he said "does not exist in the usage and law of merchants." This doctrine, which he put forward in *Pillans v. Van Mierop* (3 Burr. 1663), would have made all written agreements enforceable, though they were not under seal. But the traditions of the common law were here too strong even for Mansfield's great prestige. Thirteen years later the House of Lords in *Rann v. Hughes* (7 T.R. 350), after consulting the judges, overruled his opinion and established the need for consideration in all contracts other than those embodied in a deed. "All contracts", the judges declared, "are by the laws of England distinguished into agreements by specialty and agreements by parol; nor is there any such third class as . . . contracts in writing. If they be merely written and not specialties, they are parol and a consideration must be proved."

But, although Mansfield's doctrine that no consideration at all was required to support a written agreement was soon overthrown, his opinion that a merely moral obligation was sufficient to constitute a consideration received general assent throughout the eighteenth century. It was not finally displaced until 1840, when Lord Denman pointed out in *Eastwood v.*

Kenyon (11 Ad. & E. 438) that it would "annihilate the necessity for any consideration at all, inasmuch as the mere fact of giving of promise creates a moral obligation to perform it."

William John Victor Windeyer, Lectures on Legal History 237–40 (2d ed. rev. 1957).

Joe Webb v. N. Floyd and Joseph F. McGowin

Court of Appeals of Alabama, 1935.
27 Ala.App. 82.

■ BRICKEN, PRESIDING JUDGE. This action is in assumpsit. The complaint as originally filed was amended. The demurrers to the complaint as amended were sustained, and because of this adverse ruling by the court the plaintiff took a nonsuit, and the assignment of errors on this appeal are predicated upon said action or ruling of the court.

A fair statement of the case presenting the questions for decision is set out in appellant's brief, which we adopt.

"On the 3d day of August, 1925, appellant while in the employ of W.T. Smith Lumber Company, a corporation, and acting within the scope of his employment, was engaged in clearing the upper floor of mill No. 2 of the company. While so engaged he was in the act of dropping a pine block from the upper floor of the mill to the ground below; this being the usual and ordinary way of clearing the floor, and it being the duty of the plaintiff in the course of his employment to so drop it. The block weighed about 75 pounds.

"As appellant was in the act of dropping the block to the ground below, he was on the edge of the upper floor of the mill. As he started to turn the block loose so that it would drop to the ground, he saw J. Greeley McGowin, testator of the defendants, on the ground below and directly under where the block would have fallen had appellant turned it loose. Had he turned it loose it would have struck McGowin with such force as to have caused him serious bodily harm or death. Appellant could have remained safely on the upper floor of the mill by turning the block loose and allowing it to drop, but had he done this the block would have fallen on McGowin and caused him serious injuries or death. The only safe and reasonable way to prevent this was for appellant to hold to the block and divert its direction in falling from the place where McGowin was standing and the only safe way to divert it so as to prevent its coming into contact with McGowin was for appellant to fall with it to the ground below. Appellant did this, and by holding to the block and falling with it to the ground below, he diverted the course of its fall in such way that McGowin was not injured. In thus preventing the injuries to McGowin appellant himself received serious bodily injuries, resulting in his right leg being broken, the heel of his right foot torn off and his right arm broken. He was badly crippled for life and rendered unable to do physical or mental labor.

"On September 1, 1925, in consideration of appellant having prevented him from sustaining death or serious bodily harm and in consideration of the injuries appellant had received, McGowin agreed with him to care for and maintain him for the remainder of appellant's life at the rate of $15 every two weeks from the time he sustained his injuries to and during the remainder of appellant's life; it being agreed that McGowin would pay this sum to appellant for his maintenance. Under the agreement McGowin paid or caused to be paid to appellant the sum so agreed on up until McGowin's death on January 1, 1934. After his death the payments were continued to and including January 27, 1934, at which time they were discontinued. Thereupon plaintiff brought suit to recover the unpaid installments accruing up to the time of the bringing of the suit."

* * *

1. The averments of the complaint show that appellant saved McGowin from death or grievous bodily harm. This was a material benefit to him of infinitely more value than any financial aid he could have received. Receiving this benefit, McGowin became morally bound to compensate appellant for the services rendered. Recognizing his moral obligation, he expressly agreed to pay appellant as alleged in the complaint and complied with this agreement up to the time of his death; a period of more than 8 years.

Had McGowin been accidentally poisoned and a physician, without his knowledge or request, had administered an antidote, thus saving his life, a subsequent promise by McGowin to pay the physician would have been valid. Likewise, McGowin's agreement as disclosed by the complaint to compensate appellant for saving him from death or grievous bodily injury is valid and enforceable.

Where the promisee cares for, improves, and preserves the property of the promisor, though done without his request, it is sufficient consideration for the promisor's subsequent agreement to pay for the service, because of the material benefit received. . . .

In *Boothe v. Fitzpatrick*, 36 Vt. 681, the court held that a promise by defendant to pay for the past keeping of a bull which had escaped from defendant's premises and been cared for by plaintiff was valid, although there was no previous request, because the subsequent promise obviated that objection; it being equivalent to a previous request. On the same principle, had the promisee saved the promisor's life or his body from grievous harm, his subsequent promise to pay for the services rendered would have been valid. Such service would have been far more material than caring for his bull. Any holding that saving a man from death or grievous bodily harm is not a material benefit sufficient to uphold a subsequent promise to pay for the service, necessarily rests on the assumption that saving life and preservation of the body from harm have only a sentimental value. The converse of this is true. Life and preservation of the body have material, pecuniary values, measurable in dollars and cents. Because of this, physicians practice their profession charging for services rendered in saving life and curing the body of its ills, and surgeons perform operations. The same is true as to the law of negligence, authorizing the assessment of damages in personal injury cases based upon the extent of the injuries, earnings, and life expectancies of those injured.

In the business of life insurance, the value of a man's life is measured in dollars and cents according to his expectancy, the soundness of his body, and his ability to pay premiums. The same is true as to health and accident insurance.

It follows that if, as alleged in the complaint, appellant saved J. Greeley McGowin from death or grievous bodily harm, and McGowin subsequently agreed to pay him for the service rendered, it became a valid and enforceable contract.

2.   It is well settled that a moral obligation is a sufficient consideration to support a subsequent promise to pay where the promisor has received a material benefit, although there was no original duty or liability resting on the promisor. . . . State ex rel. Bayer v. Funk, 105 Or. 134, 25 A.L.R. 625, 634. . . . In the case of *State ex rel. Bayer v. Funk*, supra, the court held that a moral obligation is a sufficient consideration to support an executory promise where the promisor has received an actual pecuniary or material benefit for which he subsequently expressly promised to pay.

The case at bar is clearly distinguishable from that class of cases where the consideration is a mere moral obligation or conscientious duty unconnected with receipt by promisor of benefits of a material or pecuniary nature. . . . Here the promisor received a material benefit constituting a valid consideration for his promise.

3.   Some authorities hold that, for a moral obligation to support a subsequent promise to pay, there must have existed a prior legal or equitable obligation, which for some reason had become unenforceable, but for which the promisor was still morally bound. This rule, however, is subject to qualification in those cases where the promisor, having received a material benefit from the promisee, is morally bound to compensate him for the services rendered and in consideration of this obligation promises to pay. In such cases the subsequent promise to pay is an affirmance or ratification of the services rendered carrying with it the presumption that a previous request for the service was made. . . .

Under the decisions above cited, McGowin's express promise to pay appellant for the services rendered was an affirmance or ratification of what appellant had done raising the presumption that the services had been rendered at McGowin's request.

4.   The averments of the complaint show that in saving McGowin from death or grievous bodily harm, appellant was crippled for life. This was part of the consideration of the contract declared on. McGowin was

benefitted. Appellant was injured. Benefit to the promisor or injury to the promisee is a sufficient legal consideration for the promisor's agreement to pay. . . .

5.   Under the averments of the complaint the services rendered by appellant were not gratuitous. The agreement of McGowin to pay and the acceptance of payment by appellant conclusively shows the contrary.

* * *

From what has been said, we are of the opinion that the court below erred in the ruling complained of; that is to say, in sustaining the demurrer, and for this error the case is reversed and remanded.

Reversed and remanded.

■ SAMFORD, JUDGE (concurring). The questions involved in this case are not free from doubt, and perhaps the strict letter of the rule, as stated by judges, though not always in accord, would bar a recovery by plaintiff, but following the principle announced by Chief Justice Marshall in *Hoffman v. Porter*, Fed.Cas. No. 6,577, 2 Brock 156, 159, where he says "I do not think that law ought to be separated from justice, where it is at most doubtful," I concur in the conclusions reached by the court.[2]

NOTES

(1)   Is *Webb v. McGowin* an example of the old saying that "hard cases make bad law?" Can the decision be reconciled with *Mills v. Wyman*? Read carefully the rule stated in Restatement (Second) § 86.

(2)   Recall the doctrine of restitution (also known as "quasi-contract" or "unjust enrichment"), which was at issue in *Bailey v. West*, one of the cases in Chapter One. An action for restitution lies where there is no contract between the parties, but one has been unjustly enriched at the expense of the other. Might there be an argument for restitution based on the facts of *Webb v. McGowin*?

The drafters of the Second Restatement argued for a link between the relatively new rule for moral obligation and the well-established doctrine of restitution or quasi-contract:

> Although in general a person who has been unjustly enriched at the expense of another is required to make restitution, restitution is denied in many cases in order to protect persons who have had benefits thrust upon them. . . . In other cases restitution is denied by virtue of rules designed to guard against false claims, stale claims, claims already litigated, and the like. In many such cases a subsequent promise to make restitution removes the reason for the denial of relief, and the policy against unjust enrichment then prevails. . . . Enforcement of the subsequent promise sometimes makes it unnecessary to decide a difficult question as to the limits on quasi-contractual relief.

---

[2]   [Certiorari denied by Alabama Supreme Court, 232 Ala. 374 (1936).—Eds.]

Restatement (Second) § 86 cmt. b.

(3)   California law is of particular interest since it contains statutes of long standing which appear to provide alternatives to consideration. Section 1550 of the California Civil Code provides that there must be either "sufficient cause or consideration." "Cause," or *causa*, is a concept employed in civil law countries, notably in Europe and South America. See Ernest G. Lorenzen, Causa *and Consideration in the Law of Contracts*, 28 Yale L.J. 621 (1919). Moreover, section 1606 of the California code states: "An existing legal obligation resting upon the promisor, *or a moral obligation originating in some benefit conferred upon the promisor, or prejudice suffered by the promisee,* is . . . good consideration for a promise, to an extent corresponding with the extent of the obligation, but no further or otherwise." (Emphasis added.)

(4)   Section 5–1105 of the New York General Obligations Law provides:

A promise in writing and signed by the promisor or by his agent shall not be denied effect as a valid contractual obligation on the ground that consideration for the promise is past or executed, if the consideration is expressed in the writing and is proved to have been given or performed and would be a valid consideration but for the time when it was given or performed.

See *Dick v. Dick*, 167 Conn. 210 (1974), where it was held that the above quoted statute required proof that any consideration stated in the writing was actually paid.

Comment: Restatement (Second) § 86 and the Future of "Moral Obligation"

The First Restatement dealt with the issues of past consideration and moral obligation under the umbrella of the bargain theory, set forth in Section 75. Provision was made for the limited enforcement of "second" promises made to pay antecedent debts barred by the statute of limitations or discharged in bankruptcy. But beyond this, forays into the realm of *Webb v. McGowin* ran up against the "bargained for and given in exchange" requirement. The Second Restatement took a more innovative approach with Section 86, "Promise for Benefit Received":

(1)   A promise made in recognition of a benefit previously received by the promisor from the promisee is binding to the extent necessary to prevent injustice.

(2)   A promise is not binding under Subsection (1)

(a)   if the promisee conferred the benefit as a gift or for other reasons the promisor has not been unjustly enriched; or

(b)   to the extent that its value is disproportionate to the benefit.

This section eschews such terminology as "past consideration" and "moral obligation," preferring to explain it as an effort to preclude an unjust enrichment that might have occurred if the courts were limited to traditional principles of quasi-contract.

In speaking of cases such as *Webb v. McGowin*, the first Reporter, Robert Braucher, observed: "What you have, really, is a line of distinction between essentially gratuitous transactions and cases which are on the borderline of quasi-contracts, where promise removes the difficulty which otherwise would bar quasi-contractual relief." He conceded that the section "bristles with nonspecific concepts," but insisted that it captured the principle that can be sustained by the cases. 42 ALI Proceedings 273–74 (1965). Be this as it may, Grant Gilmore argued that Section 86 "gives overt recognition to an important principle whose existence *Restatement* ignored and, by implication denied." He suggested that "by the time we get to Restatement (Third) it may well be that § 89A will have flowered like Jack's bean-stalk in the same way that § 90 did between Restatement and Restatement (Second)." Grant Gilmore, The Death of Contract 76 (1974).

A 2010 study of the cases employing the moral obligation rule reported the following:

> Since the adoption of Section 86 of the Restatement (Second) of Contracts, there have been only eight cases applying the material benefit rule to enforce a promise. Even if one looks back an additional ten years, to the point when the Restatement drafts were widely circulated, there have only been a handful of additional cases—six to be precise—applying the material benefit rule to enforce a promise. The vast majority of these fourteen cases—ten of them—fall into the wavier or ratification exceptions to the rule against past consideration. They are, in other words, promises to repay a debt discharged under bankruptcy rules or otherwise rendered unrecoverable because of some procedural bar like the statute of limitations.

> Of the remaining four cases, one of them can be justified on very similar grounds to the ratification or waiver exception to past consideration. * * *

> The final three cases . . . are from Louisiana. The impact of these decisions is negligible, however, because Louisiana is the only civil law state. Although the reasoning in these cases suggests that a more thoroughgoing moral obligation principle is at work, none of them cite Section 86 of the Restatement (Second) of Contracts and they do not contain the sort of direct assault on the doctrine of consideration that the Restatement drafters might have endorsed.

Edwin Butterfoss & H. Allen Blair, *Where Is Emily Litella When You Need Her?: The Unsuccessful Effort to Craft A General Theory of Obligation of Promise for Benefit Received*, 28 Quinnipiac L. Rev. 385, 415–16 (2010). The authors conclude: "Robert Braucher, the Reporter for the Restatement (Second) of Contracts, once suggested that the material benefit rule 'probably has more theoretical interest than practical significance.' We could not agree more. Practically, the rule has proven to have almost no significance." Id. at 428 (quoting Robert Braucher, *Freedom of Contract and the Second Restatement*, 78 Yale L.J. 598, 604 (1969)).

(E) MIXED MOTIVES AND ADEQUACY OF CONSIDERATION

We return now to the primary basis of contract liability in the United States: consideration. We saw in the previous section one limit on what will count as consideration. Nominal consideration, which reflects the mere pretense of a bargain, is generally insufficient to support a contractual obligation. We now examine several other possible limits.

Samuel Thomas v. Eleanor Thomas

Queen's Bench, 1842.
2 Q.B. 851.

Assumpsit. The declaration stated an agreement between plaintiff and defendant that the defendant should, when thereto required by the plaintiff, by all necessary deeds, conveyances, assignments, or other assurances, grants, etc., or otherwise, assure a certain dwelling house and premises, in the county of Glamorgan, unto plaintiff for her life * * *.

At the trial, before Coltman, J., at the Glamorganshire Lent Assizes, 1841, it appeared that John Thomas, the deceased husband of the plaintiff, at the time of his death, in 1837, was possessed of a row of seven dwelling houses in Merthyr Tidvil, in one of which, being the dwelling house in question, he was himself residing; and that by his will he appointed his brother Samuel Thomas (since deceased) and the defendant executors thereof, to take possession of all his houses, etc., subject to certain payments in the will mentioned, among which were certain charges in money for the benefit of the plaintiff. In the evening before the day of his death he expressed orally a wish to make some further provision for his wife; and on the following morning he declared orally, in the presence of two witnesses, that it was his will that his wife should have either the house in which he lived and all that it contained, or an additional sum of £100 instead thereof.

This declaration being shortly afterward brought to the knowledge of Samuel Thomas and the defendant, the executors and residuary legatees, they consented to carry the intentions of the testator so expressed into effect; and, after the lapse of a few days, they and the plaintiff executed the agreement declared upon; which, after stating the parties, and briefly reciting the will, proceeded as follows:

"And, whereas the said testator, shortly before his death, declared in the presence of several witnesses, that he was desirous his said wife should have and enjoy during her life, or so long as she continue his widow, all and singular the dwelling house," etc., "or £100 out of his personal estate," in addition to the respective legacies and bequests given her in and by his said will; "but such declaration and desire was not reduced to writing in the lifetime of the said John Thomas and read over to him; but the said Samuel Thomas and Benjamin Thomas are fully convinced and satisfied that such was the desire of the said testator, and are willing and desirous that such intention should be carried into full effect. Now these presents witness, and it is hereby agreed and declared by and between the parties, that, in consideration of such desire and of the premises," the executors would convey the dwelling house, etc., to the plaintiff and her assigns during her life, or for so long a time as she should continue a widow and unmarried: "provided nevertheless, and it is hereby further agreed and declared, that the said Eleanor Thomas, or her assigns, shall and will, at all times during which she shall have possession of the said dwelling house, etc., pay to the said Samuel Thomas and Benjamin Thomas, their executors, etc., the sum of £1 yearly toward the ground rent payable in respect of the said dwelling house and other premises thereto adjoining, and shall keep the said dwelling house and premises in good and tenantable repair"; with other provisions not affecting the questions in this case.

The plaintiff was left in possession of the dwelling house and premises for some time; but the defendant, after the death of his coexecutor, refused to execute a conveyance tendered to him for execution pursuant to the agreement, and, shortly before the trial, brought an ejectment, under which he turned the plaintiff out of possession. It was objected for the defendant that, a part of the consideration proved being omitted in the declaration, there was a fatal variance. The learned judge overruled the objection, reserving leave to move to enter a non-suit. Ultimately a verdict was found for the plaintiff on all the issues; and, in Easter Term last, a rule *nisi* was obtained pursuant to the leave reserved.

* * *

■ LORD DENMAN, C.J. There is nothing in this case but a great deal of ingenuity, and a little wilful blindness to the actual terms of the instrument itself. There is nothing whatever to show that the ground rent was payable to a superior landlord; and the stipulation for the payment of it is not a mere proviso, but an express agreement. * * * This is in terms an express agreement, and shows a sufficient legal consideration quite independent of the moral feeling which disposed the executors to enter into such a contract. * * *

■ PATTESON, J. * * * Motive is not the same thing with consideration. Consideration means something which is of some value in the eye of the law, moving from the plaintiff; it may be some benefit to the plaintiff, or some detriment to the defendant; but at all events it must be moving from the plaintiff. Now that which is suggested as the consideration here, a pious respect for the wishes of the testator, does not in any way move from the plaintiff; it moves from the testator; therefore, legally speaking, it forms no part of the consideration. Then it is said that, if that be so, there is no consideration at all, it is a mere voluntary gift; but when we look at the agreement we find that this is not a mere proviso that the donee shall take the gift with the burthens; but it is an express agreement to pay what seems to be a fresh apportionment of a ground rent, and which is made payable not to a superior landlord, but to the executors. So that this rent is clearly not something incident to the assignment of the house, for in that case, instead of being payable to the executors, it would have been payable to the landlord. Then as to the repairs, these houses may very possibly be held under a lease containing covenants to repair; but we know nothing about it, for anything that appears the liability to repair is first created by this instrument. The proviso certainly struck me at first * * * that the rent and repairs were merely attached to the gift by the donors; and, had the instrument been executed by the donors only, there might have been some ground for that construction; but the fact is not so. * * *

■ COLERIDGE, J. The concessions made in the course of the argument have, in fact, disposed of the case. It is conceded that mere motive need not be stated, and we are not obliged to look for the legal consideration in any particular part of the instrument, merely because the consideration is usually stated in some particular part; *ut res magis valeat*, we may look to any part. In this instrument, in the part where it is usual to state the consideration, nothing certainly is expressed but a wish to fulfil the intentions of the testator, but in another part we find an express agreement to pay an annual sum for a particular purpose, and also a distinct agreement to repair. If these had occurred in the first part of the instrument, it could hardly have been argued that the declaration was not well drawn and supported by the evidence. As to the suggestion of this being a voluntary conveyance, my impression is that this payment of £1 annually is more than a good consideration, it is a valuable consideration, it is clearly a thing newly created and not part of the old ground rent.

Rule discharged.

NOTES

(1)   Why did the executors enter into the agreement with their dead brother's spouse? That is, what was their motive in allowing her to remain in the house? What was the purpose of the £1 annual rent? Does your answer depend on the value of a Pound in 1837? Why was the provision regarding upkeep inserted? Could one argue that it was simply a condition on a gift?

(2)   Restatement (Second) § 81(1) provides that "[t]he fact that what is bargained for does not of itself induce the making of a promise does not prevent it from being consideration for the promise." Section 81(2) makes the same points about the motives of the promisee. The parties may have more than one motive, even in a commercial exchange. But doesn't this suppose that the performance was bargained for? As comment b puts the point:

"Unless both parties know that the purported consideration is mere pretense, it is immaterial that the promisor's desire for the consideration is incidental to other objectives and even that the other party knows this to be so." See First Commerce Corp. v. United States, 60 Fed. Cl. 570, 584–85 (2004) (citing and applying section 81 with approval); Austell v. Rice, 5 Ga. 472 (1848) (if promisors got what they bargained for, their motive was irrelevant).

PROBLEM: THE CASE OF THE FINE PENNY

Your client, Pauline, is a second-year student at Yale Law School. Pauline's Uncle Fred, a Harvard Law graduate, owns a first edition of Langdell's *Cases on Contracts*, published in 1871. The value of the book is $5,000. Pauline expressed an interest in the book (to add to a growing collection) and, at Thanksgiving, Uncle Fred made a statement at the dinner table that he would give the book to her for Christmas. The next day, Uncle Fred was shown Pauline's coin collection and discovered that she had two 1909s-VDB pennies, one in very fine condition (valued at $1,000) and one in fine condition (valued at $500). Fred confessed that he needed such a penny to round out his collection of Lincoln pennies, and Pauline stated that she would give him the penny in "fine" condition for Christmas.

Shortly after the first of the year, Pauline visited your office and presented a writing, dated December 1, of the same year, which stated: "In consideration of one penny, receipt of which is hereby acknowledged, I promise to give my niece Pauline my first edition of Langdell on Christmas day of this year." The writing, which had been mailed to Pauline, was signed by Fred. She further said that on Christmas Day she tendered the "fine" 1909s-VDB penny to Fred, and he took it. Fred, however, refused to tender the Langdell to Pauline, saying he was a bit short of cash and that he had sold it to the Harvard Law Library for $7,500. He did thank Pauline for her "wonderful gift."

Advise Pauline of her rights.

Robert C. Browning v. O. Arthur Johnson

Supreme Court of Washington, 1967.
70 Wash.2d 145.

■ LANGENBACH, JUDGE. This is the tale of two osteopaths who attempted a business transaction. The heart of the case is a certain promise which Dr. Browning made to Dr. Johnson. The sole issue is whether Dr. Browning is to be bound by his promise.

Browning and Johnson entered into a contract of sale whereby Browning was to sell his practice and equipment to Johnson. Both parties and their attorneys believed the contract made to be completely valid and enforceable. Before the contract's effective date, Browning changed his mind about selling and sought to be released from the obligations he had undertaken. Johnson, at first, demurred. Later, however, upon Browning's promise to pay Johnson $40,000 if Johnson would give up the contract of sale, the parties entered into a contract (the contract here in issue) canceling the contract of sale.

Some months later Browning tired of his bargain and brought this action for declaratory judgment and restitution. In the course of this action the trial court concluded that the canceled sale contract had lacked mutuality and had been too indefinite in its terms for enforcement. Nevertheless, it concluded that the contract canceling the sale contract was supported by "adequate consideration." Browning has appealed from that decision. He brought 24 errors which pertain mainly to the trial court's failure to adopt his proposed findings. He insists that his promise to pay Johnson was unsupported by consideration and that the promise was a child of mutual mistake.

We should first say a word about terminology. Courts are loath to inquire into the "adequacy" of consideration, that is, into the comparative value of the promises and acts exchanged. As we said in *Rogich v. Dressel*, 45 Wash.2d 829, 843 (1954):

> [W]e must apply the rule followed in this state that parties who are competent to contract will not be relieved from a bad bargain they make unless the consideration is so inadequate as to be constructively fraudulent * * *.

But "adequacy" of consideration, into which courts seldom inquire, is to be distinguished from the legal "sufficiency" of any particular consideration. The latter phrase is concerned not with comparative value but with that which will support a promise. "[A]nything which fulfils the requirements of consideration will support a promise whatever may be the comparative value of the consideration, and of the thing promised." 1 Williston, Contracts § 115, cited in Puget Mill Co. v. Kerry, 183 Wash. 542, 558 (1935). "[T]he relative values of a promise and the consideration for it, do not affect the sufficiency of consideration." Restatement, Contracts § 81 (1932). This distinction is sometimes lost sight of. In the instant case, Browning bargained for Johnson's act of giving up the contract of sale. The issue is whether the law regards Johnson's act of giving up that contract as legally "sufficient" consideration to support Browning's promise to pay him for such an act. The trial court concluded that giving up the contract of sale was "adequate" consideration for Browning's promise.

Whether there exists something which will support a promise and which therefore may be called legally sufficient consideration is obviously prior to the question of whether that consideration is adequate when compared to the value of the promise given in exchange for it. Therefore, whether the trial court meant (1) that giving up the contract of sale was a bargained-for act legally sufficient to support Browning's promise, or (2) that giving up the contract of sale was sufficient consideration, *and* moreover, consideration not so inadequate as to be constructively fraudulent is not important. We hold that Browning's promise was supported by sufficient consideration and there is nothing in this case which induces us, under the *Rogich* formulation, to consider the relative values of the things exchanged.

This is a unilateral contract. . . . A unilateral contract is one in which a promise is given in exchange for an act or forbearance. Here, Browning gave Johnson a promise to pay $40,000 in exchange for Johnson's act of giving up the contract of sale. Sufficiency of consideration in unilateral contracts is discussed by Professor Williston in his treatise, Contracts § 102 (3d ed. 1957). There he indicates that the requirement of sufficient consideration to support a promise is met by a detriment incurred by the promisee (Johnson) or a benefit received by the promisor (Browning) at the request of the promisor. "That a detriment suffered by the promisee at the promisor's request and as the price for the promise is sufficient, though the promisor is not benefited, is well settled." Williston, supra. This has been the law in Washington for over 50 years. . . . The question then becomes the nature of a detriment. Detriment is defined by Williston as the giving up of "something which immediately prior thereto the promisee was privileged to retain, or doing or refraining from doing something which he was then privileged not to do, or not to refrain from doing." Williston, supra, § 102A. We have already had occasion to quote this definition with approval. * * *

The problem presented by this case is not a new one. Over a century ago, in England, Brooks obtained a certain document from Haigh believing that it was a guarantee, and promised to pay a certain sum of money in consideration of Haigh's giving it up. The guarantee proved to be unenforceable. Haigh sued Brooks for the money promised. The court said:

> [T]he plaintiffs were induced by the defendant's promise to part with something which they might have kept, and the defendant obtained what he desired by means of that promise. Both being free and able to judge for themselves, how can the defendant be justified in breaking this promise, by discovering afterwards that the thing in consideration of which he gave it did not possess that value which he supposed to belong to it? It cannot be ascertained that that value was what he most regarded. He may have had other objects and motives; and of their weight he was the only judge.

Haigh v. Brooks, 10 A. & E. 309, 320 (1839). Similarly here, of Browning's objects and motives, he was the only judge.[1]

---

[1] On December 20, 1962, Browning wrote Johnson a six-page letter which read, in part: "Dear Art, * * * All I can honestly say is that it would have been a real error to have gone through with it [the Everett venture] * * *. [T]he area south of Everett in regard to housing, schools and recreation [is] far below what we have here in Greater Tacoma. Young Steve has been having a real bad time of it this year at the Academy and it is most imperative, because of this, that he remain * * * there * * *. Muriel and the children are very happy we are staying * * * they didn't want to leave * * *. I will be most content to be back in Tacoma in practice an [sic] able to live and play here as well. We are looking forward to boating again come spring. * * * I want to be back among the people who know me * * *. Sincerely Bob."

* * *

In 1935 the case of Puget Mill Co. v. Kerry, supra, came before this court. The following discussion (appearing in 183 Wash. pp. 556, 559, 49 P.2d pp. 63, 64), while not entirely necessary there is persuasive here.

* * *

Then, it is well settled that a consideration sufficient to support a promise need not always, in the last analysis, have an actual value. In this instance, it may be assumed that whether or not respondent had the right to refuse its consent to an assignment of the lease could only be determined by the courts. The giving of its consent by respondent would constitute a valuable consideration for a promise, even though a possibility existed that at the end of protracted litigation, it might be held that respondent had lost its right to accept or reject a new tenant. Of course, a consideration cannot be sham or frivolous or manifestly false; but in the case at bar, we are satisfied that a real controversy might have been waged before the courts as to the rights of respondent as they existed in 1923.

* * *

That the parties cited none of the above cases in their briefs makes these cases no less appropriate. It is clear that at the time of contracting, the parties, equally informed, of equal bargaining power and equally assisted by able counsel, freely bargained for, and freely settled upon an exchange which each felt would be beneficial to him. Their mutual assent proved this mutual expectation of benefit for the law must presume that no man bargains against his own interest. Subsequent events revealed that the contract, fully acceptable to both parties when made, was less beneficial to the promisor than he and his attorney had, at the time of contracting, thought. But this *alone* can not be reason enough for allowing the promisor to avoid it. There was no misrepresentation, no fraud, and no duress. The promisor Browning wanted Johnson to give up the sale contract and to secure the performance of that act, he solemnly promised to pay Johnson $40,000. Johnson, induced by Browning's urgent pleas and solemn promise, gave up the sale contract. The legal detriment suffered by Johnson through Browning's inducement will support Browning's promise to pay.

Finally, we reach Browning's argument that the parties entered into this contract under the influence of a mutual mistake. There is no doubt that a contract can be supported by sufficient consideration and yet be voidable for mistake. But we do not reach that issue. [The court declined to consider the issue because it was not pled below.]

* * *

The judgment is affirmed.

NOTES

(1)   How does one "give up" a contract? What was it about the contract given up that caused Browning to claim that consideration was inadequate? What is the court's answer to this argument?

(2)   The court in *Browning v. Johnson* draws a distinction between "sufficient" and "adequate" consideration. The Second Restatement has not preserved this distinction on the ground that it was "confusing." See Section 71, Reporter's Note. Rather, if a performance, such as the "destruction of a legal relation," is bargained for, there is consideration, Section 71(3), and if the "requirement of consideration is met, there is no additional requirement of . . . equivalence in the values exchanged." Section 79(b).

(3)   Section 74(1) of the Second Restatement provides the following rule for settlements of claims:

> Forbearance to assert or the surrender of a claim or defense which proves to be invalid is not consideration unless (a) the claim or defense is in fact doubtful because of uncertainty as to the facts or the law, or (b) the forbearing or surrendering party believes that the claim or defense may be fairly determined to be valid.

Is this consistent with the outcome in *Browning v. Johnson*? Recall that the plaintiff in *Hamer v. Sidway* was suing not on the uncle's first promise to pay his nephew $5,000 for good behavior, but on his second promise to pay the money later with interest. Does section 74(1) provide an alternative ground for the outcome in *Hamer*? What about in *In re Greene*, in which the court held that the claimant's purported release of claims was not consideration? Is that holding consistent with the rule in section 74(1)?

(4)   The First Restatement required that the claimant have both an honest *and* a reasonable belief in the validity of a claim. Restatement § 76. The Restatement (Second) § 74(1)(b) suggests that an honest belief is enough, even if it is unreasonable. Which is the better rule? Can the two standards be sharply delineated? Might not unreasonableness of the alleged belief itself be some evidence of bad faith? A Missouri appellate court addressed the problem:

> The law favors compromise of doubtful claims, and forbearance may be a sufficient consideration for such compromise, even though the claim upon which it is based should develop to be ill-founded. The fact that, had the parties proceeded to litigate the claim, one of them would certainly have won, does not destroy the consideration for the compromise, for the consideration is said to be the settlement of the dispute.
>
> But there are certain essentials to the validity of such consideration. For one thing, and by all authority, the claim upon which the settlement is based must be one made in good faith. . . . Secondly, the claim must have *some* foundation. As to this second consideration we find the courts using varying language. The claim cannot be "utterly baseless." It has been said that it must have a "tenable ground" or a "reasonable, tenable ground." It must be

based on a "colorable right," or on some "legal foundation." It must have at least an appearance of right sufficient to raise a "possible doubt" in favor of the party asserting it. . . .

It is difficult to reconcile the antinomous rules and statements which are applied to the "doubtful claims" and to find the words which will exactly draw the line between the compromise (on the one hand) of an honestly disputed claim which has some fair element of doubt and is therefore to be regarded as consideration and (on the other hand) a claim, though honestly made, which is so lacking in substance and virility as to be entirely baseless. The Missouri courts have struggled and not yet found apt language. We think we had best leave definitions alone, confident that, as applied to each individual case, the facts will make the thing apparent. But if we should make further effort to distinguish we would say that if the claimant, *in good faith*, makes a mountain out of a mole hill the claim is "doubtful." But if there is no discernible mole hill in the beginning, then the claim has no substance.

Duncan v. Black, 324 S.W.2d 483, 486–88 (Mo.App. 1959).

Robert C. Apfel v. Prudential-Bache Securities, Inc.
Court of Appeals of New York, 1993.
81 N.Y.2d 470.

■ SIMONS, JUDGE. Defendant, an investment bank, seeks to avoid an agreement to purchase plaintiffs' idea for issuing and selling municipal bonds. Its principal contention is that plaintiffs had no property right in the idea because it was not novel and, therefore, consideration for the contract was lacking. For reasons which follow, we conclude that a showing of novelty is not required to validate the contract. The decisive question is whether the idea had value, not whether it was novel.

I

In 1982, plaintiffs, an investment banker and a lawyer, approached defendant's predecessor with a proposal for issuing municipal securities through a system that eliminated paper certificates and allowed bonds to be sold, traded, and held exclusively by means of computerized "book entries". Initially, the parties signed a confidentiality agreement that allowed defendant to review the techniques as detailed in a 99-page summary. Nearly a month of negotiations followed before the parties entered into a sale agreement under which plaintiffs conveyed their rights to the techniques and certain trade names and defendant agreed to pay a stipulated rate based on its use of the techniques for a term from October 1982 to January 1988. Under the provisions of the contract, defendant's obligation to pay was to remain even if the techniques became public knowledge or standard practice in the industry and applications for patents and trademarks were denied. Plaintiffs asserted that they had not previously disclosed the techniques to anyone and they agreed to maintain them in confidence until they became public.

From 1982 until 1985, defendant implemented the contract, although the parties dispute whether amounts due were fully paid. Defendant actively encouraged bond issuers to use the computerized "book entry" system and, for at least the first year, was the sole underwriter in the industry employing such a system. However, in 1985, following a change in personnel, defendant refused to make any further payments. It maintained that the ideas conveyed by plaintiffs had been in the public domain at the time of the sale agreement and that what plaintiffs sold had never been theirs to sell. Defendant's attempts to patent the techniques proved unsuccessful. By 1985, investment banks were increasingly using computerized systems, and by 1990 such systems were handling 60% of the dollar volume of all new issues of municipal securities.

Plaintiffs commenced this litigation seeking $45 million in compensatory and punitive damages. They asserted 17 causes of action based on theories of breach of contract, breach of a fiduciary duty, fraud, various torts arising from defendant's failure to obtain patents, and unjust enrichment. Defendant's answer interposed defenses and counterclaims for breach of contract, breach of warranty, waiver, fraud, estoppel, laches, mutual mistake, rescission, and a lack of consideration. Plaintiffs then moved for partial summary judgment, defendant cross-moved for summary judgment dismissing the complaint, and plaintiffs responded with a motion seeking dismissal of the affirmative defenses.

Supreme Court concluded that triable issues existed on the questions of whether defendant breached the contract by refusing to make payments and whether plaintiffs committed a breach by allegedly disclosing the techniques to another company. The court also found defendant had raised a triable issue on whether plaintiffs had partially waived their right to payment by forgoing certain claims to compensation. The remainder of the pleadings were found to be legally insufficient. Accordingly, the court dismissed all the causes of action except the first, which alleges breach of contract, and struck all defendant's defenses and counterclaims except those relating to breach of contract and the partial defense of waiver. The Appellate Division modified the order by reinstating defendant's claim that the sale agreement lacked consideration. [183 A.D.2d 439.] It held that novelty was required before an idea could be valid consideration but concluded that the question was one of fact to be decided at trial. It also reinstated the cause of action for unjust enrichment, holding that the presence of an express contract did not foreclose recovery on a theory of quasi contract.

On this appeal, defendant's principal contention is that no contract existed between the parties because the sale agreement lacked consideration. Underlying that argument is its assertion that an idea cannot be legally sufficient consideration unless it is novel. . . . Plaintiffs insist that their system was indeed novel, but contend that, in any event, novelty is not required to validate the contract at issue here.

II

Defendant's cross motion for summary judgment insofar as it sought to dismiss the first cause of action alleging breach of contract was properly denied. Additionally, plaintiffs' motion to dismiss the lack of consideration defenses and counterclaims should be granted.

Under the traditional principles of contract law, the parties to a contract are free to make their bargain, even if the consideration exchanged is grossly unequal or of dubious value. . . . It is enough that something of "real value in the eye of the law" was exchanged. . . . The fact that the sellers may not have had a property right in what they sold does not, by itself, render the contract void for lack of consideration. . . .

Manifestly, defendant received something of value here; its own conduct establishes that. After signing the confidentiality agreement, defendant thoroughly reviewed plaintiffs' system before buying it. Having done so, it was in the best position to know whether the idea had value. It decided to enter into the sale agreement and aggressively market the system to potential bond issuers. For at least a year, it was the only underwriter to use plaintiffs' "book entry" system for municipal bonds, and it handled millions of such bond transactions during that time. Having obtained full disclosure of the system, used it in advance of competitors, and received the associated benefits of precluding its disclosure to others, defendant can hardly claim now the idea had no value to its municipal securities business. Indeed, defendant acknowledges it made payments to plaintiffs under the sale agreement for more than two years, conduct that would belie any claim it might make that the idea was lacking in value or that it had actually been obtained from some other source before plaintiffs' disclosure.

Thus, defendant has failed to demonstrate on this record that the contract was void or to raise a triable issue of fact on lack of consideration.

III

[The court, after reviewing the New York cases, held that novelty of the idea was not required for the idea to serve as consideration. Rather, it was sufficient to prove that the party to whom the idea was disclosed was not aware of the idea.]

These decisions do not support defendant's contention that novelty is required in all cases involving disclosure of ideas. Indeed, we have explicitly held that it is not. . . . [The] decisions involve a distinct factual pattern: the buyer and seller contract for *disclosure* of the idea with payment based on use, but no separate postdisclosure contract for *use* of the idea has been made. Thus, they present the issue of whether the idea the buyer was using, was, in fact, the seller's.

Such transactions pose two problems for the courts. On the one hand, how can sellers prove that the buyer obtained the idea from them, and nowhere else, and that the buyer's use of it thus constitutes misappropriation of property? Unlike tangible property, an idea lacks title and boundaries and cannot be rendered exclusive by the acts of the one who first thinks it. On the other hand, there is no equity in enforcing a seemingly valid contract when, in fact, it turns out upon disclosure that the buyer already possessed the idea. In such instances, the disclosure, though freely bargained for, is manifestly without value. A showing of novelty, at least novelty as to the buyer, addresses these two concerns. Novelty can then serve to establish both the attributes of ownership necessary for a property-based claim and the value of the consideration—the disclosure—necessary for contract-based claims.

There are no such concerns in a transaction such as the one before us. Defendant does not claim that it was aware of the idea before plaintiffs disclosed it but, rather, concedes that the idea came from them. When a seller's claim arises from a contract to use an idea entered into *after* the disclosure of the idea, the question is not whether the buyer misappropriated property from the seller, but whether the idea had value to the buyer and thus constitutes valid consideration. In such a case, the buyer knows what he or she is buying and has agreed that the idea has value, and the Court will not ordinarily go behind that determination. The lack of novelty, in and of itself, does not demonstrate a lack of value. . . . To the contrary, the buyer may reap benefits from such a contract in a number of ways—for instance, by not having to expend resources pursuing the idea through other channels or by having a profit-making idea implemented sooner rather than later. The law of contracts would have to be substantially rewritten were we to allow buyers of fully disclosed ideas to disregard their obligation to pay simply because an idea could have been obtained from some other source or in some other way.

* * *

Accordingly, the order of the Appellate Division should be modified, without costs, in accordance with this opinion, and, as so modified, affirmed, and the certified question answered in the negative.

NOTES

According to the court in *Kurtz v. Lelchuk*, 12 Misc.3d 1182 (N.Y.Sup.Ct. 2006):

> A transaction is supported by consideration when something of real value to the parties is exchanged. . . . The adequacy of consideration is not the proper subject of judicial scrutiny when some benefit was received. . . . The slightest consideration is sufficient to support the most onerous obligations * * * The prudence or fairness of [the] deal is not the subject of judicial scrutiny in the absence of fraud or unconscionability. . . .

Comment: Adequacy of Consideration

By now it should be clear that if there is consideration, the courts will generally resist a request to inquire into the adequacy of the agreed exchange. This has been regarded as a corollary of freedom of contract, buttressed by laissez-faire economics. Reflecting this approach, the First Restatement flatly stated that "the relative values of a promise and the consideration for it, do not affect the sufficiency of consideration." § 81. Similarly, the Second Restatement provides that there is no requirement of "equivalence in the values exchanged." § 79(b). This general respect for private autonomy, encompassing a broad recognition of the power of contracting parties to determine their own obligations, can be discerned throughout contemporary contract law. See Robert Braucher, *Freedom of Contract and the Second Restatement*, 78 Yale L.J. 598 (1969).

Should courts ever protect contracting parties from "bad bargains," i.e. agreed exchanges which, in retrospect, involve materially disparate values? If so, does the current rule leave any room for them to do so?

One approach is to find that the exchange was not bargained for because the promisor was not aware of the disparity and therefore did not in fact bargain for it. If there is no consideration, the insulation of "adequacy" from judicial review does not arise.

If there was a bargained for exchange, another approach is to examine the quality of the bargaining process that preceded the agreement. Was the promisor's access to information or choice impaired by fraud or duress by the other party, or by mistake? These are process-based exceptions to the adequacy principle and will be considered in Chapter Four. The doctrine of unconscionability is concerned with process where there is no fraud, duress, or mistake. As noted in *Jones v. Star Credit*, the hallmarks of unconscionability are "unfair surprise" and "oppression." We will return to see how this plays out in other cases, such as those involving so-called "contracts of adhesion," i.e., form "contracts" drafted exclusively by one party and offered to the other on a "take-it-or-leave-it" basis.

Another approach is to refuse enforcement where the outcome of the exchange "shocks the conscience," without explicitly examining the process by which it was made. This was the general medieval attitude, influenced in part by Roman law antecedents, which sought to insure equivalency of value in all exchanges. Concepts of "just price," for example, were formulated to inhibit unfair advantage in bargaining, even where the disadvantage arose from inadvertence, inexperience, carelessness or the like. See Alphonse Squillante, *The Doctrine of Just Price—Its Origin and Development*, 74 Com. L.J. 333 (1969). By the doctrine of *laesio enormis*, a vendor could rescind a transaction where the price received was less than one-half its value. This was limited to real estate transactions under Roman law, but extended to others by the canonists. There are some vestiges of the lesion doctrine in civil law countries, but the trend has been in the other direction. See Amos and Walton, Introduction to French Law 163–5 (2d ed. 1963).

PROBLEM: THE CASE OF THE HOME-RUN BALL

On July 16, 2009, Ryan Howard of the Philadelphia Phillies hit his 200th career home run at Land Shark Stadium. It was a record-breaking ball—Howard had just reached this milestone in fewer games than any other player in the history of the major leagues.

Lucky game attendee Jennifer Valdivia, a 12-year-old girl from Miami, caught Howard's home-run ball. Because Howard hoped to retrieve the ball, Phillies affiliates ushered Jennifer to the clubhouse after her fateful catch. They convinced her to trade the record ball for an ordinary autographed ball.

Two and a half months later, Jennifer discovered her error. Her Fort Lauderdale attorney, Norm Kent, who also happened to be a memorabilia enthusiast, informed Jennifer and her family that the record ball was worth significantly more than the autographed ball.

Kent filed suit against the Phillies on behalf of Jennifer and her family. On the same day the suit was filed, the Phillies agreed to return the home-run ball to Jennifer. See Adam H. Beasley and Emily Michot, *Historic baseball safe at home in Miami girl's hands*, Miami Herald, October 7, 2009, at A1.

Suppose the Phillies had not returned the ball to Jennifer. Bracketing the question of whether Jennifer was old enough to enter into a binding contract to exchange the balls (a minor's capacity to contract is discussed in Chapter Four), are there any other arguments that the exchange was not binding? Suppose you are given the unenviable task of representing the Phillies in the lawsuit. What would be your best arguments?

(F) PREEXISTING DUTY RULE

The preexisting duty rule provides that the performance or the promise to perform a preexisting legal duty does not constitute consideration. This rule has important consequences both for agreements to discharge obligations and for agreements to modify them. Perhaps no common law rule has been subjected to more critical evaluation than this staple of contract law. Courts have exercised considerable ingenuity in fashioning exceptions, and there is a significant reorientation of the matter in the Uniform Commercial Code. See UCC §§ 1–306 and 2–209(1).

The preexisting duty rule was first applied to cases involving the discharge of obligations. To illustrate: Debtor owes Creditor $1,000. The parties agree that Creditor will accept $500 in full settlement. Debtor pays the agreed $500; Creditor sues for the remaining $500. Creditor wins.

Based upon the previous cases in this chapter, is this a predictable result? Is it a good result? What additional facts might influence your judgment as to the proper outcome?

As the rule developed, it was also applied to one-sided modification of existing contracts, in which one party undertook to do something additional and the other side's obligations or performance remained the same. For example, Contractor agrees to build a garage, and Owner promises to pay $5,000. Contractor encounters unforeseen costs and refuses to perform unless Owner agrees to pay an additional $1,000. Owner promises to pay the additional amount. Is this promise enforceable? The traditional answer is "no." There is no consideration for Owner's promise to pay the $1,000 because Contractor did no more than that which it was already obliged to do.

Is a result favorable to Owner the logical outcome under the concept of consideration as elaborated in the preceding cases? Is it a fair result? Again, what additional factual data would be helpful?

Reflection upon these questions suggests the limitations of the classical theory of consideration. In reading the materials that follow, pay attention to the tools courts (and legislatures) have used to craft limited exceptions to the consideration requirement in order to address the practical needs of parties and to reach just results.

William Levine v. Anne Blumenthal

Supreme Court of New Jersey, 1936.
117 N.J.L. 23.

■ HEHER, JUSTICE. By an indenture dated April 16th, 1931, plaintiff leased to defendants, for the retail merchandising of women's wearing apparel, store premises situate in the principal business district of the city of Paterson. The term was two years, to commence on May 1st next ensuing, with an option of renewal for the further period of three years; and the rent reserved was $2,100 for the first year, and $2,400 for the second year, payable in equal monthly installments in advance.

The state of the case settled by the District Court judge sets forth that defendants adduced evidence tending to show that, in the month of April, 1932, before the expiration of the first year of the term, they advised plaintiff that "it was absolutely impossible for them to pay any increase in rent; that their business had so fallen down that they had great difficulty in meeting the present rent of $175 per month; that if the plaintiff insisted upon the increase called for in the lease, they would be forced to remove from the premises or perhaps go out of business altogether;" and that plaintiff "agreed to allow them to remain under the same rental 'until business improved.'" While conceding that defendants informed him that "they could not pay the increase called for in the lease because of adverse business conditions," plaintiff, on the other hand, testified that he "agreed to accept the payment of $175 each month, on account." For eleven months of the second year of the term rent was paid by defendants, and accepted by plaintiff, at the rate of $175 per month. The option of renewal was not exercised; and defendants surrendered the premises at the expiration of the term leaving the last month's rent unpaid. This action was brought to recover the unpaid balance of the rent reserved by the lease for the second year—$25 per month for eleven months, and $200 for the last month.

The District Court judge found, as a fact, that "a subsequent oral agreement had been made to change and alter the terms of the written lease, with respect to the rent paid," but that it was not supported by "a lawful consideration," and therefore was wholly ineffective.

The insistence is that the current trade depression had disabled the lessees in respect of the payment of the full rent reserved, and a consideration sufficient to support the secondary agreement arose out of these special circumstances; and that, in any event, the execution of the substituted performance therein provided is a defense at law, notwithstanding the want of consideration. . . . It is said also that, "insofar as the oral agreement has become executed as to the payments which had fallen due and had been paid and accepted in full as per the oral agreement," the remission of the balance of the rent is sustainable on the theory of gift, if not of accord and satisfaction. . . .

It is not suggested that the primary contract under consideration was of a class which may not lawfully be modified by parol, except to the extent that the substituted performance has been actually and fully executed and accepted; and we are not therefore called upon to consider that question. . . . The point made by respondent is that the subsequent oral agreement to reduce the rent is *nudum pactum*, and therefore created no binding obligation.

It is elementary that the subsequent agreement, to impose the obligation of a contract, must rest upon a new and independent consideration. The rule was laid down in very early times that even though a part of a matured liquidated debt or demand has been given and received in full satisfaction thereof, the creditor may yet recover the remainder. The payment of a part was not regarded in law as a satisfaction of the whole, unless it was in virtue of an agreement supported by a consideration. . . . The principle is firmly imbedded in our jurisprudence that a promise to do what the promisor is already legally bound to do is an unreal consideration. . . . It has been criticised [sic], at least in some of its special applications, as "mediaeval" and wholly artificial—one that operates to defeat the "reasonable bargains of business men." See Professor Ames' Treatise, *Two Theories of Consideration*, 12 Harv. L. Rev. 515, 521; . . . But these strictures are not well grounded. They reject the basic principle that a consideration, to support a contract, consists either of a benefit to the promisor or a detriment to the promisee—a doctrine that has always been fundamental in our conception of consideration. It is a principle, almost universally accepted, that an act or forbearance required by a legal duty owing to the promisor that is neither doubtful nor the subject of honest and reasonable dispute is not a sufficient consideration. . . .

Yet any consideration for the new undertaking, however insignificant, satisfies this rule. . . . For instance, an undertaking to pay part of the debt before maturity, or at a place other than where the obligor was legally bound to pay, or to pay in property, regardless of its value, or to effect a composition with creditors by the payment of less than the sum due, has been held to constitute a consideration sufficient in law. The test is whether there is an additional consideration adequate to support an ordinary contract, and consists of something which the debtor was not legally bound to do or give. . . .

And there is authority for the view that, where there is no illegal preference, a payment of part of a debt, "accompanied by an agreement of the debtor to refrain from voluntary bankruptcy," is a sufficient consideration for the creditor's promise to remit the balance of the debt. But the mere fact that the creditor "fears that the debtor will go into bankruptcy, and that the debtor contemplates bankruptcy proceedings," is not enough; that alone does not prove that the creditor requested the debtor to refrain from such proceedings. . . .

The cases to the contrary either create arbitrary exceptions to the rule, or profess to find a consideration in the form of a new undertaking which in essence was not a tangible new obligation or a duty not imposed by the lease, or, in any event, was not the price "bargained for as the exchange for the promise" (see Coast National Bank v. Bloom, 113 N.J.Law 597), and therefore do violence to the fundamental principle. They exhibit the modern tendency, especially in the matter of rent reductions, to depart from the strictness of the basic common law rule and give effect to what has been termed a "reasonable" modification of the primary contract. . . .

So tested, the secondary agreement at issue is not supported by a valid consideration; and it therefore created no legal obligation. General economic adversity, however disastrous it may be in its individual consequences, is never a warrant for judicial abrogation of this primary principle of the law of contracts.

It remains to consider the second contention that, in so far as the agreement has been executed by the payment and acceptance of rent at the reduced rate, the substituted performance stands, regardless of the want of consideration. This is likewise untenable. Ordinarily, the actual performance of that which one is legally bound to do stands on the same footing as his promise to do that which he is legally compellable to do. Anson on Contracts (Turck Ed.) 234; Williston on Contracts (Rev. Ed.) §§ 130, 130a. This is a corollary of the basic principle. Of course, a different rule prevails where *bona fide* disputes have arisen respecting the relative rights and duties of the parties to a contract, or the debt or demand is unliquidated, or the contract is wholly executory on both sides. Anson on Contracts (Turck Ed.) 240, 241.

It is settled in this jurisdiction that, as in the case of other contracts, a consideration is essential to the validity of an accord and satisfaction. . . . On reason and principle, it could not be otherwise. This is the general rule. . . . It results that the issue was correctly determined.

Judgment affirmed, with costs.

Alaska Packers' Association v. Domenico

United States Court of Appeals, Ninth Circuit, 1902.
117 Fed. 99.

[On March 26, 1900, appellees entered into a written contract with appellant in San Francisco, under which they agreed to sail on a vessel provided by appellant to Pyramid Harbor, Alaska for the 1900 fishing season and then to return. Appellant had a salmon cannery at that location in which it had invested $150,000. Appellees agreed, as sailors and fishermen, to do "regular ship's duty, both up and down, discharging and loading; and to do any other work whatsoever when requested to do so by the captain or agent of the Alaska Packers' Association." For this work, some appellees were to be paid $50 and others $60 for the season, and all were to be paid "two cents for each red salmon in the catching of which he took part."]

[The appellees arrived at Pyramid Harbor in April 1900 and began to unload the ship and fit up the cannery. On May 19, however, "they stopped work in a body, and demanded of the company's superintendent there in charge $100 for services in operating the vessel to and from Pyramid Harbor, instead of the sums stipulated for in and by the contracts; stating that unless they were paid this additional wage they would stop work entirely, and return to San Francisco." The evidence showed that the superintendent stated that he had no authority to modify the contract and was unable to induce the appellees to continue working. Because of the remoteness of the location and the shortness of the season, he was also unable to obtain replacements. On May 22, the superintendent "yielded to their demands" and substituted $100 for the previously agreed seasonal rates in a document that was signed by the appellees before a shipping commissioner who had been brought in for the occasion. After completing the season and returning to San Francisco, the appellees were informed by appellant that they would be paid only the amounts agreed to in March. Some of the appellees sued to enforce the agreed modification and received a judgment in the district court.]

■ Ross, Circuit Judge. * * * The real questions in the case as brought here are questions of law, and, in the view that we take of the case, it will be necessary to consider but one of those. Assuming that the appellant's superintendent at Pyramid Harbor was authorized to make the alleged contract of May 22d, and that he executed it on behalf of the appellant, was it supported by a sufficient consideration? From the foregoing statement of the case, it will have been seen that the libelants agreed in writing, for certain stated compensation, to render their services to the appellant in remote waters where the season for conducting fishing operations is extremely short, and in which enterprise the appellant had a large amount of money invested; and, after having entered upon the discharge of their contract, and at a time when it was impossible for the appellant to secure other men in their places, the libelants, without any valid cause, absolutely refused to continue the services they were under contract to perform unless the appellant would consent to pay them more money. Consent to such a demand, under such circumstances, if given, was, in our opinion, without consideration, for the reason that it was based solely upon the libelants' agreement to render the exact services, and none other, that they were already under contract to render. The case shows that they willfully and arbitrarily broke that obligation. As a matter of course, they were liable to the appellant in damages, and it is quite probable, as suggested by the court below in its opinion, that they may have been unable to respond in damages. But we are unable to agree with the conclusions there drawn, from these facts, in these words:

> "Under such circumstances, it would be strange, indeed, if the law would not permit the defendant to waive the damages caused by the libelants' breach, and enter into the contract sued upon,—a contract mutually beneficial to all the parties thereto, in that it gave to the libelants reasonable compensation for their labor, and enabled the defendant to employ to advantage the large capital it had invested in its canning and fishing plant."

Certainly, it cannot be justly held, upon the record in this case, that there was any voluntary waiver on the part of the appellant of the breach of the original contract. The company itself knew nothing of such breach until the expedition returned to San Francisco, and the testimony is uncontradicted that its superintendent at Pyramid Harbor, who, it is claimed made on its behalf the contract sued on, distinctly informed the libelants that he had no power to alter the original or to make a new contract; and it would, of course, follow that if he had no power to change the original, he would have no authority to waive any rights thereunder. The circumstances of the present case bring it, we think, directly within the sound and just observations of the supreme court of Minnesota in the case of *King v. Railway Co.*, 61 Minn. 482:

> "No astute reasoning can change the plain fact that the party who refuses to perform, and thereby coerces a promise from the other party to the contract to pay him an increased compensation for doing that which he is legally bound to do, takes an unjustifiable advantage of the necessities of the other party. Surely it would be a travesty on justice to hold that the party so making the promise for extra pay was estopped from asserting that the promise was without consideration. A party

cannot lay the foundation of an estoppel by his own wrong, where the promise is simply a repetition of a subsisting legal promise. There can be no consideration for the promise of the other party, and there is no warrant for inferring that the parties have voluntarily rescinded or modified their contract. The promise cannot be legally enforced, although the other party has completed his contract in reliance upon it."

In *Lingenfelder v. Brewing Co.*, 103 Mo. 578, the court, in holding void a contract by which the owner of a building agreed to pay its architect an additional sum because of his refusal to otherwise proceed with the contract, said:

"It is urged upon us by respondents that this was a new contract. New in what? Jungenfeld was bound by his contract to design and supervise this building. Under the new promise, he was not to do anything more or anything different. What benefit was to accrue to Wainwright? He was to receive the same service from Jungenfeld under the new, that Jungenfeld was bound to tender under the original, contract. What loss, trouble, or inconvenience could result to Jungenfeld that he had not already assumed? No amount of metaphysical reasoning can change the plain fact that Jungenfeld took advantage of Wainwright's necessities, and extorted the promise of five per cent. on the refrigerator plant as the condition of his complying with his contract already entered into. Nor had he even the flimsy pretext that Wainwright had violated any of the conditions of the contract on his part. Jungenfeld himself put it upon the simple proposition that 'if he, as an architect, put up the brewery, and another company put up the refrigerating machinery, it would be a detriment to the Empire Refrigerating Company,' of which Jungenfeld was president. To permit plaintiff to recover under such circumstances would be to offer a premium upon bad faith, and invite men to violate their most sacred contracts that they may profit by their own wrong. That a promise to pay a man for doing that which he is already under contract to do is without consideration is conceded by respondents. The rule has been so long imbedded in the common law and decisions of the highest courts of the various states that nothing but the most cogent reasons ought to shake it. [Citing a long list of authorities.] But it is 'carrying coals to Newcastle' to add authorities on a proposition so universally accepted, and so inherently just and right in itself. The learned counsel for respondents do not controvert the general proposition. Their contention is, and the circuit court agreed with them, that, when Jungenfeld declined to go further on his contract, the defendant then had the right to sue for damages, and not having elected to sue Jungenfeld, but having acceded to his demand for the additional compensation, defendant cannot now be heard to say his promise is without consideration. While it is true Jungenfeld became liable in damages for the obvious breach of his contract, we do not think it follows that defendant is estopped from showing its promise was made without consideration. * * * "

* * *

It results from the views above expressed that the judgment must be reversed, and the cause remanded, with directions to the court below to enter judgment for the [appellant], with costs. It is so ordered.

Alaska Packers' Association Boats

NOTES

(1) Consideration is normally regarded as something which is bargained for and given in exchange for a promise. Was not the bargain requirement satisfied in *Levine*? Why, then, does the court reject the defendants' position? Would the decision have been different were it clearly established that the lessor importuned the lessees to stay on under the new arrangement?

(2) Is there a reasonable basis for distinguishing *Levine* and *Alaska Packers* on consideration theory? Assuming the consideration argument was unavailing in *Alaska Packers*, could you argue persuasively for a similar result predicated on other grounds?

(3) When will a court invoke the strict preexisting duty rule, and when will it permit some flexibility? In *Levine* the rule was invoked to protect the lessor-creditor against a modification made in the midst of a depression. In *Labriola v. Pollard Group, Inc.*, 152 Wash.2d 828 (2004), the rule was invoked to protect an at-will employee against a non-competition agreement made with the employer after five years of employment. The court required an "independent" consideration for the modification and found no new

benefit for the employee and no further obligations of the employer to provide continued employment or additional training.

(4) *Net Present Value.* In *Alaska Packers*, the fishermen tried to prove that the nets furnished to them were not serviceable because they permitted the smaller salmon to slip through. The district court concluded that the contention was not proven (a finding affirmed in the full opinion of the Ninth Circuit), reasoning in part that Alaska Packers had every incentive to supply nets adequate to the task. Is this right? Given the payment structure in the contract, did Alaska Packers and the fishermen have the same incentives with respect to the size of the holes in the nets?

The district court nevertheless held that an executory contract could be validly modified by substituting the modifying agreement for the original contract (a novation) and that there was no duress to prevent enforcement. On appeal, the Ninth Circuit rejected the novation theory, holding that new consideration was required to validate the modification. Moreover, the court of appeals appears to conclude that the modification was extracted under duress—by an unlawful threat to breach the contract, leaving the Packers without any viable alternatives and some very uncertain damage remedies. See Restatement (Second) § 73 (performance of a legal duty "neither doubtful nor the subject of honest dispute is not consideration"). Is the appellate court's further suggestion of duress appropriate, given the findings of the trial court?

For an interesting context study of this case that completes the record and develops some alternative stories about what likely occurred, see Debora L. Threedy, *A Fish Story:* Alaska Packers' Association v. Domenico, 2000 Utah L. Rev. 185 (2000). Threedy suggests that the fishermen, because of differences in language and experience, might have misunderstood that the nets were serviceable. While this would not justify a strike, it tends to neutralize the claim of duress. Id. at 205–07. Threedy also suggests that nets which appear unserviceable to those hoping to catch more fish (the fishermen) would be perfect for the Packers who were concerned about catching too many fish or perhaps wanted to cut corners on equipment.

(5) Facially neutral rules can be used for non-neutral purposes. Reva Siegal and Jill Hasday have each cataloged US courts' hostility to agreements between spouses involving payment for services, which almost always involve a wife suing a husband or his estate for money owed. Their analyses suggest that U.S. courts have commonly refused enforcement in these cases on the ground either that the agreement is without consideration, since the spouse has a preexisting duty to provide the bargained-for services, or that it is unenforceable on the grounds of public policy, since enforcement would allow the market to intrude into the marriage relationship. Jill Elaine Hasday, *Intimacy and Economic Exchange*, 119 Harv. L. Rev. 491, 500–02 (2005); Reva B. Siegel, *The Modernization of Marital Status Law: Adjudicating Wives' Rights to Earnings*, 1860–1930, 82 Geo. L.J. 2127, 2174–96 (1994).

Alfred L. Angel v. John E. Murray, Jr.

Supreme Court of Rhode Island, 1974.
113 R.I. 482.

■ ROBERTS, CHIEF JUSTICE. This is a civil action brought by Alfred L. Angel and others against John E. Murray, Jr., Director of Finance of the City of Newport, the city of Newport, and James L. Maher, alleging that Maher had illegally been paid the sum of $20,000 by the Director of Finance and praying that the defendant Maher be ordered to repay the city such sum. The case was heard by a justice of the Superior Court, sitting without a jury, who entered a judgment ordering Maher to repay the sum of $20,000 to the city of Newport. Maher is now before this court prosecuting an appeal.

The record discloses that Maher has provided the city of Newport with a refuse-collection service under a series of five-year contracts beginning in 1946. On March 12, 1964, Maher and the city entered into another such contract for a period of five years commencing on July 1, 1964, and terminating on June 30, 1969. The contract provided, among other things, that Maher would receive $137,000 per year in return for collecting and removing all combustible and noncombustible waste materials generated within the city.

In June of 1967 Maher requested an additional $10,000 per year from the city council because there had been a substantial increase in the cost of collection due to an unexpected and unanticipated increase of 400 new dwelling units. Maher's testimony, which is uncontradicted, indicates the 1964 contract had been predicated on the fact that since 1946 there had been an average increase of 20 to 25 new dwelling units per year. After a public meeting of the city council where Maher explained in detail the reasons for his request and was questioned by members of the city council, the city council agreed to pay him an additional $10,000 for the year ending on June 30, 1968. Maher made a similar request again in June of 1968 for the same reasons, and the city council again agreed to pay an additional $10,000 for the year ending on June 30, 1969.

The trial justice found that each such $10,000 payment was made in violation of law. His decision, as we understand it, is premised on two independent grounds. First, he found that the additional payments were unlawful because they had not been recommended in writing to the city council by the city manager. Second, he found that Maher was not entitled to extra compensation because the original contract already required him to collect all refuse generated within the city and, therefore, included the 400 additional units. The trial justice further found that these 400 additional units were within the contemplation of the parties when they entered into the contract. It appears that he based this portion of the decision upon the rule that Maher had a preexisting duty to collect the refuse generated by the 400 additional units, and thus there was no consideration for the two additional payments.

[The court concluded that the charter provision did not preclude the city council from acting without the city manager's recommendation in altering the written contract.]

Having found that the city council had the power to modify the 1964 contract without the written recommendation of the city manager, we are still confronted with the question of whether the additional payments were illegal because they were not supported by consideration.

* * *

It is generally held that a modification of a contract is itself a contract, which is unenforceable unless supported by consideration. See Simpson, [Contracts § 93 (2d ed. 1965)]. In *Rose v. Daniels*, 8 R.I. 381 (1866), this court held that an agreement by a debtor with a creditor to discharge a debt for a sum of money less than the amount due is unenforceable because it was not supported by consideration.

Rose is a perfect example of the preexisting duty rule. Under this rule an agreement modifying a contract is not supported by consideration if one of the parties to the agreement does or promises to do something that he is legally obligated to do or refrains or promises to refrain from doing something he is not legally privileged to do. . . . In *Rose* there was no consideration for the new agreement because the debtor was already legally obligated to repay the full amount of the debt.

Although the preexisting duty rule is followed by most jurisdictions, a small minority of jurisdictions, Massachusetts, for example, find that there is consideration for a promise to perform what one is already legally obligated to do because the new promise is given in place of an action for damages to secure performance. See Swartz v. Lieberman, 323 Mass. 109 (1948); Munroe v. Perkins, 26 Mass. (9 Pick.) 298 (1830). *Swartz* is premised on the theory that a promisor's forbearance of the power to breach his original agreement and be sued in an action for damages is consideration for a subsequent agreement by the promisee to pay extra compensation. This rule, however, has been widely criticized as an anomaly. . . .

The primary purpose of the preexisting duty rule is to prevent what has been referred to as the "hold-up game." See 1A Corbin, [Contracts § 171 (1963)]. A classic example of the "hold-up game" is found in *Alaska Packers' Ass'n v. Domenico*, 117 F. 99 (9th Cir. 1902). * * *

Another example of the "hold-up game" is found in the area of construction contracts. Frequently, a contractor will refuse to complete work under an unprofitable contract unless he is awarded additional compensation. The courts have generally held that a subsequent agreement to award additional compensation is unenforceable if the contractor is only performing work which would have required of him under the original contract. . . .

These examples clearly illustrate that the courts will not enforce an agreement that has been procured by coercion or duress and will hold the parties to their original contract regardless of whether it is profitable or unprofitable. However, the courts have been reluctant to apply the preexisting duty rule when a party to a contract encounters unanticipated difficulties and the other party, not influenced by coercion or duress, voluntarily agrees to pay additional compensation for work already required to be performed under the contract. For example, the courts have found that the original contract was rescinded, Linz v. Schuck, 106 Md. 220 (1907); abandoned, Connelly v. Devoe, 37 Conn. 570 (1871); or waived, Michaud v. McGregor, 61 Minn. 198 (1895).

Although the preexisting duty rule has served a useful purpose insofar as it deters parties from using coercion and duress to obtain additional compensation, it has been widely criticized as a general rule of law. With regard to the preexisting duty rule, one legal scholar has stated:

> "There has been a growing doubt as to the soundness of this doctrine as a matter of social policy. * * * In certain classes of cases, this doubt has influenced courts to refuse to apply the rule, or to ignore it, in their actual decisions. Like other legal rules, this rule is in process of growth and change, the process being more active here than in most instances. The result of this is that a court should no longer accept this rule as fully established. It should never use it as the major premise of a decision, at least without giving careful thought to the circumstances of the particular case, to the moral deserts of the parties, and to the social feelings and interests that are involved. It is certain that the rule, stated in general and all-inclusive terms, is no longer so well-settled that a court must apply it though the heavens fall."

1A Corbin, supra, § 171; see also Calamari and Perillo, [Contracts § 61 (1970)].

The modern trend appears to recognize the necessity that courts should enforce agreements modifying contracts when unexpected or unanticipated difficulties arise during the course of the performance of a contract, even though there is no consideration for the modification, as long as the parties agree voluntarily.

Under the Uniform Commercial Code, § 2–209(1), which has been adopted by 49 states, "[a]n agreement modifying a contract [for the sale of goods] needs no consideration to be binding." See G.L.1956 (1969 Reenactment) § 6A–2–209(1). Although at first blush this section appears to validate modifications obtained by coercion and duress, the comments to this section indicate that a modification under this section must meet the test of good faith imposed by the Code, and a modification obtained by extortion without a legitimate commercial reason is unenforceable.

The modern trend away from a rigid application of the preexisting duty rule is reflected by § 89D(a) [§ 89(a) in the final draft—Eds.] of the American Law Institute's Restatement Second of the Law of Contracts, which provides: "A promise modifying a duty under a contract not fully performed on either side is binding (a) if the modification is fair and equitable in view of circumstances not anticipated by the parties when the contract was made * * *."

We believe that § 89D(a) is the proper rule of law and find it applicable to the facts of this case. It not only prohibits modifications obtained by coercion, duress, or extortion but also fulfills society's expectation that agreements entered into voluntarily will be enforced by the courts.[3] See generally Horwitz, *The Historical Foundations of Modern Contract Law*, 87 Harv. L. Rev. 917 (1974). Section 89D(a), of course, does not compel a modification of an unprofitable or unfair contract; it only enforces a modification if the parties voluntarily agree and if (1) the promise modifying the original contract was made before the contract was fully performed on either side, (2) the underlying circumstances which prompted the modification were unanticipated by the parties, and (3) the modification is fair and equitable.

The evidence, which is uncontradicted, reveals that in June of 1968 Maher requested the city council to pay him an additional $10,000 for the year beginning on July 1, 1968, and ending on June 30, 1969. This request was made at a public meeting of the city council, where Maher

---

[3] The drafters of § 89D(a) of the Restatement Second of the Law of Contracts use the following illustrations in comment (b) as examples of how this rule is applied to certain transactions:

"1. By a written contract A agrees to excavate a cellar for B for a stated price. Solid rock is unexpectedly encountered and A so notifies B. A and B then orally agree that A will remove the rock at a unit price which is reasonable but nine times that used in computing the original price, and A completes the job. B is bound to pay the increased amount.

"2. A contracts with B to supply for $300 a laundry chute for a building B has contracted to build for the Government for $150,000. Later A discovers that he made an error as to the type of material to be used and should have bid $1,200. A offers to supply the chute for $1,000, eliminating overhead and profit. After ascertaining that other suppliers would charge more, B agrees. The new agreement is binding.

"3. A is employed by B as a designer of coats at $90 a week for a year beginning November 1 under a written contract executed September 1. A is offered $115 a week by another employer and so informs B. A and B then agree that A will be paid $100 a week and in October execute a new written contract to that effect simultaneously tearing up the prior contract. The new contract is binding.

"4. A contracts to manufacture and sell to B 2,000 steel roofs for corn cribs at $60. Before A begins manufacture a threat of a nationwide steel strike raises the cost of steel about $10 per roof, and A and B agree orally to increase the price to $70 per roof. A thereafter manufactures and delivers 1,700 of the roofs, and B pays for 1,500 of them at the increased price without protest, increasing the selling price of the corn cribs by $10. The new agreement is binding.

"5. A contracts to manufacture and sell to B 100,000 castings for lawn mowers at 50 cents each. After partial delivery and after B has contracted to sell a substantial number of lawn mowers at a fixed price, A notifies B that increased metal costs require that the price be increased to 75 cents. Substitute castings are available at 55 cents, but only after several months delay. B protests but is forced to agree to the new price to keep its plant in operation. The modification is not binding."

explained in detail his reasons for making the request. Thereafter, the city council voted to authorize the Mayor to sign an amendment to the 1964 contract which provided that Maher would receive an additional $10,000 per year for the duration of the contract. Under such circumstances we have no doubt that the city voluntarily agreed to modify the 1964 contract.

Having determined the voluntariness of this agreement, we turn our attention to the three criteria delineated above. First, the modification was made in June of 1968 at a time when the five-year contract which was made in 1964 had not been fully performed by either party. Second, although the 1964 contract provided that Maher collect all refuse generated within the city, it appears this contract was premised on Maher's past experience that the number of refuse-generating units would increase at a rate of 20 to 25 per year. Furthermore, the evidence is uncontradicted that the 1967–1968 increase of 400 units "went beyond any previous expectation." Clearly, the circumstances which prompted the city council to modify the 1964 contract were unanticipated.[4] Third, although the evidence does not indicate what proportion of the total this increase comprised, the evidence does indicate that it was a "substantial" increase. In light of this, we cannot say that the council's agreement to pay Maher the $10,000 increase was not fair and equitable in the circumstances.

The judgment appealed from is reversed, and the cause is remanded to the Superior Court for entry of judgment for the defendants.

NOTES

(1)   Is the "unexpected or unanticipated difficulties" exception referred to in the instant case a mere technical evasion? Or is there a sound basis in policy for upholding modifications under such circumstances?

---

[4]   The trial justice found that § 2(a) of the 1964 contract precluded Maher from recovering extra compensation for the 400 additional units. Section 2(a) provided: "*The Contractor, having made his proposal after his own examinations and estimates, shall take all responsibility for, and bear, any losses resulting to him in carrying out the contract;* and shall assume the defence of, and hold the City, its agents and employees harmless from all suits and claims arising from the use of any invention, patent, or patent rights, material, labor or implement, by or from any act, omission or neglect of, the Contractor, his agents or employees, in carrying out the contract." (Emphasis added). The trial justice, quoting the italicized portion of § 2(a), found that this section required that any losses incurred in the performance of the contract were Maher's responsibility. In our opinion, however, the trial justice overlooked the thrust of § 2(a) when read in its entirety.

It is clearly a contractual provision requiring the contractor to hold the city harmless and to defend it in any litigation arising out of the performance of his obligations under the contract, whether a result of affirmative action or some omission or neglect on the part of Maher or his agents or employees. We are persuaded that the portion of § 2(a) specifically referred to by the court refers to losses resulting to Maher from some action or omission on the part of his own agents or employees. It cannot be disputed, however, that any losses that resulted from an increase in the cost of collecting from the increased number of units generating refuse in no way resulted from any action on the part of either Maher or his employees. Rather, whatever losses he did entail by reason of the requirement of such extra collection resulted from actions completely beyond his control and thus unanticipated.

(2) *Modification under the Uniform Commercial Code.* Section 2–209(1) of the UCC provides: "An agreement modifying a contract within this Article needs no consideration to be binding." The drafters appended the following commentary:

> Subsection (1) provides that an agreement modifying a sales contract needs no consideration to be binding.

> However, modifications made thereunder must meet the test of good faith imposed by this Act. The effective use of bad faith to escape performance on the original contract terms is barred, and the extortion of a "modification" without legitimate commercial reason is ineffective as a violation of the duty of good faith. Nor can a mere technical consideration support a modification made in bad faith.

> The test of "good faith" between merchants or as against merchants includes "observance of reasonable commercial standards of fair dealing in the trade" (Section 2–103), and may in some situations require an objectively demonstrable reason for seeking a modification. But such matters as a market shift which makes performance come to involve a loss may provide such a reason even though there is no such unforeseen difficulty as would make out a legal excuse from performance under Sections 2–615 and 2–616.

Section 2–209(1) is obviously a departure from the common law and, as elaborated in the comments, basically reorients the subject. The emphasis is no longer upon consideration, but upon good faith. For example, it is noted that a "mere technical consideration" cannot support a "modification made in bad faith." To what extent should the Code apply in analogous transactions, for example, in construction contracts or employment contracts? Would the Code furnish a superior method of approach in these cases, or would the more traditional view(s) appear more conducive to the attainment of satisfactory results?

(3) Although the case of *Angel v. Murray* is rarely cited by courts outside of Rhode Island, the case and the challenges posed by the Restatement test are frequently discussed by commentators. The challenge, in the absence of a consideration requirement, is to draw a workable line between good faith and duress. See, e.g., Meredith R. Miller, *Revisiting Austin v. Loral: A Study in Economic Duress, Contract Modification, and Framing*, 2 Hastings Bus. L.J. 357 (2006). We return to this problem in Chapter Four.

PROBLEM: THE CASE OF THE DISSATISFIED ENTERTAINER

(You are a justice of a state appellate court, and the following is the beginning of an opinion which you are to complete for submission to your colleagues.)

This is an appeal from a judgment entered in the Circuit Court, after a jury trial in which the plaintiff, Oliver Ajax, received a verdict for $30,000 in a breach of contract action against the defendant, James Bond.

On February 15, Ajax and Bond entered into a written contract whereby the former, a professional entertainer, was to perform at Bond's resort hotel for the week of July 1–7 for $20,000. In late spring, Ajax had a hit record which virtually overnight made him a star who could command at least $50,000 for a one-week engagement. In early June, he contacted Bond to renegotiate their contract, demanding $50,000 for the July 1–7 period. Initially, Bond refused to renegotiate, but when Ajax said he would not perform, Bond relented. After discussion, Bond dictated a new contract to his stenographer, in the exact words of the original contract and running for the same period, but with the compensation changed to $50,000. As they signed the new contract, they tore up the old one. Thereafter, Ajax kept the engagement, but Bond refused to pay him more than $20,000. Whereupon, Ajax filed the instant suit for $30,000.

Over defendant's objection, the trial judge instructed the jury as follows: "If you find that the '$20,000 contract' was prior to or at the time of the execution of the '$50,000 contract' cancelled and revoked by the parties by their mutual consent, then it is your duty to find that there was consideration for the making of the contract in suit and, in that event, the plaintiff is entitled to your verdict in the amount of $30,000." On this appeal, the defendant contends that the giving of this instruction constituted reversible error.

PROBLEM: THE CASE OF THE SUBCONTRACTOR'S ADDED INDUCEMENT

Edward Woodward is the owner of a large smelting operation in Metropolis. On August 7, Woodward entered into a written contract with Peter Rogers, a general contractor, for the construction of an additional power plant at the operation.

On August 14, Rogers entered into a written subcontract with John Newman for the erection of all structural steel work required for the power plant. For the purpose of performing his work, Newman rented certain equipment for use until the job was completed. The work continued until October 7, when a strike occurred among Newman's employees, and work was discontinued for a period of approximately nine weeks. During this time, Newman was obliged to pay rent for the equipment and other sums to insure its safekeeping.

A meeting was called to adjust differences. In attendance were Newman, Rogers, Woodward and a representative of the union of the strikers. As a result of lengthy discussion, the strike was called off. However, Newman refused to continue performance unless he was paid for the rentals and charges accruing during the time of the strike. Woodward then promised to pay this amount so that the work could proceed.

The work was completed under the contracts, but Woodward refused to pay the rentals and charges. Newman consults you. Advise him. See Restatement (Second) § 73.

(G) DISCRETION, MUTUALITY, AND IMPLIED OBLIGATIONS

What happens when an agreement, or some rule of law, permits one party to withdraw sometime after performance begins for reasons totally or partially within that party's control? Such agreements can seem to create a consideration problem. Suppose Anne promises to appear on Friday to paint Paul's house, and Paul agrees to pay $1,000 when the job is completed "if I feel like it." If Anne fails to show and Paul sues for breach, there is no question but that Anne can defend on the ground that Paul gave no consideration for her promise. Paul's apparent promise was in fact illusory. Or, to put the matter more traditionally: in the attempted bilateral contract, there was no mutuality of obligation, and therefore no consideration! But now flip the facts around, and suppose Anne appeared and painted the house in a proper manner, and then Paul refused to pay. Could Anne recover the agreed price? The reasonable value of her services? Paul will argue that he made no promise to pay and that Anne, therefore, assumed the risk. Should that argument succeed? Or should the court read into Anne and Paul's agreement some implied limitation on Paul's discretion, such as a duty to act in good faith, so as to protect Anne's investment and render the agreement enforceable?

Rehm-Zeiher Co. v. F.G. Walker Co.

Court of Appeals of Kentucky, 1913.
156 Ky. 6.

■ CARROLL, J. The appellant, a corporation, in the years 1908, 1909, 1910, 1911, and 1912, and prior thereto, was engaged in the business of selling whisky; that is to say, it purchased from distillers certain brands and quantities of whisky, and then sold the whisky so bought to the trade. The appellee, during the years named, and prior thereto, owned and operated a distillery. In 1908 the parties entered into the following contract:

> "This contract made and entered into this November 17, 1908, by and between the F.G. Walker Company, of Bardstown, Nelson county, Kentucky, a corporation, party of the first part, and the Rehm-Zeiher Company, of Louisville, Jefferson county, Kentucky, party of the second part. The party of the first part has this day sold to the party of the second part 2,000 cases of old Walker whisky put up under a private brand, to be delivered during the years 1909, 3,000 cases to be delivered during the year 1910, 4,000 cases to be delivered during the year 1911, and 5,000 cases to be delivered during the year 1912, at the following prices: Quarts bottled in bond, $6.70; pints bottled in bond, $7.20; half pints bottled in bond, $7.70. Should the party of the first part lose by fire the whisky with which this bottling is to be done or the bottling room during the life of this contract, then they are to be held excusable for not filling same. If for any

unforeseen reason the party of the second part find that they cannot use the full amount of the above-named goods, the party of the first part agrees to release them from the contract for the amount desired by party of the second part."

In 1912 the appellant brought this suit against the appellee to recover damages for its failure to furnish 2,596 cases of the 4,000 cases of whisky it was provided in the contract should be furnished in 1911. The petition averred that during the year 1911 the appellant demanded that the appellee furnish to it 4,000 cases of old Walker whisky, but that in violation of its contract the appellee only furnished 1,044 cases, and refused to furnish the remainder, to its damage in the sum of $6,798, which sum it averred was the loss it sustained by the failure of the appellee to furnish the 2,596 cases it failed and refused to furnish.[3]

After a demurrer had been overruled, an answer was filed setting up various defenses, which were controverted by a reply, and the parties went to trial before a jury. After the evidence for the appellant had been concluded, the lower court directed a verdict in favor of the appellee, upon the ground that the contract was lacking in mutuality, and therefore could not be made the subject of an action for its breach by either party. On this appeal the only question we need concern ourselves with is the one upon which the trial judge rested his opinion that the appellant could not recover.

It appears without contradiction that in 1909 the appellant only ordered and received 786 cases of the 2,000 called for by the contract, and that in 1910 it only ordered and received 1,200 cases of the 3,000 cases called for by the contract, and that the appellee did not demand or request that it should take in either of these years the full number of cases specified in the contract or any greater number than it did take. It further appears that in the early part of 1911 whisky advanced in price, and the appellee refused to deliver to the appellant whisky it ordered. After this, however, the appellee, upon request, furnished to the appellant 1,044 cases of the 1911 whisky; but in September, 1911, it peremptorily refused to furnish any more, and thereupon this suit was brought.

* * *

There is a line of cases holding that, where, for example, A. and B. enter into a contract by which A. agrees to furnish to B. all the coal that B. will require in the operation of an established factory, the contract is not lacking in mutuality, as B. may require A. to furnish him all the coal he needs to operate his factory, and A. may insist that B. shall take from him all the coal he needs for this purpose.

An illustration of this class of cases is *Crane v. Crane*, 105 Fed. 869, where the court said:

---

[3]   [Sic. 1,044 + 2,596 ≠ 4,000.—Eds.]

"It is within legal competency for one to bind himself to furnish another with such supplies as may be needed during some certain period for some certain business or manufacture, or with such commodities as the purchaser has already bound himself to furnish another. Reasonable provision in business requires that such contracts, though more or less indefinite, should be upheld. Thus a foundry may purchase all the coal needed for the season, or a furnace company its requirements in the way of iron, or a hotel its necessary supply of ice. * * * So, too, a dealer in coal in any given locality may contract for such coal as he may need to fulfill his existing contracts, regardless of whether delivery by him to his customers is to be immediate or in the future. * * * In all these cases contracts looking towards the future, and embodying subject-matter necessarily indefinite in quantity, have been upheld; but it will be observed that, although the quantity under contract is not measured by any certain standard, it is capable of an approximately accurate forecast. The capacity of the furnace, the needs of the railroad, or the requirements of the hotel are, within certain limits, ascertainable by the vendor."

* * *

The facts of this case, however, do not bring it within the scope of the principle announced in [*Crane*]. * * * If the contract had specified that the Rehm-Zeiher Company was only obliged to take so much of the whisky as it "desired to take," or as it "pleased to take," it would not any more certainly have given the company the right to exercise its pleasure as to how much whisky it would take than do the words "unforeseen reason." The unforeseen reason that would excuse the company from only taking so much of the whisky as it desired to take, if any, left the amount it should take entirely to its discretion. The contract places no limitation whatever upon the meaning of the words "unforeseen reason," so that any reason that the company might assign for not taking the whisky would relieve it of any obligation to do so. It was not necessary that the reason should be a good reason or a reasonable reason.

If the Walker Company had sought by a suit to compel the Rehm-Zeiher Company to take in any of the years the amount of whisky specified in the contract, or any part of it, it is clear that the Rehm-Zeiher Company could have defeated this suit by pleading that some unforeseen reason had arisen that justified them in not taking any of the whisky, and therefore they were not obliged to do so. If, as we think, the contract was nonenforceable by the Walker Company, either in whole or in part, it was certainly lacking in such mutuality of obligation as rendered it nonenforceable by the Rehm-Zeiher Company.

* * *

Some importance seems to be attached to the circumstance that the Walker Company furnished in 1909, 1910, and 1911 a part of the whisky mentioned in the contract, for which the Rehm-Zeiher Company paid the prices agreed upon. We do not think, however, that this circumstance is entitled to any controlling weight in determining the rights of the parties in the present litigation. The Walker Company was not obligated to furnish any whisky in the years named, nor was the Rehm-Zeiher Company obliged to take any, and the mere fact that the Walker Company voluntarily chose to furnish some of the whisky did not deny to it the privilege of refusing at its election to furnish the remainder of the whisky. In other words, its conduct in furnishing part of the whisky did not affect in any manner the rights of the parties to the contract, or amount to an election on the part of the Rehm-Zeiher Company, to accept unconditionally the terms of the contract. In short, the obstacle in the way of the Rehm-Zeiher Company in this case is that they are seeking to enforce a contract that was never at any time binding upon them. Their acceptance of a part of the whisky provided for in the contract in the years 1909 and 1910 did not oblige them to take any of it in the subsequent years.

* * *

Upon the whole case our conclusion is that the judgment of the lower court was correct, and it is affirmed.

NOTES

Frequently, parties do business for an extended period of time under an arrangement where some of the terms are agreed but neither party makes a promise to the other. Here there is no contract until one party offers to sell or to buy and the other accepts that proposal. Under these arrangements, either party can refuse to deal without risk of liability. For such a case, see *Mid-South Packers v. Shoney's, Inc.*, 761 F.2d 1117 (5th Cir. 1985). Is *Rehm-Zeiher* such a case? Suppose the market price of whisky had dropped, and the seller had demanded that the buyer take and pay for the 4,000 cases. Could the buyer defend on the ground that the seller had made no promise—that the seller's unexercised option to declare "unforeseen reasons" made the purported promise illusory? The answer depends upon how the phrase "unforeseen reason" is interpreted by the court. Does the phrase give the seller unfettered discretion (a "free way out"), or is that discretion limited by what is foreseen and what is not? And what is "unforeseen" in this business context? A rise in liquor prices? Hardly. In the words of an unknown economist, "on a clear day you can foresee forever."

W. M. McMichael v. Harley T. Price

Supreme Court of Oklahoma, 1936.
177 Okla. 186.

■ OSBORN, VICE CHIEF JUSTICE. This action was instituted in the district court of Tulsa county by Harley T. Price, doing business as Sooner Sand Company, hereinafter referred to as plaintiff, against W.M. McMichael, hereinafter referred to as defendant, as an action to recover damages for the breach of a contract. The cause was tried to a jury and a verdict returned in favor of plaintiff for $7,512.51. The trial court ordered a remittitur of $2,500, which was duly filed. Thereafter the trial court rendered judgment upon the verdict for $5,012.51, from which judgment defendant has appealed.

The pertinent provisions of the contract, which is the basis of this action, are as follows:

* * *

"In consideration of the mutual promises herein contained, first party agrees to purchase and accept from second party all of the sand of various grades and quality which the said first party can sell, for shipment to various and sundry points outside of the City of Tulsa, Oklahoma, provided that the sand so agreed to be furnished and loaded by the said second party shall at least be equal to in quality and comparable with the sand of various grades sold by other sand companies in the City of Tulsa, Oklahoma, or vicinity. First party agrees to pay and the second party agrees to accept as payment and compensation for said sand so furnished and loaded, a sum per ton which represents sixty percent (60%) of the current market price per ton of concrete sand at the place of destination of said shipment. It is agreed that statements are to be rendered by second party to first party every thirty days; the account is payable monthly by first party with a discount to be allowed by second party of four cents per ton for payment within ten days after shipment of any quantity of sand. * * *

"This contract and agreement shall cover a period of ten years from the date hereof. . . ."

* * *

Defendant contends that the contract between the parties was a mere revocable offer and is not a valid and binding contract of purchase and sale for want of mutuality. The general rule is that in construing a contract where the consideration on the one side is an offer or an agreement to sell, and on the other side an offer or agreement to buy, the obligation of the parties to sell and buy must be mutual, to render the contract binding on either party, or, as it is sometimes stated, if one of the parties, not having suffered any previous detriment, can escape future liability under the contract, that party may be said to have a "free way out" and the contract lacks mutuality. Consolidated Pipe Line Co. v. British American Oil Co., 163 Okl. 171. Attention is directed to the specific language used in the contract binding the defendant to "furnish all of the sand of various grades and qualities which the first party can sell" and whereby plaintiff is bound "to purchase and accept from second party all of the sand of various grades and qualities which the said first party [plaintiff] can sell." It is urged that plaintiff had no established business and was not bound to sell any sand whatever and might escape all liability under the terms of the contract by a mere failure or refusal to sell sand. In this connection it is to be noted that the contract recites that plaintiff is "engaged in the business of selling and shipping sand from Tulsa, Oklahoma, to various points." The parties based their contract on this agreed predicate.

* * *

At the time the contract involved herein was executed, plaintiff was not the owner of an established sand business. The evidence shows, however, that he was an experienced salesman of sand, which fact was well known to defendant, and that it was anticipated by both parties that on account of the experience, acquaintances, and connections of plaintiff, he would be able to sell a substantial amount of sand to the mutual profit of the contracting parties. The record discloses that for the nine months immediately following the execution of the contract plaintiff's average net profit per month was $516.88.

By the terms of the contract the price to be paid for sand was definitely fixed. Plaintiff was bound by a solemn covenant of the contract to purchase all the sand he was able to sell from defendant and for a breach of such covenant could have been made to respond in damages. The argument of defendant that the plaintiff could escape liability under the contract by going out of the sand business is without force in view of our determination, in line with the authorities hereinabove cited, that it was the intent of the parties to enter into a contract which would be mutually binding.

* * *

The judgment is affirmed.

NOTES

(1)   Should any degree of limitation upon freedom of action be sufficient to insulate an agreement against a defense based on lack of mutuality? For instance, what if Price had not been an experienced sand dealer, but was merely contemplating entering the business?

(2)   Seller makes an agreement with Buyer for the sale of a certain boat then owned by a third party. It was stipulated in the written contract of purchase that Seller's obligation was contingent upon his acquiring the boat from said third party. Thereafter, Seller did purchase the boat, but refuses to abide by his commitment to Buyer. He insists that the contract lacks mutuality of obligation, as he might have chosen not to satisfy the condition of his supposed obligation to sell by refusing to purchase the boat from the third party; therefore, neither party is bound. Do you agree? Cf. Scott v. Moragues Lumber Co., 202 Ala. 312 (1918).

(3)   *Requirements and Output Contracts.* As will be discussed in Chapter Three, the Uniform Commercial Code is quite sympathetic to the use of "open price" terms. Section 2–305. Similarly, the code promotes an

additional measure of "certainty with flexibility" regarding quantity terms in its treatment of requirements and output contracts. UCC § 2–306(1) provides: "A term which measures the quantity by the output of the seller or the requirements of the buyer means such actual output or requirements as may occur in good faith, except that no quantity unreasonably disproportionate to any stated estimate or in the absence of a stated estimate to any normal or otherwise comparable prior output or requirements may be tendered or demanded." Is the agreement in *McMichael v. Price* an output contract or a requirements contract? How does the rule in section 2–306(1) address earlier concerns about whether such contracts are supported by consideration?

Benjamin Nathan Cardozo: Born in 1870, Benjamin Cardozo earned both a bachelor's and a law degree from Columbia University. Cardozo practiced law for 23 years before being elected to the New York Supreme Court in 1913. After serving just a month on the bench, Judge Cardozo was appointed to the state's highest court, the Court of Appeals. He held that seat until 1927, when he was elected Chief Judge. During his tenure, his prolific writings (including several influential books) and quotable opinions made him perhaps the most famous state judge in the nation. President Hoover appointed Cardozo to the Supreme Court in 1932, where he served until his death in 1938. Among Cardozo's famous opinions are *Meinhard v. Salmon* (partners owe each other "not honesty alone, but the punctilio of an honor the most sensitive") and *Palsgraf v. Long Island Rail Road* (developing the tort concept of proximate cause). See Richard A. Posner, Cardozo: A Study in Reputation (1990); Andrew L. Kaufman, Cardozo (1998).

Otis F. Wood v. Lucy, Lady Duff-Gordon

Court of Appeals of New York, 1917.
222 N.Y. 88.

■ CARDOZO, J. The defendant styles herself "a creator of fashions." Her favor helps a sale. Manufacturers of dresses, millinery and like articles are glad to pay for a certificate of her approval. The things which she designs, fabrics, parasols, and what not, have a new value in the public mind when issued in her name. She employed the plaintiff to help her to turn this vogue into money. He was to have the exclusive right, subject always to her approval, to place her indorsements on the designs of others. He was also to have the exclusive right to place her own designs on sale, or to license others to market them. In return, she was to have one-half of "all profits and revenues" derived from any contracts he might make. The exclusive right was to last at least one year from April 1, 1915, and thereafter from year to year unless terminated by notice of ninety days. The plaintiff says that he kept the contract on his part, and that the defendant broke it. She placed her indorsement on fabrics, dresses and millinery without his knowledge, and withheld the profits. He sues her for the damages, and the case comes here on demurrer.

The agreement of employment is signed by both parties. It has a wealth of recitals. The defendant insists, however, that it lacks the elements of a contract. She says that the plaintiff does not bind himself to anything. It is true that he does not promise in so many words that he will use reasonable efforts to place the defendant's indorsements and market her designs. We think, however, that such a promise is fairly to be implied. The law has outgrown its primitive stage of formalism when the precise word was the sovereign talisman, and every slip was fatal. It takes a broader view today. A promise may be lacking, and yet the whole writing may be "instinct with an obligation," imperfectly expressed (SCOTT, J., in McCall Co. v. Wright, 133 App.Div. 62; . . .). If that is so, there is a contract.

The implication of a promise here finds support in many circumstances. The defendant gave an *exclusive* privilege. She was to have no right for at least a year to place her own indorsements or market her own designs except through the agency of the plaintiff. The acceptance of the exclusive agency was an assumption of its duties. . . . We are not to suppose that one party was to be placed at the mercy of the other. . . . Many other terms of the agreement point the same way. We are told at the outset by way of recital that "the said Otis F. Wood possesses a business organization adapted to the placing of such indorsements as the said Lucy, Lady Duff-Gordon has approved." The implication is that the plaintiff's business organization will be used for the purpose for which it is adapted. But the terms of the defendant's compensation are even more significant. Her sole compensation for the grant of an exclusive agency is to be one-half of all the profits resulting from the plaintiff's efforts. Unless he gave his efforts, she could never get anything. Without an implied promise, the transaction cannot have such business "efficacy as both parties must have intended that at all events it should have" (BOWEN, L.J., in The Moorcock, 14 P.D. 64, 68). But the contract does not stop there. The plaintiff goes on to promise that he will account monthly for all moneys received by him, and that he will take out all such patents and copyrights and trademarks as may in his judgment be necessary to protect the rights and articles affected by the agreement. It is true, of course, as the Appellate Division has said, that if he was under no duty to try to market designs or to place certificates of indorsement, his promise to account for profits or take out copyrights would be valueless. But in determining the intention of the parties, the promise *has* a value. It helps to enforce the conclusion that the plaintiff *had* some duties. His promise to pay the defendant one-half of the profits and revenues resulting from the exclusive agency and to render accounts monthly, was a promise to use reasonable efforts to bring profits and revenues into existence. For this conclusion, the authorities are ample. . . .

The judgment of the Appellate Division should be reversed, and the order of the Special Term affirmed, with costs in the Appellate Division and in this court.

NOTES

(1) *You Picked a Fine Time to Leave Me, Lucille.* In *Lucy,* what did each party expressly promise? Why were these express commitments insufficient, of themselves, to satisfy the demand that each be under some type of obligation? Does the finding of implied promise do violence to the expressed understanding of the parties?

Compare UCC § 2–306(2): "A lawful agreement by either the seller or the buyer for exclusive dealing in the kind of goods concerned imposes unless otherwise agreed an obligation by the seller to use best efforts to supply the goods and by the buyer to use best efforts to promote their sale." Would the "best efforts" rule change the outcome in *Rehm-Zeiher*? If not, why not?

(2) Lawrence A. Cunningham argues that the *Lucy* opinion exhibits Cardozo's concerns about the "risks of interparty exploitation and the judicial need to balance freedom of contract with other social values." Cunningham suggests that the implication of a promise to use best efforts "now seems so intuitive as to be commonplace, yet at the time, the opinion amounted to an extraordinary innovation." In short, Judge Cardozo's approach was an "attempt to keep law congruent with commercial reality" and the "finding of consideration" was just a "kernel of the opinion and just one illustration of [his] wider ability to work within the received doctrine and to achieve a richer balance of both fairness and the efficiency of consensual exchange." Lawrence A. Cunningham, *Cardozo and Posner: A Study in Contracts*, 36 Wm. & Mary L. Rev. 1379, 1395–98 (1995).

Lady Duff-Gordon

(3) *Lucy, Lady Duff-Gordon: Creator of Fashions.* Lucy, Lady Duff-Gordon led a charmed life. She and her husband, Sir Cosmo Duff-Gordon, booked separate first class cabins on the maiden voyage of Titanic. After Titanic hit the iceberg, she and her husband managed to board a lifeboat and survive. Although Sir Cosmo never quite overcame the stigma of being a male survivor in a half-full lifeboat, Lucy (as the following description by Walter Pratt reveals) remained an important innovator:

As she did with the general development of the period, Lucy personified the particular changes in the economy and in contract practice. Very much independent, Lucy renounced the traditions of her generation when she began her own business, designing women's clothing. Like many of the entrepreneurs of the period, Lucy started with little capital. Nevertheless, after overcoming early difficulties, she established herself by 1900 as one of the pre-eminent designers of fashion for women. In a manner typical of the personal style of the American economy during the Reconstruction era, Lucy at first designed only for individual women for specific grand occasions such as coronations and state funerals. Because her designs were created for one woman to wear on a particular occasion, they became known as "personality" dresses.

As the times changed, so did Lucy. First, she became a company, with the name "Lucille." Later, in 1910, she opened a branch office in New York City where she continued to embody the economic changes by depersonalizing her services. In common with much of the production in the United States, Lucy no longer personally designed each dress for each customer. Instead, she hired others to design and sew; she even began to produce more than one dress of each design. With the change in style and the concentration of population in urban areas, Lucy could now profit from marketing multiple copies of the same design. In addition, Lucy hired a manager for her branch office, further increasing the distance between herself and her customers; she would no longer be able to devote personal attention to each client for each occasion.

Lucy also came to appreciate that something as ephemeral as her name could be of value in the emerging consumer society of the United States. As seller after seller saw production overtake demand in the last years of the nineteenth century, advertising became increasingly important both to inform buyers of products and to persuade customers to buy. To take advantage of that new demand, Lucy turned to an advertising agent, yet another intermediary between herself and her clients.

* * *

[Lucy] brought Wood's lawsuit upon herself when, in one of the more innovative decisions of her career, she arranged with Sears, Roebuck and Company to sell her dresses through its catalogues. Sears published the first catalogue (which it called a "portfolio") of Lucy's designs for the fall and winter of 1916–1917. That Lucy was once again at the forefront of commercial practice was evident from a comment in the trade journal *Printer's Ink*, which reported that the announcement of the agreement threw "a bomb into the camp of rival mail-order houses." The announcement, the journal further explained, was "by far the most spectacular bid for prestige which this daring advertiser [Sears] has made since it first announced the new handy edition of the Encyclopedia Britannica."

Walter Pratt, *American Contract Law at the Turn of the Century*, 39 S.C. L. Rev. 415, 429–432, 439 (1988).

Omni Group, Inc. v. Seattle-First National Bank

Court of Appeals of Washington, 1982.
32 Wash.App. 22.

■ JAMES, JUDGE. Plaintiff Omni Group, Inc. (Omni), a real estate development corporation, appeals entry of a judgment in favor of John B. Clark, individually, and as executor of the estate of his late wife, in Omni's action to enforce an earnest money agreement for the purchase of realty owned by the Clarks. We reverse.

In December 1977, Mr. and Mrs. Clark executed an exclusive agency listing agreement with the Royal Realty Company of Bellevue (Royal) for the sale of approximately 59 acres of property. The list price was $3,000 per acre.

In early May, Royal offered the Clark property to Omni. On May 17, following conversations with a Royal broker, Omni signed an earnest money agreement offering $2,000 per acre. Two Royal brokers delivered the earnest money agreement to the Clarks. The Clarks signed the agreement dated May 19, but directed the brokers to obtain further consideration in the nature of Omni's agreement to make certain improvements on adjacent land not being offered for sale. Neither broker communicated these additional terms to Omni.

In pertinent part, the earnest money agreement provides:

> This transaction is subject to purchaser receiving an engineer's and architect's feasibility report prepared by an engineer and architect of the purchaser's choice. Purchaser agrees to pay all costs of said report. If said report is satisfactory to purchaser, purchaser shall so notify seller in writing within fifteen (15) days of seller's acceptance of this offer. If no such notice is sent to seller, this transaction shall be considered null and void.

Exhibit A, ¶ 6. Omni's purpose was to determine, prior to actual purchase, if the property was suitable for development.

On June 2, an Omni employee personally delivered to the Clarks a letter advising that Omni had decided to forgo a feasibility study. They were further advised that a survey had revealed that the property consisted of only 50.3 acres. The Clarks agreed that if such were the case, they would accept Omni's offer of $2,000 per acre but with a minimum of 52 acres ($104,000). At this meeting, the Clarks' other terms (which had not been disclosed by Royal nor included in the earnest money agreement signed by the Clarks) were discussed. By a letter of June 8, Omni agreed to accept each of the Clarks' additional terms. The Clarks, however, refused to proceed with the sale after consulting an attorney.

The Clarks argued and the trial judge agreed, that by making its obligations subject to a satisfactory "engineer's and architect's feasibility report" in paragraph 6, Omni rendered its promise to buy the property illusory. Omni responds that paragraph 6 created only a condition precedent to Omni's duty to buy, and because the condition was for its benefit, Omni could waive the condition and enforce the agreement as written. We conclude Omni's promise was not illusory.

A promise for a promise is sufficient consideration to support a contract. E.g., Cook v. Johnson, 37 Wash.2d 19 (1950). If, however, a promise is illusory, there is no consideration and therefore no enforceable contract between the parties. Interchange Associates v. Interchange, Inc., 16 Wash.App. 359 (1976). Consequently, a party cannot create an enforceable contract by waiving the condition which renders his promise illusory. But that a promise given for a promise is dependent upon a condition does not necessarily render it illusory or affect its validity as consideration. . . . Furthermore,

> a contractor can, by the use of clear and appropriate words, make his own duty expressly conditional upon his own personal satisfaction with the quality of the performance for which he has

bargained and in return for which his promise is given. Such a limitation on his own duty does not invalidate the contract as long as the limitation is not so great as to make his own promise illusory.

3A A. Corbin, Contracts § 644 at 78–79 (1960).

Paragraph 6 may be analyzed as creating two conditions precedent to Omni's duty to buy the Clarks' property. First, Omni must receive an "engineer's and architect's feasibility report." Undisputed evidence was presented to show that such "feasibility reports" are common in the real estate development field and pertain to the physical suitability of the property for development purposes. Such a condition is analogous to a requirement that a purchaser of real property obtain financing, which imposes upon the purchaser a duty to make a good faith effort to secure financing. . . . In essence, this initial language requires Omni to attempt, in good faith, to obtain an "engineer's and architect's feasibility report" of a type recognized in the real estate trade.

The second condition precedent to Omni's duty to buy the Clarks' property is that the feasibility report must be "satisfactory" to Omni. A condition precedent to the promisor's duty that the promisor be "satisfied" may require performance personally satisfactory to the promisor or it may require performance acceptable to a reasonable person. Whether the promisor was actually satisfied or should reasonably have been satisfied is a question of fact. In neither case is the promisor's promise rendered illusory. 3A A. Corbin, Contracts § 644 (1960).

In *Mattei v. Hopper*, 51 Cal.2d 119 (1958), plaintiff real estate developer contracted to buy property for a shopping center "[s]ubject to Coldwell Banker & Company obtaining leases satisfactory to the purchaser." Plaintiff had 120 days to consummate the purchase, including arrangement of satisfactory leases for shopping center buildings, before he was committed to purchase the property. The trial judge found the agreement "illusory." The California Supreme Court reversed. The court's language is apposite:

> [I]t would seem that the factors involved in determining whether a lease is satisfactory to the lessor are too numerous and varied to permit the application of a reasonable man standard as envisioned by this line of cases. Illustrative of some of the factors which would have to be considered in this case are the duration of the leases, their provisions for renewal options, if any, their covenants and restrictions, the amounts of the rentals, the financial responsibility of the lessees, and the character of the lessees' businesses.

Comparable factors doubtless determine whether an "engineer's and architect's feasibility report" is satisfactory. But

> [t]his *multiplicity* of factors which must be considered in evaluating a lease shows that this case more appropriately falls

within the second line of authorities dealing with "satisfaction" clauses, being those involving fancy, taste, or judgment. Where the question is one of judgment, the promisor's determination that he is not satisfied, when made in good faith, has been held to be a defense to an action on the contract. . . . Although these decisions do not expressly discuss the issues of mutuality of obligation or illusory promises, they necessarily imply that the promisor's duty to exercise his judgment in good faith is an adequate consideration to support the contract. None of these cases voided the contracts on the ground that they were illusory or lacking in mutuality of obligation. Defendant's attempts to distinguish these cases are unavailing, since they are predicated upon the assumption that the deposit receipt was not a contract making plaintiff's performance conditional on his satisfaction. As seen above, this was the precise nature of the agreement.

Further,

[e]ven though the "satisfaction" clauses discussed in the above-cited cases dealt with performances to be received as parts of the agreed exchanges, the fact that the leases here which determined plaintiff's satisfaction were not part of the performance to be rendered is not material. The standard of evaluating plaintiff's satisfaction—good faith—applies with equal vigor to this type of condition and prevents it from nullifying the consideration otherwise present in the promises exchanged.

Mattei v. Hopper, supra at 123–24. Thus, even the fact that "[i]t was satisfaction with the leases that [the purchaser] was himself to obtain" was immaterial. 3A A. Corbin, Contracts § 644 at 84. . . . We conclude that the condition precedent to Omni's duty to buy requiring receipt of a "satisfactory" feasibility report does not render Omni's promise to buy the property illusory.

Paragraph 6 further provides, "If said report is satisfactory to purchaser, purchaser shall so notify seller in writing within fifteen (15) days of seller's acceptance of this offer"; otherwise, the transaction "shall be considered null and void." We read this language to mean that Omni is required ("shall") to notify the Clarks of its acceptance if the feasibility report was "satisfactory." As we have stated, this determination is not a matter within Omni's unfettered discretion.

Omni has, by the quoted language, reserved to itself a power to cancel or terminate the contract. . . . Such provisions are valid and do not render the promisor's promise illusory, where the option can be exercised upon the occurrence of specified conditions. . . . Here, Omni can cancel by failing to give notice only if the feasibility report is not "satisfactory." Otherwise, Omni is bound to give notice and purchase the property. Accordingly, we conclude paragraph 6 does not render Omni's promise illusory. The May 18 earnest money agreement was supported by consideration.

* * *

The judgment is reversed and remanded with instructions to enter a decree ordering specific performance of the earnest money agreement.

NOTES

(1) *The "Mutuality" Requirement.* It is commonplace for agreements to provide a "way out" for one or both of the parties. It may be provided that performance is conditional upon the purchaser obtaining satisfactory leases, securing suitable financing, etc. Or, there may be a reserved power of termination, exercisable by one or both of the parties. Cases of this type have traditionally been addressed in terms of "mutuality of obligation," though it is perhaps clearer to simply say that the problem is one of an illusory promise. See Restatement (Second) § 79(c) and cmt. f. If, in the words of the California Supreme Court, cited above, a party is "free to perform or to withdraw from the agreement at his own unrestricted pleasure, the promise is deemed illusory and it provides no consideration." Mattei v. Hopper, 51 Cal.2d 119, 122 (1958).

The parties do not have a "free way out" if there is some check on their discretion, such as the duty of good faith, a requirement that the party's dissatisfaction be reasonable or in good faith or, in the case of a termination right, announced with advance notice.

(2) *Subjective vs. Objective Satisfaction Tests.* "When it is a condition of an obligor's duty that he be satisfied with respect to the obligee's performance or with respect to something else, and it is practicable to determine whether a reasonable person in the position of the obligor would be satisfied, an interpretation is preferred under which the condition occurs if such a reasonable person in the position of the obligor would be satisfied." Restatement (Second) § 228. What is the test for when it is not practicable to determine when a reasonable person would be satisfied? See § 228 cmt. b.

In order to decide the case, the *Omni* court did not have to determine whether paragraph 6 required "performance personally satisfactory to" Omni or "performance acceptable to a reasonable person," for it held that in neither case was the promise illusory. Given the facts of the transaction and the language of paragraph 6, do you think the clause should be read as requiring that the reports be objectively satisfactory, or subjectively satisfactory to Omni?

Suppose you are negotiating a contract on behalf of a seller, and the buyer wants a satisfaction clause. How would you rank the following five possible phrasings with respect to your client's interests?

(a) "If purchaser is satisfied with report, purchaser shall. . ."

(b) "If the report is satisfactory, purchaser shall. . ."

(c) "If the report is satisfactory to purchaser, purchaser shall. . ."

(d)   "If the report is reasonably satisfactory, purchaser shall. . ."

(e)   "If the report is personally satisfactory, purchaser shall. . ."

(3)   *Obligation and UCC § 2–204.* In seeking to salvage an obligation, counsel must frequently press beyond the words of the written agreement. For example, in *Warrick Beverage Corp. v. Miller Brewing Co.*, 170 Ind.App. 114 (1976), the court considered an "arrangement" between a brewery and a beer distributor. A letter from the brewery to the distributor provided, in part, the following: "Our relationship is that of seller and buyer and in no other respect is any relationship established between us. You are not required to place orders, nor are we required to accept orders for beer. As is the custom in our industry, these sales are made on a shipment-to-shipment basis only, and either of us can terminate this relationship at any time without incurring liability to the other." Upon being "terminated" by the brewer, the distributor sought the advantage of an Indiana statute which made it unlawful to "cancel or terminate an agreement or contract between a beer wholesaler and a brewer for the sale of beer, unfairly and without due regard for the equities of the other party." In rejecting the brewer's mutuality of obligation argument, the court referred to conduct after the execution of the writing which, in effect, recognized the existence of some type of contractual obligation. Principal reliance was upon UCC § 2–204(1): "A contract for sale of goods may be made in any manner sufficient to show agreement, including conduct by both parties which recognizes the existence of such a contract."

(4)   Why do you think that Omni might have chosen to forgo the feasibility study? Is the reason perhaps related to the explanation why the Clarks wanted to back out of the transaction?

PROBLEM: THE CASE OF THE ILLUSORY BONUS

John was an agent for Super Life, an insurance company, and was paid a salary and commissions for writing life insurance policies. In early February 1997, Super Life issued a bulletin addressed to all agents. The bulletin was titled "Extra Earnings Agreement" and stated that "you will receive at the end of each 12 month period a bonus" in accordance with a formula based upon the percentage of policies that you are able to renew after lapse. The lower the lapse ratio, the higher the bonus. Thus, if an agent's lapse ratio were between 0 and 10%, the bonus would be 150% of the average monthly premiums in force, but if the lapse ratio were, say, between 40 and 50%, the bonus would be only 60% of the premiums. If the lapse ratio were over 70%, there would be no bonus. In paragraph 7 (there were 12 paragraphs in all), the following term appeared in the same type size as the rest of the bulletin:

> This renewal bonus is a *voluntary* contribution on the part of Super Life. It is agreed by you and by us that it may be withheld, increased, decreased or discontinued, individually or collectively, with or without actual notice. Further, this Renewal Bonus is contingent upon you actually writing policies for this Company as a licensed agent at the time such Bonus is to be paid.

The agents were exhorted to give their "best efforts" and requested to sign and return the "enclosed copy of this agreement." John complied.

In February 1998, John reported that his lapse ratio over the last twelve months was between 20 and 30% and that, under the schedule, he was entitled to a bonus of 100% of the average monthly premiums in force, some $10,000. Without giving any notice or reasons, however, Super Life discontinued the bonus plan on February 15, 1998 without paying any bonuses.

John and other agents sued for the bonuses. Super Life filed a motion to dismiss and argued: (1) No promise was made, since the "voluntary" contribution clause reserved complete and unfettered discretion to the company; (2) The plain and ordinary language of the clause, which the agents as "White Collar" workers should reasonably understand, should be implemented; and (3) Even if a promise was made, there was no consideration since the Agents were already obligated to sell and renew life insurance policies.

In opposing the motion to dismiss, John's attorney made the following argument. "Your honor, we think that a literal interpretation of the bonus plan language should be avoided, especially where extra efforts were expended by the agents. Super Life is subject to a duty of good faith in the performance of the contract, and that duty should be imposed upon the exercise of the reserved discretion to terminate the plan, unless both parties intended Super Life to have unfettered discretion. The question is whether this interpretation was within the fair contemplation of the parties, and the answer is not found in the 'four corners' of the writing or the 'plain meaning' of the language. If no such intention is found, the next question is whether Super Life acted in bad faith and this, at a minimum, requires an examination of Super Life's reasons for withdrawing the plan. Thus, factual questions about intention and bad faith are presented, and the motion to dismiss should be dismissed." John's brief cited *Nolan v. Control Data Corp.*, 243 N.J.Super. 420 (App.Div. 1990) to support this argument.

How would you rule?

2. PROMISSORY ESTOPPEL: PROMISE PLUS UNBARGAINED FOR RELIANCE

Our inquiry concerning legally enforceable agreements has so far focused on the doctrine of consideration, which forms the center of the traditional Anglo-American theory of contract. To be sure, for centuries a promise under seal was enforceable (and still is in a few jurisdictions), and Pennsylvania has its Written Obligations Act. But in the main, the common law courts traditionally enforced bargains and only bargains. Something, whether of benefit to the promisor or detrimental to the promisee, must be bargained for and given in exchange for the promise.

There have always been discernible traces of uneasiness respecting a strong consideration requirement. Much of the dissatisfaction relates to transactions where there is substantial *unbargained-for* reliance. If the outcome in *Kirksey v. Kirksey* was unsatisfactory, it was because the plaintiff, in reliance on her brother-in-law's promise to provide her with a place to live, gave up her own property and moved her family. In the early twentieth century, the problem of unbargained-for reliance was addressed by the new doctrine of promissory estoppel.

Andrew D. Ricketts v. Katie Scothorn

Supreme Court of Nebraska, 1898.
57 Neb. 51.

■ SULLIVAN, J. In the district court of Lancaster county the plaintiff, Katie Scothorn, recovered judgment against the defendant, Andrew D. Ricketts, as executor of the last will and testament of John C. Ricketts, deceased. The action was based upon a promissory note, of which the following is a copy:

"May the first, 1891. I promise to pay to Katie Scothorn on demand, $2,000, to be at 6 per cent per annum. J.C. Ricketts."

In the petition the plaintiff alleges that the consideration for the execution of the note was that she should surrender her employment as bookkeeper for Mayor Bros., and cease to work for a living. She also alleges that the note was given to induce her to abandon her occupation, and that, relying on it, and on the annual interest, as a means of support, she gave up the employment in which she was then engaged. These allegations of the petition are denied by the executor. The material facts are undisputed. They are as follows: John C. Ricketts, the maker of the note, was the grandfather of the plaintiff. Early in May—presumably on the day the note bears date—he called on her at the store where she was working. What transpired between them is thus described by Mr. Flodene, one of the plaintiff's witnesses:

"A. Well the old gentleman came in there one morning about 9 o'clock—probably a little before or a little after, but early in the morning—and he unbuttoned his vest and took out a piece of paper in the shape of a note; that is the way it looked to me; and he says to Miss Scothorn, 'I have fixed out something that you have not got to work any more.' He says, 'None of my grandchildren work and you don't have to.'

"Q. Where was she?

"A. She took the piece of paper and kissed him; and kissed the old gentleman and commenced to cry."

It seems Miss Scothorn immediately notified her employer of her intention to quit work, and that she did soon after abandon her occupation. The mother of the plaintiff was a witness and testified that she had a conversation with her father, Mr. Ricketts, shortly after the note was executed, in which he informed her that he had given the note to the plaintiff to enable her to quit work; that none of his grandchildren worked, and he did not think she ought to. For something more than a year the plaintiff was without an occupation; but in September, 1892, with the consent of her grandfather, and by his assistance, she secured a position as bookkeeper with Messrs. Funke & Ogden. On June 8, 1894, Mr. Ricketts died. He had paid one year's interest on the note, and a short time before his death expressed regret that he had not been able to pay the balance. In the summer or fall of 1892 he stated to his daughter, Mrs. Scothorn, that if he could sell his farm in Ohio he would pay the note out of the proceeds. He at no time repudiated the obligation.

We quite agree with counsel for the defendant that upon this evidence there was nothing to submit to the jury, and that a verdict should have been directed peremptorily for one of the parties. The testimony of Flodene and Mrs. Scothorn, taken together, conclusively establishes the fact that the note was not given in consideration of the plaintiff pursuing, or agreeing to pursue, any particular line of conduct. There was no promise on the part of the plaintiff to do, or refrain from doing, anything. Her right to the money promised in the note was not made to depend upon an abandonment of her employment with Mayer Bros. and future abstention from like service. Mr. Ricketts made no condition, requirement, or request. He exacted no *quid pro quo*. He gave the note as a gratuity and looked for nothing in return. So far as the evidence discloses, it was his purpose to place the plaintiff in a position of independence where she could work or remain idle as she might choose. The abandonment by Miss Scothorn of her position as bookkeeper was altogether voluntary. It was not an act done in fulfillment of any contract obligation assumed when she accepted the note. The instrument in suit, being given without any valuable consideration, was nothing more than a promise to make a gift in the future of the sum of money therein named. Ordinarily, such promises are not enforceable even when put in the form of a promissory note. . . . But it has often been held that an action on a note given to a church, college, or other like institution, upon the faith of which money has been expended or obligations incurred, could not be successfully defended on the ground of a want of consideration. . . . In this class of cases the note in suit is nearly always spoken of as a gift or donation, but the decision is generally put on the ground that the expenditure of money or assumption of liability by the donee, on the faith of the promise, constitutes a valuable and sufficient consideration. It seems to us that the true reason is the preclusion of the defendant, under the doctrine of estoppel, to deny the consideration. Such seems to be the view of the matter taken by the supreme court of Iowa in the case of *Simpson Centenary College v. Tuttle*, 71 Ia. 596, where Rothrock, J., speaking for the court, said: "Where a note, however, is based on a promise to give for the support of the objects referred to, it may still be open to this defense [want of consideration], unless it shall appear that the donee has, prior to any revocation, entered into engagements or made expenditures based on such promise, so that he must suffer loss or injury if the note is not paid. This is based on the equitable principle that, after allowing the donee to incur obligations on the faith that the note would be paid, the donor would be estopped from pleading want of consideration." And in the case of *Reimensnyder v. Gans*, 110 Pa.St. 17, which was an action on a note given as a donation to a charitable object, the court said: "The fact is that, as we may see from the case of *Ryerss v. Trustees*, 33 Pa.St. 114, a contract of the kind here involved is enforceable rather by way of estoppel than on the ground of consideration in the original undertaking." It has been held that a note given in expectation of the payee performing certain services, but without any contract binding him to serve, will not support an action. . . . But when the payee changes his position to his disadvantage, in reliance on the promise, a right of action does arise. . . .

Under the circumstances of this case, is there an equitable estoppel which ought to preclude the defendant from alleging that the note in controversy is lacking in one of the essential elements of a valid contract? We think there is. An estoppel *in pais* is defined to be "a right arising from acts, admissions, or conduct which have induced a change of position in accordance with the real or apparent intention of the party against whom they are alleged." Mr. Pomeroy has formulated the following definition: "Equitable estoppel is the effect of the voluntary conduct of a party whereby he is absolutely precluded, both at law and in equity, from asserting rights which might perhaps have otherwise existed, either of property, or contract, or of remedy, as against another person who in good faith relied upon such conduct, and has been led thereby to change his position for the worse, and who on his part acquires some corresponding right either of property, of contract, or of remedy." (2 Pomeroy, Equity Jurisprudence 804.) According to the undisputed proof, as shown by the record before us, the plaintiff was a working girl, holding a position in which she earned a salary of $10 per week. Her grandfather, desiring to put her in a position of independence, gave her the note, accompanying it with the remark that his other grandchildren did not work, and that she would not be obliged to work any longer. In effect, he suggested that she might abandon her employment and rely in the future upon the bounty which he promised. He, doubtless, desired that she should give up her occupation, but whether he did or not, it is entirely certain that he contemplated such action on her part as a reasonable and probable consequence of his gift. Having intentionally influenced the plaintiff to alter her position for the worse on the faith of the note being paid when due, it would be grossly inequitable to permit the maker, or his executor, to resist payment on the ground that the promise was given without consideration. The petition charges the elements of an equitable estoppel, and the evidence conclusively establishes them. If errors intervened at the trial, they could not have been prejudicial. A verdict for the defendant would be unwarranted. The judgment is right and is

Affirmed.

Comment: The Evolution of Promissory Estoppel

It has long been recognized that a defendant's conduct may estop (from the Old French *stopper*, to stop or bar) or preclude one from raising an otherwise available defense or contesting the accuracy of a representation of fact. As the California Supreme Court has explained:

> The doctrine of equitable estoppel is founded on concepts of equity and fair dealing. It provides that a person may not deny the existence of a state of facts if he intentionally led another to believe a particular circumstance to be true and to rely upon such belief to his detriment. The elements of the doctrine are that (1) the party to be estopped must be apprised of the facts; (2) he must intend that his conduct shall be acted upon, or must so act that the party asserting the estoppel has a right to believe it was so intended; (3) the other party must be ignorant of the true state of facts; and (4) he must rely upon the conduct to his injury.

Strong v. County of Santa Cruz, 15 Cal.3d 720, 725 (1975). In *Lambertini v. Lambertini*, 655 So.2d 142 (Fla. Dist. Ct. App. 1995), for example, the court held that the plaintiff was equitably estopped from claiming that a Mexican marriage was invalid after holding himself and defendant out as being married for thirty years.

The use of estoppel in *Ricketts* was unusual for two reasons. First, courts have traditionally been reluctant to extend equitable estoppel to statements concerning future facts, predictions or promises, as distinguished from existing facts. Second, the doctrine of equitable estoppel is commonly understood to provide a shield, not a sword. Estoppel is a defense that prevents another from raising certain facts. In *Ricketts*, the doctrine is applied to support a cause of action that would otherwise not exist.

Was the *Ricketts* court simply confused about the meaning of "equitable estoppel"? One might instead read the opinion as a good example of judicial craft under the common law. The court observed a form of injustice that the law might remedy. Finding no clear legal grounds at hand, and facing the bar of the doctrine of consideration, it took a neighboring legal category—estoppel—and stretched it a bit to do new work.

The modern term "promissory estoppel" dates from Samuel Williston's 1920 treatise on contract law. Williston was one of the champions of the bargain theory of consideration. But his careful study of the case law also convinced him that the consideration doctrine could not explain all of the case outcomes. Williston collected in the treatise a number of cases, including *Ricketts*, in which reliance seemed to be doing the job of consideration. Recognizing the differences between the well-established doctrine of equitable estoppel and the doctrine invoked by this collection of cases, Williston suggested a new name for the latter:

"promissory estoppel." Williston was later chosen to serve as the Reporter on the First Restatement of Contracts, which included the famous section 90:

> A promise which the promisor should reasonably expect to induce action or forbearance of a definite and substantial character on the part of the promisee and which does induce such action or forbearance is binding if injustice can be avoided only by enforcement of the promise.

The section's number remained the same in the Second Restatement, though there were some changes to the rule:

> A promise which the promisor should reasonably expect to induce action or forbearance on the part of the promisee or a third person and which does induce such action or forbearance is binding if injustice can be avoided only by enforcement of the promise. The remedy granted for breach may be limited as justice requires.

What are the differences between the First and Second Restatement formulations?

In his 1974 book, *The Death of Contract*, Grant Gilmore characterized promissory estoppel as the "unwanted stepchild of" the First Restatement which, by the time of the Second Restatement, had "swallowed up the bargain principle of § 75." Over thirty-five years later, Gilmore's claims appear a bit overblown. Liability based on the classical bargain theory of consideration remains alive and well, and continues to provide the core model for enforcing promises. The most important difference between an action in contract and an action based on promissory estoppel is the remedy available in each. As Restatement (Second) § 90 indicates, damages in a promissory estoppel case can be significantly less than damages for an analogous breach of contract. Perhaps because recovery is based on the plaintiff's reliance, courts in promissory estoppel cases sometimes (though not always!) limit recovery to reliance damages rather than awarding the expectation measure.

That said, promissory estoppel has grown into a significant alternative form of liability, one that, as we will see in later chapters, can apply not only when there is a failure of consideration, but also when there is a failure of agreement or a lack of a required writing.

William F. Langer v. Superior Steel Corp.

Superior Court of Pennsylvania, 1932.
Supra at 77.

NOTES

(1) *Reliance.* "It would seem * * * that the framers of section 90 recognized the fact that there is a class of cases where gratuitous promises should be enforced for compelling reasons of justice, where the promisee

incurs a substantial detriment on the faith of such promises, and this, whether the promisor intended the detriment or not. The test seems to be whether the promisor could reasonably have expected the detriment to be incurred on the strength of the promise. If the detriment is incurred, and there is no other way of avoiding injustice, the promise is enforceable. Of course, as pointed out by Judge Baldrige, in *Langer v. Superior Steel Corp*. . . . and also by Professor Williston in his work on 'Contracts' not every gratuitous promise and reliance thereon is enforceable. The doctrine must be limited in its application to that group of cases where the reliance on the promise brought about such a substantial, changed condition on the part of the promisee that enforcement of the promise is the only way to avoid injustice. What constitutes injustice has not been defined; that, it would seem, must be determined from all the surrounding circumstances of each case. Professor Williston hints that injustice does not necessarily mean pecuniary loss. As he points out, the meaning is 'purposely left somewhat indefinite,' which means that the equities of each case must point the way to its solution under this doctrine of promissory estoppel." Trexler's Estate, 27 Pa.D. & C. 4, 13 (Pa.Orph. 1936).

(2) *Employment Contracts*. Promissory estoppel is frequently invoked in the context of employment contracts. In some cases, like *Langer*, the question is whether a promise to pay a lifetime annuity induced early retirement. Some of these cases turn on a finding that the employer promised to pay in exchange for the employee's early retirement or agreed restrictions on the employee's post-retirement conduct. See Osborne v. Locke Steel Chain Co., 153 Conn. 527 (1966) (retired officer was to be available for consultation and to refrain from competition with former employer); Lowndes Cooperative Association v. Lipsey, 240 Miss. 71 (1961) (promise conditioned upon early retirement and post-retirement cooperation); Specht v. Eastwood-Nealley Corp., 34 N.J.Super. 156 (1955) (promise conditioned upon non-disclosure of trade secrets, non-competition, etc.). Other decisions, like *Langer*, find that the pension promise can be enforced on the basis of *either* consideration or promissory estoppel. See Hessler, Inc. v. Farrell, 226 A.2d 708 (Del.1967) (employee induced to forego other offers and remain with company); Wickstrom v. Vern E. Alden Co., 99 Ill.App.2d 254 (1968) (employee induced to retire early).

Promissory estoppel might also be invoked where an employee has relied upon a promise by the employer to change the "at will" status of the employment, for example by quitting an existing job or rejecting another job offer. An example is *Blinn v. Beatrice Community Hospital*, reproduced in Chapter Three. See also Grouse v. Group Health Plan, Inc., 306 N.W.2d 114 (Minn. 1981) (employee entitled to good faith opportunity to undertake "at will" employment); Ravelo v. County of Hawaii, 66 Haw. 194 (1983) (county police department's rescission of their acceptance of plaintiff's application for employment could constitute a cognizable claim under promissory estoppel).

(3) *Contemporary Pension Plans*. It is common practice for employers to establish private pension plans for the benefit of their employees. Prior to the passage of The Employee Retirement Income Security Act of 1974 (ERISA), vesting provisions for these plans often set a high bar that

relatively few employees cleared. ERISA was enacted to improve and strengthen the protection for the majority of the participants of contemporary plans by providing statutory protection for participants in both private employee benefit plans and welfare benefit plans. ERISA's statutory protection and enforcement procedures in this area preempt state law that would otherwise enforce vesting plans on theories of contract or promissory estoppel. However, these theories still apply to unfunded plans and other types of plans exempt from ERISA coverage.

Allegheny College v. National Chautauqua County Bank of Jamestown

Court of Appeals of New York, 1927.
246 N.Y. 369.

■ CARDOZO, CHIEF JUSTICE. The plaintiff, Allegheny College, is an institution of liberal learning at Meadville, Pennsylvania. In June 1921, a "drive" was in progress to secure for it an additional endowment of $1,250,000. An appeal to contribute to this fund was made to Mary Yates Johnston of Jamestown, New York. In response thereto, she signed and delivered on June 15, 1921, the following writing:

"Estate Pledge, Allegheny College Second Century Endowment

"Jamestown, N.Y., June 15, 1921.

"In consideration of my interest in Christian Education, and in consideration of others subscribing, I hereby subscribe and will pay to the order of the Treasurer of Allegheny College, Meadville, Pennsylvania, the sum of Five Thousand Dollars; $5,000.

"This obligation shall become due thirty days after my death, and I hereby instruct my Executor, or Administrator, to pay the same out of my estate. This pledge shall bear interest at the rate of _____ per cent per annum, payable annually, from _____ till paid. The proceeds of this obligation shall be added to the Endowment of said Institution, or expended in accordance with instructions on reverse side of this pledge.

"Name   MARY YATES JOHNSTON,

"Address   306 East 6th Street,

                                              "Jamestown N.Y.

"Dayton E. McClain   Witness
"T.R. Courtis   Witness
            "to authentic signature."

On the reverse side of the writing is the following indorsement: "In loving memory this gift shall be known as the Mary Yates Johnston Memorial Fund, the proceeds from which shall be used to educate students preparing for the Ministry, either in the United States or in the Foreign Field.

"This pledge shall be valid only on the condition that the provisions of my Will, now extant, shall be first met. MARY YATES JOHNSTON."

The subscription was not payable by its terms until thirty days after the death of the promisor. The sum of $1,000 was paid, however, upon account in December, 1923, while the promisor was alive. The college set the money aside to be held as a scholarship fund for the benefit of students preparing for the ministry. Later, in July, 1924, the promisor gave notice to the college that she repudiated the promise. Upon the expiration of thirty days following her death, this action was brought against the executor of her will to recover the unpaid balance.

The law of charitable subscriptions has been a prolific source of controversy in this State and elsewhere. We have held that a promise of that order is unenforceable like any other if made without consideration. . . . On the other hand, though professing to apply to such subscriptions the general law of contract, we have found consideration present where the general law of contract, at least as then declared, would have said that it was absent. . . .

A classic form of statement identifies consideration with detriment to the promisee sustained by virtue of the promise (Hamer v. Sidway, 124 N.Y. 538; Anson, Contracts [Corbin's ed.] 116; 8 Holdsworth, History of English Law 10). So compendious a formula is little more than a half truth. There is need of many a supplementary gloss before the outline can be so filled in as to depict the classic doctrine. "The promise and the consideration must purport to be the motive each for the other, in whole or at least in part. It is not enough that the promise induces the detriment or that the detriment induces the promise if the other half is wanting" (Wisc. & Mich. Ry. Co. v. Powers, 191 U.S. 379, 386; McGovern v. City of N.Y., 234 N.Y. 377, 389; Walton Water Co. v. Village of Walton, 238 N.Y. 46, 51; 1 Williston, Contracts § 139; Langdell, Summary of the Law of Contracts 82–88). If A promises B to make him a gift, consideration may be lacking, though B has renounced other opportunities for betterment in the faith that the promise will be kept.

The half truths of one generation tend at times to perpetuate themselves in the law as the whole truths of another, when constant repetition brings it about that qualifications, taken once for granted, are disregarded or forgotten. The doctrine of consideration has not escaped the common lot. As far back as 1881, Judge Holmes in his lectures on the Common Law (p. 292), separated the detriment which is merely a consequence of the promise from the detriment which is in truth the motive or inducement, and yet added that the courts "have gone far in obliterating this distinction." The tendency toward effacement has not lessened with the years. On the contrary, there has grown up of recent days a doctrine that a substitute for consideration or an exception to its ordinary requirements can be found in what is styled "a promissory estoppel" (Williston, Contracts §§ 139, 116). Whether the exception has made its way in this State to such an extent as to permit us to say that the general law of consideration has been modified accordingly, we do not now attempt to say. Cases such as *Siegel v. Spear & Co.* (234 N.Y. 479) and *DeCicco v. Schweizer* (221 N.Y. 431) may be signposts on the road. Certain, at least, it is that we have adopted the doctrine of promissory estoppel as the equivalent of consideration in connection with our law of charitable subscriptions. So long as those decisions stand, the question is not merely whether the enforcement of a charitable subscription can be squared with the doctrine of consideration in all its ancient rigor. The question may also be whether it can be squared with the doctrine of consideration as qualified by the doctrine of promissory estoppel.

We have said that the cases in this State have recognized this exception, if exception it is thought to be. Thus, in *Barnes v. Perine* (12 N.Y. 18) the subscription was made without request, express or implied, that the church do anything on the faith of it. Later, the church did incur expense to the knowledge of the promisor, and in the reasonable belief that the promise would be kept. We held the promise binding, though consideration there was none except upon the theory of a promissory estoppel. In *Presbyterian Society v. Beach* (74 N.Y. 72) a situation substantially the same became the basis for a like ruling. So in *Roberts v. Cobb* (103 N.Y. 600) and *Keuka College v. Ray* (167 N.Y. 96) the moulds of consideration as fixed by the old doctrine were subjected to a like expansion. Very likely, conceptions of public policy have shaped, more or less subconsciously, the rulings thus made. Judges have been affected by the thought that "defences of that character" are "breaches of faith toward the public, and especially toward those engaged in the same enterprise, and an unwarrantable disappointment of the reasonable expectations of those interested" (W.F. Allen, J., in Barnes v. Perine, supra and cf. Eastern States League v. Vail, 97 Vt. 495, 505, and cases there cited). The result speaks for itself irrespective of the motive. Decisions which have stood so long, and which are supported by so many considerations of public policy and reason, will not be overruled to save the symmetry of a concept which itself came into our law, not so much from any reasoned conviction of its justice, as from historical accidents of practice and procedure (8 Holdsworth, History of English Law 7 et seq.). The concept survives as one of the distinctive features of our legal system. We have no thought to suggest that it is obsolete or on the way to be abandoned. As in the case of other concepts, however, the pressure of exceptions has led to irregularities of form.

It is in this background of precedent that we are to view the problem now before us. The background helps to an understanding of the implications inherent in subscription and acceptance. This is so though we may find in the end that without recourse to the innovation of promissory estoppel the transaction can be fitted within the mould of consideration as established by tradition.

The promisor wished to have a memorial to perpetuate her name. She imposed a condition that the "gift" should "be known as the Mary

Yates Johnston Memorial Fund." The moment that the college accepted $1,000 as a payment on account, there was an assumption of a duty to do whatever acts were customary or reasonably necessary to maintain the memorial fairly and justly in the spirit of its creation. The college could not accept the money, and hold itself free thereafter from personal responsibility to give effect to the condition. . . . More is involved in the receipt of such a fund than a mere acceptance of money to be held to a corporate use. . . . The purpose of the founder would be unfairly thwarted or at least inadequately served if the college failed to communicate to the world, or in any event to applicants for the scholarship, the title of the memorial. By implication it undertook, when it accepted a portion of the "gift" that in its circulars of information and in other customary ways, when making announcement of this scholarship, it would couple with the announcement the name of the donor. The donor was not at liberty to gain the benefit of such an undertaking upon the payment of a part and disappoint the expectation that there would be payment of the residue. If the college had stated after receiving $1,000 upon account of the subscription that it would apply the money to the prescribed use, but that in its circulars of information and when responding to prospective applicants it would deal with the fund as an anonymous donation, there is little doubt that the subscriber would have been at liberty to treat this statement as the repudiation of a duty impliedly assumed, a repudiation justifying a refusal to make payments in the future. Obligation in such circumstances is correlative and mutual. * * * We do not need to measure the extent either of benefit to the promisor or of detriment to the promisee implicit in this duty. "If a person chooses to make an extravagant promise for an inadequate consideration it is his own affair" (8 Holdsworth, History of English Law 17). It was long ago said that "when a thing is to be done by the plaintiff, be it ever so small, this is a sufficient consideration to ground an action" (Sturlyn v. Albany, 1587 Cro.Eliz. 67, quoted by Holdsworth, supra; cf. Walton Water Co. v. Village of Walton, 238 N.Y. 46, 51). The longing for posthumous remembrance is an emotion not so weak as to justify us in saying that its gratification is a negligible good.

We think the duty assumed by the plaintiff to perpetuate the name of the founder of the memorial is sufficient in itself to give validity to the subscription within the rules that define consideration for a promise of that order. When the promisee subjected itself to such a duty at the implied request of the promisor, the result was the creation of a bilateral agreement. . . . There was a promise on the one side and on the other a return promise, made it is true, by implication, but expressing an obligation that had been exacted as a condition of the payment. A bilateral agreement may exist though one of the mutual promises be a promise "implied in fact," an inference from conduct as opposed to an inference from words (Williston, Contracts §§ 90, 22–a; Pettibone v. Moore, 75 Hun. 461, 464). We think the fair inference to be drawn from the acceptance of a payment on account of the subscription is a promise by the college to do what may be necessary on its part to make the scholarship effective. The plan conceived by the subscriber will be mutilated and distorted unless the sum to be accepted is adequate to the end in view. Moreover, the time to affix her name to the memorial will not arrive until the entire fund has been collected. The college may thus thwart the purpose of the payment on account if at liberty to reject a tender of the residue. It is no answer to say that a duty would then arise to make restitution of the money. If such a duty may be imposed, the only reason for its existence must be that there is then a failure of "consideration." To say that there is a failure of consideration is to concede that a consideration has been promised since otherwise it could not fail. No doubt there are times and situations in which limitations laid upon a promisee in connection with the use of what is paid by a subscriber lacks the quality of a consideration, and are to be classed merely as conditions (Williston, Contracts § 112; Page, Contracts § 523). "It is often difficult to determine whether words of condition in a promise indicate a request for consideration or state a mere condition in a gratuitous promise. An aid, though not a conclusive test in determining which construction of the promise is more reasonable is an inquiry whether the happening of the condition will be a benefit to the promisor. If so, it is a fair inference that the happening was requested as a consideration" (Williston, supra § 112). Such must be the meaning of this transaction unless we are prepared to hold that the college may keep the payment on account, and thereafter nullify the scholarship which is to preserve the memory of the subscriber. The fair implication to be gathered from the whole transaction is assent to the condition and the assumption of a duty to go forward with performance. . . . The subscriber does not say: I hand you $1,000, and you make up your mind later, after my death, whether you will undertake to commemorate my name. What she says in effect is this: I hand you $1,000, and if you are unwilling to commemorate me, the time to speak is now.

The conclusion thus reached makes it needless to consider whether, aside from the feature of a memorial, a promissory estoppel may result from the assumption of a duty to apply the fund, so far as already paid, to special purposes not mandatory under the provisions of the college charter (the support and education of students preparing for the ministry), an assumption induced by the belief that other payments sufficient in amount to make the scholarship effective would be added to the fund thereafter upon the death of the subscriber (Ladies' Collegiate Inst. v. French, 16 Gray 196; Barnes v. Perine, 12 N.Y. 18, and cases there cited).

The judgment of the Appellate Division and that of the Trial Term should be reversed, and judgment ordered for the plaintiff as prayed for in the complaint, with costs in all courts.

■ KELLOGG, J (dissenting). The Chief Judge finds in the expression, "In loving memory this gift shall be known as the Mary Yates Johnston

Memorial Fund" an offer on the part of Mary Yates Johnston to contract
with Allegheny College. The expression makes no such appeal to me.
Allegheny College was not requested to perform any act through which
the sum offered might bear the title by which the offeror states that it
shall be known. The sum offered was termed a "gift" by the offeror.
Consequently, I can see no reason why we should strain ourselves to
make it, not a gift, but a trade. Moreover, since the donor specified that
the gift was made "In consideration of my interest in Christian education,
and in consideration of others subscribing," considerations not adequate
in law, I can see no excuse for asserting that it was otherwise made in
consideration of an act or promise on the part of the donee, constituting
a sufficient *quid quo pro* to convert the gift into a contract obligation. To
me the words used merely expressed an expectation or wish on the part
of the donor and failed to exact the return of an adequate consideration.
But if an offer indeed was present, then clearly it was an offer to enter
into a unilateral contract. The offeror was to be bound provided the
offeree performed such acts as might be necessary to make the gift offered
become known under the proposed name. This is evidently the thought
of the Chief Judge, for he says: "She imposed a condition that the 'gift'
should be known as the Mary Yates Johnston Memorial Fund." In other
words, she proposed to exchange her offer of a donation in return for acts
to be performed. Even so there was never any acceptance of the offer and,
therefore, no contract, for the acts requested have never been performed.
The gift has never been made known as demanded. Indeed, the requested
acts, under the very terms of the assumed offer, could never have been
performed at a time to convert the offer into a promise. This is so for the
reason that the donation was not to take effect until after the death of
the donor, and by her death her offer was withdrawn. (Williston on
Contracts § 62.) Clearly, although a promise of the college to make the
gift known, as requested, may be implied, that promise was not the
acceptance of an offer which gave rise to a contract. The donor stipulated
for acts, not promises. "In order to make a bargain it is necessary that
the acceptor shall give in return for the offer or the promise exactly the
consideration which the offeror requests. If an act is requested, that very
act and no other must be given. If a promise is requested, that promise
must be made absolutely and unqualifiedly." (Williston on Contracts
§ 73.) "It does not follow that an offer becomes a promise because it is
accepted; it may be and frequently is, conditional, and then it does not
become a promise until the conditions are satisfied; and in case of offers
for a consideration, the performance of the consideration is always
deemed a condition." (Langdell, Summary of the Law of Contracts § 4). It
seems clear to me that there was here no offer, no acceptance of an offer,
and no contract. Neither do I agree with the Chief Judge that this court
"found consideration present where the general law of contract, at least
as then declared, would have said it was absent" in the cases of *Barnes
v. Perine* (12 N.Y. 18), *Presbyterian Society v. Beach* (74 N.Y. 72) and
Keuka College v. Ray (167 N.Y. 96). * * * However, even if the basis of the

decisions be a so-called "promissory estoppel," nevertheless they initiated no new doctrine. A so-called "promissory estoppel," although not so termed, was held sufficient by Lord Mansfield and his fellow judges as far back as the year 1765. (Pillans v. Van Mierop, 3 Burr. 1663.) Such a doctrine may be an anomaly; it is not a novelty. Therefore, I can see no ground for the suggestion that the ancient rule which makes consideration necessary to the formation of every contract is in danger of effacement through any decisions of this court. To me that is a cause for gratulation rather than regret. However, the discussion may be beside the mark, for I do not understand that the holding about to be made in this case is other than a holding that consideration was given to convert the offer into a promise. With that result I cannot agree and, accordingly, must dissent.

Congregation Kadimah Toras-Moshe
v. Robert A. DeLeo

Supreme Judicial Court of Massachusetts, 1989.
405 Mass. 365.

■ LIACOS, CHIEF JUSTICE. Congregation Kadimah Toras-Moshe (Congregation), an Orthodox Jewish synagogue, commenced this action in the Superior Court to compel the administrator of an estate (estate) to fulfil the oral promise of the decedent to give the Congregation $25,000. The Superior Court transferred the case to the Boston Municipal Court, which rendered summary judgment for the estate. The case was then transferred back to the Superior Court, which also rendered summary judgment for the estate and dismissed the Congregation's complaint. We granted the Congregation's application for direct appellate review. We now affirm.

The facts are not contested. The decedent suffered a prolonged illness, throughout which he was visited by the Congregation's spiritual leader, Rabbi Abraham Halbfinger. During four or five of these visits, and in the presence of witnesses, the decedent made an oral promise to give the Congregation $25,000. The Congregation planned to use the $25,000 to transform a storage room in the synagogue into a library named after the decedent. The oral promise was never reduced to writing. The decedent died intestate in September, 1985. He had no children, but was survived by his wife.

The Congregation asserts that the decedent's oral promise is an enforceable contract under our case law, because the promise is allegedly supported either by consideration and bargain, or by reliance. . . . We disagree.

The Superior Court judge determined that "[t]his was an oral gratuitous pledge, with no indication as to how the money should be used, or what [the Congregation] was required to do if anything in return for this promise." There was no legal benefit to the promisor nor detriment to the promisee, and thus no consideration. . . . Furthermore, there is no evidence in the record that the Congregation's plans to name a library after the decedent induced him to make or to renew his promise. Contrast *Allegheny College v. National Chautauqua County Bank,* 246 N.Y. 369, 377–379 (1927) (subscriber's promise became binding when charity implicitly promised to commemorate subscriber).

As to the lack of reliance, the judge stated that the Congregation's "allocation of $25,000 in its budget[,] for the purpose of renovating a storage room, is insufficient to find reliance or an enforceable obligation." We agree. The inclusion of the promised $25,000 in the budget, by itself, merely reduced to writing the Congregation's expectation that it would have additional funds. A hope or expectation, even though well founded, is not equivalent to either legal detriment or reliance. . . .

The Congregation cites several of our cases in which charitable subscriptions were enforced. These cases are distinguishable because they involved written, as distinguished from oral, promises and also involved substantial consideration or reliance. [The court reviewed the cases.]

The Congregation asks us to abandon the requirement of consideration or reliance in the case of charitable subscriptions. The Congregation cites the Restatement (Second) of Contracts § 90 (1981), which provides, in subsection (2): "A charitable subscription . . . is binding under Subsection (1) without proof that the promise induced action or forbearance." Subsection (1), as modified in pertinent part by subsection (2), provides: "A promise which the promisor should reasonably expect to induce action or forbearance on the part of the promisee or a third person . . . is binding if injustice can be avoided only by enforcement of the promise. . . ."

Assuming without deciding that this court would apply § 90, we are of the opinion that in this case there is no injustice in declining to enforce the decedent's promise. Although § 90 dispenses with the absolute requirement of consideration or reliance, the official comments illustrate that these are relevant considerations. Restatement (Second) of Contracts, supra at § 90 comment f. The promise to the Congregation is entirely unsupported by consideration or reliance. Furthermore, it is an oral promise sought to be enforced against an estate. To enforce such a promise would be against public policy.

Judgment affirmed.

NOTES

(1) Does Judge Cardozo in *Allegheny College* purport to find consideration for the promise being sued upon? Is the conclusion that Mrs. Johnston bargained for and received a promise by the college, implied from the conduct of accepting the $1,000 payment and putting it aside in order to set up and publicize the fund when the final payment was made, convincing?

For a line-by-line analysis, see Alfred Konefsky, *How to Read, Or at Least Not Misread, Cardozo in the* Allegheny College *Case*, 36 Buff. L. Rev. 645 (1989).

(2) *Charitable Subscriptions.* Cases enforcing promises to charities on the basis of unbargained-for reliance can be counted among the historical antecedents of modern promissory estoppel theory. See Benjamin Boyer, *Promissory Estoppel: Principle from Precedents*, 50 Mich. L. Rev 639, 873 (1952). There are references to some of these decisions in *Ricketts* and *Allegheny College*. Hence, even if a court is unwilling to stretch to find consideration, as Judge Cardozo did in *Allegheny College*, there may be an alternative basis of recovery. But this alternative basis traditionally required a showing of reliance on the part of the promisee, and it may be impossible for a charity to establish any specific reliance on a particular promised gift. To obviate this difficulty, the drafters of Restatement (Second) propose to dispense with the necessity of proving reliance. Subsection (2) of section 90 provides: "A charitable subscription . . . is binding . . . without proof that the promise induced action or forbearance." For a case adopting the Restatement position, see Salsbury v. Northwestern Bell Telephone Co., 221 N.W.2d 609 (Iowa 1974). The Iowa Supreme Court commented as follows: "We believe public policy supports this view. It is more logical to bind charitable subscriptions without requiring a showing of consideration or detrimental reliance. Charitable subscriptions often serve the public interest by making possible projects which otherwise could never come about. * * * [W]here a subscription is unequivocal the pledgor should be made to keep his word." 221 N.W.2d at 613.

Why was this reasoning rejected in *Congregation Kadimah*? Does the answer lie in the peculiar facts of the case?

(3) *Promissory Estoppel in New York.* The development of promissory estoppel in New York was traced in *Cyberchron Corp. v. Calldata Systems Development, Inc.*, 47 F.3d 39, 44–46 (2d Cir. 1995). According to the federal court, prior to 1980 New York courts limited promissory estoppel as a "substitute for consideration" to specific contexts, such as charitable subscriptions and bailments and disputes over the statute of frauds. After 1980, some lower courts embraced the more general principle but imposed higher standards than those expressed in section 90 of the Second Restatement. Thus, the promise must be "clear and unambiguous," reliance must be foreseeable to the promisor and reasonable by the promisee, and the resulting injury must be "unconscionable." Some have argued that Judge Cardozo impeded the development of promissory estoppel in New York by his decision in *Allegheny College*. See Phuong N. Pham, Comment, *The Waning of Promissory Estoppel*, 79 Cornell L. Rev. 1263 (1994).

Comment: Promissory Estoppel in Particular Contexts

Enforcing Gratuitous Promises in Tort, Agency and Bailment. In *King v. Riveland*, 886 P.2d 160, 168–169 (1994), prisoners convicted of sex offenses were convinced to enter a state-run sex offender treatment program by a promise that whatever was divulged in the program would be confidential. The prisoners sought an injunction against a threatened disclosure, which the court granted. Although the court concluded that there was no consideration, it relied on section 90 to hold that the promise did induce reliance, and justice required its enforcement.

In *Abresch v. Northwestern Bell Telephone Co.*, 246 Minn. 408 (1956), the plaintiff sought damages he suffered when his building was destroyed by fire. Upon discovering the fire, he phoned the telephone operator, requesting her to call the fire department. The court noted that "while the telephone company is under no duty to assume responsibility of delivering messages in cases of emergency, if it does voluntarily assume such responsibility and thereby leads others to rely on such assumption of duty and to refrain from taking other and more direct action to protect themselves, the company is required to exercise reasonable care in performing the duty so assumed for a failure of which it may become liable in a tort action." 246 Minn. at 416. "It is ancient learning that one who assumes to act, even though gratuitously, may thereby become subject to the duty of acting carefully, if he acts at all." *Glanzer v. Shepard*, 233 N.Y. 236, 239 (1922). See Restatement (Second) of Torts § 323.

Litigants have sought to enhance prospects of recovery by attempting to show that the defendant was or undertook to become an agent or bailee of the plaintiff. Certain obligations adhere to the principal-agent and bailor-bailee relationships by operation of law quite apart from the explicit agreement or understanding of the parties. In *Lester v. Marshall*, 143 Colo. 189 (1960), for example, a real estate broker engaged by the plaintiffs to find a home for them also gratuitously undertook to "take care of everything" prior to and after closing, assuring plaintiffs they would get title free of encumbrances. The court relied upon the revised Restatement of Agency, which in section 378 provides as follows: "One who, by a gratuitous promise or other conduct which he should realize will cause another reasonably to rely upon the performance of definite acts of service by him as the other's agent, causes the other to refrain from having such acts done by other available means is subject to a duty to use care to perform such service or, while other means are available, to give notice that he will not perform." Restatement of Agency (Second) § 378.

While still a relatively undeveloped area, there is some possibility of liability for malfeasance (the negligent performance of a promised act) as well as for misfeasance (the non-performance of a promised act). For it is recognized that the underlying basis of liability is the reasonable reliance, which clearly can follow a negligent performance of a promised act, as well as a failure to perform the promised act altogether. See Restatement (Second) of Torts § 323, comment d.

Promissory Estoppel and Entertainment Contracts. After The Ohio Players struck it big with their hit single "Funky Worm," they sought to back out of the recording agreement they had with Westbound Records,

Inc. alleging a lack of consideration. They maintained that although they were bound to record exclusively for Westbound, the latter was not, by the express terms of the agreement, obliged to make any records using the group. The Appellate Court of Illinois found consideration in a $4,000 advance against royalties and prescinded from any inquiry into adequacy. Bonner v. Westbound Records, Inc., 76 Ill.App.3d 736 (1979). Moreover, the court met an objection based on lack of mutuality of obligation by implying an obligation by Westbound to act in good faith and, following *Wood v. Lucy, Lady Duff-Gordon*, a duty to use its best efforts. Finally, the court found that liability could be predicated upon promissory estoppel "as a substitute for consideration." In reliance upon the recording agreement, Westbound undertook a substantial business risk, incurring more than $80,000 in expenses which it could recoup only if the recordings were successful. "The Ohio Players now seek to deny Westbound the sole reward of its success. Their aim is to keep for themselves the fame and money which, judging by their past experience, they could not have acquired without Westbound's aid, by asserting that Westbound did not originally promise to do what it has already actually done. This the plaintiffs are estopped to do; even if the agreements were not originally supported by consideration, they became enforceable when Westbound performed in reliance on the promises of The Ohio Players, and indeed advanced additional monies not called for by the contract, to protect its investment." 76 Ill.App.3d at 749.

Promissory Estoppel and Corporate Relocation. In recent years, corporations who decided to close or move business operations have been sued by employees, a union or a local government unit on a promissory estoppel theory. The claim was that the plaintiff had relied upon a corporate promise to remain or to stay open and that injustice could be prevented only by giving an appropriate remedy, whether damages or an injunction. These claims have all foundered because a clear and definite promise by the corporation could not be proved. See, e.g., Abbington v. Dayton Malleable, Inc., 738 F.2d 438 (6th Cir. 1984); Local 1330, United Steel Workers v. United States Steel Corp., 631 F.2d 1264 (6th Cir. 1980); Marine Transport Lines, Inc. v. International Organization of Masters, Mates & Pilots, 636 F.Supp. 384 (S.D.N.Y. 1986). See also, Charter Twp. of Ypsilanti v. General Motors Corp., 201 Mich.App. 128 (1993), *appeal denied*, 443 Mich. 882 (1993). The assumption in these cases is, however, that if the requisite promise and reliance were established, the court would inquire into the "injustice" question. Should a court do this?

But What Are Courts Actually Doing? Promissory estoppel was spawned in Williston's Treatise and the Restatements of Contracts. How do courts actually apply the doctrine? There have been numerous attempts at empirical research into the case law, many of which come to divergent results. See, e.g., Daniel A. Farber and John H. Matheson, *Beyond Promissory Estoppel: Contract Law and the "Invisible Handshake,"* 52 U. Chi. L. Rev. 903 (1985) (finding that reliance is no longer the key to promissory estoppel cases); Randy Barnett and Mary Becker, *Promissory Estoppel, Contract Formalities, and Misrepresentation*, 15 Hofstra L. Rev. 443 (1987) (finding that courts impose promissory estoppel liability not on the basis of reliance, but on facts involving misrepresentation or where the parties intended to be legally bound); Mary E. Becker, *Promissory Estoppel Damages*, 16 Hofstra L. Rev 131 (1987) (finding that courts routinely award expectation damages in promissory estoppel cases); W. David Slawson, *The Role of Reliance in Contract Damages*, 76 Cornell L. Rev. 197 (1990) (finding expectation damages are usually awarded); Edward Yorio and Steve Thel, *The Promissory Basis of Section 90*, 101 Yale L.J. 111 (1991) (finding a preference for awards of specific performance or expectation damages); Phoung N. Pham, Note, *The Waning of Promissory Estoppel*, 79 Cornell L. Rev. 1263 (1994) (finding courts reluctant to employ promissory estoppel); Eric M. Holmes, *Restatement of Promissory Estoppel*, 32 Williamette L. Rev. 263 (1996) (finding some but not all jurisdictions limiting damages to reliance); Sidney W. DeLong, *The New Requirement of Enforcement Reliance in Commercial Promissory Estoppel: Section 90 as Catch-22*, 1997 Wis. L. Rev. 943 (finding that promissory estoppel is not a significant force in commercial disputes); Robert Hillman, *Questioning the "New Consensus" on Promissory Estoppel: An Empirical and Theoretical Study*, 98 Colum. L. Rev. 580 (1998) (finding that courts flexibly award either expectation or reliance damages); Sidney W. DeLong, *Placid, Clear-Seeming Words: Some Realism about the New Formalism (With Particular Attention to Promissory Estoppel)*, 38 San Diego L. Rev. 13 (2001) (identifying techniques merchants and courts use to avoid promissory estoppel liability); Marco Jimenez, *The Many Faces of Promissory Estoppel: An Empirical Analysis under the Restatement (Second) of Contracts*, 57 UCLA L. Rev. 669 (2010) (finding that promissory estoppel is a more significant theory of recovery than has been previously thought and is positioned to grow further in importance).

Promissory Estoppel in England. No unitary principle of promissory estoppel has emerged in English or Commonwealth contract law. Perhaps the reliance interest has been, or could be, protected under the more flexible definition of consideration as either a benefit to the promisor or a detriment to the promisee. The bargain rhetoric does not dominate discussions of consideration in English case law. See G. Treitel, The Law of Contract, Chapter 3 (11th ed. 2003). For a more general argument about the relationship between consideration and freedom of contract in England, see Patrick S. Atiyah, The Rise and Fall of Freedom of Contracts (1979).

PROBLEM: THE CASE OF THE DISAPPOINTED MORTGAGEE

Brad wanted to buy some land from Harold and build a new home. Harold was willing to sell 3 acres in his subdivision for $6,000. Company, in another state, was willing to sell Brad a prefabricated home for $40,000, to be delivered to the site and set up by Brad. Bank agreed to loan Brad $6,000 to pay Harold for the land and created a first mortgage in the property. Company was willing to sell the home to Brad for $3,000 down with a promise to pay the balance in installments, but Company, knowing of Bank's involvement, wanted a second mortgage in the land. Company reasoned that the land with a home would be valuable and that even if Brad defaulted, the proceeds from any foreclosure sale would exceed the amount of Bank's loan. The second mortgage was executed, but before shipping the home to Brad, Company obtained a written promise from Bank that if Brad was seriously in default to Bank, Bank would promptly notify Company. Company shipped the home, which Brad attempted to set up. Before the work was done, Brad was seriously in default to Bank. Bank, however, did not notify Company. Rather, Bank sold Brad's note and the first mortgage to Harold for $5,500, the amount due under the loan. Harold then foreclosed the mortgage and, at the foreclosure sale, bid on the property and purchased it for $6,000. Harold then completed construction of the home for $10,000 and sold the lot and completed home to Frank for $30,000.

Company has been advised that it cannot upset the foreclosure sale to Frank (it had notice of the sale but did not attend) and accepts that advice. But it wants to sue Bank for the failure to give notice of Brad's default. Is Bank's promise enforceable? If so, what damages should Company recover? See Miles Homes Division of Insilco Corp. v. First State Bank of Joplin, 782 S.W.2d 798 (Mo.App. 1990).

PROBLEM: THE CASE OF FRIENDLY FORD'S LOANER VEHICLE

Richard Keller purchased a new Taurus station wagon from Friendly Ford, Inc. which he returned to the dealer and for which he sought a refund "because obviously it was a lemon." Thereafter, he needed a car to drive his daughter to college in another state, and Friendly Ford's sales manager assured him on the phone that he could "have a loaner vehicle" for the journey. But when he came to pick up the "loaner," the company president refused to supply the car. At that point Keller said he had no choice but to drive the Taurus "and hope and pray it didn't break down on the trip." But break down it did, causing Keller considerable inconvenience and expense (e.g., rental of a van to complete the trip). Should Keller be able to recover from Friendly Ford for these expenses? See Keller v. Friendly Ford, Inc., 782 S.W.2d 170 (Mo.App. 1990).

Comment: Promissory Estoppel and the Choice of Remedies

From one point of view, distinctly Willistonian, the full range of contract remedies should always be available, whether the reason for enforcement is consideration or reliance. A contract is a contract is a contract. Thus, grandfather's promise to pay granddaughter $2,000, the employer's promise to pay retirement benefits, and the donor's promise to make a charitable subscription should each be performed in full, even though the promisee's detriment was induced rather than bargained for and, if quantified and valued, that reliance would be worth less than the value of the promised performance. Section 90 of the First Restatement was silent on this point, stating only that a promise which induces foreseeable reliance "of a definite and substantial character . . . is binding if injustice can be avoided only by enforcement of the promise." But the overall structure of the First Restatement—with its definition of contract as "a promise . . . for the breach of which the law gives a remedy," (§ 1), its expectation-oriented approach to remedies (§§ 326–384), and the comments of its Reporter, Williston, see 4 A.L.I. Proceedings 97–106 (1926)—supports the conclusion that expectation damages were meant to be the rule rather than the exception. See G. Gilmore, The Death of Contract 59–65 (1974).

From another point of view, recovery under promissory estoppel should often be limited to the amount of the plaintiff's reliance, whether this be measured in terms of "out of pocket" expenditures, foregone opportunities or both. Historically the doctrine of estoppel was defensive. The representor was simply estopped from denying the accuracy of what had been stated. When the representation is by promise, "promissory estoppel acts defensively so as to prevent an attack upon the enforceability of a contract." Wheeler v. White, 398 S.W.2d 93, 97 (Tex. 1965). The *Wheeler* court went on, however, to state: "Under this theory, losses of expected profits will not be allowed even if expected profits are provable with certainty." Id. According to (now Judge) Richard Posner, these limitations are consistent with the theory of economic efficiency in contract law. For example, Posner asserts that it "obscures analysis to equate reliance with consideration in circumstances where no exchange is contemplated" and suggests that a "better approach would be to treat the breach of promise likely to induce reliance as a form of actionable negligence under tort law." R. Posner, Economic Analysis of Law 70 (2d ed. 1977).

Recognizing this other point of view, Restatement (Second) § 90 eliminated the First Restatement's requirement that the reliance be "definite and substantial" and provided that the "remedy granted for breach may be limited as justice requires." The assumption is that one starts from a position of full-scale enforcement, but that the "same factors which bear on whether any relief should be granted also bear on the extent and character of the remedy." (See *Sullivan v. O'Connor* in Chapter One.) Thus recovery might "sometimes be limited to restitution or to damages or specific relief measured by the extent of the promisee's reliance rather than by the terms of the promise." § 90 cmt. d. Factors that should be relevant in the decision include policies implicit in the transaction type (e.g., charitable subscriptions, retirement promises, family relations), the reason for the non-performance (financial reverses might suggest a lesser while dishonest conduct might support a greater remedy), the degree of disproportion associated with enforcement of the promise (e.g., the promise to obtain insurance), and any historical patterns of enforcement associated with the transaction type (e.g., the bailment).

Melvin Eisenberg, among others, has argued that if the reason for enforcing the promise is reliance rather than bargain, then the scope of remedial protection should be limited by the reliance interest. As he put it, it is a "nice question how much difference there is between a rule that donative promises are unenforceable unless reasonably relied upon, and a rule that donative promises are enforceable but only to the extent reasonably relied upon." Melvin A. Eisenberg, *Donative Promises*, 47 U. Chi. L. Rev. 1, 33 (1979). This argument is part of a broader assertion that the primary reason for protecting the expectation interest in bargain contracts is to insure that "hidden" reliance, frequently in the form of hard-to-measure-and-prove opportunity costs, is fully compensated. In short, protecting the expectation interest is a surrogate for protecting reliance in the bargain contract. Thus, in a non-bargain contract, the assumption should be that the court will protect the reliance interest, with expectation damages awarded only when necessary to insure that "hidden" reliance is fully compensated. See Melvin A. Eisenberg, *The Bargain Principle and its Limits*, 95 Harv. L. Rev. 741, 785–98 (1982); *The Principles of Consideration*, 67 Cornell L. Rev. 640, 656–59 (1982).

The Seventh Circuit's decision in *Walters v. Marathon Oil Co.*, 642 F.2d 1098 (7th Cir. 1981), is instructive here. Relying on defendant's promise to supply gasoline and "continuing negotiations," plaintiff purchased and made improvements on a vacant service station site. After the negotiations were completed, however, defendant refused to sign the dealership agreement because of a newly announced moratorium on dealerships. The trial court found for plaintiff on the theory of promissory estoppel and awarded damages based upon the profits that plaintiff would have made on the sale of gasoline during the first year under the promised dealership. On appeal, defendant argued that plaintiff's damages should be measured by its reliance on the promise, namely, the investment in and improvements on the service station. As such, defendant claimed, there should be no recovery because the fair market value of the improved service station exceeded plaintiff's out-of-pocket expenditure. The Court of Appeals affirmed the trial court's rejection of this theory. The court noted that the plaintiff had suffered "a loss of profits as a direct result of their reliance . . . and the amount of the lost profits was ascertained with reasonable certainty." Moreover, "in reliance upon appellant's promise, they had foregone the opportunity to make the investment elsewhere." Characterizing promissory estoppel as "an equitable matter," the court concluded that the award of lost profits was necessary to "secure complete justice." As the court put it: "An equity court possesses some discretionary power to award damages in order to do complete justice. . . . Furthermore, since it is the historic purpose of equity to secure complete justice, the courts are able to adjust the remedies so as to grant the necessary relief, . . . and a district court sitting in equity may even devise a remedy which extends or exceeds the terms of a prior agreement between the parties, if it is necessary to make the injured party whole." 642 F.2d at 1100. But see Walser v. Toyota Motor Sales, U.S.A., Inc., 43 F.3d 396, 400–402 (8th Cir. 1994) (damages for breach of promise to grant dealership were properly limited to out-of-pocket expenditures).

PROBLEM: THE CASE OF THE INDEPENDENT CAB DRIVER

During a lull in the proceedings of a Legion convention, a few of the participants made their way to a nearby bar for refreshments and conversation.

One of the men, Marty Lawless, began bemoaning the lot of a cab driver. Since his discharge from the Army, Marty had been driving a cab in a metropolitan area for a large company. "If I could only lay my hands on twenty thousand bucks," he remarked, "I could really make out. I could get a cab and license of my own and start working for myself, instead of the other guy."

In the group was Jim Craven, who had attended law school after his discharge and had built up a lucrative personal injury practice. After questioning Marty a bit more regarding what the latter could do with a cab of his own, Jim said to him: "I'll loan you the money. Pay it back when you want, up to ten years. And it won't cost you a thing. I owe you a lot more than that, heaven knows." (This last remark referred to the fact that Jim credits Marty with saving his life in battle.)

But Marty was hesitant. He didn't want any "charity." He answered: "I appreciate your offer, Jim. I really do. But I couldn't take it. I think a bank will loan me the money."

"Aw, Lawless, you're crazy to pass up a deal like that," said John Coburn, another member of the group.

Jim spoke up: "Now hold on. It's not charity, if that's what you're thinking. We'll make it carry one percent interest. How's that?"

This was too good to pass up, thought Marty. And, after all, Craven could afford it. So he replied: "Thanks a lot, Jim. It will sure give me a boost. And don't worry, you'll be repaid."

Jim then raised a glass and said to everyone present: "All right, everybody. Let's drink to the world's newest independent cab driver!" Everyone complied.

Upon returning home, one of Marty's first stops was to the office of his employer, where he resigned his job.

But a few days later he received a letter from Craven in which Craven said he had a "big deal" come up and didn't have the money to loan now. He expressed his regrets and said he hoped they "can get together real soon."

Lawless has hastened to your office and now awaits your advice. Advise him.

CHAPTER THREE

AGREEMENT

1. THE AGREEMENT PROCESS: MANIFESTATION OF MUTUAL ASSENT

In any exchange transaction, the parties' two primary objectives are to reach agreement on the terms of the exchange and then to realize a satisfactory completion of it. Depending on the parties' situation, the transaction and other market or legal constraints, negotiation over terms may precede the final expression of agreement. Negotiations happen only when parties' options are subject to their own choice rather than predetermined by law or circumstances. Parties might negotiate over willingness to deal one with the other, the description, quality and quantity of what it is that one party is to provide, the price and method of payment, the time and method of performance, which party bears what risks, the duration of the relationship and so forth. It is assumed that individual bargainers will define their wants in a rational way and seek to satisfy them through a process of voluntary exchange. If there is adequate information and sufficient choice, both parties will gain from the completed exchange—that is, both parties will conclude that the transaction has increased if not maximized their satisfactions.

The purpose of this section is to explore how courts tell when there has been sufficient agreement to create a contract. The issue typically arises when, after negotiations have commenced and before any performance of the proposed exchange has occurred, one party withdraws from the transaction. The other then asserts that their agreement had reached a point where a contract was formed and that the withdrawal breached it. How the withdrawing party responds to this and the extent to which the law of contracts supports these responses at various stages of the agreement process is the central problem to be considered. At stake is the general issue of freedom *from* contract. Individuals in our society can typically refuse to deal or to negotiate with another without liability. At some point, however, a contract is formed. When does that happen?

(A) ASCERTAINING ASSENT: THE "OBJECTIVE" TEST

What is the overall approach that a court should take to ascertaining whether the parties have assented to a bargain and what their relevant intentions were in the process? The traditional answer and some of the problems associated with it are suggested in the following two cases and discussed in the notes.

Embry v. Hargadine, McKittrick Dry Goods Co.

St. Louis Court of Appeals, Missouri, 1907.
127 Mo.App. 383.

■ GOODE, J. [Appellant's written employment contract with Appellee expired on December 15, 1903. He had been unsuccessful in obtaining a meeting with Appellee's president before the expiration date. On December 23, during peak season, Appellant met with the president, Mr. McKittrick, and, according to his testimony, stated that unless he had another contract for the next year he would "quit" then and there. According to Appellant, the president replied: "Go ahead, you're all right; get your men out and don't let that worry you." Appellant thought that the contract had been renewed and made no further effort to find employment. When his employment was terminated on March 1, 1904, Appellant sued for breach of contract. At the trial, the president denied making the "you're all right statement" and testified that he was pressed to prepare for a board meeting, did not intend at that point to renew the contract and had deferred the renewal issue until a later date.]

It is assigned for error that the court required the jury, in order to return a verdict for appellant, not only to find the conversation occurred as appellant swore, but that both parties intended by such conversation to contract with each other for plaintiff's employment for the year from December, 1903, at a salary of $2,000. * * * [I]t remains to determine whether or not this part of the instruction was a correct statement of the law in regard to what was necessary to constitute a contract between the parties; that is to say, whether the formation of a contract by what, according to Embry, was said, depended on the intention of both Embry and McKittrick. Or, to put the question more precisely, did what was said constitute a contract of re-employment on the previous terms irrespective of the intention or purpose of McKittrick?

Judicial opinion and elementary treatises abound in statements of the rule that to constitute a contract there must be a meeting of the minds of the parties, and both must agree to the same thing in the same sense. Generally speaking, this may be true; but it is not literally or universally true. That is to say, the inner intention of parties to a conversation subsequently alleged to create a contract cannot either make a contract of what transpired, or prevent one from arising, if the words used were sufficient to constitute a contract. In so far as their intention is an influential element, it is only such intention as the words or acts of the parties indicate; not one secretly cherished which is inconsistent with those words or acts. The rule is thus stated by a text-writer, and many decisions are cited in support of his text: "The primary object of construction in contract law is to discover the intention of the parties. This intention in express contracts is, in the first instance, embodied in the words which the parties have used and is to be deduced therefrom. This rule applies to oral contracts, as well as to contracts in writing, and is the rule recognized by courts of equity." 2 Page, Contracts,

§ 1104. So it is said in another work: "Now this measure of the contents of the promise will be found to coincide, in the usual dealings of men of good faith and ordinary competence, both with the actual intention of the promisor and with the actual expectation of the promisee. But this is not a constant or a necessary coincidence. In exceptional cases, a promisor may be bound to perform something which he did not intend to promise, or a promisee may not be entitled to require that performance which he understood to be promised to him." Walds-Pollock, Contracts (3d Ed.) 309. In Brewington v. Mesker, 51 Mo.App. 348, 356, it is said that the meeting of minds, which is essential to the formation of a contract, is not determined by the secret intention of the parties, but by their expressed intention, which may be wholly at variance with the former. * * * In view of those authorities, we hold that, though McKittrick may not have intended to employ Embry by what transpired between them according to the latter's testimony, yet if what McKittrick said would have been taken by a reasonable man to be an employment, and Embry so understood it, it constituted a valid contract of employment for the ensuing year.

The next question is whether or not the language used was of that character, namely, was such that Embry, as a reasonable man, might consider he was re-employed for the ensuing year on the previous terms, and act accordingly. * * * Embry was demanding a renewal of his contract, saying he had been put off from time to time, and that he had only a few days before the end of the year in which to seek employment from other houses, and that he would quit then and there unless he was re-employed. McKittrick inquired how he was getting along with the department, and Embry said they (i.e., the employees of the department) were very busy getting out salesmen; whereupon McKittrick said: "Go ahead, you are all right; get your men out and do not let that worry you." We think no reasonable man would construe that answer to Embry's demand that he be employed for another year, otherwise than as an assent to the demand, and that Embry had the right to rely on it as an assent. The natural inference is, though we do not find it testified to, that Embry was at work getting samples ready for the salesmen to use during the ensuing season. Now, when he was complaining of the worry and mental distress he was under because of his uncertainty about the future, and his urgent need, either of an immediate contract with respondent, or a refusal by it to make one, leaving him free to seek employment elsewhere, McKittrick must have answered as he did for the purpose of assuring appellant that any apprehension was needless, as appellant's services would be retained by the respondent. The answer was unambiguous, and we rule that if the conversation was according to appellant's version, and he understood he was employed, it constituted in law a valid contract of re-employment, and the court erred in making the formation of a contract depend on a finding that both parties intended to make one. It was only necessary that Embry, as a reasonable man, had a right to and did so understand.

Some other rulings are assigned for error by the appellant, but we will not discuss them because we think they are devoid of merit.

The judgment is reversed, and the cause remanded. All concur.

W.O. Lucy v. A.H. Zehmer

Supreme Court of Appeals of Virginia, 1954.
196 Va. 493.

■ BUCHANAN, JUSTICE. This suit was instituted by W.O. Lucy and J.C. Lucy, complainants, against A.H. Zehmer and Ida S. Zehmer, his wife, defendants, to have specific performance of a contract by which it was alleged the Zehmers had sold to W.O. Lucy a tract of land owned by A.H. Zehmer in Dinwiddie county containing 471.6 acres, more or less, known as the Ferguson farm, for $50,000. J.C. Lucy, the other complainant, is a brother of W.O. Lucy, to whom W.O. Lucy transferred a half interest in his alleged purchase.

The instrument sought to be enforced was written by A.H. Zehmer on December 20, 1952, in these words: "We hereby agree to sell to W.O. Lucy the Ferguson Farm complete for $50,000.00, title satisfactory to buyer," and signed by the defendants, A.H. Zehmer and Ida S. Zehmer.

The answer of A.H. Zehmer admitted that at the time mentioned W.O. Lucy offered him $50,000 cash for the farm, but that he, Zehmer, considered that the offer was made in jest; that so thinking, and both he and Lucy having had several drinks, he wrote out "the memorandum" quoted above and induced his wife to sign it; that he did not deliver the memorandum to Lucy, but that Lucy picked it up, read it, put it in his pocket, attempted to offer Zehmer $5 to bind the bargain, which Zehmer refused to accept, and realizing for the first time that Lucy was serious, Zehmer assured him that he had no intention of selling the farm and that the whole matter was a joke. Lucy left the premises insisting that he had purchased the farm.

Depositions were taken and the decree appealed from was entered holding that the complainants had failed to establish their right to specific performance, and dismissing their bill. The assignment of error is to this action of the court.

[At the trial, Lucy testified that he was a farmer and had known Zehmer for 15 to 20 years. He stated that he knew the farm well and, seven years earlier, Zehmer had rejected his offer to purchase it for $20,000. Lucy claimed that he wanted to try again to buy the farm and said to Zehmer, "bet you won't take $50,000." Zehmer responded, "yes, but you wouldn't give it" and expressed doubt that Lucy could raise the money. Lucy then told Zehmer to write an agreement and, after 30–40 minutes of discussion and modification, all of the parties, including Mrs. Zehmer, signed. Zehmer then refused Lucy's tender of $5 to seal the bargain. Lucy conceded that there was a bottle on the table between them and that they had had a "couple of drinks." He also testified that the next day, in order to raise the $50,000, he persuaded his brother to put up half of the money. He also had the title examined. Upon stating that he was ready to proceed, Zehmer told him that there was no contract.

[Zehmer's testimony was that he had purchased the farm eleven years ago for $11,000 and had refused many offers to buy it. It was just before Christmas, there was "lots of drinking," and he was "high as a Georgia pine." When Lucy approached him about selling the farm, Zehmer doubted that Lucy had $50,000. He claimed he was just "needling" and stated that after the writing was signed he told Lucy that it was just "liquor talking" and that he would not sell. Zehmer's wife testified that she would not sign the writing until told it was a joke, that both men were "tight" and that the husband told Lucy before he left that there was no sale. This latter fact was corroborated by a waitress, who witnessed the transaction.]

* * *

The defendants insist that the evidence was ample to support their contention that the writing sought to be enforced was prepared as a bluff or dare to force Lucy to admit that he did not have $50,000; that the whole matter was a joke; that the writing was not delivered to Lucy and no binding contract was ever made between the parties.

It is an unusual, if not bizarre, defense. When made to the writing admittedly prepared by one of the defendants and signed by both, clear evidence is required to sustain it.

In his testimony Zehmer claimed that he "was high as a Georgia pine," and that the transaction "was just a bunch of two doggoned drunks bluffing to see who could talk the biggest and say the most." That claim is inconsistent with his attempt to testify in great detail as to what was said and what was done. It is contradicted by other evidence as to the condition of both parties, and rendered of no weight by the testimony of his wife that when Lucy left the restaurant she suggested that Zehmer drive him home. The record is convincing that Zehmer was not intoxicated to the extent of being unable to comprehend the nature and consequences of the instrument he executed, and hence that instrument is not to be invalidated on that ground. . . . It was in fact conceded by defendants' counsel in oral argument that under the evidence Zehmer was not too drunk to make a valid contract.

The evidence is convincing also that Zehmer wrote two agreements, the first one beginning "I hereby agree to sell." Zehmer first said he could not remember about that, then that "I don't think I wrote but one out." Mrs. Zehmer said that what he wrote was "I hereby agree," but that the "I" was changed to "We" after that night. The agreement that was written and signed is in the record and indicates no such change. Neither are the mistakes in spelling that Zehmer sought to point out readily apparent.

The appearance of the contract, the fact that it was under discussion for forty minutes or more before it was signed; Lucy's objection to the first draft because it was written in the singular, and he wanted Mrs. Zehmer to sign it also; the rewriting to meet that objection and the signing by Mrs. Zehmer; the discussion of what was to be included in the sale, the provision for the examination of the title, the completeness of the instrument that was executed, the taking possession of it by Lucy with no request or suggestion by either of the defendants that he give it back, are facts which furnish persuasive evidence that the execution of the contract was a serious business transaction rather than a casual, jesting matter as defendants now contend.

* * *

If it be assumed, contrary to what we think the evidence shows, that Zehmer was jesting about selling his farm to Lucy and that the transaction was intended by him to be a joke, nevertheless the evidence shows that Lucy did not so understand it but considered it to be a serious business transaction and the contract to be binding on the Zehmers as well as on himself. The very next day he arranged with his brother to put up half the money and take a half interest in the land. The day after that he employed an attorney to examine the title. The next night, Tuesday, he was back at Zehmer's place and there Zehmer told him for the first time, Lucy said, that he wasn't going to sell and he told Zehmer, "You know you sold that place fair and square." After receiving the report from his attorney that the title was good he wrote to Zehmer that he was ready to close the deal.

Not only did Lucy actually believe, but the evidence shows he was warranted in believing, that the contract represented a serious business transaction and a good faith sale and purchase of the farm.

In the field of contracts, as generally elsewhere, "We must look to the outward expression of a person as manifesting his intention rather than to his secret and unexpressed intention. 'The law imputes to a person an intention corresponding to the reasonable meaning of his words and acts.'" First Nat. Exchange Bank of Roanoke v. Roanoke Oil Co., 169 Va. 99, 114.

* * *

The mental assent of the parties is not requisite for the formation of a contract. If the words or other acts of one of the parties have but one reasonable meaning, his undisclosed intention is immaterial except when an unreasonable meaning which he attaches to his manifestations is known to the other party. Restatement of the Law of Contracts, Vol. I, § 71, p. 74.

" * * * The law, therefore, judges of an agreement between two persons exclusively from those expressions of their intentions which are communicated between them. * * *." Clark on Contracts, 4 ed., § 3, p. 4.

An agreement or mutual assent is of course essential to a valid contract but the law imputes to a person an intention corresponding to the reasonable meaning of his words and acts. If his words and acts, judged by a reasonable standard, manifest an intention to agree, it is immaterial what may be the real but unexpressed state of his mind. . . .

So a person cannot set up that he was merely jesting when his conduct and words would warrant a reasonable person in believing that he intended a real agreement. . . .

Whether the writing signed by the defendants and now sought to be enforced by the complainants was the result of a serious offer by Lucy and a serious acceptance by the defendants, or was a serious offer by Lucy and an acceptance in secret jest by the defendants, in either event it constituted a binding contract of sale between the parties.

* * *

The complainants are entitled to have specific performance of the contract sued on. The decree appealed from is therefore reversed and the cause is remanded for the entry of a proper decree requiring the defendants to perform the contract in accordance with the prayer of the bill.

Reversed and remanded.

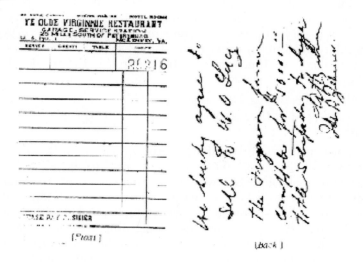

The "Contract" in Lucy v. Zehmer

NOTES

(1) *Some History.* At one time common law judges, along with their counterparts in civil law countries, claimed to adhere to the subjective theory, which required a "meeting of minds." For example, if A made an offer to B, allowing the offeree until later in the afternoon to accept or reject, B's assent to the proposal within that period would be ineffective if A could establish he or she was not then of a mind to contract. An offeror need not communicate a withdrawal (revocation) of the offer; all that was needed was to prove that the offeror no longer intended to contract when the other party tried to accept. See Cooke v. Oxley, 100 Eng.Rep. 785 (1790). Secret,

unmanifested intention could defeat what outwardly was an expression of assent. For if actual assent was the decisive factor, the outward manifestation was not controlling.

It must not be supposed that under the subjective theory the outward expression was of no consequence. One would obviously have some explaining to do if it were maintained in court that when one said "I promise to pay $5,000," one actually meant to say "I promise to pay $4,000." Just as in other fields of law where the central inquiry is the ascertainment of actual intent, circumstances may be very persuasive.

The early Twentieth Century saw a shift in common law decisions toward greater acceptance of the objective theory. For example: "While ordinarily present, it is not the meeting of minds of the parties, but the expression of their mutual assent that * * * is the culmination of the contract-making process * * *. It is not the subjective thing known as meeting of the minds, but the objective thing, manifestation of mutual assent, which is essential." Field-Martin Company v. Fruen Milling Company, 210 Minn. 388 (1941).

The avowed reason was to protect the stability of contractual relationships by enabling the parties to act upon reasonable appearance. We might also think of the change as altering who bears the risk of error. Under the subjective theory, the hearer (who cannot be absolutely certain of the speaker's subjective intent) bears the risk that what was said was different from what was meant. Under the objective approach, the speaker bears that risk.

(2) *How Objective is Objective?* The following statement by Justice Learned Hand is a rather extreme statement of the objective theory of agreement:

> A contract has, strictly speaking, nothing to do with the personal, or individual, intent of the parties. A contract is an obligation attached by mere force of law to certain acts of the parties, usually words, which ordinarily accompany and represent a known intent. If, however, it were proved by twenty bishops that either party, when he used the words, intended something else than the usual meaning which the law imposes upon them, he would still be held, unless there were some mutual mistake or something else of the sort.

Hotchkiss v. National City Bank of New York, 200 Fed. 287, 293 (S.D.N.Y. 1911). More recently, Frank Easterbrook has offered this explanation:

> * * * Walters stoutly maintains that he subjectively intended to be bound and he wants to invite a jury to infer the same about Telstar. * * * Yet 'intent' does not invite a tour through Walters's cranium, with Walters as the guide. * * * 'The intent of the parties [to be bound] must necessarily be derived from a consideration of their words, written and oral, and their actions.' * * * Secret hopes and wishes count for nothing. The status of a document as a contract depends on what the parties express to each other and to the world, not on what they keep to themselves. * * * The objective approach

is an essential ingredient to allowing the parties jointly to control the effect of their document. If unilateral or secret intentions could bind, parties would become wary, and the written word would lose some of its power. The ability to fix the consequences with certainty is especially important in commercial transactions that are planned with care in advance.

Skycom Corporation v. Telstar Corporation, 813 F.2d 810, 814–5 (7th Cir. 1987).

There is, however, "a 'subjective' as well as an 'objective' side" to the law of contracts, and "although the 'objective' theory has now become fashionable," it is "erroneous to regard it as a complete statement of the law." Glanville Williams, *Mistake as to Party in the Law of Contract,* 23 Can. B. Rev. 271, 380, 387 (1945). Lawrence Solan puts the point as follows:

> Most problematic for the objective account is that when both parties agree that a commitment has been made, the promisor is bound, and when neither believes that a promise has been made, the promisor is not bound. Objective considerations are irrelevant. Even when a reasonable person would construe the promisor's statement as a commitment, courts will not enforce a statement to which neither party subscribed. By the same token, courts will enforce a promise to which both parties agreed, even if a reasonable person would not have understood it as a promise.

Lawrence M. Solan, *Contract as Agreement*, 83 Notre Dame L. Rev. 353, 354 (2007). If both parties subjectively believe that an agreement has been made, should the law refuse enforcement just because an "objective" reasonable person in their shoes would disagree? For more on this, see the next case, *Raffles v. Wichelhaus* and the accompanying notes.

(3) *The Meaning of "Objective": Words and Context.* Objective approaches to interpretation need not be formalist. The objective meaning of a party's words and actions could be the meaning that a reasonable person would attach to them *in those circumstances*. Those circumstances can include the parties' background knowledge, their past dealings, the purpose of the conversation, and so forth. As one court has put it:

> It is a fundamental and well recognized rule that in construing contracts, courts must look not only to the specific language employed but also to the subject matter contracted about, the relationship of the parties, the circumstances surrounding the transaction, or in other words place themselves in the same position the parties occupied when the contract was entered into and view the terms and intent of the agreement in the same light in which the parties did when the same was formulated and accepted.

Miller v. Miller, 134 F.2d 583, 588 (10th Cir. 1943). Does this comport with the court's reasoning in *Embry v. Hargadine*? In *Lucy v. Zehmer*?

(4) *Consequences of "Objective" Approach.* What is at stake in the choice between a "subjective" and an "objective" approach to contract? One consequence is revealed in the two cases just considered. If Mr. McKittrick

did not intend to renew Mr. Embry's contract and Mr. Zehmer did not intend to sell the land to Mr. Lucy and both acted honestly, the objective test excludes as irrelevant what they actually intended. It protects the plaintiff's reasonable understanding based upon what was said and done rather than what was thought. Put another way, if the court and jury find that the plaintiff's expectations based upon what was said or done were reasonable and the other requisites for contract formation are present, those expectations are protected. Thus, in *Embry*, Mr. Embry reasonably thought that his contract had been renewed. He remained on the job, thereby foregoing other opportunities, and was not informed about Mr. McKittrick's real intention until over two months later.

But are the facts so compelling in *Lucy?* At what point was Mr. Lucy first clearly informed that Zehmer did not intend to sell? Had Mr. Lucy changed his position in any substantial way at that time? Should that make any difference? Malcolm P. Sharp argues that in light of the costs to individual freedom, the objective test should be employed only where the defendant has carelessly used language that induced actual and justified reliance by the plaintiff. "Contracts" in *Mr. Justice Holmes: Some Modern Views,* 31 U. Chi. L. Rev. 268, 272–74 (1964).

A broader consequence is that the "objective" test affords the courts an opportunity to control or regulate individual exchange behavior through use of that great "collectivist," the "reasonable" person. As J. Willard Hurst puts it, the test satisfied a "particular need" in a market society "to create and maintain a framework of reasonably well defined and assured expectations as to the likely official and nonofficial consequences of private venture and decision." J.W. Hurst, Law and the Conditions of Freedom in Nineteenth Century America 21–22 (1956).

Grant Gilmore is more critical and argues that the objective test represents a move toward absolute liability. Under the guidance of O.W. Holmes, Jr. and Williston, it became the "great metaphysical solvent—the critical test for distinguishing between the false and the true." G. Gilmore, The Death of Contract 42–43 (1974). Morton Horwitz suggests that the development in the nineteenth century of an objective approach based on the external manifestation of mutual assent was a pro-commercial market attack on the theory of intrinsic value that lay at the base of the eighteenth century equity idea of contract. It expressed a market ideology, downplayed justice and gave courts an opportunity to prefer certain groups and interests as more reasonable than others. Morton Horwitz, *The Historical Foundations of Modern Contract Law*, 87 Harv. L. Rev. 917 (1974).

A final and more practical consequence concerns the problem of proof. As we shall see in the following materials, the focus is upon what was said and done rather than what was thought, and the question is what the plaintiff could reasonably understand or, in some cases, what the defendant knew or should have known that the plaintiff understood. Throughout, a question concerning the range of "objective" evidence relevant to the question of what the parties knew or should have known becomes critical. Also, who should make the critical determination of reasonableness, the court or the jury? Would you conclude, for example, that it would be sounder to limit extrinsic evidence to the words, written or spoken, of the parties and let the court decide who is reasonable? Or to have a more expansive concept of relevance with the jury as the ultimate arbiter of reasonableness?

(5) The objective approach has perhaps reached its apotheosis in the form of electronic contracting. Section 14 of the Uniform Electronic Transactions Act (UETA) (1999) provides:

> In an automated transaction, the following rules apply:
>
> (1) A contract may be formed by the interaction of electronic agents of the parties, even if no individual was aware of or reviewed the electronic agents' actions or the resulting terms and agreements.
>
> (2) A contract may be formed by the interaction of an electronic agent and an individual, acting on the individual's own behalf or for another person, including by an interaction in which the individual performs actions that the individual is free to refuse to perform and which the individual knows or has reason to know will cause the electronic agent to complete the transaction or performance.
>
> (3) The terms of the contract are determined by the substantive law applicable to it.

At the time of publication, the UETA had been enacted by forty-seven states.

(6) *A New "Toy Yoda."* Former Hooters waitress Jodee Berry sued her ex-employer for breaching its promise to give her a new car. Berry alleged that her manager, Jared Blair, had promised that the waitresses who sold the most beer at each participating Hooters during April 2001 would be entered in a drawing for a new Toyota. After Berry won the drawing, Blair presented her with a "toy Yoda." Berry sued for breach of contract and promissory fraud. Hooters ultimately settled the case. See *New Toyota to Replace Toy Yoda*, Bradenton Herald, May 10, 2002 ("Berry can now go to a local car dealership and pick out whatever type of Toyota she wants"). See also Keith A. Rowley, *You Asked for It, You Got It . . . Toy Yoda: Practical Jokes, Prizes and Contract Law*, 3 Nevada L.J. 526 (2003).

Comment: Objectivity Through the Looking Glass

Glanville Williams provides the following illustration of the objective approach in action:

> At that moment Alice's attention was distracted by the entry of a fluffy white figure. It was the White Rabbit, and a hum of conversation broke out from the gathering as he entered. He was dressed in immaculate morning dress, with a white camellia in the buttonhole, and immediately went up to where the little Lizard was sitting.
>
> Alice suddenly realized the reason for the whole proceeding. The White Rabbit was to be married to the Lizard. That was why he had been so agitated about the time. "Of course," Alice said aloud to herself when she made this discovery.
>
> "My dear, then I am so happy," said the Tortoise.

"Happy about what?" asked Alice.

"Happy that you will marry me," said the Tortoise.

"I will do nothing of the kind," replied Alice with dignity.

"But you just said so. I asked you to marry me and you replied 'Of course.'"

"I didn't hear you asking me to marry you, and I was talking to myself."

"Oh, Oh," cried the Tortoise, weeping bitterly. "I didn't know that. You couldn't expect me to." He sighed gustily, and looked up at Alice with a face all smeary with tears.

"Still," he added, brightening, "you have promised to marry me, you know."

"I have done nothing of the sort," said Alice.

"Yes you have," replied the Tortoise. "I thought you promised, therefore you did promise."

"How could I make you a promise," asked Alice, "when I was not speaking to you?"

"Anyway," said the Tortoise, "promise or not, I thought you were promising, and it was quite natural that I should think so. So you really ought to marry me."

Alice had never before considered marrying a Tortoise, but she had once kept one in her garden and had thought it quite a nice creature.

She did not feel at all certain what was the right thing to do in the circumstances, but the easiest thing seemed to be to do as the Tortoise wanted, and to see what would happen. Accordingly she replied, "Oh, all right," which made the Tortoise look contented.

Glanville Williams, *A Lawyer's Alice,* 9 Cambridge L.J. 171, 172 (1945).

PROBLEM: THE CASE OF THE HOLE-IN-ONE

Amos was playing in the East End Open Golf Tournament on the Fairview Golf Course. Fairview was a popular public course and hosted several corporate outings a month. When Amos arrived at the ninth tee, a 185 yard par three playing into the wind, he saw a new Chevrolet Beretta with signs posted reading as follows: "HOLE-IN-ONE Wins this 2003 Chevrolet Beretta GT Courtesy of Tiger Buick Chevy Pontiac $49 OVER FACTORY INVOICE." There were no observers on either the tee or at the green. Amos aced the hole (with a new hybrid club) and claimed the automobile as his prize. Tiger refused. It had offered the car as a prize for a charity golf tournament sponsored by the local Sertoma Club two days earlier and had neglected to remove the car and signs. Amos sues. What result?

The backdrop for the next cases is the American Civil War which disrupted the supply of cotton to England and spurred fluctuations in the commodity's price.

Raffles v. Wichelhaus

Court of Exchequer, 1864.
159 Eng.Rep. 375.

Declaration. For that it was agreed between the plaintiff and the defendants, to wit, at Liverpool, that the plaintiff should sell to the defendants, and the defendants buy of the plaintiff, certain goods, to wit, 125 bales of Surat cotton, guaranteed middling fair merchant's Dhollorah, to arrive ex "Peerless" from Bombay; and that the cotton should be taken from the quay, and that the defendants would pay the plaintiff for the same at a certain rate, to wit, at the rate of 17¼d. per pound, within a certain time then agreed upon after the arrival of said goods in England. Averments: that the said goods did arrive by the said ship from Bombay in England, to wit, at Liverpool, and the plaintiff was then and there ready and willing and offered to deliver the said goods to the defendants, & c. Breach: that the defendants refused to accept the said goods or pay the plaintiff for them.

Plea. That the said ship mentioned in the said agreement was meant and intended by the defendants to be the ship called the "Peerless," which sailed from Bombay, to wit, in October; and that the plaintiff was not ready and willing, and did not offer to deliver to the defendants any bales of cotton which arrived by the last-mentioned ship, but instead thereof was only ready and willing, and offered to deliver to the defendants 125 bales of Surat cotton which arrived by another and different ship, which was also called the "Peerless," and which sailed from Bombay, to wit, in December.

Demurrer, and joinder therein.

Milward, in support of the demurrer. The contract was for the sale of a number of bales of cotton of a particular description, which the plaintiff was ready to deliver. It is immaterial by what ship the cotton was to arrive, so that it was a ship called the "Peerless." The words "to arrive ex 'Peerless,'" only mean that if the vessel is lost on the voyage, the contract is to be at an end. [Pollock, C.B. It would be a question for the jury whether both parties meant the same ship called the "Peerless."] That would be so if the contract was for the sale of a ship called the "Peerless"; but it is for the sale of cotton on board a ship of that name. [Pollock, C.B. The defendant only bought that cotton which was to arrive by a particular ship. It may as well be said, that if there is a contract for the purchase of certain goods in warehouse A., that is satisfied by the delivery of goods of the same description in warehouse B.] In that case there would be goods in both warehouses; here it does not appear that the plaintiff had any goods on board the other "Peerless." [Martin, B. It is imposing on the defendant a contract different from that which he entered into. Pollock, C.B. It is like a contract for the purchase of wine coming from a particular estate in France or Spain, where there are two estates of that name.] The defendant has no right to contradict by parol evidence a written contract good upon the face of it. He does not impute misrepresentation or fraud, but only says that he fancied the ship was a different one. Intention is of no avail, unless stated at the time of the contract. [Pollock, C.B. One vessel sailed in October and the other in December.] The time of sailing is no part of the contract.

Mellish (Cohen with him), in support of the plea. There is nothing on the face of the contract to shew that any particular ship called the "Peerless" was meant; but the moment it appears that two ships called the "Peerless" were about to sail from Bombay there is a latent ambiguity, and parol evidence may be given for the purpose of shewing that the defendant meant one "Peerless," and the plaintiff another. That being so, there was no consensus ad idem, and therefore no binding contract. He was then stopped by the Court.

■ PER CURIAM. There must be judgment for the defendants.

Judgment for the defendants.

The October Peerless. One of the ships named "Peerless."

NOTES

(1) *Misunderstanding vs. Mistake.* As we will see in the next chapter, the common law holds that one or both parties' mistake about a material fact can render a contract voidable by the disadvantaged party. That is, the disadvantaged party has the power to undo the contract. The common law has distinguished misunderstanding, such as that in the *Peerless* case.

Misunderstanding involves not an erroneous belief about the world, but parties who attach different meanings to the same word or words. And courts have attached different legal effects to misunderstanding: rather than a voidable contract, where there is a material misunderstanding no contract comes into existence at all.

Is this a sensible distinction? More to the point, is the distinction between mistake and misunderstanding one that should make a legal difference?

(2) *How Objective is Objective (Again)?* The Second Restatement describes the *Peerless* rule as follows:

(1) There is no manifestation of mutual assent to an exchange if the parties attach materially different meanings to their manifestations and (a) neither party knows or has reason to know the meaning attached by the other; or (b) each party knows or each party has reason to know the meaning attached by the other.

(2) The manifestations of the parties are operative in accordance with the meaning attached to them by one of the parties if (a) that party does not know of any different meaning attached by the other, and the other knows the meaning attached by the first party; or (b) that party has no reason to know of any different meaning attached by the other, and the other has reason to know the meaning attached by the first party.

Restatement (Second) § 20; see also Id. § 201. Relatively few cases are decided under conditions of symmetric ignorance § 20(1)(a) and even fewer under conditions of symmetric "reason to know" § 20(1)(b). But see *Acme Investment, Inc. v. Southwest Tracor*, Inc., 911 F.Supp. 1261 (D. Neb. 1995) ("parties reasonably and objectively attached different meanings to the words ['within 30 days before' in option provision], and neither party knew or had reason to know of the meaning attached to the words by the other party"). Article 8(1) of the CISG provides: "For purposes of this Convention, statements made by and other conduct of a party are to be interpreted according to his intent where the other party knew or could not have been unaware what that intent was." Do these rules comport with the objective test for assent?

(3)   Oliver Wendell Holmes, the great proponent of the objective theory, attempted the following reconciliation with the *Peerless* decision:

It is commonly said that such a contract is void, because of mutual mistake as to the subject matter, and because therefore the parties did not consent to the same thing. But this way of putting it seems to me misleading. The law has nothing to do with the actual state of the parties' minds. In contract, as elsewhere, it must go by externals, and judge parties by their conduct. If there had been but one 'Peerless,' and the defendant had said 'Peerless' by mistake, meaning 'Peri,' he would have been bound. The true ground of the decision was not that each party meant a different thing from the other, as is implied by the explanation which has been mentioned, but that each said a different thing. The plaintiff offered one thing, the defendant expressed his assent to another.

O.W. Holmes, The Common Law 242 (Howe ed. 1963). Grant Gilmore observed that "[e]ven for Holmes this was an extraordinary tour de force. * * * The magician who could 'objectify' *Raffles v. Wichelhaus* could, the need arising, objectify anything." G. Gilmore, The Death of Contract 41 (1974).

Gilmore, in the course of tracing the development of the objective test, suggests that a break in the price of cotton on the Liverpool market between the arrival dates of the two ships Peerless may explain why the buyer rejected the goods and that the court, despite the probing of plaintiff's counsel Milward, remained unshaken in its conclusion that "Peerless" was a material term in the bargain in that it manifested the time for delivery of the goods.

> In any event it does not necessarily follow that a ship sailing from Bombay in October would have made port in Liverpool before a ship sailing in December. Either Peerless may have been a sailing vessel, subject to the vagaries of wind and weather—or both of them may have been—and either one (or both) may have called at intermediate ports. Since the buyer did not in his plea raise any issue about the time of the seller's tender in Liverpool, we may, I think, safely assume that there was no such issue to be raised. Furthermore, as Milward * * * correctly pointed out, there was no provision in the contract relating to the time of sailing from Bombay. * * * None of the judges thought of asking Mellish what would seem to be obvious questions. Would a reasonably well-informed cotton merchant in Liverpool have known that there were two ships called Peerless? Ought this buyer to have known? If in fact the October Peerless had arrived in Liverpool first, had the buyer protested the seller's failure to tender the cotton?

The failure to probe Mellish with the same zeal exhibited toward Milward suggests to Gilmore that the court was "entirely content to let the case go off on the purely subjective failure of the minds to meet at the time the contract was entered into." G. Gilmore, The Death of Contract 35–39 (1974).

The legal historian A.W.B. Simpson, in turn, had this to say about Gilmore's explanation:

> What of Grant Gilmore's discussion of the case in *The Death of Contract*? His speculations as to the background are inevitably misconceived, being unrelated to evidence. But his principal point was that the judges in the case foolishly failed to grasp, in spite of Clement Milward's attempts to put the point to them, that in terms of commercial understanding the identity of the carrying ship was immaterial. Its only relevance was to the risk of loss. He backs this claim up with a classic statement of the ahistorical attitude to legal sources: "In commercial understanding, that is exactly what the terms mean today and there is no reason to believe that they meant anything else a hundred years ago." And to be sure, Gilmore is correct in saying that there is no reason if we pay no attention

whatever to the historical context in which the dispute arose. But from what I have said, it is perfectly plain that in arrival contracts where ship and port were named, the identity of the carrying vessel was of central importance. It was the identity of the carrying vessel that fixed the time of arrival and delivery. In the volatile cotton market, that time was critical to the success or failure of the speculation. The reason why time was not specified directly was technological, and as the technology changed, 'shipments' were to be superseded by a new form of contract, 'deliveries,' which did directly specify time. Out of transactions involving this newer form of arrival contract was to develop the practice of futures trading, but that is another story.

A.W.B. Simpson, *Contracts for Cotton to Arrive: The Case of the Two Ships Peerless,* 11 Cardozo L. Rev. 287, 324 (1989).

(4) *Do We Need the* Peerless *Doctrine?* Farnsworth argues that the *Peerless* doctrine is unnecessary. Restatement (Second) § 20 effectively requires that each party's understanding be reasonable. In *Peerless* cases, neither party can prove that its interpretation is the right one. The buyer in *Peerless* will not be able to prove that the contract referred to the October ship named "Peerless," and the seller will not be able to prove that it referred to the December ship. If neither side can sustain its burden of proof, the contract is for practical purposes unenforceable. 2 E. Allan Farnsworth, Contracts, 4th ed. § 7.9 (2004).

(B) IMPLIED-IN-FACT AGREEMENT

Wrench, LLC v. Taco Bell Corp.

United States District Court, Western District of Michigan, 1999.
51 F.Supp.2d 840, reversed on other grounds, 256 F.3d 446 (6th Cir. 2001).

■ QUIST, DISTRICT JUDGE. This case is about two dogs: Gidget, a live female Chihuahua who stars in Defendant, Taco Bell Corp.'s ("Taco Bell"), popular television commercials as the suave male Chihuahua with a taste for Taco Bell food and known for the line, "Yo quiero Taco Bell" ("I want some Taco Bell"), and "Psycho Chihuahua," Plaintiffs' caricature of a feisty, edgy, confident Chihuahua with a big dog's attitude. The question at the bottom of this dispute is whether Taco Bell's live Chihuahua is Psycho Chihuahua incarnate. Plaintiffs contend that Taco Bell used their ideas based on Psycho Chihuahua to create the live Chihuahua character featured in Taco Bell's current advertising campaign and have sued Taco Bell alleging claims for breach of implied contract, misappropriation, conversion, and unfair competition. Now before the Court is Taco Bell's motion for summary judgment.

Facts

[Plaintiffs Thomas Rinks and David Shields, doing business as Wrench LLC, ("Wrench"), developed the character Psycho Chihuahua in 1995 as a clever, feisty dog, with a "do-not-back-down" attitude. Ed Alfaro and Rudy Pollack worked respectively as the Creative Services Manager and Vice President of Administration and Employee Programs of Taco Bell. After seeing Wrench's Psycho Chihuahua materials at a trade show in June 1996, Alfaro and Pollack began discussions with Wrench about using Psycho Chihuahua, a dog with an "insatiable craving" for Taco Bell. Shortly after, Alfaro (who was not part of the marketing group) began promoting within Taco Bell the idea of using Psycho Chihuahua as a corporate icon. Wrench sent art boards, marketing boards, merchandise, point of purchase drawings, and commercial scripts to Alfaro, and travelled to engage in several meetings regarding the Psycho Chihuahua character.

In November 1996, Wrench's licensing agents met with Alfaro, Pollack, and two others in Alfaro's Creative group to discuss potential advertising opportunities. After the meeting, Pollack requested a proposal of terms to use Psycho Chihuahua. Wrench's licensing agent sent a proposal on November 18. The proposal provided that Taco Bell would pay Wrench a percentage based upon the amount of money spent on advertising, a percentage of Taco Bell's retail licensing sales, and a percentage based on the cost of premiums, such as toys sold in Taco Bell restaurants. Taco Bell did not accept the proposal, although it did not explicitly reject it or indicate that it was ceasing further discussions. Alfaro held a meeting with Rinks and Shields in February 1997 to prepare a presentation for Alfaro's group. Alfaro continued to meet with Wrench and accept their materials through June of 1997.

In March 1997, Taco Bell hired a new advertising agency TBWA Chiat/Day. Chiat/Day assigned Chuck Bennett and Clay Williams as creative directors on the account. Bennett and Williams had previously used dogs, including a Chihuahua, in a commercial for Nissan. On June 2, 1997, Bennett and Williams presented several ideas to Taco Bell, including a commercial using a male Chihuahua who would pass up a female Chihuahua to get to a person eating Taco bell food. According to Bennett and Williams, they conceived the idea on a Sunday afternoon while having lunch at a Mexican restaurant. Chiat/Day presented the duo's Taco Bell Chihuahua commercial concept to focus groups.

In late June or July, at Alfaro's insistence, Wrench's Chihuahua materials were passed along to Chiat/Day with a note suggesting Psycho Chihuahua as an icon. In July, focus group reports showed positive response to Bennett and Williams' Chihuahua commercial, and Taco Bell launched its national campaign with their content in December 1997. Taco Bell continued to use the Chihuahua in its marketing through the time of the litigation.]

Discussion

In its prior opinion issued on June 18, 1998, this Court granted in part and denied in part Taco Bell's motion to dismiss, leaving intact the breach of implied contract, misappropriation, conversion, and unfair competition claims. * * *

In its present motion, Taco Bell contends that it is entitled to summary judgment because: (1) Plaintiffs have not established an implied in fact contract, or alternately, if they have, their claims are preempted by the Copyright Act because the implied contract creates legal rights that are equivalent to the rights within the general scope of copyright; (2) the concept of using a live Chihuahua in Taco Bell commercials was independently created by Chiat/Day; and (3) Plaintiffs' ideas were not novel.

As discussed below, the Court concludes that although Plaintiffs have presented sufficient evidence to establish an implied in fact contract, those claims are subject to copyright preemption. Although the Court concludes that Plaintiffs' claims are preempted, it will also address Taco Bell's independent creation and novelty arguments.

I.   Implied in Fact Contract

A contract between two parties may be implied in fact when the intention to enter into a contract "is not manifested by direct or explicit words between the parties," but instead is "gathered by implication or proper deduction from the conduct of the parties, language used, or things done by them, or other pertinent circumstances attending the transaction." Miller v. Stevens, 224 Mich. 626, 632 (1923); see also Featherston v. Steinhoff, 226 Mich. App. 584, 589 (1997) (noting that "where the parties do not explicitly manifest their intent to contract by words, their intent may be gathered by implication from their conduct, language, and other circumstances attending the transaction"). "An implied contract, like other contracts, requires mutual assent and consideration" and is treated in all other respects like an express contract. Spruytte v. Department of Corrections, 82 Mich. App. 145, 147 (1978). Therefore, "in determining whether there is a contract implied in fact, the courts look to the acts and conduct of the parties to determine whether the essential elements of an express contract have been established." Lawrence v. Ingham County Health Dep't Family Planning/Pre-Natal Clinic, 160 Mich. App. 420, 422 n.1 (1987).

Implied in fact contracts often arise where one accepts a benefit from another for which compensation is customarily expected. Thus, where evidence shows that the parties understood that compensation would be paid for services rendered, a promise to pay fair value may be implied, even if no agreement was reached as to price, duration, or other terms of the contract. See In re Estate of Morris, 193 Mich. App. 579, 583 (1992).

Taco Bell concedes that there is sufficient evidence in the record to support Plaintiff's allegation that the parties had a basic understanding that if Taco Bell used the Psycho Chihuahua idea, concept, or image, that Taco Bell would compensate Plaintiffs for the fair value of such use. However, Taco Bell argues that Plaintiffs cannot prove the existence of an implied in fact contract because the parties did not agree on any of the essential terms that would normally be included in a licensing agreement, such as price, duration, scope of use, and exclusivity.

Plaintiffs agree that no agreement was reached on the terms that would normally be included in a licensing agreement, but argue that their understanding with Alfaro that Taco Bell would pay Plaintiffs for the use of the Psycho Chihuahua materials if Taco Bell decided to use the Psycho Chihuahua idea is, by itself, sufficient to support an implied in fact contract.

Courts in several jurisdictions have agreed with Plaintiffs' contention that an implied in fact contract may be found when the parties have an understanding that the recipient of a valuable idea has accepted and used the idea, knowing that compensation is expected for use of the idea, without paying the purveyor of the idea. For example, in *Desny v. Wilder*, 46 Cal. 2d 715 (1956), the plaintiff, at defendant's request, prepared an abbreviated movie script for defendant. Plaintiff communicated a synopsis of the script to defendant's secretary. Shortly thereafter, the defendant produced a movie that closely resembled the plaintiff's story, but did not pay plaintiff for it. The California Supreme Court concluded that there was a genuine issue of material fact as to whether an implied in fact contract existed. See also Landsberg v. Scrabble Crossword Game Players, Inc., 802 F.2d 1193, 1196 (9th Cir. 1986) (stating that "California law allows for recovery for the breach of an implied-in-fact contract when the recipient of a valuable idea accepts the information knowing that compensation is expected, and subsequently uses the idea without paying for it").

The Alaska Supreme Court reached a similar conclusion in *Reeves v. Alyeska Pipeline Service Co.*, 926 P.2d 1130 (Alaska 1996) (per curiam). Citing 3 David Nimmer, Nimmer on Copyright, § 16.05[D], at 16–40 (1994), the court noted that "a request by the recipient for disclosure usually implies a promise to pay for the idea if the recipient uses it." *Reeves*, 926 P.2d at 1141. The court held that a reasonable jury could find that an implied in fact contract was created because the plaintiff had shown that the defendant solicited the plaintiff's idea and later asked for a written proposal. * * *

The Court agrees with the analysis in these cases and finds that Plaintiffs have presented sufficient evidence to create a genuine issue of material fact regarding whether an implied in fact contract existed between the parties. The cases establish that a plaintiff may support a claim of implied in fact contract by showing that the plaintiff disclosed an idea to the defendant at the defendant's request and the defendant understood that the plaintiff expected compensation for use of his ideas. Because Taco Bell concedes that there is sufficient evidence to support such an understanding in this case, Taco Bell's assertion that Plaintiffs cannot establish an implied in fact contract must be rejected.

* * *

[In Parts II, III, IV of the decision, the court found that despite the potential existence of an implied-in-fact contract, the plaintiff's claims were preempted by the federal Copyright Act. Plaintiffs state contract claim therefore could not be sustained, and the court granted summary judgment to the defendant Taco Bell.]

Conclusion

For the foregoing reasons, the Court will grant summary judgment to Taco Bell on all of Plaintiffs' claims.

"Gidget," the Taco Bell Chihuahua

NOTES

(1) Can you think of contexts where people volunteer information without expectation of seeking compensation? Any business contexts? Why didn't Taco Bell's rejection of Scanlan's proposal destroy the possibility of an implied-in-fact contract?

There is a rich history of claims that script ideas were stolen without compensation—on such movies as "The Last Samurai," "Coming to America," "Rounders," and even "America's Funniest Home Videos." Allison Weiner, *Lawyer Is Upping the Ante in Claims of Idea Theft in Hollywood*, New York Times A8 (July 27, 2006).

(2) *A Helpful Example?* The Second Restatement provides the following illustration of an implied-in-fact contract:

A, on passing a market, where he has an account, sees a box of apples marked "25 cts. each." A picks up an apple, holds it up so that a clerk of the establishment sees the act. The clerk nods, and A passes on. A has promised to pay twenty-five cents for the apple.

Restatement (Second) of Contracts § 4, ill. 2.

(3) *The Importance of Context.* Disputes frequently arise when an employer terminates an employee "at will." Assuming that the employer acted in good faith (this may be a limitation on the power to terminate), the

employee may try to prove that the original employment was for a stated duration, say three years, or that there was an implied promise not to terminate arbitrarily given during the employment in exchange for "independent" consideration by the employee. Such a case was *Pugh v. See's Candies, Inc.*, 116 Cal.App.3d 311 (1981), where the court concluded:

> Here . . . there were facts in evidence from which the jury could determine the existence of such an implied promise: the duration of appellant's employment, the commendations and promotions he received, the apparent lack of any direct criticism of his work, the assurances he was given, and the employer's acknowledged policies. While oblique language will not, standing alone, be sufficient to establish agreement, it is appropriate to consider the totality of the parties' relationship: Agreement may be " 'shown by the acts and conduct of the parties, interpreted in the light of the subject matter and of the surrounding circumstances.' " (Marvin v. Marvin (1976) 18 Cal.3d 660, 678, fn. 16) We therefore conclude that it was error to grant respondents' motions for nonsuit as to See's.

(4)   *Federal Preemption.* The federal Copyright Act is often an obstacle to bringing claims like those in *Wrench v. Taco Bell*. The Act preempts state implied-in-fact contract claims when the plaintiff's claim is "equivalent to any of the exclusive rights within the general scope of copyright." Del Madera Props. v. Rhodes & Gardner, Inc., 820 F.2d 973, 976 (9th Cir. 1987). But the 9th Circuit has enhanced the viability of such litigation by finding non-equivalence:

> The dispositive preemption issue in this case is whether the rights protected by [an implied-in-fact contract] claim are equivalent to the rights protected by copyright. To survive preemption, the state cause of action must protect rights that are qualitatively different from the rights protected by copyright: the complaint must allege an "extra element" that changes the nature of the action. Our prior decision in *Landsberg v. Scrabble Crossword Game Players, Inc.*, 802 F.2d 1193, 1196–97 (9th Cir. 1986), supports treating the implied promise to pay required . . . as an "extra element" for preemption purposes. In *Landsberg*, the defendants used the plaintiff's idea for a Scrabble strategy book without paying the expected compensation, and we applied California law to affirm a judgment of liability on a *Desny* claim. We explained that: "The contract claim turns not upon the existence of a [copyright] . . . but upon the implied promise to pay the reasonable value of the material disclosed." Id. at 1196.

Grosso v. Miramax Film Corp., 383 F.3d 965, 968 (9th Cir. 2004). The Sixth Circuit reversed the District Court's decision in *Wrench v. Taco Bell* on grounds that the Copyright Act did not in this case preempt the state contract claim. Wrench LLC v. Taco Bell Corp., 256 F.3d 446 (6th Cir. 2001). In 2003, a jury awarded plaintiffs $30.1 million in damages.

(C) WHAT IS AN OFFER?

An agreement requires communications between two parties. The common law traditionally viewed the process of reaching an agreement as requiring two steps: an offer by one party, and an acceptance by the other. While not every agreement has this structure, see UCC § 2–204, many do take the form of offer followed by acceptance. And the offer-acceptance framework helps us distinguish between different types of issues that relate to the agreement process. We begin with offers.

Joseph Lonergan v. Albert Scolnick

Court of Appeals of California, 1954.
129 Cal.App.2d 179.

■ BARNARD, PRESIDING JUSTICE. This is an action for specific performance or for damages in the event specific performance was impossible.

The complaint alleged that on April 15, 1952, the parties entered into a contract whereby the defendant agreed to sell, and plaintiff agreed to buy a 40-acre tract of land for $2,500; that this was a fair, just and reasonable value of the property; that on April 28, 1952, the defendant repudiated the contract and refused to deliver a deed; that on April 28, 1952, the property was worth $6,081; and that plaintiff has been damaged in the amount of $3,581. The answer denied that any contract had been entered into, or that anything was due to the plaintiff.

By stipulation, the issue of whether or not a contract was entered into between the parties was first tried, reserving the other issues for a further trial if that became necessary. The issue as to the existence of a contract was submitted upon an agreed statement, including certain letters between the parties, without the introduction of other evidence.

The stipulated facts are as follows: During March, 1952, the defendant placed an ad in a Los Angeles paper reading, so far as material here, "Joshua Tree vic. 40 acres, * * * need cash, will sacrifice." In response to an inquiry resulting from this ad the defendant, who lived in New York, wrote a letter to the plaintiff dated March 26, briefly describing the property, giving directions as to how to get there, stating that his rock-bottom price was $2,500 cash, and further stating that "This is a form letter." On April 7, the plaintiff wrote a letter to the defendant saying that he was not sure he had found the property, asking for its legal description, asking whether the land was all level or whether it included certain jutting rock hills, and suggesting a certain bank as escrow agent "should I desire to purchase the land." On April 8, the defendant wrote to the plaintiff saying "From your description you have found the property"; that this bank "is O.K. for escrow agent"; that the land was fairly level; giving the legal description; and then saying, "If you are really interested, you will have to decide fast, as I expect to have a buyer in the next week or so." On April 12, the defendant sold the property to a third party for $2,500. The plaintiff received defendant's letter of April 8, on April 14. On April 15 he wrote to the defendant thanking him for his letter "confirming that I was on the right land", stating that he would immediately proceed to have the escrow opened and would deposit $2,500 therein "in conformity with your offer", and asking the defendant to forward a deed with his instructions to the escrow agent. On April 17, 1952, the plaintiff started an escrow and placed in the hands of the escrow agent $100, agreeing to furnish an additional $2,400 at an unspecified time, with the provision that if the escrow was not closed by May 15, 1952, it should be completed as soon thereafter as possible unless a written demand for a return of the money or instruments was made by either party after that date. It was further stipulated that the plaintiff was ready and willing at all times to deposit the $2,400.

The matter was submitted on June 11, 1953. On July 10, 1953, the judge filed a memorandum opinion stating that it was his opinion that the letter of April 8, 1952, when considered with the previous correspondence, constituted an offer of sale which offer was, however, qualified and conditioned upon prompt acceptance by the plaintiff; that in spite of the condition thus imposed, the plaintiff delayed more than a week before notifying the defendant of his acceptance; and that since the plaintiff was aware of the necessity of promptly communicating his acceptance to the defendant his delay was not the prompt action required by the terms of the offer. Findings of fact were filed on October 2, 1953, finding that each and all of the statements in the agreed statement are true, and that all allegations to the contrary in the complaint are untrue. As conclusions of law, it was found that the plaintiff and defendant did not enter into a contract as alleged in the complaint or otherwise, and that the defendant is entitled to judgment against the plaintiff. Judgment was entered accordingly, from which the plaintiff has appealed.

The appellant contends that the judgment is contrary to the evidence and to the law since the facts, as found, do not support the conclusions of law upon which the judgment is based. It is argued that there is no conflict in the evidence, and this court is not bound by the trial court's construction of the written instruments involved; that the evidence conclusively shows that an offer was made to the plaintiff by the defendant, which offer was accepted by the mailing of plaintiff's letter of April 15; that upon receipt of defendant's letter of April 8th plaintiff had a reasonable time within which to accept the offer that had been made; that by his letter of April 15 and his starting of an escrow the plaintiff accepted said offer; and that the agreed statement of facts establishes that a valid contract was entered into between the parties. In his briefs the appellant assumes that an offer was made by the defendant, and confined his argument to contending that the evidence shows that he accepted that offer within a reasonable time.

There can be no contract unless the minds of the parties have met and mutually agreed upon some specific thing. This is usually evidenced by one party making an offer which is accepted by the other party. Section 25 of the Restatement of the Law on Contracts reads:

"If from a promise, or manifestation of intention, or from the circumstances existing at the time, the person to whom the promise or manifestation is addressed knows or has reason to know that the person making it does not intend it as an expression of his fixed purpose until he has given a further expression of assent, he has not made an offer."

The language used in *Niles v. Hancock*, 73 P. 840, 842, "It is also clear from the correspondence that it was the intention of the defendant that the negotiations between him and the plaintiff were to be purely preliminary," is applicable here. The correspondence here indicates an intention on the part of the defendant to find out whether the plaintiff was interested, rather than an intention to make a definite offer to the plaintiff. The language used by the defendant in his letters of March 26 and April 8 rather clearly discloses that they were not intended as an expression of fixed purpose to make a definite offer, and was sufficient to advise the plaintiff that some further expression of assent on the part of the defendant was necessary.

The advertisement in the paper was a mere request for an offer. The letter of March 26 contains no definite offer, and clearly states that it is a form letter. It merely gives further particulars, in clarification of the advertisement, and tells the plaintiff how to locate the property if he was interested in looking into the matter. The letter of April 8 added nothing in the way of a definite offer. It merely answered some questions asked by the plaintiff, and stated that if the plaintiff was really interested he would have to act fast. The statement that he expected to have a buyer in the next week or so indicated that the defendant intended to sell to the first-comer, and was reserving the right to do so. From this statement, alone, the plaintiff knew or should have known that he was not being given time in which to accept an offer that was being made, but that some further assent on the part of the defendant was required. Under the language used the plaintiff was not being given a right to act within a reasonable time after receiving the letter; he was plainly told that the defendant intended to sell to another, if possible, and warned that he would have to act fast if he was interested in buying the land.

Regardless of any opinion previously expressed, the court found that no contract had been entered into between these parties, and we are in accord with the court's conclusion on that controlling issue. The court's construction of the letters involved was a reasonable one, and we think the most reasonable one, even if it be assumed that another construction was possible.

The judgment is affirmed.

J.W. Southworth v. Joseph Oliver

Supreme Court of Oregon, 1978.
284 Or. 361.

[The defendant first approached the plaintiff, who was a neighbor, to determine his possible interest in purchasing grazing land identified on a map. The plaintiff was definitely interested, but price, other terms, and the treatment of certain grazing permits in which a neighbor was interested were not determined. Subsequently, the plaintiff telephoned the defendant to inquire how things were going and to renew his interest in the land and confirm that he had the money ready for a purchase. The defendant stated that he was making progress and would soon have information to establish the land value.]

* * * Several days later plaintiff received from defendants a letter dated June 17, 1976, which stated:

"Enclosed please find the information about the ranch sales that I had discussed with you previously.

"These prices are the market value according to the records of the Grant County Assessor.

"Please contact me if there are any questions."

There were two enclosures with that letter. The first was as follows:

"JOSEPH C. and ARLENE G. OLIVER

"200 Ford Road

"John Day, OR 97845

"Selling approximately 2933 Acres in Grant County in T. 16 S., R. 31 E., W.M. near Seneca, Oregon at the assessed market value of:

"LAND	$306,409
"IMPROVEMENTS	18,010
"Total	$324,419

"Terms available—29% down—balance over 5 years at 8% interest. Negotiate sale date for December 1, 1976 or January 1, 1977.

"Available after hay is harvested and arrangements made for removal of hay, equipment and supplies.

"ALSO: Selling

"Little Bear Creek allotment permit . . . 100 head @ $225

"Big Bear Creek allotment permit . . . . . 200 head @ $250"

The second enclosure related to "selling approximately 6365 acres" in Grant County near John Day—another ranch owned by the Oliver family.

Defendant Joseph Oliver testified that this letter and enclosures were "drafted" by his wife, defendant Arlene Oliver; that he then read and signed it; that he sent it not only to plaintiff, but also to Clyde Holliday and two other neighbors; that it was sent because "I told them I would send them all this information and we would go from there," that it was not made as an offer, and that it was his intention that the "property" and "permits" be transferred "together."

Upon receiving that letter and enclosures, plaintiff immediately responded by letter addressed to both defendants, dated June 21, 1976, as follows:

> "Re the land in Bear Valley near Seneca, Oregon that you have offered to sell; I accept your offer."

* * *

[On June 24 (apparently after consulting an attorney), the defendant mailed the following letter to the plaintiff:]

> "We received your letter of June 21, 1976. You have misconstrued our prior negotiations and written summaries of the lands which we and J.C. wish to sell. That was not made as or intended to be a firm offer of sale, and especially was not an offer of sale of any portion of the lands and permits described to any one person separately from the rest of the lands and permits described.

> "The memorandum of ours was for informational purposes only and as a starting point for further negotiation between us and you and the others also interested in the properties.

> "It is also impossible to tell from the attachment to our letter of June 17, 1976, as to the legal description of the lands to be sold, and would not in any event constitute an enforceable contract.

> "We are open to further negotiation with you and other interested parties, but do not consider that we at this point have any binding enforceable contract with you."

This lawsuit then followed.

* * *

In *Kitzke v. Turnidge*, 209 Or. 563, 573 (1957), this court quoted with approval the following rule as stated in 1 Williston on Contracts 49–50, § 22A (1957):

> " ' * * * In the early law of assumpsit stress was laid on the necessity of a promise in terms, but the modern law rightly construes both acts and words as having the meaning which a reasonable person present would put upon them in view of the surrounding circumstances. Even where words are used, "a contract includes not only what the parties said, but also what is necessarily to be implied from what they said." And it may be

said broadly that any conduct of one party, from which the other may reasonably draw the inference of a promise, is effective in law as such.' "

* * *

As also stated in 1 Restatement of Contracts § 25, Comment (a) (1932) as quoted by this court with approval in *Metropolitan Life Ins. Co. v. Kimball*, 163 Or. 31, 58 (1939):

> "It is often difficult to draw an exact line between offers and negotiations preliminary thereto. It is common for one who wishes to make a bargain to try to induce the other party to the intended transaction to make the definite offer, he himself suggesting with more or less definiteness the nature of the contract he is willing to enter into. Besides any direct language indicating an intent to defer the formation of a contract, the definiteness or indefiniteness of the words used in opening the negotiation must be considered, as well as the usages of business, and indeed all accompanying circumstances."

The difficulty in determining whether an offer has been made is particularly acute in cases involving price quotations, as in this case. It is recognized that although a price quotation, standing alone, is not an offer, there may be circumstances under which a price quotation, when considered together with facts and circumstances, may constitute an offer which, if accepted, will result in a binding contract. It is also recognized that such an offer may be made to more than one person. Thus, the fact that a price quotation is sent to more than one person does not, of itself, require a holding that such a price quotation is not an offer.

We agree with the analysis of this problem as stated in Murray on Contracts 37–40, § 24 (1977), as follows:

> "If *A* says to *B,* "I am going to sell my car for $500," and *B* replies, "All right, here is $500, I will take it," no contract results, assuming that *A's* statement is taken at its face value. *A's* statement does not involve any promise, commitment or undertaking; it is at most a statement of *A's present intention.* * * *

> " * * * However, a price quotation or advertisement may contain sufficient indication of willingness to enter a bargain so that the party to whom it is addressed would be justified in believing that his assent would conclude the bargain. * * *

> " * * * The basic problem is found in the expressions of the parties. People very seldom express themselves either accurately or in complete detail. Thus, difficulty is encountered in determining the correct interpretation of the expression in question. Over the years, some more or less trustworthy guides to interpretation have been developed.

"The first and strongest guide is that the particular expression is to be judged on the basis of what a reasonable man in the position of the offeree has been led to believe. This requires an analysis of what the offeree should have understood under all of the surrounding circumstances, with all of his opportunities for comprehending the intention of the offeror, rather than what the offeror, in fact, intended. This guide may be regarded as simply another manifestation of the objective test. Beyond this universally accepted guide to interpretation, there are other guides which are found in the case law involving factors that tend to recur. The most important of the remaining guides is the language used. If there are no words of promise, undertaking or commitment, the tendency is to construe the expression to be an invitation for an offer or mere preliminary negotiations in the absence of strong, countervailing circumstances. Another guide which has been widely accepted is the determination of the party or parties to whom the purported offer has been addressed. If the expression definitely names a party or parties, it is more likely to be construed as an offer. If the addressee is an indefinite group, it is less likely to be an offer. The fact that this is simply a guide rather than a definite rule is illustrated by the exceptional cases which must be noted. The guide operates effectively in relation to such expressions as advertisements or circular letters. The addressee is indefinite, and, therefore, the expression is probably not an offer. However, in reward cases, the addressee is equally indefinite and, yet, the expression is an offer. Finally, the definiteness of the proposal itself may have a bearing on whether it constitutes an offer. In general, the more definite the proposal, the more reasonable it is to treat the proposal as involving a commitment. * * * " (Footnotes omitted)

Upon application of these tests to the facts of this case we are of the opinion that defendants' letter to plaintiff dated June 17, 1976, was an offer to sell the ranch lands. We believe that the "surrounding circumstances" under which this letter was prepared by defendants and sent by them to plaintiff were such as to have led a reasonable person to believe that defendants were making an offer to sell to plaintiff the lands described in the letter's enclosure and upon the terms as there stated.

That letter did not come to plaintiff "out of the blue," as in some of the cases involving advertisements or price quotations. Neither was this a price quotation resulting from an inquiry by plaintiff. According to what we believe to be the most credible testimony, defendants decided to sell the lands in question and defendant Joseph Oliver then sought out the plaintiff who owned adjacent lands. Defendant Oliver told plaintiff that defendants were interested in selling that land, inquired whether plaintiff was interested, and was told by plaintiff that he was "very interested in the land," after which they discussed the particular lands to be sold. That conversation was terminated with the understanding that Mr. Oliver would "determine" the value and price of that land, i.e., "what he wanted for the land," and that plaintiff would undertake to arrange financing for the purchase of that land. In addition to that initial conversation, there was a further telephone conversation in which plaintiff called Mr. Oliver "to ask him if his plans for selling . . . continued to be in force" and was told "yes"; that there had been some delay in getting information from the assessor, as needed to establish the value of the land; and that plaintiff then told Mr. Oliver that "everything was in order" and that "he had the money available and everything was ready to go."

Under these facts and circumstances, we agree with the finding and conclusion by the trial court, in its written opinion, that when plaintiff received the letter of June 17th, with enclosures, which stated a price of $324,419 for the 2,933 acres in T 16 S, R 31 E., W.M., as previously identified by the parties with reference to a map, and stating "terms" of 29 percent down—balance over five years at eight percent interest—with a "sale date" of either December 1, 1976, or January 1, 1977, a reasonable person in the position of the plaintiff would have believed that defendants were making an offer to sell those lands to him.

This conclusion is further strengthened by "the definiteness of the proposal," not only with respect to price, but terms, and by the fact that "the addressee was not an indefinite group." See Murray, supra at 40.

As previously noted, defendants contend that they "obviously did not intend [the letter] as an offer." While it may be proper to consider evidence of defendants' subjective intent under the "objective test" to which this court is committed, it is the manifestation of a previous intention that is controlling, rather than a "person's actual intent." We do not agree with defendants' contention that it was "obvious" to a reasonable person, under the facts and circumstances of this case that the letter of January 17th was not intended to be an offer to sell the ranch lands to plaintiff.

We recognize, as contended by defendants, that the failure to use the word "offer," the fact that the letter included the "information" previously discussed between the parties, and the fact that plaintiff knew that the same information was to be sent to others, were important facts to be considered in deciding whether plaintiff, as a reasonable person, would have been led to believe that this letter was an "offer." See also Murray, supra, at 40. We disagree, however, with defendants' contention that these and other factors relied upon by defendants "preponderate" so as to require a holding that the letter of January 17th was not an offer.

The failure to add the word "offer" and the use of the word "information" are also not controlling, and, as previously noted, an offer may be made to more than one person. The question is whether, under all of the facts and circumstances existing at the time that this letter was received, a reasonable person in the position of the plaintiff would have understood the letter to be an offer by defendants to sell the land to him.

Defendants also contend that "plaintiff knew of the custom of transferring [Forest Service grazing] permits with the land and had no knowledge from the writing or previous talk that defendants were selling any cattle" (so as to provide such a basis for a transfer of the permits). Plaintiff testified, however, that at the time of the initial conversation, Mr. Oliver told plaintiff that he thought plaintiff "would be interested in the land and that Clyde would be interested in the permits." In addition, defendant Joseph Oliver, in response to questions by the trial judge, although denying that at that time he told plaintiff that he was "going to offer the permits to Mr. Holliday," admitted that he "knew Mr. Holliday was interested in the permits" and "could have" told plaintiff that he was "going to talk to Mr. Holliday about him purchasing the permits."

On this record we believe that plaintiff's knowledge of the facts noted by defendants relating to the transfer of such permits did not require a holding that, as a reasonable man, he did not understand or should not have understood that defendants' letter of June 17th was an offer to sell the ranch lands to him.

* * *

For all of these reasons, the decree of the trial court [granting specific performance] is affirmed.

NOTES

(1) What explains the different outcomes in *Lonergan* and *Southworth*? How does the analysis of the appellate court in *Lonergan* differ from that of the trial court in the case?

(2) Would the result likely have been different in *Lonergan* if the March 26th letter had not contained the sentence "This is a form letter"? Or, if the concluding sentence of the April 8th letter ("If you are really interested . . .") had been omitted? What if such language had been in the *Southworth* letter of June 24?

(3) *What is an offer?* Section 25 of the First Restatement, quoted in *Lonergan,* formulates what may be called the "fixed purpose" test. Is the focus upon the intention of the one who makes the manifestation, or is it upon the reasonable impression created in the mind of the other? The corresponding Restatement (Second) § 26 reads as follows: "A manifestation of willingness to enter into a bargain is not an offer if the person to whom it is addressed knows or has reason to know that the person making it does not intend to conclude a bargain until he has made a further manifestation of assent." More affirmatively, Section 24 of the Restatement defines an offer as "the manifestation of willingness to enter into a bargain, so made as to justify another person in understanding that his assent to that bargain is invited and will conclude it."

(4)   An offer has an immediate and significant legal effect. It enables or empowers the offeree to accept and thereby place the parties in a contractual relationship. Thus, an offer is said to confer upon the offeree a "power of acceptance." See Corbin § 11 (original edition). The power to offer is therefore a dangerous thing. By exercising it, one gives another the ability to put one under a new legal obligation. Does this suggest a narrow or a broad test for when an offer has been made?

PROBLEM: WHEN IS A PRICE SOLICITATION AN OFFER?

On September 21, 2002, Defendant, a grain dealer in Oregon, mailed a sample of clover seed to numerous parties, including Plaintiff, a grain wholesaler in Wisconsin. The following language appeared on the face of the envelope containing the seed: "Red clover. 50,000 lbs. like sample. I am asking 24 cents per pound, f.o.b. Amity, Oregon." Plaintiff acknowledged receipt of the sample and advised Defendant that it had accumulated quite a stock of clover seed and preferred to wait a while before "operating further."

After rains created unfavorable hulling conditions, Defendant, on October 4, contacted Plaintiff again and Plaintiff responded: "Special delivery sample received. Your price is too high. Wire firm offer, naming absolutely lowest f.o.b." On October 8, Defendant telegraphed Plaintiff as follows: "I am asking 23 cents per pound for the car of red clover seed from which your sample was taken. No. 1 seed, practically no plantain whatever. Have an offer 22¾ per pound, f.o.b. Amity."

Plaintiff promptly telegraphed "We accept your offer" and gave shipment instructions. Plaintiff also resold the clover seed to a third party at a profit. Defendant, however, sold the carload to another buyer and refused to deliver.

Plaintiff sued Defendant for damages. The court held that Defendant had made no offer and dismissed the petition. In essence, the trial court concluded that from the language "am asking" in the telegram of October 8 Defendant should have known that Plaintiff was still soliciting offers to buy rather than making an offer to sell. Even though all other material terms were stated, the implication was that Defendant must say "I will sell to you" before any offer to sell was made.

The case is now on appeal. A partner in the firm you work for has asked you, her associate, to help develop a theory to reverse the trial court. She has given you a Memo to get you going:

Memo:

1.   This case is governed by Article 2 of the UCC, but the code does not define offer. See UCC §§ 2–204, 2–205, 2–206, 2–207. How do we decide what is an offer in a purported contract to sell goods? My impression is that if Article 2 does not displace the common law, common law concepts apply under UCC § 1–103(b). If that is correct, what definition would apply? That in Restatement (Second) § 24? This result finds support in *Cannavino & Shea, Inc. v. Water Works Supply Corp.*, 361 Mass. 363 (1972) and, more recently, in

Architectural Metal Systems, Inc. v. Consolidated Systems, Inc., 58 F.3d 1227 (7th Cir. 1995) (Illinois law).

2.   The trial court's decision is somewhat rigid. Is there any way to persuade the appellate court that the reasonable meaning of language used early in the negotiations, i.e., "am asking," may change as the discussions proceed? For example, if the seller uses "am asking" late in the negotiations and knows or has reason to know that the buyer will take him seriously, is there any responsibility to clarify that the seller is still soliciting?

Morris Lefkowitz v. Great Minneapolis Surplus Store

Supreme Court of Minnesota, 1957.
251 Minn. 188.

■ MURPHY, JUSTICE. This is an appeal from an order of the Municipal Court of Minneapolis denying the motion of the defendant for amended findings of fact, or, in the alternative, for a new trial. The order for judgment awarded the plaintiff the sum of $138.50 as damages for breach of contract.

This case grows out of the alleged refusal of the defendant to sell to the plaintiff a certain fur piece which it had offered for sale in a newspaper advertisement. It appears from the record that on April 6, 1956, the defendant published the following advertisement in a Minneapolis newspaper:

"Saturday 9 A.M. Sharp 3 Brand New Fur Coats
Worth to $100.00 First Come
First Served $1 Each"

On April 13, the defendant again published an advertisement in the same newspaper as follows:

"Saturday 9 A.M. 2 Brand New Pastel Mink 3-Skin
Scarfs Selling for $89.50 Out they go Saturday.
Each . . . $1.00 1 Black Lapin Stole Beautiful, worth $139.50
. . . $1.00 First Come First Served"

The record supports the findings of the court that on each of the Saturdays following the publication of the above-described ads the plaintiff was the first to present himself at the appropriate counter in the defendant's store and on each occasion demanded the coat and the stole so advertised and indicated his readiness to pay the sale price of $1. On both occasions, the defendant refused to sell the merchandise to the plaintiff, stating on the first occasion that by a "house rule" the offer was intended for women only and sales would not be made to men, and on the second visit that plaintiff knew defendant's house rules.

The trial court properly disallowed plaintiff's claim for the value of the fur coats since the value of these articles was speculative and uncertain. The only evidence of value was the advertisement itself to the effect that the coats were "Worth to $100.00," how much less being speculative especially in view of the price for which they were offered for sale. With reference to the offer of the defendant on April 13, 1956, to sell the "1 Black Lapin Stole * * * worth $139.50 * * * " the trial court held that the value of this article was established and granted judgment in favor of the plaintiff for that amount less the $1 quoted purchase price.

1.   The defendant contends that a newspaper advertisement offering items of merchandise for sale at a named price is a "unilateral offer" which may be withdrawn without notice. He relies upon authorities which hold that, where an advertiser publishes in a newspaper that he has a certain quantity or quality of goods which he wants to dispose of at certain prices and on certain terms, such advertisements are not offers which become contracts as soon as any person to whose notice they may come signifies his acceptance by notifying the other that he will take a certain quantity of them. Such advertisements have been construed as an invitation for an offer of sale on the terms stated, which offer, when received, may be accepted or rejected and which therefore does not become a contract of sale until accepted by the seller; and until a contract has been so made, the seller may modify or revoke such prices or terms. . . . Craft v. Elder & Johnston Co., 34 Ohio L.A. 603; Annotation, 157 A.L.R. 746.

The defendant relies principally on *Craft v. Elder & Johnston Co.* supra. In that case, the court discussed the legal effect of an advertisement offering for sale, as a one-day special, an electric sewing machine at a named price. The view was expressed that the advertisement was (34 Ohio L.A. 605) "not an offer made to any specific person but was made to the public generally. Thereby it would be properly designated as a unilateral offer and not being supported by any consideration could be withdrawn at will and without notice." It is true that such an offer may be withdrawn before acceptance. Since all offers are by their nature unilateral because they are necessarily made by one party or on one side in the negotiation of a contract, the distinction made in that decision between a unilateral offer and a unilateral contract is not clear. On the facts before us we are concerned with whether the advertisement constituted an offer, and, if so, whether the plaintiff's conduct constituted an acceptance.

There are numerous authorities which hold that a particular advertisement in a newspaper or circular letter relating to a sale of articles may be construed by the court as constituting an offer, acceptance of which would complete a contract. . . .

The test of whether a binding obligation may originate in advertisements addressed to the general public is "whether the facts show that some performance was promised in positive terms in return for something requested." 1 Williston Contracts (Rev. ed.) § 27.

The authorities above cited emphasize that, where the offer is clear, definite, and explicit, and leaves nothing open for negotiation, it constitutes an offer, acceptance of which will complete the contract. The most recent case on the subject is *Johnson v. Capital City Ford Co.*, La.App., 85 So.2d 75, in which the court pointed out that a newspaper advertisement relating to the purchase and sale of automobiles may constitute an offer, acceptance of which will consummate a contract and create an obligation in the offeror to perform according to the terms of the published offer.

Whether in any individual instance a newspaper advertisement is an offer rather than an invitation to make an offer depends on the legal intention of the parties and the surrounding circumstances. . . . We are of the view on the facts before us that the offer by the defendant of the sale of the Lapin fur was clear, definite, and explicit, and left nothing open for negotiation. The plaintiff having successfully managed to be the first one to appear at the seller's place of business to be served, as requested by the advertisement, and having offered the stated purchase price of the article, he was entitled to performance on the part of the defendant. We think the trial court was correct in holding that there was in the conduct of the parties a sufficient mutuality of obligation to constitute a contract of sale.

2. The defendant contends that the offer was modified by a "house rule" to the effect that only women were qualified to receive the bargains advertised. The advertisement contained no such restriction. This objection may be disposed of briefly by stating that, while an advertiser has the right at any time before acceptance to modify his offer, he does not have the right, after acceptance, to impose new or arbitrary conditions not contained in the published offer. . . .

Affirmed.

NOTES

(1) *Advertisement: Making an Offer or Inviting an Offer?* Does the ordinary advertisement indicate a "fixed purpose" by the advertiser to be bound without a further expression of assent? In the view of most courts, the answer is no unless there are exceptional circumstances and the words are "plain and clear." Thus, in *O'Keefe v. Lee Calan Imports, Inc.*, 128 Ill.App.2d 410 (1970), the court held that the presumption against an offer was not overcome where a dealer's newspaper ad to sell a used car contained an error in the price (the intended price was $1,795; the advertised price was $1,095), the error was not the fault of the dealer, and there was "no reference to several material matters relating to the purchase of an automobile, such as equipment to be furnished or warranties to be offered by defendant. Indeed the terms were so incomplete and so indefinite that they could not be regarded as a valid offer."

On the other hand, in *Donovan v. RRL Corporation*, 26 Cal.4th 261 (2001) the court held that a proposal by a car dealer in a newspaper ad to sell a 1995 Jaguar XJ6 Vanden Plas for a stated price was an offer even though it did not request performance of a specific act (such as "first come first serve") to conclude the bargain. But the court interpreted the ad with provisions of the California Vehicle Code, which regulated the content of dealer advertising. As the court put it, "legislation can affect consumer expectations and cause reasonable individuals to regard certain retail advertisements for the sale of goods as offers to complete a bargain." 27 P.3d at 711. Since the ad mistakenly understated the intended price by $12,000, however, the court permitted the dealer to avoid the contract for mistake. See also Jay M. Feinman and Stephen R. Brill, *Is an Advertisement an Offer?: Why It Is, and Why It Matters*, 58 Hastings L.J. 61 (2006).

(2)   *False Advertising.* Did the fact that the plaintiff had been told of the "house" rule have any bearing on the outcome of *Lefkowitz*? Should it have? Did the court regard the advertisement as legally objectionable? In the *O'Keefe* case, supra note 1, *Lefkowitz* was distinguished on the ground that the defendant "deliberately used misleading advertising." States have statutes, modeled generally upon Section 5 of the Federal Trade Commission Act, prohibiting "unfair" and "deceptive" trade practices or acts. A few outlaw false advertising in general terms, while others specify types of prohibited advertising in a "laundry list" of per se violations. See generally J. Sheldon, Unfair and Deceptive Acts and Practices (4th ed. 2000). For more on these UDAP statutes, see Chapter Four, Section B.4.

(3)   *Bait and Switch.* If, in *Lefkowitz,* the advertisement was not used as a bona fide device to make or solicit offers but, rather, as a means of obtaining leads, we have an illustration of so-called "bait advertising." This practice can also be evidenced by a seller's refusal to show the advertised product, a demonstration of a defective product, a failure to have available for sale a sufficient quantity of the advertised product to meet reasonably anticipated demands, or a sales or compensation plan which has the effect of discouraging sales personnel from selling the advertised product. The Federal Trade Commission's Guides Against Bait Advertising, 16 C.F.R. § 238, define the practice as follows: "Bait advertising is an alluring but insincere offer to sell a product or service which the advertiser in truth does not intend or want to sell. Its purpose is to switch consumers from buying the advertised merchandise, in order to sell something else, usually at a higher price or on a basis more advantageous to the advertiser. The primary aim of a bait advertisement is to obtain leads as to persons interested in buying merchandise of the type so advertised." Neither the law of contracts nor ordinary judicial remedies have been of great help to the unwary consumer who is persuaded to make the switch. Some state legislatures have declared bait advertising to be a misdemeanor, subjecting the violator to criminal sanctions. Others have defined the practice as within their consumer protection statutes and thus made relief available to private parties harmed by the proscribed activity. The Federal Trade Commission, however, has been responsible for most of the litigation and activity in this area. It issues cease and desist orders and frequently seeks injunctive relief. See J. Sheldon, Unfair and Deceptive Acts and Practices § 4.6.1 (4th ed. 2000); Annot., *Validity, Construction, and Effect of State Legislation Regulating or Controlling "Bait-and-Switch" or Disparagement Advertising or Sales Practices*, 50 A.L.R.3d 1008 (1973). The prohibition of insincere

offers is analogous to the prohibition of insincere promises. See infra Chapter Four, Section B.4. Comment on Promissory Fraud.

PROBLEM: THE CASE OF THE STATUE OF LIBERTY COMMEMORATIVE COINS

In 1985, Congress authorized the sale of a limited number of specially-minted commemorative coins "to restore and renovate the Statue of Liberty and the facilities used for immigration at Ellis Island." Pursuant to this authorization, the U.S. Mint mailed certain advertising materials to previous customers/coin collectors. The materials, which included an order form, represented that if the Mint received "your reservation by December 31, 1985, you will enjoy a favorable Pre-Issue Discount saving you up to 16% on your coins." Payment could be made either by check, money order, or credit card.

Demand for the five-dollar gold coins far exceeded the 500,000 supply. News of the sell-out caused keen disappointment to would-be purchasers, especially in view of the fact that the gold coins had increased in value by approximately 200% within the first few months of 1986.

Mary and Anthony Mesaros were among the many disappointed parties. They had forwarded an order to the Mint on November 26, 1985, but the order was not filled, ostensibly because of an inability to process their credit card but really because of the deluge of orders. Mr. and Mrs. Mesaros filed a class action lawsuit against the government. Based on *Lefkowitz,* what are the prospects of recovery? See Mesaros v. United States, 845 F.2d 1576 (Fed.Cir. 1988).

John Leonard v. Pepsico, Inc.

United States District Court, Southern District of New York, 1999.
88 F.Supp.2d 116, aff'd, 210 F.3d 88 (2d Cir. 2000).

■ KIMBA M. WOOD, DISTRICT JUDGE. Plaintiff brought this action seeking, among other things, specific performance of an alleged offer of a Harrier Jet, featured in a television advertisement for defendant's "Pepsi Stuff" promotion. Defendant has moved for summary judgment pursuant to Federal Rule of Civil Procedure 56. For the reasons stated below, defendant's motion is granted.

I.   Background

This case arises out of a promotional campaign conducted by defendant, the producer and distributor of the soft drinks Pepsi and Diet Pepsi. The promotion, entitled "Pepsi Stuff," encouraged consumers to collect "Pepsi Points" from specially marked packages of Pepsi or Diet Pepsi and redeem these points for merchandise featuring the Pepsi logo. . . . While living in Seattle, plaintiff saw the Pepsi Stuff commercial that he contends constituted an offer of a Harrier Jet.

A.   The Alleged Offer

Because whether the television commercial constituted an offer is the central question in this case, the Court will describe the commercial in detail. The commercial opens upon an idyllic, suburban morning, where the chirping of birds in sun-dappled trees welcomes a paperboy on his morning route. As the newspaper hits the stoop of a conventional two-story house, the tattoo of a military drum introduces the subtitle, "MONDAY 7:58 AM." The stirring strains of a martial air mark the appearance of a well-coiffed teenager preparing to leave for school, dressed in a shirt emblazoned with the Pepsi logo, a red-white-and-blue ball. While the teenager confidently preens, the military drumroll again sounds as the subtitle "T-SHIRT 75 PEPSI POINTS" scrolls across the screen. Bursting from his room, the teenager strides down the hallway wearing a leather jacket. The drumroll sounds again, as the subtitle "LEATHER JACKET 1450 PEPSI POINTS" appears. The teenager opens the door of his house and, unfazed by the glare of the early morning sunshine, puts on a pair of sunglasses. The drumroll then accompanies the subtitle "SHADES 175 PEPSI POINTS." A voiceover then intones, "Introducing the new PepsiStuff catalog," as the camera focuses on the cover of the catalog.[2]

The scene then shifts to three young boys sitting in front of a high school building. The boy in the middle is intent on his Pepsi Stuff Catalog, while the boys on either side are each drinking Pepsi. The three boys gaze in awe at an object rushing overhead, as the military march builds to a crescendo. The Harrier Jet is not yet visible, but the observer senses the presence of a mighty plane as the extreme winds generated by its flight create a paper maelstrom in a classroom devoted to an otherwise dull physics lesson. Finally, the Harrier Jet swings into view and lands by the side of the school building, next to a bicycle rack. Several students run for cover, and the velocity of the wind strips one hapless faculty member down to his underwear. While the faculty member is being deprived of his dignity, the voiceover announces: "Now the more Pepsi you drink, the more great stuff you're gonna get."

The teenager opens the cockpit of the fighter and can be seen, helmetless, holding a Pepsi. "[L]ooking very pleased with himself," (Pl. Mem. at 3,) the teenager exclaims, "Sure beats the bus," and chortles. The military drumroll sounds a final time, as the following words appear: "HARRIER FIGHTER 7,000,000 PEPSI POINTS." A few seconds later, the following appears in more stylized script: "Drink Pepsi—Get Stuff." With that message, the music and the commercial end with a triumphant flourish.

Inspired by this commercial, plaintiff set out to obtain a Harrier Jet. Plaintiff explains that he is "typical of the 'Pepsi Generation' . . . he is

---

2   At this point, the following message appears at the bottom of the screen: "Offer not available in all areas. See details on specially marked packages."

young, has an adventurous spirit, and the notion of obtaining a Harrier Jet appealed to him enormously." Plaintiff consulted the Pepsi Stuff Catalog. The Catalog features youths dressed in Pepsi Stuff regalia or enjoying Pepsi Stuff accessories, such as "Blue Shades" ("As if you need another reason to look forward to sunny days."), "Pepsi Tees" ("Live in 'em. Laugh in 'em. Get in 'em."), "Bag of Balls" ("Three balls. One bag. No rules."), and "Pepsi Phone Card" ("Call your mom!"). The Catalog specifies the number of Pepsi Points required to obtain promotional merchandise. The Catalog includes an Order Form which lists, on one side, fifty-three items of Pepsi Stuff merchandise redeemable for Pepsi Points (the "Order Form"). Conspicuously absent from the Order Form is any entry or description of a Harrier Jet. The amount of Pepsi Points required to obtain the listed merchandise ranges from 15 (for a "Jacket Tattoo" ("Sew 'em on your jacket, not your arm.")) to 3300 (for a "Fila Mountain Bike" ("Rugged. All-terrain. Exclusively for Pepsi.")). It should be noted that plaintiff objects to the implication that because an item was not shown in the Catalog, it was unavailable.

The rear foldout pages of the Catalog contain directions for redeeming Pepsi Points for merchandise. These directions note that merchandise may be ordered "only" with the original Order Form. The Catalog notes that in the event that a consumer lacks enough Pepsi Points to obtain a desired item, additional Pepsi Points may be purchased for ten cents each; however, at least fifteen original Pepsi Points must accompany each order.

Although plaintiff initially set out to collect 7,000,000 Pepsi Points by consuming Pepsi products, it soon became clear to him that he "would not be able to buy (let alone drink) enough Pepsi to collect the necessary Pepsi Points fast enough." Reevaluating his strategy, plaintiff "focused for the first time on the packaging materials in the Pepsi Stuff promotion," and realized that buying PepsiPoints would be a more promising option. Through acquaintances, plaintiff ultimately raised about $700,000.

B.   Plaintiff's Efforts to Redeem the Alleged Offer

On or about March 27, 1996, plaintiff submitted an Order Form, fifteen original Pepsi Points, and a check for $700,008.50. Plaintiff appears to have been represented by counsel at the time he mailed his check; the check is drawn on an account of plaintiff's first set of attorneys. At the bottom of the Order Form, plaintiff wrote in "1 Harrier Jet" in the "Item" column and "7,000,000" in the "Total Points" column. In a letter accompanying his submission, plaintiff stated that the check was to purchase additional Pepsi Points "expressly for obtaining a new Harrier jet as advertised in your Pepsi Stuff commercial."

On or about May 7, 1996, defendant's fulfillment house rejected plaintiff's submission and returned the check, explaining that:

The item that you have requested is not part of the Pepsi Stuff collection. It is not included in the catalogue or on the order form, and only catalogue merchandise can be redeemed under this program. The Harrier jet in the Pepsi commercial is fanciful and is simply included to create a humorous and entertaining ad. We apologize for any misunderstanding or confusion that you may have experienced and are enclosing some free product coupons for your use.

Plaintiff's previous counsel responded on or about May 14, 1996, as follows:

Your letter of May 7, 1996 is totally unacceptable. We have reviewed the video tape of the Pepsi Stuff commercial . . . and it clearly offers the new Harrier jet for 7,000,000 Pepsi Points. Our client followed your rules explicitly. . . . This is a formal demand that you honor your commitment and make immediate arrangements to transfer the new Harrier jet to our client. If we do not receive transfer instructions within ten (10) business days of the date of this letter you will leave us no choice but to file an appropriate action against Pepsi. . . .

This letter was apparently sent onward to the advertising company responsible for the actual commercial, BBDO New York ("BBDO"). In a letter dated May 30, 1996, BBDO Vice President Raymond E. McGovern, Jr., explained to plaintiff that:

I find it hard to believe that you are of the opinion that the Pepsi Stuff commercial ("Commercial") really offers a new Harrier Jet. The use of the Jet was clearly a joke that was meant to make the Commercial more humorous and entertaining. In my opinion, no reasonable person would agree with your analysis of the Commercial. * * *

Litigation of this case initially involved two lawsuits, the first a declaratory judgment action brought by PepsiCo in this district (the "declaratory judgment action"), and the second an action brought by Leonard in Florida state court (the "Florida action"). PepsiCo brought suit in this Court on July 18, 1996, seeking a declaratory judgment stating that it had no obligation to furnish plaintiff with a Harrier Jet. * * * The Florida suit was transferred to this Court. * * *

* * *

B.   Defendant's Advertisement Was Not an Offer

1.   Advertisements as Offers

The general rule is that an advertisement does not constitute an offer. The Restatement (Second) of Contracts explains that:

Advertisements of goods by display, sign, handbill, newspaper, radio or television are not ordinarily intended or understood as offers to sell. The same is true of catalogues, price lists and circulars, even though the terms of suggested bargains may be stated in some detail. It is of course possible to make an offer by an advertisement directed to the general public, but there must ordinarily be some language of commitment or some invitation to take action without further communication.

Restatement (Second) of Contracts § 26 cmt. b (1979). Similarly, a leading treatise notes that:

> It is quite possible to make a definite and operative offer to buy or sell goods by advertisement, in a newspaper, by a handbill, a catalog or circular or on a placard in a store window. It is not customary to do this, however; and the presumption is the other way. . . . Such advertisements are understood to be mere requests to consider and examine and negotiate; and no one can reasonably regard them as otherwise unless the circumstances are exceptional and the words used are very plain and clear.

1 Arthur Linton Corbin & Joseph M. Perillo, Corbin on Contracts § 2.4, at 116–17 (rev. ed.1993). * * *

An advertisement is not transformed into an enforceable offer merely by a potential offeree's expression of willingness to accept the offer through, among other means, completion of an order form. * * * The exception to the rule that advertisements do not create any power of acceptance in potential affairs is where the advertisement is "clear, definite, and explicit, and leaves nothing open for negotiation," in that circumstance, "it constitutes an offer, acceptance of which will complete the contract." Lefkowitz v. Great Minneapolis Surplus Store, 251 Minn. 188 (1957). [The court discussed the *Lefkowitz* case, supra.]

The present case is distinguishable from *Lefkowitz*. First, the commercial cannot be regarded in itself as sufficiently definite, because it specifically reserved the details of the offer to a separate writing, the Catalog. The commercial itself made no mention of the steps a potential offeree would be required to take to accept the alleged offer of a Harrier Jet. The advertisement in *Lefkowitz*, in contrast, "identified the person who could accept." Second, even if the Catalog had included a Harrier Jet among the items that could be obtained by redemption of Pepsi Points, the advertisement of a Harrier Jet by both television commercial and catalog would still not constitute an offer. As the *Mesaros* court explained, the absence of any words of limitation such as "first come, first served," renders the alleged offer sufficiently indefinite that no contract could be formed. See Mesaros, 845 F.2d at 1581. "A customer would not usually have reason to believe that the shopkeeper intended exposure to the risk of a multitude of acceptances resulting in a number of contracts exceeding the shopkeeper's inventory." Farnsworth, supra, at 242. There was no such danger in *Lefkowitz*, owing to the limitation "first come, first served."

The Court finds, in sum, that the Harrier Jet commercial was merely an advertisement. The Court now turns to the line of cases upon which plaintiff rests much of his argument.

2.   Rewards as Offers

In opposing the present motion, plaintiff largely relies on a different species of unilateral offer, involving public offers of a reward for performance of a specified act. Because these cases generally involve public declarations regarding the efficacy or trustworthiness of specific products, one court has aptly characterized these authorities as "prove me wrong" cases. See Rosenthal v. Al Packer Ford, 36 Md.App. 349 (1977). The most venerable of these precedents is the case of *Carlill v. Carbolic Smoke Ball Co.*, 1 Q.B. 256 (Court of Appeal, 1892), a quote from which heads plaintiff's memorandum of law: "[I]f a person chooses to make extravagant promises . . . he probably does so because it pays him to make them, and, if he has made them, the extravagance of the promises is no reason in law why he should not be bound by them." Carbolic Smoke Ball, 1 Q.B. at 268 (Bowen, L.J.).

Other "reward" cases underscore the distinction between typical advertisements, in which the alleged offer is merely an invitation to negotiate for purchase of commercial goods, and promises of reward, in which the alleged offer is intended to induce a potential offeree to perform a specific action, often for noncommercial reasons. In *Newman v. Schiff*, 778 F.2d 460 (8th Cir. 1985), for example, the Fifth Circuit held that a tax protestor's assertion that, "If anybody calls this show . . . and cites any section of the code that says an individual is required to file a tax return, I'll pay them $100,000," would have been an enforceable offer had the plaintiff called the television show to claim the reward while the tax protestor was appearing. . . . The court noted that, like *Carbolic Smoke Ball*, the case "concerns a special type of offer: an offer for a reward." *James v. Turilli*, 473 S.W.2d 757 (Mo.Ct.App. 1971), arose from a boast by defendant that the "notorious Missouri desperado" Jesse James had not been killed in 1882, as portrayed in song and legend, but had lived under the alias "J. Frank Dalton" at the "Jesse James Museum" operated by none other than defendant. Defendant offered $10,000 "to anyone who could prove me wrong." The widow of the outlaw's son demonstrated, at trial, that the outlaw had in fact been killed in 1882. On appeal, the court held that defendant should be liable to pay the amount offered.

In the present case, the Harrier Jet commercial did not direct that anyone who appeared at Pepsi headquarters with 7,000,000 Pepsi Points on the Fourth of July would receive a Harrier Jet. Instead, the commercial urged consumers to accumulate Pepsi Points and to refer to the Catalog to determine how they could redeem their Pepsi Points. The commercial sought a reciprocal promise, expressed through acceptance of, and compliance with, the terms of the Order Form. As noted previously, the Catalog contains no mention of the Harrier Jet. Plaintiff states that he "noted that the Harrier Jet was not among the items described in the catalog, but this did not affect [his] understanding of the offer." It should have.[10]

* * *

C.   An Objective, Reasonable Person Would Not Have Considered the Commercial an Offer

Plaintiff's understanding of the commercial as an offer must also be rejected because the Court finds that no objective person could reasonably have concluded that the commercial actually offered consumers a Harrier Jet.

1.   Objective Reasonable Person Standard

In evaluating the commercial, the Court must not consider defendant's subjective intent in making the commercial, or plaintiff's subjective view of what the commercial offered, but what an objective, reasonable person would have understood the commercial to convey. * * *

If it is clear that an offer was not serious, then no offer has been made: What kind of act creates a power of acceptance and is therefore an offer? It must be an expression of will or intention. It must be an act that leads the offeree reasonably to conclude that a power to create a contract is conferred. * * *

2.   Necessity of a Jury Determination

Plaintiff also contends that summary judgment is improper because the question of whether the commercial conveyed a sincere offer can be answered only by a jury. Relying on dictum from *Gallagher v. Delaney*, 139 F.3d 338 (2d Cir. 1998), plaintiff argues that a federal judge comes from a "narrow segment of the enormously broad American socio-economic spectrum," and, thus, that the question whether the commercial constituted a serious offer must be decided by a jury composed of, inter alia, members of the "Pepsi Generation," who are, as plaintiff puts it, "young, open to adventure, willing to do the unconventional." Plaintiff essentially argues that a federal judge would view his claim differently than fellow members of the "Pepsi Generation."

Plaintiff's argument that his claim must be put to a jury is without merit. Gallagher involved a claim of sexual harassment in which the defendant allegedly invited plaintiff to sit on his lap, gave her inappropriate Valentine's Day gifts, told her that "she brought out feelings that he had not had since he was sixteen," and "invited her to help him feed the ducks in the pond, since he was 'a bachelor for the evening.'" Gallagher, 139 F.3d at 344. The court concluded that a jury determination was particularly appropriate because a federal judge lacked "the current real-life experience required in interpreting subtle

---

[10]   In his affidavit, plaintiff places great emphasis on a press release written by defendant, which characterizes the Harrier Jet as "the ultimate Pepsi Stuff award." Plaintiff simply ignores the remainder of the release, which makes no mention of the Harrier Jet even as it sets forth in detail the number of points needed to redeem other merchandise.

sexual dynamics of the workplace based on nuances, subtle perceptions, and implicit communications." Id. at 342. This case, in contrast, presents a question of whether there was an offer to enter into a contract, requiring the Court to determine how a reasonable, objective person would have understood defendant's commercial. Such an inquiry is commonly performed by courts on a motion for summary judgment.

3.   Whether the Commercial Was "Evidently Done In Jest"

Plaintiff's insistence that the commercial appears to be a serious offer requires the Court to explain why the commercial is funny. Explaining why a joke is funny is a daunting task; as the essayist E.B. White has remarked, "Humor can be dissected, as a frog can, but the thing dies in the process. . . ." The commercial is the embodiment of what defendant appropriately characterizes as "zany humor." * * *

First, the . . . implication of the commercial is that Pepsi Stuff merchandise will inject drama and moment into hitherto unexceptional lives. . . . A reasonable viewer would understand such advertisements as mere puffery, not as statements of fact, see, e.g., Hubbard v. General Motors Corp., 95 Civ. 4362 (S.D.N.Y. May 22, 1996) (advertisement describing automobile as "Like a Rock," was mere puffery, not a warranty of quality); and refrain from interpreting the promises of the commercial as being literally true.

Second, the callow youth featured in the commercial is a highly improbable pilot. . . .

Third, the notion of traveling to school in a Harrier Jet is an exaggerated adolescent fantasy. . . .

Fourth, . . . [i]n light of the Harrier Jet's well-documented function in attacking and destroying surface and air targets, armed reconnaissance and air interdiction, and offensive and defensive anti-aircraft warfare, depiction of such a jet as a way to get to school in the morning is clearly not serious even if, as plaintiff contends, the jet is capable of being acquired "in a form that eliminates [its] potential for military use."

Fifth, the number of Pepsi Points the commercial mentions as required to "purchase" the jet is 7,000,000. To amass that number of points, one would have to drink 7,000,000 Pepsis (or roughly 190 Pepsis a day for the next hundred years—an unlikely possibility), or one would have to purchase approximately $700,000 worth of Pepsi Points. The cost of a Harrier Jet is roughly $23 million dollars, a fact of which plaintiff was aware when he set out to gather the amount he believed necessary to accept the alleged offer. Even if an objective, reasonable person were not aware of this fact, he would conclude that purchasing a fighter plane for $700,000 is a deal too good to be true.

Plaintiff argues that a reasonable, objective person would have understood the commercial to make a serious offer of a Harrier Jet because there was "absolutely no distinction in the manner" in which the items in the commercial were presented. Plaintiff also relies upon a press release highlighting the promotional campaign, issued by defendant, in which "[n]o mention is made by [defendant] of humor, or anything of the sort." * * * In light of the obvious absurdity of the commercial, the Court rejects plaintiff's argument that the commercial was not clearly in jest.

* * * Finally, plaintiff's assertion that he should be afforded an opportunity to determine whether other individuals also tried to accumulate enough Pepsi Points to "purchase" a Harrier Jet is unavailing. The possibility that there were other people who interpreted the commercial as an "offer" of a Harrier Jet does not render that belief any more or less reasonable. The alleged offer must be evaluated on its own terms. Having made the evaluation, the Court concludes that summary judgment is appropriate on the ground that no reasonable, objective person would have understood the commercial to be an offer.

* * *

For the reasons stated above, the Court grants defendant's motion for summary judgment. The Clerk of Court is instructed to close these cases. Any pending motions are moot.

NOTES

(1)   Of what relevance should be the commercial's characterization of "*Offer* not available in all areas"?

(2)   *The Big Check.* In December 1995, the Republican National Committee ran full page advertisements in *USA Today* and *Roll Call* which showed a picture of RNC Chair Haley Barbour holding an oversized $1 million check. The copy of the ad read in part: "Heard the one about Republicans 'cutting' Medicare? The fact is Republicans are increasing Medicare spending by more than half. I'm Haley Barbour, and I'm so sure of that fact I'm willing to give you this check for a million dollars if you can prove me wrong." In another portion of the add enclosed with the filigree of a legal form, entitled "Million Dollar Medicare Challenge," the advertisement said:

> The Republican National Committee will present a cashier's check for $1 million to the first American who can prove the following statement is false: "In November 1995, the U.S. House and Senate passed a balanced budget bill. It increases total federal spending on Medicare by more than 50% from 1995 to 2002 pursuant to Congressional Budget Office standards."

More than 80 people sent in responses claiming the prize. Douglas Frymire, a 70-year-old from Idaho, claimed the statement was false because Congress cannot guarantee budget numbers for more than one year. Leslie Kee, a 42-year old high school teacher from Wyoming, argued that if you compare the Republican plan with what would already have been allocated to Medicare under existing law, the GOP proposal would actually *reduce* spending. Charles Resor argued that a bill doesn't actually increase anything until it becomes law. Representative Gene Taylor argued the statement was false because the "balanced budget bill" did not actually balance the budget. The RNC refused to pay and one of the claimants, Bob Shireman, an analyst at the U.S. Office of Management and Budget, filed a breach-of-contract suit against Barbour and the RNC in Washington, D.C. Superior Court. The RNC responded in 1997 by filing a declaratory judgment action against all 80 claimants in Jackson, Mississippi. The suit argues that the advertisement was a "mere puff." The District Court for the District of Columbia refused to grant summary judgment that the ad "was merely a 'parody' and not binding on the RNC" but did grant summary judgment because "the Challenge Statement was not false." Republican National Committee and Haley Barbour v. Taylor, 299 F.3d 887 (D.C.Cir. 2002). See John Solomon, *Prize Fight*, The New Republic 23 (Nov. 15, 1999).

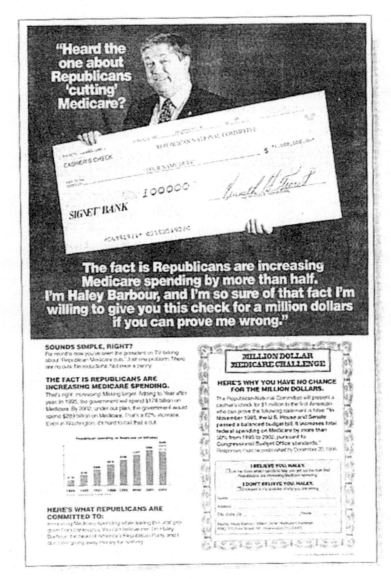

PROBLEM: THE CASE OF THE "HIS AND HERS" MERCEDES

In 1993, Nationwide Insurance announced a contest to create a theme or a slogan for the 1994 South Central Regional Offices claims convention. Employees were urged to submit a slogan limited to not more than eight words. Prizes were involved:

> Here's what you could win: His and Hers Mercedes. An all expense paid trip for two around the world. Additional prizes to be announced. (All prizes subject to availability).

Mears submitted the slogan "At the top and still climbing," and shortly thereafter left the employ of Nationwide. Later he was informed that he had won the contest and (according to Mears) was told that he had won two Mercedes-Benz automobiles. Still later, he was told that he might not receive the autos because the theme might change before the Convention, he was no longer employed by Nationwide, and the contest was a joke. Nationwide, however, did use the theme (it dominated the convention) but refused to deliver the cars. Rather, they offered Mears a restaurant gift.

Mears, claiming that he had accepted an offer, sued for breach of contract, claiming either the autos themselves or damages. What result? See *Mears v. Nationwide Mutual Insurance Co.*, 91 F.3d 1118 (8th Cir. 1996).

Comment: Auctions and Sealed Bidding

An auction is a contracting technique invoked most frequently by sellers of goods or land to stimulate price competition. The seller, by soliciting bids from a group of prospective buyers, seeks to develop a market whose prices are determined by on-the-spot competitive bidding. Auctions dispose of real estate, livestock, household goods, antiques, wine, and works of art. In addition to owners, they are used by repossessing creditors, public officials, such as the sheriff, and executors of decedents' estates. The terms and procedures of an auction are usually determined by the advertisement, trade usage or practice and statutes. The terms of the sale are normally set out in advertisements and other writings before the auction is conducted. See, e.g., Dulman v. Martin Fein & Co., Inc., 411 N.Y.S.2d 358 (1978); Restatement (Second) § 28(2). Often, auction disputes involve a combination of advertisement, trade usage and statutory controls and raise issues of agency law (the auctioneer is agent for a principal who may be undisclosed) and property ownership (sometimes stolen goods are sold by auction).

In most auctions the only important term left for agreement is price. The prospective buyer should understand that the function of an auction is to generate price competition and that there is, therefore, some risk that the property will be withdrawn before being sold. The law supports the seller: the consistent legal conclusion has been that, in the absence of agreement to the contrary, an advertisement describing property to be sold to the highest bidder at a stated time and place is not an offer, even though the power to withdraw the goods is *not* expressly reserved. The advertisement merely solicits offers that the seller is privileged to accept or reject. See UCC § 2–328(3); Restatement (Second) § 28(1)(a); Weinstein v. Green, 347 Mass. 580 (1964). Unless otherwise agreed, the offer is accepted when the auctioneer "so announces by the fall of the hammer or in other customary manner." UCC § 2–328(2).

On the other hand, if the sale is announced to be "without reserve," then the sale must be made to the highest bidder. In the language of UCC § 2–328(3): "In an auction without reserve, after the auctioneer calls for bids on an article or lot, that article or lot cannot be withdrawn unless no bid is made within a reasonable time." Accord Pitchfork Ranch Co. v. Bar TL, 615 P.2d 541 (Wyo. 1980); Zuhak v. Rose, 264 Wis. 286 (1953) (high bidder gets specific performance after dissatisfied owner of land discharges auctioneer). Moreover, in an auction without reserve the seller cannot bid. See Pyles v. Goller, 109 Md.App. 71 (1996).

Does this mean that the advertisement is converted into an offer that is accepted by the bidder, subject to discharge if a higher bid is made? Or, has the high bidder simply made an offer that the auctioneer has a legal duty to accept? One court has stated that the best explanation is "that the owner, by making such an announcement, enters into a collateral contract with all persons bidding at the auction that he will not withdraw the property for sale, regardless of how low the highest bid may be." Drew v. John Deere Company of Syracuse, 241 N.Y.S.2d 267, 269 (1963). But to further complicate matters, UCC § 2–328(3) provides that the high bidder "may retract this bid until the auctioneer's announcement of completion of the sale" and that the retraction does not revive any previous bids that have lapsed upon the making of a higher bid. Accord Restatement (Second) § 28(1)(c). Thus, if it is a "collateral" contract, it binds the auctioneer but not the high bidder—at least until the hammer falls.

At first blush these rules appear to be anomalous deviations from normal contract formation procedures. But they serve a useful purpose in auctions. The "without reserve" language informs prospective bidders that the owner is dispensing with a broad power to withdraw goods once they are put up for sale—that he or she is willing to take the highest bid produced by competition. This information may induce greater reliance on the part of individual bidders in attending the auction. The bidder's withdrawal privilege affords some measure of protection from a hasty bid made in the heat of competition. There is some time to reflect and repent before the hammer falls. In view of this, is the fact that bidders have more mobility than sellers in "without reserve" auctions disturbing? Anomalous?

A bid in a sealed auction of "X dollars over the highest bid" is commonly referred to as a "sharp" bid, and the practice has been soundly condemned. Such a bid is said to be unfair to other bidders, by allowing the "sharp" bidder to appropriate the judgment of the other bidders, as well as unfair to the seller, in that, if allowed, it would discourage and drive off sum-certain bidders. *Webster v. French*, 11 Ill. 254 (1849) (contrary to public policy and void); *Casey v. Independence County,* 109 Ark. 11 (1913) ("no bid at all," being both unfair and incomplete). Sharp bidding is clearly a fraudulent practice, and with respect to a public sale, such a bid is void from its inception. It is illegal *per se.* In case of a private sale, it has been held that while concealed sharp bidding taints a resulting contract with fraud, it is not void but voidable at the election of the defrauded parties. Ordinarily, the defrauded parties would be the seller and the highest sum-certain bidder. See Short v. Sun Newspapers, Inc., 300 N.W.2d 781 (Minn. 1980).

Government entities at all levels employ other competitive procedures in procuring supplies and services. The Competition in Contracting Act, enacted by Congress in 1984, is designed to further encourage competitive practice by the federal government. Title VII of Division B of the Deficit Reduction Act of 1984, P.L. 98–369, 98 Stat. 494. Under the Act, "sealed bidding" must be utilized (1) if time permits the solicitation, submission, and evaluation of sealed bids, (2) the award will be made on the basis of price and other price-related factors, (3) it is not necessary to conduct discussion with the responding sources about their bids, and (4) there is a reasonable expectation of receiving more than one sealed bid. Otherwise, the contract is negotiated through the solicitation of competitive proposals from private contractors.

A variation of the auction technique, sealed bidding unfolds in a series of distinct steps. First, contracting officials prepare an invitation for bids (IFB) which describes the government's needs, states the basic terms and conditions (quantity, time and place of delivery, method of payments, etc.), and incorporates by reference applicable standard forms of the government. Second, the IFB is distributed or otherwise publicized to a sufficient number of prospects so as to ensure adequate competition. Third, bidders prepare and submit their bids. This bid is the offer. To be eligible for acceptance, it must be submitted on time and conform in every material respect to the IFB. That is, the bidder must submit a responsive bid. Fourth, the bids are opened and evaluated by the government. After bid opening, the bidder cannot change the bid or withdraw the offer unless a mistake has been made and some rather rigid conditions are satisfied. Unlike the private auction, the offeror may not withdraw after bids are opened, but the offeree may reject all bids if there is a "compelling" reason for doing so; e.g., supplies or services contracted for are no longer required; bids indicate that the needs of the government can be satisfied by a less expensive article differing from that for which the bids were invited. Federal Acquisitions Regulation 14.404. Fifth, if everything is in order, an award is made, either by written notice of award or by furnishing the successful bidder with an executed award document. FAR 14.407. The award is, of course, the acceptance, a matter to be examined a "little bid later."

Sealed bidding minimizes the questions as to whether an offer was made and, if so, by whom. This highly structured process is designed to produce full and complete agreement on all material terms without negotiation and clearly designates the bidder as offeror. Litigation over traditional questions of offer and acceptance in government contracts is rare.

(D) MODES OF ACCEPTANCE

Assuming that there is an offer, how can it be accepted? As we will see below, the common law distinguishes between two modes of acceptance: acceptance by performance and acceptance by return promise. This basic division gives rise to any number of other questions: When may an offeree accept in one way or another? When has an offeree accepted by return promise? At what point is an acceptance by performance effective? Can silence ever count as acceptance?

The answer to many of these questions will be default rules. The overarching rule, which we will see in the first two cases in this section, is that the offeror is the master of the offer. In other words, the offeror gets to decide what counts as acceptance of the offer. In thinking about many of the rules governing acceptance, it is therefore important to ask why the law prefers that default rather than another.

The different modes of acceptance described in this section are also relevant to the legal effects of the offer—for example, whether or when the offeror may revoke the offer. Those aspects are covered in the next section.

(1)   WHO DECIDES WHAT COUNTS AS ACCEPTANCE?

La Salle National Bank v. Mel Vega

Appellate Court of Illinois, Second District, 1988.
167 Ill.App.3d 154.

■ PRESIDING JUSTICE LINDBERG delivered the opinion of the court:

* * *

Plaintiff's first amended complaint alleged the existence of a contract for the sale of real estate between it and Mel [Vega] and sought specific performance of the alleged contract and damages from defendants for willfully and intentionally breaching it. Borg was permitted to intervene and filed a counterclaim naming plaintiff and defendants as counterdefendants. As finally amended, the counterclaim sought specific performance of a different contract for sale of the same real estate to Borg; a judgment declaring the alleged contract between Mel and plaintiff void and holding it for naught; and, if the alleged contract with plaintiff was "held to be a valid and enforceable contract," damages from defendants for fraud for failure to disclose the contract with plaintiff to Borg.

Borg moved for partial summary judgment (Ill.Rev.Stat.1985, ch. 110, par. 2–1005(d)) requesting a determination by the court that the alleged contract between plaintiff and Mel was unenforceable because it was not "signed in accordance with its terms and provisions" and because plaintiff abandoned it. The trial court granted partial summary judgment on the basis of the first ground argued by Borg.

In its verified first amended complaint, plaintiff alleged, *inter alia:*

"The Defendant, MEL VEGA, on March 12, 1985, in his own behalf and in behalf of all the owners of record, entered into a Real Estate Sale Contract (herein 'Contract') with the Plaintiff, a true and correct copy of said Contract is attached hereto and incorporated herein as Exhibit A."

Exhibit A is a document, drafted by counsel for plaintiff, entitled "Real Estate Sale Contract." On the first page of this document appears the date March 12, 1985, and the statement that "Attached Rider is part of this Contract." One of the Rider's provisions states:

"This contract has been executed and presented by an authorized agent for the purchaser, the beneficiaries of the La Salle National Bank, under Trust No. 109529, as Trustee aforesaid for the benefit of the Trust only and not personally. Upon execution of this contract by the Seller, this contract shall be presented to the trust for full execution. Upon the trust's execution, this contract will then be in full force and a copy of a fully executed contract along with evidence of the earnest money deposit will be delivered back to Seller."

The document was signed by Bernard Ruekberg as the purchaser's purchasing agent and by Mel Vega (on March 19, 1985, according to the date by his signature on the Rider) as the seller but not by the trustee for the purchaser.

* * *

It has long been settled that a contract is " 'an agreement between competent parties, upon a consideration sufficient in law, to do or not to do a particular thing.' " (Steinberg v. Chicago Medical School (1977), 69 Ill.2d 320, 329, quoting People v. Dummer (1916), 274 Ill. 637, 640.) The formation of a contract requires an offer, an acceptance, and consideration. . . . The trial court held that there was no genuine issue of material fact that no contract was formed because the offer was made by Mel, the offer could only be accepted by execution of the document at issue by the trust, and the document was not executed by the trust. * * *

Whether a contract was formed without execution of the document by the trust may now be considered. This requires first an analysis of the events which occurred with respect to the document in terms of offer and acceptance.

The pertinent provision of the document stated:

[The court quoted the attached rider, supra.]

Thus, a specific order of events was contemplated, after which the contract would be in full force. Ruekberg (the purchasing agent) was to execute the document and present it to Mel (the seller). Then Mel was to execute it. After Mel executed it, the document was to be presented to the trust for execution. Finally, "upon the trust's execution," the contract would be in full force.

An offer is an act on the part of one person giving another person the legal power of creating the obligation called a contract. . . . From the provisions contained in the document at bar, particularly the language quoted, it is apparent that there was to be no contract (i.e., the "contract" was not to be in full force) until it was executed by the trust. Thus, Ruekberg's presentation of the document he had executed to Mel was not an offer because it did not give Mel the power to make a contract by accepting it. On the other hand, when Mel executed the document and gave it back to Ruekberg he made an offer which could be accepted by execution of the document by the trust.

An offeror has complete control over an offer and may condition acceptance to the terms of the offer. . . . The language of an offer may moreover govern the mode of acceptance required, and, where an offer requires a written acceptance, no other mode may be used. . . . In the case at bar, the document at issue stated clearly that the contract would be in full force upon the trust's execution. This indicates that the only mode by which Mel's offer could be accepted was execution of the document by the trust. The trust not having executed the document, there was no acceptance of the offer, and so there was no contract. . . .

* * *

The judgment of the circuit court of Du Page County is accordingly affirmed.

NOTES

(1) *Offeror's Mastery of Offer.* The offeror is master of the offer. As illustrated by *La Salle Bank*, this means first and foremost that a potential offeror can stipulate whether a communication is an offer, that is, whether it gives the recipient the power of acceptance. A communication that does not confer the power of acceptance is not an offer, but a mere solicitation of an offer.

When there is an offer, the offeror can also stipulate the terms upon which he or she is willing to bargain and prescribe the method by which the offeree may accept. The offeror fashions the power of acceptance that is conferred upon the offeree and can expressly limit the ways in which that power may be exercised. Hence, it follows that an examination of the terms of the offer is a first step in determining the validity of an alleged acceptance.

(2)   Consider *La Salle Bank* and answer the following questions: (a) What did the offeror indicate as to the permissible manner of acceptance? Was that manner invited or required? (b) Did the offeree accept in either case? Why not? (c) Suppose that the bank had executed the written offer by signature before Vega revoked it. Would there then be a contract or would notice to Vega of the signature be required?

(2)   ACCEPTANCE BY PERFORMANCE AND ACCEPTANCE BY PROMISE

Steve Hendricks v. Eugene Behee

Missouri Court of Appeals, Southern District, 1990.
786 S.W.2d 610.

■ FLANIGAN, PRESIDING JUDGE. Plaintiff Steve L. Hendricks, d/b/a Hendricks Abstract & Title Co., instituted this interpleader action, Rule 52.07, V.A.M.R., against defendants Eugene Behee, Artice Smith, and Pearl Smith. Plaintiff was the escrowee of $5,000 which had been paid by defendant Behee as a deposit accompanying Behee's offer to purchase real estate owned by defendants Artice Smith and Pearl Smith, husband and wife, in Stockton, Missouri. A dispute between Behee and the Smiths as to whether their dealings resulted in a binding contract prompted the interpleader action. Behee filed a cross-claim against the Smiths.

After a nonjury trial, the trial court awarded plaintiff $997.50 to be paid out of the $5,000 deposit. None of the parties challenges that award. The trial court awarded the balance of $4,002.50 to defendant Behee. Defendants Smith appeal.

In essence the Smiths contend that the dealings between them and Behee ripened into a contract and entitled the Smiths to the balance of $4,002.50, and that the trial court erred in ruling otherwise.

After Behee, as prospective buyer, and the Smiths, as prospective sellers, had engaged in unproductive negotiations, Behee, on March 2, 1987, made a written offer of $42,500 for the real estate and $250 for a dinner bell and flower pots. On March 3 that offer was mailed to the Smiths, who lived in Mississippi, by their real estate agent. There were two real estate agents involved. The trial court found that both were the agents of the Smiths, and that finding has not been disputed by the Smiths in this appeal. For simplicity, the two agents will be considered in this opinion as one agent who acted on behalf of the Smiths.

On March 4 the Smiths signed the proposed agreement in Mississippi. Before Behee was notified that the Smiths had accepted the offer, Behee withdrew the offer by notifying the real estate agent of the withdrawal. That paramount fact is conceded by this statement in the Smiths' brief: "On either March 5, 6 or 7, 1987, Behee contacted [the Smiths' real estate agent] and advised her that he desired to withdraw his offer to purchase the real estate. Prior to this communication, Behee had received no notice that his offer had been accepted by the Smiths."

There is no contract until acceptance of an offer is communicated to the offeror. . . . An uncommunicated intention to accept an offer is not an acceptance. . . . When an offer calls for a promise, as distinguished from an act, on the part of the offeree, notice of acceptance is always essential. . . . A mere private act of the offeree does not constitute an acceptance. . . . Communication of acceptance of a contract to an agent of the offeree is not sufficient and does not bind the offeror. . . .

Unless the offer is supported by consideration, . . . an offeror may withdraw his offer at any time "before acceptance and communication of that fact to him." . . . To be effective, revocation of an offer must be communicated to the offeree before he has accepted. . . .

Notice to the agent, within the scope of the agent's authority, is notice to the principal, and the agent's knowledge is binding on the principal. . . .

Before Behee was notified that the Smiths had accepted his offer, Behee notified the agent of the Smiths that Behee was withdrawing the offer. The notice to the agent, being within the scope of her authority, was binding upon the Smiths. Behee's offer was not supported by consideration and his withdrawal of it was proper. * * *

The judgment is affirmed.

NOTES

(1) A signature, if invited or required as a method of acceptance, constitutes assent to the proposed bargain, including a promise to perform the agreement. A signature is not part performance of the proposed exchange. But is the signature alone enough? Consider this statement of the rule:

> If we are to proceed on an objective theory of mutual assent, it would seem to be too clear for argument that the offeree's assent should be communicated or manifested to the offeror before a contract can come into being. This is so because, it is what the one party has caused the other to believe he intends, that is important, rather than what he actually intends or what he has caused the world at large to believe he intends. Moreover, where the offer is one that calls for the making of a promise as the requested return, there is an additional reason for reaching this conclusion. The very idea of promise involves communication. In other words, a promise is a communicated undertaking.

Grismore, Contracts § 45 (1st ed. 1947). Compare Restatement (Second) § 56:

> Except [in cases where acceptance is possible through silence] or where the offer manifests a contrary intention, it is essential to an acceptance by promise either that the offeree exercise reasonable diligence to notify the offeror of acceptance or that the offeror receive the acceptance seasonably.

What is the difference? Why might an offeror want to allow an acceptance by return promise to be effective upon signing and without notification? The comments to Section 56 give the following illustration:

> A makes written application for life insurance through an agent for B Insurance Company, pays the first premium, and is given a receipt stating that the insurance "shall take effect as of the date of approval of the application" at B's home office. Approval at the home office in accordance with B's usual practice is an acceptance of A's offer even though no steps are taken to notify A.

Restatement (Second) § 56 ill. 2.

(2)   The rule in Restatement (Second) § 56 is a default rule. In other words, the offeror can opt-out of it, making acceptance effective upon signing rather than upon notification. Why not make acceptance upon signing the default? Which rule is more favorable to offerors? Which do most parties want? For some ideas on this subject, see Comment: How Should the Law Set "Default" Rules?, infra Part 2.C.

Louisa Elizabeth Carlill v. Carbolic Smoke Ball Co.

Court of Appeal, 1893.
[1893] 1 Q.B. 256.

The defendants, who were the proprietors and vendors of a medical preparation called "The Carbolic Smoke Ball," inserted in the *Pall Mall Gazette* of November 13, 1891, and in other newspapers, the following advertisement: "100£. reward will be paid by the Carbolic Smoke Ball Company to any person who contracts the increasing epidemic influenza, colds, or any disease caused by taking cold, after having used the ball three times daily for two weeks according to the printed directions supplied with each ball. 1000£. is deposited with the Alliance Bank, Regent Street, shewing our sincerity in the matter.

"During the last epidemic of influenza many thousand carbolic smoke balls were sold as preventives against this disease, and in no ascertained case was the disease contracted by those using the carbolic smoke ball.

"One carbolic smoke ball will last a family several months, making it the cheapest remedy in the world at the price, 10*s.*, post free. The ball can be refilled at a cost of 5*s.* Address, Carbolic Smoke Ball Company, 27 Princes Street, Hanover Square, London."

The plaintiff [Lilli Carlill], a lady, on the faith of this advertisement, bought one of the balls at a chemist's, and used it as directed, three times a day, from November 20, 1891, to January 17, 1892, when she was attacked by influenza. Hawkins, J., held that she was entitled to recover the 100£. The defendants appealed. The appeal was dismissed.

* * *

■ LINDLEY, L.J. * * * The first observation I will make is that we are not dealing with any inference of fact. We are dealing with an express promise to pay 100£. in certain events. Read the advertisement how you will, and twist it about as you will, here is a distinct promise expressed in language which is perfectly unmistakable—"100£. reward will be paid by the Carbolic Smoke Ball Company to any person who contracts the influenza after having used the ball three times daily for two weeks according to the printed directions supplied with each ball."

We must first consider whether this was intended to be a promise at all, or whether it was a mere puff which meant nothing. Was it a mere puff? My answer to that question is No, and I base my answer upon this passage: "1000£. is deposited with the Alliance Bank, shewing our sincerity in the matter." Now, for what was that money deposited or that statement made except to negative the suggestion that this was a mere puff and meant nothing at all? The deposit is called in aid by the advertiser as proof of his sincerity in the matter—that is, the sincerity of his promise to pay this 100£. in the event which he has specified. I say this for the purpose of giving point to the observation that we are not inferring a promise; there is the promise, as plain as words can make it.

Then it is contended that it is not binding. In the first place, it is said that it is not made with anybody in particular. Now that point is common to the words of this advertisement and to the words of all other advertisements offering rewards. They are offers to anybody who performs the conditions named in the advertisement, and anybody who does perform the condition accepts the offer. In point of law this advertisement is an offer to pay 100£. to anybody who will perform these conditions, and the performance of the conditions is the acceptance of the offer.

* * *

We, therefore, find here all the elements which are necessary to form a binding contract enforceable in point of law, subject to two observations. First of all it is said that this advertisement is so vague that you cannot really construe it as a promise—that the vagueness of the language shews that a legal promise was never intended or contemplated. The language is vague and uncertain in some respects, and particularly in this, that the 100£. is to be paid to any person who contracts the increasing epidemic after having used the balls three times daily for two weeks. It is said, When are they to be used? According to the language of the advertisement no time is fixed, and, construing the offer most strongly against the person who has made it, one might infer that any time was meant. I do not think that was meant, and to hold the contrary would be pushing too far the doctrine of taking language most strongly against the person using it. I do not think that business people or reasonable people would understand the words as meaning that if you took a smoke ball and used it three times daily for two weeks you were to be guaranteed against influenza for the rest of your life, and I think it would be pushing the language of the advertisement too far to construe it as meaning that. But if it does not mean that, what does it mean? It is for the defendants to shew what it does mean; and it strikes me that there are two, and possibly three, reasonable constructions to be put on this advertisement, any one of which will answer the purpose of the plaintiff. Possibly it may be limited to persons catching the "increasing epidemic" (that is, the then prevailing epidemic), or any colds or diseases caused by taking cold, during the prevalence of the increasing epidemic. That is one suggestion; but it does not commend itself to me. Another suggested meaning is that you are warranted free from catching this epidemic, or colds or other diseases caused by taking cold, whilst you are using this remedy after using it for two weeks. If that is the meaning, the plaintiff is right, for she used the remedy for two weeks and went on using it till she got the epidemic. Another meaning, and the one which I rather prefer, is that the reward is offered to any person who contracts the epidemic or other disease within a reasonable time after having used the smoke ball. Then it is asked, What is a reasonable time? It has been suggested that there is no standard of reasonableness; that it depends upon the reasonable time for a germ to develop! I do not feel pressed by that. It strikes me that a reasonable time may be ascertained in a business sense and in a sense satisfactory to a lawyer, in this way; find out from a chemist what the ingredients are; find out from a skilled physician how long the effect of such ingredients on the system could be reasonably expected to endure so as to protect a person from an epidemic or cold, and in that way you will get a standard to be laid before a jury, or a judge without a jury, by which they might exercise their judgment as to what a reasonable time would be. It strikes me, I confess, that the true construction of this advertisement is that 100£. will be paid to anybody who uses this smoke ball three times daily for two weeks according to the printed directions, and who gets the influenza or cold or other diseases caused by taking cold within a reasonable time after so using it; and if that is the true construction, it is enough for the plaintiff. . . .

It appears to me, therefore, that the defendants must perform their promise, and, if they have been so unwary as to expose themselves to a great many actions, so much the worse for them.

■ BOWEN, L.J. I am of the same opinion.

* * * One cannot doubt that, as an ordinary rule of law, an acceptance of an offer made ought to be notified to the person who makes the offer, in order that the two minds may come together. Unless this is done the two minds may be apart, and there is not that consensus which is necessary according to the English law—I say nothing about the laws of other countries—to make a contract. But there is this clear gloss to be made upon the doctrine, that as notification of acceptance is required for the benefit of the person who makes the offer, the person who makes the offer may dispense with notice to himself if he thinks it desirable to do so and I suppose there can be no doubt that where a person in an offer made by him to another person, expressly or impliedly intimates a particular mode of acceptance as sufficient to make the bargain binding, it is only necessary for the other person to whom such offer is made to follow the indicated method of acceptance; and if the person making the offer, expressly or impliedly intimates in his offer that it will be sufficient to

act on the proposal without communicating acceptance of it to himself, performance of the condition is a sufficient acceptance without notification.

* * *

Now, if that is the law, how are we to find out whether the person who makes the offer does intimate that notification of acceptance will not be necessary in order to constitute a binding bargain? In many cases you look to the offer itself. In many cases you extract from the character of the transaction that notification is not required, and in the advertisement cases it seems to me to follow as an inference to be drawn from the transaction itself that a person is not to notify his acceptance of the offer before he performs the condition, but that if he performs the condition notification is dispensed with. It seems to me that from the point of view of common sense no other idea could be entertained. If I advertise to the world that my dog is lost, and that anybody who brings the dog to a particular place will be paid some money, are all the police or other persons whose business it is to find lost dogs to be expected to sit down and write me a note saying that they have accepted my proposal? Why, of course, they at once look after the dog, and as soon as they find the dog they have performed the condition. The essence of the transaction is that the dog should be found, and it is not necessary under such circumstances, as it seems to me, that in order to make the contract binding there should be any notification of acceptance. It follows from the nature of the thing that the performance of the condition is sufficient acceptance without the notification of it, and a person who makes an offer in an advertisement of that kind makes an offer which must be read by the light of that common sense reflection. He does, therefore, in his offer impliedly indicate that he does not require notification of the acceptance of the offer.

A further argument for the defendants was that this was a nudum pactum—that there was no consideration for the promise—that taking the influenza was only a condition, and that the using the smoke ball was only a condition, and that there was no consideration at all; in fact that there was no request, express or implied, to use the smoke ball. * * * Can it be said here that if the person who reads this advertisement applies thrice daily, for such time as may seem to him tolerable, the carbolic smoke ball to his nostrils for a whole fortnight, he is doing nothing at all—that it is a mere act which is not to count towards consideration to support a promise (for the law does not require us to measure the adequacy of the consideration). Inconvenience sustained by one party at the request of the other is enough to create a consideration. I think, therefore, that it is consideration enough that the plaintiff took the trouble of using the smoke ball. But I think also that the defendants received a benefit from this user, for the use of the smoke ball was contemplated by the defendants as being indirectly a benefit to them, because the use of the smoke balls would promote their sale. * * *

I cannot picture to myself the view of the law on which the contrary could be held when you have once found who are the contracting parties. If I say to a person, "If you use such and such a medicine for a week I will give you 5£.," and he uses it, there is ample consideration for the promise.

■ A.L. SMITH, L.J. * * * [I]t was argued, that if the advertisement constituted an offer which might culminate in a contract if it was accepted, and its conditions performed, yet it was not accepted by the plaintiff in the manner contemplated, and that the offer contemplated was such that notice of the acceptance had to be given by the party using the carbolic ball to the defendants before user [*sic.*], so that the defendants might be at liberty to superintend the experiment. All I can say is, that there is no such clause in the advertisement, and that, in my judgment, no such clause can be read into it; and I entirely agree with what has fallen from my Brothers, that this is one of those cases in which a performance of the condition by using these smoke balls for two weeks three times a day is an acceptance of the offer.

* * *

Lastly, it was said that there was no consideration, and that it was *nudum pactum*. There are two considerations here. One is the consideration of the inconvenience of having to use this carbolic smoke ball for two weeks three times a day; and the other more important consideration is the money gain likely to accrue to the defendants by the enhanced sale of the smoke balls, by reason of the plaintiff's user of them. There is ample consideration to support this promise. I have only to add that as regards the policy and the wagering points, in my judgment, there is nothing in either of them.

Appeal dismissed.

NOTES

(1) What manner of acceptance was invited by the offer? Could a member of the public, for example, create a contract by promising to buy and use the Smoke Ball? At what point did a contract come into existence? Was notification of the offeror a requisite of contractual obligation?

(2) In a section of the *Leonard v. Pepsico* opinion not reprinted above, Judge Wood discusses *Carbolic Smoke Ball* at some length. 88 F.Supp.2d at 125–26. What are the similarities? What are the differences?

(3) *A Unilateral Contract Sampler.* Although not used in the Restatement (Second), the phrase "unilateral contract" refers to an offer that invites acceptance by performance of the bargained for exchange and does not invite acceptance by a promise. See Section 53(3). Unilateral contract analysis has been utilized in resolving an important employment contract issue. See, e.g., Pine River State Bank v. Mettille, 333 N.W.2d 622 (Minn. 1983) (whether terms of employee handbook become part of contract). But even if a unilateral contract case lacks real importance, it is seldom lacking in human interest. For example:

Barnes v. Treece, 15 Wash.App. 437 (1976) (Offer by punch board distributor to pay $100,000 to anyone who found a "crooked" punchboard.)

Las Vegas Hacienda, Inc. v. Gibson, 77 Nev. 25 (1961) (Offer by owner of golf course to pay $5,000 to anyone shooting a hole-in-one.)

James v. Turilli, 473 S.W.2d 757 (Mo.App. 1971) (Offer by owner of "Jesse James Museum" in Stanton, Missouri, to pay $10,000 to anyone who could disprove his claim that the man shot and buried in 1882 as Jesse James was an impostor, and that the real Jesse James, under the name of J. Frank Dalton, lived at the offeror's museum for many years.)

Newman v. Schiff, 778 F.2d 460 (8th Cir. 1985) (Offer on CBS Nightwatch program to pay $100,000 to anyone who called the show and cited any section of the Internal Revenue Code "that says an individual is required to file a tax return".)

Harris v. Time, Inc., 191 Cal.App.3d 449 (1987) (Offer to give a calculator watch free "just for opening this envelope" was accepted by opening envelope, but plaintiff failed to give defendant notice of acceptance within a reasonable time).

(4) *Can A Newspaper Contract Around New York Times v. Sullivan?* In *Cohen v. Cowles Media*, which appears in Chapter Two, the court found that a reporter's confidentiality promise did not create a contract because the parties did not intend it to be legally enforceable. But imagine a newspaper, the *Servanda*, that on the front page of each issue (i) expressly promises to compensate any individual that it mentions who is injured by the newspaper's negligent misrepresentation and (ii) expressly represents that it intends this promise to be legally enforceable. Like the Carbolic Smoke Ball Co., *Servanda* believes that it can sell more newspapers if it warrants the quality of its product. Putting aside consideration problems, would it be constitutional to enforce the contract? Is *New York Times v. Sullivan*, 376 U.S. 254 (1964) (requiring actual malice for libel liability), merely a default rule? If so, could the legislature flip the default and require newspapers that didn't want to stand behind the truthfulness of their statements to opt out of liability by including a short disclaimer somewhere in the publication?

Corinthian Pharmaceutical Systems, Inc. v. Lederle Laboratories

United States District Court, Southern District, Indiana, 1989.
724 F.Supp. 605.

■ MCKINNEY, DISTRICT JUDGE. * * * Defendant Lederle Laboratories is a pharmaceutical manufacturer and distributor that makes a number of drugs, including the DTP vaccine. Plaintiff Corinthian Pharmaceutical is a distributor of drugs that purchases supplies from manufacturers such as Lederle Labs and then resells the product to physicians and other providers. One of the products that Corinthian buys and distributes with some regularity is the DTP vaccine.

* * *

[From 1984 on] Lederle continued to manufacture and sell the vaccine, and Corinthian continued to buy it from Lederle and other sources. Lederle periodically issued a price list to its customers for all of its products. Each price list stated that all orders were subject to acceptance by Lederle at its home office, and indicated that the prices shown "were in effect at the time of publication but are submitted without offer and are subject to change without notice." The price list further stated that changes in price "take immediate effect and unfilled current orders and back orders will be invoiced at the price in effect at the time shipment is made."

From 1985 through early 1986, Corinthian made a number of purchases of the vaccine from Lederle Labs. During this period of time, the largest single order ever placed by Corinthian with Lederle was for 100 vials. When Lederle Labs filled an order it sent an invoice to Corinthian.

* * *

During this period of time, product liability lawsuits concerning DTP increased, and insurance became more difficult to procure. As a result, Lederle decided in early 1986 to self-insure against such risks. In order to cover the costs of self-insurance, Lederle concluded that a substantial increase in the price of the vaccine would be necessary.

In order to communicate the price change to its own sales people, Lederle's Price Manager prepared "PRICE LETTER NO. E–48." This document was dated May 19, 1986, and indicated that effective May 20, 1986, the price of the DTP vaccine would be raised from $51.00 to $171.00 per vial. Price letters such as these were routinely sent to Lederle's sales force, but did not go to customers. Corinthian Pharmaceutical did not know of the existence of this internal price letter until a Lederle representative presented it to Corinthian several weeks after May 20, 1986.

Additionally, Lederle Labs also wrote a letter dated May 20, 1986, to its customers announcing the price increase and explaining the liability and insurance problems that brought about the change. Corinthian somehow gained knowledge of this letter on May 19, 1986, the date before the price increase was to take effect. In response to the knowledge of the impending price increase, Corinthian immediately ordered 1000 vials of DTP vaccine from Lederle. Corinthian placed its order on May 19, 1986, by calling Lederle's "Telgo" system. The Telgo system is a telephone computer ordering system that allows customers to place orders over the phone by communicating with a computer. After Corinthian placed its order with the Telgo system, the computer gave Corinthian a tracking number for its order. On the same date, Corinthian sent Lederle two written confirmations of its order. On each form Corinthian stated that this "order is to receive the $64.32 per vial price."

On June 3, 1986, Lederle sent invoice 1771 to Corinthian for 50 vials of DTP vaccine priced at $64.32 per vial. The invoice contained the standard Lederle conditions noted above. The 50 vials were sent to Corinthian and were accepted. At the same time, Lederle sent its customers, including Corinthian, a letter regarding DTP vaccine pricing and orders. This letter stated that the "enclosed represents a partial shipment of the order for DTP vaccine, which you placed with Lederle on May 19, 1986." The letter stated that under Lederle's standard terms and conditions of sale the normal policy would be to invoice the order at the price when shipment was made. However, in light of the magnitude of the price increase, Lederle had decided to make an exception to its terms and conditions and ship a portion of the order at the lower price. The letter further stated that the balance would be priced at $171.00, and that shipment would be made during the week of June 16. The letter closed, "If for any reason you wish to cancel the balance of your order, please contact [us] . . . on or before June 13."

Based on these facts, plaintiff Corinthian Pharmaceutical brings this action seeking specific performance for the 950 vials of DTP vaccine that Lederle Labs chose not to deliver. In support of its summary judgment motion, Lederle urges a number of alternative grounds for disposing of this claim, including that no contract for the sale of 1000 vials was formed, that if one was formed, it was governed by Lederle's terms and conditions, and that the 50 vials sent to Corinthian were merely an accommodation.

* * *

[T]his is a straightforward sale of goods problem resembling those found in a contracts or sales casebook. The fundamental question is whether Lederle Labs agreed to sell Corinthian Pharmaceuticals 1,000 vials of DTP vaccine at $64.32 per vial. As shown below, the undisputed material facts mandate the conclusion as a matter of law that no such agreement was ever formed.

* * *

The starting point in this analysis is where did the first offer originate. An offer is "the manifestation of willingness to enter into a bargain, so made as to justify another person in understanding that his assent to that bargain is invited and will conclude it." H. Greenberg, Rights and Remedies Under U.C.C. Article 2 § 5.2 at 50 (1987) [hereinafter "Greenberg, U.C.C. Article 2"], (quoting 1 Restatement (Second), Contracts § 4 (1981)). The only possible conclusion in this case is that Corinthian's "order" of May 19, 1986, for 1,000 vials at $64.32 was the first offer. Nothing that the seller had done prior to this point can be interpreted as an offer.

* * *

Thus, as a matter of law, the first offer was made by Corinthian when it phoned in and subsequently confirmed its order for 1,000 vials at the lower price. The next question, then, is whether Lederle ever accepted that offer.

Under the Code, an acceptance need not be the mirror-image of the offer. U.C.C. § 2–207. However, the offeree must still do some act that manifests the intention to accept the offer and make a contract. Under § 2–206, an offer to make a contract shall be construed as inviting acceptance in any manner and by any medium reasonable in the circumstances. The first question regarding acceptance, therefore, is whether Lederle accepted the offer prior to sending the 50 vials of vaccine.

The record is clear that Lederle did not communicate or do any act prior to shipping the 50 vials that could support the finding of an acceptance. When Corinthian placed its order, it merely received a tracking number from the Telgo computer. Such an automated, ministerial act cannot constitute an acceptance. . . . Thus, there was no acceptance of Corinthian's offer prior to the deliver of 50 vials.

The next question, then, is what is to be made of the shipment of 50 vials and the accompanying letter. Section 2–206(b) of the Code speaks to this issue:

> [A]n order or other offer to buy goods for prompt or current shipment shall be construed as inviting acceptance either by a prompt promise to ship or by the prompt or current shipment of conforming or non-conforming goods, *but such a shipment of non-conforming goods does not constitute an acceptance if the seller seasonably notifies the buyer that the shipment is offered only as an accommodation to the buyer.*

§ 2–206 (emphasis added). Thus, under the Code a seller accepts the offer by shipping goods, whether they are conforming or not, but if the seller ships non-conforming goods and seasonably notifies the buyer that the shipment is a mere accommodation, then the seller has not, in fact, accepted the buyer's offer. See Greenberg, U.C.C. Article 2 § 5.5 at 53.

In this case, the offer made by Corinthian was for 1,000 vials at $64.32. In response, Lederle Labs shipped only 50 vials at $64.32 per vial, and wrote Corinthian indicating that the balance of the order would be priced at $171.00 per vial and would be shipped during the week of June 16. The letter further indicated that the buyer could cancel its order by calling Lederle Labs. Clearly, Lederle's shipment was non-conforming. . . . The narrow issue, then, is whether Lederle's response to the offer was a shipment of non-conforming goods not constituting an acceptance because it was offered only as an accommodation under § 2–206.

An accommodation is an arrangement or engagement made as a favor to another. Black's Law Dictionary (5th ed. 1979). The term implies no consideration. Id. In this case, then, even taking all inferences favorably for the buyer, the only possible conclusion is that Lederle Labs' shipment of 50 vials was offered merely as an accommodation; that is to say, Lederle had no obligation to make the partial shipment, and did so only as a favor to the buyer. The accommodation letter, which Corinthian is sure it received, clearly stated that the 50 vials were being sent at the lower price as an exception to Lederle's general policy, and that the balance of the offer would be invoiced at the higher price. The letter further indicated that Lederle's proposal to ship the balance of the order at the higher price could be rejected by the buyer. Moreover, the standard terms of Lederle's invoice stated that acceptance of the order was expressly conditioned upon buyer's assent to the seller's terms.

Under these undisputed facts, § 2–206(1)(b) was satisfied. Where, as here, the notification is properly made, the shipment of nonconforming goods is treated as a counteroffer just as at common law, and the buyer may accept or reject the counteroffer under normal contract rules. 2 W. Hawkland, Uniform Commercial Code Series § 2–206:04 (1987).

Thus, the end result of this analysis is that Lederle Lab's price quotations were mere invitations to make an offer, that by placing its order Corinthian made an offer to buy 1,000 vials at the low price, that by shipping 50 vials at the low price Lederle's response was non-conforming, but the non-conforming response was a mere accommodation and thus constituted a counteroffer. Accordingly, there being no genuine issues of material fact on these issues and the law being in favor of the seller, summary judgment must be granted for Lederle Labs.

* * *

For all these reasons, the defendant's motion for summary judgment is granted.

IT IS SO ORDERED.

NOTES

(1) Read UCC § 2–206 carefully. What are the different ways that an offer can be accepted under this section? Had Lederle Labs not given notice to Corinthian that the 50 vials were shipped as an accommodation, what would have been the legal effect of such shipment? Is it possible, under UCC § 2–206, to have an "acceptance" that is also a "breach"?

(2) Read UCC § 2–204 carefully. How does this section relate to UCC § 2–206? Does it recognize that a contract for sale may be formed by offer and acceptance? By what other ways can a contract be formed?

(3) If the offeror specifies that "the signed acceptance of this proposal shall constitute a contract," the requisite signature would seem to conclude a contract whether or not the offeror knew the action had been taken and despite the lack of any attempt by the offeree to so inform the offeror. For the offeror's mastery of the offer enables one to prescribe how the power of acceptance can be exercised, and one may, if one sees fit, agree to be bound at the moment of signing. By necessary inference the offeror appears to dispense with the necessity of communication of the offeree's assent, and one

can be placed in a contractual relationship without knowing it. But what if the offeror does not expressly indicate when the acceptance is to become operative? Are we to assume, then, that there must be a communication, just as there would seem to be no operative offer until it is communicated?

Industrial America, Inc. v. Fulton Industries, Inc.

Supreme Court of Delaware, 1971.
285 A.2d 412.

■ HERRMANN, JUSTICE. [The plaintiff, "Industrial America," Inc., was a broker specializing in the sale or merger of businesses. Bush Hog, Inc. (B-H) was a farm machinery company which had informed several brokers, including the plaintiff, of its desire to consummate a merger. With B-H's authorization, and armed with documentary data furnished by it, the plaintiff's president, Millard B. Deutsch, first approached the Borg Warner Corporation with the B-H merger possibility; but nothing came of that effort. Next, again with B-H's authorization and updated material, Deutsch attempted to interest the Wickes Corporation in the merger possibility. After negotiations were carried on for several months between the two corporations, Deutsch participating actively therein, the talks ceased in early 1965. During the Wickes discussions, Deutsch outlined to B-H the commission arrangement he would expect if the merger were consummated. After the Wickes negotiations ended, according to B-H, it decided not to deal further with Deutsch or any other broker; but this decision was never communicated to Deutsch.

In the fall of 1965, while eating lunch with an accountant friend, Deutsch learned that Fulton Industries, Inc., (and its successor, Allied Products Corporation), the defendant herein, was an "acquisition minded" company. Deutsch forthwith took from his own office files a copy of the following ad in the *Wall Street Journal:*

> WANTED—PRODUCT LINES! Heavy or Medium Machinery of Industrial Products. One of Fulton Industries' divisions desires additional products to manufacture. Its modern manufacturing facility of more than 250,000 sq. ft. includes grey iron foundry, heavy and light machining, sheet metal forming, and capable engineering, sales and service staffs.

> Fulton will buy outright, or acquire by merger, active product line with annual sales of $2 million or more. Will take over manufacture, sales, service and key people. Brokers fully protected.

On October 7, 1965, Deutsch wrote to Fulton, describing but not naming B-H as a prospective acquisition; the response, dated October 14, was a request for financial data. On October 19, Deutsch replied by naming B-H as the prospect and transmitting financial data supplied to him by B-H. By letter dated October 22, Fulton stated it was "very much interested," and requested Deutsch to arrange a visit by the Fulton people to the B-H plant. By letter of October 26, with copy to Fulton, Deutsch advised B-H of Fulton's interest and suggestion for a visit. At some time after October 26 and prior to November 2, Fulton's executive vice president telephoned B-H's president directly and arranged a meeting for November 4. Deutsch first learned of this when, on November 3, he inquired of B-H regarding its failure to reply to his letter of October 26. Despite his repeated efforts and offers to assist, neither B-H nor Fulton dealt further with Deutsch; they both ignored his inquiries except for B-H's promise to keep him informed. Negotiations between B-H and Fulton continued until March 11, 1966, when a merger agreement between them was consummated.

After a series of hearings and appeals, the plaintiff was successful in getting a judgment for his broker's commission against B-H ($125,000) on the grounds that it was the procuring cause. The plaintiff, however, was unsuccessful in recovering judgment against Fulton; through special interrogatories, the trial court found that the plaintiff had never accepted Fulton's "offer."]

The basic question for decision in this appeal, in our view, is whether the plaintiff had the burden of proving a subjective intent on the part of Deutsch to accept the offer of guaranty which had been made in the advertisement by Fulton under the jury's findings.

We are of the opinion that Deutsch's subjective intent was not a relevant issue; that, rather, the relevant issues were (1) whether Fulton's offer of guaranty invited acceptance by performance; (2) whether Deutsch knew of the offer; and (3) whether Deutsch's course of action constituted a performance amounting to an acceptance.

It is basic that overt manifestation of assent—not subjective intent—controls the formation of a contract; that the "only intent of the parties to a contract which is essential is an intent to say the words or do the acts which constitute their manifestation of assent"; that "the intention to accept is unimportant except as manifested." Restatement of Contracts, § 20; . . .

Where an offeror requests an act in return for his promise and the act is performed, the act performed becomes the requisite overt manifestation of assent if the act is done intentionally; i.e., if there is a "conscious will" to do it. Restatement of Contracts, § 20; 1 Williston on Contracts (3d Ed.) § 68. But "it is not material what induces the will," Restatement of the Law of Contracts, § 20, Comment (a). Otherwise stated, motive in the manifestation of assent is immaterial. There may be primary and secondary reasons or motives for a performance constituting manifestation of assent to an offer inviting acceptance by performance; and the "chief reason" or the prevailing motive need not necessarily be the offer itself. A unilateral contract may be enforceable when the promisor has received the desired service even though the service was primarily motivated by a reason other than the offer. The "motivating causes of human action are always complex and are frequently not clearly thought out or expressed by the actor himself. This being true, it is desirable that not much weight should be given to the motives of an offeree and that no dogmatic requirement should be embodied in a stated rule of law." 1 Corbin on Contracts, § 58, p. 244, § 59, p. 246. It follows that a unilateral contract may arise even though at the time of performance the offeree did not "rely" subjectively upon, i.e., was not primarily motivated by, the offer. See Simmons v. United States 308 F.2d 160 (4th Cir. 1962); Eagle v. Smith 4 Houst. 293 (Del. 1871); Carlill v. Carbolic Smoke Ball Co. [1893] Q.B. 256; Restatement of Contracts, § 55, Comment b (1932): " * * * contracts may exist where if the offer is in any sense a cause of the acceptor's action it is so slight a factor that a statement that the acceptance is caused by the offer is misleading."

The clear trend and development of the law in this connection is demonstrated by a proposed change in the status of Section 55 of the Restatement of Contracts (1932).[2] The development of this facet of the law of contracts became apparent in Section 55 of the 1964 Tentative Draft of Restatement of Contracts (Second).[3] A comparison of the 1932 and the 1964 versions of Section 55 indicates that under the currently developing rule of law, an offer that invites an acceptance by performance will be deemed accepted by such performance unless there is a manifestation of intention to the contrary. See 1 Williston on Contracts (3d Ed.) § 67. Thus, in the establishment of a contractual obligation, the favored rule shifts the emphasis away from a manifestation of intent to accept to a manifestation of intent not to accept; thereby establishing, it would appear, a rebuttable presumption of acceptance arising from performance when the offer invites acceptance by performance. See Braucher, *Offer and Acceptance in Second Restatement*, 74 Yale L.J. 302, 308 (1964). The law thus rightfully imputes to a person an intention corresponding to the reasonable meaning of his words and deeds.

The defendants contend that, because an offer of guaranty is here involved, the issue is whether the plaintiff gave to Fulton the necessary notice of acceptance of the offer, citing 1 Williston on Contracts (3d Ed.)

---

[2]   Section 55 provided:

"ACCEPTANCE OF OFFER FOR UNILATERAL CONTRACT; NECESSITY OF INTENT TO ACCEPT

"If an act or forbearance is requested by the offeror as the consideration for a unilateral contract, the act or forbearance must be given with the intent of accepting the offer."

[3]   The Draft contains the following:

"ACCEPTANCE BY PERFORMANCE; MANIFESTATION OF INTENTION NOT TO ACCEPT

"(1) An offer may be accepted by the rendering of a performance only if the offer invites such an acceptance. (2) Except as stated in § 72, the rendering of a performance does not constitute an acceptance if within a reasonable time the offeree exercises reasonable diligence to notify the offeror of nonacceptance. (3) Where an offer of a promise invites acceptance by performance and does not invite a promissory acceptance, the rendering of the invited performance does not constitute an acceptance if before the offeror performs his promise the offeree manifests an intention not to accept." [This is § 53 in the final draft.—Eds.]

§ 69AA, p. 223. The position is untenable in the light of the following portion of the Williston statement upon which the defendants rely:

"Ordinarily there is no occasion to notify the offeror of the acceptance of such an offer, if the doing of the act is sufficient acceptance, and the promisor knows that he is bound when he sees that action has been taken on the faith of his offer. * * *."

See also Restatement of Contracts, § 56 (1932); 1 Corbin on Contracts, § 68, f. n. 91. The facts of this case meet the test. In this connection, the Trial Judge ruled that Fulton's knowledge of the plaintiff's submission of B-H's name to it was notice to Fulton of an act constituting acceptance of its offer. We concur in that ruling.

Applying the law we find applicable to the facts of this case: we conclude that the Trial Court erred in submitting the issue of subjective reliance to the jury under Interrogatory No. 4. We hold that there was no relevant issue of fact as to the plaintiff's subjective reliance upon Fulton's offer. As a matter of law, it appears unquestionable that Fulton's offer invited acceptance by performance; it is uncontroverted that Deutsch knew of the offer at the time of performance; by the jury's finding of procuring cause, it has been established that the plaintiff did in fact and in law perform. It follows as a matter of law, in the absence of any manifestation of intention to the contrary, that the plaintiff's performance constituted an acceptance of the offer of Fulton which was found by the jury to be an offer of guaranty outstanding and viable at the time of the performance.

The necessary result of the foregoing chain is that the plaintiff is entitled to judgments against Fulton and Allied as a matter of law upon the basis of the judgment against B-H, unless there is validity in any of the grounds of the defendants' appeals herein.

* * *

Accordingly, upon the bases of the jury's answers to the special interrogatories and of the conclusions we have reached herein, we conclude that as a matter of law the plaintiff is entitled to judgments against Fulton and Allied as well as against B-H upon the verdict of $125,000. The cause is remanded for further proceedings consistent herewith.

NOTES

To understand this case, note that there were two possible offers that the plaintiff could have accepted by finding the buyer that resulted in the sale. Try to identify the two offers. Next, consider which offer the plaintiff intended to accept by its conduct of full performance. The defendant argued that the plaintiff intended to accept the other offer, not its ad in the Wall Street Journal. How does the court deal with this argument?

Mary Glover v. Jewish War Veterans of United States

Municipal Court of Appeals for the District of Columbia, 1949.
68 A.2d 233.

■ CLAGETT, ASSOCIATE JUDGE. The issue determinative of this appeal is whether a person giving information leading to the arrest of a murderer without any knowledge that a reward has been offered for such information by a non-governmental organization is entitled to collect the reward. The trial court decided the question in the negative and instructed the jury to return a verdict for defendant. Claimant appeals from the judgment on such instructed verdict.

The controversy grows out of the murder on June 5, 1946, of Maurice L. Bernstein, a local pharmacist. The following day, June 6, Post No. 58, Jewish War Veterans of the United States, communicated to the newspapers an offer of a reward of $500 "to the person or persons furnishing information resulting in the apprehension and conviction of the persons guilty of the murder of Maurice L. Bernstein." Notice of the reward was published in the newspaper June 7. A day or so later Jesse James Patton, one of the men suspected of the crime, was arrested and the police received information that the other murderer was Reginald Wheeler and that Wheeler was the "boy friend" of a daughter of Mary Glover, plaintiff and claimant in the present case. On the evening of June 11 the police visited Mary Glover, who in answer to questions informed them that her daughter and Wheeler had left the city on June 5. She told the officers she didn't know exactly where the couple had gone, whereupon the officers asked for names of relatives whom the daughter might be visiting. In response to such questions she gave the names and addresses of several relatives, including one at Ridge Spring, South Carolina, which was the first place visited by the officers and where Wheeler was arrested in company with plaintiff's daughter on June 13. Wheeler and Patton were subsequently convicted of the crime.

Claimant's most significant testimony, in the view that we take of the case, was that she first learned that a reward had been offered on June 12, the day after she had given the police officers the information which enabled them to find Wheeler. Claimant's husband, who was present during the interview with the police officers, also testified that at the time of the interview he didn't know that any reward had been offered for Wheeler's arrest, that nothing was said by the police officers about a reward and that he didn't know about it "until we looked into the paper about two or three days after that."

We have concluded that the trial court correctly instructed the jury to return a verdict for defendant. While there is some conflict in the decided cases on the subject of rewards, most of such conflict has to do with rewards offered by governmental officers and agencies. So far as rewards offered by private individuals and organizations are concerned, there is little conflict on the rule that questions regarding such rewards are to be based upon the law of contracts.

Since it is clear that the question is one of contract law, it follows that, at least so far as private rewards are concerned, there can be no contract unless the claimant when giving the desired information knew of the offer of the reward and acted with the intention of accepting such offer; otherwise the claimant gives the information not in the expectation of receiving a reward but rather out of a sense of public duty or other motive unconnected with the reward. "In the nature of the case," according to Professor Williston, "it is impossible for an offeree actually to assent to an offer unless he knows of its existence." After stating that courts in some jurisdictions have decided to the contrary, Williston adds, "It is impossible, however, to find in such a case [that is, in a case holding to the contrary] the elements generally held in England and America necessary for the formation of a contract. If it is clear the offeror intended to pay for the service, it is equally certain that the person rendering the service performed it voluntarily and not in return for a promise to pay. If one person expects to buy, and the other to give, there can hardly be found mutual assent. These views are supported by the great weight of authority, and in most jurisdictions a plaintiff in the sort of case under discussion is denied recovery."

The American Law Institute in its Restatement of the Law of Contracts follows the same rule, thus: "It is impossible that there should be an acceptance unless the offeree knows of the existence of the offer." The Restatement gives the following illustration of the rule just stated: "A offers a reward for information leading to the arrest and conviction of a criminal. B, in ignorance of the offer, gives information leading to his arrest and later, with knowledge of the offer and intent to accept it, gives other information necessary for conviction. There is no contract."

We have considered the reasoning in state decisions following the contrary rule. Mostly, as we have said, they involve rewards offered by governmental bodies and in general are based upon the theory that the government is benefited equally whether or not the claimant gives the information with knowledge of the reward and that therefore the government should pay in any event. We believe that the rule adopted by Professor Williston and the Restatement and in the majority of the cases is the better reasoned rule and therefore we adopt it. We believe furthermore that this rule is particularly applicable in the present case since the claimant did not herself contact the authorities and volunteer information but gave the information only upon questioning by the police officers and did not claim any knowledge of the guilt or innocence of the criminal but only knew where he probably could be located.

Affirmed.

NOTES

(1)   Compare the following two statements:

The liability for a reward of this kind must be created, if at all, by contract. There is no rule of law which imposes it except that which enforces contracts voluntarily entered into. A mere offer or promise to pay does not give rise to a contract. That requires the assent or meeting of two minds, and therefore is not complete until the offer is accepted. Such an offer as that alleged may be accepted by anyone who performs the service called for when the acceptor knows that it has been made and acts in performance of it, but not otherwise. He may do such things as are specified in the offer, but, in so doing, does not act in performance of it, and therefore does not accept it, when he is ignorant of its having been made. There is no such mutual agreement of minds as is essential to a contract. The offer is made to anyone who will accept it by performing the specified acts, and it only becomes binding when another mind has embraced and accepted it. The mere doing of the specified things without reference to the offer is not the consideration for which it calls. This is the theory of the authorities which we regard as sound.

Broadnax v. Ledbetter, 100 Tex. 375, 375–77 (1907).

If the offer was made in good faith, why should the defendant inquire whether the plaintiff knew that it had been made? Would the benefit to him be diminished by the discovery that the plaintiff, instead of acting from mercenary motives, has been impelled solely by the desire to prevent the larceny from being profitable to the person who had committed it?

Dawkins v. Sappington, 26 Ind. 199, 201 (1866).

(2)   Do you think the result would have been different in *Glover* if the reward had been offered by a public authority, such as the District of Columbia? This problem came before the court two years later. See Glover v. District of Columbia, 77 A.2d 788 (D.C.Mun.Ct.App. 1951).

(3)   Assume Mary Glover knew of the reward, but when she furnished the information she did so reluctantly and with no desire to assist apprehension. Would she be entitled to the reward?

(4)   Again, assuming Mary Glover knew of the reward, but it was her information combined with information from another person that led to the apprehension. What, if anything, should she recover? See Reynolds v. Charbeneau, 744 S.W.2d 365 (Tex. Ct. App. 1988).

(5)   Assume that the reward claimant was a District police officer, who furnished the information in the course of his usual employment. Would he be eligible for the reward? Would your answer be the same if it were established that he had not been assigned to the Bernstein murder case, nor had he participated in the official investigation thereof, but had worked on the matter, with the hope of obtaining the reward, during off-duty hours? See Maryland Casualty Co. v. Mathews, 209 F.Supp. 822 (S.D.W.Va. 1962).

Cf. Denney v. Reppert, 432 S.W.2d 647 (Ky. 1968) (Deputy sheriff who assisted in arrest outside of his jurisdiction held entitled to reward.)

PROBLEM: THE CASE OF THE LITTLE LEAGUE SPONSORS

Charley, a public spirited citizen, placed an advertisement in the Suburbia *Press,* stating that he would give $1,000 to anyone who sponsored a little league baseball club in the area for the ensuing season.

Baker, unaware of the advertisement, sponsored a little league club that year in Suburbia. He did not learn of the ad until the season was over, but at the instigation of his son, a first-year law student, brought suit against Charley for the $1,000. Any recovery? Assume, instead, that Baker had seen the advertisement before the season began but did not give it another thought until the season was concluded. Would he then be entitled to claim the $1,000?

Abel, owner of a Suburbia restaurant, sponsored a local club that season, the same as he had in previous years. He did not learn of the advertisement until midseason, at which time he determined to claim the $1,000. At the end of the season he filed suit against Charley. What result?

Ever-Tite Roofing Corp. v. G.T. Green

Court of Appeal of Louisiana, 1955.
83 So.2d 449.

■ AYRES, JUDGE. This is an action for damages allegedly sustained by plaintiff as the result of the breach by the defendants of a written contract for the re-roofing of defendants' residence. Defendants denied that their written proposal or offer was ever accepted by plaintiff in the manner stipulated therein for its acceptance, and hence contended no contract was ever entered into. The trial court sustained defendants' defense and rejected plaintiff's demands and dismissed its suit at its costs. From the judgment thus rendered and signed, plaintiff appealed.

Defendants executed and signed an instrument June 10, 1953, for the purpose of obtaining the services of plaintiff in re-roofing their residence situated in Webster Parish, Louisiana. The document set out in detail the work to be done and the price therefor to be paid in monthly installments. This instrument was likewise signed by plaintiff's sale representative, who, however, was without authority to accept the contract for and on behalf of the plaintiff. This alleged contract contained these provisions:

"This agreement shall become binding only upon written acceptance hereof, by the principal or authorized officer of the Contractor, *or upon commencing performance of the work.* This contract is Not Subject to Cancellation. . . ."(Emphasis supplied.)

Inasmuch as this work was to be performed entirely on credit, it was necessary for plaintiff to obtain credit reports and approval from the lending institution which was to finance said contract. With this procedure defendants were more or less familiar and knew their credit rating would have to be checked and a report made. On receipt of the proposed contract in plaintiff's office on the day following its execution, plaintiff requested a credit report, which was made after investigation and which was received in due course and submitted by plaintiff to the lending agency. Additional information was requested by this institution, which was likewise in due course transmitted to the institution, which then gave its approval.

The day immediately following this approval, which was either June 18 or 19, 1953, plaintiff engaged its workmen and two trucks, loaded the trucks with the necessary roofing materials and proceeded from Shreveport to defendants' residence for the purpose of doing the work and performing the services allegedly contracted for the defendants. Upon their arrival at defendants' residence, the workmen found others in the performance of the work which plaintiff had contracted to do. Defendants notified plaintiff's workmen that the work had been contracted to other parties two days before and forbade them to do the work.

Formal acceptance of the contract was not made under the signature and approval of an agent of plaintiff. It was, however, the intention of plaintiff to accept the contract by commencing the work, which was one of the ways provided for in the instrument for acceptance, as will be shown by reference to the extract from the contract quoted hereinabove. Prior to this time, however, defendants had determined on a course of abrogating the agreement and engaged other workmen without notice thereof to plaintiff.

The basis of the judgment appealed was that defendants had timely notified plaintiff before "commencing performance of work". The trial court held that notice to plaintiff's workmen upon their arrival with the materials that defendants did not desire them to commence the actual work was sufficient and timely to signify their intention to withdraw from the contract. With this conclusion we find ourselves unable to agree.

Defendants' attempt to justify their delay in thus notifying plaintiff for the reason they did not know where or how to contact plaintiff is without merit. The contract itself, a copy of which was left with them, conspicuously displayed plaintiff's name, address and telephone number. Be that as it may, defendants at no time, from June 10, 1953, until plaintiff's workmen arrived for the purpose of commencing the work, notified or attempted to notify plaintiff of their intention to abrogate, terminate or cancel the contract.

Defendants evidently knew this work was to be processed through plaintiff's Shreveport office. The record discloses no unreasonable delay on plaintiff's part in receiving, processing or accepting the contract or in commencing the work contracted to be done. No time limit was specified in the contract within which it was to be accepted or within which the work was to be begun. It was nevertheless understood between the parties that some delay would ensue before the acceptance of the contract and the commencement of the work, due to the necessity of compliance with the requirements relative to financing the job through a lending agency. The evidence as referred to hereinabove shows that plaintiff proceeded with due diligence.

The general rule of law is that an offer proposed may be withdrawn before its acceptance and that no obligation is incurred thereby. This is, however, not without exceptions. For instance, Restatement of the Law of Contracts stated:

"(1) The power to create a contract by acceptance of an offer terminates at the time specified in the offer, or, if no time is specified, at the end of a reasonable time.

"What is a reasonable time is a question of fact depending on the nature of the contract proposed, the usages of business and other circumstances of the case which the offeree at the time of his acceptance either knows or has reason to know."

* * *

Therefore, since the contract did not specify the time within which it was to be accepted or within which the work was to have been commenced, a reasonable time must be allowed therefor in accordance with the facts and circumstances and the evident intention of the parties. A reasonable time is contemplated where no time is expressed. What is a reasonable time depends more or less upon the circumstances surrounding each particular case. The delays to process defendants' application were not unusual. The contract was accepted by plaintiff by commencement of the performance of the work contracted to be done. This commencement began with the loading of the trucks with the necessary materials in Shreveport and transporting such materials and the workmen to defendants' residence. Actual commencement or performance of the work therefore began before any notice of dissent by defendants was given plaintiff. The proposition and its acceptance thus became a completed contract.

By their aforesaid acts defendants breached the contract. They employed others to do the work contracted to be done by plaintiff and forbade plaintiff's workmen to engage upon that undertaking. By this breach defendants are legally bound to respond to plaintiff in damages. . . .

* * *

Plaintiff expended the sum of $85.37 in loading the trucks in Shreveport with materials and in transporting them to the site of defendants' residence in Webster Parish and in unloading them on their return, and for wages for the workmen for the time consumed. Plaintiff's Shreveport manager testified that the expected profit on this job was $226. None of this evidence is controverted or contradicted in any manner.

* * *

For the reasons assigned, the judgment appealed is annulled, avoided, reversed and set aside and there is now judgment in favor of plaintiff, Ever-Tite Roofing Corporation, against the defendants, G.T. Green and Mrs. Jessie Fay Green, for the full sum of $311.37, with 5 per cent per annum interest thereon from judicial demand until paid, and for all costs.

Reversed and rendered.

NOTES

(1)   How did the offer stipulate that it could be accepted—by promise or by performance? Given the answer to that question, what was the legal effect of the beginning of performance? See Restatement (Second) § 62. What would have been the legal effect if the offer had permitted acceptance by performance only? See Restatement (Second) § 45.

The terms of the offer in this case were probably written by Ever-Tite, who was the offeree. Why was the agreement structured in this way? Given the differences between § 45 and § 62, did Ever-Tite structure the offer in the way that was most favorable to it? Any benefits to Ever-Tite from structuring the offer to require acceptance by performance only? We return to these issues in Section 1.E. See Comment: Acceptance by Performance Under the Second Restatement.

(2)   Granted that an acceptance by "commencement of performance" was invited in *Ever-Tite,* was there, on the facts stated, such a commencement? At what point could one say the work commenced? With the loading of the trucks? When the trip to Webster Parish began? Restatement (Second) § 45 cmt. f provides the following guidance:

> What is begun or tendered must be part of the actual performance invited in order to preclude revocation under this Section. Beginning preparations, though they may be essential to carrying out the contract or to accepting the offer, is not enough. Preparations to perform may, however, constitute justifiable reliance sufficient to make the offeror's promise binding under § 87(2).

See also § 62 cmt. d.

Given that under Restatement (Second) § 62 the beginning of performance operated as a return promise, was notification necessary? Compare the rules in Restatement (Second) §§ 53, 54 and 56.

(3)   Homeowner submitted an order to Manufacturer on a form prepared by Manufacturers for the purchase of aluminum storm doors and windows. The order contained the following stipulation: "This contract is not binding on manufacturer until accepted by signature of authorized agent at the home office. It shall then be a binding contract as to all parties, and is not, thereafter, subject to cancellation." When the order was received at the home office, Manufacturer checked Homeowner's credit and found it satisfactory. Whereupon, it began fabricating the doors and windows. At no

time, however, was the order signed by Manufacturer, nor did the latter notify Homeowner that work had commenced. Homeowner telephoned Manufacturer that he had changed his mind and wanted to cancel the order. Was his revocation timely? See Venters v. Stewart, 261 S.W.2d 444 (Ky. 1953). Would your answer be the same if Homeowner had been aware that work had begun?

PROBLEM: THE CASE OF THE LASER SALE

Swift Ray is a manufacturer of industrial lasers. After extended negotiations with Swift Ray, Brice Electronics mailed, on October 7, a written detailed offer to Swift Ray which concluded as follows: "If you will agree to manufacture the lasers according to the above stated terms, we will pay the stipulated contract price upon delivery next January." When Swift Ray received the offer on October 9, the president told his purchasing agent: "It's a good deal. Buy the necessary materials to fill the order." The order to suppliers was placed the next day. Similarly, the sales manager prepared and signed an acknowledgment. However, on October 12, before the acknowledgment was mailed, the purchasing agent from Brice Electronics telephoned Swift Ray and cancelled the order. An unexpected cutback in business was given as the justification.

Swift Ray sued Brice for damages whereupon Brice filed a motion to dismiss the complaint for failure to state a cause of action. At the hearing on the motion, Brice argued that the written offer clearly invited acceptance by a promise to perform. As such, the offeree failed to complete every act essential to the making of the promise before the revocation was received, i.e., the offeree did not actually notify or exercise reasonable diligence to notify the offeror of his agreement. Swift Ray argued that the written offer did not unambiguously narrow the method and manner of acceptance to that asserted by Brice. Rather, the offer should be interpreted as inviting the offeree to accept either by promise or by rendering part of the performance. Since the offer did not request notification, no notification of acceptance by performance was required unless the offeree had reason to know that the offeror had no adequate way of learning of the acceptance and then failed to exercise due diligence in notification.

(1)   What result under UCC § 2–206?

(2)   Suppose that Swift Ray mailed the acknowledgment on October 9. Thereafter but before the acknowledgment arrived, Brice telephoned Swift Ray and canceled the deal. Is there a contract? See UCC § 2–206(1).

(3)   ACCEPTANCE BY CONDUCT OR SILENCE

Theodore Russell v. Texas Co.

United States Court of Appeals, Ninth Circuit, 1956.
238 F.2d 636.

■ HALBERT, DISTRICT JUDGE. Plaintiff-appellant, Russell, claims title to certain real property, which will be referred to in this opinion as section

23. Russell's predecessors in interest acquired their interest in this property from the Northern Pacific Railway Company, defendant-appellee herein, through a contract followed by a warranty deed executed in 1918. In both the contract and the deed was a reservation of mineral rights by the grantor. The Texas Company, defendant-appellee and cross-appellant herein, has been conducting extensive operations on section 23 since 1952 under an oil and gas lease granted by Northern Pacific Railway Company. The Texas Company has also made use of the surface of section 23 in connection with operations carried on by it on lands other than section 23.

* * *

(B) The sums alleged to be due under a revocable license commencing on October 30, 1952, which obligated The Texas Company to pay Russell $150.00 a day for the continued use of section 23 in connection with its operations on adjacent lands, a use admittedly in excess of the easement flowing from the mineral reservation in the original deed.

The evidence shows that The Texas Company received on October 30, 1952, an offer from Russell for a revocable license to cover the use of section 23 in connection with operations on adjacent lands for the sum of $150.00 a day, which offer contained the express proviso that, "your continued use of the roadway, water and/or materials will constitute your acceptance of this revocable permit." The evidence further shows that The Texas Company did so continue to use section 23 until November 22, 1952, and it was not until sometime in December of that year that Russell finally received a communication from the Company to the effect that the offer was rejected. Neither party depends in any material respect on this purported rejection.

* * *

Judgment was entered in favor of Russell and against The Texas Company in the amount of $3,837.60, which consisted of $3,600.00 due under the revocable license and $237.60 due for the use of the land under the terms of the mineral reservation.

The Texas Company appeals from that portion of the judgment which awarded Russell $3,600.00 as the amount due under the terms of the revocable license, contending that the court erred as a matter of law in finding that the offer for the said license was accepted.

Russell appeals from that portion of the judgment against The Texas Company which awarded him $237.60, claiming that the court, in arriving at the measure of compensation, applied the wrong rule of damages. * * *

The Texas Company argues that the revocable license, which Russell offered to it in connection with its wrongful use of section 23, was never accepted, because the Company had no intention of accepting it. Appellant presents for our consideration numerous passages from the

Restatement of Contracts and Williston on Contracts dealing with the necessity of the offeree's intent to accept where an ambiguous act is selected by the offeror to signify acceptance, or where silence and inaction can be considered an acceptance. None of these citations deal with the precise question that we are confronted with in this case. The question here is whether an offeree may vitiate a contract by a claim of lack of intention to accept an offer when he accepts and retains the benefits offered to him by the offeror, with a positive and affirmative proviso by the offeror that such acceptance of the benefits will, in and of itself, be deemed by the offeror to be an acceptance. To put the problem in homely terms, may an offeree accept all of the benefits of a contract and then declare that he cannot be held liable for the burdens because he secretly had said, "King's Ex"? We think not. A rule with such effect would be unconscionable and is not in line with either fairness or justice. The correct rule, we believe, is found in § 72(2) of the Restatement of Contracts, wherein it is stated:

> "Where the offeree exercises dominion over things which are offered to him, such exercise of dominion in the absence of other circumstances showing a contrary intention is an acceptance. *If circumstances indicate that the exercise of dominion is tortious the offeror may at his option treat it as an acceptance, though the offeree manifests an intention not to accept.*" (Emphasis added).

Russell's offer of the license in clear and unambiguous terms stated that the continued use of section 23 in connection with activities and operations on other lands would constitute an acceptance of the offer of the license. The trial court found on the evidence that The Texas Company did so continue to use section 23, and hence unequivocally came within the terms specified for acceptance. It is a well established principle of property law that the right to use the surface of land as an incident of the ownership of mineral rights in the land, does not carry with it the right to use the surface in aid of mining or drilling operations on other lands. . . . That such use by The Texas Company was tortious admits of no doubt. But even in the absence of a tortious use, the true test would be whether or not the offeror was reasonably led to believe that the act of the offeree was an acceptance, and upon the facts of this case it seems evident that even this test is met.

* * *

The conclusion reached by the trial court on this phase of the case was correct.

* * *

The judgment is affirmed as to both appellants. [The Court's discussion of issues raised by Russell's appeal is omitted.]

NOTES

(1)   The court refers to authority dealing with "the necessity of the offeree's intent to accept where an ambiguous act is selected by the offeror to signify acceptance." Is the decision in *Industrial America*, reprinted earlier in this Chapter, inconsistent with this view?

(2)   Was there a "meeting of minds" in *Russell?* Was there a manifestation of mutual assent?

(3)   *Waiver of Tort and Suit in Assumpsit.* Offeror offers goods to Offeree upon specified terms. Offeree, without responding expressly to the offer, proceeds to exercise dominion over the goods, as, for example, by using them. What legal recourse is available to Offeror? Offeror might sue Offeree for the tort of conversion and recover damages. Might Offeror, however, sue for breach of contract? Prevailing authority indicates that this option might be available. Restatement (Second) § 69 provides: "An offeree who does any act inconsistent with the offeror's ownership of offered property is bound in accordance with the offered terms unless they are manifestly unreasonable. But if the act is wrongful as against the offeror it is an acceptance only if ratified by him." The use of the goods, albeit a wrongful use, can be construed as an implied acceptance of the offer. In effect, Offeror can treat Offeree as either a tortfeasor or a contract breaker.

The foregoing option grew out of a common law procedural alternative called "waiver of tort and suit in assumpsit." This process encompassed not only "implied acceptance" situations, but also those in which there was no outstanding offer. For instance, *A* steals goods belonging to *B* and sells them to *C*. It came to be recognized that *B* could "waive" the tort and sue in "assumpsit" under the fictitious assumption that *A* promised to restore to *B* benefits received from *C*. The remedy was essentially restitutionary in nature, designed to prevent *A*'s unjust enrichment. Since the objective was the disgorgement of *A*'s benefit, the amount of recovery might, if *A* made an advantageous sale to *C,* exceed the market value of the goods, the tort measure of recovery. Problems in this area are taken up in other law school courses.

(4)   "We have not been cited to a case in this state involving the liability of a person who, though not having subscribed for a newspaper, continues to accept it by receiving it through the mail. There are, however, certain well-understood principles in the law of contracts that ought to solve the question. It is certain that one cannot be forced into contractual relations with another and that therefore he cannot, against his will, be made the debtor of a newspaper publisher. But it is equally certain that he may cause contractual relations to arise by necessary implication from his conduct. The law in respect of contractual indebtedness for a newspaper is not different from that relating to other things which have not been made the subject of an express agreement. Thus one may not have ordered supplies for his table, or other household necessities, yet if he continue to receive and use them, under circumstances where he had no right to suppose they were a gratuity, he will be held to have agreed, by implication, to pay their value. In this case defendant admits that, notwithstanding he ordered the paper discontinued

at the time when he paid a bill for it, yet plaintiff continued to send it, and he continued to take it from the post office to his home. This was an acceptance and use of the property, and, there being no pretense that a gratuity was intended, an obligation arose to pay for it." Austin v. Burge, 156 Mo.App. 286 (1911).

(5) *The Problem of Unordered Merchandise.* The widespread practice of sending unordered merchandise to prospective purchasers has elicited legislative responses at both the state and federal levels. As with the problem of "bait advertising," discussed above in the notes to *Lefkowitz,* general contract law has not operated as an effective control of the abusive practice. The Federal Trade Commission has become increasingly active in the area through issuance of cease and desist orders. These are based on findings that the methods employed constitute unfair and deceptive acts and practices in violation of Section 5 of the Federal Trade Commission Act. In addition, there is now a federal statute covering the shipment of unsolicited merchandise through the mails. It provides as follows:

(a) Except for (1) free samples clearly and conspicuously marked as such, and (2) merchandise mailed by a charitable organization soliciting contributions, the mailing of unordered merchandise or of communications prohibited by subsection (c) of this section constitutes an unfair method of competition and an unfair trade practice in violation of section 45(a)(1) of title 15 [§ 5 of Federal Trade Commission Act].

(b) Any merchandise mailed in violation of subsection (a) of this section, or within the exceptions contained therein, may be treated as a gift by the recipient, who shall have the right to retain, use, discard, or dispose of it in any manner he sees fit without any obligation whatsoever to the sender. All such merchandise shall have attached to it a clear and conspicuous statement informing the recipient that he may treat the merchandise as a gift to him and has the right to retain, use, discard, or dispose of it in any manner he sees fit without any obligation whatsoever to the sender.

(c) No mailer of any merchandise mailed in violation of subsection (a) of this section, or within the exceptions contained therein, shall mail to any recipient of such merchandise a bill for such merchandise or any dunning communications.

(d) For the purposes of this section, "unordered merchandise" means merchandise mailed without the prior expressed request or consent of the recipient.

39 U.S.C.A. § 3009. See Annot., *Validity, Construction, and Application of 39 U.S.C.A. § 3009, Making It an Unfair Trade Practice to Mail Unordered Merchandise,* 39 A.L.R.Fed. 674 (1978).

State authorities have also been responsive to this problem. An Illinois statute, for instance, reads as follows: "Unless otherwise agreed, where unsolicited goods are delivered to a person, he has a right to refuse to accept delivery of the goods and is not bound to return such goods to the sender. If such unsolicited goods are either addressed to or intended for the recipient, they shall be deemed a gift to the recipient, who may use them or dispose of them in any manner without any obligation to the sender." Smith-Hurd Ill.Ann.Stat. ch. 121½, § 351.

ap

R.L. Ammons v. Wilson & Co.

Supreme Court of Mississippi, 1936.
176 Miss. 645.

■ ANDERSON, JUSTICE. Appellant brought this action in the circuit court of Bolivar county against appellee, a Delaware corporation engaged in the meat packing business with its principal office at Kansas City, Kansas, to recover the sum of six hundred and fifty-eight dollars and seventy-four cents—damages claimed by appellant and alleged to have been caused by appellee's breach of contract to ship appellant nine hundred and forty-two cases of shortening. Appellant testified in his own behalf, and was the only witness who testified in the case. At the conclusion of the evidence, on appellee's motion, the court excluded it and directed a verdict and judgment for appellee which were accordingly entered. From that judgment appellant prosecutes this appeal.

Appellant was engaged in the wholesale grocery business at Beulah in Bolivar county. Appellee, as stated, was engaged in the business of meat packing, part of which was the manufacture and sale of shortening. Appellant made the following case by his evidence: Appellee had one Tweedy as its traveling salesman in the territory including Bolivar county. On or about the 9th, 10th or 11th of August, 1934 (appellant could not make it more definite in his testimony), Tweedy "booked" him for sixty thousand pounds of shortening at seven and one-half cents per pound tierce basis. The booking meant nothing more than the appellee was willing to receive orders from appellant for shortening up to that amount at seven and one-half cents per pound tierce basis, such orders subject to acceptance by appellee, and that by the booking appellant was not bound to order all or any part of the sixty thousand pounds, nor was appellee bound to accept orders for all or any part thereof. In other words, the evidence showed that the booking neither constituted a contract nor an absolute offer to contract—it was merely tentative. On the 23rd and 24th of August appellant, through appellee's traveling salesman Tweedy, ordered for prompt shipment nine hundred and forty-two cases of shortening, aggregating forty-three thousand, nine hundred and sixteen pounds. These orders were sent in by Tweedy. Appellant heard nothing from them until the 4th of September following, when he was advised by appellee, in response to his inquiry as to when the shipment would be made, that the orders had been declined. At that time the price of shortening was nine cents instead of seven and one-half cents a pound. In other words, appellee waited twelve days from the time the orders were given before declining to accept them. Tweedy had represented appellee in that territory for six or eight months and during that time he had taken several orders from appellant for certain of appellee's products, which orders in every case had been accepted and shipped not later than one week from the time they were given.

The orders here involved, as well as prior ones, were in writing and contained this provision: "This order taken subject to acceptance by seller's authorized agent at point of shipment." Under this stipulation the orders constituted mere offers to purchase on appellant's part and were not binding on appellee until received and accepted. It is also true, as contended by appellee, that its traveling salesman Tweedy was without authority to make a binding contract for it. The extent of his authority was to solicit and transmit orders to his principal for approval. . . .

The question in the case is whether or not, under the law, appellee should be charged with an implied acceptance of the orders by its silence. As above stated, all of appellant's previous orders had been accepted and the goods shipped not later than a week from the giving of such orders, while appellee was silent for twelve days after the giving of the orders here involved, and then refused to accept them in response to appellant's request for shipment. We think the sound governing principles are laid down in Restatement, Contracts, subsection 1(c) of section 72, the applicable part of which is as follows:

"(1) Where an offeree fails to reply to an offer, his silence and inaction operate as an acceptance in the following cases and in no others: * * *

"(c) Where because of previous dealings or otherwise, the offeree has given the offeror reason to understand that the silence of [or] inaction is intended by the offeree as a manifestation of assent, and the offeror does so understand."

"Illustration of Subsection (1, c): 5. A, through salesmen, has frequently solicited orders for goods from B, the orders to be subject to A's personal approval. In every case A has shipped the goods ordered within a week and without other notification to B than billing the goods to him. A's salesman solicits and receives another order from B. A receives the order and remains silent. B relies on the order and forbears to buy elsewhere for a week. A is bound to fill the order."

We are not aware of any decisions of our court in conflict with these principles; certainly those relied on by appellee are not.

We are of the opinion that it was a question for the jury whether or not appellee's delay of twelve days before rejecting the orders, in view of the past history of such transactions between the parties, including the booking, constituted an implied acceptance. The evidence was rather uncertain as to the damages suffered by appellant on account of the alleged breach of contract. If there was a breach, appellant was entitled to at least nominal damages. If there were actual damages, it devolves on appellant to trace them directly to the breach of the contract and make them definite enough to comply with the governing rules of law.

Reversed and remanded.

NOTES

(1) *Silence as Assent.* If *A* offers to sell *B* a certain book for $5, and the latter remains silent, is the silence indicative of assent? Not necessarily. *B* may be weighing the proposal, mentally determining whether to accept or reject, or may be thinking about something else altogether. Hence, there is the general refusal of courts to regard silence, standing alone, as constituting acceptance. But what if *A* adds: "If you say nothing I will know you accept." What objection is there then to holding *B* to a contract? Should the offeree be obliged to reply in order to prevent a contract? Finally, would there be any reason for objection to contract if *B,* taking *A* at his or her word, remained silent with the intention of accepting the offer?

(2) Would the result in *Ammons* have been the same even if there had been no previous dealings? Most likely there would have been no contract. What, then, was the effect of the prior course of dealing? The court in *Ammons* held that the jury should decide whether there was an implied acceptance.

Restatement (Second) § 69, pertaining to acceptance by silence or exercise of dominion, provides as follows:

(1) Where an offeree fails to reply to an offer, his silence and inaction operate as an acceptance in the following cases only:

(a) Where an offeree takes the benefit of offered services with reasonable opportunity to reject them and reason to know that they were offered with the expectation of compensation.

(b) Where the offeror has stated or given the offeree reason to understand that assent may be manifested by silence or inaction, and the offeree in remaining silent and inactive intends to accept the offer.

(c) Where because of previous dealings or otherwise, it is reasonable that the offeree should notify the offeror if he does not intend to accept.

(2) An offeree who does any act inconsistent with the offeror's ownership of offered property is bound in accordance with the offered terms unless they are manifestly unreasonable. . . . .

Subparagraph (a) describes what might alternatively be characterized as a partially implied-in-fact contract, where the offeree's taking of the benefit operates as acceptance. Subparagraph (c) covers circumstances where the parties' prior dealing establishes silence as acceptance. But subparagraph (b) is troubling from an objectivist standpoint because on its face there is no requirement of prior dealing or subsequent action to signal an offeree's assent. The few cases following the paragraph grow out of prior contractual dealings. See, e.g., *Golden Eagle Ins. Co. v. Foremost Ins. Co.*, 20 Cal.App.4th 1372 (1993) (offer of continued insurance was accepted by insured's silence).

(3) *An Agent's Authority.* In *Ammons,* Tweedy, the traveling salesman, was an agent of Wilson & Co., but did not have the authority to bind the latter contractually. When does an agent have such authority? In brief, when the principal confers the authority (actual) or holds the agent out as having the authority (apparent).

As defined by the Restatement of Agency, authority is "the power of the agent to affect the legal relations of the principal by acts done in accordance with the principal's manifestations of consent to him." Restatement (Second) of Agency § 7 (1958). This actual authority may be express (i.e., spelled out by the principal in directions to the agent) or implied (i.e., inferred from directions to the agent, customs of trade, etc.)

Whereas actual authority, express or implied, derives from what the principal tells the agent, apparent authority results from the principal's manifestations to third persons. "To bind the principal * * * the one dealing with the agent must prove that the principal was responsible for the appearance of authority by doing something or permitting the agent to do something which reasonably led others, including the plaintiff, to believe that the agent had the authority he purported to have. If this is proved, the principal should have realized that his conduct would cause others to believe that the agent was authorized, and the principal and the other party are bound by the ordinary rules of contract, unless the other has notice that the agent was unauthorized." Seavey, Handbook of the Law of Agency 13 (1964). Obviously, the objective theory of contracts and the agency doctrine of apparent authority are compatible ideas.

S. Allen Schreiber v. Olan Mills

Superior Court of Pennsylvania, 1993.
627 A.2d 806.

■ POPOVICH, JUDGE. We are asked to review the appeal of the order of September 15, 1992, granting the preliminary objections in the nature of a demurrer of the defendant, Olan Mills, and dismissing the complaint of the plaintiff/appellant, S. Allen Schreiber. We affirm.

On appeal from an order sustaining preliminary objections in the nature of demurrers, [we] must confine our analysis to the complaint and decide whether sufficient facts have been pleaded which would permit recovery if ultimately proven.

We begin our analysis with the observation that the defendant, a Tennessee-based corporation, operates a nationwide chain of family portrait studios. In securing business, the defendant relies heavily upon "telemarketing". This practice of soliciting customers, because of the compelling quality of the telephone as a desirable medium for disseminating information, has spawned a rapidly growing billion dollar industry which includes "telemarketing", phone surveying and soliciting by phone. Nadel, Mark S., *Rings of Privacy: Unsolicited Telephone Calls and the Right of Privacy,* 4 Yale J. on Reg. 99 (1986).

Instantly, a representative of the defendant phoned the plaintiff on November 29, 1989, the result of which prompted the following letter:

Mrs. Linda Borelli

Olan Mills 547

Clairton Blvd.

Pittsburgh, Pa. 15236

Dear telemarketer:

Today, you called us attempting to sell a product or a service. We have no interest in the product or service that you are selling. Please don't call us again. Please remove us from your telemarketing list and notify the provider of the list to also remove our name and number since we do not appreciate receiving telemarketing phone calls.

We rely on the availability of our phone lines which have been installed for our convenience and not for the convenience of telemarketers. We pay for these phone lines and instruments. You do not. Please don't tie up our phone lines.

Should we receive any more phone calls from you or from anyone connected with your firm of a telemarketing nature, we will consider that you have entered into a contract with us for our listening services and that you have made those calls to us and expect us to listen to your message on a "for hire" basis.

If we receive any additional telemarketing phone calls from you, you will be invoiced in accordance with our rates which are $100.00 per hour or fraction thereof with a $100.00 minimum charge. Payment will be due on a net seven (7) day basis.

Late payment charge of 1-1/2% per month or fraction thereof on the unpaid balance subject to a minimum late charge of $9.00 per invoice per month or fraction thereof will be billed if payment is not made as outlined above. This is an annual percentage rate of 18%. In addition, should it become necessary for us to institute collection activities, all costs in connection therewith including, but not limited to, attorney fees will also be due and collectible.

Thereafter, two phone contacts caused the plaintiff to bill the defendant for services, which, when not paid, resulted in the institution of a suit [before the arbitration division of the Court of Common Pleas] to collect $479.00 in fees. Preliminary objections were filed by the defendant in which it argued that the facts alleged in the complaint did not show an intent, on the part of either party or their representative, to enter into a contract.

The court concluded from a review of the record and law that the parties did not enter into a contract for the purchase of the plaintiff's "listening services." Not only did the court find that there was "no true and actual meeting of the minds," but, under the circumstances, there was no "ordinary course of dealing and the common understanding of men[ ] show[ing] a mutual intention to contract." Lower Court Opinion at 3, citing *Ingrassia Construction Co. v. Walsh*, 337 Pa.Super. 58 (1984). Thus, the defendant's preliminary objections were granted and this appeal followed.

The sole issue we need to concern ourselves with, in disposing of the case at bar, is whether a binding contract was effectuated between the parties so as to obligate the defendant to pay the plaintiff for his "listening-for-hire" services.

[W]hen seeking to enforce an agreement, one may look to the "conduct" of the parties to ascertain the acceptance of the agreement. A panel of this Court, when confronted with the question of whether "conduct" is sufficient to constitute "acceptance" of an "offer" for services provided, has held:

> It is settled that for an agreement to exist, there must be a "meeting of the minds," . . .; the very essence of an agreement is that the parties mutually assent to the same thing, ... The principle that a contract is not binding unless there is an offer and an acceptance is to ensure that there will be mutual assent. . . . Notwithstanding the aforesaid, it is equally well-established that "an offer may be accepted by conduct and what the parties d[o] pursuant to th[e] offer" is germane to show whether the offer is accepted. *Accu-Weather, Inc. v. Thomas Broadcasting Co.,* 425 Pa.Super. 335 (1993).

Instantly, it is evident from the tenor of the plaintiff's communique to the defendant that it was in the nature of a "cease and desist" request rather than an "offer" to "listen . . . 'for hire' " to the solicitations of the defendant. As observed by the court on this point:

> The sole purpose of the November 29, 1989 letter was to encourage Olan Mills to remove plaintiff from its calling lists and not to solicit a purchaser for "listening services." The sole purpose of any additional calls that Olan Mills made to plaintiff was to solicit orders and not to obtain "listening services." Consequently, as a matter of law the parties did not enter into a contract.

Lower Court Opinion at 3. We agree.

[T]here obviously can be no bargained-for-exchange ("consideration") if one of the parties acts without any intention of binding itself to a contract for "listening services." There was no "unconditional" manifestation on the part of Olan Mills or its representative that a contract was acknowledged by behavior of the defendant.

Unlike *Accu-Weather, Inc.,* supra, at bar there was no "offer", "acceptance', "consideration" or "mutual meeting of the minds" to effectuate the elemental aspects of a contract.

Order affirmed.

NOTES

(1)   Is it clear that the "sole purpose" of Schreiber's letter was to remove plaintiff from its calling lists? Could future Schreibers change the language of their letter to make it an offer for "listening services"? Is this a case like *Cohen v. Cowles Media Co,* supra Chapter 2, where the court for public policy reasons wants to bar certain types of offers. Would consumers be better off if consumer offers for unilateral contracts against manufacturers were enforced?

(2)   Even though offerors are masters of their offers, they are not allowed to name modes of acceptance that would force offerees to deviate from their normal life activities. For example, imagine that Will says to Grace, "I offer to buy your car for $50, and I will take your going to work sometime next week as accepting my offer." If Grace goes to her place of employment in the next week, she has not manifested assent (because she was going there anyway). Would a better rationale for this ruling be that calling = acceptance was an unreasonable condition of acceptance for Schreiber to impose?

(3)   The FTC's Do-Not-Call Registry was not launched until 2003. Would Schreiber have a stronger argument that his letter plus subsequent telemarketing call constituted a contract if Schreiber had the right to register his home number? If he had exercised that right?

Comment: The Role of Conduct as Evidence of Agreement in UCC Article 2

UCC § 1–201(b)(3) defines "agreement" as the "bargain of the parties in fact as found in their language or by implication from other circumstances including course of dealing or usage of trade or course of performance as provided in this Act (Section 1–303, . . .)." "Contract" is defined as the "total legal obligation which results from the parties' agreement as affected by this Act and any other applicable rules of law." UCC § 1–201(b)(12). Where a claimed sale of goods or a lease of goods are involved, whether an agreement as defined in Article 1 is a contract depends upon the application of Article 2 or Article 2A of the UCC. In answering the formation question in a "code covered" transaction, e.g., an alleged sale of goods, Article 1 and Article 2 may be read together.

Consider again the facts in *Ammons v. Wilson & Co.,* supra. The seller's agent, Tweedy, solicited an order of a specific quantity of goods at a fixed price from Ammons for "prompt shipment." This order was then treated as an offer.

Under UCC § 2–206(1)(b), the offer could be accepted by a "prompt promise to ship" or by the "prompt or current shipment of conforming goods. . . ." Thus, an invited method of acceptance is the conduct of shipment. Moreover, the "beginning of a requested performance", if reasonable, may also create a contract. UCC § 2–206(2). This, however, is not the *Ammons* case.

To vary the facts a bit more, suppose the offer was for 942 cases of shortening and the seller responded by telephone that it could ship only 800 cases. At this point there is no contract but the seller has made a counteroffer to ship 800 cases which the buyer can accept or reject. Suppose the buyer initially says no to the counteroffer but the seller, nevertheless, ships 800 cases and the buyer accepts them without objection. Is there a contract? See UCC § 2–204(1). If so, what are the terms? More pointedly, what is the agreement upon which the contract rests? Clearly, it is at a minimum an agreement to buy 800 cases.

Return to *Ammons* where the offer was to buy 942 cases at 7½ cents per pound. Since Wilson neither shipped nor promised to ship (and in fact ultimately rejected the offer), is the failure to reject within a reasonable time an acceptance under Article 2? The answer depends on whether the seller has agreed to the buyer's proposed bargain and this turns on how one uses the prior course of dealing between the parties. Read UCC § 1–303. Is that course of dealing "other circumstances" from which the seller's agreement to accept orders by silence unless a prompt rejection is given can be implied? If not, may the buyer turn to the protective arm of Section 69(1)(c) of the Restatement (Second)? We think that the answer to the first question is "probably not" but that the answer to the second question is "yes."

Beneficial National Bank, U.S.A. v. Obie Payton

United States District Court, S.D. Mississippi, 2001.
214 F.Supp.2d 679.

■ TOM S. LEE, CHIEF JUDGE. Two motions are currently pending in this court for decision. Defendant Obie Payton has moved to dismiss the case for lack of subject matter jurisdiction, and plaintiffs Beneficial National Bank, U.S.A. (Beneficial) and Household Bank (SB), N.A. (Household) have moved to compel arbitration pursuant to § 4 of the Federal Arbitration Act (FAA), 9 U.S.C. § 4. Having considered these motions, together with the parties' responses and accompanying memoranda of authorities and attachments, the court * * * concludes that plaintiffs' motion to compel arbitration is well taken and should be granted.

In April 1995, the defendant purchased a home satellite system which he financed through a revolving credit card account with Beneficial. That account was later assigned to Household. In February 2001, Payton filed suit against Beneficial and Household in the Circuit Court of Kemper County, Mississippi alleging that his participation in this transaction was induced by fraudulent misrepresentations and other wrongful conduct on the part of Household and its agents. Shortly after Payton filed suit, Household and Beneficial brought this action in federal court to compel arbitration in accordance with § 4 of the FAA, contending that the claims asserted against them by Payton in the state court action are governed by an arbitration agreement that is a part of Payton's cardholder agreement.

* * *

To fully appreciate the parties' arguments, it is important to first understand the factual setting underlying plaintiffs' contention that Payton's agreement includes a provision for mandatory arbitration and Payton's contention that it does not. Payton's signature on the credit application with Beneficial appears directly below the following statement:

> You acknowledge that you have received and read a copy of the BNB USA Cardholder Agreement attached hereto and made a part of this Application (including the instructions in the Account Information paragraph) and understand and agree to its terms and conditions. . . .

The accompanying "Cardholder Agreement and Disclosure Statement" recites, in relevant part, as follows:

> NOTICE TO CARDHOLDER:
>
> Do not use your Cardholder Account ("the Account") before you read this Agreement. You are entitled to an exact copy of this Agreement. Keep it to protect your legal rights. You have the right to pay amounts owed under your Account in full or in part at any time without penalty.
>
> Agreement: You have applied for an Account with us. The Account can only be used to obtain advances to purchase goods and services ("Purchase Advances") from participating merchants and to which merchants we will advance funds for such purchases. You will be required to sign a Sales Slip or other written authorization for such purchases. By applying for an Account or signing the Application or using this Account, you agree to the terms and conditions contained in this Agreement and the terms and conditions contained in the Application, which you and we agree is a part of this Agreement.
>
> . . .
>
> Change in Terms: We may change the terms of this Agreement with respect to both existing balances and future purchases. To the extent required by law, we will mail you written notice of any change at least 30 days prior to its effective date. The change will then occur automatically on its effective date. If the change will increase your periodic interest or interest charges,

the change will occur on its effective date, unless you notify us in writing within that 30 day period, that you do not accept the change. If you so notify us, we will allow you to pay off your remaining balance under current terms, however we may close your Account to further charges. At our option, we may choose to make any change effective only if you use your Account on or after a specified date.

. . .

Applicable Law: This Agreement is governed by the law of the State of Delaware and applicable federal laws.

In 1996, the year after Payton applied for and was approved for the Beneficial account, Beneficial sent a notice to all its cardholders, including Payton, advising that changes were being made to the Cardholder Agreement, and specifically, that a provision for mandatory arbitration was to become a part of the agreement unless the cardholder rejected the change. The notice stated as follows:

NOTICE TO CARDHOLDERS

This will notify you that changes are being made to your Cardholder Agreement and Disclosure Statement ("Agreement") for your private label credit card account with Beneficial National Bank USA. Effective in thirty days, the following section will be added to your agreement:

Arbitration: Any claim, dispute or controversy (whether in contract, tort or otherwise) arising from or relating to this Agreement or the relationships which result from this Agreement, including the validity or enforceability of this arbitration clause or the entire Agreement ("Claim"), shall be resolved, upon the election of you or us, by binding arbitration pursuant to this arbitration provision and the Code of Procedure of the National Arbitration Forum in effect at the time the Claim is filed. Any such election may be made at any time, regardless of whether a law suit has been filed or not, unless such a law suit him resulted in a judgment. Rules and forms of the National Arbitration Forum may be obtained by calling (800) 474–2371 and all Claims shall be filed at any National Arbitration Forum office or at Post Office Box 50191, Minneapolis, Minnesota 55404. Any participatory arbitration hearing that you attend will take place in the federal judicial district of your residence. At your request, we will advance the filing and hearing fees for any Claim which you may file against us. The arbitrator will decide whether we or you will ultimately be responsible for paying these fees.

This arbitration agreement is made pursuant to a transaction involving interstate commerce, and shall be governed by the Federal Arbitration Act, 9 U.S.C. Sections 1–16. The arbitrator shall apply relevant law and provide written, reasoned findings of fact and conclusions of law. Judgment upon the award may be entered in any court having jurisdiction.

. . .

Notwithstanding the foregoing, you have the option to notify us before the aforesaid 30 day period has elapsed that you do not agree to accept these changes by writing to us at BNB USA, P.O. Box 15521, Wilmington, Delaware, whereupon you shall have the right to continue to pay off the credit card account in the same manner and under the same terms and conditions as now in effect. In the absence of your giving us such notice, you will be deemed to consent to the changes.

It is undisputed that Payton did not notify Beneficial within the thirty day period that he did not agree to accept these changes, and thus according to plaintiffs, the changes became effective November 8, 1996.

About a year-and-a-half later, in May 1999, Payton's account with Beneficial was assigned to Household Bank. Cardholders were notified of the assignment by a billing statement insert. The insert . . . included a provision for arbitration substantially like that set forth in Beneficial's 1996 notice of changes.

Plaintiffs maintain that the arbitration provision added in 1996 to the original Beneficial Cardholder Agreement was and is valid and enforceable inasmuch as Payton agreed to the original cardholder agreement which authorized Beneficial to change the terms of the agreement upon giving any notice required by law. They submit further that because Payton continued to maintain his account after it was transferred to Household and after being apprized of the terms of Household's Cardholder Agreement, he thereby became bound by the arbitration provision contained in the Household Cardholder Agreement.

In his response to plaintiffs' motion to compel arbitration, Payton insists that he never agreed to arbitrate any disputes with plaintiffs, as the original agreement did not grant Beneficial the right to add altogether new terms to the parties' existing agreement, and since he never affirmatively accepted the terms of either the Beneficial Amended Cardholder Agreement or took any of the steps required to bind him to the terms of the Household Cardholder Agreement. * * * [He] insists that the "change of terms" provision only authorized Beneficial to change existing terms of the agreement and did not give Beneficial the right to add altogether new terms.

In *Bank One v. Coates*, 125 F.Supp.2d 819 (S.D. Miss. 2001), this court considered whether an arbitration provision could be added to an existing agreement pursuant to a provision in the parties' original agreement authorizing the lender to "change or amend the terms" of the agreement upon notification to the borrower defendant. The defendant argued that despite this provision, he could not have anticipated that the lender could amend the agreement to add an arbitration agreement, since the original agreement contained no mention of arbitration and the "amendment" provision referenced only changes to payments, charges, fees and the interest rate. The court rejected the defendant's argument because "[t]he agreement . . . stated simply, unambiguously and without limitation, that [the lender] could 'change or amend the terms of th[e] Agreement.'" The court stated,

> Given . . . that the original cardholder agreement permitted amendments, the arbitration provision is not rendered unenforceable simply by virtue of the fact that Bank One undertook to add the arbitration provision via amendment. Consistent with the terms of the original agreement, Bank One could validly amend its agreement to add an arbitration clause, just as it could have amended the agreement to add or change any other term on the agreement. See, e.g., Samuels v. Old Kent Bank, No. 96 C 6667, 1997 WL 458434 (N.D.Ill. Aug.1, 1997) (canceling Card Miles bonus program).[8]

Defendant submits that Coates is distinguishable since the provision in the original agreement in Coates authorized the lender to "change or amend" the terms of the parties' agreement whereas the agreement at issue here allowed Beneficial only to "change" the terms of the agreement. In the court's opinion, however, there is no practical distinction between a "change" and an "amendment" to the terms of the agreement. The agreement authorized Beneficial to "change the terms of the agreement," which Beneficial did by mailing to its cardholders, including Payton, a notice of the change in terms which included an arbitration provision. The notice to Payton specifically informed him that he had the right to reject the arbitration provision, and yet the record reflects that he did not avail himself of that right.

Payton next argues, though, that irrespective of the terms of the "Notice to Cardholders" which clearly required customers to affirmatively reject the arbitration agreement if they did not wish it to become a part of their contracts with Beneficial, his failing to take affirmative steps to opt out of the arbitration provision is immaterial

---

[8]   See also Marsh v. First USA Bank, N.A., 103 F.Supp.2d 909, 921 (N.D.Tex. 2000) (enforcing arbitration agreement added by way of amendment to credit card agreement); Herrington v. Union Planters Bank N.A., 113 F.Supp.2d 1026, 1031 (S.D.Miss. 2000) (enforcing arbitration agreement added to account agreement via amendment); Stiles v. Home Cable Concepts, Inc., 994 F.Supp. 1410, 1419 (M.D.Ala. 1998) (enforcing arbitration provision added to a credit card agreement via amendment where original agreement provided that it was subject to change, the plaintiff acknowledged that he had received notice of the amendment and he agreed that he had failed to return the postage-paid card provided by the company for customers who chose to reject the arbitration provision); cf. Goetsch v. Shell Oil Co., 197 F.R.D. 574 (W.D.N.C. 2000) (enforcing amendments to credit card agreement which first added and then modified the added arbitration agreement where original agreement provided for amendment by notice to cardholder); Hill v. Gateway 2000, Inc., 105 F.3d 1147 (7th Cir.), cert. denied, 522 U.S. 808, 118 S.Ct. 47, 139 L.Ed.2d 13 (1997) (arbitration clause which was included with product (computer) mailed to customer with a proviso that the customer could return the product within 30 days was binding on customer who did not return the computer).

since a valid and binding arbitration agreement may not be predicated on nothing more than his failure to reject the arbitration provision. For this proposition, defendant relies on *Long v. Fidelity Water Systems, Inc.*, (N.D.Cal. 2000), in which the court suggested that acceptance of an arbitration agreement may not be found based merely on a party's failure to reject such an agreement. In Coates, however, this court considered the California court's opinion in *Long*, and found it unpersuasive. * * *

Defendant next maintains that even if the arbitration provision became a part of his contract, his claims against plaintiffs do not fall within the scope of the arbitration provision since they relate to allegedly wrongful acts that were committed prior to the purported effective date of the arbitration agreement. He argues, in other words, that the arbitration provision may not be applied retroactively to events which predated the alleged arbitration agreement. Based on the following, the court must disagree. As numerous courts have recognized,

> if [an] arbitration clause contains retroactive time-specific language, e.g., a phrase reading "this agreement applies to all transactions occurring before or after this agreement," then [the court] may apply the arbitration provision to events relating to past events. Or, if the arbitration clause contains language stating that it applies to "all transactions between us" or "all business with us," then [the court] may apply the arbitration clause retroactively.

Kenworth of Dothan v. Bruner-Wells Trucking, Inc., 745 So.2d 271, 275 (Ala. 1999). In the case at bar, while the Beneficial arbitration provision contains no "retroactive time-specific language," in the court's opinion, it is sufficiently broad to cover the dispute between the parties in the state court action, particularly considering that ambiguity as to the availability of arbitration is to be resolved in favor of arbitration. * * *

In a final attempt to avoid arbitration, Payton asserts that the arbitration provision at issue is substantively unconscionable because it designates the National Arbitration Forum (NAF) as the arbitral forum. However, as this court stated in Coates, "the rules governing the conduct of NAF arbitrations belie [Payton's] speculation that suspected bias by the NAF has any realistic potential for affecting decisions of arbitrators in NAF arbitrations." Coates, 125 F.Supp.2d at 835. Defendant may not avoid arbitration on this basis.

For all of the foregoing reasons, the court concludes that plaintiffs' motion to compel arbitration should be granted.

NOTES

(1) The *Payton* case concerns the increasingly common "change of term" provision which allows banks, credit-card issuers, cellular service carriers, airlines with frequent-flier programs, cable television companies, Internet service companies and other sellers of consumer products and

services to unilaterally modify the terms of an agreement. An important aspect of these "change of term" provisions is that consumer silence operates as acceptance. The concern is that consumers will not pay attention to the junk mail that changes substantive provisions, including the price, of their services. See David Horton, *The Shadow Terms: Contract Procedure and Unilateral Amendments*, 57 UCLA L. Rev. 605 (2010).

(2)   One way to understand the issue in *Payton* is in terms of defaults and altering rules. The default in contract law is that there is usually no acceptance by silence. When the parties enter into an agreement, should they be allowed to change that default with respect to their subsequent dealings? If you answer "No," then you think the silence rule should be a mandatory one. If you answer "Yes," there remains a further question: What should the parties have to do in order to opt-out of the default? That is, what is the altering rule? In *Payton*, this comes down to the question: Should the language in the Cardholder Agreement and Disclosure Statement be enough to allow the credit card company to unilaterally change terms, or should the law require additional steps?

(3)   As of the writing of this edition, eleven states have passed versions of Uniform Consumer Credit Code § 3.205, which makes "silence as acceptance" the default: "Whether or not a change is authorized by prior agreement, a creditor may change the terms of an open-end credit account applying to any balance incurred before or after the effective date of the change." This language suggests that creditors can unilaterally modify the contracts even when there is no express change of term provision in the initial contract.

(4)   The Credit Card Accountability Responsibility and Disclosure Act of 2009 limits the types of unilateral modification that can be made to credit card contracts (for example, the statute prohibits interest hikes on existing balances unless the cardholder falls 60 days behind on the minimum payments). Oren Bar-Gill and Kevin Davis have proposed that unilateral modification only be enforced if approved by "Change Approval Boards." Oren Bar-Gill and Kevin Davis, *Empty Promises*, 84 S. Cal. L. Rev. 1 (2010). See also Ian Ayres and Barry Nalebuff, *A Market Test for Credit Cards*, Forbes 34 (July 13, 2009) (proposing that "[a]t the time when the lender proposes a unilateral change, it would be required to put the existing account balance up for auction on a LendingTree-like service that would allow other credit card issuers to bid for a chance to issue a new card and take over the existing balance.").

(5)   The new terms at issue in *Beneficial National Bank* stipulated arbitration by the National Arbitration Forum (NAF). In 2008, the San Francisco City Attorney sued Bank of America's credit card subsidiary for its use of the NAF. The suit alleged that the NAF operated an "arbitration mill, churning out arbitration awards in favor of debt collectors and against California consumers, often without regard to whether consumers actually owed the money sought by debt collectors." The case was settled for a payment of $5 million and an agreement by Bank of America not to work with the NAF for at least five years. See Amy Yarbrough, "BOFA 'arbitration mill' case reaches settlement," Daily Journal (August 22, 2011).

(6)   In a footnote above, the court cites *Hill v. Gateway 2000, Inc.*, 105 F.3d 1147 (7th Cir. 1997). This Seventh Circuit's opinion in that case is reproduced in Section 2.B below.

(E) TERMINATION OF OFFERS

We have observed that an offer is a dangerous thing. To make an offer is to give the offeree the power to accept—the power, through the offeree's unilateral act, to bind the offeror to the contract. When does the offeree's power to accept end? Suppose the offeror has a change of heart before the offeree has had a chance to accept. Should the offeror be able to withdraw the offer? If so, how? Alternatively, suppose an offeror wants to make a binding offer—one that he or she cannot withdraw. Should we give offerors the power to make such offers? If so, when and how?

This section discusses these and related questions. As we will see, the law's answers to them have been influenced by the consideration doctrine. The answers also differ depending on the mode of acceptance—whether the offer invites acceptance by return promise, by performance, or by either. And the answers sometimes turn on the issue of reliance, as found in the doctrine of promissory estoppel. The legal questions discussed in this section may seem relatively narrow. All have to do only with the duration of offers. But their answers illustrate the place of offers in contract law as a whole and require an understanding of a number of other rules. Here, as elsewhere in contract, no rule is an island unto itself. All are connected to the whole.

Steve Hendricks v. Eugene Behee
Missouri Court of Appeals, Southern District, 1990.
Supra at 239.

George Dickinson v. John Dodds
Court of Appeal, Chancery Division, 1876.
2 Ch.D. 463.

On Wednesday, the 10th of June, 1874, the Defendant John Dodds signed and delivered to the Plaintiff, George Dickinson, a memorandum, of which the material part was as follows:—

"I hereby agree to sell to Mr. George Dickinson the whole of the dwelling-houses, garden ground, stabling, and outbuildings thereto belonging, situate at Croft, belonging to me, for the sum of 800. As witness my hand this tenth day of June, 1874.

"£800.(Signed) John Dodds."

"P.S.—This offer to be left over until Friday, 9 o'clock, A.M. J.D. (the twelfth), 12th June, 1874.

"(Signed) J. Dodds."

The bill alleged that Dodds understood and intended that the Plaintiff should have until Friday 9 A.M. within which to determine whether he would or would not purchase, and that he should absolutely have until that time the refusal of the property at the price of £800, and that the Plaintiff in fact determined to accept the offer on the morning of Thursday, the 11th of June, but did not at once signify his acceptance to Dodds, believing that he had the power to accept it until 9 A.M. on the Friday.

In the afternoon of the Thursday the Plaintiff was informed by a Mr. Berry that Dodds had been offering or agreeing to sell the property to Thomas Allan, the other Defendant. Thereupon the Plaintiff, at about half-past seven in the evening, went to the house of Mrs. Burgess, the mother-in-law of Dodds, where he was then staying, and left with her a formal acceptance in writing of the offer to sell the property. According to the evidence of Mrs. Burgess this document never in fact reached Dodds, she having forgotten to give it to him.

On the following (Friday) morning, at about seven o'clock, Berry, who was acting as agent for Dickinson, found Dodds at the Darlington railway station, and handed to him a duplicate of the acceptance by Dickinson, and explained to Dodds its purport. He replied that it was too late, as he had sold the property. A few minutes later Dickinson himself found Dodds entering a railway carriage, and handed him another duplicate of the notice of acceptance, but Dodds declined to receive it, saying, "You are too late. I have sold the property."

It appeared that on the day before, Thursday, the 11th of June, Dodds had signed a formal contract for the sale of the property to the Defendant Allan for £800, and had received from him a deposit of £40.

The bill in this suit prayed that the Defendant Dodds might be decreed specifically to perform the contract of the 10th of June, 1874; that he might be restrained from conveying the property to Allan; that Allan might be restrained from taking any such conveyance; that, if any such conveyance had been or should be made, Allan might be declared a trustee of the property for, and might be directed to convey the property to, the Plaintiff; and for damages.

The cause came on for hearing before Vice-Chancellor Bacon on the 25th of January, 1876.

[A decree for specific performance was entered, and the Defendants appealed.]

■ JAMES, L.J., after referring to the document of the 10th of June, 1874, continued:—

The document, though beginning "I hereby agree to sell," was nothing but an offer, and was only intended to be an offer, for the Plaintiff himself tells us that he required time to consider whether he would enter into an agreement or not. Unless both parties had then agreed there was no concluded agreement then made; it was in effect and substance only an offer to sell. The Plaintiff, being minded not to complete the bargain at that time, added this memorandum—"This offer to be left over until Friday, 9 o'clock A.M., 12th June, 1874." That shews it was only an offer. There was no consideration given for the undertaking or promise, to whatever extent it may be considered binding, to keep the property unsold until 9 o'clock on Friday morning; but apparently Dickinson was of opinion, and probably Dodds was of the same opinion, that he (Dodds) was bound by that promise, and could not in any way withdraw from it, or retract it, until 9 o'clock on Friday morning, and this probably explains a good deal of what afterwards took place. But it is clear settled law, on one of the clearest principles of law, that this promise, being a mere nudum pactum, was not binding, and that at any moment before a complete acceptance by Dickinson of the offer, Dodds was as free as Dickinson himself. Well, that being the state of things, it is said that the only mode in which Dodds could assert that freedom was by actually and distinctly saying to Dickinson, "Now I withdraw my offer." It appears to me that there is neither principle nor authority for the proposition that there must be an express and actual withdrawal of the offer, or what is called a retraction. It must, to constitute a contract, appear that the two minds were at one, at the same moment of time, that is, that there was an offer continuing up to the time of the acceptance. If there was not such a continuing offer, then the acceptance comes to nothing. Of course it may well be that the one man is bound in some way or other to let the other man know that his mind with regard to the offer has been changed; but in this case, beyond all question, the Plaintiff knew that Dodds was no longer minded to sell the property to him as plainly and clearly as if Dodds had told him in so many words, "I withdraw the offer." This is evident from the Plaintiff's own statements in the bill.

The Plaintiff says in effect that, having heard and knowing that Dodds was no longer minded to sell to him, and that he was selling or had sold to some one else, thinking that he could not in point of law withdraw his offer, meaning to fix him to it, and endeavouring to bind him, "I went to the house where he was lodging, and saw his mother-in-law, and left with her an acceptance of the offer, knowing all the while that he had entirely changed his mind. I got an agent to watch for him at 7 o'clock the next morning, and I went to the train just before 9 o'clock, in order that I might catch him and give him my notice of acceptance just before 9 o'clock, and when that occurred he told my agent, and he told me, you are too late, and he then threw back the paper." It is to my mind quite clear that before there was any attempt at acceptance by the Plaintiff, he was perfectly well aware that Dodds had changed his mind, and that he had in fact agreed to sell the property to Allan. It is impossible, therefore, to say there was ever that existence of the same mind between the two parties which is essential in point of law to the making of an agreement. I am of opinion, therefore, that the Plaintiff has failed to prove that there was any binding contract between Dodds and himself.

■ MELLISH, L.J.:—I am of the same opinion. The first question is, whether this document of the 10th of June, 1874, which was signed by Dodds, was an agreement to sell, or only an offer to sell, the property therein mentioned to Dickinson; and I am clearly of opinion that it was only an offer, although it is in the first part of it, independently of the postscript, worded as an agreement. I apprehend that, until acceptance, so that both parties are bound, even though an instrument is so worded as to express that both parties agree, it is in point of law only an offer, and, until both parties are bound, neither party is bound. It is not necessary that both parties should be bound within the Statute of Frauds, for, if one party makes an offer in writing, and the other accepts it verbally, that will be sufficient to bind the person who has signed the written document. But, if there be no agreement, either verbally or in writing, then, until acceptance, it is in point of law an offer only, although worded as if it were an agreement. But it is hardly necessary to resort to that doctrine in the present case, because the postscript calls it an offer, and says, "This offer to be left over until Friday, 9 o'clock A.M." Well, then, this being only an offer, the law says—and it is a perfectly clear rule of law—that, although it is said that the offer is to be left open until Friday morning at 9 o'clock, that did not bind Dodds. He was not in point of law bound to hold the offer over until 9 o'clock on Friday morning. He was not so bound either in law or in equity. Well, that being so, when on the next day he made an agreement with Allan to sell the property to him, I am not aware of any ground on which it can be said that that contract with Allan was not as good and binding a contract as ever was made. Assuming Allan to have known (there is some dispute about it, and Allan does not admit that he knew of it, but I will assume that he did) that Dodds had made the offer to Dickinson, and had given him till Friday morning at 9 o'clock to accept it, still in point of law that could not prevent Allan from making a more favourable offer than Dickinson, and entering at once into a binding agreement with Dodds.

Then Dickinson is informed by Berry that the property has been sold by Dodds to Allan. Berry does not tell us from whom he heard it, but he says that he did hear it, that he knew it, and that he informed Dickinson of it. Now, stopping there, the question which arises is this—If an offer has been made for the sale of property, and before that offer is accepted, the person who has made the offer enters into a binding agreement to sell the property to somebody else, and the person to whom the offer was first made receives notice in some way that the property has been sold to another person, can he after that make a binding contract by the acceptance of the offer? I am of opinion that he cannot. The law may be right or wrong in saying that a person who has given to another a certain time within which to accept an offer is not bound by his promise to give that time; but, if he is not bound by that promise, and may still sell the property to some one else, and if it be the law that, in order to make a contract, the two minds must be in agreement at some one time, that is, at the time of the acceptance, how is it possible that when the person to whom the offer has been made knows that the person who has made the offer has sold the property to someone else, and that, in fact, he has not remained in the same mind to sell it to him, he can be at liberty to accept the offer and thereby make a binding contract? It seems to me that would be simply absurd. If a man makes an offer to sell a particular horse in his stable, and says, "I will give you until the day after to-morrow to accept the offer," and the next day goes and sells the horse to somebody else, and receives the purchase-money from him, can the person to whom the offer was originally made then come and say, "I accept," so as to make a binding contract, and so as to be entitled to recover damages for the non-delivery of the horse? If the rule of law is that a mere offer to sell property, which can be withdrawn at any time, and which is made dependent on the acceptance of the person to whom it is made, is a mere nudum pactum, how is it possible that the person to whom the offer has been made can by acceptance make a binding contract after he knows that the person who has made the offer has sold the property to some one else? It is admitted law that, if a man who makes an offer dies, the offer cannot be accepted after he is dead, and parting with the property has very much the same effect as the death of the owner, for it makes the performance of the offer impossible. I am clearly of opinion that, just as when a man who has made an offer dies before it is accepted it is impossible that it can then be accepted, so when once the person to whom the offer was made knows that the property has been sold to some one else, it is too late for him to accept the offer, and on that ground I am clearly of opinion that there was no binding contract for the sale of this property by Dodds to Dickinson, and even if there had been, it seems to me that the sale of the property to Allan was first in point of time. However, it is not necessary to consider, if there had been two binding contracts, which of them would be entitled to priority in equity, because there is no binding contract between Dodds and Dickinson.

NOTES

(1)   Why wasn't the offer in *Dickinson* irrevocable, given the postscript that "this offer to be left over until Friday . . . 12th June, 1874"? Is this a sensible application of the doctrine of consideration?

(2)   Section 42 of the First Restatement, following *Dickinson,* provided: "Where an offer is for the sale of an interest in land or in other things, if the offeror, after making the offer, sells or contracts to sell the interest to another person, and the offeree acquires reliable information of that fact, before he has exercised his power of creating a contract by acceptance of the offer, the offer is revoked." Should this rule of "indirect revocation" be limited to cases involving "the sale of an interest in land or in other things"? The drafters of the Second Restatement extended the scope of the corresponding section: "An offeree's power of acceptance is terminated when the offeror takes definite action inconsistent with an intention to enter into the proposed contract and the offeree acquires reliable information to that effect." Restatement (Second) § 43.

(3)   Do the opinions clearly disclose whether Berry told Dickinson that Dodds had actually contracted to sell to another or had merely made an offer to sell? Would, or should, the result be the same in either case?

Suppose that Dodds learned from a reliable third person that Dickinson was no longer interested in the offer and had agreed to purchase other property instead. Could Dickinson, assuming he had not spoken with Dodds about the matter, change his mind and accept the offer of Dodds?

(4)   Is *Dickinson* consistent with the objective theory of contracts? Here is Holmes in a different context:

> It seems to us a reasonable requirement that, to disable the plaintiffs from accepting their offer, the defendants should bring home to them actual notice that it has been revoked. By their choice and act they brought about a relation between themselves and the plaintiffs, which the plaintiffs could turn into a contract by an act on their part, and authorized the plaintiffs to understand and to assume that that relation existed. When the plaintiffs acted in good faith on the assumption, the defendants could not complain. Knowingly to lead a person reasonably to suppose that you offer, and to offer, are the same thing. . . . The offer must be made before the acceptance, and it does not matter whether it is made a longer or shorter time before, if, by its express or implied terms, it is outstanding at the time of the acceptance. Whether much or little time has intervened, it reaches forward to the moment of the acceptance, and speaks then. It would be monstrous to allow an inconsistent act of the offeror, not known or brought to the notice of the offeree, to affect the making of the contract; for instance, a sale by an agent elsewhere one minute after the principal personally has offered goods which are accepted within five minutes by the person to whom he is speaking. The principle is the same when the time is longer, and the act relied on a step looking to, but not yet giving notice.

Brauer v. Shaw, 168 Mass. 198, 198–200 (1897). See G. Gilmore, The Death of Contract 28–34 (1974).

(5)   Restatement (Second) § 36: "(1) An offeree's power of acceptance may be terminated by (a) rejection or counter-offer by the offeree, or (b) lapse of time, or (c) revocation by the offeror, or (d) death or incapacity of the offeror or offeree. (2) In addition, an offeree's power of acceptance is terminated by the non-occurrence of any condition of acceptance under the terms of the offer."

(6)   *Rewards.* Additional considerations are involved in determining how a general offer may be revoked. If, for example, the offeror in *Glover v. Jewish War Veterans*, supra Section 1.D.2, had decided to withdraw its offer, how could it have done so? It would scarcely be feasible to notify directly all offerees, nor would "indirect revocation" reach the vast majority of those who had read the advertisements. The authorities favor a practical rule that, in general, obliges the offeror to give the notice of revocation publicity equal to

that given the offer. See Restatement (Second) § 46; Corbin § 41; Williston §§ 59–59A.

(7) *Lapse of Offer.* An offer "lapses" of its own terms after the expiration of the time stipulated in the offer or upon the occurrence of a stipulated event, or if there is no such stipulation, after a reasonable period of time. See Restatement (Second) § 41. What is reasonable will depend upon the circumstances. For example, one would expect an offer to sell securities that are subject to rapid price fluctuations to lapse after a shorter period of time than an offer to sell unimproved real estate. Where the offer stipulates that it will be open for a stated period (e.g., ten days), generally the period will begin when the offer is received, not when it is dispatched. Caldwell v. Cline, 109 W.Va. 553 (1930). Finally, an offer made by one to another in face-to-face conversation is ordinarily deemed to continue only to the close of their conversation and cannot be accepted thereafter. Akers v. J.B. Sedberry, Inc., 39 Tenn.App. 633 (1955). See also Newman v. Schiff, 778 F.2d 460 (8th Cir. 1985) (Schiff's statement on the live CBS Nightwatch program that he would pay $100,000 to anyone who called the show and cited any section of the Internal Revenue Code "that says an individual is required to file a tax return" constituted an offer, but it did not extend beyond the time of the program).

PROBLEM: THE CASE OF THE DEAD GUARANTOR

You are an Associate Justice of the Supreme Court of Nowhere. The case of *Millcreek Corporation v. Simmons, Executor,* is now under advisement. Set out below are draft opinions by our colleagues. You are the swing vote in the case. Prepare a short opinion in which you either affirm or reverse the courts below and give reasons for your decision.

Beginning in 1989 the plaintiff, a wholesaler of building supplies, sold on credit a number of items to Bishop, a house painter. Bishop was slow in paying and appeared to be in some financial difficulty, and so in 1990, Millcreek refused to sell to Bishop unless he paid cash or provided suitable security. Bishop's father was a retired building contractor of some wealth who lived some 300 miles away. Bishop provided Millcreek a written guaranty agreement, dated February 1, 1990, in which his father promised that if, in the next six months, Millcreek extended credit to Bishop in an amount not to exceed $8,000, he (the father) would pay Bishop's obligation to Millcreek if Bishop failed to do so when the obligation was due. After calling the elder Bishop's attorney to verify the signature, Millcreek accepted the guaranty as appropriate security.

From February 5 through March 13, Millcreek made five separate credit sales to Bishop. Three occurred after March 8, when, unknown to Millcreek (but known to Bishop), the elder Bishop had died. The amount involved in these three transactions totaled $5,000. On March 13, Millcreek received a letter from the elder Bishop's executor, informing it of the death and requesting a surrender of the guaranty. Later, after Bishop failed to pay the $5,000 obligations due to insolvency, Millcreek brought suit against the executor to recover on the guaranty contract. The trial court, at the conclusion of the evidence, granted the executor's motion for a judgment on the ground that the guaranty constituted an offer for a series of separate contracts and that the death of the offeror on March 8 automatically terminated the offer with regard to sales made thereafter. The intermediate appellate court affirmed and Millcreek has appealed.

■ ALTMAN, J. (for affirmance). I am of the opinion that the judgment below should be affirmed. The law is clear. An offer is terminated by the death of the offeror before an acceptance occurs, even if the offeree is unaware of that death. This rule finds consistent support in the precedents of this and other states and in the Restatement of Contracts of the American Law Institute. See, e.g., Restatement (First) § 48; Jordan v. Dobbins, 122 Mass. 168 (1877). As one court put it: "This rule has been criticized on the ground that under the modern view of the formation of contracts, it is not the actual meeting of minds of the contracting parties that is the determining fact, but rather the apparent state of mind of the parties embodied in an expression of mutual consent; so that the acceptance by an offeree of an offer, which is apparently still open, should result in an enforceable contract notwithstanding the prior death of the offeror unknown to the offeree. On the other hand, it has been forcibly suggested that ordinarily the condition is implied in an offer that the offeror will survive to supervise the performance if his offer is accepted, and therefore an acceptance after death is ineffective even though the acceptor be ignorant of the offeror's death. . . . These conflicting views, however, were given consideration in the preparation of the Restatement, and the rule announced was adopted as representing the weight of authority and professional opinion." Chain v. Wilhelm, 84 F.2d 138, 140 (4th Cir. 1936). Accord Restatement (Second) § 48.

The guaranty, properly interpreted, was an offer looking forward to a series of separate acceptances. No contract was formed until Millcreek had actually extended credit to Bishop within the limits of the guaranty. Although the decedent agreed that the guaranty should last for six months, Millcreek gave no consideration to support this promise. As such, the agreement to keep the offer of guaranty open for six months was not enforceable.

From these rules it logically follows that the offer to guarantee Bishop's debts was terminated by the offeror's death on March 8, and the judgment below is affirmed.

■ OLIVER, J. (for affirmance). I concur in the majority opinion written by Justice Altman, but for different reasons. Surely we can agree that a sound judicial decision cannot be made from logic and logic alone. As Justice Holmes said, "the life of the law has been experience, not logic." I feel strongly that law in general and contract law in particular exists to serve human needs and that the rules of contract must constantly be adjusted and adapted to the human conditions which produce the disputes. But there is no evidence of those "human conditions" in this case and the court has no way of knowing what impact the rather clear rule that death terminates an unaccepted offer has had upon the planning and other relevant behavior of contracting parties. Do the parties take this rule into account when they negotiate guaranty contracts? What would be the impact upon business practices if the rule were overturned? There are no answers to these questions contained in the record before us. Since the rule has a long history of acceptance in the law and since the effect of its alteration by this court is uncertain, I am hesitant to intervene at this time and change the law. The risk of death is well known to all and surely the plaintiff in this case is just as capable as the decedent to make provision in the agreement or otherwise against the risk of death. If change is needed it should come from the legislature, not the court.

■ ROSCOE, J. (against affirmance). It is obviously unfair to leave the risk of death upon the plaintiff in this case. The plaintiff relied in good faith upon a written promise of guaranty without actual knowledge that the guarantor had died. The plaintiff had no reason to know of the death—the guarantor lived 300 miles away and no method of quick notice was available. A basic policy of the law of contracts is to protect the reasonable expectations of parties to whom promises have been made. See Corbin § 54. Application of the old rule in this case would impair this policy and produce an unfair result in this case. Neither result would, in my mind, be sound.

But we do not have to change the law in this case. A realistic construction of the writing signed by the decedent persuades me that an offer looking forward to a bilateral contract accepted by the first extension of credit was made. Thus, when the plaintiff made the first extension of credit on February 5, he impliedly promised that during the life of the guaranty he would extend credit up to the $8,000 limit to Bishop. See Restatement (Second) §§ 53(1), 54(1) and 62. Thus, the decedent died during the performance of an existing bilateral contract, not before an outstanding offer had been accepted. Or, if the bilateral contract analysis is unsound, the court should, after the first extension of credit is made, imply a promise to hold the guaranty open for six months. Restatement (Second) § 87(2). See § 88. In either case, thus, the question is whether obligations to pay money incurred after death but when the plaintiff had no knowledge of the death are enforceable against the Estate. The answer is "yes." See Restatement (Second) § 262. Although death of one contracting party may discharge some contracts, when the other party has fully performed and the obligation is to pay money alone, the obligation will not be discharged. In my view, the court below erroneously construed the guaranty writing and committed other material errors of law. The judgment below should be reversed and a final judgment entered for the plaintiff.

■ EARL, J. (against affirmance). The rule of law in dispute here is of ancient vintage and, presumably, served some legitimate purpose in a time when contracts were more personal and a "subjective" theory of relationships seemed to dominate. But in this day of impersonal, complicated and widespread commerce, the old rule is anachronistic. It is but another example of "slow moving" law getting out of joint with ever changing life. At the same time, the rule seems to provide a rather arbitrary protection to promisors who die without considering the interests of promisees—those who rely on promises. Assuming that both parties have legitimate interests to protect, if they have not provided for the risk of death clearly in the agreement, the question is whether the current rule provides a fair allocation of risk in the circumstances.

The question is not without difficulty. If we limit, as we must, the problem to contracts of guaranty (and not try to over-generalize), we find almost no evidence in the record about business practices and methods of risk allocation in this particular setting. Perhaps it is enough to say that the burden is on the plaintiff to show clearly that the old rule produces disruptive and unfair results when applied to guaranty contracts, especially when the decedent was not compensated for the risk he assumed. As the defendant Executor forcefully argued, why should the estate make payments to the detriment of lawful heirs for credit extensions which occurred after death and for which the estate received no valuable exchange? This makes the point of Justice Oliver in a slightly different manner.

Even so, it seems clear that in the absence of clear agreement by the parties allocating the risk and other compelling social policies, the general purpose to be achieved by these rules of offer and acceptance should be to facilitate and promote ongoing commercial transactions. Without a strained construction of the writing, the parties contemplated a six-month period where the plaintiff probably would be extending credit to Bishop. They were at a distance, and it is unrealistic to expect the plaintiff to telephone the decedent or check the obituary column in the newspaper before every extension of credit. The plaintiff honestly and without reason to know of death, did precisely what the written guaranty permitted—extended credit to Bishop in reliance upon the decedent's promise. In this context, at least, where both parties were equally capable of providing against the risk in the contract, there seems to be no reason for the arbitrary preference given to the decedent. The broader policy concern for smooth, dependable commercial activity supports the plaintiff's contention that the rule should be changed, and we would so hold. In guaranty contracts, at least, where death occurs before the extension of credit but the promisee acts in good faith and without reason to know, the estate must pay these obligations. This rule is realistically attuned to the needs and problems of the parties. It rejects mechanical applications of the old and strained constructions in order to put the law more solidly into the life around it. The result is not clearly inefficient unless the plaintiff was the "least cost" risk avoider. See Murray on Contracts 124–25 (4th ed. 2001) (a relic of the obsolete view that contract requires a "meeting of the minds"). See also Val D. Ricks, *The Death of Offers*, 79 Ind. L. J. 667 (2004).

Humble Oil & Refining Co. v. Westside Investment Corp.

Supreme Court of Texas, 1968.
428 S.W.2d 92.

■ SMITH, JUSTICE. Petitioner, Humble Oil & Refining Company, filed this suit on February 10, 1965, against Westside Investment Corporation seeking a judgment commanding specific performance based on a written option and contract for the sale of real estate. Petitioner, Marvin H.

Mann, a realtor, as a third-party plaintiff, filed a plea in intervention, seeking a judgment for $1260.00 against Westside as brokerage charges in connection with the transaction. Westside, Humble and Mann each filed a motion for summary judgment. The court granted Westside's motion, and overruled the motions of Humble and Mann. The court of civil appeals affirmed. 419 S.W.2d 448. We reverse the judgments of the courts below. We hold that Humble is entitled to specific performance of the option contract and render judgment for Humble. We hold that a material issue of fact exists as to whether Mann is entitled to a brokerage commission and remand that portion of the case to the district court for trial.

The facts, most of which are either stipulated or established by affidavits, are these:

On April 5, 1963, Westside as seller and Humble as buyer agreed and entered into a written contract whereby Westside gave and granted to Humble an exclusive and irrevocable option to purchase for a consideration of $35,000.00 a tract of land situated outside of the city limits of San Antonio, Bexar County, Texas, being all of lots 19, 20, 21, 22 and 23 of Block 2, Lackland Heights Subdivision.

The option contract was supported by a consideration. The contract provided that Humble might exercise the option by giving notice at any time prior to 9:00 p.m. on the 4th day of June, 1963, and by paying to Westside at the time of such notice or within ten (10) days following such notice the sum of $1750.00 as earnest money. This sum of money, together with the sum of Fifty Dollars ($50.00) as consideration paid at the time of the execution of the option contract, made a total of $1800.00 paid by Humble, leaving a balance of $33,200.00 yet to be paid as purchase money in accordance with the option contract.

On May 14, 1963, within the time period provided for in the option contract, Humble paid the above mentioned sum of $1750.00 to the designated escrow agent, Commercial Abstract & Title Company.

Westside admits in its pleadings that it entered into the option contract with Humble, but contends that the option agreement was "rejected, repudiated, and terminated by Humble." Westside contends that summary judgment proof of rejection of the option contract is contained in letters written by Humble to Westside on May 2, 1963, and May 14, 1963. The pertinent portion of the May 2nd letter reads:

"Humble Oil & Refining Company hereby exercises its option to purchase Lots 19, 20, 21, 22 and 23, Block 2, Lackland Heights Subdivision, in or near the City of San Antonio, Bexar County, Texas, granted in Option and Purchase Contract dated April 5, 1963. As additional inducement for Humble to exercise its option to purchase, you have agreed that all utilities (gas, water, sewer and electricity) will be extended to the property prior to the closing of the transaction. The contract of sale is hereby amended to provide that Seller shall extend all utility lines to the property before the date of closing.

"Please sign and return one copy of this letter in the space indicated below to signify your agreement to the amendment to the purchase contract."

The May 14th communication provided, in part, as follows:

"Humble * * * hereby notifies you of its intention to exercise the option granted in option and purchase contract dated April 5, 1963, covering Lots 19, 20, 21, 22 and 23, Block 2, Lackland Heights Subdivision in or near the City of San Antonio, Bexar County, Texas. *The exercise of said option is not qualified and you may disregard the proposed amendment to the contract suggested in letter of May 2, 1963.* * * * "(Emphasis added.)

We conclude from this record that the parties are in agreement that Humble's letter of May 14, 1963, and the payment of earnest money within 10 days thereof was in law a timely exercise of the option to purchase *unless* Humble's letter of May 2, 1963, terminated and rendered unenforceable the option contract. The narrow question to be determined is whether or not the letter of May 2, 1963, constitutes a rejection of the option contract. If it does, the trial court properly granted Westside's motion for summary judgment and the court of civil appeals correctly affirmed such judgment.

Westside contends that Humble's letter of May 2nd was a conditional acceptance which amounted in law to a rejection of the option contract. Westside argues that the letter of May 2nd "clearly evidences Humble's intent to accept the offer *only if* Westside would agree to an amendment to the terms of its original offer." (Emphasis added.) It further argues that Humble's letter of May 14, 1963, reflects that Humble itself understood that its letter of May 2, 1963, contained a qualified acceptance, and did not form a contract. The basis for this conclusion is the sentence in the May 14 letter which reads: "The exercise of said option is not qualified and you may disregard the proposed amendment to the contract suggested in letter dated May 2, 1963, from the undersigned. * * * " We cannot agree with Westside's contentions.

The mere fact that the parties may choose to negotiate before accepting an option does not mean that the option contract is repudiated. As stated in James on Option Contracts § 838:

"It is laid down in the law of offers that a qualified or conditional acceptance is a rejection of the offer. It is clearly established by the decisions that a qualified or conditional acceptance of an offer does not raise a contract because the minds of the parties do not meet in agreement upon the same terms. It is said that such an acceptance is a counter-proposal for a new contract, to give legal life to which requires the assent or acceptance of the other party. It is in this sense that a qualified or conditional acceptance is a rejection of the offer first made because the original negotiations are dropped and negotiations for a new and different contract begun.

"An option is a contract, the negotiations for the making of which are concluded by the execution and delivery of the option. The minds of the parties have met in agreement, the distinctive feature of which is that the optionor, for a consideration, binds himself to keep the option open for election by the optionee, for and during the time stipulated, or implied by law.

"Under an option, the act necessary to raise a binding promise to sell, is not, therefore, an acceptance of the offer, but rather the performance of the condition of the option contract. If this is true, then the rule peculiar to offers to the effect that a conditional acceptance is, in itself, in every case, a rejection of the offer, is not applicable to an option contract, supported by a consideration and fixing a time limit for election."

* * *

We hold that Humble's letter of May 2, 1963, did not terminate the option contract. Humble, for a valuable consideration, purchased the right to keep the option contract open for the time specified, and the right to create a contract of purchase. Although Humble did have the right to *accept* or *reject* the option in the sense that it was free to take the action required to close the transaction, Humble was not foreclosed from negotiating relative to the contract of sale as distinguished from the option. The option, considered as an independent completed agreement, gave the optionee the right to purchase the property within the time specified. The option contract bound Humble to do nothing but granted it the right to accept or reject the option in accordance with its terms within the time and in the manner specified in the option. Westside was bound to keep the option open and could not act in derogation of the terms of the option. By the letter of May 2, 1963, Humble did not surrender or reject the option. The option to purchase was still a binding obligation between the parties when Humble exercised it on May 14, 1963. . . .

Our holding falls within the rule stated in 1 Corbin on Contracts § 91. According to Corbin:

"If the original offer is an irrevocable offer, creating in the offeree a 'binding option,' the rule that a counter offer terminates the power of acceptance does not apply. Even if it is reasonable to hold that it terminates a revocable power, it should not be held to terminate rights and powers created by a contract. A 'binding option' is such a contract (usually unilateral); and an offer in writing, that allows a time for acceptance (either definite or reasonable) and that is irrevocable by virtue of a statute, is itself a unilateral contract. A counter offer by such an offeree, or other negotiation not resulting in a contract, does not terminate the power of acceptance."

* * *

NOTES

(1)   Critically evaluate the following statement from Langdell, Law of Contracts § 178 (2d ed. 1880): "An offer is merely one of the elements of a contract; and it is indispensable to the making of a contract that the wills of the contracting parties do, in legal contemplation, concur at the moment of making it. An offer, therefore, which the party making it has no power to revoke, is a legal impossibility."

(2)   *Option Varieties.* Restatement (Second) § 25 defines an "option contract" as follows: "An option contract is a promise which meets the requirements for the formation of a contract and limits the promisor's power to revoke an offer." This may take the form of a collateral contract not to revoke an existing offer. ("In consideration of $1, I promise not to revoke for thirty days my offer to sell Blackacre for $10,000. . . .") Another method is a contract between the parties whereby, for a consideration (usually a nominal payment), the owner promises to sell and convey the property for a stated price on condition of either notice of acceptance or actual payment within a specified time. ("In consideration of $1, I promise to convey Blackacre, if within thirty days you pay me $10,000. . . .") This type of "option contract" is actually a conditional contract to sell; it does not take the form of an offer accompanied by an enforceable promise not to revoke. By prevailing law the practical effect is the same in both cases; *viz.,* the offeror has no power to revoke, and any attempt to do so is ineffectual. See Corbin § 262. An option may also appear as part of a larger transaction, as, for example, a renewal option in a lease. See, e.g., 1020 Park Ave., Inc. v. Raynor, 411 N.Y.S.2d 172 (1978).

(3)   *Recital of Consideration as Implied Promise to Pay.* "The majority of cases from other jurisdictions hold that the offeror may prove that the consideration had not been paid and that no other consideration had taken its place. Bard v. Kent, 19 Cal.2d 449 (1942); Calamari and Perillo, Law of Contracts, § 58 (1970). However, the minority rule, and what we consider to be the best view, is that even if it is shown that the dollar was not paid it does not void the contract. We have held many times that the recital of the one dollar consideration gives rise to an implied promise to pay which can be enforced by the other party." Smith v. Wheeler, 233 Ga. 166, 168 (1974). Accord 1464-Eight, Ltd. v. Joppich, 154 S.W.3d 101 (Tex. 2004). Contra Board of Control of Eastern Michigan University v. Burgess, 45 Mich.App. 183 (1973) (recited consideration of $1 must be paid or tendered).

Restatement (Second) § 87(1)(a) provides: "An offer is binding as an option contract if it (a) is in writing and signed by the offeror, recites a purported consideration for the making of the offer, and proposes an exchange on fair terms within a reasonable time."

(4)   *Irrevocability by Statute.* Certain offers are made irrevocable by statute. For example, UCC § 2–205 provides: "An offer by a merchant to buy

or sell goods in a signed writing which by its terms gives assurance that it will be held open is not revocable, for lack of consideration, during the time stated or if no time is stated for a reasonable time, but in no event may such period of irrevocability exceed three months; but any such term of assurance on a form supplied by the offeree must be separately signed by the offeror." See also Article 16 of the United Nations Convention on Contracts for the International Sale of Goods: "(1) Until a contract is concluded an offer may be revoked if the revocation reaches the offeree before he has dispatched an acceptance. (2) However, an offer cannot be revoked: (a) if it indicates, whether by stating a fixed time limit or otherwise, that it is irrevocable; or (b) if it was reasonable for the offeree to rely on the offer as being irrevocable and the offeree has acted in reliance on the offer."

(5) *Effect of Rejection by Optionee.* "Where an offer is supported by a binding contract that the offeree's power of acceptance shall continue for a stated time, will a communicated rejection terminate the offeree's power to accept within the time? On principle, there is no reason why it should. The offeree has a contract right to accept within the time. At most, rejection is a waiver of this right, but waiver not supported by consideration or an estoppel by change of position can have no effect upon subsequent assertion of the right. So an option holder may complete a contract by communicating his acceptance despite the fact that he has previously rejected the offer. Where, however, before the acceptance the offeror has materially changed his position in reliance on the communicated rejection, as by selling or contracting to sell the subject matter of the offer elsewhere, the subsequent acceptance will be inoperative. Here the rejection is a waiver of the offeree's contract right to accept the offer, binding the offeree by estoppel, so his power to accept is gone." Simpson on Contracts, 2d ed., § 23, quoted in Ryder v. Wescoat, 535 S.W.2d 269, 270 (Mo. Ct. App. 1976). See also Restatement (Second) § 37: "[T]he power of acceptance under an option contract is not terminated by rejection or counter-offer, by revocation, or by death or incapacity of the offeror, unless the requirements are met for the discharge of a contractual duty." For a criticism of the majority view that rejection or counter-offer by offeree-optionee should not, of itself, terminate the latter's power of acceptance, see Cozzillio, *The Option Contract: Irrevocable Not Irrejectable,* 39 Cath. U. L. Rev. 491 (1990).

PROBLEM: EFFECT OF FIRST REFUSAL

Defendant owned a tract of land containing three lots, all of which were zoned commercial. In June, 2010, Defendant sold two of the lots to Plaintiff for $400,000. As part of the transaction, Defendant granted Plaintiff a "first refusal" on the third lot for a period to end on July 1, 2012. In June 2012, Defendant, without informing Plaintiff, solicited offers on the third lot from third parties. A written offer to buy for $175,000 cash was made by a third party. Plaintiff learned of the offer and, on June 25, 2012, informed Defendant that it intended to exercise the right of "first refusal" and tendered a certified check for $175,000. Defendant rejected both the third party offer and Plaintiff's tender and did not sell the property.

It is now July 10, 2012. The property has not been sold. Plaintiff claims that it exercised its right of "first refusal" before July 1, 2012 and that it is entitled to specific performance for the third lot. As authority, it cites *Humble Oil,* supra, and other authorities on option contracts. What result?

PROBLEM: CREATION OF RELIANCE OPTIONS

Peter owned real estate in New York City worth $100,000. Patrick held an installment promissory note in the amount of $50,000 upon which Peter was the maker. The note was secured by a first mortgage on the property. Peter had paid $40,000 on the note, plus interest and the balance was due in 12 months, on October 1, 2012. On July 1, 2012, Patrick telephoned Peter and said he would be willing to cancel the note and the mortgage if Peter would pay him $8,500 in cash within 7 days. Peter said he was a bit short of cash and would have to think about it. Patrick then said "if you pay me $8,500 cash by 4 PM on July 8, I will cancel the note and release the mortgage." Peter hung up after thanking Patrick and saying he would try to raise the money.

On July 7, Peter was able to sell his valuable coin collection to a dealer for $10,000. On the morning of July 8, Peter agreed in writing to sell his New York property to Priscilla free of any mortgage for $100,000. With the cash in his brief case, Peter began to look for Patrick. He was not in his office and could not be found at his favorite pub. The bartender, however, said that Patrick had gone to his home in the Bronx and that some deal was brewing with Paul about some mortgage. Peter then took a taxi to the Bronx, arriving at Patrick's home about 3:45 PM. As he walked up the driveway, he saw Patrick at the open window, waved his briefcase and yelled: "Good news, I've got the money to pay off the mortgage." Patrick responded, "You are too late, I sold the note and the mortgage to Paul this morning." Patrick then closed the window and refused to open the door.

Crestfallen, Peter consults you for advice. Consider the materials we have studied so far and those to come in the balance of this section. What is the strongest argument for Peter? Will it be successful?

Ever-Tite Roofing Corp. v. G.T. Green

Court of Appeal of Louisiana, 1955.
Supra at 259.

A.A. Marchiondo v. Frank Scheck

Supreme Court of New Mexico, 1967.
78 N.M. 440.

■ WOOD, JUDGE, Court of Appeals. The issue is whether the offeror had a right to revoke his offer to enter a unilateral contract.

Defendant, in writing, offered to sell real estate to a specified prospective buyer and agreed to pay a percentage of the sales price as a commission to the broker. The offer fixed a six-day time limit for acceptance. Defendant, in writing, revoked the offer. The revocation was received by the broker on the morning of the sixth day. Later that day, the broker obtained the offeree's acceptance.

Plaintiff, the broker, claiming breach of contract, sued defendant for the commission stated in the offer. On the above facts, the trial court dismissed the complaint.

We are not concerned with the revocation of the offer as between the offeror and the prospective purchaser. With certain exceptions . . . , the right of a broker to the agreed compensation, or damages measured thereby, is not defeated by the refusal of the principal to complete or consummate a transaction. . . .

Plaintiff's appeal concerns the revocation of his agency. As to that revocation, the issue between the offeror and his agent is not whether defendant had the power to revoke; rather, it is whether he had the right to revoke. . . .

When defendant made his offer to pay a commission upon sale of the property, he offered to enter a unilateral contract; the offer was for an act to be performed, a sale. 1 Williston on Contracts, § 13 at 23 (3rd ed. 1957); Hutchinson v. Dobson-Bainbridge Realty Co., 31 Tenn.App. 490 (1946).

Many courts hold that the principal has the right to revoke the broker's agency at any time before the broker has actually procured a purchaser. See Hutchinson v. Dobson-Bainbridge Realty Co., supra, and cases therein cited. The reason given is that until there is performance, the offeror has not received that contemplated by his offer, and there is no contract. Further, the offeror may never receive the requested performance because the offeree is not obligated to perform. Until the offeror receives the requested performance, no consideration has passed from the offeree to the offeror. Thus, until the performance is received, the offeror may withdraw the offer. Williston, supra, § 60; Hutchinson v. Dobson-Bainbridge Realty Co., supra.

Defendant asserts that the trial court was correct in applying this rule. However, plaintiff contends that the rule is not applicable where there has been part performance of the offer.

Hutchinson v. Dobson-Bainbridge Realty Co., supra, states:

> "A greater number of courts, however, hold that part performance of the consideration may make such an offer irrevocable and that where the offeree or broker manifests his assent to the offer by entering upon performance and spending time and money in his efforts to perform, then the offer becomes irrevocable during the time stated and binding upon the principal according to its terms. * * * "

Defendant contends that the decisions giving effect to a part performance are distinguishable. He asserts that in these cases the offer was of an exclusive right to sell or of an exclusive agency. Because neither factor is present here, he asserts that the "part performance" decisions are not applicable.

Many of the decisions do seem to emphasize the exclusive aspects of the offer. . . .

Such emphasis reaches its extreme conclusion in *Tetrick v. Sloan*, 170 Cal.App.2d 540 (1959), where no effect was given to the part performance because there was neither an exclusive agency, nor an exclusive right to sell.

Defendant's offer did not specifically state that it was exclusive. Under § 70–1–43, N.M.S.A.1953, it was not an exclusive agreement. It is not the exclusiveness of the offer that deprives the offeror of the right to revoke. It is the action taken by the offeree which deprives the offeror of that right. Until there is action by the offeree—a partial performance pursuant to the offer—the offeror may revoke even if his offer is of an exclusive agency or an exclusive right to sell. . . .

Once partial performance is begun pursuant to the offer made, a contract results. This contract has been termed a contract with conditions or an option contract. This terminology is illustrated as follows:

> "If an offer for a unilateral contract is made, and part of the consideration requested in the offer is given or tendered by the offeree in response thereto, the offeror is bound by a contract, the duty of immediate performance of which is conditional on the full consideration being given or tendered within the time stated in the offer, or, if no time is stated therein, within a reasonable time." Restatement of Contracts, § 45 (1932).

Restatement (Second) Contracts § 45, Tent.Draft No. 1, (approved 1964, Tent.Draft No. 2, p. vii) states:

> "(1) Where an offer invites an offeree to accept by rendering a performance and does not invite a promissory acceptance, an option contract is created when the offeree begins the invited performance or tenders part of it.[73]

> "(2) The offeror's duty of performance under any option contract so created is conditional on completion or tender of the invited performance in accordance with the terms of the offer."

Restatement (Second) Contracts § 45, Tent.Draft No. 1, comment (g), says:

> "This Section frequently applies to agency arrangements, particularly offers made to real estate brokers. * * * "

See Restatement (Second) Agency § 446, comment (b).

---

[73] [The final draft replaces the final three words, "part of it," with "a beginning of it."—Eds.]

The reason for finding such a contract is stated in *Hutchinson v. Dobson-Bainbridge Realty Co.*, supra, as follows:

> "This rule avoids hardship to the offeree, and yet does not hold the offeror beyond the terms of his promise. It is true by such terms he was to be bound only if the requested act was done; but this implies that he will let it be done, that he will keep his offer open till the offeree who has begun can finish doing it. At least this is so where the doing of it will necessarily require time and expense. In such a case it is but just to hold that the offeree's part performance furnishes the 'acceptance' and the 'consideration' for a binding subsidiary promise not to revoke the offer, or turns the offer into a presently binding contract conditional upon the offeree's full performance."

We hold that part performance by the offeree of an offer of a unilateral contract results in a contract with a condition. The condition is full performance by the offeree. Here, if plaintiff-offeree partially performed prior to receipt of defendant's revocation, such a contract was formed. Thereafter, upon performance being completed by plaintiff, upon defendant's failure to recognize the contract, liability for breach of contract would arise. Thus, defendant's right to revoke his offer depends upon whether plaintiff had partially performed before he received defendant's revocation. * * *

What constitutes partial performance will vary from case to case since what can be done toward performance is limited by what is authorized to be done. Whether plaintiff partially performed is a question of fact to be determined by the trial court.

The trial court denied plaintiff's requested finding concerning his partial performance. It did so on the theory that partial performance was not material. In this the trial court erred. * * *

The cause is remanded for findings on the issue of plaintiff's partial performance of the offer prior to its revocation, and for further proceedings consistent with this opinion and the findings so made.

It is so ordered.

NOTES

(1)   In *Marchiondo*, the offer looked forward to a performance (finding a ready, able and willing buyer) as the only method of acceptance. A promise would not do. That buyer was not found before the agency was terminated. Do the facts support the court's theory?

(2)   It will be noted the first Restatement does not state that the offer becomes irrevocable after part performance, but that the offeror is "bound by a contract," etc. The formulation of the rule in this manner by Williston, principal author of the Restatement, was challenged at a discussion of the tentative draft. The following colloquy took place:

JUDGE CARDOZO: Are there any suggestions as to * * * Section 45?
* * *

MR. WILLIS: I wonder if there is not an inaccuracy in Section 45 in lines 22, 23 and 24 as follows: "the offeror is bound by a contract, liability upon which is conditional on the completion by the offeree of the requested performance within the time stated in the offer, etc." Under such circumstances as we find in Section 45, we do not have a contract of course. The statement in line 23 does not say that we have a contract, and yet it says the offeror is bound by a contract. I wonder if that is not misleading. The actual fact is that in our most recent cases and the modern development of the law the power of revocation on the part of the offeror is destroyed, and therefore the offeree has the power to go on if he wants to and complete his acceptance. If he does we finally get a contract, but if he does not go on and perform the rest of the work of course there is no contract. * * *

MR. WILLISTON: I call an irrevocable offer a contract. The offeror has promised to do something and he is liable if he does not do it.

MR. WILLIS: I beg your pardon, you do not want to call this an irrevocable offer, do you?

MR. WILLISTON: That is what you called it, did you not?

MR. WILLIS: Oh, no.

MR. WILLISTON: You stated the power to revoke is destroyed.

MR. WILLIS: It becomes irrevocable—

MR. WILLISTON: All right. When it becomes irrevocable it is an irrevocable offer.

MR. WILLIS: But it does not seem to me that that is so; it seems to me that a contract is one thing and an irrevocable offer is another.

MR. WILLISTON: We are apart on that. An irrevocable [offer] is not *the* contract which the offer proposes, but being a binding promise, it is a contract.

3 ALI Proceedings 204–5 (1925).

(3) The drafters of the first Restatement appended the following commentary to § 45: "The main offer includes as a subsidiary promise, necessarily implied, that if part of the requested performance is given, the offeror will not revoke his offer, and that if tender is made it will be accepted. Part performance or tender may thus furnish consideration for the subsidiary promises. Moreover, merely acting in justifiable reliance on an offer may in some cases serve as sufficient reason for making a promise binding (see § 90)." Is this comment consistent with the "black letter" of Section 45?

Comment: Acceptance by Performance Under the Second Restatement

In the first Restatement, a sharp dichotomy between bilateral and unilateral contracts was maintained. Although Section 31 established a presumption in favor of the bilateral contract, it was supposed that every offer invited acceptance by either a promise or by full performance. This view was criticized by Karl Llewellyn, *Our Case Law of Contract—Offer and Acceptance,* 48 Yale L.J. 779, 786 (1939), and was explicitly rejected by UCC § 2–206(1)(a), which provides that "unless otherwise unambiguously indicated," an offer "shall be construed as inviting acceptance in any manner and by any medium reasonable in the circumstances." Thus, if a buyer offers to purchase goods for "prompt or current shipment," and the language or circumstances do not unambiguously indicate that acceptance by shipment is required, the offer "shall be construed as inviting acceptance either by a prompt promise to ship or by the prompt or current shipment" of goods. UCC § 2–206(1)(b). The rule of construction operates to give an offeree a choice among reasonable methods of acceptance and by expanding the power to create a contract protects the offeree's reasonable reliance.

Restatement (Second) has followed this lead by abolishing the labels "bilateral" and "unilateral" and by charting a middle ground for acceptance between assent expressed by words of promise and assent expressed by completing a performance that the offeror required exclusively for acceptance. For a critical view of this development, see Mark Pettit, *Modern Unilateral Contracts,* 63 B.U. L. Rev. 551 (1983). This middle ground emerges in a case where acceptance by "rendering a performance" is invited or required by the offer but where the offeree also has power to accept by making a promise. To accept the offer, the offeree must at least perform or tender part of the performance invited. Section 50(2). More importantly, this tender or beginning of performance is an acceptance which "operates as a promise to render complete performance." Section 62(2). It does not create an option contract, à la Section 45. Rather, it creates a full-blown reciprocal commitment, which used to be called a "bilateral" contract. Finally, "no notification is necessary to make such an acceptance effective unless the offer requests" it. Section 54(1). The contractual duties may be discharged if the offeree "has reason to know that the offeror has no adequate means of learning of the performance with reasonable promptness" and fails to exercise "reasonable diligence to notify the offeror of acceptance." Section 54(2)(a). But the contract, under these circumstances, is formed by the conduct of part performance or tender, not the giving or the effort to give notice to the offeror.

The intricate Restatement (Second) maze can be illustrated by three examples.

1.   A, who lives in the city, owns 100 acres of farm land some 100 miles away. In the past, B, a farmer, has plowed the field

for A in the Spring. On Monday, A telephoned B and said: "If you will agree by 4 PM tomorrow to plow my field, I will pay you $500 when the job is done." B said he would "consider it." The next day, B started to plow the field at 3 PM but had not notified A by 4 PM and, in fact, did not inform A until the next morning. There is no contract if the court accepts the following version of the case. The offer invited or required B's acceptance to be made "by an affirmative answer in words" and did not invite acceptance by performance. Section 30. Put another way, the language and circumstances clearly limited the manner of acceptance to an affirmative promise in words. See Section 32. As such, B did not "complete every act essential to the making of the promise," Section 50(3), or exercise "reasonable diligence to notify the offeror of acceptance," Section 56, before the offer lapsed at 4 PM. What about B's reliance (and A's enrichment, to the extent the field was plowed)? In theory, at least, if B knew that the only way to accept was to "say yes" before 4 PM and failed to do so, he plowed at his peril.

2.   Suppose, in Example #1, that A had telephoned B and said: "When and only when you plow my 100 acres by 4 PM next Monday, I will pay you $500." B replied: "I'll do it. You can count on it." A responded: "I want a plowed field not a promise. Plow it or we have no deal." B started to plow the field on Friday, completing 20% by sunset. The next day, A telephoned before 7 AM and revoked the offer. B ignored A and completed the plowing before 4 PM on Monday. There is a contract if the court accepts the following version of the case. A's offer required acceptance by rendering a completed performance but did not invite acceptance by promise. These limitations were clear and unambiguous. As such, B's commencing performance does not operate as a "promise to render complete performance." See Section 62. But it did create an option contract under Section 45 when B began the invited performance. And, under Section 45(2), B properly completed the performance "in accordance with the terms of the offer," thus imposing on A the duty to pay $500. Note that Section 45 applies only where the offer "invites an offeree to accept by rendering a performance and does *not* invite a promissory acceptance."

3.   Suppose, in Example #1, that A had telephoned B and said: "If you will plow my field by 4 PM next Monday I will pay you $500." B replied: "I'll consider it." The next day, B started to plow the field and was 20% completed when, in the evening, A called to revoke the offer. There is a contract if the court accepts the following version of the case. The offer empowered B to make a choice between acceptance by promise (he could have said yes over the telephone) and acceptance by performance. Section 30.

There are no language or circumstances clearly to the contrary, and Section 32 provides that "in case of doubt an offer is interpreted as inviting the offeree to accept either by promising to perform what the offer requests or by rendering the performance, as the offeree chooses." Thus, the offer was accepted when part-performance occurred, Section 50(2), and the acceptance by performance operated as a promise to complete the plowing. Section 62(2). Notice of acceptance to A was not required, Section 54(1), and, anyway, A learned of the performance when he telephoned to revoke the offer. Note that where the offer invites a choice between a performance and a promise, the reliance in part performance creates a promise to complete (yes, a "bilateral" contract) rather than an option under Section 45.

PROBLEM: THE CASE OF PROFESSOR FUZZY'S WELL

The well of Professor Fuzzy's suburban homesite ran dry during an extended drought period. He hastened to make arrangements for the drilling of a new one, contacting among others the Retaw Drilling Company. He told of his plight, but a company representative said they were so committed they could not assist him. Fuzzy countered by saying he was desperate and would give them $1,000 if they would drill a well for him, a sum about double the estimated cost. The drilling company agent said, "Well, we can't guarantee you anything, but if we can pull a rig off another job, we'll try to help you out."

It happened the following day that a rig did become available, and the company, at considerable expense, moved drilling equipment onto Professor Fuzzy's property.

Meanwhile, however, the professor's neighbor informed him that a connection could be made to the municipal water supply system and it was a waste of money to drill a new well. Fuzzy verified the fact that he was eligible to so purchase water from the city and decided this was his best course. Accordingly, he told the company not to drill. The company transferred its equipment to another location but sent him a bill. The latter asserted he "did not owe a cent." The Retaw Drilling Company sues for damages. Any recovery?

Assume, instead, that after transfer of the equipment to Fuzzy's property, circumstances arose which prompted the drilling company to claim the absence of obligation to proceed. (E.g., a more profitable job came along.) Would Fuzzy have any legal recourse?

(Billings) Learned Hand: In more than 40 years as a federal judge, Learned Hand wrote more than 2,000 opinions, many of which made lasting impacts on antitrust (United States v. ALCOA), torts (United States v. Carroll Towing), and the First Amendment (Masses Publishing v. Patten). Hand was educated at Harvard where he earned his A.B. in philosophy, a master's degree in philosophy, and finally a law degree. He began practicing law in New York in 1897 and was appointed by President Taft to the U.S. District Court for the Southern District of New York in 1909. At age 37, he was one of the youngest federal judges ever appointed. President Coolidge elevated Hand to the Court of Appeals for the Second Circuit in 1924, where he served until he retired in 1951.

James Baird Co. v. Gimbel Brothers, Inc.

United States Court of Appeals, Second Circuit, 1933.
64 F.2d 344.

■ L. HAND, CIRCUIT JUDGE. The plaintiff sued the defendant for breach of a contract to deliver linoleum under a contract of sale; the defendant denied the making of the contract; the parties tried the case to the judge under a written stipulation and he directed judgment for the defendant. The facts as found, bearing on the making of the contract, the only issue necessary to discuss, were as follows: The defendant, a New York merchant, knew that the Department of Highways in Pennsylvania had asked for bids for the construction of a public building. It sent an employee to the office of a contractor in Philadelphia, who had possession of the specifications, and the employee there computed the amount of the linoleum which would be required on the job, underestimating the total yardage by about one-half the proper amount. In ignorance of this mistake, on December twenty-fourth the defendant sent to some twenty or thirty contractors, likely to bid on the job, an offer to supply all the linoleum required by the specifications at two different lump sums, depending upon the quality used. These offers concluded as follows: "If successful in being awarded this contract, it will be absolutely guaranteed, * * * and * * * we are offering these prices for reasonable" (sic), "prompt acceptance after the general contract has been awarded." The plaintiff, a contractor in Washington, got one of these on the twenty-eighth, and on the same day the defendant learned its mistake and telegraphed all the contractors to whom it had sent the offer, that it withdrew it and would substitute a new one at about double the amount of the old. This withdrawal reached the plaintiff at Washington on the afternoon of the same day, but not until after it had put in a bid at Harrisburg at a lump sum, based as to linoleum upon the prices quoted by the defendant. The public authorities accepted the plaintiff's bid on December thirtieth, the defendant having meanwhile written a letter of confirmation of its withdrawal, received on the thirty-first. The plaintiff formally accepted the offer on January second, and, as the defendant persisted in declining to recognize the existence of a contract, sued it for damages on a breach.

Unless there are circumstances to take it out of the ordinary doctrine, since the offer was withdrawn before it was accepted, the acceptance was too late. Restatement of Contracts, § 35. To meet this the plaintiff argues as follows: It was a reasonable implication from the defendant's offer that it should be irrevocable in case the plaintiff acted upon it, that is to say, used the prices quoted in making its bid, thus putting itself in a position from which it could not withdraw without great loss. While it might have withdrawn its bid after receiving the revocation, the time had passed to submit another, and as the item of linoleum was a very trifling part of the cost of the whole building, it would have been an unreasonable hardship to expect it to lose the contract on that account, and probably forfeit its deposit. While it is true that the plaintiff might in advance have secured a contract conditional upon the success of its bid, this was not what the defendant suggested. It understood that the contractors would use its offer in their bids, and would thus in fact commit themselves to supplying the linoleum at the proposed prices. The inevitable implication from all this was that when the contractors acted upon it, they accepted the offer and promised to pay for the linoleum, in case their bid were accepted.

It was of course possible for the parties to make such a contract, and the question is merely as to what they meant; that is, what is to be imputed to the words they used. Whatever plausibility there is in the argument, is in the fact that the defendant must have known the predicament in which the contractors would be put if it withdrew its offer after the bids went in. However, it seems entirely clear that the contractors did not suppose that they accepted the offer merely by putting in their bids. If, for example, the successful one had repudiated the contract with the public authorities after it had been awarded to him, certainly the defendant could not have sued him for a breach. If he had become bankrupt, the defendant could not prove against his estate. It seems plain therefore that there was no contract between them. And if there be any doubt as to this, the language of the offer sets it at rest. The phrase, "if successful in being awarded this contract," is scarcely met by the mere use of the prices in the bids. Surely such a use was not an "award" of the contract to the defendant. Again the phrase, "we are offering these prices for * * * prompt acceptance after the general contract has been awarded," looks to the usual communication of an acceptance, and precludes the idea that the use of the offer in the bidding shall be the equivalent. It may indeed be argued that this last language contemplated no more than an early notice that the offer had been accepted, the actual acceptance being the bid, but that would wrench its natural meaning too far, especially in the light of the preceding phrase. The contractors had a ready escape from their difficulty by insisting upon a contract before they used the figures; and in commercial transactions it does not in the end promote justice to seek strained interpretations in aid of those who do not protect themselves.

But the plaintiff says that even though no bilateral contract was made, the defendant should be held under the doctrine of "promissory estoppel." This is to be chiefly found in those cases where persons subscribe to a venture, usually charitable, and are held to their promises after it has been completed. It has been applied much more broadly, however, and has now been generalized in section 90, of the Restatement of Contracts. We may arguendo accept it as it there reads, for it does not apply to the case at bar. Offers are ordinarily made in exchange for a consideration, either a counter-promise or some other act which the promisor wishes to secure. In such cases they propose bargains; they presuppose that each promise or performance is an inducement to the other. . . . But a man may make a promise without expecting an equivalent; a donative promise, conditional or absolute. The common law provided for such by sealed instruments, and it is unfortunate that these are no longer generally available. The doctrine of "promissory estoppel" is to avoid harsh results of allowing the promisor in such a case to repudiate, when the promisee has acted in reliance upon the promise. . . . But an offer for an exchange is not meant to become a promise until a consideration has been received, either a counterpromise or whatever else is stipulated. To extend it would be to hold the offeror regardless of the stipulated condition of his offer. In the case at bar the defendant offered to deliver the linoleum in exchange for the plaintiff's acceptance, not for its bid, which was a matter of indifference to it. That offer could become a promise to deliver only when the equivalent was received; that is, when the plaintiff promised to take and pay for it. There is no room in such a situation for the doctrine of "promissory estoppel."

Nor can the offer be regarded as of an option, giving the plaintiff the right seasonably to accept the linoleum at the quoted prices if its bid was accepted, but not binding it to take and pay, if it could get a better bargain elsewhere. There is not the least reason to suppose that the defendant meant to subject itself to such a one-sided obligation. True, if so construed, the doctrine of "promissory estoppel" might apply, the plaintiff having acted in reliance upon it, though, so far as we have found, the decisions are otherwise. . . . As to that, however, we need not declare ourselves.

Judgment affirmed.

Roger J. Traynor: Roger Traynor served as an Associate Justice of the California Supreme Court from 1940 until 1964, and then as the Court's Chief Justice until his retirement in 1970. Traynor made notable contributions to contract and criminal law. But he is perhaps best known for his tort and product liability opinions, which helped establish the principle of strict liability. Traynor graduated from the University of California at Berkeley in 1923, earning both his Ph.D. (1926) and his J.D. (1927) there as well. He was editor-in-chief of the California Law Review and taught political science at Berkeley from 1926 until his appointment to the bench in 1940. Traynor was born in Park City, Utah in 1900. He died in 1983.

William Drennan v. Star Paving Co.

Supreme Court of California, 1958.
51 Cal.2d 409.

■ TRAYNOR, JUSTICE. Defendant appeals from a judgment for plaintiff in an action to recover damages caused by defendant's refusal to perform certain paving work according to a bid it submitted to plaintiff.

On July 28, 1955, plaintiff, a licensed general contractor, was preparing a bid on the "Monte Vista School Job" in the Lancaster school district. Bids had to be submitted before 8:00 p.m. Plaintiff testified that it was customary in that area for general contractors to receive the bids of subcontractors by telephone on the day set for bidding and to rely on them in computing their own bids. Thus on that day plaintiff's secretary, Mrs. Johnson, received by telephone between fifty and seventy-five subcontractors' bids for various parts of the school job. As each bid came in, she wrote it on a special form, which she brought into plaintiff's office. He then posted it on a master cost sheet setting forth the names and bids of all subcontractors. His own bid had to include the names of subcontractors who were to perform one-half of one percent or more of the construction work, and he had also to provide a bidder's bond of ten percent of his total bid of $317,385 as a guarantee that he would enter the contract if awarded the work.

Late in the afternoon, Mrs. Johnson had a telephone conversation with Kenneth R. Hoon, an estimator for defendant. He gave his name and telephone number and stated that he was bidding for defendant for the paving work at the Monte Vista School according to plans and specifications and that his bid was $7,131.60. At Mrs. Johnson's request he repeated his bid. Plaintiff listened to the bid over an extension telephone in his office and posted it on the master sheet after receiving the bid form from Mrs. Johnson. Defendant's was the lowest bid for the paving. Plaintiff computed his own bid accordingly and submitted it with the name of defendant as the subcontractor for the paving. When the bids were opened on July 28th, plaintiff's proved to be the lowest, and he was awarded the contract.

On his way to Los Angeles the next morning plaintiff stopped at defendant's office. The first person he met was defendant's construction engineer, Mr. Oppenheimer. Plaintiff testified: "I introduced myself and he immediately told me that they had made a mistake in their bid to me the night before, they couldn't do it for the price they had bid, and I told him I would expect him to carry through with their original bid because I had used it in compiling my bid and the job was being awarded them. And I would have to go and do the job according to my bid and I would expect them to do the same."

Defendant refused to do the paving work for less than $15,000. Plaintiff testified that he "got figures from other people" and after trying for several months to get as low a bid as possible engaged L & H Paving Company, a firm in Lancaster, to do the work for $10,948.60.

The trial court found on substantial evidence that defendant made a definite offer to do the paving on the Monte Vista job according to the plans and specifications for $7,131.60, and that plaintiff relied on defendant's bid in computing his own bid for the school job and naming defendant therein as the subcontractor for the paving work. Accordingly, it entered judgment for plaintiff in the amount of $3,817.00 (the difference between defendant's bid and the cost of the paving to plaintiff) plus costs.

Defendant contends that there was no enforceable contract between the parties on the ground that it made a revocable offer and revoked it before plaintiff communicated his acceptance to defendant.

There is no evidence that defendant offered to make its bid irrevocable in exchange for plaintiff's use of its figures in computing his bid. Nor is there evidence that would warrant interpreting plaintiff's use of defendant's bid as the acceptance thereof, binding plaintiff, on condition he received the main contract, to award the subcontract to defendant. In sum, there was neither an option supported by consideration nor a bilateral contract binding on both parties.

Plaintiff contends, however, that he relied to his detriment on defendant's offer and that defendant must therefore answer in damages for its refusal to perform. Thus the question is squarely presented: Did plaintiff's reliance make defendant's offer irrevocable?

Section 90 of the Restatement of Contracts states: "A promise which the promisor should reasonably expect to induce action or forbearance of a definite and substantial character on the part of the promisee and which does induce such action or forbearance is binding if injustice can be avoided only by enforcement of the promise." This rule applies in this state. . . .

Defendant's offer constituted a promise to perform on such conditions as were stated expressly or by implication therein or annexed thereto by operation of law. . . . Defendant had reason to expect that if its bid proved the lowest it would be used by plaintiff. It induced "action * * * of a definite and substantial character on the part of the promisee."

Had defendant's bid expressly stated or clearly implied that it was revocable at any time before acceptance we would treat it accordingly. It was silent on revocation, however, and we must therefore determine whether there are conditions to the right of revocation imposed by law or reasonably inferable in fact. In the analogous problem of an offer for a unilateral contract, the theory is now obsolete that the offer is revocable at any time before complete performance. Thus section 45 of the Restatement of Contracts provides: "If an offer for a unilateral contract is made, and part of the consideration requested in the offer is given or tendered by the offeree in response thereto, the offeror is bound by a contract, the duty of immediate performance of which is conditional on the full consideration being given or tendered within the time stated in the offer, or, if no time is stated therein, within a reasonable time." In explanation, comment *b* states that the "main offer includes as a subsidiary promise, necessarily implied, that if part of the requested performance is given, the offeror will not revoke his offer, and that if tender is made it will be accepted. Part performance or tender may thus furnish consideration for the subsidiary promise. Moreover, merely acting in justifiable reliance on an offer may in some cases serve as sufficient reason for making a promise binding (see § 90)."

Whether implied in fact or law, the subsidiary promise serves to preclude the injustice that would result if the offer could be revoked after the offeree had acted in detrimental reliance thereon. Reasonable reliance resulting in a foreseeable prejudicial change in position affords a compelling basis also for implying a subsidiary promise not to revoke an offer for a bilateral contract.

The absence of consideration is not fatal to the enforcement of such a promise. It is true that in the case of unilateral contracts the Restatement finds consideration for the implied subsidiary promise in the part performance of the bargained-for exchange, but its reference to section 90 makes clear that consideration for such a promise is not always necessary. The very purpose of section 90 is to make a promise binding even though there was no consideration "in the sense of something that is bargained for and given in exchange." (See 1 Corbin, Contracts 634 et seq.) Reasonable reliance serves to hold the offeror in lieu of the consideration ordinarily required to make the offer binding. In a case involving similar facts the Supreme Court of South Dakota stated that "we believe that reason and justice demand that the doctrine [of section 90] be applied to the present facts. We cannot believe that by accepting this doctrine as controlling in the state of facts before us we will abolish the requirement of a consideration in contract cases, in any different sense than an ordinary estoppel abolishes some legal requirement in its application. We are of the opinion, therefore, that the defendants in executing the agreement [which was not supported by consideration] made a promise which they should have reasonably expected would induce the plaintiff to submit a bid based thereon to the Government, that such promise did induce this action, and that injustice can be avoided only by enforcement of the promise." Northwestern Engineering Co. v. Ellerman, 69 S.D. 397, 408; see also, Robert Gordon, Inc. v. Ingersoll-Rand Co., 7 Cir., 117 F.2d 654, 661; cf. James Baird Co. v. Gimbel Bros., 2 Cir., 64 F.2d 344.

When plaintiff used defendant's offer in computing his own bid, he bound himself to perform in reliance on defendant's terms. Though defendant did not bargain for this use of its bid neither did defendant make it idly, indifferent to whether it would be used or not. On the contrary it is reasonable to suppose that defendant submitted its bid to obtain the subcontract. It was bound to realize the substantial possibility that its bid would be the lowest, and that it would be included by plaintiff in his bid. It was to its own interest that the contractor be awarded the general contract; the lower the subcontract bid, the lower the general contractor's bid was likely to be and the greater its chance of acceptance and hence the greater defendant's chance of getting the paving subcontract. Defendant had reason not only to expect plaintiff to rely on its bid but to want him to. Clearly defendant had a stake in plaintiff's reliance on its bid. Given this interest and the fact that plaintiff is bound by his own bid, it is only fair that plaintiff should have at least an opportunity to accept defendant's bid after the general contract has been awarded to him.

It bears noting that a general contractor is not free to delay acceptance after he has been awarded the general contract in the hope of getting a better price. Nor can he reopen bargaining with the subcontractor and at the same time claim a continuing right to accept the original offer. . . . In the present case plaintiff promptly informed defendant that plaintiff was being awarded the job and that the subcontract was being awarded to defendant.

Defendant contends, however, that its bid was the result of mistake and that it was therefore entitled to revoke it. * * * Plaintiff, however, had no reason to know that defendant had made a mistake in submitting its bid, since there was usually a variance of 160 per cent between the highest and lowest bids for paving in the desert around Lancaster. He committed himself to performing the main contract in reliance on defendant's figures. Under these circumstances defendant's mistake, far from relieving it of its obligation, constitutes an additional reason for enforcing it, for it misled plaintiff as to the cost of doing the paving. Even had it been clearly understood that defendant's offer was revocable until accepted, it would not necessarily follow that defendant had no duty to exercise reasonable care in preparing its bid. It presented its bid with knowledge of the substantial possibility that it would be used by plaintiff; it could foresee the harm that would ensue from an erroneous underestimate of the cost. Moreover, it was motivated by its own business interest. Whether or not these considerations alone would justify recovery for negligence had the case been tried on that theory (see Biakanja v. Irving, 49 Cal.2d 647, 650), they are persuasive that defendant's mistake should not defeat recovery under the rule of section 90 of the Restatement of Contracts. As between the subcontractor who made the bid and the general contractor who reasonably relied on it, the loss resulting from the mistake should fall on the party who caused it.

* * *

The judgment is affirmed.

NOTES

(1) In *Drennan,* Judge Traynor observes that "there was neither an option supported by consideration nor a bilateral contract binding on both parties." He then proceeds to create an option under promissory estoppel doctrine. How does he avoid Judge Hand's reasoning in *Baird?* For what reasons and by what methodology is the option created? What is the scope of the protection afforded the general contractor by the option?

(2) Did the general contractor, in *Drennan,* know or have reason to know that a mistake had been made? Would such knowledge affect the outcome?

(3) The position adopted by Judge Traynor has come to predominate. See Pavel v. A.S. Johnson, 342 Md. 143, 152–160 (1996); Bishop, *The Subcontractor's Bid: An Option Contract Arising through Promissory Estoppel,* 34 Emory L.J. 42 (1985). The Second Restatement appears not only to follow *Drennan,* but to extend it. Section 87(2) provides: "An offer which the offeror should reasonably expect to induce action or forbearance of a substantial character by the offeree before acceptance and which does induce such action or forbearance is binding as an option contract to the extent necessary to avoid injustice." But what is the likely impact of limiting the binding effect of the option "to the extent necessary to avoid injustice"? Cf. Loranger Construction Corp. v. E.F. Hauserman Co., 376 Mass. 757 (1978). In an opinion by Judge Braucher, first Reporter of Second Restatement, the court eschews promissory estoppel analysis ("it tends to confusion rather than clarity"), preferring to base liability on a "typical bargain."

(4) Oil Lease Owner offered to enter a "farmout agreement" with Oil Driller. The offer stated that it was irrevocable for a period of 120 days, plus a 30 day extension. Driller, who was to accept the offer by drilling on a designated parcel, paid nothing for the option. Before acceptance, Driller in reliance on the option drilled a test well on another parcel. Data from this drilling would help to evaluate whether to accept the offer. Before acceptance, however, Owner attempted to change the terms of the offer. Held: Under Section 90 of the Restatement (Second), Driller's reliance upon the written option promise made the offer irrevocable and Driller could create a contract on the original terms of the offer. Strata Production v. Mercury Exploration, 121 N.M. 622, 627–630 (1996).

(5) *Protection for the Subcontractor?* Under *Drennan,* a general contractor, armed with an award of the overall project, can solicit a new round of subcontractor bids. Subcontractors thus anxious about the prospect of obtaining certain subcontracts for the project are susceptible to pressures to lower their bids. Since the overall project contract has already been awarded at this point, only the general contractor, not the project owner, will profit from this "bid shopping." How can a subcontractor protect itself from bid shopping by the general contractor?

Recognizing a potential for abuse, in 1963 the California legislature adopted the Subletting and Subcontracting Fair Practices Act, West's Ann.Cal.Gov.Code §§ 4100–08. This statute provides that a general contractor bidding on "any public work or improvement" must disclose in its bid the name of any subcontractor whose bid is incorporated into and exceeds ½ of 1% of the price of the general contractor's bid. The statute further provides that a general contractor whose bid on a public project is accepted shall not replace a subcontractor listed in his bid with another subcontractor, except where a listed subcontractor refuses to execute or perform a written contract for the work, becomes insolvent, or fails to satisfy bonding requirements. In addition, replacement of a listed subcontractor under any of these circumstances requires the awarding authority's consent. In *Southern California Acoustics Co. v. C.V. Holder, Inc.*, 71 Cal.2d 719 (1969), the California Supreme Court held that public authorities have a duty to listed subcontractors under the Act not to consent to wrongful substitutions. See also W.J. Lewis Corp. v. C. Harper Construction Co., Inc., 116 Cal.App.3d 27 (1981). Florida has enacted similar legislation. See West's Fla.Stat.Ann. § 286.27. See E.M. Watkins & Co. v. Board of Regents, 414 So.2d 583 (Fla. Dist. Ct. App. 1982).

(6) "Generally, the mere use of a subcontractor's bid by a general contractor bidding on a prime contract does not constitute acceptance of the subcontractor's bid and imposes no obligation upon the prime contractor to accept the subcontractor's bid. . . . Moreover, ECM concedes that the mere solicitation of bids by a general contractor is not an offer and does not impose any obligations upon the general contractor. But ECM points out that even if it were obligated not to revoke its bid, it was not obligated to bid in the first place. ECM alleged in its complaint that it initially refused Maeda's solicitation to bid and only subsequently bid because Maeda promised that if ECM undertook the time and expense to prepare and submit an electrical subcontractor's bid, Maeda would award ECM the subcontract if its bid were the lowest. While this is an issue of first impression, we believe that where a subcontractor allegedly agreed to bid only after receiving the general contractor's promise to accept the bid if it were the low bid and if the general contractor were awarded the prime contract, there is consideration for the general contractor's promise. The consideration for Maeda's promise was ECM's submission of a bid—an act for which Maeda bargained and that ECM was not under a legal duty to perform. See Restatement (Second) of Contracts §§ 71–73 (any bargained for performance other than the performance of a legal duty owed to the promisor is consideration for a promise) . . .". Electrical Construction & Maintenance Co. v. Maeda Pacific Corp., 764 F.2d 619 (9th Cir. 1985).

PROBLEM: THE CASE OF THE BID-SHOPPING CONTRACTOR

School Corporation decided to build an annex to its senior high school. Plans and specifications were prepared, and various building firms were invited to submit bids. Among those contacted was Contractor. The latter, in turn, determined to submit a bid and proceeded to contact potential subcontractors relative to various components of the project.

Subcontractor *A* telephoned a bid for the excavating work. Since this was the low bid of the responding excavating subcontractors, Contractor used *A*'s figure in computing his bid to School Corporation. Subcontractor *B* submitted a bid in writing for the electrical work, which Contractor also used in computing the general bid since *B*'s price was the lowest of the electrical subcontractors. Subcontractor *C*'s bid was low for the plumbing component, and it, too, was used by Contractor in preparing the prime bid.

At the bid opening on March 18, Contractor was found to be the lowest bidder, and two days later was awarded the contract. Armed with this award, Contractor immediately sought out other excavating subcontractors in an effort to get a lower figure, but he was unsuccessful. On March 22, he wired an acceptance to A. He fared better, however, with respect to the electrical work. He secured, on March 23, the agreement of subcontractor *D* to do the work for $15,000 less than specified by *B*. He took no further action regarding *B*'s bid.

At the bid opening Contractor mentioned to another general contractor that he thought *C*'s bid on the plumbing work was too high and that he could do much better elsewhere. Two days later the other contractor told *C* of this conversation, and the latter, thinking Contractor would not want him to do the work, accepted an outstanding offer from another. However, Contractor did not seek out other plumbing subcontractors, and on March 24 undertook to accept *C*'s offer.

Contractor is now beset with problems. *A* and *C* refuse to perform; *B* insists he has a binding contract for the electrical work. Contractor consults you. Advise him both as to his present difficulties and as to how he should proceed in future post-award negotiations.

(F) TIMING ISSUES

Adams v. Lindsell

Court of King's Bench, 1818.
106 Eng.Rep. 250.

Action for non-delivery of wool according to agreement. At the trial at the last Lent Assizes for the county of Worcester, before Burrough, J., it appeared that the defendants, who were dealers in wool, at St. Ives, in the county of Huntingdon, had, on Tuesday the 2d of September 1817, written the following letter to the plaintiffs, who were woolen manufacturers residing in Bromsgrove, Worcestershire. "We now offer you eight hundred tods of weather fleeces, of a good fair quality of our country wool, at 35s. 6d. per tod, to be delivered at Leicester, and to be paid for by two months' bill in two months, and to be weighed up by your agent within fourteen days, receiving your answer in course of post."

This letter was misdirected by the defendants, to Bromsgrove, Leicestershire, in consequence of which it was not received by the plaintiffs in Worcestershire till 7 P.M. on Friday, September 5th. On that evening the plaintiffs wrote an answer, agreeing to accept the wool on the terms proposed. The course of the post between St. Ives and Bromsgrove is through London, and consequently this answer was not received by the defendants till Tuesday, September 9th. On the Monday September 8th, the defendants not having, as they expected, received an answer on Sunday September 7th, (which in case their letter had not been misdirected, would have been in the usual course of post,) sold the wool in question to another person. Under these circumstances, the learned Judge held, that the delay having been occasioned by the neglect of the defendants, the jury must take it, that the answer did come back in due course of post; and that then the defendants were liable for the loss that had been sustained; and the plaintiffs accordingly recovered a verdict.

Jervis having in Easter term obtained a rule nisi for a new trial, on the ground that there was no binding contract between the parties.

Dauncey, Puller, and Richardson, showed cause. They contended, that at the moment of the acceptance of the offer of the defendants by the plaintiffs, the former became bound. And that was on the Friday evening, when there had been no change of circumstances. They were then stopped by the Court, who called upon Jervis and Campbell in support of the rule. They relied on Payne v. Cave (3 T.R. 148), and more particularly on Cooke v. Oxley (Ibid. 653). In that case, Oxley, who had proposed to sell goods to Cooke, and given him a certain time at his request, to determine whether he would buy them or not, was held not liable to the performance of the contract, even though Cooke, within the specified time, had determined to buy them, and given Oxley notice to that effect. So here the defendants who have proposed by letter to sell this wool, are not to be held liable, even though it be now admitted that the answer did come back in due course of post. Till the plaintiffs' answer was actually received, there could be no binding contract between the parties; and before then, the defendants had retracted their offer, by selling the wool to other persons. But—

The Court said, that if that were so, no contract could ever be completed by the post. For if the defendants were not bound by their offer when accepted by the plaintiffs till the answer was received, then the plaintiffs ought not to be bound till after they had received notification that the defendants had received their answer and assented to it. And so it might go on ad infinitum. The defendants must be considered in law as making, during every instant of the time their letter was travelling, the same identical offer to the plaintiffs; and then the contract is completed by the acceptance of it by the latter. Then as to the delay in notifying the acceptance, that arises entirely from the mistake of the defendants, and it therefore must be taken as against them, that the plaintiffs' answer was received in course of post.

Rule discharged.

NOTES

(1)   Exactly what did *Adams v. Lindsell* hold, that the contract was formed when the letter of acceptance was posted or something else?

(2)   *Justifications for the Mailbox Rule.* The so-called "mailbox" rule, derived from *Adams v. Lindsell*, has gained almost universal acceptance in common law jurisdictions. Thus Restatement (Second) § 63(a) provides: "Unless the offer provides otherwise, (a) an acceptance made in a manner and by a medium invited by an offer is operative and completes the manifestation of mutual assent as soon as put out of the offeree's possession, without regard to whether it ever reaches the offeror; * * *."

An English court provided the following justification in 1879:

> There is no doubt that the implication of a complete, final, and absolutely binding contract being formed, as soon as the acceptance of an offer is posted, may in some cases lead to inconvenience and hardship. But such there must be at times in every view of the law. It is impossible in transactions which pass between parties at a distance, and have to be carried on through the medium of correspondence, to adjust conflicting rights between innocent parties, so as to make the consequences of mistake on the part of a mutual agent fall equally upon the shoulders of both. At the same time I am not prepared to admit that the implication in question will lead to any great or general inconvenience or hardship. *An offeror, if he chooses, may always make the formation of the contract which he proposes dependent upon the actual communication to himself of the acceptance.* If he trusts to the post he trusts to a means of communication which, as a rule, does not fail, and if no answer to his offer is received by him, and the matter is of importance to him, he can make inquiries of the person to whom his offer was addressed. On the other hand, if the contract is not finally concluded, except in the event of the acceptance actually reaching the offeror, the door would be opened to the perpetration of much fraud, and, putting aside this consideration, considerable delay in commercial transactions, in which despatch, is as a rule, of the greatest consequence, would be occasioned; for the acceptor would never be entirely safe in acting upon his acceptance until he had received notice that his letter of acceptance had reached its destination.

Household Fire & Carriage Accident Insurance Co., Ltd. v. Grant (1879) 4 Ex.D. 216, 223–24 (emphasis added). Is this persuasive? See G.H. Treitel, The Law of Contracts 23–29 (10th ed.1999) (describing the rule as arbitrary but workable).

The mailbox rule is a default rule: the offeror can always require receipt of the acceptance before the contract is formed. For a recent example, see *Crane v. Timberbrook Village*, Ltd., 774 P.2d 3 (Utah App. 1989). Perhaps the reason for the rule lies in the fact that it is the offeror who has the power to opt-out of any default. If the offeror wants a rule that is more advantageous to him- or herself, the offeror must expressly opt-out of the mailbox rule, thereby giving notice to the offeree.

Another thought concerns the optimal number of confirmations. As recognized in *Crook v. Cowan*, 64 N.C. 743 (1870), the last person to confirm will always be at an informational disadvantage because she will not know whether her confirmation got through:

> [I]f an offer and acceptance—an unconditional and specific order, and an exact fulfillment, as in this case, does not complete the contract, how would it be possible to complete a contract by mail? A sends an unconditional order to B, and instead of B's filling the order, he writes back that he accepts the order and will fill it, but in the meantime, A may have changed his mind, and lest he has, he must write back to B and so on, for ever. . . . [If we were to require such serial re-confirmations], no contract could ever be completed by post. For if the defendant was not bound by his offer, when accepted by the plaintiff, until the answer was received, then the plaintiff ought not to be bound until after he had received the notification that the defendant had received his answer and assented to it. And so it might go on *ad infinitum.*

Id. at 746. Additional confirmations do not reduce the chance of mistake, but merely shift it to the other side and waste social resources to boot. See Eric Talley, *Interdisciplinary Gap Filling*, 22 L. & Soc. Inquiry 1055 (1997).

(3)   *Scope of the Mailbox Rule.* To what methods of communication and to what kind of facts should the "mailbox" rule be limited? For example, if an offer is sent by telegraph is a contract formed when an acceptance is mailed? Sent by carrier pigeon? Spoken into a telephone receiver? See UCC § 2–206(1); *Szollosy v. Hyatt Corp.*, 396 F.Supp.2d 159, 164, n. 11 (D.Conn. 2005) ("Analogizing the mailbox rule to newer electronic forms of communication, the Court finds that the Szollosys also may be considered to have formed a contract at the moment their reservation form was faxed to the travel agency and then to the Hyatt Regency. Under whatever reasoning, Connecticut warranty law will govern these counts.").

(4)   There have been attempts at other rules. In *Rhode Island Tool Co. v. United States*, 130 Ct.Cl. 698 (1955), the offeror, who had made a mistake in its bid, communicated a withdrawal of the offer to the contracting officer after written notice of award was mailed but before it was received. The court held that no contract was created, relying substantially upon revised postal regulations that gave the sender control over a letter up to delivery: "The acceptance, therefore, is not final until the letter reaches destination, since the sender has the absolute right of withdrawal from the post office, and even the right to have the postmaster at the delivery point return the letter at any time before actual delivery." Is this reasoning persuasive?

(5)   *Electronic Communication and the Demise of the "Mailbox" Rule?* As time goes on, more and more contracting will be by electronic transmission where communication is virtually instantaneous. Under such circumstances, there is good reason for holding that an acceptance is effective when received, not when transmitted. The authors of an influential study observed that an important premise upon which the "mailbox" rule is predicated is the notion that delayed media, such as mailed writings, do not provide either party the ability to verify in a timely fashion that receipt of a message has occurred and that the message as received is without error.

Hence, they maintain that electronic transmission should be governed by the same rules that apply when parties are in the presence of each other and the acceptance should be deemed effective when received. See *The Commercial Use of Electronic Data Interchange—A Report and Model Trading Partner Agreement,* 45 Bus. Law. 1645, 1666–67 (1990). On the other hand, one scholar, after an extensive review of the literature, has concluded that the mailbox rule should be retained for any "non-instantaneous method of communication." See Valerie Watnick, *The Electronic Formation of Contracts and the Common Law "Mail Box" Rule,* 56 Baylor L. Rev. 175 (2004). Section 15 of the Uniform Electronic Transactions Act provides rules for determining when an electronic record has been sent or received.

(6) Assume that upon receipt of a written "Offer and Acceptance" signed by Purchaser, Vendor signed as seller and deposited the writing in the mail, properly addressed to Purchaser. Before the letter arrived Vendor telephoned Purchaser that he had decided not to sell. Was there a binding contract? Cf. Morrison v. Thoelke, 155 So.2d 889 (Fla.App. 1963).

Comment: Other Timing Rules

Acceptances are not the only legal acts that figure into the formation (or non-formation) of a contract. The mailbox issue also arises with regard to rejections, counteroffers and revocations. As distinguished from acceptances, the common law makes these communications effective when received. Restatement (Second) §§ 40, 42. Why? Maybe because these rules are also defaults that are set against the person who has a unilateral power to opt out.

What happens if an offeree sends a rejection or counteroffer and then, before that missive is received, sends an acceptance. Restatement (Second) § 40 provides that the rejection or counteroffer "limits the power so that a letter or telegram of acceptance started after the sending of an otherwise effective rejection or counter-offer is only a counter-offer unless the acceptance is received by the offeror before he receives the rejection or counter-offer." Interpret!

What about firm offers, that is, option contracts? Restatement (Second) § 63 provides that "an acceptance under an option contract is not effective until received by the offeror." In the view of the drafters, since the option contract provides for irrevocability of the offer, the primary reason for the rule of *Adams v. Lindsell* and its progeny is absent. Corbin explains:

> If in an option contract the duty of the promisor is conditional on notice within 30 days, does this mean notice received or notice properly mailed? It is believed that, in the absence of an expression of contrary intention, it should be held that the notice must be received. As above explained, the notice is in one respect a notice of acceptance of an offer; but in another aspect it is a condition of the promisor's already existing conditional duty. It is more likely to be regarded in this latter aspect by the

parties themselves. The rule that an acceptance by post is operative on mailing was itself subjected to severe criticism; and, even though it may now be regarded as settled, it should not be extended to notice of acceptance in already binding option contracts.

Corbin § 264. See Romain v. A. Howard Wholesale Co., 506 N.E.2d 1124 (Ind. Ct. App. 1987). Not all courts follow this powerful tandem, however. See, e.g., Worms v. Burgess, 620 P.2d 455 (Okla. App. 1980).

What about non-U.S. jurisdictions? While generalization is risky, it seems that other legal systems, particularly the civil law, are more willing to enforce an offeror's statement that the offer is "irrevocable" without the presence of formality, bargain or reliance than the common law. See 1 Rudolph Schlesinger, Formation of Contracts: A Study of the Common Core of Legal Systems 109–11, 747–91 (1968). And there appears to be some correlation between the irrevocability of an offer and a legal system's willingness to hold that a contract is created when the acceptance is mailed. Thus, in Austria and Germany where offers are normally irrevocable, a contract is not formed until the acceptance is received by the offeror since there is "no necessity for fixing an earlier moment for the acceptance in order to protect the offeree against possible speculations of the offeror." Schlesinger, supra at 159.

Could it be that the "mailbox" rule evolved as a common law substitute for the civil law doctrine of irrevocability? Put another way, does the "mailbox" rule make the most sense when employed to protect the offeree's opportunity to make a sound decision against an unexpected revocation? If so, should it be extended to fact patterns where no threat of revocation is involved? Given that the doctrine of promissory estoppel is increasingly invoked to protect the relying offeree against precipitous revocation, is there any real need for a "mailbox" rule?

Articles 16(2) and 18(2) of the Convention on Contracts for the International Sale of Goods (CISG) are more consistent with the civil law. Note that while Article 18(2) states that an acceptance is not effective until it "reaches" the offeror, Article 16(2) states that an offer cannot be revoked after the offeree has "dispatched" the acceptance. The UNIDROIT Principles of International Commercial Contracts are in accord. See Articles 2.4(2) and 2.6(2).

PROBLEM: ACCEPTANCE OF RESIGNATION BY MAIL

In July 1990, Carol was hired as a special education teacher by the Huron School District for the 1990–91 school year. On August 15, 1990, Carol handed to Ed, her supervisor, a letter of resignation effective on August 17, 1990. In the letter she requested that her final check be mailed to an address some fifty miles away (her parents' home). Ed gave the letter to Mary, the superintendent with authority to hire and fire, on August 20. That same day, Mary prepared and mailed a letter properly addressed to Carol at her parents accepting the resignation. The next day Carol hand-delivered a letter to Mary withdrawing her resignation. Mary told Carol that the resignation had been accepted and handed her a copy of the letter mailed the day before. That letter did not reach Carol's parents' home until August 24. Carol claims that the resignation had been withdrawn in time because the acceptance letter should have been handed to her.

(1) What are the strongest arguments for the School District? How should the court decide? See Cantu v. Central Education Agency, 884 S.W.2d 565 (Tex. Ct. App. 1994).

(2) Suppose Carol had sent a telegram of resignation from her parents' home and Mary had mailed a letter of acceptance to that address. Before the letter arrived, Carol revoked the resignation by e-mail.

(3) Suppose Carol had telephoned Mary, but when Mary was "not available to take your call," Carol left the resignation on Mary's voice mail. How should Mary accept the resignation on these facts? Suppose the resignation came by facsimile? See Equity Fire & Casualty Co. v. Traver, 330 Ark. 102 (1997) (where offer by fax stated that acceptance must be received, mailing an acceptance did not create a contract).

PROBLEM: THE CASE OF THE REJECTION, REVOCATION AND ACCEPTANCE RACE

On July 4, A mailed to B a written offer to sell ten shares of an unlisted stock at $60.00 per share. B was given four days from the date of the letter to accept. The offer was received on July 6, at 2 PM. At 3 PM on July 6, B mailed a letter to A that stated, in part: "will purchase ten shares at $55.00 per share. . . ." At 11 AM on July 6, however, A had sold the ten shares to C for $65.00 and at 1 PM of the same day had mailed a letter to B revoking the offer. B, who was blissfully unaware of A's activity, learned at 4 PM on July 6 that the market price of the shares might increase and, at 5 PM on the same day, telegraphed A to "disregard letter . . . will take offered stock for $60.00 per share." B's telegram of July 6 was received by A at 9 AM on July 7. B's letter of July 6 was received by A at 2 PM on July 8. A's letter of July 6 was received by B at 2 PM on July 8.

(1) B claims that he has a contract with A for the purchase of the stock. Is this contention correct?

(2) Suppose at 3 PM on July 6 that B mailed a letter to A that "accepted your offer." Shortly thereafter the market for the shares of stock dropped sharply and, at 5 PM, B telegraphed A to "disregard" my prior letter, I have "decided not to buy." The telegram was received by A on July 7 at 9 AM, whereupon A sold the shares to C. B's letter of acceptance was received on July 8 at 2 PM. Is there a contract? What are A's options?

(3) Draft a new section for the proposed Restatement (Third) Contracts that would resolve this question.

2. SPECIAL PROBLEMS IN THE AGREEMENT PROCESS

The above discussion has covered the basic rules that govern the agreement process. As complicated as those rules are, their application raises even thornier questions. The remainder of this chapter describes four examples: (1) situations in which the parties have clearly agreed to transact with one another, but their communications contain different terms; (2) terms that a consumer does not receive until he or she opens the box, or are provided via a link on a website; (3) agreements that are indefinite or missing terms; and (4) precontractual liability for acts during the course of negotiations.

(A) COUNTEROFFERS, FORM BATTLES AND UCC § 2–207

Minneapolis & St. Louis Railway Co. v. Columbus Rolling-Mill Co.

Supreme Court of the United States, 1886.
119 U.S. 149.

This was an action by a railroad corporation established at Minneapolis in the State of Minnesota against a manufacturing corporation established at Columbus in the State of Ohio. The petition alleged that on December 19, 1879, the parties made a contract by which the plaintiff agreed to buy of the defendant, and the defendant sold to the plaintiff, two thousand tons of iron rails of the weight of fifty pounds per yard, at the price of fifty-four dollars per ton gross, to be delivered free on board cars at the defendant's rolling mill in the month of March, 1880, and to be paid for by the plaintiff in cash when so delivered. The answer denied the making of the contract. It was admitted at the trial that the following letters and telegrams were sent at their dates, and were received in due course, by the parties, through their agents.

December 5, 1879. Letter from plaintiff to defendant: "Please quote me prices for 500 to 3000 tons 50 lb. steel rails, and for 2000 to 5000 tons 50 lb. iron rails, March 1880 delivery."

December 8, 1879. Letter from defendant to plaintiff: "Your favor of the 5th inst. at hand. We do not make steel rails. For iron rails, we will sell 2000 to 5000 tons of 50 lb. rails for fifty-four ($54.00) dollars per gross ton for spot cash, F.O.B. cars at our mill, March delivery, subject as follows: In case of strike among our workmen, destruction of or serious damage to our works by fire or the elements, or any causes of delay beyond our control, we shall not be held accountable in damages. If our offer is accepted, shall expect to be notified of same prior to Dec. 20th, 1879."

December 16, 1879. Telegram from plaintiff to defendant: "Please enter our order for twelve hundred tons rails, March delivery, as per your favor of the eighth. Please reply."

December 16, 1879. Letter from plaintiff to defendant: "Yours of the 8th came duly to hand. I telegraphed you to-day to enter our order for twelve hundred (1200) tons 50 lb. iron rails for next March delivery, at fifty-four dollars ($54.00) F.O.B. cars at your mill. Please send contract.

Also please send me templet of your 50 lb. rail. Do you make splices? If so, give me prices for splices for this lot of iron."

December 18, 1879. Telegram from defendant to plaintiff received same day: "We cannot book your order at present at that price."

December 19, 1879. Telegram from plaintiff to defendant: "Please enter an order for two thousand tons rails, as per your letter of the sixth. Please forward written contract. Reply." (The word "sixth" was admitted to be a mistake for "eighth.")

December 22, 1879. Telegram from plaintiff to defendant: "Did you enter my order for two thousand tons rails, as per my telegram of December nineteenth? Answer."

After repeated similar inquiries by the plaintiff, the defendant, on January 19, 1880, denied the existence of any contract between the parties.

The jury returned a verdict for the defendant, under instructions which need not be particularly stated; and the plaintiff alleged exceptions, and sued out this writ of error.

■ MR. JUSTICE GRAY, after making the foregoing statement of the case, delivered the opinion of the court.

The rules of law which govern this case are well settled. As no contract is complete without the mutual assent of the parties, an offer to sell imposes no obligation until it is accepted according to its terms. So long as the offer has been neither accepted nor rejected, the negotiation remains open, and imposes no obligation upon either party; the one may decline to accept, or the other may withdraw his offer; and either rejection or withdrawal leaves the matter as if no offer had ever been made. A proposal to accept, or an acceptance, upon terms varying from those offered, is a rejection of the offer, and puts an end to the negotiation, unless the party who made the original offer renews it, or assents to the modification suggested. The other party, having once rejected the offer, cannot afterwards revive it by tendering an acceptance of it. . . . If the offer does not limit the time for its acceptance, it must be accepted within a reasonable time. If it does, it may, at any time within the limit and so long as it remains open, be accepted or rejected by the party to whom, or be withdrawn by the party by whom, it was made. . . .

The defendant, by the letter of December 8, offered to sell to the plaintiff two thousand to five thousand tons of iron rails on certain terms specified, and added that if the offer was accepted the defendant would expect to be notified prior to December 20. This offer, while it remained open, without having been rejected by the plaintiff or revoked by the defendant, would authorize the plaintiff to take at his election any number of tons not less than two thousand nor more than five thousand, on the terms specified. The offer, while unrevoked, might be accepted, or rejected by the plaintiff at any time before December 20. Instead of accepting the offer made, the plaintiff, on December 16, by telegram and letter, referring to the defendant's letter of December 8, directed the defendant to enter an order for twelve hundred tons on the same terms. The mention, in both telegram and letter, of the date and the terms of the defendant's original offer, shows that the plaintiff's order was not an independent proposal, but an answer to the defendant's offer, a qualified acceptance of that offer, varying the number of tons, and therefore in law a rejection of the offer. On December 18, the defendant by telegram declined to fulfill the plaintiff's order. The negotiation between the parties was thus closed, and the plaintiff could not afterwards fall back on the defendant's original offer. The plaintiff's attempt to do so, by the telegram of December 19, was therefore ineffectual and created no rights against the defendant.

Such being the legal effect of what passed in writing between the parties, it is unnecessary to consider whether, upon a fair interpretation of the instructions of the court, the question whether the plaintiff's telegram and letter of December 16 constituted a rejection of the defendant's offer of December 8 was ruled in favor of the defendant as a matter of law, or was submitted to the jury as a question of fact. The submission of a question of law to the jury is no ground of exception if they decide it aright. . . .

Judgment affirmed.

NOTES

(1) *Common Law Mirror Image Rule.* "When the plaintiffs submitted this offer in their letter of April 4th to the defendant, only one of two courses of action was open to the defendant. It could accept the offer made and thus manifest that assent which was essential to the creation of a contract, or it could reject the offer. There was no middle course. * * * A proposal to accept the offer it modified or an acceptance subject to other terms and conditions was equivalent to an absolute rejection of the offer made by the plaintiffs." Poel v. Brunswick-Balke-Collender Co., 216 N.Y. 310, 319 (1915). In so speaking the New York Court of Appeals reaffirmed the settled doctrine that for a valid bargain contract there must be an offer and an acceptance, with the acceptance expressing unconditional assent to the terms of the offer. An offeree cannot pick and choose from among the terms, agreeing here and disagreeing there, and then assert the existence of an operative acceptance. If the terms are varied or changed, there is a counter-offer. No contract can arise until agreement is reached as to those changes; i.e., until the counter-offer has itself been accepted. Traditionally, courts have insisted upon total congruence between offer and acceptance, the latter required to be the "mirror image" of the former. Under the mirror-image rule, even a non-material variation is fatal. See Minar v. Skoog, 235 Minn. 262, 265 (1951) (valid acceptance must embrace terms of offer with exactitude and unequivocally express an intent to create without more a contract).

(2) *Effect of Requests or Suggestions.* According to Restatement (Second) section 59, a reply that purports to be an acceptance but which adds qualifications or requires performance of conditions is not an acceptance, but

a counter-offer. But an acceptance that *requests* a change or addition to the terms of the offer is not invalidated unless the acceptance is made to depend on an assent to the changed or added terms. Restatement (Second) § 61. There is a considerable body of law differentiating a so-called "conditional" acceptance, which is really no acceptance at all, from a genuine acceptance accompanied by mere "inquiries," "requests," or "suggestions" of the offeree. See, e.g., Valashinas v. Koniuto, 308 N.Y. 233 (1954). Finally, it must be borne in mind that an added term or qualifier in the acceptance may be no more than a repetition of what is already contained, expressly or impliedly, in the offer. *United States v. National Optical Stores* Co., 407 F.2d 759 (7th Cir. 1969) is illustrative. The federal government's notice of acceptance was made subject to approval of credit and antitrust clearance by the Department of Justice. But these two conditions were found to be incorporated in the bid itself. The court concluded: "Since defendant's bid promise included the credit data and antitrust conditions and was accepted by the Government, both parties then became bound in accordance with the mutual assent they had expressed. * * * The Government's letter * * * imposed no additional or different terms from those offered and was therefore not a counter-offer." 407 F.2d at 761.

(3) *Whose Default?* Like many of the formation rules, the idea that a counteroffer terminates an offeree's power of acceptance is a default rule which can be contracted around unilaterally by *either* the offeror or offeree: "An offeree's power of acceptance is terminated by his making of a counter-offer, unless the offeror has manifested a contrary intention or unless the counter-offer manifests a contrary intention of the offeree." Restatement (Second) of Contracts § 39(2). But what happens if the original offer explicitly states that any counteroffer terminates the offer, but the offeree nonetheless counteroffers expressly manifesting an intention to retain her power of acceptance? Cf. Restatement (Second) of Contracts § 36(2). See Ian Ayres, *Never Say No: The Law, Economics, and Psychology of Counteroffers*, 25 Ohio State J. on Dispute Resolution 603 (2010).

(4) *The "Grumbling" Acceptance.* In *Panhandle Eastern Pipe Line Co. v. Smith*, 637 P.2d 1020 (Wyo. 1981), an employer (Panhandle) fired an employee (Smith). The latter, following the grievance procedure of a collective bargaining agreement, unsuccessfully challenged the dismissal. However, Mr. Smith's union representative requested Panhandle to reconsider, and the latter responded with a letter to Smith in which it offered to withdraw the discharge if he would comply with certain terms and conditions. Smith signed under the typewritten words, "Understood, Agreed to and Accepted," added some handwritten notations, and again signed his name. The notations contained a request by Smith to see his personnel file and to contest any mistakes he found there. Panhandle contended that Smith, by adding the request to see his personnel file and to contest mistakes, made a counter-offer. The Wyoming Supreme Court disagreed. There was testimony that all Panhandle employees had a right to see their personnel files, and while the court acknowledged that the acceptance was what Corbin once referred to as a "grumbling" acceptance, it was an acceptance nonetheless.

(5) *The Battle of Forms, Mirror Image and UCC § 2–207.* In *Minneapolis & St. Louis Railway Co*, supra, the parties, who were at a distance, exchanged letters and telegrams. The terms of these writings were read and responded to. But the contract failed because of a disagreement over a material, negotiated term: the quantity of steel to be sold.

In many transactions, the writings of the parties may be a bit more complex. The buyer's purchase order and the seller's acknowledgment may be standard forms that contain terms that are not read or negotiated over by the other party. Put differently, these terms are in preprinted boilerplate drafted by one party in its own interest. Sometimes these terms add to terms in the offer of the other party or to an agreement previously reached. Sometimes these terms contradict other terms. In all cases, however, the party drafting the terms will claim that they are part of the agreement. Consider the words of one court:

> The problem underlying any "battle of the forms" is that parties engaged in commerce have failed to incorporate into one formal, signed contract the terms of their contractual relationship. Instead, each has been content to rely upon standard terms which each has included in its purchase orders or acknowledgments, terms which often conflict with those in the other party's documents. Usually, these standard terms mean little, for a contract looks to its fulfillment and rarely anticipates its breach. Hope springs eternal in the commercial world and expectations are usually, but not always, realized. It is only when the good faith expectations of the parties are frustrated that the legal obligations and rights of the parties must be precisely determined. This case presents a situation typical in any battle of the forms: it is not that the parties' forms have said too little, but rather that they have said too much yet have expressly agreed upon too little.

McJunkin Corporation v. Mechanicals, Inc., 888 F.2d 481, 482 (6th Cir. 1989).

UCC § 2–207 was drafted to provide a more rational resolution to such battles of the forms. In thinking through it in the following cases, keep three questions in mind: (1) Was any contract formed between the parties; (2) If so, what are its terms; and (3) What commercial policies explain (or should explain) UCC § 2–207?

DTE Energy Technologies, Inc v. Briggs Electric, Inc.

Eastern District of Michigan, 2007.
2007 WL 674321.

■ PATRICK J. DUGGAN, UNITED STATES DISTRICT JUDGE. DTE Energy Technologies, Inc. ("Plaintiff") initiated this diversity lawsuit after Briggs Electric, Inc. ("Defendant") allegedly breached a contract for the sale of electric generator systems. Plaintiff, in its amended complaint, seeks: (1) damages based on Defendant's alleged failure to pay invoices and (2) declaratory relief prohibiting Defendant from both obtaining incidental or consequential damages and forcing Plaintiff to mediate this dispute in California. Presently before the Court is Defendant's motion to dismiss for lack of personal jurisdiction and improper venue, filed pursuant to Rule 12 of the Federal Rules of Civil Procedure, and alternatively, to transfer. * * *

I. *Background*

In May 2002, Plaintiff, a Michigan corporation with its principal place of business in Farmington Hills, Michigan, began negotiations with Hoag Memorial Hospital Presbyterian ("Hoag") for the sale of electric generator systems to be installed as part of a construction project ("Project") at Hoag's site in Newport Beach, California. On May 6, 2003, Hoag and DPR Construction, Inc. ("DPR") entered into a contract where DPR would act as general contractor for the Project. Subsequently, on August 1, 2003, Hoag informed Plaintiff that it would not be entering into a contract with Plaintiff and "instead directed [Plaintiff] to attempt to negotiate a subcontract for the sale of the electric generator systems with an unspecified subcontractor of DPR." . . .

Defendant later won the bid as the subcontractor. Part of Defendant's obligation as subcontractor was to perform the electrical work on the Project, which included "procuring and installing the electric generator systems." . . . On October 21, 2003, Defendant sent a Purchase Order to Plaintiff. Defendant contends that the Purchase Order constituted an offer. Furthermore, Defendant argues that Plaintiff accepted its Purchase Order on November 10, 2003 when Rick Cole sent an email to Ron Calkins, a representative of Defendant, stating:

Ron,

Per our discussion.

Rick

The e-mail also contained a forwarded message, bearing the subject line "Waukesha extended warranty," from Rick Cole to James Easley, a representative of Hoag. This forwarded message states in relevant part:

Jim,

We have received our order from Briggs Electric for the three Waukesha engine generator sets. I wanted to take this opportunity to thank you again for allowing DTE to participate on this project. We have assigned a project manager and two engineers to the project and we are completing the submittals now.

The bid documents required that we offer a price for extended warranty which was quoted at $21,000 per year. Waukesha's warranty policy requires that we include the extended warranty coverage at the time we enter our order. I need to know if Hoag is planning to accept the extended warranty and, if so, how to bill the cost.

Thus, according to Defendant, this forwarded message acknowledging the receipt of the Purchase Order is evidence that Plaintiff accepted the Purchase Order, through its conduct.

Plaintiff submitted an Order Acknowledgment to Defendant on December 4, 2003. . . . Plaintiff contends that the Order Acknowledgment and the Standard Terms and Conditions of Sale attached to the Order Acknowledgment should be construed as an offer. Plaintiff argues that Defendant did not object to the terms of this alleged offer, and Defendant accepted the alleged offer when it sent payment to Plaintiff. The Standard Terms and Conditions of Sale attached to the Order Acknowledgment contain the following forum-selection and choice-of-law clause:

> The provisions of this Agreement shall be construed in accordance with and governed by the laws of the State of Michigan as applicable to contracts made and performed entirely within that State, and any action thereon may be brought only in a court of competent jurisdiction located in Michigan.

Plaintiff contends that it delivered the electric generator systems and provided other related services at Defendant's request. Furthermore, Plaintiff argues that Defendant has breached its obligation to pay Plaintiff under the agreement and "owes [Plaintiff] in excess of $880,000 for the generator systems, for related service, and for additional work which [Plaintiff] performed at [Defendant's] request." Rather than paying the amount owed, Plaintiff alleges that Defendant has made a demand to Plaintiff for damages that "purportedly arise out of delays in completion of the Project." Specifically, Plaintiff alleges that "[o]n or about October 6, 2006, [Defendant] allegedly submitted a demand for mediation against [Plaintiff], Hoag, and [the general contractor] with JAMS in California seeking a declaration of the contractual rights and duties of the parties arising out of the same transaction and occurrence of events pled in this Complaint."

Defendant acknowledges that the Order Acknowledgment contains a forum-selection and choice of law clause. However, Defendant contends that it did not agree to the forum-selection clause.

II. *Defendant's Motion to Dismiss for Lack of Personal Jurisdiction*

* * *

Plaintiff argues that Defendant has consented to personal jurisdiction based on a forum-selection clause in the parties' sales agreement. Under Michigan law, consent is a basis for a court to exercise personal jurisdiction over a non-resident corporation as long as the limitations in Section 600.745 are satisfied. Mich. Comp. Laws § 600.711. Section 600.745 states in relevant part:

> If the parties agreed in writing that an action on a controversy may be brought in this state and the agreement provides the only basis

for the exercise of jurisdiction, a court of this state shall entertain the action if all the following occur:

(a) The court has power under the law of this state to entertain the action.

(b) This state is a reasonably convenient place for the trial of the action.

(c) The agreement as to the place of the action is not obtained by misrepresentation, duress, the abuse of economic power, or other unconscionable means.

(d) The defendant is served with process as provided by court rules. Id. § 600.745(2).

According to Plaintiff, Defendant consented to personal jurisdiction when it accepted the forum-selection clause in the December 4, 2003 Order Acknowledgment, which Plaintiff contends was the offer. Defendant argues that the Order Acknowledgment was not the offer and contends that the Purchase Order it sent Plaintiff on October 21, 2003 was the offer. Once the Court determines which document operated as the offer, it can decide whether the forum-selection clause is binding.

In their briefs and at the hearing held on this motion, the parties refer to Michigan's version of the Uniform Commercial Code ("UCC"). The UCC provides that "[a] contract for the sale of goods may be made in any manner sufficient to show agreement, including conduct by both parties which recognizes the existence of such a contract." Mich. Comp. Laws § 440.2204(1). More specifically, "[a]n offer to make a contract shall be construed as inviting acceptance in any manner and by any medium reasonable in the circumstances." Id. § 440.2206(1)(a). "As a general rule orders are considered as offers to purchase."

* * *

Plaintiff asserts two other reasons why the Purchase Order should not be construed as an offer. First, Plaintiff argues that Defendant did not formally become the subcontractor on the Project until November 5, 2003; thus, the Purchase Order could not have operated as an offer. Second, Plaintiff argues that the Purchase Order is "indefinite, incomplete, and contradictory." . . . This Court disagrees with these arguments. First, the fact that Defendant submitted the Purchase Order before it was formally the subcontractor has no bearing on whether the Purchase Order constituted an offer. Second, the Court does not believe the Purchase Order was "indefinite, incomplete, and contradictory." The Purchase Order contained a quantity, price, and delivery terms.

This Court believes the October 21, 2003 Purchase Order constituted an offer. The Purchase Order was the initial communication between Plaintiff and Defendant, and it was sent to Plaintiff after Hoag informed Plaintiff that it would need to negotiate a deal with the subcontractor. Furthermore, the Order Acknowledgment references, by number, the

Purchase Order and lists the exact price as that listed in the Purchase Order. Because the Court believes the Purchase Order was an offer, the Court must now determine the effect of the Order Acknowledgment, and more specifically, whether the forum-selection clause is enforceable against Defendant.

"Michigan courts recognize that '[a] contractual forum selection clause, though otherwise valid, may not be enforced against one not bound by the contract.' . . ." "It is for Michigan courts to determine in the first instance whether a forum selection clause is contractually binding." In deciding whether Defendant is bound by the forum selection clause, the Court is guided by Michigan Compiled Laws Section 440.2207, which is identical to Section 2–207 of the UCC. Compare Mich. Comp. Laws § 440.2207 with UCC § 2–207. "[T]he purpose of Section 2–207 is to interpret a contract that has been made, not to determine that one exists." James J. White, *Contracting Under Amended 2–207,* 2004 Wis. L. Rev. 723, 723 (2004). As stated above, the parties do not dispute whether a contract for the sale of the electric generators exists; rather, the parties disagree as to whether the forum-selection clause is part of their contract.

[Section 440.2207] alters the common law "mirror image rule" by establishing a general rule that a written confirmation operates as an acceptance even though its terms are not identical to those contained in the offer. James J. White & Robert S. Summers, Uniform Commercial Code 55–56 (5th ed. 2006). This general rule contains an exception. In order to avoid accepting an offer by sending a written confirmation containing additional or different terms, a party can state that "acceptance is expressly made conditional on assent to the additional or different terms." Mich. Comp. Laws § 440.2207(1). The Sixth Circuit has stated: "[i]n order to fall within this [exception], it is not enough that acceptance is expressly conditional on additional or different terms; rather, an acceptance must be *expressly* conditional on offeror's *assent* to those terms." Dorton v. Collins & Aikman Corp., 453 F.2d 1161, 1168 (6th Cir. 1972) (emphasis in original).

Plaintiff argues that even if the Purchase Order constituted an offer, it expressly rejected the offer in its Order Acknowledgment. Plaintiff contends that the following clause contained in the Standard Terms and Conditions of Sale attached to the Order Acknowledgment is an express rejection:

> 1. Entire Agreement. These Standard Terms and Conditions of Sale, together with the Sale Agreement into which they are incorporated and Schedule 1 thereof (collectively the "Agreement"), set forth and forms the entire understanding between DTE Energy Technologies, Inc. ("Seller") and Buyer with respect to the products described in the Sale Agreement. All prior other and collateral agreements, representations, warranties, promises and conditions relating to the subject

matter of this Agreement are superseded by this Agreement. No additions to or variations from these Terms and Conditions shall be binding unless in a writing executed by Seller's President or one of Seller's Vice Presidents and Buyer. If Buyer's purchase order is referenced, it is solely for inclusion of a purchase order number and none of the terms and conditions of any purchase order or other Buyer document shall apply.

This Court does not believe this provision amounts to an express rejection under Section 440.2207(1).

As stated above, in order for a written confirmation of an offer to amount to a rejection and/or a counteroffer, the written confirmation must be *"expressly* made conditional on *assent* to the additional or different terms." Dorton, 453 F.2d at 1168. Furthermore, Section 440.2207 is "intended to apply only to an acceptance which clearly reveals that the offeree is unwilling to proceed with the transaction unless he is assured of the offeror's assent to the additional or different terms therein." Id. The provision Plaintiff contends is an express rejection does not contemplate the buyer's assent to the additional or different terms. Rather, it makes any additional or different terms binding with or without the buyer's assent.[6]

Because the Order Acknowledgment was not expressly conditional on Defendant's assent to the additional terms, "[t]he additional terms are to be construed as proposals for addition to the contract." Mich. Comp. Laws § 440.2207(2). Furthermore, absent the application of a specified exception, the additional terms become part of the contract when the contracting parties are both "merchants."

Defendant, invoking one of the specified exceptions pertaining to merchants, argues that the forum-selection clause is an additional term and that it "materially alters" the terms of the parties' contract. Id. § 440.2207(2)(b). Recently, another court in the Eastern District of Michigan addressed this exact issue. In *Metro. Alloys Corp. v. State Metals Indus., Inc.,* 416 F.Supp.2d 561 (E.D. Mich. 2006), the defendant, a New Jersey corporation, argued that personal jurisdiction did not exist based on the plaintiff's consent to a New Jersey forum-selection clause set forth on the reverse side of the defendant's "Sales Contract." Id. at 564. The court recognized that the determinative issue was whether the plaintiff was bound by the forum-selection clause. Id. at 566. After finding that the Michigan state courts had not directly addressed the issue, the Court, taking into consideration the objectives of the UCC and

---

[6]   Even if the Order Acknowledgment was an express rejection, Defendant did not accept the forum-selection clause by merely accepting and paying for the electric generators. PCS Nitrogen Fertilizer, L.P. v. The Christy Refractories, L.L.C., 225 F.3d 974, 980 (8th Cir. 2000) (stating "mere acceptance of and payment for goods does not constitute acceptance of all the terms in the seller's counter-offer") (citing Ralph Shrader, Inc. v. Diamond Int'l Corp., 833 F.2d 1210, 1215 (6th Cir. 1987)).

the Michigan courts' policy of looking to interpretations of other jurisdictions to resolve undecided contractual issues, held:

> if faced with the issue, the Michigan Supreme Court would rule that a unilateral addition of a forum selection clause to a contract governed by the UCC is a material alteration of the contract that does not become part of the contract by operation of M.C.L. 440.2207(2)(b).

After reviewing the reasoning of the court in *Metro. Alloys Corp.*, this Court concludes that Defendant is not bound by the forum-selection clause. The forum-selection clause was contained in the fine print attached to an Order Acknowledgment sent by Plaintiff after Defendant had submitted an offer. Assuming the Order Acknowledgment operated as an acceptance, which on these facts the Court believes is an interpretation most favorable to Plaintiff and an interpretation that does not take into consideration Defendant's controverted factual assertions, this Court finds that the forum-selection clause at issue in the present case materially altered the parties' contract and is not enforceable against Defendant.

* * *

In conclusion, this Court does not believe Plaintiff has satisfied its burden of establishing a prima facie showing that personal jurisdiction exists over Defendant. * * *

Accordingly, IT IS ORDERED, that Defendant's motion to dismiss is GRANTED.

NOTES

(1)   Which party made the offer in this case, the seller (plaintiff) or the buyer (defendant)? Were you persuaded by the court's decision? The court does not provide a working definition of offer and does not explain how the plaintiff, who was competing for the subcontract, knew or had reason to know that the defendant was inviting it to accept.

(2)   If the defendant made the offer, how did the plaintiff accept it under UCC § 2–207(1)? If there was no express condition (the court so holds), how can plaintiff accept the offer and still propose an additional materially altering term, the forum selection clause?

(3)   How does UCC § 2–207(2) deal with the plaintiff's materially altering term? Is it part of the contract? What is the effect of the parties' conduct, i.e., the seller ships the goods and the buyer accepts and pays for them. Does the buyer's conduct (without objection) accept the forum selection clause?

In *Deer Stags, Inc. v. Garrison Indus.*, 2000 WL 1800491 (S.D.N.Y. 2000), the seller's written confirmation of an oral agreement UCC § 2–207(1) contained an additional term, namely, an arbitration clause. The buyer accepted the goods without objection. The court held that under UCC § 2–207(2), the arbitration clause was not material and became part of the contract. The court reasoned that because the parties had engaged in more than 50 transactions in the past with the same terms, there was no unfair surprise or hardship to the buyer to include the term. Is this a proper reading of the statute?

(4) Suppose that the purchase order contained a term agreeing to mediate disputes in California under specified procedures. If the seller accepts the offer in the acknowledgment and proposes a Michigan forum selection clause, the seller has proposed a different rather than an additional term. How is this issue resolved under UCC § 2–207(2)?

(5) Although disputes like that in *DTE Energy* are frequently called a "battle of the forms," UCC § 2–207 neither defines "standard forms" nor limits its application to standard form contracts. Does this mean that UCC § 2–207 applies to disputes like that in *Minneapolis & St. Louis Ry. Co.*, supra? If so, how would the dispute in that case be resolved under UCC § 2–207? Can there ever be a "definite acceptance" when the purported acceptance materially varies the quantity or price terms?

Comment: Problems in the Interpretation of UCC § 2–207

Routes to Contract Formation. There are at least four distinct routes to contract formation in and around UCC § 2–207. It is useful to distinguish among the different routes because the test for the terms of the contract depends on the particular path to formation.

Non-matching Acceptance: The first route appears before the comma in subsection (1) and involves mismatched expressions of acceptance. § 2–207 changes the common law "mirror image" rule. Now mismatched expressions of acceptance can "operate as an acceptance" so long as the acceptance is not expressly made conditional on assent to the additional or different terms.

Additional Assent: The second route appears after the comma in subsection (1). Suppose the offeree sends a response with additional or different terms and states that "this acceptance is conditioned upon the offeror agreeing to [the additional or different terms]." This "acceptance" is a counteroffer. See UCC § 2–207(1), after the comma. How can it be accepted? If the goods are not shipped to and accepted by the buyer, acceptance of the counteroffer would have to be by words of assent. Silence would not do it. See Textile Unlimited v. A. BMH & Co., reprinted below.

Suppose, however, the offeree, a seller, ships the goods and the buyer accepts them. Does the buyer's conduct accept the counteroffer? Or is this a case for the application of UCC § 2–207(3)? Although early decisions interpreting UCC § 2–207 held that the counteroffer was accepted by conduct, the preferred view is that UCC § 2–207(3) controls in all cases where no contract is formed under subsection (1) and the seller ships and the buyer accepts the goods. See JOM, Inc. v. Adell Plastics, Inc., 193 F.3d 47, 52–59 (1st Cir. 1999). So the second route to formation is where the offeree's expression of acceptance is treated as a counteroffer because it is expressly made conditional on other side's assent to the additional terms, and the other side does expressly assent.

Non-Matching Confirmation: The third route to formation concerns a non-matching confirmation of a prior agreement, typically oral. It has been said that UCC § 2–207(1) is "unusually poorly drafted as it applies to written confirmations." Utz, *More on the Battle of the Forms: The Treatment of "Different" Terms Under the Uniform Commercial Code*, 16 UCC L.J. 103, 105, n. 5 (1983). According to the text of UCC § 2–207(1), the written confirmation operates as an acceptance even though it states terms at variance with those agreed upon. But if the parties reached a prior agreement, hasn't there already been an acceptance? Once a contract is formed, there can be no further acceptance. There can only be a confirmation. Note, however, that a written confirmation might satisfy the writing requirement of a statue of frauds, salvaging an agreement that would otherwise be unenforceable. UCC § 2–201(2).

Conduct: The fourth and final route to formation can be found in subsection (3). If there is no formation under any of the first three formation routes, but the conduct of the parties nonetheless recognizes the existence of a contract (for example, by the tender and acceptance of goods), then there is formation by conduct. So if an offeree sends a mismatched expression of acceptance that is made expressly conditional on additional assent by the offeror and that assent never comes, but the parties nevertheless ship and accept the goods, then there is subsection (3) formation by conduct.

What Are the Terms of the Contract? In most cases under UCC § 2–207 a contract has been formed by one route or another and the dispute is over what terms are part of the contract. It is important to pay attention to the route to formation because different routes trigger different rules for whether additional or different terms are included in the contract. If there is additional assent to a counteroffer (route 2) formation, then the terms in the counteroffer become part of the contract. If there is either formation by non-matching acceptance or non-matching confirmation (formation routes 1 and 3), the inclusion of the terms will be decided by subsection (2). And if there is conduct formation (route 4), the mismatched terms are knocked out by subsection (3) and replaced by the UCC default provisions.

What are the terms of the following contracts:

(a) B makes an offer to buy goods on a purchase order which, on the back in smaller type, provides that seller shall pay "liquidated damages" in the amount of $500 for each day of delayed delivery. Assume that clause, if agreed to, would be enforceable. See UCC § 2–718(1). S responds by telegram and "accepts" the offer. There are no additional or different terms. S breaches the contract by a 20-day delay in delivery.

(b)   B makes an offer to buy goods on a purchase order. S sends an acknowledgment that accepts the offer and contains a form clause on the back that purports to exclude all liability for consequential damages resulting from the delay. Assume that the clause, if agreed to, would be enforceable. See UCC § 2–719(3). S ships the goods and B accepts and uses them. Due to non-conformities, B suffers consequential losses of $50,000. Is the "excluder" term part of the contract? Should the question be answered under UCC § 2–207(2) or 2–207(3)? What is the difference?

(c)   Suppose B makes an offer to buy goods. On the back of the purchase order is a form clause that S shall pay $500 per day for consequential damages caused by delay in delivery. S responds by an acknowledgment that accepts the offer, but the acknowledgment provides (on the back in a form term) that the seller shall not be liable for consequential damages caused by any delay in delivery. S is 20 days late in delivery and B, invoking its liquidated damage clause, sues for $10,000. Should the question be answered under UCC § 2–207(2) or (3)? What is the difference?

Different terms. UCC § 2–207(1) uses the phrase "terms additional to or different from," whereas subsection (2) refers to "additional" terms only. It is generally assumed that both types of variant terms should be disposed of in accordance with the rules of subsection (2). However, the omission of "different" from subsection (2) has influenced some courts to apply a so-called "knock out" doctrine, whereby even if a contract is formed under subsection (1), the terms of the contract are not those contained in the "offer" plus whatever terms are added by reason of subsection (2), but those upon which the "forms" agree. That is, the differing terms cancel each other. See, e.g., Northrop Corp. v. Litronic Industries, 29 F.3d 1173 (7th Cir. 1994); Daitom, Inc. v. Pennwalt Corp., 741 F.2d 1569 (10th Cir. 1984). Where is the statutory basis for either reading?

International Contracts and Sales. Despite the fact that form contracts and terms are used by both seller and buyer in international sales, CISG rejected the approach of UCC § 2–207. Thus, Article 19(1) provides:

> A reply to an offer which purports to be an acceptance but contains additions, limitations or other modifications is a rejection of the offer and constitutes a counter-offer.

Article 19(2) states that a contract may be created if a purported acceptance "contains additional or different terms which do not materially alter the terms of the offer," and Article 19(3) attempts to state the terms that are considered to alter the terms of an offer materially. A notable inclusion is terms relating to the settlement of disputes, such as arbitration provisions.

Article 2.1.11 of the UNIDROIT Principles of International Commercial Contracts follows CISG Art. 19 up to a point. Special rules, however, are applicable to contracting under standard terms. See Art. 2.1.19 through 2.1.22. Article 2.1.22 deals specifically with the "battle of the forms":

> Where both parties use standard terms and reach agreement except on those terms, a contract is concluded on the basis of the agreed terms and of any standard terms which are common in substance unless one party clearly indicates in advance, or later and without undue delay informs the other party, that it does not intend to be bound by such a contract.

To the extent that there is no agreement, the disputed standard terms are "knocked out."

PROBLEM: JUST ANOTHER STANDARD TERMS CASE

After negotiations without an agreement, Buyer in California sends Seller in New York an offer to buy described factory machinery. On the back of the offer a standard term provided that "all disputes arising out of or relating to this contract shall be arbitrated in Los Angeles under the Rules of the American Arbitration Association." Seller sends Buyer an acknowledgment of the order and then ships the goods by carrier. On the back of the acknowledgment, which Buyer received, there was a standard term that provided "all disputes relating to the conformity of the described goods to the contract shall be arbitrated in New York City under the rules of the International Chamber of Commerce." The goods were destroyed by fire in transit and a dispute arose over who had the risk of loss. Seller initiated arbitration against Buyer in New York to recover the price. Buyer sought an order staying the litigation pending arbitration and an order compelling arbitration in Los Angeles.

(1)   How would this come out under current UCC § 2–207?

(2)   If Seller's place of business was in Toronto, Canada, how would this come out under CISG?

Textile Unlimited, Inc. v. A..BMH and Company, Inc.

United States Court of Appeals, Ninth Circuit, 2001.
240 F.3d 781.

■ THOMAS, CIRCUIT JUDGE. In this appeal, we consider, *inter alia,* the proper venue for a suit to enjoin an arbitration. Under the circumstances presented by this case, we conclude that the Federal Arbitration Act does not require venue in the contractually-designated arbitration locale.

I

Textile Unlimited, Inc. ("Textile") claims that A..BMH and Company, Inc. ("A..BMH") is, in the parlance of the industry, spinning a yarn by contending that the two companies had agreed to settle contract disputes by binding arbitration in Georgia. A..BMH counters that Textile is warping the facts.

Over the course of ten months of this tangled affair, Textile bought goods from A..BMH in approximately thirty-eight transactions. Each followed a similar pattern. Textile would send a purchase order to a broker in California containing the date, item number, item description, quantity ordered, and price. A..BMH would respond with an invoice, followed by shipment of the yarn and an order acknowledgment. Both the invoice and the order acknowledgment contained a twist: additional terms tucked into the back of the invoice and the face of the acknowledgment, terms that had not adorned Textile's purchase order. Specifically, the A..BMH documents provided:

> *Terms.* All sales of yarn by A..BMH & Co., Inc. ("Seller") are governed by the terms and conditions below. Seller's willingness to sell yarn to you is conditioned on your acceptance of these Terms of Sale. If you do not accept these terms, you must notify Seller in writing within 24 hours of receiving Seller's Order Confirmation. If you accept delivery of Seller's yarn, you will be deemed to have accepted these Terms of Sale in full. You expressly agree that these Terms of Sale supersede any different terms and conditions contained in your purchase order or in any other agreement.
>
> . . .
>
> *Arbitration.* All disputes arising in connection with this agreement shall be settled in Atlanta, Georgia by binding arbitration conducted under the Commercial Arbitration Rules of the American Arbitration Association. The arbitrator will not be permitted to award punitive damages with respect to any dispute. Judgment upon the award rendered may be entered, and enforcement sought, in any court having jurisdiction. The total costs of arbitration, including attorneys' fees, will be paid by the losing party.
>
> *Governing Law and Venue.* This transaction shall be governed by and construed in accordance with the laws of the State of Georgia. If any court action is brought to enforce the provisions of this agreement, venue shall lie exclusively in the Superior Court of Fulton County, Georgia. You expressly consent to personal jurisdiction in the Superior Court of Fulton County, Georgia, and waive the right to bring action in any other state or federal court.

Textile did not request any alterations. However, after receiving a shipment in September 1998, Textile refused to pay, alleging that the yarn was defective. A..BMH submitted the matter to arbitration in Atlanta, Georgia. The American Arbitration Association ("AAA") notified both parties on January 10, 2000, that it had received the arbitration request. Textile did not object to the arbitration within the time provided by AAA rules. Textile eventually protested, contending that the arbitration clause had not been woven into the contract. Textile also argued that the objection period should have been lengthened because the initial notice had been sent to an attorney no longer with its law firm. Textile reserved the right to challenge the jurisdiction of the AAA, and indicated that nothing in the letter should be deemed a waiver.

With arbitration looming, Textile filed an action on April 10, 2000 in the United States District Court for the Central District of California to enjoin the arbitration. Unruffled, the AAA Arbitrator found on May 5, 2000 that the case was arbitrable. On June 26, 2000, Textile moved for a stay of the arbitration pending in Georgia. On July 17, 2000, the district court preliminarily enjoined both the pending arbitration and A..BMH from any further action regarding arbitration of the dispute in question. A..BMH timely appealed the district court's order.

II

The district court correctly concluded that venue was proper in the Central District of California under 28 U.S.C. § 1391. Contrary to A..BMH's arguments, nothing in the Federal Arbitration Act ("FAA" or "the Act"), 9 U.S.C. § 1 *et seq.,* requires that Textile's action to enjoin arbitration be brought in the district where the contract designated the arbitration to occur. [The court reviewed the judicial decisions interpreting the venue provisions of the Federal Arbitration Act.]

In sum, the district court correctly determined that venue was proper in the Central District of California. * * * This result is consistent with the underpinnings of arbitration theory. One of the threads running through federal arbitration jurisprudence is the notion that "arbitration is a matter of contract and a party cannot be required to submit to arbitration any dispute which he has not agreed so to submit." AT&T Techs., Inc. v. Communications Workers, 475 U.S. 643, 648 (1986) (quoting United Steelworkers v. Warrior and Gulf Navigation Co., 363 U.S. 574, 582 (1960)). Requiring a party to contest the very existence of an arbitration agreement in a forum dictated by the disputed arbitration clause would run counter to that fundamental principle.

III

The district court did not abuse its discretion in granting the preliminary injunction. . . .

The district court found that Textile would suffer irreparable harm if the arbitration were not stayed, that the balance of hardships tipped in Textile's favor and that it was in the public interest to stay arbitration. These findings were not clearly erroneous, and A..BMH does not contest them on appeal.

Thus, to obtain a preliminary injunction, Textile needed only to show that serious questions were raised. The district court determined that not only were serious questions raised, but that Textile had shown a probability of success on the merits. The district court did not err in that assessment.

A

Section 2207 of the California Commercial Code controls contract interpretation when the parties have exchanged conflicting forms. * * *

Under § 2207(1), an acceptance will operate to create a contract even if additional or different terms are stated *unless* the acceptance is expressly conditioned on assent to the new terms. If a contract is created under § 2207(1), then § 2207(2) defines the terms of the contract. . . . However, if the acceptance is expressly conditioned on the offeror's assent to the new terms, the acceptance operates as a counteroffer. If the counteroffer is accepted, a contract exists and the additional terms become part of the contract. . . . To qualify as an acceptance under § 2207(1), an offeror must "give specific and unequivocal assent" to the supplemental terms. [The court relied upon *Diamond Fruit Growers, Inc. v. Krack Corp.*, 794 F.2d 1440 (9th Cir. 1986), interpreting the Oregon enactment of UCC § 2–207.] If the new provisos are not accepted, then no contract is formed. However, even when the parties' written expressions do not establish a binding agreement under § 2207(1), a contract may arise based upon their subsequent conduct pursuant to § 2207(3). Id.

A..BMH argues that a contract including the arbitration clause was formed pursuant to § 2207(1) because the fine print provided that Textile was "deemed to have accepted these terms in full" if Textile did not respond in 24 hours. This contention is foreclosed . . . because Textile did not "give specific and unequivocal assent" to the supplemental conditions. Thus, a contract containing the new terms that A..BMH attempted to pin on Textile was not formed under § 2207(1).

Part of . . . the rationale [in *Diamond Fruit Growers*, supra] was to avoid a rule which would allow one party to obtain "all of its terms simply because it fired the last shot in the exchange of forms." Id. at 1444. In short, modern commercial transactions conducted under the U.C.C. are not a game of tag or musical chairs. Rather, if the parties exchange incompatible forms, "all of the terms on which the parties' forms do not agree drop out, and the U.C.C. supplies the missing terms."

A..BMH also claims that a contract formed under § 2207(1) because its acceptance was not expressly made conditional on Textile's assent to the additional or different terms. Thus, A..BMH reasons, a contract was formed under § 2207(1) and we must turn to § 2207(2) to ascertain the contract terms. However, A..BMH's assertion is belied by the plain words of its documents which provide that "Seller's willingness to sell yarn to you is conditioned on your acceptance of these Terms of Sale." Thus, A..BMH's claim is unavailing.

B

Because no contract was formed under § 2207(1), our interpretation of the agreement must be guided by § 2207(3) which examines the conduct of the parties to determine whether a contract for sale has been established and the terms thereof. The parties do not dispute that through their actions, they formed a contract under § 2207(3).

The terms of an agreement formed pursuant to § 2207(3) are those terms upon which the parties expressly agreed, coupled with the standard "gap-filler" provisions of Article Two. The U.C.C. does not contain a "gap-filler" provision providing for arbitration. . . .

Under § 2207(3), the disputed additional items on which the parties do not agree simply "drop out" and are trimmed from the contract. . . . Thus, the supplemental terms proposed by A..BMH, including the arbitration clause, do not festoon the contract between the parties.

* * *

In sum, this action was properly venued in the Central District of California. The district court did not abuse its discretion in granting the preliminary injunction. To the contrary, the district court's reasoning was correct in all respects.

NOTES

(1)   The court concludes that no contract to arbitrate was made under UCC § 2–207(1) and that the seller made a counteroffer. If the buyer accepted the goods without objection, isn't that an acceptance of the counteroffer with the arbitration clause? How did the court interpret UCC § 2–207 to avoid this result? Do you see any support for that interpretation in the text or the comments? In the purpose of the statute?

Comment: Revised Section 2–207 and What Might Have Been

Commentary upon UCC § 2–207 is voluminous, much of it critical. See e.g., Daniel Keating, *Exploring the Battle of Forms in Action,* 98 Mich. L. Rev. 2678 (2000), and other articles in that Symposium.

The 2003 Amendments to UCC, which were enacted by no state and have since been withdrawn, would have completely overhauled Section 2–207:

Subject to Section 2–202, if (i) conduct by both parties recognizes the existence of a contract although their records do not otherwise establish a contract, (ii) a contract is formed by an offer and acceptance, or (iii) a contract formed in any manner is confirmed by a record that contains terms additional to or different from those in the contract being confirmed, the terms of the contract are:

(a) terms that appear in the records of both parties;

(b) terms, whether in a record or not, to which both parties agree; and

(c) terms supplied or incorporated under any provision of this Act.

(The 2003 Amendments defined a "record" as "information that is inscribed on a tangible medium or that is stored in an electronic or other medium and is retrievable in perceivable form." UCC 1–201(b)(31).) Revised Section 2–206(3) would have provided that a "definite and seasonable expression of acceptance in a record operates as an acceptance even if it contains terms additional to or different from the offer." Do the withdrawn revisions to 2–207 prove that we do not in fact live in the best of all possible worlds?

(B) SHRINKWRAP AND BROWSEWRAP

Frank H. Easterbrook: Frank Easterbrook graduated from Swarthmore College in 1970 and the University of Chicago Law School in 1973. After serving as a clerk to Judge Levin H. Campbell of the First Circuit Court of Appeals, he worked in the solicitor general's office-first as an assistant to the solicitor general (1974–77), and then as deputy solicitor general of the United States (1978–79). He left the government to join the University of Chicago faculty, where he was a professor until 1985, when President Reagan appointed him to the Seventh Circuit Court of Appeals. Judge Easterbrook is a titan of law and economics. He has written extensively on antitrust and corporate law.

Rich Hill v. Gateway 2000

United States Court of Appeals, Seventh Circuit, 1997.
105 F.3d 1147.

■ EASTERBROOK, JUDGE. A customer picks up the phone, orders a computer, and gives a credit card number. Presently a box arrives, containing the computer and a list of terms, said to govern unless the customer returns the computer within 30 days. Are these terms effective as the parties' contract, or is the contract term-free because the order-taker did not read any terms over the phone and elicit the customer's assent?

One of the terms in the box containing a Gateway 2000 system was an arbitration clause. Rich and Enza Hill, the customers, kept the computer more than 30 days before complaining about its components and performance. They filed suit in federal court arguing, among other things, that the product's shortcomings make Gateway a racketeer (mail and wire fraud are said to be the predicate offenses), leading to treble damages under RICO for the Hills and a class of all other purchasers. Gateway asked the district court to enforce the arbitration clause; the judge refused, writing that "[t]he present record is insufficient to support a finding of a valid arbitration agreement between the parties or that the plaintiffs were given adequate notice of the arbitration clause." Gateway [appealed].

The Hills say that the arbitration clause did not stand out: they concede noticing the statement of terms but deny reading it closely enough to discover the agreement to arbitrate, and they ask us to conclude that they therefore may go to court. Yet an agreement to arbitrate must be enforced "save upon such grounds as exist at law or in equity for the revocation of any contract." 9 U.S.C. § 2. *Doctor's Associates, Inc. v. Casarotto,* 517 U.S. 681 (1996), holds that this provision of the Federal Arbitration Act is inconsistent with any requirement that an arbitration clause be prominent. A contract need not be read to be effective; people who accept take the risk that the unread terms may in retrospect prove unwelcome. Terms inside Gateway's box stand or fall together. If they constitute the parties' contract because the Hills had an opportunity to return the computer after reading them, then all must be enforced.

ProCD, Inc. v. Zeidenberg, 86 F.3d 1447 (7th Cir. 1996), holds that terms inside a box of software bind consumers who use the software after an opportunity to read the terms and to reject them by returning the product. Likewise, *Carnival Cruise Lines, Inc. v. Shute,* 499 U.S. 585 (1991), enforces a forum-selection clause that was included among three pages of terms attached to a cruise ship ticket. *ProCD* and *Carnival Cruise Lines* exemplify the many commercial transactions in which people pay for products with terms to follow. The district court concluded in *ProCD* that the contract is formed when the consumer pays for the software; as a result, the court held, only terms known to the consumer at that moment are part of the contract, and provisos inside the box do not count. Although this is one way a contract could be formed, it is not the only way: "A vendor, as master of the offer, may invite acceptance by conduct, and may propose limitations on the kind of conduct that constitutes acceptance. A buyer may accept by performing the acts the vendor proposes to treat as acceptance." Id. at 1452. Gateway shipped computers with the same sort of accept-or-return offer ProCD made to users of its software. *ProCD* relied on the Uniform Commercial Code rather than any peculiarities of Wisconsin law; both Illinois and South Dakota, the two states whose law might govern relations between Gateway and the Hills, have adopted the UCC; neither side has pointed us to any atypical doctrines in those states that might be pertinent; *ProCD* therefore applies to this dispute.

Plaintiffs ask us to limit *ProCD* to software, but where's the sense in that? *ProCD* is about the law of contract, not the law of software. Payment preceding the revelation of full terms is common for air transportation, insurance, and many other endeavors. Practical considerations support allowing vendors to enclose the full legal terms with their products. Cashiers cannot be expected to read legal documents to customers before ringing up sales. If the staff at the other end of the phone for direct-sales operations such as Gateway's had to read the four-page statement of terms before taking the buyer's credit card number, the droning voice would anaesthetize rather than enlighten many potential buyers. Others would hang up in a rage over the waste of their time. And oral recitation would not avoid customers' assertions (whether true or feigned) that the clerk did not read term X to them, or that they did not remember or understand it. Writing provides benefits for both sides of commercial transactions. Customers as a group are better off when vendors skip costly and ineffectual steps such as telephonic recitation, and use instead a simple approve-or-return device. Competent adults are bound by such documents, read or unread. For what little it is worth, we add that the box from Gateway was crammed with software. The computer came with an operating system, without which it was useful only as a boat anchor. Gateway also included many application programs. So the Hills' effort to limit *ProCD* to software would not avail them factually, even if it were sound legally—which it is not.

For their second sally, the Hills contend that *ProCD* should be limited to executory contracts (to licenses in particular), and therefore does not apply because both parties' performance of this contract was complete when the box arrived at their home. This is legally and factually wrong: legally because the question at hand concerns the *formation* of the contract rather than its *performance*, and factually because both contracts were incompletely performed. . . . One element of the transaction was the warranty, which obliges sellers to fix defects in their products. The Hills have invoked Gateway's warranty and are not satisfied with its response, so they are not well positioned to say that

Gateway's obligations were fulfilled when the motor carrier unloaded the box.

Next the Hills insist that *ProCD* is irrelevant because Zeidenberg was a "merchant" and they are not. Section 2–207(2) of the UCC, the infamous battle-of-the-forms section, states that "additional terms [following acceptance of an offer] are to be construed as proposals for addition to a contract. Between merchants such terms become part of the contract unless . . .". Plaintiffs tell us that *ProCD* came out as it did only because Zeidenberg was a "merchant" and the terms inside ProCD's box were not excluded by the "unless" clause. This argument pays scant attention to the opinion in *ProCD,* which concluded that, when there is only one form, "sec. 2–207 is irrelevant." 86 F.3d at 1452. The question in *ProCD* was not whether terms were added to a contract after its formation, but how and when the contract was formed—in particular, whether a vendor may propose that a contract of sale be formed, not in the store (or over the phone) with the payment of money or a general "send me the product," but after the customer has had a chance to inspect both the item and the terms. *ProCD* answers "yes," for merchants and consumers alike. . . .

Perhaps the Hills would have had a better argument if they were first alerted to the bundling of hardware and legal-ware after opening the box and wanted to return the computer in order to avoid disagreeable terms, but were dissuaded by the expense of shipping.

What the remedy would be in such a case—could it exceed the shipping charges?—is an interesting question, but one that need not detain us because the Hills knew before they ordered the computer that the carton would include *some* important terms, and they did not seek to discover these in advance. Gateway's ads state that their products come with limited warranties and lifetime support. How limited was the warranty—30 days, with service contingent on shipping the computer back, or five years, with free onsite service? What sort of support was offered? Shoppers have three principal ways to discover these things. First, they can ask the vendor to send a copy before deciding whether to buy. The Magnuson-Moss Warranty Act requires firms to distribute their warranty terms on request, 15 U.S.C. § 2302(b)(1)(A); the Hills do not contend that Gateway would have refused to enclose the remaining terms too. Concealment would be bad for business, scaring some customers away and leading to excess returns from others. Second, shoppers can consult public sources (computer magazines, the Web sites of vendors) that may contain this information. Third, they may inspect the documents after the product's delivery. Like Zeidenberg, the Hills took the third option. By keeping the computer beyond 30 days, the Hills accepted Gateway's offer, including the arbitration clause.

The decision of the district court is vacated, and this case is remanded with instructions to compel the Hills to submit their dispute to arbitration.

William Klocek v. Gateway

United States District Court, D. Kansas, 2000.
104 F.Supp.2d 1332, order vacated for lack of subject matter jurisdiction, 2000 WL
1372886 (D. Kan. 2000), aff'd, 2001 WL 1568346 (D. Kan. 2001).

■ VRATIL, DISTRICT JUDGE. * * * Plaintiff brings individual and class action claims against Gateway, alleging that it induced him and other consumers to purchase computers and special support packages by making false promises of technical support. Individually, plaintiff also claims breach of contract and breach of warranty, in that Gateway breached certain warranties that its computer would be compatible with standard peripherals and standard internet services.

Gateway asserts that plaintiff must arbitrate his claims under Gateway's Standard Terms and Conditions Agreement ("Standard Terms"). Whenever it sells a computer, Gateway includes a copy of the Standard Terms in the box which contains the computer battery power cables and instruction manuals. At the top of the first page, the Standard Terms include the following notice:

NOTE TO THE CUSTOMER:

This document contains Gateway 2000's Standard Terms and Conditions. By keeping your Gateway 2000 computer system beyond five (5) days after the date of delivery, you accept these Terms and Conditions.

The notice is in emphasized type and is located inside a printed box which sets it apart from other provisions of the document. The Standard Terms are four pages long and contain 16 numbered paragraphs. Paragraph 10 provides the following arbitration clause:

DISPUTE RESOLUTION. Any dispute or controversy arising out of or relating to this Agreement or its interpretation shall be settled exclusively and finally by arbitration. The arbitration shall be conducted in accordance with the Rules of Conciliation and Arbitration of the International Chamber of Commerce. The arbitration shall be conducted in Chicago, Illinois, U.S.A. before a sole arbitrator. Any award rendered in any such arbitration proceeding shall be final and binding on each of the parties, and judgment may be entered thereon in a court of competent jurisdiction.

* * *

The Uniform Commercial Code ("UCC") governs the parties' transaction under both Kansas and Missouri law. . . . Regardless whether plaintiff purchased the computer in person or placed an order and received shipment of the computer, the parties agree that plaintiff paid for and received a computer from Gateway. This conduct clearly demonstrates a contract for the sale of a computer. . . . Thus the issue is whether the contract of sale includes the Standard Terms as part of the agreement.

State courts in Kansas and Missouri apparently have not decided whether terms received with a product become part of the parties' agreement. Authority from other courts is split. . . . It appears that at least in part, the cases turn on whether the court finds that the parties formed their contract *before* or *after* the vendor communicated its terms to the purchaser. . . .

Gateway urges the Court to follow the Seventh Circuit decision in *Hill* [Hill v. Gateway, supra]. That case involved the shipment of a Gateway computer with terms similar to the Standard Terms in this case, except that Gateway gave the customer 30 days—instead of 5 days—to return the computer. In enforcing the arbitration clause, the Seventh Circuit relied on its decision in *ProCD*, where it enforced a software license which was contained inside a product box. . . . In *ProCD*, the Seventh Circuit noted that the exchange of money frequently precedes the communication of detailed terms in a commercial transaction. Citing UCC § 2–204, the court reasoned that by including the license with the software, the vendor proposed a contract that the buyer could accept by using the software after having an opportunity to read the license. . . . Specifically, the court stated:

> A vendor, as master of the offer, may invite acceptance by conduct, and may propose limitations on the kind of conduct that constitutes acceptance. A buyer may accept by performing the acts the vendor proposes to treat as acceptance. . . .

The *Hill* court followed the *ProCD* analysis, noting that "[p]ractical considerations support allowing vendors to enclose the full legal terms with their products." Hill, 105 F.3d at 1149. . . .[9]

The Court is not persuaded that Kansas or Missouri courts would follow the Seventh Circuit reasoning in *Hill* and *ProCD*. In each case the Seventh Circuit concluded without support that UCC § 2–207 was irrelevant because the cases involved only one written form. . . . This conclusion is not supported by the statute or by Kansas or Missouri law. Disputes under § 2–207 often arise in the context of a "battle of forms," . . . but nothing in its language precludes application in a case which involves only one form. * * *

---

[9] Legal scholars have criticized the reasoning of the Seventh Circuit See, e.g., Jean R. Sternlight, *Gateway Widens Doorway to Imposing Unfair Binding Arbitration on Consumers,* Fla. Bar J., Nov. 1997, at 8, 10–12 (outcome in *Gateway* is questionable on federal statutory, common law and constitutional grounds and as a matter of contract law and is unwise as a matter of policy because it unreasonably shifts to consumers search cost of ascertaining existence of arbitration clause and return cost to avoid such clause); Thomas J. McCarthy et al., *Survey: Uniform Commercial Code,* 53 Bus. Law. 1461, 1465–66 (Seventh Circuit finding that UCC § 2–207 did not apply is inconsistent with official comment); Batya Goodman, *Honey, I Shrink-Wrapped the Consumer: the Shrinkwrap Agreement as an Adhesion Contract,* 21 Cardozo L. Rev. 319, 344–352 (Seventh Circuit failed to consider principles of adhesion contracts); Jeremy Senderowicz, *Consumer Arbitration and Freedom of Contract: A Proposal to Facilitate Consumers' Informed Consent to Arbitration Clauses in Form Contracts,* 32 Colum. J.L. & Soc. Probs. 275, 296–299 (judiciary (in multiple decisions, including *Hill*) has ignored issue of consumer consent to an arbitration clause) [The court cited several cases that have followed *Hill.*]

By its terms, § 2–207 applies to an acceptance or written confirmation. It states nothing which requires another form before the provision becomes effective. In fact, the official comment to the section specifically provides that §§ 2–207(1) and (2) apply "where an agreement has been reached orally . . . and is followed by one or both of the parties sending formal memoranda embodying the terms so far agreed and adding terms not discussed." Official Comment 1 of UCC § 2–207. Kansas and Missouri courts have followed this analysis. . . . Thus, the Court concludes that Kansas and Missouri courts would apply § 2–207 to the facts in this case. . . .

In addition, the Seventh Circuit provided no explanation for its conclusion that "the vendor is the master of the offer. . . ." In typical consumer transactions, the purchaser is the offeror, and the vendor is the offeree. . . . While it is possible for the vendor to be the offeror, . . . Gateway provides no factual evidence which would support such a finding in this case. The Court therefore assumes for purposes of the motion to dismiss that plaintiff offered to purchase the computer (either in person or through catalog order) and that Gateway accepted plaintiff's offer (either by completing the sales transaction in person or by agreeing to ship and/or shipping the computer to plaintiff). . . .

Under § 2–207, the Standard Terms constitute either an expression of acceptance or written confirmation. As an expression of acceptance, the Standard Terms would constitute a counter-offer only if Gateway expressly made its acceptance conditional on plaintiff's assent to the additional or different terms. . . . Gateway provides no evidence that at the time of the sales transaction, it informed plaintiff that the transaction was conditioned on plaintiff's acceptance of the Standard Terms. Moreover, the mere fact that Gateway shipped the goods with the terms attached did not communicate to plaintiff any unwillingness to proceed without plaintiff's agreement to the Standard Terms. . . .

Because plaintiff is not a merchant, additional or different terms contained in the Standard Terms did not become part of the parties' agreement unless plaintiff expressly agreed to them. See K.S.A. § 84–2–207, Kansas Comment 2 (if either party is not a merchant, additional terms are proposals for addition to the contract that do not become part of the contract unless the original offeror expressly agrees).[13] Gateway argues that plaintiff demonstrated acceptance of the arbitration provision by keeping the computer more than five days after the date of delivery. Although the Standard Terms purport to work that result, Gateway has not presented evidence that plaintiff expressly agreed to those Standard Terms. Gateway states only that it enclosed the Standard Terms inside the computer box for plaintiff to read afterwards. It provides no evidence that it informed plaintiff of the five-day review-and-return period as a condition of the sales transaction, or that the parties

---

[13] The Court's decision would be the same if it considered the Standard Terms as a proposed modification under UCC § 2–209. . . .

contemplated additional terms to the agreement.[14] . . . The Court finds that the act of keeping the computer past five days was not sufficient to demonstrate that plaintiff expressly agreed to the Standard Terms. . . . Thus, because Gateway has not provided evidence sufficient to support a finding under Kansas or Missouri law that plaintiff agreed to the arbitration provision contained in Gateway's Standard Terms, the Court overrules Gateway's motion to dismiss.

NOTES

(1)   Which of the above opinions, Judge Easterbrook's or Judge Vratil's, gets the UCC right? The UCC aside, which establishes the better rule?

(2)   The decision in *Hill v. Gateway* builds on Easterbrook's earlier opinion in the famous *ProCD, Inc. v. Zeidenberg*, 86 F.3d 1447 (7th Cir. 1996). Mark Lemley provides a brief overview the case and its influence.

> Until 1996, every court to consider the validity of a shrinkwrap license held it unenforceable. The tide began to turn with Judge Easterbrook's 1996 opinion upholding a shrinkwrap license in *ProCD, Inc. v. Zeidenberg*. ProCD held Zeidenberg bound to terms he first saw when he loaded ProCD's software into his computer, even though he paid for the software before being made aware of the terms. The court's legal reasoning is certainly questionable. Judge Easterbrook relied on U.C.C. § 2–204, which provides that a contract can be formed in any way the parties agree. But arguably he should have treated the additional terms as a proposed modification to the contract Zeidenberg entered into when he handed money to a store clerk in exchange for a box containing software. Under U.C.C. § 2–209, such proposed new terms can become part of the contract without additional consideration, but not if they make material changes to the contract, as ProCD's terms likely did. *ProCD* also distinguished U.C.C. § 2–207, which deals with the situation of standard forms exchanged by the parties. The court reasoned that Section 2–207 could not apply unless the parties exchanged at least two forms, an interpretation that finds some support in the language of the section but that leads to the peculiar result that merchant buyers get more protection against a seller's standard form than consumers do. Despite these and other problems, the *ProCD* opinion has proved influential. While a number of courts since 1996 have continued to reject shrinkwrap licenses, still more courts have followed *ProCD* and enforced those licenses.

Mark A. Lemley, *Terms of Use*, 91 Minn. L. Rev. 459, 468–69 (2006). The Draft Restatement (Third) of Consumer Contracts reports that an empirical analysis of cases shows "a clear trend towards increased enforcement of [pay-

---

[14]   The Court is mindful of the practical considerations which are involved in commercial transactions, but it is not unreasonable for a vendor to clearly communicate to a buyer—at the time of sale—either the complete terms of the sale or the fact that the vendor will propose additional terms as a condition of sale, if that be the case.

now-terms-later] contracts and an increased influence of the landmark cases, *ProCD* and *Hill*, that pioneered their enforcement." Council Draft No. 3, § 2, Reporters' Notes, at 34 (December 20, 2016).

(3) *Shrinkwrap, Unconscionability and the Continuing Relevance of* Hill v. Gateway. In *Trujillo v. Apple Computer, Inc.*, 578 F.Supp.2d 979 (N.D.Ill. 2008), an Illinois District Court revisited the Seventh Circuit's decision in *Hill v. Gateway*, in light of the Illinois Supreme Court's intervening decision in *Razor v. Hyundai Motor Am.*, 222 Ill.2d 75 (2006). The District Court described the *Razor* holding as follows:

> In *Razor*, the Illinois Supreme Court concluded that a warranty containing a disclaimer of consequential damages had not been "made available to the plaintiff at or before the time she signed the sale contract for an automobile, because it was contained in an owner's manual in the automobile's glove compartment, where it was unavailable to the consumer until after she took delivery." [222 Ill.2d at 100–10.] Though the court acknowledged that the waiver was in understandable language and was easy to read—a contention likewise made by [the defendant] in the present case— these facts "simply do[ ] not matter," the court said, "if the consumer did not have the opportunity to *see* the language before entering into the contract to purchase the car." Id. at 101, (emphasis in original). The waiver was ineffective, the court said, because it was not "provided to the purchaser at or before the time that the purchase occurs." Id. at 103.

578 F.Supp.2d at 992–93. The court concluded that *Hill* was no longer controlling in a case that involved AT&T's wireless service agreement, which the plaintiff was given when he first turned on his (already purchased) iPhone and which included an arbitration clause.

> Although it was presumably just as true in *Razor* as in *Hill* that the consumer could have asked in advance for a copy of any applicable agreement, or could have checked a website, the Illinois Supreme Court did not hint that this was at all significant as a matter of Illinois unconscionability law. Given this significant intervening decision from Illinois' highest court, this Court must rely on *Razor*, to the extent it is contrary to *Hill*, in determining what Illinois law holds in this context.

Id. at 994. The court held that the plaintiff had "established, in the particular circumstances of his case, the procedural unconscionability—and thus the unenforceability—of [the defendant's] arbitration requirement." Id. at 995. The unconscionability doctrine is discussed in Chapter Four.

Is it appropriate for the Draft Restatement (Third) of Consumer Contracts to rely on the Seventh Circuit's decision in *Hill* if there is contrary authority from the Illinois Supreme Court?

(4) *Regulating "Rolling Contracts"*. Rolling contracts involve exchange relationships that evolve over time with one party providing terms in batches. The question is when is some contract formed between the parties. If the contract is formed early in the deal (when money is exchanged for the

goods), then terms subsequently proposed by the seller are offers to modify the contract—an offer which the buyer can accept or reject. If the contract is formed late in the deal, then no contract is formed until the seller has proposed the last batch or terms, which the buyer, of course, can accept or reject. The odds are, however, that the buyer will accept the terms by conduct (without reading them). If the terms are rejected, then no contract was formed and goods and money will have to be returned. Stephen Friedman suggests that instead of embracing or rejecting rolling contracts, lawmakers should embrace a requirement of "template" notice where a seller, instead of providing all terms at the time of the initial order, would need to notify the buyer that important terms would be sent subsequently and that buyer would have a right to reject such terms and avoid the transaction. Stephen E. Friedman, *Improving the Rolling Contract*, 56 Am. U. L. Rev. (2006).

Christopher Specht v. Netscape Communications Corporation

United States Court of Appeals, Second Circuit, 2002.
306 F.3d 17.

■ SOTOMAYOR, CIRCUIT JUDGE.

* * *

BACKGROUND

I.   Facts

In three related putative class actions, plaintiffs alleged that, unknown to them, their use of SmartDownload transmitted to defendants private information about plaintiffs' downloading of files from the Internet, thereby effecting an electronic surveillance of their online activities in violation of two federal statutes, the Electronic Communications Privacy Act, 18 U.S.C. §§ 2510 *et seq.,* and the Computer Fraud and Abuse Act, 18 U.S.C. § 1030.

Specifically, plaintiffs alleged that when they first used Netscape's Communicator—a software program that permits Internet browsing—the program created and stored on each of their computer hard drives a small text file known as a "cookie" that functioned "as a kind of electronic identification tag for future communications" between their computers and Netscape. Plaintiffs further alleged that when they installed SmartDownload—a separate software "plug-in" that served to enhance Communicator's browsing capabilities—SmartDownload created and stored on their computer hard drives another string of characters, known as a "Key," which similarly functioned as an identification tag in future communications with Netscape. According to the complaints in this case, each time a computer user employed Communicator to download a file from the Internet, SmartDownload "assume[d] from Communicator the task of downloading" the file and transmitted to Netscape the address of the file being downloaded together with the cookie created by Communicator and the Key created by SmartDownload. These processes, plaintiffs claim, constituted unlawful "eavesdropping" on users of Netscape's software products as well as on Internet websites from which users employing SmartDownload downloaded files.

In the time period relevant to this litigation, Netscape offered on its website various software programs, including Communicator and SmartDownload, which visitors to the site were invited to obtain free of charge. It is undisputed that five of the six named plaintiffs—Michael Fagan, John Gibson, Mark Gruber, Sean Kelly, and Sherry Weindorf—downloaded Communicator from the Netscape website. These plaintiffs acknowledge that when they proceeded to initiate installation of Communicator, they were automatically shown a scrollable text of that program's license agreement and were not permitted to complete the installation until they had clicked on a "Yes" button to indicate that they accepted all the license terms.[4] If a user attempted to install Communicator without clicking "Yes," the installation would be aborted. All five named user plaintiffs expressly agreed to Communicator's license terms by clicking "Yes." The Communicator license agreement that these plaintiffs saw made no mention of SmartDownload or other plug-in programs, and stated that "[t]hese terms apply to Netscape Communicator and Netscape Navigator" and that "all disputes relating to this Agreement (excepting any dispute relating to intellectual property rights)" are subject to "binding arbitration in Santa Clara County, California."

Although Communicator could be obtained independently of SmartDownload, all the named user plaintiffs, except Fagan, downloaded and installed Communicator in connection with downloading SmartDownload. Each of these plaintiffs allegedly arrived at a Netscape webpage captioned "SmartDownload Communicator" that urged them to "Download With Confidence Using SmartDownload!" At or near the bottom of the screen facing plaintiffs was the prompt "Start Download" and a tinted button labeled "Download." By clicking on the button, plaintiffs initiated the download of SmartDownload. Once that process was complete, SmartDownload, as its first plug-in task, permitted plaintiffs to proceed with downloading and installing Communicator, an operation that was accompanied by the clickwrap display of Communicator's license terms described above.

---

4   This kind of online software license agreement has come to be known as "clickwrap" (by analogy to "shrinkwrap," used in the licensing of tangible forms of software sold in packages) because it "presents the user with a message on his or her computer screen, requiring that the user manifest his or her assent to the terms of the license agreement by clicking on an icon. The product cannot be obtained or used unless and until the icon is clicked." Specht, 150 F.Supp.2d at 593–94. Just as breaking the shrinkwrap seal and using the enclosed computer program after encountering notice of the existence of governing license terms has been deemed by some courts to constitute assent to those terms in the context of tangible software, see, e.g., ProCD, Inc. v. Zeidenberg, 86 F.3d 1447, 1451 (7th Cir. 1996), so clicking on a webpage's clickwrap button after receiving notice of the existence of license terms has been held by some courts to manifest an Internet user's assent to terms governing the use of downloadable intangible software.

The signal difference between downloading Communicator and downloading SmartDownload was that no clickwrap presentation accompanied the latter operation. Instead, once plaintiffs Gibson, Gruber, Kelly, and Weindorf had clicked on the "Download" button located at or near the bottom of their screen, and the downloading of SmartDownload was complete, these plaintiffs encountered no further information about the plug-in program or the existence of license terms governing its use. The sole reference to SmartDownload's license terms on the "SmartDownload Communicator" webpage was located in text that would have become visible to plaintiffs only if they had scrolled down to the next screen.

Had plaintiffs scrolled down instead of acting on defendants' invitation to click on the "Download" button, they would have encountered the following invitation: "Please review and agree to the terms of the *Netscape SmartDownload software license agreement* before downloading and using the software." Plaintiffs Gibson, Gruber, Kelly, and Weindorf averred in their affidavits that they never saw this reference to the SmartDownload license agreement when they clicked on the "Download" button. They also testified during depositions that they saw no reference to license terms when they clicked to download SmartDownload, although under questioning by defendants' counsel, some plaintiffs added that they could not "remember" or be "sure" whether the screen shots of the SmartDownload page attached to their affidavits reflected precisely what they had seen on their computer screens when they downloaded SmartDownload.

In sum, plaintiffs Gibson, Gruber, Kelly, and Weindorf allege that the process of obtaining SmartDownload contrasted sharply with that of obtaining Communicator. Having selected SmartDownload, they were required neither to express unambiguous assent to that program's license agreement nor even to view the license terms or become aware of their existence before proceeding with the invited download of the free plug-in program. Moreover, once these plaintiffs had initiated the download, the existence of SmartDownload's license terms was not mentioned while the software was running or at any later point in plaintiffs' experience of the product.

Even for a user who, unlike plaintiffs, did happen to scroll down past the download button, SmartDownload's license terms would not have been immediately displayed in the manner of Communicator's clickwrapped terms. Instead, if such a user had seen the notice of SmartDownload's terms and then clicked on the underlined invitation to review and agree to the terms, a hypertext link would have taken the user to a separate webpage entitled "License & Support Agreements." The first paragraph on this page read, in pertinent part:

> The use of each Netscape software product is governed by a license agreement. You must read and agree to the license agreement terms BEFORE acquiring a product. Please click on

the appropriate link below to review the current license agreement for the product of interest to you before acquisition. For products available for download, you must read and agree to the license agreement terms BEFORE you install the software. If you do not agree to the license terms, do not download, install or use the software.

Below this paragraph appeared a list of license agreements, the first of which was *"License Agreement for Netscape Navigator and Netscape Communicator Product Family* (Netscape Navigator, Netscape Communicator and Netscape SmartDownload)." If the user clicked on that link, he or she would be taken to yet another webpage that contained the full text of a license agreement that was identical in every respect to the Communicator license agreement except that it stated that its "terms apply to Netscape Communicator, Netscape Navigator, and Netscape SmartDownload." The license agreement granted the user a nonexclusive license to use and reproduce the software, subject to certain terms:

> BY CLICKING THE ACCEPTANCE BUTTON OR INSTALLING OR USING NETSCAPE COMMUNICATOR, NETSCAPE NAVIGATOR, OR NETSCAPE SMARTDOWNLOAD SOFTWARE (THE "PRODUCT"), THE INDIVIDUAL OR ENTITY LICENSING THE PRODUCT ("LICENSEE") IS CONSENTING TO BE BOUND BY AND IS BECOMING A PARTY TO THIS AGREEMENT. IF LICENSEE DOES NOT AGREE TO ALL OF THE TERMS OF THIS AGREEMENT, THE BUTTON INDICATING NON-ACCEPTANCE MUST BE SELECTED, AND LICENSEE MUST NOT INSTALL OR USE THE SOFTWARE.

Among the license terms was a provision requiring virtually all disputes relating to the agreement to be submitted to arbitration:

> Unless otherwise agreed in writing, all disputes relating to this Agreement (excepting any dispute relating to intellectual property rights) shall be subject to final and binding arbitration in Santa Clara County, California, under the auspices of JAMS/EndDispute, with the losing party paying all costs of arbitration.

* * *

DISCUSSION
* * *

III. Whether the User Plaintiffs Had Reasonable Notice of and Manifested Assent to the SmartDownload License Agreement

Whether governed by the common law or by Article 2 of the Uniform Commercial Code ("UCC"), a transaction, in order to be a contract, requires a manifestation of agreement between the parties. . . .[13] Mutual manifestation of assent, whether by written or spoken word or by conduct, is the touchstone of contract. . . . Although an onlooker observing the disputed transactions in this case would have seen each of the user plaintiffs click on the SmartDownload "Download" button, . . . a consumer's clicking on a download button does not communicate assent to contractual terms if the offer did not make clear to the consumer that clicking on the download button would signify assent to those terms. . . . California's common law is clear that "an offeree, regardless of apparent manifestation of his consent, is not bound by inconspicuous contractual provisions of which he is unaware, contained in a document whose contractual nature is not obvious." . . .

Arbitration agreements are no exception to the requirement of manifestation of assent. This principle of knowing consent applies with particular force to provisions for arbitration. . . . Clarity and conspicuousness of arbitration terms are important in securing informed assent. If a party wishes to bind in writing another to an agreement to arbitrate future disputes, such purpose should be accomplished in a way that each party to the arrangement will fully and clearly comprehend that the agreement to arbitrate exists and binds the parties thereto. . . . Thus, California contract law measures assent by an objective standard that takes into account both what the offeree said, wrote, or did and the transactional context in which the offeree verbalized or acted.

A.   The Reasonably Prudent Offeree of Downloadable Software

Defendants argue that plaintiffs must be held to a standard of reasonable prudence and that, because notice of the existence of SmartDownload license terms was on the next scrollable screen, plaintiffs were on "inquiry notice" of those terms. We disagree with the proposition that a reasonably prudent offeree in plaintiffs' position would necessarily have known or learned of the existence of the SmartDownload license agreement prior to acting, so that plaintiffs may be held to have assented to that agreement with constructive notice of its terms. . . . But courts are quick to add: "An exception to this general rule exists when the writing does not appear to be a contract and the terms are not called to the attention of the recipient. In such a case, no contract is formed with respect to the undisclosed term." . . .

Most of the cases cited by defendants in support of their inquiry-notice argument are drawn from the world of paper contracting. . . .

---

[13] The district court concluded that the SmartDownload transactions here should be governed by "California law as it relates to the sale of goods, including the Uniform Commercial Code in effect in California." Specht, 150 F.Supp.2d at 591. It is not obvious, however, that UCC Article 2 ("sales of goods") applies to the licensing of software that is downloadable from the Internet. * * *

We need not decide today whether UCC Article 2 applies to Internet transactions in downloadable products. The district court's analysis and the parties' arguments on appeal show that, for present purposes, there is no essential difference between UCC Article 2 and the common law of contracts. We therefore apply the common law, with exceptions as noted.

As the foregoing cases suggest, receipt of a physical document containing contract terms or notice thereof is frequently deemed, in the world of paper transactions, a sufficient circumstance to place the offeree on inquiry notice of those terms. "Every person who has actual notice of circumstances sufficient to put a prudent man upon inquiry as to a particular fact, has constructive notice of the fact itself in all cases in which, by prosecuting such inquiry, he might have learned such fact." Cal. Civ.Code § 19. These principles apply equally to the emergent world of online product delivery, pop-up screens, hyperlinked pages, clickwrap licensing, scrollable documents, and urgent admonitions to "Download Now!". What plaintiffs saw when they were being invited by defendants to download this fast, free plug-in called SmartDownload was a screen containing praise for the product and, at the very bottom of the screen, a "Download" button. Defendants argue that under the principles set forth in the cases cited above, a "fair and prudent person using ordinary care" would have been on inquiry notice of SmartDownload's license terms. . . .

We are not persuaded that a reasonably prudent offeree in these circumstances would have known of the existence of license terms. Plaintiffs were responding to an offer that did not carry an immediately visible notice of the existence of license terms or require unambiguous manifestation of assent to those terms. Thus, plaintiffs' "apparent manifestation of . . . consent" was to terms "contained in a document whose contractual nature [was] not obvious. . . ." Moreover, the fact that, given the position of the scroll bar on their computer screens, plaintiffs may have been aware that an unexplored portion of the Netscape webpage remained below the download button does not mean that they reasonably should have concluded that this portion contained a notice of license terms. In their deposition testimony, plaintiffs variously stated that they used the scroll bar "[o]nly if there is something that I feel I need to see that is on—that is off the page," or that the elevated position of the scroll bar suggested the presence of "mere [ ] formalities, standard lower banner links" or "that the page is bigger than what I can see." Plaintiffs testified, and defendants did not refute, that plaintiffs were in fact unaware that defendants intended to attach license terms to the use of SmartDownload.

We conclude that in circumstances such as these, where consumers are urged to download free software at the immediate click of a button, a reference to the existence of license terms on a submerged screen is not sufficient to place consumers on inquiry or constructive notice of those terms. The SmartDownload webpage screen was "printed in such a manner that it tended to conceal the fact that it was an express acceptance of [Netscape's] rules and regulations." Internet users may have, as defendants put it, "as much time as they need[ ]" to scroll through multiple screens on a webpage, but there is no reason to assume that viewers will scroll down to subsequent screens simply because screens are there. When products are "free" and users are invited to download them in the absence of reasonably conspicuous notice that they are about to bind themselves to contract terms, the transactional circumstances cannot be fully analogized to those in the paper world of arm's-length bargaining. * * *

B.   Shrinkwrap Licensing and Related Practices

Defendants cite certain well-known cases involving shrinkwrap licensing and related commercial practices in support of their contention that plaintiffs became bound by the SmartDownload license terms by virtue of inquiry notice. * * * [The court cited and discussed several cases.] These cases do not help defendants. To the extent that they hold that the purchaser of a computer or tangible software is contractually bound after failing to object to printed license terms provided with the product, [they] do not differ markedly from the cases involving traditional paper contracting discussed in the previous section. * * * In sum, the foregoing cases [because the purchaser was clearly aware of the terms at issue before using the computer] are clearly distinguishable from the facts of the present action.

C.   Online Transactions

Cases in which courts have found contracts arising from Internet use do not assist defendants, because in those circumstances there was much clearer notice than in the present case that a user's act would manifest assent to contract terms. . . .[17]

---

[17] Although the parties here do not refer to it, California's consumer fraud statute, Cal. Bus. & Prof.Code § 17538, is one of the few state statutes to regulate online transactions in goods or services. The statute provides that in disclosing information regarding return and refund policies and other vital consumer information, online vendors must legibly display the information either:

> (i) [on] the first screen displayed when the vendor's electronic site is accessed, (ii) on the screen on which goods or services are first offered, (iii) on the screen on which a buyer may place the order for goods or services, (iv) on the screen on which the buyer may enter payment information, such as a credit card account number, or (v) for nonbrowser-based technologies, in a manner that gives the user a reasonable opportunity to review that information.

Id. § 17538(d)(2)(A). The statute's clear purpose is to ensure that consumers engaging in online transactions have relevant information before they can be bound. Although consumer fraud as such is not alleged in the present action, and § 17538 protects only California residents, we note that the statute is consistent with the principle of conspicuous notice of the existence of contract terms that is also found in California's common law of contracts.

In addition, the model code, UCITA [the Uniform Computer Information Transactions Act—Eds.] generally recognizes the importance of conspicuous notice and unambiguous manifestation of assent in online sales and licensing of computer information. For example, § 112, which addresses manifestation of assent, provides that a user's opportunity to review online contract terms exists if a "record" (or electronic writing) of the contract terms is "made available in a manner that ought to call it to the attention of a reasonable person and permit review." UCITA, § 112(e)(1) (rev. ed. Aug. 23, 2001) (available at www.ucitaonline.com/ucita.html). Section 112 also provides, in pertinent part, that "[a] person manifests assent to a record or term if the person, acting with knowledge of, or after having an opportunity to review the record or term or a copy of it ... intentionally engages in conduct or makes statements with reason to know that the other party or its electronic agent may infer from the conduct or statement that the person assents to the record or term." *Id.* § 112(a)(2). In the case of a "mass-market license," a party adopts the terms of the license only by manifesting assent "before or during the party's initial performance or use of or access to the information." *Id.* § 209(a).

After reviewing the California common law and other relevant legal authority, we conclude that under the circumstances here, plaintiffs' downloading of SmartDownload did not constitute acceptance of defendants' license terms. Reasonably conspicuous notice of the existence of contract terms and unambiguous manifestation of assent to those terms by consumers are essential if electronic bargaining is to have integrity and credibility. We hold that a reasonably prudent offeree in plaintiffs' position would not have known or learned, prior to acting on the invitation to download, of the reference to SmartDownload's license terms hidden below the "Download" button on the next screen. We affirm the district court's conclusion that the user plaintiffs, including Fagan, are not bound by the arbitration clause contained in those terms.

* * *

CONCLUSION

For the foregoing reasons, we affirm the district court's denial of defendants' motion to compel arbitration and to stay court proceedings.

Cairo, Inc. v. Crossmedia Services, Inc.

United States District Court, N.D. California, 2005.
2005 WL 756610.

Order Granting Defendant's Motion to Dismiss

I.   INTRODUCTION

■ WARE, J. Plaintiff Cairo, Inc. ("Plaintiff" or "Cairo") has filed a complaint for declaratory relief against Defendant Crossmedia Services, Inc. ("Defendant" or "CMS") seeking a declaratory judgment from this Court that (1) its web site does not infringe any copyrightable material belonging to CMS; (2) its web site does not infringe any registered federal trademark held by CMS; (3) its web site does not infringe any California trademark held by CMS; (4) its web site does not constitute an unfair trade practice under federal or California law; (5) its conduct does not breach any enforceable contract with CMS; (6) it has not committed trespass as to CMS's personal property; (7) it has not misappropriated property or assets belonging to CMS; and (8) it has not wrongfully interfered with CMS's business relationships. Defendant moves to dismiss Plaintiff's Complaint for improper venue, pursuant to Fed. R. Civ. P. 12(b)(3). On Tuesday, March 29, 2005, this Court held a hearing regarding Defendant's motion. Based upon counsels' comments at the hearing and upon all papers filed to date, this Court GRANTS CMS's motion to dismiss.

---

* * *

We hasten to point out that UCITA, which has been enacted into law only in Maryland and Virginia, does not govern the parties' transactions in the present case, but we nevertheless find that UCITA's provisions offer insight into the evolving online "circumstances" that defendants argue placed plaintiffs on inquiry notice of the existence of the SmartDownload license terms. UCITA has been controversial as a result of the perceived breadth of some of its provisions. * * *

II. BACKGROUND

Cairo is a Delaware corporation with its principal place of business in San Ramon, California. CMS is a Delaware Corporation with its principal place of business in Chicago, Illinois. Both parties operate web sites that allow users to search for products on sale at local retailers.

A. CMS's Business

CMS's business has two aspects: its SmartCircular Service and its ShopLocal Network. The SmartCircular Service and ShopLocal Network enable CMS's retail customers to distribute their promotional information via the Internet to shoppers in local geographic markets and enable these shoppers to identify sales, specials, and promotions at local retailers. CMS enters into agreements with retailers and other businesses to make their promotional materials available on CMS's web sites.

Using its SmartCircular Service, which allegedly consists of proprietary processes and technology, CMS takes its customers' promotional materials and creates interactive electronic versions of those materials. CMS hosts these materials on more than 250 web sites that it operates. A shopper may access the interactive promotional materials created by CMS through CMS's ShopLocal Network or through the retailers' own web sites. When a shopper clicks on a link on a retailer's web site to view the retailer's promotional materials, the shopper is directed to a web site hosted by CMS.

CMS's ShopLocal Network provides shoppers with access to the interactive promotional materials that CMS has created for its customers with its SmartCircular Services technology. A shopper can use the ShopLocal Network by visiting any one of a number of web sites, including CMS's shoplocal.com, saleshound.com, and realmalls.com; more than 140 local newspaper sites; and certain "portals" and "destination sites."

When a shopper visits the web site of one of CMS's retail customers and clicks on a link for sales or specials, the shopper is directed to a CMS web page that asks her to enter her zip code, or city and state, to find the sales, specials, and promotions in her area. Once the location information is entered, the shopper is directed to a page displaying CMS's customers' interactive promotional material.

Except for the web pages that CMS operates for Target Corporation, every web page hosted by CMS displays the CMS name and logo and the following notice: "By continuing past this page and/or using this site, you agree to abide by the Terms of Use for this site, which prohibit commercial use of any information on this site." "Terms of Use" appears in an underlined and highlighted format which signals in a common Internet convention that users can view the terms by clicking on the hyperlink. Once a user clicks on the link, a user sees the full CMS Terms of Use. The introductory provision of the Terms of Use reads as follows:

"These terms of use constitute a binding legal agreement (the "Agreement") between the user and CrossMedia Services, Inc. ("CrossMedia"), the owner and operator of the Website. If you do not accept the terms stated here, do not use the Website."

CMS allows users to "view and download a single copy of content on [CrossMedia web sites] solely for lawful, non-commercial and personal use by users and other authorized users as expressly permitted by and subject to the restrictions" imposed by its Terms of Use. CMS's Terms of Use prohibit users from deep-linking to CMS's web sites for any purpose unless specifically authorized by CMS. They also bar users from accessing CMS web sites with "any robot, spider or other automatic device or process to monitor or copy any portion" of those sites.

CMS's Terms of Use contain a forum selection clause:

> Jurisdiction for any claims arising under this Agreement shall lie exclusively with the state or federal courts in Chicago, Illinois where CrossMedia has its principal place of business.

B. Cairo's Business

Cairo's web site allows a user to search its database of in-store sales information. By entering her zip code, a user can search for products on sale at local retail stores by typing in a particular product in which she is interested, by selecting a product category prepared by Cairo, by selecting a retailer from a prepared list, or by selecting a specific brand from a list prepared by Cairo. The user's search results include the name of the specific product on sale accompanied by a small image of the retailer's newspaper weekly circular. If the user clicks on the name of the product, the user is directed to the retailer's web page with information about that particular product. Alternatively, if the user clicks on the image of the circular, she is directed to the retailer's weekly circular web page.

Cairo compiles information from retailers' weekly circular web pages, some of which are enabled by CMS. Cairo collects sale information from retailers' web sites by means of computer programs variously referred to as "robots," "spiders," or "crawlers," which automatically visit retailers' web sites, record the relevant sales information from the retailers' weekly circular web pages, and then return that information to a database maintained by Cairo.

Cairo's computer search programs cannot read the Terms of Use posted on a web site, and they do not report the presence of such Terms of Use back to Cairo. On a day-to-day basis, Cairo does not actually know whether the web pages it searches contain Terms of Use, much less what the specific content of those Terms of Use is.

C. The Dispute

Within days after Cairo launched its web site in October 2004, CMS discovered by reviewing its server logs and by reviewing the Cairo site that Cairo was copying promotional materials from CMS's SmartCircular web pages and posting a version of those materials on the Cairo site. CMS alleges that Cairo's scraper program submits requests to the servers hosting CMS's web pages and in response, the servers provide a copy of the requested web pages to the scraper. When users of the Cairo site search a particular product or brand, Cairo displays as the search results the promotional material it has copied from the CMS pages in the form of thumbnail images with accompanying text. A user of the Cairo site who clicks on some of the thumbnail images or associated text links is connected to a CMS web page via a "deep link" where she will find a larger, searchable, interactive version of the image and text, created and displayed by CMS.

On November 1, 2004, CMS's counsel sent a letter to the President and the Vice President of Products of Cairo informing Cairo that its conduct constituted a breach of the Terms of Use and demanding that Cairo cease such conduct. Despite the November 1, 2004 letter, CMS alleges that Cairo has continued its scraping of and deep-linking to CMS's web pages. CMS alleges that its records show that Cairo's scraper is accessing CMS's web pages many thousands of times per month.

On November 12, 2004, Cairo filed a declaratory relief action against CMS in the United States District Court for the Northern District of California. On January 14, 2005, CMS filed a Motion to Dismiss for improper venue, alleging that the forum selection clause in CMS's Terms of Use requires Cairo to file lawsuits against CMS in the state and federal courts in Chicago, Illinois, rendering venue in this Court improper. Cairo argues that no one at Cairo was aware of the forum selection clause in CMS's Terms of Use until CMS filed its Motion to Dismiss, and that no one at Cairo was aware of CMS's Terms of Use until immediately prior to CMS sending its letter threatening legal action on November 1, 2004. Further, Cairo argues that no agreement exists between the parties at all, and that Cairo has not assented to CMS's Terms of Use or the forum selection clause therein. Additionally, CMS argues that even if the Court finds that CMS's Terms of Use are binding on Cairo, CMS's forum selection clause does not apply to Cairo's federal copyright claim nor to its federal and state trademark claims.

* * *

IV. DISCUSSION

* * *

A.   The Forum Selection Clause in CMS's Terms of Use is Enforceable as to Cairo

Cairo makes no allegations of fraud or overreaching underlying the forum selection clause that would render its enforcement unreasonable. Instead, the issue before the Court is whether Cairo is bound by CMS's Terms of Use in the first instance.

As a preliminary matter, Cairo asserts that the question of whether a contract exists to bind Cairo to CMS's terms should not be resolved on a pleadings motion because Cairo would be required to prove its case on the merits prior to conducting any discovery. The Court agrees that the merits of any potential contractual dispute between the parties should be reserved for and decided by the trial court that will eventually preside over this case. However, strictly for purposes of Defendant's Motion to Dismiss, this Court has before it all facts necessary to resolve the issue of whether Cairo is bound by CMS's terms.

Cairo asserts that since it never explicitly agreed to CMS's Terms of Use, it is not contractually bound by the forum selection provision. Further, Cairo denies being aware of CMS's forum selection clause at the time it filed this case. CMS correctly cites *Register.com, Inc. v. Verio, Inc.*, 356 F.3d 393 (2d Cir. 2004) to counter Cairo's argument. In that case, the defendant Verio contended that it was never contractually bound to the conditions imposed by Register.com, a web site it was accessing via robot software. In response, the Second Circuit stated:

> While new commerce on the Internet has exposed courts to many new situations, it has not fundamentally changed the principles of contract. It is standard contract doctrine that when a benefit is offered subject to stated conditions, and the offeree makes a decision to take the benefit with knowledge of the terms of the offer, the taking constitutes acceptance of the terms, which accordingly become binding on the offeree.

Id. at 403 (citations omitted). Similar to the circumstance in *Register.com*, Cairo's visits to CMS's web sites with knowledge of CMS's Terms of Use constituted acceptance of the terms, which accordingly are binding on Cairo.

Cairo argues that forum selection clauses must be reasonably communicated for a party to be bound by its terms, seeking support from *Specht v. Netscape Communications Corp.*, 306 F.3d 17 (2d Cir. 2002). In that case, the Second Circuit ruled that users who downloaded Netscape's software from Netscape's web site were not bound by an agreement to arbitrate disputes with Netscape because users would not have seen Netscape's terms without scrolling down their computer screens, and there was no reason for them to do so. The evidence did not demonstrate that one who had downloaded Netscape's software had necessarily seen the terms of its offer. Unlike the circumstances in *Specht*, Cairo admits to actual knowledge of CMS's Terms as of at least "the day before CMS sent its letter threatening legal action on November 1, 2004." Moreover, Cairo's repeated and automated use of CMS's web pages can form the basis of imputing knowledge to Cairo of the terms on which CMS's services were offered even before Cairo's notice of CMS's cease and desist letter. See *Register.com*, 356 F.3d at 401–02 (imputing knowledge of web site's terms of use to repeated user of Register.com's database). Thus, even accepting Cairo's allegation that it did not explicitly agree to CMS's Terms of Use, the Court finds that Cairo's use of CMS's web site under circumstances in which Cairo had actual or imputed knowledge of CMS's terms effectively binds Cairo to CMS's Terms of Use and the forum selection clause therein.

Cairo argues that if the Court finds that CMS's Terms of Use are binding on Cairo, the terms themselves are ambiguous as to where the litigation should take place and the Court should not decide the issue of the contract's interpretation on a Rule 12(b) motion. Cairo asserts that because some versions of CMS's terms include provisions requiring that all disputes be litigated in the state and federal courts in Chicago and be subjected to binding arbitration, the agreement is ambiguous as to the very question before the Court: whether or not to require that this dispute be litigated in Chicago. To the extent that ambiguity exists with regard to which of the two contradictory provisions should govern, this Court declines to interpret which provision should be given effect. However, it is clear that neither provision allows for the resolution of disputes in the Northern District of California. Allowing the litigation to proceed in this Court would be contrary to any interpretation of the terms.

* * *

V.   CONCLUSION

For the reasons set forth above, Defendant's Motion to Dismiss is GRANTED. All findings in this Order are made for the limited purpose of assessing whether venue in this Court is proper. Nothing in this Order is intended to address the merits of any claim, contractual or otherwise.

NOTES

(1)   *Shrinkwrap, Clickwrap and Browsewrap.* The shrinkwrap cases of the 1990s and early 2000s set the stage, and the nomenclature, for judicial understanding of what, with the emergence of the Internet, might well be the more significant issues of clickwrap and browsewrap. As Judge (now Justice) Sotomayor notes in *Specht*, "clickwrap" refers to an electronic agreement in which a user indicates agreement to terms by clicking on a radio button, checking a box or the like, usually as a condition of using a device or piece of software. The term "browsewrap" refers to terms of use, often found via a link on a website's main page, that purport to bind a user solely by virtue of his or her continued use of the site.

(2)   In *Register.com, Inc. v. Verio, Inc.*, Judge Leval (also on the panel in *Specht*) drew the following analogy to explain why repeated use of a website with actual knowledge of browsewrap terms might bind a user:

> The situation might be compared to one in which plaintiff P maintains a roadside fruit stand displaying bins of apples. A visitor, defendant D, takes an apple and bites into it. As D turns to leave, D sees a sign, visible only as one turns to exit, which says "Apples—50 cents apiece." D does not pay for the apple. D believes

he has no obligation to pay because he had no notice when he bit into the apple that 50 cents was expected in return. D's view is that he never agreed to pay for the apple. Thereafter, each day, several times a day, D revisits the stand, takes an apple, and eats it. D never leaves money.

P sues D in contract for the price of the apples taken. D defends on the ground that on no occasion did he see P's price notice until after he had bitten into the apples. D may well prevail as to the first apple taken. D had no reason to understand upon taking it that P was demanding the payment. In our view, however, D cannot continue on a daily basis to take apples for free, knowing full well that P is offering them only in exchange for 50 cents in compensation, merely because the sign demanding payment is so placed that on each occasion D does not see it until he has bitten into the apple.

356 F.3d 393, 401 (2d Cir. 2004). Does the analogy work? Is there any danger in analogical reasoning when it comes to new technologies? What incentives does an actual-knowledge rule create?

(3) *Applicable Law.* The question of applicable law continues to plague Internet transaction. If the contract was for the sale of goods, UCC Article 2 will apply even if the contract was concluded electronically. But what are goods? For example, should there be any difference between a CD boxed and sold in a store and the content of that CD downloaded from a website? And what about goods like smartphones that are operated by software?

The Uniform Computer Information Transactions Act (UCITA), adopted by the NCCUSL in 1999, was designed to solve the problem. The model act was designed to govern "computer information transactions," § 103(a), and defined "computer information" as "information in electronic form which is obtained from or through the use of a computer or which is in a form capable of being processed by a computer," § 102(a)(10). Section 112(a) would have dealt with clickwrap and browsewrap, providing that "A person manifests assent to a record or term if the person, acting with knowledge of, or after having an opportunity to review the record or term or a copy of it: (1) authenticates the record or term with intent to adopt or accept it; or (2) intentionally engages in conduct or makes statements with reason to know that the other party or its electronic agent may infer from the conduct or statement that the person assents to the record or term." Only two states, Virginia and Maryland, enacted UCITA, and the project was abandoned by the National Conference of Commissioners after several states enacted legislation prohibiting UCITA from regulating transactions within their borders.

In 2009, the American Law Institute adopted Principles of the Law of Software Contracts. "In light of the many percolating legal issues that pertain to the formation and enforcement of software agreements," the drafters did not attempt to restate existing law, but instead instituted a " 'Principles' project [that] accounts for the case law and recommends best practices, without unduly hindering the law's adaptability to future developments." Principles of the Law of Software Contracts Intro. (2010). Section 1.01(*l*) defines "standard-form transfer of generally available software" as "a transfer using a standard form of (1) a small number of copies of software to an end user; or (2) the right to access software to a small number of end users if the software is generally available to the public under substantially the same standard terms." Section 2.02 provides:

(b) A transferee adopts a standard form as a contract when a reasonable transferor would believe the transferee intends to be bound to the form.

(c) A transferee will be deemed to have adopted a standard form as a contract if

(1) the standard form is reasonably accessible electronically prior to initiation of the transfer at issue;

(2) upon initiating the transfer, the transferee has reasonable notice of and access to the standard form before payment or, if there is no payment, before completion of the transfer;

(3) in the case of an electronic transfer of software, the transferee signifies agreement at the end of or adjacent to the electronic standard form, or in the case of a standard form printed on or attached to packaged software or separately wrapped from the software, the transferee does not exercise the opportunity to return the software unopened for a full refund within a reasonable time after the transfer; and

(4) the transferee can store and reproduce the standard form if presented electronically.

(d) Subject to § 1.10 (public policy), § 1.11 (unconscionability), and other invalidating defenses supplied by these Principles or outside law, a standard term is enforceable if reasonably comprehensible.

(e) If a transferee asserts that it did not adopt a standard form as a contract under subsection (b) or asserts a failure of the transferor to comply with subsection (c) or (d), the transferor has the burden of production and persuasion on the issue of compliance with the subsections.

As of the date of publication, it remains to be seen how much influence, if any, the principles will have on judicial decisions.

(3) *Clickwrap*. Courts are in general agreement that a click is enough to signify agreement to an electronic transaction. See, e.g., Centrifugal Force, Inc. v. Softnet Communication, Inc., 2011 WL 744732 at *7 (S.D.N.Y. 2011) ("In New York, clickwrap agreements are valid and enforceable contracts."); Segal v. Amazon.com, Inc., 763 F. Supp. 2d 1367, 1369 (S.D. Fla. 2011) ("In Florida and the federal circuits clickwrap agreements are valid and enforceable contracts."); Van Tassell v. United Marketing Group, LLC, 795 F.Supp.2d 770, 790 (N.D. Ill. 2011) ("Because clickwrap agreements require affirmative action on the part of the user to manifest assent, courts regularly uphold their validity when challenged.").

But Robert Hillman and Jeffrey J. Rachlinski argue that while an individual's opportunity to protect herself against one-sided standard forms is arguably greater when contracting by computer than when contracting through written forms, the "cognitive perspective that consumers tend to adopt with respect to contractual risks makes it unlikely that many will take advantage of these new [electronic] tools . . . [and] the electronic environment gives businesses new opportunities to exploit consumers." *Standard-Form Contracting in the Electronic Age*, 77 N.Y.U. L. Rev. 429, 495 (2002). In short, almost no one reads the terms of the clickwrap license before assenting to the program. Florencia Marotta-Wurgler studied the clickstream data for 47,399 households over a one-month period to see whether users read end-user license agreements (EULAs). She found that

> contract accessibility does not result in an economically significant increase in readership. Mandating assent by requiring consumers to agree to terms by clicking on an "I agree" box next to the terms increases contract readership by at best on the order of 1 percent. Averaging across six different estimates of shoppers' readership rates, I estimate that clickwraps are read only 0.36 percent more often than browsewraps, and the overall average rate of readership of EULAs is on the order of 0.1 percent to 1 percent. This low average rate of readership is conservative in that I assume that all shoppers who access a EULA page for at least one second can be said to have read it, despite the fact that the average EULA is 2,300 words long and written in complex language.

Does Increased Disclosure Help? Evaluating the Recommendations of the ALI's 'Principles of the Law of Software Contracts', 78 U. Chi. L. Rev 165, 168 (2011). This explains why the British software retailer GameStation was able to successfully add an "immortal soul clause" to its EULA that read:

> By placing an order via this Web site on the first day of the fourth month of the year 2010 Anno Domini, you agree to grant Us a non transferable option to claim, for now and for ever more, your immortal soul. Should We wish to exercise this option, you agree to surrender your immortal soul, and any claim you may have on it, within 5 (five) working days of receiving written notification from gamesation.co.uk or one of its duly authorised minions.

7,500 Online Shoppers Unknowingly Sold Their Souls, foxnews.com (April 15, 2010).

(C) INDEFINITE AGREEMENTS AND GAPS

George Varney v. Issac Ditmars

Court of Appeals of New York, 1916.
217 N.Y. 223.

■ CHASE J. This is an action brought for an alleged wrongful discharge of an employee. The defendant is an architect employing engineers, draftsmen, and other assistants. The plaintiff is an architect and draftsman. In October, 1910, he applied to the defendant for employment and when asked what wages he wanted, replied that he would start for

$40 per week. He was employed at $35 per week. A short time thereafter he informed the defendant that he had another position offered to him, and the defendant said that if he would remain with him and help him through the work in his office he thought he could offer him a better future than anybody else. He continued in the employ of the defendant and became acquainted with a designer in the office, and said designer and the plaintiff from time to time prior to the 1st of February, 1911, talked with the defendant about the work in his office. On that day by arrangement the two remained with the defendant after the regular office hours, and the defendant said: "I am going to give you $5 more a week; if you boys will go on and continue the way you have been and get me out of this trouble and get these jobs started that were in the office three years, on the 1st of next January I will close my books and give you a fair share of my profits." That was the result of the conversation. That was all of that conversation.

The plaintiff was given charge of the drafting. Thereafter suggestions were made by the plaintiff and said designer about discharging many of the defendant's employees and employing new men, and such suggestions were carried out and the two worked in the defendant's office overtime and many Sundays and holidays. At least one piece of work that the defendant said had been in his office for three years was completed. The plaintiff on his cross-examination told the story of the employment of himself and said designer as follows: "And he says at that time, 'I am going to give you $5 more a week starting this week.' This was about Thursday. He says, 'You boys go on and continue the work you are doing and the first of January next year I will close my books and give you a fair share of my profits.' Those were his exact words."

Thereafter the plaintiff was paid $40 a week. On November 6, 1911, the night before the general election in this state, the defendant requested that all of his employees that could do so, should work on election day. The plaintiff told the defendant that he wanted to remain at home to attend an election in the village where he lived. About 4 o'clock in the afternoon of election day he was taken ill and remained at his house ill until a time that as nearly as can be stated from the evidence was subsequent to December 1, 1911. On Saturday, November 11th, the defendant caused to be delivered to the plaintiff a letter in which he said: "I am sending you herewith your pay for one day's work of seven hours, performed on Monday, the 6th inst. On Monday night, I made it my special duty to inform you that the office would be open all day Election Day and that I expected you and all the men to report for work. Much to my surprise and indignation, on Tuesday you made no appearance and all of the men remained away, in obedience of your instructions to them of the previous evening. An act of this kind I consider one of extreme disloyalty and insubordination and I therefore am obliged to dispense with your services."

After the plaintiff had recovered from his illness and was able to do so he went to the defendant's office (the date does not appear) and told him that he was ready, willing, and able to continue his services under the agreement. The defendant denied that he had any agreement with him, and refused to permit him to continue in his service. Thereafter and prior to January 1, 1912, the plaintiff received for special work about $50.

The plaintiff seeks to recover in this action for services from November 7, 1911, to December 31, 1911, inclusive, at $40 per week and for a fair and reasonable percentage of the net profits of the defendant's business from February 1, 1911, to January 1, 1912, and demands judgment for $1,680.

At the trial he was the only witness sworn as to the alleged contract, and at the close of his case the complaint was dismissed.

The statement alleged to have been made by the defendant about giving the plaintiff and said designer a fair share of his profits is vague, indefinite, and uncertain, and the amount cannot be computed from anything that was said by the parties or by reference to any document, paper, or other transaction. The minds of the parties never met upon any particular share of the defendant's profits to be given the employees or upon any plan by which such share could be computed or determined. The contract so far as it related to the special promise or inducement was never consummated. It was left subject to the will of the defendant or for further negotiation. It is urged that the defendant by use of the word "fair," in referring to a share of his profits, was as certain and definite as people are in the purchase and sale of a chattel when the price is not expressly agreed upon, and that if the agreement in question is declared to be too indefinite and uncertain to be enforced, a similar conclusion must be reached in every case where a chattel is sold without expressly fixing the price therefor.

The question whether the words "fair" and "reasonable" have a definite and enforceable meaning when used in business transactions is dependent upon the intention of the parties in the use of such words and upon the subject-matter to which they refer. In cases of merchandising and in the purchase and sale of chattels the parties may use the words "fair and reasonable value" as synonymous with "market value." A promise to pay the fair market value of goods may be inferred from what is expressly agreed by the parties. The fair, reasonable, or market value of goods can be shown by direct testimony of those competent to give such testimony. The competency to speak grows out of experience and knowledge. The testimony of such witnesses does not rest upon conjecture. The opinion of this court in *United Press v. N.Y. Press Co.*, 164 N.Y. 406, was not intended to assert that a contract of sale is unenforceable, unless the price is expressly mentioned and determined.

In the case of a contract for the sale of goods or for hire without a fixed price or consideration being named it will be presumed that a reasonable price or consideration is intended, and the person who enters into such a contract for goods or service is liable therefor as on an implied contract. Such contracts are common, and when there is nothing therein to limit or prevent an implication as to the price they are, so far as the terms of the contract are concerned, binding obligations.

The contract in question, so far as it relates to a share of the defendant's profits, is not only uncertain, but it is necessarily affected by so many other facts that are in themselves indefinite and uncertain that the intention of the parties is pure conjecture. A fair share of the defendant's profits may be any amount from a nominal sum to a material part according to the particular views of the person whose guess is considered. Such an executory contract must rest for performance upon the honor and good faith of the parties making it. The courts cannot aid parties in such a case when they are unable or unwilling to agree upon the terms of their own proposed contract.

It is elementary in the law that, for the validity of a contract, the promise, or the agreement, of the parties to it must be certain and explicit, and that their full intention may be ascertained to a reasonable degree of certainty. Their agreement must be neither vague nor indefinite, and, if thus defective, parol proof cannot be resorted to. * * *

The rule stated from the *United Press* Case does not prevent a recovery upon quantum meruit in case one party to an alleged contract has performed in reliance upon the terms thereof, vague, indefinite, and uncertain though they are. In such case the law will presume a promise to pay the reasonable value of the services. Judge Gray, who wrote the opinion in the *United Press* Case, said therein: "I entertain no doubt that, where work has been done, or articles have been furnished, a recovery may be based upon quantum meruit, or quantum valebant; but, where a contract is of an executory character and requires performance over a future period of time, as here, and it is silent as to the price which is to be paid to the plaintiff during its term, I do not think that it possesses binding force. As the parties had omitted to make the price a subject of covenant, in the nature of things, it would have to be the subject of future agreement, or stipulation." . . .

In *Petze v. Morse Dry Dock & Repair Co.*, 109 N.Y.S. 328, 331, the court said: "There is no contract so long as any essential element is open to negotiation." In that case a contract was made by which an employee in addition to certain specified compensation was to receive 5 per cent. of the net distributable profits of a business, and it was further provided: "That 'the method of accounting to determine the net distributable profits is to be agreed upon later when the company's accounts have developed for a better understanding.'"

The parties never agreed as to the method of determining the net profits and the plaintiff was discharged before the expiration of the term. The court in the opinion say: "That 'the plaintiff could recover for what he had done on a quantum meruit, and the employment must be deemed to have commenced with a full understanding on the part of both parties that that was the situation.' "

The judgment of the Appellate Division was unanimously affirmed without opinion in this court. 195 N.Y. 584.

So, in this case, while I do not think that the plaintiff can recover anything as extra work, yet if the work actually performed as stated was worth more than $40 per week he, having performed until November 7, 1910, could, on a proper complaint, recover its value less the amount received. . . .

* * *

The judgment should be affirmed, with costs.

■ CARDOZO, J., (dissenting). I do not think it is true that a promise is always and of necessity too vague to be enforced. . . . The promise must, of course, appear to have been made with contractual intent. . . . But if that intent is present, it cannot be said from the mere form of the promise that the estimate of the reward is inherently impossible. The data essential to measurement may be lacking in the particular instance, and yet they may conceivably be supplied. It is possible, for example, that in some occupations an employee would be able to prove a percentage regulated by custom. The difficulty in this case is not so much in the contract as in the evidence. Even if the data required for computation might conceivably have been supplied, the plaintiff did not supply them. He would not have supplied them if all the evidence which he offered and which the court excluded had been received. He has not failed because the nature of the contract is such that damages are of necessity incapable of proof. He has failed because he did not prove them.

There is nothing inconsistent with this view in *United Press v. N.Y. Press Co.*, 164 N.Y. 406. The case is often cited as authority for the proposition that an agreement to buy merchandise at a fair and reasonable price is so indefinite that an action may not be maintained for its breach in so far as it is still executory. Nothing of the kind was decided, or with reason could have been. What the court did was to construe a particular agreement, and to hold that the parties intended to reserve the price for future adjustment. If instead of reserving the price for future adjustment, they had manifested an intent on the one hand to pay and on the other to accept a fair price, the case is far from holding that a jury could not determine what such a price would be and assess the damages accordingly. Such an intent, moreover, might be manifested not only through express words, but also through reasonable implication. It was because there was neither an express statement nor a reasonable implication of such an intent that the court held the agreement void to the extent that it had not been executed.

On the ground that the plaintiff failed to supply the data essential to computation, I concur in the conclusion that profits were not to be included as an element of damages. I do not concur, however, in the conclusion that he failed to make out a case of damage to the extent of his loss of salary. The amount may be small, but none the less it belongs to him. The hiring was not at will. . . . The plain implication was that it should continue until the end of the year when the books were to be closed. The evidence would permit the jury to find that the plaintiff was discharged without cause, and he is entitled to damages measured by his salary for the unexpired term.

The judgment should be reversed, and a new trial granted, with costs to abide the event.

Judgment affirmed.

Morris Lefkowitz v. Great Minneapolis Surplus Store
Supreme Court of Minnesota, 1957.
Supra at 219.

NOTES

(1) If the majority opinion in *Varney* represents the traditional approach to judging definiteness in contracting, how would you characterize that approach? What is the difference between the majority and the dissent of Judge Cardozo? The "traditional approach," to the extent that *quantum meruit*, aka unjust enrichment, does not fully protect the employee, provides the wrong incentives for employers. Does Judge Cardozo's approach provide better incentives?

(2) *The Modern Rule.* Should courts attempt to fill gaps or resolve ambiguities in a contract? When does doing so amount to "making the contract for the parties"? There has been a shift from a strict view that no contract can be formed until clear and complete agreement is reached on material terms to more flexible standards such as those announced in UCC § 2–204 and Restatement (Second) §§ 33 and 34. Section 33 recommends the following rule:

> (1) Even though a manifestation of intention is intended to be understood as an offer, it cannot be accepted so as to form a contract unless the terms of the contract are reasonably certain. (2) The terms of a contract are reasonably certain if they provide a basis for determining the existence of a breach and for giving an appropriate remedy. (3) The fact that one or more terms of a proposed bargain are left open or uncertain may show that a manifestation of intention is not intended to be understood as an offer or as an acceptance.

How do *Varney* and *Lefkowitz* come under the section 33 test?

(3) *Two Theoretical Perspectives.* There are several arguments for the relaxation of the definiteness requirement. Ian Macneil argues that one reason lies in a better understanding of contractual relationships. Ian R. Macneil, *Restatement (Second) of Contracts and Presentiation,* 60 Va. L. Rev. 589 (1974). Traditional contract theory thinks of transactions as "one-shot deals," in which strangers come together to engage in a single exchange, and

then have no further dealings with one another. The assumption in such transactions is that the parties could and should "presentiate," that is, express all of the material elements of the future exchange *ex ante*, in the contract. But this picture does not describe many long-term, relational contracts, such as those between a supplier and a manufacturer, a union and a corporation, the government and a defense contractor, or a franchisor and a franchisee. These parties may wish to have the protection of contract but be unwilling or unable to articulate all terms of the future exchange in an initial agreement. If that protection is extended to them, new techniques must be developed to manage the inevitable disputes that will arise as the parties attempt to perform and to adjust these open-ended relationships. For an example of such a relationship and "new technique," see the next case, *Oglebay Norton Company v. Armco, Inc.*

Economists have suggested a different reason why courts should be willing to fill gaps or resolve ambiguities. Reaching a complete express agreement on all terms is a costly enterprise. At a certain point, the transaction costs of specifying every term of the agreement exceed the benefits of having a complete contract. The law can help by allowing courts to fill gaps and resolve ambiguities that the parties left behind. Of course *ex post* judicial gap-filling and interpretation has its costs as well. These include both the out-of-pocket costs of lawyers, judges and courtrooms and more difficult to quantify error costs—the costs of courts getting it wrong. From this economic perspective, the question is which is cheaper: greater *ex ante* specification by the parties (taking into account that the issue might never arise) or *ex post* judicial gap filling (on the off chance that the issue does arise and the parties cannot resolve it without litigation).

(4) *Contracts vs. Offers.* Should a different rule govern indefinite offers than covers indefinite contracts? Consider Ian Ayres and Robert Gertner, *Filling Gaps in Incomplete Contracts: An Economic Theory of Default Rules*, 99 Yale L.J. 87, 106 (1989):

> In applying the common-law standard that indefinite contracts are unenforceable, the [*Lefkowitz*] court ignored the likely market response to the non-enforceability default. [N]on-enforceability can be viewed as a penalty default that encourages both parties to come forward and fill in the gap; that is, refusing to enforce indefinite contracts drives out indefinite contracts. In *Lefkowitz*, however, the court's refusal to enforce the indefinite offer leads to exactly the opposite result. Ask yourself the simple question: What kind of ad is the Great Minneapolis Surplus Store going to run the week following the court's decision? By lending its imprimatur to the indefinite ad, the court allows retailers to induce inefficient consumer reliance with impunity. The *Lefkowitz* case dramatically illustrates that only by enforcing indefinite offers against the offeror can one drive out indefinite offers.

(5) *Varieties of Indefiniteness.* There is never a shortage of litigation contesting contractual validity on the basis of alleged indefiniteness of terms. Each term must, of course, be considered contextually, as Judge Cardozo insisted in *Varney*. But even when so considered, many fail to pass muster.

For a sampling of cases, see Union State Bank v. Woell, 434 N.W.2d 712 (N.D. 1989) (promise of bank to provide future financing if borrower could market a particular product nationally); Roy v. Danis, 553 A.2d 663 (Me. 1989) (promise of purchaser of transmission business to employ the seller for life to do "anything [purchaser] asked," such as "putting [seller] on the road * * * running errands"; promise of purchaser to seller that if latter started another shop, purchaser would "send him some work"); Trimmer v. Van Bomel, 434 N.Y.S.2d 82 (1980) (promise of wealthy widow to her former companion and paid escort to pay latter an amount sufficient to cover "costs and expenses for sumptuous living and maintenance for the remainder of his life"); Champaign National Bank v. Landers Seed Co., Inc., 165 Ill.App.3d 1090 (1988) (promise of bank not to collect on note "as long as [debtor] make[s] progress toward profitability"); Cobble Hill Nursing Home, Inc. v. Henry and Warren, 74 N.Y.2d 475 (1989) (promise of nursing home owner to sell property to New York Department of Health "at a price to be determined by the Department in accordance with the Public Health Law and all applicable rules and regulations of the Department").

(6)   *Quasi Contract.* The majority in *Varney v. Ditmars* suggests that if the plaintiff cannot recover in contract, he might recover in *quantum meruit*, if he could show that the reasonable value of the services was greater than the amount he had been paid. For more on the idea behind this, see the discussion of unjust enrichment at the end of this chapter.

Oglebay Norton Company v. Armco, Inc.

Supreme Court of Ohio, 1990.
52 Ohio St.3d 232.

On January 9, 1957, Armco Steel Corporation, n.k.a. Armco, Inc., appellant, entered into a long-term contract with Columbia Transportation Company, which later became a division of Oglebay Norton Company, appellee. The principal term of this contract required Oglebay to have adequate shipping capacity available and Armco to utilize such shipping capacity if Armco wished to transport iron ore on the Great Lakes from mines in the Lake Superior district to Armco's plants in the lower Great Lakes region.

In the 1957 contract, Armco and Oglebay established a primary and a secondary price rate mechanism which stated:

> "*Armco agrees to pay * * ** for all iron ore transported hereunder *the regular net contract rates for the season* in which the ore is transported, *as recognized by the leading iron ore shippers* in such season for the transportation of iron ore * * *. *If,* in any season of navigation hereunder, *there is no regular net contract rate recognized by the leading iron ore shippers* for such transportation, *the parties shall mutually agree upon a rate* for such transportation, *taking into consideration the contract rate being charged for similar transportation* by the leading

independent vessel operators engaged in transportation of iron ore from The Lake Superior District." (Emphasis added.)

During the next twenty-three years, Armco and Oglebay modified the 1957 contract four times. With each modification Armco agreed to extend the time span of the contracts beyond the original date. Both parties acknowledged that the ever-increasing requirements capacity Armco sought from Oglebay would require a substantial capital investment from Oglebay to maintain, upgrade, and purchase iron ore carrier vessels.

The fourth amendment, signed in 1980, required Oglebay to modify and upgrade its fleet to give each Oglebay vessel that Armco utilized a self-unloading capability. It is undisputed that Oglebay began a $95 million capital improvement program at least in part to accommodate Armco's new shipping needs. For its part, Armco agreed to pay an additional twenty-five cents per ton for ore shipped in Oglebay's self-unloading vessels and agreed to extend the running of the contract until December 31, 2010.

During trial, the court recognized Armco's and Oglebay's close and long-standing business relationship, which included a seat for Armco on Oglebay's Board of Directors, Armco's owning Oglebay Norton stock, and a partnership in another venture. In fact, one of Oglebay's vessels was named "The Armco."

This relationship is perhaps best characterized by the language contained in the 1962 amendment, wherein the parties provided:

> " * * * Armco has a vital and unique interest in the continued dedication of * * * [Oglebay's] bulk vessel fleet * * * since such service is a necessary prerequisite to Armco's operation as a major steel producer. * * * Armco's right to require the dedication of * * * [Oglebay's] bulk vessels to Armco's service * * * is the essence of this Agreement * * *."

The amendment also granted to Armco the right to seek a court order for specific performance of the terms of the contract.

From 1957 through 1983 the parties established the contract shipping rate that Oglebay charged Armco by referring to a specified rate published in "Skillings Mining Review," in accordance with the 1957 contract's primary price mechanism. The published rate usually represented the price that Innerlake Steamship Company, a leading independent iron ore shipper, charged its customers for a similar service. Oglebay would quote this rate to Armco, which would then pay it to Oglebay.

Unfortunately, in 1983 the iron and steel industry suffered a serious downturn in business. Thus, in late 1983, when Oglebay quoted Armco the shipping rate for the 1984 season, Armco challenged that rate. Due to its weakened economic position, Armco requested that Oglebay reduce the rate Oglebay was going to charge Armco. The parties then negotiated a mutually satisfactory rate for the 1984 season.

In late 1984 the parties were unable to establish a mutually satisfactory shipping rate for the 1985 season. Oglebay billed Armco $7.66 ($.25 self-unloading vessel surcharge included) per gross ton, and Armco reduced the invoice amount to $5 per gross ton. Armco then paid the $5 per ton figure, indicating payment in full language on the check to Oglebay, and explaining its position in an accompanying letter. In late 1985, the parties again attempted to negotiate a rate, this time for the 1986 season. Again they failed to reach a mutually satisfactory rate.

On April 11, 1986, Oglebay filed a declaratory judgment action requesting the court to declare the rate set forth in the contract to be the correct rate, or in the absence of such a rate, to declare a reasonable rate for Oglebay's services. Armco's answer denied that the $7.41 rate sought by Oglebay was the "contract rate," and denied that the trial court had jurisdiction to declare this rate of its own accord, as a "reasonable rate" or otherwise.

During the 1986 season, Oglebay continued to ship iron ore for Armco. Armco paid Oglebay $4.22 per gross ton for ore shipped prior to August 1, 1986 and $3.85 per gross ton for ore shipped after August 1, 1986.

On August 12, 1987, Armco filed a * * * counterclaim seeking a declaration that the contract was no longer enforceable, because the contract had failed of its purpose due to the complete breakdown of the rate pricing mechanisms.

After a lengthy bench trial, the trial court on November 20, 1987 issued its declaratory judgment, which made four basic findings of fact and law. First, the court held that it was apparent from the evidence presented that Oglebay and Armco intended to be bound by the 1957 contract, even though the rate or price provisions in the contract were not settled.

Second, the court held that where the parties intended to be bound, but where a service contract pricing mechanism based upon the mutual agreement of the parties fails, " * * * then the price shall be the price that is 'reasonable' under all the circumstances at the time the service is rendered."

Third, the trial court held that the parties must continue to comply with the alternative pricing provision contained within paragraph two of the 1957 contract. That alternative pricing provision mandates that the parties consider rates charged for similar services by leading independent iron ore vessel operators.

Fourth, the trial court held that if the parties were unable to agree upon a rate for the upcoming seasons, then the parties must notify the court immediately. Upon such notification, the court, through its equitable jurisdiction, would appoint a mediator and require the parties' chief executive officers " * * * to meet for the purpose of mediating and determining the rate for such season, i.e., that they 'mutually agree upon a rate.'"

The court of appeals affirmed the judgment of the trial court.

The cause is now before the court upon the allowance of a motion to certify the record.

■ PER CURIAM. This case presents three mixed questions of fact and law. First, did the parties intend to be bound by the terms of this contract despite the failure of its primary and secondary pricing mechanisms? Second, if the parties did intend to be bound, may the trial court establish $6.25 per gross ton as a reasonable rate for Armco to pay Oglebay for shipping Armco ore during the 1986 shipping season? Third, may the trial court continue to exercise its equitable jurisdiction over the parties, and may it order the parties to utilize a mediator if they are unable to mutually agree on a shipping rate for each annual shipping season? We answer each of these questions in the affirmative and for the reasons set forth below affirm the decision of the court of appeals.

I

Appellant Armco argues that the complete breakdown of the primary and secondary contract pricing mechanisms renders the 1957 contract unenforceable, because the parties never manifested an intent to be bound in the event of the breakdown of the primary and secondary pricing mechanisms. Armco asserts that it became impossible after 1985 to utilize the first pricing mechanism in the 1957 contract, i.e., examining the published rate for a leading shipper in the "Skillings Mining Review," because after 1985 a new rate was no longer published. Armco asserts as well that it also became impossible to obtain the information necessary to determine and take into consideration the rates charged by leading independent vessel operators in accordance with the secondary pricing mechanism. This is because that information was no longer publicly available after 1985 and because the trial court granted the motions to quash of non-parties, who were subpoenaed to obtain this specific information.[4] Armco argues that since the parties never consented to be bound by a contract whose specific pricing mechanisms had failed, the trial court should have declared the contract to be void and unenforceable.

The trial court recognized the failure of the 1957 contract pricing mechanisms. Yet the trial court had competent, credible evidence before

---

[4] Oglebay Norton sought subpoenas from independent vessel operators and captive fleets to obtain information about rates those carriers were charging for the transportation of iron ore to lower lake ports. The other carriers resisted the subpoenas, requesting that the court quash the subpoenas or issue a protective order. The subpoenas were quashed prior to trial. The trial court's reasons for sustaining the motion to quash rather than issuing a protective order are unclear. It would appear that such information taken pursuant to a protective order under Civ.R. 26(C) might have been appropriate, given the dearth of reliable information concerning past and future controversies regarding rates.

it to conclude that the parties intended to be bound despite the failure of the pricing mechanisms. The evidence demonstrated the long-standing and close business relationship of the parties, including joint ventures, interlocking directorates and Armco's ownership of Oglebay stock. As the trial court pointed out, the parties themselves contractually recognized Armco's vital and unique interest in the combined dedication of Oglebay's bulk vessel fleet, and the parties recognized that Oglebay could be required to ship up to 7.1 million gross tons of Armco iron ore per year.

Whether the parties intended to be bound, even upon the failure of the pricing mechanisms, is a question of fact properly resolved by the trier of fact. Since the trial court had ample evidence before it to conclude that the parties did so intend, the court of appeals correctly affirmed the trial court regarding the parties' intent. We thus affirm the court of appeals on this question.

II

Armco also argues that the trial court lacked jurisdiction to impose a shipping rate of $6.25 per gross ton when that rate did not conform to the 1957 contract pricing mechanisms. The trial court held that it had the authority to determine a reasonable rate for Oglebay's services, even though the price mechanism of the contract had failed, since the parties intended to be bound by the contract. The court cited 1 Restatement of the Law 2d, Contracts (1981) 92, Section 33, and its relevant comments to support this proposition. Comment *e* to Section 33 explains in part:

> " * * * Where * * * [the parties] * * * intend to conclude a contract for the sale of goods * * * and the price is not settled, the price is a reasonable price at the time of delivery if * * * (c) the price is to be fixed in terms of some agreed market or other standard as set or recorded by a third person or agency and it is not so set or recorded. Uniform Commercial Code § 2–305(1)." Id. at 94–95.

* * *

The court therefore determined that a reasonable rate for Armco to pay to Oglebay for transporting Armco's iron ore during the 1986 shipping season was $6.00 per gross ton with an additional rate of twenty-five cents per gross ton when self-unloading vessels were used. The court based this determination upon the parties' extensive course of dealing, " * * * the detriment to the parties respectively, and valid comparisons of market price which reflect [the] economic reality of current depressed conditions in the American steel industry."

The court of appeals concluded that the trial court was justified in setting $6.25 per gross ton as a "reasonable rate" for Armco to pay Oglebay for the 1986 season, given the evidence presented to the trial court concerning various rates charged in the industry and given the intent of the parties to be bound by the agreement.

The court of appeals also held that an open price term could be filled by a trial court, which has the authority to review evidence and establish a "reasonable price," when the parties clearly intended to be bound by the contract. To support this holding, the court cited Restatement of the Law 2d, Contracts, supra, at 92, Section 33, and its comments, and 179, Section 362, and its comments.

* * *

The court of appeals concluded that the $6.25 per gross ton figure fell acceptably between the rate range extremes proven at trial. The court found this to be a reasonable figure. We find there was competent, credible evidence in the record to support this holding and affirm the court of appeals on this question.

III

Armco also argues that the trial court lacks equitable jurisdiction to order the parties to negotiate or in the failure of negotiations, to mediate, during each annual shipping season through the year 2010. The court of appeals ruled that the trial court did not exceed its jurisdiction in issuing such an order.

3 Restatement of the Law 2d, Contracts (1981) 179, Section 362, entitled "Effect of Uncertainty of Terms," is similar in effect to Section 33 and states:

> "Specific performance or an injunction will not be granted unless the terms of the contract are sufficiently certain to provide a basis for an appropriate order."

Comment *b* to Section 362 explains:

> " * * * Before concluding that the required certainty is lacking, however, a court will avail itself of all of the usual aids in determining the scope of the agreement. * * * Expressions that at first appear incomplete may not appear so after resort to usage * * * or the addition of a term supplied by law * * *." Id. at 179.

Ordering specific performance of this contract was necessary, since, as the court of appeals pointed out, " * * * the undisputed dramatic changes in the market prices of great lakes shipping rates and the length of the contract would make it impossible for a court to award Oglebay accurate damages due to Armco's breach of the contract." We agree with the court of appeals that the appointment of a mediator upon the breakdown of court-ordered contract negotiations neither added to nor detracted from the parties' significant obligations under the contract.

It is well-settled that a trial court may exercise its equitable jurisdiction and order specific performance if the parties intend to be bound by a contract, where determination of long-term damages would be too speculative. See 3 Restatement of the Law 2d, Contracts, supra, at 171–172, Section 360(a), Comment *b*; Columbus Packing Co. v. State, ex rel. Schlesinger (1919), 100 Ohio St. 285, 294. Indeed, the court of appeals pointed out that under the 1962 amendment, Armco itself had the contractual right to seek a court order compelling Oglebay to specifically perform its contractual duties.

The court of appeals was correct in concluding that ordering the parties to negotiate and mediate during each shipping season for the duration of the contract was proper, given the unique and long-lasting business relationship between the parties, and given their intent to be bound and the difficulty of properly ascertaining damages in this case. The court of appeals was also correct in concluding that ordering the parties to negotiate and mediate with each shipping season would neither add to nor detract from the parties' significant contractual obligations. This is because the order would merely facilitate in the most practical manner the parties' own ability to interact under the contract. Thus we affirm the court of appeals on this question.

The court of appeals had before it competent, credible evidence from which to conclude that the parties intended to be bound by the terms of the contract, to conclude that the $6.25 per gross ton figure was a "reasonable rate" under the circumstances, and to conclude that the trial court's exercise of continuing equitable jurisdiction was proper in this situation. Accordingly, we affirm the decision of the court of appeals.

Judgment affirmed.

NOTES

(1) *Relational Contract Theory.* The *Oglebay Norton* facts reveal a contract with relational characteristics. The relationship was to last for 50 years; the price term, which was intended to track the market over time (rather than to allocate risk), depended ultimately upon cooperative behavior by the parties (agreeing to fix the price); the carrier was asked to and made "transaction specific investments" in modifying the vessels for Armco's needs; and close relationships between the parties (almost but not quite a joint venture) developed. As such, a court might be reluctant to terminate the contract unless both parties clearly wanted to and might try to preserve the relationship. How did the court respond to Armco's failure to agree on the price and its apparent desire to exit from the contract (presumably because of a very bad market for steel)? Did the court consider Armco to be in breach of contract? If so, what was the breach? If not, how could the court appoint a mediator and order specific performance? See Richard E. Speidel, *The Characteristics and Challenges of Relational Contracts,* 94 Nw. U. L. Rev. 823, 833–37 (2000) (analyzing the opinion).

(2) *Indefiniteness and Open Terms under the UCC.* Although the contract in *Oglebay Norton* was not for the sale of goods, the court applies UCC provisions, seemingly by analogy. These provisions break decisively with the traditional approach to open and indefinite terms. UCC § 2–204(3), which states the basic principle as to open-terms agreements underlying other sections, reads: "Even though one or more terms are left open a

contract for sale does not fail for indefiniteness if the parties have intended to make a contract and there is a reasonably certain basis for giving an appropriate remedy." Subsection (3) establishes two further requirements: (1) the parties must have intended to make a contract; and (2) there must be a reasonably certain basis for giving an appropriate remedy.

Whether there is a reasonably certain basis for giving a remedy depends in part on whether the gap can be filled. The UCC Statute of Frauds section 2–201(1) limits enforcement to the quantity of goods shown in the writing. Thus, even with an intent to contract, lack of written agreement on the quantity term will often mean that the contract fails "for indefiniteness."

With regard to the *price* term, the standard is supplied by section 2–305. If the parties intend "not to be bound unless the price be fixed or agreed and it is not fixed or agreed there is no contract." UCC § 2–305(4). If the requisite intent is present and the "price is left to be agreed by the parties and they fail to agree," the "price is a reasonable price at the time for delivery." UCC § 2–305(1)(b). At this point, section 2–305 is not concerned with why the parties failed to agree or with whether either or both of them negotiated in good faith. The fact of a failure to agree coupled with the requisite intent to contract justifies the court's intervention to fill the "gap" with a "reasonable price." Although it is easier for a court to ascertain reasonable price than reasonable quantity, success is not guaranteed. Thus, in *North Central Airlines, Inc. v. Continental Oil Co.*, 574 F.2d 582 (D.C. Cir. 1978), a contract for the sale of oil failed for indefiniteness when the agreed pricing standard became inoperable and there was no reasonable basis for determining a substitute price. But see *D.R. Curtis Co. v. Mathews*, 103 Idaho 776 (Ct. App. 1982), where the court upheld the trial court's substitute price, determined after the parties failed to agree, as not unreasonable.

(3)   *Intent to Contract.* As discussed in Chapter Two, Section 1.B, the general rule in U.S. law is that "[n]either real nor apparent intention that a promise be legally binding is essential for the formation of a contract." Restatement (Second) § 21. Restatement (Second) § 33(1) and UCC §§ 2–204(3) and 2–305 seem to make an exception for agreements that are missing important terms. Such agreements will be enforced only if the parties intended to be bound. Why should the rule be different for indefinite agreements? And doesn't every agreement contain some gaps? If this is so, how do we tell when a showing of intent is required?

One review of the cases concluded as follows:

While a few courts have * * * read Sections 2–204(3) and 2–305 to condition enforcement on the parties' intent to contract, many more apply the rules without a separate inquiry into the parties' contractual intent. And it is difficult to find any cases in which the parties' intent makes a difference in the outcome—in which the court holds that incomplete terms are "reasonably certain," but then refuses enforcement because the parties did not intend to be legally bound. Though the gestures towards an intent-to-contract test for incomplete and indefinite agreements suggest the justificatory role such intent might play, without more evidence it cannot be said to be the law.

Gregory Klass, *Intent to Contract*, 95 Va. L. Rev. 1437, 1452–53 (2009).

(4)   Liability and remedy issues are often intertwined in disputes over indefiniteness. The agreement may be too indefinite to warrant specific performance but not money damages, or, as in *Oglebay,* the court may, in the exercise of its equitable jurisdiction, appoint a mediator and order the parties to negotiate. Similarly, damages measured by lost expectations may be unwarranted, but not damages measured by costs reasonably incurred in reliance upon the other's promise. Finally, the plaintiff should have a restitutionary remedy for the value of benefits conferred on the defendant through part performance.

Comment: Open Terms Other than Price

Article 2 of the UCC is predominantly a collection of default rules. The phrase "unless otherwise agreed" appears dozens of times in the text. And § 1–302 makes clear that by default UCC provisions should be interpreted as defaults:

> Except as otherwise provided . . . the effect of provisions of [the Uniform Commercial Code] may be varied by agreement. . . . The presence in certain provisions . . . of the phrase "unless otherwise agreed", or words of similar import, does not imply that the effect of other provisions may not be varied by agreement under this section.

Moreover, § 2–204(3) clearly suggests that the code has an inclination toward filling gaps rather than striking down open-ended contracts for indefiniteness:

> Even though one or more terms are left open a contract for sale does not fail for indefiniteness if the parties have intended to make a contract and there is a reasonably certain basis for giving an appropriate remedy.

Not all provisions, however, are contractable. Most importantly, the obligation of "good faith" may not be disclaimed even by express agreement. UCC § 1–302(b). But even here the code allows some contractual flexibility:

> The parties, by agreement, may determine the standards by which [good faith] is to be measured if those standards are not manifestly unreasonable. Id.

There are a number of Code sections, other than the one dealing with open price contracts, which help make contracts more complete if the contract is silent. For example, unless otherwise agreed, the Code ordains:

> 1.   All of the goods are to be delivered at one time, not in several lots. UCC § 2–307.

2.   The buyer has the option of selecting the assortment of the goods; the seller has the option of determining the specifications or arrangements relating to shipment. UCC § 2–311(2). This is subject to the mandatory rule, however, that such specifications "must be made in good faith and within limits set by commercial reasonableness." UCC § 2–311(1).

3.   The time for shipment or delivery or any other action under a contract . . . shall be a reasonable time. UCC § 2–309(1).

4.   The place for delivery of goods is the seller's place of business or residence. UCC § 2–308.

5.   If the agreement authorizes the seller to send the goods to the buyer (and the location of buyer and seller in distant cities could amount to this authorization), the seller may use documents of title and ship under reservation. UCC § 2–310(b).

6.   Payment of the price is due on receipt of the goods, UCC §§ 2–301, 2–310(a), 2–507.

7.   The seller warrants that the title conveyed shall be good. UCC § 2–312.

8.   A merchant seller warrants that the goods are "merchantable." UCC § 2–314.

9.   With certain qualifications, duties may be delegated and rights may be assigned to third parties UCC § 2–210.

The result of these rules can be summarized as follows:

The parties are free to work out the terms of their own contract. As long as those terms fall within the boundaries of conscionability and fair dealing, the courts will enforce those terms. However, failure to agree on each and every term will not result in an unenforceable agreement. The Code fleshes out the skeletal contract by providing terms which the drafters thought would most probably be in the minds of the parties.

Nordstrom, Handbook of the Law of Sales 105–110 (1970). This comment grows out of Nordstrom's discussion.

Comment: How Should the Law Set "Default" Rules?

If the parties have intended to contract but the agreement is incomplete, what "default" rules should be inserted to fill the gaps? The traditional answer is give the parties what they would have contracted for if they had expressly contracted. But this "hypothetical contracting" rule is often devilishly difficult to apply in practice. It is hard to know what terms two parties would have arrived at given their individual interests, relative bargaining power, other opportunities, and so forth. Often the best a court can do is to adopt instead a "majoritarian approach" and seek out which terms most parties in similar circumstances would prefer. Consider again default price provision in

UCC § 2–305. Most parties, and probably these parties, probably contract for a reasonable price—which is normally going to be cashed out as closely related to the market price. Indeed, anytime you see the word "reasonable" included in the description of a defaults, there is a good chance that hypothetical gap filler is at work.[74]

But the law sometimes chooses to fill gaps with terms that do not accord with the hypothetical contracting approach. Whereas the UCC will fill in a missing price with the reasonable price, it does not fill quantity gaps by trying to divine what would have been a reasonable quantity. Instead, the impact of the UCC statute of frauds is often to create de facto a quantity default of zero.[75] The *contra proferentem* rule (which says to resolve contractual ambiguity by interpreting the contract against the drafting party) seems to aim to penalize sloppy drafting rather than attempting to divine what the parties would have expressly contracted for if they had been asked to resolve the ambiguity themselves. Indeed, any of the interpretive "rules of construction" (which strive to resolve ambiguity on some basis other than an attempt to uncover the parties' intent)[76] can be seen as departing from the hypothetical contracting standard.

Ian Ayres and Rob Gertner have argued that these departures might at times make good sense. "Penalty" or "information-forcing" defaults that intentionally penalize a contractor failing to fill a gap can further both equity and efficiency by giving contracting parties an incentive to expressly say what they want. Ayres and Gertner, *Filling Gaps in Incomplete Contracts: An Economic Theory of Default Rules,* 99 Yale L.J. 87 (1989). A penalty default rule is a rule that the contractors would not have wanted. Its presence in the right case will provide contractors "an incentive to contract around the default rule and therefore to choose affirmatively the contract provision they prefer. In contrast to the received wisdom, penalty defaults are purposely set at what the parties would not want—in order to encourage the parties to reveal information to each other or to third parties (especially the courts)." Id. at 91. "When strategic considerations cause a more knowledgeable party not to raise issues that could improve contractual efficiency, a default that penalizes

---

[74] However, § 204 of the Restatement (Second) of Contract provides that terms that are "reasonable in the circumstances" should be used to fill "omitted essential terms," but expressly disclaims reliance on the hypothetical approach in the accompanying comment:

Sometimes it is said that the search is for the term the parties would have agreed to if the question had been brought to their attention. Both the meaning of the words used and the probability that a particular term would have been used if the question had been raised may be factors in determining what term is reasonable in the circumstances. But where there is in fact no agreement, the court should supply a term which comports with community standards of fairness and policy rather than analyze a hypothetical model of the bargaining process.

[75] UCC § 2–201 ("A writing is not insufficient because it omits or incorrectly states a term agreed upon; [but] the contract is not enforceable . . . beyond the quantity of goods shown in such writing").

[76] See, e.g., Restatement (Second) of Contract § 207 ("In choosing among the reasonable meanings of a promise . . . a meaning that serves the public interest is generally preferred").

the more informed party may encourage the revelation of information." Id. at 128.

In fact, there are a host of reasons besides "information forcing" that can justify a "minoritarian" default—that is, a default that only a minority of contracting parties would actually prefer. Minoritarian rules might be justified by:

(1) differences in the private costs of contracting,

(2) differences in the private costs of failing to contract,

(3) differences in the public costs of filling gaps, and

(4) differences in private information about the law.

"The choice of an efficient default does not boil down merely to a choice between the majoritarian rule (for which most contractors would have contracted) and a penalty default designed to induce a contractor to reveal information about her type. Instead, efficiency-minded lawmakers will often need to consider [other] factors to decide whether it is more efficient to choose a default that only a minority values." Ian Ayres and Rob Gertner, *Majoritarian v. Minoritarian Defaults*, 51 Stan. L. Rev. 1591 (1999).

Robert Blinn v. Beatrice Community Hospital and Health Center, Inc.

Supreme Court of Nebraska, 2006.
270 Neb. 809.

* * *

II. BACKGROUND

1. Facts

The following facts are taken from Blinn's deposition testimony, received into evidence at the hearing on Beatrice's motion for summary judgment. As pertinent, Blinn testified that in June 2002, he had received a job offer from a Kansas hospital. The Kansas job would have been at a larger hospital and would have offered more responsibility and income potential than Blinn's job of executive director, medical staff development, at Beatrice. It was Blinn's understanding that the Kansas offer was for a position that Blinn could keep until he retired. Blinn was 67 years old at the time he received the offer. Blinn then went to the Beatrice administrator, Larry Emerson, seeking assurances about the permanency of Blinn's position with Beatrice, and drafted a resignation letter he intended to submit to Beatrice unless he received full assurances that Beatrice wanted him to stay. Blinn said:

> Well, I went in and asked him if I could visit, and I shut the door in his office and handed him this letter, and he read it, and he told me that he did not want me to leave. He assured me that I was doing a good job, and most importantly, he said, "Bob, we've

got at least five more years of work to do." And I left his office feeling fully assured and fully confident that he had no negatives, "cause I gave him total opportunity here to tell me."

I left his office feeling he wanted me there, that he wanted me to stay there and that I should stay there and that we had plenty of work to do and that I could get the job done.

Blinn also asked for Emerson's permission to talk to the chairman of Beatrice's board of directors to seek similar assurances. Blinn testified that the chairman of the board said: "We want you to stay," and I said, "Well, it's really important to me, because whether I stay here or whether I go to [the Kansas hospital], I want it to be the last job I ever have," and [the chairman] assured me he wanted me to stay there and I could stay there until I retired.

However, Blinn was asked to resign by Beatrice in January 2003, and his employment with Beatrice was terminated in February.

2.   Procedural History

Blinn sued Beatrice, alleging several theories of recovery based upon the termination of his employment. Blinn had been hired by Beatrice as an at-will employee, but alleged that his at-will employment status had been modified by oral agreement to a term of employment of "at least five more years," which was not completed before Blinn's termination. The substance of Blinn's petition in the district court was that his at-will employment status had been modified by representations of Beatrice promising Blinn would be employed for a period of at least 5 years, that the representations induced Blinn to forgo another employment opportunity, and that Beatrice then terminated Blinn's employment approximately 6 months after the alleged representations. As pertinent, Blinn alleged theories of recovery based upon breach of an oral contract and promissory estoppel. * * *

Beatrice filed a motion for summary judgment. The district court determined the alleged oral modification of Blinn's contract was not definite or specific enough to modify his at-will employment status, and entered summary judgment for Beatrice. * * *

The Court of Appeals reversed the district court's summary judgment. * * * The Court of Appeals concluded that because there was evidence that Beatrice had assured Blinn he could work there " 'until [he] retired,' " the alternate theory of employment until retirement could be considered to have been tried by implied consent. . . . The Court of Appeals further reasoned that the evidence created a genuine issue of material fact about whether Beatrice offered to extend Blinn's employment until he chose to retire. * * * Finally, the Court of Appeals concluded that the evidence created a genuine issue of material fact on Blinn's theory of recovery for promissory estoppel. The Court of Appeals reversed the order granting summary judgment and remanded the cause for further proceedings. We granted Beatrice's petition for further review. * * *

V. ANALYSIS

* * *

(a) Breach of Contract

We turn first to Blinn's breach of contract claim, which rests on Blinn's contention that the representations made to him by his superiors were sufficient to modify his status as an at-will employee. When employment is not for a definite term and there are no contractual, statutory, or constitutional restrictions upon the right of discharge, an employer may lawfully discharge an employee whenever and for whatever cause it chooses. . . . Oral representations may, standing alone, constitute a promise sufficient to create contractual terms which can modify the at-will status of an employee. . . . However, the burden of proving the existence of an employment contract and all the facts essential to the cause of action is upon the person who asserts the contract. . . .

The question is whether the assurances allegedly given to Blinn were sufficiently definite in form to constitute an offer of a unilateral contract. The language which forms the basis of an alleged employment contract, whether oral or written, must constitute an offer definite in form which is communicated to the employee, and the offer must be accepted and consideration furnished for its enforceability. . . . Under those circumstances, the employee's retention of employment constitutes acceptance of the offer of a unilateral contract because by continuing to stay on the job although free to leave, the employee supplies the necessary consideration for the job. . . .

The question under such circumstances is whether the employer manifests a clear intent to make a promise as an offer of employment other than employment at will, and to be bound by it, so as to justify an employee in understanding that a commitment has been made. . . . Whether a proposal is meant to be an offer for a unilateral contract is determined by the outward manifestations of the parties, not by their subjective intentions. . . . There must be a meeting of the minds or a binding mutual understanding between the parties to the contract.

Here, even viewed in the light most favorable to Blinn, the assurances offered to him were not sufficiently definite in form to constitute an offer of a unilateral contract. The statement that "we've got at least five more years of work to do" is not a clear offer of definite employment and does not manifest an intent to create a unilateral contract. . . . An employee's subjective understanding of job security is insufficient to establish an implied contract of employment to that effect, . . . and the record here does not establish sufficient evidence to conclude that any employee of Beatrice intended to offer a contract of employment on terms other than employment at will.

For that reason, the Court of Appeals erred in concluding that there was a genuine issue of material fact with respect to Blinn's breach of contract claim.

(b)   Promissory Estoppel

Recovery on a theory of promissory estoppel is based upon the principle that injustice can be avoided only by enforcement of a promise. . . . Under the doctrine of promissory estoppel, a promise which the promisor should reasonably expect to induce action or forbearance is binding if injustice can be avoided only by enforcement of the promise. . . .

Under Nebraska law, the doctrine of promissory estoppel does not require that the promise giving rise to the cause of action must meet the requirements of an offer that would ripen into a contract if accepted by the promisee. . . . Simply stated, there is no requirement of "definiteness" in an action based upon promissory estoppel. Instead of requiring reasonable definiteness, promissory estoppel requires only that reliance be reasonable and foreseeable.

Here, we agree with the determination made by the Court of Appeals that there is a genuine issue of material fact with respect to Blinn's promissory estoppel claim. While the statements allegedly made by Blinn's superiors were insufficiently definite to offer a contract of employment on terms other than employment at will, there is a genuine issue of material fact as to whether Blinn was promised terms of employment that could reasonably have been expected to induce Blinn to forgo the job opportunity in Kansas of which he had informed Beatrice. Under the circumstances, when considering the lesser requirement that Nebraska law imposes on a promise that forms the basis of a promissory estoppel cause of action, we conclude that the district court erred in not finding a genuine issue of material fact.

* * *

Under the Restatement view, a "promise" for purposes of promissory estoppel must meet the same requirements as a "promise" for purposes of contract formation. Compare Restatement (Second) of Contracts §§ 2 and 90 (1981). Generally speaking, under the Restatement, when a promise is made, but a contract is not formed because of a lack of consideration, reasonable reliance by the promisee can still render the promisor liable for breach of the promise. . . . In short, analysis of the promise is the same as that for a contract, except that the promisee's reliance on the promise replaces the missing consideration. See, generally, Restatement, supra, § 90, comment a.

But in Nebraska, we have rejected that view. As noted earlier, we have held that there is no requirement of "definiteness" in an action based upon promissory estoppel. Rosnick v. Dinsmore, 235 Neb. 738 (1990). In Rosnick, we departed from the Restatement view that a promise for estoppel purposes requires the same definiteness as a promise for contract purposes. In Whorley v. First Westside Bank, 240

Neb. 975 (1992), we expressly considered the Restatement view, cited conflicting authority, and reaffirmed our holding in *Rosnick*. Contrary to the Restatement view, the law in Nebraska is that a promissory estoppel action may be based on an alleged promise that is insufficiently definite to form a contract, but upon which the promisee's reliance is reasonable and foreseeable. . . . The difference between contract and promissory estoppel, then, is that a contract requires that the promisor intend to make a binding promise—a binding mutual understanding or "meeting of the minds"—while promissory estoppel requires only that the promisee's reliance on the promise be reasonable and foreseeable, even if the promisor did not intend to be bound. A promisor need not intend a promise to be binding in order to foresee that a promisee may reasonably rely on it.

Contrary to that jurisprudence, the dissent mistakenly concludes that since Beatrice did not make a sufficiently definite promise for an offer of a unilateral contract, the promise must have been for, at best, continued at-will employment. Because promissory estoppel does not require definiteness, an employer need not intend to contractually modify an employee's at-will employment in order for an employee to reasonably and foreseeably believe that his or her terms of employment have been changed and, therefore, act in reliance on that belief. Here, there is insufficient evidence to conclude that Beatrice intended to offer Blinn a unilateral contract. But there is sufficient evidence, if believed by the trier of fact, to conclude that Blinn reasonably and foreseeably relied on Beatrice's assurances of a fixed term of employment, and Beatrice breached that promise. There is a genuine issue of material fact to be decided, and the Court of Appeals correctly reversed the district court's judgment on this issue.

NOTES

(1)   Given the court's holding that Emerson's statement was "not a clear offer of definite employment and [did] not manifest an intent to create a unilateral contract," how is it that it could have supported an action for promissory estoppel? In an action for promissory estoppel there must be a promise. Restatement (Second) § 90. Isn't that just what is required to create a contract as well, and what was missing in *Blinn*?

(2)   When Williston introduced the doctrine of promissory estoppel, he argued that reliance can sometimes serve as a "substitute" for consideration. 1 Samuel Williston, The Law of Contracts § 139 (1920). On this view, a relied-upon promise in an action for promissory estoppel creates a contract, the only difference being that the reason for enforcement is reliance rather than consideration. That approach suggests that all of the other conditions of contractual validity still apply, including the rule for indefiniteness.

As the promissory estoppel doctrine has developed, it has become more difficult to view reliance as simply a substitute for consideration in promissory estoppel cases. Most obviously, whereas the First Restatement said nothing about the remedy in promissory estoppel cases, the Second Restatement provides that the remedy "may be limited as justice requires." Restatement (Second) § 90. If an action for promissory estoppel is simply another sort of action for breach of contract, why should the remedy be different? Contrariwise, if the action for promissory estoppel is not an action for breach of contract (after all the remedy is different), why should we insist on satisfaction of the other conditions of contractual validity. Hence we arrive at cases like *Blinn*, in which the bar to enforcement in contract is not lack of consideration (Emerson got something in exchange for his assurances), but indefiniteness of terms.

(3)   What remedy is appropriate in cases like this? Should it be based on what Blinn would have earned from the promisor or what he lost in rejecting of other offer or employment?

(D) PRECONTRACTUAL LIABILITY

Metro-Goldwyn-Mayer, Inc. v. Roy Scheider
Court of Appeals of New York, 1976.
40 N.Y.2d 1069.

■ PER CURIAM. Following a nonjury trial and confronted with sometimes conflicting evidence, the court found that the parties had entered into an oral contract by which appellant had agreed to be principal actor in a pilot film and in the television series which might develop therefrom. After performing in the pilot and being fully compensated therefor, appellant refused to perform in the subsequent television series.

The core issue on this appeal is whether the determination that there was a complete contract between the parties is to be upheld. The negotiations of the parties extended over many weeks. Initially the broad outlines of the contract and its financial dimensions were agreed to in September, 1971, with explicit expectations that further agreements were to follow. Additional important provisions were negotiated over the following weeks. It was during this period that appellant went to Europe for the filming of the pilot. All culminated in supplemental agreements concluded in February, 1972. The only essential term as to which there was no finding of articulated understanding was the starting date for filming the television series. This term was supplied by a finding of the trial court based on proof of established custom and practice in the industry, of which both parties were found to be aware, set in the context of the other understandings reached by them. As Mr. Justice Arnold L. Fein wrote at Trial Term (347 N.Y.S.2d 755, 761): "[W]here the parties have completed their negotiations of what they regard as essential elements, and performance has begun on the good faith understanding that agreement on the unsettled matters will follow, the court will find and enforce a contract even though the parties have expressly left these other elements for future negotiation and agreement, if some objective method of determination is available, independent of either party's mere wish or desire. Such objective criteria may be found in the agreement itself, commercial practice or other usage and custom. If the contract can be rendered certain and complete, by reference to something certain, the court will fill in the gaps" (see Restatement 2d, Contracts, § 230, esp. Comment *d*; § 247; Corbin, Contracts, § 95, pp. 401–404; cf. May Metropolitan Corp. v. May Oil Burner Corp., 290 N.Y. 260).

The findings of fact by the trial court were expressly approved and adopted at the Appellate Division. In this procedural posture such findings, supported as they are by evidence in this record, are now beyond the scope of our review.

Noting that the defense predicated in the courts below on the Statute of Frauds has been abandoned on the appeal to us, we have examined appellant's objection to the Appellate Division's remand for a second trial on the issue of damages and his other contentions and find them to be without merit.

Accordingly, the judgment of Supreme Court should be affirmed.

Joseph Martin, Jr., Delicatessen, Inc. v. Henry Schumacher

Court of Appeals of New York, 1981.
52 N.Y.2d 105.

■ FUCHSBERG, JUDGE. This case raises an issue fundamental to the law of contracts. It calls upon us to review a decision of the Appellate Division, 419 N.Y.S.2d 558, which held that a realty lease's provision that the rent for a renewal period was "to be agreed upon" may be enforceable.

The pertinent factual and procedural contexts in which the case reaches this court are uncomplicated. In 1973, the appellant, as landlord, leased a retail store to the respondent for a five-year term at a rent graduated upwards from $500 per month for the first year to $650 for the fifth. The renewal clause stated that "[t]he Tenant may renew this lease for an additional period of five years at annual rentals to be agreed upon; Tenant shall give Landlord thirty (30) days written notice, to be mailed certified mail, return receipt requested, of the intention to exercise such right." It is not disputed that the tenant gave timely notice of its desire to renew or that, once the landlord made it clear that he would do so only at a rental starting at $900 a month, the tenant engaged an appraiser who opined that a fair market rental value would be $545.41.

The tenant thereupon commenced an action for specific performance in Supreme Court, Suffolk County, to compel the landlord to extend the lease for the additional term at the appraiser's figure or such other sum as the court would decide was reasonable. For his part, the landlord in due course brought a holdover proceeding in the local District Court to evict the tenant. On the landlord's motion for summary judgment, the Supreme Court, holding that a bald agreement to agree on a future rental was unenforceable for uncertainty as a matter of law, dismissed the tenant's complaint. Concordantly, it denied as moot the tenant's motion to remove the District Court case to the Supreme Court and to consolidate the two suits.

It was on appeal by the tenant from these orders that the Appellate Division, expressly overruling an established line of cases in the process, reinstated the tenant's complaint and granted consolidation. In so doing, it reasoned that "a renewal clause in a lease providing for future agreement on the rent to be paid during the renewal term is enforceable if it is established that the parties' intent was not to terminate in the event of a failure to agree." It went on to provide that, if the tenant met that burden, the trial court could proceed to set a "reasonable rent." One of the Justices, concurring, would have eliminated the first step and required the trial court to proceed directly to the fixation of the rent. Each party now appeals by leave of the Appellate Division pursuant to CPLR 5602 (subd. [b], par. 1). The tenant seeks only a modification adopting the concurrer's position. The question formally certified to us by the Appellate Division is simply whether its order was properly made. Since we conclude that the disposition at the Supreme Court was the correct one, our answer must be in the negative.

We begin our analysis with the basic observation that, unless otherwise mandated by law (e.g., residential emergency rent control statutes), a contract is a private "ordering" in which a party binds himself to do, or not to do, a particular thing (Fletcher v. Peck, 6 Cranch [10 U.S.] 87, 136. Hart and Sachs, Legal Process, 147–148 [1958]). This liberty is no right at all if it is not accompanied by freedom not to contract. The corollary is that, before one may secure redress in our courts because another has failed to honor a promise, it must appear that the promisee assented to the obligation in question.

It also follows that, before the power of law can be invoked to enforce a promise, it must be sufficiently certain and specific so that what was promised can be ascertained. Otherwise, a court, in intervening, would be imposing its own conception of what the parties should or might have undertaken, rather than confining itself to the implementation of a bargain to which they have mutually committed themselves. Thus, definiteness as to material matters is of the very essence in contract law. Impenetrable vagueness and uncertainty will not do * * *.

Dictated by these principles, it is rightfully well settled in the common law of contracts in this State that a mere agreement to agree, in which a material term is left for future negotiations, is unenforceable. . . . This is especially true of the amount to be paid for the sale or lease of real property * * *. The rule applies all the more, and not the less, when, as here, the extraordinary remedy of specific performance is sought * * *.

This is not to say that the requirement for definiteness in the case before us now could only have been met by explicit expression of the rent to be paid. The concern is with substance, not form. It certainly would have sufficed, for instance, if a methodology for determining the rent was to be found within the four corners of the lease, for a rent so arrived at would have been the end product of agreement between the parties themselves. Nor would the agreement have failed for indefiniteness because it invited recourse to an objective extrinsic event, condition or standard on which the amount was made to depend. All of these, *inter alia,* would have come within the embrace of the maxim that what can be made certain is certain (9 Coke, 47a). * * *

But the renewal clause here in fact contains no such ingredients. Its unrevealing, unamplified language speaks to no more than "annual rentals to be agreed upon." Its simple words leave no room for legal construction or resolution of ambiguity. Neither tenant nor landlord is bound to any formula. There is not so much as a hint at a commitment to be bound by the "fair market rental value" which the tenant's expert reported or the "reasonable rent" the Appellate Division would impose, much less any definition of either. Nowhere is there an inkling that either of the parties directly or indirectly assented, upon accepting the clause, to subordinate the figure on which it ultimately would insist, to one fixed judicially, as the Appellate Division decreed be done, or, for that matter, by an arbitrator or other third party.

Finally in this context, we note that the tenant's reliance on *May Metropolitan Corp. v. May Oil Burner Corp.*, 290 N.Y. 260 is misplaced. There the parties had executed a franchise agreement for the sale of oil burners. The contract provided for annual renewal, at which time each year's sales quota was "to be mutually agreed upon". In holding that the defendant's motion for summary judgment should have been denied, the court indicated that the plaintiff should be given an opportunity to establish that a series of annual renewals had ripened into a course of dealing from which it might be possible to give meaning to an otherwise uncertain term. This decision, in the more fluid sales setting in which it occurred, may be seen as a precursor to the subsequently enacted Uniform Commercial Code's treatment of open terms in contracts for the sale of goods (see Uniform Commercial Code, § 1–205, subd. [1]; § 2–204, subd. [3]; see, also, Restatement, Contracts 2d, § 249). As the tenant candidly concedes, the code, by its very terms, is limited to the sale of goods. The *May* case is therefore not applicable to real estate contracts. Stability is a hallmark of the law controlling such transactions * * *.

For all these reasons, the order of the Appellate Division should be reversed, with costs, and the orders of the Supreme Court, Suffolk County, reinstated. The certified question, therefore, should be answered in the negative. As to the plaintiff's appeal, since that party was not aggrieved by the order of the Appellate Division, the appeal should be dismissed (CPLR 5511), without costs.

■ MEYER, JUDGE (concurring). While I concur in the result because the facts of this case do not fit the rule of *May Metropolitan Corp. v. May Oil Burner Corp.*, 290 N.Y. 260, I cannot concur in the majority's rejection of that case as necessarily inapplicable to litigation concerning leases. That the setting of that case was commercial and that its principle is now incorporated in a statute (the Uniform Commercial Code) which by its terms is not applicable to real estate is irrelevant to the question whether the principle can be applied in real estate cases.

As we recognized in *Farrell Lines v. City of New York*, 30 N.Y.2d 76, 82, quoting from *A.Z.A. Realty Corp. v. Harrigan's Cafe*, 185 N.Y.S. 212, 217: "An agreement of lease possesses no peculiar sanctity requiring the application of rules of construction different from those applicable to an ordinary contract." To the extent that the majority opinion can be read as holding that no course of dealing between the parties to a lease could make a clause providing for renewal at a rental "to be agreed upon" enforceable I do not concur.

■ JASEN, JUDGE (dissenting in part). While I recognize that the traditional rule is that a provision for renewal of a lease must be "certain" in order to render it binding and enforceable, in my view the better rule would be that if the tenant can establish its entitlement to renewal under the lease, the mere presence of a provision calling for renewal at "rentals to be agreed upon" should not prevent judicial intervention to fix rent at a reasonable rate in order to avoid a forfeiture. Therefore, I would affirm the order of the Appellate Division for the reasons stated in the opinion of Justice Leon D. Lazer at the Appellate Division.

NOTES

The *Schumacher* doctrine still prevails in New York, particularly in real estate transactions. As one court put it: "If an agreement is not reasonably certain in its material terms, there can be no legally enforceable contract. The price and terms of payment are essential elements in a contract for the sale of real property. . . . Where an element of the contemplated contract, such as price, is unsettled and left to future negotiations, the agreement is unenforceable under the statute of frauds." Pino v. Harnischfeger, 840 N.Y.S.2d 504, 507–08 (2007). On the other hand, another court suggested that if the "*Schumacher* doctrine is applied with a heavy hand it may defeat the reasonable expectations of the parties in entering into the contract . . . therefore, striking down a contract as indefinite . . . is at best a last resort." Best Way Realty v. Perlegis, 831 N.Y.S.2d 351 (N.Y.Sup. 2006).

James "Buster" Douglas hitting Mike Tyson

PROBLEM: THE CASE OF THE LEGAL BOUT

James "Buster" Douglas and his manager John Johnson, entered into a boxing promotion agreement on December 31, 1988 (the "Promotional Agreement" or "Agreement"), with Don King Productions, Inc. (DKP). The Promotional Agreement provided for payment of $25,000 to Douglas in return for DKP's exclusive right to promote his professional boxing bouts for three years. The Agreement provided that this term would be automatically extended in the event Douglas was recognized as world champion, "to cover the entire period you are world champion and a period of two years following" loss of the title. Compensation for individual bouts was to be agreed upon, with the negotiated terms to be set forth in the individually-negotiated bout agreements. The Promotional Agreement specified a floor level of compensation of $50,000 plus $10,000 in training expenses for Douglas' fights, except that in the case of a title bout or defense, no floor was provided, but such a purse was to be "negotiated and mutually agreed upon."

During the first year of the agreement, Douglas participated in three bouts arranged by DKP, the last of which was the heavyweight championship bout held in Tokyo on February 10, 1990, in which Douglas "shocked the world" by defeating Mike Tyson. In accordance with the Promotional Agreement, Douglas and Johnson had entered into a bout agreement on August 14, 1989 (the "Bout Agreement") pursuant to which Douglas was to be paid $1.3 million. This Bout Agreement granted DKP an "exclusive option: to promote [Douglas'] next three bouts following the Tokyo bout, such option to be exercised by giving notice to Douglas no later than 30 days after the Tokyo bout." The Bout Agreement provided that Douglas would receive $1 million for each of these bouts, except that in the event Douglas was the winner of the Tokyo bout, subsequent bouts would be subject to negotiation of a higher purse.

DKP sought to exercise its option and hold a rematch between Douglas and Tyson in June, 1990 at Trump Plaza in Atlantic City. However, on

February 21, 1990, Douglas and Johnson executed a contract with Golden Nugget, Inc. and The Mirage Casino-Hotel (collectively, "Mirage") to stage Douglas' next two fights at the Mirage in Las Vegas, with a guaranteed minimum purse of $25 million each. This contract was made contingent upon Douglas obtaining a release from DKP or a judicial declaration that the Promotional and Bout Agreements were void or unenforceable.

In seeking such a declaration, Douglas and Johnson contend that they are not bound by the Promotional and Bout Agreements because those agreements "are indefinite as to the essential term of consideration." Assuming New York law controls, how would you expect a court to rule? See Don King Productions, Inc. v. Douglas (James "Buster"), 742 F.Supp. 741 (S.D.N.Y. 1990).

Joseph Hoffman v. Red Owl Stores, Inc.

Supreme Court of Wisconsin, 1965.
26 Wis.2d 683.

The complaint alleged that Lukowitz, as agent for Red Owl, represented to and agreed with plaintiffs that Red Owl would build a store building in Chilton and stock it with merchandise for Hoffman to operate in return for which plaintiffs were to put up and invest a total sum of $18,000; that in reliance upon the above mentioned agreement and representations plaintiffs sold their bakery building and business and their grocery store and business; also in reliance on the agreement and representations Hoffman purchased the building site in Chilton and rented a residence for himself and his family in Chilton; plaintiffs' action in reliance on the representations and agreement disrupted their personal and business life; plaintiffs lost substantial amounts of income and expended large sums of money as expenses. Plaintiffs demanded recovery of damages for the breach of defendants' representations and agreements.

The action was tried to a court and jury. The facts hereafter stated are taken from the evidence adduced at the trial. Where there was a conflict in the evidence the version favorable to plaintiffs has been accepted since the verdict rendered was in favor of plaintiffs.

Hoffman assisted by his wife operated a bakery at Wautoma from 1956 until sale of the building late in 1961. The building was owned in joint tenancy by him and his wife. Red Owl is a Minnesota corporation having its home office at Hopkins, Minnesota. It owns and operates a number of grocery supermarket stores and also extends franchises to agency stores which are owned by individuals, partnerships and corporations. Lukowitz resides at Green Bay and since September, 1960, has been divisional manager for Red Owl in a territory comprising Upper Michigan and most of Wisconsin in charge of 84 stores. Prior to September, 1960, he was district manager having charge of approximately 20 stores.

In November, 1959, Hoffman was desirous of expanding his operations by establishing a grocery store and contacted a Red Owl representative by the name of Jansen, now deceased. Numerous conversations were had in 1960 with the idea of establishing a Red Owl franchise store in Wautoma. In September, 1960, Lukowitz succeeded Jansen as Red Owl's representative in the negotiations. Hoffman mentioned that $18,000 was all the capital he had available to invest and he was repeatedly assured that this would be sufficient to set him up in business as a Red Owl store. About Christmas time, 1960, Hoffman thought it would be a good idea if he bought a small grocery store in Wautoma and operated it in order that he gain experience in the grocery business prior to operating a Red Owl store in some larger community. On February 6, 1961, on the advice of Lukowitz and Sykes, who had succeeded Lukowitz as Red Owl's district manager, Hoffman bought the inventory and fixtures of a small grocery store in Wautoma and leased the building in which it was operated.

After three months of operating this Wautoma store, the Red Owl representatives came in and took inventory and checked the operations and found the store was operating at a profit. Lukowitz advised Hoffman to sell the store to his manager, and assured him that Red Owl would find a larger store for him elsewhere. Acting on this advice and assurance, Hoffman sold the fixtures and inventory to his manager on June 6, 1961. Hoffman was reluctant to sell at that time because it meant losing the summer tourist business, but he sold on the assurance that he would be operating in a new location by fall and that he must sell this store if he wanted a bigger one. Before selling, Hoffman told the Red Owl representatives that he had $18,000 for "getting set up in business" and they assured him that there would be no problems in establishing him in a bigger operation. The makeup of the $18,000 was not discussed; it was understood plaintiff's father-in-law would furnish part of it. By June, 1961, the towns for the new grocery store had been narrowed down to two, Kewaunee and Chilton. In Kewaunee, Red Owl had an option on a building site. In Chilton, Red Owl had nothing under option, but it did select a site to which plaintiff obtained an option at Red Owl's suggestion. The option stipulated a purchase price of $6,000 with $1,000 to be paid on election to purchase and the balance to be paid within 30 days. On Lukowitz's assurance that everything was all set plaintiff paid $1,000 down on the lot on September 15th.

On September 27, 1961, plaintiff met at Chilton with Lukowitz and Mr. Reymund and Mr. Carlson from the home office who prepared a projected financial statement. Part of the funds plaintiffs were to supply as their investment in the venture were to be obtained by sale of their Wautoma bakery building.

On the basis of this meeting Lukowitz assured Hoffman: " * * * [E]verything is ready to go. Get your money together and we are set." Shortly after this meeting Lukowitz told plaintiffs that they would have to sell their bakery business and bakery building, and that their retaining this property was the only "hitch" in the entire plan. On November 6, 1961, plaintiffs sold their bakery building for $10,000. Hoffman was to retain the bakery equipment as he contemplated using it to operate a bakery in connection with his Red Owl store. After sale of the bakery Hoffman obtained employment on the night shift at an Appleton bakery.

* * *

On November 22nd or 23rd, Lukowitz and plaintiffs met in Minneapolis with Red Owl's credit manager to confer on Hoffman's financial standing and on financing the agency. Another projected financial statement was there drawn up entitled, "Proposed Financing For An Agency Store." This showed Hoffman contributing $24,100 of cash capital of which only $4,600 was to be cash possessed by plaintiffs. Eight thousand was to be procured as a loan from a Chilton bank secured by a mortgage on the bakery fixtures, $7,500 was to be obtained on a 5 percent loan from the father-in-law, and $4,000 was to be obtained by sale of the lot to the lessor at a profit.

A week or two after the Minneapolis meeting Lukowitz showed Hoffman a telegram from the home office to the effect that if plaintiff could get another $2,000 for promotional purposes the deal could go through for $26,000. Hoffman stated he would have to find out if he could get another $2,000. He met with his father-in-law, who agreed to put $13,000 into the business provided he could come into the business as a partner. Lukowitz told Hoffman the partnership arrangement "sounds fine" and that Hoffman should not go into the partnership arrangement with the "front office." On January 16, 1962, the Red Owl credit manager teletyped Lukowitz that the father-in-law would have to sign an agreement that the $13,000 was either a gift or a loan subordinate to all general creditors and that he would prepare the agreement. On January 31, 1962, Lukowitz teletyped the home office that the father-in-law would sign one or other of the agreements. However, Hoffman testified that it was not until the final meeting some time between January 26th and February 2nd, 1962, that he was told that his father-in-law was expected to sign an agreement that the $13,000 he was advancing was to be an outright gift. No mention was then made by the Red Owl representatives of the alternative of the father-in-law signing a subordination agreement. At this meeting the Red Owl agents presented Hoffman with the following projected financial statement:

"Capital required in operation:

"Cash	$ 5,000.00
"Merchandise	20,000.00
"Bakery	18,000.00
"Fixtures	17,500.00

"Promotional Funds		1,500.00
"TOTAL:		$62,000.00
"Source of funds:		
"Red Owl 7-day terms		$ 5,000.00
"Red Owl Fixture contract (Term 5 years)		14,000.00
"Bank loans (Term 9 years Union State Bank of Chilton		8,000.00
"(Secured by Bakery Equipment)		
"Other loans (Term No-pay) No interest Father-in-law		13,000.00
"(Secured by None)		
"(Secured by Mortgage on		2,000.00
"Wautoma Bakery Bldg.)		
"Resale of land		6,000.00
"Equity Capital:	$ 5,000.00 -Cash	
"Amount owner has	17,500.00 -Bakery	
Equip. to invest:		22,500.00
"TOTAL:		$70,500.00"

Hoffman interpreted the above statement to require of plaintiffs a total of $34,000 cash made up of $13,000 gift from his father-in-law, $2,000 on mortgage, $8,000 on Chilton bank loan, $5,000 in cash from plaintiff, and $6,000 on the resale of the Chilton lot. Red Owl claims $18,000 is the total of the unborrowed or unencumbered cash, that is, $13,000 from the father-in-law and $5,000 cash from Hoffman himself. Hoffman informed Red Owl he could not go along with this proposal, and particularly objected to the requirement that his father-in-law sign an agreement that his $13,000 advancement was an absolute gift. This terminated the negotiations between the parties.

[At the conclusion of the trial, the trial court determined that Hoffman and Red Owl had engaged in negotiations looking toward the establishment of a franchise and that they had not reached final agreement on all details at the time Hoffman withdrew from negotiations. The jury, in response to specific questions, found that Red Owl represented that if Hoffman met certain conditions he would get a franchise, that Hoffman reasonably relied upon these representations and that Hoffman had fulfilled all conditions required at the time negotiations terminated. The jury also determined that $3,265 would reasonably compensate Hoffman for the sale of the bakery building, taking up the Chilton option and various moving and rental expenses and that $16,735 should be awarded for the sale of the Wautoma store fixtures and inventory. After appropriate motions, the trial court vacated the finding concerning the Wautoma store, affirmed the other findings and ordered a new trial on the Wautoma damage issue. Red Owl appealed the awarding of any compensation and Hoffman appealed the order for a new trial. After stating the issues to be (1) whether the facts support a cause of action for promissory estoppel and (2) whether the jury's findings with respect to damages were sustained by the evidence, the court, speaking through Chief Justice Currie, endorsed and adopted for Wisconsin "the doctrine of promissory estoppel . . . which supplies a needed tool which courts may employ in a proper case to prevent injustice."]

* * *

Applicability of Doctrine to Facts of this Case

The record here discloses a number of promises and assurances given to Hoffman by Lukowitz in behalf of Red Owl upon which plaintiffs relied and acted upon to their detriment.

Foremost were the promises that for the sum of $18,000 Red Owl would establish Hoffman in a store. After Hoffman had sold his grocery store and paid the $1,000 on the Chilton lot, the $18,000 figure was changed to $24,100. Then in November, 1961, Hoffman was assured that if the $24,100 figure were increased by $2,000 the deal would go through. Hoffman was induced to sell his grocery store fixtures and inventory in June, 1961, on the promise that he would be in his new store by fall. In November, plaintiffs sold their bakery building on the urging of defendants and on the assurance that this was the last step necessary to have the deal with Red Owl go through.

We determine that there was ample evidence to sustain the answers of the jury to the questions of the verdict with respect to the promissory representations made by Red Owl, Hoffman's reliance thereon in the exercise of ordinary care, and his fulfillment of the conditions required of him by the terms of the negotiations had with Red Owl.

There remains for consideration the question of law raised by defendants that agreement was never reached on essential factors necessary to establish a contract between Hoffman and Red Owl. Among these were the size, cost, design, and layout of the store building; and the terms of the lease with respect to rent, maintenance, renewal, and purchase options. This poses the question of whether the promise necessary to sustain a cause of action for promissory estoppel must embrace all essential details of a proposed transaction between promisor and promisee so as to be the equivalent of an offer that would result in a binding contract between the parties if the promisee were to accept the same.

Originally the doctrine of promissory estoppel was invoked as a substitute for consideration rendering a gratuitous promise enforceable as a contract. See Williston, Contracts (1st ed.), p. 307, sec. 139. In other words, the acts of reliance by the promisee to his detriment provided a substitute for consideration. If promissory estoppel were to be limited to only those situations where the promise giving rise to the cause of action must be so definite with respect to all details that a contract would result were the promise supported by consideration, then the defendants' instant promises to Hoffman would not meet this test. However, sec. 90 of Restatement, 1 Contracts, does not impose the requirement that the promise giving rise to the cause of action must be so comprehensive in scope as to meet the requirements of an offer that would ripen into a contract if accepted by the promisee. Rather the conditions imposed are:

(1) Was the promise one which the promisor should reasonably expect to induce action or forbearance of a definite and substantial character on the part of the promisee?

(2) Did the promise induce such action or forbearance?

(3) Can injustice be avoided only by enforcement of the promise?

We deem it would be a mistake to regard an action grounded on promissory estoppel as the equivalent of a breach of contract action. As Dean Boyer points out, it is desirable that fluidity in the application of the concept be maintained. 98 University of Pennsylvania Law Review (1950), 459, at page 497. While the first two of the above listed three requirements of promissory estoppel present issues of fact which ordinarily will be resolved by a jury, the third requirement, that the remedy can only be invoked where necessary to avoid injustice, is one that involves a policy decision by the court. Such a policy decision necessarily embraces an element of discretion.

We conclude that injustice would result here if plaintiffs were not granted some relief because of the failure of defendants to keep their promises which induced plaintiffs to act to their detriment.

* * *

Since the evidence does not sustain the large award of damages arising from the sale of the Wautoma grocery business, the trial court properly ordered a new trial on this issue.

Order affirmed. Because of the cross-appeal, plaintiffs shall be limited to taxing but two-thirds of their costs.

**A typical mid-western Red Owl store of the period.
Remodeled Red Owl Store**

NOTES

(1)   In a portion of the opinion we have omitted, the Wisconsin Supreme Court considered whether Hoffman could "recover for any loss of future profits for the summer months following the sale" of the Wautoma grocery store. Reasoning that "[w]here damages are awarded in promissory estoppel instead of specifically enforcing the promisor's promise, they should be only such as in the opinion of the court is necessary to prevent injustice," the court held that those lost profits were not recoverable. The court emphasized that the purchase of the Wautoma store was meant as a temporary experiment, and concluded: "Justice does not require that the damages awarded [Hoffman], because of selling these assets at the behest of [Red Owl], should exceed any actual loss sustained measured by the difference between the sales price and the fair market value."

Recall the Massachusetts Supreme Court's discussion in *Sullivan v. O'Connor* about whether doctors should be held liable in contract for breach of promise to their patients, and its analysis of the appropriate remedy for breach of such promise. How are the two questions related? In the case of *Red Owl*, does or should it matter in deciding the liability question whether damages are measured by Hoffman's expectation interest or by his reliance interest?

(2)   *Red Owl* might be called the high water mark in the development of promissory estoppel and has received considerable attention in the literature. See, e.g., Barnett & Becker, Promissory Estoppel, Contract Formalities, and Misrepresentation, 15 Hofstra L. Rev. 443, 485–495 (1987); Feinman, *Critical Approaches to Contract Law,* 30 UCLA L. Rev. 829, 852–57 (1983). The case represents the farthest advance of contract, i.e., promise-based theory, into policing conduct in pre-contract negotiations. Neither Rev.

UCC § 1–304 nor Restatement (Second) § 205 impose a duty of good faith in the negotiation of a contract, although protection may be achieved through such doctrines as unconscionability and through remedies in restitution or tort. See Restatement (Second) § 205, Comment c. The remedy under *Red Owl* and similar cases has usually been limited to protection of the reliance interest. Profits that would have been earned if the contract had been formed have not been allowed. See, e.g., Wheeler v. White, 398 S.W.2d 93 (Tex. 1965); Restatement (Second) § 90, Comment d. But for a case awarding lost profits where liability was based upon promissory estoppel, see Walters v. Marathon Oil Co., 642 F.2d 1098 (7th Cir. 1981).

(3) In 1984, Ashton Springer, a Broadway producer, sought to produce a musical based on the life of Mahalia Jackson. Springer wanted Aretha Franklin for the title role, and Franklin was receptive to the idea. The parties negotiated over a period of several months, working out many details, including a handsome compensation package. Drafts of a proposed agreement were circulated, but a final draft was never executed. Meanwhile, Springer, on the basis of Franklin's assurance, incurred substantial expenses making other arrangements for the production. After negotiations broke down, Springer sued. The court found that the parties were not to be bound contractually until the draft agreement was signed, but proceeded to base recovery on promissory estoppel. Elvin Associates v. Franklin, 735 F.Supp. 1177 (S.D.N.Y. 1990). "It is difficult to imagine a more fitting case for applying [promissory estoppel]. Although for her own business purposes Franklin insisted that the formal contract be with the corporate entity through which her services were to be 'furnished,' in the real world the agreement was with her, and we find that she had unequivocally and intentionally committed herself to appear in the production long before the day on which it was intended that the finished agreement with her corporation would be signed. * * * [U]nder the circumstances * * * it would be unconscionable not to compensate [plaintiff] for the losses he incurred through his entirely justified reliance on Franklin's oral promises." Id. at 1182.

(4) Robert Scott and Alan Schwartz have argued that in fact *Red Owl* is an outlier.

> In order to evaluate systematically how contemporary American courts treat reliance investments made before the parties have written a complete contract, we analyzed a sample of 105 cases litigated between 1999 and 2003 that directly presented the issue of recovery for precontractual reliance. Our goal was to disaggregate the precontractual reliance cases by uncovering the commercial patterns that generated litigation and identifying the legal consequences courts attached to those patterns.

> * * *

> [T]he sample shows that courts consistently have denied recovery for precontractual reliance unless the parties, by agreeing on something significant, indicated their intention to be bound. The key issues thus involve reliance behavior that follows the

conclusion of an agreement that is incomplete in some respects. Litigation results because the agreement does not represent the final stage in the contracting process. Central to these cases, therefore, are the following questions: First, what criteria do courts use to decide whether parties have made an enforceable preliminary agreement? Second, what does enforcement entail?

Alan Schwartz and Robert E. Scott, *Precontractual Liability and Preliminary Agreements*, 120 Harv. L. Rev. 661, 671–73 (2007). For answers to these questions, see the following Comment and case.

Comment: Preliminary Agreements

In an important 1987 article, Allan Farnsworth identified a line of cases that distinguished agreements to agree, such as that at issue in *Schumacher*, from agreements to negotiate.

Agreement to Negotiate

1. *Nature of the Regime.*—The regime under an agreement to negotiate is similar to that under an agreement with open terms in that it imposes on the parties a duty to negotiate. But it differs in that should negotiations fail, there will be no agreement. Under an agreement with open terms, the parties negotiate with the knowledge that if they fail to reach agreement on the open terms, they will be bound by an ultimate agreement containing the terms on which they have agreed together with those terms that a court will supply. Under an agreement to negotiate, the parties negotiate with the knowledge that if they fail to reach ultimate agreement they will not be bound. The parties to an agreement to negotiate do, however, undertake a general obligation of fair dealings in their negotiations. This often happens when there is a division of responsibility between managers and lawyers.

What is the remedy for breach of such an obligation? The situation here differs from that under the regimes of ultimate agreement and agreement with open terms. There, the obligation of fair dealing is but one obligation that is part of a larger agreement, so that a breach of that obligation might, in an extreme case, be treated as a total breach of that agreement with a resulting claim to damages based on lost expectation. Here, there is no larger agreement and so no possibility of a claim for lost expectations under such an agreement. Furthermore, here there is no way of knowing what the terms of the ultimate agreement would have been, or even whether the parties would have arrived at an ultimate agreement, so there is no possibility of a claim for lost expectation under such an agreement.

Because of the uncertain scope of an undertaking to negotiate, a court cannot be expected to order its specific performance, though a court might enjoin a party that had undertaken to negotiate exclusively from negotiating with others. Usually the injured party's recourse is to refuse to negotiate and to seek monetary relief. In some situations recovery measured by the restitution interest will be appropriate, as under the regime of negotiation. Generally, however, recovery will be measured by the reliance interest. Reliance damages are particularly appropriate here since a party generally perceives an agreement to negotiate as protecting just that interest, should the other pull out of the negotiations. And the case for counting lost opportunities is strengthened because, in contrast to the regime of negotiation, here the parties explicitly subject themselves to the regime by undertaking to negotiate.

2. *Enforceability of the Agreement.*—Courts have often balked at enforcing agreements to negotiate even if the parties have made it clear that they want to subject themselves to this regime. * * *

In the United States, where many of the leading cases involve mergers and acquisitions, courts have been of two minds. Some have, like English courts, refused to accord parties the freedom to impose this regime on themselves. Federal courts applying New York law have been the most prominent in refusing on the ground of indefiniteness to enforce explicit agreements to negotiate, whether expressed in terms of "good faith" [or "best efforts."]

Other courts have been willing to give effect to the parties' expressed intention. *Itek Corp. v. Chicago Aerial Industries* [248 A.2d 625 (Del. 1968)] is the leading example. During negotiations for the purchase of Itek's assets by California Aerial Industries (CAI), the parties executed a "letter of intent" confirming the terms of the sale and providing that they "shall make every reasonable effort to agree upon and have prepared . . . a contract providing for the foregoing purchase . . . embodying the above terms and such other terms and conditions as the parties shall agree upon." [Id. at 627.] Itek later consented to a modification of the agreed terms, but CAI, evidently having received a more favorable offer, telegraphed that it would not go ahead with the transaction. Itek sued CAI, which had summary judgment. The Supreme Court of Delaware reversed, reasoning that the letter in which "the parties obligated themselves to 'make every reasonable effort' to agree upon a formal contract . . . obligated each side to attempt in good faith to reach final and formal agreement." [Id. at 629] It was error to grant summary judgment because there was evidence that in order to accept a more favorable offer, "CAI willfully failed to negotiate in good faith and to make 'every reasonable effort' to agree upon a formal contract, as it was required to do." [Id.]

This view has gained a substantial following. A few courts have gone to considerable lengths in spelling out an obligation to negotiate from unclear language and suggestive circumstances. There have even been intimations that such an obligation might be implied in law in the absence of any actual assent by the parties. One may doubt the wisdom of those courts that have strained to find an agreement to negotiate in the absence of a clear indication of assent, for if carried to an extreme this would enable courts to impose a general obligation of fair dealing. But there is no compelling justification for those decisions that, in line with the English precedents, have refused to give effect to the intention of the parties when they have made an explicit agreement to negotiate.

E. Allan Farnsworth, *Precontractual Liability and Preliminary Agreements: Fair Dealing and Failed Negotiations*, 87 Colum. L. Rev. 217, 263–67 (1987).

The same year, a federal District Court decided what has become a leading case in this line, *Teachers Insurance and Annuity Association of America v. Tribune Company*, 670 F.Supp. 491 (S.D.N.Y. 1987). The case concerned the failed negotiations for a 14-year, $76 million dollar loan from Teachers Insurance and Annuity Association to the Tribune Company. It turned on the legal effect of a commitment letter, prepared by Teachers Insurance and signed by Tribune.

The letter, mailed on September 22, included a two page Summary of Proposed Terms drawn from the term sheet included in Tribune's Offering Circular and the ensuing conversations. Teacher's term sheet covered all the basic economic terms of a loan. Neither the term sheet nor the covering commitment letter made reference to offset accounting. The letter stated that the agreement was "contingent upon the preparation, execution and delivery of documents . . . in form and substance satisfactory to TIAA and to TIAA's special counsel . . . ," and that the transaction documents would contain the "usual and customary" representations and warranties, closing conditions, other covenants, and events of default "as we and our special counsel may deem reasonably necessary to accomplish this transaction." It concluded by inviting Tribune to "evidence acceptance of the conditions of this letter by having it executed below by a duly authorized officer . . . ," and finally stated:

> Upon receipt by TIAA of an accepted counterpart of this letter, our agreement to purchase from you and your agreement to issue sell and deliver to us . . . the captioned securities, shall become a binding agreement between us.

When Tribune received this commitment letter, the "binding agreement" language caused serious concern to its lawyers. Tribune's outside counsel, Alfred Spada of the firm of Reuben & Proctor, advised Smith [Tribune's VP and Treasurer] not to sign a letter containing "binding agreement" language. But, having been turned down by five other institutions, Smith did not want to risk losing Teacher's commitment. He made no comment orally or in writing to Teachers questioning the "binding agreement" language. He executed and returned the letter on behalf of Tribune Company adding the notation that it was subject to certain modifications outlined in his accompanying letter. In the accompanying letter Smith wrote,

> [O]ur acceptance and agreement is subject to approval by the Company's Board of Directors and the preparation and execution of legal documentation satisfactory to the Company.

Smith's acceptance letter made no mention of offset accounting.

Id. at 494. The parties were not able to come to agreement on the remaining terms, and Teachers Insurance sued. Teachers Insurance argued that Tribune withdrew from negotiations because of a sharp decline in interest rates, and because of a change in regulatory practices with respect to offset accounting, an accounting practice that Tribune wanted to use in the deal. Tribune maintained that its commitment had always been contingent on the availability of offset accounting, that the change in interest rates had nothing to do with its refusal to consummate the transaction, and that the reservation regarding the Board of Directors' right of approval rendered the commitment letter nonbinding.

Judge Pierre Leval set out the following test to determine whether the parties had entered into a binding agreement to negotiate:

> In seeking to determine whether such a preliminary commitment should be considered binding, a court's task is, once again, to determine the intentions of the parties at the time of their entry into the understanding, as well as their manifestations to one another by which the understanding was reached. Courts must be particularly careful to avoid imposing liability where binding obligation was not intended. There is a strong presumption against finding binding obligation in agreements which include open terms, call for future approvals and expressly anticipate future preparation and execution of contract documents. Nonetheless, if that is what the parties intended, courts should not frustrate their achieving that

objective or disappoint legitimately bargained contract expectations.

Id. at 499. Leval identified five factors to determine whether the parties intended the commitment letter to be binding: (1) the language of agreement, (2) the context of negotiations, with particular attention to the parties' motives, (3) the number of open terms, (4) the extent to which the agreement had been performed, and (5) usage of trade. Id. at 499–503. Based on highly detailed factual findings about the transaction and the surrounding circumstances, Leval found that the commitment letter "represented a binding preliminary commitment and obligated both sides to seek to conclude a final loan agreement upon the agreed terms by negotiating in good faith to resolve such additional terms as are customary in such agreements." Id. at 499.

Schwartz and Scott have criticized the fact-specific approach in *Teachers Insurance*.

> This modern approach provides too little normative guidance. The cases endorse a multifactor analysis that invokes the language of the agreement; the existence, number, and character of open terms; the extent of any reliance investments or partial performance; and the customary practice regarding formalities. The court is to consider, in addition, the context of the negotiations resulting in the preliminary agreement. Any list of relevant factors confines a court's discretion to some extent, but it leaves the decision process largely obscure when, as with these factors, courts fail to attach weights to the factors or to specify the relationship among them. For example, focusing on the number of terms that remain open is unhelpful: courts cannot easily determine whether many terms or only a few remain to be negotiated.

Alan Schwartz and Robert E. Scott, *Precontractual Liability and Preliminary Agreements*, 120 Harv. L. Rev. 661, 675–76 (2007). Does the next case provide a better approach?

Empro Manufacturing Co., Inc. v. Ball-Co Manufacturing, Inc.

United States Court of Appeals, Seventh Circuit, 1989.
870 F.2d 423.

■ EASTERBROOK, CIRCUIT JUDGE. We have a pattern common in commercial life. Two firms reach concord on the general terms of their transaction. They sign a document, captioned "agreement in principle" or "letter of intent", memorializing these terms but anticipating further negotiations and decisions—an appraisal of the assets, the clearing of a title, the list is endless. One of these terms proves divisive, and the deal collapses. The party that perceives itself the loser then claims that the preliminary document has legal force independent of the definitive contract. Ours is such a dispute.

Ball-Co Manufacturing, a maker of specialty valve components, floated its assets on the market. Empro Manufacturing showed interest. After some preliminary negotiations, Empro sent Ball-Co a three-page "letter of intent" to purchase the assets of Ball-Co and S.B. Leasing, a partnership holding title to the land under Ball-Co's plant. Empro proposed a price of $2.4 million, with $650,000 to be paid on closing and a 10-year promissory note for the remainder, the note to be secured by the "inventory and equipment of Ball-Co." The letter stated "[t]he general terms and conditions of such proposal (which will be subject to and incorporated in a formal, definitive Asset Purchase Agreement signed by both parties)". Just in case Ball-Co might suppose that Empro had committed itself to buy the assets, paragraph four of the letter stated that "Empro's purchase shall be subject to the satisfaction of certain conditions precedent to closing including, but not limited to" the definitive Asset Purchase Agreement and, among five other conditions, "[t]he approval of the shareholders and board of directors of Empro".

Although Empro left itself escape hatches, as things turned out Ball-Co was the one who balked. The parties signed the letter of intent in November 1987 and negotiated through March 1988 about many terms. Security for the note proved to be the sticking point. Ball-Co wanted a security interest in the land under the plant; Empro refused to yield.

When Empro learned that Ball-Co was negotiating with someone else, it filed this diversity suit. Contending that the letter of intent obliges Ball-Co to sell only to it, Empro asked for a temporary restraining order. The district judge set the case for a prompt hearing and, after getting a look at the letter of intent, dismissed the complaint under Fed.R.Civ.P. 12(b)(6) for failure to state a claim on which relief may be granted. Relying on *Interway, Inc. v. Alagna*, 85 Ill.App.3d 1094 (1st Dist. 1980), the district judge concluded that the statement, appearing twice in the letter, that the agreement is "subject to" the execution of a definitive contract meant that the letter has no independent force.

Empro insists on appeal that the binding effect of a document depends on the parties' intent, which means that the case may not be dismissed—for Empro says that the parties intended to be bound, a factual issue. Empro treats "intent to be bound" as a matter of the parties' states of mind, but if intent were wholly subjective there would be no parol evidence rule, no contract case could be decided without a jury trial, and no one could know the effect of a commercial transaction until years after the documents were inked. That would be a devastating blow to business. Contract law gives effect to the parties' wishes, but they must express these openly. Put differently, "intent" in contract law is objective rather than subjective—a point *Interway* makes by holding that as a matter of law parties who make their pact "subject to" a later definitive agreement have manifested an (objective) intent not to be bound, which under the parol evidence rule becomes the definitive intent even if one party later says that the true intent was different. As the Supreme Court of Illinois said in *Schek v. Chicago Transit Authority*, 42 Ill.2d 362, 364 (1969), "intent must be determined solely from the language used when no ambiguity in its terms exists". . . . Parties may decide for themselves whether the results of preliminary negotiations bind them, . . . but they do this through their words.

Because letters of intent are written without the care that will be lavished on the definitive agreement, it may be a bit much to put dispositive weight on "subject to" in every case, and we do not read *Interway* as giving these the status of magic words. They might have been used carelessly, and if the full agreement showed that the formal contract was to be nothing but a memorial of an agreement already reached, the letter of intent would be enforceable. Borg-Warner Corp. v. Anchor Coupling Co., 16 Ill.2d 234 (1958). Conversely, Empro cannot claim comfort from the fact that the letter of intent does not contain a flat disclaimer, such as the one in *Feldman* pronouncing that the letter creates no obligations at all. The text and structure of the letter—the objective manifestations of intent—might show that the parties agreed to bind themselves to some extent immediately. *Borg-Warner* is such a case. One party issued an option, which called itself "firm and binding"; the other party accepted; the court found this a binding contract even though some terms remained open. After all, an option to purchase is nothing if not binding in advance of the definitive contract. The parties to *Borg-Warner* conceded that the option and acceptance usually would bind; the only argument in the case concerned whether the open terms were so important that a contract could not arise even if the parties wished to be bound, a subject that divided the court. See 156 N.E.2d at 930–36 (Schaefer, J., dissenting).

A canvass of the terms of the letter Empro sent does not assist it, however. "Subject to" a definitive agreement appears twice. The letter also recites, twice, that it contains the "general terms and conditions", implying that each side retained the right to make (and stand on) additional demands. Empro insulated itself from binding effect by listing, among the conditions to which the deal was "subject", the "approval of the shareholders and board of directors of Empro". The board could veto a deal negotiated by the firm's agents for a reason such as the belief that Ball-Co had been offered too much (otherwise the officers, not the board, would be the firm's final decisionmakers, yet state law vests major decisions in the board). The shareholders could decline to give their assent for any reason (such as distrust of new business ventures) and could not even be required to look at the documents, let alone consider the merits of the deal. See Earl Sneed, *The Shareholder May Vote As He Pleases: Theory and Fact,* 22 U. Pittsburgh L. Rev. 23, 31–36, 40–42 (1960) (collecting cases). Empro even took care to require the return of its $5,000 in earnest money "without set off, in the event this transaction is not closed", although the seller usually gets to keep the earnest money if the buyer changes its mind. So Empro made clear that it was free to walk.

Neither the text nor the structure of the letter suggests that it was to be a one-sided commitment, an option in Empro's favor binding only Ball-Co. From the beginning Ball-Co assumed that it could negotiate terms in addition to, or different from, those in the letter of intent. The cover letter from Ball-Co's lawyer returning the signed letter of intent to Empro stated that the "terms and conditions are generally acceptable" but that "some clarifications are needed in Paragraph 3(c) (last sentence)", the provision concerning Ball-Co's security interest. "Some clarifications are needed" is an ominous noise in a negotiation, foreboding many a stalemate. Although we do not know what "clarifications" counsel had in mind, the specifics are not important. It is enough that even on signing the letter of intent Ball-Co proposed to change the bargain, conduct consistent with the purport of the letter's text and structure.

The shoals that wrecked this deal are common hazards in business negotiations. Letters of intent and agreements in principle often, and here, do no more than set the stage for negotiations on details. Sometimes the details can be ironed out; sometimes they can't. Illinois, . . . allows parties to approach agreement in stages, without fear that by reaching a preliminary understanding they have bargained away their privilege to disagree on the specifics. Approaching agreement by stages is a valuable method of doing business. So long as Illinois preserves the availability of this device, a federal court in a diversity case must send the disappointed party home empty-handed. Empro claims that it is entitled at least to recover its "reliance expenditures", but the only expenditures it has identified are those normally associated with pre-contractual efforts: its complaint mentions the expenses "in negotiating with defendants, in investigating and reviewing defendants' business, and in preparing to acquire defendants' business." Outlays of this sort cannot bind the other side any more than paying an expert to tell you whether the painting at the auction is a genuine Rembrandt compels the auctioneer to accept your bid.

NOTES

(1) Both *Red Owl* and the *Teachers Insurance-Empro* line of cases deal with liability during negotiations before a final contract has been concluded. What are the differences between the approaches in each? While *Red Owl* has had a limited impact, the *Teachers Insurance-Empro* line is today the dominant approach to precontractual liability. Is it the better one?

(2) The decisions in *Teachers Insurance*, described in the above Comment, and *Empro* agree on this: In order to determine whether a preliminary agreement is binding, a court should ask whether the parties objectively intended it to be so. But Judge Leval's approach to determining

the parties' intent in *Teachers Insurance* is very different from Judge Easterbrook's approach in *Empro*. What are the pros and cons of each?

Judge Easterbrook observes that " 'intent' in contract law is objective rather than subjective," from which he concludes: "Parties may decide for themselves whether the results of preliminary negotiations bind them, . . . but they do this through their words." Does the objective theory of contract mean that a court should look only at the parties' words to determine their intent?

(3)   Gregory Klass has analyzed the problem of identifying the parties' intent in terms of default and altering rules. Klass argues for a no-enforcement default for preliminary agreements with an express altering rule.

> Parties entering into a preliminary agreement are best positioned to know whether they will benefit from legal liability than is a court during later litigation. By conditioning legal liability on an express contemporary statement of that preference, the law can give the parties a reason to share that information with the court and each other—to generate simple and reliable evidence of their intent. Imposing this minimal ex ante cost on parties who want legal liability obviates the need for [an] expensive ex post judicial inquiry into efficiency.

> What of the other variables relevant to determining the best rule for interpreting the parties' contractual intent? A few facts bear mention. Most preliminary agreement cases involve sophisticated parties represented by lawyers in negotiations over high-value transactions. The negotiations are typically lengthy, complex, and relatively adversarial. And in most cases that reach the courts, the preliminary agreement has been reduced to writing. Taken together, these facts suggest that it is generally clear to the parties that they are moving toward a legally enforceable agreement. What remains uncertain is whether they have yet reached one.

> These observations suggest that neither the out-of-pocket costs of an express opt-out nor party error costs should be especially worrisome. Particularly where the preliminary agreement is already in writing, the costs of adding words to the effect of "This is a legally enforceable agreement" are minimal. And if the parties are sophisticated players represented by counsel, there is little chance they will forget to add those words or expect enforcement in their absence. Nor are the relational costs particularly high. In most preliminary agreements, the scope of legal liability is among the issues under discussion. Legal enforcement is already on the table. This diminishes the relational costs of having to say precisely when enforcement shall attach.

Gregory Klass, *Intent to Contract*, 95 Va. L. Rev. 1437, 1486–87 (2009).

Frank Dixon v. Wells Fargo Bank, N.A.

United States District Court, District of Massachusetts, 2011.
798 F.Supp. 2d 336.

■ YOUNG, DISTRICT JUDGE.

I.   INTRODUCTION

Frank and Deana Dixon (collectively "the Dixons") bring this cause of action against Wells Fargo Bank, N.A. ("Wells Fargo"), seeking (1) an injunction prohibiting Wells Fargo from foreclosing on their home; (2) specific performance of an oral agreement to enter into a loan modification; and (3) damages. Wells Fargo, having removed the action from state court, now moves for dismissal of the Dixons' complaint under Fed.R.Civ.P. 12(b)(6), arguing that the allegations are insufficient to invoke the doctrine of promissory estoppel.

* * *

The Dixons reside at their home in Scituate, Plymouth County, Massachusetts. Wells Fargo is a corporation doing business in the Commonwealth of Massachusetts. Wells Fargo alleges that it is the holder of a mortgage on the Dixons' home.

On or about June 8, 2009, the Dixons orally agreed with Wells Fargo to take the steps necessary to enter into a mortgage loan modification. As part of this agreement, Wells Fargo instructed the Dixons to stop making payments on their loan. It was contemplated that the unpaid payments would be added to the note as modified. In addition, Wells Fargo requested certain financial information, which the Dixons promptly supplied.

Notwithstanding the Dixons' diligent efforts and reliance on Wells Fargo's promise, Wells Fargo has failed, and effectively refused, to abide by the oral agreement to modify the existing mortgage loan.

On or about December 8, 2010, the Dixons received notice from the Massachusetts Land Court that Wells Fargo was proceeding with a foreclosure on their home. The return date on the order of notice in the Land Court was January 10, 2011, and so the Dixons sought a temporary restraining order in the Superior Court to prevent the loss of their home.

The Dixons state that, on information and belief, the fair market value of their home is in excess of the mortgage loan balance and any arrearage.

II.   ANALYSIS

* * *

B.   Promissory Estoppel

The gravamen of the Dixons' complaint is that Wells Fargo promised to engage in negotiations to modify their loan, provided that they took certain "steps necessary to enter into a mortgage modification." On the basis of Wells Fargo's representation, the Dixons stopped making payments on their loan and submitted the requested financial information—only to learn subsequently that the bank had initiated foreclosure proceedings against them. They contend that Wells Fargo ought have anticipated their compliance with the terms of its promise to consider them for a loan modification. Not only was it reasonable that they would rely on the promise, but also their reliance left them considerably worse off, for by entering into default they became vulnerable to foreclosure.

The question whether these allegations are sufficient to state a claim for promissory estoppel requires a close look at the doctrine's evolution in the law of Massachusetts. In *Loranger Const. Corp. v. E.F. Hauserman Co.,* 376 Mass. 757 (1978), the Supreme Judicial Court recognized the enforceability of a promise on the basis of detrimental reliance, but declined to "use the expression 'promissory estoppel,' since it tends to confusion rather than clarity." Id. at 760–61. The court reasoned that "[w]hen a promise is enforceable in whole or in part by virtue of reliance, it is a 'contract,' and it is enforceable pursuant to a 'traditional contract theory' antedating the modern doctrine of consideration." Id. at 761. Since *Loranger,* the court has adhered to its view that "an action based on reliance is equivalent to a contract action, and the party bringing such an action must prove all the necessary elements of a contract other than consideration." Rhode Island Hosp. Trust Nat'l Bank v. Varadian, 419 Mass. 841, 850 (1995).

"An essential element in the pleading and proof of a contract claim is, of course, the 'promise' sought to be enforced." Kiely v. Raytheon Co., 914 F.Supp. 708, 712 (D.Mass. 1996) (O'Toole, J.). Thus, even where detrimental reliance acts as a substitute for consideration, the promise on which a claim for promissory estoppel is based must be interchangeable with an offer "in the sense of 'commitment.'" Cataldo Ambulance Serv., Inc. v. City of Chelsea, 426 Mass. 383, 386 n. 6 (1998). * * *

In addition to demonstrating a firm commitment, the putative promise, like any offer, must be sufficiently "definite and certain in its terms" to be enforceable. Moore v. La-Z-Boy, Inc., 639 F.Supp.2d 136, 142 (D.Mass. 2009) (Stearns, J.) (quoting Kiely, 914 F.Supp. at 712). "[I]f an essential element is reserved for the future agreement of both parties, as a general rule, the promise can give rise to no legal obligation until such future agreement." 1 Richard A. Lord, Williston on Contracts § 4:29 (4th ed. 1990). * * *

The longstanding reluctance of courts to enforce open-ended "agreements to agree" reflects a belief that, unless a "fall-back standard" exists to supply the missing terms, there is no way to know what ultimate agreement, if any, would have resulted. E. Allan Farnsworth, *Precontractual Liability and Preliminary Agreements: Fair Dealing and Failed Negotiations,* 87 Colum. L. Rev. 217, 255–56 (1987). * * *

Moreover, parties ought be allowed to step away unscathed if they are unable to reach a deal. Cf. R.W. Int'l Corp. v. Welch Food, Inc., 13 F.3d 478, 484–85 (1st Cir. 1994). To impose rights and duties at "the stage of 'imperfect negotiation,'" *Lafayette Place Assocs.*, 427 Mass. at 517, would be to interfere with the liberty to contract—or not to contract. Thus, the concern is that if a court were to order specific performance of an agreement to agree, where the material terms of the final agreement were left open by the parties, not only would there be "little, if anything, to enforce," Lambert v. Fleet Nat'l Bank, 449 Mass. 119, 123 (2007), but also future negotiations would be chilled. * * *

Wells Fargo would have this Court end its inquiry here. The complaint plainly alleges that the parties had an "agreement to enter into a loan modification agreement," but as matter of law "[a]n agreement to reach an agreement is a contradiction in terms and imposes no obligations on the parties thereto." Rosenfield, 290 Mass. at 217. As such, the complaint would appear to fail to state a claim.

During the course of opposing Wells Fargo's motion to dismiss, however, the Dixons have made clear that they do not seek specific performance of a promised loan modification. They admit that there was no guarantee of a modification by Wells Fargo, only a verbal commitment to determine their eligibility for a modification if they followed the bank's prescribed steps. Thus, the Dixons' request that Wells Fargo be held to its promise to consider them for a loan modification is not a covert attempt to bind the bank to a final agreement it had not contemplated. There is no risk that this Court, were it to uphold the promissory estoppel claim, would be "trapping" Wells Fargo into a vague, indefinite, and unintended loan modification masquerading as an agreement to agree. Teachers Ins. & Annuity Ass'n of Am. v. Tribune Co., 670 F.Supp. 491, 497 (S.D.N.Y. 1987).

Furthermore, because the parties had not yet begun to negotiate the terms of a modification, the Court questions whether Wells Fargo's promise ought even be characterized as a preliminary agreement to agree. Instead, it more closely resembles an "agreement to negotiate." See Farnsworth, supra at 263–69 . . .

To be sure, Massachusetts courts have tended to treat agreements to negotiate as variants of open-ended agreements to agree. The view that "[a]n agreement to negotiate does not create a binding contract," *Sax,* 639 F.Supp.2d at 171, again reflects a concern that a promise of further negotiations is too indefinite, too undefined in scope, to be enforceable. See Bell, 359 Mass. at 763 (finding an agreement to negotiate "for as long as the parties agreed" to be "void for vagueness"). This is particularly true where the parties have not specified the terms on which they will continue negotiating. See Farnsworth, supra at 264. Conventional wisdom holds that courts ought not "strain[ ] to find an agreement to negotiate in the absence of a clear indication of assent" by the parties to a governing standard of conduct, e.g., "good faith" or "best efforts," Id. at 266–67, because "there is no meaningful content in a general duty to negotiate, standing alone," Steven J. Burton & Eric G. Anderson, Contractual Good Faith § 8.4.2, at 361 (1995). . . . As with open-ended agreements to agree, judicial enforcement of vague agreements to negotiate would risk imposing on parties contractual obligations they had not taken on themselves.

In this case, Wells Fargo and the Dixons had not yet contemplated the terms of a loan modification, but they had contemplated negotiations. Their failure to elaborate on the boundaries of that duty to negotiate, however, would seem to militate against enforcement of it. Yet, Wells Fargo made a specific promise to consider the Dixons' eligibility for a loan modification if they defaulted on their payments and submitted certain financial information. * * * Importantly, it was not a promise made in exchange for a bargained-for legal detriment, as there was no bargain between the parties; rather, the legal detriment that the Dixons claim to have suffered was a direct consequence of their reliance on Wells Fargo's promise. . . . Under the theory of promissory estoppel, "[a] negotiating party may not with impunity break a promise made during negotiations if the other party has relied on it." Farnsworth, supra at 236.

Promissory estoppel has developed into "an attempt by the courts to keep remedies abreast of increased moral consciousness of honesty and fair representations in all business dealings." Peoples Nat'l Bank of Little Rock v. Linebarger Constr. Co., 219 Ark. 11 (1951). While it began as "a substitute for (or the equivalent of) consideration" in the context of an otherwise binding contract, Perillo, supra § 6.1, at 218, "promissory estoppel has come to be a doctrine employed to rescue failing contracts where the cause of the failure is not related to consideration," Id. § 6.3, at 229. It now "provides a remedy for many promises or agreements that fail the test of enforceability under many traditional contract doctrines," Id. § 6.1, at 218, but whose enforcement is "necessary to avoid injustice," Restatement (Second) of Contracts § 90, comment (b).

Admittedly, the courts of Massachusetts have yet to formally embrace promissory estoppel as more than a consideration substitute. See, e.g., Varadian, 419 Mass. at 850. Nonetheless, without equivocation, they have adopted section 90 of the Restatement (Second) of Contracts. Nowhere in the comments to section 90 nor in section 2 of the Restatement, which defines the word "promise," is there an explicit "requirement that the promise giving rise to the cause of action must be so comprehensive in scope as to meet the requirements of an offer that would ripen into a contract if accepted by the promisee." Hoffman v. Red Owl Stores, Inc., 26 Wis.2d 683 (1965).

* * *

Massachusetts's continued insistence that a promise be definite—at least to a degree likely not met in the present case—is arguably in tension with its adoption of the Restatement's more relaxed standard. This tension is not irreconcilable, however. Tracing the development of promissory estoppel through the case law reveals a willingness on courts' part to enforce even an indefinite promise made during preliminary negotiations where the facts suggest that the promisor's words or conduct were designed to take advantage of the promisee. The promisor need not have acted fraudulently, deceitfully, or in bad faith. McLearn v. Hill, 276 Mass. 519, 524–25 (1931). Rather, "[f]acts falling short of these elements may constitute conduct contrary to general principles of fair dealing and to the good conscience which ought to actuate individuals and which it is the design of courts to enforce." Id. at 524. * * * Typically, where the Massachusetts courts have applied the doctrine of promissory estoppel to enforce an otherwise unenforceable promise, "there has been a pattern of conduct by one side which has dangled the other side on a string." Pappas Indus. Parks, Inc. v. Psarros, 24 Mass.App.Ct. 596, 598 (1987).

* * *

In the present case, Wells Fargo convinced the Dixons that to be eligible for a loan modification they had to default on their payments, and it was only because they relied on this representation and stopped making their payments that Wells Fargo was able to initiate foreclosure proceedings. While there is no allegation that its promise was dishonest, Wells Fargo distinctly gained the upper hand by inducing the Dixons to open themselves up to a foreclosure action. In specifically telling the Dixons that stopping their payments and submitting financial information were the "steps necessary to enter into a mortgage modification," Wells Fargo not only should have known that the Dixons would take these steps believing their fulfillment would lead to a loan modification, but also must have intended that the Dixons do so. The bank's promise to consider them for a loan modification if they took those steps necessarily "involved as matter of fair dealing an undertaking on [its] part not to [foreclose] based upon facts coming into existence solely from" the making of its promise. McLearn, 276 Mass. at 523–24. Wells Fargo's decision to foreclose without warning was unseemly conduct at best. In the opinion of this Court, such conduct presents "an identifiable occasion for applying the principle of promissory estoppel." Greenstein, 19 Mass.App.Ct. at 356–57.

* * *

There remains the concern that, by imposing precontractual liability for specific promises made to induce reliance during preliminary negotiations, courts will restrict parties' freedom to negotiate by reading in a duty to bargain in good faith not recognized at common law. While this concern does not fall on deaf ears, it can be effectively minimized by limiting the promisee's recovery to his or her reliance expenditures. * * *

Moreover, because the promisee's reliance must be not only reasonable and foreseeable but also detrimental, such that injustice would result if the promise were not binding, "the doctrine renders the motive of the promisor a secondary consideration in deciding whether to award relief." Metzger and Phillips, supra at 888. Although some sense that the promisor has acted to take unfair advantage of the promisee is typically what prompts courts to enforce promises made during preliminary negotiations, the foreseeability and injustice requirements of section 90 render inquiry into whether the promisor acted in bad faith unnecessary, which, in turn, obviates any need to impose a precontractual duty to negotiate in good faith.[1] * * *

Finally, contrary to the conventional wisdom that precontractual liability unduly restricts the freedom to negotiate, a default rule allowing recovery but limiting it to reliance expenditures may in fact promote more efficient bargaining. . . . "[T]he existence of liability does not chill the parties' incentives to enter negotiation," [Lucian Arye Bebchuk & Omri Ben-Shahar, *Precontractual Reliance*, 30 J. Legal Stud. 423, 457 (2001)], as "[r]ational parties will pursue efficient projects and abandon inefficient projects. . . . disagree[ing], if at all, over whether a party should be compensated for a reliance expense," [Alan Schwartz & Robert E. Scott, *Precontractual Liability and Preliminary Agreements*, 120 Harv. L. Rev. 661, 667 (2007)]. It is only under the current regime of either no liability or strict liability that negotiating parties are discouraged from making early and "exploratory investments that are a necessary precondition to the later writing of efficient final contracts." Id. at 690; see Bebchuk & Ben-Shahar, supra at 457; [Avery Katz, *When Should an Offer Stick? The Economics of Promissory Estoppel in Preliminary Negotiations*, 105 Yale L.J. 1249, 1267 (1996)]. * * *

This Court, therefore, holds that the complaint states a claim for promissory estoppel: Wells Fargo promised to engage in negotiating a loan modification if the Dixons defaulted on their payments and provided certain financial information, and they did so in reasonable reliance on that promise, only to learn that the bank had taken advantage of their default status by initiating foreclosure proceedings. Assuming they can prove these allegations by a preponderance of the evidence, their damages appropriately will be confined to the value of their expenditures in reliance on Wells Fargo's promise.[2]

---

[1]   * * * The Dixons have not alleged that a duty of good faith governed their negotiations with Wells Fargo over a loan modification, and thus this Court need not address the issue. The fact that the parties already were bound to the special contractual relationship of mortgagor-mortgagee, however, lends support to today's conclusion that Wells Fargo's conduct, at a minimum, was "shabby and doubtless would not be followed by conscientious mortgagees." Williams, 417 Mass. at 385.

[2]   The Court need not decide at this early juncture what the measurement of the Dixons' reliance damages would be were they to prevail at trial. A balancing of the equities, however, would seem to weigh in favor of limiting recovery to the detriment sustained. As the Texas Supreme Court said in *Wheeler v. White,* 398 S.W.2d 93 (Tex. 1966):

> Where the promisee has failed to bind the promisor to a legally sufficient contract, but where the promisee has acted in reliance upon a promise to his detriment, the promisee is to be allowed to recover no more than reliance damages measured by the detriment sustained. Since the promisee in such cases is partially responsible for his failure to bind the promisor to a legally sufficient contract, it is reasonable to conclude that all that is required to achieve justice is to put the promisee in the position he would have been had he not acted in reliance upon the promise.

Without question, this is an uncertain result. But the "type of life-situation" out of which the Dixons' case arises—a devastating and nationwide foreclosure crisis that is crippling entire communities—cannot be ignored. Karl N. Llewellyn, Jurisprudence Realism in Theory and Practice 219–20 (1962). Distressed homeowners are turning to the courts in droves, hoping for relief for what they perceive as misconduct by their mortgage lenders. Many of these cases are factually similar, if not identical to, the Dixons' case. Yet, with the notable exception of three Massachusetts federal district court cases,[77] virtually no other court has upheld a claim for promissory estoppel premised on such facts.[78]

To the extent that today's result is an anomaly, this Court has sought to explain its decision "openly and with respect for precedent, not by sleight of hand." David L. Shapiro, *Mr. Justice Rehnquist: A Preliminary View,* 90 Harv. L.Rev. 293, 355 (1976); see Robert E. Keeton, Keeton on Judging in the American Legal System 5 (1999) ("Judging is choice. . . . Judicial choice, at its best, is reasoned choice, candidly explained."). It is the view of this Court that "[f]oreclosure is a powerful act with significant consequences," Ibanez, 458 Mass. at 655, 941 N.E.2d 40 (Cordy, J., concurring), and where a bank has obtained the opportunity to foreclose by representing an intention to do the exact opposite—i.e., to negotiate a loan modification that would give the homeowner the right to stay in his or her home—the doctrine of promissory estoppel is properly invoked under Massachusetts law to provide at least reliance-based recover.

NOTES

(1) *A New* Red Owl*?* When *Red Owl* was decided, some thought that its application of promissory estoppel in the precontractual setting might point the way toward a more general obligation of good faith in precontractual negotiations. That potential was not realized, and *Red Owl* has not had a broad effect. Does *Dixon v. Wells Fargo* show that *Red Owl* is not dead yet?

Judge Young was clearly aware of the *Teachers Insurance-Empro* line of preliminary agreement cases. Why did he not apply them to this case?

Id. at 97. The Dixons allege that, before Wells Fargo's promise induced them to stop making their payments, they were not in default. Returning their loan to non-default status would put them back in their previous position. By the same reasoning, they would be required to resume their mortgage payments in their original amount, with the missed payments being added into the loan balance amortized over the life of the loan. If the Dixons were unable to resume their payments, Wells Fargo could then proceed in foreclosure. But all of this remains speculative; assuming liability, the evidence presented at trial will no doubt illuminate the proper measure of reliance damages that the Court ought fashion. See Fuller and Perdue, supra at 53 (commenting that, "when courts work on the periphery of existing doctrine," it becomes "obvious" that the "the process of 'measuring' and 'determining' [damages] is really a part of the process of creating them").

[77] [The court listed: In re Bank of Am. Home Affordable Modification Program (HAMP) Contract Litig., 2011 WL 2637222 (D.Mass. 2011); Bosque v. Wells Fargo Bank, N.A., 762 F.Supp.2d 342, 351 (D.Mass. 2011); Durmic v. J.P. Morgan Chase Bank, NA, 2010 WL 4825632 (D.Mass. 2010).—Eds.]

[78] [The court listed twenty-five cases decided between 2009 and 2011 reaching the opposite result.—Eds.]

Could he have? Why did Judge Young turn instead to the doctrine of promissory estoppel?

(2)   *Federal Courts and State Law.* Much contemporary law regarding precontractual liability has been developed by federal courts applying state law. *Teachers Insurance* is especially noteworthy in this regard. Judge Leval's decision was innovative in at least two respects. First, it ran against the spirit of *Schumacher* and other previous New York cases, which sharply limited precontractual liability. Second, the broad-ranging factual inquiry into the parties' intent differed from the tendency of New York courts to put greater weight on the written word. See, e.g., IDT Corp. v. Tyco Group, 13 N.Y.3d 209, 214 (2009) ("A contract is to be construed in accordance with the parties' intent, which is generally discerned from the four corners of the document itself."). Judge Young addressed the issue in a footnote in *Dixon v. Wells Fargo*:

> A federal district court may certify a question for decision by the Supreme Judicial Court "if there are involved in any proceeding before it questions of law of [the Commonwealth of Massachusetts] which may be determinative of the cause then pending in the certifying court and as to which it appears to the certifying court there is no controlling precedent in the decisions of [the Supreme Judicial Court]." Mass. S.J.C. Rule 1:03, § 1 (2010). This Court has elected not to certify the question whether the Dixons' allegations are sufficient to state a claim for promissory estoppel, but acknowledges that, with the exception of *McLearn*, 276 Mass. 519, the cases relied on herein are primarily those of the Massachusetts Appeals and Superior Courts, not the Supreme Judicial Court. . . . Should either Wells Fargo or the Dixons wish to bring a motion for certification, this Court will entertain it. Mass. S.J.C. Rule 1:03, § 2 (a question may certified "upon the motion of any party to the cause").

Not every state permits certification of a question by a federal court. In states that do, should federal courts be more willing to certify undecided questions of state law? See Guido Calabresi, *Federal and State Courts: Restoring a Working Balance*, 78 N.Y.U. L. Rev. 1293 (2003).

(E) ACCORD AND SATISFACTION

Vincent J. Douthwright v. Northeast Corridor Foundations

Appellate Court of Connecticut, 2002.
72 Conn. App. 319.

■ PETERS, J. This case concerns the applicability of the doctrine of accord and satisfaction, a common-law doctrine that, for negotiable instruments such as checks, has now been codified in article three of the Uniform

Commercial Code, General Statutes § 42a–3–311.[2] Invoking this doctrine, a debtor maintains that its belated payment of the principal amount of a debt discharged it of any obligation to pay interest on the debt because its payment check was accompanied by a letter stating that the check was tendered as an accord and satisfaction.

A precondition of an enforceable accord and satisfaction is that the tender of payment occur in the context of a good faith dispute about the amount of an unpaid debt. This was the rule at common law and, for checks, it is now the rule of § 42a–3–311(a). . . . The trial court found that the debtor did not prove that it had satisfied this precondition because, at the time when the check was sent, the amount of the debt, both as to principal and as to interest, was liquidated and therefore not subject to a good faith dispute.

In its appeal, the debtor contests the validity of the court's refusal to apply the doctrine of accord and satisfaction. We, however, are persuaded that the court's decision is amply supported by the facts of record at trial. Accordingly, we affirm the judgment of the court ordering the payment of interest for the time between the accrual of the debt and the acceptance of the check.

On February 13, 2001, the plaintiff Vincent Douthwright filed a motion pursuant to General Statutes § 52–195c for a default judgment arising out of the failure of the named defendant et al. to pay their full share of an oral settlement agreement. The agreement entitled the plaintiff to recover $3.2 million as settlement of his tort action to recover damages for serious injuries that he received when concrete pylons rolled off a truck and crushed his leg. Pursuant to the agreement, the defendants were obligated to pay $2.5 million of that sum. Although the defendants' primary insurer had paid $1 million, the defendants' excess insurance carrier had refused to pay the remaining $1.5 million.

The plaintiff sought a default judgment in the amount of $1.5 million plus interest. In response, on March 13, 2001, the defendants denied that the settlement agreement imposed upon them an obligation to pay the plaintiff immediately.

---

[2]   General Statutes § 42a–3–311 provides in relevant part: "Accord and satisfaction by use of instrument. (a) If a person against whom a claim is asserted proves that (i) that person in good faith tendered an instrument to the claimant as full satisfaction of the claim, (ii) the amount of the claim was unliquidated or subject to a bona fide dispute, and (iii) the claimant obtained payment of the instrument, the following subsections apply.

"(b) Unless subsection (c) applies, the claim is discharged if the person against whom the claim is asserted proves that the instrument or an accompanying written communication contained a conspicuous statement to the effect that the instrument was tendered as full satisfaction of the claim. . . .

"(d) A claim is discharged if the person against whom the claim is asserted proves that within a reasonable time before collection of the instrument was initiated, the claimant, or an agent of the claimant having direct responsibility with respect to the disputed obligation, knew that the instrument was tendered in full satisfaction of the claim."

On March 26, 2001, the parties appeared before the court for an initial hearing on the motion for default.[6] Subsequent to that hearing, the defendants sent the plaintiff a check in the amount of $1.5 million, accompanied by a cover letter. The amount of the check represented the principal sum then due. It did not include any payment of interest.

On May 8, 2001, after an evidentiary hearing, the trial court rendered judgment in favor of the plaintiff in the amount of $40,931.45. That amount represented interest at the rate of 12 percent per year as specified in § 52–195c(d) for the period between February 2, 2001, when the defendants' payment became due, and April 25, 2001, when the defendants paid $1.5 million.

As the basis for its judgment, the court made two central findings of fact. One concerned the terms of the settlement agreement and the other concerned the date when the defendants' obligation to pay became due. The defendants' appeal challenges the propriety of these findings as they relate to their claim of accord and satisfaction.

Our review of the defendants' appeal is governed by the well established principle that an appellate court will overturn the factual findings of a trial court only if these findings are clearly erroneous. * * *

To support their claim of accord and satisfaction, the defendants maintain that the trial court improperly determined the terms of an oral settlement agreement to which the parties had agreed on December 15, 2000. The court found that the agreement unconditionally entitled the plaintiff to receive $3.2 million in full settlement of his claims against the defendants and New England Pipe Corporation. On an interim basis, the agreement allocated $2.5 million of this payment to the defendants. Further, the agreement provided that the ultimate allocation of payments between the defendants and New England Pipe Corporation would be decided by a subsequent arbitration. The court's final and most significant finding was that the settlement agreement entitled the plaintiff to immediate payment and that this payment was *not* conditioned on the execution of the contemplated arbitration agreement. The defendants disagree with the finding that the plaintiff should have been paid immediately.

The court based its finding on the testimony of all the participants in the settlement proceedings. The defendants' counsel testified that, at the time of the settlement negotiations, he had made it clear that the settlement was contingent upon the execution of the contemplated arbitration agreement between the defendants and New England Pipe Corporation. This testimony was flatly contradicted by the testimony of the other four attorneys who participated in the mediation that led to the settlement agreement. One of these attorneys was the mediator. The

---

[6]   At that time, the defendants indicated that they would issue a check to the plaintiff for $1.5 million. The plaintiff reasserted his right to interest on the delayed payment.

court expressly found that, even though the defendants' counsel believed his testimony to be accurate, the testimony was not credible.

* * *

Having determined that the settlement agreement entitled the plaintiff to immediate payment, the trial court found that the defendants' debt matured upon the plaintiff's delivery of the appropriate releases and the withdrawal of his complaint. See General Statutes § 52–195c(a). The plaintiff fulfilled his responsibilities on January 2, 2001. Accordingly, the defendants' debt became due and payable on February 2, 2001. The defendants' only challenge to this finding is their aforementioned contention that the settlement agreement was not unconditional. That claim we have already rejected.

The court's finding that the plaintiff was unconditionally entitled to payment on February 2, 2001 knocked out the underpinnings of the defendants' claim that their obligation to pay interest was discharged by their tender and payment of a check in the principal amount of their indebtedness.[8] In order to obtain such a discharge, the defendants bore the burden of proving not only that there was "a dispute" between the parties, but also that the amount of the plaintiff's claim was "unliquidated or subject to a bona fide dispute. . . ." General Statutes § 42a–3–311(a)(ii).

After February 2, 2001, there was no basis for a *good faith* dispute about the defendants' indebtedness to the plaintiff. Likewise, there was no basis for a *good faith* dispute about the amount of the defendants' indebtedness for interest. Section 52–195c unequivocally required the defendants to pay interest at the rate of 12 percent per year after February 2, 2001. Under these circumstances, the court found that the defendants' letter stating that the check was tendered as full satisfaction of its indebtedness had no legal effect.[9]

We are persuaded that the court's findings must be sustained. The defendants did not satisfy the burden of proof assigned to them by § 42a–3–311(a) or by the common law. We conclude, therefore, that the

---

[8] The check was accompanied by a letter, dated April 24, 2001, stating: "As you know, it is our position that any settlement of the above-referenced matter was expressly contingent upon the defendants reaching an agreement with respect to arbitration. We understand you disagree with that position and, as a result, seek interest on the settlement amount to be paid by my clients. We dispute that any interest is owing.

"Despite our dispute, we hereby enclose . . . [a] check . . . on behalf of defendants . . . in the amount of $1.5 million . . . in full and final settlement of the referenced matter."

The plaintiff's counsel responded . . . in a letter stating: "I received the check for Mr. and Mrs. Douthwright in the amount of $1,500,000 on Wednesday, April 25, 2001 by Federal Express delivery. While I cannot agree that this is a full and final settlement in view of the pending motion, I do thank you for sending the check at this time."

[9] General Statutes § 42a–3–311(b) further conditions a discharge on the debtor's proof of "a conspicuous statement to the effect that the instrument was tendered as full satisfaction" of the disputed debt. The court found that the letter sent by the defendant did not communicate its intent to seek discharge of its principal obligation as well as of its indebtedness for interest. Presumably, this failure of communication means that the requirements of subsection (b) were also not met.

defendants have not provided any sustainable basis for their argument that the trial court's judgment should be set aside. None of the court's findings of fact was clearly erroneous.

* * *

The judgment is affirmed.

NOTES

(1) In *County Fire Door Corp. v. C. F. Wooding Co.*, 202 Conn. 277, 281–82 (1987), Justice Ellen Peters found:

> When there is a good faith dispute about the existence of a debt or about the amount that is owed, the common law authorizes the debtor and the creditor to negotiate a contract of accord and satisfaction to settle the outstanding claim. Such a contract is often initiated by the debtor, who offers an accord by tendering a check as "payment in full" or "in full satisfaction." If the creditor knowingly cashes such a check, or otherwise exercises full dominion over it, the creditor is deemed to have assented to the offer of accord. Upon acceptance of the offer of accord, the creditor's receipt of the promised payment discharges the underlying debt and bars any further claim relating thereto, if the contract of accord is supported by consideration. * * *

> A contract of accord and satisfaction is sufficiently supported by consideration if it settles a monetary claim that is unliquidated in amount. . . . [A] claim is unliquidated when the debtor tenders payment in an amount that does not exceed that to which the creditor is concededly entitled. . . . Where the claim is unliquidated any sum, given and received in settlement of the dispute, is a sufficient consideration.

The court also noted that if the debtor offers "in good faith to settle an unliquidated debt by tendering, in full satisfaction, the payment of an amount less than that demanded" by the creditor, the creditor cannot "simultaneously cash such a check and disown the condition on which it had been tendered." Id. at 282–83. In short, the tender is an offer to settle that the offeree must accept in full or not at all.

(2) *Law Reform*. Before 1990, UCC § 1–207 provided:

> A party who with explicit reservation of rights performs or promises performance or assents to performance in a manner demanded or offered by the other party does not thereby prejudice the rights reserved. Such words as "without prejudice", "under protest" or the like are sufficient.

Some courts and commentators read this language as a modification of the common law rule. In essence, the reading was that the tender of a full payment check was an offer of "performance" by the debtor to which the creditor could assent without prejudice to any rights explicitly reserved. Thus, in the case of an unliquidated debt, if the debtor tendered a check for $10,000 in "full settlement" of the amount, and the creditor cashed the check with an explicit reservation of rights to sue for the claimed excess, there was no accord and satisfaction. Mixed with an interpretation of the UCC was a judicial concern for small creditors dealing with strong debtors who might be forced to take a lesser amount because the money was needed and litigation was expensive. See AFC Interiors v. DiCello, 46 Ohio St. 3d 1 (1989).

Other commentators and courts disagreed, including Chief Justice Peters, who in the *County Fire Door* decision interpreted UCC § 1–207 in a way that preserved the common law rule.

The 1990 amendments to Article 1 changed UCC § 1–207 (now codified as UCC § 1–308) to make clear that the reservation of rights does not apply to a payment made as an accord and satisfaction. Also, a new section, 3–311, was placed in Article 3 to deal with an accord and satisfaction when a negotiable instrument was involved:

> (a) If a person against whom a claim is asserted proves that (i) that person in good faith tendered an instrument to the claimant as full satisfaction of the claim, (ii) the amount of the claim was unliquidated or subject to a bona fide dispute, and (iii) the claimant obtained payment of the instrument, the following subsections apply.

> (b) Unless subsection (c) applies, the claim is discharged if the person against whom the claim is asserted proves that the instrument or an accompanying written communication contained a conspicuous statement to the effect that the instrument was tendered as full satisfaction of the claim.

> (c) Subject to subsection (d), a claim is not discharged under subsection (b) if either of the following applies:

>> (1) The claimant, if an organization, proves that (i) within a reasonable time before the tender, the claimant sent a conspicuous statement to the person against whom the claim is asserted that communications concerning disputed debts, including an instrument tendered as full satisfaction of a debt, are to be sent to a designated person, office, or place, and (ii) the instrument or accompanying communication was not received by that designated person, office, or place.

>> (2) The claimant, whether or not an organization, proves that within 90 days after payment of the instrument, the claimant tendered repayment of the amount of the instrument to the person against whom the claim is asserted. This paragraph does not apply if the claimant is an organization that sent a statement complying with paragraph (1)(i).

> (d) A claim is discharged if the person against whom the claim is asserted proves that within a reasonable time before collection of the instrument was initiated, the claimant, or an agent of the claimant having direct responsibility with respect to the disputed obligation, knew that the instrument was tendered in full satisfaction of the claim.

Some questions: (1) How does UCC § 3–311 differ from the common law of accord and satisfaction? (2) Under what circumstances would a full payment check cashed by the creditor not be an accord and satisfaction?

PROBLEM: MODIFICATION OR DISCHARGE OF DUTY TO PAY MONEY

(1)   LE leased a store from LR for 36 months at $2,000 per month to operate a small deli. After 18 months, a general recession had set in, and LE's business had dropped by 50%. LE came to LR and stated that due to the drop in business, she could not continue to lease the premises at the agreed rent. There was a risk that she would have to vacate the premises and declare bankruptcy. LR said, "Oh, don't do that. Surely we can work something out." LE then stated that she would pay LR $20,000 cash today in full settlement of the balance of the rent and would remain in the premises until the lease terminated. LR agreed and took the cash. The economy improved, and LE's business began to flourish. At the end of the lease, LR refused to renew and sued LE for $16,000, the alleged balance due on the rent. May LR recover?

(2)   Suppose, instead, that the lease terminated after the third year with LE owing $10,000 back rent. LE proposed to pay LR $5,000 cash in full settlement of the back rent, and LR took the money. Later, LR sued LE for $5,000. What result? Would it make any difference if LE had tendered and LR had cashed a check for $5,000 "in full payment of all of my indebtedness"?

(3)   If you represented LE in the two transactions above, how would you structure the deals to maximize the chances of enforcement?

3.   RECOVERY WITHOUT AGREEMENT: UNJUST ENRICHMENT (AND QUASI-CONTRACTS AND IMPLIED-IN-LAW CONTRACTS)

Howard E. Bailey v. Richard E. West

Supreme Court of Rhode Island, 1969.
Supra at 12.

Peter Kossian v. American National Insurance Co.

Court of Appeal, Fifth District, California, 1967.
254 Cal.App.2d 647.

■ STONE, ASSOCIATE JUSTICE. On February 19, 1964, fire destroyed a portion of the Bakersfield Inn, owned by one Reichert. At the time, the property was subject to a first deed of trust in which defendant was the beneficiary. Pursuant to the requirements of the deed of trust, defendant's interest in the property was protected by policies of fire insurance. On March 16, 1964, Reichert, as owner in possession, entered into a written contract with plaintiff whereby plaintiff agreed to clean up and remove the debris from the fire damaged portion of the Inn for the sum of $18,900. Defendant had no knowledge of the execution of the agreement between plaintiff and Reichert.

Plaintiff commenced work in the middle of March 1964, and completed it in early April. During the entire time work was in progress Reichert was in possession of the premises as owner, although defendant caused a notice of Reichert's default under the deed of trust to be filed four days after the contract for demolition was entered into between plaintiff and Reichert. The record does not reflect that plaintiff had actual knowledge of the notice of default until after the work was completed.

Some time after plaintiff had fully performed the contract, Reichert filed a petition in bankruptcy. The trustee in bankruptcy abandoned the premises comprising the Bakersfield Inn, together with any interest in the four fire insurance policies up to the amount of $424,000. Each policy contained a provision insuring against the cost of cleaning up and removing debris caused by fire damage.

Following abandonment of the policies by the trustee in bankruptcy, Reichert and his wife assigned their interest in them to defendant in accordance with the terms of the deed of trust. Defendant submitted proofs of loss, claiming a total of $160,000, including the sum of $18,000 as the estimated cost for removing and cleaning up debris. These claims were rejected by the carriers; negotiations followed; the compromise figure of $135,620 was agreed upon and this amount paid to defendant. We do not have an itemization of the adjusted claims of loss upon which the compromised loss settlement was made, so that the record is not clear as to what part of the $18,900 cost of debris removal defendant received. It is clear, however, that the insurance payment included at least a part of the cost of debris removal and demolition.

Defendant demonstrates, by a careful analysis of the facts, that there was no direct relationship between plaintiff and defendant in regard to either the work performed on the property after the fire or in relation to the fire insurance policies. The contract for debris removal was between plaintiff and Reichert, and defendant did not induce plaintiff, directly or indirectly, to enter into that contract. Plaintiff had no lien against the property resulting from his work, and if he had such a lien it would have been wiped out by defendant's foreclosure of its first deed of trust.

Had the circumstances been simply that defendant, by foreclosure, took the property improved by plaintiff's debris removal, there would be a benefit conferred upon defendant by plaintiff, but no unjust enrichment. (See Griffith Co. v. Hofues, 201 Cal.App.2d 502.) It is the additional fact that defendant made a claim to the insurance carriers for the value of work done by plaintiff that is the nub of the case.

Defendant argues that plaintiff was not a party to the insurance contracts, while defendant had a contract right to collect indemnity for losses resulting from the fire, including the debris removal cost. This contract right was embodied in the insurance policies. Defendant relies upon *Russell v. Williams*, 58 Cal.2d 487, 490, where it is said:

> 'It is a principle of long standing that a policy of fire insurance does not insure the property covered thereby, but is a personal contract indemnifying the insured against loss resulting from the destruction of or damage to his interest in that property. (Citations.) This principle gives rise to the supplemental rule that, in the absence of a special contract, the proceeds of a fire insurance policy are not a substitute for the property the loss of which is the subject of indemnity.'

Defendant says it made no agreement, express or implied, with plaintiff that it would pay for the debris removal or that any part of the insurance proceeds would be applied for that purpose. Therefore, conclude defendant, there being no privity of relationship between it and plaintiff, and no fraud or deceit alleged or proved, defendant has the right to the property benefited by plaintiff's work and labor expended in removing the debris and to the insurance payments as well.

Plaintiff makes no claim to the insurance 'fund' upon the ground he relied thereon similar to the reliance of a mechanic or materialman that forms the basis of an equitable claim to a building fund. . . He relies upon the basic premise that defendant should not be allowed to have the fruits of plaintiff's labor and also the money value of that labor. This, of course, is a simplified pronouncement of the doctrine of unjust enrichment, a theory which can, in some instances, have validity without privity of relationship. The most prevalent implied-in-fact contract recognized under the doctrine of unjust enrichment is predicated upon a relationship between the parties from which the court infers an intent. However, the doctrine also recognizes an obligation imposed by law regardless of the intent of the parties. In these instances there need be no relationship that gives substance to an implied intent basic to the 'contract' concept, rather the obligation is imposed because good conscience dictates that under the circumstances the person benefited should make reimbursement. . .

Plaintiff's claim does not rest upon a quasi contract implied in fact, but upon an equitable obligation imposed by law. It is true that defendant's right to the insurance payment was a contract right embodied in the policies of insurance, as explicated in *Russell v. Williams*, supra, 58 Cal.2d 487, nevertheless the indemnity payment was based in part upon a claim of loss that did not exist because plaintiff had already remedied the loss by his work for which he was not paid.

We are cited no California cases that are close aboard, and independent research reveals none. Lack of precedent applicable to the facts peculiar to this case is not surprising, however, as the authors of the Restatement recognize that the essential nature of equity cases concerned with problems of restitution makes definitive precedent unlikely. We are guided by the 'Underlying Principles' delineated in the Restatement on Restitution:

> 'The rules stated in the Restatement of this Subject depend for their validity upon certain basic assumptions in regard to what is required by justice in the various situations. In this Topic, these are stated in the form of principles. They cannot be stated as rules since either they are too indefinite to be of value in a specific case or, for historical or other reasons, they are not universally applied. They are distinguished from rules in that they are intended only as general guides for the conduct of the courts * * *.' (P. 11.)

The governing principle is expressed in the opening sentence of the Restatement on Restitution, as follows:

> 'The Restatement of this Subject deals with situations in which one person is accountable to another on the ground that otherwise he would unjustly benefit or the other would unjustly suffer loss.' (P. 1.)

The question, simply stated, is whether in a jurisdiction that recognizes the equitable doctrine of unjust enrichment one party should be indemnified twice for the same loss, once in labor and materials and again in money, to the detriment (forfeiture) of the party who furnished the labor and materials. We conclude that the doctrine of unjust enrichment is applicable to the facts of this case, and that plaintiff is entitled to reimbursement out of the insurance proceeds paid defendant for work done by plaintiff.

The facts concerning the amount of insurance recovered by defendant and the percentage of the total proof of loss attributable to plaintiff's work are not altogether clear, probably because this is a proceeding for summary judgment before trial of the action. In any event, it is clear that defendant, in addition to taking over the property which plaintiff cleared of debris, also received indemnity insurance payments covering at least part of the cost for clearing that property of debris. The amount can be made certain by a trial on the merits, and if it develops that defendant recovered only a part of the cost for debris removal, this fact does not preclude a partial recovery by plaintiff. We learn from the Restatement, page 611:

> 'Where a person is entitled to restitution from another because the other, without tortious conduct, has received a benefit, the measure of recovery for the benefit thus received is the value of what was received * * *.'

Thus, to the extent defendant received insurance for debris removal performed by plaintiff, plaintiff should recover. If defendant received less than the value of plaintiff's work, as defendant seems to contend, then plaintiff should recover Pro tanto.

The judgment is reversed.

NOTES

(1)   What explains the failure of the plaintiff's unjust enrichment claim in *Bailey v. West*? Why was the claim successful in *Kossian v. American Standard*?

(2)   Section 1 of the Restatement (Third) of Restitution and Unjust Enrichment, adopted by the American Law Institute in 2010, provides, "A person who is unjustly enriched at the expense of another is subject to liability in restitution." Restitution as a cause of action must be distinguished from restitution as a measure of damages. The cause of action defines when legal liability attaches; the measure of damages describes a type of remedy, which might be available for different causes of action. Our present concern is only restitution as a cause of action, sometimes termed "quasi-contract," "implied-in-law contract," "quantum meruit" or "unjust enrichment." The preferred terms today are "restitution" and "unjust enrichment." As one court has explained:

> [A] contract implied in law [or quasi-contract] is not a contract at all, but an obligation imposed by law for the purpose of bringing about justice and equity without reference to the intent or the agreement of the parties and, in some cases, in spite of an agreement between the parties. . . . It is a non-contractual obligation that is to be treated procedurally as if it were a contract, and is often referred to as quasi contract, unjust enrichment, implied in law contract or restitution. * * * [T]he essence of a contract implied in law lies in the fact that the defendant has received a benefit which it would be inequitable for him to retain.

Continental Forest Products, Inc. v. Chandler Supply Co., 95 Idaho 739, 743 (1974).

(3)   *When is Enrichment Unjust?* When is one person's enrichment at the expense of another unjust? While the action for quantum meruit originated in part in the courts of law, it has a strong equitable flavor, making it difficult to formulate a crisp rule. As the drafters of the Restatement (Third) of Restitution explain:

> It is by no means obvious, as a theoretical matter, how "unjust enrichment" should best be defined; whether it constitutes a rule of decision, a unifying theme, or something in between; or what role the principle would ideally play in our legal system.

§ 1 cmt. a. Thus whereas the contract Restatements are largely structured in terms the elements of the cause of action ("Capacity," "Mutual Assent," "Consideration," and so forth), the major chapters and subchapters of the Restatement (Third) of Restitution are structured to identify fact patterns, such as "Benefits Conferred by Mistake," "Defective Consent or Authority," "Emergency Intervention," and "Restitution for Wrongs." In this book, of course, we are primarily concerned with when restitution can fill the gap left by a failed contract.

Though it is difficult to formulate a simple rule for when restitution is justified, we can identify some important factors in the inquiry.

Assume party A has conferred a measurable benefit on party B. One question is whether A had a reasonable expectation of compensation. In *Bailey v. West*, the answer was "No." Bailey conferred a measurable benefit on West's horse by feeding and caring for it for over four months. But after West knew of the benefit, he refused to receive it by abandoning the horse. In such a case, Bailey could not reasonably expect compensation. The outcome might be different had Bailey been performing a duty imposed upon West by law, such as the duty of a parent to provide necessary medical care to a dependent child. See State, Division of Family Services v. Hollis, 639 S.W.2d 389 (Mo. Ct. App. 1982). But West had no legal duty to provide necessaries to his horse, dependent or not.

Another question is whether there was an opportunity for A to obtain B's consent before conferring the benefit. If A first obtains B's consent, then liability will likely be based on contract rather than unjust enrichment (unless the contract fails for other reasons). If A did not obtain B's consent, the question is whether there was a reasonable excuse for A's failure to do so.

> There is no liability in restitution for an unrequested benefit voluntarily conferred, unless the circumstances of the transaction justify the claimant's intervention in the absence of contract.

Restatement (Third) Restitution, § 2(3). Intervention in the absence of a contract is justified when contracting is impracticable. A classic illustration is medical exigencies, such as where aid is given to an unconscious patient who could not have consented to contract. In *Bailey v. West* those circumstances did not exist. The life or well being of the horse was not in jeopardy, and Bailey could easily have contacted West before performing services. Thus, Bailey's intervention was "officious" and West's enrichment, to the extent it existed, was not unjust.

(4) *What Measure of Recovery?* The point of an unjust enrichment award is to return a benefit conferred. Thus the most common measure of money damages is restitution—the value of the benefit conferred. When there has been the transfer of a thing, the remedy might involve restoration of the thing to the original owner. Where the benefit has been wrongfully obtained, the remedy can include not only restitution of the benefits directly conferred but also disgorgement of any additional gains by the defendant made possible by that benefit. See Restatement (Third) Restitution §§ 49–61.

(5) *Restitution and Contract.* Many breaches of contract involve the wrongful enrichment of one party at the expense of the other. It does not follow that those contract plaintiffs can also, or instead, bring an action for unjust enrichment. The existence of a contract prevents an action for unjust enrichment. "A valid contract defines the obligations of the parties as to matters within its scope, displacing to that extent any inquiry into unjust enrichment." Restatement (Third) Restitution § 2(2). In fact, as noted above, even the opportunity to contract can defeat a claim for restitution. Restitution is designed for those cases in which a voluntary exchange is not possible, or recovery in contract is for other reasons not available.

Although restitution is usually seen as an alternative to contract, the drafters of the Restatement (Third) of Restitution suggest that it might be available for certain wrongful breaches. Section 39 provides:

> (1) If a deliberate breach of contract results in profit to the defaulting promisor and the available damage remedy affords inadequate protection to the promisee's contractual entitlement, the promisee has a claim to restitution of the profit realized by the promisor as a result of the breach. Restitution by the rule of this section is an alternative to a remedy in damages.
>
> (2) A case in which damages afford inadequate protection to the promisee's contractual entitlement is ordinarily one in which damages will not permit the promisee to acquire a full equivalent to the promised performance in a substitute transaction.
>
> (3) Breach of contract is profitable when it results in gains to the defendant (net of potential liability in damages) greater than the defendant would have realized from performance of the contract. Profits from breach include saved expenditure and consequential gains that the defendant would not have realized but for the breach, as measured by the rules that apply in other cases of disgorgement.

There is sparse support for this proposition in U.S. caselaw, though there is some from foreign jurisdictions. At present it is unclear whether U.S. courts will follow the new Restatement's lead in this section. In *Kansas v. Nebraska*, 135 S.Ct. 1042 (2015), a fairly unusual case involving a water compact between two states, Justice Kagan, writing for the majority, relied on § 39 to affirm a disgorgement remedy. Writing in dissent, Justice Scalia observed:

> Section 39 . . . constitutes a " 'novel extension' " of the law that finds little if any support in case law. Restatement sections such as that should be given no weight whatever as to the current state of the law, and no more weight regarding what the law ought to be than the recommendations of any respected lawyer or scholar.

Id. at 1064. For criticism of the Restatement on this point, see Daniel Markovits and Alan Schwartz, *The Myth of Efficient Breach: New Defenses of the Expectation Interest*, 97 Va. L. Rev. 1939 (2011); Caprice L Roberts, *Restitutionary Disgorgement for Opportunistic Breach of Contract and Mitigation of Damages*, 42 Loyola (LA) L. Rev. 131 (2008).

(6) *Restitution as a Put Option.* The opportunity to confer a restitution-worthy benefit is a kind of legal "put" option. The option to confer a benefit is the option to sell—to force a purchase from the putative beneficiary. A potential rescuer who comes across an unconscious victim, has the option to be paid for conferring a benefit. See Abraham Bell and Gideon Parchomovsky, *Givings*, 111 Yale L.J. 547 (2001); Ian Ayres, Optional Law: The Structure of Legal Entitlements (2003).

CHAPTER FOUR

FORMATION DEFENSES

This chapter explores ways that a party can avoid, due to events or conditions *at the time of formation*, a legal obligation to perform an agreement that otherwise satisfies the conditions of contractual validity. Courts might refuse to enforce an agreement for consideration because of the absence of a required writing, because of a lack of capacity of one or both parties, because of mistake, fraud, duress or unconscionability, or because terms in the agreement make performance illegal or against public policy. In Chapter Five, we explore several *post*-formation events that can allow a party to avoid liability, such as supervening impracticability or breach by the other side.

While it is possible to contract around many of the rules of agreement (e.g., the mailbox rule), performance (e.g., payment of a reasonable price) and liability (e.g., expectation damages), the rules in this Chapter are for the most part mandatory or immutable. Parties do not have the freedom to waive these defenses. It is generally accepted that there are two sorts of justifications for mandatory restrictions on freedom of contract: paternalism and negative externalities. Legal immutability can protect parties inside the contract from entering into ill-advised bargains (paternalism) or can protect parties outside the contract from suffering the effects of someone else's contract (negative externalities). As you explore the mandatory rules in this chapter, it is worth asking which, if any, can be justified by paternalism or negative externalities.

Yet a third sort of justification, which works for many of the mandatory rules in this chapter, turns on the idea of *revealed preferences*. Under certain conditions, the process of contracting can produce evidence that the transaction is value creating. If Cardozo agrees to buy Traynor's belt for $15, third parties can infer from Cardozo's actions that he prefers the belt to having $15. Analogously, if Traynor agrees to the deal, his agreement reveals a preference for having $15 instead of the belt. These revealed preferences allow third parties, including courts, to infer that the contract creates value—in the sense that after the exchange, Traynor has assets that he values more, and Cardozo has assets that he values more. This inference, however, is only valid if Cardozo and Traynor were adequately informed and had the capacity to freely decide whether agreeing to the contract would improve their lots in life. The formation defenses in this chapter can be thought of as ways that the law supports the revealed preference inference of value creation. The inference requires adequate proof of an agreement (the Statute of Frauds), parties who are capable of deciding what is in their best interests (capacity), parties who are sufficiently informed about the deal (no mistake, misrepresentation or failure to disclose), and parties who are exercising true choice (no duress). The revealed preference inference can then work together with the court's own evaluation of the parties' actual interests (under some readings, the reason for the unconscionability doctrine) and of the agreement's effects on third parties (see the rules for illegality and public policy) to reach a (hopefully) accurate and predictable judgment as to the social value of the transaction.

A Brief Comment on Vocabulary. As we will see in this Chapter, courts distinguish between contracts that are *void*, contracts that are *voidable* and contracts that are *unenforceable*. To say that a contract is "void" is something of a misnomer, since what is meant is that the transaction has created no contractual obligations at all. A contract is described as "voidable" when one or both parties have the power to dissolve the legal relationship. The exercise of that power is termed "rescission," "disaffirmance" or "avoidance." Until and unless a party with the power to rescind exercises it, a voidable contract remains in effect. A contract that is "unenforceable" remains in existence, but under certain circumstances courts will not enforce it.

1.   FORMAL REQUIREMENTS: THE STATUTE OF FRAUDS

Chapter Two considered whether a formal writing, such as a sealed instrument, can ever be *sufficient* for legal enforcement of a promise *without* consideration. Here we examine when a formal writing is *necessary* for legal enforcement of an agreement *for* consideration. The necessity, if any, stems from the Statute of Frauds.

(A) GENERAL STATUTES OF FRAUDS

Comment: Introduction to the Statute of Frauds

Origins. Samuel Goldwyn reportedly said that an oral contract is not worth the paper it is written on. One can hardly gainsay the desirability of reducing a contract to writing. But in Anglo-American law, the existence of a writing has never been a general prerequisite for legal enforcement. In 1677, however, Parliament enacted legislation requiring that certain contracts be in writing and "signed by the party to be charged." The English law, called the "Statute of Frauds," was a comprehensive "Act for Prevention of Frauds and Perjuries" and applied to a wide range of transactions. Sections 4 and 17 pertained to contracts:

Section 4: [N]o action shall be brought

(1) whereby to charge any executor or administrator upon any special promise, to answer for damages out of his own estate;

(2) or whereby to charge the defendant upon any special promise to answer for the debt, default or miscarriage of another person;

(3) or to charge any person upon any agreement made upon consideration of marriage;

(4) or upon any contract or sale of lands, tenements or hereditaments, or any interest in or concerning them;

(5) or upon any agreement that is not to be performed within the space of one year from the making thereof;

unless the agreement upon which such action shall be brought, or some memorandum or note thereof, shall be in writing, and signed by the party to be charged therewith or some other person thereunto by him lawfully authorized.

Section 17: And be it further enacted [that] no contract for the sale of any goods, wares and merchandizes, for the price of ten pounds sterling or upwards, shall be allowed to be good, except the buyer shall accept part of the goods so sold, and actually receive the same, or give something in earnest to bind the bargain, or in part of payment, or that some note or memorandum in writing of the said bargain be made and signed by the parties to be charged by such contract, or their agents thereunto lawfully authorized.

Section 4 was widely copied in this country, although the language was sometimes altered, and other transactions, such as contracts to make a will or to pay a commission to a real estate agent, were sometimes added. Delaware's Statute of Frauds is representative:

(a) No action shall be brought to charge any person upon any agreement made upon consideration of marriage, or upon any contract or sale of lands, tenements, or hereditaments, or any interest in or concerning them, or upon any agreement that is not to be performed within the space of one year from the making thereof, or to charge any person to answer for the debt, default, or miscarriage, of another, in any sum of the value of $25 and upwards, unless the contract is reduced to writing, or some memorandum, or notes thereof, are signed by the party to be charged therewith, or some other person thereunto by the party lawfully authorized in writing. * * *

(b) A contract, promise, undertaking or commitment to loan money or to grant or extend credit, or any modification thereof, in an amount greater than $100,000, not primarily for personal, family, or household purposes, made by a person engaged in the business of lending or arranging for the lending of money or the extending of credit shall be invalid unless it or some note or memorandum thereof is in writing and subscribed by the party to be charged or by the party's agent. * * *

(c) For the purposes of this section, "writing" includes microphotography, photography and photostating, and a microphotographic, photographic or photostatic copy of any agreement covered by this section. * * *

6 Del. C. § 2714. See also Restatement (Second) § 110 (summarizing classes of contracts covered by typical statutes of frauds).

Section 17 of the English Statute of Frauds dealt with the sale of goods and found its counterpart in section 4 of the Uniform Sales Act:

> (1) A contract to sell or a sale of any goods or choses in action of the value of five hundred dollars or upwards shall not be enforceable by action unless the buyer shall accept part of the goods or choses in action so contracted to be sold or sold, and actually receive the same, or give something in earnest to bind the contract or in part payment, or unless some note or memorandum in writing of the contract or sale be signed by the party to be charged or his agent in that behalf.

> (2) The provisions of this section apply to every such contract or sale notwithstanding that the goods may be intended to be delivered at some future time or may not at the time of such contract or sale be actually made, procured, or provided, or fit, or ready for delivery, or some act may be requisite for the making or completing thereof, or rendering the same fit for delivery; but if the goods are to be manufactured by the seller especially for the buyer and are not suitable for sale to others in the ordinary course of the seller's business, the provisions of this section shall not apply.

> (3) There is an acceptance of goods within the meaning of this section when the buyer, either before or after delivery of the goods, expresses by words or conduct his assent to becoming the owner of those specific goods.

Section 4 of the Uniform Sales Act has now been replaced by section 2–201 of the Uniform Commercial Code, which is the subject of study below.

Debate over the Statute. An enormous amount of litigation has arisen respecting the Statute of Frauds. Judicial treatment has tracked divergent opinions about the utility of the legislation. Controversy arose early and continues unabated. A commission of the Lord Chancellor gave this brief sketch of English opinion:

> Lord Kenyon's verdict: "One of the wisest laws in our Statute Book" (Chaplin v. Rogers, 1800, 1 East at p. 194), and, "I lament extremely that exceptions were ever introduced in construing the Statute" (Chester v. Beckett, 7 T.R. at p. 204) contrasts with that pronounced by Wilmot J., and concurred in by Lord Mansfield (in Simon v. Metivier, 1766, 1 Bl.W. at p. 601): "Had the Statute of Frauds been always carried into execution according to the letter, it would have done ten times more mischief than it has done good, by protecting, rather than by preventing, frauds."

Law Revision Committee, Sixth Interim Report 6 (1937).

The repeated claim that the Statute's writing requirement might, as Lord Campbell argued, "promote more fraud than it prevents" turns on a distinction between two different types of fraud. On the one hand, a plaintiff can falsely assert the existence of a promise, where the defendant in fact had not promised. The writing requirement reduces fraudulent assertions of this sort by imposing what is in effect a heightened evidentiary requirement. On the other hand, a defendant can falsely deny the existence of a contract, where in fact she had previously made an oral promise. The writing requirement can exacerbate the fraudulent denials of this second sort. It gives parties to oral agreements a degree of freedom to disclaim their promises without legal penalty.

It might therefore seem that we do as well with the Statute of Frauds as without it—the presence or the absence of a writing requirement would exacerbate one of the two types of fraud. With a writing requirement, however, a party can protect herself from an oral promisor's false denial by simply demanding that the oral promise be reduced to writing. Without the requirement, on the contrary, a party cannot effectively protect herself against false assertions that a promise was made. It's theoretically easier for potential victims of false denials to protect themselves than for potential victims of false assertions. The problem comes when promisees—notwithstanding the writing requirement—fail to demand a writing and nonetheless rely.[1]

American opinion has also been divided. Karl Llewellyn, the primary drafter of the Uniform Commercial Code, gave this salute: "That statute is an amazing product. In it de Leon might have found his secret of perpetual youth. After two centuries and a half the statute stands, in essence better adapted to our need than when it first was passed." Karl N. Llewellyn, *What Price Contract?—An Essay in Perspective*, 40 Yale L.J. 704, 747 (1931). Others have condemned the contract clauses of the Statute of Frauds as anachronistic:

> The original reasons for a Statute of Frauds—to prevent men from being held by means of perjury on promises they had never made—were first the uncontrolled discretion of the jury, second, the rule as to competency of witnesses, and, third, the immaturity of contract law in the seventeenth century.
>
> While the process of the evolution of the jury, from a tribunal where the jurors were witnesses and decided the facts in cases on their own knowledge, to a tribunal where the jurors were judges of the facts and decided cases on evidence given in open court, was just about completed, the modern control of the court over the jury, in the matter of limits and elements of injury, the rules by which compensation for pecuniary injuries

---

[1] The parol evidence rule, discussed infra in Chapter 6, raises parallel issues. There the core question is not whether a contract exists, but whether a particular oral agreement adding additional terms was part of the contract. Again, there are two types of fraud—false assertions and false denials. The presence or absence of a writing requirement (now with regard to the asserted additional term) will reduce one type of fraud and exacerbate another. Finally, potential victims of false denials can protect themselves by demanding that oral agreements be reduced to writing.

shall be ascertained, and in cases of passion and prejudice, was only just beginning. It was therefore a wise precaution at this time to require certain kinds of evidence as proof of certain contracts in order to place a limitation upon the uncontrolled power of the jury, which would be exercised only in this way. . . .

At the time of the enactment of the original Statute of Frauds neither the parties to the action, nor any person who had any interest in the result of the litigation, were competent witnesses. . . . Such a state of the law of evidence was a temptation to plaintiffs to procure perjured testimony, and exposed defendants to outrageous liabilities; and it probably was in this state of the law a wise precaution to require for such liability, either writing or other adequate evidence, at least where it was feasible to do so as in the case of contracts.

Hugh Evander Willis, *The Statute of Frauds—A Legal Anachronism*, 3 Ind. L.J. 427, 429–31 (1928). It has been suggested, however, that even if the original reasons are no longer persuasive, there are other reasons to insist on a writing in some situations. This was Llewellyn's view, and it no doubt partly accounts for the retention of a statute of frauds provision, albeit in a significantly modified form, in the Uniform Commercial Code:

The statute serves a useful purpose in so far as it contributes to the business habit of requiring a writing. The lay tradition, often encountered, that a writing signed by the party must be had to make a contract binding probably is to a certain extent derived from the statute of frauds. Not only is a writing useful to prevent fraud by deliberate overreaching regarding the terms of the bargain, but the presence of a writing prevents to a large extent otherwise possible innocent misunderstanding of what actually were the terms of the bargain. It also preserves the exact wording of the terms, rather than leaving them to the recollection of their general purport preserved in the elusive and treacherous memory of interested parties.

Lawrence Vold, *The Application of the Statute of Frauds under the Uniform Sales Act*, 15 Minn. L. Rev. 391, 393–95 (1931).

Proponents of abolition scored a victory in England in 1954, when Parliament repealed all but the sections relating to promises to answer for the debts of another (suretyship clauses) and contracts for the sale of land. Law Reform (Enforcement of Contracts) Act, 1954, 2 & 3 Eliz. II, c. 34. There does not seem to be a likelihood of general repeal in the United States in the near future. Instead, "a cautious approach to the Statute of Frauds seems to be in harmony with American professional opinion." Robert Braucher, *The Commission and the Law of Contracts*, 40 Cornell L.Q. 696, 705 (1955). It is likely that some erosion will continue through judicial interpretations restricting statutory coverage, easing the requirements for statutory compliance and making assertion of the statutory defense more difficult.

Professional Bull Riders, Inc. v. AutoZone, Inc.

Supreme Court of Colorado, en banc, 2005.
113 P.3d 757.

■ COATS, JUSTICE. Pursuant to 10th Cir. R. 27.1, The United States Court of Appeals for the Tenth Circuit certified to this court the following question:

> Under Col.Rev.Stat. § 38–10–112(1)(a), is an oral agreement void when: (1) the agreement contemplates performance for a definite period of more than one year but (2) allows the party to be charged an option to terminate the agreement by a certain date less than a year from the making of the agreement and when (3) the party to be charged has not exercised that option to terminate the agreement?

[handwritten margin note: issue?]

Pursuant to C.A.R. 21.1, we agreed to answer the question and do so now (in the context provided us) in the negative.

I.

The certifying court provided the following statement of factual and procedural circumstances, giving context to the question.

In the years leading up to this dispute, the defendant AutoZone sponsored events conducted by the plaintiff Professional Bull Riders (PBR). For the years 2001 and 2002, PBR prepared a written agreement to provide for AutoZone's sponsorship. Section I of that agreement states:

> The term of this agreement shall commence as of December 29, 2000 and end on December 31, 2002, unless terminated earlier in accordance with the provisions of this Agreement. Notwithstanding the preceding sentence, AutoZone may, at its option, elect to terminate this Agreement and its sponsorship of PBR and the Series effective as of the end of the Finals in 2001, by giving PBR written notice of termination by no later than August 15, 2001.

AutoZone never signed this agreement. However, PBR alleges that by its actions, AutoZone tacitly accepted its terms set forth in the proposed written agreement and that, as a result, the parties entered into an oral agreement mirroring the terms set forth in writing.

There appears to be a factual dispute as to the communications between the parties during 2001. However, it appears undisputed that in January 2002, AutoZone notified PBR that AutoZone would not be sponsoring PBR events in 2002. However, despite this notice, AutoZone alleges, "PBR continued to use AutoZone's protected trade name and service mark for an indeterminate period of time in its programs."

PBR then sued AutoZone for breach of the oral sponsorship agreement. * * *

As to PBR's breach of contract claim, the district court granted summary judgment to AutoZone. The court reasoned that the oral contract could not be performed within one year and was therefore unenforceable under the Colorado statute of frauds, Col.Rev.Stat. § 38–10–112, which provides, in part:

> (1) Except for contracts for the sale of goods . . . and lease contracts . . . , in the following cases every agreement shall be void, unless such agreement or some note or memorandum thereof is in writing and subscribed by the party charged therewith:
>
> > (a) Every agreement that by the terms is not to be performed within one year after the making thereof.

The district court explained:

> Although no Colorado court has ruled on the question of whether the statute of frauds governs an oral contract which, by its express terms, is to last for more than one year but which contains a provision allowing one party to terminate the contract before the end of the first year, case law from other jurisdictions indicates that the statute of frauds will bar an action on verbal agreements that the parties intend to put into writing. * * *

The district court reasoned that the purported oral contract provided for a term of two years and was thus unenforceable.

II.

* * * The overriding purpose of the Statute of Frauds was to prevent the perpetration of fraud by the device of perjury. Kiely [v. St. Germain, 670 P.2d 764, 768 (Colo. 1983)]. While the English statute of frauds has since been repealed, almost every state has enacted (and currently has in force) a statute containing language substantially similar to portions of the original act. Id.

Few indicators of the precise intent of the framers of the original English provisions exist. Commentators have noted that the purpose of the one-year provision is especially puzzling. Due to this provision's questionable effectiveness in carrying out the general purposes of the statute, under virtually any rationale,[4] courts have tended to construe it

---

[4]   Farnsworth states:

The one-year provision is ill-contrived if it is based on the tendency of memory to fail and of evidence to go stale with the passage of time. The one-year period does not run from the time that the contract is made to the time for proof that it was made, but from the time that the contract was made to the time for completion of performance. If an oral contract that cannot be performed within a year is broken the day after it making, the provision applies though the terms of the contract are fresh in the minds of the parties. But if an oral contract that can be performed within a year is broken and suit is not brought until nearly six years (the usual statute of limitations for contract

narrowly, to void the fewest number of oral contracts. The provision is therefore universally understood to apply only to agreements that, by their terms, are incapable of being performed within one year.

Nevertheless, courts and commentators have disagreed sharply about the effect of various contingencies that may result in termination of an agreement in less than a year. Debate persists about whether particular kinds of termination amount to performance or merely a defeasance short of breach, such as annulment, frustration of the purposes of the contract, or excuse for nonperformance. Disagreement among authorities is particularly prevalent concerning options for one or both parties to terminate merely by giving notice. See 2 Farnsworth, § 6.4, at 129–130 (stating that while some courts have held that a contract is within the statute even though it provides that one or both parties have the power to terminate the contract within one year of its making, there is a strong contrary view, with a growing number of courts coming to regard a contract as not within the statute if one party can terminate within a year); Caroline N. Brown, 4 Corbin on Contracts § 19.6, at 603–04 (Joseph M. Perillo ed., Revised ed. 1997) (stating that a contract with an option to terminate within a year should "be held not within the one year clause but a good many cases take the contrary view").

While there is little agreement whether an option to terminate should itself be considered an alternative way of performing, compare Hopper v. Lennen & Mitchell, Inc., 146 F.2d 364 (9th Cir. 1944) (holding that "the contract would be fulfilled in a sense originally contemplated by the parties," either by performing without exercising option to terminate or by performing until exercising option), and Johnston v. Bowersock, 62 Kan. 148 (1900) (holding that if termination is authorized then it is not a breach and "if not a breach, it must be performance"), with French v. Sabey Corp., 134 Wash.2d 547 (1998) (holding that option to end contract within a year does not take it out of the statute if, independent of option, the agreement cannot be performed within a year), there is, at the same time, little question that a promise of two or more performances, in the alternative, does not fall within the one-year provision if any one of the alternatives could be fully performed within one year. . . .

Whether a contract actually contemplates alternate performance obligations or merely provides an excuse for nonperformance, however, necessarily depends on the purposes of the parties, as expressed in the terms of the contract. . . . It does not matter which party has the right to name the alternative . . . , as long as the agreement contemplates that the election will establish the performance obligations of the parties rather than merely relieving the electing party of its obligations under

---

actions) after the breach, the provision does not apply, even though the terms of the contract are no longer fresh in the minds of the parties. * * *

2 Farnsworth, § 6.4, at 130–31.

the agreement. In keeping with the accepted narrow construction of the one-year provision of the statute of frauds, no contract that may be "fairly and reasonably interpreted such that it may be performed within one year," Cron v. Hargro Fabrics, Inc., 91 N.Y.2d 362 (1998), will be voided by it.

III.

Colorado enacted the one-year provision of the statute of frauds in 1861, drawing heavily from the English statute, and the language of that provision has never been amended. See Sec. 12, 1861 Colo. Sess. Laws 241 (currently § 38–10–112(1)(a), C.R.S. (2004)). Although we have not before expressly addressed an option like the one presented by the certification, we have long construed the one-year provision narrowly, to bring within the statute only those agreements that exclude, by their very terms, the possibility of performance within one year. . . . If the agreement "could have been performed" within one year, the statute is inapplicable. Kuhlmann v. McCormack, 116 Colo. 300, 302 (1947). That an agreement was not actually performed within one year of its making is, by this construction, clearly of no consequence in determining the applicability of the statute of frauds.

As described by the Tenth Circuit, the agreement that is the subject of its certification required AutoZone to sponsor "PBR and the Series." With regard to the length of AutoZone's required sponsorship, however, the agreement provided an election. By its own terms, the sponsorship agreement was to run for two seasons, unless sooner terminated as contemplated by the agreement itself. The agreement then expressly left to AutoZone the choice to terminate not only the Agreement, but also its obligation of sponsorship, effective upon the conclusion of only one season.

While the agreement was couched in terms of an agreement to sponsor for two seasons, with an option to terminate after sponsoring for only one season, it cannot be reasonably understood as other than an agreement of sponsorship for either one or two seasons, at AutoZone's choice. The agreement did not purport to grant AutoZone an option to terminate the agreement at will or upon the occurrence of some particular event; rather it provided AutoZone with two alternative ways of satisfying its obligations as contemplated by the agreement. Although the agreement contemplated performance for two seasons (a definite period of more than one year), if AutoZone chose that option, it also contemplated that AutoZone could completely perform its obligation by sponsoring PBR for one full season. Whether or not AutoZone effectively elected its option to limit its sponsorship obligation to only one season, the agreement expressly provided, by its owns terms, an alternative performance that could be completed in less than one year.

Under the circumstances of this case, it is unnecessary for us to decide whether an option to terminate a contract must always be construed as an alternative and sufficient means of performance. . . .

Where the terms of an agreement can fairly and reasonably be interpreted to define alternate obligations, one or more of which can be performed within one year, the agreement in question may be fairly and reasonably interpreted such that it may be performed within one year. The one-year provision therefore does not bring such an agreement within the statute of frauds. And at least where, as here, the word "terminate" not only applies to the agreement itself but expressly limits the electing party's performance obligation to a specific task—sponsorship for one season—an interpretation of the election as defining alternate obligations is not only fair and reasonable, it is clear.

IV.

Because exercise of the option to terminate could reasonably be construed, by the terms of the agreement, to constitute complete performance of AutoZone's sponsorship obligation, whether or not it effectively exercised that option, nothing in § 38–10–112(1)(a), C.R.S. (2004), renders the agreement void. We therefore answer the certified question in the negative.

NOTES

(1) What do you think the result in *PBR v. AutoZone* would have been if the oral contract had given AutoZone the ability to terminate at any time with 30 days' notice, rather than at the end of the first season? Is this a difference that should make a difference in the outcome of cases?

(2) *Judicial Readings of the One-Year Provision.* Judicial doubts about the writing requirement can be seen in the very narrow interpretation given the one-year provision:

> [Courts] have observed the exact words of this provision and have interpreted them literally and very narrowly. The words are "agreement that is not to be performed." They are not "agreement that is not in fact performed" or "agreement that may not be performed" or "agreement that is not at all likely to be performed." To fall within the words of the provision, therefore, the agreement must be one of which it can truly be said at the very moment that it is made, "This agreement is not to be performed within one year"; in general, the cases indicate that there must not be the slightest possibility that it can be fully performed within one year.

Goodwin v. Southtex Land Sales, 243 S.W.2d 721, 725 (Tex.Civ.App. 1951).

(3) *Other Forms of Termination.* Suppose that E and R orally agreed that if E quits E's job with R, E will not compete with R within a 20-mile radius for five years, but if E does compete, E will pay R a liquidated damage sum of $10,000. E left the job and, after two years, started to compete with R. Six months later, E was killed by lightning on a golf course. Alleging the oral agreement, R sued E's estate for $10,000. E's executor moved to dismiss, arguing that the one-year provision made the alleged oral agreement unenforceable. R argued that E's death rendered E's performance complete, citing *Young v. Ward*, 917 S.W.2d 506 (Tex.App. 1996), and since death could

have occurred within one year of the alleged oral agreement, the one-year provision did not apply. E's executor responded that R's argument failed to distinguish between performance of the contract and an excuse for non-performance, citing *Frantz v. Parke*, 111 Idaho 1005, 1008 (App. 1986): "[T]he great weight of authority holds that a contract not to compete would be 'terminated,' not fully performed, by death of the promisor. . . . Indeed, if the unstated but omnipresent possibility of death could take an agreement for a definite time outside the statute of frauds, it would eviscerate the statute in virtually all contracts for definite terms between mortals." Assuming that the covenant not to compete and the liquidated damage provision are otherwise enforceable, how should the Statute of Frauds defense be decided?

(4)   *One Side Rule.* Section 198 of the First Restatement provided: "Where any of the promises in a bilateral contract cannot be fully performed within a year from the time of the formation of the contract, all promises in the contract are within [the one-year clause of the Statute of Frauds], unless and until one party to such a contract completely performs what he has promised. When there has been such complete performance, none of the promises in the contract is [within such provision]." Restatement (Second) § 130 is less transparent, but in accord. As one court explained: "Why, in the present case, should not a plaintiff be entitled to recover upon a contract which he has completely performed? The defendant has received the full benefit—not of an implied contract, but of an express one. He has received everything that the express contract stipulated that he should receive and nothing remains to be done on his part but the payment of money. Nor do we see any substance in the minority rule. In almost every case where a recovery on the contract has been refused it has been suggested that a recovery could be had under quantum meruit or quantum valebant counts." Emerson v. Universal Products Co., 162 A. 779, 781 (Del. Super. 1932). Other states, however, refuse to apply the "part performance" exception to the one-year section of the Statute. See, e.g., Coca-Cola Co. v. Babyback's Int'l, Inc., 841 N.E.2d 557 (Ind. 2006).

(5)   *Cumulative Effect of Statute of Frauds Provisions.* In *Freedman v. Chemical Construction Corporation*, 372 N.E.2d 12 (N.Y. 1977), the plaintiff, "a self-described retired industrialist," sued on an alleged oral agreement to pay him a 5% fee ($2,500,000) for his participation in the obtaining by the defendant of a $41,000,000 contract to build a plant in Saudi Arabia. Payment was to be made upon completion of the plant. Plaintiff's services extended over a three-year period, and it took another six years to build the plant. Nonetheless, the alleged contract was not within the "one year" clause, for "[i]t matters not * * * that it was unlikely or improbable that a $41 million plant would be constructed within one year." 372 N.E.2d at 15. However, the court held that the action was barred by another statute of frauds provision covering "a contract to pay compensation for services rendered in negotiating a loan, or in negotiating the purchase, sale, exchange, renting or leasing of any real estate or interest therein, *or of a business opportunity*, business, its good will, inventory, fixtures or an interest therein. * * * " N.Y. Gen. Obl. L. § 5–701(10) (emphasis added). Statute of frauds provisions are "cumulative." It takes but one provision to bar enforcement.

There is, however, support for the view that if an oral contract for the sale of goods meets the requirements of UCC § 2–201, which does not include a one-year provision, it is enforceable despite the fact that it might be unenforceable under the one-year provision of the state's general statute of frauds. See the Comment on Special Aspects of UCC § 2–201 below.

PROBLEM: THE CASE OF JANE FONDA'S ATTORNEY

In 1968, Jane Fonda retained the services of a New York law firm to represent her in general business matters, orally agreeing to pay five percent of her earnings as compensation for the firm's services. Richard Rosenthal, a member of the firm, assumed responsibility for a large share of the firm's activities on Fonda's behalf.

In 1971, the law firm dissolved and in 1972, Rosenthal began to represent her as an independent private practitioner. In April of 1972, he and Fonda entered into an oral contract whereby he agreed to continue performing a variety of services for her and she, in return, agreed to pay him ten percent of all gross professional income derived from the projects that were initiated during his tenure.

Rosenthal continued to represent Fonda from his New York office until, in 1978, he and his family moved to California, at Fonda's request, so that he could represent her more effectively.

Approximately two years later, on May 30, 1980, Fonda discharged Rosenthal. Rosenthal sued to recover commissions on projects that were initiated during his tenure and produced or continued to produce income after his termination. What result? See Rosenthal v. Fonda, 862 F.2d 1398 (9th Cir. 1988).

Nate L. Crabtree v. Elizabeth Arden Sales Corp.

Court of Appeals of New York, 1953.
305 N.Y. 48.

■ FULD, JUDGE. In September of 1947, Nate Crabtree entered into preliminary negotiations with Elizabeth Arden Sales Corporation, manufacturers and sellers of cosmetics, looking toward his employment as sales manager. Interviewed on September 26th, by Robert P. Johns, executive vice-president and general manager of the corporation, who had apprised him of the possible opening, Crabtree requested a three-year contract at $25,000 a year. Explaining that he would be giving up a secure well-paying job to take a position in an entirely new field of endeavor—which he believed would take him some years to master—he insisted upon an agreement for a definite term. And he repeated his desire for a contract for three years to Miss Elizabeth Arden, the corporation's president. When Miss Arden finally indicated that she was prepared to offer a two-year contract, based on an annual salary of $20,000 for the first six months, $25,000 for the second six months and $30,000 for the second year, plus expenses of $5,000 a year for each of those years, Crabtree replied that that offer was "interesting". Miss

Arden thereupon had her personal secretary make this memorandum on a telephone order blank that happened to be at hand:

"EMPLOYMENT AGREEMENT WITH

NATE CRABTREE   Date Sept. 26–1947

At 681—5th Ave   6: PM

* * *

Begin   20000.

6 months   25000.

6 "   30000.

5000.—per year

Expense Money

[2 years to make good]

Arrangement with Mr. Crabtree

By Miss Arden

Present

    Miss Arden

    Mr. John

    Mr. Crabtree

    Miss O'Leary"

A few days later, Crabtree phoned Mr. Johns and telegraphed Miss Arden; he accepted the "invitation to join the Arden organization", and Miss Arden wired back her "welcome". When he reported for work, a "pay-roll change" card was made up and initialed by Mr. Johns, and then forwarded to the payroll department. Reciting that it was prepared on September 30, 1947, and was to be effective as of October 22d, it specified the names of the parties, Crabtree's "Job Classification" and, in addition, contained the notation that "This employee is to be paid as follows:

"First six months of employment	$20,000.	per	Annum
Next six months of employment	25,000.	"	"
After one year of employment	30,000.	"	"

Approved by,   RPJ   [initialed]"

After six months of employment, Crabtree received the scheduled increase from $20,000 to $25,000, but the further specified increase at the end of the year was not paid. Both Mr. Johns and the comptroller of the corporation, Mr. Carstens, told Crabtree that they would attempt to straighten out the matter with Miss Arden, and, with that in mind, the comptroller prepared another "pay-roll change" card, to which his signature is appended, noting that there was to be a "Salary increase" from $25,000 to $30,000 a year, "per contractual arrangements with Miss Arden". The latter, however, refused to approve the increase and, after further fruitless discussion, plaintiff left defendant's employ and commenced this action for breach of contract.

At the ensuing trial, defendant denied the existence of any agreement to employ plaintiff for two years, and further contended, that, even if one had been made, the statute of frauds barred its enforcement. The trial court found against defendant on both issues and awarded plaintiff damages of about $14,000, and the Appellate Division, two justices dissenting, affirmed. Since the contract relied upon was not to be performed within a year, the primary question for decision is whether there was a memorandum of its terms, subscribed by defendant, to satisfy the statute of frauds (Personal Property Law, § 31).

Each of the two payroll cards—the one initialed by defendant's general manager, the other signed by its comptroller—unquestionably constitutes a memorandum under the statute. That they were not prepared or signed with the intention of evidencing the contract, or that they came into existence subsequent to its execution, is of no consequence . . .; it is enough, to meet the statute's demands, that they were signed with intent to authenticate the information contained therein, and that such information does evidence the terms of the contract. . . . Those two writings contain all of the essential terms of the contract—the parties to it, the position that plaintiff was to assume, the salary that he was to receive—except that relating to the duration of plaintiff's employment. Accordingly, we must consider whether that item, the length of the contract, may be supplied by reference to the earlier unsigned office memorandum, and, if so, whether its notation, "2 years to make good", sufficiently designates a period of employment.

The statute of frauds does not require the "memorandum * * * to be in one document. It may be pieced together out of separate writings, connected with one another either expressly or by the internal evidence of subject matter and occasion." Marks v. Cowdin, 226 N.Y. 138, 145. . . . Where each of the separate writings has been subscribed by the party to be charged, little if any difficulty is encountered. See, e.g., Marks v. Cowdin, supra, at 144–145. Where, however, some writings have been signed, and others have not—as in the case before us—there is basic disagreement as to what constitutes a sufficient connection permitting the unsigned papers to be considered as part of the statutory memorandum. The courts of some jurisdictions insist that there be a reference, of varying degrees of specificity, in the signed writing to that unsigned, and, if there is no such reference, they refuse to permit consideration of the latter in determining whether the memorandum satisfies the statute. . . . That conclusion is based upon a construction of the statute which requires that the connection between the writings and defendant's acknowledgment of the one not subscribed, appear from examination of the papers alone, without the aid of parol evidence. The other position—which has gained increasing support over the years—is that a sufficient connection between the papers is established simply by a reference in them to the same subject matter or transaction. . . . The statute is not pressed "to the extreme of a literal and rigid logic" (Marks v. Cowdin, supra, at 144) and oral testimony is admitted to show the connection between the documents and to establish the acquiescence, of the party to be charged, to the contents of the one unsigned. . . .

The view last expressed impresses us as the more sound, and, indeed—although several of our cases appear to have gone the other way . . . —this court has on a number of occasions approved the rule, and we now definitively adopt it, permitting the signed and unsigned writings to be read together, provided that they clearly refer to the same subject matter or transaction. . . .

The language of the statute—"Every agreement * * * is void, unless * * * some note or memorandum thereof be in writing, and subscribed by the party to be charged" (Personal Property Law, § 31)—does not impose the requirement that the signed acknowledgment of the contract must appear from the writings alone, unaided by oral testimony. The danger of fraud and perjury, generally attendant upon the admission of parol evidence, is at a minimum in a case such as this. None of the terms of the contract are supplied by parol. All of them must be set out in the various writings presented to the court, and at least one writing, the one establishing a contractual relationship between the parties, must bear the signature of the party to be charged, while the unsigned document must on its face refer to the same transaction as that set forth in the one that was signed. Parol evidence—to portray the circumstances surrounding the making of the memorandum—serves only to connect the separate documents and to show that there was assent, by the party to be charged, to the contents of the one unsigned. If that testimony does not convincingly connect the papers, or does not show assent to the unsigned paper, it is within the province of the judge to conclude, as a matter of law, that the statute has not been satisfied. True, the possibility still remains that, by fraud or perjury, an agreement never in fact made may occasionally be enforced under the subject matter or transaction test. It is better to run that risk, though, than to deny enforcement to all agreements, merely because the signed document made no specific mention of the unsigned writing. As the United States Supreme Court declared, in sanctioning the admission of parol evidence to establish the connection between the signed and unsigned writings, "There may be cases in which it would be a violation of reason and common sense to ignore a reference which derives its significance from such [parol] proof. If there is ground for any doubt in the matter, the general rule should be enforced. But where there is no ground for doubt, its enforcement would aid, instead of discouraging, fraud." Beckwith v. Talbot, 95 U.S. 289, 292. . . .

Turning to the writings in the case before us—the unsigned office memo, the payroll change form initialed by the general manager Johns, and the paper signed by the comptroller Carstens—it is apparent, and most patently, that all three refer on their face to the same transaction. The parties, the position to be filled by plaintiff, the salary to be paid him, are all identically set forth; it is hardly possible that such detailed information could refer to another or a different agreement. Even more, the card signed by Carstens notes that it was prepared for the purpose of a "Salary increase per contractual arrangements with Miss Arden". That certainly constitutes a reference of sorts to a more comprehensive "arrangement," and parol is permissible to furnish the explanation.

The corroborative evidence of defendant's assent to the contents of the unsigned office memorandum is also convincing. Prepared by defendant's agent, Miss Arden's personal secretary, there is little likelihood that that paper was fraudulently manufactured or that defendant had not assented to its contents. Furthermore, the evidence as to the conduct of the parties at the time it was prepared persuasively demonstrates defendant's assent to its terms. Under such circumstances, the courts below were fully justified in finding that the three papers constituted the "memorandum" of their agreement within the meaning of the statute.

Nor can there be any doubt that the memorandum contains all of the essential terms of the contract. . . . Only one term, the length of the employment, is in dispute. The September 26th office memorandum contains the notation, "2 years to make good". What purpose, other than to denote the length of the contract term, such a notation could have, is hard to imagine. Without it, the employment would be at will . . . , and its inclusion may not be treated as meaningless or purposeless. Quite obviously, as the courts below decided, the phrase signifies that the parties agreed to a term, a certain and definite term, of two years, after which, if plaintiff did not "make good", he would be subject to discharge. And examination of other parts of the memorandum supports that construction. Throughout the writings, a scale of wages, increasing plaintiff's salary periodically, is set out; that type of arrangement is hardly consistent with the hypothesis that the employment was meant to be at will. The most that may be argued from defendant's standpoint is that "2 years to make good", is a cryptic and ambiguous statement. But, in such a case, parol evidence is admissible to explain its meaning. . . . Having in mind the relations of the parties, the course of the negotiations and plaintiff's insistence upon security of employment, the purpose of the phrase—or so the trier of the facts was warranted in finding—was to grant plaintiff the tenure he desired.

The judgment should be affirmed, with costs.

NOTES

(1) Which writings constituted the requisite memorandum? To what extent was parol evidence needed to show actual connection?

(2)   Restatement (Second) § 132, influenced by *Crabtree*, provides: "The memorandum may consist of several writings if one of the writings is signed and the writings in the circumstances clearly indicate that they relate to the same transaction."

(3)   Suppose a memo sufficient to satisfy the statute is made before the alleged oral contract. Section 136 of the Second Restatement provides that "[a] memorandum sufficient to satisfy the Statute may be made or signed at any time before or after the formation of the contract." How can a writing generated during the course of negotiations be evidence of a subsequent oral agreement?

Comment: Satisfying the Statute

Statutes of frauds require a signed writing. What counts as a signature? Courts have traditionally taken a broad view. A signature need not be in ink, and may be stamped or typewritten. Section 134 of the Second Restatement provides that the signature "may be any symbol made or adopted with an intention, actual or apparent, to authenticate the writing as that of the signer." Similarly, the comments to the UCC's writing requirement provide that "signed" means "any authentication which identifies the party to be charged." UCC § 1–201 cmt. 1.

With the advent of the Internet and the massive shift toward electronic business, it has become imperative for the law to create certainty about the validity of electronically formed contracts. Both state and federal lawmakers have responded. In 1999, the National Conference of Commissioners on Uniform State Law approved the Uniform Electronic Transactions Act (UETA), which has been adopted by 41 states. UETA defines an "electronic signature" as "an electronic sound, symbol, or process attached to or logically associated with a record and executed or adopted by a person with the intent to sign the record," and provides that "[a] record or signature may not be denied legal effect or enforceability solely because it is in electronic form." UETA §§ 2(8), 7(a).

In 2000, Congress enacted the Electronic Signatures in Global and National Commerce Act (E-Sign), 15 U.S.C. §§ 7001 et seq. E-Sign also makes clear that a contract may not be denied legal effect solely because it is in electronic form or because an electronic signature or electronic record was used in its formation. It similarly defines "electronic signature" to mean "an electronic sound, symbol, or process, attached to or logically associated with a contract or other record and executed or adopted by a person with the intent to sign the record." 15 U.S.C. § 7006(5). Except for a few specified provisions, including state enactments of UETA, E-Sign preempts other state law with respect to what counts as a signature. 15 U.S.C. § 7002.

For some thoughts on the potential consequences of the move to electronic contracting, see Margaret Jane Radin, *Online Standardization and the Integration of Text and Machine*, 70 Fordham L. Rev. 1125 (2002).

Joan Sullivan v. Merval Porter, Jr.

Supreme Judicial Court of Maine, 2004.
861 A.2d 625.

■ SAUFLEY, C.J. Merval and Susan Porter appeal from a judgment in the Superior Court (Hancock County, HJELM, J.) entered in favor of Joan Sullivan and David Andrews in which the jury found that the parties had entered into an oral contract for the sale of the Porters' farm and the trial court ordered the Porters to transfer the property to Sullivan and Andrews. The Porters argue that (1) the evidence was insufficient for a jury to find that the parties entered into an oral contract for the sale of real estate; (2) the evidence of "part performance" and "reasonable reliance" was insufficient to remove the oral contract for the sale of real estate from the statute of frauds; * * * and (5) the court erred in entering an order of specific performance. We affirm the judgment.

I.   BACKGROUND

Accepting the facts in the light most favorable to Sullivan and Andrews, as we must, . . . the jury and the court could have relied on the following facts. In December 1999, Sullivan began managing a horse stable located on property owned by Merval and Susan Porter in Bar Harbor. In July 2000, Merval informed Sullivan that he planned to move, and asked if she would like to rent the property to run a horse trail riding and lesson business. The property included a farmhouse, large barn, and over fifty-two acres of land.

Sullivan and Andrews expressed an interest in the proposal, but after touring the property decided to rent only the barn and fields because the farmhouse required too much rehabilitation. Sullivan and Andrews never had a chance to explain their decision to Merval because, when the parties met in August 2000, Merval offered to sell the property to them for $350,000. At the same time, he also offered to owner-finance the sale at an interest rate between five and seven percent for a period between twenty and thirty years, and asked for a $20,000 down payment. Sullivan and Andrews orally accepted his offer. Merval told Sullivan and Andrews that he would contact his attorney to start the paperwork. Sullivan and Andrews informed Merval that they would refinance their house to obtain the down payment for the property.

When the Porters moved out of the farmhouse in September 2000, they gave the keys to Sullivan and Andrews. Sullivan and Andrews took possession of the property and began improving the stable and trails. The parties continued on this course without incident until November 24, 2000, when Merval arrived at the farm with a real estate agent. When questioned by Sullivan, Merval informed her that there was interest from another buyer, but told Sullivan that he would honor their agreement. The parties agreed to meet the following day for presentation of half of the down payment.

When the parties met the next day, Merval again reaffirmed his intention to honor the agreement. Sullivan offered him $10,000 in cash toward the down payment, but Merval stated that he did not feel right accepting the money until the paperwork was prepared. Nonetheless, he and his wife eventually accepted $3000 toward the down payment.

After the November 25, 2000 meeting, Sullivan and Andrews began extensive renovations of the farmhouse, which included removing four tons of horsehair plaster from the walls and replacing it with insulation and sheet rock, rewiring the electricity, installing new plumbing, erecting new fencing, and removing trash. They also started their new business, joined the chamber of commerce, repaired horse trails, began giving riding lessons and rehabilitating horses, placed advertisements in the local newspaper, and paid for an appraisal of the property. During the renovation process, Merval visited the property regularly and received updates about the renovations. When asked about the necessary paperwork, Merval always responded that he was too busy to contact his attorney.

In June 2001, Sullivan forwarded a copy of an appraisal of the Porters' property, valuing the property at $250,000, and a letter stating that Sullivan and Andrews planned to "stick to the $350,000 price [they] agreed on." Merval responded to this correspondence by offering to sell the property to Sullivan and Andrews for $450,000 with a $50,000 down payment. After the parties were unable to resolve the issues privately, Sullivan and Andrews filed a complaint alleging, among other things, the existence of a contract and promissory estoppel, and requesting specific performance. The Porters asserted the statute of frauds as an affirmative defense.

The parties agreed to allow the jury to decide whether a contract existed and to have the jury sit in an advisory capacity relating to the statute of frauds, promissory estoppel, and specific performance. After the close of evidence, the trial court provided instructions to the jury including an ordinary contract instruction articulating the burden of proof for the existence of a contract and the part performance of that contract as a preponderance of the evidence. The court thereafter instructed that the alternative claim for promissory estoppel required proof by clear and convincing evidence. Both parties agreed to the court's prepared jury instructions before they were delivered to the jury.

The jury found that the parties entered into a contract for the sale of the farm. Acting in an advisory capacity, the jury found in favor of Andrews and Sullivan on the issues of the part performance doctrine, promissory estoppel, and specific performance. Although not bound by the jury's decision, the court concluded that the jury's assessment of the equitable issues was warranted. The court also found that the evidence at trial established that the parties agreed to a $350,000 purchase price and that the Porters agreed to finance the sale at an interest rate between five and seven percent for a term of between twenty and thirty years. The court ordered the Porters to execute a purchase and sale agreement for $350,000 to be financed by the Porters unless otherwise agreed, and required them to provide notice of the terms of repayment and interest rate in the range found by the court within ten days of the judgment.

II. DISCUSSION

A. Statute of Frauds

We begin with the axiom that, absent extraordinary circumstances, a contract for the sale of land must be in writing to be enforceable. 33 M.R.S.A. § 51(4) (1999) (statute of frauds).[4] A transfer of real property without a written instrument may be enforced only if the party seeking to enforce the contract proves by clear and convincing evidence that an oral contract exists and that an exception to the statute of frauds applies. . . . One exception to the statute of frauds is found in the part performance doctrine.

The part performance doctrine requires the party seeking to enforce the contract to establish both that she acted in partial performance of her contractual duties and that the other party made misrepresentations that induced that partial performance. . . . Thus, to remove the contract from the operation of the statute of frauds pursuant to this doctrine, the party seeking to enforce the contract must establish by clear and convincing evidence (1) that the parties did enter into a contract; (2) that the party seeking to enforce the contract partially performed the contract; and (3) that the performance was induced by the other party's misrepresentations, which may include acquiescence or silence. . . .

1. Existence of a Contract

Because any action to enforce a contract depends on the existence of the contract itself, we begin by addressing the Porters' argument that there was insufficient evidence for the jury to find the existence of a contract for the sale of their farm to Sullivan and Andrews. * * *

* * *

[The court concluded that there was sufficient evidence of an oral agreement.]

2. Part Performance

In addition to arguing that there was insufficient evidence to support the existence of the contract, the Porters also argue that Sullivan and Andrews failed to prove part performance.

---

[4] Maine's statute of frauds provides, in relevant part, that

[n]o action shall be maintained . . . [u]pon any contract for the sale of lands . . . unless the promise, contract or agreement on which such action is brought, or some memorandum or note thereof, is in writing and signed by the party to be charged therewith, or by some person thereunto lawfully authorized; but the consideration thereof need not be expressed therein, and may be proved otherwise.

33 M.R.S.A. § 51(4) (1999).

The part performance doctrine is grounded in the principle of equitable estoppel. . . . Equitable estoppel, also referred to as estoppel *in pais*, "involves misrepresentations, including misleading statements, conduct, or silence, that induce detrimental reliance," . . . "After having induced or knowingly permitted another to perform in part an agreement, on the faith of its full performance by both parties and for which he could not well be compensated except by specific performance, the other shall not insist that the agreement is void." . . . Accordingly, the party asserting partial performance must demonstrate not only meaningful partial performance, but also the other party's inducement of that performance through misrepresentation.

a.   Proof of Performance

Sullivan and Andrews took possession of the farm in September 2000 with the understanding that Merval would begin the necessary paperwork to effectuate the sale of the farm. Sullivan and Andrews made extensive repairs to the farmhouse, stables, and grounds. They also offered $10,000 toward the down payment, $3000 of which the Porters actually accepted, and devoted time and money to their new business on the property. This evidence supports a conclusion that Sullivan and Andrews partially performed their contractual obligations.

b.   Proof of Inducement by Misrepresentation

The evidence also supports the finding that the Porters induced Sullivan and Andrews's partial performance by misrepresentation. The Porters relinquished possession of the farm to Sullivan and Andrews. They remained silent upon learning that Sullivan and Andrews planned to refinance their home to obtain the funds for the agreed upon down payment. After accepting $3000 as a partial down payment for the farm, the Porters remained silent while they observed Sullivan and Andrews beginning extensive renovations and building their business on the property. Merval also repeatedly represented that he was having his lawyer draw up the paperwork for the sale of the farm. Taken collectively, the Porters' actions and silent acquiescence resulted in a misrepresentation that induced Sullivan and Andrews to partially perform their contractual obligations in faith that the Porters were going to perform the contract.

In sum, the evidence supports the findings that (1) the Porters entered into a contract with Sullivan and Andrews to sell the farm; (2) Sullivan and Andrews partially performed their duties under the contract; and (3) the Porters made misrepresentations through their actions and omissions that induced Sullivan and Andrews's partial performance. We therefore affirm the court's finding, consistent with the jury's advisory finding on the issue, that the parties' oral contract for the sale of land was removed from the statute of frauds based on the part performance doctrine.

* * *

D. Remedy

It is within the trial court's equitable powers to apply the remedy of specific performance when a legal remedy is either inadequate or impractical. . . . An order of specific performance may be appropriate to enforce a contract for the sale of land because of the uniqueness of each parcel of real property. . . . The terms of a contract must be reasonably certain in order to be enforceable by specific performance. . . . We review a trial court's order of specific performance for an unsustainable exercise of discretion. . . .

The trial court did not exceed the bounds of its discretion by finding that the nature of the property, Sullivan and Andrews's substantial investment of time and money to renovate the farmhouse and grounds, and the resources they devoted to establishing a new business, made Lakewood Farm so unique that there was no adequate remedy other than an order of specific performance. Finally, the trial court did not exceed the bounds of its discretion by finding that the terms of the contract were sufficiently certain to allow the court to order specific performance in the form of a purchase and sale agreement.[9]

The entry is: Judgment affirmed.

NOTES

All statutes of frauds cover agreements to convey an interest in land. Section 127 of the Second Restatement explains that an "interest in land" in such statutes includes "any right, privilege, power or immunity, or combination thereof, which is an interest in land under the law of property and is not 'goods' within the Uniform Commercial Code." Although there are some disputes about the scope of this section and when a writing satisfies it, most courts recognize that action in reliance on an oral promise to transfer an interest in land can take the case "out of the statute." Section 129 of the Second Restatement requires that the reliance be reasonable, the "continuing assent of the party against whom enforcement is sought," and a sufficient change of position so that "injustice can be avoided only by specific enforcement."

(B) THE WRITING REQUIREMENT IN CONTRACTS FOR THE SALE OF GOODS

UCC § 2–201 provides a statute of frauds for contracts for the sale of goods:

> (1)   Except as otherwise provided in this section a contract for the sale of goods for the price of $500 or more is not enforceable by way of action or defense unless there is some writing sufficient to indicate that a contract for sale has been made between the parties

---

[9]   Because we affirm the finding of an express contract that is removed from the statute of frauds by the part performance doctrine, we need not address whether the promissory estoppel doctrine applies to an oral contract for the sale of real estate.

and signed by the party against whom enforcement is sought or by his authorized agent or broker. A writing is not insufficient because it omits or incorrectly states a term agreed upon but the contract is not enforceable under this paragraph beyond the quantity of goods shown in such writing.

(2) Between merchants if within a reasonable time a writing in confirmation of the contract and sufficient against the sender is received and the party receiving it has reason to know its contents, it satisfies the requirements of subsection (1) against such party unless written notice of objection to its contents is given within ten days after it is received.

(3) A contract which does not satisfy the requirements of subsection (1) but which is valid in other respects is enforceable

(a) if the goods are to be specially manufactured for the buyer and are not suitable for sale to others in the ordinary course of the seller's business and the seller, before notice of repudiation is received and under circumstances which reasonably indicate that the goods are for the buyer, has made either a substantial beginning of their manufacture or commitments for their procurement; or

(b) if the party against whom enforcement is sought admits in his pleading, testimony or otherwise in court that a contract for sale was made, but the contract is not enforceable under this provision beyond the quantity of goods admitted; or

(c) with respect to goods for which payment has been made and accepted or which have been received and accepted (Sec. 2–606).

Section 2–201 is not the only statute of frauds provision in the Code. UCC § 2A–201 governs leases of goods. In addition, there are sections that, although not ordinarily referred to as statute of frauds provisions, prescribe a writing as a formal requisite of liability. Examples include negotiable instruments (UCC § 3–104(a)), letters of credit (UCC § 5–104), and security agreements (UCC § 9–203(b) (2000)). Beyond this, there are numerous statutory provisions of a regulatory nature that not only insist upon a signed writing as a *sine qua non* of legal obligation but also prescribe in considerable detail the content of the writing. Examples are statutes dealing with insurance, small loans, and retail installment sales. Note that the residual statute of frauds, UCC § 1–206, formerly found in Article 1, has been repealed in Revised Article 1.

PROBLEMS: § 2–201

Are there enforceable contracts under the following scenarios? Are there any additional facts you would need to know before answering?

(1) September 1, 2011: B, manager of a retail outdoor sports store, calls S, chief sales representative of a major boat building company, on the phone

and orders 5 kayaks for $500 each, delivery on December 1, 2011, payment upon receipt.

(2)   September 1, 2011: B calls S and orders 15 kayaks at $500 each, delivery on December 1, 2011, payment upon receipt. The next day, S faxes B a signed letter reading: "This confirms 9/1/11 kayak order and your price of $500/boat." B signs the bottom of the letter and faxes it back to S.

(3)   September 1, 2011: B calls S and orders 10 canoes at $400 each, delivery on December 1, 2011, payment upon receipt. The next day, B sends S an email reading: "10 units confirmed. Sincerely, B." S replies to the email: "Yes.—S"

(4)   September 1, 2011: B calls S and orders 20 canoes at $400 each, delivery on December 1, 2011, payment upon receipt. On September 15, S faxes a signed confirmation letter to B. Consider each of the following scenarios:

(a)   B does nothing.

(b)   On September 28, B telephones S and denies ordering the canoes.

(c)   In response to the September 15 confirmation, on September 16, B sends S a fax reading in pertinent part: "This is unacceptable to me. I am cancelling my order.—B"

(d)   In response to the September 15 confirmation, on September 25, B sends S an email denying the order.

(5)   September 1, 2011: B sees S at the whitewater boating convention, orally orders 30 canoes at $400 each, seals the deal with a handshake, and pays S half the purchase price ($6,000) up-front, the remainder to be paid upon delivery.

(6)   September 1, 2011: S meets C, extreme whitewater kayak champion, at the convention and suggests a 5-year endorsement deal, whereby C is to be paid $500 per year. C accepts, and they seal it with a handshake.

(7)   September 1, 2011: C meets S at the convention and, over drinks, describes the ultimate kayak. S says she can build it for $5,000. C says, "Build it and I'll buy it for that." Two months later, C calls S and says: "Forget it, I don't have the cash."

(8)   September 1, 2011: C orders the ultimate whitewater kayak from S at the convention as above. On September 7, S sends C a note confirming the order. On October 1, C calls S to say he didn't think they had reached an agreement about the kayak. S has been interviewing job applicants to help build C's boat, but has not yet begun building it.

(9)   September 1, 2011: At the whitewater convention, B orally orders 20 canoes at $400 each from S, delivery on December 1, 2011. S attempts to deliver on December 1; B refuses to accept the goods. S sues for breach.

(a)   B argues in defense that the contract is unenforceable under the Statute of Frauds. When asked in court, B testifies: "Yes I made the oral agreement, but I figured it was unenforceable because it wasn't in writing."

(b)   B argues in defense that the contract is unenforceable under the Statute of Frauds. S introduces a signed letter from B to D, another boat builder, dated October 1, 2011, that reads: "I'm sorry, I won't be ordering any canoes from you this year. I just put in an order for 20 canoes with S."

(c)   B claims in defense that the agreement is unenforceable under the Statute of Frauds. B then testifies: "Yes I made the order, but it was only for 15 canoes." S calls D, E, F and G, all of whom were present when the oral agreement was made. Each testifies that the order was for 20 canoes.

(d)   B's attorney files an answer to the complaint. Point 1 states: "Assuming *arguendo* that there was an oral promise, it did not comply with the Statute of Frauds and is therefore not enforceable." B then moves to dismiss for noncompliance with the Statute of Frauds. S opposes the motion, arguing that B has admitted that there was a contract.

(e)   Same as in (d), except that in S's opposition to the motion to dismiss, S seeks permission to compel B to testify as to whether there was an oral promise.

Comment: Special Aspects of UCC § 2–201

Missing Terms and Quantity. UCC § 2–201(1) provides that "[a] writing is not insufficient because it omits or incorrectly states a term agreed upon but the contract is not enforceable under this paragraph beyond the quantity of goods shown in such writing." The drafters added the following commentary: "The required writing need not contain all the material terms of the contract and such material terms as are stated need not be precisely stated. All that is required is that the writing afford a basis for believing that the offered oral evidence rests on a real transaction. . . . The only term which must appear is the quantity term which need not be accurately stated. . . . The price, time and place of payment or delivery, the general quality of the goods, or any particular warranties may all be omitted." UCC § 2–201 cmt. 1. Courts have tended to be strict respecting the need for a statement of quantity in the writing. See, e.g., Thomas J. Kline, Inc. v. Lorillard, Inc., 878 F.2d 791 (4th Cir. 1989). Why is quantity different from terms like price, time, or place of delivery or warranties?

Custom Goods. The Code provides a separate rule for goods that are specially manufactured or custom made. Goods specially manufactured *for* the buyer (even if not manufactured *by* the seller) are *not* within the scope of UCC § 2–201 if (1) they are not suitable for sale to others in the ordinary course of the seller's business and (2) the seller, before notice of repudiation is received and under circumstances which indicate that the goods are for the buyer, has made either a substantial beginning of their manufacture or commitments for their procurement. UCC § 2–201(3)(a).

For example, a contract for the sale of standard white shirts would be covered by the goods section of the Statute of Frauds. Not so, however, if the seller was required to add the buyer's business name and logo to the shirts. See, e.g., Smith-Scharff Paper Co. v. P. N. Hirsch & Co. Stores, Inc., 754 S.W.2d 928 (Mo.App. 1988) (paper bags imprinted with buyer's logo not covered by the Statute); Flowers Baking Co. of Lynchburg, Inc. v. R-P Packaging, Inc., 229 Va. 370 (1985) (cellophane wrapping material manufactured to custom size and imprinted with buyer's name and unique artwork not covered). What if the seller is in the business of manufacturing custom designed goods, and the goods, with some alteration, could be marketed? Should the seller be able to claim the advantage of the specially manufactured goods exception? See Impossible Electronic Techniques, Inc. v. Wackenhut Protective Systems, Inc., 669 F.2d 1026 (5th Cir. 1982) ("specially manufactured" refers to the nature of the goods, not to the manufacturing process).

The One-Year Provision. What of contracts for the sale of goods that cannot be performed within a year? Section 2–201 says nothing about the issue. Does the one-year rule from a state's general statute of frauds apply where the UCC is silent?

The answer must be found in UCC § 1–103(b), which provides that "[u]nless displaced by the particular provisions of [the Uniform Commercial Code], the principles of law and equity, including the law merchant and the law relative to capacity to contract, principal and agent, estoppel, fraud, misrepresentation, duress, coercion, mistake, bankruptcy, and other validating or invalidating cause supplement its provisions." The question, then, is whether section 2–201's silence on the issue is enough to displace the general rule. Most courts addressing the question have held that the highly detailed requirements of section 2–201 do in fact displace the provisions of the generic Statute of Frauds, including with respect to issues on which section 2–201 is silent. As a Minnesota court explained:

> Section 336.2–201 is a special legislative attempt to tailor the enforcement and exceptions of the statute of frauds to the unique characteristics of a transaction for the sale of goods. Conversely, Minn.Stat. § 531.01 is the "general" statute of frauds provision historically encompassing a wide variety of contractual obligations. Because of Minnesota's policy of interpreting special statutes as exceptions to more general provisions, and because the transactions in question fall squarely within the scope of the sale of goods provisions of the UCC, the oral agreements need only satisfy the requirements of section 336.2–201.

Glacial Plains Co-op v. Lindgren, 759 N.W.2d 661 (Minn. App. 2009). The 2003 amendments to section 2–201, which have since been withdrawn, would have addressed the question by adding a new subsection 4, which would have read: "[a] contract that is enforceable under this section is not rendered unenforceable merely because it is not capable of being performed within one year or any other applicable period after its making."

PROBLEM: THE CORN CASE

Farmer and Dealer have done business together for over 10 years. In 2012, their transaction followed the usual pattern. In March, Farmer telephoned Dealer and offered to sell 5,000 bushels of #1 Yellow Corn for $6.00 per bushel, October delivery. After some discussion, there was an oral agreement to sell at $5.40 per bushel. As Farmer knew it would, Dealer immediately resold the corn to a cereal producer for $7.60 per bushel, November 2012 delivery. Dealer also mailed to Farmer a written, signed memorandum stating simply: "This is to confirm our agreement to sell and buy your output of corn for October 2012 delivery." Farmer received the memo and did not respond. In September 2012, Farmer harvested 6,000 bushels from the farm and tendered 1,000 bushels to Dealer, which Dealer accepted. Because of bad weather elsewhere, the market price of #1 Yellow Corn had risen to $10.00 per bushel. Farmer then sold the balance of the crop on the open market for $10.00 per bushel and refused to deliver any more to Dealer. Farmer's attorney argued that the alleged oral agreement, if any, was unenforceable under UCC § 2–201.

You represent Dealer. Review section 2–201 carefully. Make a list of the issues that must be resolved before Dealer can prevail. How should the case come out?

(C) EFFECT OF NON-COMPLIANCE

An oral contract that is within and does not satisfy the Statute of Frauds is not a complete nullity. The vast majority of the cases have held that such a contract is "not void in the strict sense that no contract has come into being at all, but [is] merely unenforceable at the option of the party against whom enforcement is sought." Borchardt v. Kulick, 234 Minn. 308, 319 (1951). This means that the defense may be waived. In addition, if there has been complete performance, there is no cause to "undo" the transaction.

Although waivable, the defense has traditionally been relatively easy to raise. One has been able, for example, to admit *arguendo* the existence of an oral agreement while insisting upon its nonenforceability. One has not been required to deny the existence of the alleged oral contract before being permitted to assert the statutory defense. Some have questioned the ethical propriety of this procedure. See, e.g., Robert Stevens, *Ethics and the Statute of Frauds*, 37 Cornell L. Rev. 355 (1952). The issue has become more prominent, particularly with respect to contracts for the sale of goods, by reason of UCC § 2–201(3)(b), which provides that a contract not satisfying the requirements of subsection (1) but valid in other respects *is* enforceable "if the party against whom enforcement is sought admits in his pleading, testimony or otherwise in court that a contract for sale was made, but the contract is not enforceable under this provision beyond the quantity of goods admitted." As is discussed in the next case, this new rule raises new issues with respect to when or whether a case may be dismissed for failure to comply with the Statute of Frauds, as well as questions about when or whether a defendant may be compelled to testify about an alleged oral agreement. Should the party against whom enforcement is sought be forced to deny that a contract was made under oath in a sworn answer or declaration? In a deposition?

In addition to the questions raised by section 2–201(3)(b), there are also important questions about how statutes of frauds interact with non-contractual grounds of recovery, such as promissory estoppel and restitution. To what extent can the defense be avoided on grounds of estoppel, equitable or promissory? May a plaintiff who is unsuccessful in removing the bar of the statute still seek restitution for benefits conferred? These are discussed later in this subsection.

Richard Allen Posner: Richard Posner is the most prolific and most cited law professor of our time. He is perhaps best known as one of the founders of the law and economics movement of the 1970s, which applies the analytical tools of economics to areas of the law as diverse as racial discrimination, privacy law and family law. Born in 1939 and raised in the suburbs of New York, Judge Posner earned his bachelor's degree from Yale and his law degree from Harvard, where he was president of the Harvard Law Review. Judge Posner clerked for Justice William Brennan, Jr. and worked in government for several years before entering academia. He joined the faculty of the University of Chicago in 1969. President Reagan appointed him to the Seventh Circuit Court of Appeals in 1981. Judge Posner has authored more than 30 books and hundreds of articles. See Larissa MacFarquhar, *The Bench Burner: An Interview with Richard Posner*, The New Yorker, December 10, 2001, at 78 ("I have exactly the same personality as my cat. I am cold, furtive, callous, snobbish, selfish, and playful, but with a streak of cruelty.").

DF Activities Corp. v. Dorothea F. Brown

United States Court of Appeals, Seventh Circuit, 1988.
851 F.2d 920.

■ POSNER, CIRCUIT JUDGE. This appeal in a diversity breach of contract case raises an interesting question concerning the statute of frauds, in the context of a dispute over a chair of more than ordinary value. The plaintiff, DF Activities Corporation (owner of the Domino's pizza chain), is controlled by a passionate enthusiast for the work of Frank Lloyd Wright. The defendant, Dorothy Brown, a resident of Lake Forest (a suburb of Chicago) lived for many years in a house designed by Frank Lloyd Wright—the Willits House—and became the owner of a chair that Wright had designed, the Willits Chair. This is a stark, high-backed, uncomfortable-looking chair of distinguished design that DF wanted to add to its art collection. In September and October 1986, Sarah-Ann Briggs, DF's art director, negotiated with Dorothy Brown to buy the Willits Chair. DF contends—and Mrs. Brown denies—that she agreed in a phone conversation with Briggs on November 26 to sell the chair to DF for $60,000, payable in two equal installments, the first due on December 31 and the second on March 26. On December 3 Briggs wrote Brown a letter confirming the agreement, followed shortly by a check for $30,000. Two weeks later Brown returned the letter and the check with the following handwritten note at the bottom of the letter: "Since I did not hear from you until December and I spoke with you the middle of November, I have made other arrangements for the chair. It is no longer available for sale to you." Sometime later Brown sold the chair for $198,000, precipitating this suit for the difference between the price at which the chair was sold and the contract price of $60,000. Brown moved under Fed.R.Civ.P. 12(b)(6) to dismiss the suit as barred by the statute of frauds in the Uniform Commercial Code. See UCC § 2–201. (The Code is, of course, in force in Illinois, and the substantive issues in this case are, all agree, governed by Illinois law.) Attached to the motion was Brown's affidavit that she had never agreed to sell the chair to DF or its representative, Briggs. The affidavit also denied any recollection of a conversation with Briggs on November 26, and was accompanied by both a letter from Brown to Briggs dated September 20 withdrawing an offer to sell the chair and a letter from Briggs to Brown dated October 29 withdrawing DF's offer to buy the chair.

The district judge granted the motion to dismiss and dismissed the suit. DF appeals, contending that although a contract for a sale of goods at a price of $500 or more is subject to the statute of frauds, the (alleged) oral contract made on November 26 may be within the statutory exception for cases where "the party against whom enforcement is sought admits in his pleading, testimony or otherwise in court that a contract for sale was made." UCC § 2–201(3)(b). DF does not argue that Brown's handwritten note at the bottom of Briggs' letter is sufficient acknowledgment of a contract to bring the case within the exemption in section 2–201(1).

At first glance DF's case may seem quite hopeless. Far from admitting in her pleading, testimony, or otherwise in court that a contract for sale was made, Mrs. Brown denied under oath that a contract had been made. DF argues, however, that if it could depose her, maybe she would admit in her deposition that the affidavit was in error, that she had talked to Briggs on November 26, and that they had agreed to the sale of the chair on the terms contained in Briggs' letter of confirmation to her.

There is remarkably little authority on the precise question raised by this appeal—whether a sworn denial ends the case or the plaintiff may press on, and insist on discovery. In fact we have found no authority at the appellate level, state or federal. Many cases hold, it is true, that the defendant in a suit on an oral contract apparently made unenforceable by the statute of frauds cannot block discovery aimed at extracting an admission that the contract was made, simply by moving to dismiss the suit on the basis of the statute of frauds or by denying in the answer to the complaint that a contract had been made. . . . There is also contrary authority. . . . The clash of views is well discussed in *Triangle Marketing, Inc. v. Action Industries, Inc.*, 630 F.Supp. 1578, 1581–83 (N.D.Ill. 1986), which, in default of any guidance from Illinois courts, adopted the *Boylan* position. We need not take sides on the conflict. When there is a bare motion to dismiss, or an answer, with no evidentiary materials, the possibility remains a live one that, if asked under oath whether a contract had been made, the defendant would admit it had been. The only way to test the proposition is for the plaintiff to take the defendant's deposition, or, if there is no discovery, to call the defendant as an adverse witness at trial. But where as in this case the defendant swears in an affidavit that there was no contract, we see no point in keeping the lawsuit alive. Of course the defendant *may* blurt out an admission in a deposition, but this is hardly likely, especially since by doing so he may be admitting to having perjured himself in his affidavit. Stranger things have happened, but remote possibilities do not warrant subjecting the parties and the judiciary to proceedings almost certain to be futile.

A plaintiff cannot withstand summary judgment by arguing that although in pretrial discovery he has gathered no evidence of the defendant's liability, his luck may improve at trial. . . . The statement in a leading commercial law text that a defense based on the statute of fraud must always be determined at trial because the defendant might in cross-examination admit the making of the contract, see White & Summers, Handbook of the Law Under the Uniform Commercial Code 67 (1980), reflects a misunderstanding of the role of summary judgment; for the statement implies, contrary to modern practice, that a party unable to generate a genuine issue of fact at the summary judgment stage, because he has no evidence with which to contest an affidavit of his adversary, see Fed.R.Civ.P. 56(e), may nevertheless obtain a trial of the issue. He may not. By the same token, a plaintiff in a suit on a contract within the statute of frauds should not be allowed to resist a motion to dismiss, backed by an affidavit that the defendant denies the contract was made, by arguing that his luck may improve in discovery. Just as summary judgment proceedings differ from trials, so the conditions of a deposition differ from the conditions in which an affidavit is prepared; affidavits in litigation are prepared by lawyers, and merely signed by affiants. Yet to allow an affiant to be deposed by opposing counsel would be to invite the unedifying form of discovery in which the examining lawyer tries to put words in the witness's mouth and construe them as admissions.

The history of the judicial-admission exception to the statute of frauds, well told in Stevens, *Ethics and the Statute of Frauds,* 37 Cornell L.Q. 355 (1952), reinforces our conclusion. The exception began with common-sense recognition that if the defendant admitted in a pleading that he had made a contract with the plaintiff, the purpose of the statute of frauds—protection against fraudulent or otherwise false contractual claims—was fulfilled. (The situation would be quite otherwise, of course, with an oral admission, for a plaintiff willing to testify falsely to the existence of a contract would be equally willing to testify falsely to the defendant's having admitted the existence of the contract.) Toward the end of the eighteenth century the courts began to reject the exception, fearing that it was an invitation to the defendant to perjure himself. Later the pendulum swung again, and the exception is now firmly established. The concern with perjury that caused the courts in the middle period to reject the exception supports the position taken by Mrs. Brown in this case. She has sworn under oath that she did not agree to sell the Willits Chair to DF. DF wants an opportunity to depose her in the hope that she can be induced to change her testimony. But if she changes her testimony this will be virtually an admission that she perjured herself in her affidavit (for it is hardly likely that her denial was based simply on a faulty recollection). She is not likely to do this. What is possible is that her testimony will be sufficiently ambiguous to enable DF to argue that there should be still further factual investigation— perhaps a full-fledged trial at which Mrs. Brown will be questioned again about the existence of the contract.

With such possibilities for protraction, the statute of frauds becomes a defense of meager value. And yet it seems to us as it did to the framers of the Uniform Commercial Code that the statute of frauds serves an important purpose in a system such as ours that does not require that all contracts be in writing in order to be enforceable and that allows juries of lay persons to decide commercial cases. The methods of judicial fact-finding do not distinguish unerringly between true and false testimony, and are in any event very expensive. People deserve some protection against the risks and costs of being hauled into court and accused of owing money on the basis of an unacknowledged promise. And being deposed is scarcely less unpleasant than being cross-examined—indeed, often it is more unpleasant, because the examining lawyer is not inhibited by the presence of a judge or jury who might resent hectoring tactics. The transcripts of depositions are often very ugly documents.

Some courts still allow the judicial-admission exception to be defeated by the defendant's simple denial, in a pleading, that there was a contract; this is the position well articulated in Judge Shadur's opinion in the *Triangle Marketing* case. To make the defendant repeat the denial under oath is already to erode the exception (as well as to create the invitation to perjury that so concerned the courts that rejected the judicial-admission exception altogether), for there is always the possibility, though a very small one, that the defendant might be charged with perjury. But, in any event, once the defendant has denied the contract under oath, the safety valve of section 2–201(3)(b) is closed. The chance that at a deposition the defendant might be badgered into withdrawing his denial is too remote to justify prolonging an effort to enforce an oral contract in the teeth of the statute of frauds. If Dorothy Brown did agree on November 27 to sell the chair to DF at a bargain price, it behooved Briggs to get Brown's signature on the dotted line, posthaste.

AFFIRMED.

■ FLAUM, CIRCUIT JUDGE (dissenting). Because I disagree with the majority's holding that additional discovery is prohibited whenever a defendant raises a statute of frauds defense and submits a sworn denial that he or she formed an oral contract with the plaintiff, I respectfully dissent. Neither would I hold, however, that a plaintiff is automatically entitled to additional discovery in the face of a defendant's sworn denial that an agreement was reached. Rather, in my view district courts should have the authority to exercise their discretion to determine the limits of permissible discovery in these cases. This flexibility is particularly important where, as here, the defendant's affidavit does not contain a conclusive denial of contract formation. While district courts have broad discretion in discovery matters, I believe the district court abused that discretion in the present case.

* * *

Because in my view the district court abused its discretion when it prohibited further discovery, I would remand this case to the district court with instructions to permit discovery to continue at least to the point where DF is given an opportunity to depose Brown. If Brown then denies under oath during her deposition that any oral contract was made, summary judgment might well be appropriate at that time.

NOTES

(1) *To Demur or Not to Demur?* Judge Posner notes that the court did not have to take sides as to whether a defendant in a suit on an oral contract

can block discovery aimed at extracting an admission by moving to dismiss. But (alas) you do, at least for classroom purposes. Before deciding, consider these examples of the "clash of views" to which Judge Posner alludes:

(a)   "The admission exception now included in the Statute of Frauds governing sales would be meaningless were the defendant permitted by the simple expedient of a motion to dismiss to deprive plaintiff of the opportunity to obtain from defendant either an admission 'in his pleading, testimony or otherwise in court' or a sworn denial of the existence of a contract. . . . If a pre-pleading motion to dismiss is permitted to defeat a cause of action on an oral sales contract before plaintiff has had an opportunity to elicit from defendant a statement in court of any kind, only malpractice by defendant's attorney would subject the defendant to the statute's ameliorative purpose. The Legislature in adopting the Uniform Commercial Code and the drafters of the Code cannot reasonably be thought to have intended that the exception have such limited application." Meyer, J., dissenting in Boylan v. G.L. Morrow Co., 63 N.Y.2d 616, 623 (1984).

(b)   "But those 'admissions' are not really admissions in the factual sense at all. Parties who move to dismiss do not truly say: 'I admit the things you allege are true fact, but I am entitled to judgment on the law.' They rather say something more like: 'Even if your allegations were true, I am entitled to judgment on the law.' Thus a motion to dismiss 'admits' the complaint's allegations only in a 'technical' sense inadequate to meet Section 2–201(3)(b)'s admission requirement. . . ." Shadur, J. in Triangle Marketing, Inc. v. Action Industries, Inc., 630 F.Supp. 1578, 1583–1584 (N.D.Ill. 1986).

(2)   If the defense is provided by statute, should there not be a convenient procedure by which to raise the defense? If so, what should it be? More specifically, how should courts answer the following questions:

(a)   May the defendant demur or move to dismiss on the ground that the agreement as alleged is unenforceable?

(b)   May the defendant move for summary judgment on the basis that the pleadings and supporting affidavits show an unenforceable oral agreement?

(c)   When may the plaintiff "compel" admissions, either in a deposition or by cross-examination in open court, and thereby render the contract enforceable?

(d)   Must the admission conclusively prove the existence of the contract? Or is it sufficient if it merely evidences the contract?

Comment: The Statute of Frauds and Estoppel

Assume that Farmer and Dealer made an oral contract in March for the sale of 5,000 bushels of #1 Yellow Corn for $5.40 per bushel, delivery in October. Relying on Farmer's oral promise, Dealer promptly resold the corn to a third person for $7.00 per bushel. Farmer, based upon their prior course of dealing, knew that this resale would probably occur. When the market price rose to $10.00 per bushel in September, Farmer refused to deliver. Dealer, alleging the oral contract and the resale, claims damages. Farmer moves to dismiss on the ground of the Statute of Frauds. UCC § 2–201. Dealer argues that the Statute of Frauds should be avoided because of his reliance upon Farmer's oral promise to deliver. Should this argument be accepted?

An affirmative answer appears to be in direct conflict with the purpose and policy of the Statute. There are no misrepresentations of fact by Farmer here, and no representation that Farmer will not insist upon a writing. Rather, it is the oral promise (which should have been in writing) that induced the reliance by Dealer. Thus, one court has argued: "[T]he moral wrong of refusing to be bound by an agreement because it does not comply with the Statute of Frauds, does not of itself authorize the application of the doctrine of estoppel, for the breach of a promise which the law does not regard as binding is not a fraud. . . . To hold otherwise would be to render the statute entirely nugatory." Ozier v. Haines, 411 Ill. 160, 162–63 (1952).

Reflecting the scarcity of case law in which a plaintiff has successfully employed estoppel in a Statute of Frauds case, the drafters of the First Restatement did not include a specific section on the subject. They did, however, provide the following comment: "Though there has been no satisfaction of the Statute, an estoppel may preclude objection on that ground in the same way that objection to the non-existence of other facts essential for the establishment of a right or a defense may be precluded. A misrepresentation that there has been such satisfaction if substantial action is taken in reliance on the representation, precludes proof by the party who made the representation that it was false; and a promise to make a memorandum, if similarly relied on, may give rise to an effective promissory estoppel if the Statute would otherwise operate to defraud." Restatement § 178 cmt. f.

The Second Restatement, in contrast, includes a separate provision for the application of promissory estoppel in cases falling under the Statute of Frauds. Section 139 provides:

> (1) A promise which the promisor should reasonably expect to induce action or forbearance on the part of the promisee or a third person and which does induce the action or forbearance is enforceable notwithstanding the Statute of Frauds if injustice can be avoided only by enforcement of the promise. The remedy granted for breach is to be limited as justice requires.

> (2) In determining whether injustice can be avoided only by enforcement of the promise, the following circumstances are significant: (a) the availability and adequacy of other remedies, particularly cancellation and restitution; (b) the definite and

substantial character of the action or forbearance in relation to the remedy sought; (c) the extent to which the action or forbearance corroborates evidence of the making and terms of the promise, or the making and terms are otherwise established by clear and convincing evidence; (d) the reasonableness of the action or forbearance; (e) the extent to which the action or forbearance was foreseeable by the promisor.

Section 139 complements Section 90 and, like that section, states a flexible standard. It also acknowledges, however, that "the requirement of consideration is more easily displaced than the requirement of a writing." Restatement (Second) § 139 cmt. b. Some courts have nonetheless expressed concern that section 139 tends to protect reliance on the very oral promise that is within the Statute. Courts in Indiana, for example, have held that not only must reliance on the oral promise be reasonable, but the reliance injury also must be somewhat independent of the oral promise and be so substantial as to constitute an unjust and unconscionable injury or loss. Coca-Cola Co. v. Babyback's Int'l, Inc., 841 N.E.2d 557 (Ind. 2006).

Section 139, however, might give some hope to Dealer in the above hypothetical, especially if subsection (2)(c) can be satisfied. Should the fact that this is a UCC case make a further difference? There is disagreement over whether promissory estoppel is available to save an oral sales contract under UCC § 2–201. The legislative history, the language and the structure of Section 2–201 all indicate that promissory estoppel was not to be used to evade the rather simple requirements of the section. See Michael Gibson, *Promissory Estoppel, Article 2 of the U.C.C., and the Restatement (Third) of Contracts*, 73 Iowa L. Rev. 659, 695 (1988). Hawkland further argues that "[g]iven the liberalizing force of the rules of Section 2–201(2) and (3), it is somewhat difficult to imagine situations where additional relief should be given by way of estoppel." 1 Hawkland UCC Series § 2–201:8 (2011).

That said, as Hawkland points out, the application of promissory estoppel to transactions falling under UCC § 2–201 remains unclear. Some courts refuse to use promissory estoppel in this area. Some apply it whenever fraud or unconscionability is present. Still others, like the Seventh Circuit in *R.S. Bennett & Co. v. Economy Mechanical Industries, Inc.*, 606 F.2d 182 (7th Cir. 1979), will evidently apply it whenever the ordinary elements of promissory estoppel are present. See generally Jeffrey Kagan, Comment, *The Indelibility of Invisible Ink: A Critical Survey of the Enforcement of Oral Contracts Without the Statute of Frauds under the Uniform Commercial Code*, 19 Whittier L. Rev. 423 (1997).

PROBLEM: THE CASE OF THE LAKE WOBEGON LOT PURCHASE

For years, Paula Purchaser has sought to buy a lot on Lake Wobegon owned by Vincent Vendor. Last week, Paula made yet another attempt to purchase the land—a one-acre lot with lake frontage and the only property Vince owned—and this time he was agreeable. While discussing the matter at Vince's house, they agreed upon all of the essential terms, including the cash price of $10,000. After "shaking on it," Paula wrote a check for $1,000, down payment on the purchase. The check was made out to Vincent Vendor and contained the following legend: "$1,000 down on lot on Lake Wobegon, balance due $9,000." The following week, however, Vince changed his mind about selling and tendered the check back to Paula. Does Paula have legal recourse? What if Paula, in the meantime, had made a commitment to a bank to borrow funds to complete the purchase?

Assume, instead, that after agreeing upon the essential terms, including the cash price of $10,000, Paula wrote out the $1,000 check as down payment (but without the legend, as above) and gave it to Vince. Vince immediately cashed the check. Thereafter, Paula determined not to go through with the deal and wants her down payment returned. Vince, however, is willing to complete the transaction whenever agreeable to Paula. Is Paula entitled to a return of the $1,000? See Restatement (Second) § 375.

2. CAPACITY TO CONTRACT

Not everyone can contract. A person must have legal capacity to enter into a contract. At various times under U.S. law, minors, the insane, intoxicated persons, married women, convicts, spendthrifts, the aged, corporations and Native Americans each lacked the legal capacity to contract.

In thinking about capacity, there are several questions to consider:

(1) Under what circumstances is a person so incapacitated that either no contract can arise from the bargain (in which case, the contract is said to be "void") or the contract that arises can be rescinded or avoided (in which case, the contract is "voidable")?

(2) What must be done to effectively rescind a voidable contract?

(3) What are the appropriate remedies available to each party involved in the transaction where either no contract has arisen or the contract has been rescinded?

A broader consideration is the extent to which the capacity cases reflect both (1) the objective of achieving fairness and broader social changes, as evidenced by, for example, the legislative trend toward lowering the age of majority from twenty-one to eighteen and (2) changes in the understanding and treatment of mental illness and drug addiction.

(A) INFANCY

"Unless a statute provides otherwise, a natural person has the capacity to incur only voidable contractual duties until the beginning of the day before the person's eighteenth birthday." Restatement (Second) § 14. In *Davis v. Clelland*, an Ohio Court of Appeals reaffirmed the orthodox doctrine:

We recognize what seems to be an injustice to the defendant to permit the minor-plaintiff to possess and enjoy the use of the automobile for almost a year, drive it into a telephone pole and wreck it, then haul it into a yard and elect to rescind the whole transaction. However, this is not an equitable proceeding and is controlled entirely by legal principles under which a minor has the right as to contracts made during minority to affirm or disaffirm his contracts other than those for necessaries. Those who deal with a minor must do so charged with the knowledge of the controlling principle of law which, as here, may work some injustice in individual cases but affords, in general, the protection of minors against their own improvidence at a time when they are presumed to be incapable of protecting themselves.

92 N.E.2d 827, 829 (Ohio App. 1950). The minor—or "infant," the term frequently used in the legal literature—has long been accorded special contractual immunity. The extent of protection has diminished somewhat in recent years, both by decision and by statute. But nowhere is the minor recognized as possessing full legal capacity to contract. In general, a minor's contracts are voidable. A minor can avoid his or her contractual obligations by timely and appropriate disaffirmance. The other party, if an adult, is bound, reflecting the risk of contracting with one who is under age. Once the age of majority is reached, the former minor can ratify, or affirm, the contract.

Larry Bowling v. Max Sperry

Appellate Court of Indiana, 1962.
133 Ind.App. 692.

■ MYERS, JUDGE. This is an appeal from a judgment of the Noble Circuit Court in a civil action brought by appellant, Larry Bowling, by Norma Lemley as next friend, hereinafter referred to as Larry, against appellee, Max E. Sperry, d/b/a Sperry Ford Sales, to disaffirm and set aside a contract for the purchase of an automobile on the grounds of infancy.

Larry was a minor, sixteen years of age. On June 29, 1957, he purchased from appellee a 1947 Plymouth automobile for the sum of $140 cash. He paid $50 down on that day and returned on July 1, 1957, to pay the balance of $90 and take possession of the car. Appellee delivered to him a certificate of title and a written receipt. This receipt stated that as of June 29, 1957, Max Sperry Ford Sales sold to Larry Bowling a 1947 Plymouth for the amount of $140, cash, paid in full.

Larry drove the car several times during the following week and discovered that the main bearing was burned out. He had the car brought back to appellee's place of business where he was informed that it would cost him from $45 to $95 to make repairs. He declined to pay this amount and left the car on appellee's lot. Subsequently, he mailed a letter to appellee to the effect that he disaffirmed the contract of purchase and demanded the return of his money. Upon appellee's refusal to pay back the $140, this lawsuit followed.

Larry's complaint is based upon the fact that appellee sold him a car knowing that he was a minor; that he tendered back the car, rescinded the contract, and demanded the sum of $140. Appellee's answer was in two paragraphs, the first being in the nature of a general denial, pursuant to the provisions of Supreme Court Rule 1–3, and the second being an allegation that Larry was accompanied by his grandmother and aunt at the time of the purchase, and that the aunt paid appellee the sum of $90 of the purchase price. Upon trial of the case by the court, judgment was rendered in favor of appellee and against Larry.

It has been the rule in Indiana for many years that the contracts of minors are voidable and may be disaffirmed. It is not necessary that the other party be placed in *statu quo,* nor is it necessary that the minor tender back the money or property he has received before suing for the value or possession of the money or property given by him to the adult. All such voidable contracts by a minor in regard to personal property may be avoided at any time during his minority or upon his arrival at full age. . . .

The evidence showed that Larry's grandmother and aunt accompanied him to appellee's used car lot on June 29, 1957, when he selected the automobile, and that his aunt drove the car around the lot at that time. Furthermore, it was revealed that his aunt had loaned him $90 in order to make final payment on the car and that he had commenced to pay this back at $10 a week thereafter.

These facts, however, do not change the general rule. In so far as the agreement and sale is concerned, there was sufficient evidence to show that it was made between appellee and Larry, and no one else. It is of no consequence that his aunt and grandmother accompanied him at the time of purchase; and the fact that his aunt made payment of the $90 balance due could have no effect upon Larry's right to take advantage of his minority in an action to recover such payment. . . . Appellee was fully aware of Larry's age when the sale was negotiated. The written receipt was in Larry's name alone. This contract was squarely between an adult and a minor and falls within the rule pronounced above. Larry had every right to disaffirm it and set it aside.

Appellee claims there is doubt as to whether Larry received a certificate of title from appellee with his name on it. It is contended that the certificate was delivered in blank. As was said in the case of *Wooldridge v. Hill,* 124 Ind.App. 11, 14 . . . "It is of little consequence whether title to the property involved had passed to the infant or not." The certificate of title is only evidence of ownership, and in this case it would make no difference whether Larry had received a certificate in blank or with his name on it. . . .

Appellee argues that an inference may be drawn from the evidence to show that the burned-out bearing was caused by Larry's operation of the car and his failure to put oil in the crankcase. Even if this were true, it is no defense to this action. There is no requirement in Indiana that before a disaffirmance is effected the parties must be placed in *statu quo*. . . .

The question of whether or not the automobile was a necessary was injected into the trial of the case although appellee did not plead it as a defense. Some argument on this subject was made by the parties in the briefs. Section 58–102, Burns' Ind.Stat., 1961 Replacement, reads as follows:

> "Capacity to buy and sell is regulated by the general law concerning capacity to contract, and to transfer and acquire property.

> "Where necessaries are sold and delivered to an infant, or to a person who by reason of mental incapacity or drunkenness is incompetent to contract, he must pay a reasonable price therefor.

> "Necessaries in this section means goods suitable to the condition in life of such infant or other person, and to his actual requirements at the time of delivery."

In the case of *Price v. Sanders*, 60 Ind. 310, 314 (1878), the following is stated:

> " 'Necessaries,' in the technical sense, mean such things as are necessary to the support, use or comfort of the person of the minor, as food, raiment, lodging, medical attendance, and such personal comforts as comport with his condition and circumstances in life, including a common school education; but it has been pithily and happily said, that necessaries do not include 'horses, saddles, bridles, liquors, pistols, powder, whips and fiddles.' "

Whether the goods are necessaries is a question of law, and if they are deemed as such, their quantity, quality and reasonable value are matters of fact. . . .

* * *

The evidence revealed that at the time of this transaction, Larry was living with his grandmother in Cromwell, Indiana, where he had lived for the past fifteen years; that his mother was dead and his father resided in Fort Wayne; that he was a student at Cromwell High School, but was on vacation; that he had a summer job working at a restaurant in the town of Syracuse, Indiana, which was eight or nine miles away from his home; that his usual means of transportation back and forth was with the cook; that on occasion he could "bum" rides with other people.

The acting manager for appellee, who had dealt with Larry, testified that when Larry's aunt and grandmother came to the sales lot on June 29, 1957, "they" said Larry needed something for him to get back and forth to work. He said it was his "understanding" that the car was needed for that purpose. Larry stated that during the short period of time he had possession of it, he only used it for pleasure, and did not drive it to work.

We are well aware of the overwhelming increase in the use and number of automobiles in this country since World War II. What once was a great luxury for only the wealthy has become a matter of common necessity for the ordinary workingman, farmer and businessman. The automobile is as important to the modern household as food, clothing and shelter. The problem here is whether the car in question was so needed by Larry, in view of his situation in life, his social status and his financial position, that he could not be maintained properly or suitably without it. The burden of showing this was upon appellee. . . . From the evidence presented, we do not think appellee met this burden. While every high school boy today wants a car of his own, and many of them own automobiles which under given circumstances may be considered as necessaries, we do not consider the car in this case so vital to Larry's existence that it could be classified as a necessary.

Judgment reversed, and cause remanded with instructions that the trial court sustain appellant's motion for a new trial on the ground that the judgment is contrary to law.

NOTES

(1)   After this brief excursion into the world of minors' contracts, what are your reactions? Are just results being achieved? What reforms, if any, are in order? In which respects might contractual immunity be legally disadvantageous to the minor?

How would you advise an adult client who proposed to contract with a minor? In *Bowling*, for example, would Sperry have been protected if Larry's grandmother had agreed to become jointly liable for Larry's contract?

(2)   *Legal Responsibility of Emancipated Minors.* In *Kiefer v. Fred Howe Motors, Inc.*, the Wisconsin Supreme Court addressed the law's treatment of the emancipated minor:

The underpinnings of the general rule allowing the minor to disaffirm his contracts were undoubtedly the protection of the minor. It was thought that the minor was immature in both mind and experience and that, therefore, he should be protected from his own bad judgments as well as from adults who would take advantage of him. The doctrine of the voidability of minors' contracts often seems commendable and just. If the beans that the young naïve Jack purchased from the crafty old man in the fairy tale "Jack and the Bean Stalk" had been worthless rather than magical, it would have been only fair to allow Jack to disaffirm the bargain and reclaim his cow. However, in today's modern and sophisticated society the "infancy doctrine" seems to lose some of its gloss.

Paradoxically, we declare the infant mature enough to shoulder arms in the military, but not mature enough to vote; mature enough to marry and be responsible for his torts and crimes, but not mature enough to assume the burden of his own contractual indiscretions. In Wisconsin, the infant is deemed mature enough to use a dangerous instrumentality—a motor vehicle—at sixteen, but not mature enough to purchase it without protection until he is twenty-one.

No one really questions that a line as to age must be drawn somewhere below which a legally defined minor must be able to disaffirm his contracts for nonnecessities. The law over the centuries has considered this age to be twenty-one. Legislatures in other states have lowered the age. We suggest that the appellant might better seek the change it proposes in the legislative halls rather than this court. A recent law review article in the Indiana Law Journal explores the problem of contractual disabilities of minors and points to three different legislative solutions leading to greater freedom to contract. The first approach is one gleaned from the statutes of California and New York, which would allow parties to submit a proposed contract to a court which would remove the infant's right of disaffirmance upon a finding that the particular contract is fair. This suggested approach appears to be extremely impractical in light of the expense and delay that would necessarily accompany the procedure. A second approach would be to establish a rebuttable presumption of incapacity to replace the strict rule. This alternative would be an open invitation to litigation. The third suggestion is a statutory procedure that would allow a minor to petition a court for the removal of disabilities. Under this procedure a minor would only have to go to court once, rather than once for each contract as in the first suggestion.

Undoubtedly, the infancy doctrine is an obstacle when a major purchase is involved. However, we believe that the reasons for allowing that obstacle to remain viable at this point outweigh those for casting it aside. Minors require some protection from the pitfalls of the market place. Reasonable minds will always differ on the extent of the protection that should be afforded. For this court to adopt a rule that the appellant suggests and remove the contractual disabilities from a minor simply because he becomes emancipated, which in most cases would be the result of marriage, would be to suggest that the married minor is somehow vested with more wisdom and maturity than his single counterpart. However, logic would not seem to dictate this result especially when today a youthful marriage is oftentimes indicative of a lack of wisdom and maturity.

39 Wis.2d 20, 24–25 (1968). Why do you think this discussion took place in 1968?

Today, "[a] minor's emancipation, whether by judicial decree or by circumstance or operation of law generally has the effect of granting the minor the 'capacity' to contract while at the same time removing the minor's ability to avoid contracts entered into after his or her emancipation." Thomas Jacobs, Children and the Law: Rights and Obligations § 11:9 (2007).

(3) *Restoration or Restitution? Bowling* adheres to the prevailing view as to the degree of restitution required of a minor upon disaffirmance. The minor is obliged to return what he or she still has, i.e., *in specie*. There is no obligation to account for use or depreciation or to return an equivalent of what was received. Thus, the requirement is one of restoration, not restitution. See, e.g., Star Chevrolet Co. v. Green, 473 So.2d 157 (Miss. 1985) (minor who wrecked vehicle not obliged to account for proceeds received from insurance company); but see Valencia v. White, 134 Ariz. 139 (App. 1982) (discussion of various departures from the majority rule in cases from New Hampshire, Minnesota, Pennsylvania, New York and New Jersey).

(4) *Disaffirmance and Ratification.* "An infant cannot affirmatively ratify until he comes of age. After that date any manifestation by him of an intent to regard the bargain as binding will deprive him of the power to avoid the contract. . . . Mere silence or inaction by a former infant after attaining majority does not amount to ratification. . . . However, an infant should be required to disaffirm within a reasonable time after coming of age. . . . Disavowal of a contract by an infant need not be by any prescribed form or ceremony; the filing of an answer by him or in his behalf disaffirming the contract is sufficient in itself to accomplish the result." Mechanics Finance Co. v. Paolino, 29 N.J.Super. 449, 455–56 (1954). No new consideration is required for the ratification of a previously voidable contract. See Restatement (Second) § 85. Should ratification be added to the list of exceptions to the consideration requirement?

In *Bobby Floars Toyota, Inc. v. Smith*, 48 N.C.App. 580 (1980), a minor made eleven monthly payments on the purchase of an automobile, ten of them after his eighteenth birthday. After noting that a reasonable time for disaffirmance depends upon the circumstances of each case, no hard-and-fast rule regarding time limits being capable of definition, the court concluded that ten months was enough time within which to elect between disaffirmance and ratification with respect to an item of personal property that is constantly depreciating in value. Cf. Keser v. Chagnon, 159 Colo. 209 (1966) (minor did not ratify contract by using car for sixty days after reaching his majority, before disaffirming and returning car ten days later).

(5) *Recovery for Necessaries Furnished.* The law is replete with instances where the effect of a strict rule is mitigated by successful assertions of claims of unjust enrichment. For example, a contract may be within the Statute of Frauds, and for that reason be unenforceable, but the plaintiff may be able to proceed on a theory of restitution. Granting relief on this basis does not, in the ordinary situation, thwart statutory purposes. In much the same way, a recovery for necessaries furnished to a minor is not viewed as inconsistent with the policy of contractual immunity. The suit is not on the contract. Rather, as one court put it, the minor "is held on a promise implied by law, and not, strictly speaking, on his actual promise. . . .

[H]e is liable to pay only what the necessaries were reasonably worth, and not what he may improvidently have agreed to pay for them." Trainer v. Trumbull, 141 Mass. 527, 530 (1886). If necessaries are involved, recovery is limited to restitution. But courts have been unwilling to expand the category of necessaries to include, for example, automobiles. Accord: Warwick Municipal Employees Credit Union v. McAllister, 110 R.I. 399 (1972). If the goal is to preclude an unjust enrichment, then why limit recovery to necessary items? See Steven Wolfe, *A Reevaluation of the Contractual Rights of Minors*, 57 UMKC L. Rev. 145 (1988).

(6) *Specific Contract Types.* In addition to the general rule for necessaries, state legislatures have passed rules that give minors the capacity to enter into specific types of contracts. Common examples are contracts for enlistment in the military or for loans to be used for higher education. In Oregon, a statute authorizes unemancipated homeless minors to contract for housing and utilities. Or. Rev. Stat. § 109. Several jurisdictions allow minors of a certain age to contract for auto, life, health, or disability insurance. For more detail, see Thomas Jacobs, Children and the Law: Rights and Obligations § 11:9 (2007).

(7) *Effect of Misrepresentation of Age: Tort and Estoppel.* If the minor is silent as to her age, the risk of her incapacity strictly falls on the other party. In effect, a contractor has a duty to ascertain that the other side is not an infant—possibly by securing a representation from the other side about her age.

There are a number of approaches to minors' misrepresentations of age. At one extreme is the Massachusetts rule that minors are "not liable in tort for deceit arising from false representations as to . . . age or for damages to the machines while in their possession and used by them." Raymond v. General Motorcycle Co., 230 Mass. 54, 55 (1918). In the middle are the cases holding that misrepresentation will not estop the minor from disaffirming but will justify damages in tort. See, e.g., Mestetzko v. Elf Motor Co., 119 Ohio St. 575 (1929); Creer v. Active Automobile Exchange, 99 Conn. 266 (1923). At the other extreme is estoppel: "When a minor has reached that stage of maturity which indicates that he is of full age, and enters into a contract falsely representing himself to be of age, accepting the benefits of the contract, he will be estopped to deny that he is not of age when the obligation of the contract is sought to be enforced against him." Johnson v. McAdory, 228 Miss. 453, 457 (1956).

The estoppel approach has been codified by statute in Indiana: "When, in case of any loan or sale made by seller, creditor or secured party, the borrower, or any other person furnishing security on behalf of the borrower, shall, as an inducement to the seller, creditor or secured party to make the loan or sale, represent to it, in writing, that he or she is eighteen (18) years of age or older, whereas in fact such person or persons are under the age of eighteen (18) years, or shall otherwise make any false statement or representation to the seller, creditor or secured party and the seller, creditor or secured party is thereby deceived, and the loan or sale is made in reliance upon such representation, neither the person so representing, nor any one in his or her behalf, nor any person otherwise legally liable to pay such loan or sale, shall afterwards be allowed, as against such seller, creditor or secured party, to take advantage of the fact that the person making the representation was under eighteen (18) years of age, but each such person shall be estopped by such representation." Ind. Code 28–1–26.5–1.

PROBLEM: THE CASE OF THE BOLD GRADUATES

After receiving their high school diplomas, Matt and Pat, each age seventeen, determined to strike out on their own. They decided to rent an apartment together, find jobs, and see if they could make it in the "real world." Their parents were pleased but somewhat dubious. They assured the boys that "they would always be welcome at home."

On June 15, the boys signed a one-year lease with Landlord, Inc., calling for a $250 monthly rental, payable in advance, plus a security deposit of $250. They paid the first month's rent and the security deposit. However, they vacated the premises on July 15 and demanded a return of all monies paid. Were they entitled to repayment?

Tiring of life in the real world, the boys took off in the fall for State U. They again executed a one-year lease (monthly rental of $400 plus $400 security deposit). But, alas, their educational careers were short-lived, and they again decided to strike out for other parts. They confronted the landlord with a demand for the return of all payments. The landlord refused. He conceded that they were paid up for the period of their stay, but he insisted they were breaching the lease and were accountable for damages that would be sustained. How should the matter be resolved?

(B) MENTAL INCOMPETENCE AND INTOXICATION

Restatement (Second) § 15 provides:

(1) A person incurs only voidable contractual duties by entering into a transaction if by reason of mental illness or defect [if] (a) he is unable to understand in a reasonable manner the nature and consequences of the transaction, or (b) he is unable to act in a reasonable manner in relation to the transaction and the other party has reason to know of his condition.

(2) Where the contract is made on fair terms and the other party is without knowledge of the mental illness or defect, the power of avoidance under Subsection (1) terminates to the extent that the contract has been so performed in whole or in part or the circumstances have so changed that avoidance would be unjust. In such a case a court may grant relief as justice requires.

What is the difference between the condition in (1)(a) and that in (1)(b)? Subsection (1)(a) relates to "cognitive" incapacity (the inability to understand), while subsection (1)(b) relates to "volitional" incapacity (the inability to act in a reasonable manner). Contractors who suffer from volitional incapacity may understand the terms of the contract but may not be able to keep themselves from manifesting assent. Why does only volitional incapacity add on the requirement that the other party had "reason to know of the condition"? One possibility is that the other party can more easily protect against contracting with someone who is cognitively impaired simply by testing whether they understand the terms of the contract. But someone who is acting under a volitional compulsion might be able to explain the terms of the contract and might be under a compulsion not to disclose that the Devil is making her manifest assent.

The drafters explain that the section is an effort to reconcile "two conflicting policies: the protection of justifiable expectations and of the security of transactions, and the protection of persons unable to protect themselves against imposition." Id. cmt. a. If a guardian is appointed, the problem is resolved: "A person has no capacity to incur contractual duties if his property is under guardianship. . . ." Restatement (Second) § 13. Without a guardian, the search for a mediating principle is complicated by the "wide variety of types and degrees of mental incompetency." This means that a "person may be able to understand almost nothing, or only simple or routine transactions, or he may be incompetent only with respect to a particular type of transaction." Also, even if his "understanding is complete, he may lack capacity to control his acts in the way that the normal individual can and does control them; in such cases the incapacity makes the contract voidable only if the other person has reason to know of his condition." Restatement (Second) § 15 cmt. b.

In *Ortelere v. Teachers' Retirement Board*, 25 N.Y.2d 196 (1969), the New York Court of Appeals rejected the traditional standard of measurement, a "cognitive test," in which the focus was on whether an individual could comprehend and understand the nature of the transaction, and instead fashioned an alternative test based upon Restatement (Second) § 15(1)(b). According to *Ortelere*, a contract may be voided where a person, "by reason of mental illness or defect" is "unable to act in a reasonable manner in relation to the transaction." 25 N.Y.2d at 202, quoting from Restatement (Second) § 15(1)(b). Thus, in New York, the test for contractual incapacity includes not only those who do not understand the nature and consequences of their actions but also those " 'whose contracts are merely uncontrolled reactions to their mental illness.' " Id. at 205.

A few courts take the position that a contract with an incompetent should be enforced if the exchange is fair, unless the other party recognizes the other's incapacity. If so, the other party is guilty of a fraud. The more common rule is that the incompetent should be able to avoid the contract only if he or she can restore the other party to the other party's pre-contract position. This rule also takes into account whether the other party acted in good faith and was unaware of the incapacity. Why the difference from the rule for minors?

Heights Realty, Ltd. v. E.A. Phillips

Supreme Court of New Mexico, 1988.
106 N.M. 692.

■ STOWERS, JUSTICE. This case involves an exclusive listing contract between plaintiff-appellant, Heights Realty, Ltd. (Heights Realty), and Johnye Mary Gholson (Mrs. Gholson), the original named defendant. Heights Realty filed an amended complaint seeking its commission for having performed under the terms of the contract by having provided a buyer to purchase Mrs. Gholson's property. During the pendency of this action, Mrs. Gholson was adjudicated incompetent and E.A. Phillips (Phillips), the present defendant-appellee, was appointed conservator of her estate. Following a bench trial, the district court found Mrs. Gholson lacked the mental capacity to have validly executed the listing contract and entered judgment in favor of Phillips. On appeal, Heights Realty argues that the presumption of competency was not overcome by clear and convincing evidence. We disagree and affirm the judgment of the district court.

In 1984, Mrs. Gholson was interested in selling her North Valley property. She telephoned Heights Realty and spoke with Pat Eichenberg, a real estate broker and owner of Heights Realty and also an acquaintance of hers, who brought Mrs. Gholson an exclusive listing agreement. Mrs. Gholson was approximately eighty-four years old when she signed the contract on September 26, 1984, listing the property for one year in the amount of $250,000 with a cash down payment of $75,000. No other terms were included in the agreement. Subsequently, Mrs. Gholson changed her mind about the amount of the down payment and on October 10, 1984, signed an addendum increasing it to $100,000. In November 1984 an offer was made to purchase the property for $255,000. Mrs. Gholson did not accept that offer.

The question to be determined is whether substantial evidence was presented from which the trial court could properly conclude that the presumption of competency was overcome by clear and convincing evidence.

On appeal, this court reviews the record to determine whether there is substantial evidence to support the trial court's findings of fact. . . .

The test of mental capacity is whether a person is capable of understanding in a reasonable manner the nature and effect of the act in which the person is engaged. . . . The law presumes that every person is competent. To show the contrary, the burden of proof rests on the person asserting lack of capacity to establish the same by clear and convincing proof. . . . The burden remains on those alleging incompetency unless the case is brought within the exception in which previous incompetency is admitted or sufficiently shown and thus changes that burden. If incompetency of a general permanent nature has been shown to once exist for a period of time prior to the execution of the instrument under attack, it is presumed to continue until there is a showing by the person relying on the validity of that instrument that proves the existence of a lucid interval at the time of its execution. . . .

Although the test of mental capacity is applied as of the date that the attacked instrument is executed, evidence of a person's prior or subsequent condition is admissible to show the condition at the time in issue. . . . The combined weight of all the evidence in each case determines the result. The court is entitled to take into consideration the individual's physical condition; the adequacy of consideration; whether or not the transaction was improvident; the relation of trust and confidence between the parties to the transaction and the weakness of the mind of the alleged incompetent person as judged by all other acts within a reasonable time prior and subsequent to the act in question. . . .

Only Mrs. Eichenberg and Mrs. Gholson were present at the time of the signing of the exclusive listing agreement on September 26, 1984, and its addendum on October 10, 1984. Mrs. Eichenberg testified that Mrs. Gholson was "just as sharp as a tack" when the agreement was executed. She further testified that on the date the addendum was signed, Mrs. Eichenberg read the contents of it to Mrs. Gholson who had been lying down on the couch because she had injured her foot and that Mrs. Gholson appeared to have no problems understanding the addendum since she even corrected a misspelling in her name.

Testimony was presented that Mrs. Gholson owned approximately twelve acres with a residence in Albuquerque's North Valley at the time she decided to sell the property for financial reasons. Mrs. Gholson stated that she set the asking price of $250,000 by guessing at the value of the property and left open all other terms vital to the contract. Mrs. Gholson also testified that she had no recollection of signing the addendum because she "couldn't think of anything in sequence at that time." Evidence showed that no family or lawyer assisted her in executing the agreements. It appears from the record that the trial court discounted Mrs. Eichenberg's testimony.

Additional testimony as to Mrs. Gholson's mental capacity was elicited from her son-in-law, Phillips, and granddaughter, Louise Loomis, both of whom had for many years observed Mrs. Gholson's speech and conduct. Phillips testified that he first noticed behavior evidencing her gradual mental decline in 1959, after the death of her husband. He recounted a number of incidents: for example, beginning in May 1983, Mrs. Gholson began to mismanage the payment of her bills, confusing credit with debit balances; she set off her burglar alarm and left it running; she locked herself out of her automobile while the engine was still on; and she failed to recall the death of her younger brother, with whom she had been extremely close, on September 19, 1984. Phillips characterized her as being constantly confused.

Louise Loomis testified that she always maintained a close and intimate relationship with her grandmother. She described the degeneration of Mrs. Gholson's mind over a period of years. In particular, she stated that around 1979 or 1980, her grandmother began to have problems comprehending matters. Mrs. Loomis testified that by the summer of 1984 on a trip to Utah, her grandmother was unable to communicate with people or dial a telephone number for room service and that shortly thereafter, Mrs. Gholson could not carry on her personal affairs nor make appointments with the hairdresser. She also developed erratic eating habits and was incapable of dealing with restaurant bills. Continuing, Mrs. Loomis testified that her grandmother became much more confused after she broke her foot in September of 1984. She opined that her grandmother did not have the mental capacity to understand a listing agreement.

Two psychiatrists testified, Dr. Farber for Heights Realty, and Dr. Muldawer on behalf of Mrs. Gholson. Dr. Farber neither met with nor examined Mrs. Gholson and only reviewed documents about her. Dr. Farber indicated that primarily he relied on Dr. Muldawer's handwritten notes and his deposition. Dr. Farber averred that he neither had sufficient evidence nor had he made a timely examination of her to enable him to say that she was incompetent, and therefore the presumption of competency had to prevail.

Dr. Muldawer testified that he examined Mrs. Gholson on January 11, 1985, reviewed relevant documents, and thereafter conferred with her relatives. He found that Mrs. Gholson showed a general decline in her cognitive skills about 1979 or 1980 involving her judgment, reasoning and memory. He further stated that this decline was slow and subtle and was evidenced by increasing forgetfulness and the general inability to take care of her own needs. He concluded that when she signed the listing agreement "she certainly didn't fully understand the terms" even though "in a broader sense she knew she was disposing of property." He then stated he could not use the word "conclusively" to describe Mrs. Gholson's lack of contractual capacity on September 26, 1984, but he could state that she was incompetent on that date within "reasonable medical probability."

A review of the trial record indicates, as properly found by the court below, that "on September 26, 1984 and thereafter Mrs. Gholson was suffering from a progressive, deteriorating mental disease which prevented her from understanding the nature and consequences of the * * * agreement and the Addendum thereto"; and that "on September 26, 1984 and thereafter, Mrs. Gholson was without lucid intervals."

There was a conflict in the general medical testimony adduced from Dr. Muldawer, who observed Mrs. Gholson, and Dr. Farber, who never observed her but relied on observations of another party. This type of medical testimony therefore, in and of itself, is not sufficient to overcome the presumption of competency. . . . The opinions expressed by Phillips and Mrs. Loomis were predicated on their many experiences with Mrs. Gholson tending to afford them opportunities to observe her mental capacity. Thus, there was substantial evidence presented from those who were in a position to observe Mrs. Gholson's conduct before and after the day the instrument in question was executed.

Even though some of the evidence adduced was conflicting, this goes to the question of credibility, a question solely for resolution by the trier of fact, who after hearing the testimony resolved the question in favor of Mrs. Gholson. This court will not resolve conflicts or substitute its judgment where the record as a whole substantially supports the trial court's findings of fact. . . .

Although the trial court did not specifically state in its findings that the presumption of competency was overcome by clear and convincing evidence, it is implicit in those findings when the evidence is viewed in its entirety that this burden of proof had been sustained. We hold that substantial evidence was presented from which the trial court could properly conclude that the presumption of competency was overcome by clear and convincing evidence; consequently, Mrs. Gholson lacked mental capacity to enter into the exclusive listing agreement and its addendum. The judgment of the district court is affirmed.

IT IS SO ORDERED.

NOTES

(1) Is adequacy of consideration relevant to the issue of mental capacity? See Restatement (Second) § 15 cmt. b: "Where a person has some understanding of a particular transaction which is affected by mental illness or defect, the controlling consideration is whether the transaction in its result is one which a reasonably competent person might have made." What evidence was there in *Heights Realty v. Phillips* that the listing agreement was improvident or unfair?

(2) *Inadequacy of Consideration Plus Something Else.* "[I]nadequacy of price *within itself*, and disconnected from all other facts, cannot be a ground for setting aside a contract, or affording relief against it. There must be something else besides the mere inadequacy of consideration or inequality in the bargain, to justify a court in granting relief by setting aside the contract. *What this something else besides the inadequacy* should be, perhaps no court ought to say, lest the wary and cunning, by employing other means than those named, should escape with their fraudulent gains. I, however, will venture to say, that it ought, in connection with the inadequacy of consideration, to superinduce the belief that there had been either a suppression of the truth, the suggestion of falsehood, abuse of confidence, a violation of duty arising out of some fiduciary relation between the parties, the exercise of undue influence, or the taking of an unjust and inequitable advantage of one whose peculiar situation at the time would be calculated to render him an easy prey to the cunning and the artful. But if no one of these appears, or if no fact is proved that will lead the mind to the conclusion, that the party against whom relief is sought has suppressed some fact that he ought to have disclosed, or that he has suggested some falsehood, or abused

in some manner the confidence reposed in him, or that some fiduciary relation existed between the parties, or that the party complaining was under his influence, or at the time of the trade was in a condition, *from any cause*, that would render him an easy victim to the unconscientious, then relief cannot be afforded; for inadequacy of consideration, *standing alone and unsupported by any thing else, can authorize no court, governed by the rules of the English law, to set aside a contract. . . .*" Judge v. Wilkins, 19 Ala. 765, 772 (1851).

(3) What result if the conservator, pleased with the offer procured by Heights Realty, had proceeded to sell to the offeror? Would this rule out the incompetency defense? Would there be a basis for recovery by the realty company?

(4) *The Case of the Adjudged Incompetent.* Manzelle Johnson was declared incompetent, and her nephew, Obbie Neal, was appointed her guardian. Obbie persuaded Mrs. Johnson to deed real property to him in his individual capacity, and he, in turn, conveyed the property to Charles Weatherly, a bona fide purchaser. Obbie was later removed as guardian, and the new guardian sued to cancel the deeds and to collect profits from the land that accrued to Weatherly. Weatherly counterclaimed for the amount of consideration paid for the land and the value of improvements which he had made. What result? See Beavers v. Weatherly, 250 Ga. 546 (1983).

Jacqueline Ervin v. Hosanna Ministry, Inc.

Superior Court of Connecticut, 1995.
1995 WL 681532 (Unpublished).

■ SKOLNICK, JUDGE. The plaintiffs, Jacqueline Ervin and Curtis Ervin, commenced this action against the defendant Hosanna Ministry, Inc., a/k/a Hosanna Ministries, Inc., ("Hosanna Ministry"), and Obie Ponton, on October 3, 1994. The plaintiffs allege that on or about December, 1992, Jacqueline Ervin was admitted into the care and custody of the defendant Hosanna Ministry for treatment and rehabilitation with respect to her alcohol/drug addictions. The plaintiffs further allege that funds were paid for Jacqueline Ervin's acceptance and admittance into the program. * * *

[The plaintiffs alleged *inter alia* "negligence on the part of Hosanna for its failure to maintain its premises in reasonably safe condition resulting in injury to the plaintiff."]

On July 11, 1995, the defendants filed a motion for summary judgment on the basis that Jacqueline Ervin waived her right to bring any claim based upon the defendants' intentional, reckless, or negligent conduct by "freely" and "with full comprehension" signing a general release on January 17, 1993. . . .

On July 26, 1995, the plaintiffs filed an objection to the defendants' motion for summary judgment along with the affidavit of Jacqueline Ervin. The objection to summary judgment essentially asserts that the plaintiff has no recollection of signing the release, was in a diminished capacity if she did sign the release, and that there were fraudulent misrepresentations made to the plaintiff at the time of admittance into Hosanna Ministry's drug/alcohol rehabilitation program, and these misrepresentations induced her to enroll in the program.

* * *

The court feels that there are several issues of material fact for a trier to determine such as whether the plaintiff actually signed the general release,[1] or, in the alternative, whether she signed the release "freely" or "with full comprehension."[2]

"Whether or not a provision forms part of a contract is ordinarily a factual question for the trier." Carter v. Reichlin Furriers, 34 Conn. Sup. 661, 665 (Appellate Sess. 1977). . . . The court believes that plaintiff's affidavit raises a genuine issue of material fact as to her assent to the general release. As plaintiff's affidavit indicates that she has no "recollection" of signing a waiver or release, an issue of fact exists as to whether she actually signed the release and assented to its terms.

Even if the court were to conclude, for the purposes of summary judgment consideration, that Jacqueline Ervin actually signed the general release, an issue of material fact would remain as to whether Jacqueline Ervin's signature was made "freely" and with "full comprehension." If, as claimed in her affidavit, she was under the influence of drugs, she may have lacked the mental capacity to execute such a general release of all claims. If the plaintiff was intoxicated or lacked mental capacity due to her addictions, then an issue exists as to whether she assented to the agreement.

"[I]n Connecticut a party may avoid certain contractual obligations on the ground that at the time they were entered into he or she was mentally incapacitated." Cottrell v. Connecticut Bank & Trust Co., 175

---

[1]   The relevant portion of the general release is as follows:

"I, the undersigned, being an adult, being *completely free of the influence of alcohol and drugs* of any kind whatsoever, and having had explained to me the importance of this paper as evidence of my present and future intent to forgive and release Hosanna Ministry, Inc., and all its officers, director employees and agents of and from all claims which I, at any time, may have against it, them or any of them;

AND IN CONSIDERATION of and for my being freely admitted into the Hosanna ministry; the free lodging, board, vocational biblical, educational and general training and education which I shall receive; the *free rehabilitation from drug and alcohol dependence* and from other forms of socially deviant behavior which I shall receive; . . . the free social and spiritual guidance and counseling which I shall receive and fully intending to be legally bound;

AND ON BEHALF of myself and my heirs, executors, administrators and assigns I do hereby *fully forgive, release and discharge* Hosanna Ministry, Inc. and its officers, directors, employees and agents. . . ." (Emphasis added.)

[2]   The relevant portions of the plaintiff's affidavit are as follows:

"For some time prior to December 1992/January 1993, I suffered from addictions to drugs (crack-cocaine) and alcohol. . . . Due to the fact that I was suffering from the aforementioned drug/alcohol addictions, I have no recollection of signing a waiver or release. . . . Due to the aforementioned fraudulent representations made to me as well as my drug/alcohol addiction, I do not recall and do not consider valid the release of claims purportedly signed by me and dated January 17, 1993. . . ."

Conn. 257, 261 (1978). According to the Restatement (Second), Contracts, a party cannot be bound to a contract if they were intoxicated when they entered into the contract. The rationale for this is that "compulsive alcoholism may be a form of mental illness. . . . If drunkenness is *so extreme* as to prevent any manifestation of assent, there is no capacity to contract." (Emphasis added.) Restatement (Second) § 16 cmt. (a) (1981). "Otherwise the other party is affected only by intoxication of which he has reason to know." Id. § 16 cmt. (b). * * *

Due to her alcohol/drug addictions the plaintiff attests that she has no recollection of signing a waiver or release of claims dated January 17, 1993. Therefore, an issue of material fact exists as to whether Jacqueline Ervin had the mental capacity to execute such a release.

"The test of mental capacity to make a contract or deed is whether at the time of execution of the instrument the maker possessed understanding sufficient to comprehend the nature, extent and consequences of the transaction." Nichols v. Nichols, 79 Conn. 644, 657 (1907). Evidence may be considered as to the mind of the alleged incompetent "before, at, and after his contract, in order to ascertain his real condition at the moment of entering into an agreement." Cooper v. Burby, 7 CSCR 591, 592 (1992), quoting Grant v. Thompson, 4 Conn. 203, 208 (1822).

* * *

Because of the existence of several issues of material fact, the defendants' motion for summary judgment is hereby denied.

NOTES

Incapacity Due to Intoxication. "Our rule regarding intoxication is much the same. The drunkenness of a party at the time of making a contract may render the contract voidable, but it does not render it void; and to render the contract voidable, it must be made to appear that the party was intoxicated to such a degree that he was, at the time of the contracting, incapable of exercising judgment, understanding the proposed engagement, and of knowing what he was about when he entered into the contract sought to be avoided. . . . Proof merely that the party was drunk on the day the sale was executed does not *per se*, show that he was without contractual capacity; there must be some evidence of a resultant condition indicative of that extreme impairment of the faculties which amounts to contract incapacity." Williamson v. Matthews, 379 So.2d 1245, 1247–48 (Ala. 1980).

Restatement (Second) § 16 glosses the rule as follows:

A person incurs only voidable contractual duties by entering into a transaction if the other party has reason to know that by reason of intoxication

(a) he is unable to understand in a reasonable manner the nature and consequences of the transaction, or

(b) he is unable to act in a reasonable manner in relation to the transaction.

How is this different from the Second Restatement rule for mental incompetence? Why the difference?

PROBLEM: THE CASE OF THE DRUG-INFLUENCED SELLER

Alvin, a graduate student, age 25, owned a gold and silver belt that was given to his grandfather when he was welterweight champion of the world. The belt was worth about $500, but had great sentimental value to Alvin. On the evening of October 20, Alvin, alone in his apartment, took a dose of LSD. Shortly thereafter, he began to hallucinate. In this state, he experienced a feeling of oneness with the universe and determined that he should sell the belt and donate the proceeds to charity. Alvin went promptly to Bart's Pawnshop and sold the belt for $475. When the effects of the drug had worn off, Alvin realized what had happened. Bart refused to return the belt, claiming that he "bought it fair and square."

Alvin brought suit to rescind the contract for sale and to recover the belt. At the trial, Plaintiff's expert testified that LSD, like other hallucinogens, can produce a range of mental states, including hallucinations, delusions and partial amnesia. He also stated that the effects of the drug may range from a loss of time and space perception to panic, paranoid delusions and symptoms very similar to those of schizophrenia. He then concluded that at the time of the sale, Plaintiff was under the influence of the drug and "was not aware of the quality and nature of his act." On cross-examination, it was shown that Plaintiff had no mental disease or defect and that he had used LSD on previous occasions. Defendant's testimony, corroborated by another witness, was that Plaintiff entered his store, offered to sell the belt for $600 and after about ten minutes of bargaining, agreed to take $475. Defendant testified that Plaintiff acted "a little strange" but that he was lucid and bargained very well. At the close of the evidence, Defendant made a motion for a directed verdict, which the trial court granted. In an oral opinion from the bench, the judge stated that he was relying on Restatement (Second) § 16 on "intoxicated persons" and that although he believed that Plaintiff was, at the time of the sale, unable to understand in a reasonable manner the nature and consequences of the transaction, he found that Defendant had no reason to know about the lessened capacity. Also, the judge opined that Plaintiff must bear some of the responsibility since he had elected to take LSD. Accordingly, the motion was granted, and a judgment was entered for Defendant.

On appeal, what result?

3. MISTAKE

The Statute of Frauds and the rules for capacity establish, in the first instance, relatively formal requirements. Both impose rule-like conditions on enforcement or contractual validity—the existence of a writing or the age or mental capacity of the parties. Neither rule begins with the history or details of the transaction.

We now turn to defenses that involve the quality of the bargaining process or the substance of the deal between the parties. These are the rules for mistake, fraud, nondisclosure, duress, undue influence, unconscionability, and public policy. Like the Statute of Frauds and capacity requirements, these defenses provide an escape from legal liability where the conditions of contractual validity are otherwise satisfied. Unlike those rules, they involve an inquiry into the specifics of the individual transaction.

We begin with mistake. The fact that one or both parties were mistaken about a "basic assumption on which the contract was made" undermines our confidence that the bargaining process will produce an equitable or efficient outcome. Mistake, as the term is used here, involves "a belief that is not in accord with the facts." Restatement (Second) § 151. It is to be distinguished from misunderstanding, which as we saw in the last Chapter exists when parties "attach materially different meanings to their manifestations" of assent. Id. § 20. In cases of misunderstanding, the law says that there is no agreement and therefore no contract. In cases of mistake, as we shall see, the rule is that there is a contract, but that it is voidable by the adversely affected party.

Boise Junior College District v. Mattefs Construction Co.

Supreme Court of Idaho, 1969.
92 Idaho 757.

■ SPEAR, JUSTICE. The issue presented is whether, under the circumstances of this case, a contractor is entitled to the equitable relief of rescission when it has submitted a bid which contains a material clerical mistake. We conclude that such relief is available.

Mattefs Construction Company (hereinafter termed respondent) was one of ten bidders on a construction contract to be let by Boise Junior College District (hereinafter referred to as appellant). Along with its bid respondent submitted the customary bid bond containing a promise to pay the difference between its bid and the next higher bid actually accepted if respondent refused to enter into a contract with appellant. Contract specifications also provided that the bid could not be withdrawn for 45 days after it was opened.

The architect's estimate of costs on the building project was $150,000, but when the bids were opened seven of them ran in excess of $155,000 while three of them were less than $150,000. Fulton Construction Company bid $134,896. The respondent bid $141,048. The third bid by Cain and Hardy, Inc., was $148,915. When Fulton refused to sign a contract it was tendered to respondent who likewise refused to sign it. Ultimately the contract was awarded to Cain and Hardy, Inc., the third lowest bidder and appellant proceeded to attempt collection on respondent's bid bond.

One who errs in preparing a bid for a public works contract is entitled to the equitable relief of rescission if he can establish the following conditions: (1) the mistake is material; (2) enforcement of a contract pursuant to the terms of the erroneous bid would be unconscionable; (3) the mistake did not result from violation of a positive legal duty or from culpable negligence; (4) the party to whom the bid is submitted will not be prejudiced except by the loss of his bargain; and (5) prompt notice of the error is given. These principles are established by substantial authority, i.e., Annot., 52 A.L.R.2d 792 § III. . . . That appellant recognizes these principles is evident, because it has raised questions as to the existence of each one of these elements by its assignments of error. Therefore, we shall consider each of these conditions necessary for equitable relief, in the context of the objections raised.

I

Appellant contends that the trial court erred in determining that omission of the glass bid was a material mistake. The trial court found:

> "This was the second largest sub bid item in the whole contract, only the mechanical sub bid being larger. It amounted to about 14% of the contract and was thus a material item."

Thus, the issue is whether, as a matter of law, a 14% error in bid is a material error. We have no difficulty in reaching the conclusion that omission of an item representing 14% of the total bid submitted is substantial and material. Appellant cites a number of cases wherein courts have directly or indirectly determined that material error was not involved, in spite of mistakes which ranged up to 50%, i.e., Modany Bros. v. State Public School Building Authority, 417 Pa. 39 (1965). . . . However, we are persuaded we should adopt a rule which is not so harsh and turn instead to authority such as Elsinore Union Elementary School Dist. v. Kastorff, 54 Cal.2d 380 (1960), in which the court stated:

> "Plaintiff suggests that in any event the amount of the plumbing bid omitted from the total was immaterial. The bid as submitted was in the sum of $89,994, and whether the sum for the omitted plumbing was $6,500 or $9,285 (the two sub bids), the omission of such a sum is plainly material to the total. In [*Lemoge Electric v. County of San Mateo*, 46 Cal.2d 659, 661–662 (1956)] the error which it was declared would have entitled plaintiff to rescind was the listing of the cost of certain materials as $104.52, rather than $10,452, in a total bid of $172,421. Thus the percentage of error here was larger than in *Lemoge*, and was plainly material."

II

An error in the computation of a bid may be material, representing a large percentage of the total bid submitted, and yet requiring compliance with the bid may not be unconscionable. Thus, omission of a

$25,000 item in a $100,000 bid would be material, but if the $100,000 bid included $50,000 in profit, no hardship would be created by requiring the contractor to comply with the terms of his bid.

This does not represent the case at bar. Here the record reveals that if respondent were forced to comply with the terms of its bid it would lose at least $10,000. Respondent's costs, including the omitted item, would be roughly $151,000 while the total amount of its bid was only $141,000. Enforcement of the bid is deemed unconscionable as working a substantial hardship on the bidder where it appears he would incur a substantial pecuniary loss. Donaldson v. Abraham, 68 Wash. 208 (1912). This is particularly so where, as here, no injury is caused by withdrawal of the bid. (See sec. IV, infra.)

III

One who seeks equitable relief from error must establish that such error does not result from violation of a positive legal duty or from culpable negligence.

" * * * [This] generally means carelessness or lack of good faith in calculation which violates a positive duty in making up a bid, so as to amount to gross negligence, or wilful negligence, when it takes on a sinister meaning and will furnish cause, if established, for holding a mistake of the offending bidder to be one not remediable in equity. *It is thus distinguished from a clerical or inadvertent error in handling items of a bid either through setting them down or transcription.*" (emphasis added) Annot., 52 A.L.R.2d 792, 794.

In several of its assignments appellant contends that the trial court erred in not finding that respondent was negligent to the point of being grossly negligent. . . .

* * *

On the basis of these facts the trial court concluded:

"There was no willful or even negligent act by plaintiff's agents which prevented knowledge of the error from reaching Mr. Mattefs prior to the opening. In preparing the bid Mattefs Construction Company proceeded in the usual way and under the same last minute pressures that are experienced by all general contractors bidding on bids of this kind. Under the evidence I conclude that it was using ordinary care in its methods of bid preparation; that is, the same care that other contractors in the area use in making bids of the kind here involved. There was no evidence of any gross negligence or fraudulent or willful intent to omit this item for the purpose of obtaining any advantage in the bidding."

It is appellant's contention that the trial court erred in making these findings. It has long been the rule of this court that:

"Where the findings of the trial court are supported by
substantial and competent, though conflicting, evidence, such
findings will not be disturbed on appeal."

Riley v. Larson, 91 Idaho 831 (1967) . . . . Additionally, the trial judge is
the arbiter of conflicting evidence; his determination of the weight,
credibility, inference and implications thereof is not to be supplanted by
this court's impressions or conclusions from the written record. . . . Also
findings of fact shall not be set aside unless clearly erroneous. I.R.C.P.
52(a).

Thus, the finding of the trial court that the mistake of respondent
was not due to the required type of negligence must be affirmed. As was
held in the *Kemper* case:

"The type of error here involved is one which will sometimes
occur in the conduct of reasonable and cautious businessmen,
and, under all the circumstances, we cannot say as a matter of
law that it constituted a neglect of legal duty such as would bar
the right to equitable relief."

M.F. Kemper Const. Co. v. City of Los Angeles, 235 P.2d 7, 11 (Cal. 1951).

IV

It is well settled by the authorities that a bid may not be withdrawn
if such withdrawal would work a substantial hardship on the offeree.
Many situations can be hypothesized where such a hardship would
result. However, none appears here, nor has appellant attempted to
prove any hardship. Appellant expected to pay $150,000 for the work it
solicited. Its actual cost will be $149,000. It complains because it cannot
have the work done for $141,000. Thus, appellant's injury consists of a
failure to save $9,000 on its construction rather than saving $1,000.

" * * * [T]he city will not be heard to complain that it cannot be
placed in *statu quo* because it will not have the benefit of an
inequitable bargain. [citations]" * * * Kemper Const. Co., supra,
at 11. See also Kutsche v. Ford, 222 Mich. 442 (1923).

The most appellant can argue is that its damage is presumed by the
requirement of a bid bond and that release of a bid bond and that release
of a bidder whenever he makes a mistake will impair the purposes for
which a bid bond is required. . . .

* * *

The proper purpose of a provision against withdrawal of a bid was
fully explained by the Maryland Court of Appeals, quoting from *Geremia
v. Boyarsky*, 107 Conn. 387 (1928):

" 'It is objected that the rule should be different where, as here,
there is a proviso forbidding the withdrawal of bids. To be sure,
this puts a bidder on notice that there is a certain finality about
bidding for a government contract. But this by no means should
enable a governmental agency to take an unconscionable

advantage of its special status as a government body. * * * The proper effect of the requirement that bids remain unrevoked is to assure the State that a bidder will be relieved of his obligation only when it is legally justifiable. That means that the State is in the same position as any acceptor when there is a question of rectifying an error. * * * Of course, it is obvious, as the State contends, that the system of public bidding, developed by experience and usual in public contracts, should not be broken down by lightly permitting bidders to withdraw because of change of mind. Such a course would be unfair to other straightforward bidders, as well as disruptive of public business. But it can hardly be a substantial impairment of such system to grant the relief—which would clearly be given as between private citizens—in a case where a bona fide mistake is proven and was known to the State before acceptance or any loss to it.' "

City of Baltimore v. De Luca-Davis Construction Co., 124 A.2d 557, 565 (1956).

V

The final element of the right to equitable relief raised by appellant is actually an adjunct of the previous question of whether the offeree will be damaged by withdrawal of the bid. The requirement of prompt notice is separately stated here because appellant earnestly argues that it was not given such prompt notice. This contention is not supported by the evidence.

* * * Relief from mistaken bids is consistently allowed where the acceptor has actual notice of the error prior to its attempted acceptance and the other elements necessary for equitable relief are present. M.F. Kemper Const. Co., 235 P.2d at 10. We see no reason to deviate from this rule where, as here, the party opposing the grant of equitable relief can show no damage other than loss of benefit of an inequitable bargain. We conclude that appellant's position is no better here than it was when similar arguments were presented to the U.S. Supreme Court nearly 70 years ago. In quoting from the circuit court opinion, the court held:

" ' * * * If the defendants [appellants] are correct in their contention there is absolutely no redress for a bidder for public work, no matter how aggravated or palpable his blunder. The moment his proposal is opened by the executive board he is held as in a grasp of steel. There is no remedy, no escape. If, through an error of his clerk, he has agreed to do work worth $1,000,000 for $10, he must be held to the strict letter of his contract, while equity stands by with folded hands and sees him driven into bankruptcy. The defendants' [appellants'] position admits of no compromise, no exception, no middle ground.' "

Moffett, Hodgkins & Clarke Co. v. City of Rochester, 178 U.S. 373 (1900).

This reasoning is equally applicable to the cause at bar.

Judgment affirmed. Costs to respondent.

NOTES

(1)   Was the Boise Junior College District at fault for the mistaken bid? If not, why shouldn't it get the benefits of the bargain that it expected? James Gordley argues that the key question in mistake cases is "when should [a party] be bound to a contract which is disadvantageous to him, given that the purpose of a contract is to advantage both parties"? James A. Gordley, *Mistake in Contract Formation*, 52 Am. J. Comp. Law. 433, 468 (2004). What do you think?

(2)   *Effect Where There Is Knowledge of Mistake.* Since the offeree appeared to have actual notice of the error prior to acceptance, why was this knowledge not sufficient to terminate the power of acceptance?

Under the court's analysis in *Boise*, would the result have been the same if the offer had been accepted before the offeree knew of the error? Restatement (Second) § 153 takes the position that a material mistake by one party as to a "basic assumption on which he made the contract" makes the contract "voidable by him if . . . the effect of the mistake is such that enforcement of the contract would be unconscionable, or . . . the other party had reason to know of the mistake or his fault caused the mistake."

The offeree's actual or constructive knowledge of a mistake is often an important factor in judicial opinions granting relief to the mistaken party. Relief typically takes the form of rescission, an equitable remedy invalidating the contract. Thus, it is evidently conceded that a contract of some sort has been formed. Yet if the offeree knew or should have known about the mistake, it is arguable that he or she had no power to accept the offer at all. In *Rushlight Automatic Sprinkler Co. v. City of Portland*, 189 Or. 194 (1950), the plaintiff's bid was substantially below the others because the cost of steel was mistakenly omitted. In allowing rescission, the court observed:

> We believe that in this State an offer and acceptance are deemed to effect a meeting of the minds, even though the offeror made a material mistake in compiling his offer, provided the acceptor was not aware of the mistake and had no reason to suspect it. But if the offeree knew of the mistake, and it was basic, or if the circumstances were such that he, a reasonable man, should have inferred that a basic mistake was made, a meeting of the minds does not occur. The circumstances which should arouse the suspicions of the fair-minded offeree are many, as stated in § 94 of Williston on Contracts, Rev.Ed.: " * * * And the same principle is applicable in any case where the offeree should know that the terms of the offer are unintended or misunderstood by the offeror. The offeree will not be permitted to snap up an offer that is too good to

be true; no contract based on such an offer can then be enforced by the acceptor."

189 Or. at 244.

Where the remedy of rescission is sought, it may make little difference whether the court concludes that there was no mutual assent or that the contract was voidable. But are there cases in which this would not be true? Is *Boise* such a case? See *Problem: The Case of the Four Million Labels* infra. In *Wil-Fred's Inc. v. Metropolitan Sanitary District of Greater Chicago*, 57 Ill.App.3d 16 (1978), the court considered the distinction traditionally made between a clerical or mathematical error and an error in business judgment: "Generally, relief is refused for errors in judgment and allowed for clerical or mathematical mistakes. . . . Nonetheless, we believe, in fairness to the individual bidder, that the facts surrounding the error, not the label, i.e. 'mistake of fact' or 'mistake of judgment,' should determine whether relief is granted." 57 Ill.App.3d at 24. The court pointed out that the plaintiff's error in judgment derived, at least in part, from misleading specifications furnished by the defendant. But the court went on to state: "Furthermore, it was established that Wil-Fred's quotation was $233,775 lower than the next lowest bid. It is apparent that such a sizable discrepancy should have placed the Sanitary District on notice that plaintiff's bid contained a material error. . . . Accordingly equity will not allow the District to take advantage of Wil-Fred's low offer." Id. There is a hint here that a "palpable" error, however derived, may be sufficient to warrant relief. For a thorough treatment of the mistaken bid problem, see Ernest Jones, *The Law of Mistaken Bids*, 48 U. Cin. L. Rev. 43 (1979).

(3) *Bidder Negligence.* Consider the following judicial analysis:

The very term "mistake" connotes some degree of negligent conduct. * * * In most circumstances it would be illogical, if not impossible, to require a bidder who made a mistake in calculating a bid to establish that the mistake was one most reasonable bidders would make under the same or substantially similar circumstances. Requiring proof of freedom from negligence focuses substantial attention on the cause of the mistake; the question of the availability of equitable relief from a mistaken bid should focus primarily on the consequences of the mistake. * * * Numerous courts and commentators have concluded that in public construction contract cases in which a bidder seeks equitable relief from bond forfeiture provisions because of a mistaken bid, the fundamental issue is whether the bidder made an honest or good faith mistake and any question of gross or extreme negligence of the bidder should be considered only as evidence of the bidder's lack of good faith. * * * This approach recognizes that a bidder should not be allowed to rescind a mistaken bid if the bid were made in bad faith and emphasizes the desirability of ensuring that public projects proceed on the basis of accurate cost estimates. A contrary rule would encourage manipulative bidding practices and undermine the stability of the bidding process. Furthermore, evenhanded application of a good faith standard ensures fair treatment of all parties involved in dealings with municipal authorities, thereby enhancing the integrity of the bidding process.

Powder Horn Constructors, Inc. v. City of Florence, 754 P.2d 356, 362 (Colo. 1988).

(4) *Mistakes in Bids and Federal Government Contracting.* Applicable regulations oblige a contracting officer to examine all bids for mistakes. Federal Acquisition Regulation (FAR) 14.407–1. In cases of apparent mistakes and in cases where the contracting officer has reason to believe that a mistake may have been made, the contracting officer is required to request from the bidder a verification of the bid, calling attention to the suspected mistake. Id. The contracting officer may correct any clerical mistake apparent on the face of the bid before the award. FAR 14.407–4. If a bidder requests permission to correct a mistake, and clear and convincing evidence establishes both the existence of the mistake and the bid actually intended, the agency head may make a determination permitting the bidder to correct the mistake—provided that if this correction would result in displacing one or more lower bids, such a determination shall not be made unless the existence of the mistake and the bid actually intended are ascertainable substantially from the invitation and the bid itself. FAR 14.407–3.

Relief from the mistake is, of course, more difficult to obtain after the award of the contract. Here one is, in general, obliged to show by clear and convincing evidence either mutual mistake or a unilateral mistake of which the contracting officer had actual or constructive knowledge, i.e., he or she knew or should have known of the error. FAR 14.407–4. For such mistakes, agencies are authorized to (1) rescind the contract or (2) reform the contract so as to delete the items involved in the mistake, or to increase the price if the contract price, as corrected, does not exceed that of the next lowest acceptable bid under the original invitation for bids. Id. The United States Claims Court has denied relief from an accepted bid on a latrine repair project, where the 13% price disparity was quite close to the government's own estimate and where the government's representative neither knew nor had reason to know of the mistake. Fadeley v. United States, 15 Cl.Ct. 706 (1988). The court observed: "The granting of equitable relief is based upon a concern with the overreaching of a contractor by a contracting officer who suspects a mistake in the bid and is willing to accept it nevertheless. That is not the situation here." 15 Cl.Ct. at 712. On the other hand, in *Information Intern. Associates, Inc. v. United States*, 74 Fed. Cl. 192 (2006), reformation of a bid was granted where the bidder omitted employee salaries from the final bid price, a mistake of which the contracting officer should have been aware. The court concluded that the bid was a clear-cut clerical rather than a judgmental error, of which the contracting officer should have been aware and have requested verification under FAR 14.407–4.

(5) *Mistaken College Admissions.* Consider the following from the *Princeton Alumni Weekly*, May 27, 1975:

Two of the 9,691 envelopes that were mailed last month to applicants to next year's freshman class contained the wrong letter, and two high school seniors who were supposed to be sent rejection notices received acceptances. "Somebody must have pulled the form letter off the wrong pile," explained Spencer J. Reynolds '61, associate director of admission. To his knowledge, he said, this was the first such error in his nine years at Princeton, during which time some 76,000 applications have been processed.

In one of the cases, the mistake was discovered when the recipient visited the campus and noticed that his name was not included in the list of admitted students posted in the admissions office. The other case came to light when the student called because his envelope had not contained a reply card. Since legally a letter of admission may be considered a binding contract, the university decided to honor the acceptances. One of the students is viewed as academically unqualified and has been advised that he probably could not handle the workload, while the other has been informed that he is thought capable of doing the work. As of Memorial Day, neither had yet notified the university of his decision.

What result under Restatement (Second) § 153?

PROBLEM: THE CASE OF THE FOUR MILLION LABELS

Reed, operator of a small photography store, had need of adhesive pricing labels. He began to prepare a purchase order for five different types of labels. In handwriting, he filled in the blank spaces for four different types and in the quantity column noted opposite each "2M." At that point he was interrupted by a customer, and it was not until later that he finished writing the order. He described the fifth label as "Label as Attached," attached a copy of the desired label and in the quantity column wrote "4MM." He then mailed the completed order to Monarch, a nationwide manufacturer and supplier of pricing and product identification labels.

The designation "M" is understood in the label industry to mean one thousand. "MM" stands for one million. Reed intended to order 4,000 of the fifth type; his use of "MM" was a mistake.

In previous transactions, the largest order Monarch had received from Reed for any one item was 4,000. Indeed, the largest order Monarch ever received previously from any source was for one million labels. Without checking further, Monarch proceeded to fill the order. The first four items were in stock and were mailed to Reed. The fifth required a special printing. Reed did not become aware of any problem until a truck drove up to his store with seven cartons of labels weighing 622 pounds!

Reed refused to receive the merchandise; Monarch sued for the $2,680 purchase price. What result? Consider the matter pro and con before consulting *Reed's Photo Mart v. Monarch Marking System Co.*, 475 S.W.2d 356 (Tex.Civ.App. 1971), reversed 485 S.W.2d 905 (Tex. 1972).

Beachcomber Coins, Inc. v. Ron Boskett

Superior Court of New Jersey, Appellate Division, 1979.
166 N.J.Super. 442.

■ CONFORD, P.J.A.D. (retired and temporarily assigned). Plaintiff, a retail dealer in coins, brought an action for rescission of a purchase by it from defendant for $500 of a dime purportedly minted in 1916 at Denver. Defendant is a part-time coin dealer. Plaintiff asserts a mutual mistake of fact as to the genuineness of the coin as Denver-minted, such a coin being a rarity and therefore having a market value greatly in excess of its normal monetary worth. Plaintiff's evidence at trial that the "D" on the coin signifying Denver mintage was counterfeited is not disputed by defendant. Although at trial defendant disputed that the coin tendered back to him by plaintiff was the one he sold, the implicit trial finding is to the contrary, and that issue is not raised on appeal.

The trial judge, sitting without a jury, held for defendant on the ground that the customary "coin dealing procedures" were for a dealer purchasing a coin to make his own investigation of the genuineness of the coin and to "assume the risk" of his purchase if his investigation is faulty. The judge conceded that the evidence demonstrated satisfaction of the ordinary requisites of the rule of rescission for mutual mistake of fact that both parties act under a mistake of fact and that the fact be "central" (material) to the making of the contract. The proofs were that the seller had himself acquired this coin and two others of minor value for a total of $450 and that his representative had told the purchaser that he would not sell the dime for less than $500. The principal of plaintiff firm spent from 15 to 45 minutes in close examination of the coin before purchasing it. Soon thereafter he received an offer of $700 for the coin subject to certification of its genuineness by the American Numismatic Society. That organization labeled it a counterfeit, and as a result plaintiff instituted the present action.

The evidence and trial judge's findings establish this as a classic case of rescission for mutual mistake of fact. As a general rule,

> * * * where parties on entering into a transaction that affects their contractual relations are both under a mistake regarding a fact assumed by them as the basis on which they entered into the transaction, it is voidable by either party if enforcement of it would be materially more onerous to him than it would have been had the fact been as the parties believed it to be.

Restatement, Contracts § 502 at 961 (1932);[1] 13 Williston on Contracts (3 ed. 1970) § 1543, 74–75. By way of example, the Restatement posits the following:

---

[1]   No substantial change in the rule was effected by Restatement, Contracts (Second) § 294(1), Tent. Dr. No. 10 (1975) at 10. This provides:

(1) Where a mistake of both parties at the time a contract was made as to a basic assumption on which the contract was made has a material effect on the agreed

> A contracts to sell to B a specific bar of silver before them. The parties supposed that the bar is sterling. It has, however, a much larger admixture of base metal. The contract is voidable by B.

Op. cit. at 964.

Moreover, "negligent failure of a party to know or to discover the facts as to which both parties are under a mistake does not preclude rescission or reformation on account thereof." Restatement § 502 at 977. The law of New Jersey is in accord. See Riviere v. Berla, 89 N.J.Eq. 596, 597 (E. & A. 1918); Dencer v. Erb, 142 N.J.Eq. 422, 429 (Ch. 1948). In the *Riviere* case relief was denied only because the parties could not be restored to the *status quo ante*. In the present case they can be. It is undisputed that both parties believed that the coin was a genuine Denver-minted one. The mistake was mutual in that both parties were laboring under the same misapprehension as to this particular, essential fact. The price asked and paid was directly based on that assumption. That plaintiff may have been negligent in his inspection of the coin (a point not expressly found but implied by the trial judge) does not, as noted above, bar its claim for rescission. Cf. Smith v. Zimbalist, 2 Cal.App.2d 324 (D.Ct.App. 1934).

Defendant's contention that plaintiff assumed the risk that the coin might be of greater or lesser value than that paid is not supported by the evidence. It is well established that a party to a contract can assume the risk of being mistaken as to the value of the thing sold. 13 Williston, Contracts § 1543A at 85. The Restatement states the rule this way:

> Where the parties know that there is doubt in regard to a certain matter and contract on that assumption, the contract is not rendered voidable because one is disappointed in the hope that the facts accord with his wishes. The risk of the existence of the doubtful fact is then assumed as one of the elements of the bargain.

Restatement § 502 cmt. f at 964. See also Restatement, Contracts (Second) § 296(b) cmt. c at 4. However, for the stated rule to apply, the parties must be conscious that the pertinent fact may not be true and make their agreement at the risk of that possibility. . . . In this case both parties were certain that the coin was genuine. They so testified. Plaintiff's principal thought so after his inspection, and defendant would not have paid nearly $450 for it otherwise. A different case would be presented if the seller were uncertain either of the genuineness of the coin or of its value [if] genuine, and had accepted the expert buyer's judgment on these matters.

---

exchange of performances, the contract is voidable by the adversely affected party unless he bears the risk of the mistake under the rule stated in § 296.

The exceptions in § 296 are not here applicable. [Section 294(1) is § 152(1) in the final draft.—Eds.]

The trial judge's rationale of custom of the trade is not supported by the evidence. It depended upon the testimony of plaintiff's expert witness who on cross-examination as to the "procedure" on the purchase by a dealer of a rare coin, stated that the dealer would check it with magnification and then "normally send it to the American Numismatic Certification Service for certification." This testimony does not in our opinion establish that practice as a usage of trade "having such regularity of observance in a * * * trade as to justify an expectation that it will be observed with respect to the transaction in question," within the intent of the Uniform Commercial Code, N.J.S.A. 12A:1–205(2).[2]

The cited code provision contemplates that the trade usage is so prevalent as to warrant the conclusion that the parties contracted with reference to, and intended their agreement to be governed by it. . . . Our reading of the testimony does not indicate any basis for findings either that this was a trade usage within the Code definition at all or that these parties in fact accepted it as such to the extent that they were agreeing that because of it the sale was an "as is" transaction. Indeed, the same witness testified there was a "normal policy" among coin dealers throughout the United States of a "return privilege" for altered coins.

* * *

Reversed.

T.C. Sherwood v. Hiram Walker

Supreme Court of Michigan, 1887.
66 Mich. 568.

■ MORSE, J. Replevin for a cow. Suit commenced in justice's court; judgment for plaintiff; appealed to circuit court of Wayne county, and verdict and judgment for plaintiff in that court. The defendants bring error, and set out 25 assignments of the same.

The main controversy depends upon the construction of a contract for the sale of the cow. * * * The Walkers are importers and breeders of polled Angus cattle. The plaintiff is a banker living at Plymouth, in Wayne County. He called upon the defendants at Walkerville for the purchase of some of their stock, but found none there that suited him. Meeting one of the defendants afterwards, he was informed that they had a few head upon their Greenfield farm. He was asked to go out and look at them, with the statement that they were probably barren, and would not breed. May 5, 1886, plaintiff went out to Greenfield, and saw the cattle. A few days thereafter, he called upon one of the defendants with the view of purchasing a cow, known as "Rose 2d of Aberlone." After considerable talk, it was agreed that defendants would telephone

---

[2]   Note, also, that evidence of a trade usage is not admissible unless the offering party gives the other party advance notice to prevent unfair surprise. N.J.S.A. 12A:1–105(6). Plaintiff received no notice that the judge intended to decide this case on the basis of the alleged trade usage.

Sherwood at his home in Plymouth in reference to the price. The second morning after this talk he was called up by telephone, and the terms of the sale were finally agreed upon. He was to pay five and one-half cents per pound, live weight, fifty pounds shrinkage. . . . He requested defendants to confirm the sale in writing, which they did. . . .

* * *

On the twenty-first of the same month the plaintiff went to defendants' farm at Greenfield, and presented the order and [confirmation letter to an employee of the Walkers], who informed him that the defendants had instructed him not to deliver the cow. Soon after, the plaintiff tendered to Hiram Walker, one of the defendants, $80, and demanded the cow. Walker refused to take the money or deliver the cow. The plaintiff then instituted this suit. * * *

* * * [At trial,] defendants . . . introduced evidence tending to show that at the time of the alleged sale it was believed by both the plaintiff and themselves that the cow was barren and would not breed; that she cost $850, and if not barren would be worth from $750 to $1,000; that after the date of the letter . . . the defendants were informed by [an employee] that in his judgment the cow was with calf, and therefore they instructed him not to deliver her to plaintiff. . . . The cow had a calf in the month of October following. . . .

* * *

It appears from the record that both parties supposed this cow was barren and would not breed, and she was sold by the pound for an insignificant sum as compared with her real value if a breeder. She was evidently sold and purchased on the relation of her value for beef, unless the plaintiff had learned of her true condition, and concealed such knowledge from the defendants. . . . The question arises whether [defendants] had a right to [refuse to perform the contract]. . . . I am of the opinion that the [circuit] court erred in . . . holding [that the contract should have been performed at the agreed upon price]. I know that this is a close question, and the dividing line between the adjudicated cases is not easily discerned. But it must be considered as well settled that a party who has given an apparent consent to a contract of sale may refuse to execute it, or he may avoid it after it has been completed, if the assent was founded, or the contract made, upon the mistake of a material fact,— such as the subject-matter of the sale, the price, or some collateral fact materially inducing the agreement; and this can be done when the mistake is mutual. . . .

If there is a difference or misapprehension as to the substance of the thing bargained for; if the thing actually delivered or received is different in substance from the thing bargained for, and intended to be sold,—then there is no contract; but if it be only a difference in some quality or accident, even though the mistake may have been the actuating motive to the purchaser or seller, or both of them, yet the contract remains binding. . . . It has been held, in accordance with the principles above stated, that where a horse is bought under the belief that he is sound, and both vendor and vendee honestly believe him to be sound, the purchaser must stand by his bargain, and pay the full price, unless there was a warranty.

It seems to me, however, in the case made by this record, that the mistake or misapprehension of the parties went to the whole substance of the agreement. If the cow was a breeder, she was worth at least $750; if barren, she was worth not over $80. The parties would not have made the contract of sale except upon the understanding and belief that she was incapable of breeding, and of no use as a cow. It is true she is now the identical animal that they thought her to be when the contract was made; there is no mistake as to the identity of the creature. Yet the mistake was not of the mere quality of the animal, but went to the very nature of the thing. A barren cow is substantially a different creature than a breeding one. There is as much difference between them for all purposes of use as there is between an ox and a cow that is capable of breeding and giving milk. If the mutual mistake had simply related to the fact whether she was with calf or not for one season, then it might have been a good sale, but the mistake affected the character of the animal for all time, and for its present and ultimate use. She was not in fact the animal, or the kind of animal, the defendants intended to sell or the plaintiff to buy. * * * The court should have instructed the jury that if they found that the cow was sold, or contracted to be sold, upon the understanding of both parties that she was barren, and useless for the purpose of breeding, and that in fact she was not barren, but capable of breeding, then the defendants had a right to rescind, and to refuse to deliver, and the verdict should be in their favor.

The judgment of the court below must be reversed, and a new trial granted, with costs of this court to defendants.

■ SHERWOOD, J. (dissenting) * * * There is no question but that the defendants sold the cow representing her of the breed and quality they believed the cow to be, and that the purchaser so understood it. And the buyer purchased her believing her to be of the breed represented by the sellers, and possessing all the qualities stated, and even more. He believed she would breed. There is no pretense that the plaintiff bought the cow for beef, and there is nothing in the record indicating that he would have bought her at all only that he thought she might be made to breed. Under the foregoing facts . . . it is held that because it turned out that the plaintiff was more correct in his judgment as to one quality of the cow than the defendants, and a quality, too, which could not by any possibility be positively known at the time by either party to exist, the contract may be annulled by the defendants at their pleasure. . . .

* * * If the owner of a Hambletonian horse had speeded him, and was only able to make him go a mile in three minutes, and should sell him to another, believing that was his greatest speed, for $300, when the

purchaser believed he could go much faster, and made the purchase for that sum, and a few days thereafter, under more favorable circumstances, the horse was driven a mile in 2 min. 16 sec., and was found to be worth $20,000, I hardly think it would be held, either at law or in equity, by any one, that the seller in such case could rescind the contract. . . .

In this case neither party knew the actual quality and condition of this cow at the time of the sale. . . . The defendants thought [the cow could not be made to breed], but the plaintiff says that he thought she could be made to breed, but believed she was not with calf. The defendants sold the cow for what they believed her to be, and the plaintiff bought her as he believed she was, after the statements made by the defendants. No conditions whatever were attached to the terms of sale by either party. . . . It is not the duty of courts to destroy contracts when called upon to enforce them, after they have been legally made. . . . There was no difference between the parties, nor misapprehension, as to the substance of the thing bargained for, which was a cow supposed to be barren by one party, and believed not to be by the other. As to the quality of the animal, subsequently developed, both parties were equally ignorant, and as to this each party took his chances. . . .

* * * In this case the cow sold was the one delivered. What might or might not happen to her after the sale formed no element in the contract. . . .

* * *

The judgment should be affirmed.

Hiram Walker, cattle breeder and distiller

Lenawee County Board of Health v. William and Martha Messerly

Supreme Court of Michigan, 1982.
417 Mich. 17.

■ RYAN, JUSTICE. In March of 1977, Carl and Nancy Pickles, appellees, purchased from appellants, William and Martha Messerly, a 600-square-foot tract of land upon which is located a three-unit apartment building. Shortly after the transaction was closed, the Lenawee County Board of Health condemned the property and obtained a permanent injunction which prohibits human habitation on the premises until the defective sewage system is brought into conformance with the Lenawee County sanitation code.

We are required to determine whether appellees should prevail in their attempt to avoid this land contract on the basis of mutual mistake and failure of consideration. We conclude that the parties did entertain a mutual misapprehension of fact, but that the circumstances of this case do not warrant rescission.

I

The facts of the case are not seriously in dispute. In 1971, the Messerlys acquired approximately one acre plus 600 square feet of land. A three-unit apartment building was situated upon the 600-square-foot portion. The trial court found that, prior to this transfer, the Messerlys' predecessor in title, Mr. Bloom, had installed a septic tank on the property without a permit and in violation of the applicable health code. The Messerlys used the building as an income investment property until 1973 when they sold it, upon land contract, to James Barnes who likewise used it primarily as an income-producing investment.

Mr. and Mrs. Barnes, with the permission of the Messerlys, sold approximately one acre of the property in 1976, and the remaining 600 square feet and building were offered for sale soon thereafter when Mr. and Mrs. Barnes defaulted on their land contract. Mr. and Mrs. Pickles evidenced an interest in the property, but were dissatisfied with the terms of the Barnes-Messerly land contract. Consequently, to accommodate the Pickleses' preference to enter into a land contract directly with the Messerlys, Mr. and Mrs. Barnes executed a quit-claim deed which conveyed their interest in the property back to the Messerlys. After inspecting the property, Mr. and Mrs. Pickles executed a new land contract with the Messerlys on March 21, 1977. It provided for a purchase price of $25,500. A clause was added to the end of the land contract form which provides:

> "17. Purchaser has examined this property and agrees to accept same in its present condition. There are no other or additional written or oral understandings."

Five or six days later, when the Pickleses went to introduce themselves to the tenants, they discovered raw sewage seeping out of the ground. Tests conducted by a sanitation expert indicated the inadequacy of the sewage system. The Lenawee County Board of Health subsequently condemned the property and initiated this lawsuit in the Lenawee Circuit Court against the Messerlys as land contract vendors, and the Pickleses, as vendees, to obtain a permanent injunction proscribing human habitation of the premises until the property was brought into conformance with the Lenawee County sanitation code. The injunction was granted, and the Lenawee County Board of Health was permitted to withdraw from the lawsuit by stipulation of the parties.

When no payments were made on the land contract, the Messerlys filed a cross-complaint against the Pickleses seeking foreclosure, sale of the property, and a deficiency judgment. Mr. and Mrs. Pickles then counterclaimed for rescission against the Messerlys, and filed a third-party complaint against the Barneses, which incorporated, by reference, the allegations of the counterclaim against the Messerlys. In count one, Mr. and Mrs. Pickles alleged failure of consideration. Count two charged Mr. and Mrs. Barnes with willful concealment and misrepresentation as a result of their failure to disclose the condition of the sanitation system. Additionally, Mr. and Mrs. Pickles sought to hold the Messerlys liable in equity for the Barneses' alleged misrepresentation. The Pickleses prayed that the land contract be rescinded.

After a bench trial, the court concluded that the Pickleses had no cause of action against either the Messerlys or the Barneses as there was no fraud or misrepresentation. This ruling was predicated on the trial judge's conclusion that none of the parties knew of Mr. Bloom's earlier transgression or of the resultant problem with the septic system until it was discovered by the Pickleses, and that the sanitation problem was not caused by any of the parties. The trial court held that the property was purchased "as is", after inspection and, accordingly, its "negative * * * value cannot be blamed upon an innocent seller". Foreclosure was ordered against the Pickleses, together with a judgment against them in the amount of $25,943.09.

Mr. and Mrs. Pickles appealed from the adverse judgment. The Court of Appeals unanimously affirmed the trial court's ruling with respect to Mr. and Mrs. Barnes but, in a two-to-one decision, reversed the finding of no cause of action on the Pickleses' claims against the Messerlys. . . . It concluded that the mutual mistake between the Messerlys and the Pickleses went to a basic, as opposed to a collateral, element of the contract, and that the parties intended to transfer income-producing rental property but, in actuality, the vendees paid $25,500 for an asset without value.[7]

---

[7] The trial court found that the only way that the property could be put to residential use would be to pump and haul the sewage, a method which is economically unfeasible, as the cost of such a disposal system amounts to double the income generated by the property. * * * The trial court and the Court of Appeals both found that the property was valueless, or had a negative value.

We granted the Messerlys' application for leave to appeal. 411 Mich. 900 (1981).

II

We must decide initially whether there was a mistaken belief entertained by one or both parties to the contract in dispute and, if so, the resultant legal significance.

A contractual mistake "is a belief that is not in accord with the facts." Restatement Contracts (Second) § 151. The erroneous belief of one or both of the parties must relate to a fact in existence at the time the contract is executed. Richardson Lumber Co. v. Hoey, 219 Mich. 643 (1922); Sherwood v. Walker, 66 Mich. 568, 580 (1887) (Sherwood, J., dissenting). That is to say, the belief which is found to be in error may not be, in substance, a prediction as to a future occurrence or non-occurrence. . . .

The Court of Appeals concluded, after a *de novo* review of the record, that the parties were mistaken as to the income-producing capacity of the property in question. . . . We agree. The vendors and the vendees each believed that the property transferred could be utilized as income-generating rental property. All of the parties subsequently learned that, in fact, the property was unsuitable for any residential use.

* * *

Having determined that when these parties entered into the land contract they were laboring under a mutual mistake of fact, we now direct our attention to a determination of the legal significance of that finding.

A contract may be rescinded because of a mutual misapprehension of the parties, but this remedy is granted only in the sound discretion of the court. . . . Appellants argue that the parties' mistake relates only to the quality or value of the real estate transferred, and that such mistakes are collateral to the agreement and do not justify rescission, citing *A & M Land Development Co. v. Miller*, 354 Mich. 681 (1959).

In that case, the plaintiff was the purchaser of 91 lots of real property. It sought partial rescission of the land contract when it was frustrated in its attempts to develop 42 of the lots because it could not obtain permits from the county health department to install septic tanks on these lots. This Court refused to allow rescission because the mistake, whether mutual or unilateral, related only to the value of the property.

> "There was here no mistake as to the form or substance of the contract between the parties, or the description of the property constituting the subject matter. The situation involved is not at all analogous to that presented in *Scott v. Grow*, 301 Mich. 226 (1942). There the plaintiff sought relief by way of reformation of a deed on the ground that the instrument of conveyance had not been drawn in accordance with the intention and agreement of

the parties. It was held that the bill of complaint stated a case for the granting of equitable relief by way of reformation. In the case at bar plaintiff received the property for which it contracted. The fact that it may be of less value than the purchaser expected at the time of the transaction is not a sufficient basis for the granting of equitable relief, neither fraud nor reliance on misrepresentation of material facts having been established." 354 Mich. 693–694.

Appellees contend, on the other hand, that in this case the parties were mistaken as to the very nature of the character of the consideration and claim that the pervasive and essential quality of this mistake renders rescission appropriate. They cite in support of that view *Sherwood v. Walker*, 66 Mich. 568 (1887), the famous "barren cow" case. In that case, the parties agreed to the sale and purchase of a cow which was thought to be barren, but which was, in reality, with calf. When the seller discovered the fertile condition of his cow, he refused to deliver her. In permitting rescission, the Court stated:

[The court quoted the last paragraph of the majority opinion in *Sherwood*.]

As the parties suggest, the foregoing precedent arguably distinguishes mistakes affecting the essence of the consideration from those which go to its quality or value, affording relief on a *per se* basis for the former but not the latter. . . .

However, the distinctions which may be drawn from *Sherwood* and *A & M Land Development Co.* do not provide a satisfactory analysis of the nature of a mistake sufficient to invalidate a contract. Often, a mistake relates to an underlying factual assumption which, when discovered, directly affects value, but simultaneously and materially affects the essence of the contractual consideration. It is disingenuous to label such a mistake collateral. . . .

Appellant and appellee both mistakenly believed that the property which was the subject of their land contract would generate income as rental property. The fact that it could not be used for human habitation deprived the property of its income-earning potential and rendered it less valuable. However, this mistake, while directly and dramatically affecting the property's value, cannot accurately be characterized as collateral because it also affects the very essence of the consideration. "The thing sold and bought [income generating rental property] had in fact no existence." Sherwood, 66 Mich. at 578.

We find that the inexact and confusing distinction between contractual mistakes running to value and those touching the substance of the consideration serves only as an impediment to a clear and helpful analysis for the equitable resolution of cases in which mistake is alleged and proven. Accordingly, the holdings of *A & M Land Development Co.*

and *Sherwood* with respect to the material or collateral nature of a mistake are limited to the facts of those cases.

Instead, we think the better-reasoned approach is a case-by-case analysis whereby rescission is indicated when the mistaken belief relates to a basic assumption of the parties upon which the contract is made, and which materially affects the agreed performances of the parties. . . . Restatement Contracts (Second) § 152.[11] Rescission is not available, however, to relieve a party who has assumed the risk of loss in connection with the mistake. . . .

All of the parties to this contract erroneously assumed that the property transferred by the vendors to the vendees was suitable for human habitation and could be utilized to generate rental income. The fundamental nature of these assumptions is indicated by the fact that their invalidity changed the character of the property transferred, thereby frustrating, indeed precluding, Mr. and Mrs. Pickles' intended use of the real estate. Although the Pickleses are disadvantaged by enforcement of the contract, performance is advantageous to the Messerlys, as the property at issue is less valuable absent its income-earning potential. Nothing short of rescission can remedy the mistake. Thus, the parties' mistake as to a basic assumption materially affects the agreed performances of the parties.

Despite the significance of the mistake made by the parties, we reverse the Court of Appeals because we conclude that equity does not justify the remedy sought by Mr. and Mrs. Pickles.

Rescission is an equitable remedy which is granted only in the sound discretion of the court. . . . A court need not grant rescission in every case in which the mutual mistake relates to a basic assumption and materially affects the agreed performance of the parties.

In cases of mistake by two equally innocent parties, we are required, in the exercise of our equitable powers, to determine which blameless party should assume the loss resulting from the misapprehension they shared.[13] Normally that can only be done by drawing upon our "own notions of what is reasonable and just under all the surrounding circumstances."[14]

---

[11] The parties have invited our attention to the first edition of the Restatement of Contracts in their briefs, and the Court of Appeals cites to that edition in its opinion. However, the second edition was published subsequent to the issuance of the lower court opinion and the filing of the briefs with this Court. Thus, we take it upon ourselves to refer to the latest edition to aid us in our resolution of this case. * * *

[13] This risk-of-loss analysis is absent in both *A & M Land Development Co.* and *Sherwood*, and this omission helps to explain, in part, the disparate treatment in the two cases. Had such an inquiry been undertaken in *Sherwood*, we believe that the result might have been different. Moreover, a determination as to which party assumed the risk in *A & M Land Development Co.* would have alleviated the need to characterize the mistake as collateral so as to justify the result denying rescission. Despite the absence of any inquiry as to the assumption of risk in those two leading cases, we find that there exists sufficient precedent to warrant such an analysis in future cases of mistake.

[14] *Hathaway v. Hudson*, 256 Mich. 702, quoting 9 C.J., p. 1161.

Equity suggests that, in this case, the risk should be allocated to the purchasers. We are guided to that conclusion, in part, by the standards announced in § 154 of the Restatement of Contracts 2d, for determining when a party bears the risk of mistake. . . . Section 154(a) suggests that the court should look first to whether the parties have agreed to the allocation of the risk between themselves. While there is no express assumption in the contract by either party of the risk of the property becoming uninhabitable, there was indeed some agreed allocation of the risk to the vendees by the incorporation of an "as is" clause into the contract which, we repeat, provided:

> "Purchaser has examined this property and agrees to accept same in its present condition. There are no other or additional written or oral understandings."

That is a persuasive indication that the parties considered that, as between them, such risk as related to the "present condition" of the property should lie with the purchaser. If the "as is" clause is to have any meaning at all, it must be interpreted to refer to those defects which were unknown at the time that the contract was executed. Thus, the parties themselves assigned the risk of loss to Mr. and Mrs. Pickles.

We conclude that Mr. and Mrs. Pickles are not entitled to the equitable remedy of rescission and, accordingly, reverse the decision of the Court of Appeals.

Messerly home: Dispute house in *Lenawee County v. Messerly*

NOTES

(1) The *Sherwood* court held that the parties' mistake was not of the "mere quality of the animal, but went to the very nature of the thing."

Moreover, "the thing sold and bought had in fact no existence." Are these distinctions helpful?

What are the competing policy considerations in cases of this type? Does Section 152 of the Second Restatement better address them? Can *Beachcomber* and *Lenawee* be reconciled on the basis of the Restatement rule?

Sherwood v. Walker is a famous staple of the first year Contracts course. For further consideration in verse, see Robert Birmingham, *A Rose by Any Other Word: Mutual Mistake in* Sherwood v. Walker, 21 U.C. Davis L. Rev. 198 (1987).

(2) What are the appropriate remedies in cases like *Sherwood v. Walker* when a court refuses to enforce a contract on grounds of mutual mistake? Restitution? Reliance? Gideon Parchomovsky, Peter Siegleman and Steve Thel have argued that the best remedy in cases like *Sherwood* is to split the difference, meaning that each party shares the loss equally. *Equal Wrongs and Half Rights*, 82 N.Y.U. L. Rev. 738, 741–42 (2007). Isn't this the fairer outcome when neither party is at fault? Or are there advantages to putting all the risk on one party?

(3) *An Anomalous Situation.* In a case presenting an "anomalous" situation, the *sellers* sought to rescind a contract for the sale of land based on a defect (leaking underground gasoline storage tanks) discovered after the agreement. The transaction involved the sale for $320,000 of a gas station and automobile parts store in East Lansing for use as a 7-Eleven store. The agreement contained an "as is" clause. The sellers sought to rescind because state environmental statutes make previous owners of sites liable for environmental contamination and responsible for cleanup. The court upheld the sellers' right to rescind based on mutual mistake. Garb-Ko, Inc. v. Lansing-Lewis Services, Inc., 423 N.W.2d 355 (Mich.App. 1988). Asserting that the "as is" clause held no significance since the buyer was not the adversely affected party, the court noted: "[The sellers] have a continuing obligation and responsibility for the contaminated property. One expert estimated that the cost of cleanup could be anywhere from $100,000 to $1,000,000. In order to contain further cleanup costs and third-party claims arising from use of the contaminated land, [the sellers] need control over the use of the property. Sale to plaintiff would not give them such control." 423 N.W.2d at 358.

(4) *The Treasure in the Dunghill: A Rabbinical Account.* The *Midrash Rabbah* includes the following account:

> Alexander of Macedon visited King Kazia beyond the dark mountains. He came forth, offering him golden bread on a golden tray. "Do I then need your gold?" he demanded. "Had you then nothing to eat in your own country that you have come here?" he retorted. "I came only because I wished to see how you dispense justice," was the reply. As he sat with him a man came with a complaint against his neighbour. "This man," he stated, "sold me a dunghill and I found a treasure in it." The buyer argued, "I bought a dunghill only," while the vendor maintained, "I sold the dunghill

and all it contained." Said he [the king] to one: "Have you a son?" "Yes," replied he. "And have you a daughter?" he asked the other. "Yes," was the answer. "Then marry them and let the treasure belong to both." He noticed him [Alexander] sitting astonished, and asked him, "Have I then not judged well?" "Yes," he replied. "Had this happened among you, how would you have judged?" "I would have slain both and kept the treasure for myself."

1 Midrash Rabbah, ch. XXXIII (H. Freedman trans. 3d ed. 1983). How might the case have come out under the Second Restatement?

PROBLEMS: THE CASES OF THE UNKNOWN OIL DEPOSITS, MESTROVIC'S DRAWINGS, AND UNKNOWN INJURIES

(a) Seller, a farmer, agreed in writing to sell forty acres of land to Purchaser, a neighbor, for $40,000 ($1,000 per acre). Before closing, it was discovered that the land contained valuable oil deposits which, if found before the time of contracting, would have justified a price of $400,000 ($10,000 per acre). Does Seller have a case for rescission? Cf. Tetenman v. Epstein, 66 Cal.App. 745 (1924).

(b) The 1st Source Bank, as executor of the estate of Olga Mestrovic, deceased widow of renowned Yugoslavian sculptor Ivan Mestrovic, entered into a contract to sell the family home to Terrence and Antoinette Wilkin. No mention was made of any works of art. After closing, the Wilkins complained that the premises were left in a cluttered condition and needed extensive cleaning. The Bank proposed that they would arrange to have the cleaning done by a rubbish removal service, or that the Wilkins could clean the house themselves and retain any items of personal property which remained. The Wilkins opted to do the work themselves and, in so doing, found eight drawings and a sculpture apparently created by Ivan Mestrovic. Neither the Bank nor the Wilkins suspected that any works of art remained on the premises. In a contest of ownership between the Bank and the Wilkins, who wins? See Wilkin v. 1st Source Bank, 548 N.E.2d 170 (Ind.App. 1990).

(c) O was injured in an accident at work. The employer's Insurance Company admitted liability and requested that O enter the hospital for tests on the extent of the injuries. At the conclusion of the hospital stay and after evaluating the doctor's report, Insurance Company offered O $40,000 in full settlement of any and all claims under the policy. O accepted the offer and signed a release that, among other things, stated that it was a "general release of all claims for personal injuries, known or unknown." O later became seriously ill due to an internal trauma not detected in the medical examination. O claims that the release should be set aside for mutual mistake. Do you agree? Compare Obaitan v. State Farm, 1997 WL 208959 (Del.Ch. 1997) with Gortney v. Norfolk & Western Ry. Co., 216 Mich.App. 535 (1996).

OneBeacon America Insurance Co. v. Travelers Indemnity Co. of Illinois

United States Court of Appeals, First Circuit, 2006.
465 F.3d 38.

■ LIPEZ, CIRCUIT JUDGE. In this diversity case, appellee Travelers Indemnity Company of Illinois ("Travelers") seeks to recover under a motor vehicle liability policy that OneBeacon America Insurance Company and Pennsylvania General Insurance Company (collectively, "OneBeacon") had issued to Leasing Associates, Inc. and LAI Trust (collectively "LAI"), a vehicle leasing agency. Travelers settled a vehicle liability suit for $5,000,000 on behalf of Capform, Inc., which had leased the vehicle involved from LAI. Citing the OneBeacon/LAI policy, Travelers demanded that OneBeacon reimburse Travelers $1,000,000, the policy's limit. Although OneBeacon has admitted that its policy with LAI may be read to extend coverage to the Capform vehicle, it protested that the parties never intended such a result. Accordingly, OneBeacon asked the district court to reform the policy in light of "mutual mistake." On cross-motions for summary judgment, the district court refused to reform the policy and ordered OneBeacon to pay the $1,000,000 to Travelers. We reverse.

I.

OneBeacon is an insurance company headquartered in Massachusetts. LAI, a Texas-based company that leases cars and trucks to businesses, contracted with OneBeacon for general insurance coverage for the company's vehicles. The policy defines an "insured" to include:

a.   You for any covered auto.

b.   Anyone else while using with your permission a covered auto you own. . . .

Although OneBeacon acknowledges that this language may be read to extend coverage to LAI's lessees, it says that neither it nor LAI intended that coverage.

Capform, Inc. is a Texas and Florida construction company that leased some of its vehicles from LAI. LAI's standard lease required lessees to insure the leased vehicles, at their own expense, either by applying to be added to the OneBeacon policy or through another insurer. Capform chose to insure its vehicles with Travelers. In 2001, a Capform employee in Florida, driving a Capform truck on long-term lease from LAI, struck and severely injured a pedestrian, Manuel Pedreira. Travelers defended Capform and eventually settled Pedreira's personal injury suit for $5,000,000.

During the settlement process, Travelers became aware of the policy OneBeacon had issued to LAI and read it to grant coverage for Pedreira's case. Travelers asked OneBeacon to contribute $1,000,000, the policy's single-occurrence limit, to the Pedreira settlement. OneBeacon refused and instead filed suit against both Travelers and LAI seeking a declaratory judgment that Capform was not covered by its policy. Alternatively, OneBeacon asked that the insurance contract be reformed to match the parties' intent that it would cover only those lessees who had specifically applied for, and been approved for, coverage under the OneBeacon policy. LAI was dismissed as a defendant after stating, in an "Agreement for Judgment" ("the Agreement"), that its OneBeacon policy did not cover lessees who purchased the required insurance coverage for their leased vehicles from insurers other than OneBeacon.

Both parties subsequently moved for summary judgment. OneBeacon argued that the Agreement, taken together with evidence of the course of conduct between it and LAI, and of the insurance obligations LAI imposed on its lessees, established that the parties were mutually mistaken when they executed a contract that did not exclude from coverage vehicles that lessees had chosen to insure independently. Travelers sought summary judgment based primarily on the policy language.

The district court initially refused to grant judgment for either party, prompting the two companies to submit a joint motion for reconsideration stating their belief that "there are no material facts that require a trial" and asserting that "this action can and should be resolved through [the parties'] Motions for Summary Judgment." In response, the district court issued a two-page order granting summary judgment for Travelers, concluding that "OneBeacon has failed to 'present full, clear, and decisive proof of mistake.' " . . . Without elaborating, the court cited three factors for its decision: the "clear and unambiguous policy language," OneBeacon's inability to identify "any policy language that was included by mistake . . . or endorsement that was omitted by mistake," and "the Massachusetts public policy concerning motor-vehicle liability insurance."

II.

On appeal, OneBeacon challenges the district court's conclusion that the evidence was insufficient to warrant reformation, arguing that the undisputed facts conclusively show that neither OneBeacon nor LAI intended insurance coverage under the OneBeacon policy for LAI lessees who did not individually apply for, and pay for, that coverage. The insurer also contends that there was no public policy justification for refusing to reform the policy to conform to the parties' intent. For reasons we shall explain, we agree.

* * *

B.   Mutual mistake and contract reformation under Massachusetts law

Under Massachusetts law, a written contract may be reformed if its language "does not reflect the true intent of both parties." . . . Massachusetts courts have referenced the approach to mutual mistake articulated in the Restatement (Second) of Contracts. . . . The Restatement summarizes the applicable principles as follows:

> Where a writing that evidences or embodies an agreement in whole or in part fails to express the agreement because of a mistake of both parties as to the contents or effect of the writing, the court may at the request of a party reform the writing to express the agreement, except to the extent that rights of third parties such as good faith purchasers for value will be unfairly affected.

Restatement (Second) of Contracts § 155 (2006). When a party asks for reformation of a contract, it is not asking the court to interpret the contract but rather to change it to conform to the parties' intent. See id. cmts. a, b. Accordingly, the usual restrictions on contract interpretation, such as the parol evidence rule, do not apply to a court's inquiry into the parties' intent. . . . In a reformation case, it does not matter that a contract unambiguously says one thing. A court still will accept extrinsic evidence in evaluating a claim that both parties to the contract intended it to say something else.

The critical limitation in a contract reformation case is the burden of proof: to be entitled to reformation, a party must "establish that the undisputed material facts fully, clearly, and decisively show[ ] a mutual mistake,". . . . Although "[t]he classic case for reformation" is when the mutual mistake can be traced to a typo or transcription error, a scrivener's error is not a prerequisite for reformation. E. Allan Farnsworth, Farnsworth on Contracts § 7.5 (2001). Mutual mistakes justifying contract reformation may result simply from the parties' inattention. . . . Such is the mistake urged by OneBeacon, which claims that neither it nor LAI realized—or intended—that the policy's broad definition of an "insured" extended coverage to LAI's lessees who had not independently insured the vehicles with OneBeacon.

The mistake that OneBeacon must demonstrate—to a high degree of certainty—is not that the outcome of its agreement differed from its expectations, but rather that the contract language did not express the agreement as originally intended. See Restatement (Second) § 155 cmt. a ("The province of reformation is to make a writing express the agreement that the parties intended it should."). The distinction is between a contract that does not accurately reflect (hence misrepresents) the agreement of the parties and a contract that accurately reflects the intent of the parties but is premised on some mistaken fact. Reformation is not available to correct mistaken factual assumptions about the parties' bargain, but may be used to correct misrepresentations of the parties' contractual intent. The distinction is perhaps best understood through an illustration. If, for example, two parties intended their agreement to cover the sale of 100 acres in Boston, but the contract erroneously identified a different piece of property in Providence, their mutual mistake could provide the basis for reformation. If, however, the contract correctly referred to the intended sale of 100 acres in Boston, but the parcel turned out to be only 90 acres, the mistake would not concern the representation of their intent—and reformation could not be used to amend the original agreement. See Restatement (Second) § 155 cmts. a, b. In short, reformation fixes a mistaken writing; it is not meant to fix a mistaken agreement.

Even if a mutual mistake in representation is proven, however, reformation may not necessarily be awarded. "Since the remedy of reformation is equitable in nature, a court has the discretion to withhold it . . . on grounds that have traditionally justified courts of equity in withholding relief." Restatement (Second) § 155 cmt. d; . . . . For example, where the "rights of third parties such as good faith purchasers for value will be unfairly affected," reformation may be withheld even if otherwise appropriate. Id. § 155.

C.   The evidence of mutual mistake

The parties have both asserted that the facts are undisputed, and Travelers has offered no evidence beyond the policy language concerning the intent of OneBeacon and LAI at the time they entered into that agreement. Consequently, in reviewing the grant of summary judgment for Travelers, our inquiry must focus on whether the court properly concluded that the undisputed facts on intent presented by OneBeacon were insufficient to establish "full, clear, and decisive proof of mistake," . . .; in other words, given the undisputed facts, did the district court err in concluding that OneBeacon fell short of meeting the legal standard for reformation?

OneBeacon submitted various forms of evidence, including affidavits, the Agreement for Judgment, and lease documents that reflected the course of conduct between LAI and its lessees. Together, they paint a consistent picture showing that LAI intended to shift responsibility for liability coverage on its vehicles to the long-term lessees of those vehicles and that OneBeacon also operated on the assumption that it provided such coverage only when a lessee individually applied and was approved.

* * *

Travelers disparages virtually all of this evidence—challenging the basis for the affiants' knowledge and criticizing the "self-serving judgment" against LAI as unworthy of the court's consideration. We note initially that while Travelers properly may debate the potency of OneBeacon's proffered evidence on the issue of mutual mistake, arguing that it does not constitute "full, clear, and decisive proof of mistake," . . . Travelers' representation to the court that no material factual disputes existed forecloses it from challenging the factual assertions made by the affiants and contained in the Agreement for Judgment. Indeed, in keeping with this protocol, Travelers does not offer conflicting evidence, but attempts only to diminish the significance of OneBeacon's offerings.

In our view, however, the affiants were sufficiently involved in LAI's acquisition of insurance from OneBeacon to be considered reliable. * * *

* * * Moreover, the affiants' statements are consistent with the undisputed documentary evidence—the standard lease forms—showing that LAI and OneBeacon operated in the belief that the policy extended only to lessees who specifically applied for coverage.

* * *

Travelers has identified no evidence that undermines the uniform picture painted by OneBeacon's evidentiary submissions. It asserts that OneBeacon has not pointed to "any specific endorsement, exclusion or other limiting language that they contend was mistakenly omitted when these policies were issued to LAI," noting that "[t]his is hardly surprising, inasmuch as the language in the policies" providing coverage to specified "insureds" is part of the boilerplate contained in standard auto industry policies. However, OneBeacon does, in fact, claim a critical omission of limiting language that would have excluded from coverage vehicles operated by long-term lessees who had not directly sought and obtained coverage under the policy.

In sum, the evidence submitted by OneBeacon is both ample and persuasive, and we therefore conclude that it has met its burden to provide "full, clear, and decisive proof of mistake," . . . . Accordingly, barring any equitable concerns, OneBeacon is entitled to reformation of the relevant policies to exclude coverage for LAI-owned vehicles on long-term leases, unless the lessee has followed the requisite application procedures and obtained its own coverage under the OneBeacon policy.

D.   Equitable considerations

We see no equitable barriers here. Travelers makes a strained argument that reforming the insurance policy as OneBeacon requests would leave vehicles uninsured in violation of Massachusetts law and public policy. LAI's general lease form does not permit a vehicle to be acquired and operated by a lessee, however, unless the lessee has secured insurance coverage, either independently or under LAI's policy with OneBeacon. Assuming that Massachusetts law were to apply to vehicles under long-term lease that are registered and operated outside the state, Massachusetts' requirement that motor vehicle operators carry liability insurance would in no way be frustrated by the OneBeacon/LAI system.

In addition, the record contains no evidence showing detrimental reliance on an assumption that the OneBeacon policy covered Capform's leased vehicles. A representative for Travelers, Shirong Chen, testified in deposition that the company was unaware of the OneBeacon policy during the underwriting process for Capform, and Capform did not look to OneBeacon for coverage after the accident. From all that appears in the record, this was a case where everyone's expectations were the same—until Travelers read the boilerplate in the OneBeacon policies. In this instance, equity favors reforming the policy to reflect the contracting parties' intent.

Therefore, the district court's summary judgment for appellee Travelers is reversed, and the court is directed to enter summary judgment for appellant OneBeacon providing for reformation of the policy consistent with our ruling.

So ordered.

NOTES

(1) *The Case for Reformation.* Reformation, like rescission, is an equitable remedy. Unlike rescission, however, reformation is designed to restore the efficacy of a writing that does not reflect the agreement of the parties, frequently oral, that they intended the writing to embody. Reformation has been described as a "way station" to some other remedy, in that the ultimate objective of the plaintiff (assuming it is the plaintiff who requests reformation) is to enforce the writing as reformed. In the classic case for reformation, the plaintiff must show by clear and convincing evidence that the parties had actually reached agreement regarding the term at issue, that both intended the term to be included in a subsequent writing, and that because of "mutual mistake" in expression, the term was not included. Since the defendant will probably deny that he intended the term to be included in the writing, the plaintiff has an uphill struggle to establish the mistake. In the plaintiff's favor, neither the plaintiff's fault in not carefully reading the writing nor the fault of the plaintiff's agent will bar reformation. See Treadaway v. Camellia Convalescent Hospitals, Inc., 43 Cal.App.3d 189 (1974). At the same time, if the "mutual" mistake is in the formulation rather than the expression of the agreement, the proper remedy is rescission rather than reformation. See Restatement (Second) §§ 153–155; National Resort Communities v. Cain, 526 S.W.2d 510 (Tex. 1975) (mutual mistake in formulation).

(2) *More Recent Developments.* As time passes, a broader basis for reformation may be emerging in the case law. Under the traditional view, reformation is granted only where there is a mutual mistake in expression. See, e.g., Hoffman v. Chapman, 182 Md. 208 (1943) (finding that rescission is the proper remedy for unilateral mistake, fraud, duress or other inequitable conduct). A slightly broader rule is found in New York, where the "classic" cases for reformation are said to include mutual mistake in expression or "a mistake on plaintiff's part and a fraud by defendant." Brandwein v. Provident Mutual Life Insurance Co., 3 N.Y.2d 491, 492 (1957). See also Barash v. Pennsylvania Terminal Real Estate Corp., 26 N.Y.2d 77 (1970). An even broader basis for reformation is stated in *Kufer v. Carson*:

> Ultimately equity will grant relief if an instrument as written fails to express the true agreement between the parties without regard to the cause of the failure to express the agreement as actually made, whether it is due to fraud, mistake in the use of language, or anything else which prevented the instrument from expressing the true intention of the parties.

230 N.W.2d 500, 504 (Iowa 1975). The Federal Circuit has held, however, that reformation for mutual mistake is not available where the facts upon which the mistake was based were not knowable at the time of contracting. "It is true that even though the outcome of a fact is unknowable, the parties can make a mistake concerning that fact. But where the existence of a fact is unknowable, the parties cannot have a belief concerning that fact, and they cannot make a mistake about it." Atlas Corp. v. United States, 895 F.2d 745, 751 (Fed.Cir. 1990).

Finally, some courts have "reformed" contracts in order to purge them of defects such as illegality and unconscionability. See Karpinski v. Ingrasci, 28 N.Y.2d 45 (1971) (illegality); Jones v. Star Credit Corp., reprinted in Chapter Two (adjusting the agreed price to the amount already paid under the contract on grounds of unconscionability). See also UCC § 2–302(1); §§ 2–719(2) & (3). At least one court has "reformed" a contract in order to relieve a party whose duty of performance was excused due to mutual mistake and commercial impracticability. See Aluminum Co. of America v. Essex Group, Inc., 499 F.Supp. 53 (W.D.Pa. 1980). In these developments, courts purport to grant reformation in order to remedy problems other than mistake in the expression of agreements and, as you can plainly see, these remedies have little to do with the parties' intentions.

Ayer v. Western Union Telegraph Co.
Supreme Judicial Court of Maine, 1887.
79 Me. 493.

■ EMERY, J. On report. The defendant telegraph company was engaged in the business of transmitting messages by telegraph between Bangor and Philadelphia, and other points. The plaintiff, a lumber dealer in Bangor, delivered to the defendant company in Bangor, to be transmitted to his correspondent in Philadelphia, the following message: "Will sell 800 M laths, delivered at your wharf, two ten net cash. July shipment. Answer quick." The regular tariff rate was prepaid by the plaintiff for such transmission. The message delivered by the defendant company to the Philadelphia correspondent was as follows: "Will sell 800 M laths, delivered at your wharf, two net cash. July shipment. Answer quick." It will be seen that the important word "ten" in the statement of price was omitted. The Philadelphia party immediately returned by telegraph the following answer: "Accept your telegraphic offer on laths. Cannot increase price spruce." Letters afterwards passed between the parties, which disclosed the error in the transmission of the plaintiff's message. About two weeks after the discovery of the error, the plaintiff shipped the laths, as per the message received by his correspondent, to-wit, at two dollars per M. He testified that his correspondent insisted he was entitled to the laths at that price, and they were shipped accordingly.

The defendant telegraph company offered no evidence whatever, and did not undertake to account for or explain the mistake in the transmission of the message. The presumption therefore is that the mistake resulted from the fault of the telegraph company. * * *

The fault and consequent liability of the defendant company being thus established, the only remaining question is the extent of that liability in this case. The plaintiff claims it extends to the difference between the market price of laths and the price at which they were shipped. The defendant claims its liability is limited to the amount paid for the transmission of the message. . . .

* * *

The defendant company . . . claims that the plaintiff was not in fact damaged to a greater extent than the price paid by him for the transmission. It contends that the plaintiff was not bound by the erroneous message delivered by the company to the Philadelphia party, and hence need not have shipped the laths at the lesser price. This raises the question whether the message written by the sender, and intrusted to the telegraph company for transmission, or the message written out and delivered by the company to the receiver at the other end of the line, as and for the message intended to be sent, is the better evidence of the rights of the receiver against the sender. The question is important and not easy of solution. It would be hard that the negligence of the telegraph company, or an error in transmission resulting from uncontrollable causes, should impose upon the innocent sender of a message a liability he never authorized nor contemplated. It would be equally hard that the innocent receiver, acting in good faith upon the message as received by him, should through such error lose all claim upon the sender. If one, owning merchandise, write a message offering to sell at a certain price, it would seem unjust that the telegraph company could bind him to sell at a less price, by making that error in the transmission. On the other hand, the receiver of the offer may in good faith, upon the strength of the telegram as received by him, have sold all the merchandise to arrive, perhaps at the same rate. It would seem unjust that he should have no claim for the merchandise. If an agent receives instructions by telegraph from his principal, and in good faith acts upon them as expressed in the message delivered him by the company, it would seem he ought to be held justified, though there were an error in the transmission.

It is evident that in case of an error in the transmission of a telegram either the sender or receiver must often suffer loss. As between the two, upon whom should the loss finally fall? We think the safer and more equitable rule, and the rule the public can most easily adapt itself to, is that, as between the sender and receiver, the party who selects the telegraph as the means of communication shall bear the loss caused by the errors of the telegraph. The first proposer can select one of many modes of communication, both for the proposal and the answer. The receiver has no such choice, except as to his answer. If he cannot safely act upon the message he received through the agency selected by the proposer, business must be seriously hampered and delayed. The use of the telegraph has become so general, and so many transactions are based on the words of the telegram received, that any other rule would now be impracticable.

Of course, the rule above stated presupposes the innocence of the receiver, and that there is nothing to cause him to suspect an error. If there be anything in the message, or in the attendant circumstances, or in the prior dealings of the parties, or in anything else, indicating a probable error in the transmission, good faith on the part of the receiver may require him to investigate before acting. Neither does the rule include forged messages, for in such case the supposed sender did not make any use of the telegraph. [The court cites authority, including *Western Union v. Shotter*, 71 Ga. 760 (1884), supporting a finding that the sender of the telegraph must bear the loss due to transmission error over the receiver, but that the sender may recover the loss from the telegraph company at fault.]

It follows that the plaintiff in this case is entitled to recover the difference between the two dollars and the market price, as to laths. The evidence shows that the difference was 10 cents per M. Judgment for plaintiff for $80, with interest from the date of the writ.

NOTES

(1) Why is it that the existence of a contract between the sender and the recipient of the message is put at issue in this case against the telegraph company? If Ayer had refused to sell the laths at the reduced price, and the *buyer* had sued Western Union for the difference, would Western Union have made the same argument regarding the existence of the contract?

(2) Was Ayer in any way responsible for the mistake? If not, is there justification for holding him to a contract on the altered terms? Do reasons of business policy support the decision? Does the case accord with the objective theory of contractual assent? What about economic efficiency?

PROBLEM: MISTAKES IN TRANSMISSION AND THE OUTER FRINGES OF THE OBJECTIVE TEST

Sam, a breeder of race horses, owned Flasher and Dasher, who, as two-year-olds, had shown great promise. Brenda, a sportsperson, was interested in buying one or both. She visited Sam's farm and, after some discussion, offered to buy Dasher for $5,000 and Flasher for $6,000. Sam replied that "under no circumstances" would he sell Flasher, who was promised to his daughter on her next birthday, but that he would sell Dasher to Brenda for $7,000. Brenda replied that the price on Dasher was "too high," but that if Sam could lower it a bit, please contact her at home some 500 miles away.

(1) The next day, Sam decided to sell Dasher to Brenda for $6,000. Accordingly, he typed out an offer to sell and placed it in a properly addressed, stamped envelope. On his way to the mailbox, Sam had a change of mind. Before he could return to his office, however, Sam was struck by a bicycle and knocked unconscious. A stranger, seeing the letter on the

sidewalk, mailed it. Upon receipt the next day, Brenda promptly telegraphed an acceptance and resold Dasher to Thad, a friend, for $8,000. Later, Sam telephoned to say that he did not intend to sell Dasher. Is there a contract to sell Dasher?

(2)   Suppose that Sam had indicated an offer to sell Dasher for $6,000, but his secretary typed "Flasher" instead, and Sam signed the letter without reading. Upon receipt, Brenda promptly telegraphed "accept your offer to sell Flasher" and resold Flasher to Thad for $8,000. Is there a contract to sell Flasher? How about Dasher? Compare Restatement (Second) § 20(2) with CISG Art. 8(1).

(3)   Suppose that Sam went to a telegraph office and on a standard form clearly wrote the following: "Will sell Dasher to you for $6,000." The form contained a limitation of liability approved by the Federal Communications Commission declaring that the company would not be liable for mistakes or delays in transmission beyond the sum of $500, unless the message was sent at repeated message rates or was specially valued. The outer limit of liability for a repeated message was $5,000. Sam read the limitation and chose not to pay the extra charge for a repeated or specially valued message. Due to a mistake of the telegraph company, the telegram as sent offered to sell Dasher for $5,000. Brenda promptly telegraphed her acceptance and resold Dasher to Thad for $8,000. Is there a contract to sell Dasher for $5,000? Assuming that the telegraph company was negligent, what is its liability, if any, to Sam? To Brenda? To Thad?

4.   MISREPRESENTATION AND NONDISCLOSURE

The basic rule for the effect of misrepresentation or nondisclosure on a contract is fairly simple. As stated in Section 164(1) of the Second Restatement:

> If a party's manifestation of assent is induced by either a fraudulent or a material misrepresentation by the other party upon which the recipient is justified in relying, the contract is voidable by the recipient.

As Section 162 explains, and simplifying a bit, a misrepresentation is fraudulent if it is made intentionally or recklessly; a misrepresentation is material "if it would be likely to induce a reasonable person to manifest his assent." The rule in Section 164 sets a lower bar than does the tort of deceit, which requires that a misrepresentation be *both* fraudulent *and* material. The black-letter rule in contract law is that either is enough. Farnsworth reports, however, that "although there is no shortage of cases allowing avoidance where the misrepresentation was both material and fraudulent, or material but not fraudulent, it is difficult to find cases that have done so where the misrepresentation was fraudulent but not material." 1 Farnsworth § 4.12, at 481.

While these general rules are fairly easy to state, there are of course complications. As we will see below, the real action in these cases often concerns what counts as a misrepresentation under the rule.

Misrepresentations can also give rise to claims of breach of warranty and in some cases to tort or statutory liability. We discuss these rules in Chapter Five, Section 3.

Peter Laidlaw v. Hector M. Organ

Supreme Court of the United States, 1817.
15 U.S. 178.

ERROR to the district court for the Louisiana district.

[Organ, the plaintiff/buyer, filed suit against Laidlaw, the defendant/seller, seeking to recover possession of 111 hogsheads of tobacco that Laidlaw had taken from Organ's possession. Laidlaw, as the seller, had initially delivered the tobacco to plaintiff under a contract for the price of $7,544.69, but later repossessed the tobacco by force. Laidlaw alleged in defense that fraud in the formation of the contract nullified Laidlaw's duty to sell. Organ and Laidlaw had been negotiating over the tobacco in question on the evening of Saturday, February 18, 1815. Late that same day, messengers "brought from the British fleet the news that a treaty of peace had been signed at Ghent by the American and British commissioners," ending the War of 1812 and consequently the British blockade of New Orleans. Having learned the news through private channels, Organ (the buyer) called Laidlaw (the seller) shortly after sunrise on Sunday. Laidlaw "asked if there was any news which was calculated to enhance the price or value of the article about to be purchased." Organ apparently remained silent and "the . . . purchase was then and there made." The news was made public in a handbill that same morning at 8 o'clock. "[I]n consequence of said news the value of said article had risen from 30 to 50 per cent." The lower court found for the plaintiff, Organ.]

■ INGERSOLL, for the plaintiffs in error. The first question is, whether the sale, under the circumstances of the case, was a valid sale; whether fraud, which vitiates every contract, must be proved by the communication of positive misinformation, or by withholding information when asked. Suppression of material circumstances within the knowledge of the vendee, and not accessible to the vendor, is equivalent to fraud, and vitiates the contract. Pothier, in discussing this subject, adopts the distinction of the forum of conscience, and the forum of law; but he admits that *fides est servanda*. The parties treated on an unequal footing, as the one party had received intelligence of the peace of Ghent, at the time of the contract, and the other had not. This news was unexpected, even at Washington, much more at New Orleans, the recent scene of the most sanguinary operations of the war. In answer to the question, whether there was any news calculated to enhance the price of the article, the vendee was silent. This reserve, when such a question was asked, was equivalent to a false answer, and as much calculated to deceive as the communication of the most fabulous intelligence. Though the plaintiffs in error, after they heard the news of peace, still went on, in ignorance of their legal rights, to complete the contract, equity will protect them. * * *

■ KEY, contra. * * * The only real question in the cause is, whether the sale was invalid because the vendee did not communicate information which he received precisely as the vendor *might* have got it had he been equally diligent or equally fortunate? And, surely, on this question there can be no doubt. Even if the vendor had been entitled to the disclosure, he waived it by not insisting on an answer to his question; and the silence of the vendee might as well have been interpreted into an *affirmative* as a *negative* answer. But, on principle, he was not bound to disclose. Even admitting that his conduct was unlawful, in *foro conscientiae*, does that prove that it was so in the civil forum? Human laws are imperfect in this respect, and the sphere of morality is more extensive than the limits of civil jurisdiction. The maxim of *caveat emptor* could never have crept into the law, if the province of ethics had been co-extensive with it. There was, in the present case, no circumvention or manoeuvre practised by the vendee, unless rising earlier in the morning, and obtaining by superior diligence and alertness that intelligence by which the price of commodities was regulated, be such. It is a romantic equality that is contended for on the other side. Parties never can be precisely equal in knowledge, either of facts or of the inferences from such facts, and both must concur in order to satisfy the rule contended for. The absence of all authority in England and the United States, both great commercial countries, speaks volumes against the reasonableness and practicability of such a rule.

■ INGERSOLL, in reply. Though the record may not show that any thing tending to mislead by positive assertion was said by the vendee, in answer to the question proposed by Mr. Girault, yet it is a case of manoeuvre; of mental reservation; of circumvention. The information was monopolized by the messengers from the British fleet, and not imparted to the public at large until it was too late for the vendor to save himself. The rule of law and of ethics is the same. It is not a romantic, but a practical and legal rule of equality and good faith that is proposed to be applied. * * *

■ MARSHALL, CHIEF JUSTICE, delivered the opinion of the court. The question in this case is, whether the intelligence of extrinsic circumstances, which might influence the price of the commodity, and which was exclusively within the knowledge of the vendee, ought to have been communicated by him to the vendor? The court is of opinion that he was not bound to communicate it. It would be difficult to circumscribe the contrary doctrine within proper limits, where the means of intelligence are equally accessible to both parties. But at the same time, each party must take care not to say or do any thing tending to impose upon the other. The court thinks that the absolute instruction of the judge was erroneous, and that the question, whether any imposition was practised by the vendee upon the vendor ought to have been submitted to the jury.

For these reasons the judgment must be reversed, and the cause remanded to the district court of Louisiana, with directions to award a *venire facias de novo.*

Venire de novo awarded.

Hector Organ was represented in the Supreme Court by Francis Scott Key. In this painting, Key beholds the American flag still flying over Fort McHenry at dawn, September 14, 1814. This event inspired Key to write "The Star-Spangled Banner."

NOTES

(1)   What is the holding of *Laidlaw v. Organ*? Who won?

On the one hand, Marshall clearly states the rule that the buyer "was not bound to communicate" the news that the war had ended. On the other, Marshall also holds that "whether any imposition was practised by the vendee upon the vendor ought to have been submitted to the jury" and remands the case on that basis. If the buyer was under no duty to disclose, what other "imposition" might there have been?

(2)   The first holding in *Laidlaw*, that the buyer did not have a general duty to disclose that the war had ended, was quite influential in the development of U.S. law. It was not until the second half of the twentieth century that U.S. courts began recognizing a duty to disclose in arms-length transactions, often on the heels of legislative disclosure requirements. Thus, the Ninth Circuit could write as late as 1967, "businessmen dealing at arm's length are rarely under a duty to speak." Simpson Timber Co. v. Palmberg Constr. Co., 377 F.2d 380, 385 (9th Cir. 1967). Today, courts are more willing to recognize a duty to disclose in arms-length transactions. For an example, see *Hill v. Jones*, later in this section, as well as Restatement (Second) § 161.

Laidlaw is unusual because it is a circumstance where a buyer's non-disclosure (in response to a question) could be an unlawful imposition. Typically the law requires disclosures from sellers, not buyers. Even though we often say caveat emptor, the law by placing few disclosure duties on buyers creates a marketplace where sellers must beware (caveat venditor).

(3) *Laidlaw* teaches that by asking a question, one party can create for the other a duty to disclose. Can a party create such a duty simply by making a representation herself—a representation that the other knows is false? See Restatement (Second) § 161(b) (disclosure required if necessary to "correct a mistake of the other party as to a basic assumption on which that party is making the contract").

(4) In a large "block trade" of securities, a seller may insist on including a "big boy" provision in the sales contract indicating that the seller is making no representation concerning whether seller has material non-public information—so that the buyer cannot later sue for a failure to disclose such information. Edwin Eshmoili, *Big Boy Letters: Trading on Inside Information*, 94 CORNELL L. REV. 133 (2008). If you were a buyer, how would the existence of such a provision impact your willingness to pay? Alternatively, buyers sometimes demand an explicit representation from the seller that seller has no material non-public information concerning the block trade. In the absence of these provisions, what should be the default seller (or buyer) representation regarding material non-public information? Does the existence of both types of provisions suggest that the legal default is uncertain?

Marina District Development Co., LLC v. Phillip Ivey

United States District Court, District of New Jersey, 2016.
2016 WL 6138239.

> [*Every breaking wave on the shore*
> *Tells the next one "there'll be one more"*
> *Every gambler knows that to lose*
> *Is what you're really there for*
>
> U2, "Every Breaking Wave,"—Eds.]

■ HILLMAN, DISTRICT JUDGE

As a general matter, gambling is illegal. This is because the law considers gambling *malum per se*, a function of the age-old belief, arising perhaps from Judeo-Christian doctrine, that gambling is an immoral vice. Hence, it is prohibited by both the state and the federal government.

But like most vices, which would exist in some measure whether banned by governments or not, many states choose to allow, regulate, and tax some versions of it while preserving the ban on unregulated enterprises. The theory is a simple one. State-sanctioned gambling will be cleansed of its most unsavory elements and the games will be conducted under a defined set of published rules overseen by an administrative body. . . .

In this case, the uncontroverted facts establish that defendants Phillip D. Ivey and Cheng Yin Sun, "high-stakes" professional gamblers, set out to shift the odds of the casino game of Baccarat away from the house and in their favor. They achieved this, and profited handsomely from it, by the use of an elaborate and hidden "edge-sorting" scheme to create, and thereafter use, a deck of cards aligned in such a way as to reveal to them the face value of a card before it was turned over. Knowing the value of the card beforehand (here within a range they chose) dramatically increased the odds their resulting bets would beat the house. And beat the house they did.

Not surprisingly, when the scheme was revealed, the Plaintiff Marina District Development Co., LLC, which does business as Borgata Hotel Casino & Spa in Atlantic City, New Jersey, cried "fraud," among other things, and brought this suit. * * * For the reasons expressed below, the Court will grant-in-part and deny-in-part Ivey and Sun's motion for summary judgment and Borgata's cross-motion for summary judgment.

BACKGROUND

In April 2012, Ivey contacted Borgata to arrange a visit to play high-stakes Baccarat. Ivey made five requests: (1) a private area or "pit" in which to play; (2) a casino dealer who spoke Mandarin Chinese; (3) a guest (defendant Sun) to sit with him at the table while he played; (4) one 8-deck shoe of purple Gemaco Borgata playing cards to be used for the entirety of each session of play; and (5) an automatic card shuffling device to be used to shuffle the cards after each shoe was dealt. Borgata agreed to Ivey's requests. In return, Ivey agreed to wire a "front money" deposit of $1 million to Borgata, and that the maximum bet would be $50,000 per hand. Under these parameters, Ivey played [four times winning $9,626,000].

According to [Borgata] the mechanics of "edge sorting" are as follows:

The backs of casino playing cards generally contain a repeating diamond or geometrical pattern. If the cards are not cut symmetrically during the manufacturing process, the two long edges of the cards will not be identical. In other words, one edge will have more of the geometrical pattern than the other.

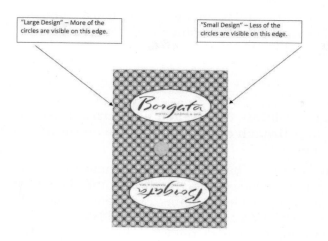

During play, Ivey and Sun used the accommodations they requested from Borgata to "turn" strategically important cards so that they could be distinguished from all other cards in the deck. The dealer would first lift the card so that Sun could see its value before it was flipped over all the way and placed on the table. If Sun told the dealer "Hao" (pronounced "how"), which translates to English as "good card," he was instructed to continue to flip the card over so that the orientation of the long edges of the card would stay on the same side when flipped. * * *

If Sun told the dealer "Buhao" (pronounced "boohow"), which translates into English as "bad card," he was instructed to flip the card side to side, so that the long edges would be reversed when flipped. * * * By telling the dealer "good card" or "bad card" in Mandarin, the dealer would place the cards on the table so that when the cards were cleared and put in the used card holder, the leading edges of the strategically important cards could be distinguished from the leading edges of the other cards in the deck.

[Ivey and Sun "turned" the cards with the highest values], so that they could be distinguished from all other cards in the deck. . . . Ivey and Sun knew that if an automatic card shuffler was used, the edges of the cards would remain facing in the same direction after they were shuffled.

Ivey also knew that if the same cards were not reused for each shoe, there would be no benefit to "edge sorting." That is why Ivey requested that the same cards be reused for each shoe.

The leading edge of the first card in the shoe is visible before the cards are dealt. Once the "edge sorting" was completed, Ivey and Sun were able to see the leading edge of the first card in the shoe before it was dealt, giving them "first card knowledge." [Their] "first card knowledge" changed the overall odds of the game from an approximate 1.06% house advantage to an approximately 6.765% advantage for Ivey. * * *

(Amend. Compl.)

DISCUSSION

* * *

1. Borgata's Claims for Breach of Contract, Breach of Implied Contract, and Breach of the Implied Covenant of Good Faith and Fair Dealing

Borgata's contract-based claims are premised on the contention that when Ivey and Sun played Baccarat at Borgata, Borgata agreed to fulfill its obligations to provide a gaming experience in compliance with the New Jersey Casino Control Act ("CCA"), and Ivey and Sun agreed to play the game in compliance with the CCA. Because Borgata complied with the CCA, while Ivey and Sun did not, Ivey and Sun breached their agreement with Borgata.

In assessing the viability of Borgata's claim when resolving Ivey and Sun's motion to dismiss, the Court observed that the only way gambling at a casino is lawful is if the patrons and the casino follow the strictures of the CCA, and that contractual agreements, whether express or implied, involving casino gambling in New Jersey must therefore include a provision that both parties agree to abide by the CCA.

* * *

Borgata contends that the turning of the cards was "marking cards," the request to use the automatic shuffling machine constitutes a "cheating device," and that the edge sorting technique is "cheating and swindling." * * * The Court finds that Ivey and Sun breached their contract with Borgata to play Baccarat in compliance with the CCA by violating N.J.S.A. 5:12–115(a)(2) and (b) when they knowingly engaged in a scheme to create a set of marked cards and then used those marked cards to place bets based on the markings. * * *

In this case, there is no dispute that Ivey and Sun did not mark the cards used in the Baccarat playing sessions in a traditional way. Ivey and Sun did not physically touch any of the cards at any time, and they did not have access to the card decks prior to their playing sessions. These factors support Ivey and Sun's argument that they did not mark any cards or knowingly use or possess any marked cards in violations of the CCA.

Ivey and Sun's view of what constitutes a "marked" card is too narrow. Such an interpretation would undermine in a fundamental way the purpose behind the regulatory ban on marked cards. "Marking" a card is to surreptitiously identify the value of the card to a player—and that player alone. The physical acts of a card being drawn on, daubed, or crimped are several ways to inform a player of its value. But, as demonstrated by Ivey and Sun's edge sorting technique, a physical act is not necessary to alert a player surreptitiously of a card's value. Asking a card dealer to turn a card a particular way so that the pattern on the edge of the card will distinguish it from other cards such that it will inform the player of that card's value also constitutes "marking" within the meaning and intent of the regulatory ban. The term "marking" therefore can be defined as having something done to the card that identifies the value of the card to a player but to no one else.[11]

Moreover, it is not the act of "marking" a card that violates the CCA, but rather the "use" or "possession" of the marked card that violates the CCA. That is because using or possessing a marked card that reveals the value of that card leads to an artificial adjustment of the set odds in the player's favor. * * *

By using cards, they caused to be maneuvered in order to identify their value only to them, Ivey and Sun adjusted the odds of Baccarat in their favor. * * * Ivey and Sun's violation of the card marking provision in the CCA constitutes a breach of their mutual obligation with Borgata to play by the rules of the CCA. Consequently, summary judgment must be entered in Borgata's favor, and against Ivey and Sun, on Borgata's contract-based claims.

2. Borgata's fraud and RICO conspiracy claims

In addition to its breach of contract claims, Borgata has alleged fraud, RICO and conspiracy-based claims against Ivey and Sun arguing that they misrepresented that they intended to abide by the rules of honest play established and required by the CCA, and they intentionally misrepresented their true reasons, motivation and purpose for the playing accommodations they sought. * * *

To state a claim of fraud under the common law, a plaintiff must allege facts that, if proven, would establish the following: " '(1) a material misrepresentation of a presently existing or past fact; (2) knowledge or belief by the defendant of its falsity; (3) an intention that the other person rely on it; (4) reasonable reliance thereon by the other person; and (5) resulting damages.' " Hoffman v. Hampshire Labs, Inc., 963 A.2d 849, 855 (N.J. Super. App. Div. 2009). * * *

The parties agree that Baccarat is a game, and all games have rules. The fundamental tenet of all games is that the players abide by the rules, otherwise any win garnered through broken rules would be unfair. In this case, none of the actual rules of Baccarat were broken, and nothing except for Ivey and Sun's motivation for certain requests was hidden from Borgata. . . . Therefore, the ultimate question is whether Ivey and Sun committed fraud by misrepresenting their true reasons for their five requests and card turning, even while none of the game's rules had been

---

[11] The basic dictionary definitions of the verb "mark" support this meaning as well. See *Merriam-Webster Dictionary* (defining "mark" as "to take notice of, to take careful notice"); *Black's Law Dictionary* (10th ed. 2014) ("MARK: A symbol, impression, or feature on something, usu. to identify it or distinguish it from something else.").

technically broken. The Court finds that the answer to that question is no.

The rules of Baccarat do not prohibit a player from manipulating the cards. In certain Baccarat games, referred to as "Macau" style, the customers are allowed to squeeze, crease, bend, or tear the cards. Baccarat is a casino game well known for unique and superstitious rituals, including asking dealers to let the players "peek" at cards before they are placed on the gaming table. Thus, Sun telling the dealer to turn a card in a certain way did not raise any red flags for Borgata.

Borgata's fraud claims hinge on Ivey and Sun's misrepresentation that their five requests, along with Sun's instructions to the dealer on how to turn a card, were because they were superstitious. Obviously, if Ivey and Sun had explained to Borgata that they were directing the dealer to turn a card a certain way so that they could later identify the card's value by the pattern on the back of the card, the "misrepresentation" element of establishing fraud would be lacking. And also obviously, if Ivey and Sun had told Borgata the real reason they wanted the cards turned, Borgata would have never let them play.

The Court notes these obvious points for a reason—a reason that is dispositive to the finding that Ivey and Sun did not commit fraud. Even though Ivey and Sun manufactured an explanation for their instruction to the dealer to turn the cards, the rules of Baccarat do not require an explanation to permit a player to manipulate the cards. In other words, a player could crease, tear, bend, or have a card turned without any explanation at all and not violate Baccarat's rules of play.

To meet the elements of fraud, Borgata must show that Ivey and Sun made a material misrepresentation and that Borgata relied upon that misrepresentation to its detriment. Ivey and Sun's five specific requests to Borgata, and their instruction to the dealer to turn the cards a certain way, did not violate any rules or regulations. Ivey and Sun did not need to claim superstition to make their requests and card turning instructions permissible—they already were. If Ivey and Sun had simply made their requests without explanation, Borgata was still empowered to grant or deny those requests. That Borgata chose to believe that Ivey and Sun were superstitious does not amount to detrimental reliance, when no explanation at all could have resulted in the same course of events. Stated differently, Borgata allowed defendants to give a silly, nonsensical reason for the card turning. That is tantamount to allowing defendants to give no reason at all. Borgata is estopped in such circumstances from alleging that the misrepresentation was material.[19]

---

[19] Borgata's argument devolves into a contention that defendants acted fraudulently because they did not reveal their fraudulent intent. Fraud is not so easy to prove. It is well to remember that fraud is both a crime and a tort and the elements are the same. While the element of a material misrepresentation may be satisfied by an omission under some circumstances, failing to confess to your victim is not one of them. Such a legal requirement would certainly be efficient, but it is not our jurisprudence. Rather the law requires either a misrepresentation that is material or an omission where there is a separate duty to disclose.

Borgata casts itself as an innocent victim who altruistically provided Ivey with his five requests, including allowing Sun to play with him, because it trusted Ivey. Borgata, however, is a for-profit business whose commodity is gambling, and whose methodology is to use the odds of casino games in its favor, among other techniques, to win as much money from its patrons as it can. Ivey is a professional gambler whose business is to play high-stakes casino games to win as much of the casino's money as he can. In exchange for agreeing to Ivey's five requests, Borgata required millions of dollars in front money from Ivey. Borgata also wanted Ivey to gamble at its casino so that his celebrity status would attract more gamblers to the casino. Borgata and Ivey had the same goal when they entered into their arrangement—to profit at the other's expense. Trust is a misplaced sentiment in this context.

Even though Ivey and Sun did not reveal to Borgata the true purpose behind their requests and actions, they were not required to provide a reason. This does not amount to legal fraud. Ivey and Sun are therefore entitled to summary judgment on all of Borgata's fraud-based claims against them.

CONCLUSION

Ivey and Sun, and perhaps others, view their actions to be akin to cunning, but not rule-breaking, maneuvers performed in many games, such as a play-action pass in American football or the "Marshall swindle" in chess.[24] Sun's mental acumen in distinguishing the minute differences in the patterns on the back of the playing cards is remarkable.

But, even though Ivey and Sun's cunning and skill did not break the rules of Baccarat, what sets Ivey and Sun's actions apart from deceitful maneuvers in other games is that those maneuvers broke the rules of gambling as defined in this state. Borgata and Ivey and Sun were obligated to follow the proscriptions of the CCA in order to lawfully gamble in the first place, and then they were also obligated to follow the rules of Baccarat. Ivey and Sun breached their primary obligation.

NOTES[2]

(1) *Fair Dealing?* Does the court's ruling that edge sorting is a kind of card marking reasonable? Did Ivey and Sun have reasonable notice of this restriction?

Here, no duty to disclose why the defendants wanted to turn the cards was imposed by the CCA, the casino rules of the game, or as a result of the arrangements made with the defendants.

[24] Even though the word "swindle" connotes "a diabolically clever move or combination that turns the tables on the opponent," a swindle "is not a kind of cheating or a contravening of the rules of the game." Robert Byrne, *Chess; The Marshall Swindle*, N.Y. Times, January 4, 1987. * * *

[2] Ivey and Sun argue that the edge sorting technique is just like card counting, which has not been held to be a violation of the CCA or any casino games. * * * The difference between card counting and edge sorting is that a card counter uses memory and statistics, not a manipulation of the cards, to create an advantage for himself.

(2) The court finds that giving "a silly, nonsensical reason" is "tantamount to allowing defendants to give no reason at all." Are all believers in superstition or the supernatural silly and nonsensical? Is the court's reasoning consistent with *Laidlaw*? Couldn't misrepresenting their reason impose upon the casino by throwing them off the trail of uncovering the real reason for the offered conditions—edge sorting? Is it appropriate for the court to decide this issue on summary judgment?

(3) Borgata learned about Ivey's edge sorting from a media report that a casino in London, Crockfords, was "withholding £7.3 million won by Ivey playing Punto Banco, which is essentially the same game as Baccarat." Ivey made the same five requests to Crockfords as he had to Borgata. Ivey sued Crockfords and in 2014 a High Court in London ruled against Ivey finding that employing the edge sorting technique constituted cheating under English civil law.

Audrey E. Vokes v. Arthur Murray, Inc.

District Court of Appeal of Florida, Second District, 1968.
212 So.2d 906.

■ PIERCE, JUDGE. This is an appeal by Audrey E. Vokes, plaintiff below, from a final order dismissing with prejudice, for failure to state a cause of action, her fourth amended complaint, hereinafter referred to as plaintiff's complaint.

Defendant Arthur Murray, Inc., a corporation, authorizes the operation throughout the nation of dancing schools under the name of "Arthur Murray School of Dancing" through local franchised operators, one of whom was defendant J.P. Davenport whose dancing establishment was in Clearwater.

Plaintiff Mrs. Audrey E. Vokes, a widow of 51 years and without family, had a yen to be "an accomplished dancer" with the hopes of finding "new interest in life". So, on February 10, 1961, a dubious fate, with the assist of a motivated acquaintance, procured her to attend a "dance party" at Davenport's "School of Dancing" where she whiled away the pleasant hours, sometimes in a private room, absorbing his accomplished sales technique, during which her grace and poise were elaborated upon and her rosy future as "an excellent dancer" was painted for her in vivid and glowing colors. As an incident to this interlude, he sold her eight ½-hour dance lessons to be utilized within one calendar month therefrom, for the sum of $14.50 cash in hand paid, obviously a baited "come-on".

Thus she embarked upon an almost endless pursuit of the terpsichorean art during which, over a period of less than sixteen months, she was sold fourteen "dance courses" totalling in the aggregate 2302 hours of dancing lessons for a total cash outlay of $31,090.45, all at Davenport's dance emporium. All of these fourteen courses were evidenced by execution of a written "Enrollment Agreement—Arthur Murray's School of Dancing" with the addendum in heavy black print,

"No one will be informed that you are taking dancing lessons. Your relations with us are held in strict confidence", setting forth the number of "dancing lessons" and the "lessons in rhythm sessions" currently sold to her from time to time, and always of course accompanied by payment of cash of the realm.

These dance lesson contracts and the monetary consideration therefor of over $31,000 were procured from her by means and methods of Davenport and his associates which went beyond the unsavory, yet legally permissible, perimeter of "sales puffing" and intruded well into the forbidden area of undue influence, the suggestion of falsehood, the suppression of truth, and the free exercise of rational judgment, if what plaintiff alleged in her complaint was true. From the time of her first contract with the dancing school in February, 1961, she was influenced unwittingly by a constant and continuous barrage of flattery, false praise, excessive compliments, and panegyric encomiums, to such extent that it would be not only inequitable, but unconscionable, for a Court exercising inherent chancery power to allow such contracts to stand.

She was incessantly subjected to overreaching blandishment and cajolery. She was assured she had "grace and poise"; that she was "rapidly improving and developing in her dancing skill"; that the additional lessons would "make her a beautiful dancer, capable of dancing with the most accomplished dancers"; that she was "rapidly progressing in the development of her dancing skill and gracefulness", etc., etc. She was given "dance aptitude tests" for the ostensible purpose of "determining" the number of remaining hours of instructions needed by her from time to time.

At one point she was sold 545 additional hours of dancing lessons to be entitled to award of the "Bronze Medal" signifying that she had reached "the Bronze Standard", a supposed designation of dance achievement by students of Arthur Murray, Inc.

Later she was sold an additional 926 hours in order to gain the "Silver Medal", indicating she had reached "the Silver Standard", at a cost of $12,501.35.

At one point, while she still had to her credit about 900 unused hours of instructions, she was induced to purchase an additional 24 hours of lessons to participate in a trip to Miami at her own expense, where she would be "given the opportunity to dance with members of the Miami Studio".

She was induced at another point to purchase an additional 126 hours of lessons in order to be not only eligible for the Miami trip but also to become "a life member of the Arthur Murray Studio", carrying with it certain dubious emoluments, at a further cost of $1,752.30.

At another point, while she still had over 1,000 unused hours of instruction she was induced to buy 151 additional hours at a cost of

$2,049.00 to be eligible for a "Student Trip to Trinidad", at her own expense as she later learned.

Also, when she still had 1100 unused hours to her credit, she was prevailed upon to purchase an additional 347 hours at a cost of $4,235.74, to qualify her to receive a "Gold Medal" for achievement, indicating she had advanced to "the Gold Standard".

On another occasion, while she still had over 1200 unused hours, she was induced to buy an additional 175 hours of instruction at a cost of $2,472.75 to be eligible "to take a trip to Mexico".

Finally, sandwiched in between other lesser sales promotions, she was influenced to buy an additional 481 hours of instruction at a cost of $6,523.81 in order to "be classified as a Gold Bar Member, the ultimate achievement of the dancing studio".

All the foregoing sales promotions, illustrative of the entire fourteen separate contracts, were procured by defendant Davenport and Arthur Murray, Inc., by false representations to her that she was improving in her dancing ability, that she had excellent potential, that she was responding to instructions in dancing grace, and that they were developing her into a beautiful dancer, whereas in truth and in fact she did not develop in her dancing ability, she had no "dance aptitude", and in fact had difficulty in "hearing the musical beat". The complaint alleged that such representations to her "were in fact false and known by the defendant to be false and contrary to the plaintiff's true ability, the truth of plaintiff's ability being fully known to the defendants, but withheld from the plaintiff for the sole and specific intent to deceive and defraud the plaintiff and to induce her in the purchasing of additional hours of dance lessons". It was averred that the lessons were sold to her "in total disregard to the true physical, rhythm, and mental ability of the plaintiff". In other words, while she first exulted that she was entering the "spring of her life", she finally was awakened to the fact there was "spring" neither in her life nor in her feet.

The complaint prayed that the Court decree the dance contracts to be null and void and to be cancelled, that an accounting be had, and judgment entered against the defendants "for that portion of the $31,090.45 not charged against specific hours of instruction given to the plaintiff". The Court held the complaint not to state a cause of action and dismissed it with prejudice. We disagree and reverse.

The material allegations of the complaint must, of course, be accepted as true for the purpose of testing its legal sufficiency. Defendants contend that contracts can only be rescinded for fraud or misrepresentation when the alleged misrepresentation is as to a material fact, rather than an opinion, prediction or expectation, and that the statements and representations set forth at length in the complaint were in the category of "trade puffing", within its legal orbit.

It is true that "generally a misrepresentation, to be actionable, must be one of fact rather than of opinion." Tonkovich v. South Florida Citrus Industries, Inc., 185 So.2d 710 (Fla.App. 1966); Kutner v. Kalish, 173 So.2d 763 (Fla.App. 1965). But this rule has significant qualifications, applicable here. It does not apply where there is a fiduciary relationship between the parties, or where there has been some artifice or trick employed by the representor, or where the parties do not in general deal at "arm's length" as we understand the phrase, or where the representee does not have equal opportunity to become apprised of the truth or falsity of the fact represented. 14 Fla.Jur. Fraud and Deceit § 28; Kitchen v. Long, 67 Fla. 72 (1914). As stated by Judge Allen of this Court in *Ramel v. Chasebrook Construction Co.*, 135 So.2d 876 (Fla.App. 1961):

> " * * * A statement of a party having * * * superior knowledge may be regarded as a statement of fact although it would be considered as opinion if the parties were dealing on equal terms."

It could be reasonably supposed here that defendants had "superior knowledge" as to whether plaintiff had "dance potential" and as to whether she was noticeably improving in the art of terpsichore. And it would be a reasonable inference from the undenied averments of the complaint that the flowery eulogiums heaped upon her by defendants as a prelude to her contracting for 1944 additional hours of instruction in order to attain the rank of the Bronze Standard, thence to the bracket of the Silver Standard, thence to the class of the Gold Bar Standard, and finally to the crowning plateau of a Life Member of the Studio, proceeded as much or more from the urge to "ring the cash register" as from any honest or realistic appraisal of her dancing prowess or a factual representation of her progress.

Even in contractual situations where a party to a transaction owes no duty to disclose facts within his knowledge or to answer inquiries respecting such facts, the law is if he undertakes to do so he must disclose the *whole truth.* . . . From the face of the complaint, it should have been reasonably apparent to defendants that her vast outlay of cash for the many hundreds of additional hours of instruction was not justified by her slow and awkward progress, which she would have been made well aware of if they had spoken the "whole truth."

In *Hirschman v. Hodges, etc.*, 59 Fla. 517 (1910), it was said that—

> " * * * what is plainly injurious to good faith ought to be considered as a fraud sufficient to impeach a contract,"

and that an improvident agreement may be avoided—

> " * * * because of surprise, or mistake, *want of freedom, undue influence, the suggestion of falsehood, or the suppression of truth.*" (Emphasis supplied.)

We repeat that where parties are dealing on a contractual basis at arm's length with no inequities or inherently unfair practices employed, the Courts will in general "leave the parties where they find themselves." But in the case *sub judice*, from the allegations of the unanswered complaint, we cannot say that enough of the accompanying ingredients, as mentioned in the foregoing authorities, were not present which otherwise would have barred the equitable arm of the Court to her. In our view, from the showing made in her complaint, plaintiff is entitled to her day in Court.

It accordingly follows that the order dismissing plaintiff's last amended complaint with prejudice should be and is reversed.

Reversed.

1922 advertisement

NOTES

(1) What exactly were the alleged misrepresentations in *Vokes v. Murray*? What does the court need to assume to make them actionable? Is the procedural posture of this case relevant?

(2) *Fraud: Kaleidoscopic and Infinite.* Consider the following classical statement of the need for a broad rule for fraud. "Fraud is kaleidoscopic, infinite. Fraud being infinite and taking on protean form at will, were courts to cramp themselves by defining it with a hard and fast definition, their jurisdiction would be cunningly circumvented at once by new schemes beyond the definition. Messieurs, the fraud-feasors, would like nothing half so well as for courts to say they would go thus far, and no further in its pursuit. * * * Accordingly definitions of fraud are of set purpose left general and flexible, and thereto courts match their astuteness against the versatile inventions of fraud-doers." Stonemets v. Head, 248 Mo. 243, 263 (1913).

Sam Buell has argued that criminal fraud functions to deter and punish novel wrongful acts that evade narrow legal definitions, and therefore it must remain adaptive. "Open-textured law that grows and innovates in competition with those who seek to evade it appears to be characteristic of any legal order that seeks to control harmful human behavior, at least in any society mature enough to have a large economy." Samuel W. Buell, *Novel*

Criminal Fraud, 81 N.Y.U. L. Rev. 1971, 1991 (2006). But see Skilling v. United States, 561 U.S. 358 (2010) (adopting a narrow interpretation of federal mail and wire fraud statutes).

(3) *Statutory Protection.* Not only is fraud "kaleidoscopic," so are the judicial attempts to reach the varieties of deceptive practices. The court in *Vokes* drew upon a tradition of case law under which the agreement might be rescinded. In a similar case, a Texas court awarded treble damages and attorney's fees, pursuant to a statute entitled "Deceptive Trade Practices— Consumer Protection Act." Bennett v. Bailey, 597 S.W.2d 532 (Tex.Civ.App. 1980). Statutes of this type figure prominently in contemporary litigation, granting additional rights not only to consumers but, in some instances, to commercial parties as well.

(4) Is it relevant that the plaintiff in the instant case was a woman?

It is difficult to ignore the fact that people resisting contract enforcement in many canonical undue influence cases are female. In *Vokes v. Arthur Murray Dance Studios*, the plaintiff was a lonely widow tricked into buying $31,000 of dance lessons by high praise for her nonexistent dancing abilities from Arthur Murray Dance Studios. Does it matter that this doctrine tends to protect women? In particular, does it undercut autonomy-based definitions of contract? Is it significant that American law protects these parties without explicitly referring to their gender, while English law explicitly extends "special tenderness" to wives in guarantee cases?

Martha M. Ertman, *Legal Tenderness: Feminist Perspectives on Contract Law*, 18 Yale J. L. & Feminism 545, 570–71 (2006).

(5) *Bah, Humbug!* Many people think that the term, humbug, is a synonym for "nonsense." But when Ebenezer Scrooge deployed the term, he was not saying that Christmas traditions were merely devoid of sense, he was suggesting they were verging on the fraudulent. P.T. Barnum, who styled himself the "Prince of Humbugs," took issue with Webster's definition that "humbug, as a noun, is an 'imposition under fair pretences;' and as a verb, it is 'to deceive; to impose on.' " Instead, Barnum defined the term by example:

> An honest man who arrests public attention will be called a "humbug," but he is not a swindler or an impostor. If, however, after attracting crowds of customers by his unique displays, a man foolishly fails to give them a full equivalent for their money, they . . . very properly denounce him as a swindler, a cheat, an impostor; they do not, however, call him a "humbug." He fails, not because he advertises his wares in an outre manner, but because, after attracting crowds of patrons, he stupidly and wickedly cheats them.

P.T. BARNUM, THE HUMBUGS OF THE WORLD AN ACCOUNT OF HUMBUGS, DELUSIONS, IMPOSITIONS, QUACKERIES, DECEITS AND DECEIVERS GENERALLY, IN ALL AGES (1866). For Barnum, a certain degree of deception in inducement was honorable so long as the customer was in some sense in on the deception and so long as the humbug gave "a full equivalent of their money." Is it possible that Arthur Miller Dance Studies was selling humbug?

(6) *Tellin' Fortunes Better Than They Do.* In 2015, a fortune teller, Christina Delmaro was indicted for grand larceny after taking more than $700,000 from a client over the course of two years. The client alleged that Delmaro first promised to reunite him with an unrequited love interest, then promised to resurrect a dead love interest and also to return most of the money when she had completed her psychic tasks. *A Manhattan Fortuneteller Cost Him Fortune After Fortune,* N.Y. TIMES (June 5, 2015). Since 1967 New York has made fortune telling for a fee a Class B misdemeanor:

> A person is guilty of fortune telling when, for a fee or compensation which he directly or indirectly solicits or receives, he claims or pretends to tell fortunes, or holds himself out as being able, by claimed or pretended use of occult powers, to answer questions or give advice on personal matters or to exorcise, influence or affect evil spirits or curses; except that this section does not apply to a person who engages in the afore described conduct as part of a show or exhibition solely for the purpose of entertainment or amusement.

New York Penal Law § 165.35

Comment: Misrepresentation, Rescission and Restitution

What is a misrepresentation? A misrepresentation is a falsehood, "an assertion that is not in accord with the facts." Restatement (Second) § 159. The apparent simplicity of this definition masks the complexity of its judicial application.

To begin with, as noted in *Vokes*, courts have held that the misrepresentation must be an assertion or affirmation of an existing fact, as distinguished from an expression of opinion, a promise to do something in the future, or a prediction of future events. But as *Vokes* shows, a statement of opinion can be a misrepresentation if the parties are in a special relationship of trust or the speaker has superior knowledge. See Restatement (Second) § 169. A statement of opinion also represents at least that the speaker holds that opinion, which is to say "that the facts known to that person are not incompatible with his opinion." Restatement (Second) § 168. Similarly, a prediction, while it is arguably neither true nor false at the time it is made, at least represents something about the speaker's present beliefs. And, as we will see with the doctrine of promissory fraud, discussed in Chapter Five, section 3(B), a promise typically implicitly represents that the speaker presently intends to perform the promised act.

A statement might also be literally true but contain false implications in context. The classic example of this is the half-truth. For example, in *V.S.H. Realty, Inc. v. Texaco, Inc.,* 757 F.2d 411, 414–15 (1st Cir. 1985), after repeated inquiries by the buyer of an oil storage facility, the seller disclosed the existence of one leak but not others of which it allegedly knew. The First Circuit held that the disclosure of the one leak carried with it "some implication of exclusivity," that is, an implication that Texaco knew of no other leaks. For more on the doctrine of half-truths, see Donald C. Langevoort, *Half-Truths: Protecting Mistaken Inferences by Investors and Others*, 52 Stan. L. Rev. 87 (1999). Half-truths are only one species of implicit misrepresentation. Consider again the facts and holding in *Laidlaw v. Organ*. Here, where the seller allegedly asked whether there was any news, the buyer's mere silence may have implicitly misrepresented what he knew.

Courts have interpreted "misrepresentation" so broadly as to also include acts of concealment and failures to disclose. Concealment is the covering up of some fact, such as painting over water damage on basement walls or hiding evidence of termite damage. While concealment is not exactly a falsehood—the seller might not say a word about leaks or termites—courts have held that such acts constitute actionable falsehoods. See, e.g., Salzman v. Maldaver, 24 N.W.2d 161, 167 (Mich. 1946) (seller allegedly placed undamaged aluminum plates on the top of bundles to conceal corroded ones beneath). Finally, as we will see in *Hill v. Jones*, even the failure to disclose some fact, where there is a duty to do so, can count as a misrepresentation. See Restatement (Second) § 161. For more on the different ways that the law identifies misrepresentations, see Gregory Klass, *Meaning, Purpose and Cause in the Law of Deception*, 100 Geo. L.J. 449 (2012).

The Consequences of Misrepresentation. Once the court has identified a misrepresentation, there are several other elements required for the defense. The other side must have justifiably relied on that misrepresentation in deciding to enter into the contract, and the misrepresentation must be either fraudulent or material.

The usual effect of wrongful misrepresentation is to render the contract "voidable" by the deceived party. But courts have identified a kind of fraud in the "execution," as distinguished from the ordinary fraud in the "inducement," that precludes the formation of any contract at all. An example is where a party secures another's signature by misrepresenting the character of the document. See Restatement (Second) § 163.

A good statement of the law of "innocent misrepresentation" is found in *Norton v. Poplos*, 443 A.2d 1, 4–5 (Del. 1982):

> Essentially, the equitable remedy of rescission results in abrogation or "unmaking" of an agreement, and attempts to return the parties to the *status quo*. Common grounds for rescission of a contract for the sale of real property include fraud, misrepresentation and mistake. . . . But in addition to rescission for fraudulent misrepresentation, rescission also may be granted under certain circumstances for innocent misrepresentations made by a seller. Thus, as stated by Professor Williston:

"It is not necessary, in order that a contract may be rescinded for fraud or misrepresentation, that the party making the misrepresentation should have known that it was false. Innocent misrepresentation is sufficient for though the representation may have been made innocently, it would be unjust and inequitable to permit a person who has made false representations, even innocently, to retain the fruits of a bargain induced by such representations."

Williston on Contracts § 1500, at 400–401 (3d ed. 1970). Similarly, . . . Restatement (Second) of Contracts, § 164, states that,

"If a party's manifestation of assent is induced by either a fraudulent *or material* misrepresentation by the other party upon which the recipient is justified in relying, the contract is voidable by the recipient." (Emphasis added.)

See also Restatement (First) § 476 (1932). Most American jurisdictions which have addressed this issue appear to recognize that an innocent material misrepresentation by a vendor which induces the sale of the property is ground for rescission of the contract. . . . In addition to ordering rescission, a court will generally direct that a down payment by a buyer be returned on a theory of restitution. . . .

Remedies. One remedy for misrepresentation is to rescind the contract. The purpose of rescission, whether through a legal or equitable action, is restitutionary; i.e., there is a dissolution or "undoing" of the contract and a restoration of the parties to their pre-contract positions (*status quo ante*). Originally, rescission was exclusively an equitable remedy, but eventually law courts recognized the right to utilize rescission as a way of securing appropriate restitutionary relief. Whether equitable or legal rescission, an "adjustment of the equities" of the parties is a matter of major concern. For example, "when a party elects to rescind the contract, he is only entitled to a return to the *status quo*. This usually requires a plaintiff to restore *any benefit* he received under the contract, *including a return* in specie *of any property received and a reasonable rental value for the use of the property*, plus damages for waste if any. Likewise, *the defendant must restore any money paid by the plaintiff under the contract plus interest*, monetary reimbursement for reasonable repairs, expenditures and improvements made on the property by the plaintiff, and, where a business has been sold, a reasonable amount of compensation for the value of the plaintiff's labor and services rendered during the period of time which he operated and possessed the property." Smeekens v. Bertrand, 262 Ind. 50, 58 (1974) (emphasis in original).

Express Warranties. So far we have identified two possible legal effects of a misrepresentation made in the course of formation. The misrepresentation might give rise to an action in tort, and it might also or instead give the deceived party the power to rescind the contract. In the next Chapter, we discuss yet a third. Sometimes a statement of fact made during negotiations can create a warranty, giving the other party an action for breach should that representation turn out to be false. For example, in contracts for the sale of goods, a seller's "affirmations of fact" to the buyer about the nature or quality of the goods which become part of the "basis of the bargain" constitute express warranties even if they are innocently mistaken. They are terms of the contract. UCC § 2–313. If the goods do not conform to the express warranties, the buyer may reject the goods upon tender, recover so much of the contract price as has been paid and sue the seller for breach of contract damages. UCC § 2–711. Why does the law give contracting parties these three separate types of protection against falsehoods?

Warren G. and Gloria R. Hill v. Ora G. and Barbara R. Jones

Court of Appeals of Arizona, 1986.
151 Ariz. 81.

■ MEYERSON, JUDGE. Must the seller of a residence disclose to the buyer facts pertaining to past termite infestation? This is the primary question presented in this appeal. Plaintiffs Warren G. Hill and Gloria R. Hill (buyers) filed suit to rescind an agreement to purchase a residence. Buyers alleged that Ora G. Jones and Barbara R. Jones (sellers) had made misrepresentations concerning termite damage in the residence and had failed to disclose to them the existence of the damage and history of termite infestation in the residence. The trial court dismissed the claim for misrepresentation based upon a so-called integration clause in the parties' agreement.

Sellers then sought summary judgment on the "concealment" claim arguing that they had no duty to disclose information pertaining to termite infestation and that even if they did, the record failed to show all of the elements necessary for fraudulent concealment. The trial court granted summary judgment, finding that there was "no genuinely disputed issue of material fact and that the law favors the . . . defendants." The trial court awarded sellers $1,000.00 in attorney's fees. Buyers have appealed from the judgment and sellers have cross-appealed from the trial court's ruling on attorney's fees.

I.   FACTS

In 1982, buyers entered into an agreement to purchase sellers' residence for $72,000. The agreement was entered after buyers made several visits to the home. The purchase agreement provided that sellers were to pay for and place in escrow a termite inspection report stating that the property was free from evidence of termite infestation. Escrow was scheduled to close two months later.

One of the central features of the house is a parquet teak floor covering the sunken living room, the dining room, the entryway and portions of the halls. On a subsequent visit to the house, and when sellers were present, buyers noticed a small "ripple" in the wood floor on the step leading up to the dining room from the sunken living room. Mr. Hill asked if the ripple could be termite damage. Mrs. Jones answered that it was water damage. A few years previously, a broken water heater in the house had in fact caused water damage in the area of the dining room and steps which necessitated that some repairs be made to the floor. No further discussion on the subject, however, took place between the parties at that time or afterwards.

Mr. Hill, through his job as maintenance supervisor at a school district, had seen similar "ripples" in wood which had turned out to be termite damage. Mr. Hill was not totally satisfied with Mrs. Jones's explanation, but he felt that the termite inspection report would reveal whether the ripple was due to termites or some other cause.

The termite inspection report stated that there was no visible evidence of infestation. The report failed to note the existence of physical damage or evidence of previous treatment. The realtor notified the parties that the property had passed the termite inspection. Apparently, neither party actually saw the report prior to close of escrow.

After moving into the house, buyers found a pamphlet left in one of the drawers entitled "Termites, the Silent Saboteurs." They learned from a neighbor that the house had some termite infestation in the past. Shortly after the close of escrow, Mrs. Hill noticed that the wood on the steps leading down to the sunken living room was crumbling. She called an exterminator who confirmed the existence of termite damage to the floor and steps and to wood columns in the house. The estimated cost of repairing the wood floor alone was approximately $5,000.

Through discovery after their lawsuit was filed, buyers learned the following. When sellers purchased the residence in 1974, they received two termite guarantees that had been given to the previous owner by Truly Nolen, as well as a diagram showing termite treatment at the residence that had taken place in 1963. The guarantees provided for semi-annual inspections and annual termite booster treatments. The accompanying diagram stated that the existing damage had not been repaired. The second guarantee, dated 1965, reinstated the earlier contract for inspection and treatment. Mr. Jones admitted that he read the guarantees when he received them. Sellers renewed the guarantees when they purchased the residence in 1974. They also paid the annual fee each year until they sold the home.

On two occasions during sellers' ownership of the house but while they were at their other residence in Minnesota, a neighbor noticed "streamers" evidencing live termites in the wood tile floor near the entryway. On both occasions, Truly Nolen gave a booster treatment for termites. On the second incident, Truly Nolen drilled through one of the wood tiles to treat for termites. The neighbor showed Mr. Jones the area where the damage and treatment had occurred. Sellers had also seen termites on the back fence and had replaced and treated portions of the fence.

Sellers did not mention any of this information to buyers prior to close of escrow. They did not mention the past termite infestation and treatment to the realtor or to the termite inspector. There was evidence of holes on the patio that had been drilled years previously to treat for termites. The inspector returned to the residence to determine why he had not found evidence of prior treatment and termite damage. He indicated that he had not seen the holes in the patio because of boxes stacked there. It is unclear whether the boxes had been placed there by buyers or sellers. He had not found the damage inside the house because a large plant, which buyers had purchased from sellers, covered the area. After investigating the second time, the inspector found the damage and evidence of past treatment. He acknowledged that this information should have appeared in the report. He complained, however, that he should have been told of any history of termite infestation and treatment before he performed his inspection and that it was customary for the inspector to be given such information.

Other evidence presented to the trial court was that during their numerous visits to the residence before close of escrow, buyers had unrestricted access to view and inspect the entire house. Both Mr. and Mrs. Hill had seen termite damage and were therefore familiar with what it might look like. Mr. Hill had seen termite damage on the fence at this property. Mrs. Hill had noticed the holes on the patio but claimed not to realize at the time what they were for. Buyers asked no questions about termites except when they asked if the "ripple" on the stairs was termite damage. Mrs. Hill admitted she was not "trying" to find problems with the house because she really wanted it.

* * *

III. DUTY TO DISCLOSE

The principal legal question presented in this appeal is whether a seller has a duty to disclose to the buyer the existence of termite damage in a residential dwelling known to the seller, but not to the buyer, which materially affects the value of the property. For the reasons stated herein, we hold that such a duty exists.

This is not the place to trace the history of the doctrine of caveat emptor. Suffice it to say that its vitality has waned during the latter half of the 20th century. . . . The modern view is that a vendor has an affirmative duty to disclose material facts where:

1.   Disclosure is necessary to prevent a previous assertion from being a misrepresentation or from being fraudulent or material;

2.   Disclosure would correct a mistake of the other party as to a basic assumption on which that party is making the contract and if nondisclosure amounts to a failure to act in good faith and in accordance with reasonable standards of fair dealing;

3.   Disclosure would correct a mistake of the other party as to the contents or effect of a writing, evidencing or embodying an agreement in whole or in part;

4.   The other person is entitled to know the fact because of a relationship of trust and confidence between them.

Restatement (Second) of Contracts § 161 (1981) (Restatement); see Restatement (Second) of Torts § 551 (1977).

Arizona courts have long recognized that under certain circumstances there may be a "duty to speak.". . . . As the supreme court noted in the context of a confidential relationship, "[s]uppression of a material fact which a party is bound in good faith to disclose is equivalent to a false representation." Leigh v. Loyd, 74 Ariz. 84, 87 (1952);. . . .

Thus, the important question we must answer is whether under the facts of this case, buyers should have been permitted to present to the jury their claim that sellers were under a duty to disclose their (sellers') knowledge of termite infestation in the residence. This broader question involves two inquiries. First, must a seller of residential property advise the buyer of material facts within his knowledge pertaining to the value of the property? Second, may termite damage and the existence of past infestation constitute such material facts?

The doctrine imposing a duty to disclose is akin to the well-established contractual rules pertaining to relief from contracts based upon mistake. Although the law of contracts supports the finality of transactions, over the years courts have recognized that under certain limited circumstances it is unjust to strictly enforce the policy favoring finality. Thus, for example, even a unilateral mistake of one party to a transaction may justify rescission. Restatement § 153.

There is also a judicial policy promoting honesty and fair dealing in business relationships. This policy is expressed in the law of fraudulent and negligent misrepresentations. Where a misrepresentation is fraudulent or where a negligent misrepresentation is one of material fact, the policy of finality rightly gives way to the policy of promoting honest dealings between the parties. See Restatement § 164(1).

Under certain circumstances nondisclosure of a fact known to one party may be equivalent to the assertion that the fact does not exist. For example "[w]hen one conveys a false impression by the disclosure of some facts and the concealment of others, such concealment is in effect a false representation that what is disclosed is the whole truth." State v. Coddington, 135 Ariz. 480, 481 (App. 1983). Thus, nondisclosure may be equated with and given the same legal effect as fraud and misrepresentation. One category of cases where this has been done involves the area of nondisclosure of material facts affecting the value of property, known to the seller but not reasonably capable of being known to the buyer.

Courts have formulated this "duty to disclose" in slightly different ways. For example, the Florida Supreme Court recently declared that "where the seller of a home knows of facts materially affecting the value of the property which are not readily observable and are not known to the buyer, the seller is under a duty to disclose them to the buyer." Johnson v. Davis, 480 So.2d 625, 629 (Fla. 1985) (defective roof in three-year old home). In California, the rule has been stated this way:

> [W]here the seller knows of facts materially affecting the value or desirability of the property which are known or accessible only to him and also knows that such facts are not known to, or within the reach of the diligent attention and observation of the buyer, the seller is under a duty to disclose them to the buyer.

Lingsch v. Savage, 213 Cal.App.2d 729, 735 (1963); contra Ray v. Montgomery, 399 So.2d 230 (Ala. 1980); see generally W. Prosser & W. Keeton, The Law of Torts § 106 (5th ed. 1984).[2] We find that the Florida formulation of the disclosure rule properly balances the legitimate interests of the parties in a transaction for the sale of a private residence and accordingly adopt it for such cases.

As can be seen, the rule requiring disclosure is invoked in the case of material facts.[3] Thus, we are led to the second inquiry—whether the existence of termite damage in a residential dwelling is the type of material fact which gives rise to the duty to disclose. The existence of termite damage and past termite infestation has been considered by other courts to be sufficiently material to warrant disclosure. See generally Annot., 22 A.L.R.3d 972 (1968).

* * *

Although sellers have attempted to draw a distinction between live termites and past infestation, the concept of materiality is an elastic one which is not limited by the termites' health. "A matter is material if it is one to which a reasonable person would attach importance in determining his choice of action in the transaction in question." Lynn v. Taylor, 7 Kan.App.2d 369, 371 (1982). For example, termite damage substantially affecting the structural soundness of the residence may be material even if there is no evidence of present infestation. Unless reasonable minds could not differ, materiality is a factual matter which must be determined by the trier of fact. The termite damage in this case may or may not be material. Accordingly, we conclude that buyers should be allowed to present their case to a jury.

---

[2] There are variations on this same theme. For example, Pennsylvania has limited the obligation of disclosure to cases of dangerous defects. Glanski v. Ervine, 269 Pa.Super. 182, 191 (1979).

[3] Arizona has recognized that a duty to disclose may arise where the buyer makes an inquiry of the seller, regardless of whether or not the fact is material. Universal Inv. Co. v. Sahara Motor Inn, Inc., 127 Ariz. 213, 215 (1980). The inquiry by buyers whether the ripple was termite damage imposed a duty upon sellers to disclose what information they knew concerning the existence of termite infestation in the residence.

Sellers argue that even assuming the existence of a duty to disclose, summary judgment was proper because the record shows that their "silence . . . did not induce or influence" the buyers. This is so, sellers contend, because Mr. Hill stated in his deposition that he intended to rely on the termite inspection report. But this argument begs the question. If sellers were fully aware of the extent of termite damage and if such information had been disclosed to buyers, a jury could accept Mr. Hill's testimony that had he known of the termite damage he would not have purchased the house.

Sellers further contend that buyers were put on notice of the possible existence of termite infestation and were therefore "chargeable with the knowledge which [an] inquiry, if made, would have revealed." Godfrey v. Navratil, 3 Ariz.App. 47, 51 (1966). . . . It is also true that "a party may . . . reasonably expect the other to take normal steps to inform himself and to draw his own conclusions." Restatement § 161 cmt. d. Under the facts of this case, the question of buyers' knowledge of the termite problem (or their diligence in attempting to inform themselves about the termite problem) should be left to the jury.[5]

By virtue of our holding, sellers' cross-appeal is moot. Reversed and remanded.

NOTES

(1) *Duty of Disclosure in Contract Negotiations.* What is the scope of the duty to disclose material facts during contract negotiations?

For the traditional approach taken by U.S. courts, see *Laidlaw v. Organ*, reprinted supra. A more recent statement can be found in *Simpson Timber Co. v. Palmberg Construction Co.*, 377 F.2d 380, 385 (9th Cir. 1967): "It is well settled that in the absence of a duty to speak, silence as to a material fact does not of itself constitute fraud. . . . On the other hand, once a duty to disclose has arisen, suppression of a material fact is tantamount to an affirmative misrepresentation. . . . However, businessmen dealing at arm's length are rarely under a duty to speak." As another court frankly, and somewhat cynically, observed, in the absence of rather special circumstances, the standards of conduct rise "no higher than the morals of the market place." Rader v. Boyd, 252 F.2d 585, 587 (10th Cir. 1957).

The existence of a fiduciary or confidential relationship is a traditional reason for augmenting a party's duty to disclose. The presence of a confidential relationship "imposes a duty on the party in whom the confidence is reposed to exercise the utmost good faith and to refrain from obtaining any advantage at the expense of the confiding party." Hyde v. Hyde, 78 S.D. 176, 186 (1959). This status is open-ended and arises from special relationships of trust or confidence or from an agreement, express or implied. Its existence is a question of fact, proof of which may be aided by

---

[5] Sellers also contend that they had no knowledge of any existing termite damage in the house. An extended discussion of the facts on this point is unnecessary. Simply stated, the facts are in conflict on this issue.

presumptions that the party in a position of superior knowledge must rebut. Its presence gives rise to a duty to speak and more. For example, in *Vai v. Bank of America National Trust & Savings Association*, 56 Cal.2d 329 (1961), a community property settlement was invalidated where the husband failed to disclose property value information to his wife. Even more striking is *Jackson v. Seymour*, 71 S.E.2d 181 (Va. 1952), where the court ordered a deed from sister to brother canceled and the *status quo* restored when it appeared that the brother, after the deed was recorded, had cut and marketed timber from the land, worth at least ten times the agreed price for the property. The court stated:

> This is not the ordinary case in which the parties dealt at arm's length and the shrewd trader was entitled to the fruits of his bargain. The parties were brother and sister. He was a successful business man and she a widow in need of money and forced by circumstances ... to sell a part of the lands which she had inherited. Because of their friendly and intimate relations she entrusted to him and he assumed the management and renting of a portion of this very land. He engaged tenants for such of the land as could be cultivated and collected the rents. She accepted his settlements without question.

> Moreover, it is undisputed that neither of the parties knew of the timber on the land and we have from the defendant's own lips the admission that as it turned out "afterwards" he had paid a grossly inadequate price for the property and that he would not have bought it from her for the small amount paid if he had then known of the true situation.

> To hold that under these circumstances the plaintiff is without remedy would be a reproach to the law. Nor do we think that a court of equity is so impotent.

71 S.E.2d at 184.

Another traditional kind of case involving a duty to "speak up" is where such disclosure is necessary to correct a previous statement or false impression. Here the duty to disclose interacts with the idea of implicit representations.

Beyond this, courts have traditionally been reluctant to recognize a disclosure obligation in an ordinary arm's length transaction. *Hill* is exceptional, but arguably represents the contemporary trend. Consider, again, the potential impact of the Second Restatement's formulation: "A person's non-disclosure of a fact known to him is equivalent to an assertion that the fact does not exist in the following cases only: * * * (b) where he knows that disclosure of the fact would correct a mistake of the other party as to a basic assumption on which that party is making the contract and if non-disclosure of the fact amounts to a failure to act in good faith and in accordance with reasonable standards of fair dealing. * * * " Restatement (Second) § 161(b).

Finally, some have urged the imposition of a general obligation to exercise "good faith" in the formation of contracts, a topic we explore further in Chapter Five. Thus, Eric Holmes has suggested:

> Although the concept is not precise, detailed, or rigid as compared with others generally used in formulations of contract law, it is suggested that "good faith" has a sufficiently common core of meaning, over a considerable range of applications, to make it functional in practical affairs. Properly perceived, "good faith" is a single mode of analysis comprising a spectrum of related, factual considerations. The context of its use is critically important. In the context of disclosures required in contracting, for example, the following factual elements should be considered: the nature of the undisclosed fact, accessibility of knowledge, the nature of the contract, trade customs and prior course of dealing, conduct of the party in obtaining knowledge, and the status and relationship of the parties.

Eric M. Holmes, *A Contextual Study of Commercial Good Faith: Good-Faith Disclosure in Contract Formation*, 39 U. Pitt. L. Rev. 381, 450–51 (1978). See also Friedrich Kessler and Edith Fine, Culpa in Contrahendo, *Bargaining in Good Faith, and Freedom of Contract: A Comparative Study*, 77 Harv. L. Rev. 401 (1964). What would be the relative advantages and disadvantages of such an approach?

(2) *Economic Perspectives.* Anthony Kronman in *Mistake, Disclosure, Information and the Law of Contracts*, 7 J. Legal Stud. 1 (1978), distinguishes between deliberately-acquired and casually-acquired information. Kronman argues that the law should not require contractual parties to disclose deliberately-acquired information. No disclosure requirement allows private parties to profit from this type of private information and hence encourages them to create it. See also Kimberly D. Krawiec and Kathryn Zeiler, *Common Law Disclosure Duties and the Sin of Omission*, 91 Va. L. Rev. 1795 (2005) (concluding from a review of the cases that a duty to disclose is most likely to be imposed where there is a casual acquisition of material information by one party and unequal access to information for the other).

Robert Cooter and Tom Ulen, in *Law and Economics* 258–61 (4th ed. 2004), have drawn a second useful distinction between "productive information," which they define as "information that can be used to increase wealth," and "redistributive information," which is "information creat[ing] a bargaining advantage that can be used to redistribute wealth in favor of the informed party." They argue that "the state must take special measures to reward people who discover productive information," but that it "should not create incentives to discover redistributive information." Which type of information is at stake in *Laidlaw*? See Steven Shavell, *Acquisition and Disclosure of Information Prior to Sale*, 25 Rand J. Econ. 20 (1994) (using this distinction to argue that sellers should be required to disclose so that they do not have unduly high incentives to acquire information, but that buyers should be allowed to conceal their information).

(3) *Regulatory Toolbox.* Lawmakers have more regulatory options than simply choosing between optional and mandatory disclosure. The law at times requires people to disclose what they should have known (to prevent willful ignorance). See, e.g., Omnicare, Inc. v. Laborers Dist. Council Const. Indus. Pension Fund, 135 S.Ct. 1318 (2015) (holding that statements of belief in a company's registration statement implicitly represent that company managers have a "reasonable basis" for holding that belief). At other times, the law prohibits disclosure or prohibits the uninformed from asking for information. See, e.g., *Illegal in Massachusetts: Asking Your Salary in a Job Interview*, N.Y. TIMES (Aug. 2, 2016); *Ban the Box to Promote Ex-Offender Employment*, 6 CRIM. & PUB. POL. 755 (2007) (prohibiting employers from asking whether applicants are felons). At still other times, the law undermines the credibility of disclosure (for example, by finding as a matter of law that certain facts as a matter of law are not material). Ian Ayres & F. Clayton Miller, *"I'll Sell It to You at Cost": Legal Methods to Promote Retail Markup Disclosure*, 84 NW. U. L. REV. 1047 (1990).

Comment: Unfair and Deceptive Acts and Practices Statutes and RICO

UDAP Statutes. Section 43(a)(1) of the Lanham Act prohibits the use of any "false or misleading description of fact, or false or misleading representation of fact, which . . . in commercial advertising or promotion, misrepresents the nature, characteristics, qualities, or geographic origin of his or her or another person's goods, services, or commercial activities." 15 U.S.C. § 1125(a)(1). Section 5 of the Federal Trade Commission Act additionally provides that "[u]nfair methods of competition in or affecting commerce, and unfair or deceptive acts or practices in or affecting commerce, are hereby declared unlawful." 15 U.S.C.A. § 45(a)(1). Every state has adopted legislation modeled on these provisions. See Jonathan A. Sheldon and Carolyn L. Carter, Unfair and Deceptive Acts and Practices (7th ed. 2008). Under both the Lanham Act and the FTC Act, the literal truth of an advertisement is not a defense if the implications of an advertisement are deceptive. See, e.g., Johnson & Johnson * Merck v. Smithkline Beecham, 960 F.2d 294 (1992) (considering whether an ad claim that, unlike Mylanta, Tums is "aluminum free" deceptively implies that aluminum is unhealthy). As originally enacted, these laws were designed to protect consumers, but in nearly half of the jurisdictions, the protective mantle now extends to business entities as well. David L. Belt, *The Standard for Determining "Unfair Acts or Practices" Under State Unfair Trade Practices Acts*, 80 Conn. B.J. 247 (2006). Although these "unfair and deceptive acts or practices" laws (UDAP) vary from state to state, one can identify some common features, most notably vague criteria and the use of a private remedy.

First, the proscribed actions are described in general terms; e.g., "deceptive," "unfair," "unconscionable." Some statutes also enumerate specific prohibitions, violations of which are *per se* violations of the statute. Some of these are specific in character; others are not. For example, in the Texas laundry list, the following is a deceptive trade practice: "disconnecting, turning back, or resetting the odometer of any motor vehicle so as to reduce the number of miles indicated on the odometer gauge." But so is the following: "failing to disclose information concerning goods or services which was known at the time of the transaction if such failure to disclose such information was intended to induce the consumer into a transaction into which the consumer would not have entered had the information been disclosed." Texas Business and Commerce Code §§ 17.46(b)(16), 17.46(b)(24).

Second, a private remedy is provided. Unlike the FTC Act (but like the Lanham Act), these little FTC acts provide a right of action to the aggrieved party. At a minimum, actual damages may be recovered, including, in appropriate situations, consequential damages. In addition, many of the statutes provide for a recovery of multiple damages, double or triple, for punitive purposes. Finally, most of the laws permit the recovery of attorney's fees and costs. In a case brought under the Massachusetts Unfair and Deceptive Trade Practices Act, for example, a buyer of a computer system was awarded compensatory damages of $2.3 million, which the court doubled to $4.6 million, and attorney's fees of $270,000. Computer Systems Engineering, Inc. v. Qantel Corp., 571 F.Supp. 1365 (D.Mass. 1983).

In *Linkage Corp. v. Trustees of Boston University*, 425 Mass. 1 (1997), the court found that the University's actions under a contract, principally those of its president, John Silber, and provost, John Westling, constituted willful and knowing violations of the Massachusetts Unfair and Deceptive Trade Practices Act, G.F. c. 93A. The trial court was warranted in finding that "Boston University's actions in the months leading up to, and after, the termination [of a renewal agreement] were unethical and unscrupulous, and [the president's and the provost's] conduct, in particular, was unfair, oppressive, and deceptive." More particularly: the University "repudiated binding agreements and usurped Linkage's business and work force in order to promote a purely self-serving agenda. The result was to end Linkage's vitality as a going concern, at least until it might be able to reconstitute itself with its main mission still intact." As a consequence, Linkage's damages of $2,411,852 were doubled under the punitive damages provision of G.L. c. 93A, and Linkage was permitted to recover its attorney's fees and costs, some $899,382.

There is a tension between rules and standards in this area. A specific rule provides certainty and predictability, whereas the exercise of discretion pursuant to general standards provides flexibility and adaptability. Is one a clearly superior method of governance in the commercial area? Richard Shell examined UDAP laws in the context of a general movement away from specific rules and toward open-ended standards, resulting in the dramatic expansion of business liability under such concepts as promissory estoppel, unconscionability, and good faith. Shell concludes:

> [S]tate legislatures should reform state FTC Acts to balance this impulse toward doing justice with restrictions that will curb the potential for abuse inherent in this regulatory scheme. This conclusion does not rest on a finding that ethical standards are improper vehicles for regulation, but rather derives from a recognition that such open-ended standards, when combined with liberal awards of treble damages and attorneys' fees, create incentives for litigation that are inappropriate in the commercial setting.

Richard Shell, *Substituting Ethical Standards for Common Law Rules in Commercial Cases: An Emerging Statutory Trend*, 82 Nw. U. L. Rev. 1198, 1253–54 (1988).

RICO. On October 15, 1970, Congress enacted the Racketeer Influenced and Corrupt Organizations Act (RICO). Congress's purpose was "to seek the eradication of organized crime in the United States by strengthening the legal tools in the evidence-gathering process, by establishing new penal prohibitions, and by providing enhanced sanctions and new remedies to deal with the unlawful activities of those engaged in organized crime." Pub.L. No. 91–452, 84 Stat. 922, 923 (Congressional Statement of Findings and Purpose). Under RICO, a private litigant can recover treble damages, costs, and attorney fees by establishing that the defendant's fraud constitutes a "pattern of racketeering activity" cognizable under the statute. There has been a growing realization that RICO remedies may be available in situations where no direct link to organized crime is proven. Hence, the potential of the statute in more ordinary commercial litigation is enormous and affords a defrauded party a civil remedy far more effective than that traditionally provided by, for example, federal securities law.

The widespread use of RICO by civil plaintiffs, particularly when using state and federal fraud statutes to satisfy the statute's predicate acts requirement, has generated heated controversy. Critics insist that the application of RICO to ordinary commercial disputes far exceeds Congressional intent. They maintain that RICO was intended to be used against the infiltration of legitimate business by organized crime, not ordinary commercial fraud. It is further argued that the statute's use in fraud suits has resulted in the unnecessary and unwise federalization of an area of law that should be left to the states. Finally, critics argue that the prospect of treble damages intimidates many defendants, causing them to settle frivolous claims. In sum, RICO's broad language and draconian penalties help increase uncertainty in the marketplace and tend to discourage legitimate business activity.

Proponents contend that Congress clearly intended the statute to be used against any criminal "enterprise," not just organized crime. Further, they maintain that RICO is expressly designed to supplement those federal and state fraud laws that were perceived to be inadequate. To the defenders of the statute, out of court settlements indicate the success of RICO by providing plaintiffs a statutory weapon which fills gaps left in existing legislation and the common law.

To date, RICO has largely survived efforts to weaken or remove its fraud provisions and remains popular with civil plaintiffs. See G. Robert Blakey and T. Perry, *An Analysis of the Myths that Bolster Efforts to Rewrite RICO and the Various Proposals for Reform: "Mother of God—Is This the End of RICO?"*, 43 Vand. L. Rev. 851 (1990); UTHE Technology Corp. v. Aetrium, Inc., 808 F.3d 755 (9th Cir. 2015) (recovery of compensatory damages in arbitration did not preclude recovery of treble damages under RICO). But see MLSMK Inv. Co. v. JP Morgan Chase & Co., 651 F.3d. 268 (2d Cir. 2011) (Private Securities Litigation Reform Act "bars civil RICO claims alleging predicate acts of securities fraud, even where a plaintiff cannot itself pursue a securities fraud action against the defendant.").

PROBLEMS: UNCOMMUNICATIVE PARTIES AND THE DUTY TO DISCLOSE

In answering these questions, think about whether disclosure is necessary to "correct a mistake of the other party as to a basic assumption on which that party is making the contract and [whether] non-disclosure of the fact amounts to a failure to act in good faith and in accordance with reasonable standards of fair dealing." Restatement (Second) of Contracts § 161 (1981).

(1)   Mr. Mc, prospective purchaser, enters into negotiations to purchase a house belonging to Ms. M. Mc inquires of M's agent as to whether the house has ever had termites. Her agent answers that it has been inspected for termites and is due for another inspection shortly. The agent does not disclose that the prior inspection indicated termite infestation. Should the parties enter into a contract for the sale of the property, could the purchaser rescind? See Murphy v. McIntosh, 199 Va. 254 (1957).

(2)   A Jewish congregation seeks to employ a rabbi to serve the congregation. Chaim W applies for the position. Neither in his resume nor during the employment negotiations does he disclose that he had previously been convicted of mail fraud and disbarred as an attorney. After he is hired and enters upon his duties, these facts of his past life come to light. Does the congregation have a right to rescind the contract? See Jewish Center of Sussex County v. Whale, 86 N.J. 619 (1981).

(3)   D, an elderly person living alone, purchases a house from K. Neither K nor his agent tells D that a woman and her four children were murdered there ten years earlier. D learns of the gruesome episode from a neighbor after the sale. Can she rescind? See Reed v. King, 145 Cal.App.3d 261 (1983).

(4)   Driller learns through an independent investigation that Owner's land contains valuable oil deposits. Knowing that Owner is not aware of this,

Driller persuades him to enter into a contract to sell the land at a price much less than Owner would have insisted upon had he been aware of the oil potential. Should Owner be entitled to rescind? Would your answer be different if Driller obtained the information from trespassing upon Owner's land? Or if Driller had received "inside" information from a relative at a State agency? See Restatement (Second) § 161 illus. 10.

(5) While looking through used books at a "flea market," Adam comes upon a Dickens first edition which carries a price tag of $5. Adam knows that the book will fetch several thousand dollars on the market and that Barbara, the proprietor, is unaware of this fact. Any duty to disclose?

(6) Employee interviews for a position in the accounting department of Employer. During the negotiations, no mention is made to the prospective employee that plans are already in place for the sale of the company. Employee is hired on an "at will" basis, and shortly thereafter the sale is announced and new management takes over. Employee is among those let go. Did Employer have a duty to disclose information regarding the pending sale to Employee? Cf. Stowman v. Carlson Companies, Inc., 430 N.W.2d 490 (Minn.App. 1988). Assume, instead, that Employee intends to work only until he can enter law school, but makes no mention of this to Employer. Should he be obliged to disclose this information?

(7) During an interview for summer employment, Jake, first-year law student, is questioned extensively about prior educational background and other personal matters. Jake knows that his chances for the job will be significantly reduced if he discloses that during his sophomore year in high school, he was suspended from the basketball team for disciplinary reasons. Should he have a duty to volunteer this information? Should he be obliged to disclose that in college, he was found guilty of plagiarism and placed on probation?

5. DURESS AND UNDUE INFLUENCE

In the mistake and fraud materials just considered, the aggrieved party assented to the bargain without complete or accurate information. In the materials to follow, the aggrieved party, who is accurately informed and primed to resist a proposed deal, is told by the defendant "unless you agree to this bargain, I will see that X happens." Because X is less pleasant than contracting, the aggrieved party, in the typical case, agrees to the bargain (which, by the way, may be perfectly fair) and later claims that the apparent assent was coerced. Put another way, it is claimed that one's will was overcome by the threat and, therefore, the bargain is not enforceable. Although the factors in the analysis tend to be both complicated and infused with a bias against the duress defense, we will try in this short subsection to determine when the defense that choice was impaired by threat is likely to succeed.

In an old joke, Jack Benny, who played a skinflint character on radio and television, is approached by a robber with a gun and given the choice: "Your money or your life." After a pause, the robber says, "Well, which is it?" Benny replies, "Give me a minute, I'm thinking about it." Although this extreme example would clearly constitute duress at common law (see the next case), Benny would clearly be better off if he acceded to the threat. But what if the gunman has asked for a promise, which the law refuses to enforce? According to Oren Bar Gill and Omri Ben-Shahar, when coercion is "credible," the law does the coerced party no favors by refusing to enforce the agreement. *Credible Coercion*, 83 Tex. L. Rev. 717 (2005). Failure to enforce might get Benny killed. Does this mean that Benny, if he gave his money to the robber, should not get it back after the fact?

Horace N. Rubenstein v. Natalie Rubenstein

Supreme Court of New Jersey, 1956.
20 N.J. 359.

■ HEHER, JUSTICE. The judgment of the Appellate Division of the Superior Court affirming the Chancery Division's judgment dismissing the complaint was certified here for appeal at the instance of plaintiff.

The gravamen of the complaint is that plaintiff, while "in fear of his safety and under duress" practiced by his defendant wife, by a deed of conveyance in which she joined, conveyed to her wholly-owned corporation, Natalie's Realty Co., Inc., all his right, title and interest in a farm of 126 1/2 acres containing a 14-room dwelling house and several farm buildings, situate on the Freehold-Matawan Road in Marlboro Township, Monmouth County, known as the "Marlboro Manor Farm," of the value of $90,000, and a plot of ground and a factory building on Dowd Avenue in Farmingdale, Monmouth County, of the value of $12,000, both tracts then being held by plaintiff and his wife in a tenancy by the entirety. The intervener-respondent was made a party defendant as the purchaser of 110 acres of the farm property for $23,000 by contract made with Natalie and her corporate codefendant, a price said to be "far below its present market value."

The complaint charges that by the conveyances thus made plaintiff "has divested himself of all his real property and all his assets"; that "when he made the said conveyances and thereafter" Natalie "promised and agreed that she would support" their two infant children, Leon, 5 1/2 years of age, and Norman Thomas, 2 1/2 years old, "out of the incomes" of these properties; that the farm land which Natalie "proposes to sell has been under lease," yielding $2500 annually; and that the farm property, "if properly managed, would produce sufficient revenues to provide for the support, maintenance and education of the infant children," but if 110 acres be sold at the stated price "the property will be so depreciated in value that the interest of the infants will be seriously jeopardized."

* * *

If these conveyances were procured by means of duress, they are inoperative and voidable. Actual violence is not an essential element of duress of the person, even at common law, because consent is the very essence of a contract and, if there be compulsion, there is no actual consent. And moral compulsion, such as that produced by threats to take life or to inflict great bodily harm, as well as that produced by imprisonment, came to be regarded everywhere as sufficient in law to destroy free agency, indispensable to the consent without which there can be no contract. Duress in its more extended sense means that degree of constraint or danger, either actually inflicted or threatened and impending, sufficient in severity or in apprehension to overcome the mind or will of a person of ordinary firmness, according to the earlier rule, but now, by the weight of modern authority, such as in fact works control of the will. There are two categories under the common law: duress *per minas* and duress of imprisonment. Duress *per minas* at common law "is where the party enters into a contract (1) For fear of loss of life; (2) For fear of loss of limb; (3) For fear of mayhem; (4) For fear of imprisonment"; and some of the later English cases confine the rule within these limits, while the American rule is more liberal and contracts procured by threats of battery to the person, or the destruction of property, were early held to be voidable on the ground of duress, "because in such a case there is nothing but the form of a contract, without the substance." Brown v. Pierce, 7 Wall. 205 (1869). In many cases it was found to be enough that there was moral compulsion "sufficient to overcome the mind and will of a person entirely competent, in all other respects, to contract," for "it is clear that a contract made under such circumstances is as utterly without the voluntary consent of the party menaced as if he were induced to sign it by actual violence; * * *." United States v. Huckabee, 16 Wall. 414 (1873).

It would seem to be basic to the legal concept of duress, proceeding as it does from the unreality of the apparent consent, that the controlling factor be the condition at the time of the mind of the person subjected to the coercive measures, rather than the means by which the given state of mind was induced, and thus the test is essentially subjective.

> "The test of duress is not so much the means by which the party was compelled to execute the contract as it is the state of mind induced by the means employed—the fear which made it impossible for him to exercise his own free will * * *. The threat must be of such a nature and made under such circumstances as to constitute a reasonable and adequate cause to control the will of the threatened person, and must have that effect; and the act sought to be avoided must be performed by such person while in such condition."

Fountain v. Bigham, 235 Pa. 35 (Sup.Ct. 1912). . . .

In the modern view, moral compulsion or psychological pressure may constitute duress if, thereby, the subject of the pressure is overborne and he is deprived of the exercise of his free will. The question is whether consent was coerced; that is, was the person complaining "induced by the duress or undue influence to give his consent, and would not have done so otherwise." Williston on Contracts (rev. ed.) § 1604. See Restatement, Contracts § 492. It was said in the early books that there could not be duress by threats unless the threats were such as "to put a brave man in fear"; then came the qualified standard of something sufficient to overcome the will of a person of "ordinary firmness"; but the tendency of the more recent cases, and the rule comporting with reason and principle, is that any "unlawful threats" which do "in fact overcome the will of the person threatened, and induce him to do an act which he would not otherwise have done, and which he was not bound to do, constitute duress. The age, sex, capacity, relation of the parties and all the attendant circumstances must be considered. This follows the analogy of the modern doctrine of fraud which tends to disregard the question whether misrepresentations were such as would have deceived a reasonable person, and confines the question to whether the misrepresentations were intended to deceive and did so." Williston on Contracts § 1605. Such is the trend of the cases in New Jersey. . . .

But the pressure must be wrongful, and not all pressure is wrongful. And means in themselves lawful must not be so oppressively used as to constitute, e.g., an abuse of legal remedies. Williston on Contracts §§ 1606, 1607. The act or conduct complained of need not be "unlawful" in the technical sense of the term; it suffices if it is "wrongful in the sense that it is so oppressive under given circumstances as to constrain one to do what his free will would refuse." First State Bank v. Federal Reserve Bank, 174 Minn. 535 (Sup.Ct. 1928). . . .

* * *

Here, the trial judge said: * * * "I will not allow [plaintiff] to testify to a state of mind." Again: "I think that we would be opening a door wide and entering into a very dangerous area if we were to allow a witness to say what his private thought was in response to an external force or statement. . . ." * * *

We come now to the case made by plaintiff which fell before the motion to dismiss. All was serene, apparently, in the domestic relation until the older boy developed a mental condition diagnosed in the Fall of 1952 as "childhood schizophrenia". . . . [The disclosure of the illness] led to sharp differences of opinion, e.g., as to the mode of treatment of the child, and eventually to an estrangement attended by the wife's insistent demands for the transfer of the husband's entire interest in the properties at issue, practically the whole of his possessions.

There is no occasion now to set down the plaintiff's evidence in detail. It suffices to say that he gave a circumstantial account of threats of gangster violence, arsenic poisoning, and a course of action designed to overcome his will, he affirms, culminating in his arrest for desertion and nonsupport. The arsenic threat, he said, had a background that filled him with an overpowering sense of foreboding and dread. His wife's father was then serving a life sentence in a Pennsylvania prison for murder committed while he was identified with an "arsenic ring" engaged in killings to defraud life insurers. The threats were first made in December 1952. The demand for the conveyances came in April 1953, and was refused. It was repeated at intervals until the following July, when the arsenic threat was made. He was seized with a great fear for his life and, so conditioned, he agreed the following day to make the conveyance. * * *

The trial judge said of the plaintiff: "I saw a witness who in many ways, in the way he testified, by voice, by his answers to direct questions and so on, who to me is possessed of an insecurity from within," one who "in life hasn't faced up reality frontally and boldly"; "as on the witness stand, he has in life tended to avoid important problems, and marriage was one"; the misfortune to the child had its effect, and the plaintiff "was running from it," although he "had every desire to do what he could" for the boy. And the suggestion was made that the defendant wife's "assumption of all liabilities against the (conveyed) property was not an unmixed blessing to him"; "A big load was shifted together with the assets."

These findings suggest psychological factors bearing on the subjective standard of free will.

* * *

There was a *prima facie* showing here of a compulsive yielding to the demand for the conveyances, rather than the volitional act of a free mind, which called for a full disclosure by the defendant wife; and so it was error to entertain the motion to dismiss at the close of the plaintiff's case. The testimony of plaintiff stood unchallenged. Stress is laid upon the advantage of personal observation of the plaintiff witness in the assessment of his testimony; but this is peculiarly a case for explanation by the defendant under the same scrutiny, in particular as to dominance of will. Duress is a species of fraud, although unlike fraud, duress does not necessarily depend on the intent of the person exercising it. See Restatement, Contracts § 492, Comment A.

The judgment is reversed; and the cause is remanded for further proceedings in conformity with this opinion.

Austin Instrument, Inc. v. Loral Corp.

Court of Appeals of New York, 1971.
29 N.Y.2d 124.

■ FULD, CHIEF JUDGE. The defendant, Loral Corporation, seeks to recover payment for goods delivered under a contract which it had with the plaintiff Austin Instrument, Inc., on the ground that the evidence establishes, as a matter of law, that it was forced to agree to an increase in price on the items in question under circumstances amounting to economic duress.

In July of 1965, Loral was awarded a $6,000,000 contract by the Navy for the production of radar sets. The contract contained a schedule of deliveries, a liquidated damages clause applying to late deliveries and a cancellation clause in case of default by Loral. The latter thereupon solicited bids for some 40 precision gear components needed to produce the radar sets, and awarded Austin a subcontract to supply 23 such parts. That party commenced delivery in early 1966.

In May, 1966, Loral was awarded a second Navy contract for the production of more radar sets and again went about soliciting bids. Austin bid on all 40 gear components but, on July 15, a representative from Loral informed Austin's president, Mr. Krauss, that his company would be awarded the subcontract only for those items on which it was low bidder. The Austin officer refused to accept an order for less than all 40 of the gear parts and on the next day he told Loral that Austin would cease deliveries of the parts due under the existing subcontract unless Loral consented to substantial increases in the prices provided for by that agreement—both retroactively for parts already delivered and prospectively on those not yet shipped—and placed with Austin the order for all 40 parts needed under Loral's second Navy contract. Shortly thereafter, Austin did, indeed, stop delivery. After contacting 10 manufacturers of precision gears and finding none who could produce the parts in time to meet its commitments to the Navy,[1] Loral acceded to Austin's demands; in a letter dated July 22, Loral wrote to Austin that "We have feverishly surveyed other sources of supply and find that because of the prevailing military exigencies, were they to start from scratch as would have to be the case, they could not even remotely begin to deliver on time to meet the delivery requirements established by the Government. * * * Accordingly, we are left with no choice or alternative but to meet your conditions."

Loral thereupon consented to the price increases insisted upon by Austin under the first subcontract and the latter was awarded a second subcontract making it the supplier of all 40 gear parts for Loral's second contract with the Navy. Although Austin was granted until September to resume deliveries, Loral did, in fact, receive parts in August and was able to produce the radar sets in time to meet its commitments to the Navy on both contracts. After Austin's last delivery under the second subcontract in July, 1967, Loral notified it of its intention to seek recovery of the price increases.

On September 15, 1967, Austin instituted this action against Loral to recover an amount in excess of $17,750 which was still due on the second subcontract. On the same day, Loral commenced an action against Austin claiming damages of some $22,250—the aggregate of the price increases under the first subcontract—on the ground of economic duress. The two actions were consolidated and, following a trial, Austin was

---

[1] The best reply Loral received was from a vendor who stated he could commence deliveries sometime in October.

awarded the sum it requested and Loral's complaint against Austin was dismissed on the ground that it was not shown that "it could not have obtained the items in question from other sources in time to meet its commitment to the Navy under the first contract." A closely divided Appellate Division affirmed (316 N.Y.S.2d 528, 532). There was no material disagreement concerning the facts; as Justice Steuer stated in the course of his dissent below, "[t]he facts are virtually undisputed, nor is there any serious question of law. The difficulty lies in the application of the law to these facts." (316 N.Y.S.2d at 534.)

The applicable law is clear and, indeed, is not disputed by the parties. A contract is voidable on the ground of duress when it is established that the party making the claim was forced to agree to it by means of a wrongful threat precluding the exercise of his free will. . . . The existence of economic duress or business compulsion is demonstrated by proof that "immediate possession of needful goods is threatened" . . . or, more particularly, in cases such as the one before us, by proof that one party to a contract has threatened to breach the agreement by withholding goods unless the other party agrees to some further demand. . . . However, a mere threat by one party to breach the contract by not delivering the required items, though wrongful, does not in itself constitute economic duress. It must also appear that the threatened party could not obtain the goods from another source of supply and that the ordinary remedy of an action for breach of contract would not be adequate.

We find without any support in the record the conclusion reached by the courts below that Loral failed to establish that it was the victim of economic duress. On the contrary, the evidence makes out a classic case, as a matter of law, of such duress.

It is manifest that Austin's threat—to stop deliveries unless the prices were increased—deprived Loral of its free will. As bearing on this, Loral's relationship with the Government is most significant. As mentioned above, its contract called for staggered monthly deliveries of the radar sets, with clauses calling for liquidated damages and possible cancellation on default. Because of its production schedule, Loral was, in July, 1966, concerned with meeting its delivery requirements in September, October and November, and it was for the sets to be delivered in those months that the withheld gears were needed. Loral had to plan ahead, and the substantial liquidated damages for which it would be liable, plus the threat of default, were genuine possibilities. Moreover, Loral did a substantial portion of its business with the Government, and it feared that a failure to deliver as agreed upon would jeopardize its chances for future contracts. These genuine concerns do not merit the label "self-imposed, undisclosed and subjective" which the Appellate Division majority placed upon them. It was perfectly reasonable for Loral, or any other party similarly placed, to consider itself in an emergency, duress situation.

Austin, however, claims that the fact that Loral extended its time to resume deliveries until September negates its alleged dire need for the parts. A Loral official testified on this point that Austin's president told him he could deliver some parts in August and that the extension of deliveries was a formality. In any event, the parts necessary for production of the radar sets to be delivered in September were delivered to Loral on September 1, and the parts needed for the October schedule were delivered in late August and early September. Even so, Loral had to "work * * * around the clock" to meet its commitments. Considering that the best offer Loral received from the other vendors it contacted was commencement of delivery sometime in October, which, as the record shows, would have made it late in its deliveries to the Navy in both September and October, Loral's claim that it had no choice but to accede to Austin's demands is conclusively demonstrated.

We find unconvincing Austin's contention that Loral, in order to meet its burden, should have contacted the Government and asked for an extension of its delivery dates so as to enable it to purchase the parts from another vendor. Aside from the consideration that Loral was anxious to perform well in the Government's eyes, it could not be sure when it would obtain enough parts from a substitute vendor to meet its commitments. The only promise which it received from the companies it contacted was for *commencement* of deliveries, not full supply, and, with vendor delay common in this field, it would have been nearly impossible to know the length of the extension it should request. It must be remembered that Loral was producing a needed item of military hardware. Moreover, there is authority for Loral's position that nonperformance by a subcontractor is not an excuse for default in the main contract. (See, e.g., McBride & Wachtel, Government Contracts, § 35.10, [11].) In light of all this, Loral's claim should not be held insufficiently supported because it did not request an extension from the Government.

Loral, as indicated above, also had the burden of demonstrating that it could not obtain the parts elsewhere within a reasonable time, and there can be no doubt that it met this burden. The 10 manufacturers whom Loral contacted comprised its entire list of "approved vendors" for precision gears, and none was able to commence delivery soon enough. As Loral was producing a highly sophisticated item of military machinery requiring parts made to the strictest engineering standards, it would be unreasonable to hold that Loral should have gone to other vendors, with whom it was either unfamiliar or dissatisfied, to procure the needed parts. As Justice Steuer noted in his dissent, Loral "contacted all the manufacturers whom it believed capable of making these parts" (316 N.Y.S.2d at 534), and this was all the law requires.

It is hardly necessary to add that Loral's normal legal remedy of accepting Austin's breach of the contract and then suing for damages would have been inadequate under the circumstances, as Loral would still have had to obtain the gears elsewhere with all the concomitant consequences mentioned above. In other words, Loral actually had no choice, when the prices were raised by Austin, except to take the gears at the "coerced" prices and then sue to get the excess back.

* * *

In sum, the record before us demonstrates that Loral agreed to the price increases in consequence of the economic duress employed by Austin. Accordingly, the matter should be remanded to the trial court for a computation of its damages.

The order appealed from should be modified, with costs, by reversing so much thereof as affirms the dismissal of defendant Loral Corporation's claim and, except as so modified, affirmed.

■ BERGAN, J (dissenting). Whether acts charged as constituting economic duress produce or do not produce the damaging effect attributed to them is normally a routine type of factual issue.

Here the fact question was resolved against Loral both by the Special Term and by the affirmance at the Appellate Division. It should not be open for different resolution here.

* * *

Machinery Hauling, Inc. v. Steel of West Virginia
Supreme Court of Appeals of West Virginia, 1989.
181 W.Va. 694.

■ MILLER, JUSTICE: [Plaintiff buyer contracted with defendant seller to purchase steel and have it delivered to a third party. Defendant informed plaintiff that the steel was unmerchantable and that the third party had rejected it and orally directed plaintiff to return the last three undelivered loads to defendant. Defendant's agent then (allegedly) told plaintiff that if it did not pay $31,000, the price of the undelivered loads, it would cease doing business with plaintiff, with a potential loss of over $1,000,000 per year.

[In its complaint, the plaintiff alleged that defendant and its agent "negligently attempted to extort money" from plaintiff by their joint threat to sever business relations unless payment for the defective product was made and sought monetary damages for their "extortionate demands." The circuit court denied recovery. On appeal, the Supreme Court first held that there was no cause of action under the West Virginia criminal extortion statute because the threat was not an unlawful act. "Steel was free to place its haulage business wherever it chose. Its statement to the plaintiff did not constitute an unlawful act."]

The more common analysis proceeds under a theory of business or economic loss. In the early common law, duress *per minas*, i.e., by threats, was available to void a contract where the threat involved imprisonment, mayhem, or loss of life or limb. Restatement (Second) of Torts § 871, comment f (1979); 25 Am.Jur.2d Duress & Undue Influence § 11 (1966). Through the years, there has been a steady expansion of duress principle such that direct dire harm is no longer essential, the focus instead being on whether the threat overbears the exercise of free will. Professor Williston, in discussing the status of business compulsion, has identified two basic elements: (1) the party who asserts business compulsion "must show that he has been the victim of a wrongful or unlawful act or threat," and (2) "[s]uch act or threat must be one which deprives the victim of his unfettered will." 13 Williston on Contracts § 1617 at 704 (1970).

Recently, courts have tended to avoid the term "free will" as applied to the victim, but instead have utilized the concept that the victim had "no reasonable alternative." This is found in Section 175(1) of the Restatement (Second) of Contracts (1981): "If a party's manifestation of assent is induced by an improper threat by the other party that leaves the victim no reasonable alternative, the contract is voidable by the victim." A more difficult issue is determining what type of threat is sufficient to invoke the rule. Courts tend to use as a shorthand summary, words such as "wrongful," "oppressive," or "unconscionable" to describe conduct, but the complexity of the term "threat" is demonstrated in Section 176 of the Restatement. The concept of "economic or business duress" may be generally stated as follows: Where the plaintiff is forced into a transaction as a result of unlawful threats or wrongful, oppressive, or unconscionable conduct on the part of the defendant which leaves the plaintiff no reasonable alternative but to acquiesce, the plaintiff may void the transaction and recover any economic loss. . . .

Furthermore, while economic duress principles are more prevalent in contract cases, they are not limited solely to this area. Some courts have proceeded to analyze economic duress cases in terms of a tort theory. Under this theory, the duty is deemed to be the reasonable use of the superior economic power of the defendant. The breach is using such power unlawfully or unreasonably. The proximate cause is shown by the fact that the victim had no reasonable recourse but to acquiesce in the unlawful conduct of the defendant and is damaged thereby. . . . It is apparent that this tort theory is not substantially different from the economic duress theory under a contract analysis.

In several cases, we have utilized what amounts to a "business compulsion" analysis, although we characterized it only as "duress." [The court reviewed the West Virginia cases.]

While we recognize the concept of business or economic duress, we do not find it exists in this case. There was no continuing contract between the plaintiff and the defendants. Thus, the demand by the defendants that the plaintiff pay $31,000 for the defective steel was not coupled with a threat to terminate an existing contract. Furthermore, the plaintiff did not accede to the defendants' demand and pay over the money.

The plaintiff's claim, stripped to its essentials, is that it has been deprived of its future prospects of doing business with the defendants. However, this future expectancy is not a legal right on which the plaintiff can anchor a claim of economic duress. * * *

Finally, there appears to be general acknowledgement that duress is not shown because one party to the contract has driven a hard bargain or that market or other conditions now make the contract more difficult to perform by one of the parties or that financial circumstances may have caused one party to make concessions. . . .

The questions certified to us by the Cabell County Circuit Court are, therefore, answered, and this case is dismissed from the docket.

NOTES

(1) *Duress: Wrongful Coercion.* Duress as such is seldom recognized as an independent tort. The victim does not usually maintain an action for damages. *Machinery Hauling* is exceptional in this respect. In the usual case, duress is pleaded as a defense or as a basis for avoiding a transaction and securing restitutionary relief. Moreover, the issue seldom arises in connection with initial contract formation; most often there is an attempt to bar enforcement of a contract modification or a settlement agreement.

Normally, duress by physical compulsion prevents formation of a contract, Restatement (Second) § 174, whereas duress by other threats makes a contract voidable. Restatement (Second) § 175 provides: "If a party's manifestation of assent is induced by an improper threat by the other party that leaves the victim no reasonable alternative, the contract is voidable by the victim." See Russell Korobkin, Michael Moffitt and Nancy Welsh, *The Law of Bargaining*, 87 Marq. L. Rev. 839 (2004).

(2) In *Austin Instruments*, Loral insisted that it was "left with no choice or alternative but to meet [Austin's] conditions." What, precisely, were its alternatives? Was there a "reasonable" alternative? See Meredith R. Miller, *Revisiting* Austin v. Loral Corp.: *A Study in Economic Duress, Contract Modification and Framing*, 2 Hastings Bus. L.J. 357 (2006).

(3) *When is a Threat Wrongful?* Can it ever be unlawful to threaten to do what one has a legal right to do? Quoting from an Oregon case, the court in *Machinery Hauling* states: "It is well established, however, that threats to do what the threatening person had a legal right to do does not constitute duress." This is misleading. The Oklahoma Supreme Court offered this clarification:

Ordinarily a party may threaten to do what is lawful; however, a coercer's threats may be wrongful even though the threatened action would have been legal. The key factor, therefore, must be the fact that the threatened action is an unreasonable alternative to an injurious contractual demand in a bargaining situation. The wrongfulness of the coercer's conduct must be related to the unreasonableness of the alternatives which he presents to the weaker party, and the inherent wrongfulness of either alternative is relevant only insofar as it shows the unreasonableness of the alternatives. "Unlawful" when applied to promises, agreements, contracts and considerations, means that the agreements are legally ineffective because they were obtained by bad faith coercion or compulsion, even though the acts may not be illegal *per se.*

Centric Corp. v. Morrison-Knudsen Co., 731 P.2d 411, 419 (Okl. 1986). A common example, and one referred to in *Machinery Hauling*, is the threat of criminal prosecution as an "improper means of inducing the recipient to make a contract," which constitutes "a misuse, for personal gain, of power given for other legitimate ends." Restatement (Second) § 176 cmt. c. Even a threat of civil process may, under exceptional circumstances, be abusive "if the threat is shown to have been made in bad faith." Id. cmt. d. For other examples of wrongful threats to do what one has a legal right to do, see Berger v. Berger, 466 So.2d 1149 (Fla.App. 1985) (husband threatens to inform Internal Revenue Service of wife's tax evasion if she does not sign settlement agreement); Wolf v. Marlton Corp., 57 N.J.Super. 278 (1959) (purchaser under land contract threatens to sell to an "undesirable" in order to force vendor-developer to return deposit). Does *Machinery Hauling* fit here?

(4) *Undue Influence.* The rule for duress was developed by courts of law. The rule for undue influence is similar to that for duress but was developed by the courts of equity, and its elements are somewhat easier to satisfy. Undue influence is characterized by "unfair" persuasion that may fall short of constituting actual duress. "The hallmark of such persuasion is high pressure, a pressure which works on mental, moral, or emotional weakness to such an extent that it approaches the boundaries of coercion." Odorizzi v. Bloomfield School District, 246 Cal.App.2d 123, 130 (1966). It is ordinarily limited to situations where there is a relationship of trust and confidence (e.g., parent and child; husband and wife; attorney and client), and one party is particularly susceptible to pressure by the other. Thus, Restatement (Second) § 177(1) states that "[u]ndue influence is unfair persuasion of a party who is under the domination of the person exercising the persuasion or who by virtue of the relation between them is justified in assuming that that person will not act in a manner inconsistent with his welfare." Undue influence has been found where a confidential relationship in the usual sense does not exist. The *Odorizzi* case, supra, is illustrative. In that case a school teacher was arrested on criminal charges of homosexual activity and, after conferring with school officials, submitted a letter of resignation the following day. A month later the charges were dismissed, and the teacher sued for rescission of the resignation and other appropriate relief. In upholding the teacher's position, the court observed that the pattern of "overpersuasion" usually involves several of the following elements: "(1) discussion of the transaction at an unusual or inappropriate time, (2) consummation of the transaction in an unusual place, (3) insistent demand that the business be finished at once, (4) extreme emphasis on untoward consequences of delay, (5) the use of multiple persuaders by the dominant side against a single servient party, (6) absence of third-party advisers to the

servient party, [and] (7) statements that there is no time to consult financial advisers or attorneys." 246 Cal.App.2d at 133.

6. UNCONSCIONABILITY

The defenses discussed above all concern the *how* of transactions. Were the parties of the right age or mental ability? Did they produce a writing? Were they fully informed and sufficiently truthful with one another, and were their decisions sufficiently voluntary? These defenses do not, generally speaking, concern the *what* of the deal—the terms that the parties arrived at. The last two defenses we discuss in this Chapter ask about the what, though as we shall see, the how still figures into the inquiry. The unconscionability doctrine, which is the subject of this section, inquires into the deal's fairness. The public policy defense, the subject of the next section, asks whether its terms are consistent with broader social goals.

The unconscionability doctrine we have today is only about fifty years old, its appearance closely tied to the production and enactment of the Uniform Commercial Code. That said, the doctrine had historical antecedents. As early as 1750, the Court of Chancery described an "unconscientious" bargain as one "such as no man in his senses and not under delusion would make on the one hand, and as no honest and fair man would accept on the other." Earl of Chesterfield v. Janssen, 28 Eng.Rep. 82 (1750), quoted in Hume v. United States, 132 U.S. 406 (1889). More generally, as Morton Horowitz has argued, there exists a longstanding strain of American case law wherein courts "limited and sometimes denied contractual obligation by reference to the fairness of the underlying exchange." Morton J. Horwitz, *The Historical Foundations of Modern Contract Law*, 87 Harv.L.Rev. 917, 923 (1974). These cases, however, were not brought under a single, clearly established doctrinal umbrella until the latter part of the twentieth century. Crucial in this process was the publication and enactment of UCC § 2–302, which permitted courts to deny enforcement of a contract "unconscionable at the time it was made." The comments to the 1958 official text of UCC § 2–302 explained the drafters' goals:

> This section is intended to make it possible for the courts to police explicitly against the contracts or clauses which they find to be unconscionable. In the past such policing has been accomplished by adverse construction of language, by manipulation of the rules of offer and acceptance or by determinations that the clause is contrary to public policy or the dominant purpose of the contract. This section is intended to allow the court to pass directly on the unconscionability of the contract or particular clauses therein and to make a conclusion of law as to its unconscionability.

Judicial inquiry into the substantial unfairness of contracts is, of course, in tension with the rule that courts shall not inquire into the adequacy of consideration, not to mention the general principle of freedom of contract. As the Utah Supreme Court put it, "people should be entitled to contract on their own terms without the indulgence of paternalism by courts in the alleviation of one side or another from the effects of a bad bargain * * * [and] should be permitted to enter into contracts that actually may be unreasonable or which may lead to hardship on one side." Carlson v. Hamilton, 8 Utah 2d 272, 274–75 (1958).[3] When deciding unconscionability cases, therefore, courts commonly demand proof not only of the agreement's substantive unfairness, but also of some defect in the process through which the parties arrived at it. Such defect need not rise to the level of mistake, misrepresentation, duress or one of the other defenses. Such a requirement would render the unconscionability defense redundant. But, typically, there must also be some problematic aspect of the *how* of contracting. As we will see, a key question in unconscionability cases is what weight to give to the substantive and to the procedural inquiries, and the relationship between them.

(A) CONSUMER TRANSACTIONS

Ora Lee Williams v. Walker-Thomas Furniture Co.

District of Columbia Court of Appeals, 1964.
198 A.2d 914.

■ QUINN, ASSOCIATE JUDGE. Appellant, a person of limited education separated from her husband, is maintaining herself and her seven children by means of public assistance. During the period 1957–1962 she had a continuous course of dealings with appellee from which she purchased many household articles on the installment plan. These included sheets, curtains, rugs, chairs, a chest of drawers, beds, mattresses, a washing machine, and a stereo set. In 1963 appellee filed a complaint in replevin for possession of all the items purchased by appellant, alleging that her payments were in default and that it retained title to the goods according to the sales contracts. By the writ of replevin appellee obtained a bed, chest of drawers, washing machine, and the stereo set. After hearing testimony and examining the contracts, the trial court entered judgment for appellee.

Appellant's principal contentions on appeal are (1) there was a lack of meeting of the minds, and (2) the contracts were against public policy.

Appellant signed fourteen contracts in all. They were approximately six inches in length and each contained a long paragraph in extremely

---

[3] It is worth noting that the Utah court, while it held that the contract at issue was enforceable, also paraphrased the equitable doctrine found in *Janssen*: "It is only where it turns out that one side or the other is to be penalized by the enforcement of the terms of a contract so unconscionable that no decent, fairminded person would view the ensuing result without being possessed of a profound sense of injustice, that equity will deny the use of its good offices in the enforcement of such unconscionability." 8 Utah 2d at 275.

fine print. One of the sentences in this paragraph provided that payments, after the first purchase, were to be prorated on all purchases then outstanding. Mathematically, this had the effect of keeping a balance due on all items until the time balance was completely eliminated. It meant that title to the first purchase, remained in appellee until the fourteenth purchase, made some five years later, was fully paid.

At trial appellant testified that she understood the agreements to mean that when payments on the running account were sufficient to balance the amount due on an individual item, the item became hers. She testified that most of the purchases were made at her home; that the contracts were signed in blank; that she did not read the instruments; and that she was not provided with a copy. She admitted, however, that she did not ask anyone to read or explain the contracts to her.

We have stated that "one who refrains from reading a contract and in conscious ignorance of its terms voluntarily assents thereto will not be relieved from his bad bargain." Bob Wilson, Inc. v. Swann, 168 A.2d 198, 199 (D.C.Mun.App. 1961). "One who signs a contract has a duty to read it and is obligated according to its terms." Hollywood Credit Clothing Co. v. Gibson, 188 A.2d 348, 349 (D.C.App. 1963). "It is as much the duty of a person who cannot read the language in which a contract is written to have someone read it to him before he signs it, as it is the duty of one who can read to peruse it himself before signing it." Stern v. Moneyweight Scale Co., 42 App.D.C. 162, 165 (1914).

A careful review of the record shows that appellant's assent was not obtained "by fraud or even misrepresentation falling short of fraud." Hollywood Credit Clothing Co. v. Gibson, supra. This is not a case of mutual misunderstanding but a unilateral mistake. Under these circumstances, appellant's first contention is without merit.

Appellant's second argument presents a more serious question. The record reveals that prior to the last purchase appellant had reduced the balance in her account to $164. The last purchase, a stereo set, raised the balance due to $678. Significantly, at the time of this and the preceding purchases, appellee was aware of appellant's financial position. The reverse side of the stereo contract listed the name of appellant's social worker and her $218 monthly stipend from the government. Nevertheless, with full knowledge that appellant had to feed, clothe and support both herself and seven children on this amount, appellee sold her a $514 stereo set.

We cannot condemn too strongly appellee's conduct. It raises serious questions of sharp practice and irresponsible business dealings. A review of the legislation in the District of Columbia affecting retail sales and the pertinent decisions of the highest court in this jurisdiction disclose, however, no ground upon which this court can declare the contracts in question contrary to public policy. We note that were the Maryland Retail Installment Sales Act, Art. 83 §§ 128–153, or its equivalent, in force in the District of Columbia, we could grant appellant appropriate relief. We think Congress should consider corrective legislation to protect the public from such exploitive contracts as were utilized in the case at bar.

Affirmed.

Ora Lee Williams v. Walker-Thomas Furniture Co.

United States Court of Appeals, District of Columbia Circuit, 1965.
Supra at 23.

NOTES

(1)   What is the difference between Judge Quinn's approach in the D.C. Court of Appeals and that of Judge Wright in the D.C. Circuit? What does the D.C. Circuit's holding do to the so-called "duty to read"?

State as clearly as you can Judge Wright's test for determining whether a contract is unconscionable. Would you expect the outcome of its application to vary with whether the contract was between a professional business person and an individual consumer or between two business people?

(2)   Below is another attempt to describe the test for unconscionability.

Unconscionability has been defined as "an absence of meaningful choice on the part of one of the parties, together with contract terms which are unreasonably favorable to the other party". . . . To show that a provision is conscionable, the party seeking to uphold the provision must show that the provision bears some reasonable relationship to the risks and needs of the business. . . . The indicators of procedural unconscionability generally fall into two areas: (1) lack of knowledge, and (2) lack of voluntariness. A lack of knowledge is demonstrated by a lack of understanding of the contract terms arising from inconspicuous print or the use of complex, legalistic language, . . . disparity in sophistication of parties, . . . and lack of opportunity to study the contract and inquire about contract terms. . . . A lack of voluntariness is demonstrated in contracts of adhesion when there is a great imbalance in the parties' relative bargaining power, the stronger party's terms are unnegotiable, and the weaker party is prevented by market factors, timing or other pressures from being able to contract with another party on more favorable terms or to refrain from contracting at all. . . .

Substantive unconscionability is found when the terms of the contract are of such an oppressive character as to be unconscionable. It is present when there is a one-sided agreement whereby one party is deprived of all the benefits of the agreement or left without a remedy for another party's nonperformance or breach, . . . a large disparity between the cost and price or a price far in excess of that prevailing in the market [place], . . . or terms which bear no reasonable relationship to business risks assumed by the parties. . . .

Bank of Indiana, National Association v. Holyfield, 476 F.Supp. 104, 109–10 (S.D.Miss. 1979).

(3) *Posner on "Meaningful Choice."* "There can be no objection to using the one-sidedness of a transaction as evidence of deception, lack of agreement, or compulsion, none of which is shown here. The problem with unconscionability as a legal doctrine comes in making sense out of lack of 'meaningful choice' in a situation where the promisor was not deceived or compelled and really did agree to the provision that he contends was unconscionable. Suppose that for reasons unrelated to any conduct of the promisee the promisor has very restricted opportunities. Maybe he is so poor that he can be induced to sell the clothes off his back for a pittance, or is such a poor credit risk that he can be made (in the absence of usury laws) to pay an extraordinarily high interest rate to borrow money that he wants desperately. Does he have a 'meaningful choice' in such circumstances? If not he may actually be made worse off by a rule of nonenforcement of hard bargains; for, knowing that a contract with him will not be enforced, merchants may be unwilling to buy his clothes or lend him money. Since the law of contracts cannot compel the making of contracts on terms favorable to one party, but can only refuse to enforce contracts with unfavorable terms, it is not an institution well designed to rectify inequalities in wealth." Amoco Oil Co. v. Ashcraft, 791 F.2d 519, 522 (7th Cir. 1986).

(4) *Substantive Unconscionability as Evidence of Procedural Unconscionability.* Lopsided agreements can actually be evidence of some procedural defect. If the court encounters a bargain that is so outrageous "such as no man in his senses and not under delusion would make," it may infer the presence of some defect in the bargaining process.

(5) *Remediability.* Which is easier for the law to cure—lack of information or lack of voluntariness? See UCC § 2–316(2) (modification of implied warranty of merchantability must be "conspicuous"). If a term is found to be unconscionable, it is possible that the court may be able to sever that term from the contract and enforce the balance. Courts have held that an unconscionable provision may be severed from the remainder of the agreement where disregard of the offending conditions leaves a fair agreement that will accomplish the primary objectives. Enforcement of the balance of the agreement turns on the parties' intent at the time the agreement was executed as determined by the language of the contract and the surrounding circumstances. Parilla v. IAP Worldwide Services, VI, 368 F.3d 269, 284–89 (3d Cir. 2004).

(6) *The Rise of Unconscionability.* At the risk of oversimplification, it is suggested that two developments have changed the perception of, if not the underlying assumptions about, unconscionability. The first was a tremendous expansion after World War II of the demand for and availability of consumer credit. One result was the increase in transactions between individuals, who purchased or borrowed items for personal, family or household purposes, and professional sellers or lenders. The second was the expanded use of contracts of adhesion—standard form contracts drafted by one party and offered to the other on a take-it-or-leave-it basis. Karl Llewellyn had this to say:

The answer [to the question, how does a court decide when a party is unfairly surprised by a contract term], I suggest, is this: Instead of thinking about "assent" to boiler-plate clauses, we can recognize so far as concerns the specific, there is no assent at all. What has in fact been assented to, specifically, are the few dickered terms, and the broad type of the transaction, and but one thing more. That one thing more is a blanket assent (not a specific assent) to any not unreasonable or indecent terms the seller may have on his form, which do not alter or eviscerate the reasonable meaning of the dickered terms. The fine print which has not been read has no business to cut under the reasonable meaning of those dickered terms which constitute the dominant and only real expression of agreement, but much of it commonly belongs in. * * * [A]ny contract with boiler-plate results in two several contracts: the *dickered* deal, and the collateral one of *supplementary* boiler plate. Rooted in sense, history, and simplicity, it is an answer which could occur to anyone.

Karl N. Llewellyn, The Common Law Tradition: Deciding Appeals 370–71 (1960).

Russell Korobkin, relying on the results of cognitive psychology, argues that because of an individual's limited powers of cognition, there will be "non-salient" aspects of forms that are objectively assented to, and that these non-salient features will probably reside in the supplementary boilerplate and are the most susceptible to abuse. *Bounded Rationality, Standard Form Contracts, and Unconscionability*, 70 U. Chi. L. Rev. 1203 (2003).

(7) *What Happens When Security Interests Are Seized?* Both Douglas Baird and Richard Epstein have suggested that Walker-Thomas had no right to keep all of the secured property in the event of a default. Richard A. Epstein, Unconscionability: A Critical Reappraisal, 18 J.L. & Econ. 293, 308 (1975)); Douglas G. Baird, *The Boilerplate Puzzle*, 104 Mich. L. Rev. 933, 944 n.39 (2006). While today the law would require return of any amount in excess of the amount owed, see UCC § 9–615(d), this was not so at the time of the transaction between Walker-Thomas Furniture and Ora Lee Williams. As historian Anne Fleming has explained:

Before the [Uniform Commercial] Code took effect in 1965, a seller under a "conditional sale" or "lease-purchase" agreement could sue a defaulting buyer either for the amount owed or could "treat the sale as a nullity" and recover the goods. Marvins Credit, Inc. v. Morgan, 87 A.2d 530, 531 (D.C. 1952). The District of Columbia had not enacted the Uniform Conditional Sales Act, which required creditors to return any surplus received from the seizure and sale of the goods to the buyer.

Anne Fleming, *The Rise and Fall of Unconscionability As the "Law of the Poor"*, 102 Geo. L.J. 1383, 1431 n. 317 (2014). In fact, Walker-Thomas's right to keep all of the collateral appears to have especially bothered Judge Wright.

As early drafts of the opinion reflect, Wright was particularly worried by Walker-Thomas Furniture's methods of doing business with poor borrowers. Repossession of used merchandise seemed to be part of the Walker-Thomas Furniture business model, rather than an unintended consequence of selling goods on credit to low-income buyers. Wright suspected that the company made a practice of selling unaffordable, high-priced items to its customers when their debts were nearly paid off, with the knowledge that they would likely default. The company could then repossess and resell the items to the next buyer. However, Wright decided not to raise these concerns in the opinion. Instead, after consulting with his colleagues, he shifted the focus of the decision away from the company's pattern and practice of dealing to highlight the unique problems in the transactions before the court. The final opinion portrayed Walker-Thomas Furniture's actions in the two cases as unusually exploitative and the defendants as particularly vulnerable, while understating the novelty of the legal holding.

Id. at 1391. Why might Judge Write have wanted to emphasize Mrs. William's vulnerability rather than the unfairness of Walker-Thomas's business model? Did the opinion as written provide the best guidance possible for future courts?

A more benign rationale that Walker-Thomas had in establishing a security interest is that under a local statute, "[a]ll beds, bedding, household furniture and furnishings, sewing machines, radios, stoves, cooking utensils, not exceeding $300 in value" were "free and exempt from distraint, attachment, levy, or seizure and sale on execution or decree of any court in the District of Columbia." See DC Code § 15–501. Thus Douglas Baird argues: "Walker-Thomas took the security interest in Williams' other household goods because these assets were exempt. It had to take a security interest in them in order to be able to reach them in the event of default. The cross-collateralization clause served this purpose and no other." 104 Mich. L. Rev. at 948.

(8) *Pop Bible Quiz*: Name unconscionable deals that Jacob cut with family members that were the bi-product of (1) lack of knowledge,[4] and (2) lack of voluntariness.[5] Extra credit: name other unconscionable deals with which Jacob was involved.[6]

---

[4]   "And Jacob said unto his father, I am Esau thy firstborn; I have done according as thou badest me: arise, I pray thee, sit and eat of my venison, that thy soul may bless me." Genesis 27:19.

[5]   "And Esau said to Jacob, Feed me, I pray thee, with that same red [pottage]; for I [am] faint: therefore was his name called Edom. And Jacob said, Sell me this day thy birthright. And Esau said, Behold, I [am] at the point to die: and what profit shall this birthright do to me?" Genesis 25:30–31.

[6]   See Genesis 29:16. See also Genesis 34:13–25 ("And the sons of Jacob answered Shechem and Hamor his father deceitfully, and said, because he had defiled Dinah their sister: And they said unto them, We cannot do this thing, to give our sister to one that is uncircumcised; for that were a reproach unto us. . . . And it came to pass on the third day, when they were sore, that two of the sons of Jacob, Simeon and Levi, Dinah's brethren, took each man his sword, and came upon the city boldly, and slew all the males.")

Comment: Renting-to-Own as a Modern Method to "Profit on Poverty"

Retailers can often avoid consumer credit regulation by restructuring a transaction as "renting-to-own," where the consumer has the option to stop renting before attaining ownership of the chattel. Unlike in traditional credit contracts, rent-to-own customers do not unconditionally promise to pay off a loan, and, therefore, the transaction falls outside of the definition of most consumer credit statutes. According to the Association of Progressive Rental Organizations, the rent-to-own business is today a $7 billion industry. An example of such a retailer is Rent-A-Center. The following article describes the business practices of Rent-A-Center, which in 2011 controlled approximately 35% of the U.S. market in renting-to-own.

For low-income customers, Rent-A-Center has tremendous appeal. The chain gives them immediate use of brand-name merchandise, and the weekly payments are usually less than $20. But while in theory customers can eventually own the goods outright, the company says three out of every four are unable to meet all their payments.

Their failure is partially responsible for Thorn's success. The company earns considerably more by renting, repossessing and then re-renting the same goods than it does if the first customer makes all the payments. Derrick-Myers, who was fired as manager of the Rent-A-Center store in Victorville, California, recalls one particular Philco VCR, for example, that he says retailed for about $119—but that brought in more than $5,000 in a five-year period.

That means the most profitable customers are people like Minneapolis welfare mother Angela Adams, who says Rent-A-Center salespeople cajoled her into renting more than a dozen items at a monthly cost that reached about $325. Though the salespeople knew how little she earned, "they pushed it on me," she says. When she fell behind in her payments in late 1991, Rent-A-Center sued her and repossessed the goods, ranging from a bedroom set to two VCRs. Ms. Adams is now a named plaintiff in one of the two class-action suits, this one pending in federal court in Minneapolis. Rent-A-Center declines comment.

"Even if a customer can't afford it and you know it and they know it, we'll rent to them anyway," says Rod Comeaux, a former store manager from Onley, Va., who was fired a year ago for unrelated reasons. "We can always get it back" and re-rent it to others, he says.

Rent-A-Center's Mr. Gates denies that salespeople put excessive pressure on customers or intentionally overload them with goods. On average, customers rent 2.85 items a month, at a total monthly cost of $99.07, and they are able to cancel rentals at any time without a penalty, he points out. Store managers—who are required to obtain income and other financial information from customers—ideally should act as "financial planners" for customers, he says, adding that the "worst thing" employees can do is to rent to customers whose "eyes are bigger than their stomachs."

Rent-A-Center says its customer base is 25% to 30% black and 10% to 15% Hispanic, and just 15% are on welfare or government subsidies. But former store managers consistently maintain that the total on government assistance is more than 25%, with some claiming up to 70%. Indeed, they unanimously report that sales always spiked on "Mother's Day," as they call the day when welfare mothers get their checks. * * *

According to a thick training manual, salespeople are supposed to quote the weekly and monthly rental rates. The manual doesn't instruct employees to quote the total cost, and former store managers say they made sure they never did. In fact, in 40 states, the total isn't even on the price tag. (Ten states require that it be listed on price tags, a rule Rent-A-Center says it will honor in all 50 states by next month.) Instead, the manual instructs employees to focus on "features and benefits," such as Rent-A-Center's free delivery and repair, and most of all, the low weekly price.

But the advertised weekly price is designed to yield each store about 3½ times its cost of purchasing the merchandise from Rent-A-Center headquarters. The total is jacked up further by a one-time processing fee (typically $7.50) and late fees (typically $5). The total price is usually revealed only in the rental agreement that customers sign at the end of the sales process, former store managers say.

To boost Rent-A-Center's profits, employees also push a "customer protection" plan that offers minimal benefits but that 95% of customers end up subscribing to. "It's better than insurance," saleswoman Laura Daupino of the Bloomfield, N.J. store was overheard telling an unemployed welfare mother recently. Yet, unlike insurance, it doesn't replace stolen or destroyed items, or reimburse customers for their loss. It offers customers basically one benefit: It prevents Rent-A-Center from suing customers if goods are stolen or destroyed.

For Rent-A-Center, however, the benefit is considerably larger: The protection plan is a $29 million annual revenue booster, much of which drops to the bottom line, as does most of the $27 million racked up from the other fees, according to internal company financial documents.

Rent-A-Center has long justified its high prices by citing customer defaults and the costs associated with its free repairs. But part of Rent-A-Center's secret of success is that those costs are minimal. Internal documents show its service expenses ran 3.3% of rental revenue in fiscal 1993, though Rent-A-Center says the actual figure is closer to 10%. And its total inventory losses—from junked merchandise and "skips and stolens" (as in customers who skip town)—run a bit over 2% of revenue. * * *

Thorn executives say there is nothing insidious about Rent-A-Center's strategy of courting customers who are of limited means, and of treating them well. Customers receive "fantastic" service, say Sir Colin, who professes to be "always puzzled" why the rent-to-own industry is "badly regarded." Rent-A-Center, he adds, "treats them like kings and queens."

Customers like Carol Baker, a waitress at a resort hotel in Bolton Landing, N.Y., are appreciative. "The prices could be cheaper," says Ms. Baker, whose home is almost completely furnished by Rent-A-Center, "but they treat me like I'm a somebody."

Former employees and other customers see things differently. "The Rent-A-Center philosophy," says Mr. Comeaux, the former store manager in Virginia, "is that if you treat the customer like they're royalty, you can bleed them through the nose." * * *

Inevitably, some customers take on more than they can handle. So it is that behind every Rent-A-Center salesman lurks his doppelganger: Repo man.

Repossessions are never pretty, and the pre-Thorn era was no exception. But because of the ambitious targets, people who have worked under both regimes say, employees now push harder than ever. Customers typically make their payments every Saturday and, throughout the morning, store employees work the phones exacting promises from the tardy. In these conversations, former customers say, they have been harassed, intimidated and even threatened with violence. Robert Keeling, a former manager in Gasden, Ala., who was fired in March in part for carrying a gun, says that a "favorite ploy is falsely informing customers or their relatives that a warrant for arrest has been issued for the theft of rental property." * * *

On Halloween night in 1991, three Rent-A-Center employees in Utica, NY, dressed up, respectively, as the Cookie Monster, a gorilla and an alien life form and knocked on a customer's door. Once inside, they successfully repossessed a home-entertainment system on which payments hadn't been made in almost three months. Gary Gerhardt, the store manager who blessed this plan, calls the ruse "a last-ditch effort," adding, "it was the only way we could think to get someone in the door."

At the crack of dawn one Sunday, Mr. Myers, the store manager in Victorville, Calif., until March 1992, pulled off a particularly tough repossession by enlisting three burly Hell's Angels. He adds that in other instances he vented his spleen on delinquent customers who wouldn't come to the door by slathering superglue all over their deadbolts and doorknobs. (Messrs. Gerhardt and Myers both were fired, but over unrelated matters.)

The grueling routine grates on some Rent-A-Center employees. Mr. Baker, the former Maryland store manager, quit in disgust in 1991 after one of his employees repossessed a refrigerator from a welfare mother with an infant, plunking her meat and milk on the kitchen table. * * *

Yet another tactic in Rent-A-Center's repo repertoire is the "couch payment"—sexual favors exacted by employees in lieu of cash. Of 28 former store managers interviewed, six said the practice had occurred in their areas. [S]ome store employees have boasted that they "have gone out to the customers' homes, had sex with them, and then repo-ed the merchandise anyway." * * *

Alix M. Freedman, *A Marketing Giant Uses Its Sales Prowess To Profit on Poverty*, Wall Street Journal, Sept. 22, 1993, at A12. [Reprinted by permission of Wall Street Journal, © 1993 Dow Jones & Company, Inc. All Rights Reserved Worldwide.]

Sol Wachtler: Born in 1930, Sol Wachtler was elected to the New York State Supreme Court in 1968 and later served on the New York Court of Appeals, the state's highest court, where, in 1985, he was appointed Chief Judge. Wachtler, a highly respected jurist, famously observed that prosecutors have so much control that they could convince grand juries to "indict a ham sandwich." Wachtler struck down New York's "marital exemption" to rape (which "essentially allowed a man to rape his wife, even a wife with whom he was estranged, with absolute impunity"). See John M. Caher, King of the Mountain: The Rise, Fall, and Redemption of Chief Judge Sol Wachtler (1998).

Clifton Jones v. Star Credit Corp.

Supreme Court of New York, 1969.
59 Misc.2d 189.

■ WACHTLER, J. On August 31, 1965, the plaintiffs, who are welfare recipients, agreed to purchase a home freezer unit for $900 as the result of a visit from a salesman representing Your Shop At Home Service, Inc. With the addition of the time credit charges, credit life insurance, credit property insurance, and sales tax, the purchase price totaled $1,234.80. Thus far the plaintiffs have paid $619.88 toward their purchase. The defendant claims that with various added credit charges paid for an extension of time there is a balance of $819.81 still due from the plaintiffs. The uncontroverted proof at the trial established that the freezer unit, when purchased, had a maximum retail value of approximately $300. The question is whether this transaction and the resulting contract could be considered unconscionable within the meaning of § 2–302 of the Uniform Commercial Code which provides in part:

"(1) If the court as a matter of law finds the contract or any clause of the contract to have been unconscionable at the time it was made the court may refuse to enforce the contract, or it may enforce the remainder of the contract without the unconscionable clause, or it may so limit the application of any unconscionable clause as to avoid any unconscionable result.

"(2) When it is claimed or appears to the court that the contract or any clause thereof may be unconscionable the parties shall be afforded a reasonable opportunity to present evidence as to its commercial setting, purpose and effect to aid the court in making the determination." (L.1962, chap. 553, eff. Sept. 27, 1964).

There was a time when the shield of *caveat emptor* would protect the most unscrupulous in the marketplace—a time when the law, in granting parties unbridled latitude to make their own contracts, allowed exploitive and callous practices which shocked the conscience of both legislative bodies and the courts.

The effort to eliminate these practices has continued to pose a difficult problem. On the one hand it is necessary to recognize the importance of preserving the integrity of agreements and the fundamental right of parties to deal, trade, bargain, and contract. On the other hand there is the concern for the uneducated and often illiterate individual who is the victim of gross inequality of bargaining power, usually the poorest members of the community.

Concern for the protection of these consumers against overreaching by the small but hardy breed of merchants who would prey on them is not novel. The dangers of inequality of bargaining power were vaguely recognized in the early English common law when Lord Hardwicke wrote of a fraud, which "may be apparent from the intrinsic nature and subject of the bargain itself; such as no man in his senses and not under delusion would make." The English authorities on this subject were discussed in *Hume v. United States* (132 U.S. 406 [1889]), where the United States Supreme Court characterized these as "cases in which one party took advantage of the other's ignorance of arithmetic to impose upon him, and the fraud was apparent from the face of the contracts."

The law is beginning to fight back against those who once took advantage of the poor and illiterate without risk of either exposure or interference. From the common law doctrine of intrinsic fraud we have, over the years, developed common and statutory law which tells not only the buyer but also the seller to beware. This body of laws recognizes the importance of a free enterprise system but at the same time will provide the legal armor to protect and safeguard the prospective victim from the harshness of an unconscionable contract.

Section 2–302 of the Uniform Commercial Code enacts the moral sense of the community into the law of commercial transactions. It authorizes the court to find, as a matter of law, that a contract or a clause of a contract was "unconscionable at the time it was made," and upon so finding the court may refuse to enforce the contract, excise the objectionable clause or limit the application of the clause to avoid an unconscionable result. "The principle," states the Official Comment to this section, "is one of the prevention of oppression and unfair surprise." It permits a court to accomplish directly what heretofore was often accomplished by construction of language, manipulations of fluid rules of contract law and determinations based upon a presumed public policy.

There is no reason to doubt, moreover, that this section is intended to encompass the price term of the agreement. In addition to the fact that it has already been so applied . . . , the statutory language itself makes it clear that not only a clause of the contract, but the contract *in toto*, may be found unconscionable as a matter of law. Indeed, no other provision of an agreement more intimately touches upon the question of unconscionability than does the term regarding price.

Fraud, in the instant case, is not present; nor is it necessary under the statute. The question which presents itself is whether or not, under the circumstances of this case, the sale of a freezer unit having a retail value of $300 for $900 ($1,439.69 including credit charges and $18 sales tax) is unconscionable as a matter of law. The court believes it is.

Concededly, deciding the issue is substantially easier than explaining it. No doubt, the mathematical disparity between $300, which presumably includes a reasonable profit margin, and $900, which is exorbitant on its face, carries the greatest weight. Credit charges alone exceed by more than $100 the retail value of the freezer. These alone, may be sufficient to sustain the decision. Yet, a caveat is warranted lest we reduce the import of § 2–302 solely to a mathematical ratio formula. It may, at times, be that; yet it may also be much more. The very limited financial resources of the purchaser, known to the sellers at the time of the sale, is entitled to weight in the balance. Indeed, the value disparity itself leads inevitably to the felt conclusion that knowing advantage was taken of the plaintiffs. In addition, the meaningfulness of choice essential to the making of a contract can be negated by a gross inequality of bargaining power. (Williams v. Walker-Thomas Furniture Co., 121 U.S.App.D.C. 315.)

There is no question about the necessity and even the desirability of installment sales and the extension of credit. Indeed, there are many, including welfare recipients, who would be deprived of even the most basic conveniences without the use of these devices. Similarly, the retail merchant selling on installment or extending credit is expected to establish a pricing factor which will afford a degree of protection commensurate with the risk of selling to those who might be default prone. However, neither of these accepted premises can clothe the sale of this freezer with respectability.

Support for the court's conclusion will be found in a number of other cases already decided. In *American Home Imp., Inc. v. MacIver* [201 A.2d 886], the Supreme Court of New Hampshire held that a contract to install windows, a door and paint, for the price of $2,568.60, of which $809.60 constituted interest and carrying charges and $800 was a salesman's commission was unconscionable as a matter of law. In *State by Lefkowitz v. ITM, Inc.* [275 N.Y.S.2d 303], a deceptive and fraudulent scheme was involved, but standing alone, the court held that the sale of a vacuum cleaner, among other things, costing the defendant $140 and sold by it for $749 cash or $920.52 on time purchase was unconscionable as a matter of law. Finally, in *Frosti-Fresh Corp. v. Reynoso* [281 N.Y.S.2d 964], the sale of a refrigerator costing the seller $348 for $900 plus credit charges of $245.88 was unconscionable as a matter of law.

* * *

Having already [been] paid more than $600 toward the purchase of this $300 freezer unit, it is apparent that the defendant has already been amply compensated. In accordance with the statute, the application of the payment provision should be limited to amounts already paid by the plaintiffs and the contract be reformed and amended by changing the payments called for therein to equal the amount of payment actually so paid by the plaintiffs.

Submit judgment on notice.

NOTES

(1) Upon what grounds was the price term found to be unconscionable? Although the facts reveal that the plaintiff was on welfare and that the sale was probably made at home, the court says nothing further about the relative bargaining capacities (e.g., education, language skills, health, or intelligence) of the parties. Does this support the "felt conclusion that knowing advantage was taken of the plaintiff?" If the contract price was disclosed and the plaintiff could have obtained a comparable freezer from another seller for $300, is judicial review of the adequacy of the exchange justified? What else do you need to know before that question can be answered?

(2) Frank P. Darr argues that there are three interrelated questions at work in price unconscionability cases: (1) Is there a community norm as to price, i.e., a range of reasonableness? (2) What was the quality of the bargaining process in the particular case? and (3) If the market has not set a competitive price, what is the likelihood of a market correction over time? Frank P. Darr, *Unconscionability and Price Fairness*, 30 Hous. L. Rev. 1819 (1994). In *Jones v. Star Credit*, the problem appears to be deficiencies in the bargaining process rather than the absence of a community norm or a market failure. But what are the defects? We return to the unconscionability problem in Chapter Four.

(3) *Paternalism.* According to James Gordley, the state is paternalistic when it "circumscribes or influences the choice a citizen would otherwise

make because it believes the citizen's choice is wrong, whether through a want of prudence or of some other virtue." James Gordley, *Morality and Contract: The Question of Paternalism*, 48 Wm. & Mary L. Rev. 1733, 1743 (2007). On the other hand, the state is not paternalistic when it intervenes to achieve a fair distribution of resources or fair contract terms rather than to question the value of a citizen's choice. What about the case of *Jones v. Star Credit*?

> [T]he state need not be acting paternalistically when it refuses to enforce a contract voluntarily entered into, at least on the terms to which the parties have agreed. It may merely be doing commutative justice. Take the case in which a person pays more or receives less than the market price. One could regard that price as unfair for the same reason as the late scholastics; it changes the distribution of purchasing power between the parties. The state might give relief simply because the price is unjust. In doing so, it is not questioning the judgment of the disadvantaged party as to what the other party's performance was worth. Whatever value that party personally places on that performance, he would not have paid more or accepted less than the market price except, as Lessius said, if he acted out of necessity or ignorance. In the case of necessity, he did not have access to the market. An example of necessity is the person in distress who must deal with only one possible rescuer. In the case of ignorance, he did not know the market price. In a well known American case, a court gave relief to a party who bought a refrigerator from a door-to-door salesman for three times its local retail price. It is possible, of course, that the disadvantaged party found himself acting out of necessity or ignorance because of his own imprudence or some other vice. He may need to be rescued because he was imprudent or rash. He may not know the market price because he imprudently failed to investigate or lacked the will power or courage to tell the door-to-door salesman to go away until he had had time to do so. But if he had access to the market or had known the market price, he would never have paid what he did. The state can conclude it is unjust to take advantage of his necessity or ignorance without ever questioning his own judgment of how he should spend his money or what performance is worth to him personally. In giving relief, the state is not acting paternalistically in the sense described earlier.

Gordley, *Morality and Contract*, 48 Wm. & Mary L. Rev. at 1745–46 (footnotes omitted).

(4) The Federal Trade Commission, by regulation, requires a "cooling off period" for door-to-door sales. The seller must inform the consumer in writing and in conspicuous type of the following: "You, the buyer, may cancel this transaction at any time prior to midnight of the third business day after the date of this transaction. See the attached notice of cancellation form for an explanation of this right." 16 C.F.R. § 429.1(a) (March 1, 2012).

Section 4(c) of the Uniform Consumer Sales Practices Act provides that "in determining whether an act or practice is unconscionable, the court shall consider circumstances such as the following of which the supplier knew or had reason to know: (1) that he took advantage of the inability of the consumer reasonably to protect his interests because of his physical infirmity, ignorance, illiteracy, inability to understand the language of an agreement or similar factors; (2) that when the consumer transaction was entered into the price grossly exceeded the price at which similar property or services were readily obtainable in similar transactions by like consumers; . . . (4) that when the consumer transaction was entered into there was no reasonable probability of payment of the obligation in full by the consumer."

(5) In *California Grocers v. Bank of America*, 22 Cal.App.4th 205 (1994), defendant bank charged customers a $3 fee for certain returned deposit items (DIRs). The California Grocers Association, a trade group of retail and wholesale grocers, attacked the fee. In holding that the fee was not unconscionable ("not so high as to shock the conscience"), the court relied upon two determinations: First, there was "free" competition among banks in California and the $3 fee was at the low end of similar fees charged by other banks; second, the "$3 fee is not so exorbitant as to shock the conscience." Even though the cost of processing a DIR was only $1.50, the markup was "only 100 percent." "This may be a generous profit, but it is wholly within the range of commonly accepted notions of fair profitability." The court noted that price unconscionability cases "generally involve much greater price-value disparities" and cited *Jones v. Star Credit* for the proposition that a "sale of a freezer at triple its retail value" was unconscionable. 22 Cal.App.4th at 216.

(6) The Supreme Court of Arizona has read UCC § 2–302 in conjunction with UCC § 2–719(3) to conclude that "a claim of unconscionability can be established with a showing of substantive unconscionability alone, especially in cases involving either price-cost disparity or limitation of remedies." Further: "If only procedural irregularities are present, it may be more appropriate to analyze the claims under the doctrines of fraud, misrepresentation, duress, and mistake, although such irregularities can make a case of procedural unconscionability." Maxwell v. Fidelity Financial Services, 184 Ariz. 82, 90 (1995). Do you agree with this reading of the Code?

In re Louis Fleet v. United States Consumer Council

United States District Court, Eastern District of Pennsylvania, 1989.
95 B.R. 319.

■ FULLAM, CHIEF JUDGE.

* * *

IV. THE FEE CHARGED BY USCC CONSTITUTED AN UNCONSCIONABLE PRICE AND A FRAUD IN VIOLATION OF NJ UDAP

The NJ UDAP [unfair and deceptive acts and practices statute, N.J.S.A. 56:8–1 et seq.] prohibits any "unconscionable commercial practice," as well as deceptive and fraudulent conduct used in the sale or advertisement of merchandise. . . .

While the term "unconscionability" is not specifically defined in either the NJ UDAP or the UCC, it has been characterized as "an amorphous concept obviously designed to establish a broad business ethic." Kugler v. Romain, 279 A.2d 640, 651 (N.J. 1971). Thus, the New Jersey Supreme Court, in *Romain*, concluded that the legislature expected the courts to interpret the concept of unconscionability "liberally so as to effectuate the public purpose, and to pour content into it on a case-by-case basis." Id. at 651 . . . As one commentator noted:

> The Courts have always avoided hampering themselves by defining or laying down as a general proposition what shall be held to constitute fraud. Fraud is infinite in variety. The fertility of man's invention in devising new schemes of fraud is so great, that the courts have always declined to define it, or to define undue influence, which is one of its many varieties, reserving to themselves the liberty to deal with it under whatever form it may present itself.

Kerr, Fraud and Mistake (7th ed. 1952). . . .

Despite the amorphous nature of the concept of unconscionability, it has been defined as establishing a standard of conduct contemplating "good faith, honesty in fact, and observance of fair dealings." . . . As the Court in *Romain* noted, "[t]he need for application of the standard is most acute when the professional seller is seeking the trade of those most subject to exploitation—the uneducated, the inexperienced and the people of low incomes." 279 A.2d at 652.[20] The Uniform Consumer Sales Practice Act (hereinafter "UCSPA") provides that, in determining whether an act or practice is unconscionable, the court should consider, among other factors, whether "the price grossly exceeded the price at which similar property or services were readily obtainable in similar transactions by like consumers." UCSPA, § 4(c)(2). . . .

The Plaintiffs maintain that the fee charged by USCC was an unconscionable price for the services provided. The seminal New Jersey case on price unconscionability is *Romain*. That case involved the door-to-door sales of so-called educational books for children. . . . Sales efforts were directed at minority group consumers and consumers of limited education and economic means. . . . The seller was charging between $250.00 and $280.00 for books with a value of about $110.00. . . . Evidence was presented that the books sold were of little or no

---

[20] The court in *Romain* recognized that "[t]he deception, misrepresentation, and unconscionable practices engaged in by professional sellers seeking mass distribution of many types of consumer goods frequently produce an adverse effect on large segments of disadvantaged and poorly educated people, who are wholly devoid of expertise and least able to understand or to cope with the ' "sale-oriented," ' ' "extroverted" ' and unethical solicitors bent on capitalizing upon their weakness, who therefore most need protection against predatory practices." 279 A.2d at 652.

educational value to children in the age-group and socio-economic position targeted by the seller. . . .

The *Romain* court found the seller's price to be unconscionable, and further held that such price unconscionability constituted a consumer fraud prohibited by NJ UDAP. . . . In so holding, the court reasoned that:

> [i]n deciding whether defendant, contrary to the statute, used any deception, fraud, false pretense, or misrepresentation, or whether he concealed, suppressed or omitted any material fact in connection with the sales to book purchaser, the price charged the consumer is only one element to be consider [sic]. If the price is grossly excessive in relation to the seller's costs, and if in addition the good sold have little or no value to the consumer for the purpose for which he was persuaded to buy them and which the seller pretended they would serve, the price paid by the consumer takes on even more serious characteristics of imposition.

279 A.2d at 644.

We find the facts in the present case to be even more indicative of imposition. The consumers who turned to USCC for help were financially troubled and distraught. Some were unemployed or disabled. Many were facing the loss of their homes through foreclosure. USCC, through its marketing scheme, represented that it could provide help to these consumers, help which USCC could not and did not provide. USCC then charged consumers $195.00 to $260.00 simply for referring them to an attorney. Such a referral could be obtained for free through a bar association lawyer referral service. . . .

In light of the circumstances of the present case, we have no difficulty concluding that the fee charged by USCC constitutes an unconscionable price for its services and a fraud in violation of NJ UDAP.

* * *

NJ UDAP also provides that, when a practice is found to be unlawful under the Act, then the court shall award treble damages plus attorneys fees, filing fees and reasonable costs to any person who has suffered any ascertainable loss of moneys or property. N.J.S.A. 56:8–19. . . . We therefore conclude that assessment of such damages and costs is not only appropriate but statutorily mandated in the present matter.

* * *

NOTES

(1) Litigants claiming price unconscionability have fared better under regulatory statutes than under UCC § 2–302 standing alone. See, e.g., McRaild v. Shepard Lincoln Mercury, 141 Mich.App. 406 (1985) (trade of an automobile valued at $17,000 plus $11,000 paid in cash for a house determined to have a minimum value of $43,000 violated Michigan

Consumer Protection Act); People by Abrams v. Two Wheel Corp., 71 N.Y.2d 693 (1988) (sale of 100 generators at inflated prices ranging from 4% to 67% over the base prices violated New York price-gouging statute); Ramirez-Eames v. Hover, 108 N.M. 520 (1989) (agreement to pay $850 monthly rental for apartment, where market value was $725, violated Uniform Owner-Resident Relations Act).

(2)   Whereas most state UDAP statutes target "unfair and deceptive" acts and practices, when it passed the Dodd-Frank Act, Congress charged the Consumer Financial Protection Bureau with protecting consumers "from unfair, deceptive, or abusive acts and practices." 12 U.S.C. § 5511(b)(2). It remains to be seen whether the CFPB will interpret "abusive" to extend beyond the familiar adjectives "unfair" and "deceptive."

Comment: Procedural Aspects of UCC § 2–302

UCC § 2–302(1) provides that if "the court as a matter of law" finds the contract to have been unconscionable "at the time it was made," it may refuse to enforce it. Thus, unconscionability is an issue of law to be decided by the court, and the court's focus is upon the situation as it existed at the time the contract was made. Because unconscionability is a question of law, review by an appellate court is *de novo*.

Ordinarily, a party will plead unconscionability as an affirmative defense, though a court may raise the issue *sua sponte*. Maxwell v. Fid. Fin. Servs., Inc., 184 Ariz. 82, 87 n.2 (1995). Although in some cases the pleadings may be sufficient to permit a court to resolve the issue, in the usual case there will be a hearing at which the parties present evidence for the trial judge's consideration. What kind of evidence? The Code does not say, other than that it should pertain to the contract's "commercial setting, purpose and effect." UCC § 2–302(2). This suggests a broad inquiry. As an Arizona court commented:

> It was the obvious intention of the drafters and our Legislature that the court have the widest latitude in hearing evidence on the issue of commercial setting in cases where unconscionability was claimed, either in whole or in part. * * * In this context, while serious questions can be raised, and have indeed been raised here, concerning the admissibility of some of the evidence under general contract law terms (the parol evidence rule), the trial court was obviously correct in allowing the widest latitude in receiving evidence on the issue of commercial setting and unconscionability.

Raybond Electronics, Inc. v. Glen-Mar Door Manufacturing Co., 22 Ariz.App. 409, 416 (1974). The right of the parties to present evidence of the contract's commercial setting, purpose, and effect may be of particular importance to one who seeks to defend against unconscionability, for evidence of commercial context may demonstrate that a contract or clause which superficially seems to be one-sided in character is actually quite reasonable when viewed in the totality of the circumstances. See, e.g., In re Elkins-Dell Manufacturing Co., 253 F.Supp. 864 (E.D.Pa. 1966).

The burden of proof is said to be upon the one who claims the unconscionability. This means, in practice, that one claiming an unconscionability defense must come forward with the evidence showing a *prima facie* case. The burden would then seem to shift to the other party to persuade the court that the contract or clause was conscionable.

Finally, if there is a judicial finding of unconscionability, what are the remedial consequences? The Code states that the court "may refuse to enforce the contract, or it may enforce the remainder of the contract without the unconscionable clause, or it may so limit the application of any unconscionable clause as to avoid any unconscionable result." UCC § 2–302(1). Essentially, the aggrieved party is limited to defensive weapons. As illustrated in *Jones*, however, the court may do more than simply refuse to enforce the contract or clause. There the court effectively reformed the contract by holding that the price was to be equal to the amount already paid. See also Vockner v. Erickson, 712 P.2d 379 (Alaska 1986) (changing amount of installment payment in land purchase agreement which was deemed unconscionable under section 208 of the revised Restatement).

There is, evidently, no right to recover damages under UCC § 2–302. See, e.g., Cowin Equipment Co. v. General Motors Corp., 734 F.2d 1581 (11th Cir. 1984); Best v. United States National Bank, 78 Or.App. 1 (1986). Although UCC § 2–302 does not specifically authorize money damages, it does authorize a court to "enforce the contract without the unconscionable clause." Thus, after striking an unconscionable clause, a court may then award damages for breach of the contract without that clause. Langemeier v. National Oats, Inc., 775 F.2d 975 (8th Cir. 1985). Finally, as illustrated by *In re Fleet*, damages might be recovered under a state's deceptive trade practices statute, thirteen of which expressly prohibit unconscionable practices generally. See Jonathan A. Sheldon and Carolyn L. Carter, Unfair and Deceptive Acts and Practices, Unfair and Deceptive Acts and Practices, Appendix A (7th ed. 2008) (Alabama; Arkansas; Florida; Idaho; Kansas; Kentucky; Michigan; New Jersey; New Mexico; Ohio; Oregon; Texas; Utah).

PROBLEM: THE CASE OF THE LIFE-CARE CONTRACT

Kathleen MacKay, age 79, visited a number of retirement facilities in the Santa Fe and Albuquerque areas. She liked La Vida Llena the best. She took several weeks to study the Residence Agreement that the facility used and discussed the proposed agreement with her friends, though not with an attorney. On March 2, she signed the agreement and made a deposit toward the entry fee; on June 16, upon payment of the remainder of the $36,950 entry fee, she moved in. She became sick on December 29th of that year, and two days later she died.

Under the Residence Agreement, the entry fee entitled Mrs. MacKay to occupy a one-bedroom unit for the rest of her life, and guaranteed her admission to the La Vida Llena Nursing Care Center whenever required. She was also obliged to pay a monthly service fee of $537.00 to cover meals, laundry, etc. She had the right to terminate the agreement upon 30-days' notice if she was unable to live alone and if monthly payments were current. La Vida Llena would then refund the entrance fee less "10% plus 1% for each month of residency." There was no refund of entry fee upon a resident's death.

Mrs. MacKay's personal representative sought a refund of the entrance fee on the ground that the agreement was an unconscionable adhesion contract. What result? See Guthmann v. LaVida Llena, 103 N.M. 506 (1985).

Comment: Beyond Commercial Transactions—Separation Agreements

After fifteen years of marriage and the birth of three children, Charles and Kathleen Williams experienced marital difficulties and decided to separate. Kathleen's lawyer prepared a separation agreement which Charles signed without the advice of counsel, evidently with the hope that his signing might help lead to a resolution of their problems and bring about a reconciliation. Under the agreement, Charles was required to transfer his interest in their home to Kathleen, together with the contents of the house and their automobile. In addition, Charles agreed to pay the mortgage on the house, the car loan and all other marital obligations. In sum, under the agreement, the wife was to receive property valued at approximately $131,000, while the husband was to retain property valued at about $1,100. Indeed, his total weekly financial obligations under the agreement exceeded his weekly net salary.

In a later divorce action, Charles sought to have the separation agreement set aside; Kathleen asked that it be incorporated into the divorce decree. The trial court found the agreement to be unconscionable, and this was upheld on appeal with the court citing Restatement (Second) § 208: "If a contract or term thereof is unconscionable at the time the contract is made a court may refuse to enforce the contract, or may enforce the remainder of the contract without the unconscionable term, or may so limit the application of any unconscionable term as to avoid any unconscionable result." Williams v. Williams, 306 Md. 332, 338 (1986).

A Virginia court has had this to say on the topic:

In separation agreements particularly, unconscionability may be of heightened importance. While no fiduciary duty exists between the parties, marriage and divorce create a relationship which is particularly susceptible to overreaching and oppression. . . . Professor Homer Clark suggests three reasons for this special emphasis. First, the relationship between husband and wife is not the usual relationship that exists between parties to ordinary commercial contracts. Particularly when the negotiation is between the parties rather than between their lawyers, the relationship creates a situation ripe for subtle overreaching and misrepresentation. Behavior that might not constitute fraud or duress in an arm's length context may suffice to invalidate a grossly inequitable agreement where the relationship is utilized to overreach or take advantage of a situation in order to achieve an oppressive result. Second, Clark notes that unlike commercial contracts, the state itself has an interest in the terms and enforceability of separation agreements. If either spouse is left in necessitous circumstances by a separation agreement, that spouse and any children might become public charges. Finally, Clark notes that courts have recognized that the law should encourage the resolution of property issues through the process of negotiation rather than through litigation. "These processes are more likely to succeed if the parties and their lawyers know in advance that . . . fairness will be insisted upon by the courts when they are called upon to approve the agreement." Clark [The Law of Domestic Relations in the United States, 1987] § 19.2.

Derby v. Derby, 8 Va.App. 19, 29 (1989).

Misty Ferguson v. Countrywide Credit Industries, Inc.

United States Court of Appeals, Ninth Circuit, 2002.
298 F.3d 778.

■ PREGERSON, CIRCUIT JUDGE. Misty Ferguson ("Ferguson") filed a complaint against Countrywide Credit Industries, Inc. ("Countrywide") and her supervisor, Leo DeLeon ("DeLeon"), alleging causes of action under federal and state law for sexual harassment, retaliation, and hostile work environment. Countrywide filed a petition for an order compelling arbitration of Ferguson's claims. The district court denied Countrywide's petition on the grounds that Countrywide's arbitration agreement is unenforceable based on the doctrine of unconscionability and that Ferguson cannot be compelled to arbitrate her Title VII employment discrimination claims. Countrywide appeals this decision. We have jurisdiction under 9 U.S.C. § 16(a)(1)(B). We review *de novo* a district court's denial of a motion to compel arbitration, . . . and affirm on the ground that the arbitration agreement is unconscionable.

I. FACTUAL and PROCEDURAL HISTORY

Ferguson filed a complaint against Countrywide and DeLeon, alleging causes of action for sexual harassment, retaliation, and hostile work environment under Title VII of the Civil Rights Act of 1964 and 1991, 42 U.S.C. §§ 2000e–2(a), 2000e 3 & 1981a(c), and the California Fair Employment and Housing Act, Cal. Gov't Code §§ 12900 et seq. ("FEHA").

Countrywide filed a petition to compel arbitration of Ferguson's claims. When Ferguson was hired she was required to sign Countrywide's Conditions of Employment, which states in relevant part: "I understand that in order to work at Countrywide I must execute an arbitration agreement." Countrywide's arbitration agreement ("the arbitration agreement") contains the following relevant clauses:

Paragraph 1. Agreement to Arbitrate; Designated Claims:

"Except as otherwise provided in this Agreement, the Company and Employee hereby consent to the resolution by arbitration of all claims or controversies for which a federal or state court . . . would be authorized to grant relief. . . ."

The arbitration agreement then outlines which claims are covered by the agreement[1] and which claims are not covered.[2]

[In the agreement, the parties agreed, *inter alia*, to (i) waive all rights to a "trial before a jury;" (ii) have arbitration as "the parties' exclusive remedy;" and (iii) limit discovery "to three depositions and an aggregate of 30 discovery requests of any kind."]

In her answer to Countrywide's petition to compel arbitration, Ferguson denied that she signed the arbitration agreement and requested a jury trial on that issue, pursuant to section 4 of the Federal Arbitration Act ("FAA"). Countrywide filed reply documents in support of the petition, and submitted evidence that Ferguson entered the agreement.

The district court . . . denied Countrywide's petition to compel arbitration. Although the court found that Ferguson raised a genuine dispute regarding the making of the arbitration agreement, it ruled that, assuming the agreement does exist: (1) the arbitration agreement is unenforceable because it is unconscionable under *Armendariz v. Foundation Health Psychcare Services, Inc.*, 24 Cal.4th 83 (Cal. 2000); and (2) under the Ninth Circuit's holding in *Duffield v. Robertson Stephens & Co.*, 144 F.3d 1182, 1190 (9th Cir. 1998), Ferguson cannot be compelled to arbitrate her Title VII claims. . . .

---

[1] *Agreement to Arbitrate; Designated Claims:* "The Claims covered by this Agreement include, but are not limited to, claims for wages or other compensation due; claims for breach of any contract or covenant, express or implied; tort claims; claims for discrimination or harassment on bases which include but are not limited to race, sex, sexual orientation, religion, national origin, age, marital status, disability or medical condition; claims for benefits . . . and claims for violation of any federal, state or other governmental constitution, statute, ordinance, regulation, or public policy."

[2] *Claims Not Covered by This Agreement:* "This Agreement does not apply to or cover claims for workers' compensation or unemployment compensation benefits; claims resulting from the default of any obligation of the Company or the Employee under a mortgage loan which was granted and/or serviced by the Company; claims for injunctive and/or other equitable relief for intellectual property violations, unfair competition and/or the use and/or unauthorized disclosure of trade secrets or confidential information; or claims based upon an employee pension or benefit plan that either (1) contains an arbitration or other non-judicial resolution procedure, in which case the provisions of such plan shall apply, or (2) is underwritten by a commercial insurer which decides claims."

II. UNCONSCIONABILITY

A. The district court correctly concluded that Countrywide's arbitration agreement was unenforceable because it is unconscionable under California law.

The FAA compels judicial enforcement of a wide range of written arbitration agreements. Section 2 of the FAA provides, in relevant part, that arbitration agreements "shall be valid, irrevocable, and enforceable, save upon such grounds that exist at law or in equity for the revocation of any contract." 9 U.S.C. § 2. In determining the validity of an agreement to arbitrate, federal courts "should apply ordinary state-law principles that govern the formation of contracts." First Options of Chicago, Inc. v. Kaplan, 514 U.S. 938, 944 (1995). "Thus, generally applicable defenses, such as . . . unconscionability, may be applied to invalidate arbitration agreements without contravening § 2 [of the FAA]." Doctor's Assocs., Inc. v. Casarotto, 517 U.S. 681, 687 (1996).

California courts may invalidate an arbitration clause under the doctrine of unconscionability. This doctrine, codified by the California Legislature in California Civil Code § 1670.5(a), provides:

> if the court as a matter of law finds the contract or any clause of the contract to have been unconscionable at the time it was made, the court may refuse to enforce the contract, or may enforce the remainder of the contract without the unconscionable clause, or it may so limit the application of any unconscionable clause as to avoid any unconscionable result.

This statute, however, does not define unconscionability. Instead, we look to the California Supreme Court's decision in *Armendariz*, 24 Cal.4th 83, which provides the definitive pronouncement of California law on unconscionability to be applied to mandatory arbitration agreements, such as the one at issue in this case. In order to render a contract unenforceable under the doctrine of unconscionability, there must be both a procedural and substantive element of unconscionability. . . . These two elements, however, need not both be present in the same degree. . . . Thus, for example, "the more substantively oppressive the contract term, the less evidence of procedural unconscionability is required to come to the conclusion that the term is unenforceable." Armendariz, 6 P.3d at 690.

1. Procedural Unconscionability

Procedural unconscionability "concerns the manner in which the contract was negotiated and the circumstances of the parties at that time." Kinney v. United Healthcare Servs., Inc., 83 Cal.Rptr.2d 348, 352–53 (Ct.App. 1999). A determination of whether a contract is procedurally unconscionable focuses on two factors: oppression and surprise. " 'Oppression' arises from an inequality of bargaining power which results in no real negotiation and an absence of meaningful choice. 'Surprise' involves the extent to which the supposedly agreed-upon terms of the bargain are hidden in the prolix printed form drafted by the party seeking to enforce the disputed terms." Stirlen v. Supercuts, Inc., 60 Cal.Rptr.2d 138, 145 (Ct.App. 1997).

In *Circuit City Stores, Inc. v. Adams*, 279 F.3d 889, 892 (9th Cir. 2002), cert. denied, 122 S.Ct. 2329 (2002), we held that the arbitration agreement at issue satisfied the elements of procedural unconscionability under California law. We found the agreement to be procedurally unconscionable because:

> Circuit City, which possesses considerably more bargaining power than nearly all of its employees or applicants, drafted the contract and uses it as its standard arbitration agreement for all of its new employees. The agreement is a prerequisite to employment, and job applicants are not permitted to modify the agreement's terms—they must take the contract or leave it. . . .

In the present case, as in *Circuit City*, the arbitration agreement was imposed as a condition of employment and was non-negotiable.

Countrywide contends that there was no element of "surprise" or "oppression" in its arbitration agreement because Ferguson had "ample time to consider alternatives to Countrywide's terms of employment" and the contract was "written in plain language." A California appellate court recently rejected these arguments, holding that whether the plaintiff had an opportunity to decline the defendant's contract and instead to enter into a contract with another party that does not include the offending terms is not the relevant test for procedural unconscionability. . . . Instead, California courts have consistently held that where a party in a position of unequal bargaining power is presented with an offending clause without the opportunity for meaningful negotiation, oppression and, therefore, procedural unconscionability, are present. * * * Because Ferguson was in a position of unequal bargaining power and was presented with offending contract terms without an opportunity to negotiate, the district court in the instant case correctly found Countrywide's arbitration agreement procedurally unconscionable.

2.   Substantive Unconscionability

Substantive unconscionability "focuses on the terms of the agreement and whether those terms are so one-sided as to shock the conscience. . . ."

* * *

a.   One-sided coverage of arbitration agreement

Countrywide's arbitration agreement specifically covers claims for breach of express or implied contracts or covenants, tort claims, claims of discrimination or harassment based on race, sex, age, or disability, and claims for violation of any federal, state, or other governmental constitution, statute, ordinance, regulation, or public policy. On the other hand, the arbitration agreement specifically excludes claims for workers' compensation or unemployment compensation benefits, injunctive and/or other equitable relief for intellectual property violations, unfair competition and/or the use and/or unauthorized disclosure of trade secrets or confidential information. . . .

Countrywide's arbitration agreement was unfairly one-sided and, therefore, substantively unconscionable because the agreement compels arbitration of the claims employees are most likely to bring against Countrywide . . . [but] exempts from arbitration the claims Countrywide is most likely to bring against its employees. Further, we . . . conclude that Countrywide's justifications for its one-sided arbitration agreement are not persuasive.

b.   Arbitration Fees

In *Armendariz*, the California Supreme Court held that:

> when an employer imposes mandatory arbitration as a condition of employment, the arbitration agreement or arbitration process cannot generally require the employee to bear any *type* of expense that the employee would not be required to bear if he or she were free to bring the action in court. This rule will ensure that employees bringing [discrimination] claims will not be deterred by costs greater than the usual costs incurred during litigation, costs that are essentially imposed on an employee by the employer.

Armendariz, 6 P.3d at 687.

Countrywide's arbitration agreement has a provision that requires the employee to "pay to NAF [National Arbitration Forum] its filing fee up to a maximum of $125.00 when the Claim is filed. The Company shall pay for the first hearing day. All other arbitration costs shall be shared equally by the Company and the Employee." Countrywide argues that this provision is not so one-sided as to "shock the conscience" and, therefore, is enforceable. However, *Armendariz* holds that a fee provision is unenforceable when the employee bears *any* expense beyond the usual costs associated with bringing an action in court. Id. As indicated in Ferguson's opposition to the petition to compel arbitration and in her brief, NAF imposes multiple fees which would bring the cost of arbitration for Ferguson into the thousands of dollars.[7] Moreover, on remand in *Circuit City*, we held that a fee allocation scheme which requires the employee to split the arbitrator's fees with the employer would alone render an arbitration agreement substantively unconscionable. . . .

* * *

---

[7]   . . . Parties to arbitration are often charged two or three thousand dollars per day in arbitration "forum fees," since arbitrators typically charge $300–400 per hour. . . .

c. One-sided discovery provision

Ferguson also argues that the discovery provision in the arbitration agreement is one-sided and, therefore, unconscionable. The discovery provision states that "[a] deposition of a corporate representative shall be limited to no more than four designated subjects," but does not impose a similar limitation on depositions of employees. Ferguson also notes that the arbitration agreement sets mutual limitations (e.g., no more than three depositions) and mutual advantages (e.g., unlimited expert witnesses) which favor Countrywide because it is in a superior position to gather information regarding its business practices and employees' conduct, and has greater access to funds to pay for expensive expert witnesses.

Ferguson urges this court to affirm the district court's ruling that the discovery provision is unconscionable on the ground that the limitations and mutual advantages on discovery are unfairly one-sided and have no commercial justification other than "maximizing employer advantage," which is an improper basis for such differences under *Armendariz*, 99 Cal.Rptr.2d 745. Countrywide argues to the contrary that the arbitration agreement provides for ample discovery by employees.

In *Armendariz*, the California Supreme Court held that employees are "at least entitled to discovery sufficient to adequately arbitrate their statutory claims, including access to essential documents and witnesses." Armendariz, 6 P.3d at 684. Adequate discovery, however, does not mean unfettered discovery. As *Armendariz* recognized, an arbitration agreement might specify "something less than the full panoply of discovery provided in [California] Code of Civil Procedure." Id.

[The court found that Countrywide's discovery provisions may afford Ferguson adequate discovery to vindicate her claims.]

Nevertheless, we recognize an insidious pattern in Countrywide's arbitration agreement. Not only do these discovery provisions appear to favor Countrywide at the expense of its employees, but the entire agreement seems drawn to provide Countrywide with undue advantages should an employment-related dispute arise. Aside from merely availing itself of the cost-saving benefits of arbitration, Countrywide has sought to advantage itself substantively by tilting the playing field.

* * * [I]n the context of an arbitration agreement which unduly favors Countrywide at every turn, we find that their inclusion reaffirms our belief that the arbitration agreement as a whole is substantively unconscionable.

B. The offending provisions of Countrywide's arbitration agreement cannot be severed or limited.

Countrywide argues that, if we conclude that certain provisions of its arbitration agreement are unconscionable, we should sever those offending provisions and enforce the remainder of the contract. Under California Civil Code § 1670.5(a):

> If the court as a matter of law finds the contract or any clause of the contract to have been unconscionable at the time it was made the court may refuse to enforce the contract, or it may enforce the remainder of the contract without the unconscionable clause, or it may so limit the application of any unconscionable clause as to avoid any unconscionable result.

Under this section, however, a court may, in its discretion, "refuse to enforce the contract as a whole if it is permeated by the unconscionability." Legislative Committee Comment on § 1670.5.

In *Armendariz*, the California Supreme Court declined to sever the unconscionable provisions of an arbitration agreement for two reasons, both of which are applicable to Countrywide's arbitration agreement. First, the court found that there was more than one unlawful provision and that "such multiple defects indicate a systematic effort to impose arbitration on an employee not simply as an alternative to litigation, but as an inferior forum that works to the employer's advantage." Armendariz, 6 P.3d at 696–97. Second, the agreement's lack of mutuality so permeated the contract that "the court would have to, in effect, reform the contract, not through severance or restriction, but by augmenting it with additional terms." Id. at 697.

In the instant case, the lack of mutuality regarding the type of claims that must be arbitrated, the fee provision, and the discovery provision, so permeate Countrywide's arbitration agreement that we are unable to sever its offending provisions. * * * For these . . . reasons, we find that Countrywide's arbitration agreement is so permeated with unconscionable clauses that we cannot remove the unconscionable taint from the agreement. . . .

The district court's denial of Countrywide's petition to compel arbitration on the ground that Countrywide's arbitration agreement is unenforceable under the doctrine of unconscionability is AFFIRMED.

NOTES

(1) *Employment Arbitration.* The *Ferguson* case is but one example of a judicial determination that a standard form arbitration clause contained in a standard form contract is both procedurally and substantively unconscionable. The reality is that standard form arbitration clauses are present in more and more contracts between individuals and organizations. In addition to employment contracts, they appear in contracts between investors and broker-dealers, customers and banks, holders and credit card issuers, and patients and HMOs, to name a few.

It is difficult to argue that these clauses are per se substantively unconscionable. Arbitration clauses remove disputes from crowded court dockets to arbitrators, who are required to apply the law and able to reach a decision more quickly and with less expense. In fact, there is a strong policy favoring arbitration under the FAA. In short, arbitration clauses are a far cry from the "cross-collateral" and "add-on" clauses found in the contracts of Mrs. Williams in *Walker-Thomas*.

One problem with this is, of course, that the individual, even if well informed, cannot bargain over the clause and cannot obtain the job, or the investment opportunity, or the bank account, or the credit card without assenting to the clause. Another problem is that to the extent that agreements to arbitrate include regulatory provisions designed to protect the individual, such as Title VII claims (which they frequently do), the courts have sent them to arbitration, where decisions of the arbitrators on the merits are usually not subject to judicial review. The final problem is one identified by the court in *Ferguson*: arbitration clauses sometimes impose unreasonable cost burdens and are frequently drafted to favor the organization. They don't prevent the individual's rights from being vindicated before the arbitrators, but they impose limitations and burdens that impede vindication. Thus, the adhesion aspect of the consent and the (potentially) one-sided nature of the clause itself, when coupled with a core characteristic of arbitration, waiver of the right to a jury trial, no class actions and limited judicial review of the decision, can undercut the initial assumption that "arbitration is good."

(2) *Empirical Evidence.* A 2011 study of 3,945 employment arbitration cases administered by the American Arbitration Association found the following:

> (1) the employee win rate among the cases was 21.4 percent, which is lower than employee win rates reported in employment litigation trials; (2) in cases won by employees, the median award amount was $36,500 and the mean was $109,858, both of which are substantially lower than award amounts reported in employment litigation; (3) mean time to disposition in arbitration was 284.4 days for cases that settled and 361.5 days for cases decided after a hearing, which is substantially shorter than times to disposition in litigation; (4) mean arbitration fees were $6,340 per case overall, $11,070 for cases disposed of by an award following a hearing, and in 97 percent of these cases the employer paid 100 percent of the arbitration fees beyond a small filing fee, pursuant to AAA procedures. * * * The results [also] provide strong evidence of a repeat employer effect in which employee win rates and award amounts are significantly lower where the employer is involved in multiple arbitration cases, which could be explained by various advantages accruing to larger organizations with greater resources and expertise in dispute resolution procedures. The results also indicate the existence of a significant repeat-employer-arbitrator pairing effect in which employees on average have lower win rates and receive smaller damage awards where the same arbitrator is involved in more than one case with the same employer, a finding supporting some of the fairness criticisms directed at mandatory employment arbitration.

Alexander J. S. Colvin, *An Empirical Study of Employment Arbitration: Case Outcomes and Processes*, 8 J. Emp. Legal Stud. 1, 1 (2011).

(3) The Federal Arbitration Act was passed in response to judicial hostility at the state level toward the idea of arbitration more generally. What we find in unconscionability cases like *Ferguson* is the use of state law to effectively restrict how parties can contract for arbitration. Is there a limit under the FAA to how far California or other states should be able to go with the unconscionability doctrine in arbitration cases? In *AT&T Mobility LLC v. Concepcion*, which we consider in Chapter Five, the Supreme Court held that the FAA preempted a California judicial rule holding that waivers of class arbitration in consumer contracts were unconscionable. 131 S.Ct. 1740 (2011).

Comment: Contracts of Adhesion

Standard form contracts presented on a take-it-or-leave-it basis are often referred to as "contracts of adhesion." At common law, contracts of adhesion have been presumptively enforceable. In *Carnival Cruise Lines v. Shute*, for example, the U.S. Supreme Court rejected the position that "a nonnegotiated forum-selection clause in a form ticket contract is never enforceable simply because it is not the subject of bargaining." 499 U.S. 585, 593 (1991). Todd Rakoff describes the traditional rule: "in the absence of extraordinary circumstances, the adherent can establish an excuse only by showing affirmative participation by the drafting party in causing misunderstanding." *Contracts of Adhesion: An Essay in Reconstruction*, 96 Harv. L. Rev. 1173, 1185 (1983). That said, section 211(3) of the Second Restatement provides the following rule for "Standardized Agreements": "Where the other party has reason to believe that the party manifesting . . . assent would not do so if he knew that the writing contained a particular term, the term is not part of the agreement." What sort of evidence could be used to prove that section 211(3) was satisfied? Perhaps consumer surveys?

California courts have taken the lead in holding that the adhesiveness of a contract is enough to establish procedural unconscionability. The question is then whether the bargain is sufficiently substantively unconscionable to warrant non-enforcement.

> A finding of a contract of adhesion is essentially a finding of procedural unconscionability. This conclusion does not end our inquiry, however, because "[t]he determination that a contract is adhesive . . . does not necessarily mean that an arbitration provision contained therein is unenforceable." An arbitration provision in an adhesion contract is legally enforceable unless the provision (1) does not fall within the reasonable expectations of the weaker party, or (2) is unduly oppressive or unconscionable. . . . [T]he courts scrutinize such contracts with care and refuse to honor the selection if to do so would result in substantial injustice to the adherent.

Ehlers Elevators, Inc. v. Beta Seed Co., 2002 WL 31492719 at *7 (Cal.App. 2002). California courts have also found, however, varying degrees of procedural unconscionability. For example:

> While the agreement was adhesive, there was no greater oppression in its presentation to Olson than is inherent in any arbitration agreement presented to any employee by any employer. . . . The agreement, however, is less than a model of clarity and could have more completely explained its implications, e.g., that Olson was giving up her right to a court trial or jury trial. On the other hand the agreement was not made opaque by technical or obscure language and its meaning was discoverable from its terms. . . . The agreement was, therefore, procedurally unconscionable but the degree of that unconscionability was relatively low.

Olson v. ARV Assisted Living, Inc., 2002 WL 31174254 at *3 (Cal.App. 2002). The result is a "sliding scale" of unconscionability: "if there exists gross procedural unconscionability then not much be needed by way of substantive unconscionability, and that the same 'sliding scale' be applied if there be great substantive unconscionability but little procedural unconscionability." Funding Systems Leas. Corp. v. King Louie Intern., 597 S.W.2d 624, 634 (Mo.Ct.App.1979); see also Sitogum Holdings, Inc. v. Ropes, 800 A.2d 915, 921–22 (N.J. Super. 2002) (collecting cases).

Thus, while the phrase "contract of adhesion" is generally used in a pejorative sense, it is important to keep in mind that most adhesive contracts will be judicially enforced. Merely arguing that your client signed a standardized contract that was presented on a take-it-or-leave-it basis will not normally be sufficient to avoid the finding of an enforceable agreement. Since different consumers will have varying costs of reading and understanding "boilerplate," sellers can use standard form contracts to strategically impose transaction costs to segment and discriminate against consumers. See David Gilo and Ariel Porat, *The Hidden Role of Boilerplate and Standard Form Contracts*, 104 Mich. L. Rev. 983 (2006).

Comment: The Draft Restatement (Third) of Consumer Contracts

At the writing of this edition, the American Law Institute will soon considering Council Draft No. 3 of a Restatement (Third) of Consumer Contracts (December 20, 2016). The drafters describe the law of consumer contracts as having arrived at a "grand bargain": "fairly unrestricted freedom for business to draft and affix their terms to the transaction, balanced by a set of substantive boundary restrictions, prohibiting businesses from going to far." Introductory Note, Council Draft 3, at 4. The basic terms of the bargain can be seen in the interplay between sections 2 and 5.

Section 2 describes an extremely permissive formation rule: "Standard contract terms are adopted as part of a consumer contract if, after receiving reasonable notice of the standard contract terms and a meaningful opportunity to review them, the consumer signifies assent to the transaction." The comments confirm that the rule means that a contract can be formed by clickwrap, shrinkwrap or browsewrap, which we discussed in Chapter Three, Section 2(B). All that is required is notice and an opportunity to exit. Section 3 provides a similar rule for modifications. Businesses can modify the terms of the contract with notice to the consumer so long as the modification is in good faith Again, notice and an opportunity to exit are enough. There is no requirement that the consumer affirmatively assent.

These very permissive formation rules are combined with several restrictions on the substance of consumer contracts. The most significant is the section 5 rule for unconscionability, which codifies the judicially created two-pronged test: procedural and substantive. Procedural unconscionability is defined as "unfair surprise or depriving consumers of meaningful choice." But the real action is in comment 6.

> The essence of the procedural-unconscionability test is consumer awareness in a market context. The question is whether an ordinary consumer would be aware of the term. When consumers are aware of a term, it affects their contracting decisions. In these situations, the reasons for intervention in the substance of the deal are diminished. The question, then, in applying the procedural unconscionability test, is whether a term affects the contracting decisions of a large enough number of consumers. (If the market is segmented, the question is whether a term affects the contracting decisions of consumers in the relevant segment.) A term that does not affect the contracting decisions of a substantial number of consumers is presumed to be procedurally unconscionable.

* * *

> It is presumed that standard contract terms do not affect the contracting decisions of a substantial number of consumers. This presumption applies most forcefully when the standard contract term is part of a long-list of fine-print terms; it is rebutted when the standard contract term is, e.g., a conspicuous price or delivery fee. This presumption can be rebutted by the business using survey evidence, as commonly used in litigation involving aspects of unfair competition.

Under this approach, price and other "salient" terms—terms consumers are likely to pay attention to—are not procedurally unconscionable. Most other terms in standard consumer contracts—warranty limitations, choice of law clauses, arbitration clauses, and so forth, all of which we know consumers are unlikely to read—are presumed to be procedurally unconscionable, opening the door to review for substantive fairness.

Section 5 defines "substantive unconscionability" as "fundamentally unfair or unreasonably one-sided." It further identifies three categories of terms presumed substantively unconscionable: exclusions of consumer remedies for death or personal injury for which the business would otherwise be liable, purported limitations on the business's liability for intentional or negligent acts or omissions, and terms that "[u]nreasonably limit the consumer's ability to pursue a complaint or seek reasonable redress for a violation of a legal right."

The draft relies in part on empirical studies of the case law. But the approach also rests on two broader claims. First, both consumers and businesses are likely to benefit from allowing businesses to craft standard contract terms. Second, consumers almost never read these terms, no matter how prominently they are displayed and no matter what the form of consumer assent. Taken together, these claims suggest allowing businesses to draft the consumer contracts they want while guarding against overreach through ex post judicial review.

(B) MERCHANT TRANSACTIONS

Should the defense of unconscionability be limited to consumer cases, that is, cases in which individuals buy goods or services for personal, family or household purposes? Or might it be used as well in transactions between businesses? If so, should it make any difference whether the person in commerce is an individual or a small business or a large corporation?

To date, merchants have not been notably successful in invoking the defense. Thus, in *Myers v. Nebraska Investment Council*, the Nebraska Supreme Court held:

> A contract is not substantively unconscionable unless the terms are grossly unfair under the circumstances that existed when the parties entered the contract. . . . In a commercial setting, however, substantive unconscionability alone is usually insufficient to void a contract or clause. . . . A court must also consider whether the contract formation procedure was procedurally unconscionable. * * * In general, we have been reluctant to rewrite contracts between parties experienced in business, as opposed to contracts between consumers and skilled corporate parties.

272 Neb. 669, 692–93 (2006). See also W.L. May Co., Inc. v. Philco-Ford Corp., 273 Or. 701, 708 (1975) ("It may also be noted that both parties to the contract were sophisticated business people. This is clearly not the case of an innocent consumer who has unsuspectingly signed an adhesion contract."); County Asphalt, Inc. v. Lewis Welding & Engineering Corp., 323 F.Supp. 1300, 1308 (S.D.N.Y. 1970) ("[I]t is the exceptional commercial setting where a claim of unconscionability will be allowed."); Stanley A. Klopp, Inc. v. John Deere Co., 510 F.Supp. 807, 810 (E.D.Pa.

1981) ("Although commercial contracts can be unenforceable in whole or in part for unconscionability, it would be improper to borrow, without differentiation, concepts developed to protect consumers and employ them in favor of one commercial party over another.").

Nevertheless, neither the Code nor case law specifically limits section 2–302 or the principles underlying it for consumer transactions, and, as illustrated in the materials to follow, commercial entities can sometimes derive protection under unconscionability theory. Arguments based upon unconscionability appear regularly in commercial litigation, and courts are being called upon to examine the issue in a wide variety of contexts.

Elaine Zapatha v. Dairy Mart, Inc.

Supreme Judicial Court of Massachusetts, 1980.
381 Mass. 284.

■ WILKINS, JUSTICE. We are concerned here with the question whether Dairy Mart, Inc. (Dairy Mart), lawfully undertook to terminate a franchise agreement under which the Zapathas operated a Dairy Mart store on Wilbraham Road in Springfield. The Zapathas brought this action seeking to enjoin the termination of the agreement, alleging that the contract provision purporting to authorize the termination of the franchise agreement without cause was unconscionable and that Dairy Mart's conduct was an unfair and deceptive act or practice in violation of G.L. c. 93A. The judge ruled that Dairy Mart did not act in good faith, that the termination provision was unconscionable, and that Dairy Mart's termination of the agreement without cause was an unfair and deceptive act. We granted Dairy Mart's application for direct appellate review of a judgment that stated that Dairy Mart could terminate the agreement only for good cause and that the attempted termination was null and void. We reverse the judgments.

Mr. Zapatha is a high school graduate who had attended college for one year and had also taken college evening courses in business administration and business law. From 1952 to May, 1973, he was employed by a company engaged in the business of electroplating. He rose through the ranks to foreman and then to the position of operations manager, at one time being in charge of all metal finishing in the plant with 150 people working under him. In May, 1973, he was discharged and began looking for other opportunities, in particular a business of his own. Several months later he met with a representative of Dairy Mart. Dairy Mart operates a chain of franchised "convenience" stores. The Dairy Mart representative told Mr. Zapatha that working for Dairy Mart was being in business for one's self and that such a business was very stable and secure. Mr. Zapatha signed an application to be considered for a franchise. In addition, he was presented with a brochure entitled

"Here's a Chance," which made certain representations concerning the status of a franchise holder.[3]

Dairy Mart approved Mr. Zapatha's application and offered him a store in Agawam. On November 8, 1973, a representative of Dairy Mart showed him a form of franchise agreement, entitled Limited Franchise and License Agreement, asked him to read it, and explained that his wife would have to sign the agreement as well.

Under the terms of the agreement, Dairy Mart would license the Zapathas to operate a Dairy Mart store, using the Dairy Mart trademark and associated insignia, and utilizing Dairy Mart's "confidential" merchandising methods. Dairy Mart would furnish the store and the equipment and would pay rent and gas and electric bills as well as certain other costs of doing business. In return Dairy Mart would receive a franchise fee, computed as a percentage of the store's gross sales. The Zapathas would have to pay for the starting inventory, and maintain a minimum stock of saleable merchandise thereafter. They were also responsible for wages of employees, related taxes, and any sales taxes. The termination provision, which is set forth in full in the margin,[4] allowed either party, after twelve months, to terminate the agreement without cause on ninety days' written notice. In the event of termination initiated by it without cause, Dairy Mart agreed to repurchase the saleable merchandise inventory at retail prices, less 20%.

The Dairy Mart representative read and explained the termination provision to Mr. Zapatha. Mr. Zapatha later testified that, while he understood every word in the provision, he had interpreted it to mean that Dairy Mart could terminate the agreement only for cause. The Dairy Mart representative advised Mr. Zapatha to take the agreement to an attorney and said "I would prefer that you did." However, he also told Mr. Zapatha that the terms of the contract were not negotiable. The Zapathas signed the agreement without consulting an attorney. When the Zapathas took charge of the Agawam store, a representative of Dairy

---

[3] It included the following statements: ". . . you'll have the opportunity to own and run your own business . . ."; "We want to be sure we're hooking up with the right person. A person who sees the opportunity in owning his own business . . . who requires the security that a multi-million dollar parent company can offer him . . . who has the good judgment and business sense to take advantage of the unique independence that Dairy Mart offers its franchisees. . . . We're looking for a partner . . . who can take the tools we offer and build a life of security and comfort. . . ."

[4] "(9) The term of this Limited Franchise and License Agreement shall be for a period of Twelve (12) months from date hereof, and shall continue uninterrupted thereafter. If DEALER desires to terminate after 12 months from date hereof, he shall do so by giving COMPANY a ninety (90) day written notice by Registered Mail of his intention to terminate. If COMPANY desires to terminate, it likewise shall give a ninety (90) day notice, except for the following reasons which shall not require any written notice and shall terminate the Franchise immediately:

"(a) Failure to pay bills to suppliers for inventory or other products when due.

"(b) Failure to pay Franchise Fees to COMPANY.

"(c) Failure to pay city, state or federal taxes as said taxes shall become due and payable.

"(d) Breach of any condition of this Agreement."

Mart worked with them to train them in Dairy Mart's methods of operation.

In 1974, another store became available on Wilbraham Road in Springfield, and the Zapathas elected to surrender the Agawam store. They executed a new franchise agreement, on an identical printed form, relating to the new location.

In November, 1977, Dairy Mart presented a new and more detailed form of "Independent Operator's Agreement" to the Zapathas for execution. Some of the terms were less favorable to the store operator than those of the earlier form of agreement.[5] Mr. Zapatha told representatives of Dairy Mart that he was content with the existing contract and had decided not to sign the new agreement. On January 20, 1978, Dairy Mart gave written notice to the Zapathas that their contract was being terminated effective in ninety days. The termination notice stated that Dairy Mart "remains available to enter into discussions with you with respect to entering into a new Independent Operator's Agreement; however, there is no assurance that Dairy Mart will enter into a new Agreement with you, or even if entered into, what terms such Agreement will contain." The notice also indicated that Dairy Mart was prepared to purchase the Zapathas' saleable inventory.

The judge found that Dairy Mart terminated the agreement solely because the Zapathas refused to sign the new agreement. He further found that, but for this one act, Dairy Mart did not behave in an unconscionable manner, in bad faith, or in disregard of its representations. * * *

[Because the franchise agreement involved mostly transactions in services, the court was disinclined to find that the transaction was a "sale of goods" exclusively covered by the U.C.C. However, the court applied the U.C.C.'s statement of policy concerning good faith and unconscionability, together with their common law counterparts, by analogy.]

We consider first the plaintiffs' argument that the termination clause of the franchise agreement, authorizing Dairy Mart to terminate the agreement without cause, on ninety days' notice, was unconscionable by the standards expressed in G.L. c. 106, § 2–302. The same standards are set forth in Restatement (Second) of Contracts § 234 (Tent. Drafts Nos. 1–7, 1973). The issue is one of law for the court, and the test is to be made as of the time the contract was made. * * * In measuring the unconscionability of the termination provision, the fact that the law

---

[5]   In his testimony, Mr. Zapatha said that he objected to a new provision under which Dairy Mart reserved the option to relocate an operator to a new location and to a requirement that the store be open from 7 A.M. to 11 P.M. every day. Previously the Zapathas' store had been open from 8 A.M. to 10 P.M.

There were other provisions, such as an obligation to pay future increases in the cost of heat and electricity, that were more burdensome to a franchisee. A few changes may have been to the advantage of the franchisee.

imposes an obligation of good faith on Dairy Mart in its performance under the agreement should be weighed. . . .

The official comment to § 2–302 states that "[t]he basic test is whether, in the light of the general commercial background and the commercial needs of the particular trade or case, the clauses involved are so one-sided as to be unconscionable under the circumstances existing at the time of the making of the contract. . . . The principle is one of prevention of oppression and unfair surprise . . . and not of disturbance of allocation of risks because of superior bargaining power." Official Comment 1 to U.C.C. § 2–302.[11] Unconscionability is not defined in the Code, nor do the views expressed in the official comment provide a precise definition. The annotation prepared by the Massachusetts Advisory Committee on the Code states that "[t]he section appears to be intended to carry equity practice into the sales field." See 1 R. Anderson, Uniform Commercial Code § 2–302:7 (1970) to the same effect. This court has not had occasion to consider in any detail the meaning of the word "unconscionable" in § 2–302. Because there is no clear, all-purpose definition of "unconscionable," nor could there be, unconscionability must be determined on a case by case basis . . . , giving particular attention to whether, at the time of the execution of the agreement, the contract provision could result in unfair surprise and was oppressive to the allegedly disadvantaged party.

We start with a recognition that the Uniform Commercial Code itself implies that a contract provision allowing termination without cause is not *per se* unconscionable. . . . Section 2–309(3) provides that "[t]ermination of a contract by one party except on the happening of an agreed event requires that reasonable notification be received by the other party and an agreement dispensing with notification is invalid if its operation would be unconscionable." G.L. c. 106, § 2–309, as appearing in St.1957, c. 765, § 1. This language implies that termination of a sales contract without agreed "cause" is authorized by the Code, provided reasonable notice is given. . . . There is no suggestion that the ninety days' notice provided in the Dairy Mart franchise agreement was unreasonable.

We find no potential for unfair surprise to the Zapathas in the provision allowing termination without cause. We view the question of unfair surprise as focused on the circumstances under which the agreement was entered into.[13] The termination provision was neither

---

[11] The comment has been criticized as useless and at best ambiguous (J. White & R. Summers, The Uniform Commercial Code, 116 [1972]), and § 2–302 has been characterized as devoid of any specific content. Leff, *Unconscionability and the Code—The Emperor's New Clause*, 115 U. Pa. L. Rev. 485, 487–489 (1967). On the other hand, it has been said that the strength of the unconscionability concept is its abstraction, permitting judicial creativity. See Ellinghaus, *In Defense of Unconscionability*, 78 Yale L.J. 757 (1969).

[13] As we shall note subsequently, the concept of oppression deals with the substantive unfairness of the contract term. This two-part test for unconscionability involves determining whether there was "an absence of meaningful choice on the part of one of the parties, together with contract terms which are unreasonably favorable to the other party." Williams v. Walker-

obscurely worded, nor buried in fine print in the contract. Contrast Williams v. Walker-Thomas Furniture Co., 350 F.2d 445, 449 (D.C.Cir. 1965). The provision was specifically pointed out to Mr. Zapatha before it was signed; Mr. Zapatha testified that he thought the provision was "straightforward," and he declined the opportunity to take the agreement to a lawyer for advice. The Zapathas had ample opportunity to consider the agreement before they signed it. Significantly, the subject of loss of employment was paramount in Mr. Zapatha's mind. He testified that he had held responsible jobs in one company from 1952 to 1973, that he had lost his employment, and that he "was looking for something that had a certain amount of security; something that was stable and something I could call my own." We conclude that a person of Mr. Zapatha's business experience and education should not have been surprised by the termination provision and, if in fact he was, there was no element of unfairness in the inclusion of that provision in the agreement. . . .

We further conclude that there was no oppression in the inclusion of a termination clause in the franchise agreement. We view the question of oppression as directed to the substantive fairness to the parties of permitting the termination provisions to operate as written. The Zapathas took over a going business on premises provided by Dairy Mart, using equipment furnished by Dairy Mart. As an investment, the Zapathas had only to purchase the inventory of goods to be sold but, as Dairy Mart concedes, on termination by it without cause Dairy Mart was obliged to repurchase all the Zapathas' saleable merchandise inventory, including items not purchased from Dairy Mart, at 80% of its retail value. There was no potential for forfeiture or loss of investment. * * *

[The court also held that Dairy Mart terminated the contract in good faith and that neither the termination clause nor process constituted a deceptive practice or an unfair trade practice.]

Judgments reversed.

NOTES

(1) Section 208 of Restatement (Second) provides:

If a contract or term thereof is unconscionable at the time the contract is made a court may refuse to enforce the contract, or may enforce the remainder of the contract without the unconscionable term, or may so limit the application of any unconscionable terms as to avoid any unconscionable result.

(2) Note that Justice Wilkins concludes that "oppression" relates to substantive rather than procedural unconscionability. This differs from more recent discussions of unconscionability, e.g., the *Ferguson* case supra, where oppression is put in the procedural camp. What difference does this make?

Thomas Furniture Co., 350 F.2d 445, 449 (D.C.Cir. 1965). . . . The inquiry involves a search for components of "procedural" and "substantive" unconscionability. See generally Leff, *Unconscionability and the Code—The Emperor's New Clause*, 115 U. Pa. L. Rev. 485 (1967). * * *

Which approach makes it easier to establish unconscionability under UCC § 2–302?

Floyd E. and Michael B. Coursey v. Caterpillar, Inc.

United States Court of Appeals, Sixth Circuit, 1995.
1995 WL 492923.

[One of the questions before the court was whether a term in a commercial contract that excluded the seller's liability for consequential damages was unconscionable. UCC § 2–719(3). The court first held that implied warranties had been properly disclaimed by the seller under UCC § 2–316(2) and that the seller had made an express warranty that the goods were free from defects in material and workmanship. However, the contract provided that repair and replacement for breach of that warranty was the exclusive remedy.]

■ PER CURIAM. * * * Except in cases in which consumer goods cause personal injuries, the buyer carries the burden of proving the unconscionability of a limitation-of-remedy clause. . . . Unconscionability is rarely found to exist in a commercial setting. . . .

The various factors considered by courts in deciding questions of unconscionability have been divided by the commentators into "procedural" and "substantive" categories. . . . Under the "procedural" rubric are facts which involve the "meeting of the minds" of the contracting parties: age, education, intelligence, business acumen and experience, relative bargaining power, who drafted the contract, whether the terms were explained to the weaker party, whether alterations in the printed terms were possible, and whether there were alternate sources of supply for the goods in question. The "substantive" heading embraces the contractual terms themselves, and requires a determination whether they were commercially reasonable. Most courts have taken a "balancing approach" to the unconscionability question and seem to require a certain quantum of procedural plus a certain quantum of substantive unconscionability to tip the scales in favor of unconscionability.

The plaintiffs failed to come forward with any evidence that the disclaimer of consequential damages was either procedurally or substantively unconscionable. The warranty provided for replacement of parts and labor in the event of mechanical failure and plaintiffs availed themselves of that warranty several times. If they did not like the terms of the warranty, they were free to purchase a tractor elsewhere. Nor have the plaintiffs demonstrated that the limitation of damages to replacement parts and labor is commercially unreasonable. The limitations clause was a conspicuous and unambiguous part of the sales transaction between two commercial entities. It was a limitation not unusual or unexpected in a commercial setting. Accordingly, the disclaimer of the remedy of consequential damages was valid and effective, and defendants were entitled to summary judgment with respect to plaintiffs' claim for consequential damages.

   * * * AFFIRMED.

NOTES

What happens to the clause excluding liability for consequential damages if the seller is unable or unwilling to perform or satisfy the limited express warranty? Suppose, for example, after several tries the seller is unable to supply a needed replacement part and the machinery will not operate. Read UCC § 2–719(2). If the limited remedy (repair and replacement) fails of its essential purpose, is the buyer entitled to consequential damages regardless of UCC § 2–719(3)? These questions are explored in Chapter Six.

7. ILLEGALITY AND PUBLIC POLICY

In some cases, a transaction satisfies the conditions established by the general law of contracts, but one of the parties or the court argues that the bargain itself, its performance or the objectives to be achieved are illegal or against public policy, and therefore it ought not be enforced. Assuming the court holds this to be the case, a further question will then be whether the court should award restitution for any benefits one side conferred on the other.

Section 512 of the First Restatement took a firm position on such cases, with a predictable result: "A bargain is illegal . . . if either its formation or its performance is criminal, tortious, or otherwise opposed to public policy." If both parties were equally involved in the illegality, section 598 stated that neither could "recover damages for breach thereof nor, by rescinding the bargain, recover the performance that he has rendered thereunder or its value." But the jump from the conclusion that the bargain or its performance is a crime, a tort or is "otherwise opposed to public policy" to the conclusion that it should not be enforced, and restitution should be denied, is not without difficulty. The statute, regulation or other source of public policy may say nothing about contracts and their enforceability. Suppose, for example, that one party is ignorant of the illegality. Or suppose the crime is a misdemeanor rather than a felony. Or perhaps the public policy is strong enough to deny enforcement, but not to deny restitution.

The drafters of the Second Restatement proposed instead a balancing approach. Section 178(1) provides, first, that a "promise or other term of an agreement is unenforceable on grounds of public policy if legislation provides that it is unenforceable. . . ." Thus, if a constitution, statute, administrative regulation or local ordinance preempts the enforceability question by clear language, the court's job is to implement that legislative decision. If there is no clear legislative mandate, the promise or term is unenforceable if the "interest in its enforcement is clearly outweighed in the circumstances by a public policy against the enforcement of such terms." Section 178(1).

What are the factors to be weighed in the balance? Section 178(2) provides that in "weighing the interest in the enforcement of a term, account is taken of (a) the parties' justified expectations, (b) any forfeiture that would result if enforcement were denied, and (c) any special public interest in the enforcement of the particular term." Section 178(3) provides that in "weighing a public policy against enforcement of a term, account is taken of (a) the strength of that policy as manifested by legislation or judicial decisions, (b) the likelihood that a refusal to enforce the term will further that policy, (c) the seriousness of any misconduct involved and the extent to which it was deliberate, and (d) the directness of the connection between that misconduct and the term." The virtue of the Restatement (Second) test is that it would seem to provide more flexibility in cases that are not clear-cut. Similarly, the Second Restatement recommends more discretion for a court to grant restitution to the plaintiff even though the bargain itself is unenforceable. See Restatement (Second) §§ 197–199.

A more fundamental policy question is: What is the purpose to be served in denying enforcement and restitution when the contract is against public policy? Assuming here that punishment may come through the criminal law, why do we need to further "punish" the parties by refusing to award damages for breach? Is it for additional deterrence? Or is there some other reason for refusing a damage award? Corbin suggests the reason lies in a "pious fear that the 'judicial ermine' might otherwise be soiled." Corbin on Contracts § 1534, at 1058 (1950).

Another reason might be to encourage opportunism in these situations, or in other words, to undermine honor among thieves. Many doctrines of contract law, such as the duty of good faith or the tort of promissory fraud, can be viewed as attempts to constrain contractual opportunism. The refusal to enforce illegal contracts or order restitution for their breach has the socially valuable effect of *encouraging* opportunism with regard to substantively illegal agreements. See Juliet Kostritsky, *Illegal Contracts and Efficient Deterrence: A Study in Modern Contract Theory*, 74 Iowa L. Rev. 115 (1988). But in some contexts, non-enforcement will increase the amount of the unwanted activity. For example, imagine that employers of undocumented workers are allowed to get away without paying wages. If employers know about this rule but undocumented workers do not, it is possible that there will be more "illegal" work. We might have less undocumented work if we enforced the employer's wage promise. Indeed, we might have even less if we required employers (the side that is more likely to know about the law) to pay three times the contract wage to any worker whom was subsequently found to be undocumented.

John W. Sinnar v. Harry K. Le Roy

Supreme Court of Washington, Department 2, 1954.
44 Wash.2d 728.

■ WEAVER, J. Plaintiff brings this action to recover four hundred fifty dollars which he delivered to defendant upon the latter's promise either to get a beer license for plaintiff or return the money. Defendant appeals from a judgment against him.

Respondent owns and operates a grocery store on Jackson street, in Seattle. Prior to the transaction involved, he made application to the Washington state liquor control board for a license to sell beer, and paid sixty dollars license fee; the license was denied and the license fee returned.

Appellant, a customer, neighbor, and friend of respondent, is a business machine operator at Boeing Airplane Company. When the license was denied, the parties discussed the matter. Appellant testified:

> "Well, I talked to—I told John [respondent] that I knew a fellow that worked for the—well, at that time I didn't know that the license come from the state, I thought beer licenses like these come from the city, and I knew this Mr. Lewis worked for the city in this County-City Building here for a number of years, and so then I talked to Mr. Lewis and he said that—(interrupted) . . . after I told him I thought I could get the license, I told him I'd see about it, and then I called about it, and I called him, after telephone conversations back and forth to me, and then I called John [respondent] . . . and I told him that it would cost him $450.00, and that's all I said and then I went on to work."

Both parties knew that a third party was to be involved. Appellant testified that he gave respondent's four hundred fifty dollars cash to a Mr. Lewis, who is not identified except as reference was made to him in appellant's testimony, herein quoted. Respondent did not receive a beer license.

He testified:

> "Well, I told him to be careful who he gives the money to. I found out that this was just a sucker game, and knowing him as well as I did, I thought he'd do me some good. Q. What, if any, conditions were attached to the delivery of the money? A. Well, he told me the license or the money back. He said it was good as in the bank. . . . I didn't care how. . . . I didn't care what he done with it, whether he bought a retired license or what."

Respondent testified several times that he told appellant to be "careful who he gave the money to." There is no indication in the evidence that the money was paid for professional services.

Appellant's assignments of error are presented upon the theory that this was an illegal transaction. The defense of illegality not having been pleaded, respondent argues that appellant is foreclosed from raising the question. We cannot agree with this conclusion.

> "Illegality, if of a serious nature, need not be pleaded. If it appears in evidence the court of its own motion will deny relief to the plaintiff. The defendant cannot waive the defense if he wishes to do so. Indeed, if the court suspects illegality, it may examine witnesses and develop facts not brought out by the parties, and thereby establish illegality that precludes recovery by the plaintiff. If, however, the illegality is not serious, and neither public policy nor statute clearly requires denial of relief, courts refuse to give effect to facts showing illegality unless those facts are essential to establish a *prima facie* right of recovery or are pleaded by defendant."

Restatement, Contracts § 600, Comment a.

The only place such a license might have been secured was from the Washington state liquor control board. Laws of 1937, chapter 217, § 1, § 23–U, p. 1066, Rem.Rev.Stat., Sup., § 7306–23U, cf. RCW 66.24.010, provides:

> "The holder of one or more licenses may assign and transfer the same to any qualified person under such rules and regulations as the board may prescribe: *Provided, however,* That no such assignment and transfer shall be made which will result in both a change of licensee and change of location; the fee for such assignment and transfer shall be ten dollars ($10.00)."

The illegality, which is claimed and argued in the instant case, is of a serious nature. The situation involves a beer license, which can be secured only from an agency of the state; it purports to deal with a matter which is exclusively within the realm of public policy. A party to such a situation cannot waive his right to set up the defense of illegality, and, if the evidence produced in support of the cause of action also establishes the illegality of the transaction, it should be considered by the trier of the facts, even though illegality has not been pleaded as a defense. . . .

* * *

In principle, we cannot distinguish the instant case from *Goodier v. Hamilton*, 172 Wash. 60, 63 (1933), wherein we said:

> "It is within the realm of contemplation that a contract of this nature would readily suggest to one desirous of securing a highly compensatory result, to employ means which the law, good morals and public policy do not sanction. To anticipate and prevent a subversion of a proper administration of justice, the law should make it impossible for any such temptation to be carried into fruition by condemning a contract that contains the germ of possible corruption."

The record not only discloses that this transaction "contains the germ of possible corruption," but the evidence, and all inferences which may be drawn, lead us to conclude that the parties contemplated the use of means other than legal to accomplish the end desired.

A court will not knowingly aid in the furtherance of an illegal transaction, but will leave the parties where it finds them.

The judgment is reversed, with instructions to dismiss the action. Since the parties are *in pari delicto*, it is consistent with our decision that each bear his own costs.

NOTES

(1)   Exactly where was the illegality in *Sinnar*—in the making of the contract, its performance, the objective to be achieved or what? Would the court come out differently on the enforceability issue using the balancing test described in Section 178 of the Second Restatement?

(2)   *Sua Sponte.* The Second Restatement clearly supports the power of a court to raise the public policy issue *sua sponte*:

> Even if neither party's pleading or proof reveals the contravention, the court may ordinarily inquire into it and decide the case on the basis of it if it finds it just to do so, subject to any relevant rules of pleading or proof by which it is bound.

Restatement (Second), Chapter 8, Topic 1, Introductory Note.

(3)   *Restitutionary Exceptions.* The result in *Sinnar v. Le Roy* is that the defendant (or some unknown third person) is permitted to keep the plaintiff's $450. Yet both were equally involved in the wrongdoing. What policy justifies this result?

Courts recognize that rigorous application of the *in pari delicto* maxim may at times lead to results which are hardly consonant with sound public policy. Hence we see the appearance of ameliorative doctrines, such as "partial illegality" discussed above, which permit enforcement of the legal portion. To quote Judge Cardozo, speaking of an unrelated matter but in a way which is apropos, courts are hesitant "to visit venial fault with oppressive retribution." Jacob & Youngs v. Kent, reprinted in Chapter Five. An effective method of avoiding application of the strict rule is to establish that the parties are not equally at fault; i.e., they are not *in pari delicto*. An illustration is *Webb v. Fulchire*, 25 N.C. (3 Ired.) 485 (1843), where the victim of a "shell game" successfully sued to recover his losses. "Surely, the artless fool, who seems to have been alike bereft of his senses and his money, is not to be deemed a partaker in the same crime, *in pari delicto*, with the juggling knave, who gulled and fleeced him." 25 N.C. at 487. One may be able to establish a lack of parity of blame by showing one's ignorance of the illegality, the other party's fraud or deception, or membership in a class the public policy is designed to protect. Finally, one may avoid strict application by withdrawing from the contract before its illegal purpose has been attained. This is known as the doctrine of *locus poenitentiae*.

The modern rule can be found in Sections 197 through 199 of the Second Restatement. Section 197 provides the general rule that "a party has no claim in restitution for performance that he has rendered under or in return for a promise that is unenforceable on grounds of public policy unless denial of restitution would cause disproportionate forfeiture." Sections 198 and 199 then provide two exceptions: (1) where the plaintiff was excusably ignorant of facts or of legislation "of a minor character, in the absence of which the promise would be enforceable," or was "not equally in the wrong with the promisor," and (2) where the plaintiff did not "engage in serious misconduct and . . . withdraws from the transaction before the improper purpose has been achieved."

For a recent application, see *White v. McBride*, 937 S.W.2d 796 (Tenn. 1996), where the court found a contingency fee contract between a lawyer and his client "clearly excessive" under the applicable Code of Professional Responsibility and denied enforcement. The court also denied the plaintiff's claim for the reasonable value of the services rendered, and distinguished this case from the "innocent snafu" that might render a fee contract unenforceable:

> A violation of [the applicable rule] is an ethical transgression of a most flagrant sort as it goes directly to the heart of the fiduciary relationship that exists between attorney and client. To permit an attorney to fall back on the theory of *quantum meruit* when he unsuccessfully fails to collect a clearly excessive fee does absolutely nothing to promote ethical behavior. On the contrary, this interpretation would encourage attorneys to enter exorbitant fee contracts, secure that the safety net of *quantum meruit* is there in case of a subsequent fall.

937 S.W.2d at 802. How does this rule compare to the availability of restitution where the contract is unenforceable because of the Statute of Frauds, or voidable under the doctrine of mistake or misrepresentation?

(4) *Mansfield on Illegal Contracts.* The following statement of Lord Mansfield in *Holman v. Johnson*, [1775] 1 Cowp. 341, is most frequently advanced to justify disallowance of recovery where the parties are *in pari delicto*:

> The objection that a contract is immoral or illegal as between plaintiff and defendant, sounds at all times very ill in the mouth of the defendant. It is not for his sake, however, that the objection is ever allowed; but it is founded in general principles of policy, which the defendant has the advantage of, contrary to the real justice as between him and the plaintiff, by accident, if I may so say. The principle of public policy is this: *Ex dolo malo non oritur actio.* No court will lend its aid to a man who founds his cause of action upon an immoral or an illegal act. If, from the plaintiff's own stating or otherwise, the cause of action appears to arise *ex turpi causa*, or the transgression of a positive law of this country, there the court says he has no right to be assisted. It is upon that ground the court goes; not for the sake of defendant, but because they will not lend their

aid to such a plaintiff. So if the plaintiff and defendant were to change sides, and the defendant was to bring his action against the plaintiff, the latter would then have the advantage of it; for where both parties are equally in fault, *potior est conditio defendentis*.

What judicial alternatives are available? Can you suggest a more acceptable approach? Mansfield recognized that the *in pari delicto* maxim should not be applied rigidly and mechanically. For example, in *Clarke v. Shee*, [1774] 1 Cowp. 197, 200, he wrote:

There are two sorts of prohibitions enacted by positive law, in respect of contracts. 1st. To protect weak or necessitous men from being overreached, defrauded or oppressed. There the rule *in pari delicto, potior est conditio defendentis*, does not hold; and an action will lie; because where the defendant imposes upon the plaintiff it is not *par delictum*. * * * The next sort of prohibition is founded upon general reasons of policy and public expedience. There both parties offending are equally guilty; *par est delictum, et potior est conditio defendentis*.

(5) *Wigmore Dissents*.

The real theory of *pari delicto* seems to be that the plaintiff loses his right by partaking in wrong-doing. * * * But the whole notion is radically wrong in principle and produces extreme injustice. If A owes B $5,000 why should he not pay it whether B has violated a statute or not? Where the issue is as to the rights of two litigants, it is unscientific to impose a penalty incidentally by depriving one of the litigants of his admitted right. It is unjust, also, for two reasons: first, one guilty party suffers, while another of equal guilt is rewarded; secondly, the penalty is usually utterly disproportionate to the offense. If there is one part of criminal jurisprudence which needs even more careful attention than it now receives it is the apportionment of penalty to offense. Yet the doctrine now under consideration requires, with monstrous injustice and blind haphazard, that the plaintiff shall be mulcted in the amount of his right, whatever that may be. Take for example the case of *Cambioso v. Maffet* (2 Wash.C.C. 98), in which plaintiff and defendant were joint owners of a vessel. To avoid paying the tax on alien owners, the vessel was registered in the name of the defendant. For this illegality the plaintiff is denied the help of the courts in making the defendant account for the vessel's profits. In this way, and in a hundred similar ways, a fine of thousands of dollars may be imposed for petty violations of law. One cannot imagine why we have so long allowed such an unworthy principle to remain.

The expedient that naturally suggests itself is merely to order the sum due to be paid into court and to deduct from it such a portion as may be named by the proper tribunal as the penalty for the violation of the law.

John H. Wigmore, *A Summary of Quasi-Contracts*, 25 Am. L. Rev. 695, 712–13 (1891).

(6) *Public Policy: An Elusive Concept.* From the dawn of the common law tradition in England, courts have refused to implement those private contractual undertakings which, when measured against the prevailing mores and moods of society, contravene judicial perceptions of public policy. See 1 E. Coke, *Institutes of the Laws of England: A Commentary upon Littleton* *19 (Thomas ed. 1827) ("*nihil quod est inconveniens est licitum*"); Percy H. Winfield, *Public Policy in the English Common Law*, 42 Harv. L. Rev. 76, 79 et seq. (1928). As the highest court in Maryland put it:

> "Public policy is that principle of the law which holds that no subject can lawfully do that which has a tendency to be injurious to the public, or against the public good, which may be termed, as it sometimes has been, the policy of the law, or public policy in relation to the administration of the law." Egerton v. Earl Brownlow, 4 H.L.Cas. 1, 196 (1853). . . . But beyond this relatively indeterminate description of the doctrine, jurists to this day have been unable to fashion a truly workable definition of public policy. Not being restricted to the conventional sources of positive law (constitutions, statutes and judicial decisions), judges are frequently called upon to discern the dictates of sound social policy and human welfare based on nothing more than their own personal experience and intellectual capacity. See 6A A. Corbin, Contracts § 1375, at 10 and 18 (1962). Inevitably, conceptions of public policy tend to ebb and flow with the tides of public opinion, making it difficult for courts to apply the principle with any degree of certainty. 1 W. Story, *A Treatise on the Law of Contracts* § 675 (5th ed. 1874). "[P]ublic policy . . . is but a shifting and variable notion appealed to only when no other argument is available, and which, if relied upon today, may be utterly repudiated tomorrow." Kenneweg v. Allegany County, 102 Md. 119, 125 (1905).

Fearing the disruptive effect that invocation of the highly elusive public policy principle would likely exert on the stability of commercial and contractual relations, Maryland courts have been hesitant to strike down voluntary bargains on public policy grounds, doing so only in those cases where the challenged agreement is patently offensive to the public good, that is, where "the common sense of the entire community would . . . pronounce it" invalid. Estate of Woods, Weeks & Co., 52 Md. 520, 536 (1879). . . . This reluctance on the part of the judiciary to nullify contractual arrangements on public policy grounds also serves to protect the public interest in having individuals exercise broad powers to structure their own affairs by making legally enforceable promises, a concept which lies at the heart of the freedom of contract principle. Restatement (Second) of Contracts, Introductory Note to Ch. 14, at 46 (Tent. Draft No. 12, 1977);. . . .

In the final analysis, it is the function of a court to balance the public and private interests in securing enforcement of the disputed promise against those policies which would be advanced were the contractual term held invalid. Enforcement will be denied only where the factors that argue against implementing the particular provision clearly and unequivocally outweigh "the law's traditional interest in protecting the expectations of the parties, its abhorrence of any unjust enrichment, and any public interest in the enforcement" of the contested term. Restatement (Second) of Contracts § 320, Comment b (Tent. Draft No. 12, 1977).

Maryland-National, etc. v. Washington National Arena, 282 Md. 588, 605–07 (1978).

PROBLEM: THE CASE OF THE GREEN DOOR TAVERN

Patricia Myers operated the Green Door tavern in Granby, Missouri. Mrs. Myers had a three-year lease with option to purchase the premises from the owner John Hurn, Jr. as well as a beer-by-the-drink license issued by the Missouri Division of Liquor Control.

Todd Clouse was a patron of the tavern. During one of his visits, Patricia's husband Jerry asked Clouse if he would be interested in purchasing an interest in the business. Negotiations followed which resulted in the signing of an "Employment/Management Contract" under which the Myers, as "Employers," agreed to hire Clouse to manage the business for a four-year period and pay him sixty percent of the net profits of the business as salary. In addition, Clouse was to receive, at the termination of the agreement or upon the exercise of the lease option to purchase, whichever came first, a sixty percent interest in the Green Door, with the Myers agreeing to exercise the option to purchase the property from Hurn within the lease period. Upon purchase of the property from Hurn, the Myers and Clouse were each to pay fifty percent of the purchase price. Finally, Clouse agreed to pay the Myers $15,000, $7,500 at the time of signing.

After executing the contract, Clouse paid the $7,500 and began operating the tavern. Two weeks later, however, the parties were summoned to the office of Larry Fuhr of the Missouri Liquor Commission. Fuhr questioned the agreement because an agreement with a licensed person (Patricia Myers) to operate a tavern is in violation of Missouri law. Fuhr also objected to Jerry Myers' name on the contract because the latter, evidently a convicted felon, could have nothing to do with the operation of the tavern. The upshot was that Patricia surrendered her license to Fuhr.

Clouse later applied for and received a liquor license to operate the tavern in his own name, and he negotiated a new lease with Hurn. Clouse then requested that the Myers return his $7,500. They refused. He sued. What result? See Clouse v. Myers, 753 S.W.2d 316 (Mo.App. 1988).

Ahmad S. Homami v. Mansoor Iranzadi

California Court of Appeal, Sixth District, 1989.
211 Cal.App.3d 1104.

■ BRAUER, ASSOCIATE JUSTICE. Ahmad Homami sued Mansoor Iranzadi to collect the balance due on a promissory note. Iranzadi claimed he had paid down the principal balance by approximately $40,000. Homami acknowledged receiving that amount but claimed the payments represented interest only. The note expressly provided: "This note shall bear no interest." But Homami testified at trial that the parties nonetheless had an oral agreement for the payment of 12 percent interest per annum. According to Homami the no interest provision on the note was only so that he could avoid reporting the income for state and federal income tax purposes.

The trial court granted judgment in favor of Homami. We reverse on the basis that Homami's claim is dependent upon an agreement for the express purpose of violating the law and defrauding state and federal governments.

FACTS

Homami and Iranzadi were brothers-in-law. At the time of this transaction, they had been involved in various business dealings together both in Iran and in the United States.

On January 9, 1984, Homami wrote a check for $250,000 to California Land Title in order to fund a real estate transaction on behalf of Iranzadi. The close of escrow was delayed until March 22, 1984. In the interim Homami kept the money available to make the loan.

The $250,000 loan was evidenced by two identical promissory notes dated March 22, 1984, in the amount of $125,000 each. Each note provided that it was all due and payable in two years and each recited that it would bear no interest. One note was secured by property known as the "Pinehill" property, and the other by property known as the "Outlook" property.

Iranzadi, who was not fluent in English, had granted Homami a power of attorney. Pursuant to this power Homami routinely wrote checks for his brother-in-law.

On March 25, 1984, three days after the loan was funded, Homami signed a check to himself for $2,104.68 on Iranzadi's account. The check bore a notation in Persian that it was for interest to March. According to Homami, this amount represented interest lost to him by virtue of the fact that he had kept the $250,000 accessible for two and a half months. He testified that Iranzadi had agreed to pay him the difference between the interest he was earning in his regular bank account and the 12 percent he would be receiving from Iranzadi.

Thereafter, checks were drawn to Homami on Iranzadi's account more or less on a monthly basis for approximately a year. For the first few months Homami signed the checks. The last six checks were signed by Iranzadi's son. With the exception of two payments, all of the checks were for $2,500. That would be the exact amount of monthly interest on a debt for $250,000 bearing a rate of 12 percent per annum. The total amount paid to Homami from Iranzadi, including the initial payment of $2,104.68, was $39,324.68.

On March 18, 1985, Homami and Iranzadi signed a document entitled "Modification Agreement" for each of the promissory notes. The modification agreements were identical except for their reference to the respective notes and deeds of trust. Each provided for the following modification of terms:

"1. The note shall be all due and payable on or before September 22, 1985.

"2. The note shall bear no interest until June 22, 1985.

"3. On June 22, 1985, interest shall commence at the rate of eighteen percent per annum; said interest shall be payable monthly commencing on July 22, 1985 and continue monthly thereafter until the maturity date expressed herein."

Thereafter, two more payments of $2,500 were made, on May 22, 1985 and June 23, 1985. No further payments of any amount were made.

On August 14, 1985, Homami filed notices of default on the ground that Iranzadi had failed to pay the monthly installment of interest due July 22, 1985. Foreclosures were commenced on both properties. Iranzadi found a buyer for the Pinehill property and escrow closed at the end of January, 1986. Homami was paid through that escrow the full principal balance of $125,000 on the one note, plus interest at 18 percent from June 22, 1985, as per the modification agreement, and foreclosure fees; however, Iranzadi expressly reserved the right to claim a credit for approximately $40,000, plus fees and costs, against the second note.

The Outlook property sold in June 1986. Homami submitted a demand for the full $125,000 plus interest on that amount from June 22, 1985, and foreclosure fees. Iranzadi, maintaining he had paid $39,324.68 on the principal balance between March 1984 and June 1985, claimed a credit in that amount. Escrow closed but the sum of $43,500 was held out of the proceeds and delivered to Albert Ham, a stakeholder, pending resolution of the dispute.

Homami filed suit October 15, 1986, alleging breach of a written contract. Attached to the complaint were the two promissory notes and modification agreements. Iranzadi filed a cross-complaint for declaratory relief, alleging that he had paid $39,324.68 towards reducing the principal, and seeking a determination of rights as to the monies held in trust. He also pleaded a cause of action for conversion of the $39,324.68 and prayed for compensatory relief and punitive damages against Homami.

At trial Homami testified that he and Iranzadi had orally agreed on an interest rate of 12 percent, and had also agreed that Iranzadi would not report interest paid and Homami would not have to report receiving the income. He testified that this arrangement was discussed and reiterated at a family meeting March 15, 1985. And he specifically stated that the reason the loan documents did not reflect any interest was so that he could avoid reporting income to the Internal Revenue Service.

Iranzadi, on the other hand, claimed that he and Homami had never discussed interest on the loan. He testified that in family dealings interest was never charged and that he had often loaned money to Homami without interest. He stated that he had authorized Homami to take $2,000 to $3,000 from his account every month to reduce the principal balance.

The trial court found that the payments made by Iranzadi to Homami totalling $39,324.68 represented interest only, and no principal reduction. Therefore Iranzadi still owed Homami that amount on the loan. The court rendered judgment in favor of Homami for $39,324.68 plus interest at 18 percent from June 30, 1986, the close of escrow, plus attorneys fees and costs. The judgment ordered that Albert Ham, the stakeholder, be awarded $588.11 for his costs and that he distribute the balance in the trust account to Homami in partial payment of the judgment.

DISCUSSION

[Iranzadi argues] that a contract which has as its object an illegal purpose is contrary to public policy and void. Since we find the last point to be dispositive, we need not address the remaining issues.

The Civil Code provides a starting place. A contract must have a lawful object. (Civ.Code, § 1550.) Any contract which has as its object the violation of an express provision of law is unlawful. (Civ.Code, § 1667, subd. 1.) The object of a contract is the thing which it is agreed, on the part of the party receiving the consideration, to do or not to do. (Civ.Code, § 1595.) The object must be lawful when the contract is made. (Civ.Code, § 1596.) And that part of the contract which is unlawful is void. (Civ.Code, § 1599.)

Courts have interpreted these statutes liberally. "The general principle is well established that a contract founded on an illegal consideration, or which is made for the purpose of furthering any matter or thing prohibited by statute, or to aid or assist any party therein, is void. This rule applies to every contract which is founded on a transaction *malum in se*, or which is prohibited by a statute on the ground of public policy." C.I.T. Corp. v. Breckenridge, 63 Cal.App.2d 198, 200 (1944).

It makes no difference whether the contract has been partially or wholly performed. Rather, the test is "whether the plaintiff requires the aid of the illegal transaction to establish his case. If the plaintiff cannot open his case without showing that he has broken the law, the court will not assist him, whatever his claim in justice may be upon the defendant." Id.

Nor does it matter that the illegality has not been pleaded. "[I]f the question of illegality develops during the course of a trial, a court must consider it whether pleaded or not. . . . 'Whenever the evidence discloses the relations of the parties to the transaction to be illegal and against public policy, it becomes the duty of the court to refuse to entertain the action.'" Russell v. Soldinger, 59 Cal.App.3d 633, 642 (1976).

Cases which have applied these principles fall into several broad categories. A common situation involves the unlicensed contractor, or other unlicensed professional, who seeks to collect money for services rendered. Courts have routinely refused to grant relief in such cases on the ground that the failure to comply with licensing requirements violates a law designed to protect and benefit the public. Therefore a party who has violated the law and entered into an agreement to perform services while unlicensed cannot obtain the aid of courts to enforce the agreement. . . .

In another factual context, courts have refused to grant relief to parties seeking to collect monies arising from illegal gambling activities. . . .

A third group of cases closer to our facts involves plaintiffs who have attempted to circumvent federal law. Generally these cases arise where nonveterans seek to obtain government benefits and entitlements available to veterans only, either by setting up a strawman veteran or otherwise by falsifying documents.

For example, in *May v. Herron*, 127 Cal.App.2d 707 (1954), the Newmans transferred property to a veteran for the sole purpose of obtaining a veteran's priority under Federal Priorities Regulation No. 33. That regulation provided that veterans who wished to build houses for their own occupancy would receive preferential treatment in obtaining construction materials. The Newmans had been advised to obtain the illegal veteran's priority by their building contractor, who then entered into a contract with the veteran to build a house which he knew the Newmans intended to occupy. When the builder sued to recover a balance due on the construction contract, the court refused to come to his aid, finding that he had "initiated, suggested and directed a conspiracy to violate and circumvent a federal regulation which had the force of law." Id. at 711. The court concluded in this vein: "To permit a recovery here on any theory would permit plaintiff to benefit from his wilful and deliberate flouting of a law designed to promote the general public welfare." Id. at 712.

* * *

The message from these cases couldn't be clearer. As the Supreme Court has expressed it: "No principle of law is better settled than that a party to an illegal contract cannot come into a court of law and ask to have his illegal objects carried out; nor can he set up a case in which he must necessarily disclose an illegal purpose as the groundwork of his claim." Lee On v. Long, 37 Cal.2d 499, 502 (1951).

We do not perceive any meaningful difference between the unlawful agreements described in the above example and the tax evasion scheme perpetrated by Homami and Iranzadi in our case. Here Homami entered into a written agreement which specifically provided that he would be paid no interest. The purpose of the provision was to enable him to avoid compliance with state and federal income tax regulations. He then secretly collected interest income which he had no intention of reporting. And when a dispute developed, he sought the aid of the court to enforce the secret agreement so that he could keep the money he had collected.

* * *

[E]ven though a written contract is legal on its face, evidence may be introduced to establish its illegal character. May v. Herron, supra, at 710–711. And if the substance of the transaction is illegal, it matters not when or how the illegality is raised in the course of the lawsuit. Whether the evidence comes from one side or the other, the disclosure is fatal to the case. . . . The fact is that Homami, in order to state his claim to the funds held out of the escrow proceeds, was obliged to testify and did testify that he collected interest secretly in order to circumvent income tax laws. As the cases have repeatedly pointed out, "the test . . . is whether the plaintiff can establish his case otherwise than through the medium of an illegal transaction to which he himself was a party." Schur v. Johnson, 2 Cal.App.2d 680, 683–684 (1934). It is clear that Homami could not do so.

* * *

Because his agreement violated the law, Homami is not entitled to the $39,624.86 he collected as unreported interest. That amount is to be credited to Iranzadi from the escrow proceeds. Distribution of the balance of the funds held in the trust account is to be determined by the court on remand. * * *

NOTES

(1)   In *Homami*, what is the public policy said to be violated? To what extent, if any, would the denial of judicial remedy promote this policy?

(2)   The court in *Homami* refers to "the importance of deterring illegal conduct." Appraise the deterrent effect of the opinion.

(3)   *Minor Infractions.* Illegality may not prevent the enforcement of a contract if the court construes the illegality not to be "serious." For example, in *Town Planning and Engineering Assoc. v. Amesbury Specialty Co.*, 369 Mass. 737 (1976), an uncredentialled engineer was hired but subsequently not paid for engineering work. Even though a Massachusetts law provides that engineering is to be performed only by registered engineers, the court found that the illegal behavior contracted for was *de minimus.*

(4) *Public Policy and the Role of the Judiciary.* If a constitutionally valid statute provides explicitly that a particular contract is illegal or otherwise opposed to public policy, the task of the court is relatively easy. The court responds, in appropriate ways, to the declared will of the legislature. Most contract illegality cases are not of this type, however. More likely the statute does not address the precise issue; there is, at most, merely an indication of general legislative policy. This means that the question of what sound policy requires regarding the allegedly illegal bargain is plainly a judicial question. The court may state that it will be "guided" by a legislative declaration of policy, but it cannot escape the responsibility of doing justice in the particular case. In short, it is the court that must perform the task of elaborating the public policy of the jurisdiction, and this, of course, is frequently a difficult undertaking. See, generally, Walter Gellhorn, *Contracts and Public Policy*, 35 Colum. L. Rev. 679 (1935).

(5) *Discrimination as Grounds for Illegality.* 42 U.S.C. § 1981 prohibits race-based discrimination in the "mak[ing] and enforce[ment]" of contracts. Prohibitions against disparate racial treatment are unusual mandatory contract rules because they cause the legality of one contract to turn on the terms of others. Only by comparing terms or offers among contracts can one establish disparate treatment. In *Patterson v. McLean Credit Union*, 491 U.S. 164 (1989), however, the Supreme Court held that Section 1981 does not regulate disparate treatment in performance of contracts. The court expressly rejected the notion that racial harassment in the conditions of employment is actionable under Section 1981 when "it amounts to a breach of contract under state law." Do employers implicitly covenant not to racially harass? Would contracting around this covenant violate public policy?

(6) *A Cautionary Note.* In an English case, *St. John Shipping Corp. v. Joseph Rank, Ltd.*, [1956] 3 All E.R. 683, the plaintiff sued for the balance of freight charges due for transporting wheat from Mobile, Alabama to Liverpool. The defendant insisted that it was not obliged to pay because the freighter had been overloaded in violation of a statute making it a criminal offense to load a ship so that the load line was submerged. In holding for the plaintiff, the court said that the question was "whether the statute is meant to prohibit the contract being sued upon." It is significant, however, that the court was influenced by practical considerations. Speaking for the court, Lord Devlin said:

> If a contract has as its whole object the doing of the very act which the statute prohibits, it can be argued that you can hardly make sense of a statute which forbids an act and yet permits to be made a contract to do it; that is a clear implication. But unless you get a clear implication of that sort, I think that a court ought to be very slow to hold that a statute intends to interfere with the rights and remedies given by the ordinary law of contract.
>
>   Caution in this respect is, I think, especially necessary in these times when so much of commercial life is governed by regulations of one sort or another which may easily be broken without wicked intent. Persons who deliberately set out to break the law cannot expect to be aided in a court of justice, but it is a different matter

when the law is unwittingly broken. To nullify a bargain in such circumstances frequently means that in a case—perhaps of such triviality that no authority would have felt it worthwhile to prosecute—a seller, because he cannot enforce his civil rights, may forfeit a sum vastly in excess of any penalty that a criminal court would impose; and the sum forfeited will not go into the public purse but into the pockets of someone who is lucky enough to pick up the windfall or astute enough to have contrived to get it. It is questionable how far this contributes to public morality. . . . It may be questionable also whether public policy is well served by driving from the seat of judgment anyone who has been guilty of a minor transgression. Commercial men who have unwittingly offended against one of a multiplicity of regulations may nevertheless feel that they have not thereby forfeited all right to justice, and may go elsewhere for it if courts of law will not give it to them. In the last resort they will, if necessary, set up their own machinery for dealing with their own disputes in the way that those whom the law puts beyond the pale, such as gamblers, have done.

3 All E.R. at 690–691. See Note, *The Doctrine of Illegality and Petty Offenders: Can Quasi-Contract Bring Justice?*, 42 Notre Dame L. Rev. 46 (1966).

PROBLEMS: IMPACT OF STATUTORY VIOLATIONS ON CONTRACT ENFORCEMENT

(a)   *The Case of the Unregistered Apartment.* Tenant signed a one-year lease with Landlord, but decided not to occupy the premises. Landlord sues for damages. Tenant argues that the lease is void because the apartment was not registered as a residential unit, nor did the Landlord secure an occupancy permit, as required by city code. What result? See Noble v. Alis, 474 N.E.2d 109 (Ind.App. 1985).

(b)   *The Case of the Unmetered Fuel Oil Deliveries.* Buyer owned two homes to which Seller delivered fuel oil on several occasions. Not all of the deliveries were metered as required by law, and for which Seller was subject to fine and/or imprisonment. Seller sues for $5,000 worth of oil delivered but not metered. What result? See Rupert's Oil Service v. Leslie, 40 Conn.Supp. 295 (1985).

(c)   *The Case of the Excessive Interest Charge.* Plaintiff, an investment company licensed by the Small Business Administration, loaned defendant $64,000. The loan was secured by a mortgage on defendant's residence. When the defendant defaulted on the loan, plaintiff sought to foreclose on the mortgage. The defendant argued that the plaintiff had charged interest above that allowed by regulations of the Small Business Administration, and this made the contract unenforceable. The trial court agreed. What result on appeal? See Lloyd Capital Corp. v. Pat Henchar, Inc., 544 N.Y.S.2d 178 (1989).

(d)   *The Case of the Uncertified Carrier.* On four occasions, Carrier transported Owner's horses in interstate commerce, but without having obtained a "certificate of public convenience and necessity" as required by the Interstate Commerce Commission Act. Can Owner interpose this statutory violation as a legal justification for not paying Carrier? See Hull and Smith Horse Vans, Inc. v. Carras, 144 Mich.App. 712 (1985).

(e) *The Case of the "No Bid" Contract.* Seller contacted Buyer, a community hospital, concerning the sale of radiator covers needed by the hospital for accreditation purposes. The county commissioners negotiated the contract with Seller but without going through the formal bidding process mandated by law. Seller sues for the $56,600 price. The county treasurer refuses to pay. Who wins? See Majestic Radiator Enclosure Co., Inc. v. County Commissioners of Middlesex, 397 Mass. 1002 (1986).

(f) *The Case of the Delayed Title Delivery.* Buyer bought a boat from Seller, but after having experienced several problems with the boat sought to avoid the sale. Buyer argued that Seller's failure to deliver a certificate of title within 20 days, as mandated by state law, made the contract unenforceable. Is Buyer correct? See Saulny v. RDY, Inc., 760 S.W.2d 813 (Tex.App. 1988).

(g) *The Case of the Missing Repair Estimate.* Owner brought his Jaguar in for service and orally agreed to pay $187 for certain repairs. When he returned to pick up the car, he agreed to pay $200 for further work which the mechanic recommended. Later, the car was delivered to his home, accompanied by a repair bill for $500. Owner refused to pay, insisting that the contract was void because the service station failed to provide a written estimate as required by statute. Does Owner make a convincing argument? See Bennett v. Hayes, 53 Cal.App.3d 700 (1975).

(h) *The Case of the Unlicensed Employment Agency.* Employer contracted with Employment Agency to find a computer programmer. The Agency found a qualified applicant, whom Employer later hired. However, Employer refused to pay the agreed upon fee, based upon Employment Agency's lack of license required by statute. What, if anything, should the Agency be able to recover? See T.E.C. & Associates, Inc. v. Alberto-Culver Co., 131 Ill.App.3d 1085 (1985). See also U.S. Nursing Corp. v. Saint Joseph Medical Center, 39 F.3d 790 (7th Cir. 1994) (unlicensed nursing service); Design Development, Inc. v. Brignole, 20 Conn.App. 685 (1990) (architect); Hoffman v. Dunn, 496 N.E.2d 818 (Ind.App. 1986) (realtor); Haberman v. Elledge, 42 Wash.App. 744 (1986) (well driller).

(i) *Political and Media Promises.* In *Cohen v. Cowles Media Co.,* reprinted in Chapter Two, the court held that a reporter's confidentiality promise did not create a contract because the parties did not intend to create a legally enforceable agreement. But what if a newspaper promises to compensate any source that it injures with negligent misrepresentations, and expressly announces that it intends this agreement to be legally enforceable? Should the contract be unenforceable as being in conflict with the holding of *New York Times v. Sullivan,* 376 U.S. 254 (1964), or do newspapers instead have a constitutional right to stand behind the truthfulness of their representations? Is *Sullivan* merely a constitutional default? Do politicians have the opportunity to make their campaign promises legally binding?: "If elected, I promise to X (and I intend for this promise to be legally enforceable)." See John Solomon, *Prize Fight*, The New Republic 23 (Nov. 15, 1999) (describing promise of RNC Chairman Haley Barbour to pay $1 million if reader can prove that Republicans are "cutting" Medicare).

Comment: Aleatory, Gambling and Insurance Contracts

An aleatory promise is a promise "under which [promisor's] duty to perform is conditional on the occurrence of a fortuitous event." Restatement (Second) § 76 cmt. c. The term derives from the Latin "alea" for die (as in Caesar's comment on crossing the Rubicon: "Alia iacta est!" "The die is cast!") The common law generally enforces such promises. For example, A can promise to sell and B to buy goods if a war ends by a certain date.

A subset of aleatory promises, however, are not enforceable. Almost every U.S. jurisdiction has a statute or constitutional provision generally prohibiting gambling and declaring gambling contracts either void or unenforceable. American common law has generally regarded gambling agreements to be voidable as against public policy. See Restatement (Second) § 178, illus. 1. Ordinarily, a party to a wagering contract can withdraw while the agreement is still executory and recover the money bet. Since wagers are against public policy, the winner of a wager cannot recover by court action money won and not paid. And money loaned or furnished for the purpose of being used in gambling cannot be recovered. Moreover, the loser in a wagering agreement cannot recover the money he lost in a court action. Finally, some states refuse to enforce gambling agreements that are legal in other jurisdictions but contrary to the laws of the forum state. Meyer v. Hawkinson, 626 N.W.2d 262 (N.D. 2001) (refusing to enforce an alleged contract to share the proceeds of a winning Western Canadian Lottery ticket).

It is, however, not always easy to distinguish illegal wagering contracts from other aleatory contracts that have a legitimate commercial or other purpose and are not considered contrary to public policy. Likewise, insurance contracts can often be recharacterized as wagers (and vice versa): "I bet you, you won't die next year" or "I'm willing to offer you insurance that the Jets win the Super Bowl." One way to distinguish between unenforceable gambling contracts and enforceable aleatory or insurance contracts is by asking whether the risk is created, or its stakes increased, by the bargain itself. Insureds tend to buy insurance to compensate them for the possible realization of an existing risk, thereby mitigating the stakes of the risk. Gamblers by their contracts tend to create the risk at issue, or at least increase the stakes of the risk. As Corbin once said: "It can hardly be conceived that prior to their betting bargain it makes any difference to either party engaged in throwing dice which faces are up when the dice stops rolling." Corbin on Contracts § 1481. So perhaps public policy condones insurance because it mitigates the stakes at risk, while gambling is against public policy because it artificially creates or increases stakes. Further, the risks that insurance mitigates are often largely monetary while those associated with gambling, if they preexisted at all, are not. Also, insureds tend to bargain for payments conditional upon something untoward happening, while gamblers tend to bargain for payments conditional upon something fortuitous happening (e.g., their favored team winning).

Comment: Public Policy and Capacity to Contract

In 2011, the state of Alabama passed an "Illegal Immigration Act" which included the following provision:

> No court of this state shall enforce the terms of, or otherwise regard as valid, any contract between a party and an alien unlawfully present in the United States, if the party had direct or constructive knowledge that the alien was unlawfully present in the United States at the time the contract was entered into, and the performance of the contract required the alien to remain unlawfully present in the United States for more than 24 hours after the time the contract was entered into or performance could not reasonably be expected to occur without such remaining.

Section 27(a) AL HB 56; Alabama Acts of the 2011 Regular Session codified at Ala.Code 1975 § 31–13–26. The section does not apply to a contract for lodging for one night, the purchase of food to be consumed by the alien, a contract for medical services, or a contract for transportation if it is intended to facilitate the alien's return to his or her country of origin. Is denying unlawful aliens the ability to enforce terms of contracts likely to decrease their presence in the state? Does the law mean that unlawful aliens don't need to pay back their loans?

Here we see an overlap between considerations of public policy and rules for capacity. How does Alabama's law compare to the rules for infancy, mental competency, and intoxication? More to the point, are the justifications for these laws similar? Are there any costs to enforcing public policy by declaring certain classes of persons to lack the capacity to contract?

In *United States v. Alabama*, 691 F.3d 1269 (11th Cir. 2012), the Eleventh Circuit held that federal law preempted Section 27. Noting that contract law "is typically within the province of the states and therefore entitled to the presumption against preemption," the court concluded that this section "constitute[d] a thinly veiled attempt to regulate immigration under the guise of contract law." Id. at 1295–6, 1297. On remand, the Northern District of Alabama permanently enjoined the state from implementing numerous sections of HB 56, including Section 27. United States v. Alabama, No. 2:11-CV-2746-SLB, 2013 WL 10799535, at *1 (N.D. Ala. Nov. 25, 2013).

Mark Broadley v. Mashpee Neck Marina, Inc.

United States Court of Appeals, First Circuit, 2006.
471 F.3d 272.

■ BOUDIN, CHIEF JUDGE. On August 25, 2002, Mark Broadley was injured at the Mashpee Neck Marina ("Marina") at Cape Cod when his foot became caught in a gap between the main dock and a floating dock where his vessel was moored. The gap between the docks is about two to three inches wide when the water is calm, but the wake of a passing boat can cause the docks to move and the gap to widen. Broadley fractured his ankle and was left with a permanent loss of function.

Broadley alleged that Marina's negligence caused the accident: the space between docks was a potential hazard that could have been mitigated either by using a flexible material to cover the gap or by tying the docks together more tightly. Marina denied liability, citing the boilerplate exculpatory clause of the contract for seasonal mooring between the parties. That clause read:

> The OWNER [Broadley] warrants and [covenants] that . . . the OWNER . . . will [not] make any claims, demands, causes of action of any kind and nature, or obtain or enforce any judgments, executions or levies thereon . . . against MARINA, its officers, directors, agents, servants, or its employees, arising out of any damage, loss, personal injury or death suffered by [him]. . . . The OWNER . . . agree[s] and covenant[s] that [he] will defend, indemnify and save MARINA harmless from any and all of such claims, demands, causes of action, judgments and executions, and the MARINA shall be entitled to responsible attorneys fees in the event of breach of the OWNER's covenant hereunder.

Marina claimed that this exculpatory clause precluded Broadley from bringing suit for personal injury due to Marina's negligence. Broadley responded that under admiralty law, a party may limit but may not completely absolve itself from liability for ordinary negligence; and that the clause was over-broad and therefore unenforceable insofar as it absolved Marina of liability for gross negligence and intentional wrongdoing. Because of its connection to maritime activities, the clause is governed by federal admiralty law. . . .

The district court issued summary judgment in Marina's favor, holding that the clause should be reformed to limit it to ordinary negligence. Broadley had conceded that Marina's negligence did not rise to the level of gross negligence, so as reformed the clause barred his claim. This appeal followed. We review grants of summary judgment *de novo*. . . .

Broadley's main argument on appeal is that, under admiralty law, a party may not completely absolve itself of liability for ordinary negligence; for support, Broadley cites the Supreme Court's decision in

Bisso v. Inland Waterways Corp., 349 U.S. 85 (1955), and our own decision in *La Esperanza de P.R., Inc. v. Perez Y Cia de P.R., Inc.*, 124 F.3d 10 (1st Cir. 1997).

Bisso could be read as laying down a flat rule, applicable to all cases, forbidding clauses that entirely exculpate a party for its own simple negligence. However, *Bisso* focused on towing contracts and the special threat of "monopolistic compulsions." 349 U.S. at 91. The Court also cited case law forbidding exculpatory clauses in common law relationships where unequal bargaining power is presumed (e.g., utilities and their customers). 349 U.S. at 90–91. Thus *Bisso* can easily be read as limited to relationships where unequal power is inherent or established.

Agreements to waive claims for mere negligence are generally enforceable at common law. See Keeton et al., Prosser & Keeton on Torts § 68, at 482–83 (5th ed. 1984). Qualifications exist—the relevant doctrines are unconscionability and contracts of adhesion—turning on factors like adequate disclosure, relative bargaining power and the like. 1–2 Farnsworth, Farnsworth on Contracts §§ 4.26, 4.28, 5.2 (3d ed. 2004). But an admiralty rule, flatly preventing parties from contracting away claims for simple negligence in all circumstances, would be surprising.

Since *Bisso*, decisions in other circuits have addressed this issue in admiralty cases but no consensus exists as to how *Bisso* should be read. Two circuits would allow a release from all liability for negligence (at least in the dockage context) and one circuit arguably would not.[2] Another circuit has upheld exculpatory clauses that limited but did not entirely preclude liability for negligence; but in our case the clause completely exculpates from such liability, so this last circuit's cases are distinguishable.[3]

As for this circuit, the main thrust of the language in *La Esperanza* was to uphold exculpatory clauses directed to mere negligence so long as "expressed clearly in contracts entered into freely by parties of equal bargaining power." The sentence ended with the phrase: "provided that the clause not provide for a total absolution of liability." 124 F.3d at 19. But this may simply mean (unexceptionally) that parties cannot contract out of gross negligence.

Nor did *La Esperanza* hold invalid a properly disclosed clause, not unfairly imposed, waiving all claims for all negligence. The decision upheld application of a clause barring recovery for lost profits or lost use of vessel caused by a shipyard's negligence. So *La Esperanza's* dicta, however read, cannot control the present case. . . . In our view, the better rule is that an exculpatory clause limited to barring liability for ordinary

---

[2]   Compare Sander v. Alexander Richardson Invs., 334 F.3d 712, 719 (8th Cir. 2003), and Morton v. Zidell Explorations, Inc., 695 F.2d 347, 350–51 (9th Cir. 1982), cert. denied, 460 U.S. 1039 (1983), with Edward Leasing Corp. v. Uhlig & Assocs., Inc., 785 F.2d 877, 888–89 (11th Cir. 1986).

[3]   Todd Shipyards Corp. v. Turbine Serv., Inc., 674 F.2d 401, 410 (5th Cir.), cert. denied sub nom, 459 U.S. 1036 (1982). * * *

negligence would be valid, assuming it were not inflicted by a monopolist or one with greatly superior bargaining power.

Broadley does not claim that Marina had undue bargaining power—presumably because there are alternative marinas in the general area—but this is not the end of the inquiry. There is no doubt that the clause as written is vastly overbroad and against public policy insofar as it purports to absolve Marina of liability for gross negligence, recklessness and intentional wrongdoing. Thus, the question remains whether a court should be willing to narrow the clause and apply it only to the extent that it excludes liability for simple negligence.

The district court said that it would "reform" the clause, narrowing it to apply only to negligence; but reformation is normally appropriate where the language somehow fails to express the actual intention of the parties and is conformed merely to reflect their actual intent or, where the contents have been fraudulently misrepresented by one party, to conform the contract to the terms conveyed to the defrauded party. See Restatement (Second) Contracts §§ 155, 166; 2 Farnsworth on Contracts § 7.5. Neither situation is present here.

The doctrine pertinent where a contract provision is unlawfully overbroad is that which *permits* a court to sever or divide provisions that are unlawful as written, retaining those provisions or applications of them that are permissible. 2 Farnsworth on Contracts § 5.8. State law is not uniform, but a modern version of the doctrine, as reflected in the Restatement (Second) of Contracts § 184 (emphasis added) provides:

> A court *may* treat only part of a term as unenforceable . . . if the party who seeks to enforce the term obtained it in good faith and in accordance with *reasonable standards of fair dealing.*

One of the illustrations makes clear that where the parties actually negotiated an overbroad exculpatory clause that clearly encompasses negligence, a good case can be made for narrowing it to apply only to negligence, id. § 184 illus. 4; but another comment, arguably more pertinent here, says that "[t]he fact that the [overbroad] term is contained in a standard form supplied by the dominant party argues against aiding him in this request." Id. § 184 cmt. b.

There is no finding in this case as to the good or bad faith of the marina owner. Quite possibly this was a form contract of a kind often furnished by trade associations seeking to give their members every advantage. In all events, we will assume that there was no subjective bad faith by Marina. Instead, the question for us is whether the clause represents fair dealing so that a judicial narrowing is sound public policy.

The substantial overbreadth of the clause has two negative consequences. Obviously such a clause can discourage perfectly legitimate claims—e.g., for gross negligence or deliberate wrongdoing—from ever being brought by the injured party. The injured slip-renter often has ample reason to hesitate about suing—time, uncertainty, expenses—especially where, as here, the contract provides for attorney's fees to Marina for breach of the agreement not to sue.

A second concern is that the clause never says that it exempts Marina from negligence. The language used, although broader, is also blander: there is no reference to fault; and, although the clause literally encompasses negligence, *Sander*, 334 F.3d at 716, it is less likely to convey an *effective* warning to the reader than would a clear and specific disclaimer of liability for *negligence*.

Finally, Marina does not suggest that there was actual negotiation about such terms. If the negligence issue had been the subject of actual bargaining and discussion, we might well have a different reaction; but this is evidently a typical case of boilerplate. Boilerplate even in contracts of adhesion is not automatically unlawful; but it is a relevant consideration in deciding whether to rescue the contract from overbreadth. See, e.g., Richards v. Richards, 181 Wis.2d 1007 (1994); Restatement (Second) Contracts § 184 cmt. b.

The case law is not very helpful in providing a controlling answer. There are two admiralty cases in other circuits sharing our reading of *Bisso* that have narrowed such clauses; but neither addresses specifically the considerations of concern to us. Cases applying state law are divided, with some courts narrowing such clauses and others declining to do so very much for the reasons we have already given. We find the latter more persuasive. [Citations omitted.]

The marina agreement in this case has, as part of the boilerplate, a severability clause. But the same public policy concerns we have described lead us to reject the application of this clause to rescue the overbroad exculpatory clause. Otherwise, the narrow and explicit language, which we think should be required, could be side-stepped by leaving the broad language in place and including the severability clause as a companion.

In declining to narrow the exculpatory clause, we rely on the extreme overbreadth of the clause and the plainness of its illegality, the boilerplate character of the contract and lack of specific negotiation, the absence of an explicit reference to negligence which would provide better warning, and the attorney's fees clause. Any competent lawyer could write a straightforward exclusion of liability for negligence that we would sustain.

Only some elements of this analysis were made by Broadley. In the district court a simple overbreadth argument was adverted to; in this court Broadley stresses lack of clarity. A litigant is not expected to guess just how a court will explain its result; but it would be easy enough for us to avoid the issue and to affirm on the ground that the overbreadth argument was not adequately developed and is therefore forfeit. United States v. Zannino, 895 F.2d 1, 17 (1st Cir.), cert. denied, 494 U.S. 1082 (1990).

But the forfeiture doctrine is not an absolute limitation on judicial power but a prudential limitation subject to the reviewing court's discretion. Indeed, a court may, although rarely will, forgive a knowing waiver where extreme injustice would be done. . . . Here, it is important that the validity issue be resolved for the sake of future case law, and invalidity is the juster result.

The only concern where the court develops issues not adequately argued is that a party not apprised may have arguments against the court's reasoning. But in this instance an overbreadth claim as such was raised in the district court and we know what Marina said in response. Similarly, we are especially open in cases of this kind to petitions for rehearing and are ready to revise reasoning and result if this is warranted.

With that qualification, we *reverse* the decision of the district court and *remand* for further proceedings. No criticism of the very able district judge is intended; we are dealing with poorly developed and confusing admiralty law in aggravated circumstances, and the district court did not receive much help. Each side will bear its own costs on this appeal. * * *

NOTES

(1) Was the exculpatory clause against public policy or was it unconscionable? What difference does that make?

(2) In *Tunkl v. Regents of the University of California*, which considered whether it was against public policy to permit a hospital to condition admission on the patient's advance waiver of rights to reasonable medical care, the California Supreme Court identified six factors courts should consider when asked to enforce an exculpatory provision.

> [T]he attempted but invalid exemption involves a transaction which exhibits some or all of the following characteristics. It concerns a business of a type generally thought suitable for public regulation. The party seeking exculpation is engaged in performing a service of great importance to the public, which is often a matter of practical necessity for some members of the public. The party holds himself out as willing to perform this service for any member of the public who seeks it, or at least for any member coming within certain established standards. As a result of the essential nature of the service, in the economic setting of the transaction, the party invoking exculpation possesses a decisive advantage of bargaining strength against any member of the public who seeks his services. In exercising a superior bargaining power the party confronts the public with a standardized adhesion contract of exculpation, and makes no provision whereby a purchaser may pay additional reasonable fees and obtain protection against negligence. Finally, as a result of the transaction, the person or property of the purchaser is placed under the control of the seller, subject to the risk of carelessness by the seller or his agents.

60 Cal.2d 92, 98–100 (1963).

(3) Under Section 402A of Restatement (Second) of Torts, a manufacturer's or seller's attempt to disclaim or limit liability for damages to person or property caused by a dangerously defective product is against public policy. See cmt. m. This policy is endorsed in Section 195(3) of the Second Restatement of Contracts for a "term exempting a seller of a product from his special tort liability for physical harm to a user or consumer . . . unless the term is fairly bargained for and is consistent with the policy underlying that liability." Comment c states that the exception is for the "rare situation in which the term is consistent with the policy underlying the liability." Where a seller's breach of warranty causes economic loss rather than damage to person or property, "disclaimers" of warranty and limitations upon remedy are enforceable if not unconscionable. See UCC §§ 2–302, 2–316(2) and 2–719(3). Put another way, there is no public policy against these risk allocation devices generally but, at the very least, they must be fairly bargained for. For a decision holding that these clauses were unconscionable in a commercial setting, see A & M Produce Co. v. FMC Corp., 135 Cal.App.3d 473 (1982).

(4) *Indemnification Clauses.* A related question concerns the validity of indemnification or "hold harmless" provisions, whereby one secures another's promise to indemnify one against one's own negligence. "An indemnity clause purports to shift responsibility for the payment of damages from one party to another. * * * As such, an indemnity clause allocates the risk of loss or injury resulting from a particular venture between the parties to the agreement. An exculpatory clause relieves one party from the consequences of its own negligence. * * * Such clause relieves one party from responsibility for injuries incurred by the other party from a particular transaction or occurrence." Whitson v. Goodbodys, Inc., 773 S.W.2d 381 (Tex.App. 1989). An agreement to indemnify another against loss from or against liability for a tort is generally enforceable. Where such a promise is likely to induce the commission of a tort, however, it will not be enforced on grounds of public policy.

PROBLEM: RELEASE OF UNKNOWN INJURIES

On November 26, 1982, Vicente Morta suffered a collision that damaged his 1976 Mazda station wagon and caused him bodily injury. According to Morta, the car was "a total loss." Morta himself was knocked unconscious and taken by ambulance to the emergency room at Guam Memorial Hospital. After treating Morta, the attending physician assured him that he was fine and could go home. Afterwards, Morta continued to have pain in his muscles, chin and chest. He was treated three days later by a second physician at the Seventh Day Adventist Clinic, who also told him he was fine, and the pain would eventually subside.

Morta sought compensation for his losses from appellant Korea Insurance Corporation (KIC), which insured the driver who had caused the accident. Morta was directed to Bernabe Santa Maria, a claims adjuster. Morta and Santa Maria happened to be from the same area of the Philippines and conversed in their native tongues, Tagalog and Ilocano. Morta testified that he had no problem understanding Santa Maria.

Santa Maria helped Morta complete the claim form, received from Morta his medical reports, examined the damaged Mazda and, acknowledging the liability of his insured, offered Morta $900. Morta testified that the settlement offer had several components: "Three Hundred Dollars for my car; $250 from loss of compensation of work, like that; and Two Hundred some for sufferings and injury that I suffered, you know. So, they told me, included also the medical bill from SDA and the towing expenses, that item."

Morta was not satisfied with that amount, claiming that the car alone had a blue-book value of $2,300. Santa Maria told him that $900 was all he could pay. Morta did not jump at the offer; he thought it over and went to see a lawyer. He showed the lawyer the medical and police reports. The lawyer evaluated Morta's claim and advised him that he would be unlikely to recover much more than the $900 KIC had offered and that any attempt to do so would delay payment. Morta returned to Santa Maria's office and accepted the $900. Because the settlement check covered damages for the car as well as for personal injuries—in short, all of Morta's claims—Morta signed a standard release, which was less than a page long. The trial court described the release as follows:

> At the top, in characters a quarter-inch tall, was the word "RELEASE"; immediately beneath, in slightly smaller letters, were the words "OF ALL CLAIMS." A few concise sentences follow, clearly and unequivocally stating that Morta releases KIC from all claims "growing out of any and all known and unknown, foreseen and unforeseen bodily and personal injuries and property damage" arising out of the accident in question. Morta also acknowledges that "the injuries sustained are or may be permanent and progressive and that recovery therefrom is uncertain and indefinite. . . ." In capital letters near the bottom is a certification that the signer has read and understands the terms of the release; immediately above the signature line, also in capitals, is a "caution" instructing the signer to read the release before signing it.

About a week after the settlement, Morta began to feel ill and dizzy. He was given medication by his doctor, but soon thereafter he collapsed unconscious, awaking in a Honolulu hospital after undergoing emergency surgery for a blood clot in his brain. The medical bills amounted to approximately $11,000, all paid for by Morta's insurer, FHP, Inc.

Morta filed suit to recover damages resulting from this injury, disavowing the release on the grounds, *inter alia*, that Santa Maria fraudulently misrepresented its contents. The jury returned a general verdict upholding the release, and the superior court entered judgment to that effect.

Morta appealed and made the following arguments as to why the release was invalid:

(1) There was a mutual mistake of fact, in that both parties assumed that there were no unknown injuries. Either the release should be avoided or reformed to exclude the phrase "unknown injuries."

(2) There was a mistake by Morta, who did not know he was signing a release or, if he did, did not know the contents of the release and was surprised to learn that it purported to release unknown claims.

(3) There was fraud by the agent, who misrepresented the contents by failing to disclose and discuss the clause.

(4) Morta was unduly influenced by the agent.

(5) The release was signed under duress, in that Morta needed the money and could not afford to refuse to sign and litigate the claim.

(6) The release was either against public policy or unconscionable.

How should these claims be resolved? See Morta v. Korea Insurance Corp., 840 F.2d 1452 (9th Cir. 1988), from which these facts were taken.

Comment: Limitations on Liability for Misrepresentation

Suppose in a bargain one party makes representations of fact, and the other party agrees that there shall be no liability if the representations of fact are false. In a contract for the sale of goods, the representations about the goods might be express warranties under UCC § 2–313(1), and a subsequent attempt to disclaim them would be ineffective to the extent that the express warranty and the disclaimer cannot be construed as consistent with each other. UCC § 2–316(1). This rule of construction seeks "to protect a buyer from unexpected and unbargained [for] language of disclaimer." Comment (1).

What about other legal effects of misrepresentation? In *Abry Partners V, L.P v. F & W*, 891 A.2d 1032 (Del. Ch. 2006), the seller of corporate assets sought to absolve itself (and foreclose the buyer's remedy of rescission) under a clause in which the buyer agreed to assume the risk of (and seek other remedies for) false or inaccurate representations. In a long and careful opinion, the court stated *inter alia*:

> [It] is appropriate for the judiciary in fashioning common law to give as much leeway to sophisticated business parties crafting acquisition agreements as is afforded to those who write the governing instruments of limited partnerships and limited liability companies. We should be reluctant to be more restrictive of freedom of contract than those elected by our citizens to write the statutory law.
>
> With that in mind, I resolve this case in the following manner. To the extent that the Stock Purchase Agreement purports to limit the Seller's exposure for its own conscious participation in the communication of lies to the Buyer, it is invalid under the public policy of this State. That is, I find that

the public policy of this State will not permit the Seller to insulate itself from the possibility that the sale would be rescinded if the Buyer can show either: 1) that the Seller knew that the Company's contractual representations and warranties were false; or 2) that the Seller itself lied to the Buyer about a contractual representation and warranty. This will require the Buyer to prove that the Seller acted with an illicit state of mind, in the sense that the Seller knew that the representation was false and either communicated it to the Buyer directly itself or knew that the Company had. In this case, that distinction is largely of little importance because of the Officer's Certificate provided by the Seller. In that certificate, the Seller certified that (1) each representation and warranty of the Company and Seller was true and correct as of the closing date; (2) the Seller and Company performed and complied in all material respects with the agreements and covenants required to be performed or complied with; and (3) between the date of signing the Stock Purchase Agreement and closing, there had been no change, event or condition of any character which had or would reasonably be expected to constitute a material adverse effect for the Company.

By contrast, the Buyer may not obtain rescission or greater monetary damages upon any lesser showing. If the Company's managers intentionally misrepresented facts to the Buyer without knowledge of falsity by the Seller, then the Buyer cannot obtain rescission or damages, but must proceed with an Indemnity Claim subject to the Indemnity Fund's liability cap. Likewise, the Buyer may not escape the contractual limitations on liability by attempting to show that the Seller acted in a reckless, grossly negligent, or negligent manner. The Buyer knowingly accepted the risk that the Seller would act with inadequate deliberation. It is an experienced private equity firm that could have walked away without buying. It has no moral justification for escaping its own voluntarily-accepted limits on its remedies against the Seller absent proof that the Seller itself acted in a consciously improper manner.

In sum, I conclude that the Seller's motion to dismiss the complaint in its entirety must be denied. But the Buyer may only obtain its desired relief—rescission or in the alternative, full compensatory damages—if it meets the burden of proof described.

891 A.2d at 1063–65. The court also recognized, however, that under Delaware law, sophisticated parties might avoid liability for misrepresentation with a non-reliance clause:

The teaching of this court . . . is that a party cannot promise, in a clear integration clause of a negotiated agreement, that it will not rely on promises and representations outside of the agreement and then shirk its own bargain in favor of a "but we did rely on those other representations" fraudulent inducement claim. The policy basis for this line of cases is, in my view, quite strong. If there is a public policy interest in truthfulness, then that interest applies with more force, not less, to contractual representations of fact. Contractually binding, written representations of fact ought to be the most reliable of representations, and a law intolerant of fraud should abhor parties that make such representations knowing they are false.

To fail to enforce non-reliance clauses is not to promote a public policy against lying. Rather, it is to excuse a lie made by one contracting party in writing—the lie that it was relying only on contractual representations and that no other representations had been made—to enable it to prove that another party lied orally or in a writing outside the contract's four corners. For the plaintiff in such a situation to prove its fraudulent inducement claim, it proves itself not only a liar, but a liar in the most inexcusable of commercial circumstances: in a freely negotiated written contract. Put colloquially, this is necessarily a "Double Liar" scenario. To allow the buyer to prevail on its claim is to sanction its own fraudulent conduct.

The enforcement of non-reliance clauses recognizes that parties with free will should say no rather than lie in a contract. The enforcement of non-reliance clauses also recognizes another reality that is often overlooked in morally-tinged ruminations on the importance of deterring fraud. That reality is that courts are not perfect in distinguishing meritorious from non-meritorious claims of fraud. Permitting the procession of fraud claims based on statements that buyers promised they did not rely upon subjects sellers to a greater possibility of wrongful liability, especially because those statements are often allegedly oral, rather than in a writing, and thus there is often an evidentiary issue about whether the supposedly false statement ever was uttered. As important, even when a court rejects a buyer's fraud claim that is grounded in a disclaimed statement, the seller does not get the full benefit of its bargain because the costs (both direct and indirect) of the litigation are rarely shifted in America to the buyer who made a meritless claim.

891 A.2d at 1057–58. This suggests that parties can effectively avoid all liability for fraud by representing no reliance. That is, a non-reliance clause has the same effect as a clause expressly limiting liability for fraud in the inducement, were the latter effective. Why allow parties to do with non-reliance clauses what the law does not allow them to do with express exculpation clauses? See Jeffrey M. Lipshaw, *Of Fine Lines, Blunt*

Instruments, and Half-Truths: Business Acquisition Agreements and the Right to Lie, 32 Del. J. Corp. L. 431 (2007).

Data Management, Inc. v. James H. Greene

Supreme Court of Alaska, 1988.
757 P.2d 62.

■ MATTHEWS, CHIEF JUSTICE.

FACTS

Data Management, Inc. employed James H. Greene and Richard Van Camp. The parties signed a contract containing a covenant not to compete. The covenant provides that the employees will not compete with Data Management in Alaska for five years after termination.[1]

Shortly after the employees' termination from Data Management, the company filed suit against them for breach of the covenant not to compete. Data Management sought a preliminary injunction enjoining Greene and Van Camp from rendering computing services to twenty-one named individuals.[2] The preliminary injunction was granted.

Subsequently, the court granted summary judgment to Greene and Van Camp. The court found that the anti-competition covenant was not severable and was wholly unenforceable. Data Management appeals.

DISCUSSION

We have not yet decided whether an overly broad covenant not to compete can be altered to render it legal. A survey of other jurisdictions reveals three different approaches.

The first approach is to hold that a covenant which is overbroad, and hence unconscionable, will not be enforced. This strict view was adopted by Arkansas in *Rector-Phillips-Morse, Inc. v. Vroman,* 489 S.W.2d 1 (1973). In that case, the court held that a three year covenant not to

---

[1] The covenant not to compete stated:

Inasmuch as the Employee will acquire or have access to information which is of a highly confidential and secret nature, it is agreed that for the terms of this agreement and for a period of 5 years after the termination of this agreement, Eployee [sic] will not, within the State of Alaska, directly or indirectly, perform any similar services for any other person or firm located within the State of Alaska, without first obtaining the written consent and approval of the Employer, and that Employee will not own, manage, operate or control, be employed by, participate in, or be connected in any manner with the ownership, management, operation or control of any business similar to the type of business conducted by the Employer at the time of the termination of this contract or in competition with, directly or indirectly, the business of the Employer. In the event of an actual or threatened breach by the Employee of the provisions of this paragraph, the Employer shall be entitled to an injunction restraining the Employee from owning, managing, operating, controling, [sic] being employed by, participating in, or being in any way so connected with any business similar to the type of business engaged in by the Employer. Nothing herein stated shall be construed as prohibiting the Employer from pursuing any other remedies available for such breach of threatened breach, including the recovery of damages from the Employee.

[2] Data Management argues that this is a reasonable modification of the covenant not to compete, and that the trial court erred in not so modifying the covenant.

compete was too long. The court rejected the employer's request to alter the covenant from three years to six months. The court held, "our rule is that when a restriction such as this one is too far-reaching to be valid, the court will not make a new contract for the parties by reducing the restriction to a shorter time or to a smaller area." 489 S.W.2d at 4. Georgia has also adopted this position. See, Rollins Protective Serv. Co. v. Palermo, 287 S.E.2d 546, 549 (1982).

We do not favor this approach. The parties' contract is a bargain. One of the elements of that bargain is the covenant not to compete. As a general rule, courts should respect the rights of parties to enter into contracts, and should not interfere with their contractual relationships. There is a need to strike a balance between protecting the rights of parties to enter into contracts, and the need to protect parties from illegal contracts. Obliterating all overbroad covenants not to compete, regardless of their factual settings, is too mechanistic and may produce unduly harsh results. In response to objections like these, a second approach was developed.

The second approach is to hold that if words in an overbroad covenant not to compete can be deleted in such a way as to render it enforceable then the court may do so. This is the so-called "blue pencil" rule. See Restatement of Contracts § 518 (1932). This position was adopted by Indiana in *Licocci v. Cardinal Associates, Inc.*, 432 N.E.2d 446, 452 (Ind.App. 1982), vacated on other grounds, 445 N.E.2d 556 (Ind. 1983), where the court stated, "if the covenant is clearly separated into parts and some parts are reasonable and others are not, the contract may be held divisible. The reasonable restrictions may then be enforced." * * *

This rule has been criticized as being too mechanical, in that it values the wording of the contract over its substance. For example, if a seller promised not to compete "anywhere in England," the whole provision would be void because the quoted clause cannot be narrowed by deleting any words. On the other hand, if the seller promised not to compete "in London or elsewhere in England," the covenant would be enforceable as to London because "elsewhere in England" could be "blue penciled." The difference is merely semantic and we reject it.

The third approach, and the one we adopt, is to hold that if an overbroad covenant not to compete can be reasonably altered to render it enforceable, then the court shall do so unless it determines the covenant was not drafted in good faith. The burden of proving that the covenant was drafted in good faith is on the employer. This is the position taken in most United States jurisdictions and by the Restatement (Second) of Contracts § 184(2) (1981).

Ohio explained this approach in *Raimonde v. Van Vlerah*, 325 N.E.2d 544 (1975).

[M]any courts have abandoned the "blue pencil" test in favor of a rule of "reasonableness" which permits courts to determine, on the basis of all available evidence, what restrictions would be reasonable between the parties. Essentially, this test differs from the "blue pencil" test only in the manner of modification allowed. It permits courts to fashion a contract reasonable between the parties, in accord with their intention at the time of contracting, and enables them to evaluate all the factors comprising "reasonableness" in the context of employee covenants.

Among the factors properly to be considered are: "[t]he absence or presence of limitations as to time and space, * * * whether the employee represents the sole contact with the customer; whether the employee is possessed with confidential information or trade secrets; whether the covenant seeks to eliminate competition which would be unfair to the employer or merely seeks to eliminate ordinary competition; whether the covenant seeks to stifle the inherent skill and experience of the employee; whether the benefit to the employer is disproportional to the detriment to the employee; whether the covenant operates as a bar to the employee's sole means of support; whether the employee's talent which the employer seeks to suppress was actually developed during the period of employment; and whether the forbidden employment is merely incidental to the main employment."

Id. at 546–47 (citations and footnote omitted).

This approach is consistent with U.C.C. § 2–302, as codified in Alaska under AS 45.02.302 * * *

One criticism of this position is that employers are encouraged to overreach; if the covenant they draft is overbroad then the court redrafts it for them. While we recognize that the problem of overreaching exists, we think it can be overcome by stressing the good faith element of the test. The trial court must determine whether an employer has overreached willfully and, if so, the court should refuse to alter the covenant.

Accordingly, we REMAND this case to the trial court so it can determine whether Data Management acted in good faith, and if so, whether the covenant not to compete can be reasonably altered.

NOTES

Covenant Not To Compete and the Concept of Partial Illegality. A prolific source of public policy litigation has been the covenant not to compete, involving either the promise of a vendor of a business not to compete with the purchaser or the promise of an employee not to compete with his or her employer after termination of the employment. There are numerous decisions and a wealth of critical commentary treating various aspects of the matter. In an opinion which must surely rank among the most exhaustive on record, an Ohio court wrote of the law on no-compete clauses:

> [It] is not one of those questions on which the legal researcher cannot find enough to quench his thirst. To the contrary there is so much authority it drowns him. It is a sea—vast and vacillating, overlapping and bewildering. One can fish out of it any kind of strange support for anything, if he lives so long. This deep and unsettled sea pertaining to an employee's covenant not to compete with his employer after termination of employment is really Seven Seas; and now that the court has sailed them, perhaps it should record those seas so that the next weary traveler may be saved the terrifying time it takes just to find them.

Arthur Murray Dance Studios of Cleveland v. Witter, 105 N.E.2d 685, 687 (Ohio Com.Pl. 1952).

In general, the courts focus upon two aspects of the covenant: (1) whether it protects some legitimate interest of the promisee; (2) whether it is reasonable in scope. Courts tend to be more favorably disposed toward covenants that are ancillary to the sale of a business than toward those which restrict an employee's competitive activities. A covenant ancillary to the sale of a business is usually seen as protective of the good will being sold. With respect to the employee covenant, where the party does not have a special or unique skill, the usual attempt is to protect by precluding the use of trade secrets, confidential information, customer lists and the like. For "[a]s a general rule, an employer is not entitled to protection from an employee's use of his knowledge, skill, or general information acquired or increased through experience or instruction while in the employment." Century Personnel, Inc. v. Brummett, 499 N.E.2d 1160, 1161 (Ind.App. 1986). Compare Field v. Alexander & Alexander of Indiana, Inc., 503 N.E.2d 627 (Ind.App. 1987) (upholding covenant not to compete by insurance salesman whereby latter was obliged for a period of two years following termination not to solicit customers with whom employee had personal contact during previous two-year period) with American Shippers Supply Co. v. Campbell, 456 N.E.2d 1040 (Ind.App. 1983) (employer did not have a protected interest in customer lists which could have been easily obtained from a telephone book or trade publication).

The reasonableness test deals primarily with the area covered and the duration. And it is here that efforts are frequently made, as in the instant case, to convince a court that the excessive parts should be excised, leaving intact that which is reasonable both as to space and time. Efforts are thus made to sever or divide the legal portion from that which is illegal. The court here discusses three judicial responses. Which do you prefer? Why?

Sue Ann Watts v. James E. Watts

Supreme Court of Wisconsin, 1987.
137 Wis.2d 506.

■ ABRAHAMSON, JUSTICE. This is an appeal from a judgment of the circuit court for Dane County, William D. Byrne, Judge, dismissing Sue Ann

Watts' amended complaint, pursuant to sec. 802.06(2)(f), Stats. 1985–86, for failure to state a claim upon which relief may be granted. * * *

The case involves a dispute between Sue Ann Evans Watts, the plaintiff, and James Watts, the defendant, over their respective interests in property accumulated during their nonmarital cohabitation relationship which spanned 12 years and produced two children. The case presents an issue of first impression and comes to this court at the pleading stage of the case, before trial and before the facts have been determined.

The plaintiff asked the circuit court to order an accounting of the defendant's personal and business assets accumulated between June 1969 through December 1981 (the duration of the parties' cohabitation) and to determine plaintiff's share of this property. * * *

The circuit court dismissed the amended complaint, concluding that sec. 767.255, Stats. 1985–86, authorizing a court to divide property, does not apply to the division of property between unmarried persons. * * *

We agree with the circuit court that the legislature did not intend sec. 767.255 to apply to an unmarried couple. We disagree with the circuit court's implicit conclusion that courts cannot or should not, without express authorization from the legislature, divide property between persons who have engaged in nonmarital cohabitation. Courts traditionally have settled contract and property disputes between unmarried persons, some of whom have cohabited. Nonmarital cohabitation does not render every agreement between the cohabiting parties illegal and does not automatically preclude one of the parties from seeking judicial relief, such as statutory or common law partition, damages for breach of express or implied contract, constructive trust and quantum meruit where the party alleges, and later proves, facts supporting the legal theory. The issue for the court in each case is whether the complaining party has set forth any legally cognizable claim.

* * *

We test the sufficiency of the plaintiff's amended complaint by first setting forth the facts asserted in the complaint and then analyzing each of the five legal theories upon which the plaintiff rests her claim for relief.

I.

The plaintiff commenced this action in 1982. The plaintiff's amended complaint alleges the following facts, which for purposes of this appeal must be accepted as true. The plaintiff and the defendant met in 1967, when she was 19 years old, was living with her parents and was working full time as a nurse's aide in preparation for a nursing career. Shortly after the parties met, the defendant persuaded the plaintiff to move into an apartment paid for by him and to quit her job. According to the amended complaint, the defendant "indicated" to the plaintiff that he would provide for her.

Early in 1969, the parties began living together in a "marriage-like" relationship, holding themselves out to the public as husband and wife. The plaintiff assumed the defendant's surname as her own. Subsequently, she gave birth to two children who were also given the defendant's surname. The parties filed joint income tax returns and maintained joint bank accounts asserting that they were husband and wife. The defendant insured the plaintiff as his wife on his medical insurance policy. He also took out a life insurance policy on her as his wife, naming himself as the beneficiary. The parties purchased real and personal property as husband and wife. The plaintiff executed documents and obligated herself on promissory notes to lending institutions as the defendant's wife.

During their relationship, the plaintiff contributed childcare and homemaking services, including cleaning, cooking, laundering, shopping, running errands, and maintaining the grounds surrounding the parties' home. Additionally, the plaintiff contributed personal property to the relationship which she owned at the beginning of the relationship or acquired through gifts or purchases during the relationship. She served as hostess for the defendant for social and business-related events. The amended complaint further asserts that periodically, between 1969 and 1975, the plaintiff cooked and cleaned for the defendant and his employees while his business, a landscaping service, was building and landscaping a golf course.

From 1973 to 1976, the plaintiff worked 20–25 hours per week at the defendant's office, performing duties as a receptionist, typist, and assistant bookkeeper. From 1976 to 1981, the plaintiff worked 40–60 hours per week at a business she started with the defendant's sister-in-law, then continued and managed the business herself after the dissolution of that partnership. The plaintiff further alleges that in 1981 defendant made their relationship so intolerable that she was forced to move from their home and their relationship was irretrievably broken. Subsequently, the defendant barred the plaintiff from returning to her business.

The plaintiff alleges that during the parties' relationship, and because of her domestic and business contributions, the business and personal wealth of the couple increased. Furthermore, the plaintiff alleges that she never received any compensation for these contributions to the relationship and that the defendant indicated to the plaintiff both orally and through his conduct that he considered her to be his wife and that she would share equally in the increased wealth.

The plaintiff asserts that since the breakdown of the relationship the defendant has refused to share equally with her the wealth accumulated through their joint efforts or to compensate her in any way for her contributions to the relationship.

* * *

[The court rejects plaintiff's contentions that (1) she is entitled to an equitable division of property under Wisconsin's Family Code and (2) defendant should be estopped from asserting lack of legal marriage.]

IV.

The plaintiff's third legal theory on which her claim rests is that she and the defendant had a contract to share equally the property accumulated during their relationship. The essence of the complaint is that the parties had a contract, either an express or implied in fact contract, which the defendant breached.

Wisconsin courts have long recognized the importance of freedom of contract and have endeavored to protect the right to contract. A contract will not be enforced, however, if it violates public policy. A declaration that the contract is against public policy should be made only after a careful balancing, in the light of all the circumstances, of the interest in enforcing a particular promise against the policy against enforcement. Courts should be reluctant to frustrate a party's reasonable expectations without a corresponding benefit to be gained in deterring "misconduct" or avoiding inappropriate use of the judicial system. . . .

The defendant appears to attack the plaintiff's contract theory on three grounds. First, the defendant apparently asserts that the court's recognition of plaintiff's contract claim for a share of the parties' property contravenes the Wisconsin Family Code. Second, the defendant asserts that the legislature, not the courts, should determine the property and contract rights of unmarried cohabiting parties. Third, the defendant intimates that the parties' relationship was immoral and illegal and that any recognition of a contract between the parties or plaintiff's claim for a share of the property accumulated during the cohabitation contravenes public policy.

The defendant rests his argument that judicial recognition of a contract between unmarried cohabitants for property division violates the Wisconsin Family Code on *Hewitt v. Hewitt*, 77 Ill.2d 49 (1979). In *Hewitt* the Illinois Supreme Court concluded that judicial recognition of mutual property rights between unmarried cohabitants would violate the policy of the Illinois Marriage and Dissolution Act because enhancing the attractiveness of a private arrangement contravenes the Act's policy of strengthening and preserving the integrity of marriage. The Illinois court concluded that allowing such a contract claim would weaken the sanctity of marriage, put in doubt the rights of inheritance, and open the door to false pretenses of marriage. Hewitt, 77 Ill.2d at 65.

We agree with Professor Prince and other commentators that the *Hewitt* court made an unsupportable inferential leap when it found that cohabitation agreements run contrary to statutory policy and that the

Hewitt court's approach is patently inconsistent with the principle that public policy limits are to be narrowly and exactly applied.[14]

Furthermore, the Illinois statutes upon which the Illinois supreme court rested its decision are distinguishable from the Wisconsin statutes. The Illinois supreme court relied on the fact that Illinois still retained "fault" divorce and that cohabitation was unlawful. By contrast, Wisconsin abolished "fault" in divorce in 1977 and abolished criminal sanctions for nonmarital cohabitation in 1983.[15]

The defendant has failed to persuade this court that enforcing an express or implied in fact contract between these parties would in fact violate the Wisconsin Family Code. The Family Code, chs. 765–68, Stats. 1985–86, is intended to promote the institution of marriage and the family. We find no indication, however, that the Wisconsin legislature intended the Family Code to restrict in any way a court's resolution of property or contract disputes between unmarried cohabitants.

The defendant also urges that if the court is not willing to say that the Family Code proscribes contracts between unmarried cohabiting parties, then the court should refuse to resolve the contract and property rights of unmarried cohabitants without legislative guidance. The defendant asserts that this court should conclude, as the *Hewitt* court did, that the task of determining the rights of cohabiting parties is too complex and difficult for the court and should be left to the legislature. We are not persuaded by the defendant's argument. Courts have traditionally developed principles of contract and property law through the case-by-case method of the common law. While ultimately the legislature may resolve the problems raised by unmarried cohabiting parties, we are not persuaded that the court should refrain from resolving such disputes until the legislature gives us direction.[16] Our survey of the cases in other jurisdictions reveals that *Hewitt* is not widely followed.

We turn to the defendant's third point, namely, that any contract between the parties regarding property division contravenes public policy because the contract is based on immoral or illegal sexual activity.
* * *

---

[14] Prince, *Public Policy Limitations in Cohabitation Agreements: Unruly Horse or Circus Pony,* 70 Minn. L. Rev. 163, 189–205 (1985).

[15] Both Illinois and Wisconsin have abolished common law marriages. In our view this abolition does not invalidate a private cohabitation contract. Cohabitation agreements differ in effect from common law marriage. There is a significant difference between the consequences of achieving common law marriage status and of having an enforceable cohabitation agreement.

In *Latham v. Latham*, 274 Or. 421, 426–27 (1976), the Oregon supreme court found that the Legislature's decriminalization of cohabitation represented strong evidence that enforcing agreements made by parties during cohabitation relationships would not be contrary to Oregon public policy.

[16] We have previously acted in the absence of express legislative direction. See Estate of Fox, 178 Wis. 369 (1922), in which the court allowed relief under the doctrine of unjust enrichment to a woman who in good faith believed that she was married when she actually was not. . . .

Courts have generally refused to enforce contracts for which the sole consideration is sexual relations, sometimes referred to as "meretricious" relationships. See In Matter of Estate of Steffes, 95 Wis.2d 490, 514 (1980), citing Restatement of Contracts Section 589 (1932). Courts distinguish, however, between contracts that are explicitly and inseparably founded on sexual services and those that are not. This court, and numerous other courts, have concluded that "a bargain between two people is not illegal merely because there is an illicit relationship between the two so long as the bargain is independent of the illicit relationship and the illicit relationship does not constitute any part of the consideration bargained for and is not a condition of the bargain." Steffes, supra, 95 Wis.2d at 514.

While not condoning the illicit sexual relationship of the parties, many courts have recognized that the result of a court's refusal to enforce contract and property rights between unmarried cohabitants is that one party keeps all or most of the assets accumulated during the relationship, while the other party, no more or less "guilty," is deprived of property which he or she has helped to accumulate. . . .

* * *

Having reviewed the complaint and surveyed the law in this and other jurisdictions, we hold that the Family Code does not preclude an unmarried cohabitant from asserting contract and property claims against the other party to the cohabitation. We further conclude that public policy does not necessarily preclude an unmarried cohabitant from asserting a contract claim against the other party to the cohabitation so long as the claim exists independently of the sexual relationship and is supported by separate consideration. Accordingly, we conclude that the plaintiff in this case has pleaded the facts necessary to state a claim for damages resulting from the defendant's breach of an express or an implied in fact contract to share with the plaintiff the property accumulated through the efforts of both parties during their relationship. Once again, we do not judge the merits of the plaintiff's claim; we merely hold that she be given her day in court to prove her claim.

V.

The plaintiff's fourth theory of recovery involves unjust enrichment. Essentially, she alleges that the defendant accepted and retained the benefit of services she provided knowing that she expected to share equally in the wealth accumulated during their relationship. She argues that it is unfair for the defendant to retain all the assets they accumulated under these circumstances and that a constructive trust should be imposed on the property as a result of the defendant's unjust enrichment. In his brief, the defendant does not attack specifically either the legal theory or the factual allegations made by the plaintiff.

Unlike claims for breach of an express or implied in fact contract, a claim of unjust enrichment does not arise out of an agreement entered into by the parties. Rather, an action for recovery based upon unjust enrichment is grounded on the moral principle that one who has received a benefit has a duty to make restitution where retaining such a benefit would be unjust. . . .

Because no express or implied in fact agreement exists between the parties, recovery based upon unjust enrichment is sometimes referred to as "quasi contract," or contract "implied in law" rather than "implied in fact." Quasi contracts are obligations created by law to prevent injustice. . . .

In Wisconsin, an action for unjust enrichment, or quasi contract, is based upon proof of three elements: (1) a benefit conferred on the defendant by the plaintiff, (2) appreciation or knowledge by the defendant of the benefit, and (3) acceptance or retention of the benefit by the defendant under circumstances making it inequitable for the defendant to retain the benefit. . . .

The plaintiff has cited no cases directly supporting actions in unjust enrichment by unmarried cohabitants, and the defendant provides no authority against it. * * *

* * *

As we have discussed previously, allowing no relief at all to one party in a so-called "illicit" relationship effectively provides total relief to the other, by leaving that party owner of all the assets acquired through the efforts of both. Yet it cannot seriously be argued that the party retaining all the assets is less "guilty" than the other. Such a result is contrary to the principles of equity. Many courts have held, and we now so hold, that unmarried cohabitants may raise claims based upon unjust enrichment following the termination of their relationships where one of the parties attempts to retain an unreasonable amount of the property acquired through the efforts of both.

In this case, the plaintiff alleges that she contributed both property and services to the parties' relationship. She claims that because of these contributions the parties' assets increased, but that she was never compensated for her contributions. She further alleges that the defendant, knowing that the plaintiff expected to share in the property accumulated, "accepted the services rendered to him by the plaintiff" and that it would be unfair under the circumstances to allow him to retain everything while she receives nothing. We conclude that the facts alleged are sufficient to state a claim for recovery based upon unjust enrichment.

As part of the plaintiff's unjust enrichment claim, she has asked that a constructive trust be imposed on the assets that the defendant acquired during their relationship. A constructive trust is an equitable device created by law to prevent unjust enrichment. Wilharms v. Wilharms, 93 Wis.2d 671, 678 (1980). To state a claim on the theory of constructive trust the complaint must state facts sufficient to show (1) unjust enrichment and (2) abuse of a confidential relationship or some other form of unconscionable conduct. The latter element can be inferred from allegations in the complaint which show, for example, a family relationship, a close personal relationship, or the parties' mutual trust. These facts are alleged in this complaint or may be inferred. Gorski v. Gorski, 82 Wis.2d 248, 254–55 (1978). Therefore, we hold that if the plaintiff can prove the elements of unjust enrichment to the satisfaction of the circuit court, she will be entitled to demonstrate further that a constructive trust should be imposed as a remedy.

* * *

NOTES

(1)   Hewitt v. Hewitt: *The Other Side.* The Wisconsin court is highly critical of *Hewitt v. Hewitt*, an opinion of the Illinois Supreme Court that espouses the traditional view regarding the enforcement of cohabitation agreements. Here is a slice of that opinion:

> The issue of whether property rights accrue to unmarried cohabitants can not, however, be regarded realistically as merely a problem in the law of express contracts. * * * There are major public policy questions involved in determining whether, under what circumstances, and to what extent it is desirable to accord some type of legal status to claims arising from such relationships. Of substantially greater importance than the rights of the immediate parties is the impact of such recognition upon our society and the institution of marriage. Will the fact that legal rights closely resembling those arising from conventional marriages can be acquired by those who deliberately choose to enter into what have heretofore been commonly referred to as "illicit" or "meretricious" relationships encourage formation of such relationships and weaken marriage as the foundation of our family-based society? In the event of death shall the survivor have the status of a surviving spouse for purposes of inheritance, wrongful death actions, workmen's compensation, etc.? And still more importantly: what of the children born of such relationships? What are their support and inheritance rights and by what standards are custody questions resolved? What of the sociological and psychological effects upon them of that type of environment? Does not the recognition of legally enforceable property and custody rights emanating from nonmarital cohabitation in practical effect equate with the legalization of common law marriage—at least in the circumstances of this case? And, in summary, have the increasing numbers of unmarried cohabitants and changing mores of our society . . . reached the point at which the general welfare of the citizens of this State is best served by a return to something resembling the judicially created common law marriage our legislature outlawed in 1905?

* * *

The real thrust of plaintiff's argument here is that we should abandon the rule of illegality because of certain changes in societal norms and attitudes. It is urged that social mores have changed radically in recent years, rendering this principle of law archaic. It is said that because there are so many unmarried cohabitants today the courts must confer a legal status on such relationships. This, of course, is the rationale underlying some of the decisions and commentaries. (See, e.g., Marvin v. [actor Lee] Marvin, 18 Cal.3d 660, 683 [1976]). . . . If this is to be the result, however, it would seem more candid to acknowledge the return of varying forms of common law marriage than to continue displaying the naïveté we believe involved in the assertion that there are involved in these relationships contracts separate and independent from the sexual activity, and the assumption that those contracts would have been entered into or would continue without that activity.

Even if we were to assume some modification of the rule of illegality is appropriate, we return to the fundamental question earlier alluded to: If resolution of this issue rests ultimately on grounds of public policy, by what body should that policy be determined? *Marvin*, viewing the issue as governed solely by contract law, found judicial policy-making appropriate. Its decision was facilitated by California precedent and that State's no-fault divorce law. In our view, however, the situation alleged here was not the kind of arm's length bargain envisioned by traditional contract principles, but an intimate arrangement of a fundamentally different kind. The issue, realistically, is whether it is appropriate for this court to grant a legal status to a private arrangement substituting for the institution of marriage sanctioned by the State. The question whether change is needed in the law governing the rights of parties in this delicate area of marriage-like relationships involves evaluations of sociological data and alternatives we believe best suited to the superior investigative and fact-finding facilities of the legislative branch in the exercise of its traditional authority to declare public policy in the domestic relations field.

Hewitt v. Hewitt, 77 Ill.2d 49, 57–61 (1979).

(2) In *Wilcox v. Trautz*, 427 Mass. 326 (1998), the court adopted the view that:

[U]nmarried cohabitants may lawfully contract containing property, financing, and other matters relevant to their relationship. Such a contract is subject to the rules of contract law and valid even if expressly made in contemplation of a common living arrangement, except to the extent that sexual services constitute the only, or dominant, consideration for the agreement, or that enforcement should be denied on some other public policy ground.

427 Mass. at 332–33. But the court further stated:

Nothing we say here today is intended to derogate from the clear distinction we have made . . . between the legal rights of married and unmarried cohabitants. . . . Nor should anything we have said be taken as a suggestion or intimation that we are retreating from our prior expressions regarding the importance of the institution of marriage and the strong public interest in ensuring that its integrity is not threatened. . . . We have never recognized common law marriage in this Commonwealth . . . nor have we permitted the incidents of the marital relationship to attach to an arrangement of cohabitation without marriage.

427 Mass. at 332. Finally, the court noted that "if the parties eventually were to marry, the [cohabitation] agreement is no longer valid, and the rules concerning antenuptial, postnuptial, or separation agreements will then govern any agreement thereafter entered into by them." 427 Mass. at 332, note 4.

(3)   *Is Marriage A Default Rule?* Until the mid-1970s, most American courts held that premarital agreements and other contracts made "in contemplation of divorce" were unenforceable as against public policy. See *In re Greene*, reprinted in Chapter Two. Courts reasoned that the agreements were void either (1) because they purported to alter the state-imposed terms of the status of marriage, which were not subject to individual alteration, or (2) because they tended to encourage divorce. The Second Restatement continues to declare: "A promise that tends unreasonably to encourage divorce or separation is unenforceable on grounds of public policy." Restatement (Second) § 190(2).

The vast majority of courts, however, now treat premarital agreements as enforceable, at least in some circumstances. Brian Bix, *Bargaining in the Shadow of Love: The Enforcement of Premarital Agreements and How We Think About Marriage*, 40 Wm. & Mary L. Rev. 145, 153 (1998). Twenty-six states have adopted the "Uniform Premarital Agreement Act," which provides that prenuptial agreements are enforceable unless "the party against whom enforcement is sought" shows that:

(1) that party did not execute the agreement voluntarily; or

(2) the agreement was unconscionable when it was executed and, before execution of the agreement, that party:

(i) was not provided a fair and reasonable disclosure of the property or financial obligations of the other party;

(ii) did not voluntarily and expressly waive, in writing, any right to disclosure of the property or financial obligations of the other party beyond the disclosure provided; and

(iii) did not have, or reasonably could not have had, an adequate knowledge of the property or financial obligations of the other party.

Uniform Premarital Agreement Act § 6(a)(1), (2) (1983). Further:

If a provision of a premarital agreement . . . causes one party to the agreement to be eligible for support under a program of public assistance at the time of separation or marital dissolution, a court, notwithstanding the terms of the agreement, may require the other party to provide support to the extent necessary to avoid that eligibility.

Id. § 6(b).

(4) In 2006, 57% of Virginia voters amended the state constitution by referendum to provide: "This Commonwealth and its political subdivisions shall not create or recognize a legal status for relationships of unmarried individuals that intends to approximate the design, qualities, significance, or effects of marriage. Nor shall this Commonwealth or its political subdivisions create or recognize another union, partnership, or other legal status to which is assigned the rights, benefits, obligations, qualities, or effects of marriage." Constitution of Virginia, Art. 1, § 15–A. Do the words of the amendment prevent courts from enforcing private agreements between unmarried couples that create the rights or effects of marriage? Child custody agreements? Medical directives? Partnership agreements?

PROBLEM: THE CASE OF DONNIS AND BENJAMIN'S COHABITATION AGREEMENT

Donnis G. Whorton and Benjamin F. Dillingham, III began dating and entered into a same-sex relationship when Whorton was a college student pursuing a Bachelor of Arts degree. When they began living together, they orally agreed that Whorton's full-time occupation was to be Dillingham's chauffeur, bodyguard, social and business secretary, and partner and counselor in real estate investments. Additionally, Whorton was to be Dillingham's constant companion, confidant, traveling and social companion, and lover. In return, Dillingham agreed to be Whorton's lover and to financially support Whorton for life, as well as to open bank accounts, grant Whorton invasionary powers to savings accounts held in Dillingham's name, and permit Whorton to charge on Dillingham's personal accounts. They also agreed that if any portion of the agreement was found to be legally unenforceable, it was severable, and the remainder of the agreement was to remain in full force and effect.

Whorton allegedly complied with all of the terms of the agreement for seven years, at which point Dillingham barred him from his premises. Dillingham refuses to perform his part of the contract, and Whorton sues. What result? See Whorton v. Dillingham, 202 Cal.App.3d 447 (1988).

Maureen Kass v. Steven Kass
Court of Appeals of New York, 1998.
91 N.Y.2d 554.

■ KAYE, CHIEF JUDGE. Although *in vitro* fertilization (IVF) procedures are now more than two decades old and in wide use, this is the first such dispute to reach our Court. Specifically in issue is the disposition of five frozen, stored pre-embryos, or "pre-zygotes,"[1] created five years ago, during the parties' marriage, to assist them in having a child. Now divorced, appellant (Maureen Kass) wants the pre-zygotes implanted, claiming this is her only chance for genetic motherhood; respondent (Steven Kass) objects to the burdens of unwanted fatherhood, claiming that the parties agreed at the time they embarked on the effort that in the present circumstances the pre-zygotes would be donated to the IVF program for approved research purposes. * * *

Facts

[Shortly after their marriage in 1988, Maureen and Steven Kass began trying to conceive a child, eventually turning to *in vitro* fertilization (IVF). As part of the IVF program, doctors created five preembryos, or "pre-zygotes," by inseminating eggs surgically removed from Maureen with sperm from Steven. At the direction of Maureen and Steven, doctors cryogenically preserved some of these pre-zygotes in liquid nitrogen. Before the procedure, both signed a series of consent forms, which stated, *inter alia*:

> We have the principal responsibility to decide the disposition of our frozen pre-zygotes. Our frozen pre-zygotes will not be released from storage for any purpose without the written consent of *both* of us, consistent with the policies of the IVF Program and applicable law. In the event of divorce, we understand that legal ownership of any stored pre-zygotes must be determined in a property settlement and will be released as directed by order of a court of competent jurisdiction.
>
> * * *
>
> In the event that we no longer wish to initiate a pregnancy or are unable to make a decision regarding the disposition of our stored, frozen pre-zygotes, we now indicate our desire for the disposition of our pre-zygotes and direct the IVF program to (choose one): * * * (b) Our frozen pre-zygotes may be examined by the IVF Program for biological studies and be disposed of by the IVF Program for approved research investigation as determined by the IVF Program[.]

(emphasis in original).

[Three weeks after signing the consent forms and initiating the procedure, Maureen and Steven drafted and signed an "uncontested divorce" agreement dissolving their marriage and directing that the "5 pre-zygotes * * * should be disposed of [in] the manner outlined in our consent form and that neither Maureen Kass[,] Steve Kass or anyone else will lay claim to custody of these pre-zygotes." Nearly two months later, Maureen commenced a matrimonial action against Steven, seeking custody of the pre-zygotes and claiming that the pre-zygotes were her

---

[1]   We use the parties' term "pre-zygotes," which are defined in the record as "eggs which have been penetrated by sperm but have not yet joined genetic material."

only chance for genetic motherhood. Steven counterclaimed for specific performance of their agreement to donate the pre-zygotes to the IVF program for research, claiming that he did not want the burdens of fatherhood. The issue was submitted to the Appellate Division, which found for Steven. Maureen appealed.]

* * *

Analysis

A.   *The Legal Landscape Generally.* We begin analysis with a brief description of the broader legal context of this dispute. In the past two decades, thousands of children have been born through IVF, the best known of several methods of assisted reproduction. Additionally, tens of thousands of frozen embryos annually are routinely stored in liquid nitrogen canisters, some having been in that state for more than 10 years with no instructions for their use or disposal. . . . As science races ahead, it leaves in its trail mind-numbing ethical and legal questions. . . .

The law, whether statutory or decisional, has been evolving more slowly and cautiously. A handful of States—New York not among them—have adopted statutes touching on the disposition of stored embryos (see, e.g., Fla. Stat. Annot. § 742.17 [couples must execute written agreement providing for disposition in event of death, divorce or other unforeseen circumstances]; N.H. Rev. Stat. Annot. §§ 168–B:13–168–B:15, 168–B:18 [couples must undergo medical exams and counseling; 14-day limit for maintenance of *ex utero* pre-zygotes]; La. Rev. Stat. Annot. §§ 9:121–9:133 [pre-zygote considered "juridical person" that must be implanted]).

In the case law, only *Davis v. Davis* (842 S.W.2d 588, 604 [Tenn. 1992], cert. denied sub nom. Stowe v. Davis, 507 U.S. 911) attempts to lay out an analytical framework for disputes between a divorcing couple regarding the disposition of frozen embryos. . . . Having declared that embryos are entitled to "special respect because of their potential for human life" (842 S.W.2d at 597, supra), *Davis* recognized the procreative autonomy of both gamete providers, which includes an interest in avoiding genetic parenthood as well as an interest in becoming a genetic parent. In the absence of any prior written agreement between the parties—which should be presumed valid, and implemented—according to *Davis*, courts must in every case balance these competing interests, each deserving of judicial respect. In *Davis* itself, that balance weighed in favor of the husband's interest in avoiding genetic parenthood, which was deemed more significant than the wife's desire to donate the embryos to a childless couple.

* * *

B.   *The Appeal Before Us.* Like the Appellate Division, we conclude that disposition of these pre-zygotes does not implicate a woman's right of privacy or bodily integrity in the area of reproductive choice; nor are the pre-zygotes recognized as "persons" for constitutional purposes (see, Roe v. Wade, 410 U.S. 113, 162 . . .). The relevant inquiry thus becomes who has dispositional authority over them. Because that question is answered in this case by the parties' agreement, for purposes of resolving the present appeal we have no cause to decide whether the pre-zygotes are entitled to "special respect. . . ."

Agreements between progenitors, or gamete donors, regarding disposition of their pre-zygotes should generally be presumed valid and binding, and enforced in any dispute between them. . . . Indeed, parties should be encouraged in advance, before embarking on IVF and cryopreservation, to think through possible contingencies and carefully specify their wishes in writing. Explicit agreements avoid costly litigation in business transactions. They are all the more necessary and desirable in personal matters of reproductive choice, where the intangible costs of any litigation are simply incalculable. Advance directives, subject to mutual change of mind that must be jointly expressed, both minimize misunderstandings and maximize procreative liberty by reserving to the progenitors the authority to make what is in the first instance a quintessentially personal, private decision. Written agreements also provide the certainty needed for effective operation of IVF programs. . . .

While the value of arriving at explicit agreements is apparent, we also recognize the extraordinary difficulty such an exercise presents. All agreements looking to the future to some extent deal with the unknown. Here, however, the uncertainties inherent in the IVF process itself are vastly complicated by cryopreservation, which extends the viability of pre-zygotes indefinitely and allows time for minds, and circumstances, to change. Divorce; death, disappearance or incapacity of one or both partners; aging; the birth of other children are but a sampling of obvious changes in individual circumstances that might take place over time.

These factors make it particularly important that courts seek to honor the parties' expressions of choice, made before disputes erupt, with the parties' over-all direction always uppermost in the analysis. Knowing that advance agreements will be enforced underscores the seriousness and integrity of the consent process. Advance agreements as to disposition would have little purpose if they were enforceable only in the event the parties continued to agree. To the extent possible, it should be the progenitors—not the State and not the courts—who by their prior directive make this deeply personal life choice.

Here, the parties prior to cryopreservation of the pre-zygotes signed consents indicating their dispositional intent. While these documents were technically provided by the IVF program, neither party disputes that they are an expression of their own intent regarding disposition of their pre-zygotes. Nor do the parties contest the legality of those agreements, or that they were freely and knowingly made. The central issue is whether the consents clearly express the parties' intent regarding disposition of the pre-zygotes in the present circumstances. Appellant claims the consents are fraught with ambiguity in this respect; respondent urges they plainly mandate transfer to the IVF program.

The subject of this dispute may be novel but the common-law principles governing contract interpretation are not. * * * Applying those principles, we agree that the informed consents signed by the parties unequivocally manifest their mutual intention that in the present circumstances the pre-zygotes be donated for research to the IVF program.

* * *

As they embarked on the IVF program, appellant and respondent—"husband" and "wife," signing as such—clearly contemplated the fulfillment of a life dream of having a child during their marriage. The consents they signed provided for other contingencies, most especially that in the present circumstances the pre-zygotes would be donated to the IVF program for approved research purposes. These parties having clearly manifested their intention, the law will honor it.

Accordingly, the order of the Appellate Division should be affirmed, with costs.

A.Z. v. B.Z.

Supreme Judicial Court of Massachusetts, 2000.
725 N.E.2d 1051.

■ COWIN, J. We transferred this case to this court on our own motion to consider for the first time the effect of a consent form between a married couple and an in vitro fertilization (IVF) clinic (clinic) concerning disposition of frozen preembryos.[1] B.Z., the former wife (wife) of A.Z. (husband), appeals from a judgment of the Probate and Family Court that included, *inter alia*, a permanent injunction in favor of the husband, prohibiting the wife "from utilizing" the frozen preembryos held in cryopreservation at the clinic. The probate judge bifurcated the issue concerning the disposition of the frozen preembryos from the then-pending divorce action. The wife appeals only from the issuance of the permanent injunction. * * *

1.   *Factual background.* We recite the relevant background facts as determined by the probate judge in his detailed findings of fact after a hearing concerning disposition of the preembryos at which both the husband and wife were separately represented by counsel. The probate judge's findings are supplemented by the record where necessary.

[Over the course of four years, B.Z. and her husband A.Z. underwent *in vitro* fertilization (IVF) treatment that resulted in the birth of twin daughters in 1992. As part of this treatment, the husband and wife consented to seven individual egg-retrieval and insemination procedures after which some of the resulting pre-zygotes, or "preembryos," were cryogenically preserved. The consent form used for each of these

---

[1]   We use the term "preembryo" to refer to the four-to-eight cell stage of a developing fertilized egg. . . .

procedures required the husband and wife to decide the disposition of the frozen preembryos for certain contingencies, including "[s]hould we become separated." Before the first IVF procedure, the wife, in the presence of her husband, filled out the consent form to indicate that if they "[s]hould become separated, [they] both agree[d] to have the embryo(s) . . . return[ed] to [the] wife for implant." They both signed the form after it was filled out. Before each of the following six IVF procedures, the husband signed a blank consent form that the wife subsequently filled out to specify that custody of the preembryos would return to the wife in the event of a separation.

[More than three years after the final IVF procedure led to the birth of the couple's twin daughters, the wife had one of the two remaining vials of preembryos thawed and implanted without the knowledge or consent of her husband. The procedure did not lead to a pregnancy. Shortly thereafter the wife received a protective order against the husband, the couple separated, and the husband filed for divorce. In the course of the divorce proceeding, the husband sought a permanent injunction prohibiting the wife from implanting the final vial of frozen preembryos. The Probate and Family Court granted the injunction and the wife appealed.]

* * *

4. *Legal analysis.* This is the first reported case involving the disposition of frozen preembryos in which a consent form signed between the donors on the one hand and the clinic on the other provided that, on the donors' separation, the preembryos were to be given to one of the donors for implantation. In view of the purpose of the form (drafted by and to give assistance to the clinic) and the circumstances of execution, we are dubious at best that it represents the intent of the husband and the wife regarding disposition of the preembryos in the case of a dispute between them. In any event, for several independent reasons, we conclude that the form should not be enforced in the circumstances of this case.

First, the consent form's primary purpose is to explain to the donors the benefits and risks of freezing, and to record the donors' desires for disposition of the frozen preembryos at the time the form is executed in order to provide the clinic with guidance if the donors (as a unit) no longer wish to use the frozen preembryos. The form does not state, and the record does not indicate, that the husband and wife intended the consent form to act as a binding agreement between them should they later disagree as to the disposition. Rather, it appears that it was intended only to define the donors' relationship as a unit with the clinic.

Second, the consent form does not contain a duration provision. The wife sought to enforce this particular form four years after it was signed by the husband in significantly changed circumstances and over the husband's objection. In the absence of any evidence that the donors agreed on the time period during which the consent form was to govern their conduct, we cannot assume that the donors intended the consent form to govern the disposition of the frozen preembryos four years after it was executed, especially in light of the fundamental change in their relationship (i.e., divorce).

Third, the form uses the term "[s]hould we become separated" in referring to the disposition of the frozen preembryos without defining "become separated." Because this dispute arose in the context of a divorce, we cannot conclude that the consent form was intended to govern in these circumstances. Separation and divorce have distinct legal meanings. Legal changes occur by operation of law when a couple divorces that do not occur when a couple separates. Because divorce legally ends a couple's marriage, we shall not assume, in the absence of any evidence to the contrary, that an agreement on this issue providing for separation was meant to govern in the event of a divorce.

The donors' conduct in connection with the execution of the consent forms also creates doubt whether the consent form at issue here represents the clear intentions of both donors. The probate judge found that, prior to the signing of the first consent form, the wife called the IVF clinic to inquire about the section of the form regarding disposition "upon separation": that section of the preprinted form that asked the donors to specify either "donated" or "destroyed" or "both." A clinic representative told her that "she could cross out any of the language on the form and fill in her own [language] to fit her wishes." Further, although the wife used language in each subsequent form similar to the language used in the first form that she and her husband signed together, the consent form at issue here was signed in blank by the husband, before the wife filled in the language indicating that she would use the preembryos for implantation on separation. We therefore cannot conclude that the consent form represents the true intention of the husband for the disposition of the preembryos.

Finally, the consent form is not a separation agreement that is binding on the couple in a divorce proceeding pursuant to G.L. c. 208, § 34. The consent form does not contain provisions for custody, support, and maintenance, in the event that the wife conceives and gives birth to a child. See G.L. c. 208, § 1A. . . . In summary, the consent form is legally insufficient in several important respects and does not approach the minimum level of completeness needed to denominate it as an enforceable contract in a dispute between the husband and the wife.

With this said, we conclude that, even had the husband and the wife entered into an unambiguous agreement between themselves regarding the disposition of the frozen preembryos, we would not enforce an agreement that would compel one donor to become a parent against his or her will.[22] As a matter of public policy, we conclude that forced

_____

[22] That is the relief sought by the wife in this case. We express no view regarding whether an unambiguous agreement between two donors concerning the disposition of frozen preembryos could be enforced over the contemporaneous objection of one of the donors, when

procreation is not an area amenable to judicial enforcement. It is well-established that courts will not enforce contracts that violate public policy. . . . While courts are hesitant to invalidate contracts on these public policy grounds, the public interest in freedom of contract is sometimes outweighed by other public policy considerations; in those cases the contract will not be enforced. . . . To determine public policy, we look to the expressions of the Legislature and to those of this court. . . .

The Legislature has already determined by statute that individuals should not be bound by certain agreements binding them to enter or not enter into familial relationships. In G.L. c. 207, § 47A, the Legislature abolished the cause of action for the breach of a promise to marry. In G.L. c. 210, § 2, the Legislature provided that no mother may agree to surrender her child "sooner than the fourth calendar day after the date of birth of the child to be adopted" regardless of any prior agreement.

Similarly, this court has expressed its hesitancy to become involved in intimate questions inherent in the marriage relationship. Doe v. Doe, 365 Mass. 556, 563 (1974). "Except in cases involving divorce or separation, our law has not in general undertaken to resolve the many delicate questions inherent in the marriage relationship. We would not order either a husband or a wife to do what is necessary to conceive a child or to prevent conception, any more than we would order either party to do what is necessary to make the other happy." Id.

In our decisions, we have also indicated a reluctance to enforce prior agreements that bind individuals to future family relationships.[25] In *R.R. v. M.H.*, 426 Mass. 501 (1998), we held that a surrogacy agreement in which the surrogate mother agreed to give up the child on its birth is unenforceable unless the agreement contained, *inter alia*, a "reasonable" waiting period during which the mother could change her mind. Id. at 510. In *Capazzoli v. Holzwasser*, 397 Mass. 158 (1986), we determined, as an expression of public policy, that a contract requiring an individual to abandon a marriage is unenforceable. And, in the same spirit, we stated in *Gleason v. Mann*, 312 Mass. 420, 425 (1942), that agreements providing for a general restraint against marriage are unenforceable.

We glean from these statutes and judicial decisions that prior agreements to enter into familial relationships (marriage or parenthood)

---

such agreement contemplated destruction or donation of the preembryos either for research or implantation in a surrogate.

We also recognize that agreements among donors and IVF clinics are essential to clinic operations. There is no impediment to the enforcement of such contracts by the clinics or by the donors against the clinics, consistent with the principles of this opinion.

[25] We have enforced agreements regarding the family relationship once the parties have freely entered into that relationship, but these cases have not involved the issue of procreation. See G.L. c. 209, § 2 (married woman may make contracts with husband); Ames v. Perry, 406 Mass. 236, 241 (1989), quoting White v. White, 141 Vt. 499, 503 (1982) (providing that "divorcing parents may in some cases bind themselves in contract on matters involving their children"); Stansel v. Stansel, 385 Mass. 510 (1982) (enforcing separation agreement); Rosenberg v. Lipnick, 377 Mass. 666, 673 (1979) (enforcing antenuptial agreement). Cf. Wilcox v. Trautz, 427 Mass. 326, 327 (1998) (enforcing agreement between unmarried cohabitants).

should not be enforced against individuals who subsequently reconsider their decisions. This enhances the "freedom of personal choice in matters of marriage and family life." Moore v. East Cleveland, 431 U.S. 494, 499 (1977), quoting Cleveland Bd. of Educ. v. LaFleur, 414 U.S. 632, 639–640 (1974).

We derive from existing State laws and judicial precedent a public policy in this Commonwealth that individuals shall not be compelled to enter into intimate family relationships, and that the law shall not be used as a mechanism for forcing such relationships when they are not desired. This policy is grounded in the notion that respect for liberty and privacy requires that individuals be accorded the freedom to decide whether to enter into a family relationship. See Commonwealth v. Stowell, 389 Mass. 171, 173 (1983). "There are 'personal rights of such delicate and intimate character that direct enforcement of them by any process of the court should never be attempted.'" Doe v. Doe, supra at 559, quoting Kenyon v. Chicopee, 320 Mass. 528, 534 (1946).

In this case, we are asked to decide whether the law of the Commonwealth may compel an individual to become a parent over his or her contemporaneous objection. The husband signed this consent form in 1991. Enforcing the form against him would require him to become a parent over his present objection to such an undertaking. We decline to do so.

NOTES

(1) What are the factual differences that made the difference between the holdings in *Kass v. Kass* and *A.Z. v. B.Z.*? Are they enough to support the difference between the rules announced in the two cases? Consider the following from Karl Llewellyn:

> The influence of the facts relative to the influence of the normally applicable rule increases roughly with the square of the peculiarity of the facts. Therefore the decision of a case really peculiar on its facts is never a safe guide to the decision of normal cases *which have not yet been* decided under its rule. *But* if a peculiar case is decided in true accordance with a rule *in use* in normal cases, that is excellent indication of the living power of that normal rule: it has overcome even tough and troublesome facts.

K.N. Llewellyn, *On Our Case-Law of Contract: Offer and Acceptance II*, 48 Yale L.J. 779, 785–86 (1938). Does this help account for the different outcomes in the two cases?

(2) *The Matter of Baby M.* Procreative promises come in many forms. Over a decade before the above cases, the nation's attention was grabbed by the "Baby M" case. In February 1985, Mary Beth Whitehead entered into a surrogacy contract with William Stern. In exchange for a payment of $10,000, Whitehead agreed to be artificially inseminated with Stern's sperm, to carry the resultant pregnancy to term, and to allow Stern and his wife to adopt the child. On March 27, 1986, Whitehead gave birth to a baby girl

whom she named "Sara Elizabeth." Whitehead realized almost at once that she could not part with the child, but surrendered the baby to the Sterns on March 30. The Sterns renamed her "Melissa."

The result was a 32-day trial before Judge Sorkow of the Superior Court of New Jersey, which culminated in an order upholding the surrogacy contract and directing that Whitehead's parental rights be terminated, with sole custody to be awarded to the Sterns. Matter of Baby M, 217 N.J.Super. 313 (1987). The Supreme Court of New Jersey arrived at a different solution. It invalidated the contract and refused to terminate Whitehead's parental rights, but agreed that custody should be awarded to the Sterns, with visitation rights for Whitehead. Matter of Baby M, 109 N.J. 396 (1988). In voiding the contract, Chief Justice Wilentz, speaking for the court, stated emphatically: "This is the sale of a child, or at the very least, the sale of a mother's right to her child, the only mitigating factor being that one of the purchasers is the father. Almost every evil that prompted the prohibition on the payment of money in connection with adoptions exists here." 109 N.J. at 437–38. Chief Justice Wilentz said further:

> Putting aside the issue of how compelling her need for money may have been, and how significant her understanding of the consequences, we suggest that her consent is irrelevant. There are, in a civilized society, some things that money cannot buy. In America, we decided long ago that merely because conduct purchased by money was "voluntary" did not mean it was good or beyond regulation and prohibition. * * * There are, in short, values that society deems more important than granting to wealth whatever it can buy, be it labor, love, or life. . . .

* * *

> The surrogacy contract is based on principles that are directly contrary to the objective of our laws. It guarantees the separation of a child from its mother; it looks to adoption regardless of suitability; it totally ignores the child; it takes the child from the mother regardless of her wishes and her maternal fitness; and it does all of this, it accomplishes all of its goals, through the use of money.

> Beyond that is the potential degradation of some women that may result from this arrangement. In many cases, of course, surrogacy may bring satisfaction, not only to the infertile couple, but to the surrogate mother herself. The fact, however, that many women may not perceive surrogacy negatively but rather see it as an opportunity does not diminish its potential for devastation to other women.

> In sum, the harmful consequences of this surrogacy arrangement appear to us all too palpable. In New Jersey the surrogate mother's agreement to sell her child is void. Its irrevocability infects the entire contract, as does the money that purports to buy it.

109 N.J. at 440–44. Compare this reasoning to that in *A.Z. v. B.Z.* How is it similar? How is it different? Does it matter that one contract involves being "compelled to enter into [an] intimate family relationship" while the other involves being forced out of one? Is this a fair distinction?

PROBLEMS: PROCREATIVE AGREEMENTS

(1) Suppose Mary Beth Whitehead had been selected in part because of her race. Would enforcement of the contract violate 42 U.S.C. § 1981? Do constitutional privacy and associational rights trump the statutory prohibitions against race discrimination in contracting?

(2) Should contracts to use or not to use contraceptives ever be enforceable (at least for money damages)? Should contracts to abort or not to abort ever be enforceable (at least for money damages)? Could a woman or a man validly promise to indemnify a sexual partner for state-imposed paternity obligations if a child is born? See Erwin L.D. v. Myla Jean L., 41 Ark.App. 16 (1993); Melanie G. McCulley, *The Male Abortion: the Putative Father's Right to Terminate His Interests in and Obligations to the Unborn Child*, 7 J.L. & Pol'y 1, 55 (1998).

(3) Assuming that a court would not enforce a promise to use birth control or to abort, what if the plaintiff could show that the defendant never intended to perform—that she intended all along to get pregnant or to carry to term, despite her promise? Should the plaintiff be able to bring a claim of promissory fraud, if not breach of contract? See the next case, and Henson v. Sorrell, 1999 WL 5630 (Tenn.Ct.App. 1999).

Peter Wallis v. Kellie Rae Smith
Court of Appeals of New Mexico, 2001.
130 N.M. 214.

■ BOSSON, JUDGE. Peter Wallis and Kellie Rae Smith were partners in a consensual sexual relationship. Allegedly, Smith misrepresented that she was practicing birth control when she was not, and Wallis unknowingly fathered her child. Wallis sued Smith for money damages, asserting four causes of action—fraud, breach of contract, conversion, and *prima facie* tort—that the district court dismissed for failure to state a claim upon which relief may be granted. Wallis appeals that dismissal. . . . We affirm the dismissal, holding that under these facts, the causes of action are not cognizable in New Mexico because they contravene the public policy of this state. . . .

BACKGROUND

The following facts are taken from Wallis's complaint, which we must assume to be true for the purpose of determining whether a complaint states a viable claim for relief. . . . Wallis and Smith began an intimate, sexual relationship some time before April 1997. They discussed contraceptive techniques and agreed that Smith would use birth control pills. Wallis and Smith further agreed that their sexual intimacy would last only as long as Smith continued to take birth control pills because Wallis made it clear that he did not want to father a child. Wallis participated in contraception only passively; he relied on Smith to use birth control and took no precautions himself.

As time went by, Smith changed her mind. She chose to stop taking birth control pills, but never informed Wallis of her decision. Wallis continued their intimate relationship, and Smith became pregnant. Smith carried the fetus to term and gave birth to a normal, healthy girl on November 27, 1998.

Wallis alleges that he has suffered, and will continue to suffer, substantial economic injury as a proximate result of his unintended fatherhood because New Mexico law requires him to pay child support for the next eighteen years. See NMSA 1978, § 40–11–15 (1997). Due to his statutory obligations, Wallis asserts that he has been injured by Smith's conduct, and requests compensatory and punitive damages from her. The district court determined that public policy prohibited the relief sought by Wallis, and dismissed the case with prejudice.

CONTRACEPTIVE FRAUD

* * * At the onset of our discussion it is important to distinguish the factual allegations of this case from other kinds of related lawsuits, and thus underscore the limited reach of this opinion. Wallis's complaint is not about sexually-transmitted disease, . . . nor does it concern the damages arising from an unwanted pregnancy that led to an abortion, . . . or an undesired pregnancy resulting in medical complications. . . . This case is not even brought to recover the expense of giving birth. . . . Wallis's complaint is limited to compensatory damages for the "economic injury" of supporting a normal, healthy child.

Although Wallis insists that he is not attempting to circumvent his child support obligations, we cannot agree. It is self-evident that he seeks to recover for the very financial loss caused him by the statutory obligation to pay child support. At oral argument when pressed by the Court to clarify what damages Wallis was seeking, his counsel stated that Wallis was seeking not punitive, but compensatory damages measured by his "out of pocket loss." Therefore, this case boils down to whether sound public policy would permit our courts to require Smith to indemnify Wallis for child support under the circumstances of this case.

* * *

Making each parent financially responsible for the conception and birth of children also illuminates a strong public policy that makes paramount the interests of the child. Our jurisprudence has abandoned the notion that the father of an "illegitimate" child could decline to accept the financial responsibility of raising that child. . . . Currently, the state exercises its *parens patriae* authority to protect the best interests of all children by ensuring that the parents provide "an adequate standard of support." NMSA 1978, § 40–4–11.1(B)(1) (1995). Placing a duty of support on each parent has the added benefit of insulating the state from the possibility of bearing the financial burden for a child. See § 40–11–15(D). In our view, it is difficult to harmonize the legislative concern for the child, reflected in the immutable duty of parental support, with Wallis's effort in this lawsuit to shift financial responsibility for his child solely to the mother.

* * *

Some courts have dismissed contraceptive fraud cases on the ground that the claims tread too far into the realm of an individual's privacy interests. . . . We agree that individuals are entitled a sphere of privacy into which courts should not tread. A person's choice whether or not to use contraceptives understandably fits into this sphere. . . . We also believe that the "privacy interests involved . . . require a cautious approach," and therefore we elect to rely primarily on the prevailing public policy of child support, while at the same time recognizing the serious privacy concerns implicated and threatened by the underlying lawsuit. . . .

Wallis's attempt to apply traditional contract and tort principles to his contraceptive agreement is unconvincing and, in the end, futile. The contract analogy fails because children, the persons for whose benefit child support guidelines are enacted, have the same needs regardless of whether their conception violated a promise between the parents. * * *

Wallis tries to make the basis for liability not so much the birth of the child, but the fact that Smith lied, and perpetrated a fraud on him. See Paula C. Murray and Brenda J. Winslett, *The Constitutional Right to Privacy and Emerging Tort Liability for Deceit in Interpersonal Relationships*, 1986 U. Ill. L. Rev. 779, 832 (advocating recognition of contraceptive fraud suits). But not all misrepresentations are actionable. * * *

Finally, Wallis argues that our courts have recognized tort claims which measure damages by the economic injury of supporting an unwanted child. See Lovelace Med. Ctr. v. Mendez, 111 N.M. 336, 345 (1991). However, *Lovelace* does not stand for the proposition that one parent can sue the other for the costs of raising a child. *Lovelace* held that a doctor has a duty to inform a couple that a surgical procedure to render one partner sterile was not successful, and the court determined the extent to which damages flow from the breach of that duty resulting in the birth of a healthy child. See id. at 342. * * *

Accordingly, we hold that the actions asserted here cannot be used to recoup the financial obligations of raising a child. We emphasize that this holding is gender neutral insofar as it precludes a monetary reimbursement for child support. . . .

* * *

■ ALARID, JUDGE (specially concurring). * * * If we recognize a claim based on intentional misrepresentation, we have started down the road towards establishing standards of conduct in reproductive relationships—one of the most important and private forms of interpersonal relations. In the absence of a clear balance favoring the imposition of legal duties of disclosure in reproductive relations between competent adult sex partners, candor in reproductive matters should be left to the ethics of the participants.

> [T]here are still many immoral acts which do not amount to torts, and the law has not yet enacted the golden rule. It is impossible to afford a lawsuit for every deed of unkindness or betrayal, and there is much evil in the world which must necessarily be left to other agencies of social control.

W. Page Keeton, Dan B. Dobbs, Robert E. Keeton, and David G. Owen, *Prosser and Keeton on Torts* § 4 at 22 (5th ed. 1984). In my view, Wallis has failed to demonstrate a clear balance in favor of recognition of a cause of action for contraceptive fraud/breach of promise to practice birth control.

* * *

Today, the Court establishes the principle that contraception is a non-delegable duty in New Mexico. I see nothing unfair in applying this rule to Wallis. Had Wallis bothered to investigate the state of the law prior to beginning a sexual relationship with Smith in April 1997, he would have learned that the overwhelming majority of jurisdictions considering the issue have refused to recognize a cause of action for economic damages stemming from contraceptive fraud/breach of promise to practice birth control. * * *

Lastly, Wallis concedes that his complaint alleges damages for purely economic loss. I express no opinion at this time as to whether privacy interests would outweigh other considerations so as to foreclose causes of action based upon tortiously-inflicted physical harm to a sex partner. See, e.g., Kathleen K. v. Robert B., 150 Cal.App.3d 992 (1984) (holding that right of privacy should not bar cause of action based upon sex partner's failure to advise other partner that he was infected with herpes).

PROBLEM: THE CASE OF THE PROMISE TO REMAIN SILENT

During a dinner party before the beginning of the fall semester, Professor A mentions that he intends to offer his used car for sale to the hordes of incoming students. Professor B, who has just arrived in town as a visiting lecturer, responds that she herself is interested in buying the car and asks if she can borrow the car to have her mechanic "check it out." Professor A agrees, but only on the condition that Professor B disclose nothing about what the mechanic finds. Professor A explains that the incoming students will not have an opportunity to have the car evaluated, and Professor A doesn't want to have to disclose negative information about the car's quality.

Professor B agrees to remain silent and takes possession of the car. The next day, Professor B calls and tells A that she does not want to buy the car. Moreover, B volunteers that the mechanic found a problem with the car. A responds, "Don't tell me." B responds, "But it's a safety problem." A responds again, "Don't tell me."

Professor A goes on to sell the car to an incoming graduate student (with limited English-speaking abilities). A does not disclose his prior agreement with B, nor does A disclose that B's mechanic found some type of a "safety problem"—but Professor A does disclose all previously acquired material information about the car.

The graduate student is subsequently injured in an accident caused by a safety problem uncovered in the initial mechanic's examination. Does Professor A face any potential legal liability for his conduct? Should the initial agreement to remain silent be unenforceable? If such agreements are unenforceable, how are future parties in Professor A's situation likely to react?

CHAPTER FIVE

PERFORMANCE

1. DETERMINING SCOPE AND CONTENT OF OBLIGATION

There is no general requirement that an agreement be in writing to be enforceable. As we have seen, the Statute of Frauds imposes that requirement for some categories of agreements. And the parties can condition liability upon a written memorialization of their agreement. Similarly, statutes occasionally require that certain types of contractually significant acts be in writing to be legally effective. See UCC § 2–205 (firm offers must be in "a signed writing") & 2–609 (either party "may in writing demand adequate assurance of performance"). On the whole, however, the modern trend is toward informality in the formation of contracts. Indeed, UCC § 1–201(b)(3) defines agreement as the "bargain of the parties in fact as found in their language or inferred from other circumstances, including course of performance, course of dealing or usage of trade." Article 11 of CISG provides "a contract of sale need not be concluded in or evidenced by writing and is not subject to any other requirement as to form. It may be proved by any means, including witnesses."

Nevertheless, many contractual agreements are expressed in writings, either in whole or in part. These writings might be the product of intensive and thorough bargaining between equal parties assisted by counsel. They might be a standard form drafted by one party and offered to the other on a take-it-or-leave-it basis. They might be the product of amateurs operating with little experience and without the advice of counsel. They might be clear or ambiguous. In short, the only sure thing is that the issues will be varied and the disputes plentiful.

In this section we are not primarily concerned with whether a contract has been formed, whether there has been a misunderstanding *à la Peerless,* whether the parties have made a mistake in reducing their oral agreement to writing, or whether any of the other contractual defenses apply. Assuming there is a written expression of the agreement, the basic questions are, first, whether a party will be given the chance to prove prior or contemporaneously agreed terms or conditions that alter or add to the writing and, second, how the court should determine the meaning of words in the writing. The first issue involves the core of the "parol evidence rule," which determines the effectiveness of a prior or contemporaneous oral or other agreements when the parties have assented to a writing. The second issue involves interpretation, or the ascertainment of the meaning to be given to contract language. As the selected materials will indicate, the two issues often overlap, both in doctrine and in practice.

(A) INTEGRATED WRITINGS AND THE PAROL EVIDENCE RULE

The parol evidence rule is about the legal effect of writings. In modern versions of the rule, that effect depends upon the parties' intention. Did the parties intend the writing as a final statement of some or all of the terms of their agreement? If they intended it to be a final statement of only the terms in the writing, without closing off the possibility of other terms, the writing is *partially integrated*. If the parties intended the writing to be a final statement of all of the terms of their agreement, it is *completely integrated*. If the writing is not integrated—if the parties did not intend it as a final statement of terms—evidence from outside the writing may be introduced for any purposes. If the parties intended the agreement to be a final statement, extrinsic evidence of additional terms maybe excluded.

So far so good. But these basic ideas are only the tip of the parol evidence iceberg. Before reading the following cases, look for answers to the following questions in sections 209–218 of the Second Restatement:

(1) What does it mean to say that a document is integrated? Completely integrated? Partially integrated?

(2) Who decides whether a contract is integrated, and if so whether partially or completely? What evidence may be considered when deciding whether an agreement is integrated, and if so whether partially or completely? Is integration a question of fact or of law?

(3) What is the effect of integration on prior agreements within the scope of integration?

(4) What extrinsic evidence is prohibited when a document is integrated? When can extrinsic evidence still be used?

Catherine C. Mitchill v. Charles Lath

Court of Appeals of New York, 1928.
247 N.Y. 377.

■ ANDREWS, JUDGE. In the fall of 1923 the Laths owned a farm. This they wished to sell. Across the road, on land belonging to Lieutenant-Governor Lunn, they had an ice house which they might remove. Mrs. Mitchill looked over the land with a view to its purchase. She found the ice house objectionable. Thereupon "the defendants orally promised and agreed, for and in consideration of the purchase of their farm by the plaintiff, to remove the said ice house in the spring of 1924." Relying upon this promise, she made a written contract to buy the property for $8,400, for cash and a mortgage and containing various provisions usual in such papers. Later receiving a deed, she entered into possession and has spent considerable sums in improving the property for use as a summer residence. The defendants have not fulfilled their promise as to the ice house and do not intend to do so. We are not dealing, however, with their moral delinquencies. The question before us is whether their oral agreement may be enforced in a court of equity.

This requires a discussion of the parol evidence rule—a rule of law which defines the limits of the contract to be construed. (Glackin v. Bennett, 226 Mass. 316.) It is more than a rule of evidence and oral testimony even if admitted, will not control the written contract (O'Malley v. Grady, 222 Mass. 202), unless admitted without objection. (Brady v. Nally, 151 N.Y. 258.) It applies, however, to attempts to modify such a contract by parol. It does not affect a parol collateral contract distinct from and independent of the written agreement. It is, at times, troublesome to draw the line. Williston, in his work on Contracts (sec. 637) points out the difficulty. "Two entirely distinct contracts," he says, "each for a separate consideration may be made at the same time and will be distinct legally. Where, however, one agreement is entered into wholly or partly in consideration of the simultaneous agreement to enter into another, the transactions are necessarily bound together. * * * Then if one of the agreements is oral and the other is written, the problem arises whether the bond is sufficiently close to prevent proof of the oral agreement." That is the situation here. It is claimed that the defendants are called upon to do more than is required by their written contract in connection with the sale as to which it deals.

The principle may be clear, but it can be given effect by no mechanical rule. As so often happens, it is a matter of degree, for, as Professor Williston also says, where a contract contains several promises on each side it is not difficult to put any one of them in the form of a collateral agreement. If this were enough written contracts might always be modified by parol. Not form, but substance, is the test.

In applying this test the policy of our courts is to be considered. We have believed that the purpose behind the rule was a wise one not easily to be abandoned. Notwithstanding injustice here and there, on the whole it works for good. Old precedents and principles are not to be lightly cast aside unless it is certain that they are an obstruction under present conditions. New York has been less open to arguments that would modify this particular rule, than some jurisdictions elsewhere. Thus in Eighmie v. Taylor (98 N.Y. 288) it was held that a parol warranty might not be shown although no warranties were contained in the writing.

Under our decisions before such an oral agreement as the present is received to vary the written contract at least three conditions must exist, (1) the agreement must in form be a collateral one; (2) it must not contradict express or implied provisions of the written contract; (3) it must be one that parties would not ordinarily be expected to embody in the writing; or put in another way, an inspection of the written contract, read in the light of surrounding circumstances must not indicate that the writing appears "to contain the engagements of the parties, and to define the object and measure the extent of such engagement." Or again, it must not be so clearly connected with the principal transaction as to be part and parcel of it.

The respondent does not satisfy the third of these requirements. It may be, not the second. We have a written contract for the purchase and sale of land. The buyer is to pay $8,400 in the way described. She is also to pay her portion of any rents, interest on mortgages, insurance premiums and water meter charges. She may have a survey made of the premises. On their part the sellers are to give a full covenant deed of the premises as described, or as they may be described by the surveyor if the survey is had, executed and acknowledged at their own expense; they sell the personal property on the farm and represent they own it; they agree that all amounts paid them on the contract and the expense of examining the title shall be a lien on the property; they assume the risk of loss or damage by fire until the deed is delivered; and they agree to pay the broker his commissions. Are they to do more? Or is such a claim inconsistent with these precise provisions? It could not be shown that the plaintiff was to pay $500 additional. Is it also implied that the defendants are not to do anything unexpressed in the writing?

That we need not decide. At least, however, an inspection of this contract shows a full and complete agreement, setting forth in detail the obligations of each party. On reading it one would conclude that the reciprocal obligations of the parties were fully detailed. Nor would his opinion alter if he knew the surrounding circumstances. The presence of the ice house, even the knowledge that Mrs. Mitchill thought it objectionable would not lead to the belief that a separate agreement existed with regard to it. Were such an agreement made it would seem most natural that the inquirer should find it in the contract. Collateral in form it is found to be, but it is closely related to the subject dealt with in the written agreement—so closely that we hold it may not be proved.

Where the line between the competent and the incompetent is narrow the citation of authorities is of slight use. Each represents the judgment of the court on the precise facts before it. How closely bound to the contract is the supposed collateral agreement is the decisive factor in each case. * * *

We do not ignore the fact that authorities may be found that would seem to support the contention of the appellant. * * * But the fixed form of a deed makes it inappropriate to insert collateral agreements, however closely connected with the sale. This may be cause for an exception. Here we deal with the contract on the basis of which the deed to Mrs. Mitchill was given subsequently, and we confine ourselves to the question whether its terms may be modified.

* * *

Our conclusion is that the judgment of the Appellate Division and that of the Special Term should be reversed and the complaint dismissed, with costs in all courts.

■ LEHMAN, JUDGE. (dissenting). I accept the general rule as formulated by Judge Andrews. I differ with him only as to its application to the facts shown in the record. * * *

Judge Andrews has formulated a standard to measure the closeness of the bond. Three conditions, at least, must exist before an oral agreement may be proven to increase the obligation imposed by the written agreement. I think we agree that the first condition that the agreement "must in form be a collateral one" is met by the evidence. I concede that this condition is met in most cases where the courts have nevertheless excluded evidence of the collateral oral agreement. The difficulty here, as in most cases, arises in connection with the two other conditions.

The second condition is that the "parol agreement must not contradict express or implied provisions of the written contract." Judge Andrews voices doubt whether this condition is satisfied. The written contract has been carried out. The purchase price has been paid; conveyance has been made; title has passed in accordance with the terms of the written contract. The mutual obligations expressed in the written contract are left unchanged by the alleged oral contract. When performance was required of the written contract, the obligations of the parties were measured solely by its terms. By the oral agreement the plaintiff seeks to hold the defendants to other obligations to be performed by them thereafter upon land which was not conveyed to the plaintiff. The assertion of such further obligation is not inconsistent with the written contract unless the written contract contains a provision, express or implied, that the defendants are not to do anything not expressed in the writing. Concededly there is no such express provision in the contract, and such a provision may be implied, if at all, only if the asserted additional obligation is "so clearly connected with the principal transaction as to be part and parcel of it," and is not "one that the parties would not ordinarily be expected to embody in the writing." The hypothesis so formulated for a conclusion that the asserted additional obligation is inconsistent with an implied term of the contract is that the alleged oral agreement does not comply with the third condition as formulated by Judge Andrews. In this case, therefore, the problem reduces itself to the one question whether or not the oral agreement meets the third condition.

I have conceded that upon inspection the contract is complete. "It appears to contain the engagements of the parties, and to define the object and measure the extent of such engagement;" it constitutes the contract between them and is presumed to contain the whole of that contract. (Eighmie v. Taylor, 98 N.Y. 288.) That engagement was on the one side to convey land; on the other to pay the price. The plaintiff asserts further agreement based on the same consideration to be performed by the defendants after the conveyance was complete, and directly affecting only other land. It is true, as Judge Andrews points out, that "the presence of the ice house, even the knowledge that Mrs. Mitchill thought it objectionable, would not lead to the belief that a separate agreement existed with regard to it;" but the question we must decide is whether or not, *assuming* an agreement was made for the removal of an unsightly ice house from one parcel of land as an inducement for the purchase of another parcel, the parties would ordinarily or naturally be expected to embody the agreement for the removal of the ice house from one parcel in the written agreement to convey the other parcel. Exclusion of proof of the oral agreement on the ground that it varies the contract embodied in the writing may be based only upon a finding or presumption that the written contract was intended to cover the oral negotiations for the removal of the ice house which lead up to the contract of purchase and sale. To determine what the writing was intended to cover "the document alone will not suffice. What it was intended to cover cannot be known till we know what there was to cover. The question being whether certain subjects of negotiation were intended to be covered, we must compare the writing and the negotiations before we can determine whether they were in fact covered." (Wigmore on Evidence [2d ed.], section 2430.)

The subject-matter of the written contract was the conveyance of land. The contract was so complete on its face that the conclusion is inevitable that the parties intended to embody in the writing all the negotiations covering at least the conveyance. The promise by the defendants to remove the ice house from other land was not connected with their obligation to convey, except that one agreement would not have been made unless the other was also made. The plaintiff's assertion of a parol agreement by the defendants to remove the ice house was completely established by the great weight of evidence. It must prevail unless that agreement was part of the agreement to convey and the entire agreement was embodied in the writing.

* * *

The rule of integration undoubtedly frequently prevents the assertion of fraudulent claims. Parties who take the precaution of embodying their oral agreements in a writing should be protected against the assertion that other terms of the same agreement were not integrated in the writing. The limits of the integration are determined by the writing, read in the light of the surrounding circumstances. A written contract, however complete, yet covers only a limited field. I do not think that in the written contract for the conveyance of land here under consideration we can find an intention to cover a field so broad as to include prior agreements, if any such were made, to do other acts on other property after the stipulated conveyance was made.

In each case where such a problem is presented, varying factors enter into its solution. Citation of authority in this or other jurisdictions is useless, at least without minute analysis of the facts. The analysis I have made of the decisions in this State leads me to the view that the decision of the courts below is in accordance with our own authorities and should be affirmed.

Rebecca D. Masterson v. Lu E. Sine

Supreme Court of California, 1968.
68 Cal.2d 222.

■ TRAYNOR, CHIEF JUSTICE. Dallas Masterson and his wife Rebecca owned a ranch as tenants in common. On February 25, 1958, they conveyed it to Medora and Lu Sine by a grant deed "Reserving unto the Grantors herein an option to purchase the above described property on or before February 25, 1968" for the "same consideration as being paid heretofore plus their depreciation value of any improvements Grantees may add to the property from and after two and a half years from this date." Medora is Dallas' sister and Lu's wife. Since the conveyance Dallas has been adjudged bankrupt. His trustee in bankruptcy and Rebecca brought this declaratory relief action to establish their right to enforce the option.

The case was tried without a jury. Over defendants' objection the trial court admitted extrinsic evidence that by "the same consideration as being paid heretofore" both the grantors and the grantees meant the sum of $50,000 and by "depreciation value of any improvements" they meant the depreciation value of improvements to be computed by deducting from the total amount of any capital expenditures made by defendants grantees the amount of depreciation allowable to them under United States income tax regulations as of the time of the exercise of the option.

The court also determined that the parol evidence rule precluded admission of extrinsic evidence offered by defendants to show that the parties wanted the property kept in the Masterson family and that the option was therefore personal to the grantors and could not be exercised by the trustee in bankruptcy.

The court entered judgment for plaintiffs, declaring their right to exercise the option, specifying in some detail how it could be exercised, and reserving jurisdiction to supervise the manner of its exercise and to determine the amount that plaintiffs will be required to pay defendants for their capital expenditures if plaintiffs decide to exercise the option.

Defendants appeal. They contend that the option provision is too uncertain to be enforced and that extrinsic evidence as to its meaning should not have been admitted. The trial court properly refused to frustrate the obviously declared intention of the grantors to reserve an option to repurchase by an overly meticulous insistence on completeness and clarity of written expression. . . . It properly admitted extrinsic evidence to explain the language of the deed . . . to the end that the consideration for the option would appear with sufficient certainty to permit specific enforcement. . . . The trial court erred, however, in excluding the extrinsic evidence that the option was personal to the grantors and therefore nonassignable.

When the parties to a written contract have agreed to it as an "integration"—a complete and final embodiment of the terms of an agreement—parol evidence cannot be used to add to or vary its terms. . . . When only part of the agreement is integrated, the same rule applies to that part, but parol evidence may be used to prove elements of the agreement not reduced to writing. . . .

The crucial issue in determining whether there has been an integration is whether the parties intended their writing to serve as the exclusive embodiment of their agreement. The instrument itself may help to resolve that issue. It may state, for example, that "there are no previous understandings or agreements not contained in the writing," and thus express the parties' "intention to nullify antecedent understandings or agreements." (See 3 Corbin, Contracts (1960) § 578, p. 411.) Any such collateral agreement itself must be examined, however, to determine whether the parties intended the subjects of negotiation it deals with to be included in, excluded from, or otherwise affected by the writing. Circumstances at the time of the writing may also aid in the determination of such integration. . . .

California cases have stated that whether there was an integration is to be determined solely from the face of the instrument . . . and that the question for the court is whether it "appears to be a complete * * * agreement * * *." (See Ferguson v. Koch (1928) 204 Cal. 342, 346, . . .) Neither of these strict formulations of the rule, however, has been consistently applied. The requirement that the writing must appear incomplete on its face has been repudiated in many cases where parol evidence was admitted "to prove the existence of a separate oral agreement as to any matter on which the document is silent and which is not inconsistent with its terms"—even though the instrument appeared to state a complete agreement. . . . Even under the rule that the writing alone is to be consulted, it was found necessary to examine the alleged collateral agreement before concluding that proof of it was precluded by the writing alone. (See 3 Corbin, Contracts (1960) § 582, pp. 444–446.) It is therefore evident that "The conception of a writing as wholly and intrinsically self-determinative of the parties' intent to make it a sole memorial of one or seven or twenty-seven subjects of negotiation is an impossible one." (9 Wigmore, Evidence (3d ed. 1940) § 2431, p. 103.) For example, a promissory note given by a debtor to his creditor may integrate all their present contractual rights and obligations, or it may be only a minor part of an underlying executory contract that would never be discovered by examining the face of the note.

In formulating the rule governing parol evidence, several policies must be accommodated. One policy is based on the assumption that written evidence is more accurate than human memory. . . . This policy, however, can be adequately served by excluding parol evidence of agreements that directly contradict the writing. Another policy is based on the fear that fraud or unintentional invention by witnesses interested in the outcome of the litigation will mislead the finder of facts. . . . McCormick has suggested that the party urging the spoken as against the written word is most often the economic underdog, threatened by severe hardship if the writing is enforced. In his view the parol evidence rule arose to allow the court to control the tendency of the jury to find through sympathy and without a dispassionate assessment of the probability of fraud or faulty memory that the parties made an oral agreement collateral to the written contract, or that preliminary tentative agreements were not abandoned when omitted from the writing. (See McCormick, Evidence (1954) § 210.) He recognizes, however, that if this theory were adopted in disregard of all other considerations, it would lead to the exclusion of testimony concerning oral agreements whenever there is a writing and thereby often defeat the true intent of the parties. (See McCormick, op. cit. supra, § 216, p. 441.)

Evidence of oral collateral agreements should be excluded only when the fact finder is likely to be misled. The rule must therefore be based on the credibility of the evidence. One such standard, adopted by section 240(1)(b) of the Restatement of Contracts, permits proof of a collateral agreement if it "is such an agreement as might *naturally* be made as a separate agreement by parties situated as were the parties to the written contract." (Italics added. . . .) The draftsmen of the Uniform Commercial Code would exclude the evidence in still fewer instances: "If the additional terms are such that, if agreed upon, they would *certainly* have been included in the document in the view of the court, then evidence of their alleged making must be kept from the trier of fact." (Com. 3, § 2–202, italics added.)[1]

The option clause in the deed in the present case does not explicitly provide that it contains the complete agreement, and the deed is silent on the question of assignability. Moreover, the difficulty of accommodating the formalized structure of a deed to the insertion of collateral agreements makes it less likely that all the terms of such an agreement were included. . . . The statement of the reservation of the option might well have been placed in the recorded deed solely to preserve the grantors' rights against any possible future purchasers and this function could well be served without any mention of the parties' agreement that the option was personal. There is nothing in the record to indicate that the parties to this family transaction, through experience in land transactions or otherwise, had any warning of the disadvantages

---

[1]   Corbin suggests that, even in situations where the court concludes that it would not have been natural for the parties to make the alleged collateral oral agreement, parol evidence of such an agreement should nevertheless be permitted if the court is convinced that the unnatural actually happened in the case being adjudicated. (3 Corbin, Contracts, § 485, pp. 478, 480; cf. Murray, The Parol Evidence Rule: A Clarification (1966) 4 Duquesne L.Rev. 337, 341–342.) This suggestion may be based on a belief that judges are not likely to be misled by their sympathies. If the court believes that the parties intended a collateral agreement to be effective, there is no reason to keep the evidence from the jury.

of failing to put the whole agreement in the deed. This case is one, therefore, in which it can be said that a collateral agreement such as that alleged "might naturally be made as a separate agreement." *A fortiori,* the case is not one in which the parties "would certainly" have included the collateral agreement in the deed.

It is contended, however, that an option agreement is ordinarily presumed to be assignable if it contains no provisions forbidding its transfer or indicating that its performance involves elements personal to the parties. . . . The fact that there is a written memorandum, however, does not necessarily preclude parol evidence rebutting a term that the law would otherwise presume. * * *

In the present case defendants offered evidence that the parties agreed that the option was not assignable in order to keep the property in the Masterson family. The trial court erred in excluding that evidence.

The judgment is reversed.

[In a dissenting opinion, Justice Burke, with whom Justice McComb concurred, insisted that the majority opinion, 1) undermined the parol evidence rule as it has been known in California since 1872, 2) rendered suspect instruments of conveyance absolute on their face, 3) materially lessened the reliance which might be placed upon written instruments affecting title to real estate, and 4) opened the door, albeit unintentionally, to a new technique for the defrauding of creditors.]

NOTES

(1) The parol evidence rule applies when the parties have expressed their agreement in a writing, and one side later wants to introduce evidence other than the writing—prior oral agreements, communications during negotiations, prior dealings between the parties, or other "parol evidence"—to prove the terms of their agreement. The first question in a parol evidence case is whether the writing was integrated, and if so, whether completely or partially. That is: Did the parties intend the writing to be a final expression of either some or all of the terms of their agreement?

(2) *Evidence of Integration: Williston vs. Corbin.* The differences between the majority and dissent in *Mitchill v. Lath*, and Traynor's decision in *Masterson v. Sine*, turn in part on their varying views of the evidence a court should consider when answering the integration question. Those varying answers replicate a disagreement between Williston and Corbin. In the first edition of his treatise, Williston quoted with approval the New York Court of Appeals:

> For if we may go outside of the instrument to prove that there was a stipulation not contained in it, and so that only part of the contract was put in writing, and then, because of that fact, enforce the oral stipulation, there will be little of value left in the rule itself. . . . If upon inspection and study of the writing, read, it may be, in the light of surrounding circumstances in order to its proper understanding and interpretation, it appears to contain the

engagements of the parties, and to define the object and measure the extent of such engagement, it constitutes the contract between them, and is presumed to contain the whole of that contract.

Samuel Williston, 2 The Law of Contracts § 606, 1165 (1920) (quoting Eighmie v. Taylor, 98 N.Y. 288, 294–95 (1885)). Against this, Corbin argued that because integration is a matter of intent, the court should always consider all relevant extrinsic evidence—including evidence of additional terms and even when the writing includes a merger clause. "[P]aper and ink possess no magic power to cause statements of fact to be true when they are actually untrue. Written admissions are evidential but they are not conclusive." "Just as no written document can prove its own execution, so none can prove that it was ever assented to as either a partial or a complete integration, supplanting and discharging what preceded it." Arthur L. Corbin, *The Parol Evidence Rule*, 53 Yale L.J. 603, 620, 642 (1944). The Second Restatement unequivocally adopts Corbin's approach. "Whether a writing has been adopted as an integrated agreement is a question of fact to be determined in accordance with all relevant evidence." Restatement (Second) § 209 cmt. c.

(3) *Evidence of Integration: Contemporary Cases.* There remains some disagreement among courts as to how to tell whether parties have altered the parol evidence default. Some jurisdictions appear still to follow the Willistonian approach. For example:

> Under New York law, a contract that appears complete on its face is an integrated agreement as a matter of law. However, in the absence of a merger clause, the court must determine whether or not there is an integration by reading the writing in the light of surrounding circumstances, and by determining whether or not the agreement was one which the parties would ordinarily be expected to embody in writing.

Indep. Energy v. Trigen Energy Corp., 944 F.Supp. 1184, 1196 (S.D.N.Y. 1996) (citations and quotation marks omitted). The rule in other jurisdictions is that a court may always consider extrinsic evidence to resolve the question of integration.

> [I]ntegration clauses, although not absolutely conclusive, are indicative of the intention of the parties to finalize their complete understanding in the written contract that there was no other prior or contemporaneous agreement not included in the written contract. Maryland law further requires, however, that the circumstances surrounding the making of the contract be considered to discover whether the integration clause in question does, in fact, express the genuine intention of the parties to make the written contract the complete and exclusive statement of their agreement. Thus, the court should consider the circumstances surrounding the making of the contract to discover whether the integration clause in question does, in fact, express the genuine intention of the parties to make the written contract the complete

and exclusive statement of their agreement. These circumstances include the length and detail of the contract, the length and nature of the negotiations preceding execution and the absence of persuasive evidence supporting a determination that the parties intended, at the time of contracting, that non-written terms be part of the overall agreement.

ARB, Inc. v. E-Systems, Inc., 663 F.2d 189, 198–199 (D.C. Cir. 1980) (citations and internal punctuation omitted).

That said, courts are often not very clear about the evidentiary rules they are applying in parol evidence cases, and cases even within a single jurisdiction demonstrate less consistency than one might hope. Thus Farnsworth observes: "Surprising little light is shed on the problem by the hundreds of decisions resolving the issue of whether an agreement is completely integrated." Farnsworth, Contracts § 7.3 (4th ed. 2004).

(4) *The Effects of Integration.* Once a court decides that a writing is integrated, when can extrinsic evidence be introduced? We can distinguish three basic cases.

First, extrinsic evidence may always be introduced to prove some invalidating cause, such as misrepresentation, duress, mistake or the like. This makes sense. If integration is a matter of agreement, defects in the agreement process are always relevant.

Second, if the agreement is only partially integrated, a party might introduce extrinsic evidence of additional consistent terms. This is why it was so important in *Masterson* to determine whether the contract was completely or partially integrated. Only if the contract was not intended to be complete could the defendants argue that the option was not assignable— a term that did not appear in the writing.

Third, when an integrated agreement is ambiguous—that is, when it has more than one plausible meaning—extrinsic evidence may be introduced to resolve the ambiguity. Thus in *Masterson*, there was no question but that extrinsic evidence could be introduced to clarify the phrases "the same consideration as being paid heretofore" and "depreciation value of any improvements."

(5) *The Functions of the Parol Evidence Rule.* On the modern view, shared by Williston and Corbin, the writing is given a special legal force because of the parties' agreement that it should have that force. Integration is, in this sense, just another term of the contract. The English Law Commission has taken this to entail that there is in fact no such thing as the parol evidence rule.

[I]t is a proposition of law which is no more than a circular statement: *when it is proved or admitted that the parties to a contract intended that all the express terms of their agreement should be a recorded in a particular document or documents, evidence will be inadmissible (because irrelevant) if it is tendered only for the purpose of adding to, varying, subtracting from or contradicting the express terms of a contract.*

Law Commission, *Law of Contract: The Parol Evidence Rule* 8 (Law Com. No. 154, 1986) Cmnd 9700.

But you cannot understand courts' approach to integration without understanding the parol evidence rule's historical functions, which also involved judgments about the reliability of various forms of evidence and about the proper division of labor between judge and jury. Consider, for example, the following description of Article Two's codification of the parol evidence rule in section 2–202:

> Courts are frequently called on to resolve disputes over terms. The novice might expect that the process of adjudication here would be the same as in any other type of case in which facts are disputed: the parties would introduce conflicting evidence as to terms, including any other writing, and the trier of fact would then determine the terms. Also there would be the usual division of labor between judge and jury. Judges would, for example, rule on relevancy and admissibility, and they would be empowered to grant a motion for a non-suit, for a directed verdict, or for a judgment *n.o.v.* Thus, the usual protections against unreasonable jury determinations would be available to help assure that in the end, the court gives effect to the contract of the parties as actually agreed.

> But Anglo-American law does not handle all disputes over contract terms in this way. Our courts apply some version of a so-called 'parol evidence rule' when some of the terms are written and some are not. This gives preference to the written version of those terms. Writings are more reliable than memories to show contract terms, and forgery is easier to detect and less common than is lying on the witness stand. These are the principal premises of a parol evidence rule. Early critics of the rule challenged these premises and emphasized that the rule is inconsistent with our usual processes of proof. If juries are to be 'trusted' in disputes over contract terms not involving writings, then why should they not hear all the evidence, even where writings are involved, and decide accordingly? One reason is the same social Darwinist reason given above for 2–201: to train contracting parties to memorialize their agreements and so to minimize disputes between them and in the courts.

James J. White and Robert S. Summers, *Uniform Commercial Code* 115–16 (6th ed. 2010).

Alaska Northern Development, Inc. v. Alyeska Pipeline Service Co.

Supreme Court of Alaska, 1983.
666 P.2d 33.

■ COMPTON, JUSTICE. Alaska Northern Development, Inc. ("AND") appeals a judgment in favor of Alyeska Pipeline Service Co. ("Alyeska") in a dispute involving contract formation and interpretation. For the reasons stated below, we affirm.

I.   FACTUAL AND PROCEDURAL BACKGROUND

In late October or early November 1976, David Reed, a shareholder and corporate president of AND, initiated discussion with Alyeska personnel in Fairbanks regarding the purchase of surplus parts. The Alyeska employees with whom Reed dealt were Juel Tyson, Clarence Terwilleger and Donald Bruce.

After a series of discussions, Terwilleger indicated that Reed's proposal should be put in writing so it could be submitted to management. With the assistance of AND's legal counsel, Reed prepared a letter of intent dated December 10, 1976. In this letter, AND proposed to purchase "the entire Alyeska inventory of Caterpillar parts." The place for the purchase price was left blank.

Alyeska responded with its own letter of intent dated December 11, 1976. The letter was drafted by Bruce and Tyson in consultation with William Rickett, Alyeska's manager of Contracts and Material Management. Again, the price term was absent. The letter contained the following language, which is the focus of this lawsuit: "Please consider this as said letter of intent, *subject to the final approval of the owner committee.*" (Emphasis added.)

Reed was given an unsigned draft of the December 11 letter, which was reviewed by AND's legal counsel. Reed then met with Rickett, and they agreed on sixty-five percent of Alyeska's price as the price term to be filled in the blank on the December 11 letter. Rickett filled in the blank as agreed and signed the letter. In March 1977, the owner committee rejected the proposal embodied in the December 11 letter of intent.

AND contends that the parties understood the subject to approval language to mean that the Alyeska owner committee would review the proposed agreement only to determine whether the price was fair and reasonable. Alyeska contends that Reed was never advised of any such limitation on the authority of the owner committee. In April 1977, AND filed a complaint alleging that there was a contract between AND and Alyeska, which Alyeska breached. The complaint was later amended to include counts for reformation and punitive damages.

Alyeska moved for summary judgment on the punitive damages and breach of contract counts. The superior court granted summary judgment in favor of Alyeska on the punitive damages count. The court initially denied Alyeska's motion for summary judgment on the breach of contract claim; however, based on a review of the case after discovery had closed, the court announced at a hearing on September 26, 1980, that it would reverse its earlier ruling and grant Alyeska's motion. The court confirmed this ruling at a hearing on November 5, 1980, after consideration of AND's Motion for Clarification.

* * *

II. APPLICATION OF THE PAROL EVIDENCE RULE

The superior court held that the parol evidence rule of the Uniform Commercial Code, section 2–202, codified as AS 45.02–202, applied to the December 11 letter and therefore no extrinsic evidence could be presented to a jury which limited the owner committee's right of approval. AND contends that the court erred in applying the parol evidence rule. We disagree.

In order to exclude parol evidence concerning the inclusion of additional terms to a writing, a court must make the following determinations. First, the court must determine whether the writing under scrutiny was integrated, i.e., intended by the parties as a final expression of their agreement with respect to some or all of the terms included in the writing. Second, the court must determine whether evidence of a prior or contemporaneous agreement contradicts or is inconsistent with the integrated portion. If the evidence is contradictory or inconsistent, it is inadmissible. If it is consistent, it may nevertheless be excluded if the court concludes that the consistent term would necessarily have been included in the writing by the parties if they had intended it to be part of their agreement. AS 45.02.202; Braund, Inc. v. White, 486 P.2d 50, 56 (Alaska 1971); U.C.C. § 2–202 comment 3 (1977).

A.   *Was the December 11 Letter a Partial Integration?*

An integrated writing exists where the parties intend that the writing be a final expression of one or more terms of their agreement. Kupka v. Morey, 541 P.2d 740, 747 n. 8 (Alaska 1975); Restatement (Second) of Contracts § 209(a) (1979). Whether a writing is integrated is a question of fact to be determined by the court in accordance with all relevant evidence. Restatement (Second) of Contracts § 209 comment c (1979).

In granting summary judgment on the breach of contract claim, the superior court stated that it had carefully considered all relevant evidence, including oral and written records of all facets of the business deal in question, to arrive at its finding that the agreement was partially integrated.[4] After the six-week trial on the reformation issue, the superior court reaffirmed this finding:

> 35. The plaintiff initially contends that the letter of December 11, 1976 (the letter) was not integrated or partially integrated

---

[4]   At the hearing on AND's Motion for Clarification, the superior court stated:

[I]t seems to me absolutely conclusive on this evidence, and I'm making this as a finding of fact, that this agreement is partially integrated, and I'm not making it by reference only to the four corners of the—of the writings but reference to all the extrinsic evidence that has been proffered to me, read everybody's deposition, considered in detail all the processes of negotiations, everything that was said and done by everybody as related by them up till the time that Rickett included the language in the letter and turned it over to Reed. So we're not here talking about the for [sic] corners or ambiguity or anything like that. We're talking about all the extrinsic evidence, meaning on balance to a conclusion more probable than not that this is a partially integrated agreement.

and therefore the court was in error in granting summary judgment in favor of defendant on the contract counts of the plaintiff's complaint on September 26, 1980.

36. After considering the evidence submitted at trial, the court reaffirms its prior conclusion that the letter was integrated as to the Owners Committee's approval clause.

37. The parties intended to write down their discussions in a comprehensive form which allowed Reed to seek financing and allow the primary actors (Tyson, Bruce, Terwilleger, Rickett) to submit the concept embodied by the letter to higher management. . . .

38. There are three subjects upon which plaintiff seeks reformation. . . . As to the first, [limiting the Owner Committee to a consideration of price] which has been plaintiff's primary focus, the court finds that such reference was integrated such that the parole [sic] evidence rule would bar any inconsistent testimony. Testimony that the owners were limited to "price" in their review is inconsistent. . . .

41. With respect to the Owners Committee's approval clause, according to the plaintiff's contention the owners were entitled to review the transaction, on whatever basis, only one time. This was testified to by both Mr. Reed and argued by plaintiff in closing. . . . It was also conceded in closing that the review by the owners, on whatever standard, would occur prior to any formal contract being negotiated and executed. . . . This is also consistent with the testimony of each of the participants.

42. In addition, Mr. Reed, in consultation with Ed Merdes and Henry Camarot, his attorneys, tendered the letter of March 4, 1977, as a document which could serve as "the contract". . . . The March 4 letter contains no further reference to the Owners Committee's approval function. . . . Therefore, I find that as to the Owners Committee's approval . . . the letter of December 11 constitutes an integration or partial integration. . . . This having been established, the analysis outlined by the court on September 26, 1980, when granting defendant's motion for summary judgment on the contract claims is applicable.

After reviewing the record, we cannot say that this finding of a partial integration was clearly erroneous.

* * *

B.   *Does the Excluded Evidence Contradict the Integrated Terms?*

Having found a partial integration, the next determination is whether the excluded evidence contradicts the integrated portion of the writing. Comment b to section 215 of the Restatement (Second) of Contracts is helpful in resolving this issue.[5] Comment b states:

> An earlier agreement may help the interpretation of a later one, but it may not contradict a binding later integrated agreement. Whether there is a contradiction depends . . . on whether the two are consistent or inconsistent. This is a question which often cannot be determined from the face of the writing; the writing must first be applied to its subject matter and placed in context. The question is then decided by the court as part of a question of interpretation. Where reasonable people could differ as to the credibility of the evidence offered and the evidence if believed could lead a reasonable person to interpret the writing as claimed by the proponent of the evidence, the question of credibility and the choice among reasonable inferences should be treated as questions of fact. But the asserted meaning must be one to which the language of the writing, read in context, is reasonably susceptible. If no other meaning is reasonable, the court should rule as a matter of law that the meaning is established.

According to comment b, therefore, a question of interpretation may arise before the contradiction issue can be resolved. If the evidence conflicts, the choice between competing inferences is for the trier of fact to resolve. . . . The meaning is determined as a matter of law, however, if "the asserted meaning [is not] one to which the language of the writing, read in context, is reasonably susceptible." Restatement (Second) of Contracts § 215 comment b (1979). . . .

AND contends that the superior court erred in granting summary judgment because the evidence conflicted as to the meaning of the owner committee approval clause. It concludes that under it was entitled to a jury trial on the interpretation issue. Alyeska contends, and the superior court ruled, that a jury trial was inappropriate because, as a matter of law, AND's asserted meaning of the clause at issue was not reasonably susceptible to the language of the writing. The superior court stated:

> The Court is making the . . . ruling that the offer of evidence to show that Rickett's letter really meant to limit owner committee approval to the price term alone . . . is not reasonably susceptible—or the writing is not reasonably susceptible to that purpose. And therefore, that extrinsic evidence operates to contradict the writing, not specific words in the writing, but the words in the context of the totality of the writing and the totality of the extrinsic evidence.

---

[5]   Restatement (Second) of Contracts § 215, which parallels the rule stated in U.C.C. § 2–202, reads: "Except as stated in the preceding Section, where there is a binding agreement, either completely or partially integrated, evidence of prior or contemporaneous agreements or negotiations is not admissible in evidence to contradict a term of the writing."

We agree that the words used in the December 11 letter are not reasonably susceptible to the interpretation advanced by AND. Therefore, we find no merit to AND's contention that it was entitled to a jury trial on the interpretation issue.

After rejecting the extrinsic evidence for purposes of interpretation, the superior court found AND's offered testimony, that the owner committee's approval power was limited to approval of the price, to be inconsistent with and contradictory to the language used by the negotiators in the December 11 letter. AND contends that the offered testimony did not contradict, but rather explained or supplemented the writing with consistent additional terms. For this contention, AND relies on the standard articulated in *Hunt Foods & Industries, Inc. v. Doliner*, 26 A.D.2d 41, 270 N.Y.S.2d 937 (N.Y.App.1966). In *Hunt Foods*, the defendant signed an option agreement under which he agreed to sell stock to Hunt Foods at a given price per share. When Hunt Foods attempted to exercise the option, the defendant contended that the option could only be exercised if the defendant had received offers from a third party. The court held that section 2–202 did not bar this evidence from being admitted because it held that the proposed oral condition to the option agreement was not "inconsistent" within the meaning of section 2–202; to be inconsistent, "the term must contradict or negate a term of the writing. A term or condition which has a lesser effect is provable." *Id.* 270 N.Y.S.2d at 940.

The narrow view of consistency expressed in *Hunt Foods* has been criticized. In *Snyder v. Herbert Greenbaum & Associates, Inc.*, 38 Md. App. 144, 380 A.2d 618 (Md. App.1977), the court held that the parol evidence of a contractual right to unilateral rescission was inconsistent with a written agreement for the sale and installation of carpeting. The court defined "inconsistency" as used in section 2–202(b) as "the absence of reasonable harmony in terms of the language *and* respective obligations of the parties." *Id.* 380 A.2d at 623 (emphasis in original) (citing U.C.C. § 1–205(4)). . . .

We agree with this view of inconsistency and reject the view expressed in *Hunt Foods*.[6] Under this definition of inconsistency, it is clear that the proffered parol evidence limiting the owner committee's right of final approval to price is inconsistent with the integrated term that unconditionally gives the committee the right to approval.

---

[6]　*Hunt Foods* was implicitly rejected in *Johnson v. Curran*, 633 P.2d 994, 996–97 (Alaska 1981) (parol evidence concerning an early termination right based on nightclub owner's dissatisfaction with the band's performance was inconsistent with parties' written contract specifying definite time without mention of any right of early termination and thus inadmissible).

Therefore, the superior court was correct in refusing to admit parol evidence on this issue.[7]

Affirmed.

NOTES

Read UCC § 2–202 and the comments. What test did the court use to determine whether the writing was partially integrated? What evidence did it consider? If the writing was not detailed and complete on its face, why did the court decide it was integrated with regard to some of the terms?

What was AND's contention with regard to the interpretation of the owner committee approval clause? On what basis did the court reject it?

Finally, what test did the court use to determine whether the oral condition was a "consistent additional term?" Is a term in "reasonable harmony" with the writing if it would have naturally and normally be made a separate agreement? Or is the test whether the oral condition "would certainly" have been included in the writing?

Comment: Other Pieces of the Parol Evidence Rule

Merger Clauses. Merger clauses, often also called "integration clauses," or "entire agreement clauses" in the United Kingdom, are common in contracts between sophisticated parties. A typical merger clause might specify that the writing "encompasses the entire agreement of the parties, and supersedes all previous understandings and agreements between the parties, whether oral or written."

The purpose of such provisions is to make clear that the agreement is a total integration—where the writing without the merger clause is, by default, more likely to be treated merely as at most partially integrated. The rules governing merger clauses are another example of altering rules: they say how parties can contract around the parol evidence default. As with integration in general, courts are divided on the use of extrinsic evidence of non-integration in the presence of a merger clause in contracts between sophisticated parties.

Collateral Agreements. What if two parties enter into two agreements, the first oral and the second in an integrated writing? Does the integrated writing affect the first oral agreement? The answer depends on the nature of the earlier agreement and the scope of the integration. Consider the following opinion applying Virginia law:

> This case involves two distinct agreements between Suburban and AMF. Suburban and AMF initially entered into the oral

---

[7] Our affirmance of the superior court's holding that the proposed version is inconsistent with the integrated clause obviates discussion of whether the addition, if consistent, would have been included in the December 11 letter. Furthermore, we decline to reach AND's contentions regarding the applicability of U.C.C. § 2–207 because AND never raised the § 2–207 argument at the superior court level. *See, e.g., Jeffries v. Glacier State Telephone Co.,* 604 P.2d 4, 11 (Alaska 1979).

franchise agreement providing for Suburban's promotion and sale of AMF products from Suburban's stores. Subsequently, the parties executed the written e-commerce agreement, which required Suburban to install and service AMF products sold by AMF through its website to its customers. Therefore, the oral franchise agreement addresses a contractual relationship between the parties that is not covered in any manner by the e-commerce agreement. As a result, the oral franchise agreement is "independent of, collateral to, and not inconsistent with" the e-commerce agreement within the meaning of *Shevel's*. *See Shevel's Inc.-Chesterfield v. Se. Assocs., Inc.*, 228 Va. 175, 182 (1984)). Thus, the parties did not intend for the e-commerce agreement to be their sole agreement such that the merger clause does not subsume the prior oral franchise agreement pursuant to Virginia's "collateral contract doctrine." Because the agreements are independent of each other, the e-commerce agreement's arbitration language cannot be attributed to the oral franchise agreement, even construing the language in favor of arbitration. Accordingly, Suburban has not agreed to arbitrate its claims in the underlying suit.

Suburban Leisure Center, Inc. v. AMF Bowling Products, Inc., 468 F.3d 523, 527 (8th Cir. 2006).

Conditions. The parol evidence rule gives special evidentiary status to a writing embodying the terms of a contract. If the writing does not constitute an enforceable contract, the rule's protective shield is unavailable. Thus, evidence establishing invalidity of the purported agreement, such as lack of consideration, fraud, mistake, duress or illegality, is always admissible.

The rule is less clear where there is a valid contract in the ordinary sense, but a party asserts an oral condition to a duty under it. Evidence of this condition does not establish the non-existence of the underlying contract, but a qualification of the duty to perform. (See infra, Section 4). If the court admits evidence of an oral condition, it must be upon a ground other than that of showing the non-existence of a contract. See Restatement (Second) § 217: "Where the parties to a written agreement agree orally that performance of the agreement is subject to the occurrence of a stated condition, the agreement is not integrated with respect to the oral condition." How do the comments to UCC 2–202 account for this rule?

PROBLEM: PAROL EVIDENCE UNDER CISG

An Italian seller of ceramic tiles and an American buyer, acting through agents, negotiated an oral agreement of sale that contained agreement on price, quality, quantity, delivery, and payment. The parties then reduced the negotiated terms to writing on a form prepared by the seller. On the front over the signature line there was language incorporating terms on the back of the writing into the contract. One of the terms on the back provided:

> Default in delay in payment within the time agreed upon gives [Seller] the right to . . . suspend or cancel the contract itself and to cancel possible other pending contracts and the buyer does not have the right to indemnification or damages.

The agents signed the writing, but there was evidence, confirmed by affidavits, that at the time of signing neither agent intended that terms on the back of the writing were part of the contract. Later, there was a dispute over late payment and the seller invoked the delay in payment term. As a defense, the buyer introduced evidence that neither party intended the back to be part of the contract, although language on the front was not modified to make this intention clear.

(1) Is this evidence admissible under CISG to exclude the default in payment clause? See CISG Art. 8. To check your reasoning, see MCC-Marble Ceramic Center, Inc. v. Ceramica Nuova d'Agostino, S.P.A., 144 F.3d 1384 (11th Cir.1998) (no parol evidence rule under CISG).

(2) If the contract was between an American seller and buyer, would the evidence be admissible under UCC § 2–202? If both parties have the same intention, should that control when it is inconsistent with a term in the writing? See Restatement (Second) § 20(2).

PROBLEM: THE CASE OF THE UNEXPECTED SPOUSE

After ten years of marriage, Ira Soper deserted his wife in Ohio under circumstances contrived to persuade that he had committed suicide. After that, he surfaced in Minneapolis under the name of John Young and became established in business and in a social way. Two years later he married a widow, but she died three years later. Two years after that he married another widow and they lived together as husband and wife for five years until Soper died, this time for real, by his own hand. Prior to his death, however, he had entered into a stock insurance plan with his business partner. Under this plan, upon the death of either partner the survivor could acquire the other's business interest from the estate and the surviving "wife" was to be compensated by life insurance to be taken out by each partner on his life, premiums to be paid by the company. The resulting written insurance "trust" provided that upon the death of the Depositor the "trust company shall deliver the stock certificates of the deceased Depositor to the surviving Depositor and it shall deliver the proceeds of the insurance on the life of the deceased Depositor to the wife of the deceased Depositor if living. . . ." The insurance proceeds were duly paid by the trust officer to Gertrude Young, the woman with whom the deceased had been living as her husband. Shortly thereafter, Adeline, the first Mrs. Soper appeared and established that she was the legal spouse of the deceased. Mrs. Soper had an administrator appointed for the estate of the deceased and brought suit against Mrs. Young to recover the insurance proceeds.

Based upon the preceding materials:

(1) What are the strongest arguments in favor of Adeline Soper?

(2)   What are the strongest arguments in favor of Gertrude Young?

(3)   How should the Court rule? See In re Soper's Estate, 196 Minn. 60 (1935).

Comment: Consumer Contracts and Integration

Section 8 of the Draft Restatement (Third) of Consumer Contracts provides:

(a) Standard contract terms presumptively constitute an integrated agreement with respect to these terms.

(b) Standard contract terms containing an express complete integration clause presumptively constitute a completely integrated agreement with respect to the transaction.

(c) The presumptions in subsections (a) and (b) are rebutted when the standard contract terms contradict or unreasonably limit an affirmation or promise, which is made part of the basis of the bargain between the business and the consumer.

Council Draft No. 3 (December 20, 2016). Section 8 must be read in light of section 7(a), which provides that "[a]n affirmation or promise made by the business, which is made part of the basis of the bargain, becomes part of the contract." Comment 3 to section 8 further explains:

Since the standard contract terms do not represent a joint effort by both parties of drafting and memorializing a negotiated agreement, there is less justification to allow them to override affirmations or promises made to the consumer. Such affirmations or promises are part of the contract under § 7 and cannot be undone by standard contract terms. * * * The presumptions in subsections (a) and (b) are rebutted even when the standard contract terms are unambiguous, when they contradict or unreasonably limit the effect of an affirmation or promise that is made part of the basis of the bargain. A further implication . . . is that in consumer contracts the "four corners test" does not apply. Still, to protect the business interest in the finality of the text, only unreasonable limitations on the effect of an affirmation or promise rebut the presumptions in subsections (a) and (b). A business is allowed to use the standard contract terms to reasonably cabin promises made and liability assumed in an affirmation or promise, especially when the format of the affirmation or promise precluded the communication of such reasonable limits (e.g., when the affirmation or promise was made in a television advertisement).

Can you imagine a situation in which, under these rules, the parol evidence rule would exclude a consumer's evidence of an inconsistent term?

(B) INTERPRETATION AND CONSTRUCTION

Having determined that the parties' agreement is enforceable as a contract and the legally relevant writings or other communications, the next question is to determine their obligations created by those writings or other communications. Insofar as those obligations are chosen, a court or other adjudicator will look to the words they used. Corbin helpfully distinguishes two stages in this process:

> By "interpretation of language" we determine what ideas that language induces in other persons. By "construction of the contract," as the term will be used here, we determine its legal operation—its effect upon the action of courts and administrative officials. If we make this distinction, then the construction of a contract starts with the interpretation of its language but does not end with it; while the process of interpretation stops wholly short of a determination of the legal relations of the parties.

Arthur Linton Corbin, 3 Corbin on Contracts: A Comprehensive Treatise on the Rules of Contract Law § 534 at 7 (1951). Although courts and commentators often use the words indiscriminately, it is worth keeping the difference between the two processes in mind. Interpretation aims to discover what the parties *meant*, construction the *legal effect* of that meaning.

(1) BASIC PRINCIPLES

Pacific Gas & Electric Co. v. G.W. Thomas Drayage & Rigging Co.

Supreme Court of California, 1968.
69 Cal.2d 33.

■ TRAYNOR, CHIEF JUSTICE. Defendant appeals from a judgment for plaintiff in an action for damages for injury to property under an indemnity clause of a contract.

In 1960 defendant entered into a contract with plaintiff to furnish the labor and equipment necessary to remove and replace the upper metal cover of plaintiff's steam turbine. Defendant agreed to perform the work "at [its] own risk and expense" and to "indemnify" plaintiff "against all loss, damage, expense and liability resulting from * * * injury to property, arising out of or in any way connected with the performance of this contract." Defendant also agreed to procure not less than $50,000 insurance to cover liability for injury to property. Plaintiff was to be an additional named insured, but the policy was to contain a cross-liability clause extending the coverage to plaintiff's property.

During the work the cover fell and injured the exposed rotor of the turbine. Plaintiff brought this action to recover $25,144.51, the amount it subsequently spent on repairs. During the trial it dismissed a count based on negligence and thereafter secured judgment on the theory that the indemnity provision covered injury to all property regardless of ownership.

Defendant offered to prove by admissions of plaintiff's agents, by defendant's conduct under similar contracts entered into with plaintiff, and by other proof that in the indemnity clause the parties meant to cover injury to property of third parties only and not to plaintiff's property. Although the trial court observed that the language used was "the classic language for a third party indemnity provision" and that "one could very easily conclude that * * * its whole intendment is to indemnify third parties," it nevertheless held that the "plain language" of the agreement also required defendant to indemnify plaintiff for injuries to plaintiff's property. Having determined that the contract had a plain meaning, the court refused to admit any extrinsic evidence that would contradict its interpretation.

When a court interprets a contract on this basis, it determines the meaning of the instrument in accordance with the " * * * extrinsic evidence of the judge's own linguistic education and experience." (3 Corbin on Contracts (1960 ed.) [1964 Supp. § 579, p. 225, fn. 56].) The exclusion of testimony that might contradict the linguistic background of the judge reflects a judicial belief in the possibility of perfect verbal expression. (9 Wigmore on Evidence (3d ed. 1940) § 2461, p. 187.) This belief is a remnant of a primitive faith in the inherent potency and inherent meaning of words.

The test of admissibility of extrinsic evidence to explain the meaning of a written instrument is not whether it appears to the court to be plain and unambiguous on its face, but whether the offered evidence is relevant to prove a meaning to which the language of the instrument is reasonably susceptible. . . .

A rule that would limit the determination of the meaning of a written instrument to its four-corners merely because it seems to the court to be clear and unambiguous, would either deny the relevance of the intention of the parties or presuppose a degree of verbal precision and stability our language has not attained.

Some courts have expressed the opinion that contractual obligations are created by the mere use of certain words, whether or not there was any intention to incur such obligations. Under this view, contractual obligations flow, not from the intention of the parties but from the fact that they used certain magic words. Evidence of the parties' intention therefore becomes irrelevant.

In this state, however, the intention of the parties as expressed in the contract is the source of contractual rights and duties. A court must ascertain and give effect to this intention by determining what the parties meant by the words they used. Accordingly, the exclusion of relevant, extrinsic evidence to explain the meaning of a written instrument could be justified only if it were feasible to determine the meaning the parties gave to the words from the instrument alone.

If words had absolute and constant referents, it might be possible to discover contractual intention in the words themselves and in the manner in which they were arranged. Words, however, do not have absolute and constant referents. "A word is a symbol of thought but has no arbitrary and fixed meaning like a symbol of algebra or chemistry * * *." (Pearson v. State Social Welfare Board (1960) 54 Cal.2d 184, 195.) The meaning of particular words or groups of words varies with the " * * * verbal context and surrounding circumstances and purposes in view of the linguistic education and experience of their users and their hearers or readers (not excluding judges). * * * A word has no meaning apart from these factors; much less does it have an objective meaning, one true meaning." (Corbin, The Interpretation of Words and the Parol Evidence Rule (1965) 50 Cornell L.Q. 161, 187.) Accordingly, the meaning of a writing " * * * can only be found by interpretation in the light of all the circumstances that reveal the sense in which the writer used the words. The exclusion of parol evidence regarding such circumstances merely because the words do not appear ambiguous to the reader can easily lead to the attribution to a written instrument of a meaning that was never intended." * * *

Although extrinsic evidence is not admissible to add to, detract from, or vary the terms of a written contract, these terms must first be determined before it can be decided whether or not extrinsic evidence is being offered for a prohibited purpose. The fact that the terms of an instrument appear clear to a judge does not preclude the possibility that the parties chose the language of the instrument to express different terms. That possibility is not limited to contracts whose terms have acquired a particular meaning by trade usage, but exists whenever the parties' understanding of the words used may have differed from the judge's understanding.

Accordingly, rational interpretation requires at least a preliminary consideration of all credible evidence offered to prove the intention of the parties. (Civ.Code, § 1647; Code Civ.Proc. § 1860; see also 9 Wigmore on Evidence, op. cit. supra, § 2470, fn. 11, p. 227.) Such evidence includes testimony as to the "circumstances surrounding the making of the agreement * * * including the object, nature and subject matter of the writing * * * " so that the court can "place itself in the same situation in which the parties found themselves at the time of contracting." (Universal Sales Corp. v. Cal. Press Mfg. Co., supra, 20 Cal.2d 751, 761) If the court decides, after considering this evidence, that the language of a contract, in the light of all the circumstances, is "fairly susceptible of either one of the two interpretations contended for * * * " (Balfour v. Fresno C. & I. Co. (1895) 109 Cal. 221, 225 . . .), extrinsic evidence relevant to prove either of such meanings is admissible.

In the present case the court erroneously refused to consider extrinsic evidence offered to show that the indemnity clause in the contract was not intended to cover injuries to plaintiff's property. Although that evidence was not necessary to show that the indemnity clause was reasonably susceptible of the meaning contended for by defendant, it was nevertheless relevant and admissible on that issue. Moreover, since that clause was reasonably susceptible of that meaning, the offered evidence was also admissible to prove that the clause had that meaning and did not cover injuries to plaintiff's property. Accordingly, the judgment must be reversed.

NOTES

(1) *Context Evidence or "Plain Meaning" Rule?* Section 212 of the Restatement (Second), in Comment b, takes a position consistent with *Pacific Gas*:

> It is sometimes said that extrinsic evidence cannot change the plain meaning of a writing, but meaning can almost never be plain except in a context. Accordingly, the rule stated in Subsection (1) [pertaining to interpretation of integrated agreements] is not limited to cases where it is determined that the language used is ambiguous. Any determination of meaning or ambiguity should only be made in the light of the relevant evidence of the situation and relations of the parties, the subject matter of the transaction, preliminary negotiations and statements made therein, usages of trade, and the course of dealing between the parties.

Chief Justice Traynor in *Pacific Gas* would have the trial judge hold a preliminary hearing to examine the proffered evidence, whether it be course of performance, a prior course of dealing, trade usage, or other circumstances, to determine whether the language of the contract is reasonably susceptible to the meaning claimed to be supported by the extrinsic evidence. If the parties have drafted a clear and complete agreement, the odds favor exclusion of all but the most compelling evidence, such as a course of performance indicating how both parties interpreted the term or a trade usage to which both parties are bound.

Whether or not you agree with Justice Traynor's theory of language, are there advantages to having a judge look at extrinsic evidence before determining whether a writing is unambiguous? The defendant in *Pacific Gas* was prepared to introduce *inter alia* admissions by the plaintiff's agents that the parties intended and understood the clause to cover injuries only to the property of third parties. Why shouldn't a court consider such evidence?

(2) The *Pacific Gas* rule is not, however, without critics. In *Trident Center v. Connecticut Gen. Life Ins. Co.*, 847 F.2d 564, 569–70 (9th Cir. 1988), Judge Alex Kozinski criticized *Pacific Gas* in extreme terms:

> Under *Pacific Gas*, it matters not how clearly a contract is written, nor how completely it is integrated, nor how carefully it is negotiated, nor how squarely it addresses the issue before the

court: the contract cannot be rendered impervious to attack by parol evidence. If one side is willing to claim that the parties intended one thing but the agreement provides for another, the court must consider extrinsic evidence of possible ambiguity. If that evidence raises the specter of ambiguity where there was none before, the contract language is displaced and the intention of the parties must be divined from self-serving testimony offered by partisan witnesses whose recollection is hazy from passage of time and colored by their conflicting interests. We question whether this approach is more likely to divulge the original intention of the parties than reliance on the seemingly clear words they agreed upon at the time.

Pacific Gas casts a long shadow of uncertainty over all transactions negotiated and executed under the law of California. As this case illustrates, even when the transaction is very sizeable, even if it involves only sophisticated parties, even if it was negotiated with the aid of counsel, even if it results in contract language that is devoid of ambiguity, costly and protracted litigation cannot be avoided if one party has a strong enough motive for challenging the contract. While this rule creates much business for lawyers and an occasional windfall to some clients, it leads only to frustration and delay for most litigants and clogs already overburdened courts.

It also chips away at the foundation of our legal system. By giving credence to the idea that words are inadequate to express concepts, *Pacific Gas* undermines the basic principle that language provides a meaningful constraint on public and private conduct. If we are unwilling to say that parties, dealing face to face, can come up with language that binds them, how can we send anyone to jail for violating statutes consisting of mere words lacking "absolute and constant referents"? How can courts ever enforce decrees, not written in language understandable to all, but encoded in a dialect reflecting only the "linguistic background of the judge"? Can lower courts ever be faulted for failing to carry out the mandate of higher courts when "perfect verbal expression" is impossible? Are all attempts to develop the law in a reasoned and principled fashion doomed to failure as "remnant[s] of a primitive faith in the inherent potency and inherent meaning of words"?

Be that as it may. While we have our doubts about the wisdom of *Pacific Gas*, we have no difficulty understanding its meaning, even without extrinsic evidence to guide us. As we read the rule in California, we must reverse and remand to the district court in order to give plaintiff an opportunity to present extrinsic evidence as to the intention of the parties in drafting the contract. It may not be a wise rule we are applying, but it is a rule that binds us.

Kozinski's reasoning has in turn been sharply criticized. See Stanley Fish, The Law Wishes to Have a Formal Existence (1992).

(3) Whereas California adheres to the *Pacific Gas* rule, other jurisdictions take the more textualist, plain meaning approach that Kozinski would prefer. A good example is *W.W.W. Associates, Inc. v. Giancontieri,* 77 N.Y.2d 157, 162–63 (1990), where the court said:

> We conclude . . . that the extrinsic evidence tendered by plaintiff is not material. In its reliance on extrinsic evidence to bring itself within the "party benefited" cases, plaintiff ignores a vital first step in the analysis: before looking to evidence of what was in the parties' minds, a court must give due weight to what was in the contract.
>
> A familiar and eminently sensible proposition of law is that, when parties set down their agreement in a clear, complete document, their writing should as a rule be enforced according to its terms. Evidence outside the four corners of the document as to what was really intended but unstated or misstated is generally inadmissible to add to or vary the writing. . . . That rule imparts "stability to commercial transactions by safeguarding against fraudulent claims, perjury, death of witnesses . . . infirmity of memory . . . [and] the fear that the jury will improperly evaluate the extrinsic evidence." [internal citation omitted]. Such considerations are all the more compelling in the context of real property transactions, where commercial certainty is a paramount concern.
>
> Whether or not a writing is ambiguous is a question of law to be resolved by the courts. . . . In the present case, the contract, read as a whole to determine its purpose and intent . . . plainly manifests the intention that defendants, as well as plaintiff, should have the right to cancel after June 1, 1987 if the litigation had not concluded by that date; and it further plainly manifests the intention that all prior understandings be merged into the contract, which expresses the parties' full agreement. * * * Thus, we conclude there is no ambiguity as to the cancellation clause in issue, read in the context of the entire agreement, and that it confers a reciprocal right on both parties to the contract.
>
> The question next raised is whether extrinsic evidence should be considered in order to create an ambiguity in the agreement. That question must be answered in the negative. It is well settled that "extrinsic and parol evidence is not admissible to create an ambiguity in a written agreement which is 'complete and clear and unambiguous upon its face.'"

Which position do you consider better?

(4) *Holmes on the Interpretation Process.* "A word is not a crystal, transparent and unchanged; it is the skin of a living thought and may vary greatly in color and content according to the circumstances and the times in which it is used." Holmes, J. in Towne v. Eisner, 245 U.S. 418, 425 (1918). For this reason, no sooner do courts advance a general rule of strict construction than are exceptions made:

Words are the conduits by which thoughts are communicated, yet scarcely any of them have such a fixed and single meaning that they are incapable of denoting more than one thought. . . . One meaning crowds a word full of significance, while another almost empties the utterance of any import. . . . Thus one is justified in saying that the language of the dictionaries is not the only language spoken in America. For instance, the word "thousand" as commonly used has a very specific meaning; it denotes ten hundreds or fifty scores, but the language of the various trades and localities has assigned to it meanings quite different from that just mentioned. Thus in the bricklaying trade a contract which fixes the bricklayer's compensation at "$5.25 a thousand" does not contemplate that he need lay actually 1,000 bricks in order to earn $5.25, but that he should build a wall of a certain size. . . . And, where the custom of a locality considers 100 dozen as constituting a thousand, one who has 19,200 rabbits upon a warren under an agreement for their sale at the price of 60 pounds for each thousand rabbits will be paid for only 16,000 rabbits. . . .

Hurst v. W.J. Lake & Co., 141 Or. 306, 310–11 (1932).

(5) *Interpretation Under the UCC.* Under the UCC, one must distinguish rules for interpreting the statute itself from rules for interpreting agreements of the parties otherwise within the scope of the statute.

With regard to the former, UCC § 1–103(a) provides that "[The Uniform Commercial Code] must be liberally construed and applied to promote" the underlying purposes and policies of the UCC, which include "to permit the continued expansion of commercial practices through custom, usage and agreement of the parties." Comment 1 further states that "[t]he text of each section should be read in the light of the purpose and policy of the rule or principle in question, as also of the Uniform Commercial Code as a whole, and the application of the language should be construed narrowly or broadly, as the case may be, in conformity with the purposes and policies involved." Like contract interpretation, there is also a hierarchy of statutory interpretation: statutory language and definitions first, the Official Comments second, judicial interpretation third, views of commentators and experts fourth, and legislative history fifth. See John M. Breen, *Statutory Interpretation and the Lessons of Llewellyn,* 33 Loy. L.A. L. Rev. 263 (2000).

With regard to contract interpretation, the UCC provides no comprehensive approach to the interpretation of agreements. However, subsection (a) of UCC § 2–202 provides that terms in an integrated writing may be *explained* or *supplemented* "by course of performance, course of dealing, or usage of trade (Section 1–303)." UCC 1–303(d) explicitly encourages the use of these important extrinsic aids in the interpretation process. "A course of performance or course of dealing between the parties or usage of trade in the vocation or trade in which they are engaged or which they are or should be aware is relevant in ascertaining, the meaning of the parties' agreement, may give particular meaning to specific terms of the agreement and may supplement or qualify the terms of the agreement."

(6)   Traynor's opinion in *Pacific Gas* appears to accept the trial court's conclusion that the plain or dictionary meaning of the indemnification clause unambiguously covered owner losses. But the intermediate appellate court concluded otherwise. Whereas the trial court perhaps focused on the words "all loss, damage, expense and liability," the Court of Appeals emphasized the meaning of "indemnify," which California statute defined as "sav[ing] another from a *legal* consequence of the conduct of one of the parties, or of some other person." Cal. Civ. Code § 2772 (emphasis added). Because the damage to the plaintiff's turbine was not a "legal consequence," the court reasoned, it fell outside of the indemnification clause's plain meaning. Pac. Gas & Elec. Co. v. G.W. Thomas Drayage & Rigging Co., 62 Cal. Rptr. 203, 204 (Ct. App. 1967). The Court of Appeals further reasoned that insofar as the indemnification clause was ambiguous, it should be interpreted against the drafter—which was the plaintiff-owner, leading to the same result. *Id.*

Comment: The Hierarchy of Contract Construction

One way to conceive of process of contract construction is as the sequential application of a hierarchical series of rules to resolve contractual meaning, ambiguity and gaps. Courts begin with the express wording of the oral or written agreement:

> If the language of the contract is plain and unambiguous, there is no room for interpretation or construction. The court merely gives effect to the intentions of the parties as clearly expressed in the contract. . . . Where no explicit, unambiguous answer as to the meaning of the contract is available from within the four corners of the instrument (or, in the absence of a writing, from the express oral agreement), the surrounding circumstances become relevant and extrinsic evidence is admissible. However, there is a hierarchy among the available "external" sources as well. . . . The next three layers of the pyramid are, accordingly, course of performance, course of dealing, and usages of trade. . . . A course of performance overrides an inconsistent course of dealing, which in turn overrides an inconsistent usage of trade. . . .

> If a question regarding the meaning of the contract is not answered by any of the above four sources, one has to resort to legal supplementary rules, either statutory or judge-made, to fill the gap. Specific rules (e.g., rules respecting commercial sales) take priority over general ones (e.g., those applicable to any contract). Traditionally, supplementary rules were conceived of as based on the parties' presumed or hypothetical intentions and were thus labeled "implied terms." Current discourse on such "default rules" and "gap fillers" also falls in line with the conventional conception of the hierarchy. Such rules—in sharp contradistinction to mandatory rules—are relevant only when no answer may be found in any of the former sources.

At times, the meaning of the contract is ascertainable neither by reference to any of the elements constituting the "bargain in fact" (the contract's language, course of performance, course of dealing, and usage of trade), nor by application of default rules. In such extreme cases the gap in the agreement and in the applicable legal rules is filled by reference to general standards of reasonableness and good faith. In such a case "a term which is reasonable in the circumstances is supplied by the court." The official comments to the Restatement stress the normative character of this task: "where there is in fact no agreement [respecting an essential issue], the court should supply a term which comports with community standards of fairness and policy rather than analyze a hypothetical model of the bargaining process." . . .

As one proceeds down the hierarchy, the level of generality and abstraction of the sources increases: first comes the specific transaction, followed by the totality of transactions made between the same parties, trade usage, legal rules applicable to similar contracts, general rules of contract law, and finally, the general standard of reasonableness. As one descends the hierarchy, there is a move away from the parties' individual will towards social values. The "community standards of fairness and policy," according to which the court should supply an omitted term, connote moral and social values of fairness, equity, decency, trust, taking the other party's interests into consideration, mutual cooperation, and good faith.

Eyal Zamir, *The Inverted Hierarchy of Contract Interpretation and Supplementation*, 97 Colum. L. Rev. 1710, 1718–19 (1997). As the article's title suggests, Zamir argues that in practice the process of construction is not so neat. According to Zamir, "to the extent that there is a hierarchy among the various sources for interpreting and supplementing contracts, this hierarchy is, and should be, the converse of the conventional one." *Id.* at 1713–14. It is important to keep the distinction between judicial practice and black-letter law in view. Here we focus on the black-letter rules for contract construction.

Black-letter law holds that after courts exhaust the attempt to discover indicia of the contractors' intent (through textualist plain meaning interpretation and then by adding extrinsic evidence), they turn then to various rules of construction—maxims such as the *contra proferentem* injunction to interpret ambiguities against the drafter (Restatement § 206) or the maxim to interpret contracts so that they "comport with community standards of fairness and policy" (Restatement § 204 cmt. d). These are pure rules of construction, not interpretation, because they are not designed to get at the actual meaning of the parties' words, or their actual intent. They operate where that meaning or intent is unclear.

A question also arises as to *who*—judge or jury—applies particular rules in the hierarchy. While judges are generally given the power to interpret the express words of the contract, juries are often given the task to interpret extrinsic evidence. See Restatement (Second) of Contracts § 212(2) (interpretation of an integrated agreement is to be determined as a question of law unless "it depends on the credibility of extrinsic evidence or on a choice among reasonable inferences to be drawn from extrinsic evidence").

But what happens if the extrinsic evidence sent to a jury is not sufficient to resolve the ambiguity? The judge should normally move on to applying the "rule of construction" tie breakers. But to do this would require a bifurcated trial (something we do not see). Mark P. Gergen, *The Jury's Role in Deciding Normative Issues in the American Common Law*, 68 Fordham L. Rev. 407 (1999).

Henry Jacob Friendly: Born in 1903, Henry Friendly attended Harvard both as an undergraduate and for his law degree. He was appointed by President Eisenhower to the Second Circuit in 1959 and served until 1974. He was widely acknowledged to be the most distinguished judge in this country during his years on the bench.

Frigaliment Importing Co. v. B.N.S. International Sales Corp.

United States District Court, S.D. New York, 1960.
190 F.Supp. 116.

■ FRIENDLY, CIRCUIT JUDGE. The issue is, what is chicken? Plaintiff says "chicken" means a young chicken, suitable for broiling and frying. Defendant says "chicken" means any bird of that genus that meets contract specifications on weight and quality, including what it calls "stewing chicken" and plaintiff pejoratively terms "fowl". Dictionaries give both meanings, as well as some others not relevant here. To support its interpretation, plaintiff sends a number of volleys over the net; defendant essays to return them and adds a few serves of its own. Assuming that both parties were acting in good faith, the case nicely illustrates Holmes' remark "that the making of a contract depends not on the agreement of two minds in one intention, but on the agreement of two sets of external signs—not on the parties' having *meant* the same thing but on their having *said* the same thing." The Path of the Law, in Collected Legal Papers, p. 178. I have concluded that plaintiff has not sustained its burden of persuasion that the contract used "chicken" in the narrower sense.

The action is for breach of the warranty that goods sold shall correspond to the description, New York Personal Property Law, McKinney's Consol. Laws, c. 41 § 95. Two contracts are in suit. In the first, dated May 2, 1957, defendant, a New York sales corporation, confirmed the sale to plaintiff, a Swiss corporation, of

> "US Fresh Frozen Chicken, Grade A, Government Inspected, Eviscerated
>
> 2½–3 lbs. and 1½–2 lbs. each
>
> all chicken individually wrapped in cryovac, packed in secured fiber cartons or wooden boxes, suitable for export
>
> 75,000 lbs. 2½–3 lbs... @ $33.00
>
> 25,000 lbs. 1½–2 lbs... @ $36.50
>
> per 100 lbs. FAS New York
>
> scheduled May 10, 1957 pursuant to instructions from Penson & Co., New York."

The second contract, also dated May 2, 1957, was identical save that only 50,000 lbs. of the heavier "chicken" were called for, the price of the smaller birds was $37 per 100 lbs., and shipment was scheduled for May 30. The initial shipment under the first contract was short but the balance was shipped on May 17. When the initial shipment arrived in Switzerland, plaintiff found, on May 28, that the 2½–3 lbs. birds were not young chicken suitable for broiling and frying but stewing chicken or "fowl"; indeed, many of the cartons and bags plainly so indicated. Protests ensued. Nevertheless, shipment under the second contract was made on May 29, the 2½–3 lbs. birds again being stewing chicken. Defendant stopped the transportation of these at Rotterdam.

This action followed. Plaintiff says that, notwithstanding that its acceptance was in Switzerland, New York law controls under the principle of Rubin v. Irving Trust Co., 1953, 305 N.Y. 288, 305, 113 N.E.2d 424, 431; defendant does not dispute this, and relies on New York decisions. I shall follow the apparent agreement of the parties as to the applicable law.

Since the word "chicken" standing alone is ambiguous, I turn first to see whether the contract itself offers any aid to its interpretation. Plaintiff says the 1½–2 lbs. birds necessarily had to be young chicken since the older birds do not come in that size, hence the 2½–3 lbs. birds must likewise be young. This is unpersuasive—a contract for "apples" of two different sizes could be filled with different kinds of apples even though only one species came in both sizes. Defendant notes that the contract called not simply for chicken but for "US Fresh Frozen Chicken, Grade A, Government Inspected." It says the contract thereby incorporated by reference the Department of Agriculture's regulations, which favor its interpretation; I shall return to this after reviewing plaintiff's other contentions.

The first hinges on an exchange of cablegrams which preceded execution of the formal contracts. The negotiations leading up to the contracts were conducted in New York between defendant's secretary, Ernest R. Bauer, and a Mr. Stovicek, who was in New York for the Czechoslovak government at the World Trade Fair. A few days after meeting Bauer at the fair, Stovicek telephoned and inquired whether defendant would be interested in exporting poultry to Switzerland. Bauer then met with Stovicek, who showed him a cable from plaintiff dated April 26, 1957, announcing that they "are buyer" of 25,000 lbs. of chicken 2½–3 lbs. weight, Cryovac packed, grade A Government inspected, at a price up to 33 per pound, for shipment on May 10, to be confirmed by the following morning, and were interested in further offerings. After testing the market for price Bauer accepted, and Stovicek sent a confirmation that evening. Plaintiff stresses that, although these and subsequent cables between plaintiff and defendant, which laid the basis for the additional quantities under the first and for all of the second contract, were predominantly in German, they used the English word "chicken"; it claims this was done because it understood "chicken" meant young chicken whereas the German word, "Huhn," included both "Brathuhn" (broilers) and "Suppenhuhn" (stewing chicken), and that defendant, whose officers were thoroughly conversant with German, should have realized this. Whatever force this argument might otherwise have is largely drained away by Bauer's testimony that he asked Stovicek what kind of chickens were wanted, received the answer "any kind of chickens," and then, in German, asked whether the cable meant "Huhn" and received an affirmative response. Plaintiff attacks this as contrary to what Bauer testified on his deposition in March, 1959, and also on the ground that Stovicek had no authority to interpret the meaning of the cable. The first contention would be persuasive if sustained by the record, since Bauer was free at the trial from the threat of contradiction by Stovicek as he was not at the time of the deposition; however, review of the deposition does not convince me of the claimed inconsistency. As to the second contention, it may well be that Stovicek lacked authority to commit plaintiff for prices or delivery dates other than those specified in the cable; but plaintiff cannot at the same time rely on its cable to Stovicek as its dictionary to the meaning of the contract and repudiate the interpretation given the dictionary by the man in whose hands it was put. . . . Plaintiff's reliance on the fact that the contract forms contain the words "through the intermediary of: ___", with the blank not filled, as negating agency, is wholly unpersuasive; the purpose of this clause was to permit filling in the name of an intermediary to whom a commission would be payable, not to blot out what had been the fact.

Plaintiff's next contention is that there was a definite trade usage that "chicken" meant "young chicken." Defendant showed that it was only beginning in the poultry trade in 1957, thereby bringing itself within the principle that "when one of the parties is not a member of the trade or other circle, his acceptance of the standard must be made to appear" by proving either that he had actual knowledge of the usage or that the usage is "so generally known in the community that his actual individual knowledge of it may be inferred." 9 Wigmore, Evidence (3d ed. 1940) § 2464. Here there was no proof of actual knowledge of the alleged usage; indeed, it is quite plain that defendant's belief was to the contrary. In order to meet the alternative requirement, the law of New York demands a showing that "the usage is of so long continuance, so well established, so notorious, so universal and so reasonable in itself, as that the presumption is violent that the parties contracted with reference to it, and made it a part of their agreement." Walls v. Bailey, 1872, 49 N.Y. 464, 472–473.

Plaintiff endeavored to establish such a usage by the testimony of three witnesses and certain other evidence. Strasser, resident buyer in New York for a large chain of Swiss cooperatives, testified that "on chicken I would definitely understand a broiler." However, the force of this testimony was considerably weakened by the fact that in his own transactions the witness, a careful businessman, protected himself by using "broiler" when that was what he wanted and "fowl" when he wished older birds. Indeed, there are some indications, dating back to a remark of Lord Mansfield, Edie v. East India Co., 2 Burr. 1216, 1222 (1761), that no credit should be given "witnesses to usage, who could not adduce instances in verification." 7 Wigmore, Evidence (3d ed.1940), § 1954; . . . While Wigmore thinks this goes too far, a witness' consistent failure to rely on the alleged usage deprives his opinion testimony of much of its effect. Niesielowski, an officer of one of the companies that had furnished the stewing chicken to defendant, testified that "chicken" meant "the male species of the poultry industry. That could be a broiler, a fryer or a roaster", but not a stewing chicken; however, he also testified that upon receiving defendant's inquiry for "chickens", he asked whether the desire was for "fowl or frying chickens" and, in fact, supplied fowl, although taking the precaution of asking defendant, a day or two after plaintiff's acceptance of the contracts in suit, to change its confirmation of its order from "chickens," as defendant had originally prepared it, to "stewing chickens." Dates, an employee of Urner-Barry Company, which publishes a daily market report on the poultry trade, gave it as his view that the trade meaning of "chicken" was "broilers and fryers." In addition to this opinion testimony, plaintiff relied on the fact that the Urner-Barry service, the Journal of Commerce, and Weinberg Bros. & Co. of Chicago, a large supplier of poultry, published quotations in a manner which, in one way or another, distinguish between "chicken," comprising broilers, fryers and certain other categories, and "fowl," which, Bauer acknowledged, included stewing chickens. This material would be impressive if there were nothing to the contrary. However, there was, as will now be seen.

Defendant's witness Weininger, who operates a chicken eviscerating plant in New Jersey, testified "Chicken is everything except a goose, a duck, and a turkey. Everything is a chicken, but then you have to say, you have to specify which category you want or that you are talking about." Its witness Fox said that in the trade "chicken" would encompass all the various classifications. Sadina, who conducts a food inspection service, testified that he would consider any bird coming within the classes of "chicken" in the Department of Agriculture's regulations to be a chicken. The specifications approved by the General Services Administration include fowl as well as broilers and fryers under the classification "chickens." Statistics of the Institute of American Poultry Industries use the phrases "Young chickens" and "Mature chickens," under the general heading "Total chickens." and the Department of Agriculture's daily and weekly price reports avoid use of the word "chicken" without specification.

Defendant advances several other points which it claims affirmatively support its construction. Primary among these is the regulation of the Department of Agriculture, 7 C.F.R. §§ 70.300–70.370, entitled, "Grading and Inspection of Poultry and Edible Products Thereof." and in particular § 70.301 which recited:

"*Chickens.* The following are the various classes of chickens:

(a) Broiler or fryer . . .

(b) Roaster . . .

(c) Capon . . .

(d) Stag . . .

(e) Hen or stewing chicken or fowl . . .

(f) Cock or old rooster . . ."

Defendant argues, as previously noted, that the contract incorporated these regulations by reference. Plaintiff answers that the contract provision related simply to grade and Government inspection and did not incorporate the Government definition of "chicken," and also that the definition in the Regulations is ignored in the trade. However, the latter contention was contradicted by Weininger and Sadina; and there is force in defendant's argument that the contract made the regulations a dictionary, particularly since the reference to Government grading was already in plaintiff's initial cable to Stovicek.

Defendant makes a further argument based on the impossibility of its obtaining broilers and fryers at the 33 cents price offered by plaintiff for the 2 1/2–3 lbs. birds. There is no substantial dispute that, in late April, 1957, the price for 2 1/2–3 lbs. broilers was between 35 and 37 cents per pound, and that when defendant entered into the contracts, it was well aware of this and intended to fill them by supplying fowl in these weights. It claims that plaintiff must likewise have known the market since plaintiff had reserved shipping space on April 23, three days before plaintiff's cable to Stovicek, or, at least, that Stovicek was chargeable with such knowledge. It is scarcely an answer to say, as plaintiff does in its brief, that the 33 cents price offered by the 2 1/2–3 lbs. "chickens" was closer to the prevailing 35 cents price for broilers than to the 30 cents at which defendant procured fowl. Plaintiff must have expected defendant to make some profit—certainly it could not have expected defendant deliberately to incur a loss.

Finally, defendant relies on conduct by the plaintiff after the first shipment had been received. On May 28 plaintiff sent two cables complaining that the larger birds in the first shipment constituted "fowl." Defendant answered with a cable refusing to recognize plaintiff's objection and announcing "We have today ready for shipment 50,000 lbs. chicken 2 1/2–3 lbs. 25,000 lbs. broilers 1 1/2–2 lbs.," these being the goods procured for shipment under the second contract, and asked immediate answer "whether we are to ship this merchandise to you and whether you will accept the merchandise." After several other cable exchanges, plaintiff replied on May 29, "Confirm again that merchandise is to be shipped since resold by us if not enough pursuant to contract chickens are shipped the missing quantity is to be shipped within ten days stop we resold to our customers pursuant to your contract chickens grade A you have to deliver us said merchandise we again state that we shall make you fully responsible for all resulting costs."[2] Defendant argues that if plaintiff was sincere in thinking it was entitled to young chickens, plaintiff would not have allowed the shipment under the second contract to go forward, since the distinction between broilers and chickens drawn in defendant's cablegram must have made it clear that the larger birds would not be broilers. However, plaintiff answers that the cables show plaintiff was insisting on delivery of young chickens and that defendant shipped old ones at its peril. Defendant's point would be highly relevant on another disputed issue—whether if liability were established, the measure of damages should be the difference in market value of broilers and stewing chicken in New York or the larger difference in Europe, but I cannot give it weight on the issue of interpretation. Defendant points out also that plaintiff proceeded to deliver some of the larger birds in Europe, describing them as "poulets"; defendant argues that it was only when plaintiff's customers complained about this that plaintiff developed the idea that "chicken" meant "young chicken." There

---

[2] These cables were in German; "chicken", "broilers" and, on some occasions, "fowl," were in English.

is little force in this in view of plaintiff's immediate and consistent protests.

When all the evidence is reviewed, it is clear that defendant believed it could comply with the contracts by delivering stewing chicken in the 2½–3 lbs. size. Defendant's subjective intent would not be significant if this did not coincide with an objective meaning of "chicken." Here it did coincide with one of the dictionary meanings, with the definition in the Department of Agriculture Regulations to which the contract made at least oblique reference, with at least some usage in the trade, with the realities of the market, and with what plaintiff's spokesman had said. Plaintiff asserts it to be equally plain that plaintiff's own subjective intent was to obtain broilers and fryers; the only evidence against this is the material as to market prices and this may not have been sufficiently brought home. In any event it is unnecessary to determine that issue. For plaintiff has the burden of showing that "chicken" was used in the narrower rather than in the broader sense, and this it has not sustained.

This opinion constitutes the Court's findings of fact and conclusions of law. Judgment shall be entered dismissing the complaint with costs.

NOTES

(1)   Judge Friendly does not discuss in *Frigaliment* whether or not the writings at issue were integrated. Do you think they were? What difference would or should it make if they were or were not integrated?

(2)   Judge Friendly concluded in *Frigaliment* that the seller should win because its understanding coincided with an "objective" meaning of "chicken," and the buyer failed to show that the word was "used in the narrower rather than in the broader sense." Corbin applauded this result, adding that the buyer also failed to prove that the seller "knew or had reason to know that plaintiff intended to buy broilers only." Arthur Corbin, *The Interpretation of Words and the Parol Evidence Rule,* 50 Cornell L.Q. 161, 169–70 (1964).

Judge Friendly, however, had second thoughts about *Frigaliment.* Dissenting in *Dadourian Export Corp. v. United States*, 291 F.2d 178, 187 n. 4 (2d Cir.1961), he suggested that the "chicken" case should have been resolved under the *Peerless* doctrine (no contract unless both parties have same meaning in mind) "with the loss still left on the plaintiff because of the defendant's not unjustifiable reliance." Does this make sense? William Young has argued that *Peerless* should be limited to cases of "true equivocation," i.e., where a full exposure to objective evidence in context fails to establish that one party's understanding is more reasonable than the other's. William Young, *Equivocation in the Making of Agreements,* 64 Colum. L. Rev. 619 (1964). Is the "chicken" case within this category?

Alan Farnsworth turns Judge Friendly's doubts around and argues that *Frigaliment* shows that we do not need the *Peerless* doctrine because in cases of true misunderstanding, neither party can satisfy a plaintiff's burden of proof. "The explanation, then, for the judgment [in *Peerless*] is not that there is no contract, but that neither party can sustain the burden of showing that its meaning should prevail." 2 Farnsworth, Contracts § 7.9 (4th ed. 2004).

(3) *Of "Cows" and "Sandwiches."* In *Shrum v. Zeltwanger*, 559 P.2d 1384 (Wyo. 1977), the court addressed the equally momentous question: "What is a cow?" The parties disagreed as to whether the term included a "heifer" which had never had a calf. The court overturned a summary judgment award for the buyer. Concluding that the word "cow" had "within the corral of this case, no plain and ordinary meaning," the matter should go to trial, presumably in order to determine which party offered the better interpretation. In *White City Shopping Center, LP v. PR Restaurants, LLC*, 21 Mass. L. Rptr. 565 (Mass. Sup. 2006), however, the court held that the term "sandwiches" in a lease, as defined by the dictionary and "dictated by common sense," did not include "burritos, tacos, and Quesadillas, which are typically made with a single tortilla and stuffed with a choice filling."

Comment: Second Restatement Rules for Interpretation and Construction

Rules of Interpretation. In the interpretation of an agreement, the key test under Restatement (Second) of whose meaning prevails is found in section 201(2):

> Where the parties have attached different meanings to a promise or agreement or a term thereof, it is interpreted in accordance with the meaning attached by one of them if at the time the agreement was made
>
> > (a) that party did not know of any different meaning attached by the other, and the other knew the meaning attached by the first party; or
> >
> > (b) that party had no reason to know of any different meaning attached by the other, and the other had reason to know the meaning attached by the first party.

Subsection 3 provides that except as provided "in this section, neither party is bound by the meaning attached by the other, even though the result may be a failure of mutual assent." Comment d states that Subsection (2) follows the terminology of § 20, referring to the understanding of each party as the meaning "attached" by him to a term of a promise of agreement, and provides the following illustration:

> A agrees to sell and B to buy a quantity of eviscerated "chicken." A tenders "stewing chicken" or "fowl;" B rejects on the ground that the contract calls for "broilers" or "fryers." Each party makes a claim for damages against the other. It is found that each acted in good faith and that neither had reason to know of the difference in meaning. Both claims fail.

Does this illustration correctly summarize the conclusion of Judge Friendly in the *Frigaliment* case?

Sections 202 and 203 of Restatement (Second) provide some general rules and standards of preference to be followed in the process of interpretation. Section 202 provides:

(1) Words and other conduct are interpreted in the light of all the circumstances, and if the principal purpose of the parties is ascertainable it is given great weight.

(2) A writing is interpreted as a whole, and all writings that are part of the same transaction are interpreted together.

(3) Unless a different intention is manifested,

(a) where language has a generally prevailing meaning, it is interpreted in accordance with that meaning;

(b) technical terms and words of art are given their technical meaning when used in a transaction within their technical field.

(4) Where an agreement involves repeated occasions for performance by either party with knowledge of the nature of the performance and opportunity for objection to it by the other, any course of performance accepted or acquiesced in without objection is given great weight in the interpretation of the agreement.

(5) Wherever reasonable, the manifestations of intention of the parties to a promise or agreement are interpreted as consistent with each other.

Contra Proferentem. Section 206 provides the Restatement (Second) version of the much used *contra proferentem* rule: "In choosing among the reasonable meanings of a promise or agreement or a term thereof, that meaning is generally preferred which operates against the party who supplies the words or from whom a writing otherwise proceeds." The *contra proferentem* rule can be seen as a "penalty altering rule," which intentionally imposes a dispreferred term on the drafter in order to give the drafter better incentives to unambiguously disclose to the non-drafting parties the rights and duties of the contract. The rule has an information-forcing effect about the terms of the contract itself. See Ian Ayres & Robert Gertner, *Filling Gaps in Incomplete Contracts: An Economic Theory of Default Rules*, 99 Yale L.J. 87 (1989).

Other Rules of Construction. Section 207 provides a second rule of construction: "In choosing among the reasonable meanings of a promise or agreement or a term thereof, a meaning that serves the public interest is generally preferred." Yet another rule of construction can be found in Section 203(a): "an interpretation which gives a reasonable, lawful, and effective meaning to all the terms is preferred to an interpretation which leaves a part unreasonable, unlawful, or of no effect." And Section 204 provides the generic rule for filling gaps: "When the parties to a bargain sufficiently defined to be a contract have not agreed with respect to a term which is essential to a determination of their rights and duties, a term which is reasonable in the circumstances is supplied by the court."

For more on the Second Restatement approach, see Robert Braucher, *Interpretation and Legal Effect in the Second Restatement of Contracts*, 81 Colum. L. Rev. 13 (1981).

Comment: Insurance Contracts

In insurance contracts, where adhesion terms dominate, courts will sometimes construe a term in light of the reasonable expectations of the individual who signed the policy. A good if somewhat dated example is *Gray v. Zurich Insurance*, 65 Cal.2d 263 (1966), in which the question was whether the insurance company had a duty to defend its insured where the claim of intentional wrongdoing, if proven, would be excluded from coverage. The court said:

> In interpreting an insurance policy we apply the general principle that doubts as to meaning must be resolved against the insurer and that any exception to the performance of the basic underlying obligation must be so stated as clearly to apprise the insured of its effect.
>
> These principles of interpretation of insurance contracts have found new and vivid restatement in the doctrine of the adhesion contract. As this court has held, a contract entered into between two parties of unequal bargaining strength, expressed in the language of a standardized contract, written by the more powerful bargainer to meet its own needs, and offered to the weaker party on a "take it or leave it basis" carries some consequences that extend beyond orthodox implications. Obligations arising from such a contract inure not alone from the consensual transaction but from the relationship of the parties.
>
> Although courts have long followed the basic precept that they would look to the words of the contract to find the meaning which the parties expected from them, they have also applied the doctrine of the adhesion contract to insurance policies, holding that in view of the disparate bargaining status of the parties we must ascertain that meaning of the contract which the insured would reasonably expect. Thus as Kessler stated in his classic article on adhesion contracts: "In dealing with standardized contracts courts have to determine what the weaker contracting party could legitimately expect by way of services according to the enterpriser's 'calling', and to what extent the stronger party disappointed reasonable expectations based on the typical life situation." (Kessler, *Contracts of Adhesion*, 43 Colum. L. Rev. 629, 637 (1943).) * * *

When we test the instant policy by these principles we find that its provisions as to the obligation to defend are uncertain and undefined; in the light of the reasonable expectation of the insured, they require the performance of that duty. At the threshold we note that the nature of the obligation to defend is itself necessarily uncertain. Although insurers have often insisted that the duty arises only if the insurer is bound to indemnify the insured, this very contention creates a dilemma. No one can determine whether the third party suit does or does not fall within the indemnification coverage of the policy until that suit is resolved; in the instant case, the determination of whether the insured engaged in intentional, negligent or even wrongful conduct depended upon the judgment in the Jones suit, and, indeed, even after that judgment, no one could be positive whether it rested upon a finding of plaintiff's negligent or his intentional conduct. The carrier's obligation to indemnify inevitably will not be defined until the adjudication of the very action which it should have defended. Hence the policy contains its own seeds of uncertainty; the insurer has held out a promise that by its very nature is ambiguous. * * *

In summary, the individual consumer in the highly organized and integrated society of today must necessarily rely upon institutions devoted to the public service to perform the basic functions which they undertake. At the same time the consumer does not occupy a sufficiently strong economic position to bargain with such institutions as to specific clauses of their contracts of performance, and, in any event, piecemeal negotiation would sacrifice the advantage of uniformity. Hence the courts in the field of insurance contracts have tended to require that the insurer render the basic insurance protection which it has held out to the insured. This obligation becomes especially manifest in the case in which the insurer has attempted to limit the principal coverage by an unclear exclusionary clause. We test the alleged limitation in the light of the insured's reasonable expectation of coverage; that test compels the indicated outcome of the present litigation. * * *

The Supreme Court of New Jersey formulated the doctrine of reasonable expectations in insurance contracts as follows: "When members of the public purchase policies of insurance they are entitled to the broad measure of protection necessary to fulfill their reasonable expectations." Kievit v. Loyal Protective Life Insurance Co., 34 N.J. 475 (1961). In Oklahoma, however, the Supreme Court has taken the position that the reasonable expectations doctrine may apply only to the construction of ambiguous insurance contracts or to contracts containing exclusions masked by technical or obscure language or hidden policy provisions. Max True Plastering Co. v. United States Fidelity &

Guaranty Co., 912 P.2d 861 (Okl. 1996). For helpful discussion, see Michelle E. Boardman, *Contra Proferentem: The Allure of Ambiguous Boilerplate*, 104 Mich. L. Rev. 1105, 1105 (2006).

In re Katrina Canal Breaches Litigation

United States Court of Appeals, Fifth Circuit, 2007.
495 F.3d 191.

■ KING, CIRCUIT JUDGE: On the morning of August 29, 2005, Hurricane Katrina struck along the coast of the Gulf of Mexico, devastating portions of Louisiana and Mississippi. In the City of New Orleans, some of the most significant damage occurred when levees along three major canals—the 17th Street Canal, the Industrial Canal, and the London Avenue Canal—ruptured, permitting water from the flooded canals to inundate the city. At one point in Katrina's aftermath, approximately eighty percent of the city was submerged in water.

Each plaintiff in this case is a policyholder with homeowners, renters, or commercial-property insurance whose property was damaged during the New Orleans flooding. Despite exclusions in their policies providing that damage caused by "flood" is not covered, the plaintiffs seek recovery of their losses from their insurers. Their primary contention is that the massive inundation of water into the city was the result of the negligent design, construction, and maintenance of the levees and that the policies' flood exclusions in this context are ambiguous because they do not clearly exclude coverage for an inundation of water induced by negligence. The plaintiffs maintain that because their policies are ambiguous, we must construe them in their favor to effect coverage for their losses.

We conclude, however, that even if the plaintiffs can prove that the levees were negligently designed, constructed, or maintained and that the breaches were due to this negligence, the flood exclusions in the plaintiffs' policies unambiguously preclude their recovery. * * *

I.   FACTUAL BACKGROUND AND PROCEDURAL HISTORY

The cases in this appeal are a handful of the more than forty currently pending cases related to Hurricane Katrina that have been consolidated for pretrial purposes in the Eastern District of Louisiana. In several of the consolidated cases, property owners are suing their insurers to obtain recovery under homeowners, renters, and commercial-property policies for the damage their property sustained during the inundation of water into the city that accompanied the hurricane.

* * *

Plaintiffs-appellees James Capella and Madeline Grenier were insured through defendant-appellant Hanover Insurance Company ("Hanover"), plaintiffs-appellees Peter Ascani III and Gregory Jackson were insured through defendant-appellant Standard Fire Insurance

Company ("Standard Fire"), and plaintiff-appellee Richard Vanderbrook was insured through defendant-appellant Unitrin Preferred Insurance Company ("Unitrin"). The Hanover, Standard Fire, and Unitrin policies provide coverage for risk of direct physical loss to structures on the property as well as for certain risks of loss to personal property, as long as the loss is not an excluded peril. The policies contain the following flood exclusion:

> We do not insure for loss caused directly or indirectly by any of the following. Such loss is excluded regardless of any other cause or event contributing concurrently or in any sequence to the loss. . . . Water Damage, meaning: . . . Flood, surface water, waves, tidal water, overflow of a body of water, or spray from any of these, whether or not driven by wind. . . .

Plaintiffs-cross-appellants Mary Jane Silva and Robert G. Harvey Sr. were insured through defendant-cross-appellee State Farm Fire and Casualty Company ("State Farm"). The State Farm policies insured against loss to the dwelling and for certain losses to personal property except as excluded by the policy. The policies contained the following flood exclusion:

> We do not insure under any coverage for any loss which would not have occurred in the absence of one or more of the following excluded events. We do not insure for such loss regardless of: (a) the cause of the excluded event; or (b) other causes of the loss; or (c) whether other causes acted concurrently or in any sequence with the excluded event to produce the loss; or (d) whether the event occurs suddenly or gradually, involves isolated or widespread damage, arises from natural or external forces, or occurs as a result of any combination of these:
>
> . . . Water Damage, meaning:
>
> (1) flood, surface water, waves, tidal water, overflow of a body of water, or spray from any of these, all whether driven by wind or not. . . .

The *Vanderbrook* action was removed to federal court on the basis of diversity jurisdiction. Hanover, Standard Fire, Unitrin, and State Farm filed Rule 12(c) motions for judgment on the pleadings, contending that the *Vanderbrook* plaintiffs' losses were excluded under their respective policies. In a single eighty-five-page order issued on November 27, 2006, the district court addressed the availability of coverage under the policies at issue in all four cases in this appeal. * * * The court determined that the policies' flood exclusions were ambiguous because the term "flood" was susceptible to two reasonable definitions: one that relates to floods resulting from natural causes only and one that relates to floods resulting from both natural causes and negligent or intentional acts. * * *

Having concluded that the term "flood" as used in the exclusions was ambiguous, the district court construed the Hanover, Standard Fire, and

Unitrin policies in the insureds' favor and concluded that the policies covered water damage caused by a ruptured levee where the rupture was due to the levee's inadequate design, construction, or maintenance. Because the plaintiffs alleged that the post-Katrina inundation of water into the City of New Orleans was caused by negligent design, construction, and maintenance of the levees alongside the city's canals, the court decided that if the plaintiffs could prove their allegations, they could prevail. Accordingly, the district court denied Hanover's, Standard Fire's, and Unitrin's motions.

With respect to State Farm's policies, however, the district court concluded that the flood exclusion's "lead-in" clause removed any ambiguity and clearly excluded coverage for all floods, whether natural or not. The "lead-in" language on which the district court relied provides in part: "We do not insure for such loss [i.e., loss resulting from flood] regardless of . . . the cause of the excluded event[ ] or . . . whether the event . . . arises from natural or external forces." The court granted State Farm's motions and dismissed the actions against it. * * *

We review de novo the district court's order on a motion to dismiss for failure to state a claim under Rule 12(b)(6). * * *

III. DISCUSSION

A. Controlling Law

In diversity cases such as these, federal courts must apply state substantive law. . . . The parties agree that in these Louisiana actions involving the interpretation of insurance policies issued in Louisiana for property located in Louisiana, Louisiana's substantive law controls.

Under Louisiana law, "[a]n insurance policy is a contract between the parties and should be construed by using the general rules of interpretation of contracts set forth in the Louisiana Civil Code." *Cadwallader v. Allstate Ins. Co.,* 848 So.2d 577, 580 (La. 2003). The Louisiana Civil Code provides that "[i]nterpretation of a contract is the determination of the common intent of the parties." La. Civ.Code Ann. art. 2045 (1987). . . . Interpretation of an insurance contract generally involves a question of law. *Bonin v. Westport Ins. Corp.,* 930 So.2d 906, 910 (La. 2006).

"The words of a contract must be given their generally prevailing meaning." La. Civ.Code Ann. art. 2047 (1987); *see also Cadwallader,* 848 So.2d at 580. "When the words of a contract are clear and explicit and lead to no absurd consequences, no further interpretation may be made in search of the parties' intent." La. Civ.Code Ann. art. 2046 (1987). "If the policy wording at issue is clear and unambiguously expresses the parties' intent, the insurance contract must be enforced as written." *Cadwallader,* 848 So.2d at 580.

Where, however, an insurance policy includes ambiguous provisions, the "[a]mbiguity . . . must be resolved by construing the policy as a whole;

one policy provision is not to be construed separately at the expense of disregarding other policy provisions." . . .

Ambiguity may also be resolved through the use of the reasonable-expectations doctrine—i.e., "by ascertaining how a reasonable insurance policy purchaser would construe the clause at the time the insurance contract was entered." . . .

"If after applying the other general rules of construction an ambiguity remains, the ambiguous contractual provision is to be construed against the drafter, or, as originating in the insurance context, in favor of the insured." *La. Ins. Guar. Ass'n,* 630 So.2d at 764. Article 2056 of the Louisiana Civil Code provides: "In case of doubt that cannot be otherwise resolved, a provision in a contract must be interpreted against the party who furnished its text. A contract executed in a standard form of one party must be interpreted, in case of doubt, in favor of the other party." La. Civ.Code Ann. art. 2056 (1987). "Under this rule of strict construction, equivocal provisions seeking to narrow an insurer's obligation are strictly construed against the insurer." *Cadwallader,* 848 So.2d at 580. "That strict construction principle applies only if the ambiguous policy provision is susceptible to two or more *reasonable* interpretations; for the rule of strict construction to apply, the insurance policy must be not only susceptible to two or more interpretations, but each of the alternative interpretations must be reasonable." *Id.* The fact that a term is not defined in the policy itself does not alone make that term ambiguous. *Am. Deposit Ins. Co. v. Myles,* 783 So.2d 1282, 1287 (La. 2001).

"An insurance contract, however, should not be interpreted in an unreasonable or strained manner under the guise of contractual interpretation to enlarge or restrict its provisions beyond what is reasonably contemplated by unambiguous terms or achieve an absurd conclusion." *Cadwallader,* 848 So.2d at 580. "Courts lack the authority to alter the terms of insurance contracts under the guise of contractual interpretation when the policy's provisions are couched in unambiguous terms." *Id.*

The policies in this case—which are homeowners, renters, and commercial-property policies—are all-risk policies. All-risk policies "create[ ] a special type of coverage that extends to risks not usually covered under other insurance; recovery under an all-risk policy will be allowed for all fortuitous losses not resulting from misconduct or fraud, unless the policy contains a specific provision expressly excluding the loss from coverage." *Alton Ochsner Med. Found. v. Allendale Mut. Ins. Co.,* 219 F.3d 501, 504 (5th Cir.2000) (applying Louisiana law). Insurers may, however, limit their liability under all-risk policies: "[A]bsent a conflict with statutory provisions or public policy, insurers, like other individuals, are entitled to limit their liability and to impose and to enforce reasonable conditions upon the policy obligations they contractually assume." . . .

B. Flood Exclusions

The plaintiffs contend that their policies' flood exclusions do not unambiguously exclude coverage for losses caused by an inundation of water resulting from a breached levee where the breach occurred in part because the levee was negligently designed, constructed, or maintained. The plaintiffs urge us to conclude that the term "flood" is ambiguous in this context and that the policies must be construed in favor of coverage. By contrast, the insurers maintain that the policies unambiguously exclude coverage for the inundation of water resulting from the breached levees.

The Louisiana Supreme Court has not interpreted a flood exclusion in the context of breached levees. We must therefore make an *Erie* guess and determine, in our best judgment, how that court would resolve the issue if presented with this case.

The plaintiffs first contend that because the term "flood" is not defined in the policies, it is ambiguous. . . . But the fact that a term used in an exclusion "is not defined in the policy itself . . . alone does not make the exclusion ambiguous; instead, [the court] will give the term its generally prevailing meaning." *Am. Deposit Ins. Co.,* 783 So.2d at 1287.

The plaintiffs also maintain that because the insurers could have more explicitly excluded floods that are caused in part by negligence, their failure to do so in these policies makes the flood exclusions ambiguous. Specifically, the plaintiffs point to evidence that before Hurricane Katrina struck, the insurer defendants knew about the availability of policy forms that more explicitly excluded floods caused in part by man but that they elected not to amend their policies' language accordingly. . . . But the fact that an exclusion could have been worded more explicitly does not necessarily make it ambiguous. . . . Nor does the fact that other policies have more explicitly defined the scope of similar exclusions. * * * We therefore reject the plaintiffs' arguments that the flood exclusions in the policies before us are ambiguous in light of more specific language used in other policies.

Furthermore, even where the scope of an exclusion is not readily apparent, we do not immediately construe that exclusion in favor of coverage. Instead, we first apply the general rules of contract construction set forth in the Civil Code. *La. Ins. Guar. Ass'n,* 630 So.2d at 764. Under those rules, we give the words of a contract their "generally prevailing meaning." La. Civ.Code Ann. art. 2047. Dictionaries, treatises, and jurisprudence are helpful resources in ascertaining a term's generally prevailing meaning. . . . Each of the dictionaries we have accessed lists more than one definition of "flood," but the existence of more than one definition of a term does not itself make the term ambiguous. *Citation Ins. Co. v. Gomez,* 688 N.E.2d 951, 953 (Mass. 1998); *see also* Webster's Third New International Dictionary Explanatory Notes at 17a n.12.4 (2002) (explaining that when a word has multiple definitions, the best definition "is the one that most aptly fits the context of an actual genuine utterance"). Likewise, when "a word has two meanings, one broad and one more restrictive included within the broader meaning, it does not follow that the narrower meaning was intended." *Comm. Union Ins. Co. v. Advance Coating Co.*, 351 So.2d 1183, 1186 (La. 1977).

The Oxford English Dictionary has two pertinent definitions of "flood": (1) "[a]n overflowing or irruption of a great body of water over land not usually submerged; an inundation, a deluge" and (2) "[a] profuse and violent outpouring of water; a swollen stream, a torrent; a violent downpour of rain, threatening an inundation." 5 Oxford English Dictionary 1075–76 (2d ed.1989). . . . Finally, of particular interest is the discussion of "flood" in the Columbia Encyclopedia, which specifically includes in the definition the inundation of water resulting from the bursting of a levee:

> [I]nundation of land by the rise and overflow of a body of water. Floods occur most commonly when water from heavy rainfall, from melting ice and snow, or from a combination of these exceeds the carrying capacity of the river system, lake, or ocean into which it runs. . . . Less predictable are *floods resulting from . . . the bursting of a natural or man-made dam or levee.* In the United States the Johnstown, Pa., flood of 1889, in which thousands of lives were lost, was caused by the breaking of an earth dam above the city.

Columbia Encyclopedia 1002 (6th ed.2000) (emphasis added).

We also consider the definitions of "flood" in treatises. Appleman's Insurance Law and Practice defines "flood waters" as "those waters above the highest line of the ordinary flow of a stream, and generally speaking they have overflowed a river, stream, or natural water course and have formed a continuous body with the water flowing in the ordinary channel." 5 John Alan Appleman & Jean Appleman, Insurance Law and Practice § 3145 (1970). And Couch on Insurance defines "flood" as "the overflow of some body of water that inundates land not usually covered with water." Steven Plitt et al., Couch on Insurance § 153:54 (3d ed.2006) [hereinafter Couch]. Couch also states that the term "flood" is generally unambiguous. *Id.* § 153:49. * * *

Where courts outside Louisiana have considered whether a flood exclusion similar to the ones here unambiguously precludes coverage for water damage resulting from the failure of a structure such as a dam or dike, they have uniformly declared that the inundation of water falls within the language of the exclusion. Russell G. Donaldson, Annotation, *What is "Flood" Within Exclusionary Clause of Property Damage Policy,* 78 A.L.R.4th 817 (1990 & Supp.2007). * * *

In light of these definitions, we conclude that the flood exclusions are unambiguous in the context of this case and that what occurred here fits squarely within the generally prevailing meaning of the term "flood."

When a body of water overflows its normal boundaries and inundates an area of land that is normally dry, the event is a flood. This is precisely what occurred in New Orleans in the aftermath of Hurricane Katrina. Three watercourses—the 17th Street, Industrial, and London Avenue Canals—overflowed their normal channels, and the levees built alongside the canals to hold back their floodwaters failed to do so. As a result, an enormous volume of water inundated the city. In common parlance, this event is known as a flood. * * *

NOTES

(1) If the plaintiff had won this case, the risk of floods caused by negligence would have been covered by the policy. Should insurance policies be interpreted the same as any other contract? What differences do you see in this case? What is the doctrine of "reasonable expectations"? Are you persuaded by the court's conclusion that the word "flood" was not ambiguous? Suppose it had been ambiguous. What next?

(2) *Who Are The Future Parties Rooting For?* If the plaintiff insureds had won this suit, what would be the probable impact on the market? Would a decision for the plaintiffs in this case mean that courts should read flood insurance policies—which insure against losses due to floods—to exclude coverage when the flood is due to a third-party's negligence?

(3) Why didn't the instant court apply the *contra proferentem* doctrine against the insurer? What is an "*Erie* guess"? Did this court have any alternative in trying to determine the substance of Louisiana law?

2. THE DUTY OF GOOD FAITH

(A) SCOPE AND CONTENT OF THE GOOD FAITH DUTY

Courts are also called upon to determine the content of the mandatory duty of good faith in the performance. In this Section we first examine the scope and content of the duty of good faith in general, then test its application in four settings where claims of bad faith are frequently made: (1) prevention, hindrance, or failure to cooperate; (2) exercise of discretion granted by the contract; (3) contract modifications; and (4) termination of the contract for reasons other than cause.

It is now well established that "every contract imposes upon each party a duty of good faith and fair dealing in its performance and its enforcement." Restatement (Second) § 205; see also UCC § 1–304. This duty "may not be disclaimed by agreement," but the parties can determine the standards of good faith if those standards are not manifestly unreasonable. UCC § 1–302(b). Although the duty of good faith is often described as a mandatory part of all contracts, it is not immutable. The parties are free to alter the duty, but have only a limited ability to disclaim it entirely. Thus, the good faith duty might more accurately be described as a default with a mandatory floor. What is not always clear is (1) to what aspects of the transaction does the duty of good faith apply, (2) what is bad faith performance, and (3) what remedies are available when one party performs in bad faith? To put the matter more practically, what is bad faith and what can the other party do about it?

While the words "good faith" conjure broad inquiries into the justice of contractor behavior, an earlier version of Article 1 limited the definition of good faith to mere "honesty in fact in the conduct or transaction involved," UCC § 1–201(b)(19) (1990). Under this meager definition, the duty of good faith seemed little more than a (redundant) prohibition against fraud. Only in Article 2 and only with regard to merchants was the duty expanded to mean "honesty in fact and the observance of reasonable commercial standards of fair dealing in the trade." UCC § 2–103(1)(b). The current version of Article 1 expands the definition beyond the sale of goods and beyond merchants (and possibly beyond the "in the trade" limitation) to define good faith for all transactions and all parties (except those within Article 5) to mean "honesty in fact and the observance of reasonable commercial standards of fair dealing." UCC § 1–201(b)(20). Is this an improvement?

The Restatement emphasizes that because the duty of good faith must be met "in a variety of contexts," its meaning should vary "somewhat with the context." Restatement (Second) § 205 cmt. a. Thus the duty of "fair dealing" means more than just honesty in fact. Comment a continues:

> Good faith performance or enforcement of a contract emphasizes faithfulness to an agreed common purpose and consistency with the justified expectations of the other party; it excludes a variety of types of conduct characterized as involving "bad faith" because they violate community standards of decency, fairness or reasonableness. The appropriate remedy for a breach of the duty of good faith also varies with the circumstances.

And, according to Comment d:

> Subterfuges and evasions violate the obligation of good faith in performance even though the actor believes his conduct to be justified. But the obligation goes further: bad faith may be overt or may consist of inaction, and fair dealing may require more than honesty. A complete catalogue of types of bad faith is impossible, but the following types are among those which have been recognized in judicial decisions: evasion of the spirit of the bargain, lack of diligence and slacking off, willful rendering of imperfect performance, abuse of power to specify terms, and interference with or failure to cooperate in the other party's performance.

Robert S. Summers, in a careful article, has applauded the Restatement (Second) approach to the duty of good faith, primarily because it permits examples of bad faith to emerge over time from context to context. Put another way, the meaning of good faith is best determined by the conduct *excluded* rather than through an *a priori,* structured definition. Robert S. Summers, *The General Duty of Good Faith—Its Recognition and Conceptualization,* 67 Cornell L. Rev. 810 (1982).

Summers' excluder theory contrasts with Steven Burton's "foregone opportunities" approach to defining good faith. Burton asserts:

> Contract formation principles require that each party undertake to forgo in some way its future freedom to pursue opportunities alternative to the contract. A party who acts after formation to recapture a forgone opportunity often is in breach of the contract by failing to perform in good faith. . . . [F]orgone opportunities [are] those alternative opportunities that would be regarded as forgone at formation by reasonable business persons operating in a commercial setting—an objective standard. Whether a party acted after formation to recapture forgone opportunities is a question of subjective intention.

Steven J. Burton, *Good Faith Performance of a Contract Within Article 2 of the Uniform Commercial Code,* 67 Iowa L. Rev. 1, 24 (1981).

Another way to aim at the same target is with the concept of "opportunism," defined by Nobel-prize winning economist Oliver Williamson to be "self-interest seeking with guile." Oliver E. Williamson, *Transaction Cost Economics: The Governance of Contractual Relations,* 22 J.L. & Econ. 233, 234, n. 3 (1979). For a recent elaboration, see Daniel Markovits, *Good Faith As Contract's Core Value, in* Philosophical Foundations of Contract Law 272 (G. Klass, et al. eds., 2014).

Centronics Corporation v. Genicom Corporation

Supreme Court of New Hampshire, 1989.
132 N.H. 133.

■ SOUTER, JUSTICE. A contract between the buyer and seller of business assets provided for arbitration of any dispute about the value of the property transferred, to which the purchase price was pegged, and required an escrow deposit of a portion of the price claimed by the seller pending final valuation. The seller has charged the buyer with breach of an implied covenant of good faith in refusing, during arbitration, to release a portion of the escrow fund claimed to be free from "dispute." The Superior Court (Hollman, J.) granted summary judgment to the buyer, which we affirm.

* * *

Distribution from the escrow fund was to be governed by two sets of provisions. Insofar as the escrow agreement relates to the issue before us, it simply provided that "[i]n accordance with Section 2.07 of the Purchase Agreement, the Escrow Agent shall hold the Escrow Fund in its possession until instructed in writing" by respective New York counsel for Centronics and Genicom "to distribute the same or some portion thereof to Centronics or [Genicom] as the case may be," whereupon the escrow agent was to make the distribution as ordered. Section 2.07 of the Purchase Agreement, entitled "Final Payment of Purchase Price," began with a provision that "[f]inal settlement and payment of the Purchase Price shall be made not later than ten days after determination of [CCNBV, consolidated closing net book value] and computation of the Purchase Price," whether by agreement of the parties or decision of the arbitrator. There followed detailed instructions for payment out of escrow and final settlement between the parties, which are of no significance in the matter before us, being intended to provide for the payment to Centronics of whatever balance it might be owed on the purchase price, and the distribution to Genicom of any amount it might be found to have overpaid.

* * *

Genicom moved for summary judgment on the theory that, given the dispute over CCNBV, the terms of the parties' agreements required payments out of escrow only upon completion of arbitration, thus barring the implication of any duty to authorize a distribution before that event. Centronics objected and sought its own summary judgment, grounded on affidavits said to indicate that Genicom's refusal was meant to pressure Centronics into conceding a disputed item worth a substantial amount.

The trial court ruled for Genicom, after construing the contract to provide that the

> "only way funds can be released is upon final determination of the purchase price, which, as the parties agree, is in the hands of the arbitrator.

> The instant suit is no more than [an] attempt on the part of [Centronics] to rewrite the contract. Essentially, [Centronics] asks this Court to read between the lines of § 2.07 and insert therein a provision regarding partial disbursal of funds from escrow in light of the protracted arbitration. While it is true that the parties contemplated a short time period for resolution of disputes through binding arbitration, the Court cannot insert a provision in the contract for partial payments where such provision does not exist.

> [Centronics] should have demanded a mechanism for partial payments from the Escrow Fund if the arbitration process lagged, or if the factual situation regarding adjustments to the final purchase price occurred as it did. The Court will not renegotiate the contract between the parties to obtain this result. To the extent [Centronics] made a less advantageous contract, it must now abide by the terms of that contract as originally agreed."

Centronics reads the foregoing order as denying that any obligation of good faith is implied in the parties' contract. We read it differently, as concluding that the express terms of the contract are inconsistent with the claim that an obligation of good faith and fair dealing, or any other sort of implied obligation, either requires Genicom to agree to an interim distribution or bars Genicom from refusing to agree except in return for Centronics's concession on a disputed item. We consequently view this appeal as raising the related questions of whether the trial judge misunderstood the implied obligation of good faith or misconstrued the contract. We conclude that he did neither.

* * *

Our own common law of good faith contractual obligation is not . . . as easily stated as we might wish, there being not merely one rule of implied good faith duty in New Hampshire's law of contract, but a series of doctrines, each of them speaking in terms of an obligation of good faith but serving markedly different functions. Since the time of our first contract decision couched in terms of good faith, Griswold v. Heat Incorporated, 108 N.H. 119 (1967), we have relied on such an implied duty in three distinct categories of contract cases: those dealing with standards of conduct in contract formation, with termination of at-will employment contracts, and with limits on discretion in contractual performance, which is at issue in the instant case. Although decisions in the first and second categories are not directly relevant here, a short detour through their cases will serve clarity by indicating the categorical distinctions.

In our decisions setting standards of conduct in contract formation, the implied good faith obligations of a contracting party are tantamount to the traditional duties of care to refrain from misrepresentation and to correct subsequently discovered error, insofar as any representation is intended to induce, and is material to, another party's decision to enter into a contract in justifiable reliance upon it. . . .

By way of contrast, the good faith enforced in the second category of our cases is an obligation implied in the contract itself, where it fulfills the distinctly different function of limiting the power of an employer to terminate a wage contract by discharging an at-will employee. Under the rule evolved from Monge v. Beebe Rubber Co., 114 N.H. 130 (1974) . . . , an employer violates an implied term of a contract for employment at-will by firing an employee out of malice or bad faith in retaliation for action taken or refused by the employee in consonance with public policy. . . . Although good faith in this context has not been rigorously defined, bad faith has been spoken of as equivalent to malice, . . . and treated virtually as a subject of equitable estoppel in labor relations, . . . Indeed, the concepts of good and bad faith applied in these cases are best understood not as elements of general contract law as such, but as expressions of labor policy. . . .

The differences between the obligations of good faith exemplified even in these first two groups of cases are enough to explain why the commentators despair of articulating any single concept of contractual good faith, even after the more than fifty years of litigation following in the wake of the American common law's first explicit recognition of an implied good faith contractual obligation in Kirke La Shelle Co. v. Paul Armstrong Co., 263 N.Y. 79, 87 (1933). . . .

Even within the narrower confines of the third category of cases, those governing discretion in contractual performance, the one notable attempt to conceptualize implied good faith in a single, general definition, Burton, *Breach of Contract and the Common Law Duty to Perform in Good Faith,* 94 Harv. L. Rev. 369 (1980), discussed infra, is opposed by the view that the obligation of good faith performance is better understood simply as excluding behavior inconsistent with common standards of decency, fairness, and reasonableness, and with the parties' agreed-upon common purposes and justified expectations, see Summers, 67 Cornell L. Rev. at 820, 826 (1982); Restatement, supra at § 205, comment a. This view is consonant with our own cases in the third category, a canvass of which should inform our consideration of what good faith may or may not demand of Genicom in the circumstances before us.

[The court reviewed the New Hampshire cases.]

* * *

Despite the variety of their fact patterns, these cases illustrate a common rule: under an agreement that appears by word or silence to invest one party with a degree of discretion in performance sufficient to deprive another party of a substantial proportion of the agreement's value, the parties' intent to be bound by an enforceable contract raises an implied obligation of good faith to observe reasonable limits in exercising that discretion, consistent with the parties' purpose or purposes in contracting. A claim for relief from a violation of the implied covenant of good faith contractual performance therefore potentially raises four questions:

1.   Does the agreement ostensibly allow to or confer upon the defendant a degree of discretion in performance tantamount to a power to deprive the plaintiff of a substantial proportion of the agreement's value? Contracts may be broken in a multitude of ways and theories of relief are correspondingly numerous, but the concept of good faith in performance addresses the particular problem raised by a promise subject to such a degree of discretion that its practical benefit could seemingly be withheld.

2.   If the ostensible discretion is of that requisite scope, does competent evidence indicate that the parties intended by their agreement to make a legally enforceable contract? * * *

3.   Assuming an intent to be bound, has the defendant's exercise of discretion exceeded the limits of reasonableness? The answer to this question depends on identifying the common

purpose or purposes of the contract, against which the reasonableness of the complaining party's expectations may be measured, and in furtherance of which community standards of honesty, decency and reasonableness can be applied.

4.   Is the cause of the damage complained of the defendant's abuse of discretion, or does it result from events beyond the control of either party, against which the defendant has no obligation to protect the plaintiff? Although this question is cast in the language of causation, it may be seen simply as the other face of question three. Suffice it to say here that its point is to emphasize that the good faith requirement is not a fail-safe device barring a defendant from the fruits of every plaintiff's bad bargain, or empowering courts to rewrite an agreement even when a defendant's discretion is consistent with the agreement's legally contractual character.

Applying this analytical sequence to the instant case takes us no further than the first of the four questions, whether the agreement effectively confers such discretion on Genicom over the timing of distributions from the escrow fund that, in the absence of some good faith limitation, Genicom could deny Centronics a substantial proportion of the contract's benefit. Was Genicom, that is, given authority to deprive Centronics indefinitely of a portion of the agreed consideration for the business assets previously transferred? The answer is obviously no. * * * [This contract] contains express and unequivocal provisions governing the timing of payment, which must occur no later than ten days after final resolution of the purchase price, presumably on conclusion of the mandatory arbitration. . . . Genicom has no discretion to withhold approval for pay-out beyond that time, or to affect the timing of the arbitration itself. If, indeed, either party were dragging its heels in the conduct of the arbitration, it should go without saying that the dilatory conduct would be seen as a breach of contract, whether expressed in the language of bad faith or in traditional terms of the obligation to act within a reasonable time. See Restatement, supra at § 205, comment d. In short, because contractual provisions mandating payment on conclusion of the valuation process determine the date on which Centronics will get its due, it is clear that what Centronics claims to be Genicom's discretion over the timing of distribution is in reality a power that each party may exercise, but only jointly with the other, to agree to remove some or all of the escrowed funds from the ambit of the otherwise mandatory pay-out provisions.

Although this discussion reflects the analytical structure of the prior good faith performance cases cited by Centronics and followed here, we should also note that the same result would obtain from applying an alternative analysis proposed by Professor Burton, referred to above, which Centronics has also urged us to employ. Burton's functional analysis of the obligation to observe good faith in discretionary contract performance applies objective criteria, see Burton, 94 Harv. L. Rev. at 390–91, to identify the unstated economic opportunities intended to be bargained away by a promisor as a cost of performance, and it identifies bad faith as a promisor's discretionary action subjectively intended, id. at 386, 389, to recapture such an opportunity, thereby refusing to pay an expected performance cost, id. at 373. Centronics argues that its uncontradicted summary judgment affidavits establish that Genicom showed bad faith in Burton's sense, because its refusal to authorize distribution of the so-called undisputed amounts was an "attempt to recapture [the] degree of control concerning the amount of the final purchase price [which] it had agreed to place . . . in the arbitrator's hands . . . and thereby unjustifiably attain funds to which it was not entitled."

Genicom, of course, denies the uncontradicted evidentiary force that Centronics claims for its affidavits. But even assuming, *arguendo*, that the affidavits are uncontradicted and tend to prove what Centronics asserts, there are two respects in which the facts would fail the Burton test of bad faith as an exercise of discretion meant to recapture an opportunity foregone at the creation of the contract.

It is significant, first, that Genicom's refusal to consent to the distribution from escrow neither recaptures nor gains Genicom anything. In and of itself, the refusal removes no issue from the contingencies of arbitration and gives Genicom no present or future right to the money it wishes to obtain. Genicom's behavior thus contrasts sharply with examples of bad faith given by Burton, in which the discretionary delay preserved the actual use of funds or other valuable resources to the party exercising the discretion. See Burton, 94 Harv. L. Rev. at 394–402. The point is that only when the discretionary act recaptures an economic opportunity does the exercise of discretion pass from the realm of applying leverage for the sake of inducing further agreement into the sphere of bad faith, in which no agreement is necessary to realize the offending party's advantage.

* * *

A second and more fundamental flaw infects Centronics's reliance on the Burton analysis, however. It will be recalled that Burton's conception of bad faith in performance is the exercise of discretion for the purpose of recapturing opportunities foregone or bargained away at the time of contracting, with the identification of such foregone opportunities depending on objective analysis of the parties' "[e]xpectations [as they] may be inferred from the express contract terms in light of the ordinary course of business and customary practice. . . ." Burton, 94 Harv. L. Rev. at 389. Hence, if an objective basis exists to infer that the parties never bargained away the right of either of them to condition any distribution on completing the arbitration of any disputes, then Genicom can not be guilty of bad faith by so insisting, whatever its subjective motive may be. We infer that the opportunity for such insistence never was bargained away.

Although the contract documents do not concisely state there will be no interim distribution, the texts come very close to such a provision. We have previously quoted the language of the escrow agreement that "[i]n accordance with Section 2.07 of the Purchase Agreement," the escrow agent shall hold the fund until instructed by the buyer's and seller's counsel to make a distribution. Section 2.07 was also quoted above. Its topic heading is "Final Payment of Purchase Price," and it provides that final payment and settlement shall be made within ten days of the final determination of net book value and purchase price, which will presumably be at the close of arbitration. "Final Payment . . ." is apparently so called to distinguish it from the "Payment to Sellers on Closing Date," required by § 2.03 of the agreement, since there is no other provision calling for any payment or distribution. The text thus supports the claim that the parties intended the escrow agent to leave the fund intact until the point of the final payment, if any, that would be due to Centronics ten days after the final price determination.

This reading is confirmed by an understanding of the evident business purposes to be served by such a restriction on payout. We explained above that the original escrow of $5,000,000 was to be increased by Genicom's deposit of an Adjustment Amount, which in effect was equal to the amount of Centronics's proposed revision of the final purchase price in excess of the preliminary purchase price. Although Centronics was obligated to follow accepted accounting procedures when it revised the balance sheet to calculate any adjustment, the revision was to be unaudited and Genicom had no control over the setting of this amount.

Genicom, however, was not left entirely subject to Centronics's natural temptation to state a higher, rather than a lower, Adjustment Amount. It is reasonable to suppose each party appreciated that the extent of disagreement and the resulting duration of arbitration would be roughly proportional to the size of the Adjustment Amount. If Centronics had to wait upon the outcome of arbitration before it received any escrowed funds, then Genicom would be able to rely on Centronics's own self-interest to limit the probable length of arbitration by limiting the amount of the adjustment potentially subject to arbitration.

It is also reasonable to assume that neither party expected the other to emerge from arbitration with the whole escrow fund. Each therefore had reason to seek some mechanism for inducing the other side to promote speedy arbitration and the prompt distribution of escrowed money. Such a mechanism would be provided by a scheme conditioning any distribution on completing arbitration, since each would thus be induced to hasten the process for their common benefit.

The probability is, therefore, that each party expected the escrow to remain intact throughout arbitration, as the reason for Genicom's agreement that Centronics would have discretion to state the amount of the adjustment, and as the inducement to a prompt effectuation of their common object of obtaining whatever would be due to each from the fund so escrowed. Whether, therefore, we rely on the analysis underlying our own prior cases, or on the rule as espoused by Burton, we affirm the trial judge's conclusion that Centronics is seeking a revision of the contract, not the enforcement of good faith in its performance.

Affirmed.

NOTES

(1) In *Centronics Corporation,* Justice Souter discussed the good faith scholarship of Robert Summers and Steven Burton. Exactly how do Summers and Burton differ in determining bad faith? Which view prevailed in *Centronics?* See Steve Burton & Eric Andersen, Contractual Good Faith 38–40 (1995), wherein Burton claims victory.

(2) Suppose Genicom had been in bad faith in refusing to release the escrow funds. What remedy would be available to Centronics? Is bad faith simply another way to describe a breach by failing to perform an agreed part of the bargain?

(3) *Good Faith Duty in Formation.* Justice Souter suggested that implied duty of good faith in formation is "tantamount to the traditional duties of care to refrain from misrepresentation and to correct subsequently discovered error." Have you seen any evidence to support this conclusion in the materials studied to here? See El Paso Natural Gas Co. v. Minco Oil & Gas, Inc., 8 S.W.3d 309 (Tex.1999) (holding that under UCC parties are not subject to the statutory duty of good faith in procuring or forming a contract).

(4) *Not a Separate Duty.* Comment 1 to UCC § 1–304 states:

> This section does not support an independent cause of action for failure to perform or enforce in good faith. Rather, this section means that a failure to perform or enforce, in good faith, a specific duty or obligation under the contract, constitutes a breach of that contract or makes unavailable, under the particular circumstances, a remedial right or power. This distinction makes it clear that the doctrine of good faith merely directs a court towards interpreting contracts within the commercial context in which they are created, performed, and enforced, and does not create a separate duty of fairness and reasonableness which can be independently breached.

Comment: Contrasting Models of Good Faith Negotiation: The UNIDROIT Principles

The American Model. American contract law imposes a mandatory duty of "good faith [and fair dealing] on the performance and enforcement of a contract." The duty does not apply to pre-contract negotiations. Nor is the duty free-floating. Rather, it applies to the performance of agreed terms in the contract. For example, if the contract contains a clear and complete termination clause and one party follows that clause in terminating the contract, a court is likely to say that the termination was in good faith. If, however, the contract reserves discretion in performance to one or both parties, the exercise of that discretion must be in good faith. On the other hand, in the absence of a term in the contract, the parties have no common-law duty to negotiate in good faith after a disruptive event such as the failure of an agreed pricing mechanism, much less a duty to agree on an adjustment.

Combined with limitations on the duty of good faith is spirited disagreement among the commentators over what constitutes bad faith and a tendency in the courts to resist a finding of bad faith even where the duty is imposed. The result is that the potential of the duty of good faith for contracts, not to mention relational contracts, has arguably not been realized in the United States.

The UNIDROIT Model. A more expansive model of good faith, one consistent with relational contract theory, is found in the UNIDROIT Principles of International Commercial Contracts.

Article 1.7(1) provides that "each party must act in accordance with good faith and fair dealing in international trade," and Comment 1 makes it clear that the "parties' behaviour throughout the life of the contract, including the negotiation process, must conform to good faith and fair dealing."

Article 2.1.15(1), however, suggests that a party is free not to negotiate (freedom from negotiation) and, if negotiations are undertaken, "is not liable for failure to reach an agreement." However, 2.1.15(2) states that a party who "negotiates or breaks off negotiations in bad faith is liable for the losses caused to the other party," and 2.1.15(3) states that it is "bad faith, in particular, for a party to enter into or continue negotiations when intending not to reach an agreement with the other party." These principles apply across the board to the formation process and the performance, adjustment, or termination of the contract.

The duty to negotiate in good faith, therefore, applies if the parties voluntarily commence negotiation or if the contract requires them to negotiate or bargain. Suppose neither of those conditions is satisfied. When is a duty to negotiate in good faith imposed?

One answer is found in Article 5.1.2, which suggests that the obligation to negotiate may be implied from the nature and purpose of the contract, from practices established between the parties, from good faith and fair dealing, or from reasonableness. This is consistent with the notion in relational contracts that norms of behavior, including a duty to negotiate in good faith, may be generated from the relationship itself.

A second answer is found in the sections of the UNIDROIT Principles dealing with the concept of hardship where "the performance of a contract becomes more onerous for one of the parties." Assuming that the definition of hardship in Article 6.2.2 is satisfied, the "disadvantaged party is entitled to request renegotiations . . . without undue delay." Article 6.2.3 states what a court may do "upon failure to reach agreement within a reasonable time," but does not explicitly say whether the nondisadvantaged party must negotiate if requested. Comment 5, however, provides: "Although nothing is said in this article to that effect, both the request for renegotiations by the disadvantaged party and the conduct of both parties during the renegotiation process are subject to the general principle of good faith (Art. 1.7) and to the duty of cooperation (Art. 5.3)."

Thus, the disadvantaged party must honestly believe that a case of hardship actually exists and not request renegotiations as a purely tactical maneuver. Similarly, once the request has been made, both parties must conduct the renegotiations in a constructive manner, in particular by refraining from any form of obstruction and by providing all the necessary information. Under a fair reading of the UNIDROIT Principles, therefore, one party has a duty to negotiate with the other in good faith, regardless of what the contract provides, in three situations: (1) where one party voluntarily commences negotiation with the other party; (2) where the duty is implied from the relationship; and (3) where, after hardship has occurred, the other (disadvantaged) party makes a timely request to renegotiate the contract or its terms. The parties, however, may fail without penalty to agree in good faith. There is no duty to agree.

(B) PREVENTION, HINDRANCE AND THE DUTY OF COOPERATION

A useful way to think about the problem posed in this section— prevention, hindrance and the duty of cooperation—is in terms of duties imposed by courts in the absence of and, maybe, in spite of an expression of contrary agreement. Whether you say that these duties are implied or imposed is not as important as understanding when and why these relational duties will be found and enforced by the courts. Thus, the doctrines of "prospective inability" to perform and "anticipatory" repudiation both emerge from the perception that the defendant has done something to impair the plaintiff's expectation of receiving due performance, and that the plaintiff's interests, whether you call them expectation, reliance or restitution, should have some protection, be it defensive, affirmative or both. Despite the "implied promise" terminology, Lord Campbell put it very well when he said "where there is a contract to do an act on a future day, there is a relation constituted between the parties in the meantime by the contract and that they impliedly promise that * * * neither will do anything to the prejudice of the other inconsistent with that relation." Hochster v. De La Tour, infra Chapter 6. This basic notion has been particularized in a contemporary decision:

> It is a fundamental principle of law that in every contract there exists an implied covenant of good faith and fair dealing. . . . Furthermore, each contract contains an implicit understanding that neither party will intentionally do anything to prevent the

other party from carrying out his part of the agreement. * * * "It is likewise implied in every contract that there is a duty of cooperation on the part of both parties. *Thus, whenever the cooperation of the promisee is necessary for the performance of the promise, there is a condition implied that the cooperation will be given."*

Lowell v. Twin Disc, Inc., 527 F.2d 767, 770 (2d Cir.1975) (emphasis in original). As with a repudiation or breach by a material nonperformance, breach by prevention or hindrance or a failure to cooperate both excuses the aggrieved party from any duty to continue performance and gives a cause of action for damages.

Benjamin Patterson v. Anna Meyerhofer

Court of Appeals of New York, 1912.
204 N.Y. 96.

■ BARTLETT, J. The parties to this action entered into a written contract whereby the plaintiff agreed to sell and the defendant agreed to buy four several parcels of land with the houses thereon for the sum of $23,000, to be paid partly in cash and partly by taking title subject to certain mortgages upon the property. When she executed this contract, the defendant knew that the plaintiff was not then the owner of the premises which he agreed to sell to her but that he expected and intended to acquire title thereto by purchasing the same at a foreclosure sale. Before this foreclosure sale took place the defendant stated to the plaintiff that she would not perform the contract on her part but intended to buy the premises for her own account without in any way recognizing the said contract as binding upon her, and this she did, buying the four parcels for $5,595 each. The plaintiff attended the foreclosure sale, able, ready and willing to purchase the premises, and he bid for the same, but in every instance of a bid made by him the defendant bid a higher sum. The result was that she acquired each lot for $155 less than she had obligated herself to pay the plaintiff therefor under the contract or $620 less in all.

In the foreclosure sale was included a fifth house, which the defendant also purchased. This was not mentioned in the written contract between the parties, but according to the complaint there was a prior parol agreement which provided that the plaintiff should buy all five houses at the foreclosure sale and should convey only four of them to the defendant, retaining the fifth house for himself.

Upon these facts the plaintiff brought the present action demanding judgment that the defendant convey to him the fifth house and declaring that he had a lien upon the premises purchased by her at the foreclosure sale and that she holds the same in trust for the plaintiff subject to the contract. The complaint also prays that the plaintiff be awarded the sum of $620 damages, being the difference between the price which the defendant paid at the foreclosure sale for the four houses mentioned in the contract and the price which she would have had to pay the plaintiff thereunder.

The learned judge who tried the case at Special Term rendered judgment in favor of the defendant, holding that under the contract of sale there was no relation of confidence between the vendor and vendee. "In the present case," he said, "each party was free to act for his own interest, restricted only by the stipulations of the contract." He was, therefore, of the opinion that "the defendant had a right to buy in at the auction and that she is entitled to hold exactly as though she had been a stranger and that the plaintiff is not entitled to recover the difference between the price paid at the auction and the contract price."

I am inclined to agree with the trial court that no relation of trust can be spelled out of the transactions between the parties. There is no finding of any parol agreement in respect to the fifth house which has been mentioned, and even if there had been such an agreement resting merely in parol, I do not see that it would have been enforceable. As to the four parcels which constituted the subject-matter of the written contract, the defendant avowed her intention to ignore that contract before bidding for them, and cannot be regarded as having gone into possession *under* the plaintiff as vendor, but did so rather in defiance of any right of his; hence, there is no likeness to the cases of Galloway v. Finley (12 Peters, [U.S.], 264) and Bush v. Marshall (6 How. [U.S.], 284) relied upon by the appellant. In those cases, it is true, vendees who had bought up better titles than those of their vendors were treated as trustees for the latter; but the contracts of sale had been carried out and the vendees were in full possession of the lands before they acquired the superior outstanding title; and both decisions were expressly placed on the ground that under such circumstances the vendor and vendee stand in the relation of landlord and tenant and the vendee cannot disavow the vendor's title.

There is no need of judicially declaring any trust in the defendant, however, to secure to the plaintiff the profit which he would have made if the defendant had not intervened as purchaser at the foreclosure sale and had fulfilled the written contract on her part. This is represented by his claim for $620 damages. That amount, under the facts as found, I think the plaintiff was entitled to recover. He has demanded it in his complaint and he should not be thrown out of court because he has also prayed for too much equitable relief.

In the case of every contract there is an implied undertaking on the part of each party that he will not intentionally and purposely do anything to prevent the other party from carrying out the agreement on his part.

This proposition necessarily follows from the general rule that a party who causes or sanctions the breach of an agreement is thereby precluded from recovering damages for its non-performance or from interposing it as a defense to an action upon the contract. . . .

"Where a party stipulates that another shall do a certain thing, he thereby impliedly promises that he will himself do nothing which may hinder or obstruct that other in doing that thing." (Gay v. Blanchard, 32 La. Ann. 497.)

By entering into the contract to purchase from the plaintiff property which she knew he would have to buy at the foreclosure sale in order to convey it to her, the defendant impliedly agreed that she would do nothing to prevent him from acquiring the property at such sale. The defendant violated the agreement thus implied on her part by bidding for and buying the premises herself. Although the plaintiff bid therefor she uniformly outbid him. Presumably if she had not interfered he could have bought the property for the same price which she paid for it. He would then have been able to sell it to her for the price specified in the contract (assuming that she fulfilled the contract), which was $620 more. This sum, therefore, represents the loss which he has suffered. It is the measure of the plaintiff's damages for the defendant's breach of contract.

I see no escape from this conclusion. It is true that the contract contemplated that the four houses should go to the defendant and they have gone to her; but that is not all. The contract contemplated that they should go to the plaintiff first. In that event the plaintiff would have received $620 which he has not got. This would have had to be paid by the defendant if she had fulfilled her contract; and she should be required to pay it now unless she can present some better defense than is presented in this record. This will place both parties in the position contemplated by the contract. The defendant will have paid no more than the contract obligated her to pay; the plaintiff will have received all to which the contract entitled him. I leave the fifth house out of consideration because as to that it seems to me there was no enforceable agreement.

For these reasons the judgments of the Appellate Division and the Special Term should be reversed and a new trial granted, with costs to abide the event.

NOTES

(1) *The Fruits of the Contract.* Whether the inquiry concerns discharge of duty, excuse for failure of condition, or action for breach, cases of this type apply the principle that "in every contract there is an implied covenant that neither party shall do anything which will have the effect of destroying or injuring the right of the other party to receive the fruits of the contract, which means that in every contract there exists an implied covenant of good faith and fair dealing." Kirke La Shelle Co. v. Paul Armstrong Co., 263 N.Y. 79, 87 (1933). See Edwin W. Patterson, *Constructive Conditions in Contracts,* 42 Colum. L. Rev. 903, 928–42 (1942) (tracing history).

(2) *The Case of the Opportunistic Tenant.* Landlord leased premises to Tenant for use as a gasoline station at a rental of five cents for each gallon of gasoline sold. Midway through the five-year term, Tenant purchased

adjoining property upon which he built and operated a new station. Prior to operation of the new station gallonage totaled approximately 40,000 per month; since that time the average has declined to around 4,000. There was no covenant in the lease prohibiting operation of a new station. Landlord consults you regarding his right, if any, to cancel the lease. What do you advise? Cf. *Seggebruch v. Stosor*, 309 Ill.App. 385 (1941).

(3) *The Case of the Interfering Homeowner.* Builder and Mr. and Mrs. Homeowner contracted for the construction of a new house, to be built according to certain plans and specifications at a cost of $100,000. Work began one week later. Almost at once Mrs. Homeowner began making daily visits to the site, each time contacting the foreman in charge relative to what, how, why, etc. was going on. After enduring this for a week, the foreman reported to Builder that he simply "couldn't stand having her around all the time, yakking and getting in the way." Builder asked if she had interfered with the work, to which he replied: "Well, yes, in a way—but the main thing is she's just a damned nuisance." Builder consults you, asking: "What can I do about this?" Advise him. Cf. *Li Volsi Construction Co. v. Shepard*, 133 Conn. 133 (1946); *Gamble v. Woodlea Construction Co.*, 246 Md. 260 (1967).

(4) *A Prevention-Hindrance Sampler: It's Bad Faith, Stupid.*

Sons of Thunder, Inc. v. Borden, Inc., 148 N.J. 396 (1997) (bad faith performance evidenced by extortion, deception, and price cutting).

Ashland Mgmt. Inc. v. Janien, 82 N.Y.2d 395 (1993) (firm's refusal to negotiate confidentiality agreement in contract with employee is bad faith).

R.J. Kuhl Corp. v. Sullivan, 17 Cal.Rptr.2d 425 (Ct. App. 1993) (collusive acts to avoid broker's fee).

Beck v. Mason, 580 N.E.2d 290 (Ind. Ct. App.1991) (vendees failed to fulfill good faith duty to obtain financing).

Cenac v. Murry, 609 So.2d 1257 (Miss.1992) (bizarre behavior by vendor who, under installment contract containing a forfeiture clause to sell country store, interferes with operation of store; bad faith is breach for which damages are recoverable).

Anthony's Pier Four, Inc. v. HBC Associates, 411 Mass. 451 (1991) (unreasonable refusal by owner under a development contract to approve developer's master plan).

United States National Bank of Oregon v. Boge, 311 Or. 550 (1991) (question of fact whether bank's refusal to give payoff information to borrower in order to prevent him from paying notes was in bad faith).

Larson v. Larson, 37 Mass. App. Ct. 106 (1994) (where separation agreement calculates support obligation on husband's earned income, bad faith for husband to retire prematurely without making some other provision for support).

(5) In *Patterson v. Meyerhofer*, the defendant took actions that prevented the plaintiff from performing the contract. What if a nonparty takes such actions? A person who is not a party to a contract cannot be held liable for breach of the contract. A third party might, however, be liable in

tort. Section 766A of the Restatement (Second) of Torts describes the rule as follows:

> One who intentionally and improperly interferes with the performance of a contract (except a contract to marry) between another and a third person, by preventing the other from performing the contract or causing his performance to be more expensive or burdensome, is subject to liability to the other for the pecuniary loss resulting to him.

In cases of this sort, A has a contract with B, C prevents B from performing, and B sues C for intentional interference. These are to be distinguished from cases, discussed in Chapter Six, in which A sues C for having induced B to breach.

PROBLEM: THE CASE OF THE UNCOOPERATIVE VENDOR

In the process of negotiating a contract for the sale of land, Vendee indicated that he hoped to secure a loan on the property to be guaranteed by the Veterans Administration. Vendor, on the other hand, was opposed to dealing with the VA and preferred other financing arrangements. The issue was resolved by the insertion of the following clauses in the contract:

> (18) It is understood and agreed that this home is to be bought and financed under the G.I. Bill of Rights and is subject to approval by Veterans Administration for a purchase price not to exceed Twenty One Thousand Nine Hundred Fifty ($21,950.00); said Eighteen Thousand Dollar First Deed of Trust herein mentioned has already been committed by the First Federal Savings & Loan Assoc. of Washington, D.C., and said loan must be placed with this company, otherwise secondary financing will be arranged.

> (21) The purchaser agrees to accept the following financing in the event the house is not financed under the aforementioned G.I. financing.

Shortly before the agreed closing date, the VA issued a certificate of "reasonable value" which appraised the property at some $4,450 less than the contract price. Since the purchase price exceeded valuation, it appeared that the VA guarantee would not be available. Vendor then informed Vendee that since the VA had disapproved the loan they should proceed in making settlement under the agreed alternative financing. Vendee then requested that Vendor furnish a schedule of his actual construction costs as a basis of appealing to the VA for a higher appraisal. Vendor refused and Vendee subsequently canceled the contract. After the settlement date passed without a closing, Vendor declared the 10% deposit forfeited and retained it as liquidated damages. Vendee sues to recover the deposit. What result?

Market Street Associates Limited Partnership v. Dale Frey

United States Court of Appeals, Seventh Circuit, 1991.
941 F.2d 588.

■ POSNER, CIRCUIT JUDGE. Market Street Associates Limited Partnership and its general partner appeal from a judgment for the defendants, General Electric Pension Trust and its trustees, entered upon cross-motions for summary judgment in a diversity suit that pivots on the doctrine of "good faith" performance of a contract. . . . Wisconsin law applies—common law rather than Uniform Commercial Code, because the contract is for land rather than for goods, UCC § 2–102; Wis.Stat. § 402.102, and because it is a lease rather than a sale and Wisconsin has not adopted UCC art. 2A, which governs leases. * * *

We come at last to the contract dispute out of which the case arises. In 1968, J.C. Penney Company, the retail chain, entered into a sale and leaseback arrangement with General Electric Pension Trust in order to finance Penney's growth. Under the arrangement Penney sold properties to the pension trust which the trust then leased back to Penney for a term of 25 years. Paragraph 34 of the lease entitles the lessee to "request Lessor [the pension trust] to finance the costs and expenses of construction of additional Improvements upon the Premises," provided the amount of the costs and expenses is at least $250,000. Upon receiving the request, the pension trust "agrees to give reasonable consideration to providing the financing of such additional Improvements and Lessor and Lessee shall negotiate in good faith concerning the construction of such Improvements and the financing by Lessor of such costs and expenses." Paragraph 34 goes on to provide that, should the negotiations fail, the lessee shall be entitled to repurchase the property at a price roughly equal to the price at which Penney sold it to the pension trust in the first place, plus 6 percent a year for each year since the original purchase. So if the average annual appreciation in the property exceeded 6 percent, a breakdown in negotiations over the financing of improvements would entitle Penney to buy back the property for less than its market value (assuming it had sold the property to the pension trust in the first place at its then market value).

One of these leases was for a shopping center in Milwaukee. In 1987 Penney assigned this lease to Market Street Associates, which the following year received an inquiry from a drugstore chain that wanted to open a store in the shopping center, provided (as is customary) that Market Street Associates built the store for it. Whether Market Street Associates was pessimistic about obtaining financing from the pension trust, still the lessor of the shopping center, or for other reasons, it initially sought financing for the project from other sources. But they were unwilling to lend the necessary funds without a mortgage on the shopping center, which Market Street Associates could not give because it was not the owner but only the lessee. It decided therefore to try to buy the property back from the pension trust. Market Street Associates' general partner, Orenstein, tried to call David Erb of the pension trust, who was responsible for the property in question. Erb did not return his calls, so Orenstein wrote him, expressing an interest in buying the property and asking him to "review your file on this matter and call me so that we can discuss it further." At first, Erb did not reply. Eventually Orenstein did reach Erb, who promised to review the file and get back to him. A few days later an associate of Erb called Orenstein and indicated an interest in selling the property for $3 million, which Orenstein considered much too high.

That was in June of 1988. On July 28, Market Street Associates wrote a letter to the pension trust formally requesting funding for $2 million in improvements to the shopping center. The letter made no reference to paragraph 34 of the lease; indeed, it did not mention the lease. The letter asked Erb to call Orenstein to discuss the matter. Erb, in what was becoming a habit of unresponsiveness, did not call. On August 16, Orenstein sent a second letter—certified mail, return receipt requested—again requesting financing and this time referring to the lease, though not expressly to paragraph 34. The heart of the letter is the following two sentences: "The purpose of this letter is to ask again that you advise us immediately if you are willing to provide the financing pursuant to the lease. If you are willing, we propose to enter into negotiation to amend the ground lease appropriately." The very next day, Market Street Associates received from Erb a letter, dated August 10, turning down the original request for financing on the ground that it did not "meet our current investment criteria": the pension trust was not interested in making loans for less than $7 million. On August 22, Orenstein replied to Erb by letter, noting that his letter of August 10 and Erb's letter of August 16 had evidently crossed in the mails, expressing disappointment at the turn-down, and stating that Market Street Associates would seek financing elsewhere. That was the last contact between the parties until September 27, when Orenstein sent Erb a letter stating that Market Street Associates was exercising the option granted it by paragraph 34 to purchase the property upon the terms specified in that paragraph in the event that negotiations over financing broke down.

The pension trust refused to sell, and this suit to compel specific performance followed. Apparently the price computed by the formula in paragraph 34 is only $1 million. The market value must be higher, or Market Street Associates wouldn't be trying to coerce conveyance at the paragraph 34 price; whether it is as high as $3 million, however, the record does not reveal.

The district judge granted summary judgment for the pension trust on two grounds that he believed to be separate although closely related. The first was that, by failing in its correspondence with the pension trust to mention paragraph 34 of the lease, Market Street Associates had prevented the negotiations over financing that are a condition precedent to the lessee's exercise of the purchase option from taking place. Second, this same failure violated the duty of good faith, which the common law of Wisconsin, as of other states, reads into every contract. * * *

We begin our analysis by setting to one side two extreme contentions by the parties. The pension trust argues that the option to purchase created by paragraph 34 cannot be exercised until negotiations over financing break down; there were no negotiations; therefore they did not break down; therefore Market Street Associates had no right to exercise the option. This argument misreads the contract. Although the option to purchase is indeed contingent, paragraph 34 requires the pension trust, upon demand by the lessee for the financing of improvements worth at least $250,000, "to give reasonable consideration to providing the financing." The lessor who fails to give reasonable consideration and thereby prevents the negotiations from taking place is breaking the contract; and a contracting party cannot be allowed to use his own breach to gain an advantage by impairing the rights that the contract confers on the other party. . . . Often, it is true, if one party breaks the contract, the other can walk away from it without liability, can in other words exercise self-help. But he is not required to follow that course. He can stand on his contract rights.

But what exactly are those rights in this case? The contract entitles the lessee to reasonable consideration of its request for financing, and only if negotiations over the request fail is the lessee entitled to purchase the property at the price computed in accordance with paragraph 34. It might seem therefore that the proper legal remedy for a lessor's breach that consists of failure to give the lessee's request for financing reasonable consideration would not be an order that the lessor sell the property to the lessee at the paragraph 34 price, but an order that the lessor bargain with the lessee in good faith. But we do not understand the pension trust to be arguing that Market Street Associates is seeking the wrong remedy. We understand it to be arguing that Market Street Associates has no possible remedy. That is an untenable position.

Market Street Associates argues, with equal unreason as it seems to us, that it could not have broken the contract because paragraph 34 contains no express requirement that in requesting financing the lessee mention the lease or paragraph 34 or otherwise alert the lessor to the consequences of his failing to give reasonable consideration to granting the request. There is indeed no such requirement (all that the contract requires is a demand). But no one says there is. The pension trust's argument, which the district judge bought, is that either as a matter of simple contract interpretation or under the compulsion of the doctrine of good faith, a provision requiring Market Street Associates to remind the pension trust of paragraph 34 should be read into the lease.

It seems to us that these are one ground rather than two. A court has to have a reason to interpolate a clause into a contract. The only reason that has been suggested here is that it is necessary to prevent

Market Street Associates from reaping a reward for what the pension trust believes to have been Market Street's bad faith. So we must consider the meaning of the contract duty of "good faith." The Wisconsin cases are cryptic as to its meaning though emphatic about its existence, so we must cast our net wider. We do so mindful of Learned Hand's warning, that "such words as 'fraud,' 'good faith,' 'whim,' 'caprice,' 'arbitrary action,' and 'legal fraud' . . . obscure the issue." *Thompson-Starrett Co. v. La Belle Iron Works*, 17 F.2d 536, 541 (2d Cir.1927). Indeed they do. . . . The particular confusion to which the vaguely moralistic overtones of "good faith" give rise is the belief that every contract establishes a fiduciary relationship. A fiduciary is required to treat his principal as if the principal were he, and therefore he may not take advantage of the principal's incapacity, ignorance, inexperience, or even naïveté. . . . If Market Street Associates were the fiduciary of General Electric Pension Trust, then (we may assume) it could not take advantage of Mr. Erb's apparent ignorance of paragraph 34, however exasperating Erb's failure to return Orenstein's phone calls was and however negligent Erb or his associates were in failing to read the lease before turning down Orenstein's request for financing.

But it is unlikely that Wisconsin wishes, in the name of good faith, to make every contract signatory his brother's keeper, especially when the brother is the immense and sophisticated General Electric Pension Trust, whose lofty indifference to small (= < $7 million) transactions is the signifier of its grandeur. In fact the law contemplates that people frequently will take advantage of the ignorance of those with whom they contract, without thereby incurring liability. *Restatement, supra,* § 161, comment d. The duty of honesty, of good faith even expansively conceived, is not a duty of candor. You can make a binding contract to purchase something you know your seller undervalues. . . . That of course is a question about formation, not performance, and the particular duty of good faith under examination here relates to the latter rather than to the former. But even after you have signed a contract, you are not obliged to become an altruist toward the other party and relax the terms if he gets into trouble in performing his side of the bargain. . . . Otherwise mere difficulty of performance would excuse a contracting party—which it does not. . . .

But it is one thing to say that you can exploit your superior knowledge of the market—for if you cannot, you will not be able to recoup the investment you made in obtaining that knowledge—or that you are not required to spend money bailing out a contract partner who has gotten into trouble. It is another thing to say that you can take deliberate advantage of an oversight by your contract partner concerning his rights under the contract. Such taking advantage is not the exploitation of superior knowledge or the avoidance of unbargained-for expense; it is sharp dealing. Like theft, it has no social product, and also like theft it induces costly defensive expenditures, in the form of overelaborate disclaimers or investigations into the trustworthiness of a prospective contract partner, just as the prospect of theft induces expenditures on locks. See generally Steven J. Burton, "Breach of Contract and the Common Law Duty to Perform in Good Faith," 94 *Harv. L. Rev.* 369, 393 (1980).

The form of sharp dealing that we are discussing might or might not be actionable as fraud or deceit. That is a question of tort law and there the rule is that if the information is readily available to both parties the failure of one to disclose it to the other, even if done in the knowledge that the other party is acting on mistaken premises, is not actionable. . . . All of these cases, however, * * * involve failure to disclose something in the negotiations leading up to the signing of the contract, rather than failure to disclose after the contract has been signed. * * * The distinction is important, as we explained in *Maksym v. Loesch,* 937 F.2d 1237, 1242 (7th Cir.1991). Before the contract is signed, the parties confront each other with a natural wariness. Neither expects the other to be particularly forthcoming, and therefore there is no deception when one is not. Afterwards the situation is different. The parties are now in a cooperative relationship the costs of which will be considerably reduced by a measure of trust. So each lowers his guard a bit, and now silence is more apt to be deceptive. . . .

Moreover, this is a contract case rather than a tort case, and conduct that might not rise to the level of fraud may nonetheless violate the duty of good faith in dealing with one's contractual partners and thereby give rise to a remedy under contract law. Burton, *supra,* at 372 n. 17. This duty is, as it were, halfway between a fiduciary duty (the duty of *utmost* good faith) and the duty merely to refrain from active fraud. Despite its moralistic overtones it is no more the injection of moral principles into contract law than the fiduciary concept itself is. . . . It would be quixotic as well as presumptuous for judges to undertake through contract law to raise the ethical standards of the nation's business people. The concept of the duty of good faith like the concept of fiduciary duty is a stab at approximating the terms the parties would have negotiated had they foreseen the circumstances that have given rise to their dispute. The parties want to minimize the costs of performance. To the extent that a doctrine of good faith designed to do this by reducing defensive expenditures is a reasonable measure to this end, interpolating it into the contract advances the parties' joint goal.

It is true that an essential function of contracts is to allocate risk, and would be defeated if courts treated the materializing of a bargained-over, allocated risk as a misfortune the burden of which is required to be shared between the parties (as it might be within a family, for example) rather than borne entirely by the party to whom the risk had been allocated by mutual agreement. But contracts do not just allocate risk. They also (or some of them) set in motion a cooperative enterprise, which may to some extent place one party at the other's mercy. * * * The office of the doctrine of good faith is to forbid the kinds of opportunistic behavior that a mutually dependent, cooperative relationship might enable in the absence of rule. " 'Good faith' is a compact reference to an implied undertaking not to take opportunistic advantage in a way that could not have been contemplated at the time of drafting, and which therefore was not resolved explicitly by the parties." *Kham & Nate's Shoes No. 2, Inc. v. First Bank, supra,* 908 F.2d at 1357. The contractual duty of good faith is thus not some newfangled bit of welfare-state paternalism or (*pace* Duncan Kennedy, "Form and Substance in Private Law Adjudication," 89 *Harv. L. Rev.* 1685, 1721 (1976)) the sediment of an altruistic strain in contract law, and we are therefore not surprised to find the essentials of the modern doctrine well established in nineteenth-century cases. * * *

The emphasis we are placing on postcontractual versus precontractual conduct helps explain the pattern that is observed when the duty of contractual good faith is considered in all its variety, encompassing not only good faith in the *performance* of a contract but also good faith in its *formation,* . . . and in its *enforcement. . . .* The formation or negotiation stage is precontractual, and here the duty is minimized. It is greater not only at the performance but also at the enforcement stage, which is also postcontractual. * * * At the formation of the contract the parties are dealing in present realities; performance still lies in the future. As performance unfolds, circumstances change, often unforeseeably; the explicit terms of the contract become progressively less apt to the governance of the parties' relationship; and the role of implied conditions—and with it the scope and bite of the good-faith doctrine—grows.

We could of course do without the term "good faith," and maybe even without the doctrine. We could, as just suggested, speak instead of implied conditions necessitated by the unpredictability of the future at the time the contract was made. Farnsworth, "Good Faith Performance and Commercial Reasonableness under the Uniform Commercial Code," 30 U. Chi. L. Rev. 666, 670 (1963). Suppose a party has promised work to the promisee's "satisfaction." As Learned Hand explained, "he may refuse to look at the work, or to exercise any real judgment on it, in which case he has prevented performance and excused the condition." *Thompson-Starrett Co. v. La Belle Iron Works, supra,* 17 F.2d at 541. . . . That is, it was an implicit condition that the promisee examine the work to the extent necessary to determine whether it was satisfactory; otherwise the performing party would have been placing himself at the complete mercy of the promisee. The parties didn't write this condition into the contract either because they thought such behavior unlikely or failed to foresee it altogether. . . . Of similar character is the implied condition that an exclusive dealer will use his best efforts to promote the supplier's goods, since otherwise the exclusive feature of the dealership contract would place the supplier at the dealer's mercy. *Wood v. Duff-Gordon,* 222 N.Y. 88 (1917) (Cardozo, J.).

But whether we say that a contract shall be deemed to contain such implied conditions as are necessary to make sense of the contract, or that a contract obligates the parties to cooperate in its performance in "good faith" to the extent necessary to carry out the purposes of the contract, comes to much the same thing. They are different ways of formulating the overriding purpose of contract law, which is to give the parties what they would have stipulated for expressly if at the time of making the contract they had had complete knowledge of the future and the costs of negotiating and adding provisions to the contract had been zero.

The two formulations would have different meanings only if "good faith" were thought limited to "honesty in fact," an interpretation perhaps permitted but certainly not compelled by the Uniform Commercial Code, see Summers, *supra,* at 207–20—and anyway this is not a case governed by the UCC. We need not pursue this issue. The dispositive question in the present case is simply whether Market Street Associates tried to trick the pension trust and succeeded in doing so. If it did, this would be the type of opportunistic behavior in an ongoing contractual relationship that would violate the duty of good faith performance however the duty is formulated. There is much common sense in Judge Reynolds' conclusion that Market Street Associates did just that. The situation as he saw it was as follows. Market Street Associates didn't want financing from the pension trust (initially it had looked elsewhere, remember), and when it learned it couldn't get the financing without owning the property, it decided to try to buy the property. But the pension trust set a stiff price, so Orenstein decided to trick the pension trust into selling at the bargain price fixed in paragraph 34 by requesting financing and hoping that the pension trust would turn the request down without noticing the paragraph. His preliminary dealings with the pension trust made this hope a realistic one by revealing a sluggish and hidebound bureaucracy unlikely to have retained in its brontosaurus's memory, or to be able at short notice to retrieve, the details of a small lease made twenty years earlier. So by requesting financing without mentioning the lease Market Street Associates might well precipitate a refusal before the pension trust woke up to paragraph 34. It is true that Orenstein's second letter requested financing "pursuant to the lease." But when the next day he received a reply to his first letter indicating that the pension trust was indeed oblivious to paragraph 34, his response was to send a lulling letter designed to convince the pension trust that the matter was closed and could be forgotten. The stage was set for his thunderbolt: the notification the next month that Market Street Associates was taking up the option in paragraph 34. Only then did the pension trust look up the lease and discover that it had been had.

The only problem with this recital is that it construes the facts as favorably to the pension trust as the record will permit, and that of course is not the right standard for summary judgment. The facts must be construed as favorably to the nonmoving party, to Market Street Associates, as the record permits (that Market Street Associates filed its own motion for summary judgment is irrelevant, as we have seen). When that is done, a different picture emerges. On Market Street Associates' construal of the record, $3 million was a grossly excessive price for the property, and while $1 million might be a bargain it would not confer so great a windfall as to warrant an inference that if the pension trust had known about paragraph 34 it never would have turned down Market Street Associates' request for financing cold. And in fact the pension trust may have known about paragraph 34, and either it didn't care or it believed that unless the request mentioned that paragraph the pension trust would incur no liability by turning it down. Market Street Associates may have assumed and have been entitled to assume that in reviewing a request for financing from one of its lessees the pension trust would take the time to read the lease to see whether it bore on the request. Market Street Associates did not desire financing from the pension trust initially—that is undeniable—yet when it discovered that it could not get financing elsewhere unless it had the title to the property it may have realized that it would have to negotiate with the pension trust over financing before it could hope to buy the property at the price specified in the lease.

On this interpretation of the facts there was no bad faith on the part of Market Street Associates. It acted honestly, reasonably, without ulterior motive, in the face of circumstances as they actually and reasonably appeared to it. The fault was the pension trust's incredible inattention, which misled Market Street Associates into believing that the pension trust had no interest in financing the improvements regardless of the purchase option. We do not usually excuse contracting parties from failing to read and understand the contents of their contract; and in the end what this case comes down to—or so at least it can be strongly argued—is that an immensely sophisticated enterprise simply failed to read the contract. On the other hand, such enterprises make mistakes just like the rest of us, and deliberately to take advantage of your contracting partner's mistake during the performance stage (for we are not talking about taking advantage of superior knowledge at the formation stage) is a breach of good faith. To be able to correct your contract partner's mistake at zero cost to yourself, and decide not to do so, is a species of opportunistic behavior that the parties would have expressly forbidden in the contract had they foreseen it. The immensely long term of the lease amplified the possibility of errors but did not license either party to take advantage of them.

The district judge jumped the gun in choosing between these alternative characterizations. The essential issue bearing on Market Street Associates' good faith was Orenstein's state of mind, a type of inquiry that ordinarily cannot be concluded on summary judgment, and could not be here. If Orenstein believed that Erb knew or would surely find out about paragraph 34, it was not dishonest or opportunistic to fail to flag that paragraph, or even to fail to mention the lease, in his correspondence and (rare) conversations with Erb, especially given the uninterest in dealing with Market Street Associates that Erb fairly radiated. To decide what Orenstein believed, a trial is necessary. As for the pension trust's intimation that a bench trial (for remember that this is an equity case, since the only relief sought by the plaintiff is specific performance) will add no illumination beyond what the summary judgment proceeding has done, this overlooks the fact that at trial the judge will for the first time have a chance to see the witnesses whose depositions he has read, to hear their testimony elaborated, and to assess their believability.

The judgment is reversed and the case is remanded for further proceedings consistent with this opinion.

NOTES

Todd Rakoff has discussed in some detail the question of whether it was bad faith for Market Street not to remind the pension trust of paragraph 34 of the contract.

> The connection between this general method and this specific conclusion seems unclear. Judge Posner's own explanation of why "tried to trick" was the "dispositive" standard was that "this would be the type of opportunistic behavior in an ongoing contractual relationship that would violate the duty of good faith performance however the duty is formulated." But the trial judge did not deny that intentional trickery would be bad faith; what he claimed was that the duty went further, requiring the lessee (regardless of motive) to remind the lessor of paragraph 34 as a precondition to later claiming rights under it. To justify the Seventh Circuit's reversal, it is not enough to allow that the duty of good faith goes as far as Judge Posner specified; one has to show that it goes no further. More is needed. * * *

> If, with Judge Posner, we start from the proposition that the doctrine of good faith is bounded on one side by intentional tort obligations and on the other side by fiduciary duties, the terrain left in the middle is very large. In it, we will find cases that are close to the tort boundary, although not quite actionable unless the parties are in a contractual relationship. These are cases, for example, in which bad faith is found in a party's deliberate use of some power it has to undercut the benefit that would in due course come to the other party from the relationship. A traditional example is *Patterson v. Meyerhofer* in which Meyerhofer, having agreed to buy from Patterson real estate that she knew he was going to first buy at auction, went to the auction herself and bought it directly, thus preventing him from earning the potential profit. A little further from the tort boundary we will see cases in which, regardless of motive, bad faith is found in one party's failure to

make an effort needed to bring forth a benefit assigned to the other party. If, for example, a sale of real estate is subject to the buyer's getting financing on stated terms, it is an actionable violation of the duty of good faith for the buyer not to apply to at least some banks or mortgage companies that might provide it. Closer to the fiduciary end of the scale we will see cases in which the court tries to even up the risks and benefits of the relationship while sticking fairly close to the commercial understanding (if not the language) of the parties' deal. Some of these are U.C.C. cases, but probably the most famous case in this category is Judge Cardozo's common law opinion in *Wood v. Lucy, Lady Duff-Gordon*. There, the court implied an obligation for an agent to use best efforts to promote his client's wares in exchange for being given an exclusive license to be paid for by a sharing of revenues. Finally, still within the realm of commercial contracts but right up against the fiduciary boundary, we will find cases in which courts treat the in-fact relationship of the parties as being something of a marriage, with the benefits and vicissitudes of the marketplace to be shared between them.

At points Judge Posner seemed to recognize the breadth of this continuum, or at least he discussed, without objection, cases that exemplify many points on it. But he also clearly rejected the portion of this continuum that comes closest to resembling the law of fiduciaries: "[E]ven after you have signed a contract, you are not obliged to become an altruist toward the other party." What appears then to have happened, if we reconstruct the force field of the opinion, is that Judge Posner's rejection of the point closest to the law of fiduciaries drove him to conclude that the correct stance was the point closest to the law of torts—the point that requires a bad, even if not tortious, intent. In other words, Judge Posner seemed to be saying that because we do not want to treat the parties as being in a sharing relationship, the only ground for relief is if one party tried to "trick" the other.

Whatever its force as a rhetorical trope, this analysis-by-ricochet does not logically follow. Because there are possibilities intermediate between sharing and intentional undercutting, the denial of the one does not suffice to establish the other. Because the trial judge chose one of these intermediate possibilities, imposing an obligation on one party without regard to motive in order to facilitate the other party's knowing performance, that logical lacuna matters. Because the hypothetical-bargain methodology that Judge Posner suggested also does not produce his result, some further force must be at work.

Todd D. Rakoff, *Good Faith in Contact Performance:* Market Street Associates Partnership v. Frey, 120 Harv. L. Rev. 1187, 1192–1196 (2007).

(C) EXERCISE OF RESERVED DISCRETION

Omni Group, Inc. v. Seattle-First National Bank
Court of Appeals of Washington, 1982.
Supra at 157.

Joseph A. Billman v. James F. Hensel
Court of Appeals of Indiana, Third District, 1979.
181 Ind.App. 272.

■ GARRARD, PRESIDING JUDGE. The Hensels, as sellers, entered into a contract to sell their home to the Billmans (the buyers) for $54,000 cash. A condition of the contract was the ability of the buyers to secure a conventional mortgage on the property for not less than $35,000 within thirty (30) days. When the buyers did not complete the purchase, the sellers commenced this suit to secure a thousand dollars ($1,000) earnest money/liquidated damage deposit required by the contract. The buyers defended upon the basis that they were relieved from performing. The case was tried by the court and judgment was entered in favor of the sellers. The sole question raised on appeal is whether the court properly determined that the buyers were not excused from performance. We affirm.

The parties do not dispute, nor do we, that the "subject to financing" clause constituted a condition precedent in the contract. . . . It is also undisputed that the buyers did not, in fact, secure a mortgage loan commitment within the contractual period.

The evidence at trial disclosed that on September 30, the day following execution of the contract, Mr. Billman met with an agent of the Lincoln National Bank and Trust Company of Fort Wayne. Billman was told that he could not obtain a mortgage loan of $35,000 unless he could show he had the difference between the purchase price and the amount of the mortgage. After totaling his available resources, including a 90 day short term note for $10,000 representing the proceeds from the sale of his present home, Billman was $6,500 short of the required $19,000 balance. On October 1st, the Hensels deposited the earnest money check into their account. Billman called Mr. Hensel to tell him that he was close on the financing and requested permission to show the home to his parents on October 3rd.

The Billmans and Mr. Billman's parents went through the house by themselves. The Hensels overheard Mr. Billman's father tell Mr. Billman that "I think I'd be careful with this . . . I'm afraid of it." The Billmans returned without the parents later that same day. Mr. Billman told the Hensels that the deal was off because his parents were unable to loan him the $5,000 needed to complete his financing. The next day, Mr. Hensel told Mr. Billman that he would reduce the price of the home by $5,000. Mr. Billman refused to consider such a reduction, stating that he still needed another $1,500. The Billmans did not deposit funds to cover the check given as earnest money, and Mrs. Billman stopped payment on the check on October 4th.

The Billmans contacted only one financial institution concerning a mortgage loan, and made no formal loan application whatever. They limited discussion to a loan of $35,000 although they subsequently claimed to have required more. When Billman told Hensels he was canceling the sale, he stated the reason was that his parents would not give him $5,000 for the purchase. However, prior to that time he had not mentioned relying upon any assistance and had instead assured Hensels they had all the money needed to complete the sale. Then when Hensels offered to reduce the price by the figure Billman had mentioned, he stated he needed yet an additional $1,500.

We believe the better view to be that such subject to financing clauses impose upon the buyers an implied obligation to make a reasonable and good faith effort to satisfy the condition. . . .

Such an interpretation not only comports with the reasonable expectations of the parties, but is a logical extension of the sound rule of contract law that a promisor cannot rely upon the existence of a condition precedent to excuse his performance where the promisor, himself, prevents performance of the condition. . . .

We recognize that the First District's decision in Blakley v. Currence (1977), Ind.App., 361 N.E.2d 921 refused to impose such an obligation where the condition was not expressed in terms of the *ability* of the buyers to secure financing. We need not reach that question on the facts before us, although we believe the rule in *Blakley* should be limited to the facts there present.

Here the condition imposed was that the buyers be *able* to secure a conventional mortgage of *not less than* $35,000. From the evidence recited above the court was justified in concluding that the sellers had carried their burden of proof by establishing that the buyers did not make a reasonable and good faith effort to secure the necessary financing,[1] and therefore could not rely upon the condition to relieve their duty to perform.

Affirmed.

Austrian Airlines Oesterreichische Luftverkehrs AG v. UT Finance Corporation

United States District Court, S.D. New York, July 18, 2008.
567 F.Supp.2d 579.

■ LEWIS A. KAPLAN, DISTRICT JUDGE. [Austrian Airlines (Austrian) sued UT Finance Corporation (UTF) for breach of contract, alleging that UTF

---

[1]   Note that ordinarily this burden will fall upon the buyer who must bring suit seeking return of his earnest money.

rejected in bad faith used aircraft based on a minor nonconformity in the fuel tanks. At the close of the bench trial, UTF moved for a judgment of dismissal.]

* * *

The UCC provides that "[e]very contract or duty within this Act imposes an obligation of good faith in its performance or enforcement," UCC § 1–203, and defines "good faith" as "honesty in fact in the conduct or transaction concerned." *Id.* § 1–201(19). Article 2 of the UCC provides a broader definition of good faith when the transaction involves merchants.[125] Good faith in those circumstances "means honesty in fact and the observance of reasonable commercial standards of fair dealing in the trade." *Id.* § 2–103(1)(b). This good faith requirement is incorporated into all contracts governed by Article 2. *See id.* § 1–203 (Official Comment). . . .

Austrian contends that one of the reasonable commercial standards of fair dealing in the aircraft trade is adherence to a custom and practice of accepting aircraft "with minor nonconformities" along with financial compensation for those shortcomings. It argues that UTF ignored this custom to avoid paying $32 million for an aircraft that had a market value of approximately $12 million. In consequence, Austrian asserts that UTF acted in bad faith and therefore breached its obligation under the [Aircraft Purchase Agreement ("APA")]. This argument is entirely without merit.

First, industry custom does not apply where the express terms of a contract mandate something different. UCC § 2–208(2). In this case, Section 2.2A, a provision unique to the APA, explicitly abrogated the alleged industry custom. It provided that UTF "*may* accept the Aircraft" in the event of noncompliance and further stated that Austrian "hereby confirms and agrees that it is obligated to deliver the Aircraft . . . in accordance with *all of the delivery conditions* contained in this Agreement and that [UTF] has *no obligation to purchase the Aircraft in the event such delivery conditions are not met.*" The parties therefore agreed that UTF could reject the Aircraft if Austrian failed to satisfy the delivery conditions in any way, no matter how insignificant.

Second, Austrian's argument, even if one were to put the APA aside and assume the existence of the alleged custom, would rest on misconceptions. It describes the industry custom as imposing on a purchaser an obligation to accept an aircraft that has minor nonconformities, defined as deviations from delivery conditions having no effect on the Aircraft's airworthiness or safety, in exchange for some quantum of financial consideration. The evidence, however, proves that the two unapproved [auxiliary center fuel tanks ("ACTs")] affected the Aircraft's airworthiness. Indeed, the Aircraft could not have received an

---

[125] Both parties concede that they are merchants.

FAA certificate of airworthiness until the ACTs were approved. The Court cannot imagine stronger proof that the deviations were not minor.

Finally, Austrian failed to prove that UTF acted in bad faith when it rejected the Aircraft. The keystone of Austrian's argument is an employee evaluation of Ferris that (1) said that his objective was to "[r]educe the exposure of the Austrian A310–300 by 1MM by 2004" and (2) concluded that he had "demonstrated extreme deftness in thwarting the airline's attempts to meet the contractual delivery conditions." On this basis, it would have the Court find that UTF rejected the Aircraft not because of the deficiencies of the tender, but to avoid what otherwise had become a disadvantageous bargain. It then relies upon *Joc Oil USA, Inc. v. Consolidated Edison Co. of New York*, 434 N.Y.S.2d 623 (Sup.Ct.N.Y.Co. 1980), *aff'd sub nom. T.W. Oil, Inc. v. Consol. Edison Co. of New York*, 447 N.Y.S.2d 572 (1st Dept.1981) (table), *aff'd* 57 N.Y.2d 574 (1982), for the proposition that such a motive would constitute bad faith and place the buyer in breach of the contract.

As a factual matter, the Court is unprepared to go as far as Austrian. The Court assumes that UTF, quite understandably, was motivated by the decline in market value to insist upon getting everything it bargained for and, if Austrian was unable to deliver in conformity with the contract, to walk away. It is common sense to recognize, for example, that the Aircraft would have been less valuable to UTF if, as was the case, it were ineligible to receive an FAA certificate of airworthiness than if it had conformed to the contract for the simple reason that the universe of potential purchasers or lessors would have been considerably smaller. Thus, insistence upon the benefit of its bargain was entirely reasonable behavior. But even if UTF was actively seeking to take advantage of Austrian's failure to tender in conformity with the APA for the dominant purpose of getting out of the deal in light of the change in the market, *Joc Oil* does not support Austrian's argument as a matter of law.

Joc Oil involved a contract for sale of a cargo of fuel oil described as having a maximum sulphur content of 0.5 percent. At the time, the buyer was purchasing from others fuel with sulphur exceeding 1 percent, mixing that fuel with other cargoes, and using fuel with average sulphur content of 0.6 to 0.8 percent. When the cargo arrived, it proved to contain 0.92 percent sulphur, and the buyer rejected on that ground. The seller promptly offered to cure the defect by substituting a conforming cargo due to arrive one week later. The buyer rejected that offer, indicating that it would purchase that substitute cargo only at the then-prevailing market price. The critical questions in the case, so far as is relevant here, were whether the seller had the right to cure its improper tender by offering a substitute conforming shipment and, if so, whether it did so reasonably and seasonably.

The court began its analysis with Section 2–508(2) of the Uniform Commercial Code, which provides that "[w]here the buyer rejects a non-conforming tender which the seller had reasonable grounds to believe would be acceptable with or without money allowance the seller may if he seasonably notifies the buyer have a further reasonable time to substitute a conforming tender." The court first concluded that the seller (1) had reasonable grounds to believe that a substitute tender would be acceptable, and (2) gave timely and reasonable notice of its intention to cure. It then noted that the substitute shipment was provided within a reasonable time, which was the relevant standard given "the absence of any contract provision or other evidence rendering time of the essence as to the original delivery." 434 N.Y.S.2d at 630. Accordingly, it held that the seller had a right to cure, that it had done so properly, and that the buyer's rejection in those circumstances placed it in breach.

In the course of discussing the question whether the seller had reason to believe that a substitute tender would be acceptable, the court focused on a variety of circumstances including the buyer's indication that it would purchase the substitute cargo, but only at the then-prevailing market price. *Id.* It concluded from that fact that the dispute centered more on price than on the sulphur content of the fuel and that "[t]here can be no doubt that this dispute would not exist if the market had risen at the time." *Id.*

Contrary to Austrian's suggestion, the *Joc Oil* court's remarks do not hold that a buyer acts in bad faith and thus breaches when it rejects a non-conforming tender because the market for the resale of the goods has declined. Rather, the issue to which the comments were addressed was whether the seller had reasonable ground to believe that the buyer would accept a nonconforming tender and thus fall within UCC Section 2–508(2) and its policy of protecting sellers against surprise rejections. Evidence that a buyer would have accepted a non-conforming tender at a lower price is relevant to that question. But that is not the issue here.

In this case, as we have seen, Section 2.2A of the APA made abundantly clear that UTF would have no obligation to accept a non-conforming tender. Thus, Austrian contracted away any right it otherwise might have had to cure its failure to perform by March 31, 2004. The fact that UTF was prepared to discuss an extension of the delivery date in exchange for financial consideration, an offer that Austrian rejected, thus is immaterial. And in any case, Austrian never made a conforming tender.

Nor would the rule for which Austrian argues make much commercial sense. Where a buyer pursuant to a contract calling for future delivery is presented with non-conforming goods, price movements intervening between the agreement and the time for delivery often are taken into consideration in determining whether to reject. It makes sense to consider them because nonconformities often go not to the ultimate utility of the goods, but to their value, especially resale value. Where the parties, as they did here, contract in terms that give the buyer the right to walk away from the deal in the event of a non-conforming tender, there is no reason not to give the buyer the benefit of its bargain. That is especially so in a case like this, which involves highly sophisticated and well advised commercial entities.[141]

Accordingly, Austrian's argument is without merit.

* * *

NOTES

(1)   How does the *Austrian Airlines* court distinguish *Jos Oil*? Of course one difference is the contract in *Austrian Airlines*, which the court reads to establish the buyer's right to reject. But the court also says the case would come out the same way without that term.

(2)   *Condition of Personal Satisfaction: Subjective or Objective Standard?* When a promisor conditions a duty to perform upon being satisfied with the other party's performance or "with respect to something else," see Restatement (Second) § 228, the expression of dissatisfaction must be in good faith. A common example of bad faith is where the promisor is dissatisfied with the overall bargain rather than the other party's performance. If, for example, the market price for goods has dropped well below the contract price, the buyer may claim dissatisfaction with the seller's performance in order to wriggle out of a bad deal. A more complex problem is the standard of good faith to be insisted upon—should it be "subjective" or "objective"? What was the test applied in *Mattei v. Hopper,* discussed in *Omni Group,* and in *Austrian Airlines*? In *Omni Group,* could an expression of honest dissatisfaction have avoided liability under the contract? Under Restatement (Second) § 228, if it is "practicable to determine whether a reasonable person in the position of the obligor would be satisfied, an interpretation is preferred under which the condition occurs if such a reasonable person in the position of the obligor would be satisfied."

Kennedy Associates, Inc. v. Fischer, 667 P.2d 174 (Alaska 1983), considered a lender's dissatisfaction with the condition of a commercial rental property under "subject to approval" clause. The court stated:

> The question of whether a court should utilize an objective rather than a subjective standard of good faith in gauging the validity of reliance upon a satisfaction clause dependent upon commercial judgment is one of first impression in this jurisdiction. It is well-established that where the condition requires satisfaction as to commercial value or quality, operative fitness, or mechanical utility, an objective standard is to be used in determining whether the clause has been satisfied. . . . On the other hand, if a judgment dependent upon personal taste or fancy, such as design of a dress or execution of a portrait is involved, a subjective test is

---

[141] Austrian's reliance on two other cases as supporting its position is misguided. *See Printing Ctr. of Texas, Inc. v. Supermind Publ'g Co.,* 669 S.W.2d 779, 784 (Tex.App.1984) (holding that "evidence of rejection of the goods *on account of a minor defect* in a falling market *would in some instances* be sufficient to support a finding that the buyer acted in bad faith when he rejected the goods") (emphasis added); *Neumiller Farms, Inc. v. Cornett,* 368 So.2d 272, 274–75 (Ala.1979) (finding that a buyer who rejected potatoes due to dissatisfaction with the way they chipped had done so in bad faith because the evidence demonstrated that the potatoes chipped satisfactorily).

appropriate. . . . The difficulty of the case before us lies in the fact that it arises in a commercial context but involves a judgment dependent upon consideration of a multiplicity of factors. . . . We conclude that the superior court should have applied an objective standard in determining whether the paragraph 14(i) condition was satisfied. Our choice of standard is predicated on the principle that a forfeiture of contractual rights is to be avoided, whenever possible. Therefore, just as "conditions" are to be construed as covenants, unless the parties have clearly agreed otherwise, so must a preference be given to application of an objective test of reasonable satisfaction whenever practicable and not precluded by the express terms of the parties' agreement.

667 P.2d at 181–82.

(3) If a buyer rejects goods in bad faith, the rejection is wrongful, enabling the seller to pursue remedies for breach under UCC § 2–703. We will have more to say about the buyer's remedies of rejection and revocation of acceptance in Chapter Six.

Comment: Lender Liability and the Duty to Act in Good Faith

A specialized context from which good faith disputes arise is the relationship between a lender and its customers; the termination of a line of credit by the lender may be bad faith, subjecting the lender to liability for the customer's commercial losses but not exemplary damages. See *Reid v. Key Bank of Southern Maine, Inc.*, 821 F.2d 9 (1st Cir. 1987), which found bad faith under the "subjective" definition of good faith (honesty in fact), where a minority customer's line of credit was abruptly terminated without notice in circumstances where there was a continuing relationship between the parties, the customer was not in default, and his overall financial position had not changed. Two other leading cases in the development of bad faith "lender liability" are *K.M.C. Co., Inc. v. Irving Trust Co.*, 757 F.2d 752 (6th Cir. 1985) (bad faith refusal to make advance under "discretionary" clause) and *999 v. C.I.T. Corp.*, 776 F.2d 866 (9th Cir. 1985) (bad faith refusal to honor commitment to finance).

Assuming that a contract exists between the parties and the contract does not clearly give the lender power to take action at any time for any reason, recurring questions include the standard of good faith to be applied and whether bad faith has been proved in the particular case. See, e.g., Gilbert Cent. Corp. v. Overland Nat'l Bank, 232 Neb. 778 (1989) (refusal of lender to perform commitment raises genuine issue of material fact on good faith); Price v. Wells Fargo Bank, 213 Cal.App.3d 465 (1989) (absent fiduciary duty, "hard line" in repayment negotiations with informed customer not bad faith). See generally, Dennis M. Patterson, *Good Faith, Lender Liability and Discretionary Acceleration: Of*

Llewellyn, Wittgenstein, and the Uniform Commercial Code, 68 Tex. L. Rev. 169 (1989).

At issue in these cases is the scope of the lender's duty to act in good faith. Should the duty be subjective or objective? If objective, should it incorporate community standards of fair dealing, including concerns about racial discrimination, see Steven J. Burton, *Racial Discrimination in Contract Performance: Patterson and a State Law Alternative,* 25 Harv. C.R.–C.L. L. Rev. 431 (1990), or should the test be limited to an interpretation of the contract terms, allowing the market to resolve other aspects of the dispute?

Consider the argument of Dan Fischel:

> Courts faced with a lender liability case must decide whether the challenged conduct of the lender was consistent with the agreement between the parties. This inquiry is primarily a matter of contract interpretation. What remains unclear, however, is whether courts should look beyond the contract itself and the usual tools of contract interpretation to some other body of authority in order to define the rights and duties between the parties. This question is important because borrowers in recent lender liability cases have argued that lenders' conduct violated the duty of good faith and fiduciary duties to the borrower. However, precisely what these concepts mean and what their relationship is to contract law is not clearly understood.

* * *

> An intermediate position is to interpret the duty of good faith as equivalent to a prohibition of opportunistic behavior. Under this view, lenders are entitled to the benefit of their bargain but are precluded from using contractual terms as a pretense for extracting benefits for which they have not bargained. For example, a lender . . . could terminate funding if the default risk increased, but, absent a risk increase, the duty of good faith would prevent the same lender from threatening to terminate funding in order to force the borrower to pay a higher interest rate.

> Once again, the rationale for imposing a duty of good faith on lenders relates to the impossibility of drafting a contract covering every possible contingency. If contracts could be negotiated and enforced without any cost, the parties could negotiate an agreement which would preclude attempts by the lender to behave opportunistically. Because of the costs of negotiating and enforcing agreements, however, the parties cannot prevent all opportunistic behavior by contract. Thus the duty of good faith acts as an implied contractual term to achieve what the parties themselves cannot given the costs involved.

While this interpretation of the duty of good faith has a certain appeal, it is not without difficulty. The problem is that distinguishing opportunistic from non-opportunistic behavior can be very complicated if not impossible. A lender will never concede that its actions were designed to obtain a benefit not bargained for in the initial agreement. On the contrary, the lender will claim that its refusal to continue funding was based on its assessment of the debtor and the probability of default. Moreover, not only will distinguishing between these two explanations be difficult, but also the attempt to distinguish them will impair the contractual protection given to the lender in the first instance.

Recall that provisions giving the lender sole discretion whether to continue funding and to call any amounts outstanding are best understood as bonding mechanisms used by the borrower to obtain more favorable credit terms. The strength of the bond, however, is weakened if the borrower can argue to a court that the exercise of discretion granted to the lender by the agreement was not done in good faith. This recourse defeats one of the key features of the bond: that the lender, and not a court, decides whether to continue the relationship with a particular borrower. On the other hand, allowing the lender absolute discretion, as discussed above, creates an incentive for the lender to behave opportunistically.

Thus there is a trade-off. The more absolute the discretion of the lender, the stronger the bond of the borrower but the greater the incentive of the lender to behave opportunistically. Conversely, the more expansive the interpretation of the duty of good faith to control opportunistic behavior by the lender, the weaker is the bond of the borrower and the less able the borrower is to use the bond to obtain more favorable credit terms.

Daniel Fischel, *The Economics of Lender Liability,* 99 Yale L.J. 131, 140–42 (1989).

Lending contracts with "demand provisions" that facially give lenders the option to demand immediate repayment of the loan give rise to questions about under what conditions is the lender option limited. UCC § 1–309 (Option to Accelerate at Will) provides:

A term providing that one party or that party's successor in interest may accelerate payment or performance or require collateral or additional collateral "at will" or when the party "deems itself insecure," or words of similar import, means that the party has power to do so only if that party in good faith believes that the prospect of payment or performance is impaired. The burden of establishing lack of good faith is on the party against which the power has been exercised.

Does § 1–309 strike the appropriate balance?

The home-mortgage crisis of 2008 gave new salience to question of lender liability. The Dodd-Frank Act subjects lenders to potential liability for making a mortgage loan unless the lenders have made "a reasonable and good faith determination, based on verified and documented information, that the consumer will have a reasonable ability to repay the loan, including any mortgage-related obligations [such as property taxes, home insurance, and homeowners' association assessments]." See 76 FR 27390 (May 11, 2011). How does this square with the obligations parties normally owe one another before entering into a contract?

Questions of lender bad faith in foreclosure actions have also arisen, especially in states like New York that require mandatory settlement conferences in residential foreclosure actions where "[b]oth the plaintiff and defendant shall negotiate in good faith to reach a mutually agreeable resolutions, including a loan modification, if possible." N.Y. C.P.L.R. 3408(f) (McKinney 2011). Under the Home Affordable Modification Program (HAMP) developed by the U.S. Department of the Treasury, and the 2009 Helping Families Save Their Homes Act, participating mortgage servicers are required to review individual loans and engage in loss mitigation including considering loan modifications before bringing a foreclosure action.

The equitable nature of the foreclosure proceeding has been used for more far-reaching scrutiny of whether lender's enforcement behavior was in good faith. For example, in *IndyMac Bank, F.S.B. v. Yano-Horoski*, 890 N.Y.S.2d 313 (N.Y. Sup. Ct. 2009), a trial court found that a bank's conduct during a foreclosure proceeding "has been and is inequitable, unconscionable, vexatious and opprobrious":

> At the conference held on September 22, 2009, Karen Dickinson, Regional Manager of Loss Mitigation for IndyMac Mortgage Services, ("IndyMac") appeared on behalf of Plaintiff. * * * At that conference, it was celeritously made clear to the Court that Plaintiff had no good faith intention whatsoever of resolving this matter in any manner other than a complete and forcible devolution of title from Defendant. Although IndyMac had prepared a two page document entitled "Mediation Yano-Horoski" which contained what purported to be a financial analysis, Ms. Dickinson's affirmative statements made it abundantly clear that no form of mediation, resolution or settlement would be acceptable to Plaintiff. . . . It was evident from Ms. Dickinson's opprobrious demeanor and condescending attitude that no proffer by Defendant (short of consent to foreclosure and ejectment of Defendant and her family) would be acceptable to Plaintiff. Even a final and desperate offer of a

deed in lieu of foreclosure was met with bland equivocation. In short, each and every proposal by Defendant, no matter how reasonable, was soundly rebuffed by Plaintiff. . . .

When the conduct of Plaintiff in this proceeding is viewed in its entirety, it compels the Court to invoke the ancient and venerable principle of *"Falsus in uno, falsus in omni"* (Latin; "false in one, false in all") upon Defendant which, after review, is wholly appropriate in the context presented, Deering v. Metcalf 74 N.Y. 501 (1878). Regrettably, the Court has been unable to find even so much as a scintilla of good faith on the part of Plaintiff. Plaintiff comes before this Court with unclean hands yet has the insufferable temerity to demand equitable relief against Defendant. * * *

Since an action claiming foreclosure of a mortgage is one sounding in equity, the very commencement of the action by Plaintiff invokes the Court's equity jurisdiction. While it must be noted that the formal distinctions between an action at law and a suit in equity have long since been abolished in New York (see Field Code Of 1848), the Supreme Court nevertheless has equity jurisdiction and distinct rules regarding equity are still extant. Speaking generally and broadly, it is settled law that "Stability of contract obligations must not be undermined by judicial sympathy . . ." However, it is true with equal force and effect that equity must not and cannot slavishly and blindly follow the law. * * * "The maxim of "clean hands" fundamentally was conceived in equity jurisprudence to refuse to lend its aid in any manner to one seeking its active interposition who has been guilty of unlawful, unconscionable or inequitable conduct in the matter with relation to which he seeks relief."

In attempting to arrive at a determination as to whether or not equity should properly intervene in this matter so as to permit foreclosure of the mortgage, the Court is required to look at the situation in toto, giving due and careful consideration as to whether the remedy sought by Plaintiff would be repugnant to the public interest when seen from the point of view of public morality. Equitable relief will not lie in favor of one who acts in a manner which is shocking to the conscience, neither will equity be available to one who acts in a manner that is oppressive or unjust or whose conduct is sufficiently egregious so as to prohibit the party from asserting its legal rights against a defaulting adversary, The compass by which the questioned conduct must be measured is a moral one and the acts complained of (those that are sufficient so as to prevent equity's intervention) need not be criminal nor actionable at law but must merely be willful and unconscionable or be of such a nature that honest and fair minded folk would roundly denounce such actions as being morally and ethically wrong. Thus, where a party acts in a manner that is offensive to good conscience and justice, he will be completely without recourse in a court of equity, regardless of what his legal rights may be. * * *

The Court is constrained, solely as a result of Plaintiff's affirmative acts, to conclude that Plaintiff's conduct is wholly unsupportable at law or in equity, greatly egregious and so completely devoid of good faith that equity cannot be permitted to intervene on its behalf. Indeed, Plaintiff's actions toward Defendant in this matter have been harsh, repugnant, shocking and repulsive to the extent that it must be appropriately sanctioned so as to deter it from imposing further mortifying abuse against Defendant. The Court cannot be assured that Plaintiff will not repeat this course of conduct if this action is merely dismissed and hence, dismissal standing alone is not a reasonable option. * * * This Court is of the opinion that cancellation of the indebtedness and discharge of the mortgage, when taken together, constitute the appropriate equitable disposition under the unique facts and circumstances presented herein.

The trial court's opinion was overturned on appeal and both the mortgage and the foreclosure were reinstated. "The reasoning of the Supreme Court that its equitable powers included the authority to cancel the mortgage and note was erroneous, since there was no acceptable basis for relieving the homeowner of her contractual obligations to the bank, particularly after a judgment had already been rendered in the plaintiff's favor." IndyMac Bank, F.S.B. v. Yano-Horoski 912 N.Y.S.2d 239, 241 (N.Y. App. Div. 2010). Do you think that the mortgage crisis makes (some) courts more willing to look for ways to grant debt relief? Should it?

Fred Feld v. Henry S. Levy & Sons, Inc.

Court of Appeals of New York, 1975.
37 N.Y.2d 466.

■ COOKE, JUDGE. Plaintiff operates a business known as the Crushed Toast Company and defendant is engaged in the wholesale bread baking business. They entered into a written contract, as of June 19, 1968, in which defendant agreed to sell and plaintiff to purchase "all bread crumbs produced by the Seller in its factory at 115 Thames Street, Brooklyn, New York, during the period commencing June 19, 1968, and terminating June 18, 1969", the agreement to "be deemed automatically renewed thereafter for successive renewal periods of one year" with the right to either party to cancel by giving not less than six months notice to the other by certified mail. No notice of cancellation was served. Additionally, pursuant to a contract stipulation, a faithful performance bond was delivered by plaintiff at the inception of the contractual relationship, and a bond continuation certificate was later submitted for the yearly term commencing June 19, 1969.

Interestingly, the term "bread crumbs" does not refer to crumbs that may flake off bread; rather, they are a manufactured item, starting with stale or imperfectly appearing loaves and followed by removal of labels, processing through two grinders, the second of which effects a finer granulation, insertion into a drum in an oven for toasting and, finally, bagging of the finished product.

Subsequent to the making of the agreement, a substantial quantity of bread crumbs, said to be over 250 tons, were sold by defendant to plaintiff but defendant stopped crumb production on about May 15, 1969. There was proof by defendant's comptroller that the oven was too large to accommodate the drum, that it was stated that the operation was "very uneconomical", but after said date of cessation no steps were taken to obtain more economical equipment. The toasting oven was intentionally broken down, then partially rebuilt, then completely dismantled in the summer of 1969 and, thereafter, defendant used the space for a computer room. It appears, without dispute, that defendant indicated to plaintiff at different times that the former would resume bread crumb production if the contract price of 6 cents per pound be changed to 7 cents, and also that, after the crumb making machinery was dismantled, defendant sold the raw materials used in making crumbs to animal food manufacturers.

Special Term denied plaintiff's motion for summary judgment on the issue of liability and turned down defendant's counter-request for a summary judgment of dismissal. From the Appellate Division's order of affirmance, by a divided court, both parties appeal.

Defendant contends that the contract did not require defendant to manufacture bread crumbs, but merely to sell those it did, and, since none were produced after the demise of the oven, there was no duty to then deliver and, consequently from then on, no liability on its part. Agreements to sell all the goods or services a party may produce or perform to another party are commonly referred to as "output" contracts and they usually serve a useful commercial purpose in minimizing the burdens of product marketing (see 1 Williston, Contracts [3d ed.], § 104A). The Uniform Commercial Code rejects the ideas that an output contract is lacking in mutuality or that it is unenforceable because of indefiniteness in that a quantity for the term is not specified. . . . Uniform Commercial Code, [2–306(1), comment] states in part: "Under this Article, a contract for output * * * is not too indefinite since it is held to mean the actual good faith output * * * of the particular party. Nor does such a contract lack mutuality of obligation since, under this section, the party who will determine quantity is required to operate his plant or conduct his business in good faith and according to commercial standards of fair dealing in the trade so that his output * * * will approximate a reasonably foreseeable figure." . . .

The real issue in this case is whether the agreement carries with it an implication that defendant was obligated to continue to manufacture bread crumbs for the full term. Section 2–306 of the Uniform Commercial Code, entitled "Output, Requirements and Exclusive Dealings" provides:

"(1) A term which measures the quantity by the output of the seller or the requirements of the buyer means such actual output or requirements as may occur in good faith except that no quantity unreasonably disproportionate to any stated estimate or in the absence of a stated estimate to any normal or otherwise comparable prior output or requirements may be tendered or demanded.

"(2) *A lawful agreement* by either the seller or the buyer *for exclusive dealing* in the kind of goods concerned *imposes* unless otherwise agreed an obligation *by the seller to use best efforts to supply the goods* and by the buyer to use best efforts to promote their sale." (Emphasis supplied.)

The Official Comment thereunder reads in part: "Subsection (2), on exclusive dealing, makes explicit the commercial rule embodied in this Act under which the parties to such contracts are held to have impliedly, even when not expressly, bound themselves to use reasonable diligence as well as good faith in their performance of the contract. * * * An exclusive dealing agreement brings into play all of the good faith aspects of the output and requirement problems of subsection (1). It also raises questions of insecurity and right to adequate assurance under this Article."

Section 2–306 is consistent with prior New York case law. . . . Under the Uniform Commercial Code, the commercial background and intent must be read into the language of any agreement and good faith is demanded in the performance of that agreement . . . , and, under the decisions relating to output contracts, it is clearly the general rule that good faith cessation of production terminates any further obligations thereunder and excuses further performance by the party discontinuing. . . .

This is not a situation where defendant ceased its main operation of bread baking. . . . Rather, defendant contends in a conclusory fashion that it was "uneconomical" or "economically not feasible" for it to continue to make bread crumbs. Although plaintiff observed in his motion papers that defendant claimed it was not economically feasible to make the crumbs, plaintiff did not admit that as a fact. In any event, "economic feasibility", an expression subject to many interpretations, would not be a precise or reliable test.

There are present here intertwined questions of fact, whether defendant performed in good faith and whether it stopped its manufacture of bread crumbs in good faith, neither of which can be resolved properly on this record. The seller's duty to remain in crumb production is a matter calling for a close scrutiny of its motives (1 Hawkland, A Transactional Guide to the Uniform Commercial Code, p.

52, see, also, p. 48), confined here by the papers to financial reasons. It is undisputed that defendant leveled its crumb making machinery only after plaintiff refused to agree to a price higher than that specified in the agreement and that it then sold the raw materials to manufacturers of animal food. There are before us no componential figures indicating the actual cost of the finished bread crumbs to defendant, statements as to the profits derived or the losses sustained, or data specifying the net or gross return realized from the animal food transactions.

The parties by their contract gave the right of cancellation to either by providing for a six months' notice to the other. The apparent purpose of such a stipulation was to provide an opportunity to either the seller or buyer to conclude their dealings in the event that the transactions were not as profitable or advantageous as desired or expected, or for any other reason. Correspondingly, such a notice would also furnish the receiver of it a chance to secure another outlet or source of supply, as the case might be. Short of such a cancellation, defendant was expected to continue to perform in good faith and could cease production of the bread crumbs, a single facet of its operation, only in good faith. Obviously, a bankruptcy or genuine imperiling of the very existence of its entire business caused by the production of the crumbs would warrant cessation of production of that item; the yield of less profit from its sale than expected would not. Since bread crumbs were but a part of defendant's enterprise and since there was a contractual right of cancellation, good faith required continued production until cancellation, even if there be no profit. In circumstances such as these and without more, defendant would be justified, in good faith, in ceasing production of the single item prior to cancellation only if its losses from continuance would be more than trivial, which, overall, is a question of fact.

The order of the Appellate Division should be affirmed, without costs.

NOTES

(1)   The *Feld* case applied section 2–306(1) of the UCC. To what extent is the exercise of discretion by an output seller or a requirements buyer governed by circumstances existing at the time of contracting? What test(s) does the court use to define bad faith at the time of performance? In any case, is the approach consistent with the view that bad faith exists when either the seller or buyer exercises discretion to recapture opportunities foregone at the time of contracting?

(2)   *The Case of Good Faith but Disproportionate Demand.* Seller and Buyer enter a five-year "requirements" contract. During the first three years, Buyer ordered and Seller supplied an average of 10,000 units. Thereafter, there was a sharp downturn in the market. During the fourth year, Buyer ordered 1,000 units and in the fifth year, no units were ordered. Seller, conceding that Buyer was in good faith, argues that the orders in both years were "substantially disproportionate" to orders during the first three years.

Accordingly, under UCC § 2–306(1), Buyer was in breach for the last two years. How should the court rule? See Posner, J. in Empire Gas Corp. v. American Bakeries Co., 840 F.2d 1333 (7th Cir.1988) (suggesting buyer has no liability because good faith is not limited by substantial disproportion language); Orange & Rockland Utilities v. Amerada Hess Corp., 397 N.Y.S.2d 814 (App. Div. 1977) (buyer's decision under requirements contract to take advantage of its cheap supply of oil by dramatically and arbitrarily increasing its requirements was not made in good faith). Cheryl R. Guttenberg, Comment, *And Then There Were None: Requirements Contracts and the Buyer Who Does Not Buy,* 64 Wash. L. Rev. 871 (1989).

(3) *Output Contracts.* In *Canusa Corporation v. A & R Lobosco, Inc.,* 986 F.Supp. 723 (E.D.N.Y. 1997), the parties entered into a five year output contract in which there was an "estimate" that Seller would ship "at a minimum" 1,500 tons of old news print per month. Seller never met this estimate and, after extended discussions and an attempt to modify, the relationship broke down and Buyer sued Seller for damages based upon the quantity in the estimate. There was evidence, however, that the amounts actually tendered were Seller's output in good faith. The court held that in an output contract under UCC § 2–306(1), good faith rather than the estimate controlled Seller's obligations: otherwise "adherence to the estimate in the contract would essentially convert all output contracts with an estimate into fixed contracts." This interpretation was extracted from the reasoning of several cases dealing with UCC § 2–306:

> First as the *Feld* court [supra] noted, good faith is the general standard by which output contracts are measured. . . . Second, as the *Empire Gas* court [*Empire Gas Corp. v. American Bakeries Co.,* note 2 supra] found, the "unreasonably disproportionate" language in sec. 2–306 is a specific construction of good faith in the context of increased output or demand, and has no relationship to a good faith analysis of a decrease. . . . In a requirements contract, the seller takes the risk that the buyer may in good faith reduce its requirements to zero. . . . Given the premise that a seller will want to maximize its output, the good faith standard provides a sufficient test to measure a reducing seller's performance against. . . . So too, in an output contract, the buyer takes the risk that the seller may reduce its production to zero. . . . Applying good faith rather than an estimate does not give a seller an un-bargained for advantage; rather, it merely preserves the essential character of contracts that lack a fixed term, albeit through the somewhat elusive concept of good faith.

On the issues posed by UCC § 2–306 and more, see Victor P. Goldberg, *Discretion in Long-Term Open Quantity Contracts: Reigning in Good Faith,* 35 U.C. Davis L. Rev. 319 (2002) (suggesting tailor-made contract clauses to reduce uncertainty without precluding flexibility).

Comment: Effect of "Best Efforts" Agreement on Contracts for Indefinite Quantity

The fact that the parties have entered an output or a requirements contract does not necessarily mean that one party must use best efforts to have output or requirements. To impose that obligation, the parties must agree, expressly or impliedly, to use best efforts. That obligation may be found in the bargain, see *Perma Research & Dev. v. Singer Co.*, 542 F.2d 111 (2d Cir.1976) (best efforts obligation implied), or presumed from the fact that the parties have entered into an exclusive dealing contract. Thus, UCC § 2–306(2) provides that a "lawful agreement by either the seller or the buyer for exclusive dealing in the kind of goods concerned imposes unless otherwise agreed an obligation by the seller to use best efforts to supply the goods and by the buyer to use best efforts to promote their sale."

The question whether a party has used "best efforts" in a particular dispute has bothered the courts and commentators. See Allan Farnsworth, *On Trying to Keep One's Promises: The Duty of Best Efforts in Contract Law,* 46 U. Pitt. L. Rev. 117 (1983). If the parties have not specified the level of best efforts in the contract, courts have, in most cases, applied an objective standard and asked whether the defendant has made reasonable efforts in the circumstances. See, e.g., Bloor v. Falstaff Brewing Corp., 601 F.2d 609 (2d Cir.1979); Victor P. Goldberg, *In Search of Best Efforts: Reinterpreting Bloor v. Falstaff,* 44 St. Louis U. L.J. 1465 (2000). This is an important inquiry for both questions of liability and remedy. Thus, if the defendant has no duty to use "best efforts" or has satisfied that duty and is otherwise in good faith, there is no breach of contract. If, however, the defendant is in good faith but has not used "best efforts," the plaintiff should recover damages. As Judge Posner put it in *Agfa-Gevaert, A.G. v. A.B. Dick Co.*, 879 F.2d 1518, 1523–24 (7th Cir. 1989):

> When a distributor obligates himself to use his best efforts to promote a product and then breaks his contract, the remedial question is indeed how much he would have sold had he used his best efforts, implying diligent and energetic promotion. . . . But when he agrees merely to take his requirements of a particular product from his seller, and breaks his contract by satisfying those requirements elsewhere, the question is how much he bought from his alternative supplier(s). . . . What he required, he bought; what he did not buy, he must not have required.

PROBLEM: PROFESSOR POST'S PUBLISHER

(Adapted from Prof. Steve Salop, Economic Reasoning for Lawyers (Georgetown University Law Center teaching materials, 2009)).

Professor Post's new internet law casebook has been published and sold directly to law students by Craven Press. The contract expressly stipulates that Craven is to use its "best efforts" to promote the book. Professor Post now has sued Craven, arguing that it failed to advertise the book sufficiently. According to the evidence submitted to the court, had Craven spent $20,000 advertising the book, it would have sold 1000 copies at a price of $50 each and Post would have earned royalties of $5,000, based on his royalty rate of 10% of gross revenue. In fact, Craven spent only about $2,000 on advertising and the book sold only 500 copies, yielding only $2,500 in royalties for Professor Post. Craven's printing, shipping and fixed overhead costs amount to $10 per copy. Post is outraged. He argues that Craven's low rate of advertising does not satisfy the best-efforts clause.

(1) Assume the law in the jurisdiction defines "best efforts" as the efforts that will maximize the parties' joint gains from the transaction (the sum of the gains of each). See Charles J. Goetz & Robert E. Scott, *Principles of Relational Contracts,* 67 Va. L. Rev. 1089, 1149–50 (1981) (arguing that "best efforts" should require that level of effort "necessary to maximize the joint net product flowing from the . . . relationship.") Explain who should win and why.

(2) Is there another way the parties could have structured the contract so that Craven would have an incentive to invest $20,000 in advertising? If so, why did the parties choose the payment structure they did?

(D) MODIFICATION BY AGREEMENT

Alfred L. Angel v. John E. Murray, Jr.

Supreme Court of Rhode Island, 1974.
Supra at 140.

Roth Steel Products v. Sharon Steel Corp.

United States Court of Appeals, Sixth Circuit, 1983.
705 F.2d 134.

■ CELEBREZZE, SENIOR CIRCUIT JUDGE. [In November, 1972, Roth contracted to purchase 200 tons of "hot rolled" steel per month from Sharon through December, 1973. The price was $148 per ton. Sharon also "indicated" that it could sell "hot rolled" steel on an "open schedule" basis for $140 and discussed the "probability" that Sharon could sell 500 tons of "cold rolled" steel at prices varying with the type ordered. At that time, the steel industry was operating at 70% of capacity, steel prices were "highly competitive" and Sharon's quoted prices to Roth were "substantially lower" than Sharon's book price for steel. In early 1973, market conditions changed dramatically due to the development of an attractive export market and an increased domestic demand for steel. During 1973 and 1974, the steel industry operated at full capacity, steel prices rose and nearly every producer experienced substantial delays in filling orders. In March, 1973, Sharon notified all purchasers, including

Roth, that it was discontinuing price concessions given in 1972. After negotiations, the parties agreed that Roth would pay the agreed price until June 30, 1973 and a price somewhere between the agreed price and Sharon's published prices for the balance of 1973. Roth was initially reluctant to agree to this modification, but ultimately agreed "primarily because they were unable to purchase sufficient steel elsewhere to meet their production requirements." Sharon was supplying one-third of Roth's requirements and all other possible suppliers were "operating at full capacity and . . . were fully booked." The parties proceeded under this modification during the balance of 1973, although Sharon experienced difficulties in filling orders on time. During 1974, the parties did business on an entirely different basis. Roth would order steel, Sharon would accept the order at the price "prevailing at the time of shipment." During 1974 and 1975, Sharon's deliveries were chronically late, thereby increasing the price to Roth in a rising market. Roth, however, acquiesced in this pattern because it believed Sharon's assurances that late deliveries resulted from shortages of raw materials and the need for equitable allocation among customers and because there was "no practical alternative source of supply." This acquiescence was jolted in May, 1974 when Roth learned that Sharon was allocating substantial quantities of rolled steel to a subsidiary for sale at premium prices. After several more months of desultory performance on both sides, Roth sued Sharon for breach of contract, with special emphasis upon the modified contract for 1973. Sharon raised several defenses, including impracticability and, in the alternative, the agreed modification. The district court, after a long trial, held, *inter alia,* that Sharon was not excused from the 1973 contract on the grounds of impracticability and that the modification was unenforceable. A judgment for $555,968.46 was entered for Roth.

On appeal, the court of appeals affirmed the district court's decision on the impracticability, modification and other issues, but remanded the case for factual findings on whether Roth gave Sharon timely notice of breach. On the impracticability defense under UCC 2–615(a), the court held that "Sharon's inability to perform was a result of its policy accepting far more orders than it was capable of fulfilling, rather than a result of the existing shortage of raw materials." In refusing to enforce the modification of the 1973 contract, the court had this to say.]

The ability of a party to modify a contract which is subject to Article Two of the Uniform Commercial Code is broader than common law, primarily because the modification needs no consideration to be binding. ORC § 1302.12 (UCC § 2–209(1)). A party's ability to modify an agreement is limited only by Article Two's general obligation of good faith. . . . In determining whether a particular modification was obtained in good faith, a court must make two distinct inquiries: whether the party's conduct is consistent with "reasonable commercial standards of fair dealing in the trade," . . . and whether the parties were in fact motivated to seek modification by an honest desire to compensate for commercial exigencies; . . . ORC § 1302.01(2) (UCC § 2–103). The first inquiry is relatively straightforward; the party asserting the modification must demonstrate that his decision to seek modification was the result of a factor, such as increased costs, which would cause an ordinary merchant to seek a modification of the contract. See Official Comment 2, ORC § 1302.12 (UCC § 2–209) (reasonable commercial standards may require objective reason); J. White & R. Summers, Handbook of Law under the UCC at 41. The second inquiry, regarding the subjective honesty of the parties, is less clearly defined. Essentially, this inquiry requires the party asserting the modification to demonstrate that he was, in fact, motivated by a legitimate commercial reason and that such a reason is not offered merely as a pretext. . . . Moreover, the trier of fact must determine whether the means used to obtain the modification are an impermissible attempt to obtain a modification by extortion or overreaching. . . .

Sharon argues that its decision to seek a modification was consistent with reasonable commercial standards of fair dealing because market exigencies made further performance entail a substantial loss. The district court, however, made three findings which caused it to conclude that economic circumstances were not the reason that Sharon sought a modification: it found that Sharon was partially insulated from raw material price increases, that Sharon bargained for a contract with a slim profit margin and thus implicitly assumed the risk that performance might come to involve a loss, and that Sharon's overall profit in 1973 and its profit on the contract in the first quarter of 1973 were inconsistent with Sharon's position that the modification was sought to avoid a loss. Although all of these findings are marginally related to the question whether Sharon's conduct was consistent with reasonable commercial standards of fair dealing, we do not believe that they are sufficient to support a finding that Sharon did not observe reasonable commercial standards by seeking a modification. In our view, these findings do not support a conclusion that a reasonable merchant, in light of the circumstances, would not have sought a modification in order to avoid a loss. For example, the district court's finding that Sharon's steel slab contract[26] insulated it from industry wide cost increases is correct, so far as it goes. Although Sharon was able to purchase steel slabs at pre-1973 prices, the district court's findings also indicate that it was not able to purchase, at those prices, a sufficient tonnage of steel slabs to meet its

---

[26] Sharon was a party to a contract with United States Steel which allowed it to make monthly purchases of slab steel ranging from a minimum of 25,000 tons per month to a maximum of 45,000 tons per month. It was also a party to a contract with Wierton Steel which allowed it to purchase slab steel in amounts varying between 10,000 to 20,000 tons per month. Both of these contracts were entered prior to 1973, at a very attractive price. When the market strengthened in 1973, however, Sharon was unable to obtain the maximum monthly tonnages permitted under these contracts: U.S. Steel delivered only 30,000 tons per month and Wierton 10,000 tons per month.

production requirements.[27] The district court also found that Sharon experienced substantial cost increases for other raw materials, ranging from 4% to nearly 20%. In light of these facts, the finding regarding the fixed-price contract for slab steel, without more, cannot support an inference that Sharon was unaffected by the market shifts that occurred in 1973. Similarly, the district court's finding that Sharon entered a contract in November, 1972 which would yield only a slim profit does not support a conclusion that Sharon was willing to risk a loss on the contract. Absent a finding that the market shifts and the raw material price increases were foreseeable at the time the contract was formed—a finding which was not made—Sharon's willingness to absorb a loss cannot be inferred from the fact that it contracted for a smaller profit than usual. Finally, the findings regarding Sharon's profits are not sufficient, by themselves, to warrant a conclusion that Sharon was not justified in seeking a modification. Clearly, Sharon's initial profit on the contract[28] is an important consideration; the district court's findings indicate, however, that at the time modification was sought substantial future losses were foreseeable.[29] A party who has not actually suffered a loss on the contract may still seek a modification if a future loss on the agreement was reasonably foreseeable. Similarly, the overall profit earned by the party seeking modification is an important factor; this finding, however, does not support a conclusion that the decision to seek a modification was unwarranted. The more relevant inquiry is into the profit obtained through sales of the product line in question. This conclusion is reinforced by the fact that only a few product lines may be affected by market exigencies;[30] the opportunity to seek modification of a contract for the sale of goods of a product line should not be limited solely because some other product line produced a substantial profit.

In the final analysis, the single most important consideration in determining whether the decision to seek a modification is justified in this context is whether, because of changes in the market or other unforeseeable conditions, performance of the contract has come to involve a loss. In this case, the district court found that Sharon suffered substantial losses by performing the contract *as modified*. See note 4,

---

[27] The district court found that Sharon suffered a continuing shortage of slab steel. It found that in 1972 (when Sharon was operating at substantially less than full capacity) it received 602,277 tons of slab steel; that in 1973, it received 506,596 tons of slab steel; and that in 1974 it received 373,898 tons. Thus, the record is clear that Sharon was in a difficult position. As demand for steel increased, and as Sharon's mills began to work at a higher capacity, its supply of slab steel steadily diminished.

[28] The district court noted that in the first three months of 1973, Sharon made $3,089.00 on sales to Roth and lost $263.00 on steel sold to Toledo. Although Sharon lost significant sums of money on its contract with the plaintiffs, Sharon enjoyed overall profits in 1973, with net earnings of $11,566,000 on net sales of $338,205,000.

[29] The evidence indicates, and the district court found, that with the exception of hot rolled sheets Sharon absorbed a loss on every rolled steel product which it sold to the defendants in 1973, even though the modified prices were in effect during the third and the fourth quarters.

[30] Apparently, Sharon's record overall profit was the result of other operations. It obtained a pre-tax profit of less than one percent on its total sales of rolled steel.

supra. We are convinced that unforeseen economic exigencies existed which would prompt an ordinary merchant to seek a modification to avoid a loss on the contract; thus, we believe that the district court's findings to the contrary are clearly erroneous. . . .

The second part of the analysis, honesty in fact, is pivotal. The district court found that Sharon "threatened not to sell Roth and Toledo any steel if they refused to pay increased prices after July 1, 1973" and, consequently, that Sharon acted wrongfully. Sharon does not dispute the finding that it threatened to stop selling steel to the plaintiffs. Instead, it asserts that such a finding is merely evidence of bad faith and that it has rebutted any inference of bad faith based on that finding. We agree with this analysis; although coercive conduct is evidence that a modification of a contract is sought in bad faith, that prima facie showing may be effectively rebutted by the party seeking to enforce the modification. . . . Although we agree with Sharon's statement of principles, we do not agree that Sharon has rebutted the inference of bad faith that rises from its coercive conduct. Sharon asserts that its decision to unilaterally raise prices was based on language in the November 17, 1972 letter which allowed it to raise prices to the extent of any general industry-wide price increase. Because prices in the steel industry had increased, Sharon concludes that it was justified in raising its prices. Because it was justified in raising the contract price, the plaintiffs were bound by the terms of the contract to pay the increased prices. Consequently, any refusal by the plaintiffs to pay the price increase sought by Sharon must be viewed as a material breach of the November, 1972 contract which would excuse Sharon from any further performance. Thus, Sharon reasons that its refusal to perform absent a price increase was justified under the contract and consistent with good faith.

This argument fails in two respects. First, the contractual language on which Sharon relies only permits, at most, a price increase for cold rolled steel; thus, even if Sharon's position were supported by the evidence, Sharon would not have been justified in refusing to sell the plaintiffs hot rolled steel because of the plaintiffs' refusal to pay higher prices for the product. More importantly, however, the evidence does not indicate that Sharon ever offered this theory as a justification until this matter was tried. Sharon's representatives, in their testimony, did not attempt to justify Sharon's refusal to ship steel at 1972 prices in this fashion. Furthermore, none of the contemporaneous communications contain this justification for Sharon's action. In short, we can find no evidence in the record which indicates that Sharon offered this theory as a justification at the time the modification was sought. Consequently, we believe that the district court's conclusion that Sharon acted in bad faith by using coercive conduct to extract the price modification is not clearly erroneous. Therefore, we hold that Sharon's attempt to modify the November, 1972 contract, in order to compensate for increased costs which made performance come to involve a loss, is ineffective because

Sharon did not act in a manner consistent with Article Two's requirement of honesty in fact when it refused to perform its remaining obligations under the contract at 1972 prices.[31] * * *

NOTES

(1)   In *Roth Steel Products,* the court held that Sharon was *not* entitled to any relief under UCC § 2–615(a). If Sharon had been entitled to "some relief," would the modification have been enforceable under UCC § 2–209(1)?

(2)   Would the modification have been enforceable under section 89 of Restatement (Second), discussed and applied in *Angel v. Murray*? How does one draw the line between "circumstances not anticipated by the parties when the contract was made," section 89(a), and the "occurrence of an event the non-occurrence of which was basic assumption on which the contract was made," section 261?

(3)   Note that *Roth Steel Products* invalidated the modification because of Sharon's bad faith rather than because of economic duress. The court suggests that proof of coercive means will not invalidate a modification made in good faith. See opinion's in last footnote. What, then, was the bad faith in *Roth Steel Products*? Is this concept consistent with the view that a modification is in bad faith when one party uses a refusal to perform as a lever to recapture an opportunity foregone at the time of contracting?

(4)   Some courts have relied exclusively upon concepts of economic duress when evaluating modifications. See, e.g., *Austin Instrument, Inc. v. Loral Corp.,* 29 N.Y.2d 124 (1971), reprinted supra Chapter 4, where the court said:

> [A] mere threat by one party to breach the contract by not delivering the required items, though wrongful, does not in itself constitute economic duress. It must also appear that the threatened party could not obtain the goods from another source of supply and that the ordinary remedy of an action for breach of contract would not be adequate.

29 N.Y.2d at 130–31.

The "economic duress" approach is strongly favored by some commentators. See, e.g., Robert Hillman, *How to Create a Commercial Calamity,* 68 Ohio St. L.J. 335 (2007); Robert Hillman, *Contract Modification Under the Restatement (Second) of Contracts,* 67 Cornell L. Rev. 680 (1982); Henry Mather, *Contract Modification under Duress,* 33 S.C. L. Rev. 615 (1982). In *Roth Steel Products,* Roth was clearly unable to obtain the promised steel from another source and ordinary damage remedies would

---

[31] The district court also found, as an alternative ground, that the modification was voidable because the plaintiffs agreed to the modification due to economic duress. See, e.g., Oskey Gasoline & Oil Co. v. Continental Oil, 534 F.2d 1281 (8th Cir.1976). Because we conclude that the modification was ineffective as a result of Sharon's bad faith, we do not reach the issue whether the contract modification was also voidable because of economic duress. We note, however, that proof that coercive means were used is necessary to establish that a contract is voidable because of economic duress. Normally, it cannot be used to void a contract modification which has been sought in good faith; if a contract modification has been found to be in good faith, then presumably no wrongful coercive means have been used to extract the modification.

appear to have been inadequate. Was Sharon's refusal (which was not excused under UCC § 2–615(a)) to deliver steel unless Roth agreed to a price modification "wrongful?"

(5) *Duty to Negotiate or Modify*? Under American law, a party advantaged by changed circumstances has no duty to negotiate with the disadvantaged party unless the contract so requires. Even then, the duty is to negotiate in good faith, not to agree to a modification. The UNIDROIT model of good faith, see supra at 678, may require a duty to negotiate in good faith upon request by the disadvantaged party but does not require a modification. Should there ever be a duty to modify the contract? If not, should a court, to restore balance, modify or revise the contract? We will return to these questions in Chapter Six, Section 4.

Beneficial National Bank, U.S.A. v. Obie Payton

United States District Court, S.D. Mississippi, 2001.
Supra at 275.

NOTES

The leading case on a business's duty of good faith in exercising a notice-only modificaiton clause is *Badie v. Bank of America*, 79 Cal. Rptr. 2d 273 (Ct. App. 1998).

> Abuse of the power to specify terms is one of the judicially-recognized types of bad faith. (Rest.2d., Contracts (1979) § 205, com. d.) While [*Perdue v. Crocker National Bank (1985) 38 Cal.3d 913*]indicated that the bank's increase in NSF check fees was to be evaluated under the "... duty of good faith and fair dealing in setting or varying such charges" (38 Cal.3d at pp. 924), other cases make it clear that the *exercise* of discretionary powers conferred on a party by contract must also be evaluated under the implied covenant to assure that the promises of the contract are effective and in accordance with the parties' legitimate expectations. (See *Carma Developers (Cal.), Inc. v. Marathon Development California, Inc.* (1992) 2 Cal.4th 342, 371–372; *Cal. Lettuce Growers v. Union Sugar Co.* (1955) 45 Cal.2d 474, 484 ["where a contract confers on one party a discretionary power affecting the rights of the other, a duty is imposed to exercise that discretion in good faith and in accordance with fair dealing"].) Thus, the trial court's conclusion that the Bank's modification of the account agreements satisfied the covenant of good faith and fair dealing because "[t]he ADR clause does not operate to deprive the customer of expected or bargained-for benefits of his or her agreement" does not withstand scrutiny. The court's focus on the ADR clause, standing alone, was misplaced: it is the Bank's exercise of its discretionary right to change the agreement, not the ADR clause in and of itself, which must first be analyzed in terms of the implied covenant. If the Bank's performance under the change of terms provision was not consonant with the duty of good faith and fair dealing, then

whether the ADR clause, considered in isolation, satisfies the implied covenant makes no difference.

* * *

Here, the Bank reserved to itself the unilateral and non-negotiable right to vary every aspect of the performance required by the parties to the account agreements. The Bank's interpretation of how broadly it may exercise that right, with no limitation on the substantive nature of the changes it may make as long as it complies with the de minimis procedural requirement of "notice," virtually eliminates the good faith and fair dealing requirement from the Bank's relationship with its credit account customers, and is thus antithetical to *Perdue,* not consistent with it, as the Bank claims. In short, we conclude the trial court erred in deciding that the implied covenant of good faith and fair dealing had been satisfied by the Bank in its performance under the change of terms provision.

Id. at 283–84. See also Cobb v. Ironwood Country Club, 233 Cal. App. 4th 960, 963 (2015) ("When one party to a contract retains the unilateral right to amend the agreement governing the parties' relationship, its exercise of that right is constrained by the covenant of good faith and fair dealing which precludes amendments that operate retroactively to impair accrued rights.").

(E) TERMINATION OF CONTRACTUAL RELATIONS OTHER THAN FOR BREACH

(1) COMMERCIAL CONTRACTS

Elaine Zapatha v. Dairy Mart, Inc.

Supreme Judicial Court of Massachusetts, 1980.
Supra at 595.

[The facts are stated above. The franchise contract contained the following termination clause:

(9) The term of this Limited Franchise and License Agreement shall be for a period of Twelve (12) months from date hereof, and shall continue uninterrupted thereafter. If DEALER desires to terminate after 12 months from date hereof, he shall do so by giving COMPANY a ninety (90) day written notice by Registered Mail of his intention to terminate. If COMPANY desires to terminate, it likewise shall give a ninety (90) day notice, except for the following reasons which shall not require any written notice and shall terminate the Franchise immediately:

(a) Failure to pay bills to suppliers for inventory or other products when due.

(b) Failure to pay Franchise Fees to COMPANY.

(c) Failure to pay city, state or federal taxes as said taxes shall become due and payable.

(d) Breach of any condition of this Agreement.

The contract also provided that in the event of a termination without cause Dairy Mart agreed to repurchase the saleable merchandise inventory at retail prices, less 20%. After holding that the termination clause was not unconscionable at the time of contracting, the Court considered whether the termination was in bad faith.]

* * *

3.   We see no basis on the record for concluding that Dairy Mart did not act in good faith, as that term is defined in the sales article ("honesty in fact and the observance of reasonable commercial standards of fair dealing in the trade"). G.L. c. 106, § 2–103(1)(b). There was no evidence that Dairy Mart failed to observe reasonable commercial standards of fair dealing in the trade in terminating the agreement. If there were such standards, there was no evidence of what they were.

The question then is whether there was evidence warranting a finding that Dairy Mart was not honest "in fact." The judge concluded that the absence of any commercial purpose for the termination other than the Zapathas' refusal to sign a new franchise agreement violated Dairy Mart's obligation of good faith. Dairy Mart's right to terminate was clear, and it exercised that right for a reason it openly disclosed. The sole test of "honesty in fact" is whether the person was honest. . . . We think that, whether or not termination according to the terms of the franchise agreement may have been arbitrary, it was not dishonest. * * *

4.   Although what we have said disposes of arguments based on application by analogy of provisions of the sales article of the Uniform Commercial Code, there remains the question whether the judge's conclusions may be supported by some general principle of law. The provisions of the Uniform Commercial Code with which we have dealt by analogy in this opinion may not have sufficient breadth to provide protection from conduct that has produced an unfair and burdensome result, contrary to the spirit of the bargain, against which the law reasonably should provide protection. . . .[17]

The law of the Commonwealth recognizes that under some circumstances a party to a contract is not free to terminate it according to its terms. In Fortune v. National Cash Register Co., 373 Mass. 96, 104–105, 364 N.E.2d 1251 (1977), we held that where an employer terminated an at will employment contract in order to deprive its employee of a

---

[17] The unconscionability provision of G.L. c. 106, § 2–302, concerns circumstances determined at the time of the making of the agreement and relates only to the unconscionability of a term or terms of the contract. The "good faith" obligation of G.L. c. 106, § 1–203, deals with "honesty in fact," a question of the state of mind of the merchant or of his adherence to whatever reasonable commercial standards there may be in his trade. A merchant's conduct might not be dishonest and might adhere to reasonable standards, if any, in his trade and thus might be in good faith under § 1–203, and yet be unfair and unreasonably burdensome.

portion of a commission due to him, the employer acted in bad faith. There, the employer correctly argued that termination of the employee was expressly permitted by the contract, and that all amounts payable under the terms of the contract at the time of termination had been paid. We concluded, however, that the law imposed an obligation of good faith on the employer and that the employer violated that obligation in terminating the relationship in order to avoid the payment of amounts earned, but not yet payable. The Legislature has limited the right of certain franchisors to terminate franchise agreements without cause.[18] On the other hand, the Legislature has not adopted limitations on the right to terminate all franchise agreements in general, and its failure to do so is understandable because of the varied nature of franchise arrangements, where such varying factors exist as the relative bargaining power of the parties, the extent of investment by franchisees, and the degree to which the franchisee's goodwill, as opposed to that of the franchisor, is involved in the business operation. * * *

We are most concerned, as was the judge below, with the introductory circular that Dairy Mart furnished Mr. Zapatha. The judge ruled that the introductory circular contained misleading information concerning the Zapathas' status as franchisees. However, we cannot find in that document any deception or unfairness that has a bearing on the right of Dairy Mart to terminate the agreement as it did. A representative read the termination clause to Mr. Zapatha before the Zapathas signed the agreement. Mr. Zapatha declined an invitation to take the agreement to a lawyer. He understood individually every word of the termination clause. Moreover, when Dairy Mart terminated the agreement, it offered to negotiate further, and the Zapathas did not take the opportunity to do so. * * *

Dairy Mart lawfully terminated the agreement because there was no showing that in terminating it Dairy Mart engaged in any unfair, deceptive, or bad faith conduct.

Judgments reversed.

NOTES

(1) In *Zapatha*, Dairy Mart reserved broad power to terminate the franchise without regard to cause and followed the clause to the letter in exercising that power. How did the court justify imposing a duty of good faith on the exercise of that power? The answer, presumably, is that Dairy Mart must exercise discretion in deciding to invoke the clause. The discretion must be exercised in good faith, and this requires an inquiry into the reasons for the exercise and suggests that there are good and bad reasons.

---

[18] See G.L. c. 93B, §§ 4(3)(e), (4) concerning the cancellation or nonrenewal of a motor vehicle dealer's franchise and requiring good cause for manufacturer's or distributor's action; G.L. c. 93E, §§ 5, 5A, requiring cause for a supplier's termination or nonrenewal of a gasoline station dealer's agreement and imposing an obligation on the supplier to repurchase merchantable products sold to the dealer. * * *

If terminating because the franchisee refuses to modify the franchise on terms more favorable to the franchisor is not bad faith, what is? Suppose that the franchisor discriminated against a minority franchisee? Suppose the termination was in retaliation because the franchisee had reported salmonella in the ice cream to state health authorities? Suppose the purpose of the termination was to capture a thriving franchise for the benefit of the president's brother-in-law?

Does it help in *Zapatha* that both parties could terminate under the clause, that a terminated party had 90 days after notice of termination to liquidate its affairs, and that Dairy Mart agreed to repurchase Zapatha's post-termination inventory?

(2) Some courts have declined to impose a duty of good faith in terminating franchise and distributorship contracts. In *Corenswet, Inc. v. Amana Refrigeration, Inc.*, 594 F.2d 129 (5th Cir. 1979), the court refused to impose a good faith limitation upon the power to terminate an exclusive distributorship where the contract permitted termination by either party "at any time for any reason" on the giving of ten days' notice. The court thought that the good faith duty always required the evaluation of the terminating party's motives and that a termination "without cause will almost always be characterizable as 'bad faith' termination." 594 F.2d at 138. Are you persuaded? Does this interpretation leave the franchisee with any protection against malicious or retaliatory terminations? See Robert Hillman, *An Analysis of the Cessation of Contractual Relations,* 68 Cornell L. Rev. 617, 642–57 (1983); Mary P. Williamson, Note, *Franchise Termination: An Analysis of the Implied Covenant of Good Faith in Franchise Agreements,* 12 Am. J. Trial Advoc. 325 (1988).

(3) Federal and state laws regulate the power to terminate some franchise relationships. For example, the Automobile Dealer's Day in Court Act, 15 U.S.C.A. § 1221 et seq., provides that a dealer may sue for damages "by reason of the failure of said automobile manufacturer . . . to act in good faith in performing or complying with any of the terms and provisions of the franchise or in terminating, canceling or not renewing the franchise with said dealer. . . ." *Id.* at § 1222. Good faith, however, is narrowly defined as the "duty of each party . . . to guarantee . . . freedom from coercion, intimidation, or threat of coercion or intimidation from the other party. . . ." *Id.* at § 1221(e). See Hubbard Chevrolet Co. v. General Motors Corp., 873 F.2d 873, 876–77 (5th Cir.1989) (federal good faith duty does not override or contradict clear reservation of power in contract). For an analysis of federal law and the effect of state "franchise relationship laws," see Thomas M. Pitegoff, *Franchise Relationship Laws: A Minefield for Franchisors,* 45 Bus. Law. 289 (1989). See also, M. Stuart Sutherland, *The Risks and Exposures Associated with Franchise Noncompliance,* 42 Bus. Law. 369 (1987).

(4) *American Model of Good Faith Revisited.* In other business relationships, terminations that follow the letter of a termination clause in the contract have been sustained even though there was evidence of opportunistic (bad faith) behavior by the terminator.

In *Sons of Thunder, Inc. v. Borden, Inc.*, 148 N.J. 396 (1997), the defendant terminated a fishing contract with the plaintiff under a termination clause "standard" in the industry. The court drew a line between bad faith performance and bad faith termination that permitted it to hold that (1) the defendant performed the contract in bad faith (by hindrance and failure to cooperate) and was liable for damages, but (2) a termination which followed the letter of the termination clause was in good faith regardless of the defendant's motives. The court stated that the "implied covenant of good faith and fair dealing cannot override an express termination clause." *Id.* at 419. The question was whether the defendant "performed its obligations [under the termination clause] in good faith." The answer was yes if the termination clause was followed.

Dennis Patterson has argued that the vice of cases like this is that control of the so-called immutable duty of good faith is given to private parties, more particularly, those who draft termination clauses and require others to assent to them. Dennis Patterson, *A Fable From The Seventh Circuit: Judge Frank Easterbrook on Good Faith,* 76 Iowa L. Rev. 503 (1991). Do you agree?

(2) EMPLOYMENT CONTRACTS

Elmer Hillesland v. Federal Land Bank Association of Grand Forks

Supreme Court of North Dakota, 1987.
407 N.W.2d 206.

■ ERICKSTAD, CHIEF JUSTICE. Elmer Hillesland appeals from a district court summary judgment dismissing his action against the Federal Land Bank Association of Grand Forks [the Association] and the Federal Land Bank of St. Paul [the Bank]. We affirm.

Hillesland began working at the Association in 1956. He received several promotions and in 1972 was named Chief Executive Officer. He held that position until his discharge on June 15, 1983.

Through his position with the Association Hillesland in early 1983 learned that Ray and Eva Westby, customers of the Association, were experiencing financial difficulties. He also learned that they had received an offer to purchase their farm from another Association customer. Hillesland contacted the Westbys to offer financial counseling. They responded by expressing their desire to sell the farm. Although the parties dispute whether Hillesland initiated the discussions of sale of the property, it is undisputed that these discussions eventually led to an offer to purchase the Westby farm by Hillesland's sons, David and Don.

In accordance with standard Association procedure, Hillesland submitted details of the proposed transaction on a "Prohibited Acts Report and Action" form to the Association board of directors for approval. After meeting in a closed session with the Westbys, the board approved the transaction. Hillesland then submitted the matter to the

Bank's Review Committee in St. Paul. In its report, the Review Committee stated that it was "not in a position to disapprove" the transaction, but it did express concern over the appearance of a conflict of interest and prohibited any further direct involvement in the transaction by Hillesland. The sale of the land to Hillesland's sons was completed shortly thereafter.

The Bank subsequently launched an investigation into the matter. On June 15, 1983, two representatives of the Bank appeared at a meeting of the Association board of directors in Grand Forks and advised Hillesland that he was being discharged from his employment with the Association. The Bank's rationale for Hillesland's termination was that he had violated written standards of conduct, had damaged the image and reputation of the Association and the Bank, and had exercised poor business judgment.

Hillesland commenced this action against the Association and the Bank alleging violation of provisions of the Farm Credit Act, breach of contract, age discrimination, and tortious interference by the Bank with Hillesland's employment contract with the Association. The district court granted summary judgment dismissing Hillesland's action, and he appeals.

[The court held, inter alia, that there was (1) no implied private right of action under the Farm Credit Act, 12 U.S.C. sec. 2227(a)(3), (2) no age discrimination, and (3) no claim against the Bank for tortious interference with contract.]

* * *

BREACH OF CONTRACT

Hillesland contends that the trial court erred in dismissing his breach of contract claim because there are material fact issues remaining which preclude summary judgment. * * *

Section 34–03–01, N.D.C.C., is North Dakota's codification of the "at will" doctrine:

> "*Termination of employment at will—Notice required.* An employment having no specified term may be terminated at the will of either party on notice to the other, except when otherwise provided by this title."

In order to support his claim for breach of an employment contract Hillesland must produce evidence that there existed a contract for employment for a specified term or that he would only be terminated for cause. Hillesland asserts that he was employed permanently, to be fired only if he did not satisfactorily perform.

The only evidence relied upon by Hillesland to support his contention that he had a contract for permanent, lifetime employment was conclusory statements in his deposition that he had received the "impression" from his job interview in 1956 that he had been hired for a "permanent type" and "career type position." Hillesland could not recall the substance of the interview but only his "impressions." Hillesland admitted that he had never been told by anyone that he would only be terminated for cause.

In *Wadeson v. American Family Mutual Insurance Co.*, 343 N.W.2d 367, 371 (N.D.1984), we held that similar statements did not create a contractual agreement to discharge only for good cause:

> "The fact that American Family 'publications' represented employment with American Family as a 'lifetime opportunity' and 'permanent and stable business', as Wadeson asserts, does not bring Wadeson's employment within the scope of cases . . . where the employer had specifically said that discharge would only be for good cause. We do not read such statements used in recruiting new agents to be promises either of permanent employment or that one will be discharged only for good cause."

Hillesland has failed to draw our attention to any evidence in the record which raises a material factual issue regarding an alleged contractual agreement taking Hillesland's employment outside the at-will rule of Section 34–03–01, N.D.C.C. We conclude that the trial court did not err in granting summary judgment on this issue.

IMPLIED COVENANT OF GOOD FAITH AND FAIR DEALING

Hillesland contends that there is an implied covenant of good faith and fair dealing in all employment contracts and that the Bank and the Association breached that covenant when they terminated his employment. Hillesland alleges that there are material factual issues to be resolved on this issue which preclude summary judgment.

A brief historical perspective of the employment-at-will doctrine is helpful at this point. Prior to the mid-nineteenth century the prevailing theory was the "English rule," which provided that an employment without a set term was presumed to be for one year. . . . Toward the end of the century the at-will rule was gaining popularity, and by the beginning of the twentieth century the at-will doctrine prevailed in the United States. . . . The classic statement of the at-will rule is that an employer may discharge an employee "for good cause, for no cause or even for cause morally wrong, without being thereby guilty of legal wrong." *Payne v. Western & Atlantic Railroad Co.*, 81 Tenn. 507, 519–520 (1884). . . .

Congress and the legislatures of many states have enacted statutory provisions intended to afford some measure of protection to employees. *See, e.g.*, § 14–02.4–03, N.D.C.C. (employer may not discharge an employee because of race, color, religion, sex, national origin, age, physical or mental handicap, or status with respect to marriage or public assistance). Judicially created exceptions to or modifications of the at-will rule have also emerged to ameliorate the sometimes harsh consequences of strict adherence to the at-will rule. The two most common modifications are the public policy exception, which allows a discharged employee to recover if his termination violates a well established and important public policy, and the imposition of an implied covenant of good faith and fair dealing into the employment contract.

As previously noted, the at-will rule is statutory in this state. Section 34–03–01, N.D.C.C., provides in pertinent part: "An employment having no specified term may be terminated at the will of either party on notice to the other." Our statute is derived from the virtually identical California statute, Cal. Lab. Code § 2922. Hillesland urges this court to imply into North Dakota employment contracts a covenant of good faith and fair dealing, as the California courts have done pursuant to that state's employment-at-will statute. Although we would normally attach great significance to a sister state's construction of a statute which served as the model for our state's provision, we decline to do so in this case.

The seminal California case is *Cleary v. American Airlines, Inc.,* 111 Cal. App. 3d 443 (1980). Cleary had been employed by American for eighteen years when he was dismissed in 1976. Although American claimed that Cleary was fired for theft, leaving his work area without authorization, and threatening a fellow employee, Cleary alleged that his termination resulted from his union activities. Cleary also asserted that American failed to follow its own regulations setting forth procedures for discipline and discharge of employees.

The Court of Appeal held that there was an implied covenant of good faith and fair dealing in every employment contract under California law and that Cleary had sufficiently pleaded facts of breach of that covenant to state a viable cause of action sounding in both tort and contract. The court relied heavily upon two factors—the length of Cleary's employment and the existence of express procedures regarding termination in the company regulations. Thus, the court held that "the longevity of the employee's service, together with the expressed policy of the employer, operate as a form of estoppel, precluding any discharge of such an employee by the employer without good cause." *Cleary v. American Airlines, Inc., supra,* 111 Cal.App.3d at 455–456.

In later cases, the California Court of Appeal has grappled with the appropriate application of *Cleary* in a variety of fact situations. For example, in *Khanna v. Microdata Corp.,* 170 Cal. App. 3d 250, 262 (1985), the First District Court of Appeal held that the application of the implied covenant was not limited to those situations where the employment was long-term and the employer acted contrary to its own stated procedures for discharge:

> "We cannot agree with appellant that the factors relied on by the court in *Cleary* are the *sine qua non* to establishing a breach of the covenant of good faith and fair dealing implied in every employment contract. The cases subsequent to *Cleary* discussing the breach of the implied covenant in employment contracts have indicated that the theory of recovery articulated

in *Cleary* is not dependent on the particular factors identified in that case. . . . To the contrary, a breach of the implied covenant of good faith and fair dealing in employment contracts is established whenever the employer engages in 'bad faith action extraneous to the contract, combined with the obligor's intent to frustrate the [employee's] enjoyment of contract rights.' . . . The facts in *Cleary* establish only one manner among many by which an employer might violate this covenant."

A few months later, the Second District Court of Appeal expressly disagreed with the holding in *Khanna,* concluding that to prove a violation of the covenant the employee "must show longevity of service, and breach of an express employer policy regarding the adjudication of employee disputes." *Foley v. Interactive Data Corp.,* 219 Cal.Rptr. 866, 871 (1985), *review granted,* 222 Cal.Rptr. 740 (1986). Noting that Foley's seven years at the company "fell short of the necessary longevity" and that Foley did not "adequately allege express formal procedures for terminating employees," the court held that dismissal of Foley's action was appropriate. *Foley, supra,* 219 Cal.Rptr. at 871.

In those other jurisdictions which have found an implied-in-law covenant of good faith and fair dealing in employment contracts the application of the rule has been far from uniform. The Arizona Supreme Court, although holding that an implied covenant of good faith and fair dealing did apply to employment contracts, disagreed with the California rule that the covenant created a duty to terminate only in good faith:

"We find neither the logic of the California cases nor their factual circumstances compelling for recognition of so broad a rule in the case before us. Were we to adopt such a rule, we fear that we would tread perilously close to abolishing completely the at-will doctrine and establishing by judicial fiat the benefits which employees can and should get *only* through collective bargaining agreements or tenure provisions. . . . While we do not reject the propriety of such a rule, we are not persuaded that it should be the result of judicial decision." *Wagenseller v. Scottsdale Memorial Hospital,* 147 Ariz. 370 (1985).

The court intimated that in Arizona the covenant would be breached only by a termination which contravened public policy. *Wagenseller, supra,* 710 P.2d at 1041.

Similarly, in *Magnan v. Anaconda Industries, Inc.,* 193 Conn. 558, 479 A.2d 781 (1984), the Supreme Court of Connecticut recognized that the covenant applied to employment contracts, but held that it should not be applied to transform an at-will employment into one terminable only for cause. To do so, the court stated, would be to "render the court a bargaining agent for every employee not protected by statute or collective bargaining agreement." *Magnan, supra,* 479 A.2d at 788. The court concluded that an at-will employee could challenge his dismissal only when the reason for discharge involved a violation of an important public policy. *Magnan, supra,* 479 A.2d at 789.

* * *

Given the somewhat erratic development of this doctrine in the courts, we decline to follow either the California formulation or any of the variant theories developed in other jurisdictions. We choose to align ourselves with the emerging majority of our sister states which have rejected the implication of a covenant of good faith and fair dealing in employment contracts. . . .

We agree entirely with the policies and reasoning enunciated by the Supreme Court of Washington, sitting en banc, in *Thompson v. St. Regis Paper Co., supra,* 685 P.2d at 1086–1087:

"A number of courts have utilized a contract theory as a means of ameliorating the harshness of the rule. One contract theory utilized by a limited number of these courts is the adoption of a 'bad faith' exception. . . . Generally, these courts hold that in every employment contract there is an implied covenant of good faith and fair dealing which limited the employer's discretion to terminate an at will employee. Appellant urges us to adopt this approach.

"We do not adopt this exception. An employer's interest in running his business as he sees fit must be balanced against the interest of the employee in maintaining his employment and this exception does not strike the proper balance. We believe that to imply into each employment contract a duty to terminate in good faith would . . . subject each discharge to judicial incursions into the amorphous concept of bad faith. . . . Moreover, while an employer may agree to restrict or limit his right to discharge an employee, to imply such a restriction on that right from the existence of a contractual right, which, by its terms has no restrictions, is internally inconsistent. . . . Such an intrusion into the employment relationship is merely a judicial substitute for collective bargaining which is more appropriately left to the legislative process." * * *

The Legislature has clearly spoken in Section 34–03–01, N.D.C.C. Adoption of the exception urged by Hillesland would effectively abrogate the at-will rule as applied in this state. We refuse to recognize a cause of action for breach of an implied covenant of good faith and fair dealing where, as in this case, the claimant relies upon an employment contract which contains no express term specifying the duration of employment. Accordingly, we conclude that the district court did not err in granting summary judgment against Hillesland on this issue.

* * *

The judgment of the district court is affirmed.

■ PEDERSON, SURROGATE JUSTICE, dissenting in part. I agree with the opinion authored by Chief Justice Erickstad in all respects except for the dicta disposition of issue number 3,—Implied Covenant of Good Faith and Fair Dealing.

As I read the pleadings in this case, the termination was not "without cause" but for the exercise of poor judgment. I believe, nevertheless, that in all relationships between civilized persons, there is an obligation to not act in bad faith. Under circumstances that are appropriate, where there is an aggravated breach, unconscionable conduct, the court should provide a remedy.

NOTES

(1) The North Dakota statute codifies the common law "termination at will" doctrine. Suppose there had been no statute. Do you think the court would have reached the same result? Assuming that the employer did have a duty to exercise the discretion to terminate at will in good faith, was there bad faith on the facts of this case?

(2) In *Wayne K. Pugh v. See's Candies, Inc.*, 116 Cal.App.3d 311 (1981), an appellate court reversed a nonsuit that had been granted against a terminated employee notwithstanding the state's employment at will doctrine. Pugh, the terminated plaintiff, had "worked his way up the corporate ladder from dishwasher to vice-president in charge of production and member of the board of directors." In 1972 he received a gold watch from See's "in appreciation of 31 years of loyal service."

> [In June 1973, Pugh] received a message directing him to fly to Los Angeles the next day and meet with [See's president] Mr. Huggins. Pugh went to Los Angeles expecting to be told of another promotion. The preceding Christmas season had been the most successful in See's history, the Valentine's Day holiday of 1973 set a new sales record for See's, and the March 1973 edition of See's Newsletter, containing two pictures of Pugh, carried congratulations on the increased production. Instead, upon Pugh's arrival at Mr. Huggins' office, the latter said, "Wayne, come in and sit down. We might as well get right to the point. I have decided your services are no longer required by See's Candies. Read this and sign it." Huggins handed him a letter confirming his termination and directing him to remove that day "only personal papers and possessions from your office," [and advising that] "No severance pay will be granted." . . . The letter contained no reason for Pugh's termination. When Pugh asked Huggins for a reason, he was told only that he should "look deep within (him) self" to find the answer, that "Things were said by people in the trade that have come back to us." Pugh's termination was subsequently announced to the industry in a letter which, again, stated no reasons.

The court, relying "on the duration of appellant's employment, the commendations and promotions he received, the apparent lack of any direct criticism of his work, the assurances he was given, and the employer's acknowledged policies," found that "the employer's conduct gave rise to an implied promise that it would not act arbitrarily in dealing with its employees." The decision is a classic example of a common-law court "hearing" an implicit promise in the parties' conduct. Does the opinion signal an interest in flipping the default—toward a just-cause presumption? If courts could use the party conduct to find an implied promise not to act arbitrarily toward employees, might a court be able to find an implied promise in car dealer negotiations not to discriminate on the basis of race or gender? Might a court be able to hear an implicit warranty that a seller knows no reason why a buyer shouldn't buy the goods at the offered price?

(3) *Is "Just Cause" a Better Default?* Pauline Kim has shown that employees are generally misinformed about the current default—believing that when contract was silent, they could only be fired for just cause. Pauline T. Kim, *Bargaining with Imperfect Information: A Study of Worker Perceptions of Legal Protection in an At-Will World*, 83 Cornell L. Rev. 105 (1997). When a contract was silent, ninety percent of employees surveyed believed that it was "unlawful" to fire an employee based on personal dislike. And over eighty percent believed that it was illegal for an employer to fire an employee in order to hire another willing to do the same job for a lower wage. See also Richard Freeman & Joel Rogers, What Workers Want 118–22 (1999) (eighty-three percent of respondents believed it was unlawful to fire an employee "for no reason").

As a repeat player, the employer is much more likely to know the default—the meaning of contractual silence. Wouldn't it make more sense to use the *contra proferentem* or a "penalty default" principle and set the default against the more knowledgeable party?

(4) *Is "Employment at Will" Really Just a Default in Missouri?* Defenses of employment at will usually stress that it is just a default— meaning that the parties are free to contract for more security if they so wish. But a few jurisdictions have erected barriers to contracting around the rule. For example, imagine that you worked in Missouri and your employer gave you a handbook that expressly stated you would only be fired "for cause." It turns out that you might still be considered an "at will" employee—who could be fired without cause. For two reasons! First, publishing an employee handbook does not constitute a contractual offer and no promise of job security can be derived from its provisions. Second, a Missouri court has rejected a written contract with an express "just-cause" clause as insufficient to overcome the at-will presumption. Main v. Skaggs Cmty. Hosp., 812 S.W.2d 185, 189 (Mo. Ct. App.1991). "Given this judicial hostility to indefinite term, just-cause contracts, it appears that in Missouri, the at-will presumption can be overcome only by a clear agreement of employment for a fixed term." Kim, 83 Cornell L. Rev. at 114. Query: Can tenured professors at Wash. U. be fired without cause?

Comment: Erosion of "Employment at Will" Doctrine

For more than a century, American courts firmly adhered to the view that an employment contract of no fixed duration was terminable "at will." This meant that an employee who was not subject to a collective bargaining agreement could quit or be fired for a good reason, a bad reason, or no reason at all. Thus, in 1884 the Tennesse Supreme Court opined:

> Obviously the law can adopt and maintain no such standards for judging human conduct; and men must be left, without interference to buy and sell where they please, and to discharge or retain employe[e]s at will for good cause or for no cause, or even for bad cause without thereby being guilty of an unlawful act per se. It is a right which an employe[e] may exercise in the same way, to the same extent, for the same cause or want of cause as the employer.

Payne v. Western & Atlantic Railroad, 81 Tenn. 507, 518–19 (1884). See Richard Epstein, *In Defense of the Contract at Will,* 51 U. Chi. L. Rev. 947 (1984).

In the second half of the twentieth century, the employer's power to discharge was increasingly limited by both statute and judicial opinion. Deborah Ballam summarizes:

> Dating from the 1960s, however, when government was focusing more of its regulations on quality of life and individual liberty issues, many exceptions to the [employment-at-will] doctrine's applicability began developing from both statutory and common law sources.
>
> Numerous statutes protect employees from discharge at the whim of their employers. The broadest protections come from the federal and state employment discrimination laws which limit the ability of employers to discharge employees if that discharge is motivated by the employee's status as a member of a protected class. More narrow protections come from statutes prohibiting discharge, for example, for jury service, filing workers' compensation or OSHA claims, and testifying in court.
>
> Common law limitations on the ability of the employer to fire at will arise from both contract and tort law. Statements in employee handbooks and oral promises made during the interview or during the initial period of employment have been found to constitute implied contracts limiting the employer's ability to fire without just cause. The significance of an implied contract exception to the at-will doctrine has been minimized in recent years, however, because of employers' attempts to state clearly, usually in the contract if there is one as well as in a prominent location in the employee handbook, that the employment relationship is an at-will relationship. Courts in some states also have used the implied covenant of good faith and fair dealing doctrine to limit the employer's ability to fire for what the courts consider to be a bad faith reason. For

example, a New Hampshire court permitted recovery under this theory for an at-will employee who had been terminated for refusing to date her foreman. However, the significance of the good-faith/fair-dealing doctrine is limited because only a few states have used it in the employment context.

The most significant limitation on the employment-at-will doctrine has arisen from tort law with a cause of action for wrongful discharge based on public policy claims. Using this theory, the terminated employee can recover from the employer if the court determines that the firing violated public policy. In one of the earliest reported cases discussing public policy in the employment context, Petermann v. International Brotherhood of Teamsters Local 396, the court held the employer liable for firing an at-will employee for refusing to commit perjury. Such a firing violates the public policy supporting truthful testimony. Unlike the contract theories which have had limited effectiveness either because of employer reaction or judicial reluctance, the public policy exception to the employment-at-will doctrine developed rapidly after the Petermann decision and has expanded into a variety of areas.

Deborah A. Ballam, *Employment-At-Will: The Impending Death of a Doctrine*, 37 Am. Bus. L.J. 653, 654–56 (2000).

In light of these developments, one can speculate on the effect of leaving such an important issue of employment relations outside of collective bargaining agreements to the law of contracts. Without the limitations of the duty of good faith, employers are protected by either the "termination at will" default rule or their power to include a termination at will provision in the contract. Even with a duty of good faith, courts are often asked to administer that vague standard in a changing labor market and to develop appropriate tort standards, such as the theory of retaliatory discharge, to protect employees' legitimate interests. These problems are challenging, to say the least.

Today attention has shifted somewhat from the end of the relationship (by termination) to the beginning, where employers are increasingly insisting that employees agree to arbitrate all claims arising out of the relationship, including rights created by statute. The vocal resistance to this move is evidenced by increased attacks on arbitration clauses in the courts. See Christine M. Reilly, *Achieving Knowing and Voluntary Consent in Pre-Dispute Mandatory Arbitration Agreements at the Contracting Stage of Employment*, 90 Cal. L. Rev. 1203 (2002).

In 1991 the NCCUSSL formally approved the Model Employment Termination Act.

[T]he "underlying theme" of the Model Act [is] "one of compromise." The quid pro quo includes the following: in exchange for the abandonment of the "at-will" standard, covered employees are granted an expanded substantive right to "good cause" protection against wrongful discharge in an arbitration setting. . . . [T]he "good cause" standard is defined as "(i) a reasonable basis related to an individual employee for termination . . . in view of relevant factors and circumstances, which may include the employee's duties, responsibilities, conduct on the job or otherwise job performance . . . , or (ii) the exercise of business judgment in good faith by the employer, including setting its economic or institutional goals." Thus, the "good cause" standard is meant to be applied somewhat differently from the traditional "just cause" standard used in collective bargaining agreements between labor unions and management. META allows the employer greater flexibility in the good faith exercise of business judgment, including setting its economic or institutional goals and determining methods to achieve those goals.

Under section 2, the scope of the Act "displaces and extinguishes all common-law rights," including a right to a jury trial, of a terminated employee against the employer and replaces them with the discharge requirement that employers meet a standard of "good cause" before an arbitrator of the state. When a successful claim is brought, the arbitration award is limited to reinstatement, with or without backpay, and severance pay when reinstatement is infeasible.

Michael S. Franczak, *The Model Employment Termination Act (META): Does It Violate the Right to Trial by Jury?*, 10 Ohio St. J. on Disp. Resol. 441, 443–449 (1996). Does this seem like a fair compromise position? In the 25 years since, no state has adopted META.

3. LIABILITY FOR REPRESENTATIONS OF FACT

(A) WARRANTIES

We are used to thinking about contract law as being primarily about promising. But it also includes binding representations of fact. As you analyze contracts, it is important to distinguish between what is being represented and what is being promised. Promises of performance tend to be forward looking ("I will deliver . . ."). Representations concern past and present facts about the world ("This car has 50,000 miles on it."). Contractually binding representations are important because they allocate risk and responsibilities. Representations that are warranted to be true allocate the risk that the assertion "is not in accord with the facts" to the representing party. Restatement (Second) § 151.

We've already seen in our discussions of uncertainty, gaps and good faith that the law sometimes imposes promissory obligations as default or mandatory terms. The same is true of representations. The law holds that unless a seller says otherwise, she implicitly represents that she owns the things that are being sold and that they are of reasonable quality. These are the default, or implied, warranties.

One might think of a warranty as a special kind of promise. Instead of promising something about the future, a warranty commits the warranting party that her representation, express or implied, is true.[1] The "seller representations and warranties" section of a contract traditionally begins with the phrase, "Seller represents and warrants . . . ." A warranty (1) is made by one party to another about existing or past facts that are knowable but not necessarily known and that (2) become a term in the contract. See UCC § 2–313(1) (to create express warranty, affirmation of fact about goods must become "part of the basis of the bargain"). For example, a seller might represent to a buyer that this painting is authentic or that "this cow is fertile and can conceive"; an owner might represent to a contractor that "there are no subsurface rock conditions that will impede construction"; or a subcontractor might represent to a prime contractor that "my workers are licensed and fully insured." If the representation is false, the recipient has an action for breach of warranty. As Judge Learned Hand once put it, a warranty "amounts to a promise to indemnify the promisee for any loss if the fact warranted proves untrue, for obviously the promisor cannot control what is already in the past." Metropolitan Coal Co. v. Howard, 155 F.2d 780, 784 (2d Cir. 1946).

Modern corporate contracts (involving, inter alia, mergers and acquisitions or sales of assets) are carefully structured around the representations and warranties of each side. By warranting that an existing fact is true, a party can expose itself to breach of contract damages if the warranty fails—and thus can better assure the other side of the product's quality. This section focuses on representations and warranties of quality in contracts for the sale of goods under Article 2 of the UCC.

(1) EXPRESS WARRANTIES

To begin, students should remember that representations are not promises, but assertions *of existing fact*. Misrepresentations of fact, however, can give rise to contractual liability when affirmations of fact become part of the bargain. The representor's legal warrant allows the recipient to count on the truth of those affirmations. Either the buyer or the seller can make representations and warrant their truthfulness—and it is standard for large corporate transactions to include both buyer and seller representations and warranties. Read carefully the rules governing express warranties in UCC § 2–313. Section 2–714(1) provides that when a seller breaches a warranty, the buyer "may recover as damages . . . the

---

[1]   At times, the word "warranty" is used imprecisely as a synonym for "promise" concerning future events—as in: "I warrant that this battery will not fail."

loss resulting in the ordinary course of events . . . as determined in any manner which is reasonable."

There is an irreducible minimum representation involved in any contract, for as a practical matter there must be some minimal description of the good or service being sold. Because courts will not enforce contracts to sell unnamed things, the minimum description of the item or service (bicycle, haircut) necessarily entails some affirmation of what is being sold.

On the other hand, statements of the type identified at the end of section 2–313(2) are excluded from the contract because they are mere puffing or sales talk, on which it is not reasonable to rely. Why does the section exclude "an affirmation merely of the value of the goods"? Aren't representations of value sometimes both falsifiable and material? Cf. Hall v. T.L. Kemp Jewelry, Inc., 322 71 N.C.App. 101 (1984) (no warranty by jewelry seller who proceed with transaction, after buyer asked "If I have $2,000.00 worth of jewelry, let's wrap it up."). A comment to section 2–313 suggests that "as to false statements of value . . . , the possibility is left open that a remedy may be provided by the law relating to fraud or misrepresentation." Cmt. 9

David Rogath v. Werner E.R. Siebenmann

United States Court of Appeals, Second Circuit, 1997.
129 F.3d 261.

■ McLAUGHLIN, CIRCUIT JUDGE.

BACKGROUND

This case revolves around a painting, entitled "Self Portrait," supposedly painted in 1972 by a well-known English artist, Francis Bacon.

In July 1993, defendant Werner Siebenmann sold the Painting to plaintiff David Rogath for $570,000. In the Bill of Sale, Siebenmann described the provenance of the Painting and warranted that he was the sole owner of the Painting, that it was authentic, and that he was not aware of any challenge to its authenticity.

Problems arose three months later when Rogath sold the Painting to Acquavella Contemporary Art, Inc., in New York, for $950,000. Acquavella learned of a challenge to the Painting's authenticity and, on November 1, 1993, requested that Rogath refund the $950,000 and take back the Painting. Rogath did so, and then sued Siebenmann in the Southern District of New York (Batts, J.) for breach of contract, breach of warranty and fraud.

Rogath moved for partial summary judgment on the breach of warranty claims, and the district court granted his motion. *See Rogath v. Siebenmann,* 941 F.Supp. 416, 422–24 (S.D.N.Y.1996). The court concluded that (1) Siebenmann was unsure of the provenance of the

Painting when he sold it to Rogath; (2) he was not the sole owner of the Painting; and (3) when he sold the Painting to Rogath he already knew of a challenge to the Painting's authenticity by the Marlborough Fine Art Gallery in London. *See id.* The court awarded Rogath $950,000 in damages, the price at which he had sold it to Acquavella. *See id.* at 424–25. The court dismissed, *sua sponte*, Rogath's remaining claims for fraud and breach of contract "in light of the full recovery on the warranties granted herein." *Id.* at 425. Finally, a few days later, the court denied Rogath's motion to attach the money that Siebenmann had remaining from the proceeds of the initial sale to Rogath.

Siebenmann appeals the grant of partial summary judgment. Rogath cross-appeals the denial of his motion for attachment and the dismissal of his fraud and breach of contract claims.

DISCUSSION

Siebenmann concedes that his promises and representations set forth in the Bill of Sale constitute warranties under New York law. He claims, however, that Rogath was fully aware when he bought the Painting that questions of authenticity and provenance had already been raised regarding the Painting. He maintains that, under New York law, Rogath therefore cannot rest claims for breach of warranty on the representations made in the Bill of Sale.

We review *de novo* the district court's disposition of Rogath's motion for partial summary judgment. *See LaFond v. General Physics Servs. Corp.,* 50 F.3d 165, 171 (2d Cir.1995). The parties agree that New York law applies.

A.   *Breach of Warranty under New York Law*

The Bill of Sale provides:

> In order to induce David Rogath to make the purchase, Seller . . . make[s] the following warranties, representations and covenants to and with the Buyer.

> 1. That the Seller is the sole and absolute owner of the painting and has full right and authority to sell and transfer same; having acquired title as described in a copy of the Statement of Provenance signed by Seller annexed hereto and incorporated herein; [and] that the Seller has no knowledge of any challenge to Seller's title and authenticity of the Painting. . . .

Because the Bill of Sale was a contract for the sale of goods, Rogath's breach of warranty claims are governed by Article Two of the Uniform Commercial Code ("UCC"). *See* N.Y.U.C.C. § 2–102 (McKinney 1993); *Foxley v. Sotheby's Inc.,* 893 F.Supp. 1224, 1232–33 (S.D.N.Y.1995). Section 2–313 of the UCC provides that "[a]ny description of the goods which is made part of the basis of the bargain creates an express warranty that the goods shall conform to the description." N.Y.U.C.C. § 2–313(1)(b) (McKinney 1993).

Whether the "basis of the bargain" requirement implies that the buyer must rely on the seller's statements to recover and what the nature of that reliance requirement is are unsettled questions. . . . Not surprisingly, this same confusion haunted the New York courts for a time. . . .

Some courts reasoned that the buyer must have relied upon the accuracy of the seller's affirmations or promises in order to recover. *See, e.g., City Mach. & Mfg. Co. v. A. & A. Mach. Corp.,* 1967 WL 8832 (E.D.N.Y.1967); *Scaringe v. Holstein; Crocker Wheeler Elec. Co. v. Johns-Pratt Co.,* 51 N.Y.S. 793, 794 (1898), *aff'd,* 164 N.Y. 593 (1900); *see also County Trust Co. v. Pilmer Edsel, Inc.,* 249 N.Y.S.2d 170, 171 (1964) (Burke, J., Van Voorhis, J., and Scileppi, J., dissenting).

Other courts paid lip service to a "reliance" requirement, but found that the requirement was met if the buyer relied on the seller's promise as part of "the basis of the bargain" in entering into the contract; the buyer need not show that he relied on the truthfulness of the warranties. *See, e.g., Ainger v. Michigan Gen. Corp.,* 476 F.Supp. 1209, 1224–27 (S.D.N.Y.1979) (interpreting, in part, § 2–313), *aff'd on other grounds,* 632 F.2d 1025 (2d Cir.1980).

Finally, some courts reasoned that there is a "reliance" requirement only when there is a dispute as to whether a warranty was in fact given by the seller. These courts concluded that no reliance of any kind is required "where the existence of an express warranty in a contract is conceded by both parties." *CPC Int'l,* 513 N.Y.S.2d at 322; *see Ainger,* 476 F.Supp. at 1226–27. In these cases, the buyer need establish only a breach of the warranty.

In 1990 New York's Court of Appeals dispelled much of the confusion when it squarely adopted the "basis of the bargain" description of the reliance required to recover for breach of an express warranty. In *CBS Inc. v. Ziff-Davis Publishing Co.,* 554 N.Y.S.2d 449 (1990), the court concluded that "[t]his view of 'reliance'—i.e., as requiring no more than reliance on the express warranty as being a part of the bargain between the parties—reflects the prevailing perception of an action for breach of express warranty as one that is no longer grounded in tort, but essentially in contract." *Id.* at 452. The court reasoned that "[t]he critical question is not whether the buyer believed in the truth of the warranted information . . . but whether [he] believed [he] was purchasing the [seller's] promise [as to its truth]." *Id.* at 452–53 (quotations omitted and some insertions altered).

CBS was not decided on the basis of the UCC, probably because the sale of the magazine business at issue did not constitute the sale of goods. . . . Nevertheless, the court relied heavily on UCC authorities, *see id.* at 452–453, expressly noting that "analogy to the Uniform Commercial Code is 'instructive'." *Id.* at 454 n. 4.

In 1992, in a case also involving the sale of a business, we followed the New York Court of Appeals and delineated fine factual distinctions in the law of warranties: a court must evaluate both the extent and the source of the buyer's knowledge about the truth of what the seller is warranting. "Where a buyer closes on a contract in the full knowledge and acceptance of facts *disclosed by the seller* which would constitute a breach of warranty under the terms of the contract, the buyer should be foreclosed from later asserting the breach. In that situation, unless the buyer expressly preserves his rights under the warranties . . . , we think the buyer has waived the breach." *Galli v. Metz,* 973 F.2d 145, 151 (2d Cir.1992) (emphasis added). . . . The buyer may preserve his rights by expressly stating that disputes regarding the accuracy of the seller's warranties are unresolved, and that by signing the agreement the buyer does not waive any rights to enforce the terms of the agreement. *See Galli,* 973 F.2d at 150.

On the other hand, if the seller is not the source of the buyer's knowledge, e.g., if it is merely "common knowledge" that the facts warranted are false, or the buyer has been informed of the falsity of the facts by some third party, the buyer may prevail in his claim for breach of warranty. In these cases, it is not unrealistic to assume that the buyer purchased the seller's warranty "as insurance against any future claims," and that is why he insisted on the inclusion of the warranties in the bill of sale. *Galli,* 973 F.2d at 151; *see CBS,* 554 N.Y.S.2d at 452–53. . . .

In short, where the seller discloses up front the inaccuracy of certain of his warranties, it cannot be said that the buyer—absent the express preservation of his rights—believed he was purchasing the seller's promise as to the truth of the warranties. Accordingly, what the buyer knew and, most importantly, whether he got that knowledge from the seller are the critical questions. *See Galli,* 973 F.2d at 151; *Chateaugay,* 155 B.R. at 650–51.

1.   *What Siebenmann Knew*

Here, as the district court pointed out, Siebenmann, the seller, produced no evidence to contradict Rogath's evidence that Siebenmann knew of the cloud that hung over the Painting's authenticity before he sold it to Rogath. * * *

2.   *What Siebenmann Told Rogath: Reasonable Inferences*

* * *

Here, the Bill of Sale states that the warranties induced Rogath to buy the Painting, but Rogath did not "expressly preserve his rights" under the Bill of Sale, as required by Galli. *See* 973 F.2d at 150. Accordingly, exactly what Siebenmann told Rogath is clearly crucial. *See Galli,* 973 F.2d at 151; *Chateaugay,* 155 B.R. at 650–51. On the other hand, what [a third party art dealer] may have told Rogath about the authenticity and provenance of the Painting is immaterial. *See Galli,* 973 F.2d at 151; *Ziff-Davis,* 554 N.Y.S.2d 449, 553 N.E.2d at 1001–002. Only if the seller, Siebenmann himself, informed Rogath of doubts about the provenance or challenges to authenticity will Rogath be deemed to have waived any claims for breach of warranty arising from the written representations appearing in the Bill of Sale. *See Galli,* 973 F.2d at 151; *Chateaugay,* 155 B.R. at 650–51.

As Rogath emphasizes, Siebenmann nowhere specifically alleges that he informed Rogath of his doubts about the authenticity and provenance of the Painting. He merely alluded to the "controversy" or "problems" with the Marlborough Gallery. Still, Siebenmann's testimony, however ambiguous, may justify the inference that Rogath knew more than he now claims to have known when he entered into the Bill of Sale.

At the very least, there is indisputable ambiguity in the affidavits about the pivotal exchange between Rogath and Siebenmann. We are satisfied that genuine issues of fact persist. In this posture, we must draw all reasonable inferences in Siebenmann's favor. *See LaFond,* 50 F.3d at 171. Accordingly, as regards the Marlborough challenge, summary judgment on Rogath's claims for breach of the warranties of provenance and no challenges to authenticity is inappropriate. . . .

* * *

C.   *Rogath's Cross-Appeal*

The district court dismissed, *sua sponte,* Rogath's claims for fraud and breach of contract "in light of the full recovery on the warranties granted herein." *Rogath,* 941 F.Supp. at 425. In light of our vacatur of Rogath's award for breach of warranty, on remand to the district court we reinstate Rogath's claims for fraud and breach of contract. Finally, on remand Rogath, if so advised, is free to move for attachment, under Federal Rule of Civil Procedure 64.

CONCLUSION

The order granting Rogath's motion for partial summary judgment is vacated, and the case is remanded to the district court for disposition not inconsistent with this opinion.

NOTES

(1)   Section 12 of the Uniform Sales Act—the precursor to Article 2 of the UCC—provided that an affirmation of fact created a warranty "if the natural tendency of such affirmation or promise is to induce the buyer to purchase the goods, and if the buyer purchases the goods relying thereon." Section 2–213 does not speak of buyer "reliance," but requires that the affirmation "become part of the basis of the bargain." Comment 3 attempts to explain:

> In actual practice affirmations of fact made by the seller about the goods during a bargain are regarded as part of the description of those goods; hence no particular reliance on such statements need be shown in order to weave them into the fabric of the agreement. Rather, any fact which is to take such affirmations, once made, out

of the agreement requires clear affirmative proof. The issue normally is one of fact.

Does the comment help?

(2)   Hawkland identifies three separate approaches courts have taken to interpreting "basis of the bargain" in section 2–313:

First, some courts do not require any showing of buyer reliance at all. Second, some courts use a presumption that the buyer relied on the representation, subject to the seller's proof that the buyer did not rely on the representation. Third, some courts require that the buyer demonstrate reliance as part of its case for breach of the express warranty.

1 Hawkland UCC Series § 2–313:4 (2016). Does the New York Court of Appeals' rule in *CBS v. Ziff-Davis* fall into one of these three boxes? What is the difference between relying on a representation and relying on the fact that a seller has warranted the representation to be true? Is it possible to warrant a fact to be true without representing that the fact is true? Why does the court in *Galli v. Metz* compare this to a type of insurance?

Section 2–313(2) provides: "It is not necessary to the creation of an express warranty that the seller use formal words such as 'warrant' or 'guarantee' or that he have a specific intention to make a warranty. . ." In other words, the seller need not have or express an intention to be legally bound by her representation in order to be so. Does the *CBS* rule mean that the buyer must understand the representation to create a legal obligation? Or does the *CBS* test state a sufficient but not necessary test for "basis of the bargain"?

(3)   White, Summers and Hillman discuss the basis for the basis-of-the-bargain requirement.

What the Code does to the pre-Code reliance requirement is quite unclear. One may argue that the exchange of the "basis of the bargain" language for the old "reliance" language will not change the outcome of any cases. Others apparently believe that the code dilutes and perhaps even emasculates the pre-Code reliance requirement. For most cases, we favor the former interpretation. Why should one who has not relied on the seller's statement have the right to sue? The plaintiff is asking for greater protection than one would get under the warranty of merchantability, far more than bargained for. We would send this party to the implied warranties.

White, Summers and Hillman, 1 Uniform Commercial Code § 10:16 (6th ed. 2012). If consumers can be bound by terms in contracts of adhesion, even though we know the vast majority of them never read, why insist that a buyer rely on a representation to create a warranty?

(4)   State as clearly as possible the New York rule for when a buyer may recover for breach of warranty despite the buyer's knowledge, at the time of formation, of facts that would constitute a breach of that warranty.

(2) IMPLIED WARRANTIES

An implied warranty is a default representation that is also by default warranted to be true. The UCC establishes three important implied warranties: the implied warranty of title, which applies in its general form to all sales; the implied warranty of merchantability, which applies only to merchants; and the implied warranty of fitness for a particular purpose, which arises after a buyer has disclosed his or her particular needs or purposes for the goods and relies upon the seller's skill and judgment to supply them. Read carefully UCC §§ 2–312, 2–314 and 2–315.

Notice that a warranty of merchantability is only implied for merchant sellers of "goods of that kind," whereas an implied warranty of fitness for a particular purpose could potentially apply to non-merchant sellers as well. The concept of "merchantability" is not self-defining, and while § 2–314(2) provides a 6-part disjunctive definition, the core representation is that the goods "are fit for the ordinary purposes for which such goods are used." UCC § 2–314(2)(c).

The official comment explains the distinction between the warranties of merchantability and of fitness:

> A "particular purpose" differs from the ordinary purpose for which the goods are used in that it envisages a specific use by the buyer which is peculiar to the nature of his business whereas the ordinary purposes for which goods are used are those envisaged in the concept of merchantability and go to uses which are customarily made of the goods in question. For example, shoes are generally used for the purpose of walking upon ordinary ground, but a seller may know that a particular pair was selected to be used for climbing mountains.

UCC § 2–315 cmt. 2. Why does the implied warranty of merchantability only apply to merchants? Why is the implied warranty of fitness for a particular purpose limited to occasions where the buyer is relying on the seller's skill or judgment?

Beyond the UCC's implied (representations and) warranties, recall from Chapter Four that implied representations can be created by a promisor's nondisclosure:

> A person's non-disclosure of a fact known to him is equivalent to an assertion that the fact does not exist in the following cases only:

> (a) Where he knows that disclosure of the fact is necessary to prevent some previous assertion from being a misrepresentation. . . .

> (b) Where he knows that disclosure of the fact would correct a mistake of the other party as to a basic assumption on which that party is making the contract and if non-disclosure of the

fact amounts to a failure to act in good faith and in accordance with reasonable standards of fair dealing. . . .

Restatement (Second) § 161. Both of these categories might be restated as a default implicit representation ("I don't know of any fact that would correct a mistake you are making as to a basic assumption."). Cf. Restatement (Second) § 153(b) (unilateral mistake if "the other party had reason to know of the mistake"). Developing the skill to "hear" these implicit or default representations is important, because contractors implicitly warrant that their implicit representations are true. The Restatement's use of the phrase "in the following cases only" suggests that courts sharply limit the class of implicit representations. But this is not true. As the above examples illustrate, contract law routinely "hears" sellers to implicitly represent that they own the goods subject to the contract, that the goods are merchantable, and that they are fit for a certain purpose.

PROBLEM: THE CASE OF THE DISAPPOINTED SKIER

Francine, an intermediate skier, went shopping for a pair of ski boots. She talked with friends and read some advertising literature and concluded that the Bordica Alpine was the ski boot for her. She then went to the Bordica outlet at the Mall and talked with Salesperson Bob. Bob fitted her with a Bordica Alpine 200 for women, telling her, inter alia, that "This is the best boot on the market—you can go anywhere with it—it is toasty on frigid days—the support on your ankles is superb." Persuaded, Francine bought a pair for $350. In January, Francine went to Vail on a ski trip. The temperature was around 0 degrees F. On the first day, she spent several hours in a back bowl over 10,000 feet high. After feeling pain and discomfort in her right foot, she started down the mountain. It was slow going. Just as she reached the top of the last easy glide to the bottom, the bindings on the left ski boot gave way, pitching her to the ground and breaking her ankle. After removing her boots, the medical attendant discovered severe frostbite on the right foot.

(1)   Francine consults you for advice. What are her best arguments that Bob made warranties to her about the boots that were breached?

(2)   If Bob breached warranties that resulted in personal injuries to Francine, are those losses recoverable under Article 2? See UCC §§ 2–715(2)(b), 2–719(3).

DRAFTING EXERCISE: ONLY DRIVEN TO CHURCH ON SUNDAY

You have decided to purchase Jerry Seinfeld's 1963 (Sunstar) Corvair. Draft a list of the seller representations and warranties you would like included in the purchase agreement for this vehicle.

(3) LIMITATIONS ON WARRANTIES

The implied warranties of § 2–314 and § 2–315 are *default rules* (presumed in the absence of express agreement to the contrary) that parties are free to contract around. But the UCC (and other statutes governing consumer contracts) also has created *altering rules* which regulate the ways that parties may contract around to disclaim or limit the warranties or their remedies. Section 2–316 says in part:

> (2) Subject to subsection (3), to exclude or modify the implied warranty of merchantability or any part of it the language must mention merchantability and in case of a writing must be conspicuous, and to exclude or modify any implied warranty of fitness the exclusion must be by a writing and conspicuous. Language to exclude all implied warranties of fitness is sufficient if it states, for example, that "There are no warranties which extend beyond the description on the face hereof."

> (3) Notwithstanding subsection (2)

>> (a) unless the circumstances indicate otherwise, all implied warranties are excluded by expressions like "as is", "with all faults" or other language which in common understanding calls the buyer's attention to the exclusion of warranties and makes plain that there is no implied warranty; and

>> (b) when the buyer before entering into the contract has examined the goods or the sample or model as fully as he desired or has refused to examine the goods there is no implied warranty with regard to defects which an examination ought in the circumstances to have revealed to him. . . .

Thus, to disclaim the implied warranty of merchantability, a seller must either conspicuously use the shibboleth "merchantability" or use words which clearly and conventionally disclaim all implicit warranties, such as "as is" or "with all faults." Even without words, implied warranties are disclaimed by operation of § 2–316(3)(b) with regard to defects which the buyer knew or should have known.

As we discuss in Chapter Six, Section 5(B), sellers often employ standard warranty limitation clauses:

> Sellers of 'hard goods'—appliances, machines—supply warranty clauses whose central features vary little across industries. These standard clauses (i) disclaim all implied warranties; (ii) expressly warrant the goods against defects in material and workmanship; (iii) limit the buyer's remedies, should the express warranty be breached, to the repair or replacement of defective parts, with the seller having the option of which remedy to use; (iv) limit the time within which claims under the express warranty can be made; (v) exclude liability for consequential damages.

Richard E. Speidel & Linda J. Rusch, Commercial Transactions: Sales, Leases and Licenses 629–667 (2d ed. 2004). Are these "central features" efficient? Equitable?

Instead of disclaiming warranties, a seller could theoretically achieve the same result by severely limiting the remedy for their breach. The ubiquity of "repair or replace" provisions, which substitute seller remedial action for damages, are a concern if the sellers don't follow through on their remedial promise. UCC § 2–719(2) responds to this concern by providing "[w]here circumstances cause an exclusive or limited remedy to fail of its essential purpose, remedy may be had as provided in this Act." For a case applying section 2–719(2) to a standard warranty package, see *Lewis Refrigeration Co. v. Sawyer Fruit, Vegetable and Cold Storage Co.*, infra Chapter Six, Section 5(B).

The UCC also limits the ability of sellers to disclaim the applicability of express or implied warranties to parties who are not in contractual privity with the seller. UCC § 2–318 offers adopting states three alternative limitations on the defense of "no privity of contract" where foreseeable users or subpurchasers are involved. Twenty-nine states have adopted "Alternative A" which extends the warranty to "any natural person who is in the family or household of [the] buyer or who is a guest in his home." Foreseeable users also have potential personal injury claims that at times are found to preempt Article 2 warranty claims. Article 2 includes as consequential damages resulting from a seller's breach "injury to person or property proximately resulting from any breach of warranty." UCC § 2–715(2)(b) and UCC § 2–719(3) provide that agreements excluding liability for personal injuries are "prima facie unconscionable."

Comment: The Parol Evidence Rule and Warranty Disclaimers

How does the parol evidence rule, UCC § 2–202, mesh with the giving and disclaiming of express or implied warranties? First, if a disclaimer is effective, the parol evidence rule is irrelevant. The warranty has been excluded from the agreement by other means. Second, suppose the seller has made an implied warranty of merchantability and it has not been disclaimed. Since the warranty is a term of the agreement, one might argue that it is subject to exclusion under UCC § 2–202 if the parties intended the writing to be a "complete and exclusive statement of the terms of the agreement." UCC § 2–202(b). But this would be a mistake. The implied warranty is not meant to be the product of the parties' agreement. It is a default that applies when the parties have not agreed one way or the other. And UCC § 2–316(2) sets out clear requirements for altering that default. A court should therefore not exclude an implied warranty of merchantability by virtue of a general "merger" clause.

More vexing problems arise when a merger clause is used to disclaim an express warranty that was promised in a pre-existing oral agreement or other communication. Normally, the UCC makes it impossible for a seller to disclaim an express warranty: if words or conduct creating an express warranty and words or conduct "tending to negate or limit warranty" cannot be construed as consistent with each other, "negation or limitation is inoperative to the extent that such construction is unreasonable." UCC § 2–316(1). But UCC § 2–316(1) also states that this limitation on disclaiming express warranties is "subject to the provisions of this Article on parol or extrinsic evidence (Section 2–202)."

Suppose, then, this situation. A used car salesman has made "affirmations of fact" about the condition of a particular used car and they become "part of the basis" of the buyer's bargain. UCC § 2–313(1). Later, the buyer signs a writing that attempts to disclaim all express warranties except a promise to share 50–50 in all repairs needed during the first 30 days and contains a general merger clause that provides: "THIS WRITING IS THE FINAL AND EXCLUSIVE STATEMENT AND EXPRESSION OF ALL OF THE TERMS OF THE AGREEMENT." Buyer signs the agreement, but 60 days later discovers a major defect inconsistent with the salesman's oral representation. Is the seller protected against the buyer's breach of warranty claim?

First, observe that the merger clause itself, even without the written disclaimer, might be read to void the earlier affirmations of fact. The question is whether the merger clause complies with the requirements of UCC § 2–316(1) for disclaiming express warranties. Does it? Of course, the seller is not protected if the court concludes that the writing was not intended as a total integration and the oral representations can be admitted as "consistent additional terms." Does the test for integration leave room for this interpretation? Does it matter what evidence the court may consider in answering the integration question? Second, the parol evidence rule does not apply at all if the representations were fraudulent. Third, there is a hint in some cases that even if a total integration was intended, the oral representation may not be excluded if the buyer was surprised by an "unexpected and unbargained for" exclusion. See Jordan v. Doonan Truck & Equipment, Inc., 220 Kan. 431 (1976); Restatement (Second) § 211.

Finally, at least one court has appealed to unconscionability in this context. "We think that it would be unconscionable to permit an inconspicuous merger clause to exclude evidence of an express oral warranty—especially in light of the policy expressed by [UCC § 2–316]. That is, a disclaimer of the implied warranties of fitness and merchantability must be conspicuous to prevent surprise." Seibel v. Layne & Bowler, Inc., 641 P.2d 668, 671 (Or. App. 1982). The court endorsed the merger clause proposed by James J. White and Robert S. Summers, *Uniform Commercial Code* 111–112 (3d ed. 1988):

> THIS AGREEMENT SIGNED BY BOTH PARTIES AND SO INITIALED BY BOTH PARTIES IN THE MARGIN OPPOSITE THIS PARAGRAPH CONSTITUTES A FINAL WRITTEN EXPRESSION OF ALL THE TERMS OF THIS AGREEMENT AND IS A COMPLETE AND EXCLUSIVE STATEMENT OF

THOSE TERMS. ANY AND ALL REPRESENTATIONS, PROMISES, WARRANTIES OR STATEMENTS BY SELLER'S AGENT THAT DIFFER IN ANY WAY FROM THE TERMS OF THIS WRITTEN AGREEMENT SHALL BE GIVEN NO FORCE OR EFFECT.

Id. n.1. Would this "merger" clause exclude implied warranties?

(B) TORT AND STATUTORY LIABILITY FOR FALSEHOODS

So far we have been considering liability for false representations in contract. But falsehoods among contracting parties can give rise to liability under other laws as well. These range from very general laws, such as false advertising and criminal fraud statutes, to very specialized ones, such as the Indian Arts and Crafts Act, which provides for civil and criminal actions against anyone who sells a good "in a manner that falsely suggests it is . . . an [American] Indian product." 18 U.S.C. § 1159.

Here we consider two especially important sources of non-contractual liability: the common law tort of deceit, together with the related action for negligent misrepresentation, and state Unfair and Deceptive Acts and Practices (UDAP) statutes, as the latter apply to deception. The tort actions for deceit and negligent misrepresentation are in some ways similar to the contract defense of misrepresentation. But whereas that rule provides a defense from liability (a shield), the torts of deception and negligent misrepresentation, like warranty rules, support an action for damages (a sword). We have already also encountered UDAP statutes, namely, in the discussion of unconscionability. But whereas there we were concerned with unfair terms, here we will look at how such statues can be applied to deceptive practices.

V.S.H. Realty, Inc. v. Texaco, Inc.

United States Court of Appeals, First Circuit, 1985.
757 F.2d 411.

■ COFFIN, CIRCUIT JUDGE.

Appellant V.S.H. Realty, Inc. (V.S.H.) claims that appellee Texaco, Inc. (Texaco) must return a $280,000 down payment V.S.H. paid on a piece of real estate in Chelsea, Massachusetts. V.S.H. claims that Texaco breached the sales agreement, fraudulently induced it into agreeing to the purchase, and violated a Massachusetts statute prohibiting unfair and deceptive acts in business dealings. The district court dismissed the case under Fed.R.Civ.P. 12(b)(6) for failure to state a claim, and denied V.S.H.'s subsequent motion to vacate judgment and to permit an amendment of the complaint. We think the court was correct in dismissing the breach of contract claim but erring in dismissing the common law and statutory deception counts.

I. Factual Background

On August 11, 1983, V.S.H. offered to purchase from Texaco a used bulk storage petroleum facility for $2.8 million. Texaco accepted the offer on September 7, and V.S.H. made a deposit of $280,000 to be applied against the purchase price. The offer to purchase required Texaco to convey the property "free and clear of all liens, encumbrances, tenancies and restrictions", except for those set forth in the offer. Attached to the offer to purchase was an acknowledgement signed by Texaco stating that, to the best of the company's knowledge and belief, it had not received "any notice, demand, or communication from any local county, state or federal department or agency regarding modifications or improvements to the facility or any part thereof." The offer also included a disclosure by Texaco that fuel oils had "migrated under [Texaco's] garage building across Marginal Street from the terminal [and that] the fuel oil underground as a result of heavy rains or high tides, seeps into the boiler room of the garage building." V.S.H., for its part, expressly stated in the offer that it had inspected the property, and accepted it "as is" without any representation on the part of Texaco as to its condition.

Problems arose when V.S.H. representatives visited the property in mid-October 1983, approximately a month after Texaco accepted the offer to purchase, and observed oil seeping from the ground at the western end of the property. During a subsequent visit, V.S.H. representatives discovered another oil seepage at the eastern end of the property. V.S.H. then notified Texaco that it would not go through with the purchase unless Texaco corrected the oil problem, provided V.S.H. with full indemnification, or reduced the purchase price. When Texaco refused, V.S.H. demanded return of its down payment. Texaco again refused, and V.S.H. filed this lawsuit on January 10, 1984.

In its three-count complaint, V.S.H. alleges first that Texaco violated Mass.Gen.Laws Ann. ch. 93A, § 2, which prohibits unfair and deceptive acts and practices, basing that assertion largely on Texaco's failure to disclose the seeping oil, and its failure to disclose an investigation of the property by the U.S. Coast Guard. V.S.H.'s second count claims relief for breach of contract, based on Texaco's alleged inability to convey the property at the specified time free of all liens, encumbrances and restrictions. V.S.H.'s contract theory is that the penalties associated with the oil seepage problem constitute an encumbrance on the property. Finally, V.S.H. charges Texaco with common law misrepresentation and deceit for failing to disclose the oil seepage problems and Coast Guard investigation "in the face of repeated inquiries by V.S.H. about the subject."

At the conclusion of a hearing on Texaco's motion to dismiss all three counts, the district court announced without explanation that the contract claims should be dismissed. It also dismissed the common law fraud count at that time, stating that V.S.H. had failed to allege the required affirmative misrepresentation or implicit misrepresentation by partial and ambiguous statements. It deferred decision on the chapter 93A count, and in a latter written decision dismissed that count on two grounds: an Attorney General's regulation upon which V.S.H. relied was not intended to apply in a transaction between two sophisticated business entities, when one party agrees to take the property "as is"; and Texaco had no duty to disclose the oil seepages to V.S.H., and so its failure to do so could not have violated chapter 93A.

Our approach to reviewing a dismissal of a complaint at such a preliminary stage of proceedings is necessarily informed by the teaching that we must consider "not whether a plaintiff will ultimately prevail but whether the claimant is entitled to offer evidence to support the claims", *Scheuer v. Rhodes,* 416 U.S. 232, 236 (1974). With that view of our task in mind, we disagree with the action taken by the district court with respect to the counts based on chapter 93A and common law misrepresentation. V.S.H.'s original complaint may well have been vague in some allegations, but we believe that it presented "enough information to 'outline the elements of the pleaders' claim' ", *Kadar Corp. v. Milbury,* 549 F.2d 230, 233 (1st Cir.1977) (quoting Wright & Miller, *Federal Practice and Procedure* § 1357). V.S.H. is therefore "entitled to be heard more fully than is possible on a motion to dismiss a complaint." *Scheuer, id.* 416 U.S. at 250. We affirm the dismissal of the count based on breach of contract. . . .

II. Sufficiency of the Complaint

A. Common Law Misrepresentation

V.S.H. bases its count for common law misrepresentation on Texaco's partial disclosure of oil seepages, the deliberate concealment of other leaks and the failure to acknowledge the U.S. Coast Guard investigation of the spills. The failure to disclose is actionable, V.S.H. argues, because it repeatedly asked Texaco about oil leaks on the premises, yet Texaco knowingly made only partial disclosure of them. V.S.H. alleges that Texaco's fragmentary disclosures induced it to enter into the contract, and caused it damage in the form of the $280,000 down payment which it otherwise would not have made.

The district court dismissed the misrepresentation count because

"[t]here was no fiduciary duty here. The parties dealt at arm's length with each other, and there was no peculiar duty to speak. There were no material misrepresentations on which the buyers relied."

What we face here, however, are allegations of partial or incomplete statements that may by their incompleteness be actionable. Restatement of Torts (Second), §§ 529, 551(2)(b). There is much case law in Massachusetts supporting the proposition that a party who discloses partial information that may be misleading has a duty to reveal all the material facts he knows to avoid deceiving the other party.

"Although there may be 'no duty imposed upon one party to a transaction to speak for the information of the other . . . if he does speak with reference to a given point of information, voluntarily or at the other's request, he is bound to speak honestly and to divulge all the material facts bearing upon the point that lie within his knowledge. Fragmentary information may be as misleading . . . as active misrepresentation, and half-truths may be as actionable as whole lies. . . .' See Harper & James, Torts, § 7.14. See also Restatement: Torts, § 529; Williston, Contracts (2d ed.) §§ 1497–1499." *Kannavos v. Annino,* 356 Mass. 42, 48 (1969).

* * *

We believe the allegations in V.S.H.'s complaint regarding partial and ambiguous statements satisfy the requirements for stating a claim of misrepresentation. V.S.H. has alleged that it made "repeated inquiries" about oil leaks on the property, to which Texaco failed to fully respond. In addition, Texaco stated in an acknowledgement attached to the contract that it had "not received any notice, demand, or communication from any local county, state or federal department or agency regarding modifications or improvements to the facility or any part thereof." Even if it is technically correct that Texaco had received no governmental communication specifically related to modifications or improvements to the facility, its failure to disclose the Coast Guard investigation of the property is arguably an actionable misrepresentation. The district court also recognized the ambiguity in Texaco's assertion, noting that "the question whether that [the Coast Guard investigation] is a notice regarding modifications or improvements of the facility is a matter of argument." Finally, and significantly, we note that Texaco affirmatively stated (with some implication of exclusivity) the existence of one leak. The combination of Texaco's affirmative disclosure of one leak, its failure to disclose the others, and its failure to acknowledge alleged Coast Guard investigation of the seepages, at a minimum, makes this case a stronger one of misrepresentation than *Nei v. Burley,* 388 Mass. 307, 310, where the Supreme Judicial Court held that the defendants "did not convey half truths nor did they make partial disclosure of the kind which so often requires a full acknowledgement to avoid deception." It is our conclusion, therefore, that the district court erred in dismissing the claim for common law misrepresentation.

B. Breach of Mass.Gen.Laws Ann. ch. 93A

Mass.Gen.Laws Ann. ch. 93A generally prohibits unfair or deceptive acts or practices in business. When it was first enacted in 1967, its primary goal was protection of consumers, *Manning v. Zuckerman,* 388 Mass. 8, 12 (1983), but the addition of section 11 in 1972 extended chapter 93A's coverage to business persons involved in transactions with other business persons. *Id.* . . . "This act is one of several legislative attempts in recent years to regulate business activities with the view to providing proper disclosure of information . . .", *Commonwealth v. DeCotis,* 366 Mass. 234, 238 (1974).

Chapter 93A § 2 provides no definition of an unfair or deceptive act or practice, and instead directs our attention to interpretations of unfair acts and practices under the Federal Trade Commission Act as construed by the Commission and the federal courts. *Commonwealth v. DeCotis,* 366 Mass. at 241; *PMP Associates, Inc. v. Globe Newspaper Co.,* 366 Mass. 593, 595 (1975). The section also empowers the Attorney General to make rules and regulations interpreting § 2(a). *See* § 2(c). V.S.H. relies heavily on one such regulation to support its allegation that Texaco violated chapter 93A.

The Attorney General's regulation in Mass.Admin.Code tit. 20, § 3.16(2) states that an act or practice violates chapter 93A if:

> "Any person or other legal entity subject to this act fails to disclose to a buyer or prospective buyer any fact, the disclosure of which may have influenced the buyer or prospective buyer not to enter into the transaction."

V.S.H.'s complaint appears to state a claim under this regulation and, in fact, mirrors its language. V.S.H. alleged in paragraph 19 of its complaint that Texaco's failure to disclose the oil leaks that V.S.H. representatives discovered in October 1983 "are facts the disclosure of which may have influenced V.S.H. not to enter into the transaction and agree to pay the sum of $2,800,000 for the premises or to pay a deposit in connection therewith of $280,000."

The district court found an inadequacy in the complaint by concluding that the disclosure language of regulation § 3.16 is incomplete.[4] The court decided that "unless a defendant has a duty to speak, his nondisclosure of a defect does not constitute a violation of chapter 93A even if the information may have influenced the buyer not to enter into the contract." The court then went on to hold that Texaco did not have a duty to disclose the oil leaks to V.S.H. We disagree for two reasons. First, even if we were to accept the court's premise that nondisclosure is a violation of chapter 93A only when there is a duty to disclose, we would find that V.S.H. has met its burden of establishing a duty by alleging that Texaco made partial or incomplete statements regarding the oil leaks on the property. *See* Restatement of Torts (Second) §§ 551, 529. *See supra* p. 415.

We are not convinced, however, that V.S.H. needs to allege more than a failure to disclose a material fact to state a cause of action under chapter 93A. In *Slaney v. Westwood Auto, Inc.,* 366 Mass. 688 (1975), the

---

[4] Texaco argues that § 3.16 actually condemns only failures to disclose that are unfair or deceptive as described by Massachusetts standards, Purity Supreme, Inc. v. Attorney General, 380 Mass. 762, 775 (1980), and that this is not such a case. While we agree with that general proposition, it is also true that "the existence of unfair acts and practices must be determined from the circumstances of each case", Commonwealth v. DeCotis, 366 Mass. at 242, 316 N.E.2d 748. . . .

Massachusetts Supreme Judicial Court examined chapter 93A at length, and emphasized the distinction between that statutory cause of action and the common law action for fraud and deceit, which would require a duty to disclose. It pointed out that "the definition of an actionable 'unfair or deceptive act or practice' goes far beyond the scope of the common law action for fraud and deceit. . . . [A] § 9 [or § 11] claim for relief . . . is not subject to the traditional limitations of preexisting causes of action such as tort for fraud and deceit." *Id.,* at 703–04. Massachusetts case law suggests that one difference between a fraud claim and the more liberal 93A is allowance of a cause of action even in the absence of a duty to disclose. *See Nei v. Boston Survey Consultants, Inc.,* 388 Mass. 320, 323–24 (1983), where the court appeared ready to find chapter 93A liability even though it found no duty to speak. . . .

The district court, however, had another reason for dismissing the claim. It concluded that chapter 93A liability was precluded because V.S.H. is a sophisticated buyer who had the opportunity to inspect the property and who agreed to purchase the property "as is". The court noted that "this type of contractual arrangement is expressly permitted under the Uniform Commercial Code, M.G.L. c. 106, § 2–316, in non-consumer sales of goods", and it thus "would be anomalous to hold that 'as is' contracts are permissible in sales of goods cases but not in commercial sales of land cases." It concluded:

> "Absent allegations of the non-detectability of defects on inspection or their fraudulent concealment by a defendant, a plaintiff who has inspected the premises to be purchased and has agreed to purchase the land 'as is' cannot rely on § 3.16(2) to establish a defendant's violation of chapter 93A."

We believe the district court's view of the law regarding "as is" clauses is incorrect. Although the Uniform Commercial Code does expressly permit disclaimers in the sale of goods between merchants, § 2–316 refers specifically to disclaimers of implied warranties, suggesting to us that it was intended only to permit a seller to limit or modify the contractual bases of liability which the Code would otherwise impose on the transaction. The section does not appear to preclude claims based on fraud or other deceptive conduct. Section 1–102(3) of Mass.Gen.Laws ch. 106 lends support to this interpretation of § 2–316. It states:

> "The effect of provisions of this chapter may be varied by agreement, except as otherwise provided in this chapter and *except that the obligations of good faith, diligence, reasonableness and care prescribed by this chapter may not be disclaimed by agreement . . .*" (emphasis added).

We find further support for our view implicit in *Marcil v. John Deere Industrial Equipment Co.,* 9 Mass.App. 625 (1980). The court in that case upheld a disclaimer of all express and implied warranties other than the warranty specified on the purchase order, finding that there was no indication that the disclaimer was unconscionable. The court went on to note that the vaguely worded allegations of the plaintiff's complaint may have stated claims for deceit or violation of chapter 93A, but the plaintiff failed to characterize them as such to the trial judge, and so he was not allowed to do so for the first time on appeal. Our reading of *Marcil* is that even if a disclaimer on its face is not unconscionable, it is subject to challenge if a plaintiff, as in this case, properly raises allegations of deceit and violation of chapter 93A.

Our conclusion here does not mean that an "as is" clause would never be given effect in real estate transactions where the buyer alleged the seller's failure to disclose a material defect in the property. The Supreme Judicial Court has held that § 3.16(2) imposes liability only when the defendant had knowledge, or should have known of the defect, and where a direct relationship existed between the parties. *See Lawton v. Dracousis,* 14 Mass.App. 164, 171 (1982) (failure to disclose building code violations not actionable where seller did not know or have reason to know of violations) ... It is possible that § 3.16(2) will be found inapplicable in other situations involving "as is" clauses.

Even more persuasive than this inferential reasoning based on the Uniform Commercial Code is the fact that Massachusetts case law unequivocally rejects assertion of an "as is" clause as an automatic defense against allegations of fraud:

> "The same public policy that in general sanctions the avoidance of a promise obtained by deceit strikes down all attempts to circumvent the policy by means of contractual devices. In the realm of fact it is entirely possible for a party knowingly to agree that no representations have been made to him, while at the same time believing and relying upon representations which in fact have been made and in fact are false but for which he would not have made the agreement." *Bates v. Southgate,* 308 Mass. 170, 182 (1941).

See also Schell v. Ford Motor Company, 270 F.2d 384, 386 (1st Cir.1959) ("under the law of Massachusetts ... *in the absence of fraud* a person may make a valid contract exempting himself from any liability to another which he may in the future incur as a result of his negligence. . . .) (emphasis added).

* * *

Although we agree that V.S.H.'s experience in the real estate business, along with the presence of an "as is" clause, is relevant to the ultimate disposition of the chapter 93A claim, we do not find that either factor makes V.S.H.'s claim insufficient as a matter of law. Sophistication of the parties is not mentioned in chapter 93A and the amendment of chapter 93A to cover business entities did not limit the statute's protection to small, unsophisticated businesses. It may be that the Massachusetts Supreme Judicial Court ultimately should decide the question of whether an "as is" clause ever should be ignored in a transaction between two sophisticated businesses and, thus, whether the existence of one should preclude a chapter 93A cause of action. We do not believe, however, that it would, or could, do so without development of a factual record. For that reason, and the absence of any contrary precedent in Massachusetts law, we conclude that the district court erred in dismissing the chapter 93A claim.

C. Breach of Contract

[The court affirmed the dismissal of V.S.H.'s breach of contract claim, concluding that the mere possibility of statutory penalties due to the oil seepages was not an encumberance" on the title.]

■ BREYER, CIRCUIT JUDGE (concurring in part and dissenting in part).

The common law misrepresentation issue is a close one given the Supreme Judicial Court's refusal to find liability in *Nei v. Burley,* 388 Mass. 307 (1983) (no misleading partial disclosure where seller gave buyer percolation test showing too much water on land while failing to disclose seasonal stream). But I agree with the panel that enough is alleged to avoid dismissal of the complaint.

I do not agree, however, with the panel's suggestion that Mass.Gen.Laws ch. 93A would allow a finding of liability for pure *nondisclosure* in a case like this one, involving sophisticated business parties and an "as is" contract. The question is difficult, and certification of this question to the Massachusetts Supreme Judicial Court might at some point be appropriate. *See* S.J.C. Rule 1:03; *Clay v. Sun Insurance,* 363 U.S. 207 (1960). But, if forced to decide the chapter 93A question, I must disagree with the panel majority; the following factors persuade me that the panel is wrong.

First, the panel's interpretation of chapter 93A virtually reads the "as is" contract out of Massachusetts law. If a seller knows he is liable for failing to disclose any material fact about which he "should have known," he will have to check the merchandise or property, and list every defect that he finds. Failure to do so certainly risks (if it does not assure) liability. Yet, it is the very purpose of an "as is" contract to shift the burden of inspection and the costs of hidden defects to the buyer. The Massachusetts Commercial Code, Mass.Gen.Laws ch. 106, § 2–316(3)(a) specifically authorizes "as is" contracts. As the district court pointed out, it is anomalous to read a different statute (chapter 93A) in a way that makes § 2–316(3)(a) of the UCC virtually meaningless. The panel majority says that perhaps the UCC's "as is" rule will still have meaningful life in other situations. Which situations? Where? How?

Second, there is a theoretical argument suggesting that applying chapter 93A here may not help—indeed it may hurt—the consumer. The basic object of chapter 93A, insofar as it requires disclosure, is to allow the consumer to make an informed choice, and thus to protect him from entering into a contract that he would not 'really' want were he more knowledgeable or sophisticated. *See generally* E. Kintner, *A Primer on the Law of Deceptive Practices* ix–xi (1978). That purpose is not directly served when the bargaining parties are knowledgeable, sophisticated businessmen. Moreover, where the contract explicitly states that the knowledgeable buyer runs the risk of, say, hidden defects (*e.g.,* where the contract says "as is"), the knowledgeable business buyer quite clearly knows what kind of situation he is getting into, and, in all likelihood, it is one (given the price) that he wants.

Under such circumstances, to allow an action under chapter 93A not only fails to serve the Act's main purpose but indeed may harm those whom the Act seeks to protect. To insist that the knowledgeable business seller disclose all material facts that the seller "should have" known (to forbid, in effect, the "as is" contract), is to prevent the buyer and seller from allocating costs and risks as they choose in both the presumably rare situation involving deceptive conduct by the seller and the more typical *non*deceptive situation. And, such a prohibition, as a general matter, may raise the price of the underlying good or service by preventing the allocation of risks (*e.g.,* of hidden defects) to the party willing to bear them most cheaply. Of course, one may think of this general price-increasing tendency as too theoretical, as ephemeral, or not worth much consideration when consumer protection is on the other side of the balance scale; but, it is, at the least, worth consideration when weighed against the need to protect those who typically need no protection (such as knowledgeable business buyers).

Third, there might be some justification for refusing to enforce an "as is" clause if the contract were ambiguous in some way that cast doubt on whether the buyer truly intended to waive his remedies against the seller. In such a case one might hesitate to find a waiver regardless of the knowledge or sophistication of the buyers. But this is not such a case: the "as is" clause in the Texaco-VSH contract could not be more clear.

* * *

The legal support for the majority's position consists of the Attorney General's regulation, which literally applies to *all* transactions, making no exception for "as is" business sales. There is no indication, however, that the Attorney General considered the "as is" business transaction when writing the regulation. At the same time, to apply the regulation literally makes a different statute—the UCC "as is" provision, § 2–316(3)(a)—nearly meaningless and seems not to further the purposes of chapter 93A. It is a common thing for statutes, rules, and regulations that purport to apply in 'all' circumstances, in fact to contain implied exceptions. . . . Under these circumstances, I agree with the district court that the regulation was not meant to override Massachusetts policy permitting "as is" contracts, at least where the contract language is clear, the contract is made by knowledgeable business parties, and the contract is untainted by any affirmative misrepresentation, fraud, or otherwise unlawful conduct.

For these reasons, I agree only in part with the panel majority.

NOTES

(1)   *The Tort of Deceit.* The common law action for deceit, also referred to as fraudulent misrepresentation, has the following elements:

> Generally, in a claim for fraudulent misrepresentation, a plaintiff must allege a misrepresentation or a material omission of fact which was false and known to be false by defendant, made for the purpose of inducing the other party to rely upon it, justifiable reliance of the other party on the misrepresentation or material omission, and injury.

Mandarin Trading Ltd. v. Wildenstein, 16 N.Y.3d 173, 178 (2011) (internal quotation marks omitted). Although the New York Court doesn't mention it, recklessness typically suffices in lieu of knowledge of falsity. What are the similarities and differences from the elements for the defense of misrepresentation in contract law as listed in Restatement (Second) § 164? Why the differences? Because it is an intentional tort, a finding of deceit can expose the defendant not only to compensatory damages, but also to punitive damages.

(2)   *State UDAP Statutes.* In the second half of the twentieth century, most states and other US jurisdictions passed unfair and deceptive acts and practices statutes, many modeled on the Federal Trade Commission Act. There are, however, large differences between the statutes and judicial interpretations of them in the various states. Most states task the state attorney general with enforcement of the statute, but also provide for private enforcement actions.

Like the tort of deceit, UDAP statutes also provide plaintiffs with the possibility of both compensatory and extracompensatory damages. The Massachusetts law, for example, provides:

> [I]f the court finds for the petitioner, recovery shall be in the amount of actual damages or twenty-five dollars, whichever is greater; or up to three but not less than two times such amount if the court finds that the use or employment of the act or practice was a willful or knowing violation of said section two or that the refusal to grant relief upon demand was made in bad faith with knowledge or reason to know that the act or practice complained of violated said section two.

Mass. Gen. Laws Ann. ch. 93A, § 9.

(3)   *Half-Truths, Nondisclosure and "As Is."* What is the difference between the V.S.H. Realty's claim of fraudulent misrepresentation and its claim that Texaco violated Massachusetts's UDAP statute?

The majority held that the "as is" clause in the sales agreement insulated the seller neither against liability in tort for its half-truths nor against liability under the UDAP statute for nondisclosure. Justice Breyer disagreed on the latter point. Why might one want to treat the effects of an "as is" clause differently for the two claims? Why not read an "as is" clause to shield parties from liability in tort or under a UDAP statute? See

Comment: Limitations on Liability for Misrepresentation, supra Chapter Four, Section 7.

Comment: Misrepresentation of Intent to Perform—Promissory Fraud

Basic Principles. Courts have long held under the doctrine of promissory fraud that a promise that the promisor does not intend to perform can satisfy the elements of deceit.

At first blush the doctrine might seem to be a non sequitur. Promising to perform in the future does not involve a representation of an existing fact. It is, rather, the undertaking of an obligation. How can the mere act of promising count as a misrepresentation? The answer, according to courts, is that the act of promising implicitly represents a *present intent* to perform the promise. And, as Lord Bowen opined, "The state of a man's mind is as much a fact as the state of his digestion." Edgington v. Fitzmaurice, 29 Ch. D. 459 (1885). The drafters of the Second Restatement of Torts stated the well accepted rule regarding such representations: "Since a promise necessarily carries with it the implied assertion of an intention to perform it follows that a promise made without such an intention is fraudulent." Restatement (Second) of Torts § 530 cmt. c. The Second Restatement of Contracts is less categorical: "If it is reasonable to do so, the promisee may properly interpret a promise as an assertion that the promisor intends to perform the promise." Restatement (Second) § 171(2). Courts generally follow the more categorical rule described in the Torts Restatement. Thus, if the promisor in fact does not intend to perform her promise, she has misrepresented her intent.

That said, the common law has been leery about giving promisees an open-ended opportunity to convert every breach of contract into a claim for punitive damages. The critical hurdle in any promissory fraud case is providing proof of the promisor's intent *at the time of formation.* Did Donald Trump really intend to build and have Mexico pay for a 2,000-mile wall when he promised during his campaign to do so? See Stephen D. Sencer, Note, *Read My Lips: Examining the Legal Implications of Knowingly False Campaign Promises*, 90 Mich. L. Rev. 428 (1991). Courts infer an initial lack of intent to perform on the basis of the following sorts of facts:

(i) lack of changed circumstances between time of promising and time of breach, as well as a short time between promise and breach;

(ii) a pattern of repeated breaching over time (for example, Herald Hill's promise in *The Music Man* to train a boy's band, or the hundreds of breached cremation promises by a Georgia funeral home);

(iii) impossibility of performance at time of promising;

(iv) internal documents indicating no intent to perform.

See Ian Ayres and Gregory Klass, Insincere Promises: The Law of Misrepresented Intent, Chapter Six, 113–41 (2005).

Judge Posner on Illinois's Scheme to Defraud Requirement. The concern that plaintiffs will use promissory fraud claims as a catch-all method of securing punitive damages has led Illinois to require plaintiffs to prove a "scheme to defraud." Judge Posner explained the requirement: "By requiring that the plaintiff show a pattern, by thus not letting him rest on proving a single promise, the law reduces the likelihood of a spurious suit; for a series of unfulfilled promises is better (though of course not conclusive) evidence of fraud than a single unfulfilled promise." Speakers of Sport, Inc. v. ProServ, Inc., 178 F.3d 862 (7th Cir. 1999).

Justice Holmes on Promissory Fraud and Bailey v. Alabama. Recall the famous "Holmesian heresy," discussed in Chapter One: "The duty to keep a contract at common law means a prediction that you must pay damages if you do not keep it,—and nothing else." Oliver Wendell Holmes, *The Path of the Law*, 10 Harv. L. Rev. 457 (1897), reprinted in 110 Harv. L. Rev. 991, 995 (1997). An adherent of this view might argue that a promisor does not implicitly represent an intent to perform the promise but, at most, an intent to perform or pay damages. And in fact, there are plenty of contexts where entering into a contract would not seem to represent an intent to perform. Merger agreements often include "breakup fees," which stipulate the damages should the shareholders reject the tender. Or think about sending in a tuition deposit to one's backup law school. Perhaps the Contracts Restatement approach is the better one: a promise represents an intent to perform only "where it is reasonable" to so interpret it. See Ayres and Klass, Insincere Promises, Chapters Two and Five, 19–45, 83–112.

In *Bailey v. Alabama*, 219 U.S. 219 (1911), however, Justice Holmes voted to affirm the conviction of an African American worker who had taken a $15 signing bonus to work for a year and then breached after a little more than a month without paying back the bonus. The Alabama criminal statute in question provided that any person who, "with intent to injure or defraud his employer" enters into a written labor contract and gets money in advance from the employer; and who then, "without refunding such money . . . refuses or fails to perform such . . . service," can be punished by a fine of double the damages suffered by the injured person. Half of the fine goes to the county, half to the "injured party." The act also established that (i) the refusal to perform or refund advanced money "shall be *prima facie* evidence of the intent to" defraud the employer, and (ii) the worker was not allowed to testify "as to his uncommunicated motives, purpose or intention." Holmes in dissent reasoned that the statute was not constitutionally infirm:

I think it a mistake to say that this statute attaches its punishment to the mere breach of a contract to labor. It does not purport to do so; what it purports to punish is fraudulently obtaining money by a false pretense of an intent to keep the written contract in consideration of which the money is advanced. (It is not necessary to cite cases to show that such an intent may be the subject of a material false representation.) But the import of the statute is supposed to be changed by the provision that a refusal to perform, coupled with a failure to return the money advanced, shall be *prima facie* evidence of fraudulent intent. I agree that if the statute created a conclusive presumption it might be held to make a disguised change in the substantive law. . . . But it only makes the conduct *prima facie* evidence,—a very different matter. Is it not evidence that a man had a fraudulent intent if he receives an advance upon a contract over night and leaves in the morning? I should have thought that it very plainly was. * * * For *prima facie* evidence is only evidence, and as such may be held by the jury insufficient to make out guilt. * * *

I do not see how the result that I have reached thus far is affected by the rule . . . that the prisoner cannot testify to his uncommunicated intentions, and therefore, it is assumed, would not be permitted to offer a naked denial of an intent to defraud. If there is an excuse for breaking the contract it will be found in external circumstances, and can be proved. * * *

To sum up, I think that obtaining money by fraud may be made a crime as well as murder or theft; that a false representation, expressed or implied, at the time of making a contract of labor that one intends to perform it and thereby obtaining an advance, may be declared a case of fraudulently obtaining money as well as any other; that if made a crime it may be punished like any other crime, and that an unjustified departure from the promised service without repayment may be declared a sufficient case to go to the jury for their judgment; all without in any way infringing the Thirteenth Amendment or the statutes of the United States.

219 U.S. at 247–50. Holmes, unfortunately, failed to acknowledge the racial dimensions of this case. There was evidence that Alabama was enforcing the criminal provisions of the statute almost exclusively against African Americans as a way of preventing their movement and depressing their wages. See Jennifer Roback, *Southern Labor Law in the Jim Crow Era: Exploitative or Competitive?* 51 U. Chi. L. Rev. 1161 (1984). The application of promissory fraud law in Alabama at the time was another example of a facially neutral rule being put to discriminatory purposes. See also Comment: The Gendered Origins of the Lumley Doctrine, infra Chapter Six, Section 4.

Promissory Fraud and the Written Word. In *Pinnacle Peak Developers v. TRW Inv. Corp.*, 631 P.2d 540 (Ariz. App. 1980), then Judge

Sandra Day O'Connor addressed the relationship between promissory fraud and promises that were not otherwise enforceable because of the Statute of Frauds or the parol evidence rule.

A summary of the problem raised in a case such as this one is succinctly stated in James and Gray, Misrepresentation (pt. II), 37 Md. Law Rev. 488, at 507–08 (1978):

> Although the notion of promissory fraud is well recognized, it may seriously collide with the policies underlying certain prophylactic legal rules like the Statute of Frauds and the parol evidence rule. Both these rules are designed to prevent fraudulent claims (or defenses) through excluding a type of evidence (viz., evidence of oral agreement) which is too easy to fabricate and too hard to meet. It could go without saying that these rules are not meant to shield fraud, but they may well have just that effect if they prevent a party from showing that he has been deceived by an oral promise, made to induce reliance and action but without the slightest intention of keeping it. Many courts allow oral proof of fraud in such a case and this seems sound because the affirmative burden of proving fraud (i.e., present intent not to keep the promise when it was made, or even the absence of an intent to keep it) would seem to be a substantial safeguard against trumped-up contracts. Moreover, the safeguard is enhanced by the prevailing procedural rules requiring clear and convincing evidence of fraud and holding that the mere nonperformance of a contract does not warrant an inference of the requisite fraudulent intent.

The cases from other states are split widely on whether to permit parol evidence which contradicts a writing when fraud in the inducement is alleged. A number of courts appear to follow the Restatement of Contracts § 238 (1932), and allow evidence of promissory fraud, notwithstanding the parol evidence rule. . . . Other courts exclude evidence of promissory fraud which contradicts the terms of the written agreement on the basis of the parol evidence rule. . . .

> The debate involves the question: is the public better served by giving effect to the parties' entire agreement written and oral, even at the risk of injustice caused by the possibility of perjury . . . , or does the security of transactions require that, despite occasional injustices, persons adopting a formal writing be required, on the penalty of voidness of their oral and written side agreements, to put their entire agreement in the formal writing?

Calamari and Perillo, A Plea For a Uniform Parol Evidence Rule and Principles of Contract Interpretation, 42 Indiana L.J. 333, 341 (1967).

* * *

A case by case study of a large number of cases nationwide dealing with the application of the parol evidence rule . . . indicate[s] that, in practice, courts generally apply the parol evidence rule to exclude allegations of prior or contemporaneous oral promises which contradict the written agreement in cases involving "formal contracts" which were the result of negotiation between parties with some expertise and business sophistication. . . . There is a much greater tendency in the reported cases to allow such evidence in "informal contracts" between people who lack sophistication in business. . . . In cases involving abuse of the bargaining process, such as unconscionable contracts or contracts involving duress, the courts almost always disregard the parol evidence rule and allow evidence of the oral promises or representations.

The pleadings and affidavits in this case reflect that the parties each had experience in business transactions and that the written option agreement was prepared as the result of negotiations between the parties, who were represented by counsel. It involved a relatively substantial and sophisticated real estate transaction. The written option agreement was a "formal contract." The contradiction of the written agreement and the oral representation is clear. . . . The facts are such that courts in most jurisdictions would exclude the evidence of the prior oral statement on the basis of a strict application of the parol evidence rule. It is our opinion on rehearing that the trial court correctly granted summary judgment to appellee on Count II quieting title to the property covered by the option agreement in appellee.

The application of the parol evidence rule moves along a continuum based on the extent of the contradiction and the relative strength and sophistication of the parties and their negotiations. . . . There are circumstances under which evidence of a prior or contemporaneous contradictory oral representation or promise would be admissible notwithstanding the subsequent integrated written agreement of the parties. . . .

631 P.2d at 544–48.

Promissory Fraud in Other Contexts. Colorable issues of promissory fraud arise in many other cases contained in this casebook. See Peevyhouse v. Garland Coal & Min Co., Chapter Six (promised land restoration perhaps known to be infeasible); Hoffman v. Red Owl Stores, Chapter Three (repeated assurances that franchise would be offered with no excuse for failure to perform); Alaska Packers' Ass'n v. Domenico, Chapter Two (employer promised modification that employer might not have intended to perform).

Promising might also implicitly represent that (i) the promisor believes that her performance is probable, and (ii) the promisor intends to compensate promisee if she breaches. See Ayres and Klass, Insincere Promises: The Law of Misrepresented Intent (2005).

All-Tech Telecom, Inc. v. Amway Corporation

United States Court of Appeals, Seventh Circuit, 1999.
174 F.3d 862.

■ POSNER, CHIEF JUDGE. A disappointed plaintiff, All-Tech Telecom, appeals from the district court's grant of summary judgment to the defendant, Amway, on All-Tech's claims of intentional and negligent misrepresentation and promissory estoppel. All-Tech was allowed to get to the jury on claims of breach of warranty, and the jury found a breach but awarded no damages. There is no challenge to the jury's verdict, only to the grant of summary judgment on the other claims. The basis of federal jurisdiction is diversity of citizenship, and the parties agree that the substantive issues are governed by Wisconsin law. * * *

[Amway, the defendant, offered a credit card based pay telephone called the TeleCharge phone to its distributors (which included the plaintiff, All-Tech). The plaintiff, All-Tech was created for the purpose of serving as an Amway distributor of TeleCharge phones. All-Tech had purchased a large number of units when Amway withdrew from the market. All-Tech claims that it relied to its detriment (in buying a large number of units) upon a series of misrepresentations by Amway regarding estimated revenue, product quality, and technical support.]

The district court threw out All-Tech's claims of misrepresentation on the basis of the "economic loss" doctrine of the common law. Originally this doctrine was merely a limitation on who could bring a tort suit for the consequences of a personal injury or damage to property: only the injured person himself, or the owner of the damaged property himself, and not also persons having commercial links to the owner, such as employees or suppliers of a merchant whose store was burned down as a result of the negligence of a third party, the tort defendant. . . . Since damage to property and even to person is a real cost and hence "economic," the doctrine would be better named the "commercial loss" doctrine. . . .

One explanation for it is that a tort may have indirect consequences that are beneficial—in the example just given, to competitors of the burned-down store—as well as harmful, and since the tortfeasor is not entitled to sue for the benefits, neither should he have to pay for the losses. . . . Another and less esoteric explanation is the desirability of confining remedies for contract-type losses to contract law. Suppliers injured in their pocketbook because of a fire at the shop of a retailer who buys and distributes their goods sustain the kind of purely business loss familiarly encountered in contract law, rather than the physical harm, whether to person or to property, with which tort law is centrally concerned. These suppliers can protect themselves from the loss caused them by the fire by buying business-loss insurance, by charging a higher price, or by including in their contract with the retailer a requirement that he buy a minimum quantity of goods from the supplier, regardless. The suppliers thus don't need a tort remedy. . . .

This point has implications for commercial fraud as well as for business losses that are secondary to physical harms to person or property. Where there are well-developed contractual remedies, such as the remedies that the Uniform Commercial Code (in force in all U.S. states) provides for breach of warranty of the quality, fitness, or specifications of goods, there is no need to provide tort remedies for misrepresentation. The tort remedies would duplicate the contract remedies, adding unnecessary complexity to the law. Worse, the provision of these duplicative tort remedies would undermine contract law. That law has been shaped by a tension between a policy of making the jury the normal body for resolving factual disputes and the desire of parties to contracts to be able to rely on the written word and not be exposed to the unpredictable reactions of lay factfinders to witnesses who testify that the contract means something different from what it says. Many doctrines of contract law, such as the parol evidence and "four corners" rules, are designed to limit the scope of jury trial of contract disputes (another example is the statute of frauds). Tort law does not have these screens against the vagaries of the jury. In recognition of this omission, the "economic loss" doctrine in the form invoked by the district judge in this case on the authority of a growing body of case law . . . forbids commercial contracting parties (as distinct from consumers, and other individuals not engaged in business) to escalate their contract dispute into a charge of tortious misrepresentation if they could easily have protected themselves from the misrepresentation of which they now complain. * * *

The function of the economic-loss doctrine in confining contract parties to their contractual remedies is particularly well illustrated by cases involving product warranties. . . . If the seller makes an oral representation that is important to the buyer, the latter has only to insist that the seller embody that representation in a written warranty. The warranty will protect the buyer, who will have an adequate remedy under the Uniform Commercial Code if the seller reneges. To allow him to use tort law in effect to enforce an oral warranty would unsettle contracts by exposing sellers to the risk of being held liable by a jury on the basis of self-interested oral testimony and perhaps made to pay punitive as well as compensatory damages. This menace is averted by channeling disputes into warranty (contract) law, where oral warranties can be expressly disclaimed, or extinguished by operation of the parol evidence rule. UCC §§ 2–202, 2–316(1) and comment 2; 1 James J. White & Robert S. Summers, *Uniform Commercial Code*, § 12–4 (3d ed. 1988). It is true that, in principle, the cheapest way to prevent fraud is to punish the fraudfeasor; but in practice, owing to the ever-present possibility of legal error, the really cheapest way in some cases may be to place a burden of taking precautions on the potential victim. Cf. Alon Harel, "Efficiency and Fairness in Criminal Law: The Case for a Criminal Law Principle of Comparative Fault," 82 *Calif. L. Rev.* 1181 (1994).

[The court discussed and doubted whether the economic loss doctrine abolished the tort of fraudulent or deliberate misrepresentation.]

But the representations challenged in this case do not press against the boundaries of the economic-loss doctrine. For they are in the nature of warranties (remember that the plaintiff made warranty claims, which the judge sent to the jury), and we cannot think of a reason why the fact that the "product" warranted was a hybrid of a product and a service should affect the application of the doctrine. A genuine stumbling block to affirming on its basis, however, is the fact that its application to cases of *intentional* misrepresentation is uncertain. *Daanen & Janssen, Inc. v. Cedarapids, Inc.*, 216 Wis.2d 395, 415 (1998), ducks the issue, and we haven't a clue as to how Wisconsin will resolve it. Other jurisdictions have divided over it, Reeder R. Fox & Patrick J. Loftus, "Riding the Choppy Waters of East River: Economic Loss Doctrine Ten Years Later," 64 *Defense Counsel J.* 260, 268–70 (1997), and the balance of the competing considerations is, as we have suggested, close. We need not choose. Amway has a solid alternative ground for affirmance: All-Tech failed to present any evidence of actionable misrepresentation. [The court found that All-Tech had failed to present any evidence of actionable misrepresentation. Moreover, some of the alleged misrepresentations were made by independent contractors, not Amway, and others were "pure puffing" on which no reasonable person would rely. There were, in short, no actionable misrepresentations.]

All-Tech's alternative claim is promissory estoppel. The doctrine of promissory estoppel provides an alternative basis to consideration for treating a promise as a contractual undertaking. When applicable, which to say when the promise is definite enough to induce a reasonable person to rely, . . . the doctrine makes the promise enforceable.

Promises are usually forward-looking; one promises to do something, necessarily in the future. The promise that All-Tech stresses as the basis for its claim of promissory estoppel—that Amway had thoroughly researched the TeleCharge program before offering it to distributors—is not of that character. It warrants a past or existing condition rather than committing to some future action and is thus more precisely described as a warranty than as a promise. UCC § 2–313(1)(a); *Restatement (Second) of Contracts* § 2 comment d (1981); . . . But a warranty is a type of promise—in this case a promise by Amway to pay for the consequences should the research that went into the development of TeleCharge not have been thorough after all. *Metropolitan Coal Co. v. Howard*, 155 F.2d 780, 784 (2d Cir.1946) (L. Hand, J.) (a warranty "amounts to a promise to indemnify the promisee for any loss if the fact warranted proves untrue, for obviously the promisor cannot control what is already in the past"); *Restatement of Contracts* § 2 (1932); cf. Oliver Wendell Holmes, Jr., *The Common Law* 298–301 (1881).

Since a warranty can induce reasonable reliance, its breach can be the basis for a claim of promissory estoppel. But only in limited circumstances. A promisee cannot be permitted to use the doctrine to do an end run around the rule that puffing is not actionable as misrepresentation, or around the parol evidence rule. . . . That rule is as applicable to a suit on an oral warranty as to a suit on any other oral promise. The Uniform Commercial Code is explicit about this. UCC § 2–316(1) and comment 2; . . .

The objections to All-Tech's claim of promissory estoppel are related to our earlier point that the economic-loss doctrine serves to protect contract doctrines and to prevent the piling on of duplicative remedies. Promissory estoppel is meant for cases in which a promise, not being supported by consideration, would be unenforceable under conventional principles of contract law. When there is an express contract governing the relationship out of which the promise emerged, and no issue of consideration, there is no gap in the remedial system for promissory estoppel to fill. . . . To allow it to be invoked becomes in those circumstances gratuitous duplication or, worse, circumvention of carefully designed rules of contract law. In our case the parties had a contract covering the relationship in the course and within the scope of which the alleged warranty of thorough research was made. This either was one of the warranties of the contract or it was not (by virtue of disclaimer, the puffing exemption, or the parol evidence rule). If it was not (and it was not), we cannot think of any reason for using the doctrine of promissory estoppel to resuscitate it. "Promissory estoppel is not a doctrine designed to give a party . . . a second bite at the apple in the event it fails to prove a breach of contract." *Walker v. KFC Corp.*, 728 F.2d 1215, 1220 (9th Cir.1984). * * *

NOTES

(1) Although its origins go back further, the economic loss rule gained prominence with two developments: the emergence of third-party liability for negligence and the expansion of strict product liability. See Dan B. Dobbs, *An Introduction to Non-Statutory Economic Loss Claims*, 48 Ariz. L. Rev. 713 (2006). In 1965 Justice Traynor explained the relation to strict liability as follows:

> Although the rules of warranty frustrate rational compensation for physical injury, they function well in a commercial setting. . . . These rules determine the quality of the product the manufacturer

promises and thereby determine the quality he must deliver. In this case, the truck plaintiff purchased did not function properly in his business. Plaintiff [buyer] therefore seeks to recover his commercial losses: lost profits and the refund of the money he paid on the trunk. White [the seller] is responsible for these losses only because it warranted the truck to be 'free from defects in material and workmanship under normal use and service.' The practical construction of this language by both parties during the eleven months that repairs were attempted establishes that plaintiff's use of the truck was a normal use within the meaning of the warranty. . . . White's failure to comply with its obligation to make "good at its factory any part or parts" of the truck after ample opportunity was given it to do so, entitles plaintiff to recover damages resulting from such breach. Had defendant not warranted the truck, but sold it 'as is,' it should not be liable for the failure of the truck to serve plaintiff's business needs.

Under the doctrine of strict liability in tort, however, the manufacturer would be liable even though it did not agree that the truck would perform as plaintiff wished or expected it to do. In this case, after plaintiff returned the truck, Southern resold it to Mr. Jack Barefield, an experienced trucker. Mr. Bearfield used the truck "to pull a 40-foot band" over state highways. After driving the truck 82,000 miles, testified that he had no unusual difficulty with it. Southern replaced two tires, added a new fifth wheel, and made minor alterations to the truck before reselling it to Mr. Barefield, so that it is possible that it found a cure for the galloping. Southern, however, replaced the tires five times, adjusted the fifth wheel, and made many other changes on the truck during the eleven months plaintiff drove it. Thus, it is more likely that the truck functioned normally when put to use in Mr. Barefield's business because his use made demands upon it different from those made by plaintiff's use. If under these circumstances defendant is strictly liable in tort for the commercial loss suffered by plaintiff, then it would be liable for business losses of other truckers caused by the failure of its trucks to meet the specific needs of their businesses, even though those needs were communicated only to the dealer. Moreover, this liability could not be disclaimed, for one purpose of strict liability in tort is to prevent a manufacturer from defining the scope of his responsibility for harm caused by his products. . . . The manufacturer would be liable for damages of unknown and unlimited scope. Application of the rules of warranty prevents this result. Defendant is liable only because of its agreement as defined by its continuing practice over eleven months. Without an agreement, defined by practice or otherwise, defendant should not be liable for these commercial losses.

Seely v. White Motor Co., 63 Cal. 2d 9, 16–17 (1965).

It is less obvious that the economic loss rule should apply to claims of misrepresentation, negligent or fraudulent. What does Posner's analysis say on the question? Should the answer depend on whether the plaintiff has claimed intentional misrepresentation?

(2) *Promissory Estoppel ... Again!* There are at least three consequences that would flow from the general adoption of Judge Posner's approach to promissory estoppel.

First, despite the tort-like rhetoric in *Cohen v. Cowles Media Co., supra,* an action on a promissory estoppel theory must be in contract rather than in tort where the induced reliance results only in economic loss. Thus, even though the promisor promised intending to induce reliance and even though there is no consent by the promisee, the law of torts does not apply.

Second, there is no place for promissory estoppel where the claimed actionable reliance was in fact bargained for by the promisor. Thus, in *Cohen v. Cowles Media,* if the agreed exchange of Cohen's disclosure for Cowles's promise of confidentiality created a contractual obligation, the presence of consideration would foreclose the use of promissory estoppel. As we shall see, however, there may be promises made within the bargain that induce unbargained-for reliance. A claim in promissory estoppel is proper in these cases.

Third, a party who makes a representation (warranty) that becomes part of a bargain also (according to the court) promises to pay damages if the warranty is not satisfied. For this proposition, Judge Posner relies on language from an opinion by Judge Learned Hand and cites the famous book by Oliver Wendell Holmes, Jr., The Common Law (1881). Put differently, the performer has a choice to satisfy the warranty or to pay damages. But note that this is not a genuine case of promised alternative performances. Arguably, the so-called promise to pay damages on breach is fictional and reflects the view that it is efficient and not immoral to breach a contract and pay damages. Support for this oft-criticized view is found (by some at least) in Holmes's "bad man" theory of law. See Robert Henry, *The Values of Oliver Wendell Holmes,* 5 Green Bag 105 (2001).

Comment: Fraud in the Performance

Courts often distinguish between two types of deceit claims: fraud in the inducement, which involves misrepresentations made before or during formation and is always actionable, and fraud in the performance, which involves misrepresentations between the parties after they have entered into a contract, actions for which face a higher hurdle.

> The distinction [between fraud in the inducement and fraud in the performance] is critical, for the essence of the 'economic loss' rule is that contract law and tort law are separate and distinct, and the courts should maintain that separation in the allowable remedies. There is a danger that tort remedies could simply engulf the contractual remedies and thereby undermine the

reliability of commercial transactions. Once the contract has been made, the parties should be governed by it.

Fraud in the inducement, however, addresses a situation where the claim is that one party was tricked into contracting. It is based on pre-contractual conduct which is, under the law, a recognized tort.

Williams Electric Co. Inc. v. Honeywell, Inc., 772 F.Supp. 1225, 1237–1238 (N.D.Fla., 1991). A leading case in the area is *Huron Tool & Engineering Co. v. Precision Consulting Services.*

> [W]e decline to adopt defendants' position that the economic loss doctrine precludes *any* fraud claim. Fraud in the inducement presents a special situation where parties to a contract appear to negotiate freely—which normally would constitute grounds for invoking the economic loss doctrine—but where in fact the ability of one party to negotiate fair terms and make an informed decision is undermined by the other party's fraudulent behavior. In contrast, where the only misrepresentation by the dishonest party concerns the quality or character of the goods sold, the other party is still free to negotiate warranty and other terms to account for possible defects in the goods.

> The distinction between fraud in the inducement and other kinds of fraud is the same as the distinction drawn by a New Jersey federal district court between fraud extraneous to the contract and fraud interwoven with the breach of contract. *Public Service Enterprise Group, Inc. v. Philadelphia Elec. Co.,* 722 F.Supp. 184, 201 (D.N.J., 1989). With respect to the latter kind of fraud, the misrepresentations relate to the breaching party's performance of the contract and do not give rise to an independent cause of action in tort.

209 Mich. App. 365, 372–73 (1995). For more on the question, see Gregory Klass, *Contracting for Cooperation in Recovery*, 117 Yale L.J. 2, 45–46 (2007); see also Dan B. Dobbs, *An Introduction to Non-Statutory Economic Loss Claims*, 48 Ariz. L. Rev. 713, 728–33 (2006).

But not all courts agree. In *Grynberg v. Citation Oil & Gas Corporation*, 573 N.W.2d 493 (S.D. 1997), South Dakota purported to apply the independent duty rule, but concluded that the defendant, which had misreported its costs in calculating the plaintiffs' royalty payments, had an independent duty to be truthful. "We hold Citation had a duty to the plaintiffs which arose outside the contract obligation, namely, the legal duty which is due from every man to his fellow, to respect his rights of property and refrain from invading them by fraud." *Id.* at 501 (internal punctuation omitted). The court explained its holding as follows:

> We believe there is a policy underpinning our conclusion that punitive damages are appropriate here upon a finding of deceit.

We agree with the reasoning of the North Carolina Supreme Court in *Oestreicher v. American National Stores Inc.*, 290 N.C. 118, 797, 809 (1976):

> In the so-called breach of contract actions that smack of tort because of the fraud and deceit involved, we do not think it is enough just to permit defendant to pay that which the . . . contract required him to pay in the first place. If this were the law, defendant has all to gain and nothing to lose. If he is not caught in his fraudulent scheme, then he is able to retain the resulting dishonest profits. If he is caught, he has only to pay back that which he should have paid in the first place.

To hold otherwise would give parties to a contract a license to steal, undercutting one of the very policy reasons for *withholding* punitives, i.e., to encourage reliance on business agreements. The twin purposes of punitive damages—deterrence and punishment—are well served in a contract where one party commits an intentional tort like deceit.

We have in the past awarded punitive damages for fraudulent inducement of a contract. * * * We find no reason at this point in time to draw a new distinction between fraud in the inducement and a fraud committed during contract performance, since the defrauded party is damaged regardless of when the fraud occurred.

Id. at 502. See also Robinson Helicopter Co. v. Dana Corp., 102 P.3d 268 (Cal. 2004) (holding that a helicopter parts supplier had an independent duty not to falsify contractually required certificates of compliance); Gregory Klass, *Contracting for Cooperation in Recovery*, 117 Yale L.J. 2, 15–18 (2007) (describing the "Catch-22" that the nonbreaching party faces if there is no extracompensatory liability for concealing or lying about breach).

Also, whereas many courts reject claims of fraud in the performance between private parties, the law governing government contracts does just the opposite. Under the False Claims Act, 31 U.S.C. §§ 3729–3733 (2006), submitting to the government a false claim for payment of money or property can be punished with treble damages and fines of between $5,000 and $10,000 per false claim. A claim is false, inter alia, when a party falsely certifies compliance with the contract—when a party falsely says that it has performed. That certification might but need not be express. Under the judicially created implied certification doctrine, the mere act of submitting a request for payment implicitly certifies that the requesting party is not in breach. See, e.g., Ab-Tech Construction v. United States, 31 Fed. Cl. 429, 434 (1994); Mikes v. Straus, 274 F.3d 687, 700 (2d Cir. 2001). In other words, the default is that by submitting a claim for payment, a contractor represents that it is in compliance with the contract. The U.S. Supreme Court has affirmed the implied certification doctrine at least with respect to half-truths—when "a defendant makes representations in submitting a claim but omits its violations of statutory, regulatory, or contractual requirements." Universal Health Servs., Inc. v. United States, 136 S.Ct. 1989, 1999 (2016). For a more in-depth treatment, see Michael Holt & Gregory Klass, *Implied Certification under the False Claims Act*, 41 Pub. Cont. L.J. 1 (2011).

For more on these themes, see Comment: *Seaman's* and Obstructive Breach, infra Chapter Six, Part 3(E).

4. CONDITIONS

(A) EXPRESS CONDITIONS

A condition on a party's contractual obligation means that the obligation is triggered only if the condition is satisfied. For example, because a life insurance company has only made a conditional promise, the insurer's duty to pay is conditional on the insured dying. Or, as we will see, that a restaurant patron's duty to pay is conditional on receiving food.

Conditions serve two broad purposes, which, following Steven Burton and Eric Anderson, we refer to as "enforcement" and "performance." *Enforcement conditions* make one side's duties to perform conditional on some level of contractual compliance by the other side. The purpose of enforcement conditions is to "enhance the security of one of the parties by providing incentives for the proper completion of performance or alternatives in its absence." Steven J. Burton & Eric G. Andersen, *The World of a Contract*, 75 Iowa L. Rev. 861 (1990). It might at first seem that the affirmative right to sue for monetary or injunctive relief would provide a stronger incentive than the defensive right to withhold your own performance. But by relieving the promisee of its duty to perform, the failure of an enforcement condition can work a great forfeiture to the non-performing promisor. For example, if a condition to a buyer's duty to pay is that the seller tender goods that perfectly comply with the terms of the agreement, then a slight deviation in performance could potentially relieve the buyer from any contractual obligation to pay for goods in its possession (although non-contractual or quasi-contractual bases such as restitution may pertain). In some contexts, the defensive protection of being able to withhold your own performance might therefore provide stronger assurance that the other side will perform her promises than the offensive right to be able to sue for damages or specific performance. But we will also see that common law courts have developed a number of ways to avoid such forfeitures.

Performance conditions typically do not make one side's duty to perform conditional on the performance of the other side, but on external conditions. The purpose of performance conditions is to either provide insurance or to limit the parties' duties to circumstances in which there are likely to be gains of trade. The life insurance example mentioned above is an example of a performance condition. The conditional duty of the insurer to pay a claim is not an enforcement condition. (The insured does not have a duty to die!) Rather the insurance function balances an unconditional premium payment against a conditional duty to pay claims. In contrast, the original contract might make both parties' duties conditional on events that are likely to impact the cost of performing or the benefits from the other side's performance. Thus, Target might contract to buy Yankees t-shirts conditional upon the Yankees winning the World Series. Or an oil company might make its promise to supply conditional upon Iran not shutting down the Strait of Hormuz.

Just as promises and representations might be express or implied, so too conditions might be express or implied. As we shall see, some implied conditions are legal defaults that pertain unless displaced by party conduct. Indeed, the substantial performance rule (which we will learn below in *Jacob & Youngs v. Kent*) is a default enforcement condition that makes a buyer's duty to pay conditional on the seller's substantial and innocent performance. In contrast, the law of impracticability, which we discuss in the next section, can be thought of as a default performance condition, making sellers duty to perform conditional on their performance not becoming impracticable.

(1) NATURE AND EFFECT

Suppose that Uncle, a noted historian, has a nephew in law school and that Nephew has absolutely no interest in "cultural" courses, such as legal history or jurisprudence. After an appropriate bit of bargaining, Uncle induces Nephew to promise to take Professor Holmes' course in Common Law Miracles by promising to pay him $500, "provided that he take the course for a grade and earn a grade of B or better." Nephew takes the course and earns a grade of C+. What is the legal position of the parties at this point? Can Uncle, if he chooses, refuse to pay the $500 without liability for breach of contract?

The argument on each side might run something like this. Uncle will argue that the "B or better" requirement was an express condition to his duty to pay $500. In Restatement (Second) parlance, it was "an event, not certain to occur, which must occur, unless its non-occurrence is excused, before performance under a contract becomes due." Restatement (Second) § 224. See, generally, Arthur Corbin, *Conditions in the Law of Contracts,* 28 Yale L.J. 739 (1919). Moreover, the event was made a condition "by agreement of the parties." Restatement (Second) § 226. Since the event did *not* occur (Nephew earned a C+), two legal consequences follow: first, Uncle's unconditional duty to pay $500 never arose; and second, the duty (and, thus, the contract) is discharged "when the condition can no longer occur." Restatement (Second) § 225(1)–(2). Uncle's legal position is purely defensive—he avoids the duty to pay because the condition failed. As a consequence, Nephew bears the risk of the investment to earn "B or better" in a situation where Uncle has received no tangible benefit from that effort.

Nephew's counter-arguments, most of which will emerge more clearly in the materials to follow, might take these forms: (1) The event was not a condition at all. Rather, it was a matter of convenience that did not affect the rights and duties of the parties. (2) The event was promised by Nephew as a part of the agreed exchange. Although Uncle's duty to pay is "constructively" conditioned upon performance of the promise, the "constructive" condition is satisfied by substantial rather than literal compliance. In short, C+ is close enough. (3) The condition was excused, i.e., deleted from the agreement, either because Uncle "waived it" or because its excuse is necessary to avoid forfeiture.

With these arguments in mind, consider the following materials. After due consideration, who has the better of it, Uncle or Nephew?

Mark Dove v. Rose Acre Farms, Inc.

Court of Appeals of Indiana, First District, 1982.
434 N.E.2d 931.

■ NEAL, JUDGE. Plaintiff—appellant Mark Dove (Dove) appeals a negative judgment of the Decatur Circuit Court in favor of defendant-appellee Rose Acre Farms, Inc. in a trial before the court without the intervention of a jury.

We affirm.

STATEMENT OF THE FACTS

The evidence most favorable to support the judgment and the facts found specially by the trial court are as follows. Dove had been employed by Rose Acre Farms, operated by David Rust (Rust), its president and principal owner, in the summers and other times from 1972 to 1979. The business of Rose Acre was the production of eggs, and, stocked with 4,000,000 hens and staffed with 300 employees, it produced approximately 256,000 dozen eggs per day. Rust had instituted and maintained extensive bonus programs, some of which were for one day only, or one event or activity only. For example, one bonus was the white car bonus; if an employee would buy a new white car, keep it clean and undamaged, place a Rose Acre sign on it, commit no tardiness or absenteeism, and attend one management meeting per month, Rose Acre would pay $100 per month for 36 months as a bonus above and beyond the employee's regular salary, to apply on payments. Any slight violation, such as being a minute late for work, driving a dirty or damaged car, or missing work for any cause, would work a forfeiture of the bonus. Other bonuses consisted of egg production bonuses, deed conversion bonuses, house management bonuses, and a silver feather bonus. This last bonus program required the participant to wear a silver feather, and a system of rewards and penalties existed for employees who participated. While the conditions of the bonuses varied, one condition existed in all bonus programs: during the period of the bonus, the employee must not be tardy for even a minute, and must not miss work any day for any cause whatever, even illness. If the employee missed any days during the week, he was sometimes permitted to make them up on Saturday and/or Sunday. Any missed work not made up within the same week worked a forfeiture of the bonus. These rules were explained to the employees and were stated in a written policy. The bonus programs were voluntary, and all the employees did not choose to participate in them. When a bonus was offered a card was issued to the participant stating his name and the terms and amount of the bonus. Upon completion of the required tasks, the card was attached to the pay sheet, and the bonus was added to the paycheck. Rust was strict about tardiness and absenteeism, whether an employee was on a bonus program or not. If an employee was tardy, his pay would be docked to the minimum wage, or he would be sent home and lose an entire day. A minute's tardiness would also deprive the employee of a day for purposes of seniority. As was stated in the evidence, bonuses were given for the "extra mile" or actions "above and beyond the call of duty." The purpose of the bonus programs and penalties was to discourage absenteeism and tardiness, and to promote motivation and dependability.

In June 1979, Rust called in Dove and other construction crew leaders and offered a bonus of $6,000 each if certain detailed construction work was completed in 12 weeks. As Dove conceded in his own testimony, the bonus card indicated that in addition to completing the work, he would be required to work at least five full days a week for 12 weeks to qualify for the bonus. On the same day Dove's bonus agreement, by mutual consent, was amended to ten weeks with a bonus of $5,000 to enable him to return to law school by September 1. Dove testified that there was no ambiguity in the agreement, and he understood that to qualify for the bonus he would have to work ten weeks, five days a week, commencing at starting time and quitting only at quitting time. Dove testified that he was aware of the provisions concerning absenteeism and tardiness as they affected bonuses, and that if he missed any work, for any reason, including illness, he would forfeit the bonus. The evidence disclosed that no exception had ever been made except as may have occurred by clerical error or inadvertence.

In the tenth week Dove came down with strep throat. On Thursday of that week he reported to work with a temperature of 104°, and told Rust that he was unable to work. Rust told him, in effect, that if he went home, he would forfeit the bonus. Rust offered him the opportunity to stay there and lay on a couch, or make up his lost days on Saturday and/or Sunday. Rust told him he could sleep and still qualify for the bonus. Dove left to seek medical treatment and missed two days in the tenth week of the bonus program.

Rust refused Dove the bonus based solely upon his missing the two days of work. While there was some question of whether the construction job was finished, Rust does not seem to have made that issue the basis of his refusal. Bonuses to other crew leaders were paid. The trial court denied Dove's recovery and, in the conclusions of law, stated that Dove had not shown that all of the conditions of the bonus contract had been met. Specifically, Dove failed to work five full days a week for ten weeks.

* * *

Dove argues that the bonus agreement was implemented to (1) insure his presence on the construction site, and (2) cut the cost of construction through maximum production by workers. He next contends that Rose Acre got what it bargained for, that is the completion of the project. He argues that he was present on the job, including the hours he worked late, at least 750 hours during the ten weeks, while regular working hours would amount to only 500 hours. Therefore, he concludes, there was substantial compliance with the agreement, and he should not be penalized because he failed to appear on the last two days because of illness.

* * *

We are constrained to observe, in the case before us, that the bonus rules at Rose Acre were well known to Dove when he agreed to the disputed bonus contract. He certainly knew Rust's strict policies and knew that any absence for any cause whatever worked a forfeiture of the bonus. With this knowledge he willingly entered into this bonus arrangement, as he had done in the past * * *; he must be held to have agreed to all of the terms upon which the bonus was conditioned. If the conditions were unnecessarily harsh or eccentric, and the terms odious, he could have shown his disdain by simply declining to participate, for participation in the bonus program was not obligatory or job dependent.

Contrary to Dove's assertion that completion of a task was the central element of the bonus program, we are of the opinion that the rules regarding tardiness and absenteeism were a central theme. Rust stated that the purpose of the bonus program was to discourage tardiness and absenteeism and to promote motivation and dependability. Indeed, some of the bonus programs such as the white car bonus and the silver feather bonus were apparently an effort on the part of Rust to establish among the employees an identity with Rose Acre and to create an *esprit de corps*. The direct tangible benefits to Rose Acre would be unmeasurable, and the burden upon the employees would be equally unmeasurable. Yet, Rust was willing to pay substantial bonuses in the implementation of his program, and the employees, including Dove, were quite as willing to take the money.

No fraud or bad faith has been shown on the part of Rose Acre, and no public policy arguments have been advanced to demonstrate why the bonus contract should not be enforced as agreed between the parties. * * *

Dove argues that he should be relieved of strict performance because his illness rendered his performance impossible.

[The court discussed and distinguished two cases]

None of these cases involved a contract for personal services, though dicta contained general language applicable to such contracts. Generally, impossibility of performance is a defense to an action for damages. . . . Dove has not demonstrated how the doctrine is applicable here. Certainly a plaintiff cannot, upon failing to perform his part of the contract, sue his adversary for damages alleging that his own non-performance was because of impossibility. Suppose Dove, because of illness, could not work at all. Could he sue for wages? * * *

For the reasons given above, we hold that Dove failed to perform all of the conditions of the contract and is not entitled to recover any portion of the bonus. The judgment is affirmed.

NOTES

(1) What is the condition in *Dove?* What was the legal effect of its non-occurrence? Is it relevant that the condition was a performance by Dove that was necessary to create a bonus contract?

(2) Dove's claim was not frivolous. Restatement (Second) § 229 provides: "To the extent that the non-occurrence of a condition would cause disproportionate forfeiture, a court may excuse the non-occurrence of that condition unless its occurrence was a material part of the agreed exchange." Was not Dove's loss of the $5,000 bonus after working 750 hours disproportionate to the costs to Rose Acre Farms of two days of Dove's work due to his illness? How does the court avoid this result?

(3) *Condition Precedent and Condition Subsequent.* A standard classification is based on the distinction between conditions that are "precedent" and those that are "subsequent." The reference point is the accrual of the cause of action; i.e., the point in time when the obligor is under a duty to render an immediate performance. Conditions precedent must be satisfied before a contractual duty of this type comes into existence; the effect of the occurrence of a condition subsequent is to extinguish or discharge such a duty. For example, in *Abolin v. Farmers' American Mutual Fire Insurance Co.*, 100 Pa.Super. 433 (1930), a fire insurance policy provided that "no suit or action on this policy for the recovery of any claim shall be sustainable in any court of law or equity * * * unless commenced within twelve months next after the fire * * * for which claim is made." After a fire occurred and proof of loss was made, both conditions precedent, the company was under a duty to make payment. But payment was not made, and the insured did not bring suit to collect within twelve months of the fire. Applying the foregoing provision, the court denied recovery. The company's duty was discharged by the failure to bring suit within the stipulated period. Such failure, in traditional usage, amounts to the occurrence of a condition subsequent in the contract.

Conditions subsequent are comparatively rare in contracts, and at times conditions which courts treat as "subsequent" are in fact clearly "precedent." See, e.g., Capitol Land Co. v. Zorn, 134 Ind.App. 431 (1962). Noting the relationship of the traditional condition subsequent to the discharge of obligation, the drafters of Restatement (Second) do not use the term and confine their use of "condition" to those of the precedent variety. See Restatement (Second) § 224 cmt. e, § 230 cmt. a.

The need for distinguishing between events which are "precedent" and "subsequent" in the above sense derives from procedural requirements. Under Rule 9(c) of the Federal Rules of Civil Procedure it is sufficient that the plaintiff allege generally in the complaint that all conditions precedent have been performed or have occurred. The defendant, on the other hand, is obliged to deny specifically and with particularity that they have not. A failure to plead accordingly will prevent using the failure of condition as a defense in the federal courts. See, e.g., Ginsburg v. Insurance Co. of N. Am., 427 F.2d 1318, 1321–22 (6th Cir.1970). Rule 9(c) does not apply to conditions subsequent. Crosney v. Edward Small Prods., 52 F. Supp. 559, 561 (S.D.N.Y. 1942). Federal courts take a different approach to conditions subsequent. If a defendant fails in a required responsive pleading to raise an issue regarding the existence of a condition subsequent, that party may not later rely on the condition subsequent as a defense. Title Guar. & Sur. Co. v. Nichols, 224 U.S. 346 (1912). Since several states have promulgated pleading requirements based on the Federal Rules or have comparable provisions relative to the pleading of conditions, similar alertness is demanded in other jurisdictions. See, e.g., Travers v. Travelers Ins. Co., 385 Mass. 811 (1982).

In re Carter's Claim
Supreme Court of Pennsylvania, 1957.
390 Pa. 365.

■ JONES, JUSTICE. This is an appeal from a judgment entered upon an arbitrator's award in a proceeding under the Act of 1927.[1]

In June 1954 the Edwin J. Schoettle Co., a Pennsylvania corporation, and its six subsidiaries were available for purchase. Lester L. Kardon, interested in purchasing the company and five of its subsidiaries, opened negotiations for that purpose. The negotiations extended from June 24, 1954 to September 17, 1954, on which latter date the parties entered into a written agreement under the terms of which Kardon (hereinafter called the buyer) purchased all the issued and outstanding capital stock of Schoettle Co. and all its subsidiaries (hereinafter called sellers). The total purchase price set forth in the agreement of sale (excluding certain real estate) was $2,100,000 of which amount $187,863.60 was set aside under paragraph 11 of the agreement to be held by the Provident Trust Company of Philadelphia as escrow

---

[1] Act of April 25, 1927, P.L. 381, No. 247, 5 P.S. § 161 et seq. [This was a Pennsylvania state arbitration act. It was repealed in 1980 when the state legislature adopted the Uniform Arbitration Act (1956).—Eds.]

agent to indemnify the buyer against "the liabilities of sellers by reason of any and all provisions of this agreement."

The present litigation arises from the fact that the buyer has presented a claim against the escrow fund for $69,998.42 as a "liability" of the seller under the agreement. Payment of this claim having been disputed by the sellers, both parties, under the provisions of the agreement, submitted to arbitration and Judge Gerald F. Flood was selected as arbitrator. On October 26, 1956 Judge Flood, as arbitrator, and after hearing, awarded to the buyer $3,182.88. Buyer's motion to correct the arbitrator's award was dismissed by the Court of Common Pleas No. 6 of Philadelphia County and judgment was entered in the amount of $3,182.88 in conformity with the arbitrator's award. From that judgment this appeal ensued.

The resolution of this controversy depends upon the interpretation of certain portions of the 25-page written agreement of September 17, 1954. The pertinent portions of this agreement are paragraphs 5(g), 9(a), 9(b), 9(c), 10(d) and 15, which read as follows:

> "5. *Representations and warranties.* Sellers *represent* and *warrant* as follows: [emphasis supplied] . . . (g) *Absence of certain changes.* Since June 30, 1954, there have not been (i) any changes in Company's or its subsidiaries' financial condition, assets, liabilities, or businesses, other than changes in the ordinary course of business, none of which have been materially adverse, and changes required or permitted hereunder; (ii) any damage, destruction, or loss, whether or not covered by insurance, materially and adversely affecting the properties or businesses of Company and its subsidiaries as an entirety; (iii) any declaration, or setting aside, or payment of any dividend or other distribution in respect of Company's capital stock or that of any subsidiary (except that prior to the date hereof, Company has declared and paid a dividend of Sixteen and Two Thirds Cents ($.16⅔) per share on all issued and outstanding shares of its said capital stock), or any direct or indirect redemption, purchase, or other acquisition of any such stock; or (iv) any increase in the compensation payable or to become payable by Company or any subsidiary to any of their officers, employees, or agents, or any bonus payment or arrangement made to or with any of them.

* * *

> "9. *Conditions precedent.* All obligations of Buyer under this agreement are subject to the fulfillment, prior to or at the closing of each of the following *conditions*: [emphasis supplied]. (a) *Financial condition at closing.* As of the time of closing the financial condition of the Company and its subsidiaries in the aggregate shall be no less favorable than the financial condition shown on the statements of said corporations dated June 30,

1954 and warranted to be true and complete in paragraph 5(e) hereof. (b) *Representations and warranties true at closing.* Sellers' representations and warranties contained in this agreement shall be true at the time of closing as though such representations and warranties were made at such time. (c) *Performance.* Sellers shall have performed and complied with all agreements and conditions required by this agreement to be performed or complied with by them prior to or at the closing.

* * *

"10. *Indemnification.* Sellers shall indemnify and hold harmless Buyer, subject to the limitations of paragraph 11 hereof, against and in respect of: * * * (d) any damage or deficiency resulting from any misrepresentation, breach of warranty, or nonfulfillment of any agreement on the part of Sellers, or any of them, under this agreement, or from any misrepresentation in or omission from any certificate or other instrument furnished or to be furnished to Buyer hereunder;

* * *

"15. *Survival of representations.* All representations, warranties and agreements made by Sellers and Buyer in this agreement or pursuant hereto shall survive closing, subject to the provisions of paragraph 11 hereof."

The buyer (appellant) contends that the financial condition on the date of purchase—September 17, 1954—was less favorable than that reflected in the company's financial statement of June 30, 1954 and, therefore, he is entitled to reimbursement out of the escrow fund for the amount of the deficiency. Sellers (appellees) deny any reduction in the financial condition and further argue that, even if there were any reduction, buyer has no right to reimbursement under the agreement unless such reduction resulted from occurrences outside the ordinary course of business or which caused a materially adverse change in the company's financial condition. Actually the buyer's position is that paragraph 9(a), supra, constituted a "warranty" on the sellers' part that the financial condition of the company and its subsidiaries was not less favorable than demonstrated by the financial statement of June 30, 1954 and, therefore, sellers having breached the warranty the buyer is entitled to claim the difference between the net worth on June 30, 1954 and September 17, 1954. On the other hand, sellers take the position that their engagement under paragraph 9(a) constituted a "condition" and not a warranty and the buyer had simply the right to refuse a consummation of the sale if the "condition" was not fulfilled; when the buyer elected to consummate the sale it waived the "condition."

* * *

This written agreement was carefully and meticulously prepared by able and competent counsel after long and thorough negotiations. Each general paragraph of the agreement is headed by a title descriptive of the contents of each paragraph. Paragraph 5, entitled "Representations and Warranties", expressly states that the sellers "represented and warranted" fifteen separate and carefully spelled out factual situations. Paragraph 9, entitled "Conditions precedent" expressly states that "All obligations of buyer under this agreement are subject to the fulfillment, prior to or at the closing, of each of the following *conditions*." It is to be noted that included among the "*conditions*" was the financial condition of the company and its subsidiaries at the time of closing, that the fulfillment of the "conditions" was to take place not subsequent to but "prior to or at the closing" and that the buyer's obligations, not the sellers', were made subject to the fulfillment of the condition. This agreement, in distinct and indubitable language, distinguishes between such engagements on the sellers' part as constitute "Warranties" and such engagements as constitute "Conditions".

Assuming, arguendo, that the company and its subsidiaries' financial condition was less favorable on September 17, 1954 than the financial condition shown on the statement dated June 30, 1954, what under this agreement was the buyer's remedy? The buyer claims that such fact constituted a breach of warranty which gave to him the right to recover the amount of the reduced net worth, while the sellers claim that the buyer had the choice on September 17, 1954 either to accept the situation or to refuse to proceed under the agreement.

The buyer argues that it was impossible to ascertain at the date of closing whether or not the net worth of the company and its subsidiaries had been reduced, and that only by an examination after date of closing could this fact be ascertained and, therefore, both parties must have intended that the buyer have a reasonable time after the date of closing to ascertain this fact. Such an argument not only finds no support in the wording of the agreement but, on the contrary, is in direct conflict with the express terms of the agreement. Such a contention would require that we read into the agreement that which is in direct variance with the clear and unambiguous language employed to express the parties' intent.

* * *

The arbitrator concluded that to construe paragraph 9(a) as creative of a promise for the breach of which the buyer could recover damages— i.e., a warranty—would be inconsistent with paragraph 5(g). With this conclusion we are in full agreement. The sellers in paragraph 5(g) represented and warranted, inter alia, that there had not been any changes in the financial condition of the company or its subsidiaries other than changes in the ordinary course of business, none of which had been materially adverse and were changes required or permitted under the agreement. Paragraph 9(a) covers an entirely different situation in that it referred to such changes in the financial condition of the company and its subsidiaries in the ordinary course of business which were materially adverse and not permitted under the agreement; if this situation arose the agreement specifically provided that the buyer was under no obligation to complete the purchase. A comparison of paragraph 5(g) with paragraph 9(a) clearly leads to this conclusion; to place upon paragraph 9(a) any other construction than that placed upon it by the arbitrator would amount to a redundancy.

A resolution of the instant controversy depends entirely upon an interpretation of the language of this agreement. The language employed by the parties is manifestly indicative of that which was intended and the meaning of the agreement—free as it is of ambiguity and doubt—is to be determined by what the agreement states. The parties carefully and scrupulously delineated between the sellers' undertakings which were intended to be "warranties" and those which were intended to be "conditions." It is crystal clear that the undertaking under paragraph 9(a) was simply a "condition" and not a "warranty" and once the buyer elected to accept this agreement the provisions of paragraph 9(a) ceased to be operative and the buyer had no right to recover any damages.

The judgment of the Court below is affirmed. Costs to be paid by appellant.

NOTES

(1)   Why was it important to differentiate warranties and conditions precedent in *In re Carter's Claim*? Note that the court appears to use the "plain meaning rule" of contract interpretation. Was that justified on these facts?

Why might it have made sense for the parties to condition the buyer's duty to purchase on the company's financial condition being "no less favorable," but not to warrant it? Why provide a warranty, then, of no material adverse changes outside of the ordinary course of business?

(2)   It is sometimes said that failure of an express condition precedent gives the promisor a "shield" but not a "sword;" he or she can avoid the contract but has no claim for damages. Why was this defensive protection denied to the buyer in *In re Carter's Claim*?

(3)   *MAC Attack.* The contractual regulation of "materially adverse" changes at the heart of *In re Carter's Claim* are one of the most hotly negotiated and litigated questions of merger law. Most friendly merger agreements contain material adverse change (MAC) and material adverse effect (MAE) clauses, which makes the buyer's duty to buy conditional on there not being a material adverse change in seller's financial condition. In recent years, merger agreements tend to include the traditional standard-like MAC and MAE terms but add explicitly negotiated "carve outs" that limit the buyer's ability to exit. The MAC and MAE provisions engender substantial litigation because it is hard for litigants to predict whether a particular negative event will be construed as "materially adverse." For example, in 2001, the Delaware Court of Chancery ruled that Tyson Foods must complete its $4.7 billion acquisition of South Dakota-based meatpacker IBP, Inc. The MAC clause in the IBP merger agreement made Tyson's duty

to buy conditional on "any event, occurrence or development of a state of circumstances or facts which has had or reasonably could be expected to have a Material Adverse Effect . . . on the condition (financial or otherwise), business, assets, liabilities or results of operations of [IBP] and [its] Subsidiaries taken as a whole." Notwithstanding a general market downturn and poor quarterly earnings, the court interpreted the provision in a manner that found no material adverse effect. General economic or even industry downturns (e.g., the adverse effect of the harsh winter on livestock markets) could not itself constitute a MAE and Tyson had failed to show that a general decline "had the required materiality of effect" on IBP itself. Second, the court held that because Tyson was not a "short-term speculator" for whom "the failure of a company to meet analysts' projected earnings for a quarter could be highly material," the downturn was not "consequential to the company's earnings power over a commercially reasonable period, which one would think would be measured in years rather than months." See Dorsey and Whitney, IBP v. Tyson Foods, Where's the Beef in Big MAC?; Ronald J. Gilson and Alan Schwartz, *Understanding MACs: Moral Hazard in Acquisitions*, 21 J.L. Econ. & Org. 330 (2005).

(4)   In some cases, the courts will construe the contract to impose a duty to give a notice that must be satisfied before the other party has a duty to perform. Failure to give the notice is a breach of contract. For example, in *Internatio-Rotterdam, Inc. v. River Brand Rice Mills, Inc.*, 259 F.2d 137 (2d Cir.1958), a buyer who had contracted to buy rice failed by twelve hours to give seller two-weeks' notice (where to ship). Because the price of rice was rising, the seller rescinded the contract. The court, examining conditions at the time the contract was made in July rather than the time of performance in December, held that the notice requirement was "the essence of the contract" and found that the defendant's refusal to sell was not a breach. In essence, the notice condition had failed and the defendant was discharged from the contract.

Robert Childres concluded that the "question should have been whether the delivery period was material; or more precisely, whether it was sufficiently material to justify seller's canceling the deal." Further, "if this had been the question, it seems clear that the buyer would have won, that the seller could not have established any material prejudice from the buyer's less than twelve-hour delay." Robert Childres, *Conditions in the Law of Contracts,* 45 N.Y.U. L. Rev. 33, 57 (1970). Do you agree with this analysis?

(5)   *Promise or Condition?* It is, of course, possible in a case like *River Brand Rice* for the parties explicitly to make a timely call or prompt sailing a condition precedent to the obligor's duty. If so and the condition fails, the promisor is discharged without regard to whether it was materially prejudiced. But if there is doubt about whether this has been done and the event is within the other party's control, Restatement (Second) § 227(2) prefers a construction that "a duty is imposed on an obligee that an event occur" rather than that the "event is made a condition of the obligor's duty." According to Comment d, the "preferred interpretation avoids the harsh results that might otherwise result from the nonoccurrence of a condition and still gives adequate protection to the obligor under the rules * * *

relating to promises for an exchange of performances * * * [where] the obligee's failure to perform his duty has, if it is material, the effect of the nonoccurrence of a condition of the obligor's duty." See Howard v. Federal Crop Ins. Corp., 540 F.2d 695 (4th Cir. 1976), where the court said:

> There is a general legal policy opposed to forfeitures. . . . Insurance policies are generally construed most strongly against the insurer. . . . When it is doubtful whether words create a promise or a condition, they will be construed as creating a promise.

This preference, however, does not apply to contracts "of a type under which only the obligor generally undertakes duties." Restatement (Second) § 227 cmt. d. Insurance is regarded as a contract of this type, where the usual interpretation is that the insured has no enforceable duty to pay premiums. Rather, if the risk insured against occurs, the insurance company's duty to pay under the policy is expressly conditioned upon the payment of premiums. Unless special arrangements with third parties have been made, however, the insured's failure to pay is a failure of condition rather than a breach of contract. See General Credit Corp. v. Imperial Casualty & Indemnity Co., 167 Neb. 833 (1959).

(6) *Time of Payment as Condition or Convenience. North American Graphite Corp. v. Allan*, 184 F.2d 387 (D.C. Cir. 1950), concerned an employment contract under which the bulk of the plaintiff's compensation was not payable until completion of a project. Following completion of most of the plaintiff's services, defendant fired him and abandoned the project. The court in *Allan* conceded that the parties could have made payment for services contingent upon successful operation of the mine, but did not clearly do so. Thus, the completion of the project language was intended as a convenient time for payment, not as a condition precedent.

The case turns upon the court's interpretation of the contract—upon "the intention of the parties" as "gathered from the language used, the situation of the parties, and the subject matter of the contract, as presented by the evidence." It should not be surprising, therefore, that in situations of this type decisions may at times be difficult to reconcile, at least on the basis of the rather meager data ordinarily appearing in an appellate court opinion. For example, in *Mascioni v. I.B. Miller, Inc.*, 261 N.Y. 1 (1933), a prime contractor's promise to a subcontractor of "[p]ayment to be made as received from the owner" was held to condition liability. However, the vast majority of decisions are in accord with *Dancy v. William J. Howard, Inc.*, 297 F.2d 686 (7th Cir. 1961), where the promise of a prime contractor to make final payment after he "has received final payment for construction" was said not to make such receipt of final payment a condition precedent, "but rather fixed it as a convenient time for payment." See also Main Elec., Ltd. v. Printz Services Corp., 980 P.2d 522 (Colo.1999) (construction against condition to avoid forfeiture). How clear must the language be to avoid the presumption against conditions?

PROBLEM: THE CASE OF THE INSOLVENT OWNER

S entered a subcontract with P for excavation work to be performed on land owned by O. P had the prime contract with O for the overall project, the development of a shopping center. The contract between S and P provided in part:

> *Article 5:* Material and work invoices submitted before the 25th of the current month will be paid by the 28th of the following month, provided the material so delivered is acceptable, and if payment for invoiced material has been received by [P] under its general contract.
>
> *Article 18:* . . . [I]f the work has been satisfactorily performed and invoice as rendered is approved and if payment for such labor and material so invoiced has been received by [P] under its general contract, the subcontractor will be paid 85% of invoice as approved, less any payments previously made on account for previous periods. No payments made shall be considered as evidence of acceptance of the work either in whole or in part until the work is completed and accepted, whereupon final payment will be made within thirty (30) days of such acceptance upon receipt of all or any bonds, guarantees required.

O became insolvent and the project was terminated before S was paid in full for work done. S filed a mechanic's lien on O's property. The trustee in the insolvency proceeding found that S was owed $84,000 for work done, but ruled that the claim against O and its land was subordinated to other creditors of O. S then sued P under the subcontract. P alleged that it had not been paid in full by O before the insolvency and argued that under the subcontract payment by O was a condition precedent to its duty to pay S. What result? See A.A. Conte, Inc. v. Campbell-Lowrie-Lautermilch, 132 Ill.App.3d 325 (1985).

DRAFTING EXERCISE: MATERIAL ADVERSE EVENT PROVISIONS

You are the general counsel of a toaster company (Smirgo, Inc.) that is the target of a friendly merger offer at an attractive share price from a buyer (Brent Outlet), a retailer of toasters and other kitchen appliances. Brent's offer includes the following "material adverse effect" provision:

> *Conditions Precedent.* All obligations of Buyer under this agreement are subject to the fulfillment, prior to or at the closing of each of the following conditions:
>
> (a) *Absence of Company Material Adverse Effect.* Except as disclosed in the Company Disclosure Letter, since the date of this Agreement there shall not have been any event, change, effect or development that, individually or in the aggregate, has had or could reasonably be expected to have a Company Material Adverse Effect.

In addition, the definitions section of the offer includes the following:

A "Company Material Adverse Effect" is a material adverse effect on the business, assets, condition (financial or otherwise), prospects or results of operations of the Company (Smirgo, Inc.) or its subsidiaries.

Your CEO is concerned that Brent's offer gives it too much freedom to claim at closing the presence of a MAE as an excuse not to purchase Smirgo at the promised share price. Draft a counteroffer, using track changes, that provides a more limited MAE provision. Among other things, be sure to consider carve outs relating to the condition of the economy and to the condition of the toaster industry. Please include a cover sheet explaining to Brent the rationale for your proposed changes.

(2) EXCUSE OF EXPRESS CONDITIONS

On the one hand, the law of conditions fosters a policy favoring freedom *from* contract. If an express condition precedent has failed, the promisor has a defense and may be discharged from the contract without any obligation to compensate the promisee for part-performance. Whether the promisor was in fact prejudiced by the failure is immaterial. On the other hand, a strict application of the law of conditions can produce a perceived forfeiture, especially where the promisor is not actually harmed by the failure of a condition and the promisee has engaged in extensive preparation to perform or part-performance. Put differently, if the condition turns out to be immaterial to the promisor and the promisee has relied or conferred a benefit on the promisor, discharging the promisor may provide a severe test for the "freedom from" contract policy.

A good example of this "severe test" is *Inman v. Clyde Hall Drilling Co.*, 369 P.2d 498 (Alaska 1962), where the court discharged an employer from a claim by a terminated employee because the employee failed to satisfy a 30-day condition of notice, even though the lawsuit was filed and service was made within the 30-day period and there was no evidence that the promisor was prejudiced by the delay. The court stated:

> Service of the complaint probably gave the Company actual knowledge of the claim. But that does not serve as an excuse for not giving the kind of written notice called for by the contract. Inman agreed that no suit would be instituted "prior to six (6) months *after the filing of the written notice of claim*." (emphasis ours) If this means what it says (and we have no reason to believe it does not), it is clear that the commencement of an action and service of the complaint was not an effective substitute for the kind of notice called for by the agreement. To hold otherwise would be to simply ignore an explicit provision of the contract and say that it had no meaning. We are not justified in doing that.

As we have seen, one way to deal with the forfeiture problem is to argue that a condition precedent was not intended. But this will not work if the contract was clearly drafted. Another way to temper forfeiture is to excuse the condition on some other ground. Some possible grounds for excuse include: (1) an agreement by both parties modifying the contract to discharge the condition; (2) conduct by the party for whose benefit the condition was made that waived the condition; (3) changed circumstances that make compliance by the promisee with the condition impracticable; and (4) discharge by the court. In this subsection, we will explore when these grounds for excuse of condition are available.

William L. Clark v. John B. West

Court of Appeals of New York, 1908.
193 N.Y. 349.

On February 12th, 1900, the plaintiff and defendant entered into a written contract under which the former was to write and prepare for publication for the latter a series of law books the compensation for which was provided in the contract. After the plaintiff had completed a three-volume work known as "Clark & Marshall on Corporations," the parties disagreed. The plaintiff claimed that the defendant had broken the contract by causing the book to be copyrighted in the name of a corporation, which was not a party to the contract, and he brought this action to recover what he claims to be due him, for an accounting and other relief. The defendant demurred to the complaint on the ground that it did not state facts sufficient to constitute a cause of action. The Special Term overruled the demurrer, but upon appeal to the Appellate Division, that decision was reversed and the demurrer sustained.

Those portions of the contract which are germane to the present stage of the controversy are as follows: "The plaintiff agreed to write a series of books relating to specified legal subjects; the manuscript furnished by him was to be satisfactory to the defendant; the plaintiff was not to write or edit anything that would interfere with the sale of books to be written by him under the contract and he was not to write any other books unless requested so to do by the defendant, in which latter event he was to be paid $3,000 a year." The contract contained a clause which provided that "The first party (the plaintiff) agrees to totally abstain from the use of intoxicating liquors during the continuance of this contract, and that the payment to him in accordance with the terms of this contract of any money in excess of $2 per page is dependent on the faithful performance of this as well as the other conditions of this contract. * * *" In a later paragraph it further recited that, "In consideration of the above promises of the first party (the plaintiff), the second party (the defendant) agrees to pay to the first party $2 per page, * * * on each book prepared by the first party under this contract and accepted by the second party, and if said first party abstains from the use of intoxicating liquor and otherwise fulfills his agreements as hereinbefore set forth, he shall be paid an additional $4 per page in manner hereinbefore stated." * * *

The plaintiff in his complaint alleges completion of the work on corporations and publication thereof by the defendant; the sale of many copies thereof from which the defendant received large net receipts; the number of pages it contained (3,469), for which he had been paid at the rate of $2 per page, amounting to $6,938; and that defendant has refused to pay him any sum over and above that amount, or any sum in excess of $2 per page. Full performance of the agreement on plaintiff's part is alleged, except that he "did not totally abstain from the use of intoxicating liquor during the continuation of said contract, but such use by the plaintiff was not excessive and did not prevent or interfere with the due and full performance by the plaintiff of all the other stipulations in said contract." The complaint further alleges a waiver on the part of the defendant of the plaintiff's stipulation to totally abstain from the use of intoxicating liquors * * *.

The defendant's breach of the contract is then alleged which is claimed to consist in his having taken out a copyright upon the plaintiff's work on corporations in the name of a publishing company which had no relation to the contract, and the relief asked for is that the defendant be compelled to account, and that the copyright be transferred to the plaintiff or that he recover its value.

The appeal is by permission of the Appellate Division and the following questions have been certified to us: 1. Does the complaint herein state facts sufficient to constitute a cause of action? 2. Under the terms of the contract alleged in the complaint, is the plaintiff's total abstinence from the use of intoxicating liquors a condition precedent which can be waived so as to render defendant liable upon the contract notwithstanding plaintiff's use of intoxicating liquors? 3. Does the complaint herein allege facts constituting a valid and effective waiver of plaintiff's non-performance of such condition precedent?

■ WERNER, J. * * * Briefly stated, the defendant's position is that the stipulation as to plaintiff's total abstinence is the consideration for the payment of the difference between $2 and $6 per page and therefore could not be waived except by a new agreement to that effect based upon a good consideration; that the so-called waiver alleged by the plaintiff is not a waiver but a modification of the contract in respect to its consideration. The plaintiff on the other hand argues that the stipulation for his total abstinence was merely a condition precedent intended to work a forfeiture of the additional compensation in case of a breach and that it could be waived without any formal agreement to that effect based upon a new consideration.

The subject-matter of the contract was the writing of books by the plaintiff for the defendant. The duration of the contract was the time necessary to complete them all. The work was to be done to the satisfaction of the defendant, and the plaintiff was not to write any other books except those covered by the contract unless requested so to do by the defendant, in which latter event he was to be paid for that particular work by the year. The compensation for the work specified in the contract was to be $6 per page, unless the plaintiff failed to totally abstain from the use of intoxicating liquors during the continuance of the contract, in which event he was to receive only $2 per page. That is the obvious import of the contract construed in the light of the purpose for which it was made, and in accordance with the ordinary meaning of plain language. It is not a contract to write books in order that the plaintiff shall keep sober, but a contract containing a stipulation that he shall keep sober so that he may write satisfactory books. When we view the contract from this standpoint it will readily be perceived that the particular stipulation is not the consideration for the contract, but simply one of its conditions which fits in with those relating to time and method of delivery of manuscript, revision of proof, citation of cases, assignment of copyrights, keeping track of new cases and citations for new editions, and other details which might be waived by the defendant, if he saw fit to do so. This is made clear, it seems to us, by the provision that, "In consideration of the above promises," the defendant agrees to pay the plaintiff $2 per page on each book prepared by him, and if he "abstains from the use of intoxicating liquor and otherwise fulfills his agreements as hereinbefore set forth, he shall be paid an additional $4 per page in manner hereinbefore stated." The compensation of $2 per page, not to exceed $250 per month, was an advance or partial payment of the whole price of $6 per page, and the payment of the two-thirds, which was to be withheld pending the performance of the contract, was simply made contingent upon the plaintiff's total abstention from the use of intoxicants during the life of the contract. * * * It is obvious that the parties thought that the plaintiff's normal work was worth $6 per page. That was the sum to be paid for the work done by the plaintiff and not for total abstinence. If the plaintiff did not keep to the condition as to total abstinence, he was to lose part of that sum. * * * This, we think, is the fair interpretation of the contract, and it follows that the stipulation as to the plaintiff's total abstinence was nothing more nor less than a condition precedent. If that conclusion is well founded there can be no escape from the corollary that this condition could be waived; and if it was waived the defendant is clearly not in a position to insist upon the forfeiture which his waiver was intended to annihilate. The forfeiture must stand or fall with the condition. If the latter was waived, the former is no longer a part of the contract. Defendant still has the right to counterclaim for any damages which he may have sustained in consequence of the plaintiff's breach, but he cannot insist upon strict performance. . . .

This whole discussion is predicated of course upon the theory of an express waiver. We assume that no waiver could be implied from the defendant's mere acceptance of the books and his payment of the sum of $2 per page without objection. It was the defendant's duty to pay that amount in any event after acceptance of the work. The plaintiff must stand upon his allegation of an express waiver and if he fails to establish that he cannot maintain his action.

The theory upon which the defendant's attitude seems to be based is that even if he has represented to the plaintiff that he would not insist upon the condition that the latter should observe total abstinence from intoxicants, he can still refuse to pay the full contract price for his work. The inequity of this position becomes apparent when we consider that this contract was to run for a period of years, during a large portion of which the plaintiff was to be entitled only to the advance payment of $2 per page, the balance being contingent, among other things, upon publication of the books and returns from sales. Upon this theory the defendant might have waived the condition while the first book was in process of production, and yet, when the whole work was completed, he would still be a position to insist upon the forfeiture because there had not been strict performance. Such a situation is possible in a case where the subject of the waiver is the very consideration of a contract, Organ v. Stewart, 60 N.Y. 413, 420, but not where the waiver relates to something that can be waived. In the case at bar, as we have seen, the waiver is not of the consideration or subject-matter, but of an incident to the method of performance. The consideration remains the same. The defendant has had the work he bargained for, and it is alleged that he has waived one of the conditions as to the manner in which it was to have been done. He might have insisted upon literal performance and then he could have stood upon the letter of his contract. If, however, he has waived that incidental condition, he has created a situation to which the doctrine of waiver very precisely applies.

The cases which present the most familiar phases of the doctrine of waiver are those which have arisen out of litigation over insurance policies where the defendants have claimed a forfeiture because of the breach of some condition in the contract, . . . but it is a doctrine of general application which is confined to no particular class of cases. A waiver has been defined to be the intentional relinquishment of a known right. It is voluntary and implies an election to dispense with something of value, or forego some advantage which the party waiving it might at its option have demanded or insisted upon. * * * While the principle may not be easily classified, it is well established that, if the words and acts of the insurer reasonably justify the conclusion that with full knowledge of all the facts it intended to abandon or not to insist upon the particular defense afterwards relied upon, a verdict or finding to that effect establishes a waiver, which, if it once exists, can never be revoked. The doctrine of equitable estoppel, or estoppel *in pais,* is that a party may be precluded by his acts and conduct from asserting a right to the detriment of another party who, entitled to rely on such conduct, has acted upon it. * * * As already said, "the doctrine of waiver is to relieve against forfeiture; it requires no consideration for a waiver, nor any prejudice or injury to the other party." . . .

It remains to be determined whether the plaintiff has alleged facts which, if proven, will be sufficient to establish his claim of an express waiver by the defendant of the plaintiff's breach of the condition to observe total abstinence. In the 12th paragraph of the complaint, the plaintiff alleges facts and circumstances which we think, if established, would prove defendant's waiver of plaintiff's performance of that contract stipulation. These facts and circumstances are that long before the plaintiff had completed the manuscript of the first book undertaken under the contract, the defendant had full knowledge of the plaintiff's non-observance of that stipulation, and that with such knowledge he not only accepted the completed manuscript without objection, but "repeatedly avowed and represented to the plaintiff that he was entitled to and would receive said royalty payments (i.e., the additional $4 per page), and plaintiff believed and relied upon such representations, * * * and at all times during the writing of said treatise on corporations, and after as well as before publication thereof as aforesaid, it was mutually understood, agreed, and intended by the parties hereto that, notwithstanding plaintiff's said use of intoxicating liquors, he was nevertheless entitled to receive and would receive said royalty as the same accrued under said contract." * * *

The three questions certified should be answered in the affirmative, the order of the Appellate Division reversed, the interlocutory judgment of the Special Term affirmed, with costs in both courts, and the defendant be permitted to answer the complaint within twenty days upon payment of costs.

NOTES

(1) *Addicted to Drinking.* A web history of Washington and Lee Law School tells us:

> In 1899, the trustees chose William L. Clark, Jr. to fill a vacancy on the law faculty. Clark was a prolific writer. Between 1894 and 1897 he authored books on the subjects of criminal law, criminal procedure, contracts, elementary law, and corporations. He co-authored (with William L. Marshall) Treatise On the Law of Crimes in 1900. Seven editions of that work have been published.

> Clark's tenure at Washington and Lee lasted only a few weeks. On October 18, 1899, President William L. Wilson wrote to Clark that, "In view of the occurrences of the past fortnight . . . I do not think it advisable for you to attempt to meet the classes in law any more." Clark tendered his resignation but requested a reason for his dismissal. In reply, Wilson wrote of Clark's being "addicted to drinking beyond what would be proper in a college professor." Notices of Clark's dismissal appeared in the Baltimore Sun and the New York Herald. Wilson thought the publicity harmful to the law school.

(2) *Waiver.* Since a condition is a term of the contract, it can be deleted or modified by a subsequent agreement between the parties. If the condition, to use Restatement (Second) language, is a "material part of the agreed

exchange," § 84(1)(a), the modification agreement must satisfy the usual modification requirements, including, upon occasion, consideration. See UCC § 2–209(1); Restatement (Second) § 89.

But a condition can sometimes be excused by conduct by one party to the contract which falls short of an agreed modification. An umbrella term for many of these situations is "waiver," which has been defined generally as the "voluntary relinquishment of a known right." E. Allan Farnsworth has argued that where express conditions are involved, waiver is associated with three recurring fact patterns, aptly illustrated by insurance contracts:

(a) *Election Waiver.* Plaintiff-insured has not satisfied an express condition that notice be given within 30 days after a covered accident, but Defendant-insurer, with full knowledge, elects to process the claim rather than to deny payment. Because of the "election" after the condition has failed, the insurer cannot thereafter insist upon the condition. See, e.g., Lee v. Casualty Co. of Am., 90 Conn. 202 (1916); Restatement (Second) § 84(1) (conduct of insurer is a "promise to perform all * * * of a conditional duty under an antecedent contract in spite of the non-occurrence of the condition"). According to Farnsworth, the insurer is precluded from raising the condition by election. E. Allan Farnsworth, Changing Your Mind: The Law of Regretted Decisions 181–192 (1998).

(b) *Estoppel Waiver.* Immediately after the accident, Defendant-insurer tells Plaintiff-insured not to worry about the 30-day notice condition. Relying on this, Plaintiff submitted notice within 45 days of the accident and Defendant refused to process the claim. The condition is waived because Plaintiff has materially changed his or her position in reliance upon Defendant's representation. See UCC § 2–209(5); Restatement (Second) §§ 84(2) & 89(c). According to Farnsworth, the insurer is precluded from raising the condition by equitable estoppel. E. Allan Farnsworth, supra at 163–173.

(c) *Waiver Without Election or Estoppel.* After Plaintiff has substantially performed the contract, Defendant states that it will not insist upon a non-material condition. The condition is waived without "election" or "estoppel." Imperator Realty Co. v. Tull, 228 N.Y. 447 (1920). More broadly, when one party has promised or represented that he or she will not insist upon express conditions, "waiver" becomes a judicial device to avoid forfeiture in particular cases where an agreed modification cannot be found. See E. Allan Farnsworth, supra at 154–162. See also, Edward Rubin, *Toward a General Theory of Waiver,* 28 UCLA L. Rev. 478 (1981).

(3) *Conditions and Duties.* Clark's abstinence from alcohol was clearly a condition of his being paid an extra four dollars per page. Did he also have a duty not to drink? If he did have a duty not to drink, did waiver of the condition affect the existence of that duty? The answers can be found in Justice Werner's opinion.

Dynamic Machine Works, Inc. v. Machine & Electrical Consultants, Inc.

Supreme Judicial Court of Massachusetts, 2005.
444 Mass. 768.

■ CORDY, J. A judge of the United States District Court for the District of Massachusetts has certified the following question: "Under the Massachusetts version of the Uniform Commercial Code, does a buyer have a right to retract a written extension allowing more time for the seller to cure defects in a delivered product absent reliance on the extension by the seller?" We answer the certified question as follows: If the written extension constitutes a modification of the agreement to purchase the product, then the buyer may not retract it unilaterally. If, on the other hand, the written extension constitutes a waiver of an executory portion of the agreement, the buyer may retract it "by reasonable notification received by the [seller] that strict performance will be required . . . unless the retraction would be unjust in view of a material change of position in reliance on the waiver." G.L. c. 106, § 2–209(5).

1. *Background.* The undisputed facts and relevant procedural history are as follows. Dynamic Machine Works, Inc. (Dynamic), is a Massachusetts manufacturer of precision components for the aerospace, chemical, military, and oil industries. Machine & Electrical Consultants, Inc. (Machine), located in Biddeford, Maine, distributes heavy machinery and turning equipment. In January, 2003, Dynamic agreed to purchase from Machine a Johnford lathe (lathe) for $355,000. The lathe was to be manufactured in Taiwan by Roundtop Machinery Industries, Co., Ltd. Under the terms of Dynamic's purchase order, Machine would receive a down payment of $29,500, a second payment of $148,000 on delivery, which was scheduled for May 15, 2003, and a final payment of $177,500 on acceptance. In the interim, Dynamic rented a Johnford ST–60B lathe (rental lathe) from Machine. In February, 2003, Dynamic informed Machine that it was experiencing problems with the rental lathe and that if these problems were not addressed and remedied in the new lathe, Dynamic would reject it.

Sometime before June, 2003, production of the lathe in Taiwan was delayed due to the "SARS" epidemic and other events beyond the control of Machine. In letters dated June 26 and July 8 (collectively the July agreement), Machine and Dynamic confirmed an oral agreement to, among other things, extend the deadline for the installation and commissioning of the lathe to September 19, 2003. The parties further agreed that any further delay would result in a $500 per day penalty assessed against Machine. On October 9, Machine delivered the lathe to Dynamic. It was subsequently installed and, throughout the month of November, the lathe was tested and readjusted in connection with its final commissioning.

On December 9, Dynamic's president, Ven Fonte, wrote a letter to the vice-president of Machine, Norman Crepeau, which advised in relevant part: "As I stated to you early this morning on the telephone, we will grant you one last and final deadline for the machine to be fully and unconditionally commissioned by the close of business day, Friday December 19, 2003." On the following day, Fonte received additional information regarding the lathe that led him to conclude that it would not be able to meet the required specifications. Dynamic promptly notified Machine that it intended to retract the deadline extension. In a letter dated December 11, counsel for Dynamic advised Machine that Dynamic was revoking acceptance of the lathe, demanded return of Dynamic's down payment and the payment of the penalty fees, and requested instructions concerning disposition of the lathe. Machine had not relied on the deadline extension granted in Fonte's letter of December 9 in any material way prior to Dynamic's written revocation of it on December 11.

* * *

Discussion. The contract in this case is one for the sale of goods. Consequently, it is governed by the Commonwealth's version of art. 2 of the Uniform Commercial Code (UCC). G.L. c. 106, §§ 2–101 et seq. Section 2–209 of the UCC provides:

(1) An agreement modifying a contract within this Article needs no consideration to be binding.

(2) A signed agreement which excludes modification or rescission except by a signed writing cannot be otherwise modified or rescinded, but except as between merchants such a requirement on a form supplied by the merchant must be separately signed by the other party.

(3) The requirements of the Statute of Frauds section of this Article (Section 2–201) must be satisfied if the contract as modified is within its provisions.

(4) Although an attempt at modification or rescission does not satisfy the requirements of subsection (2) or (3) it can operate as a waiver.

(5) A party who has made a waiver affecting an executory portion of the contract may retract the waiver by reasonable notification received by the other party that strict performance will be required of any term waived, unless the retraction would be unjust in view of a material change of position in reliance on the waiver.

The UCC does not define "waiver" or "modification," but they "are distinct concepts." . . . A modification "is the changing of the terms of the agreement which may diminish or increase the duty of either party." 2A R.A. Anderson, Uniform Commercial Code § 2–209:49 (3d ed.1997). While a waiver may be effectuated by one party, a modification "is the result of the bilateral action of both parties to the sales transaction." *Id.* *Cochran v. Quest Software, Inc.,* 328 F.3d 1, 9 (1st Cir.2003) ("Under

Massachusetts law, the parties to a contract must agree to a modification"). By the plain terms of § 2–209(5), a waiver is retractable in the absence of reliance. G.L. c. 106, § 2–209(5). A modification, in contrast, cannot be retracted unilaterally. *BMC Indus., Inc. v. Barth Indus., Inc.,* 160 F.3d 1322, 1334 (11th Cir.1998) ("while a party that has agreed to a contract modification cannot cancel the modification without giving consideration for the cancellation, a party may unilaterally retract its waiver of a contract term provided it gives reasonable notice"). . . .

Dynamic contends that its letter of December 9, 2003, is a waiver (or at least a partial waiver) of the time by which Machine had a duty to perform, and not a mutual agreement to change the terms of the contract. In support of this position, it points out that the letter does not expressly state that both parties "agreed" to the "last and final deadline" of Friday, December 19, 2003, and reflects only what Dynamic's president "stated" in that regard, without any reference to Machine's position on the matter. Moreover, it argues that the use of the word "grant," as opposed to "agree," is dispositive. Machine, on the other hand, argues that Dynamic's extension of the commissioning deadline constitutes a modification because (1) the extension satisfies the Statute of Frauds; (2) the extension was granted in a letter written and signed by Dynamic's president;[7] (3) the letter granting the extension "clearly demonstrates that both parties had discussed and agreed to the new commissioning deadline"; and (4) the terms of the letter are sufficiently definite.

Determining whether Dynamic's letter of December 9 (or the conversation to which it refers) constitutes a waiver or a modification is in large measure a question of fact. . . . As applied to this case, the answer turns on whether Dynamic and Machine mutually agreed to extend the commissioning deadline to December 19, 2003. . . . The fact that the extension was granted in a signed writing does not of itself establish that the extension was intended to be a modification, and not a waiver. A waiver "can be inferred from a party's conduct and the surrounding circumstances," but it can also be "express, . . . and there is no reason why it cannot be in writing. Conversely, the absence of consideration for the extension of the time of performance does not preclude a finding that the extension was the product of a mutual agreement to modify the contract terms, as the UCC explicitly states that '[a]n agreement modifying a contract . . . needs no consideration to be binding.' " G.L. c. 106, § 2–209(1).

---

[7] General Laws c. 106, § 2–209(2), provides that "[a] signed agreement which excludes modification or rescission except by a signed writing cannot be otherwise modified or rescinded, but except as between merchants such a requirement on a form supplied by the merchant must be separately signed by the other party." Here, the contract did not prohibit oral modifications. This case thus does not present the thorny issue whether an oral modification of a contract that forbids oral modifications constitutes an "attempt at modification" operating as a waiver under G.L. c. 106, § 2–209(4). See *Wisconsin Knife Works v. National Metal Crafters,* 781 F.2d 1280 (7th Cir.1986).

We answer only the certified question . . . and the judge has not asked us to determine whether the December 9 letter extending the time for performance constitutes a modification of the July agreement or a waiver of Machine's duty to perform by a particular date.

NOTES

(1) Like an offer—and, as we will see, like an anticipatory repudiation—a waiver does not require agreement. It is a unilateral act by one party. Here's what section 84(2) of the Second Restatement has to say on whether waivers can be withdrawn:

> If [a promise to perform in spite of the nonoccurrence of a condition] is made before the time for the occurrence of the condition has expired and the condition is within the control of the promisee or a beneficiary, the promisor can make his duty again subject to the condition by notifying the promisee or beneficiary of his intention to do so if
>
> (a) the notification is received while there is still a reasonable time to cause the condition to occur under the antecedent terms or an extension given by the promisor; and
>
> (b) reinstatement of the requirement of the condition is not unjust because of a material change of position by the promisee or beneficiary; and
>
> (c) the promise is not [otherwise] binding. . . .

Any similarities to the rules governing when an offer becomes firm? Any differences?

(2) *Is Reliance Required to Waive Terms Under UCC § 2–209?* In *Wisconsin Knife Works v. National Metal Crafters*, 781 F.2d 1280 (7th Cir.1986), Judge Posner shook up the UCC waters by concluding that reliance was required for an effective waiver under UCC § 2–209. Judge Easterbrook dissented: "The introduction of a reliance requirement into a body of law from which the doctrine of consideration has been excised is novel." *Id.* at 1290. The issue was nicely described by the Eleventh Circuit in *BMC Industries, Inc. v. Barth Industries, Inc.*, 160 F.3d 1322, 1333–34 (11th Cir.1998), which adopted Easterbrook's position.

> Our conclusion follows from the plain language of subsections 672.209(4) and (5). While subsection (4) states that an attempted modification that fails may still constitute a waiver, subsection (5) provides that the waiver may be retracted *unless* the non-waiving party relies on the waiver. Consequently, the statute recognizes that waivers may exist in the absence of detrimental reliance— these are the retractable waivers referred to in subsection (5). Only this interpretation renders meaning to subsection (5), because reading subsection (4) to require detrimental reliance for all waivers means that waivers would *never* be retractable. *See Wisconsin Knife Works v. National Metal Crafters,* 781 F.2d 1280, 1291 (7th Cir.1986) (Easterbrook, J., dissenting) (noting that

reading a detrimental reliance requirement into the UCC would eliminate the distinction between subsections (4) and (5)). Subsection (5) would therefore be meaningless. * * *

Although other courts have held that waiver requires reliance under the UCC, those courts have ignored the UCC's plain language. The leading case espousing this view of waiver is *Wisconsin Knife Works v. National Metal Crafters*, 781 F.2d 1280 (7th Cir.1986) . . . in which a panel of the Seventh Circuit addressed a contract that included a term prohibiting oral modifications, and considered whether an attempted oral modification could instead constitute a waiver. Writing for the majority, Judge Posner concluded that the UCC's subsection (2), which gives effect to "no oral modification" provisions, would become superfluous if contract terms could be waived without detrimental reliance. Judge Posner reasoned that if attempted oral modifications that were unenforceable because of subsection (2) were nevertheless enforced as waivers under subsection (4), then subsection (2) is "very nearly a dead letter." *Id.* at 1286. According to Judge Posner, there must be some difference between modification and waiver in order for both subsections (2) and (4) to have meaning. This difference is waiver's detrimental reliance requirement.[2]

Judge Posner, however, ignores a fundamental difference between modifications and waivers: while a party that has agreed to a contract modification cannot cancel the modification without giving consideration for the cancellation, a party may unilaterally retract its waiver of a contract term provided it gives reasonable notice. The fact that waivers may unilaterally be retracted provides the difference between subsections (2) and (4) that allows both to have meaning. We therefore conclude that waiver under the UCC does not require detrimental reliance.

(3) *Effect of Term Requiring Written Modification.* A contract term that prohibits a non-written modification can be waived without a writing at common law. See First Nat. Bank of Pa. v. Lincoln Nat. Life Ins. Co., 824 F.2d 277, 280 (3d Cir. 1987). UCC § 2–209(2), however, provides that "A signed agreement which excludes modification or rescission except by a signed writing cannot be otherwise modified or rescinded. . . ." Does this foreclose a non-written waiver?

(4) *Effect of Anti-Waiver Clause.* In *M.J.G. Properties, Inc. v. Hurley,* 27 Mass. App. Ct. 250 (1989), the lessee covenanted that it would use the

---

[2] Contrary to our reasoning above, Judge Posner claims that reading a reliance requirement into waiver under subsection (4) is not inconsistent with subsection (5). According to Judge Posner, subsection (5) is broader than subsection (4), covering waivers other than mere attempts at oral modification. Judge Posner argues as an example that subsection (5) covers express waivers that are written and signed. *See id.* at 1287. In dissent, however, Judge Easterbrook convincingly dissects this argument. As Judge Easterbrook explains, subsection (5) is narrower than subsection (4) limiting the effect of waivers that are not detrimentally relied upon-not the reverse as Judge Posner claims. Furthermore, Judge Easterbrook demonstrates that subsection (5) cannot cover express written and signed waivers because such writings are not waivers, but rather effective written modifications under subsection (2).

property consistent with applicable zoning ordinances. The lease also provided that upon any breach of covenant, the lessor could repossess the premises "at any time" notwithstanding any waiver. After three breaches, the lessor sought to repossess the property. The lessee argued and the trial court agreed that the lessor, despite the "anti-waiver" clause, had waived its power to repossess. On appeal, the judgment was affirmed. The court stated:

> On the record before us, the trial judge was presented with the following evidence; two breaches occurring in 1985 had been ignored by the lessor, and no mention of them had been made to the lessee; nothing was said about a third breach for seven months, after which time the lessor attempted to terminate the lease; in the meantime two actions in small claims court were brought against the lessee on other grounds (one for increased rent); rent was accepted without reservation throughout the period prior to notice of termination; notice of termination came only after the lessee had exercised the option to extend. On this evidence, considering the antiwaiver clause as relevant but not dispositive, we cannot say, especially in view of the incomplete record before us . . . that the judge erred in finding a waiver by the lessor. *Id.* at 253.

Forrest D. Ferguson v. Phoenix Assurance Company of New York

Supreme Court of Kansas, 1962.
189 Kan. 459.

■ SCHROEDER, J. This is an action against an insurance company on a Storekeepers Burglary and Robbery Policy for loss of money by *safe burglary*. The question presented on appeal is whether the loss is covered by the provisions of the policy.

The facts have been stipulated and are not in controversy. The plaintiff, Forrest D. Ferguson (appellee), was insured under a "Storekeepers Burglary and Robbery Policy" issued by the Phoenix Assurance Company of New York (defendant-appellant). He operated the Rexall drug store in Council Grove, Kansas. During the night of March 8, 1960, the insured's place of business was broken into by forcing the front door open, as evidenced by tool marks. As a result of the burglary there was actual damage to the premises in the amount of $70; narcotics were taken from a storage drawer from within the premises of the value of $32.59; and money was taken from within the safe in the sum of $433.76.

Before the case was tried the insurance company confessed judgment in the amount of $152.59. This comprised the $70, the $32.59, and $50 for the loss of money from within the safe. The only amount in dispute is the remaining $383.76 taken from the safe.

The safe used in the drug store herein had two doors, the outer one was locked by means of a combination lock and the inner one by means of a key. Both doors to the safe were locked. In gaining access to the safe the outer door was opened by manipulating the combination thereof, and the inner door was opened by punching out the lock. There were no visible marks upon the exterior of the outer door of the safe to show the use of force or violence in gaining access through this door, but the inner door did disclose marks of force and violence upon its exterior, evidencing the use of tools in gaining access.

The policy of insurance entitled "Storekeepers Burglary and Robbery Policy" limited liability to $1,000 under each of the seven "Insuring Agreements." Among them is the following:

"IV. Burglary; Safe Burglary

"To pay for loss by safe burglary of money, securities and merchandise within the premises and for loss, not exceeding $50, by burglary of money and securities within the premises."

The policy in chronological sequence then listed the "Exclusions." The only one having any bearing upon this case reads:

"This policy does not apply:

"(a) to loss due to any fraudulent, dishonest or criminal act by any insured, a partner therein, or an officer, employee, director, trustee or authorized representative thereof, [while working or otherwise and] whether acting alone or in collusion with others; provided, this exclusion does not apply to [kidnapping,] safe burglary or robbery or attempt thereat by other than an insured or a partner therein;"

This exclusion was amended by an attached rider to include the words set forth in the brackets.

The policy then set forth the "Conditions" among which was: "1. Definitions . . . (j) Safe Burglary." The definition of the term "Safe Burglary," however, was amended by a rider attached to the policy. The amended definition, which is substantially identical to the original, reads:

" 'Safe Burglary' means (1) the felonious abstraction of insured property from within a vault or safe, the door of which is equipped with a combination lock, located within the premises by a person making felonious entry into such vault or such safe and any vault containing the safe, when all doors thereof are duly closed and locked by all combination locks thereon, provided such entry shall be made by actual force and violence, *of which force and violence there are visible marks made by tools, explosives, electricity or chemicals upon the exterior of (a) all of said doors of such vault or such safe and any vault containing the safe, if entry is made through such doors*, or (b) the top, bottom or walls of such vault or such safe and any vault containing the safe through which entry is made, if not made through such doors, or (2) the felonious abstraction of such safe from within the premises." (Emphasis added.)

The trial court said there was no question but that a burglary occurred, the money was taken, and the insurance was carried for that particular purpose. It held the provision relied upon by the insurer was "an escape clause" and allowed full recovery under the policy for the money taken from the safe. Judgment was entered for $536.35, as requested in the petition, plus $300 for attorney fees to be assessed as costs against the insurance company.

Appeal has been duly perfected by the insurance company presenting as the only dispute the construction of the insurance policy in question as it relates to safe burglary.

A study of the policy discloses that if the appellee is entitled to recover the loss must fall within provision No. IV of the "Insuring Agreements."

* * * The appellant contends the definition of safe burglary in the policy is clear and unambiguous. It says, since entry was made to the safe in question through the doors thereof, and there were no visible marks of force and violence made by tools, explosives, electricity or chemicals upon the exterior of the outer door through which entry was made, the loss was not insured under the plain meaning of the policy. * * *

The appellee contends the appellant's interpretation of safe burglary within the terms of the policy is not applicable and is illogical and contrary to the public policy of this state. It is argued the appellee is entitled to recover for the loss as a result of the burglary of his safe, when the facts are that the inner door of the safe was locked by a key and the safe entered by force and violence of which there were visible marks on the exterior of such inner door.

The appellee argues if the insurance company did not intend to pay for loss of money by safe burglary under the facts in this case, it should have had another item under its "Exclusions," stating in substance "that the company will not pay for any loss if a combination to a safe has been worked by manipulation." (See the policy provisions in . . . *Assurance Corp. v. Heller*, [1953], 127 Colo. 64, 253 P. 2d 966.)

It is a generally accepted rule that insurance policies are to be construed in favor of the insured and against the company. This rule, however, is to be invoked only where there exists rational grounds for construction of the policy. . . . [But] courts are not at liberty to indulge in a construction that would give an unnatural meaning to the language in order to accomplish results that could not be shown to have been in the minds of the parties. * * *

In *Security State Bank v. Royal Indemnity Co.*, 127 Kan. 230, 273 Pac. 430, the policy of insurance required the insured to provide a guard for each custodian while conveying insured property outside the premises as a precaution to prevent loss. The insured failed to send a guard with a messenger who was robbed, and sought to recover. The court said:

> "... We are of the opinion that the failure of the plaintiff to comply with the provision of the policy with respect to sending a guard with the messenger increased the risk of loss by robbery and may reasonably be said to have constituted a direct cause of the loss in question. ..." (p. 231.)

This condition in the policy was recognized by the court as *substantive* and required fulfillment before liability attached.

It is not uncommon for insurance companies to include in theft or burglary insurance policies provisions restricting their liability to cases where the insured produces some form of specified evidence that the loss was due to theft or burglary. The reason for such restrictions, quite obviously, is to protect the companies from what are commonly known as "inside jobs," and from frauds that would inevitably result, but for such protection. (*United Sponging Co. v. Preferred Acc. Ins. Co.* [1916], 161 N. Y. S. 309.) * * *

The clause with which the court is concerned in the instant case specifies that there be "visible marks" upon the exterior of all doors of a safe, if entry is made through such doors.

The first question to be determined is whether this clause is designed to set forth a rule of evidence, or whether it is designed to set forth a rule of substantive law—a condition precedent limiting the liability of the insurance company. * * *

It is to be noted the indemnifying provision, "Insuring Agreement No. IV.," imposes no restriction or limitation. By this provision the company, under a policy entitled "Storekeepers Burglary and Robbery Policy," agrees "To pay for loss by safe burglary of money, securities and merchandise within the premises." Furthermore, no limitation or restriction is to be found among the "Exclusions," except the loss occasioned by "inside jobs"—safe burglary committed by the insured or a partner. Thereafter, as a *condition* in the policy, safe burglary is defined as the felonious abstraction of insured property from within a safe located within the insured premises by a person *making felonious entry into such safe by actual force and violence.* It requires that the door of such safe be equipped with a combination lock and that all doors thereof be duly closed and locked by all combination locks thereon.

There is no provision in the policy that force and violence are necessary to gain entry through each of the doors to the safe. The crucial clause here under consideration reads: "of which force and violence there are visible marks made by tools, explosives, electricity or chemicals upon the exterior of (*a*) all of said doors." The term "force and violence" used in this clause refers to the "actual force and violence" used in "making *felonious entry into*" the safe. The recital that there be *visible marks* upon the exterior of all of the doors to the safe has reference only to *evidence* of the force and violence used in making the felonious entry into the safe. In other words, the substantive condition of the proviso is that entry into the safe be made by actual force and violence. The further condition that there be visible marks upon the exterior of all doors to the safe, if entry is made through such doors, is merely evidentiary to show an entry into the safe by actual force and violence. * * *

As we interpret the "Storekeepers Burglary and Robbery Policy" of insurance presently before the court, the "visible marks" clause imposes a rule of evidence upon the assured to establish that entry was made into the safe by actual force and violence. Whether such force and violence need be only a contributing factor in making entry into the safe is not a point at issue. On the admitted facts here confronting the court actual force and violence were used in making entry into the appellee's safe and there were visible marks of such force and violence upon the exterior of the inner door, but there were no marks of force or violence upon the exterior of the outer door which was opened by manipulating the combination.

The question then resolves into whether an insurance company, in order to protect itself from "inside jobs" and frauds, may impose a rule of evidence which is binding upon the assured by a provision in the policy.

It is a well-established rule of insurance contracts that the insurance carrier can and must be able to select the risks it insures. But a provision intended to determine the character of evidence necessary to show liability is another matter. The cases generally hold, if the parties to an insurance contract adopt a provision which contravenes no principle of public policy and contains no element of ambiguity, the courts have no right to relieve one of them from disadvantageous terms, which he has actually made, by a process of interpretation. Upon this principle the insurance carrier has a perfect right, if it sees fit, to require proof even of so-called evidentiary facts as an indispensable basis for recovery. Where the provision is not in contravention of public policy and not ambiguous, the only inquiry can be whether the parties have assented to the incorporation in their agreement of a provision which clearly calls for such evidentiary proof. * * *

We hold that where a rule of evidence is imposed by a provision in an insurance policy, as here, the assertion of such rule by the insurance carrier, beyond the reasonable requirements necessary to prevent fraudulent claims against it in proof of the substantive conditions imposed by the policy, contravenes the public policy of this state. This becomes apparent when the statement of the rule in the policy itself, or its assertion by the insurance carrier, is designed to prevent recovery on an obviously justifiable claim.

On the facts in this case money was taken from the assured's safe by an admitted entry into the safe by actual force and violence, which was evidenced by visible marks upon the inner door of the safe. Under these circumstances the assertion by the insurance carrier of the evidentiary requirement, that there be visible marks of force and violence upon the exterior of the outer door, is obviously designed to defeat recovery on a just claim under the policy which insured the felonious abstraction of money from within the safe, by a person making felonious entry into such safe by actual force and violence, where both doors of the safe were duly closed and locked.

Had the insurance carrier desired to exclude loss by safe burglary where the combination of the outer door is worked by manipulation, such provision should have been incorporated under the "Exclusions" in the policy. The appellant asserts in its brief that the appellee is demanding payment "for a loss that clearly was *excluded* in the contract," (Emphasis added) thus recognizing the need for an *exclusion* in the policy to support its contention, but without actually having made such exclusion in the policy.

The judgment of the lower court is affirmed.

■ PRICE, J., dissenting: Concededly, this policy of insurance contains a restrictive "safe burglary" clause—just as many other types of policies contain restrictions. In this day and age a person gets just about what he pays for—whether it be insurance protection or anything else—and that is what happened here. The clause in question is *plain, clear* and *unambiguous*, and, such being the case, should be enforced according to its terms in harmony with the universal rule pertaining to insurance contracts. In my opinion this court has no business making another contract for the parties—its function is to enforce the contract as made.

I would reverse the judgment.

NOTES

(1) *A Hidden Purpose?* In the 1989 movie, *Breaking In,* Burt Reynolds plays a veteran safecracker who reluctantly takes on a novice thief. The first lesson Reynolds's character imparts to his student is to "always check the catch." People get lazy when closing safes and intentionally choose not to spin the dial so that they can easily reopen the safe by only turning the dial once (instead of three times). "Checking the catch" means to check whether someone failed to spin the dial—so that the safecracker can just open the safe without cracking it. This suggests an alternative rationale for the insurance policy's "visible marks" limitations. The policy might have not only been trying to exclude inside jobs but also outside jobs that were facilitated by the insured's negligence—failing to spin the dial.

(2) *Non-Enforcement of Insurance Policy Conditions.* Insurance statutes and regulations tend to go even further than the common law rules in avoiding forfeitures when conditions in insurance policies fail. Many states require that life and disability insurance contracts include "incontestability clauses" that preclude insurers from contesting the validity of the policy after a designated period (usually one or two years). See, e.g., Oglesby v. Penn Mut. Life Ins. Co., 889 F.Supp. 770, 775 (D. Del. 1995) (quoting Del. Code Ann. tit. 18, § 3306(a)(2) (1989)). Other statutes limit the

"failure of condition" defense to circumstances in which the failure "increased the risk of loss," N.Y. Ins. Law § 150(2) (McKinney 1985), or "contributed to the loss," Neb. Rev. Stat. § 44–358 (Reissue 1993). Should an insurance company be able to avoid paying a life insurance claim if (a) the insured intentionally misrepresented that she was a non-smoker at inception of policy; (b) intentionally started to smoke after-inception but before the claimed loss; or (c) the insured was killed in a motorcycle accident (even if company can show that smokers are more likely to die in motorcycle accidents)? Eugene R. Anderson, Richard G. Tuttle & Susannah Crego, *Draconian Forfeitures of Insurance: Commonplace, Indefensible, and Unnecessary*, 65 Fordham L. Rev. 825 (1996).

(3) Recall the distinction between performance and enforcement conditions discussed in the introduction to this section. Burton and Anderson argue that "[i]f the condition is an enforcement term, . . . it should be given effect only if doing so would advance the purpose for which it was included in the agreement, without unnecessary cost to the party against whom enforcement is sought." Steven J. Burton & Eric G. Andersen, *The World of a Contract*, 75 Iowa L. Rev. 861 (1990). Was the "visible marks" condition a performance or enforcement term?

PROBLEM: EXCUSE OF CONDITION TO AVOID DISPROPORTIONATE FORFEITURE

Harry, a dentist, leased a suite in a building from Denise. When Denise refused to renew the lease at end of term, Harry removed his equipment in such a manner that the suite was damaged. Denise's insurance company, Federal, paid for the damage and then, on December 1, 1999, as subrogee sued Harry for the loss. On December 1, 2002, Harry, for the first time, notified his insurance company, Chubb, of Federal's claim and on March 1, 2003 filed a motion to implead Chubb. This motion was granted.

Thereafter, Chubb made a motion for summary judgment, raising two defenses under terms of the insurance policy. The first of these provisions states: "In the event of an occurrence, written notice . . . shall be given by or for the insured to the company . . . as soon as practicable." The other states: "If claim is made or suit is brought against the insured, the insured shall immediately forward to the company every demand, notice, summons, or other process received by him or his representative." Harry admitted that he had not complied with these terms, but argued that they should be excused because Chubb had not alleged that it was prejudiced by the failure. Chubb, on the other hand, argued that the notice condition was for its benefit, that the condition had not been waived, and that it was entitled to a presumption that failure of the condition was prejudicial. Even so, argued Chubb, the burden is on Harry to prove that there was no prejudice. See Aetna Cas. and Sur. Co. v. Murphy, 206 Conn. 409 (1988). The trial court agreed and granted the summary judgment.

You represent Harry, who wants you to appeal the decision. Your associate has called attention to Restatement (Second) § 229, which provides: "To the extent that the non-occurrence of a condition would cause disproportionate forfeiture, a court may excuse the non-occurrence of that condition unless its occurrence was a material part of the agreed exchange." If you appeal, what are Harry's best arguments? Are they likely to prevail?

Comment: Limitations on the Waiver Doctrine

Conditions precedent, express or implied, to a promisor's duty to perform are terms of the contract: they are part of the agreed exchange. Sometimes the other party promises that they will occur but most of the time she does not. In other words, in most cases the failure of a condition is not a breach of contract by the other party. Rather, failure gives the promisor a defense only.

If the promisor waives a condition inserted for its own benefit, an alteration of the contract has occurred. But agreement by the promisee is not required. Are there any limitations on the scope of an alteration by waiver?

Suppose that P, a consultant, was retained by D, a manufacturer, to give advice on how utility rates might be reduced by increased efficiency at D's plants. Compensation depended, in part upon the degree of increased efficiency resulting from the advice. P was to advise D about the plant at St. Joseph as well as others but St. Joseph, because of evaluations already under way, was excluded by the contract from the compensation base. P made recommendations about St. Joseph and increased efficiency resulted. Relying upon an exchange of letters after the contract was formed but before the evaluation was completed, P claimed that D, by stating that compensation would be paid for St. Joseph, had waived the limitation in the contract. There was no evidence of new consideration or that P had relied upon D's letter. The court affirmed a directed verdict for the defendant.

> The theory of "waiver" upon which appellant now bases its right to recover compensation has no application to this case. A party may waive performance of a condition inserted for his benefit and thereby make unconditional the other party's duty under an agreement, but he cannot by waiver of a condition precedent to his own liability create obligation in himself where none previously existed. To create such an obligation requires a new contract and new consideration. . . . "One cannot 'waive' himself into a duty to make a gift of money. . . ."

Nat'l Util. Serv., Inc. v. Whirlpool Corp., 325 F.2d 779, 781 (2d Cir. 1963).

(B) CONSTRUCTIVE CONDITIONS OF EXCHANGE

This section investigates several default conditions that relate each side's performance to the other's. They are defaults because they apply absent the parties' agreement to the contrary. There are three basic issues.

The first is whether breach by one party relieves the other of its performance obligations. If it does, we say that the parties' contractual obligations are *dependent*. If it does not, their obligations are *independent*.

The second concerns the *order* in which the agreed exchange is to be performed. Which party is obligated to tender performance or to perform first? The question is important if the parties' obligations are dependent. In that case, if Party A must perform first, Party B will have no duty under the contract until Party A has tendered or performed. Put differently, Party A's performance of the agreed exchange is a condition precedent to Party B's duty.

If Party A is obligated to go first, the third issue is quantitative: How much performance must Party A tender or render before Party B has a duty under the contract? Is *perfect performance* required, or will *substantial performance* be sufficient? If the latter, by what standard will substantial performance be measured? Again, this is an important inquiry. If Party A's breach is substantial (material), Party B can cancel the contract and pursue remedies based upon Party A's total breach. If Party A's performance is not substantial, Party B cannot cancel and must perform, subject to an offset for any damages caused by Party A's breach.

There is a fourth, related problem: In some cases, part performance by A—perfect or substantial—might suffice to trigger part of B's duty to perform. We consider this problem in the discussion of divisible and indivisible contracts in Chapter Six, Section 3(D).

Comment: Historical Background on Independent and Dependent Promises

Suppose that an owner contracted to sell described land to a vendee for a stated price. The written agreement provided that the price was to be paid on June 1 but nothing was said about when the owner was to tender a deed. On June 1, the owner demanded payment but the vendee refused until a deed in proper form was tendered. The owner then sued for the price without tendering or alleging that the deed had been tendered. Can the owner recover? You might be surprised to learn that until the middle of the eighteenth century, the answer in England was "yes," especially where the vendee ultimately had an action against the owner for failure to convey the land. See, e.g., Pordage v. Cole, 1 Wms. Saunders 319 (K.B. 1669). In the absence of an agreement that the owner shall tender before the price was due, it was thought that the vendee "relied upon his remedy, and did not intend to make the performance a condition precedent." See Serjeant Williams' note to *Pordage v. Cole* in 1 Wms. Saunders 320. The legal result was that the exchange of promises, although mutual, was presumed to be independent rather than dependent.

Edwin Patterson explained this result by the interaction of three factors: (1) The literal-mindedness of the early law; (2) The failure of the common law courts to recognize the exchange function of many contracts; (3) The inhibiting effect of the forms of action available for contract litigation. Edwin W. Patterson, *Constructive Conditions in Contracts,* 42 Colum. L. Rev. 903, 907–910 (1943). According to Patterson, although the "courts were willing to seize upon any language which could be tortured into an express condition of exchange," in the absence of such language, they refused to "construct conditions of exchange." This was "serious because * * * procedure did not recognize the counterclaim; the defendant's remedy was to sue the plaintiff in a separate action for breach of contract." The practical effect of the rule was that the vendee was required to extend credit to the vendor and to rely upon his legal remedies if a tender of the deed was not forthcoming.

Palmer v. Fox

Supreme Court of Michigan, 1936.
274 Mich. 252.

■ TOY, JUSTICE. This is an action at law to recover the balance of the purchase price due on a land contract, made on September 28, 1925, between the Louis G. Palmer & Company, a corporation, as vendor, and the defendant, as vendee, for the sale of a certain lot in Palmer Grove Park Subdivision Number Two, in the city of Detroit. The contract provided for a purchase price of $1,650, of which $247.50 was to be paid at the execution thereof, and the balance to be paid in monthly installments of $16.50 each; the entire amount to be paid "on or before five years from the date hereof." The defendant made the initial payment and also made the monthly payments as called for in the contract up to and including that of February 11, 1931.

* * *

The defendant claimed that the vendor and its assignees failed to perform the covenants in the contract to make stated improvements in the subdivision, and especially, in failing to cinderize or gravel all the streets therein. Defendant further claimed that plaintiff could not recover because of the failure to tender a deed to the premises before commencement of this action.

The court below tried the case without a jury, and found for the plaintiff in the amount of $709.02 principal and $146.89 interest, or a total of $855.91, whereupon judgment was entered for that amount.

Defendant appeals to this court.

The land contract contained a covenant as follows: "The vendor agrees at its own expense to furnish cement sidewalks and to grade all streets; and either cinderize or gravel the streets, except Plymouth Avenue, at its election, and to furnish water mains and lateral sewers in the streets or alleys of said subdivision. If the water and sewer are put in by the city, the assessment against the property shall be paid by the vendor."

The contract also provided that upon receiving payment of principal and interest in full and upon surrender of the contract, the vendor would execute and deliver to the vendee a warranty deed of the premises, subject to certain covenants and restrictions. The contract further provided, "that time is of the essence of this contract."

The lot contracted for fronts on a street in said subdivision known as Westwood avenue (formerly Martin avenue). The testimony showed that said street had been graded but never cinderized or graveled. The proof further showed that the other improvements called for in the contract had been made, although there is some dispute as to whether certain other streets in the subdivision had been fully cinderized or graveled. However, it is conceded by both parties that Westwood avenue in said subdivision was never cinderized or graveled as covenanted in the contract. Defendant contends that the failure to cinderize this street of the subdivision, on which the lot in question abuts, is a material breach of the covenant requiring this improvement, and that such covenant being a dependent one, plaintiff cannot recover in this action.

Plaintiff contends that the covenant by defendant to pay is independent of plaintiff's covenant to furnish improvements, and that whether the covenant to put in improvements "is dependent or independent, is immaterial in view of the fact that the plaintiff's failure to cinderize the street before the defendant's lot, under said covenant, is not a material breach."

Was the covenant of vendor to make improvements, in the instant case, a dependent covenant?

In Folkerts v. Marysville Land Co., 236 Mich. 294, this court conceded that: "It appears to be a more or less difficult task in some cases to say whether the covenants are independent or dependent."

In that case the court set forth the language contained in 6 R.C.L. p. 861, as being the general rule for determining this question, and we quote therefrom, in part, as follows: "But the modern rule is that stipulations are to be construed to be dependent or independent according to the intention of the parties and the good sense of the case. Technical words should give way to such intention. Courts will not and ought not to construe covenants and agreements as independent, and still enforce performance by the other party, unless there is no other mode of construing the instrument, and unless it clearly appears to have been the deliberate intention of the parties at the time the instrument was executed. In brief, the courts will construe covenants to be dependent, unless a contrary intention clearly appears. A party should not be forced to pay out his money, unless he can get that for which he stipulated. * * * Where the acts or covenants of the parties are concurrent, and to be done or performed at the same time, the covenants are dependent, and neither party can maintain an action against the other, without averring and proving performance on his part."

Were the covenants here concurrent? We think so.

It must be remembered that plaintiff brings this action to recover the balance due under the land contract. In the contract the defendant agreed to make payment "on or before five years from the date hereof." Plaintiff agreed to make certain improvements, and although no time was stated as to when such improvements were to be made, we think that the intention of the parties, in relation thereto, clearly appears from the language of the contract, as well as from extraneous facts contained in the record, that such improvements were to be made within the five-year period. Certainly they must be made within a reasonable time. Brow v. Gibraltar Land Co., 249 Mich. 662, 229 N.W. 604.

The contract contains a provision that *after* payment and "upon the surrender of this contract," the vendor will execute and deliver to the vendee a warranty deed to the premises. Logically, it would follow, then, that if the vendee must surrender the contract, every covenant of the contract, or at least every material covenant, must necessarily be effected before such surrender. Especially does such inference apply, where the contract itself does not provide for the performing of any of the agreements after the surrender of the contract. When the contract is surrendered by the vendee, it follows that any rights he has thereunder are likewise surrendered. So, if the vendee must surrender the contract before he may receive a deed, it must have been intended that all other covenants in the contract must necessarily be performed prior to such surrender. Therefore, the covenant to improve the property must have been intended by the terms of the contract to have run concurrently with the covenant to pay the full purchase price within five years.

It further appears from the record that plaintiff put in all the improvements called for by the contract during the period of five years, excepting the cinderizing or graveling of streets, or at least of one street, as hereinbefore stated. This partial performance by the vendor indicates its knowledge of the necessity of performing its covenants.

In the case of Folkerts v. Marysville Land Co., supra, this court, after quoting the statement from Ruling Case Law, hereinbefore in part set forth, said: "Looking at the contracts which plaintiffs made, with these tests in mind, we are persuaded that the covenants to make improvements are dependent. The reasons which have moved us to this position are, in part, as follows: (a) The contract does not, upon its face, show that the covenants are independent. (b) The time stipulated for the performance by each party is concurrent. * * * (c) These plaintiffs purchased these lots for a home."

In the instant case, we have a contract that does not, upon its face, show that the covenants are independent; we also have the inferred intention of the parties that the covenants were to be performed concurrently. But here we do not have a vendee who purchased the lot for a home. On the contrary, the defendant testified that he purchased the property for investment purposes.

While, under the reasoning of this court in the case of Folkerts v. Marysville Land Co., supra, the fact that the vendees had purchased the property for a home was a circumstance considered in determining the intention of the parties, it was not conclusive. Nor does it appear that such circumstance was in and of itself decisive. While it is true that the defendant in the instant case purchased the lot for investment purposes, yet can it be consistently urged that he therefore intended that he should get less than that for which he bargained?

We infer from the record that at the time of the execution of the land contract there were no improvements in the subdivision. It does not seem plausible that defendant would have purchased the lot if it was to remain in that same condition. He had a right to expect, and in all probability did expect, that by the time he had the lot paid for, all of the improvements would be in, and that instead of owning a lot in a subdivision marked by surveyors' stakes, he would have a lot on a street in a subdivision with water mains, lateral sewers, cement sidewalks and graded and surfaced streets, all materially present and not merely outlined on a plat or prospectus. The agreed consideration was to be paid, not for the lot as it was when the contract was made, but as it would be when the stipulated improvements were completed.

The making of the improvements was an essential part of the consideration supporting defendant's agreement to pay the purchase price. That the defendant intended to buy, and that the vendor agreed to sell a lot in a subdivision with improvements, is clear from the provisions of the contract. The defendant's covenant to pay the balance of the purchase price and to surrender the contract was dependent upon the vendor's covenant to make the specified improvements and to deliver a deed to the lot.

* * *

We therefore conclude that the covenant to improve and the covenant to pay the purchase price were dependent covenants.

But, contends plaintiff, it is immaterial whether or not the covenant to make improvements is dependent or independent "in view of the fact that the plaintiff's failure to cinderize the street before the defendant's lot, under said covenant, is not a material breach." On this point, in the trial court, plaintiff introduced testimony to the effect that the cost to cinderize the street in *front* of the lot in question would be only about $7. But the contract called for more than the cinderizing of the street in front of the lot purchased by defendant. It required the vendor to "either cinderize or gravel the streets." Merely to have cinderized or not to have cinderized that portion of the street in front of defendant's lot is beside the point.

The necessity of surfacing the streets in the subdivision, in order to improve the premises, is apparent, and insofar as defendant's rights are concerned, the surfacing of the entire street upon which his lot abutted was of paramount importance to him. The putting in of water mains, sidewalks, and sewers was of little avail, if the street remained unsurfaced so that he and others might not have a convenient way to and from his property. Merely to have surfaced the street in front of the one lot would be absurd. We think that the noncompliance by plaintiff in this respect amounts to a substantial and material breach of the covenant to improve.

The plaintiff and his assignors, therefore, being guilty of a substantial breach of a dependent covenant, cannot maintain this action.

It is not necessary to decide whether or not the tender of a deed to the property in question, made in the declaration of the plaintiff and again at the time of trial, is a sufficient tender, or whether any tender was necessary to be made before instituting this action, as decision has turned on the other questions presented.

The judgment is reversed, without new trial, with costs to defendant.

NOTES

(1) Review the agreement in *Palmer v. Fox*. When was the vendee to pay the price? When was the vendor to deliver a warranty deed? When was the vendor to complete the improvements? If the vendor did not agree to complete the improvements before the vendee's final payment, how does the court conclude that completion was a condition to payment?

(2) *Presumption of Dependency.* Why is there a "presumption that mutual promises in a contract are dependent and are to be so regarded, whenever possible?" As Holmes put it: "You can always imply a condition in a contract. But why do you imply it?" Holmes, *The Path of the Law,* 10 Harv. L. Rev. 457, 466 (1897). According to one court, the "doctrine of constructive dependency of promises should * * * be rested solely on their fairness, and not on any intention of the parties where they express none." Thus, the determination of mutual dependency should arise from the "inherent justice of the situation and not the unexpressed intention of the parties." Giumarra v. Harrington Heights, Inc., 33 N.J.Super. 178, 191 (1954).

But, again, if the parties in *Palmer v. Fox* did not agree that the improvements should be completed before payment, what is the inherent injustice in requiring the vendee to pay before the improvements are completed? According to Restatement (Second), the answer turns on two general considerations: First, dependency "offers both parties maximum security against disappointment of their expectations of a subsequent exchange of performances by allowing each party to defer his own performance until he has been assured that the other will perform"; and second, dependency "avoids placing on either party the burden of financing the other before the latter has performed." Restatement (Second) § 234 cmt. a. Do these considerations justify the result in *Palmer*? Compare *Rowe v.*

Great Atlantic & Pacific Tea Co., Inc., 46 N.Y.2d 62 (1978), where the court refused to "imply" a covenant limiting the lessee's power to assign the lease.

> [A] party who asserts the existence of an implied-in-fact covenant bears a heavy burden, for it is not the function of the courts to remake the contract agreed to by the parties, but rather to enforce it as it exists. Thus, a party making such a claim must prove not merely that it would have been better or more sensible to include such a covenant, but rather that the particular unexpressed promise sought to be enforced is in fact implicit in the agreement viewed as a whole. This is especially so where, as here, the implied covenant sought to be recognized and enforced is of a type not favored by the courts. * * * Such a covenant is to be recognized only if it is clear that a reasonable landlord would not have entered into the lease without such an understanding, for it is only in such a situation that it can be said with the requisite certainty that to refuse to recognize such a covenant would be to deprive the landlord of the fruits of his bargain.

46 N.Y.2d at 69–70.

(3) *Timing.* The modern view on the order of performance is stated in Restatement (Second) § 234:

> (1) Where all or part of the performances to be exchanged under an exchange of promises can be rendered simultaneously, they are to that extent due simultaneously, unless the language or the circumstances indicate the contrary.

> (2) Except to the extent stated in Subsection (1), where the performance of only one party under such an exchange requires a period of time, his performance is due at an earlier time than that of the other party, unless the language or the circumstances indicate the contrary.

In *Bell v. Elder*, 782 P.2d 545 (Utah Ct. App. 1989), the parties contracted to buy and sell real estate. The agreement did not provide a date for performance or state which party was to perform first. Before a reasonable time for performance had passed, the vendee, without first tendering payment, brought suit to cancel the contract and obtain restitution. The court dismissed the lawsuit.

> Although the contract ... does not specify a precise deadline, performance was nevertheless due within a reasonable time. ... If neither party performed its exchanged promise within that time, both promises are discharged. ... Neither of these parties argues that the time for performance exceeds a reasonable time. Since performance of these obligations was due concurrently, neither party could claim a breach by the other until the party claiming the breach tendered performance of its concurrent obligation. The rule requiring such a tender has been explained in a case in which a real estate purchaser and seller each demanded and awaited performance by the other of their respective obligations to pay the

price and deliver the property. The Supreme Court's words in that case apply here as well:

> This is precisely the sort of deadlock meant to be resolved by the requirement of tender. . . . During the executory period of a contract whose time of performance is uncertain but which contemplates simultaneous performance by both parties, . . . neither party can be said to be in default . . . until the other party has tendered his performance. In other words, the party who desires to use legal process to exercise his legal remedies under such a contract must make a tender of his own agreed performance in order to put the other party in default.

782 P.2d at 548 (quoting Century 21 All Western Real Estate and Inv. Inc. v. Webb, 645 P.2d 52, 55–56 (Utah 1982)).

(4) *Leases.* Under what circumstances can a lessee terminate a lease upon a "material" breach of a covenant by the lessor? At common law, a lease was regarded as a conveyance of property rather than a contract. Rent was regarded as a payment "yielded" by the land, not as a contract for the payment of money. See Jersey Boulevard Corp. v. Lerner Stores Corp., 168 Md. 532 (1935). For this reason, covenants between lessor and lessee were regarded as independent unless otherwise expressly agreed. See, e.g., Rock Cnty. Sav. & Trust Co. of Janesville v. Yost's, Inc., 36 Wis.2d 360 (1967); Uniform Residential Landlord and Tenant Act § 1.102, Comment. But see, McGovern, *Dependent Promises in the History of Leases and Other Contracts,* 52 Tul. L. Rev. 659, 703 (1978), who argues that the difference between modern and medieval law on dependency in leases has been "greatly exaggerated."

The modern view in both residential and commercial leases is that the promise to pay rent is dependent upon such lessor covenants as repair, habitability or assignability and that the lessee may withhold rent or terminate the lease if "deprived of a significant inducement to the making of the lease." Restatement (Second) Property § 7.1 (1977). As one court put it, the "actual subject matter of most leases, commercial or residential, is the building leased, not the land upon which it stands, and that therefore contract law rather than property law should be applied to disputes between landlords and tenants." Pawco, Inc. v. Bergman Knitting Mills, 283 Pa.Super. 443 (1980). Thus, the duty of the lessee to pay rent or to remain in the lease is dependent upon "substantial performance" of the lessor's covenants, express or implied, with regard to the quality of the premises, thereby depriving the lessor of a traditional advantage when disputes over the lease arise. See, e.g., Teodori v. Werner, 490 Pa. 58 (1980); Shaw v. Mobil Oil Corp., 272 Or. 109 (1975), applying the "modern" view in commercial leases.

PROBLEM: THE CASE OF THE DEFAULTING PURCHASER

On March 1, Vendor contracted to sell land to Vendee for $8,000. Vendee paid $2,000 at the time of contracting and agreed to pay $1,000 by the first of each succeeding month until the total price was paid. Vendor agreed to convey the property on September 1, the day the final payment was due.

(a) Suppose Vendee failed to make the June 1 payment. Can Vendor recover the payment without tendering a deed?

(b) Assume that Vendee failed to make the July, August and September payments. Can Vendor recover these payments without tendering a deed? Can he recover the July and August payments alone? See Restatement (Second) § 234 and Illustrations 6, 7 and 12. See also Ideal Family & Youth Ranch v. Whetstine, 655 P.2d 429 (Colo. App. 1982) (vendor agreed to put deed in escrow before vendee had duty to pay installments).

Comment: The Forfeiture Problem

Suppose a contractor agrees to construct a new garage for Owner for $25,000. Nothing is said about when payment should be made. Under the modern view of constructive conditions, "where the performance of only one party under an exchange requires a period of time, his performance is due at an earlier time than that of the other party, unless the language or the circumstances indicate the contrary." Restatement (Second) § 234(2). Contractor, then, must perform first. Suppose, however, that contractor demands part payment after 50% of the work has been completed and Owner contends that contractor must either fully or substantially perform the work before any payment is due. Without more, owner is correct. Unless the contract is divisible or the parties have agreed upon installment payments or trade usage is to the contrary, contractor must first satisfy the constructive condition of exchange. As the court stated in *Stewart v. Newbury*, 220 N.Y. 379 (1917): "Where a contract is made to perform work and no agreement is made as to payment, the work must be substantially performed before payment can be demanded."

What is the "inherent fairness" in a rule that requires the construction contractor to extend credit to the owner? Is it enough to conclude that the operative rule is centuries old, the parties can, by agreement, mitigate its harshness and, in any event, "it is just as fair as the opposite rule would be?" See Restatement (Second) § 234 cmt. e.

Jacob & Youngs, Inc. v. George E. Kent
Court of Appeals of New York, 1921.
230 N.Y. 239.

■ CARDOZO, J. The plaintiff built a country residence for the defendant at a cost of upwards of $77,000, and now sues to recover a balance of $3,483.46, remaining unpaid. The work of construction ceased in June, 1914, and the defendant then began to occupy the dwelling. There was no complaint of defective performance until March, 1915. One of the specifications for the plumbing work provides that "all wrought iron pipe must be well galvanized, lap welded pipe of the grade known as 'standard pipe' of Reading manufacture." The defendant learned in March, 1915, that some of the pipe, instead of being made in Reading, was the product of other factories. The plaintiff was accordingly directed by the architect to do the work anew. The plumbing was then encased within the walls except in a few places where it had to be exposed. Obedience to the order meant more than the substitution of other pipe. It meant the demolition at great expense of substantial parts of the completed structure. The plaintiff left the work untouched, and asked for a certificate that the final payment was due. Refusal of the certificate was followed by this suit.

The evidence sustains a finding that the omission of the prescribed brand of pipe was neither fraudulent nor willful. It was the result of the oversight and inattention of the plaintiff's subcontractor. Reading pipe is distinguished from Cohoes pipe and other brands only by the name of the manufacturer stamped upon it at intervals of between six and seven feet. Even the defendant's architect, though he inspected the pipe upon arrival, failed to notice the discrepancy. The plaintiff tried to show that the brands installed, though made by other manufacturers, were the same in quality, in appearance, in market value and in cost as the brand stated in the contract—that they were, indeed, the same thing, though manufactured in another place. The evidence was excluded, and a verdict directed for the defendant. The Appellate Division reversed, and granted a new trial.

We think the evidence, if admitted, would have supplied some basis for the inference that the defect was insignificant in its relation to the project. The courts never say that one who makes a contract fills the measure of his duty by less than full performance. They do say, however, that an omission, both trivial and innocent, will sometimes be atoned for by allowance of the resulting damage, and will not always be the breach of a condition to be followed by a forfeiture. . . . The distinction is akin to that between dependent and independent promises, or between promises and conditions. . . . Some promises are so plainly independent that they can never by fair construction be conditions of one another. . . . Others are so plainly dependent that they must always be conditions. Others, though dependent and thus conditions when there is departure in point of substance, will be viewed as independent and collateral when the departure is insignificant. . . . Considerations partly of justice and partly of presumable intention are to tell us whether this or that promise shall be placed in one class or in another. The simple and the uniform will call for different remedies from the multifarious and the intricate. The margin of departure within the range of normal expectation upon a sale of common chattels will vary from the margin to be expected upon a contract for the construction of a mansion or a "skyscraper." There will be harshness sometimes and oppression in the implication of a condition when the thing upon which labor has been expended is incapable of surrender because united to the land, and equity and reason in the implication of a like condition when the subject-matter, if defective, is in shape to be returned. From the conclusion that promises may not be treated as dependent to the extent of their uttermost minutiae without a sacrifice of justice, the progress is a short one to the conclusion that they may not be so treated without a perversion of intention. Intention not otherwise revealed may be presumed to hold in contemplation the reasonable and probable. If something else is in view, it must not be left to implication. There will be no assumption of a purpose to visit venial faults with oppressive retribution.

Those who think more of symmetry and logic in the development of legal rules than of practical adaptation to the attainment of a just result will be troubled by a classification where the lines of division are so wavering and blurred. Something, doubtless, may be said on the score of consistency and certainty in favor of a stricter standard. The courts have balanced such considerations against those of equity and fairness, and found the latter to be the weightier. The decisions in this state commit us to the liberal view, which is making its way, nowadays, in jurisdictions slow to welcome it. . . . Where the line is to be drawn between the important and the trivial cannot be settled by a formula. "In the nature of the case precise boundaries are impossible" (2 Williston on Contracts, sec. 841). The same omission may take on one aspect or another according to its setting. Substitution of equivalents may not have the same significance in fields of art on the one side and in those of mere utility on the other. Nowhere will change be tolerated, however, if it is so dominant or pervasive as in any real or substantial measure to frustrate the purpose of the contract. . . . There is no general license to install whatever, in the builder's judgment, may be regarded as "just as good" (Easthampton L. & C. Co., Ltd. v. Worthington, 186 N.Y. 407, 412). The question is one of degree, to be answered, if there is doubt, by the triers of the facts . . . and, if the inferences are certain, by the judges of the law. . . . We must weigh the purpose to be served, the desire to be gratified, the excuse for deviation from the letter, the cruelty of enforced adherence. Then only can we tell whether literal fulfillment is to be implied by law as a condition. This is not to say that the parties are not free by apt and certain words to effectuate a purpose that performance of every term shall be a condition of recovery. That question is not here. This is merely to say that the law will be slow to impute the purpose, in the silence of the parties, where the significance of the default is grievously out of proportion to the oppression of the forfeiture. The willful transgressor must accept the penalty of his transgression. . . . For him there is no occasion to mitigate the rigor of implied conditions. The transgressor whose default is unintentional and trivial may hope for mercy if he will offer atonement for his wrong. . . .

In the circumstances of this case, we think the measure of the allowance is not the cost of replacement, which would be great, but the difference in value, which would be either nominal or nothing. Some of the exposed sections might perhaps have been replaced at moderate expense. The defendant did not limit his demand to them, but treated the plumbing as a unit to be corrected from cellar to roof. In point of fact, the plaintiff never reached the stage at which evidence of the extent of the allowance became necessary. The trial court had excluded evidence that the defect was unsubstantial, and in view of that ruling there was no occasion for the plaintiff to go farther with an offer of proof. We think, however, that the offer, if it had been made, would not of necessity have been defective because directed to difference in value. It is true that in most cases the cost of replacement is the measure. . . . The owner is entitled to the money which will permit him to complete, unless the cost of completion is grossly and unfairly out of proportion to the good to be attained. When that is true, the measure is the difference in value. Specifications call, let us say, for a foundation built of granite quarried in Vermont. On the completion of the building, the owner learns that through the blunder of a subcontractor part of the foundation has been built of granite of the same quality quarried in New Hampshire. The measure of allowance is not the cost of reconstruction. "There may be omissions of that which could not afterwards be supplied exactly as called for by the contract without taking down the building to its foundations, and at the same time the omission may not affect the value of the building for use or otherwise, except so slightly as to be hardly appreciable" (Handy v. Bliss, 204 Mass. 513, 519). The rule that gives a remedy in cases of substantial performance with compensation for defects of trivial or inappreciable importance, has been developed by the courts as an instrument of justice. The measure of the allowance must be shaped to the same end.

The order should be affirmed, and judgment absolute directed in favor of the plaintiff upon the stipulation, with costs in all courts.

■ McLaughlin, J. (dissenting). I dissent. The plaintiff did not perform its contract. Its failure to do so was either intentional or due to gross neglect which, under the uncontradicted facts, amounted to the same thing, nor did it make any proof of the cost of compliance, where compliance was possible.

Under its contract it obligated itself to use in the plumbing, only pipe (between 2,000 and 2,500 feet) made by the Reading Manufacturing Company. The first pipe delivered was about 1,000 feet and the plaintiff's superintendent then called the attention of the foreman of the subcontractor, who was doing the plumbing, to the fact that the specifications annexed to the contract required all pipe used in the plumbing to be of the Reading Manufacturing Company. They then examined it for the purpose of ascertaining whether this delivery was of that manufacture and found it was. Thereafter, as pipe was required in the progress of the work, the foreman of the subcontractor would leave word at its shop that he wanted a specified number of feet of pipe, without in any way indicating of what manufacture. Pipe would thereafter be delivered and installed in the building, without any examination whatever. Indeed, no examination, so far as appears, was made by the plaintiff, the subcontractor, defendant's architect, or any one else, of any of the pipe except the first delivery, until after the building had been completed. Plaintiff's architect then refused to give the certificate of completion, upon which the final payment depended, because all of the pipe used in the plumbing was not of the kind called for by the contract. After such refusal, the subcontractor removed the covering or insulation from about 900 feet of pipe which was exposed in the basement, cellar and attic, and all but 70 feet was found to have been manufactured, not by the Reading Company, but by other manufacturers, some by the Cohoes Rolling Mill Company, some by the National Steel Works, some by the South Chester Tubing Company, and some which bore no manufacturer's mark at all. The balance of the pipe had been so installed in the building that an inspection of it could not be had without demolishing, in part at least, the building itself.

I am of the opinion the trial court was right in directing a verdict for the defendant. The plaintiff agreed that all the pipe used should be of the Reading Manufacturing Company. Only about two-fifths of it, so far as appears, was of that kind. If more were used, then the burden of proving that fact was upon the plaintiff, which it could easily have done, since it knew where the pipe was obtained. The question of substantial performance of a contract of the character of the one under consideration depends in no small degree upon the good faith of the contractor. If the plaintiff had intended to, and had complied with the terms of the contract except as to minor omissions, due to inadvertence, then he might be allowed to recover the contract price, less the amount necessary to fully compensate the defendant for damages caused by such omissions. (Woodward v. Fuller, 80 N.Y. 312; Nolan v. Whitney, 88 N.Y. 648.) But that is not this case. It installed between 2,000 and 2,500 feet of pipe, of which only 1,000 feet at most complied with the contract. No explanation was given why pipe called for by the contract was not used, nor was any effort made to show what it would cost to remove the pipe of other manufacturers and install that of the Reading Manufacturing Company. The defendant had a right to contract for what he wanted. He had a right before making payment to get what the contract called for. It is no answer to this suggestion to say that the pipe put in was just as good as that made by the Reading Manufacturing Company, or that the difference in value between such pipe and the pipe made by the Reading Manufacturing Company would be either "nominal or nothing." Defendant contracted for pipe made by the Reading Manufacturing Company. What his reason was for requiring this kind of pipe is of no importance. He wanted that and was entitled to it. It may have been a mere whim on his part, but even so, he had a right to this kind of pipe, regardless of whether some other kind, according to the opinion of the contractor or experts, would have been "just as good, better, or done just as well." He agreed to pay only upon condition that the pipe installed were made by that company and he ought not to be compelled to pay unless that condition be performed. . . . The rule, therefore, of substantial performance, with damages for unsubstantial omissions, has no application. . . .

* * *

I am of the opinion the trial court did not err in ruling on the admission of evidence or in directing a verdict for the defendant.

For the foregoing reasons I think the judgment of the Appellate Division should be reversed and the judgment of the Trial Term affirmed.

Order affirmed, etc.

NOTES

(1)   The dissenting judge insists that "[t]he plaintiff did not perform its contract." Does Judge Cardozo disagree? If not, where is the express condition in this case? Arguably, the plaintiff satisfied a "constructive" condition of substantial performance that was precedent to the defendant's duty to pay the last installment.

(2)   Is the issue here one of liability, remedy, or both?

(3)   Could the contract have been drafted so as to preclude any recovery if Reading pipe was not installed? Which "apt and certain words" would you use to draft a clause that ensures the protection of Kent's idiosyncratic preference? Should Cardozo have dropped a footnote suggesting words that would suffice? See Ian Ayres, *Regulating Opt-Out: An Economic Theory of Altering Rules*, 121 Yale L.J. 2032, 2056 (2012).

(4)   The contract said that final payment was due only after plaintiff's architect gave a "certificate of completion." Is it reasonable for a buyer and seller to rely on a third-party architect (who is a repeat player in the market and subject to professional ethics and potential reputational sanctions) to determine whether or not performance was adequate? It is clear from the opinion that the architect refused to issue the certificate of payment when the plaintiff refused to "do the work anew." Except for noting that the architect failed to notice the discrepancy in the pipe until after the house was completed, the court did not consider the effect of substantial performance upon the express condition that issuance of the certificate was to precede the duty to pay. One reason for this may be the case of *Nolan v. Whitney*, 88 N.Y. 648 (1882), where the court held that when a contractor has substantially performed the contract the architect is "bound" to issue the certificate. An unreasonable and wrongful refusal excuses the necessity that the certificate be issued.

Most states, however, have followed the principle of review set forth in section 303 of the first Restatement:

Where a certificate of an architect, surveyor or engineer is a condition precedent to a duty of immediate payment for work, the condition is excused if the architect, surveyor or engineer (a) dies or becomes incapacitated, or (b) refuses to give a certificate because of collusion with the promisor, or (c) refuses to give a certificate after making examination of the work and finding it adequate, or (d) fails to make proper examination of the work, or (e) fails to exercise an honest judgment, or (f) makes a gross mistake with reference to facts on which a refusal to give a certificate is based.

An assumption here is that the architect, as a professional, should have more room for the exercise of honest judgment than that permitted if the decision were reviewable under standards of reasonableness:

> Agreements to submit specific determinations of controversies and disputes arising under a contract to a third party chosen by the contracting parties are valid. * * * The decision of the third party as to matters entrusted to him, like the award of an arbitrator, is final and binding upon the parties unless the decision is impeached for fraud, accident, or gross mistake of such a nature that fraud may be inferred. * * * Parties competent to enter into this construction contract are competent to agree that the architect, even though he is the agent of one of the contracting parties, shall determine the question of claimed losses and damages. They are also competent to agree that said designated person's determination shall be final and binding on them. * * * Anticipatory provisions for settlements of disputes are favored and have the approval of the courts.

E.H. Marhoefer, Jr., Co. v. Mount Sinai, Inc., 190 F.Supp. 355, 359–60 (E.D. Wis. 1961).

(5) While, outside the UCC, a buyer's duty to pay is normally conditioned on seller's substantial performance (unless otherwise agreed), the seller's duty to sell is normally conditioned on perfect tender of full payment. Should there be exceptions to this rule where the buyer is a day late or a dollar short? Cf. Lane Enter., Inc. v. L.B. Foster Co., 700 A.2d 465 (Pa. Super. Ct. 1997) (finding that buyer breached duty to pay by withholding "$7,082.22 out of a $133,922.40 purchase order" but that this breach was not a material breach which justified the seller's cancellation of the contract).

(6) *Trivial Breach.* In *Foundation Dev. Corp. v. Loehmann's, Inc.,* 163 Ariz. 438 (1990), Loehmann's, the anchor tenant in a shopping center under a 20-year lease failed by two days to pay a disputed charge within the ten days specified in the lease. Because of this tardy payment, the lessor exercised its contractual right to terminate the lease. The court held that lessor did not have the right to terminate for a "trivial breach" but did not explain what words would have been sufficient to make timely payment a condition of further rental. The court dismissed "stock phrases" such as "time is of the essence" as indicating an intent to create such a condition. What non-stock phrases would have been sufficient?

PROBLEM: READING PIPE AND THE WAIVER OF CONDITIONS

In *Jacob & Youngs v. Kent,* the court concluded that the installation of the particular brand of pipe, Reading pipe, was not a condition precedent to the duty of the owner to pay the balance due under the construction contract. But Judge Cardozo, speaking for the majority, did observe: "This is not to say that the parties are not free by apt and certain words to effectuate a purpose that performance of every term shall be a condition of recovery."

(1)   What if, for some reason (e.g., it is intended as a show house for Reading pipe, or his wife once won a Miss Reading Pipe contest), the owner did indeed want the installation of this brand of pipe to be a condition? Could it be done? How?

(2)   Assume that installation of Reading pipe was thus made a condition precedent, but that the contractor cannot procure Reading pipe. He approaches the owner, advising him that Cohoes pipe, a brand of equal quality, is available. Owner is agreeable to the substitution, but after installation of the substitute, stands by the original contract provision making installation of Reading pipe a condition of recovery. Will owner prevail?

(3)   Assume instead that the owner does the totally unexpected; *viz.,* he says that not only is it all right to omit the installation of Reading pipe, there is no need to install any pipe at all or to even construct the building. The owner will pay anyway. Can contractor hold owner to this commitment?

(4)   As alternative to the above scenarios, suppose that contractor went ahead with the installation of Cohoes pipe without discussing the matter with the owner. Is the latter obligated to pay? Would it make a difference if the owner, after becoming aware of the substitution, indicated that he would still pay? Even if obliged to pay, could the owner still recover damages if the Cohoes pipe was inferior to the Reading pipe?

(5)   Finally, assume that the contractor did not install any pipe at all, but the owner (again, doing the unlikely thing) said that he would still pay. Would the owner be bound by this commitment?

PROBLEM: THE OVEN CASES—PERFECT TENDER?

Recall the Ovens Case in Chapter One, in which Smirgo, an oven manufacturer, contracts to sell Bisko, a bakery, two custom made oven for $30,000, delivery November 1, payment due 90 days after delivery.

(1)   To what extent is there a doctrine of "substantial" performance under Article 2 of the UCC? What are the buyer's non-judicial remedies? Consider the following scenarios:

(a) Smirgo tendered delivery of the two ovens three days late. In addition, one of the ovens failed to conform to the specifications (a minor deviation which could be corrected for $100). Bisko wants to reject the goods, cancel the contract and sue Smirgo for damages. Would you recommend this course of action? See UCC §§ 2–601, 2–602, 2–711(1) & 2–713. Or, should Bisko accept the goods and seek damages for breach of warranty? See UCC §§ 2–606 & 2–714(2).

(b) Would your analysis in (a), above, be altered by the following factual changes:

(1) Bisko in fact has suffered no damage and has found another manufacturer who can supply the same ovens at 20% less. See

UCC §§ 1–103, 1–304, & 2–103(1)(b). Is the buyer's remedy of rejection subject to a duty of good faith?

(2) Smirgo delivered the defective oven on October 15 rather than November 4. See UCC § 2–508(1).

(3) The delay of three days was caused by Smirgo's failure promptly to notify Bisko of the shipment. See UCC § 2–504.

(4) Smirgo was to deliver the ovens in two installments, the first of which was defective. See UCC § 2–612.

(5) Bisko accepted delivery of both ovens, subsequently discovered the defect and now seeks to revoke acceptance and cancel the contract. See UCC § 2–608.

(6) If Bisko rightfully rejects the tender of delivery, Smirgo might have a right to cure the non-conformity under UCC § 2–508. Would that right exist on these facts?

(2) Suppose Bisko had paid Smirgo $15,000 upon signing the contract and agreed to pay the balance upon delivery. Consider the following questions:

(a) If Smirgo repudiated the contract before any deliveries were made, would Bisko be entitled to cancel the contract, recover the down payment *and* seek compensatory damages for breach of contract? See UCC § 2–711.

(b) Suppose Bisko repudiated the contract before delivery and it is clear that Smirgo suffered no damage from the breach. May Bisko recover the $15,000 down payment? (Assume there has been no effort to liquidate damages.) See UCC § 2–718(2) & (3).

DRAFTING EXERCISE: SELLING A BOUTIQUE

You represent Alice Rosamond, the owner of a boutique women's clothing retailer named Dahlia, located in downtown Rochester, New York. Robert Roswell has been in informal negotiations to purchase the boutique and buyer's counsel has just sent you the offer reproduced below. Your assignment is to edit the buyer's offer to create a counteroffer. Modify the existing provisions and add new provisions so that the result is more fair or favorable to your client. Do not incorporate changes you think a reasonable buyer would not accept—your submission should resemble a final contract that both parties can agree upon. For each provision modified or added, explain the rationale behind the change. For at least one of these changes, present an alternative you considered that would be more favorable to your client but that you rejected because you did not think a reasonable buyer would be receptive to the change. See generally William K. Sjostrom, Jr., *An Introduction to Contract Drafting* (2012).

DAHLIA SALE AGREEMENT

This business sale agreement (the "Agreement") is made on _____ between Alice Rosamond (the "Seller"), an individual residing at 33 Nicholson Ave., Rochester, NY, and Robert Roswell (the "Buyer"), an individual residing at 451 Bucksmills Rd., Rochester, NY.

The Seller is the sole owner of Dahlia (the "Business"), a boutique women's clothing retailer located at 52 Central St., Rochester, NY. The Seller wishes to sell the Business to the Buyer, and the Buyer wishes to purchase the Business from the Seller.

Accordingly, the parties agree as follows:

1.   Sale and Purchase of Business. The Seller hereby agrees to sell to the Purchaser the following:

   a.   Business Name. The trade name, business name, and goodwill of the Business;

   b.   Lease. The Lease to the premises at which the Business is conducted;

   c.   Inventory. All stock in trade and merchandise in Seller's inventory on the date the sale is closed; and

   d.   Fixtures. All furniture, fixtures, furnishings, and other equipment used by Seller in the conduct of the Business more fully described in the Exhibit A attached to this Agreement and made a part of it.

2.   Purchase Price. The purchase price, exclusive of inventory, is $550,000.

3.   Inventory. The Seller and the Buyer valued the inventory at $234,860 on January 19th, 2017. The purchase price for the inventory will be this value adjusted by adding all purchases made by the Seller (at the Seller's cost) from the date on which the value of the inventory was determined to the date of the closing of this sale and subtracting the value of all inventory sold by the Seller from the date on which the value of the inventory was determined to the date of the closing of this sale. However, the Buyer will not be obligated to pay more than $300,000 for the inventory.

4.   Payment. The Buyer agrees to pay the $550,000 purchase price, exclusive of inventory, on the closing of the sale by a certified check. The Buyer will pay the purchase price of the inventory after the Buyer verifies the value of the inventory, which will occur no later than one week after closing.

5.   Time and Place of Closing. The closing will take place at the office of Josiah Tulkinghorn, Esq., Seller's attorney, at 1853 Broadstairs St., Rochester, NY, on _____, at _____.

6.   Closing Documents. At the closing, the Seller shall deliver to the Buyer, properly executed and in form for recording, the following documents:

   a.   Bill of Sale. A Bill of Sale conveying the equipment, inventory, and other tangible personal property being purchased;

b.   Assignment of Business Name. An assignment of the Seller's interest in the business name "Dahlia"; and

c.   Assignment of Lease. An assignment of Lease of the premises at which the Business is conducted, being a Lease dated March 31st, 2011 between Stillwater Realty as Lessor and Seller as Lessee, along with a written consent to assignment of the Lease executed by the Lessor.

7.   Seller's Representations and Warranties. Seller represents and warrants the following:

a.   Good Title. Seller has good and marketable title to all the assets to be sold pursuant to this Agreement and they are free of any encumbrance;

b.   Business Records. All business records made available to the Buyer are true and correct;

c.   Financial Statements. The balance sheet as of December 31st, 2016 and income statement for the period from January 1st, 2016 through December 31st 2016, as contained in Exhibit B attached to this agreement, have been audited by an independent auditor in accordance with generally accepted accounting principles and are correct, complete, and fairly represent the financial condition of the Business as of the dates stated; and

d.   No Judgments or Liens. No judgments, liens, actions, or proceedings are presently outstanding or pending against the Business or Seller personally, or against any of the property that is the subject of this Agreement.

8.   Seller's Covenants. Between the date this Agreement is signed and the date of closing, the Seller warrants that it will:

a.   Continued Operations. Continue to operate the Business in the same manner as it has previously and not introduce any new method of management, operation or accounting;

b.   Maintain Facilities. Maintain the properties and facilities in present condition; and

c.   Maintain Relationships. Retain its present employees and maintain its relationships with suppliers, customers, and others having business relations with it.

Between the date this Agreement is signed and the date of closing, the Seller warrants that it will not, without the Buyer's prior written consent:

d.   Contracts. Enter into any contract or commitment, or incur or agree to incur any liability, except in the normal course of business;

e.   Capital Expenditures. Make any capital expenditures, except in the normal course of business; or

    f.   Compensation. Increase the compensation payable or to become payable to any employee or agent, or make any bonus payment to any such person;

9.   Closing Conditions. The Buyer's obligation to close the sale is subject to the satisfaction of the following conditions:

    a.   Representations and Warranties. Seller's representations and warranties must be true on the closing date;

    b.   Covenants. Seller must have performed all of the covenants to be performed by it on or before the closing date; and

    c.   Material Adverse Changes. No material adverse changes in the financial condition or prospects of the Business shall have occurred between the date this Agreement was signed and the date of closing.

10.   Covenant not to Compete. For a period of three years from the date of closing, Seller will not, directly or indirectly, either as principal, partner, agent, manager, employee, stockholder, director, officer, or in any other capacity, engage or be interested in the conduct of a business similar to the one sold pursuant to this Agreement within a radius of 100 miles from the location of the Business.

The restrictive covenant contained in this Clause will inure to the benefit of Buyer's assigns, successors, and transferees. If Buyer sells or otherwise transfers the business, Seller will remain bound by the terms of the restrictive covenant, which may be enforced by Buyer's assigns, successors, and transferees.

11.   Risk of Loss or Destruction. All risk of loss or damage to the property being purchased under this Agreement will remain with the Seller to the date of the closing of this sale and pass to the Buyer upon the closing. If any such property is lost or damaged prior to closing, Buyer may terminate this Agreement and demand the return of any sums Buyer may have paid to Seller on account of the purchase price.

12.   Governing Law. This Agreement shall be governed by and construed under the laws of the state of New York, without regard to that state's conflict of law principles.

13.   Amendments. The Agreement may be amended only by a writing that is signed by both parties to this Agreement.

14.   Waiver. No waiver to any provision of this Agreement shall be binding unless the purported waiver is set forth in writing and signed by the party. Any waiver shall be limited to the event or circumstance referenced in the writing and shall not be considered a waiver of any other term of the Agreement, or of the same event or circumstance should the event or circumstance recur.

15.   Confidentiality. Seller agrees to keep the terms of this Agreement confidential.

To evidence the parties' agreement to this Agreement's provisions, they have executed and delivered this Agreement on the date set forth in the preamble.

[signature lines]

5. CHANGED CIRCUMSTANCES: IMPRACTICABILITY AND FRUSTRATION OF PURPOSE

The law of impracticability and frustration can be thought of as another type of implied condition, this one a performance condition. One's duty to perform a contract is normally—that is, by default—conditioned not only upon the absence of a material breach by the other side, but also upon performance not becoming impracticable or frustrated due to changed circumstances.

The policy implications of this default deserve some attention. Why should a court imply a condition that excuses a promise where the parties have not provided for the event? As one court put it, the "sanctity of contract . . . requires the parties to do what they have agreed to do." Dermott v. Jones, 69 U.S. 1 (1864). If unexpected impediments lie in the way and a loss must ensue, why not leave the loss where the contract places it? Nonetheless, if the event was unexpected and the impact on performance severe, most courts are willing to consider the possibility of some relief. Under this view, the impracticability defense is "an equitable one to be applied when fair and just" and a promisor "should not be required to bear the cost of changed circumstances that could not reasonably be provided against in the contract" and have made performance "vitally different" from what was anticipated when the contract was made. Opera Co. of Boston, Inc. v. Wolf Trap Found., 817 F.2d 1094, 1099–1100 (4th Cir. 1987).

In determining when, if ever, relief from changed circumstances should be granted, analysis is aided if the following questions are asked and answered.

First, what was the nature of the risk event and what was its impact on the contractual relationship? Was the event a condition which existed at the time of contracting or a circumstance which arose thereafter? Was the impact of the event that performance as agreed was prevented or made more costly or that the incentive of one party to perform was impaired because its purpose in entering the contract was frustrated?

Second, was the party seeking relief at fault in that it caused the event or failed to take reasonable steps either to avoid it or to minimize the impact?

Third, if the party seeking relief was not at fault, did the agreement allocate the risk of the event to one or the other or both parties? The form of agreement may include an express condition, an "excuse" or *force majeure* clause[3] or a more elaborate risk allocation system, including insurance. Or it might be concluded that because the risk was discussed or foreshadowed in the negotiations, it was "tacitly" agreed to by the promisor who made an unconditional promise to perform at a fixed price.

Fourth, if there was no agreement, express or implied, allocating the risk, how is the court to fill the gap in risk allocation? One method is for the court to refuse to impose any risk allocation terms on the parties. In short, the maker of an unconditional promise bears the full risk of the event and its impact. A more flexible test, adopted by section 261 of Restatement (Second), is as follows:

> Where, after a contract is made, a party's performance is made impracticable without his fault by the occurrence of an event the non-occurrence of which was a basic assumption on which the contract was made, his duty to render that performance is discharged, unless the language or the circumstances indicate the contrary.

The section 261 test is derived from UCC § 2–615(a). See also Restatement (Second) § 266 (event existed at the time of contracting) and § 265 (frustration of purpose).

Fifth, what is the nature and scope of relief when the conditions of section 261 or UCC § 2–615(a) are satisfied? Is relief limited to discharge of the contract with appropriate restitution or must the parties continue performance under terms adjusted by the court to reflect the risk? Is there a remedial middle ground?

Sixth, suppose in a case of impracticability that the disadvantaged party offers to modify the contract by agreement. Would that modification be enforceable? Suppose that the advantaged party refused to negotiate over a proposed modification. Would that ever be bad faith?

The excuse doctrine involves a balancing act. Too much excuse undermines the stability of contracts, reallocates risks already insured against in an inefficient manner and invites courts to make contracts that the parties could and should have made for themselves. But how much is too much? Despite sound analysis and a flexible test for excuse, perhaps you will not be surprised to discover that there is considerable judicial talk about granting relief but precious little evidence that relief has been granted.

---

[3] Here is an example of a *force majeure* clause:

Shipper shall not be responsible nor deemed to be in default on account of delays in performance of this Agreement due to causes beyond Shipper's control and not occasioned by its fault or negligence, including but not being limited to civil war, insurrections, strikes, riots, fires, floods, explosions, earthquakes, serious accidents, and any act of government, acts of God or the public enemy, failure of transportation, epidemics, quarantine restrictions, failure of vendors or other shippers to perform their contracts or labor troubles causing cessation, slowdown, or interruption of work, provided such cause is beyond Shipper's control.

See Eastern Air Lines, Inc. v. McDonnell Douglas Corp., 532 F.2d 957, 988 (5th Cir. 1976).

(A) EXISTING IMPRACTICABILITY

United States v. Wegematic Corp.

United States Court of Appeals, Second Circuit, 1966.
360 F.2d 674.

■ FRIENDLY, CIRCUIT JUDGE. The facts developed at trial in the District Court for the Southern District of New York, fully set forth in a memorandum by Judge Graven, can be briefly summarized: In June 1956 the Federal Reserve Board invited five electronics manufacturers to submit proposals for an intermediate-type, general-purpose electronic digital computing system or systems; the invitation stressed the importance of early delivery as a consideration in determining the Board's choice. Defendant, a relative newcomer in the field, which had enjoyed considerable success with a smaller computer known as the ALWAC III–E, submitted a detailed proposal for the sale or lease of a new computer designated as the ALWAC 800. It characterized the machine as "a truly revolutionary system utilizing all of the latest technical advances," and featured that "maintenance problems are minimized by the use of highly reliable magnetic cores for not only the high speed memory but also logical elements and registers." Delivery was offered nine months from the date the contract or purchase order was received. In September the Board acted favorably on the defendant's proposal, ordering components of the ALWAC 800 with an aggregate cost of $231,800. Delivery was to be made on June 30, 1957, with liquidated damages of $100 per day for delay. The order also provided that in the event the defendant failed to comply "with any provision" of the agreement, "the Board may procure the services described in the contract from other sources and hold the Contractor responsible for any excess cost occasioned thereby." Defendant accepted the order with enthusiasm.

The ALWAC III–E (a big computer)

The first storm warning was a suggestion by the defendant in March 1957 that the delivery date be postponed. In April it informed the Board by letter that delivery would be made on or before October 30 rather than as agreed, the delay being due to the necessity of "a redesign which we feel has greatly improved this equipment"; waiver of the stipulated damages for delay was requested. The Board took the request under advisement. On August 30 defendant wrote that delivery would be delayed "possibly into 1959"; it suggested use of ALWAC III–E equipment in the interim and waiver of the $100 per day "penalty." The Board also took this request under advisement but made clear it was waiving no rights. In mid-October defendant announced that "due to engineering difficulties it has become impracticable to deliver the ALWAC 800 Computing System at this time"; it requested cancellation of the contract without damages. The Board set about procuring comparable equipment from another manufacturer; on October 6, 1958, International Business Machines Corporation delivered an IBM 650 computer, serving substantially the same purpose as the ALWAC 800, at a rental of $102,000 a year with an option to purchase for $410,450.

In July 1958 the Board advised defendant of its intention to press its claim for damages; this suit followed. The court awarded the United States $46,300 for delay under the liquidated damages clause, $179,450 for the excess cost of the IBM equipment, and $10,056 for preparatory expenses useless in operating the IBM system—a total of $235,806, with 6% interest from October 6, 1958.

The principal point of the defense, which is the sole ground of this appeal, is that delivery was made impossible by "basic engineering difficulties" whose correction would have taken between one and two years and would have cost a million to a million and a half dollars, with success likely but not certain. Although the record does not give an entirely clear notion what the difficulties were, two experts suggested that they may have stemmed from the magnetic cores, used instead of transistors to achieve a solid state machine, which did not have sufficient uniformity at this stage of their development. Defendant contends that under federal law, which both parties concede to govern, see Cargill, Inc. v. Commodity Credit Corp., 275 F.2d 745, 751–753 (2 Cir. 1960), the "practical impossibility" of completing the contract excused its defaults in performance.

* * *

We find persuasive the defendant's suggestion of looking to the Uniform Commercial Code as a source for the "federal" law of sales. . . .

Section 2–615 of the UCC, entitled "Excuse by failure of presupposed conditions," provides that:

"Except so far as a seller may have assumed a greater obligation * * * delay in delivery or non-delivery * * * is not a breach of his duty under a contract for sale if performance as agreed has been made impracticable by the occurrence of a contingency the nonoccurrence of which was a basic assumption on which the contract was made * * *."

The latter part of the test seems a somewhat complicated way of putting Professor Corbin's question of how much risk the promisor assumed. Recent Developments in the Law of Contracts, 50 Harv. L. Rev. 449, 465–66 (1937); 2 Corbin, Contracts § 1333, at 371. We see no basis for thinking that when an electronics system is promoted by its manufacturer as a revolutionary breakthrough, the risk of the revolution's occurrence falls on the purchaser; the reasonable supposition is that it has already occurred or, at least, the manufacturer is assuring the purchaser that it will be found to have when the machine is assembled. As Judge Graven said: "The Board in its invitation for bids did not request invitations to conduct a development program for it. The Board requested invitations from manufacturers for the furnishing of a computer machine." Acceptance of defendant's argument would mean that though a purchaser makes his choice because of the attractiveness of a manufacturer's representation and will be bound by it, the manufacturer is free to express what are only aspirations and gamble on mere probabilities of fulfillment without any risk of liability. In fields of developing technology, the manufacturer would thus enjoy a wide degree of latitude with respect to performance while holding an option to compel the buyer to pay if the gamble should pan out. . . . We do not think this the common understanding—above all as to a contract where the manufacturer expressly agreed to liquidated damages for delay and authorized the purchaser to resort to other sources in the event of non-delivery. . . . If a manufacturer wishes to be relieved of the risk that what looks good on paper may not prove so good in hardware, the appropriate exculpatory language is well known and often used.

Beyond this the evidence of true impracticability was far from compelling. The large sums predicted by defendant's witnesses must be appraised in relation not to the single computer ordered by the Federal Reserve Board, evidently for a bargain price, but to the entire ALWAC 800 program as originally contemplated. Although the record gives no idea what this was, even twenty-five machines would gross $10,000,000 if priced at the level of the comparable IBM equipment. While the unanticipated need for expending $1,000,000 or $1,500,000 on redesign might have made such a venture unattractive, as defendant's management evidently decided, the sums are thus not so clearly prohibitive as it would have them appear. What seemingly did become impossible was on-time performance; the issue whether if defendant had offered prompt rectification of the design, the Government could have refused to give it a chance and still recover not merely damages for delay but also the higher cost of replacement equipment, is not before us.

Affirmed.

NOTES

(1) Excuse issues arise under government contracts when a contractor performing a fixed-price contract claims that it is "impossible" or impracticable to achieve the promised result under the specifications. Normally, the contractor will not be excused under the contract "default" clause or other standard risk allocation clauses. See, e.g., Austin Co. v. United States, 161 Ct.Cl. 76 (1963) (holding contractor assumed the risk if default clause did not provide an excuse and contractor agreed to produce a particular result at a fixed price).

As Judge Friendly indicated in *Wegematic,* however, appropriate sections of the Uniform Commercial Code may be used as a source of federal contract law. What "test" for excuse did Judge Friendly adopt in *Wegematic?* If the risk of not achieving the promised result was properly on the contractor, was the court correct in considering whether "performance as agreed" was made impracticable?

(2) If the government has furnished detailed specifications which the contractor must follow ("design specifications") or specifications which require a particular result ("performance specifications") and the contractor is unable to perform on time, the risk is placed upon the government if the specifications were defective or an implied warranty of suitability was made. Similarly, if the contractor actually completes performance at a cost in excess of the contract price, it will commonly be excused for any delay and compensated for additional costs under a changes clause. Finally, the government may be liable for extra costs incurred in achieving promised results when contracting officials have failed to disclose material information about performance at the time of contracting under circumstances where the government knew that the contractor was unaware of the information and not likely to find out. See generally John W. Whelan & James F. Nagle, Federal Government Contracts: Cases and Materials 266–329 (3d ed. 2007).

(3) *Subsurface Conditions.* When a contractor encounters unexpected subsurface conditions upon the land of another which delay or increase the cost of performance, the usual rule is that the contractor assumes the risk unless the owner, whether a private party or the government, has agreed to assume the risk, misrepresented the conditions or failed to disclose known difficulties. See Whelan, Federal Government Contracts, supra, at 450–458; Restatement (Second) § 266, Illus. 8. Impracticability alone is not an excuse: both parties must assume that the conditions did not exist. Compare Mineral Park Land Co. v. Howard, 172 Cal. 289 (1916). In order to avoid "padded" prices by contractors and the delays incident to disputes over subsurface conditions, the government has developed a standard clause dealing with these risks:

DIFFERING SITE CONDITIONS (1984)

(a) The Contractor shall promptly, and before such conditions are disturbed, notify the Contracting Officer in writing of: (1) subsurface or latent physical conditions at the site differing materially from those indicated in this contract, or (2) unknown physical conditions at the site, of an unusual nature, differing materially from those ordinarily encountered and generally recognized as inhering in work of the character provided for in this contract. The Contracting Officer shall promptly investigate the conditions, and if he finds that such conditions do materially so differ and cause an increase or decrease in the Contractor's cost of, or the time required for, performance of any part of the work under this contract, whether or not changed as a result of such conditions, an equitable adjustment shall be made and the contract modified in writing accordingly.

(b) No claim of the Contractor under this clause shall be allowed unless the Contractor has given the notice required in (a) above; *provided,* however, the time prescribed therefor may be extended by the Government.

(c) No claim by the Contractor for an equitable adjustment hereunder shall be allowed if asserted after final payment under this contract.

(4) *Existing Impracticability v. Mutual Mistake.* Section 266(1) of Restatement (Second) provides:

> Where, at the time a contract is made, a party's performance under it is impracticable without his fault because of a fact of which he has no reason to know and the non-existence of which is a basic assumption on which the contract is made, no duty to render that performance arises, unless the language or circumstances indicate the contrary.

Section 152(1), on the other hand, provides that a contract is "voidable" by an adversely affected party "where a mistake of both parties at the time the contract was made has a material effect on the agreed exchange of performances" unless he bears the risk under the agreement, or has proceeded with limited knowledge of the facts to which the mistake relates but "treats his limited knowledge as sufficient" or the risk is allocated to him "by the court on the ground that it is reasonable in the circumstances to do so." See Roy v. Stephen Pontiac-Cadillac, Inc., 15 Conn.App. 101 (1988) (buyer "had reason to know" that seller could not deliver truck actually ordered).

Suppose that you represented the contractor in *United States v. Wegematic,* supra, and Restatement (Second) was available. Which theory of risk allocation would you pursue, existing impracticability or mutual mistake? A question to consider is whether either theory should be applied to circumstances which arise after the contract is formed. For example, is it correct to draw a distinction between facts that are knowable and not known, and facts that are not knowable and not known?

(B) SUPERVENING IMPRACTICABILITY

Taylor v. Caldwell

King's Bench, 1863.
122 Eng. Rep. 309.

■ BLACKBURN, J. In this case the plaintiffs and defendants had, on the 27th May, 1861, entered into a contract by which the defendants agreed to let the plaintiffs have the use of The Surrey Gardens and Music Hall on four days then to come, viz., the 17th June, 15th July, 5th August and 19th August, for the purpose of giving a series of four grand concerts, and day and night fetes at the Gardens and Hall on those days respectively; and the plaintiffs agreed to take the Gardens and Hall on those days, and pay £100 for each day.

The parties inaccurately call this a "letting," and the money to be paid a "rent"; but the whole agreement is such as to shew that the defendants were to retain the possession of the Hall and Gardens so that there was to be no demise of them, and that the contract was merely to give the plaintiffs the use of them on those days. Nothing however, in our opinion, depends on this. The agreement then proceeds to set out various stipulations between the parties as to what each was to supply for these concerts and entertainments, and as to the manner in which they should be carried on. The effect of the whole is to shew that the existence of the Music Hall in the Surrey Gardens in a state fit for a concert was essential for the fulfillment of the contract, such entertainment as the parties contemplated in their agreement could not be given without it.

After the making of the agreement, and before the first day on which a concert was to be given, the Hall was destroyed by fire. This destruction, we must take it on the evidence, was without the fault of either party, and was so complete that in consequence the concerts could not be given as intended. And the question we have to decide is whether, under these circumstances, the loss which the plaintiffs have sustained is to fall upon the defendants. The parties when framing their agreement evidently had not present to their minds the possibility of such a disaster, and have made no express stipulation with reference to it, so that the answer to the question must depend upon the general rules of law applicable to such a contract.

There seems no doubt that where there is a positive contract to do a thing, not in itself unlawful, the contractor must perform it or pay damages for not doing it, although in consequence of unforeseen accidents, the performance of his contract has become unexpectedly burdensome or even impossible. . . . But this rule is only applicable when the contract is positive and absolute, and not subject to any condition either express or implied; and there are authorities which, as we think, establish the principle that where, from the nature of the contract, it appears that the parties must from the beginning have known that it could not be fulfilled unless when the time for the fulfillment of the contract arrived some particular specified thing continued to exist, so that, when entering into the contract, they must have contemplated such continuing existence as the foundation of what was to be done; there, in the absence of any express or implied warranty that the thing shall exist, the contract is not to be construed as a positive contract, but as subject to an implied condition that the parties shall be excused in case, before breach, performance becomes impossible from the perishing of the thing without default of the contractor.

There seems little doubt that this implication tends to further the great object of making the legal construction such as to fulfill the intention of those who entered into the contract. For in the course of affairs men in making such contracts in general would, if it were brought to their minds, say that there should be such a condition.

Accordingly, in the Civil law, such an exception is implied in every obligation of the class which they call obligatio de certo corpore. The rule is laid down in the Digest, lib. xlv., tit. 1, d verborum obligationibus, 1. 33. "Si Stichus certo die dari promissus, ante diem moriatur: non tenetur promissor."[4] The principle is more fully developed in 1. 23. "Si ex legati causa, aut ex stipulatu hominem certum mihi debeas: non aliter post mortem ejus tenearis mihi, quam si per te steterit, quominum vivo eo eum mihi dares: quod ita fit, si aut interpellatus non didisti, aut occidisti eum."[5] The examples are of contracts respecting a slave, which was the common illustration of a certain subject used by the Roman lawyers, just as we are apt to take a horse; and no doubt the propriety, one might almost say necessity, of the implied condition is more obvious when the contract relates to a living animal, whether man or brute, than when it relates to some inanimate thing (such as in the present case a theatre) the existence of which is not so obviously precarious as that of the live animal, but the principle is adopted in the Civil law as applicable to every obligation of which the subject is a certain thing. The general subject is treated of by Pothier, who in his Traite des Obligations, partie 3, chap. 6, art. 3, § 668 states the result to be that the debtor corporis certi is freed from his obligation when the thing has perished, neither by his act, nor his neglect, and before he is in default, unless by some stipulation he has taken on himself the risk of the particular misfortune which has occurred.

Although the Civil law is not of itself authority in an English Court, it affords great assistance in investigating the principles on which the law is grounded. And it seems to us that the common law authorities

---

4   ["If Stichus is promised to be delivered on a certain day and dies before that day, the promisor will not be liable."—Eds.]

5   ["If on account of a legacy, or a stipulation you owe me a certain slave, you will not be liable to me after his death; unless you were to blame for not delivering him to me while he was living, such as if, after having been notified to deliver him, you did not do so, or you killed him."—Eds.]

establish that in such a contract the same condition of the continued existence of the thing is implied by English law.

There is a class of contracts in which a person binds himself to do something which requires to be performed by him in person; and such promises, e.g. promises to marry, or promises to serve for a certain time, are never in practice qualified by an express exception of the death of the party; and therefore in such cases the contract is in terms broken if the promisor dies before fulfillment. Yet it was very early determined that, if the performance is personal, the executors are not liable; Hyde v. The Dean of Windsor (Cro.Eliz. 552, 553). See 2 Wms.Exors. 1560, 5th ed., where a very apt illustration is given. "Thus," says the learned author, "if an author undertakes to compose a work, and dies before completing it, his executors are discharged from this contract: for the undertaking is merely personal in its nature, and, by the intervention of the contractor's death, has become impossible to be performed." For this he cites a dictum of Lord Lyndhurst in Marshall v. Broadhurst (1 Tyr. 348, 349), and a case mentioned by Patteson J. in Wentworth v. Cock (10 A. & E. 42, 45–46). In Hall v. Wright (E.B. & E. 746, 749), Crompton J., in his judgment, puts another case. "Where a contract depends upon personal skill, and the act of God renders it impossible, as, for instance, in the case of a painter employed to paint a picture who is struck blind, it may be that the performance might be excused."

It seems that in those cases the only ground on which the parties or their executors, can be excused from the consequences of the breach of the contract is, that from the nature of the contract there is an implied condition of the continued existence of the life of the contractor, and, perhaps in the case of the painter of his eyesight. In the instances just given, the person, the continued existence of whose life is necessary to the fulfilment of the contract, is himself the contractor, but that does not seem in itself to be necessary to the application of the principle; as is illustrated by the following example. In the ordinary form of an apprentice deed the apprentice binds himself in unqualified terms to "serve until the full end and term of seven years to be fully complete and ended," during which term it is covenanted that the apprentice his master "faithfully shall serve," and the father of the apprentice in equally unqualified terms binds himself for the performance by the apprentice of all and every covenant on his part. (See the form, 2 Chitty on Pleading, 370, 7th ed. by Greening.) It is undeniable that if the apprentice dies within the seven years, the covenant of the father that he shall perform his covenant to serve for seven years is not fulfilled, yet surely it cannot be that an action lie against the father? Yet the only reason why it would not is that he is excused because of the apprentice's death.

These are instances where the implied condition is of the life of a human being, but there are others in which the same implication is made as to the continued existence of a thing. For example, where a contract of sale is made amounting to a bargain and sale, transferring presently the property in specific chattels, which are to be delivered by the vendor at a future day; there, if the chattels, without fault of the vendor, perish in the interval, the purchaser must pay the price and the vendor is excused from performing his contract to deliver, which has thus become impossible.

* * *

It may, we think, be safely asserted to be now English law, that in all contracts of loan of chattels or bailments if the performance of the promise of the borrower or bailee to return the things lent or bailed, becomes impossible because it has perished, this impossibility (if not arising upon the fault of the borrower or bailee from some risk which he has taken upon himself) excuses the borrower or bailee from the performance of his promise to redeliver the chattel.

The great case of Coggs v. Bernard (1 Smith's L.C. 171, 5th ed.; 2 L.Raym. 909) is now the leading case on the law of bailments, and Lord Holt, in that case, referred so much to the Civil law that it might perhaps be thought that this principle was there derived direct from the civilians, and was not generally applicable in English law except in the case of bailments; but the case of Williams v. Lloyd (W. Jones, 179), above cited, shews that the same law had been already adopted by the English law as early as The Book of Assizes. The principle seems to us to be that, in contracts in which the performance depends on the continued existence of a given person or thing, a condition is implied that the impossibility of performance arising from the perishing of the person or thing shall excuse the performance.

In none of these cases is the promise in words other than positive, nor is there any express stipulation that the destruction of the person or thing shall excuse the performance; but that excuse is by law implied, because from the nature of the contract it is apparent that the parties contracted on the basis of the continued existence of the particular person or chattel. In the present case, looking at the whole contract, we find that the parties contracted on the basis of the continued existence of the Music Hall at the time when the concerts were to be given; that being essential to their performance.

We think, therefore, that the Music Hall having ceased to exist, without fault of either party, both parties are excused, the plaintiffs from taking the gardens and paying the money, the defendants from performing their promise to give the use of the Hall and Gardens and other things. Consequently the rule must be absolute to enter the verdict for the defendants.

Rule absolute.

The Surrey Hall and Gardens

NOTES

(1) Upon what theory does the court excuse the defendant? Does "implied condition" mean that the court is seeking the intention of the parties or providing a term regardless of that intention? See Edwin W. Patterson, *Constructive Conditions in Contracts,* 42 Colum. L. Rev. 903, 943–954 (1942). As Lord Wright put it eighty years later: "[T]he court has to decide not what the parties actually intended, but what as reasonable men they should have intended. The court personifies for this purpose the reasonable man." Joseph Constantine S.S. Line v. Imperial Smelting Corp. (1942) A.C. 154, 185. See Kinzer Constr. Co. v. State, 125 N.Y.S. 46, 54 (1910) (reviewing American cases and concluding that provisions are implied in contract by force of law and not because parties had them in mind).

(2) How is it determined that the "parties contracted on the basis of the continued existence of the Music Hall?" Suppose the defendant had another hall of similar quality and offered it to the plaintiff without additional cost. Would the plaintiff be required to accept it? Suppose the fire destroyed part of the hall but, in the judgment of the plaintiff, would not substantially affect the suitability of the hall for the proposed concerts and fetes. Is the defendant excused from the contract? If the fire destroyed the concert stage but the defendant, at a cost of £10,000, could effect repairs in time for the concert, would he be obligated to do so? If the particular hall was necessary for performance, the probable answers to the last three questions are "no", "no" and "no." See Restatement (Second) § 263, which provides:

> If the existence of a specific thing is necessary for the performance
> of a duty, its failure to come into existence, destruction, or such

deterioration as makes performance impracticable is an event the non-occurrence of which was a basic assumption on which the contract was made.

(3) *Death or Incapacity of an Essential Person.* Restatement (Second) § 262 provides:

> If the existence of a particular person is necessary for the performance of a duty, his death or such incapacity as makes performance impracticable is an event the non-occurrence of which was a basic assumption on which the contract was made.

As with Restatement (Second) § 263, the "basic assumption" question is answered by determining whether the "particular person is necessary for the performance of a duty." The question of who is "necessary" may be determined by the agreement or, if the agreement is silent, an assessment of whether the performance was a "personal matter requiring personal experience, ability, skill and judgment. . . ." Kelley v. Thompson Land Co., 112 W.Va. 454 (1932) (formation of a going corporation deemed personal on facts of case). Under this test, the death of an artist employed to paint a portrait would discharge the contract but the death of the subject of the portrait would not discharge a duty to pay the agreed price.

Another way to determine who is necessary is to ask whether the person who dies or was incapacitated could have delegated his or her duty to a third party without the other party's consent. The question is whether the other party has a "substantial interest" in having the contract performed by the particular person. See UCC § 2–210(1). If so, the contract is discharged. Compare Seitz v. Mark-O-Lite Sign Contractors, Inc., 210 N.J.Super. 646 (1986) (death of contractor does not excuse contract to do sheet metal work) with Cazares v. Saenz, 208 Cal.App.3d 279 (1989) (death of attorney discharges contract with law firm). But since people rather than corporations die or become incapacitated, the question remains whether the performance to be rendered was "so personal in nature, calling for a peculiar skill or special exercise of discretion, as to make it nondelegable." *Seitz,* supra, 210 N.J.Super. at 653.

Canadian Industrial Alcohol Co. v. Dunbar Molasses Co.

Court of Appeals of New York, 1932.
258 N.Y. 194.

■ CARDOZO, C.J. A buyer sues a seller for breach of an executory contract of purchase and sale.

The subject-matter of the contract was "approximately 1,500,000 wine gallons Refined Blackstrap [molasses] of the usual run from the National Sugar Refinery, Yonkers, N.Y., to test around 60% sugars."

The order was given and accepted December 27, 1927, but shipments of the molasses were to begin after April 1, 1928, and were to be spread out during the warm weather.

After April 1, 1928, the defendant made delivery from time to time of 344,083 gallons. Upon its failure to deliver more, the plaintiff brought this action for the recovery of damages. The defendant takes the ground that, by an implied term of the contract, the duty to deliver was conditioned upon the production by the National Sugar Refinery at Yonkers of molasses sufficient in quantity to fill the plaintiff's order. The fact is that the output of the refinery, while the contract was in force, was 485,848 gallons, much less than its capacity, of which amount 344,083 gallons were allotted to the defendant and shipped to the defendant's customer. The argument for the defendant is that its own duty to deliver was proportionate to the refinery's willingness to supply, and that the duty was discharged when the output was reduced.

The contract, read in the light of the circumstances existing at its making, or more accurately in the light of any such circumstances apparent from this record, does not keep the defendant's duty within boundaries so narrow. We may assume, in the defendant's favor, that there would have been a discharge of its duty to deliver if the refinery had been destroyed . . . or if the output had been curtailed by the failure of the sugar crop . . . or by the ravages of war . . . or conceivably in some circumstances by unavoidable strikes. . . . We may even assume that a like result would have followed if the plaintiff had bargained not merely for a quantity of molasses to be supplied from a particular refinery, but for molasses to be supplied in accordance with a particular contract between the defendant and the refiner, and if thereafter such contract had been broken without fault on the defendant's part. . . . The inquiry is merely this, whether the continuance of a special group of circumstances appears from the terms of the contract, interpreted in the setting of the occasion, to have been a tacit or implied presupposition in the minds of the contracting parties, conditioning their belief in a continued obligation. . . .

Accepting that test, we ask ourselves the question what special group of circumstances does the defendant lay before us as one of the presuppositions immanent in its bargain with the plaintiff? The defendant asks us to assume that a manufacturer, having made a contract with a middleman for a stock of molasses to be procured from a particular refinery, would expect the contract to lapse whenever the refiner chose to diminish his production, and this in the face of the middleman's omission to do anything to charge the refiner with a duty to continue. Business could not be transacted with security or smoothness if a presumption so unreasonable were at the root of its engagements. There is nothing to show that the defendant would have been unable by a timely contract with the refinery to have assured itself of a supply sufficient for its needs. There is nothing to show that the plaintiff, in giving the order for the molasses, was informed by the defendant that such a contract had not been made, or that performance would be contingent upon obtaining one thereafter. If the plaintiff had been so informed, it would very likely have preferred to deal with the refinery directly, instead of dealing with a middleman. The defendant does not even show that it tried to get a contract from the refinery during the months that intervened between the acceptance of the plaintiff's order and the time when shipments were begun. It has wholly failed to relieve itself of the imputation of contributory fault (3 Williston on Contracts, § 1959). So far as the record shows, it put its faith in the mere chance that the output of the refinery would be the same from year to year, and finding its faith vain, it tells us that its customer must have expected to take a chance as great. We see no reason for importing into the bargain this aleatory element. The defendant is in no better position than a factor who undertakes in his own name to sell for future delivery a special grade of merchandise to be manufactured by a special mill. The duty will be discharged if the mill is destroyed before delivery is due. The duty will subsist if the output is reduced because times turn out to be hard and labor charges high. . . .

* * *

The judgment should be affirmed with costs.

NOTES

(1) "A party may not, by its own conduct, create the event causing the impracticability of performance . . .; in fact it must make all reasonable efforts to avoid the 'impossibility' . . .; and, once the event occurs, it must employ any practicable means of fulfilling the contract, even if it had originally expected to meet its obligation in a particular way. . . ." Chemetron Corp. v. McLouth Steel Corp., 381 F.Supp. 245, 257 (N.D. Ill. 1974).

(2) Suppose, in the *Dunbar Molasses* case, that the contract between the plaintiff and the defendant contained the following clause:

> If the failure to perform is caused by the default of a supplier, and if such default arises out of causes beyond the control of both the seller and the supplier, and without the fault or negligence of either of them, the seller shall not be liable for any excess costs for failure to perform, unless the supplies or services to be furnished by the supplier were obtainable from other sources in sufficient time to permit the seller to meet the delivery schedule.

Would this clause alter the result?

(3) Under UCC § 2–615(a), if the parties specify a particular source of supply in the contract and that source fails, the seller will be excused if (1) both parties assumed that the source was exclusive, (2) the seller employed all due measures to assure that the source would perform, and (3) the seller turned over to the buyer any rights against the supplier corresponding to the seller's claim of excuse. UCC § 2–615 cmt. 5. On the other hand, if excuse is predicated upon a *force majeure* clause in the contract for sale rather than UCC § 2–615(a), the seller need not turn over its rights against the supplier to the buyer. See InterPetrol Bermuda Ltd. v. Kaiser Aluminum Int'l Corp., 719 F.2d 992 (9th Cir. 1983). Finally, as Judge Cardozo indicated in *Dunbar*

Molasses, the seller's responsibility, both before and after the exclusive source failure, to avoid or mitigate the loss, exists as a condition to excuse.

PROBLEMS: CASUALTY TO IDENTIFIED GOODS

(1)   F, a farmer, has 100 acres of bottom land in which he regularly plants corn. On May 1, F contracted to sell 20,000 bushels of #1 yellow corn to B, a grain dealer, for $2.40 per bushel. Delivery was expected after harvest. At the time of contracting, 50% of the land had been planted and the balance was completed within 10 days. In early July, a severe drought began and then intensified until after the usual harvest date. The crop was so bad that F ground it up for fodder. At that time, #1 yellow corn was selling at $5 per bushel. B demanded delivery of 20,000 bushels and F refused, claiming excuse under UCC §§ 2–613 through 2–616. B claims damages of $2.60 per bushel. Should he collect them? What are the statutory issues that must be resolved?

(2)   B contracted to sell 11,000 combat boots of a stated quality to a country in Africa. The price was $158,000. On July 1, B contracted with S to procure those boots from a Korean manufacturer for $95,000, with delivery no later than November 1. S immediately placed the order with the manufacturer and the boots arrived in San Francisco on October 15. The boots conformed to the contract requirements, but contained no markings identifying their origin. S immediately shipped the boots to B in New York by rail under the shipment term "FOB point of Destination." The goods were totally destroyed by fire while in the carrier's possession, and S was unable to obtain substitutes in time to meet the November 1 delivery date. B then canceled the contract for breach, and sued S for damages. S claims that performance was excused under Sections 2–612 through 2–616 of the UCC. What result? You may assume that the goods were first identified to the contract between S and B when they were shipped to B from San Francisco, see UCC 2–501(1), and that the risk of loss was on S at the time of the fire. See UCC §§ 2–319(1)(b) & 2–509(1)(b).

(3)   What result if the risk of loss was on B at the time of the fire? See *Windows, Inc. v. Jordan Panel Sys. Corp.,* 177 F.3d 114 (2d Cir. 1999) (holding that where the risk of loss is on the buyer in a "shipment" contract, the seller has performed its obligations under the contract). Under UCC § 2–709(1), the buyer would owe the price (if not previously paid) and would have to seek indemnity for loss of the goods from either its insurance company or the carrier.

Ellen Ash Peters: A 1951 graduate of Swarthmore College (B.A.), Ellen Peters earned her law degree from Yale in 1954. She then clerked for Chief Judge Charles E. Clark of the Court of Appeals for the Second Circuit, and spent a year as a Research Associate at the University of California Law School at Boalt Hall before returning to Yale to begin her teaching career. She was member of the Yale faculty for 22 years, during which she served as an advisor to the Restatement of Contracts. In 1978, Peters was appointed to the Connecticut Supreme Court and was named Chief Justice in 1984, retiring in 1996. Her writings include a casebook in contract law and numerous scholarly articles.

Timothy E. Dills v. Town of Enfield

Supreme Court of Connecticut, 1989.
210 Conn. 705.

■ PETERS, CHIEF JUSTICE. The principal issue in this appeal is whether the doctrine of commercial impracticability excuses a developer from submitting construction plans when he discovers that necessary financing has become unavailable. The plaintiffs, Timothy E. Dills and the Neecon Corporation, sued the defendants, the town of Enfield (town) and the Enfield development agency (agency), to recover a $100,000 deposit Dills had paid the agency under an option and contract for sale. The trial court referred the case to Attorney J. Read Murphy, a state trial referee appointed pursuant to General Statutes § 52–434(a)(4). Following a hearing and the parties' submission of briefs, the referee reported his findings of fact and recommended that judgment enter for the plaintiffs. The trial court rejected the referee's recommendation, instead rendering judgment for the defendants. The plaintiff Neecon

Corporation appealed to the Appellate Court and we transferred the case here pursuant to Practice Book § 4023. We find no error.

The relevant facts reported by the referee, accepted by the trial court and supported by the record, are as follows. The town of Enfield instructed its development agency to solicit private developers for the Enfield Memorial Industrial Park to be constructed on town property. Pursuant to an earlier option agreement, on May 1, 1974, the plaintiff Dills and the development agency entered into a contract for the sale of the land to be developed. Dills at that time paid a $100,000 deposit toward the contract price of $985,900. The plaintiff Neecon Corporation, owned by Dills, was to perform the necessary work, and has become, by virtue of an assignment from Dills, the only remaining plaintiff in this appeal.

Under the terms of the contract, the development agency agreed to convey the property to the developer sixty days after the fulfillment of two conditions: (1) the submission and approval of construction plans in accordance with section 301 of the contract; and (2) the submission of evidence of financial capacity in accordance with section 304 of the contract. The contract also included provisions for its termination by either party. Section 702(b) of the contract allowed the developer to withdraw and to reclaim his deposit if, after the preparation of construction plans satisfactory to the agency, the developer could not obtain the necessary mortgage financing. Section 703(b) of the contract allowed the agency to terminate the contract, retaining the deposit as liquidated damages, if the developer failed to submit acceptable construction plans.

Dills never submitted construction plans that were acceptable to the agency. A set of plans denominated "preliminary" was rejected by the agency on June 24, 1974. The agency accepted a revised set of "preliminary plans" and drawings three months later, but demanded the submission of full construction plans and specifications by early December. The referee found that the preliminary sets of plans did not themselves meet the definition of "construction plans" in section 301. The referee agreed with the agency's interpretation of section 301 of the contract as requiring the developer to submit full construction plans within 210 days of the agency's approval of preliminary plans.

The reason Dills failed to submit construction plans was that, despite diligent efforts, he was unable to obtain mortgage financing. Thereafter, both parties attempted, with proper notification, to invoke the contract's termination clauses. On December 19, 1974, the agency, having been informed by Dills of his financial difficulties, voted to terminate the agreement pursuant to section 703(b) of the contract of sale and to retain the $100,000 deposit as liquidated damages. On December 22, 1974, Dills' attorney notified the agency that, because of Dills' inability to obtain financing within the time specified in the contract,

Dills was terminating the agreement pursuant to section 702(b) of the contract of sale.

* * *

[The referee found, among other things, that Dills' duty to provide full construction plans by December, 1974 was discharged by supervening impracticability. The trial court, however, rejected the referee's recommendation that judgment be entered for Dills, concluding that unless there was impracticability in preparing and submitting construction plans rather than obtaining financing for them there was no basis for excuse.]

B

Finally we must decide whether the trial court erred as a matter of law in rejecting the referee's determination, endorsed by the plaintiff on appeal, that the impracticability doctrine excused Dills' failure to deliver construction plans to the agency. The plaintiff contends that Dills' inability to obtain such financing made submitting the construction plans a "futile" and "useless act," and therefore the doctrine of supervening impracticability discharged his duty to submit the plans. We hold, as did the trial court, that "[t]he doctrine of impracticability and impossibility . . . [is] not relevant to this case."

The impracticability doctrine represents an exception to the accepted maxim of *pacta sunt servanda,* in recognition of the fact that certain conditions cannot be met because of unforeseen occurrences. Cf. Aetna Casualty & Surety Co. v. Murphy, 206 Conn. 409, 413, 538 A.2d 219 (1988). A party claiming that a supervening event or contingency has prevented, and thus excused, a promised performance must demonstrate that: (1) the event made the performance impracticable; (2) the nonoccurrence of the event was a basic assumption on which the contract was made; (3) the impracticability resulted without the fault of the party seeking to be excused; and (4) the party has not assumed a greater obligation than the law imposes. 2 Restatement (Second), Contracts § 261; E. Farnsworth, Contracts (1982) § 9.6, p. 678. We discuss only the first two prongs of this test in disposing of the plaintiff's argument.

Although courts in recent years have liberalized the requirements for such an excuse . . . only in the most exceptional circumstances have courts concluded that a duty is discharged because additional financial burdens make performance less practical than initially contemplated. . . . Thus, the fact that preparing the construction plans would have cost Dills a great deal of money (more than the deposit he sought to recover) did not excuse him from submitting them as the contract provided.

Furthermore, the event upon which the obligor relies to excuse his performance cannot be an event that the parties foresaw at the time of the contract. We have previously held that "[t]he regular enforcement of conditions is . . . subject to the competing but equally well established principle that the occurrence of a condition may be excused in the event of impracticability '*if the occurrence of the condition is not a material part of the agreed exchange* and forfeiture would otherwise result.'" . . . Thus, the "central inquiry" is whether the nonoccurrence of the alleged impracticable condition "was a basic assumption on which the contract was made." General Statutes § 42a–2–615(a);[17] 2 Restatement (Second), Contracts § 261;[18]. . . .

In this case the contingency upon which fulfilling the contract allegedly depended was Dills' obtaining the requisite financing. We cannot conclude, however, that Dills' failure to obtain financing was "an event the non-occurrence of which was a basic assumption on which the contract was made." Indeed, section 702(b) of the contract of sale demonstrates that the parties expressly contemplated that Dills might encounter financial difficulties. The contract allowed Dills to terminate for this reason "after preparation of Construction Plans satisfactory to the Agency." If "an event is foreseeable, a party who makes an unqualified promise to perform necessarily assumes an obligation to perform, even if the occurrence of the event makes performance impracticable." E. Farnsworth, supra, p. 686.[19]

This case, like virtually every case involving discharge from an obligation to perform, concerns the issue of which party bears the loss resulting from an event that renders performance by one party uneconomical. . . . "Determining whether the non-occurrence of a particular event was or was not a basic assumption involves a judgment as to which party assumed the risk of its occurrence. . . . In making such determinations, a court will look at all circumstances, including the terms of the contract." 2 Restatement (Second), Contracts, c. 11, introductory note. "Since impossibility and related doctrines are devices for shifting risk in accordance with the parties' presumed intentions, which are to minimize the costs of contract performance, one of which is the disutility created by risk, they have no place when the contract explicitly assigns a particular risk to one party or the other." Northern Indiana Public Service Co. v. Carbon County Coal Co., 799 F.2d 265, 278 (7th Cir. 1986). . . . Where, as in this case, sophisticated contracting

---

[17] General Statutes § 42a–2–615(a) provides in pertinent part: "Delay in delivery or nondelivery in whole or in part by a seller . . . is not a breach of his duty under a contract for sale if performance as agreed has been made impracticable by the occurrence of a contingency *the nonoccurrence of which was a basic assumption on which the contract was made* or by compliance in good faith with any applicable foreign or domestic governmental regulation or order whether or not it later proves to be invalid." (Emphasis added.) While the instant case does not concern the sale of goods, and therefore the Uniform Commercial Code does not apply, § 2–615 has been adopted by the Restatement and "promises to have a substantial influence on the law of contract generally. . . ." E. Farnsworth, Contracts (1982) § 9.6, p. 677.

[18] The Restatement (Second) of Contracts § 261 provides: "Where, after a contract is made, a party's performance is made impracticable without his fault by the occurrence of an event *the non-occurrence of which was a basic assumption on which the contract was made,* his duty to render that performance is discharged, unless the language or the circumstances indicate the contrary." (Emphasis added.)

[19] Significantly, the defendants never conceded that the promised plans would have been of no use to them. Thus, it is far from certain that submitting the plans would have been a "futile act" from the defendants' point of view.

parties have negotiated termination provisions, courts should be slow to invent additional ways to excuse performance. We exercise such caution in this case.

There is no error.

NOTES

(1)   For exactly what reason did the court conclude that Dills was not excused from the contract: (a) The parties assigned the risk to Dills in the contract; or (b) Obtaining financing was *not* a basic assumption of the contract; or (c) The extra cost of performance did not make performance impracticable? Is the conclusion sound if the court relies on *all three* reasons?

(2)   Can you develop a hypothetical scenario in which Justice Peters would grant excuse?

(3)   *The Basic Assumption Test.* UCC § 2–615(a) provides that a seller in a contract for the sale of goods is excused for "delay in delivery or non-delivery * * * if performance as agreed has been made impracticable by the occurrence of a contingency the non-occurrence of which was a basic assumption on which the contract was made * * *."

Without question, the Second Restatement has jumped on the "basic assumption" bandwagon. Whether an existing or supervening event makes performance impracticable or "frustrates" the purpose of one party to the contract, the "*non-occurrence*" of that event or fact must have been "a basic assumption on which the contract was made." See, e.g., Restatement (Second) §§ 261–66. If it was not, the promisor bears the risk of any impracticability unless the risk was otherwise allocated by agreement. How, then, does one come to grips with this crucial risk allocation test?

The Reporter of the Second Restatement, E. Alan Farnsworth, offered the following guidance:

> Determining whether the non-occurrence of a particular event was or was not a basic assumption involves a judgment as to which party assumed the risk of its occurrence. In contracting for the manufacture and delivery of goods at a price fixed in the contract, for example, the seller assumes the risk of increased costs within the normal range. If, however, a disaster results in an abrupt tenfold increase in cost to the seller, a court might determine that the seller did not assume this risk by concluding that the non-occurrence of the disaster was a "basic assumption" on which the contract was made. In making such determinations, a court will look at all circumstances, including the terms of the contract. The fact that the event was unforeseeable is significant as suggesting that its non-occurrence was a basic assumption. However, the fact that it was foreseeable, or even foreseen, does not, of itself, argue for a contrary conclusion, since the parties may not have thought it sufficiently important a risk to have made it a subject of their bargaining. Another significant factor may be the relative bargaining positions of the parties and the relative ease with which

either party could have included a clause. Another may be the
effectiveness of the market in spreading such risks as, for example,
where the obligor is a middleman who has an opportunity to adjust
his prices to cover them.

Restatement (Second), Ch. 11, p. 311.

(4) *The Foreseeability Test.* At the risk of oversimplifying, consider the
argument that both parties assume that a risk event will not occur when that
event, at the time of contract, was not foreseeable as likely to occur. Put
differently, the risk event was so remote that it did not figure into the pricing
or other calculations that the parties made. See Restatement (Second) § 261
cmt. c. In short, there are limitations upon human cognition. See Melvin A.
Eisenberg, *The Limits of Cognition and the Limits of Contract,* 47 Stan. L.
Rev. 211 (1995) (analysis of the behavioral science literature and application
to selected issues); Richard E. Speidel, Contracts in Crises: Excuse Doctrine
and Retrospective Government Acts 188–90 (2007) (hereafter cited as
Contracts in Crises) (discussing cognitive biases at time of contracting).[6]

Many courts accept that the key to the analysis of "foreseeability" is the
probability that the foreseen event will occur or, if it does occur, certain
consequences will follow. As one court put it, "was the contingency which
developed one which the parties could reasonably be thought to have
foreseen as a *real possibility* which could affect performance?" Mishara
Constr. Co., Inc. v. Transit-Mixed Concrete Corp., 365 Mass. 122, 129 (1974).
If so, the court is unlikely to conclude that both parties assumed that the
event would not occur. See also Specialty Tires of Am., Inc. v. CIT
Grp./Equip. Fin., Inc., 82 F. Supp. 2d 434 (W.D. Pa. 2000) (some foreseeable
risks not deemed worthy of bargaining over); Aluminum Co. of Am. v. Essex
Grp., Inc., 499 F.Supp. 53, 70 (W.D. Pa. 1980) ("The proper question is not
simply whether the parties to a contract were conscious of uncertainty with
respect to a vital fact, but whether they believed that uncertainty was
effectively limited within a designated range so that they would deem
outcomes beyond that range to be highly unlikely.").

(5) *Economic Analysis.* In 1977, then Professor (now Judge) Richard
Posner argued that in all cases of impracticability, the key question is "who
should bear the loss resulting from an event that has rendered performance
uneconomical" and that the answer, provided by economic analysis, is the
party who is the "most efficient bearer of the particular risk in the particular
circumstances." Richard A. Posner and Andrew M. Rosenfield, *Impossibility
and Related Doctrines in Contract Law: An Economic Analysis,* 6 J. Legal.
Stud. 83, 86, 90 (1977).

The discharge question arises only in those cases where the
contract does not assign the risk in question and the event giving
rise to the discharge claim was not avoidable by any cost justified

---

[6] The foreseeability test is further challenged by what behavioral scientists call the
"hindsight bias." In essence, research suggests that judges and others "cannot ignore a known
outcome when assessing a likelihood." Put differently, if a risk event actually occurs and causes
harm, the hindsight judgment after the event may be biased: "precautions that seem reasonable
in foresight look inadequate in hindsight." Kim A. Kamin & Jeffrey J. Rachlinski, *Ex Post ≠ Ex
Ante: Determining Liability in Hindsight,* 19 Law & Hum. Behav. 89 (1995).

precautions. When these threshold conditions have been satisfied, economic analysis suggests that the loss should be placed on the party who is the superior (that is, lower-cost) risk bearer. To determine which party is the superior risk bearer three factors are relevant—knowledge of the magnitude of the loss, knowledge of the probability that it will occur, and (other) costs of self—or market—insurance.

This analysis has been criticized as unworkable as a test for deciding cases and has been absorbed by the voluminous and often conflicting literature by economists on when excuse for changed circumstances is efficient. See Speidel, Contracts in Crises at 185–87 (discussing literature). In all of this, however, one can profit by considering the "compensation principle" proposed by Steven Walt. He argues that if performance as agreed has been made impracticable, excuse is fair (and not inefficient) if the risk event was so remote or uncertain that the parties could not and did not provide against it by insurance or other terms of the contract. Steven Walt, *Expectations, Loss Distribution, and Commercial Impracticability*, 24 Ind. L. Rev. 65 (1990).

Comment: Impracticability by Government Regulation

An important category where, historically, excuse has been granted involves subsequent acts of government that prevent performance of existing contracts or make such performance illegal. Even before *Taylor v. Caldwell*, supra, courts recognized an excuse where supervening changes in domestic law made performance illegal. See A.W.B. Simpson, A History of the Common Law of Contract: The Rise of the Action of Assumpsit, 525–526 (1975). Lord Ellenborough in 1809, addressing both existing and supervening illegality:

> That no contract can properly be carried into effect, which was originally made contrary to the provisions of law; or, which being made consistently with the rules of law at the time, has become illegal in virtue of some subsequent law; are propositions which admit no doubt.

Atkinson v. Ritchie, 103 Eng. Rep. 877, 878 (K.B.1809) (charter party frustrated by outbreak of war).

The effect of government action that prevented performance rather than made it illegal was raised in *Baily v. De Crespigny*, L.R. 4 Q.B. 180 (Q.B.1869). Under a long-term lease of land, the defendant covenanted that neither he nor his assigns would permit any building on a paddock fronting the property. In 1862, however, Parliament conferred power on a railroad company to take the paddock for purposes of the railroad and defendant, faced with the fact that the railroad would take the paddock, conveyed it to them for value. When the railroad built a structure, the plaintiff sued the defendant for breach of the lease.

The court denied the claim on the ground that, under the circumstances, it was not possible for the defendant to perform the covenant without violating the law. The court found that the defendant did not assume the risk of this governmental action under the lease, and reasoned that the parties must be assumed to contract with reference to the state of law existing at the time of the contract. Although parties can agree to allocate the risk of a change in law, the presumption that the current law will continue ought to be rebutted by clear language showing a contrary intention. The general language of unconditional liability did not allocate risk to the defendant:

> [W]here the event is of such a character that it cannot reasonably be supposed to have been in the contemplation of the contracting parties when the contract was made, they will not be held bound by general words which, though large enough to include, were not used with reference to the possibility of the particular contingency which afterwards happens. . . . To hold a man liable by words, in a sense affixed to them by legislation subsequent to the contract, is to impose on him a contract he never made.

In essence, the defendant was "discharged from his covenant by the subsequent act of Parliament which put it out of his power to perform it."[7]

One sees in the opinion a regulatory context wherein the government was interested in fostering the development of railroads during the industrial revolution. This regulatory atmosphere, however, did not suffice to defeat the presumption that the current state of law would continue, at least in the absence of evidence of actual instability in the regulatory context at the time the lease was made. See Speidel, Contracts in Crises at 36–39.

Centex Corporation v. John Dalton

Supreme Court of Texas, 1992.
840 S.W.2d 952.

■ GAMMAGE, JUSTICE. We consider whether the court of appeals erred by holding that Centex Corporation's (Centex) contract with John Dalton was not invalidated by a governmental regulation. In district court, Dalton filed suit against Centex seeking to recover liquidated damages for alleged breach of contract. He later moved for summary judgment, which the district court granted, awarding him $750,000 as damages for breach of contract, plus prejudgment interest, post-judgment interest, costs and attorney's fees. The court of appeals affirmed. . . . We reverse and hold that Centex's contract with Dalton is unenforceable because a

---

[7] If, however, performance was prevented or made illegal by a change of foreign law at the place of performance, the defendant was not excused. See John D. Wladis, *Common Law and Uncommon Events: The Development of the Doctrine of Impossibility of Performance in English Contract Law*, 75 G.T. L.J. 1575, 1601, n. 126 (1987). Note that the railroad had power to "take" the property for compensation. Although the defendant was not liable for damages for failing to honor the covenant, the plaintiff might still have some recourse for the value of the compensation received.

governmental regulation prohibiting Centex's performance invalidates the contract, discharging Centex's obligation.

FACTS

The material facts are undisputed. Centex is a company engaged in residential and commercial construction and related financial services. In November 1988, Dalton was an executive of a Texas thrift institution.

In 1988, because the flagging Texas economy adversely affected the state's thrift institutions, the Federal Home Loan Bank Board (Bank Board) and other regulatory agencies determined it was in the best interest of depositors, borrowers and other creditors of the state's thrift institutions to close, merge, liquidate or sell several large thrift institutions under what came to be known as the "Southwest Plan." In November 1988, Centex, acting through its executive vice president, David Quinn, contacted Dalton to request that he assist Centex in acquiring certain thrift institutions made available through the Southwest Plan. A few weeks later, Dalton traveled to Washington, D.C., where he made an unsuccessful bid at acquiring a group of thrift institutions for Centex. While making that bid, Dalton learned that four other central Texas thrift institutions, known as the "Lamb Package," were available for purchase. Dalton informed Centex about the availability of the Lamb Package, and on December 23, 1988, Centex entered into a letter agreement with Dalton, wherein Centex promised to pay Dalton $750,000 over a three-year period if Centex were successful in acquiring the Lamb Package.

Before Centex and Dalton signed the letter agreement, Centex met with the Bank Board and advised the Bank Board of its intention to pay fees to Dalton upon completion of acquisition of the Lamb Package. The Bank Board told Centex that its payment of fees to Dalton would be acceptable as long as Centex made payment and not any of the thrift institutions in the Lamb Package or the entity formed to acquire the Lamb Package. But, on December 28, 1988, the night before Centex's acquisition of the Lamb Package closed, Quinn learned the Bank Board probably would not permit payment of the fees to Dalton. Centex, nevertheless, acquired the Lamb Package, forming a wholly-owned subsidiary known as Texas Trust Savings Bank, FSB (Texas Trust) as the acquiring entity.

At a meeting on December 29, 1988, the Bank Board approved the acquisition of the Lamb Package, conditioned on a prohibition against Texas Trust's direct or indirect payment of finder's fees. The transcript of the meeting shows that members of the Bank Board discussed Texas Trust's planned payment of fees to Dalton, made specific objection to the payment, and requested its general counsel to prepare an amendment to clarify that its prohibition against the payment of fees extended to affiliates of Texas Trust. On January 31, 1989, the Bank Board adopted the amendment proposed by its counsel.

Dalton performed the services required of him under the letter agreement, but Centex did not pay him. The evidence shows Centex refused to pay Dalton because of the prohibition imposed by the Bank Board when it approved Centex's acquisition of the Lamb Package on December 29, 1988, and because of the prohibition amendment the Bank Board adopted on January 31, 1989.

In August 1989, the Financial Institutions Reform Recovery and Enforcement Act (FIRREA) became effective, abolishing the Bank Board and creating the Office of Thrift Supervision (OTS). FIRREA gave OTS the powers that formerly had been vested in the abolished Bank Board. Pursuant to 12 U.S.C. § 1818(b)(6)(D) (1989), OTS has authority to issue cease-and-desist orders, to rescind contracts and to correct violations of Bank Board conditions. On December 11, 1990, while this case was before the court of appeals, OTS issued such a cease-and-desist order to prevent Centex or Texas Trust from paying any fees to Dalton under the letter agreement.

DISCUSSION

Centex argues that, because its performance under the letter agreement has been made impracticable by having to comply with the Bank Board's order, its duty to render that performance is discharged. We agree.

Congress gave the Bank Board power to regulate the acquisition and control of federally-insured thrifts by savings and loan holding companies. 12 U.S.C. § 1730a (1982). As a result, the Bank Board's prohibition makes it illegal for Centex to perform under the letter agreement. "Where . . . a party's performance is made impracticable . . . by the occurrence of an event the non-occurrence of which was a basic assumption on which the contract was made, his duty to render that performance is discharged. . . ." Restatement (Second) of Contracts § 261 (1981). A governmental regulation or order that makes impracticable the performance of a duty "is an event the non-occurrence of which was made a basic assumption on which the contract was made." Restatement (Second) of Contracts § 264 (1981). Consequently, to avoid inconsistency with the bank board's prohibition and conflict with federal regulatory law, we must hold that Centex is excused from performance by the doctrine of impossibility.

In *Houston Ice & Brewing Co. v. Keenan,* 99 Tex. 79, 88 S.W. 197, 199 (1905), this court approved the general doctrine of impossibility due to illegality: "the performance of a contract is excused by a supervening impossibility caused by the operation of a change in the law." . . . When courts are asked to excuse a party's performance due to supervening circumstances which made performance impracticable or impossible, they sometimes attempt to allocate the burden of risk and decide who must pay for the unanticipated occurrence. Foreseeability is one factor used to decide which party assumed the risk of supervening impossibility. . . .

The foreseeability factor has, however, gradually decreased in importance. . . . For example, the first Restatement of Contracts § 457 (1932) provided that the party seeking to be excused from performing the contract must have "had no reason to anticipate" the supervening occurrence. The updated Restatement (Second) of Contracts § 261 (1981) omitted that requirement, explaining that many factors may excuse a failure to deal with contingencies, and that even if the event was reasonably foreseeable, or even foreseen, the contracting party may still be discharged. [T]he Restatement (Second) reporters wrote that "the dangers of the mechanistic use of a foreseeability test have been noted. . . ." Here, one party, Centex, *cannot* be required to pay, regardless of the foreseeability of the Bank Board's prohibition.

* * *

The dissent urges the court to utilize the equitable remedy of quantum meruit to remand this cause and afford Dalton alternative means to collect full payment for services performed. Even if quantum meruit might have afforded Dalton an alternate ground of recovery, Dalton did not plead it, and a judgment must be based upon pleadings. . . .

Dalton knew about the federal prohibition and was on notice that Centex contended it made his contract unenforceable at the time he filed this lawsuit. When it is possible a contract claim may be held invalid, it is somewhat standard practice for a party to plead an alternative quantum meruit claim. Dalton's failure to initially plead quantum meruit as an alternative theory of recovery suggests he concluded that if the contract claim were barred, quantum meruit would also be barred. In reality, never at any point in the legal process of this case, not even in his appearance before this court, did Dalton assert a quantum meruit claim. His failure to plead quantum meruit at the first trial may *not* serve as a basis for a remand on appeal. * * *

We also note the court of appeals reasoned that, because the obligation of Centex to pay Dalton arose when the letter agreement was signed on December 23, 1988, before the Bank Board's adoption of its prohibition on December 29, 1988, the prohibition did not apply to the letter agreement. Centex, the court concluded, was not prohibited from paying Dalton his fees. The court of appeals' reasoning was incorrect because the letter agreement is premised on a condition precedent. A condition precedent is an event that must happen or be performed before a right can accrue to enforce an obligation. . . . Here, by the terms of the letter agreement, Dalton's right to enforce it could not accrue until the Bank Board approved the acquisition. Because the Bank Board, in approving the acquisition, prohibited the payment of the finder's fees, thereby invalidating the letter agreement, Dalton's right to enforce the letter agreement never accrued.

The Bank Board's order prohibits Centex's performance under the letter agreement, which otherwise would be enforceable under state contract law. Centex cannot pay Dalton and obey the governmental regulation, which has prohibited the proposed payment. Centex's duty to perform under the letter agreement is excused. Consequently, we reverse the court of appeals and render judgment for Centex.

■ MAUZY, J., dissents. The majority opinion recognizes an injustice, but fails to correct it. Having concluded that the Bank Board's prohibition invalidates the agreement between Centex and Dalton, the majority declines to provide an opportunity for an equitable remedy. As a result, Centex reaps a windfall at Dalton's expense. I dissent.

Centex agreed to pay Dalton a total of $750,000 if Centex closed a deal on a thrift by a certain date. The fee was to compensate Dalton for his services in arranging the sale. Although its representative had previously approved the agreement, the Bank Board prohibited payment to Dalton on the eve of the closing date. Centex proceeded without notice to Dalton.

The majority determines that the Board's prohibition invalidated the contract before Dalton's right to enforcement accrued. Allowing that the agreement is unenforceable, Centex should not reap a windfall for its acquiescence to the belated disapproval of the fee. Although there is no indication that Centex affirmatively sought the prohibition, there is also no indication that it made any effort to avoid the foreseeable bar to performance. At a minimum, Centex should have notified Dalton upon learning that the Board would not permit payment. Instead, Centex evidently kept the information to itself, preventing Dalton from appealing the decision while the contract was still viable.

Further, Centex need not have proceeded with the acquisition on the Board's new terms. Having chosen to do so, the resulting, inconsistent obligations were its burden. Instead of resolving those obligations, it pawned the responsibility onto Dalton.

The majority now rewards Centex with a windfall of $750,000, thus recommending a neatly profitable scheme to those in positions to influence regulatory policymaking. The decision is explained in terms of federal supremacy and the intricacies of contract law, but the plain injustice of the result is overlooked: Centex, by quietly acquiescing to the Board's new terms, unfairly escaped its debt for the benefit of Dalton's services. * * *

I would reverse the judgment of the Court of Appeals and remand this cause to the trial court. Dalton, in fairness, should have the opportunity to assert a claim under a theory that is consistent with the majority's invalidation of the agreement.

NOTES

(1) Note that the government regulation, which had retrospective effect, made the agreed performance illegal rather than preventing or hindering it. Should that distinction make any difference? In either case, the

promisor is in what might be called a "zone of coercion": The choice is to breach the contract or continue the illegal performance with the risk of sanctions against it. As one court put it, "when a contract is originally legal, but performance becomes illegal due to a change in the law, any subsequent performance is against public policy and the party who has agreed to perform is excused from doing so." White v. J.M. Brown Amusement Co., Inc., 360 S.C. 366, 371 (2004).

(2)   The Centex case does not consider the risk allocation test expressed in Restatement (Second) § 264:

> If the performance of a duty is made impracticable by having to comply with a domestic or foreign governmental regulation or order, that regulation or order is an event the non-occurrence of which was a basic assumption on which the contract was made.

Similarly, UCC § 2–615(a) bypasses the "basic assumption" test and provides that relief is granted "if performance as agreed has been made impracticable by . . . compliance in good faith with any applicable foreign or domestic governmental regulation or order whether or not it later proves to be invalid."

Thus, the Restatement and the UCC give the party seeking relief a presumption that both parties assumed that the law would not change. The presumption does not apply if, according to the Restatement, the "language or circumstances indicate the contrary," or, according to the UCC comments, unless the governmental interference "truly 'supervenes' in such a manner as to be beyond the seller's assumption of risk." If the agreement does not allocate the risk of subsequent retrospective legal change, the party seeking relief is entitled to a presumption that the other party must rebut, presumably by evidence that both parties at the time of contracting foresaw that the legal change was likely to occur. If, however, the party seeking relief acted in bad faith or caused the subsequent impairment, relief will be denied.

The evolution of this approach and relevant case law are treated in Speidel, Contracts in Crises, at 156–159, 171–73, 213–221.

Comment: The Contract Clause and Retroactive Illegality

This section has so far focused on the consequences of legislatures and courts limiting the enforceability of prospective agreements that are deemed to be illegal or against public policy. Here we ask whether the law can retroactively limit or alter the enforceability of agreements that were enforceable when made.

The Contract Clause is a provision of the U.S. Constitution that states: "No State shall . . . pass . . . Law impairing the Obligation of Contracts . . . ." U.S. Const. art. 1, § 10, cl. 1. Its primary purpose is to prohibit states from creating laws that retroactively impair contract rights. The Contract Clause protects both public and private contracts from retroactive legislative interference, as demonstrated by the seminal case *Trustees of Dartmouth College v. Woodward*, 17 U.S. 518, 643–44 (1816). *Dartmouth College* involved the attempt by the New Hampshire

Legislature to make Dartmouth College, which had been established as a private college by a royal charter, a public institution. Daniel Webster's impassioned oral argument to the Supreme Court ended with, "It is, sir, as I have said, a small college. And yet there are those who love it!" The Court found that Dartmouth's charter of incorporation was a contract, and that the New Hampshire Legislature's acts amending the charter and altering Dartmouth College's corporate structure violated the Contract Clause.

Despite the potential reach of the constitutional protection for private and public contracts, there are several important limitations to the Contract Clause's effect: (1) It only applies to the states. *Julliard v. Greenman*, 110 U.S. 421, 446 (1884). (2) It is restricted to acts by state legislatures. *New Orleans Waterworks Co. v. La. Sugar Ref. Co.*, 125 U.S. 18, 30 (1888). And (3) it involves retroactive impairments—in other words, it protects only the laws that interfere with already established contracts. Because the Contract Clause does not restrict a legislature's ability to prohibit certain types of prospective contracting, it had a narrower reach than the *Lochner*-era substantive Due Process Clause. Consequently, though the New York legislation at issue in *Lochner v. New York*, 198 U.S. 45 (1905), also impaired established contracts, the Supreme Court focused on the Due Process Clause protections of parties' freedom to create contracts, a future-oriented activity that would not invoke the Contract Clause. Given these limitations, scholars have noted the decline of Contract Clause jurisprudence in the twentieth century. *See* James W. Ely Jr., *Whatever Happened to the Contract Clause?*, 4 Charleston L. Rev. 371, 371–72 (2010) (noting the Contract Clause's recent decline in legal consciousness despite being one of the most litigated constitutional provisions during the nineteenth century).

A Rendering of Daniel Webster's Supreme Court Argument.

Notwithstanding its fading relevance in Supreme Court jurisprudence, the Contract Clause takes on special significance in eras of financial crisis. During the Great Depression, the Supreme Court carved out certain exceptions to the constitutional restrictions on legislative impairment of contracts for emergencies. For example, in *Home Building & Loan Association v. Blaisdell*, 290 U.S. 348, 444–45 (1933), the Court refused to apply the Contract Clause bar to a law temporarily prohibiting mortgage holders from foreclosing on mortgages. Since its inception the emergency exception to the Contract Clause has been used sparingly. In *U.S. Trust Co. of New York v. New Jersey*, 431 U.S. 1, 25 (1977), the Supreme Court created a balancing test to determine whether a legislative modification was permissible: the impairment must be "reasonable and necessary to serve an important public purpose."

Recently, the Contract Clause has come back to the fore with the public pension crisis facing many states. Many states' defined benefit pension plans are massively underfunded, and many states have been or soon will be unable to meet their pension obligations. See Pew Ctr. on the States, *The Trillion Dollar Gap: Underfunded State Retirement Systems and the Roads To Reform* (2010). In order to combat mounting state debts, several state legislatures passed bills adjusting the provisions of the pension promises—thereby retroactively impairing established contracts. The backlash against these provisions has resulted in new state court litigation and questions of whether this economic downturn is significant enough to justify the emergency exceptions recognized during the Great Depression. See Whitney Cloud, *State Pension Deficits, the Recession, and a Modern View of the Contracts Clause*, 121 Yale L.J. 2199 (2011).

Some courts have allowed retroactive application of new mandatory rules when the new rules are deemed to be merely procedural requirements. See Sinclair v. Sinclair, 654 A.2d 438 (Me. 1995) (retroactively applying a new statute requirement that mortgagee be given notice of her right to cure the default). UCC § 11–103 established "almost complete retroactivity" with regard to application of Revised Article 9 treatment of security interests. David Frisch, *Rational Retroactivity in a Commercial Context*, 58 Ala. L.Rev. 765, 791 (2007). Should this kind of retroactive application of mandatory rules violate the Contracts Clause? Do lawmakers have a greater ability to retroactively apply changes to default rules (than with regard to altering rules or new mandatory rules)? If so, allowing lawmakers to fill pre-existing gaps with new rules would give contractors incentives to redundantly restate the default rules so as to reduce the chance of retroactive drift.

Bolin Farms v. American Cotton Shippers Ass'n

United States District Court, Western District of Louisiana, 1974.
Supra at 19.

Comment: Post-Contract Changes in Market Price or Cost of Performance

In contracts with a fixed price, the question is when, if ever, a dramatic rise or fall in the market price for the goods will provide the basis for an excuse. As *Bolin Farms* indicates, the answer is rarely. See, e.g., R.N. Kelly Cotton Merch., Inc. v. York, 494 F.2d 41 (5th Cir. 1974) (market 300% higher than contract price); Hancock Paper Co. v. Champion Intern. Corp., 424 F.Supp. 285 (E.D. Pa. 1976) (market price drops). As comment 4 to UCC § 2–615 states, this is "exactly the type of risk which business contracts made at a fixed price are intended to cover." See Alan Schwartz, *Sales Law and Inflations,* 50 S. Cal. L. Rev. 1 (1976). Thus, if because of the pricing mechanism, both parties did not assume that market prices would remain stable, there is no excuse.

A similar result—no excuse—is usually reached when promisor's cost of performance dramatically exceeds the contract price due to supervening market shifts beyond its control and without its fault or negligence that affect the price of performance inputs. For example, in *Louisiana Power & Light v. Allegheny Ludlum Industries,* 517 F.Supp. 1319 (E.D. La. 1981), a seller refused to perform a contract for nuclear condenser tubing after an increase in metal price would have caused seller to lose $428,500 on a $1.3 million contract. The court found that the seller's non-performance was not excused by impracticability. Commercial impracticability requires an "especially severe and unreasonable loss" and the seller's plant even after loss on contract would have still cleared $589,000.

In cases involving increased costs of performance however, the risk event, whether it be an Act of God, war, extreme inflation, or an oil embargo, can, unlike market price fluctuations, be viewed as a "contingency the non-occurrence of which was a basic assumption on which the contract was made." UCC § 2–615(a). In these cases, the court should consider whether "performance as agreed has been made impracticable" by the risk event. In other words, the party seeking relief must prove that there was an extraordinary circumstance (both parties assumed it would not happen) that made performance so vitally different from what was reasonably to be expected as to alter the essential nature of that performance (impracticable). See Restatement (Second), Chapter 11, page 309; UCC § 2–615 cmt. 4 (increased cost alone does not excuse performance unless the rise in cost is due to some unforeseen contingency which alters the essential nature of the performance). Accord: Bernina Distrib., Inc. v. Bernina Sewing Mach. Co., 646 F.2d 434, 438–39 (10th Cir. 1981) (cost increase must cause "especially severe and unreasonable" loss). But see Florida Power & Light Co. v. Westinghouse Elec. Corp., 826

F.2d 239 (4th Cir. 1987) (defendant excused from obligation to remove and dispose of spent nuclear waste after government unexpectedly discontinued waste processing and use of alternative source would increase cost by $80,000,000).

Kaiser-Francis Oil Co. v. Producer's Gas Co.

United States Court of Appeals, Tenth Circuit, 1989.
870 F.2d 563.

■ BALDOCK, CIRCUIT JUDGE. Appellee and seller, Kaiser-Francis Oil Co. (Kaiser-Francis), sought to enforce the provisions of two similar gas purchase contracts (the "Ellis" and "Cronin" contracts) against appellant and buyer, Producer's Gas Co. (PGC). Under the contracts, PGC was required to take or pay for certain minimum quantities of gas from wells in which Kaiser-Francis had a percentage interest. When the resale price for natural gas declined, PGC did not pay Kaiser-Francis for gas taken on the theory that it was purchasing the gas from Kaiser-Francis' co-owners at reduced prices. PGC also declined to pay for the minimum contract quantities of the gas which were not taken. PGC's actions were based on various defenses to the contracts. The district court granted summary judgment on the issue of liability in favor of Kaiser-Francis, thereby rejecting all of PGC's defenses. The parties thereafter stipulated as to the appropriate damages, interest and attorney's fees that would accrue upon the liability determination. Thus, we consider only issues of liability under the contracts, whether the district court improperly rejected any or all of PGC's defenses to the contract.

On appeal, PGC contends that the district court erred in granting partial summary judgment in favor of Kaiser-Francis because 1) the force majeure provision in the contracts extends to a partial lack of demand caused by market forces, 2) the gas to be supplied by Kaiser-Francis failed to meet the quality specifications of the contract, 3) PGC was not purchasing gas from Kaiser-Francis, but rather from Kaiser-Francis' co-owners in various wells, and 4) any take-or-pay payments required under the contract would violate ceiling prices set by the Natural Gas Policy Act [NGPA]. We find each of these contentions without merit and affirm. Our jurisdiction to review this diversity case arises under 28 U.S.C. § 1291. Consistent with the choice of law provision in each contract, we apply Oklahoma substantive law. * * *

I.   PGC first contends that the force majeure provision[1] in each contract extends to a lack of demand for gas, thereby providing relief in

---

[1]   *14.1* Except for Buyer's obligations to make payment due for gas delivered hereunder, neither party shall be liable for failure to perform this agreement when such failure is due to "force majeure." "Force majeure" shall mean acts of God, strikes, lockouts, or industrial disputes or disturbances, civil disturbances, arrests and restraints, interruptions by government or court orders, present and future valid order of any regulatory body having proper jurisdiction, acts of the public enemy, wars, riots, insurrections, inability to secure labor or inability to secure materials, including inability to secure materials by reason of allocations promulgated by authorized governmental agencies, epidemics, fires, explosions, breakage or accident to

this case from the take-or-pay obligation[2] contained in each contract. PGC suggests that there is an issue of fact concerning the extent of the failure of demand for gas. Essentially, PGC contends that a force majeure event occurred because the demand for gas sharply decreased, with a corresponding decrease in the resale price of gas that PGC was obligated to take or pay for under the contracts. Unfortunately for PGC, however, the Oklahoma Supreme Court, in interpreting a similar force majeure provision, has determined that neither a decline in demand, nor an inability to sell gas at or above the contract price, constitutes a force majeure event. Golsen v. Ong Western, Inc., 756 P.2d 1209, 1213 (Okla. 1988) (interpreting force majeure provision extending to "failure of gas supply or markets"). That decision applies to this case.

PGC's interpretation of the force majeure provision is antithetical to the take-or-pay provision. Under its interpretation, PGC could be expected to take only when the demand for gas resulted in a resale price at or above the contract price. PGC could never be expected to take or pay when the demand for gas resulted in a resale price below the contract price. Rather than taking or paying under the take-or-pay provision, PGC would rely on the force majeure provision. Thus, Kaiser-Francis would be shut in during any drop in demand, for up to twenty years, without any ability to sell in other markets. Such a one-sided interpretation is suspect.

> The purpose of the take-or-pay clause is to apportion the risks of natural gas production and sales between the buyer and seller. The seller bears the risk of production. To compensate the seller for that risk, the buyer agrees to take, or pay for if not taken, a minimum quantity of gas. The buyer bears the risk of market demand.

---

machinery or lines of pipe, freezing of wells or pipelines, inability to obtain easements, right-of-way or other interests in realty, the making of repairs, replacements or alterations to lines of pipe or plants, partial or entire failure of gas supply or demand over which neither Seller nor Buyer have [sic] control or any other cause, whether of the kind herein enumerated or otherwise, not reasonably within the control of the party claiming "force majeure." Events of "force majeure" shall, so far as possible, be remedied with all reasonable dispatch. The settlement of industrial difficulties shall be within the discretion of the party having the difficulty, and the requirement that "force majeure" be remedied with all reasonable dispatch shall not require the settlement of industrial difficulties by acceding to the demands of any opposing party when such course is inadvisable in the discretion of the party having the difficulty.
Rec. vol. II (Attachment to Brief In Support of Kaiser-Francis Oil Company's Motion for Partial Summary Judgment—1980 Ellis & 1982 Cronin contracts) (emphasis added).

[2] *4.1* Subject to all terms and conditions of this Agreement, Seller shall sell and deliver during each Accounting Year from the lands and leases covered hereby, and Buyer shall purchase and receive from Seller or pay for if available but not taken, a quantity of gas equal to the Daily Contract Quantities herein specified.

4.7 If at the end of any Accounting Year, Buyer shall have failed to purchase during such Year the sum the applicable Daily Contract Quantities, after credit is allowed for (i) deficiency existing by *force majeure*, . . . , Buyer shall pay for the remaining deficiency as if taken.
Rec. vol. II (Attachment to Brief in Support of Kaiser-Francis Oil Company's Motion for Partial Summary Judgment—1980 Ellis and 1982 Cronin contracts).

. . . . Should the resale price decline below the contract price, PGC could still take the gas and sell it, albeit at a loss, or pay for the gas without taking it, also at a loss. The change in the general or relative resale price of gas does not constitute a "partial failure of gas demand" which would relieve PGC of its obligation to take or pay. The force majeure provision cannot substitute for a price redetermination or market-out provision which would allow PGC to reduce the price paid to Kaiser-Francis for gas, thereby ameliorating PGC's take-or-pay obligation when the resale price of natural gas declined.

* * *

NOTES

(1) Are you persuaded by the court's reasoning on why the *force majeure* clause should not excuse the defendant? Suppose the clause, as in *Golsen,* had included "failure of gas supply or markets" as a ground for excuse? What contract provision would best protect the defendant from the particular events that occurred? See generally, Harold A. Lewis, *Allocating Risk in Take-or-Pay Contracts: Are Force Majeure and Commercial Impracticability the Same Defense?* 42 Sw. L.J. 1047 (1989).

(2) *Judge Posner on Force Majeure Clauses.* "A *force majeure* clause is not intended to buffer a party against the normal risks of a contract. The normal risk of a fixed-price contract is that the market price will change. If it rises, the buyer gains at the expense of the seller (except insofar as escalator provisions give the seller some protection); if it falls * * * the seller gains at the expense of the buyer. The whole purpose of a fixed-price contract is to allocate risk in this way. A *force majeure* clause interpreted to excuse the buyer from the consequences of the risk he expressly assumed would nullify a central term of the contract." Northern Ind. Pub. Serv. Co. v. Carbon Cnty. Coal Co., 799 F.2d 265, 275 (7th Cir. 1986) (the *NIPSCO* case, reprinted infra, Chapter 6).

(3) *Judge Posner on Fixed Price Contracts.* The essence of the outcome in take-or-pay contracts was expressed in the (just-mentioned) *NIPSCO* case, 799 F.2d at 278, where the court, speaking through Judge Posner, stated:

> Since impossibility and related doctrines are devices for shifting risk in accordance with the parties' presumed intentions, which are to minimize the costs of contract performance, one of which is the disutility created by risk, they have no place when the contract explicitly assigns a particular risk to one party or the other. [A] fixed-price contract is an explicit assignment of the risk of market price increases to the seller and the risk of market price decreases to the buyer, and the assignment of the latter risk to the buyer is even clearer where * * * the contract places a floor under price but allows for escalation. If * * * the buyer forecasts the market incorrectly and therefore finds himself locked into a disadvantageous contract, he has only himself to blame and so cannot shift the risk back to the seller by invoking impossibility or

related doctrines. * * * Since "the very purpose of a fixed price agreement is to place the risk of increased costs on the promisor (and the risk of decreased costs on the promisee)," the fact that costs decrease steeply * * * cannot allow the buyer to walk away from the contract.

(4) *Take-or-Pay Contracts.* In the 1970's, producers entered long-term contracts with pipelines for the sale of natural gas. The pipelines agreed to "take or pay" for a portion of the producer's output at an agreed price, subject to escalation. The base price was set at an agreed dollar amount per unit, called MMBTU. In essence, the pipeline could either "take" the gas when produced and pay for it or pay without taking and expect the producer to "make up" deliveries in the future. Under this arrangement, the pipeline secured a long-term source of supply at a predictable price and the producer obtained a reliable source of cash with which to finance production and the development of reserves. In addition, the contract might contain a *force majeure* clause or other provisions allocating risk, such as a "market out" or a "matching price" clause. Under these clauses, the pipeline could terminate the contract if a lower long-term price for gas could be found from another source and the producer was unwilling or unable to match it. See Joe Caggiano, *Understanding Natural Gas Contracts,* 38 Oil & Gas Tax Q. 267, 267–278 (1989).

By 1983, the price of most gas at the "wellhead" had been deregulated under the Natural Gas Policy Act of 1978. At the same time, a depressed economy and lower demand for natural gas at the retail level put the pipelines in a bind. They did not need the gas they had agreed to take and the contract price that they had agreed to pay was substantially above that now available under either new long-term contracts or on the spot market. With large volumes of gas at stake, the dollar amount involved in a single contract could exceed $500,000,000. To no one's surprise, the pipelines began to search for ways to adjust or to terminate the contracts.

Without attempting here to exhaust the possibilities for agreed settlement, a survey of litigation under the UCC suggests that the pipelines were singularly unsuccessful in avoiding these contracts. A summary of the judicial outcomes:

(1) A long-term contract for the sale of natural gas is subject to Article 2 of the UCC if the gas is to be "severed by the seller." UCC § 2–107(1);

(2) Take-or-Pay provisions are not unconscionable at the time the contract is made;

(3) Take-or-Pay provisions do not provide for liquidated damages. Rather, they give the buyer a choice between alternative performances under the contract;

(4) *Force majeure* clauses are not intended to excuse the buyer from changes in the market, no matter how dramatic;

(5) UCC § 2–615 will not be applied to excuse the buyer from the contract, even though government action in deregulating natural gas prices played an important role in the market decline.

For more, see Speidel, Contracts in Crises at 229–46.

Comment: Reopener Clauses in Long-Term Supply Contracts

The uncertainties involved when a court develops and imposes a price adjustment could be partially resolved if the parties included a "gross inequities" or a "reopener" clause in the contract. These clauses operate in three stages: *first,* a "gross inequity" under the existing contract resulting from "unusual economic conditions not contemplated by the parties at the time of contracting" must exist; *second,* the parties agree to negotiate in good faith to correct or to adjust the inequity by agreement and to cooperate with each other in the process; *third,* if negotiations fail to produce an agreed adjustment, the dispute is submitted to arbitration, where the decision of the arbitrator is final and conclusive. These clauses, when included, preserve both the relative equities of the parties over time and the contract. Normally, the parties agree to continue performance under the original terms while the dispute is being resolved. See Georgia Power Co. v. Cimarron Coal Corp., 526 F.2d 101, 103–04 (6th Cir. 1975) (dispute under "gross inequities" clause subject to arbitration). These clauses vary in scope and detail with the particular industry. As one commentator has noted, contract solutions "are not self-operative and depend, in large measure, upon the good faith of both the purchaser and the seller." Sam A. Snyder, *Geothermal Sales Contracts,* 13 Land & Water L. Rev. 259, 288 (1977).

Here is an edited example of a "Fair Clause" which has been used in long-term international sales contracts in the copper industry:

Fair Clause

§ 15.1 In entering into this long-term Agreement the parties hereto recognize that it is impracticable to make provision for every contingency which may arise during the term of this Agreement and the parties declare it to be their intention that this Agreement shall operate between them with fairness.

§ 15.2 Based on the foregoing principle the provisions of this Article 15 shall apply if during the term of this Agreement a new situation arises which is beyond the reasonable control of either party and which is not covered by any of the provisions of this Agreement and if such situation results in (a) a material disadvantage to one party and a corresponding material advantage to the other or (b) severe hardship to one party without an advantage to the other party. * * *

§ 15.4(a) In situations described under § 15.2(a) a solution shall be found in order to restore a fair balance of advantages and disadvantages as between the parties.

(b) In situations described under § 15.2(b) a solution shall be found in order to remove the severe hardship for the party affected; provided, however, that the provisions of this Agreement, as changed or modified by such solution and considered as a whole, shall remain commensurate with those of other international contracts between copper mines and independent smelters/refineries at the time of such change or modification and

(i) in case [buyer] invokes the Fair Clause, shall be no less favorable to [seller] than the provisions of any other comparable international contract between [buyer] and any independent copper mine other than [seller]; and

(ii) in case [seller] invokes the Fair Clause, shall be no less favorable to [buyer] than the provisions of any other comparable international contract between [seller] and any independent copper smelter/refinery other than [buyer].

The comparison of provisions as aforesaid shall serve as a valuation basis for the adjustment of the particular provisions of this Agreement which are involved, for instance the smelting/refining charge, but shall not result in replacing the provisions of this Agreement by the provisions of any compared contract, unless agreed upon between [seller] and [buyer].

(c) In arriving at solutions for either of the situations described in § 15.2, due consideration shall be given to such benefits as may have been obtained by each party as a result of a prior invocation of this Article 15.

§ 15.5 If either party hereto shall believe that a new situation described in § 15.2 shall have arisen, then, at the request of either party hereto, the parties shall promptly consult with a view toward reaching a mutually acceptable agreement dealing with such situation. In the event that within six months after the date of such request the parties shall not reach agreement with respect to such situation, either party shall have the right, exercisable within three months after the expiration of such six-month period, to refer the matter to arbitration pursuant to § 19.1. The arbitrator or arbitrators shall determine whether the particular situation is a "new situation" described in § 15.2(a) or in § 15.2(b) and, if so, shall, in any award entered, specify the section involved and unless the parties come to a prompt solution themselves, thereafter on the request of either party also establish a solution in conformity with § 15.4. Such arbitrator or arbitrators may obtain, for the purpose of establishing such solution, the opinion of an impartial expert of recognized standing in the international copper business, who shall not be domiciled in either the United States or Germany unless the parties hereto shall otherwise consent. Promptly after the entering of such award the parties hereto shall enter into a written agreement incorporating the terms of such award and making such changes or modifications in this Agreement as may be required in order to give effect to such award.

Practice in international trade has influenced the UNIDROIT Principles of International Commercial Contracts, which recognize that events subsequent to the contract may cause hardship and require that upon request of the disadvantaged party the other party must, at a minimum, negotiate in good faith toward an equilibrium. Articles 6.2.2 and 6.2.3, Comment 5. If the parties fail to reach agreement within a reasonable time, a court, if it finds hardship, "may, if reasonable, (a) terminate the contract at a date and on terms to be fixed, or (b) adapt the contract with a view to restoring its equilibrium." Article 6.2.3(4).

(C) FRUSTRATION OF PURPOSE

In this subsection, the emphasis shifts from changed circumstances that impair or impact the capacity of a party to perform to the contract to circumstances that *frustrate the purpose* of a party in entering the contract. In economic terms, we shift from increased costs of performance for the promisor to decreased benefits from performance for the promisee. When, if ever, should relief be granted in these cases?

Prince Rupert, son of Elizabeth, Queen of Bohemia, grandson of James I, nephew of Charles I, and first cousin to Charles II, was born in Germany in 1619. He arrived in England in 1641 to serve Charles I, and from 1641–45, he was "the toast of the Royalists, the terror of the Roundheads, and the mainstay of the King's war effort."

Paradine v. Jane
King's Bench, 1647.
82 Eng. Rep. 897.

In debt the plaintiff declares upon a lease for years rendering rent at the four usual feasts; and for rent behind for three years, ending at the Feast of the Annunciation, 21 Car. brings his action; the defendant pleads, that a certain German prince, by name Prince Rupert, an alien born, enemy to the King and kingdom, had invaded the realm with an hostile army of men; and with the same force did enter upon the defendant's possession, and him expelled, and held out of possession from the 19 of July 18 Car. till the Feast of the Annunciation, 21 Car. whereby he could not take the profits; whereupon the plaintiff demurred, and the plea was resolved insufficient.

1.   Because the defendant hath not answered to one quarters rent.

2.   He hath not averred that the army were all aliens, which shall not be intended, and then he hath his remedy against them; and Bacon cited 33 H. 6. 1. e. where the gaoler in bar of an escape pleaded, that alien enemies broke the prison & c. and exception take to it, for that he ought to shew of what countrey they were, viz. Scots, & c.

3.   It was resolved, that the matter of the plea was insufficient; for though the whole army had been alien enemies, yet he ought to pay his rent. And this difference was taken, that where the law creates a duty or charge, and the party is disabled to perform it without any default in him, and hath no remedy over, there the law will excuse him. As in the case of waste, if a house be destroyed by tempest, or by enemies, the lessee is excused. Dyer, 33. a. Inst. 53. d. 283. a. 12 H. 4. 6. so of an escape. Co. 4. 84. b. 33 H. 6. 1. So in 9 E. 3. 16. a supersedeas was awarded to the justices, that they should not proceed in a cessavit upon a cesser during the war, but when the party by his own contract creates a duty or charge upon himself, he is bound to make it good, if he may, notwithstanding any accident by inevitable necessity, because he might have provided against it by his contract. And therefore if the lessee covenant to repair a house, though it be burnt by lightning, or thrown down by enemies, yet he ought to repair it. Dyer 33. a. 40 E. 3. 6. h. Now the rent is a duty created by the parties upon the reservation, and had there been a covenant to pay it, there had been no question but the lessee must have made it good, notwithstanding the interruption by enemies, for the law would not protect him beyond his own agreement, no more than in the case of reparations; this reservation then being a covenant in law, and whereupon an action of covenant hath been maintained (as Roll said) it is all one as if there had been an actual covenant. Another reason was added, that as the lessee is to have the advantage of casual profits, so he must run the hazard of casual losses, and not lay the whole burthen of them upon his lessor; and Dyer 56. 6. was cited for this purpose, that though the land be surrounded, or gained by the sea, or made barren by wildfire, yet the lessor shall have his whole rent: and judgment was given for the plaintiff.

Krell v. Henry

Court of Appeal, 1903.
[1903] 2 K.B. 740.

Appeal from a decision of DARLING, J. The plaintiff, Paul Krell, sued the defendant, C.S. Henry, for 50*l.*, being the balance of a sum of 75*l.*, for which the defendant had agreed to hire a flat at 56A, Pall Mall on the days of June 26 and 27, for the purpose of viewing the processions to be held in connection with the coronation of His Majesty. The defendant denied his liability, and counterclaimed for the return of the sum of 25*l*., which had been paid as a deposit, on the ground that, the processions not having taken place owing to the serious illness of the King, there had been a total failure of consideration for the contract entered into by him.

[The defendant was induced to contract by an announcement in the window of plaintiff's flat renting windows to view the coronation, but the contract itself contained no express reference to the coronation.]

Darling J., held, upon the authority of *Taylor v. Caldwell* . . . that there was an implied condition in the contract that the procession should take place, and gave judgment for the defendant on the claim and counter-claim. The plaintiff appealed.

■ VAUGHAN WILLIAMS L.J. read the following written judgment:—The real question in this case is the extent of the application in English law of the principle of the Roman law which has been adopted and acted on in many English decisions, and notably in the case of *Taylor v. Caldwell*. That case at least makes it clear that

> where, from the nature of the contract, it appears that the parties must from the beginning have known that it could not be fulfilled unless, when the time for the fulfilment of the contract arrived, some particular specified thing continued to exist, so that when entering into the contract they must have contemplated such continued existence as the foundation of what was to be done; there, in the absence of any express or implied warranty that the thing shall exist, the contract is not to be considered a positive contract, but as subject to an implied condition that the parties shall be excused in case, before breach, performance becomes impossible from the perishing of the thing without default of the contractor.

Thus far it is clear that the principle of the Roman law has been introduced into the English law. The doubt in the present case arises as to how far this principle extends. * * *

I do not think that the principle of the civil law as introduced into the English law is limited to cases in which the event causing the impossibility of performance is the destruction or non-existence of some thing which is the subject-matter of the contract or of some condition or state of things expressly specified as a condition of it. I think that you first have to ascertain, not necessarily from the terms of the contract, but, if required, from necessary inferences, drawn from surrounding circumstances recognised by both contracting parties, what is the substance of the contract, and then to ask the question whether that substantial contract needs for its foundation the assumption of the existence of a particular state of things. If it does, this will limit the operation of the general words, and in such case, if the contract becomes impossible of performance by reason of the nonexistence of the state of things assumed by both contracting parties as the foundation of the contract, there will be no breach of the contract thus limited. . . .

In my judgment the use of the rooms was let and taken for the purpose of seeing the Royal procession. It was not a demise of the rooms, or even an agreement to let and take the rooms. It is a license to use rooms for a particular purpose and none other. And in my judgment the taking place of those processions on the days proclaimed along the proclaimed route, which passed 56A, Pall Mall, was regarded by both contracting parties as the foundation of the contract; and I think that it cannot reasonably be supposed to have been in the contemplation of the contracting parties, when the contract was made, that the coronation would not be held on the proclaimed days, or the processions not take place on those days along the proclaimed route; and I think that the words imposing on the defendant the obligation to accept and pay for the use of the rooms for the named days, although general and unconditional, were not used with reference to the possibility of the particular contingency which afterwards occurred. It was suggested in the course of the argument that if the occurrence, on the proclaimed days, of the coronation and the procession in this case were the foundation of the contract, and if the general words are thereby limited or qualified, so that in the event of the non-occurrence of the coronation and procession along the proclaimed route they would discharge both parties from further performance of the contract, it would follow that if a cabman was engaged to take some one to Epsom on Derby Day at a suitable enhanced price for such a journey, say 10*l.*, both parties to the contract would be discharged in the contingency of the race at Epsom for some reason becoming impossible; but I do not think this follows, for I do not think that in the cab case the happening of the race would be the foundation of the contract. No doubt the purpose of the engager would be to go to see the Derby, and the price would be proportionately high; but the cab had no special qualifications for the purpose which led to the selection of the cab for this particular occasion. Any other cab would have done as well. Moreover, I think that, under the cab contract, the hirer, even if the race went off, could have said, "Drive me to Epsom; I will pay you the agreed sum; you have nothing to do with the purpose for which I hired the cab," and that if the cabman refused he would have been guilty of a breach of contract, there being nothing to qualify his promise to drive the hirer to Epsom on a particular day. Whereas in the case of the coronation, there is not merely the purpose of the hirer to see the coronation procession, but it is the coronation procession and the relative position of the rooms which is the basis of the contract as much for the lessor as the hirer; and I think that if the King, before the coronation day and after the contract, had died, the hirer could not have insisted on having the rooms on the days named. It could not in the cab case be reasonably said that seeing the Derby race was the foundation of the contract, as it was of the license in this case. Whereas in the present case, where the rooms were offered and taken, by reason of their peculiar suitability from the position of the rooms for a view of the coronation procession, surely the view of the coronation procession was the foundation of the contract, which is a very different thing from the purpose of the man who engaged the cab—namely, to see the race—being held to be the foundation of the contract. Each case must be judged by its own circumstances. In each case one must ask oneself, first, what, having regard to all the circumstances, was the foundation of the contract? Secondly, was the performance of the contract prevented? Thirdly, was the event which prevented the performance of the contract of such a character that it cannot reasonably be said to have been in the contemplation of the parties at the date of the contract? If all these questions are answered in the affirmative (as I think they should be in this case), I think both parties are discharged from further performance of the contract. I think that the coronation procession was the foundation of this contract, and that the non-happening of it prevented the performance of the contract; and, secondly, I think that the non-happening of the procession . . . was an event "of such a character that it cannot reasonably be supposed to have been in the contemplation of the contracting parties when the contract was made, and that they are not to be held bound by general words which, though large enough to include, were not used with reference to the possibility of the particular contingency which afterwards happened." The test seems to be whether the event which causes the impossibility was or might have been anticipated and guarded against. * * *

I myself am clearly of opinion that in this case, where we have to ask ourselves whether the object of the contract was frustrated by the non-happening of the coronation and its procession on the days proclaimed, parol evidence is admissible to shew that the subject of the contract was rooms to view the coronation procession, and was so to the knowledge of both parties. . . .

This disposes of the plaintiff's claim for 50*l.* unpaid balance of the price agreed to be paid for the use of the rooms. The defendant at one time set up a cross-claim for the return of the 25*l.* he paid at the date of the contract. As that claim is now withdrawn it is unnecessary to say anything about it.

Appeal dismissed.

NOTES

(1) *The Development of Frustration Under English Law.* After tracing the development of frustration in English law, G. H. Treitel concludes:

> From a practical point of view, the doctrine of frustration gives rise to two related difficulties. The first is that it may scarcely be more satisfactory to hold that the contract is totally discharged than to hold that it remains in force; often some compromise may be a more reasonable solution. * * * In the absence of * * * express provisions, this kind of solution is not open to the courts; they have no power

to *modify* contracts in the light of supervening events. The second difficulty is that the allocation of risks produced at common law by the doctrine of frustration is not always entirely satisfactory. In a case like *Taylor v. Caldwell* it may be reasonable that neither party should be liable for loss of the benefit that the other expected to derive from performance * * * [b]ut it does not follow that loss suffered by one party as a result in acting in reliance on the contract should equally lie where it falls. In *Taylor v. Caldwell* the plaintiffs did not in fact make any claim for lost profits, but only one for expenses thrown away in advertising the concerts. It is by no means self-evident that the owners of the hall (who had presumably insured it) should escape all liability for this loss; and it might be more satisfactory if loss of this kind could be apportioned. At common law this was only possible where the contract expressly so provided; * * *. A more general, but nevertheless limited power of apportionment now exists by statute, but it does not cover all cases in which some form of apportionment would seem to be desirable. [citing the Frustrated Contracts Act.]

G.H. Treitel, The Law of Contract 651–52 (6th ed. 1983).

(2) In *Krell v. Henry*, Henry had paid 25 pounds in advance but withdrew a cross-claim for restitution of that amount. In other coronation cases, the plaintiffs sought and were denied restitution of the down payment: the gains and losses were left where they lay at the time of frustration. See e.g., Chandler v. Webster, 1 K.B. 493 (1904). This result was ultimately reversed in *Fibrosa Spolka Akcyjna v. Fairbairn Lawson Combe Barbour, Ltd.*, 2 All. Eng. 122 (H.L.1942). See R.G. McElroy & Glanville Williams, *The Coronation Cases-II*, 5 Mod. L. Rev. 1 (1941) (discussing Chandler and related cases).

(3) *The Prohibition Cases.* In the late 19th and early 20th centuries (before National Prohibition), many states passed legislation either prohibiting the manufacture and sale of alcoholic beverages or giving to local government the option to enact such prohibitions. State legislation prohibiting the manufacture and sale of alcoholic beverages was upheld against attack under the 14th Amendment by the owner of a brewery in *Mugler v. Kansas*, 123 U.S. 623 (1887), decided by the Supreme Court in 1887.

After the turn of the century, the absolute liability theory of *Paradine v. Jane*, as modified by *Krell v. Henry*, appeared but was not explicitly identified in state decisions on the effect of legislative prohibitions against the sale of alcohol that had retrospective effect on existing leases. In a typical case, an owner had leased premises for a fixed term to a lessee for the purpose of operating a bar or a saloon. After state or local legislation prohibiting the sale of alcoholic beverages was enacted, the lessee defaulted on the rent obligation on the grounds of supervening illegality. The lessee's obligation to pay rent, however, was not made illegal. Rather, a main purpose for which the property was leased was prohibited. It would now be a crime to use the premises for the sale of alcoholic beverages.

In some cases, relief was denied under a *Paradine*-like absolutist principal. For example, in *Houston Ice & Brewing Co. v. Keenan,* 99 Tex. 79 (1905), relief was denied even though there was a stipulation in the lease that the premises should be used for "saloon business." The Texas Supreme Court held that even if use was so restricted, the adoption of the local option did not make the contract of lease illegal or absolve the defendant from the rent. The court embraced the hard-line reasoning of the Court of Civil Appeals which, while recognizing the principle of excuse from supervening illegality of performance, held that this case was not within the exception to the general rule that "where the performance becomes impossible subsequent to the making of the contract, the promisor is not thereby discharged." Key to the case, however, was the fact that the local option statute had been enacted but not implemented at the time the lease was signed: The "appellant must have known that [implementation] was likely to occur, and, if it did, the performance of the stipulation under discussion would be prohibited." Further, this was a "probable contingency which an ordinarily prudent man should have foreseen and provided for in his contract, and, having failed to so do, he took the risk upon himself, and must abide the consequences." To put the matter in the words of the English courts, even if the Texas court had recognized and embraced the "frustration of purpose" principal, it concluded that the subsequent government act was "contemplated" at the time of contracting and unless the risk was allocated by the agreement it would be assumed by the lessee. In a modern parlance, the legal context at the time the lease was signed was unstable and the subsequent prohibition, which had retrospective effect, was foreseeable as likely to occur.

In other cases, relief was granted under the general principle of subsequent illegality. This was done either by construing the lease to limit use to a particular purpose, operating of a saloon, or by finding that the purpose of both parties, as clearly expressed by the lease, was that the premises should be used as a saloon. Under either approach, the subsequent legislation made that common purpose illegal and discharged the contract. On the other hand, if use on the premises was not restricted or assumed to be limited to a bar or saloon (in the strict sense) and other commercial uses were possible, excuse was likely to be denied. In these cases, *Krell v. Henry* was not cited and the doctrine of "frustration of purpose" was neither identified nor discussed. But in leases at least the frustration doctrine had arrived in the United States as a possible exception to *Paradine v. Jane,* provided that the risk of subsequent, retrospective law was not foreseeably likely to occur. See Speidel, Contracts in Crises at 52–59.

(4) *The Restatement Approaches.* By the time of the First Restatement (1933), the doctrine of "Frustration of the Object or Effect of the Contract" was restated in section 288, which, curiously, was placed in Chapter 10 on "Conditions" rather than in Chapter 14 on "Impossibility." Section 288 provided:

> Where the assumed possibility of a desired object or effect to be attained by either party to a contract forms the basis on which both parties enter into it, and this object or effect is or surely will be

frustrated, a promisor who is without fault in causing the frustration, and who is harmed thereby, is discharged from the duty of performing his promises unless a contrary intention appears.

Comment (a) stated that the "object or effect to be gained must be so completely the basis of the contract that, as both parties know, without it the contract would have little meaning."

Washington State Hop Producers, Inc. v. Goschie Farms, Inc.

Supreme Court of Washington, 1989.
112 Wash.2d 694.

[From 1965 until 1985, the U.S. Department of Agriculture required hop growers to obtain federal allotments in order to market their hops. This was called "hop base." Growers could transfer excess allotments to other growers. Over time, "hop base" became a scarce, expensive commodity and a secondary market developed for trading. Plaintiff, the Trust, was organized in 1979 to acquire, lease and sell federal hop base.

Because the system restricted market entry, legal efforts to change the marketing order were commenced in 1981. The USDA considered various changes, but as late as June, 1985, substantial changes in the marketing order were not anticipated. On May 31, 1985, the Trust mailed invitations to bid on two pools of "hop base" for sale. Pool A of 633,500 pounds was available for use in 1985 and Pool B of 432,639 pounds was available for use in 1986. On June 16, 1985, bids were received ranging from $0.05 per pound to $0.76 per pound. On June 21, 1985, the Trust mailed notices of award to bids in the $0.50 to $0.76 range, including Gochie and other respondents in this case. On June 27, 1985, however, the USDA terminated the marketing order, effective December 31, 1985. All of the respondents refused to perform the contracts for sale. The Trust was able to sell nearly 50% of the "hop base" in Pool B for an average price of $0.07 per pound, compared with earlier successful bids of $0.60 per pound.

In an action by the Trust to enforce the contracts, the trial court granted summary judgment to the respondents. This was affirmed in the court of appeals which, in essence, held that the respondent's contracts were excused by the rule of supervening frustration. The Trust appealed.]

* * *

Perhaps the earliest case clearly recognizing frustration of purpose as a defense in a breach of contract action is Krell v. Henry, 2 K.B. 740 (C.A.1903). There, a lease was made to rent use of a window overlooking the route for the coronation parade of Albert Edward when he succeeded his mother, Queen Victoria. After the agreement, Edward became ill, the parade was canceled, and the purpose of renting the window was frustrated. The lessee refused to pay the agreed rent. The court held that his duty was discharged and that he was therefore not liable for breach. Both parties were capable of performing the terms of their contracts, and there was arguably still some market value in the vendor's performance. But the lessee's ultimate purpose was frustrated and he was released from his contract nonetheless.

The doctrine of "Discharge by Supervening Frustration" is recited in Restatement (Second) of Contracts § 265 (1979). * * * This is the rule and test recited and applied by the Court of Appeals.... However, Washington has not before now adopted the doctrine of supervening frustration as recited in Restatement (Second) of Contracts § 265 (1979).

Under the restatement formula, "the purpose that is frustrated must have been a principal purpose of that party in making the contract . . . without [which] the transaction would make little sense." Restatement (Second) of Contracts § 265, comment (a) (1979). The Court of Appeals found "the principal purpose of this contract was to purchase a hop allotment base provided and created pursuant to a hop marketing agreement." Washington State Hop Producers, Inc. Liquidation Trust v. Goschie Farms, Inc., 51 Wash. App. 484 (1988). We agree.

Under the conditions prevailing for nearly 20 years before the termination order, ownership of hop base provided permanent access to the hop market otherwise unavailable. After the termination, what was available to "purchase" was at most access to the 1985 crop year market. The Trust had formerly been in the business of renting 1-year access to the hop market. The Growers did not seek single-year market access, nor did they bid prices in the range of the 1-year rental (6 cents ($0.06) per pound). Without the federal requirement of hop base, there would have been no subject matter for the contracts nor any consideration from the Trust to support the transactions. Because the Growers sought to *purchase* hop base instead of renting it, the inference is that *future* market access was their principal purpose in entering the transactions. This purpose was understood by both parties. Purchase, as opposed to rental, of the hop base made little sense without future market access. The record provides sufficient undisputed facts to sustain the Court of Appeals' determination on this point.

The Court of Appeals relied upon the decline in value of hop allotments in determining that the purpose of the contracts had been frustrated by termination of the hop marketing order. The pertinent language from the appellate opinion is:

> Here, we find the principal purpose of this contract was to purchase a hop allotment base provided and created pursuant to a hop marketing agreement. As is evident when the marketing order was terminated, effective December 31, 1985, the value of that allotment decreased [in June 1985 when the termination was announced], assuming a bid of $.50 fell to $.05, i.e., one-tenth the bid price. We consider that a substantial frustration falling within the rule.

Washington State Hop Producers, Inc. Liquidation Trust v. Goschie Farms, Inc., 51 Wash. App. 484, 489 (1988). It is not clear from the language employed whether the "frustration" is the 90 percent decline in market price, or whether the decline in value is merely evidence of the substantiality of the frustration.

The decline in price was great. Before the Termination Order, hop base was a prerequisite to the sale of hops. The annual *rental* price of hop base for 1985 was 6 cents per pound before the Termination Order. Successful bids to *purchase* Pool "A" hop base before termination ranged up to 76 cents per pound. After termination, hop base would be unnecessary following the 1985 crop year. Pool "B" hop base that had commanded a pre-termination price of not less than 50 cents (when it could be sold at all after the termination was announced) commanded an average price of just 7/10 of one cent ($0.007)—a 98 percent decrease in value.

[A] rational market should have valued post-termination Pool "A" base at about 6 and 7/10 cents ($0.067) per pound.... [T]he post-termination decrease remains in the range of 92 percent. . . .

If the decline in price alone is considered to be substantial frustration, then the decision of the Court of Appeals cannot be affirmed without doing violence to established principles of contract law. See, e.g., Restatement (Second) of Contracts § 265, comment (a) (1979) ("It is not enough that the transaction has become less profitable for the affected party or even that he will sustain a loss."). The decision may be affirmed on other grounds, however. * * *

If the decline in price is regarded merely as evidence of substantiality of frustration of the purpose of the contract, then the Court of Appeals' reasoning, as well as its decision, may stand.... [I]t is not the decline in market price, but the irrelevance of control of hop base after the 1985 crop year that supplies the frustration justifying rescission.

Application of the doctrine of frustration is a question of law and not a question of fact.... Whether, as appellant states, "the value of the [Trust's] performance is ... totally or nearly totally destroyed by supervening events," as evidenced by the decline in price, seems a matter well within the sound judgment of the trial court. We will not disturb that court's determination.

In this case appellant Trust makes repeated references to "foreseeability" of the market order termination as invalidating the rescission granted by the trial court. However, as the Court of Appeals noted, "[w]hile the Trust seeks to hold the growers to knowledge that the order could be terminated at any time, it takes no responsibility for the same knowledge." Washington State Hop Producers, Inc. Liquidation Trust v. Goschie Farms, Inc., 51 Wash. App. 484, 488 (1988). The court noted that the Trust had incorporated no language in its bid form allocating the risk to the growers. The court also noted that the growers had not included any allocating language in their "acceptance." This latter reference seems not to be made to any particular document. All documents and exhibits in the record comprising the transactions between the parties consist of forms provided by the Trust. The growers simply filled in blanks on bid forms provided by the Trust. There is no indication that any restrictive language could have been added by the growers. By contrast, the Trust had every opportunity to draft the language to its own advantage. It did not do so.

Moreover, the inference is that, even to the Trust, the termination was unforeseeable or at least not foreseen. . . . In its own brief, the Trust states, "[a]s late as June, 1985 . . . it was not anticipated that any substantial change in the Marketing Order would be proposed by the Secretary of Agriculture." In its introduction to Chapter 11, the Restatement notes the significance of the "relative ease with which either party could have inserted a clause" 2 Restatement (Second) of Contracts 311 (1979). In context, this factor is equivalent to foreseeability in affecting the application of the doctrine.

Under the Restatement formula, foreseeability is merely a relevant factor in determining whether nonoccurrence of the frustrating event was a basic assumption of the frustrated party in entering the transaction. If that basic assumption is found, as it was here, the "issue" of foreseeability becomes irrelevant. . . . The trial court, implicitly, and the Court of Appeals, explicitly, found that continued need to own or control hop base in order to sell hops was an assumption central to the subject matter of the contract. The Court of Appeals concluded that "[w]e find without this basic assumption there would neither have been an offer nor an acceptance." 51 Wash. App. 484, 490.

By repeating its position, the Restatement is emphatic on the role of foreseeability. The introductory note to Chapter 11 reads:

> The fact that the [frustrating] event was unforeseeable is significant as suggesting that its non-occurrence was a basic assumption. However, the fact that it was foreseeable, or even foreseen, does not, of itself, argue for a contrary conclusion, since the parties may not have thought it sufficiently important a risk to have made it a subject of their bargaining. Another significant factor may be the relative bargaining positions of the parties and the relative ease with which either party could have included a clause.

2 Restatement (Second) of Contracts § 311 (1979).

Appellant refers to the Restatement (Second) of Contracts § 261 in support of its contention that foreseeability avoids the defense of commercial frustration. The section is inapposite because it concerns the defense of supervening impracticability. Frustration is covered in § 265.

However, even if the reference did apply, the language does not advance appellant's argument.

> A commercial practice under which a party might be expected to insure or otherwise secure himself against a risk also militates against shifting it to the other party. If the supervening event was not reasonably foreseeable when the contract was made, the party claiming discharge can hardly be expected to have provided against its occurrence. However, if it was reasonably foreseeable, or even foreseen, the opposite conclusion [i.e., that the party should not be discharged] does not necessarily follow.

Restatement (Second) of Contracts § 261 at comment (c), p. 315. Cross reference is made to § 265, comment (a), quoted above, and § 261, comment (c). Pertinent language from this latter reference includes the following: "The fact that the event was foreseeable *or even foreseen,* does not necessarily compel a conclusion that its non-occurrence was not a basic assumption." (Italics ours.) Restatement (Second) of Contracts § 261, comment (b), p. 314.

* * *

Although language suggesting that unforeseeability is a prerequisite of supervening frustration has found its way into the case law of this state, . . . the basis for this rule does not apply to this case. The Growers did not receive an estate in land, such as would be provided by a commercial lease, see Lloyd v. Murphy, 25 Cal. 2d 48 (1944), nor did they ever have the beneficial use of the subject matter of the contracts for which they request rescission. The Restatement (Second) of Contracts repeatedly refers to foreseeability as only a factor in determining whether the non-occurrence of the frustrating event was an assumption basic to the contract. Moreover, foreseeability of a possible frustrating event is meaningful only where the party seeking relief could have controlled the language of the contract to the extent of allocating the risk. Here, exclusive control of the contract language was in the hands of the Trust and the Trust did not include disclaimers in its contracts until after the termination order.

NOTES

(1) *Goschie Farms* is one of the rare American decisions granting relief under the doctrine of "frustration of purpose." For some other examples, see Chase Precast Corp. v. John J. Paonessa Co., 409 Mass. 371 (1991) (both parties assumed key items in project would continue to be used by government); Aluminum Co. of Am. v. Essex Grp., Inc., 499 F.Supp. 53, 76–77 (W.D. Pa. 1980) (supplier's "principal purpose" to make a profit substantially frustrated by changed economic conditions); Western Properties v. Southern Utah Aviation, Inc., 776 P.2d 656, 659 (Utah Ct. App. 1989) (sublessee's duty to pay rent and improve premises frustrated by government act which left property without value); Matter of Fontana D'Oro

Foods, Inc., 472 N.Y.S.2d 528 (N.Y. Sup. Ct. 1983) (purpose of one party to settlement frustrated by unforeseen conduct of insurance company which rendered assets valueless); Molnar v. Molnar, 110 Mich.App. 622 (1981) (death of child frustrates purpose in divorce property settlement). But see Arabian Score v. Lasma Arabian Ltd., 814 F.2d 529 (8th Cir. 1987) (death of stallion shortly after delivery to buyer did not discharge seller's duty to pay a fixed price for advertising and promotion over a five year period). See Contracts in Crises at 130–33, 221–225.

(2) *Frustration in Leases.* In England until 1981, *Paradine v. Jane,* supra, was still thought to be good law. Lessees to whom an interest in land was conveyed were thought to have an absolute duty to pay the rent regardless of alleged frustrating events. In 1981, the House of Lords, in *National Carriers Ltd. v. Panalpina (Northern) Ltd.,* [1981] A.C. 675, held that a lease could be discharged by frustration, but concluded that relief was not justified on the facts of the particular case and suggested that such relief would be very rare. In *National Carriers,* the tenant, under a 10-year lease of a warehouse, was denied relief even though the only access road was closed by local authorities four and one-half years before the end of the term and remained closed for 20 months. The interruption was not deemed sufficiently serious to justify discharge. See G. Treitel, The Law of Contract 832–834 (10th ed. 1999); Jeffrey Price, *The Doctrine of Frustration and Leases,* 10 J. Legal Hist. 90 (1989).

Courts in the United States have frequently noted the possibility that a lessee might be discharged due to frustration (see discussion of the Prohibition Cases, supra), but have rarely granted relief. In the well known case of *Lloyd v. Murphy,* 25 Cal.2d 48 (1944), Justice Traynor recognized that a lease might be frustrated in a proper case. Nevertheless, the court refused to discharge the lessee of prime commercial property when a governmental wartime order prevented use of the property for the sole purpose of the lease, the sale of new cars. The lessor, however, had modified the restriction to permit other uses and, although there were still restrictions, the lease was still valuable to the lessee. In short, in the absence of proof that the value of the lease was "totally destroyed," relief was denied. Accord: Mel Frank Tool & Supply Inc. v. Di-Chem Co., 580 N.W.2d 802 (Iowa 1998) (subsequent government regulation must prohibit tenant from legally using premises for originally intended purpose). See Contracts in Crises at 130–33 (analyzing Lloyd v. Murphy).

A court discharged the duty of a sub-lessee to pay rent on the following facts: Cedar City leased undeveloped land near the municipal airport to Western Properties for a 15 year term. Western, with Cedar City approval, subleased the land for part of that term to Southern Utah Aviation. Southern agreed to pay rent and to construct a maintenance building on the land, which would revert to Western at the end of the lease. Cedar City, however, had not developed a master plan for the airport and, because of this, failed to approve Southern's application for a site plan to construct the building. Southern abandoned the site without constructing the building or paying the rent due. Western sued for damages for failure to construct and for rent due. Concluding that both parties assumed that the City would approve the site plan, the court excused the duty to construct on grounds of impracticability and excused the duty to pay rent on grounds of frustration. Without confronting the common law rule restricting discharge of a duty to pay rent, the court discharged the lessee and stated: "Without a way of productively using the land, the purpose of the leasehold was effectively frustrated. * * * There was no point in leasing this land once its development became impossible." Western Properties v. Southern Utah Aviation, Inc., 776 P.2d 656, 659 (Utah Ct. App.1989).

PROBLEM: THE CASE OF FOREGONE COSTS AND BENEFITS

Hannie Leibovitz has agreed to photograph the nuptials of Serena Gomez and Justin Beeber for a fee (as yet unpaid) of $50,000 *and* a front row seat to listen to the couple's upcoming Valentine's Day "Lustin' for Justin" concert at the Hollywood Bowl. The contract specifies that Leibovitz is to use her patented sepia style so that the photographs will look "classy." Leibovitz has a morbid curiosity in attending the wedding and secretly would be willing to do the work even if she had to pay $10,000 to have the opportunity. She is also a huge Beeber fan and would be willing to pay $300,000 for the opportunity to hear what she considers will be a once-in-a-lifetime concert. Imagine that one of the following occurs one week before the wedding:

A.   The price of the photographic chemicals Leibowitz needs unexpectedly increase by $A.

B.   Tronald Dump offers Leibovitz $B to photograph Dump's 14th divorce ceremony. (Leibovitz is put off by Dump's hair and would need at least $80,000 to compensate her just for having to look at him.)

C.   Leibovitz contracts a rare hearing disorder that reduces the value of her of attending the concert by $C.

D.   Leibovitz is offered $D to photograph the beatification of Mikhail Brokhorov in Moscow on the same day as the "Lustin' For Justin" concert. If she accepts Brokhorov's offer, she will have to miss her once-in-a-lifetime opportunity.

Are there any values of $A–D that would relieve Leibovitz of her contractual obligation to photograph the wedding? A line from Billy Joel's song, *Only the Good Die Young*, describes a concept that economists would call an opportunity cost as "the price that you pay for things that you might have done." Should the law of impracticability treat increased costs the same as increased opportunity costs? Should the law of frustration treat decreased benefits the same as decreased "opportunity benefits?" See Paul J. Ferraro & Laura O. Tailor, *Do Economists Recognize An Opportunity Cost When They See One?*, 4 Contributions in Economic Analysis and Policy 7 (2005) ("An avoided benefit is a cost, and an avoided cost is a benefit.").

Comment: Forms of Relief After Impracticability or Frustration

If a claim of "existing" or "supervening" impracticability is raised during performance, the parties may agree upon an appropriate modification or adjustment of the contract and complete performance without knowing whether the promisor was entitled to "some relief" as a matter of law. The courts are unanimous that in the absence of an agreement a promisee has no duty to negotiate with the promisor in good faith over any proposed adjustment.

If the court determines that the promisor is not entitled to relief and there is no agreed adjustment, the legal situation is reasonably clear. If the promisor has failed to complete performance, it has breached the contract and is liable for damages to the promisee. If the promisor has completed performance despite the difficulty it must bear the burden of any costs incurred in excess of the contract price. See, e.g., Transatlantic Financing Corp. v. United States, 363 F.2d 312 (D.C. Cir. 1966).

If the court determines that the promisor is entitled to "some relief" from impracticability, exactly what form should that relief take? First, let us assume that despite the existing or supervening difficulty, the promisor has completed performance at additional costs but without any default. This is risky business. Even if the promisee has requested the continued performance in light of the difficulty, some courts have denied recovery for any costs incurred after the promisor knew or had reason to know that performance was impracticable. See, e.g., the "Chugach Trilogy," Northern Corp. v. Chugach Elec. Ass'n, 518 P.2d 76 (Alaska 1974), modified 523 P.2d 1243 (1974), judgment of the trial court affirmed, Chugach Elec. Ass'n v. N. Corp., 562 P.2d 1053 (1977). For the final word, see 563 P.2d 883 (1977). A rare exception is *National Presto Indus., Inc. v. United States*, 338 F.2d 99 (Ct. Cl. 1964), where the Court of Claims granted one-half of the contractor's claim for extra costs incurred in overcoming difficulties inhering in a new, experimental manufacturing process. In holding that the United States must share the excess costs, the court stressed that (1) both parties assumed that an essential step in the process would not be required but understood that time and expense would be needed to determine this with certainty, (2) the government was anxious to perfect the new process, (3) the government benefited from the perfected process and (4) if asked, the government would have agreed at the beginning of performance to share some but not all of the extra costs. As Judge Davis put it:

> For such a case it is equitable to reform the contract so that each side bears a share of the unexpected costs, instead of permitting the whole loss to remain with the party on whom it chanced to light. . . . Reformation, as the child of equity, can mold its relief to attain any fair result within the broadest perimeter of the charter the parties have established for themselves. Where that

arrangement has allocated the risk to neither side, a judicial division is fair and equitable.

338 F.2d at 112. Despite the potential, reformation in this context has not been embraced in disputes in private contracts and has been limited in government contracts to a "joint enterprise" experiment where the government is more concerned with process than end product and also benefits from the contractor's trial and error. Even without loss sharing, however, a contractor whose performance is delayed by impracticability will be excused. See UCC § 2–615(a).

Second, suppose the promisor, upon encountering claimed impracticability, refuses to continue performance. If the court determines that performance was excused, a traditional statement of the form of relief goes something like this. The promisor is discharged from the unexecuted portion of the contract. Neither party can recover damages for breach of contract. If there has been some part performance prior to discharge, either party can recover at the contract rate for a divisible or severable part of that performance. If part performance is not divisible, either party can recover in restitution for any benefit conferred on the other. But expenditures incurred in reliance on the contract, whether in preparation or part performance, are not recoverable unless they have met the "divisibility" or "benefit" tests.

The limited scope of this traditional position prompted U.K.'s Parliament to enact the "Frustrated Contracts" Act in 1943. This statute, which is reprinted below,[8] gave limited protection to the pre-discharge

---

[8] The Law Reform (Frustrated Contracts), Act 1943 (6 & 7 Geo. 6 c. 40).

1. Adjustment of rights and liabilities of parties to frustrated contracts.

(1) Where a contract governed by English law has become impossible of performance or been otherwise frustrated, and the parties thereto have for that reason been discharged from the further performance of the contract, the following provisions of this section shall, subject to the provisions of section two of this Act, have effect in relation thereto.

(2) All sums paid or payable to any party in pursuance of the contract before the time when the parties were so discharged (in this Act referred to as "the time of discharge") shall, in the case of sums so paid, be recoverable from him as money received by him for the use of the party by whom the sums were paid, and, in the case of sums so payable, cease to be so payable:

Provided that, if the party to whom the sums were so paid or payable incurred expenses before the time of discharge in, or for the purpose of, the performance of the contract, the court may, if it considers it just to do so having regard to all the circumstances of the case, allow him to retain or, as the case may be, recover the whole or any part of the sums so paid or payable, not being an amount in excess of the expenses so incurred.

(3) Where any party to the contract has, by reason of anything done by any other party thereto in, or for the purpose of, the performance of the contract, obtained a valuable benefit (other than a payment of money to which the last foregoing subsection applies) before the time of discharge, there shall be recoverable from him by the said other party such sum (if any), not exceeding the value of the said benefit to the party obtaining it, as the court considers just, having regard to all the circumstances of the case and, in particular,—

(a) the amount of any expenses incurred before the time of discharge by the benefited party in, or for the purpose of, the performance of the contract, including any sums paid or payable by him to any other party in pursuance of the contract and retained or recoverable by that party under the last foregoing subsection, and

reliance interest. See Luke Nottage, *Changing Contract Lenses: Unexpected Supervening Events in English, New Zealand, U.S., Japanese, and International Sales Law and Practice*, 14 Ind. J. Global Legal Stud. 385 (2007).

A bolder solution is proposed in section 272 of the Second Restatement. Subsection (1) states the classic view. Paraphrasing, in "any case" where relief from impracticability or frustration of purpose is justified, "either party may have a claim for relief including restitution" under the rules stated in section 240, dealing with "divisible" contracts, and section 377, dealing with restitution in cases of impracticability. There is not much change here. Subsection (2), however, provides:

> In any case governed by the rules stated in this Chapter, if those rules together with the rules stated in Chapter 16 will not avoid injustice, the court may grant relief on such terms as justice requires including protection of the parties' reliance interests.

Thus, if the contract is discharged because of impracticability, the court, in the interest of justice, may supply a term to protect the reliance interest regardless of whether the contract was properly divisible or whether the other party has benefited from the part-performance. An American court following the Restatement (Second), therefore, would have far more flexibility than an English court under the Frustrated Contracts Act to "mop up" after discharging a contract.

The court in the infamous *ALCOA* case, Aluminum Company of America v. Essex Group, Inc., 499 F.Supp. 53 (W.D. Pa. 1980), granted reformation relief from changed circumstances under a long term contract under which ALCOA was to convert Essex's alumina into aluminum. The court found that a failed price index provision frustrated a principal purpose of the contract, which was for ALCOA to "earn money". It reviewed the American cases, the Restatement (Second), various treatises and foreign authorities.

> Happily some American cases and the law of many foreign countries take a different view of the problem. The problem of serious, sustained inflation is not unique to modern America. During the Revolution and the Civil War, America witnessed serious inflation. And several other nations have recently experienced more severe inflation than America has. When the problem has arisen, here and abroad, courts and legislatures have repeatedly acted to relieve parties from great and unexpected losses. See Mann, The Legal Aspect of Money (1938);

(*b*) the effect, in relation to the said benefit, of the circumstances giving rise to the frustration of the contract.

(4) In estimating, for the purposes of the foregoing provisions of this section, the amount of any expenses incurred by any party to the contract, the court may, without prejudice to the generality of the said provisions, include such sum as appears to be reasonable in respect of overhead expenses and in respect of any work or services performed personally by the said party.

. . . The exact character of the relief granted is not important here. Neither is the exact explanation of the decisions found in the cases, because even the Civil War cases antedate the evolution of the distinct doctrine of frustration. What is important is this: first, the results of those decisions would be readily explained today in terms of frustration of purpose. * * * And second, the frustration which they involved was a frustration of the purpose to earn money or to avoid losses. Thus it appears that there is no legitimate doctrinal problem which prevents relief for frustration of this sort. There remain the customary strictures concerning risk allocation and gravity of injury. Those have been addressed above and need not be considered again here. The Court holds ALCOA is entitled to relief on its claim of frustration of purpose. [499 F.Supp. at 76–77.]

The *ALCOA* court imposed a price adjustment as a form of "equitable" reformation rather than to discharge the contract as a response to the conclusion that ALCOA was entitled to "some relief" from commercial impracticability. The court, in effect, deleted the original cost escalation clause and filled the "gap" with a new clause intended to respond to the changed circumstances. The parties did not agree to this move and there was no "equitable adjustment" clause in the contract beyond the escalation provision which had failed its intended purpose. The criticisms of this remedy have ranged from the pious assertion that it is an unprecedented and improper exercise of judicial power to "make" a contract for the parties, to the more practical concern about the feasibility of a court undertaking to provide a realistic pricing mechanism in a complex case where the parties have been unable or unwilling to agree. See John P. Dawson, *Judicial Revision of Frustrated Contracts,* 1982 Jurid. Rev. 86, 101–05. Others have applauded the case as a recognition of the realities of long-term contracts and as responsive to the dilemmas posed by the either-or approach of the common law—either the contract is discharged or it is not. In addition, the case is seen as a healthy move toward the legal requirement of cooperation rather than competition where unanticipated events produce gains and losses that have not been "paid for" in the bargaining process. See Richard E. Speidel, *Court-Imposed Price Adjustments Under Long-Term Supply Contracts,* 76 Nw. U. L. Rev. 369 (1981).

Could a court find support for the imposed price adjustment in Restatement (Second) § 272(2)? The seeds may be there. Comment c states that in "some instances" the "just solution is to 'sever' the agreement and require that some unexecuted part of it be performed on both sides, rather than to relieve both parties of all of their duties." So far, this is *ALCOA.* The Comment also states that the question is "whether the court can salvage a part of the agreement that is still executory on both sides" and supply a term which is "reasonable in the circumstances." Again, this is *ALCOA*. But section 272(2) was drafted before *ALCOA* was decided, and the illustrations do not clearly support the excision by the court of an existing contract term and the substitution of a more reasonable one.

6. ARBITRATION CLAUSES

We have already seen agreements to arbitrate appear in several cases in this book: *Beneficial National Bank v. Payton, Textile Unlimited v. A..BMH and Company, Hill v. Gateway* and *Klocek v. Gateway, Specht v. Netscape, Centronics v. Genicom, Ferguson v. Countywide Credit Industries, In re Carter's Claim.* These appearances reflect arbitration's increasing pervasiveness in US dispute resolution generally, and especially in the resolution of contract disputes.

Here we consider the special rules that govern the interpretation and construction of agreements to arbitrate. As we shall see, arbitration agreements raise a host of special issues, not in the least because of the effects of the Federal Arbitration Act and the U.S. Supreme Court's recent jurisprudence under it.

Comment: The Nature and Characteristics of Arbitration

The following is reprinted with permission from Richard E. Speidel, Arbitration of Statutory Rights Under the Federal Arbitration Act: The Case for Reform, *4 Ohio St. J. Disp. Resol. 157, 158–61 (1989).*

Arbitration: The Classic Model. Let us start with the basics. Arbitration is a form of Alternative Dispute Resolution. Unlike other methods of ADR, however, arbitration is a private adjudicatory process invoked as an alternative to filing a law suit. The classic model of arbitration can be reduced to three essential elements. First, arbitration depends upon consent. The parties must agree, either before or after the dispute arises, to arbitrate the dispute. In most cases, that agreement will be evidenced by mutual assent to a commercial or consumer contract which contains a written arbitration term.

Second, arbitration is a less formal adjudicatory process that has assumed advantages over litigation in courts or other forms of ADR. The parties expect that an unbiased and competent private arbitrator will conduct a relatively expeditious, informal, inexpensive, and private hearing and decide the merits of the dispute fairly between them.

Third, the arbitrator is empowered by the agreement and applicable arbitration rules to make a final decision on the merits of the dispute, i.e., to decide both questions of fact and of law and to provide appropriate remedies.

Unlike the judicial process, there is no review of the merits of this primary decision by the arbitrator. In the absence of fraud, bias, or process defects, the court is empowered to confirm and enforce the award as if it were a final judgment. There are, of course, incentives for negotiated settlement within the arbitral process and the arbitrator's decision will frequently contain an element of compromise. Nevertheless, in whatever contexts arbitration is invoked, the parties participate in the decisional process by presenting evidence and reasoned arguments to an arbitrator whose final decision should be responsive to the dispute as presented. As a practical matter, finality is achieved when both parties acquiesce in the arbitrator's decision with or without seeking limited judicial review.

Characteristics of Arbitration. Although an objective of arbitration is to achieve justice between the parties through less formal adjudication, the quality of justice may be different (if not less) than that achieved in civil litigation. As one court warned, arbitration is "not the most perfect alternative to adjudication" in the courts. It is "an inferior system of justice, structured without due process, rules of evidence, accountability of judgment or rules of law." In short, "parties should be aware that they get what they bargain for and that arbitration is far different from adjudication."[9]

What do the parties get when they bargain for arbitration? The characteristics of the classic model of arbitration, along with its potential strengths and limitations, emerge when it is contrasted with the judicial process. For emphasis, the differences will be stated in the extreme.

1. *Control Over Scope, Content and Arbitrator Selection.* As a voluntary dispute resolution technique, one party can avoid arbitration by refusing to agree to arbitrate an existing or future dispute. But if a decision to arbitrate is made, the parties have an opportunity to define the scope and content of the process as well as to control its procedures in the agreement. The same cannot be said for civil litigation. Similarly, the arbitrator is selected by or through procedures agreed to by the parties while the judge is imposed upon them by law and local allocation practices.

2. *Less Formality and Complexity.* Arbitration procedures and fact finding processes are not clearly defined or required by arbitration statutes. They depend upon the agreement, relevant arbitration practice or institutional procedures, such as the

---

[9]   Stroh Container Co. v. Delphi Indus., 783 F.2d 743, 751, note 12 (8th Cir.), *cert. denied*, 476 U.S. 1141 (1986).

American Arbitration Association (AAA) Arbitration Rules, and are usually less formal than those in court. The arbitrator has less authority than a judge to order discovery or to compel the attendance of witnesses or the production of evidence. The parties have less power to engage in pretrial discovery. The parties, however, may define by agreement the procedures and the powers of and even the substantive law and remedies to be applied by the arbitrator. In the absence of such agreement, arbitration procedures may be attended with a great deal of uncertainty.

3. *Duration of Proceedings.* In arbitration, the arbitrator and the parties control the timing, duration, and complexity of the hearings. In judicial proceedings, these matters may be beyond the parties' control. The potential for savings in time and cost, therefore, differs. In short, arbitration is expected (and assumed) to be quicker, less formal and less expensive than litigation in court.

4. *Arbitrator Expertise.* In arbitration, the arbitrator is expected to be an expert in or familiar with the context within which the dispute arose while a judge will, normally, have no special expertise. Furthermore, an arbitrator is not required to produce a written opinion with reasons for the decision. Presumably, this reduces the risk of disagreement over reasons by parties otherwise satisfied with the result. In court, a reasoned opinion by a judge is required.

5. *Confidentiality.* Arbitration is touted as a private process where confidence is normally maintained while the opposite is true in court.

6. *Justice Between the Parties.* A primary objective in arbitration is to achieve a just result between the parties. But arbitration seeks particularized justice rather than to foster substantive consistency and predictable results for the future. Courts, on the other hand, are concerned both about just results and announced precedent and the effect of the decision on third persons who are not parties to the litigation.

Furthermore, in arbitration, a compromise decision is possible while judicial decisions tend to be either win all or lose all. According to some observers: "The arbitration process frequently resembles three-party negotiation or mediation, with many arbitrators consciously or unconsciously identifying outside parameters of possible settlement and endeavoring to reach a decision that will at least be minimally acceptable to both parties."[10]

---

[10]   Earl Johnson, Valerie Kantor and Elizabeth Schwartz, Outside the Courts: A Survey of Diversion Alternatives in Civil Cases 55 (1977).

In sum, arbitration is a form of consensual, relatively informal, personalized adjudication where the primary objective is to obtain less expensive justice between the parties. The challenge is to obtain particularized justice in an extra-legal adjudicatory process which has potential strengths and weaknesses when compared to civil litigation.

Hall Street Associates, L.L.C. v. Mattel, Inc.

Supreme Court of the United States, 2008.
552 U.S. 576.

■ SOUTER, JUSTICE. The Federal Arbitration Act (FAA or Act) provides for expedited judicial review to confirm, vacate, or modify arbitration awards. §§ 9–11 (2006 ed.). The question here is whether statutory grounds for prompt vacatur and modification may be supplemented by contract. We hold that the statutory grounds are exclusive.

I

This case began as a lease dispute between landlord, petitioner Hall Street Associates, L.L.C., and tenant, respondent Mattel, Inc. The property was used for many years as a manufacturing site, and the leases provided that the tenant would indemnify the landlord for any costs resulting from the failure of the tenant or its predecessor lessees to follow environmental laws while using the premises.

Tests of the property's well water in 1998 showed high levels of trichloroethylene (TCE), the apparent residue of manufacturing discharges by Mattel's predecessors between 1951 and 1980. After the Oregon Department of Environmental Quality (DEQ) discovered even more pollutants, Mattel stopped drawing from the well and, along with one of its predecessors, signed a consent order with the DEQ providing for cleanup of the site.

After Mattel gave notice of intent to terminate the lease in 2001, Hall Street filed this suit, contesting Mattel's right to vacate on the date it gave, and claiming that the lease obliged Mattel to indemnify Hall Street for costs of cleaning up the TCE, among other things. Following a bench trial before the United States District Court for the District of Oregon, Mattel won on the termination issue, and after an unsuccessful try at mediating the indemnification claim, the parties proposed to submit to arbitration. The District Court was amenable, and the parties drew up an arbitration agreement, which the court approved and entered as an order. One paragraph of the agreement provided that

> "[t]he United States District Court for the District of Oregon may enter judgment upon any award, either by confirming the award or by vacating, modifying or correcting the award. The Court shall vacate, modify or correct any award: (i) where the arbitrator's findings of facts are not supported by substantial

evidence, or (ii) where the arbitrator's conclusions of law are erroneous."

Arbitration took place, and the arbitrator decided for Mattel. In particular, he held that no indemnification was due, because the lease obligation to follow all applicable federal, state, and local environmental laws did not require compliance with the testing requirements of the Oregon Drinking Water Quality Act (Oregon Act); that Act the arbitrator characterized as dealing with human health as distinct from environmental contamination.

Hall Street then filed a District Court Motion for Order Vacating Modifying And/Or Correcting Arbitration Accord, on the ground that failing to treat the Oregon Act as an applicable environmental law under the terms of the lease was legal error. The District Court agreed, vacated the award, and remanded for further consideration by the arbitrator. The court expressly invoked the standard of review chosen by the parties in the arbitration agreement, which included review for legal error, and cited *LaPine Technology Corp. v. Kyocera Corp.* (C.A.9 1997), for the proposition that the FAA leaves the parties "free . . . to draft a contract that sets rules for arbitration and dictates an alternative standard of review."

On remand, the arbitrator followed the District Court's ruling that the Oregon Act was an applicable environmental law and amended the decision to favor Hall Street. This time, each party sought modification, and again the District Court applied the parties' stipulated standard of review for legal error, correcting the arbitrator's calculation of interest but otherwise upholding the award. Each party then appealed to the Court of Appeals for the Ninth Circuit, where Mattel switched horses and contended that the Ninth Circuit's recent en banc action overruling *LaPine* in *Kyocera Corp. v. Prudential-Bache Trade Servs., Inc.*, 341 F.3d 987 (2003), left the arbitration agreement's provision for judicial review of legal error unenforceable. Hall Street countered that *Kyocera* (the later one) was distinguishable, and that the agreement's judicial review provision was not severable from the submission to arbitration.

The Ninth Circuit reversed in favor of Mattel in holding that, "[u]nder *Kyocera* the terms of the arbitration agreement controlling the mode of judicial review are unenforceable and severable." 113 Fed.Appx. 272, 272–273 (2004). The Circuit instructed the District Court on remand to "return to the application to confirm the original arbitration award (not the subsequent award revised after reversal), and . . . confirm that award, unless . . . the award should be vacated on the grounds allowable under 9 U.S.C. § 10, or modified or corrected under the grounds allowable under 9 U.S.C. § 11." *Id.* at 273.

After the District Court again held for Hall Street and the Ninth Circuit again reversed, we granted certiorari to decide whether the grounds for vacatur and modification provided by §§ 10 and 11 of the FAA are exclusive. . . . We agree with the Ninth Circuit that they are, but vacate and remand for consideration of independent issues.

II

Congress enacted the FAA to replace judicial indisposition to arbitration with a "national policy favoring [it] and plac[ing] arbitration agreements on equal footing with all other contracts." Buckeye Check Cashing, Inc. v. Cardegna, 546 U.S. 440, 443 (2006). * * * [I]n cases falling within a court's jurisdiction, the Act makes contracts to arbitrate "valid, irrevocable, and enforceable," so long as their subject involves "commerce." 9 U.S.C. § 2. * * *

The Act also supplies mechanisms for enforcing arbitration awards: a judicial decree confirming an award, an order vacating it, or an order modifying or correcting it. §§ 9–11. An application for any of these orders will get streamlined treatment as a motion, obviating the separate contract action that would usually be necessary to enforce or tinker with an arbitral award in court. § 6. Under the terms of § 9, a court "must" confirm an arbitration award "unless" it is vacated, modified, or corrected "as prescribed" in §§ 10 and 11. Section 10 lists grounds for vacating an award, while § 11 names those for modifying or correcting one.[4]

The Courts of Appeals have split over the exclusiveness of these statutory grounds when parties take the FAA shortcut to confirm, vacate, or modify an award, with some saying the recitations are exclusive, and others regarding them as mere threshold provisions open to expansion by agreement. * * * We now hold that §§ 10 and 11 respectively provide the FAA's exclusive grounds for expedited vacatur and modification.

---

[4] Title 9 U.S.C. § 10(a) (2000 ed., Supp. V) provides in part:

"In any of the following cases the United States court in and for the district wherein the award was made may make an order vacating the award upon the application of any party to the arbitration—

"(1) where the award was procured by corruption, fraud, or undue means;

"(2) where there was evident partiality or corruption in the arbitrators, or either of them;

"(3) where the arbitrators were guilty of misconduct in refusing to postpone the hearing, upon sufficient cause shown, or in refusing to hear evidence pertinent and material to the controversy; or of any other misbehavior by which the rights of any party have been prejudiced; or

"(4) where the arbitrators exceeded their powers, or so imperfectly executed them that a mutual, final, and definite award upon the subject matter submitted was not made."

Title 9 U.S.C. § 11 (2000 ed.) provides:

"In either of the following cases the United States court in and for the district wherein the award was made may make an order modifying or correcting the award upon the application of any party to the arbitration—

"(a) Where there was an evident material miscalculation of figures or an evident material mistake in the description of any person, thing, or property referred to in the award.

"(b) Where the arbitrators have awarded upon a matter not submitted to them, unless it is a matter not affecting the merits of the decision upon the matter submitted.

"(c) Where the award is imperfect in matter of form not affecting the merits of the controversy.

"The order may modify and correct the award, so as to effect the intent thereof and promote justice between the parties."

III

* * *

Hall Street says that the agreement to review for legal error ought to prevail simply because arbitration is a creature of contract, and the FAA is "motivated, first and foremost, by a congressional desire to enforce agreements into which parties ha[ve] entered." Dean Witter Reynolds, Inc. v. Byrd, 470 U.S. 213, 220 (1985). But . . . we think the argument comes up short. Hall Street is certainly right that the FAA lets parties tailor some, even many features of arbitration by contract, including the way arbitrators are chosen, what their qualifications should be, which issues are arbitrable, along with procedure and choice of substantive law. But to rest this case on the general policy of treating arbitration agreements as enforceable as such would be to beg the question, which is whether the FAA has textual features at odds with enforcing a contract to expand judicial review following the arbitration.

To that particular question we think the answer is yes, that the text compels a reading of the §§ 10 and 11 categories as exclusive. To begin with, even if we assumed §§ 10 and 11 could be supplemented to some extent, it would stretch basic interpretive principles to expand the stated grounds to the point of evidentiary and legal review generally. Sections 10 and 11, after all, address egregious departures from the parties' agreed-upon arbitration: "corruption," "fraud," "evident partiality," "misconduct," "misbehavior," "exceed[ing] . . . powers," "evident material miscalculation," "evident material mistake," "award[s] upon a matter not submitted;" the only ground with any softer focus is "imperfect[ions]," and a court may correct those only if they go to "[a] matter of form not affecting the merits." Given this emphasis on extreme arbitral conduct, the old rule of *ejusdem generis* has an implicit lesson to teach here. Under that rule, when a statute sets out a series of specific items ending with a general term, that general term is confined to covering subjects comparable to the specifics it follows. Since a general term included in the text is normally so limited, then surely a statute with no textual hook for expansion cannot authorize contracting parties to supplement review for specific instances of outrageous conduct with review for just any legal error. "Fraud" and a mistake of law are not cut from the same cloth.

That aside, expanding the detailed categories would rub too much against the grain of the § 9 language, where provision for judicial confirmation carries no hint of flexibility. On application for an order confirming the arbitration award, the court "must grant" the order "unless the award is vacated, modified, or corrected as prescribed in sections 10 and 11 of this title." There is nothing malleable about "must grant," which unequivocally tells courts to grant confirmation in all cases, except when one of the "prescribed" exceptions applies. This does not sound remotely like a provision meant to tell a court what to do just in case the parties say nothing else.

In fact, anyone who thinks Congress might have understood § 9 as a default provision should turn back to § 5 for an example of what Congress thought a default provision would look like:

> "[i]f in the agreement provision be made for a method of naming or appointing an arbitrator . . . such method shall be followed; but if no method be provided therein, or if a method be provided and any party thereto shall fail to avail himself of such method, . . . then upon the application of either party to the controversy the court shall designate and appoint an arbitrator . . . . ."

"[I]f no method be provided" is a far cry from "must grant . . . unless" in § 9.

Instead of fighting the text, it makes more sense to see the three provisions, §§ 9–11, as substantiating a national policy favoring arbitration with just the limited review needed to maintain arbitration's essential virtue of resolving disputes straightaway. Any other reading opens the door to the full-bore legal and evidentiary appeals that can "rende[r] informal arbitration merely a prelude to a more cumbersome and time-consuming judicial review process," Kyocera, 341 F.3d at 998 . . . , and bring arbitration theory to grief in post-arbitration process.

* * *

Although we agree with the Ninth Circuit that the FAA confines its expedited judicial review to the grounds listed in 9 U.S.C. §§ 10 and 11, we vacate the judgment and remand the case [to determine whether the arbitration agreement, which was entered into in the course of district-court litigation, should "be treated as an exercise of the District Court's authority to manage its cases under Federal Rules of Civil Procedure 16." (at 591)]

■ STEVENS, JUSTICE, with whom JUSTICE KENNEDY joins (dissenting). * * *

NOTES

(1) *Judicial Review of Questions of Law Decided by the Arbitrators.* The grounds for vacating arbitral awards under Section 10 of the FAA, Section 23 of the Revised Uniform Arbitration Act (a model state arbitration law), and Article V of the New York Convention (dealing with international arbitration) do not include erroneous decisions of law or fact by the tribunal. Without more, these decisions are final and are not subject to judicial review.

In the United States, at least, a non-statutory ground for vacating an award has emerged; an arbitrator's award may be vacated for "manifest disregard" of the law. According to the Second Circuit, "a party seeking vacatur must . . . demonstrate that the arbitrator knew of the relevant principle, appreciated that this principle controlled the outcome of the disputed issue, and nonetheless willfully flouted the governing law by refusing to apply it." Westerbeke Corp. v. Daihatsu Motor Co., Ltd., 304 F.3d 200, 217 (2d Cir. 2002) (stating principle and reviewing cases). Arguably, this non-statutory ground is part of the ground stated in FAA Section 10(4) that the arbitrator may not exceed his or her powers. Thus, if the parties chose the law of a state that had Rule X and the arbitrator disregarded it, the arbitrator exceeded his or her authority. But as the cases reveal, it is not this simple. Even though there are very few cases actually vacating an award for manifest disregard, one can safely conclude that a doctrine of dubious origin frequently invoked by losing parties has caused more delay and expense in the final enforcement of arbitration awards.

(2)   *Optional Arbitration.* Should the *Hall Street* analysis apply when a dispute resolution provision contemplates parallel litigation? In *Parisi v. Netlearning, Inc.*, 139 F.Supp.2d 745 (E.D. Va. 2001), the court held that the "mandatory administrative proceedings" conducted under the Uniform Domain-Name Dispute Resolution Policy (UDRP) of the Internet Corp. for Assigned Names and Numbers (ICANN) did not constitute an arbitration subject to the FAA restrictions on judicial oversight because nothing "in the UDRP restrains either party from filing suit before, after, or during the administrative proceedings."

(3)   *Default or Mandatory?* Are you persuaded by *Hall Street*'s statutory interpretation that Congress in passing the FAA intended the grounds for vacatur to be exclusive? What other aspects of the FAA are non-contractible?

(4)   The position of the English Arbitration Act of 1996, which applies to almost all arbitrations where the "seat" of arbitration is in the UK, is worth noting. First, Section 45(1) permits a court, upon a party's application, to "determine any question of law arising in the course of the proceedings which the court is satisfied substantially affects the rights of one or more of the parties." The process, however, is hedged with conditions and can be blocked if one party to the proceeding does not agree. More to the point, in addition to the grounds for challenge stated in Section 68 (serious irregularity affecting the tribunal, the proceedings or the award), a party to an arbitration proceeding may appeal to the court on a question of law arising out of the award. § 69(1). Once again, all parties must agree to the appeal, which will be granted only if the determination will substantially affect the rights of one or more parties, and the decision of the tribunal was obviously wrong or the question is one of "general public importance and the decision of the tribunal is at least open to serious doubt." § 69(3).

Michael-Curry Cos., Inc. v. Knutson Shareholders Liquidating Trust

Supreme Court of Minnesota, 1989.
449 N.W.2d 139.

■ KEITH, JUSTICE. The central issue in this case is whether an arbitration clause which provides for arbitration of, *inter alia*, "[a]ny controversy or claim arising out of or relating to * * * the making" of a contract, compels arbitration of a claim that an amendment to the contract was fraudulently induced. The trial court held in the negative. The court of appeals reversed, holding that the clause was sufficiently broad to comprehend that the issue of fraud in the inducement be submitted to arbitration. . . . We affirm.

* * *

1.   The issue of arbitrability is to be determined by ascertaining the intention of the parties through examination of the language of the arbitration agreement. . . . A reviewing court is not bound by the trial court's interpretation of the arbitration agreement and independently determines whether the trial court correctly interpreted the clause. . . .

The purchase and sale agreement in this case provided that "this Agreement shall be construed in accordance with, and governed by, the laws of the State of Minnesota." Both parties agree that Minnesota law governs the agreement and the amendment, which incorporates the terms of the agreement.

Minn.Stat. § 572.08 (1988) provides that written agreements or contract provisions to arbitrate are valid, enforceable, and irrevocable *absent grounds for revocation of the contract*. Under the procedural rules of Minn.Stat. § 572.09, if one party refuses to arbitrate, the court must order arbitration. A party wishing to stay arbitration must show that there is no agreement to arbitrate. "Such an issue, when in substantial bona fide dispute, shall be forthwith and summarily tried and the stay ordered if found for the moving party." Minn.Stat. § 572.09(b) (1988). Otherwise the court must order arbitration. Id.

A claim of fraud in the inducement puts the "making" of the contract itself in issue. This court has said that "that issue is more properly determined by those trained in the law." Atcas v. Credit Clearing Corp., 292 Minn. 334, 350 (1972). Minnesota has ruled that fraud which vitiates a contract also vitiates an arbitration clause within the contract. Id. at 349; Minn.Stat. § 572.08. By claiming fraud in the inducement, the Trust is asserting that no valid agreement to arbitrate exists under Minn.Stat. § 572.09. The court must therefore determine whether the parties agreed to arbitrate the issue of fraud in the inducement.

Parties may validly choose to arbitrate all controversies, including fraud in the inducement. . . . To determine intent to arbitrate fraud in the inducement, the court must look to the language of the arbitration clause. The language in the clause must either (1) specifically show that the parties intended to arbitrate fraud in the inducement, or (2) be "sufficiently broad to comprehend that the issue of fraudulent inducement be arbitrated. . . ." If the clause does not specifically include fraud in the inducement and is not sufficiently broad to comprehend it, then a trial must be had on the issue of fraud in the inducement. . . .

The arbitration clause in the instant case states:

13.01 *Arbitration.* Any controversy or claim arising out of, or relating to, this Agreement, or the making, performance, or interpretation thereof, shall be settled by arbitration * * *. (Emphasis supplied).

The clause does not specifically mention fraud. We find, however, that it meets the second prong of the *Atcas* test.

The clause in this case is broader than the clauses in previous cases this court has considered. First, it provides for arbitration of controversies relating to "the making" of the contract, which clauses *Atcas* and later cases did not contain. The word "making" refers to circumstances surrounding formation of the contract. See Atcas, 292 Minn. at 350 (a claim of fraudulent inducement puts "the making of the agreement itself * * * in issue"). See also . . . Prima Paint v. Flood & Conklin Mfg., 388 U.S. 395, 403–04 (1967) (under the FAA, a fraud in the inducement claim "goes to the 'making' of the agreement"). It is difficult to see how the parties in this case could have drafted a "broader" agreement.

The Trust attempts to circumvent the *Atcas* "broadly worded" option by arguing that specificity is always required. The Trust argues that the word "fraud" must appear in the arbitration clause. The Minnesota Uniform Arbitration Act changed "the common law policy of judicial hostility toward arbitration to one favoring arbitration." Layne-Minnesota Co. v. Regents of Univ. of Mn., 266 Minn. 284, 288 (1963). This policy requires the court to give effect to parties' arbitration agreements, and weighs against the Trust's assertion. The Trust's suggested standard would render meaningless the second alternative of the *Atcas* test. Requiring a specific list of all possible claims constituting grounds for rescission would be impractical, defeating the policy favoring arbitration. Further, given the realities of commercial dealings, parties would hesitate to enter into a contract when fraud is mentioned at the outset. . . .[2]

2.   We are also concerned that parties often allege fraud in the inducement as a final attempt to avoid arbitration. We therefore emphasize that, where a party applies for a stay of arbitration, "circumstances constituting fraud * * * shall be stated with particularity." See Atcas, 292 Minn. at 348. Minn.Stat. §§ 572.09(a) and (b) should not be invoked without such particularity.

For the reasons stated above, we affirm the judgment of the court of appeals and remand to the district court for an order compelling

---

[2]   In a related area, this court has held that parties who fashion a "broad" arbitration clause must enumerate specifically whatever they wish to exclude from the powers of the arbitrators.

In *David Co. v. Jim W. Miller Constr., Inc.*, 444 N.W.2d 836 (Minn. 1989), this court upheld an "innovative and unique" award fashioned by arbitrators as authorized by a broad arbitration clause, even though "it may be correct to surmise that initially neither party specifically contemplated" that such an award could be made. *Id.* at 840, 842. The parties were experienced in construction; therefore they should have been aware of the extent of the liability and possible awards involved. Thus, if the parties had desired to limit the powers of the arbitrators, they should have specifically expressed this in the broadly-worded arbitration clause. Supporting this conclusion is the "long-established policy favoring expansion of the arbitration remedy." *Id.* at 842.

arbitration pursuant to the arbitration clause in the parties' purchase agreement.

NOTES

(1) *Revised Uniform Arbitration Act.* Minnesota, like many states, has enacted legislation based upon the Uniform Arbitration Act. That legislation was revised in 2000 and has been adopted by 13 states. Section 6 of the Revision, entitled "Validity of Agreement to Arbitrate" provides:

(a) An agreement contained in a record to submit to arbitration any existing or subsequent controversy arising between the parties to the agreement is valid, enforceable, and irrevocable except upon a ground that exists at law or in equity for the revocation of a contract.

(b) The court shall decide whether an agreement to arbitrate exists or a controversy is subject to an agreement to arbitrate.

(c) An arbitrator shall decide whether a condition precedent to arbitration has been fulfilled and whether a contract containing a valid agreement to arbitrate is enforceable.

(d) If a party to a judicial proceeding challenges the existence of, or claims that a controversy is not subject to, an agreement to arbitrate, the arbitration proceeding may continue pending final resolution of the issue by the court, unless the court otherwise orders.

Revised Section 7 deals with motions to compel arbitration and to stay litigation pending arbitration. It is clear that the court, when these motions are made, has authority to determine whether there is an enforceable agreement to arbitrate and, if there is, to both order arbitration and "stay any judicial proceeding that involves a claim alleged to be subject to the arbitration. . . ." § 7(f), (g). Under Section 28(a)(1), an appeal may not be taken from an order compelling arbitration.

Minnesota enacted the Uniform Arbitration Act in 2010. Minn. Stat. Ann. § 572B.01 et seq. Would these revisions affect the *Michael-Curry* case?

(2) *Separability and Competence to Decide Arbitrability?* In most commercial contracts, the parties will agree to a "broad" arbitration clause that covers all disputes arising under or relating to the contract in which the clause is contained. Two questions recur: who has authority, courts or arbitrators, to make decisions regarding (1) attacks on the enforceability of the agreement to arbitrate (competence issues) and (2) attacks on the enforceability of the contract in which an unenforceable arbitration term is contained (separability issues)?

(a) *Competence to Decide Arbitrability.* Taking the first question, under the FAA, arbitrability issues (e.g., Was there a written agreement to arbitrate? Was the dispute within the scope of the agreement? Was the arbitration agreement induced by fraud?) are for the court to decide unless the parties have "clearly agreed" to have the arbitrator decide them. First Options of Chicago, Inc. v. Kaplan, 514 U.S. 938 (1995). This is not the case under the usual broad agreement to arbitrate, but the language used is always open to interpretation. See Bell v. Cendant Corp., 293 F.3d 563 (2d

Cir. 2002) (finding clear agreement in an exceptionally broad clause). This result is significant. If, for example, the arbitral tribunal has been selected and a challenge to their jurisdiction is then made on the grounds that the agreement to arbitrate was not enforceable, the challenging party could seek an injunction against arbitration and argue the issue to the court. Some courts have found that procedural questions of arbitrability (such as whether a claim is time-barred) should be decided by arbitrators, while substantive questions of arbitrability (i.e., whether a claim substantively falls within the scope of the arbitration agreement) are to be decided (at least unless the agreement says otherwise) by courts. See Howsam v. Dean Witter Reynolds, Inc., 537 U.S. 79 (2002).

The opposite result is reached in international arbitration. For example, Section 16(1) of the UNCITRAL Model Law on International Commercial Arbitration provides that the "arbitral tribunal may rule on its own jurisdiction, including any objections with respect to the existence or validity of the arbitration agreement." This principle is also found in the arbitration rules of the leading international arbitration institutions, such as the American Arbitration Association, the International Chamber of Commerce, and the London Court of International Arbitration. See, e.g., ICC Rules of Arbitration Art. 6(4). Section 30 of the English Arbitration Act (1996) is in accord.

(b)   *Separability*. In *Michael-Curry*, the claim was that an amendment to the contract was induced by fraud. There was no claim that the arbitration clause itself was directly induced by fraud. The court, however, suggested that fraud which vitiates the underlying contract "also vitiates an arbitration clause within the contract" and held that a *court* should first decide whether the fraud issue was within the scope of the agreement to arbitrate. Why? According to the court, the scope issue was "more properly determined by those trained in law." Once the scope issue is decided, however, whether there was fraud in fact is for the arbitrators to decide.

Is this result changed by Section 6(c) of the Revised UAA, which states that an "arbitrator shall decide whether * * * a contract containing a valid agreement to arbitrate is enforceable"?

Under the FAA, a claim that the underlying contract or an amendment thereto was induced by fraud does not constitute a direct attack on the arbitration clause, even though the vitiation of the underlying contract might vitiate the arbitration clause. Under *Prima Paint Corp. v. Flood & Conklin Mfg. Co.*, 388 U.S. 395 (1967), and its better reasoned progeny, a fraud attack on the underlying contract is for the arbitrator to decide unless the claim was beyond the scope of the agreement to arbitrate. This approach expands the scope of the arbitrator's power and, of course, assumes that the arbitrators are capable of resolving fraud and similar claims.

Suppose, however, that the party opposing arbitration claims that the underlying contract was void (never came into existence) rather than voidable. Should that make any difference? There is some authority for the proposition that a challenge to the "very existence" of a contract is an attack on the enforceability of the arbitration clause and should not be submitted to arbitration (unless the parties have clearly agreed). See Primerica Life Ins. Co. v. Brown, 304 F.3d 469, 473 (5th Cir. 2002) (concurring opinion). The Supreme Court, however, has held that under a broad arbitration clause, the claim that the underlying contract is "void" (because of state usury laws) is within the scope of the "separability" doctrine if the parties actually manifested assent to the agreement. In absence of actual assent to the underlying contract, the separability doctrine does not apply. Buckeye Check Cashing, Inc. v. Cardegna, 546 U.S. 440 (2006). With actual assent, however, it is irrelevant whether the underlying contract is classified as "void" or "voidable." For an argument that the separability doctrine under the FAA should be repealed, see Brunet, American Arbitration Law at 90–102.

This is a non-issue in international commercial arbitration, where relevant legislation and arbitration rules give the tribunal power to decide the validity of the underlying contract in all cases. For example, Section 16(1) of the UNCITRAL Model Law states that the arbitration clause that "forms part of a contract shall be treated as an agreement independent of the other terms of the contract" and that a decision by the "arbitral tribunal that the contract is null and void shall not entail *ipso jure* the invalidity of the arbitration clause." Section 7 of the English Arbitration Act is in accord.

Stolt-Nielsen S.A. v. AnimalFeeds International Corp.

Supreme Court of the United States, 2010.
559 U.S. 662.

■ ALITO, JUSTICE. We granted certiorari in this case to decide whether imposing class arbitration on parties whose arbitration clauses are "silent" on that issue is consistent with the Federal Arbitration Act (FAA), 9 U.S.C. § 1 et seq.

I

Petitioners are shipping companies that serve a large share of the world market for parcel tankers—seagoing vessels with compartments that are separately chartered to customers wishing to ship liquids in small quantities. One of those customers is AnimalFeeds International Corp. (hereinafter AnimalFeeds), which supplies raw ingredients, such as fish oil, to animal-feed producers around the world. AnimalFeeds ships its goods pursuant to a standard contract known in the maritime trade as a charter party. Numerous charter parties are in regular use, and the charter party that AnimalFeeds uses is known as the "Vegoilvoy" charter party. Petitioners assert, without contradiction, that charterers like AnimalFeeds, or their agents—not the shipowners—typically select the particular charter party that governs their shipments. Accord, Trowbridge, Admiralty Law Institute: Symposium on Charter Parties: The History, Development, and Characteristics of the Charter Concept, 49 Tulane L. Rev. 743, 753 (1975) ("Voyage charter parties are highly standardized, with many commodities and charterers having their own specialized forms").

Adopted in 1950, the Vegoilvoy charter party contains the following arbitration clause:

> "Arbitration. Any dispute arising from the making, performance or termination of this Charter Party shall be settled in New York, Owner and Charterer each appointing an arbitrator, who shall be a merchant, broker or individual experienced in the shipping business; the two thus chosen, if they cannot agree, shall nominate a third arbitrator who shall be an Admiralty lawyer. Such arbitration shall be conducted in conformity with the provisions and procedure of the United States Arbitration Act [i.e., the FAA], and a judgment of the Court shall be entered upon any award made by said arbitrator."

In 2003, a Department of Justice criminal investigation revealed that petitioners were engaging in an illegal price-fixing conspiracy. When AnimalFeeds learned of this, it brought a putative class action against petitioners in the District Court for the Eastern District of Pennsylvania, asserting antitrust claims for supracompetitive prices that petitioners allegedly charged their customers over a period of several years.

Other charterers brought similar suits. In one of these, the District Court for the District of Connecticut held that the charterers' claims were not subject to arbitration under the applicable arbitration clause * * *

In 2005, AnimalFeeds served petitioners with a demand for class arbitration, designating New York City as the place of arbitration and seeking to represent a class of "[a]ll direct purchasers of parcel tanker transportation services globally for bulk liquid chemicals, edible oils, acids, and other specialty liquids from [petitioners] at any time during the period from August 1, 1998, to November 30, 2002." The parties entered into a supplemental agreement providing for the question of class arbitration to be submitted to a panel of three arbitrators who were to "follow and be bound by Rules 3 through 7 of the American Arbitration Association's Supplementary Rules for Class Arbitrations. . . ." These rules (hereinafter "Class Rules") were developed by the American Arbitration Association (AAA) after our decision in *Green Tree Financial Corp. v. Bazzle*, 539 U. S. 444 (2003), and Class Rule 3, in accordance with the plurality opinion in that case, requires an arbitrator, as a threshold matter, to determine "whether the applicable arbitration clause permits the arbitration to proceed on behalf of or against a class."

The parties selected a panel of arbitrators and stipulated that the arbitration clause was "silent" with respect to class arbitration. Counsel for AnimalFeeds explained to the arbitration panel that the term "silent" did not simply mean that the clause made no express reference to class arbitration. Rather, he said, "[a]ll the parties agree that when a contract is silent on an issue there's been no agreement that has been reached on that issue."

After hearing argument and evidence, including testimony from petitioners' experts regarding arbitration customs and usage in the maritime trade, the arbitrators concluded that the arbitration clause allowed for class arbitration. They found persuasive the fact that other arbitrators ruling after *Bazzle* had construed "a wide variety of clauses in a wide variety of settings as allowing for class arbitration," but the panel acknowledged that none of these decisions was "exactly comparable" to the present dispute. Petitioners' expert evidence did not show an "inten[t] to preclude class arbitration," the arbitrators reasoned, and petitioners' argument would leave "no basis for a class action absent express agreement among all parties and the putative class members."

The arbitrators stayed the proceeding to allow the parties to seek judicial review, and petitioners filed an application to vacate the arbitrators' award in the District Court for the Southern District of New York. See 9 U.S.C. § 10(a)(4) (authorizing a district court to "make an order vacating the award upon the application of any party to the arbitration . . . where the arbitrators exceeded their powers"). . . . The District Court vacated the award, concluding that the arbitrators' decision was made in "manifest disregard" of the law insofar as the arbitrators failed to conduct a choice-of-law analysis. . . . Had such an analysis been conducted, the District Court held, the arbitrators would have applied the rule of federal maritime law requiring that contracts be interpreted in light of custom and usage.

AnimalFeeds appealed to the Court of Appeals, which reversed. . . . As an initial matter, the Court of Appeals held that the "manifest disregard" standard survived our decision in *Hall Street Associates, L.L.C. v. Mattel, Inc.* [supra] as a "judicial gloss" on the enumerated grounds for vacatur of arbitration awards under 9 U.S.C. § 10. Nonetheless, the Court of Appeals concluded that, because petitioners had cited no authority applying a federal maritime rule of custom and usage *against* class arbitration, the arbitrators' decision was not in manifest disregard of federal maritime law. Nor had the arbitrators manifestly disregarded New York law, the Court of Appeals continued, since nothing in New York case law established a rule against class arbitration. We granted certiorari.

II

Petitioners contend that the decision of the arbitration panel must be vacated, but in order to obtain that relief, they must clear a high hurdle. It is not enough for petitioners to show that the panel committed an error—or even a serious error. . . . "It is only when [an] arbitrator strays from interpretation and application of the agreement and effectively 'dispense[s] his own brand of industrial justice' that his decision may be unenforceable." Major League Baseball Players Assn. v. Garvey, 532 U.S. 504, 509 (2001) (*per curiam*). . . . In that situation, an arbitration decision may be vacated under § 10(a)(4) of the FAA on the ground that the arbitrator "exceeded [his] powers," for the task of an arbitrator is to interpret and enforce a contract, not to make public policy. In this case, we must conclude that what the arbitration panel did was simply to impose its own view of sound policy regarding class arbitration.[3]

In its memorandum of law filed in the arbitration proceedings, AnimalFeeds made three arguments in support of construing the arbitration clause to permit class arbitration:

> "The parties' arbitration clause should be construed to allow class arbitration because (a) the clause is silent on the issue of class treatment and, without express prohibition, class arbitration is permitted under *Bazzle*; (b) *the clause should be construed to permit class arbitration as a matter of public policy*; and (c) the clause would be unconscionable and unenforceable if it forbade class arbitration." (emphasis added)

The arbitrators expressly rejected AnimalFeeds' first argument, and said nothing about the third. Instead, the panel appears to have rested its decision on AnimalFeeds' public policy argument. Because the parties agreed their agreement was "silent" in the sense that they had not reached any agreement on the issue of class arbitration, the arbitrators' proper task was to identify the rule of law that governs in that situation. Had they engaged in that undertaking, they presumably would have looked either to the FAA itself or to one of the two bodies of law that the parties claimed were governing, i.e., either federal maritime law or New York law. But the panel did not consider whether the FAA provides the rule of decision in such a situation; nor did the panel attempt to determine what rule would govern under either maritime or New York law in the case of a "silent" contract. Instead, the panel based its decision on post-*Bazzle* arbitral decisions that "construed a wide variety of clauses in a wide variety of settings as allowing for class arbitration." The panel did not mention whether any of these decisions were based on a rule derived from the FAA or on maritime or New York law.[4]

Rather than inquiring whether the FAA, maritime law, or New York law contains a "default rule" under which an arbitration clause is construed as allowing class arbitration in the absence of express consent, the panel proceeded as if it had the authority of a common-law court to develop what it viewed as the best rule to be applied in such a situation.

---

[3]   We do not decide whether " 'manifest disregard' " survives our decision in *Hall Street* as an independent ground for review or as a judicial gloss on the enumerated grounds for vacatur set forth at 9 U.S.C. § 10. AnimalFeeds characterizes that standard as requiring a showing that the arbitrators "knew of the relevant [legal] principle, appreciated that this principle controlled the outcome of the disputed issue, and nonetheless willfully flouted the governing law by refusing to apply it." Brief for Respondent 25 (internal quotation marks omitted). Assuming, *arguendo*, that such a standard applies, we find it satisfied for the reasons that follow.

[4]   The panel's reliance on these arbitral awards confirms that the panel's decision was not based on a determination regarding the parties' intent. All of the arbitral awards were made under the AAA's Class Rules, which were adopted in 2003, and thus none was available when the parties here entered into the Vegoilvoy charter party during the class period ranging from 1998 to 2002. * * *

Perceiving a post-*Bazzle* consensus among arbitrators that class arbitration is beneficial in "a wide variety of settings," the panel considered only whether there was any good reason not to follow that consensus in this case. The panel was not persuaded by "court cases denying consolidation of arbitrations," by undisputed evidence that the Vegoilvoy charter party had "never been the basis of a class action," or by expert opinion that "sophisticated, multinational commercial parties of the type that are sought to be included in the class would never intend that the arbitration clauses would permit a class arbitration."[6] Accordingly, finding no convincing ground for departing from the post-*Bazzle* arbitral consensus, the panel held that class arbitration was permitted in this case. The conclusion is inescapable that the panel simply imposed its own conception of sound policy.

* * *

In sum, instead of identifying and applying a rule of decision derived from the FAA or either maritime or New York law, the arbitration panel imposed its own policy choice and thus exceeded its powers. As a result, under § 10(b) of the FAA, we must either "direct a rehearing by the arbitrators" or decide the question that was originally referred to the panel. Because we conclude that there can be only one possible outcome on the facts before us, we see no need to direct a rehearing by the arbitrators.

III

[The Court criticizes the arbitration panel's interpretation of the *Bazzle* opinions.]

IV

While the interpretation of an arbitration agreement is generally a matter of state law, . . . the FAA imposes certain rules of fundamental importance, including the basic precept that arbitration "is a matter of consent, not coercion." Volt Information Sciences, Inc. v. Board of Trustees of Leland Stanford Junior Univ., 489 U.S. 468, 479 (1989).

* * *

Whether enforcing an agreement to arbitrate or construing an arbitration clause, courts and arbitrators must "give effect to the contractual rights and expectations of the parties." Id. In this endeavor, "as with any other contract, the parties' intentions control. . . ." This is because an arbitrator derives his or her powers from the parties' agreement to forgo the legal process and submit their disputes to private dispute resolution. * * *

Underscoring the consensual nature of private dispute resolution, we have held that parties are "generally free to structure their arbitration agreements as they see fit. . . ." For example, we have held

---

[6] [Under] both New York law and general maritime law, evidence of "custom and usage" is relevant to determining the parties' intent when an express agreement is ambiguous. * * *

that parties may agree to limit the issues they choose to arbitrate, . . . and may agree on rules under which any arbitration will proceed. . . . They may choose who will resolve specific disputes. * * *

We think it is also clear from our precedents and the contractual nature of arbitration that parties may specify *with whom* they choose to arbitrate their disputes. * * * It falls to courts and arbitrators to give effect to these contractual limitations, and when doing so, courts and arbitrators must not lose sight of the purpose of the exercise: to give effect to the intent of the parties. . . .

From these principles, it follows that a party may not be compelled under the FAA to submit to class arbitration unless there is a contractual basis for concluding that the party *agreed* to do so. In this case, however, the arbitration panel imposed class arbitration even though the parties concurred that they had reached "no agreement" on that issue. The critical point, in the view of the arbitration panel, was that petitioners did not "establish that the parties to the charter agreements intended to *preclude* class arbitration." Even though the parties are sophisticated business entities, even though there is no tradition of class arbitration under maritime law, and even though AnimalFeeds does not dispute that it is customary for the shipper to choose the charter party that is used for a particular shipment, the panel regarded the agreement's silence on the question of class arbitration as dispositive. The panel's conclusion is fundamentally at war with the foundational FAA principle that arbitration is a matter of consent.

In certain contexts, it is appropriate to presume that parties that enter into an arbitration agreement implicitly authorize the arbitrator to adopt such procedures as are necessary to give effect to the parties' agreement. Thus, we have said that " 'procedural' questions which grow out of the dispute and bear on its final disposition' are presumptively not for the judge, but for an arbitrator, to decide." Howsam v. Dean Witter Reynolds, Inc., 537 U.S. 79, 84 (2002). . . . This recognition is grounded in the background principle that "[w]hen the parties to a bargain sufficiently defined to be a contract have not agreed with respect to a term which is essential to a determination of their rights and duties, a term which is reasonable in the circumstances is supplied by the court." Restatement (Second) of Contracts § 204 (1979).

An implicit agreement to authorize class-action arbitration, however, is not a term that the arbitrator may infer solely from the fact of the parties' agreement to arbitrate. This is so because class-action arbitration changes the nature of arbitration to such a degree that it cannot be presumed the parties consented to it by simply agreeing to submit their disputes to an arbitrator. In bilateral arbitration, parties forgo the procedural rigor and appellate review of the courts in order to realize the benefits of private dispute resolution: lower costs, greater efficiency and speed, and the ability to choose expert adjudicators to resolve specialized disputes. . . . But the relative benefits of class-action arbitration are much less assured, giving reason to doubt the parties' mutual consent to resolve disputes through class-wide arbitration. Cf. First Options of Chicago, Inc. v. Kaplan, 514 U. S. 938, 945 (1995) (noting that "one can understand why courts might hesitate to interpret silence or ambiguity on the 'who should decide arbitrability' point as giving the arbitrators that power, for doing so might too often force unwilling parties to arbitrate" contrary to their expectations).

Consider just some of the fundamental changes brought about by the shift from bilateral arbitration to class-action arbitration. An arbitrator chosen according to an agreed-upon procedure . . . no longer resolves a single dispute between the parties to a single agreement, but instead resolves many disputes between hundreds or perhaps even thousands of parties. . . . Under the Class Rules, "the presumption of privacy and confidentiality" that applies in many bilateral arbitrations "shall not apply in class arbitrations," thus potentially frustrating the parties' assumptions when they agreed to arbitrate. The arbitrator's award no longer purports to bind just the parties to a single arbitration agreement, but adjudicates the rights of absent parties as well. . . . And the commercial stakes of class-action arbitration are comparable to those of class-action litigation . . . even though the scope of judicial review is much more limited, see Hall Street, 552 U.S. at 588. We think that the differences between bilateral and class-action arbitration are too great for arbitrators to presume, consistent with their limited powers under the FAA, that the parties' mere silence on the issue of class-action arbitration constitutes consent to resolve their disputes in class proceedings.[10]

* * *

For these reasons, the judgment of the Court of Appeals is reversed, and the case is remanded for further proceedings consistent with this opinion.

■ GINSBURG, JUSTICE (dissenting), with whom JUSTICE STEVENS and JUSTICE BREYER join. When an arbitration clause is silent on the question, may arbitration proceed on behalf of a class? The Court prematurely takes up that important question and, indulging in *de novo* review, overturns the ruling of experienced arbitrators.

The Court errs in addressing an issue not ripe for judicial review. Compounding that error, the Court substitutes its judgment for that of the decisionmakers chosen by the parties. I would dismiss the petition as improvidently granted. Were I to reach the merits, I would adhere to the strict limitations the Federal Arbitration Act (FAA), 9 U.S.C. § 1 et seq., places on judicial review of arbitral awards. § 10. Accordingly, I would

---

[10] We have no occasion to decide what contractual basis may support a finding that the parties agreed to authorize class-action arbitration. * * *

affirm the judgment of the Second Circuit, which rejected petitioners' plea for vacation of the arbitrators' decision.

* * *

NOTES

(1) *The Sound of Silence.* Most contracts without arbitration provisions are also silent as to whether class actions are allowed. Should the silence in these contracts be taken to mean that the parties were opting out of Rule 23 of the Federal Rules of Civil Procedure?

(2) In *First Options of Chicago, Inc. v. Kaplan*, supra, the Supreme Court established a default that courts have the primary power to decide arbitrability:

> * * * Just as the arbitrability of the merits of a dispute depends upon whether the parties agreed to arbitrate that dispute, . . . so the question "who has the primary power to decide arbitrability" turns upon whether the parties agreed to submit that question to arbitration. * * * When deciding whether the parties agreed to arbitrate a certain matter (including arbitrability), courts generally (though with a qualification we discuss below) should apply ordinary state-law principles that govern the formation of contracts. * * *
>
> This Court, however, has (as we just said) added an important qualification, applicable when courts decide whether a party has agreed that arbitrators should decide arbitrability: Courts should not assume that the parties agreed to arbitrate arbitrability unless there is "clea[r] and unmistakabl[e]" evidence that they did so. . . . In this manner the law treats silence or ambiguity about the question "*who* (primarily) should decide arbitrability" differently from the way it treats silence or ambiguity about the question "*whether* a particular merits-related dispute is arbitrable because it is within the scope of a valid arbitration agreement"—for in respect to this latter question the law reverses the presumption.

Can the Supreme Court's default jurisprudence in *First Options* and *Stolt-Nielsen* be reconciled?

(3) *Does* Stolt-Nielsen *Matter?* In *Stolt-Nielsen* Justice Alito framed the issue as about the parties' intent. But the parties had stipulated that they did not have an intent or agreement about class arbitration *one way or the other*. In fact, the question was not about the parties' intent, but about the right default meaning of an arbitration clause that is silent on class arbitration.

This might suggest that the outcome of *Stolt-Nielsen* was not that important. After *Stolt-Nielsen*, sophisticated drafters who want class arbitration must say so in their arbitration clauses. If the case had come out the other way, sophisticated parties who didn't want class arbitration would have had to include a no-class-arbitration provision to get that result. In fact, in a 2015 major study—five years after Stolt-Neilsen—the Consumer

Financial Protection Bureau found that "[n]early all the arbitration clauses studied included provisions stating that arbitration may not proceed on a class basis." Consumer Financial Protection Bureau, Arbitration Study, March 2015, at 10.

But legal defaults are not inert. One reason: they tend to stick. If there is a social interest in permitting the aggregation of claims, we might want the default to be that class arbitration is permitted.

Nor, as will become clear in *AT&T Mobility v. Concepcion*, was Alito's reasoning in *Stolt-Nielsen* without effect. By effectively defining "arbitration" as bilateral arbitration only, *Stolt-Nielsen* set the stage for the next round.

(4)   In *Oxford Health Plans LLC v. Sutter*, 133 S. Ct. 2064 (2013), the Supreme Court held that *Stolt-Nielsen* did not prevent an arbitrator from finding that the parties had authorized class arbitration, even though the arbitration clause did not expressly address class arbitration. What was essential, according to Kagan's majority opinion, was that "the arbitrator (even arguably) interpreted the parties' contract." *Id.* at 2068. Thus an arbitrator might find an implied agreement to authorize class arbitration, so long as he "endeavor[s] to give effect to the parties' intent and articulate[s] a contractual basis for his decision." *Id.* at 2068 (internal punctuation omitted). Kagan distinguished *Stolt-Nielsen* based on the *Stolt-Nielsen* parties' stipulation that they had not agreed one way or the other with respect to class arbitration. Justice Alito concurred, but argued that the outcome was correct only because the defendant had consented to the arbitrator determining the question of class arbitrability.

Stolt-Nielsen set the default with respect to class arbitration, but did not identify the associated altering rule. That is, *Stolt-Nielsen* did not explain what parties' can or must say to contract around the no-class-arbitration default. *Oxford Health* suggests that a party who wants class arbitration does not need to say much, at least if it later has an arbitrator on its side. Is this the best rule? Note that the outcome rests partly on the deference to an arbitrator's findings of fact required by section 10(a)(4) of the FAA. "Because the parties bargained for the arbitrator's construction of their agreement, an arbitral decision even arguably construing or applying the contract must stand, regardless of a court's view of its (de)merits." 133 S.Ct. at 2069.

Misty Ferguson v. Countrywide Credit Industries, Inc.

United States Court of Appeals, Ninth Circuit, 2002.
Supra at 583.

AT&T Mobility LLC v. Vincent Concepcion

United States Supreme Court, 2011.
563 U.S. 333.

■ JUSTICE SCALIA delivered the opinion of the Court.

* * *

I

In February 2002, Vincent and Liza Concepcion entered into an agreement for the sale and servicing of cellular telephones with AT&T Mobility LCC (AT&T). The contract provided for arbitration of all disputes between the parties, but required that claims be brought in the parties' "individual capacity, and not as a plaintiff or class member in any purported class or representative proceeding." . . . .

The revised agreement provides that customers may initiate dispute proceedings by completing a one-page Notice of Dispute form available on AT&T's Web site. AT&T may then offer to settle the claim; if it does not, or if the dispute is not resolved within 30 days, the customer may invoke arbitration by filing a separate Demand for Arbitration, also available on AT&T's Web site. In the event the parties proceed to arbitration, the agreement specifies that AT&T must pay all costs for nonfrivolous claims; that arbitration must take place in the county in which the customer is billed; that, for claims of $10,000 or less, the customer may choose whether the arbitration proceeds in person, by telephone, or based only on submissions; that either party may bring a claim in small claims court in lieu of arbitration; and that the arbitrator may award any form of individual relief, including injunctions and presumably punitive damages. The agreement, moreover, denies AT&T any ability to seek reimbursement of its attorney's fees, and, in the event that a customer receives an arbitration award greater than AT&T's last written settlement offer, requires AT&T to pay a $7,500 minimum recovery and twice the amount of the claimant's attorney's fees.

The Concepcions purchased AT&T service, which was advertised as including the provision of free phones; they were not charged for the phones, but they were charged $30.22 in sales tax based on the phones' retail value. In March 2006, the Concepcions filed a complaint against AT&T in the United States District Court for the Southern District of California. The complaint was later consolidated with a putative class action alleging, among other things, that AT&T had engaged in false advertising and fraud by charging sales tax on phones it advertised as free.

In March 2008, AT&T moved to compel arbitration under the terms of its contract with the Concepcions. The Concepcions opposed the motion, contending that the arbitration agreement was unconscionable and unlawfully exculpatory under California law because it disallowed classwide procedures. The District Court denied AT&T's motion. It described AT&T's arbitration agreement favorably, noting, for example, that the informal dispute-resolution process was "quick, easy to use" and likely to "promp[t] full or . . . even excess payment to the customer *without* the need to arbitrate or litigate"; that the $7,500 premium functioned as "a substantial inducement for the consumer to pursue the claim in arbitration" if a dispute was not resolved informally; and that consumers who were members of a class would likely be worse off. Nevertheless, relying on the California Supreme Court's decision in *Discover Bank v. Superior Court,* 36 Cal.4th 148 (2005), the court found that the arbitration provision was unconscionable because AT&T had not shown that bilateral arbitration adequately substituted for the deterrent effects of class actions.

The Ninth Circuit affirmed, also finding the provision unconscionable under California law as announced in *Discover Bank. Laster v. AT&T Mobility LLC,* 584 F.3d 849, 855 (2009). It also held that the *Discover Bank* rule was not preempted by the FAA because that rule was simply "a refinement of the unconscionability analysis applicable to contracts generally in California." 584 F.3d, at 857. * * *

II

The FAA was enacted in 1925 in response to widespread judicial hostility to arbitration agreements. Section 2, the "primary substantive provision of the Act," *Moses H. Cone Memorial Hospital v. Mercury Constr. Corp.,* 460 U.S. 1 (1983), provides, in relevant part, as follows:

> "A written provision in any maritime transaction or a contract evidencing a transaction involving commerce to settle by arbitration a controversy thereafter arising out of such contract or transaction . . . shall be valid, irrevocable, and enforceable, save upon such grounds as exist at law or in equity for the revocation of any contract." 9 U.S.C. § 2.

We have described this provision as reflecting both a "liberal federal policy favoring arbitration," *Moses H. Cone, supra,* at 24, and the "fundamental principle that arbitration is a matter of contract," *Rent-A-Center, West, Inc. v. Jackson,* 130 S.Ct. 2772, 2776 (2010). In line with these principles, courts must place arbitration agreements on an equal footing with other contracts, and enforce them according to their terms.

The final phrase of § 2, however, permits arbitration agreements to be declared unenforceable "upon such grounds as exist at law or in equity for the revocation of any contract." This saving clause permits agreements to arbitrate to be invalidated by "generally applicable contract defenses, such as fraud, duress, or unconscionability," but not by defenses that apply only to arbitration or that derive their meaning from the fact that an agreement to arbitrate is at issue. The question in this case is whether § 2 preempts California's rule classifying most collective-arbitration waivers in consumer contracts as unconscionable. We refer to this rule as the *Discover Bank* rule.

Under California law, courts may refuse to enforce any contract found "to have been unconscionable at the time it was made," or may "limit the application of any unconscionable clause." Cal. Civ.Code Ann. § 1670.5(a) (West 1985). A finding of unconscionability requires "a 'procedural' and a 'substantive' element, the former focusing on 'oppression' or 'surprise' due to unequal bargaining power, the latter on 'overly harsh' or 'one-sided' results." *Armendariz v. Foundation Health Pyschcare Servs., Inc.,* 24 Cal.4th 83, 114 (2000); accord, *Discover Bank,* 36 Cal.4th, at 159–161.

In *Discover Bank,* the California Supreme Court applied this framework to class-action waivers in arbitration agreements and held as follows:

> "[W]hen the waiver is found in a consumer contract of adhesion in a setting in which disputes between the contracting parties predictably involve small amounts of damages, and when it is alleged that the party with the superior bargaining power has carried out a scheme to deliberately cheat large numbers of consumers out of individually small sums of money, then . . . the waiver becomes in practice the exemption of the party 'from responsibility for [its] own fraud, or willful injury to the person or property of another.' Under these circumstances, such waivers are unconscionable under California law and should not be enforced." *Id.,* at 162 (quoting Cal. Civ.Code Ann. § 1668).

California courts have frequently applied this rule to find arbitration agreements unconscionable.

III

* * *

The "principal purpose" of the FAA is to "ensur[e] that private arbitration agreements are enforced according to their terms." *Volt,* 489 U.S., at 478; see also *Stolt-Nielsen S.A. v. AnimalFeeds Int'l Corp.,* 130 S.Ct. 1758, 1763 (2010). This purpose is readily apparent from the FAA's text. Section 2 makes arbitration agreements "valid, irrevocable, and enforceable" as written (subject, of course, to the saving clause); § 3 requires courts to stay litigation of arbitral claims pending arbitration of those claims "in accordance with the terms of the agreement"; and § 4 requires courts to compel arbitration "in accordance with the terms of the agreement" upon the motion of either party to the agreement (assuming that the "making of the arbitration agreement or the failure . . . to perform the same" is not at issue). In light of these provisions, we have held that parties may agree to limit the issues subject to arbitration, *Mitsubishi Motors Corp. v. Soler Chrysler-Plymouth, Inc.,* 473 U.S. 614 (1985), to arbitrate according to specific rules, *Volt, supra,* at 479, and to limit *with whom* a party will arbitrate its disputes, *Stolt-Nielsen, supra,* at 1773.

The point of affording parties discretion in designing arbitration processes is to allow for efficient, streamlined procedures tailored to the type of dispute. It can be specified, for example, that the decisionmaker be a specialist in the relevant field, or that proceedings be kept confidential to protect trade secrets. And the informality of arbitral proceedings is itself desirable, reducing the cost and increasing the speed of dispute resolution.

* * *

California's *Discover Bank* rule . . . interferes with arbitration. Although the rule does not *require* classwide arbitration, it allows any party to a consumer contract to demand it *ex post*. The rule is limited to adhesion contracts, *Discover Bank,* 36 Cal.4th, at 162–163, but the times in which consumer contracts were anything other than adhesive are long past.[6] *Carbajal v. H & R Block Tax Servs., Inc.,* 372 F.3d 903, 906 (7th Cir.2004); see also *Hill v. Gateway 2000, Inc.,* 105 F.3d 1147, 1149 (C.A.7 1997). The rule also requires that damages be predictably small, and that the consumer allege a scheme to cheat consumers. *Discover Bank, supra,* at 162–163. The former requirement, however, is toothless and malleable (the Ninth Circuit has held that damages of $4,000 are sufficiently small, see *Oestreicher v. Alienware Corp.,* 322 Fed.Appx. 489, 492 (2009) (unpublished)), and the latter has no limiting effect, as all that is required is an allegation. Consumers remain free to bring and resolve their disputes on a bilateral basis under *Discover Bank,* and some may well do so; but there is little incentive for lawyers to arbitrate on behalf of individuals when they may do so for a class and reap far higher fees in the process. And faced with inevitable class arbitration, companies would have less incentive to continue resolving potentially duplicative claims on an individual basis.

Although we have had little occasion to examine classwide arbitration, our decision in *Stolt-Nielsen* is instructive. In that case we held that an arbitration panel exceeded its power under § 10(a)(4) of the FAA by imposing class procedures based on policy judgments rather than the arbitration agreement itself or some background principle of contract law that would affect its interpretation. 130 S.Ct. at 1773–1776. We then held that the agreement at issue, which was silent on the question of class procedures, could not be interpreted to allow them because the "changes brought about by the shift from bilateral arbitration to class-action arbitration" are "fundamental." *Id.,* at 1776. This is obvious as a structural matter: Classwide arbitration includes absent parties, necessitating additional and different procedures and involving higher stakes. Confidentiality becomes more difficult. And while it is theoretically possible to select an arbitrator with some expertise relevant

---

[6] Of course States remain free to take steps addressing the concerns that attend contracts of adhesion—for example, requiring class-action-waiver provisions in adhesive arbitration agreements to be highlighted. Such steps cannot, however, conflict with the FAA or frustrate its purpose to ensure that private arbitration agreements are enforced according to their terms.

to the class-certification question, arbitrators are not generally knowledgeable in the often-dominant procedural aspects of certification, such as the protection of absent parties. The conclusion follows that class arbitration, to the extent it is manufactured by *Discover Bank* rather than consensual, is inconsistent with the FAA.

* * *

The dissent claims that class proceedings are necessary to prosecute small-dollar claims that might otherwise slip through the legal system. . . . But States cannot require a procedure that is inconsistent with the FAA, even if it is desirable for unrelated reasons. Moreover, the claim here was most unlikely to go unresolved. As noted earlier, the arbitration agreement provides that AT&T will pay claimants a minimum of $7,500 and twice their attorney's fees if they obtain an arbitration award greater than AT&T's last settlement offer. The District Court found this scheme sufficient to provide incentive for the individual prosecution of meritorious claims that are not immediately settled, and the Ninth Circuit admitted that aggrieved customers who filed claims would be "essentially guarantee[d]" to be made whole, 584 F.3d, at 856, n. 9. Indeed, the District Court concluded that the Concepcions were *better off* under their arbitration agreement with AT&T than they would have been as participants in a class action, which " could take months, if not years, and which may merely yield an opportunity to submit a claim for recovery of a small percentage of a few dollars." *Laster,* 2008 WL 5216255, at *12.

* * *

Because it "stands as an obstacle to the accomplishment and execution of the full purposes and objectives of Congress," *Hines v. Davidowitz,* 312 U.S. 52, 67 (1941), California's *Discover Bank* rule is preempted by the FAA. The judgment of the Ninth Circuit is reversed, and the case is remanded for further proceedings consistent with this opinion.

JUSTICE BREYER, with whom JUSTICE GINSBURG, JUSTICE SOTOMAYOR, and JUSTICE KAGAN Join, dissenting.

* * *

The *Discover Bank* rule does not create a "blanket policy in California against class action waivers in the consumer context." *Provencher v. Dell, Inc.,* 409 F.Supp.2d 1196, 1201 (C.D.Cal.2006). Instead, it represents the "application of a more general [unconscionability] principle." *Gentry v. Superior Ct.,* 42 Cal.4th 443, 457 (2007). Courts applying California law have enforced class-action waivers where they satisfy general unconscionability standards. And even when they fail, the parties remain free to devise other dispute mechanisms, including informal mechanisms, that, in context, will not prove unconscionable.

* * *

The *Discover Bank* rule is also consistent with the basic "purpose behind" the Act. *Dean Witter Reynolds Inc. v. Byrd,* 470 U.S. 213, 219 (1985). We have described that purpose as one of "ensur[ing] judicial enforcement" of arbitration agreements. As is well known, prior to the federal Act, many courts expressed hostility to arbitration, for example by refusing to order specific performance of agreements to arbitrate. The Act sought to eliminate that hostility by placing agreements to arbitrate " 'upon the same footing as other contracts.' " *Scherk v. Alberto-Culver Co.,* 417 U.S. 506, 511 (1974) (quoting H.R.Rep. No. 96, at 2; emphasis added).

Congress was fully aware that arbitration could provide procedural and cost advantages. The House Report emphasized the "appropriate[ness]" of making arbitration agreements enforceable "at this time when there is so much agitation against the costliness and delays of litigation." *Id.,* at 2. And this Court has acknowledged that parties may enter into arbitration agreements in order to expedite the resolution of disputes. See *Preston v. Ferrer,* 552 U.S. 346, 357 (2008) (discussing "prime objective of an agreement to arbitrate").

But we have also cautioned against thinking that Congress' primary objective was to guarantee these particular procedural advantages. Rather, that primary objective was to secure the "enforcement" of agreements to arbitrate. *Dean Witter,* 470 U.S., at 221. The relevant Senate Report points to the Act's basic purpose when it says that "[t]he purpose of the [Act] is *clearly set forth in section 2,*" S.Rep. No. 536, at 2 (emphasis added), namely, the section that says that an arbitration agreement "shall be valid, irrevocable, and enforceable, save upon such grounds as exist at law or in equity for the revocation of any contract," 9 U.S.C. § 2.

Thus, insofar as we seek to implement Congress' intent, we should think more than twice before invalidating a state law that does just what § 2 requires, namely, puts agreements to arbitrate and agreements to litigate "upon the same footing."

* * *

The majority's contrary view . . . rests primarily upon its claims that the *Discover Bank* rule increases the complexity of arbitration procedures, thereby discouraging parties from entering into arbitration agreements, and to that extent discriminating in practice against arbitration. These claims are not well founded.

* * *

Where does the majority get its . . . idea—that individual, rather than class, arbitration is a "fundamental attribut[e]" of arbitration? *Ante,* at 9. The majority does not explain. And it is unlikely to be able to trace its present view to the history of the arbitration statute itself.

When Congress enacted the Act, arbitration procedures had not yet been fully developed. Insofar as Congress considered detailed forms of arbitration at all, it may well have thought that arbitration would be used primarily where merchants sought to resolve disputes of fact, not law, under the customs of their industries, where the parties possessed roughly equivalent bargaining power. This last mentioned feature of the history—roughly equivalent bargaining power—suggests, if anything, that California's statute is consistent with, and indeed may help to further, the objectives that Congress had in mind.

Regardless, if neither the history nor present practice suggests that class arbitration is fundamentally incompatible with arbitration itself, then on what basis can the majority hold California's law pre-empted?

* * *

Because California applies the same legal principles to address the unconscionability of class arbitration waivers as it does to address the unconscionability of any other contractual provision, the merits of class proceedings should not factor into our decision. If California had applied its law of duress to void an arbitration agreement, would it matter if the procedures in the coerced agreement were efficient?

Regardless, the majority highlights the disadvantages of class arbitrations, as it sees them. . . . But class proceedings have countervailing advantages. In general agreements that forbid the consolidation of claims can lead small-dollar claimants to abandon their claims rather than to litigate. I suspect that it is true even here, for as the Court of Appeals recognized, AT&T can avoid the $7,500 payout (the payout that supposedly makes the Concepcions' arbitration worthwhile) simply by paying the claim's face value, such that "the maximum gain to a customer for the hassle of arbitrating a $30.22 dispute is still just $30.22." *Laster v. AT&T Mobility LLC,* 584 F.3d 849, 855, 856 (C.A.9 2009).

What rational lawyer would have signed on to represent the Concepcions in litigation for the possibility of fees stemming from a $30.22 claim? See, *e.g., Carnegie v. Household Int'l, Inc.,* 376 F.3d 656, 661 (C.A.7 2004) ("The *realistic* alternative to a class action is not 17 million individual suits, but zero individual suits, as only a lunatic or a fanatic sues for $30"). In California's perfectly rational view, nonclass arbitration over such sums will also sometimes have the effect of depriving claimants of their claims (say, for example, where claiming the $30.22 were to involve filling out many forms that require technical legal knowledge or waiting at great length while a call is placed on hold). *Discover Bank* sets forth circumstances in which the California courts believe that the terms of consumer contracts can be manipulated to insulate an agreement's author from liability for its own frauds by "deliberately cheat[ing] large numbers of consumers out of individually small sums of money." 36 Cal.4th, at 162–163. Why is this kind of decision—weighing the pros and cons of all class proceedings alike—not California's to make?

* * *

With respect, I dissent.

NOTES

(1) *Preemptive Effect of the Federal Arbitration Act.* Suppose that state law denied enforcement to agreements to arbitrate future disputes and, allegedly, the "contract evidenced a transaction involving commerce" under FAA § 2. In *Allied-Bruce Terminix Cos., Inc. v. Dobson*, 513 U.S. 265 (1995), the Court held that the FAA's scope extended to the limits of Congress's power to regulate interstate commerce and that state law conflicting with the FAA's enforceability rules was preempted. Thus, Alabama law, which (then) did not enforce agreements to arbitrate future disputes, could not preclude the enforcement of such an agreement within the scope of the FAA.

Similarly, a state law that imposes special conditions on the enforceability of provisions to arbitrate which are not applicable to contracts generally is preempted. For example, in *Doctor's Associates, Inc. v. Casarotto*, 517 U.S. 681 (1996), the Court struck down a Montana statute which required that "notice that a contract is subject to arbitration . . . shall be typed in underlined capital letters on the first page of the contract, and unless such notice is displayed thereon, the contract may not be subject to arbitration." The vice was that the statute did not apply generally to all contracts. To pass muster under the FAA, the law (whether it be a required notice or principles of fraud, capacity or unconscionability) must have general application and not discriminatorily apply to arbitration provisions. According to the Court, Congress in enacting the FAA "precluded states from singling out arbitration provisions for suspect status" and required, instead, that arbitration terms be put on the "same footing as other contracts." *Id.* at 686–87. See Judith Resnik, *Fairness in Numbers: A Comment on* AT&T v. Concepcion, Wal-Mart v. Dukes, *and* Turner v. Rogers, 125 Harv. L. Rev. 78 (2011).

Suppose, however, that the parties choose in clear language state arbitration law that differs from the FAA, or state substantive law that singles out federal arbitration agreements for special treatment. This raises the difficult question of whether the parties can, through a choice of law clause, contract out of the FAA, or vary the effect of its provisions by agreement. In most cases the courts will recognize the power to contract out of or vary the provisions of the FAA if it is clearly expressed. See Volt Information Sciences, Inc. v. Board of Trustees of Leland Stanford Junior University, 489 U.S. 468 (1989) (choice of California law).

(2) *The Other Shoe.* In *American Express v. Italian Colors Restaurant*, 133 S.Ct. 2304 (2013), the Supreme Court considered another class-action waiver case, but one involving not a private claim for damages but a charge of antitrust violations. Here the question was whether there was an exception to the *Concepcion* rule where a class action was necessary to protect the "effective vindication" of a federal statutory right. Plaintiff, a small business, argued that because its individual claim amounted to only a few thousand dollars and the cost of bringing antitrust action typically runs into the hundreds of thousands of dollars, only via aggregation of claims would effective litigation be possible.

The Court rejected this argument. Writing for the majority, Justice Scalia explained:

> Truth to tell, our decision in *AT&T Mobility* all but resolves this case. There we invalidated a law conditioning enforcement of arbitration on the availability of class procedure because that law "interfere[d] with fundamental attributes of arbitration." . . . "[T]he switch from bilateral to class arbitration," we said, "sacrifices the principal advantage of arbitration—its informality—and makes the process slower, more costly, and more likely to generate procedural morass than final judgment." . . . We specifically rejected the argument that class arbitration was necessary to prosecute claims "that might otherwise slip through the legal system." . . .

133 S.Ct at 2312. Justice Kagan authored a dissent excoriating the majority's decision:

> Here is the nutshell version of this case, unfortunately obscured in the Court's decision. The owner of a small restaurant (Italian Colors) thinks that American Express (Amex) has used its monopoly power to force merchants to accept a form contract violating the antitrust laws. The restaurateur wants to challenge the allegedly unlawful provision (imposing a tying arrangement), but the same contract's arbitration clause prevents him from doing so. That term imposes a variety of procedural bars that would make pursuit of the antitrust claim a fool's errand. So if the arbitration clause is enforceable, Amex has insulated itself from antitrust liability—even if it has in fact violated the law. The monopolist gets to use its monopoly power to insist on a contract effectively depriving its victims of all legal recourse.
>
> And here is the nutshell version of today's opinion, admirably flaunted rather than camouflaged: Too darn bad.
>
> * * *
>
> The Court today mistakes what this case is about. To a hammer, everything looks like a nail. And to a Court bent on diminishing the usefulness of Rule 23, everything looks like a class action, ready to be dismantled. So the Court does not consider that Amex's agreement bars not just class actions, but "other forms of cost-sharing . . . that could provide effective vindication." *Ante, . . .* n. 4. In short, the Court does not consider—and does not decide—Italian Colors's (and similarly situated litigants') actual argument about why the effective-vindication rule precludes this agreement's enforcement.
>
> As a result, Amex's contract will succeed in depriving Italian Colors of any effective opportunity to challenge monopolistic conduct allegedly in violation of the Sherman Act. The FAA, the majority says, so requires. Do not be fooled. Only the Court so requires; the FAA was never meant to produce this outcome. The FAA conceived of arbitration as a "method of *resolving* disputes"—a way of using tailored and streamlined procedures to facilitate redress of injuries.

Rodriguez de Quijas, 490 U.S. 477, 481 (1917) (emphasis added). In the hands of today's majority, arbitration threatens to become more nearly the opposite—a mechanism easily made to block the vindication of meritorious federal claims and insulate wrongdoers from liability. The Court thus undermines the FAA no less than it does the Sherman Act and other federal statutes providing rights of action. I respectfully dissent.

133 S.Ct at 2313, 2320. For more on the effects of the Court's recent FAA jurisprudence, see J. Maria Glover, *Disappearing Claims and the Erosion of Substantive Law,* 124 Yale L.J. 3052 (2015); Judith Resnik, *Diffusing Disputes: The Public in the Private of Arbitration, the private in Courts, and the Erasure of Rights,* 124 Yale L.J. 2804 (2015).

(3) *Contracts of Adhesion.* Scalia's majority opinion in *Concepcion* suggests that the fact that the contract was one of adhesion shouldn't make a difference in the analysis. Do you agree? In its 2015 study of arbitration agreements, the Consumer Financial Protection Bureau found inter alia:

> Consumers are generally unaware of whether their credit card contracts include arbitration clauses. Consumers with such clauses in their agreements generally either do not know whether they can sue in court or wrongly believe that they can do so.

> Consumers beliefs about credit card dispute resolution rights bear little to no relation to the dispute resolution provisions in their credit card contracts. Most consumers whose agreements contain arbitration clauses wrongly believe that they can participate in class actions.

Consumer Financial Protection Bureau, Arbitration Study, March 2015, at 11.

As we noted in Chapter Four, the Draft Restatement (Third) of Consumer Contracts provides that terms that "[un]reasonably limit the consumer's ability to pursue a complaint or seek reasonable redress for violation of a legal right" are presumed substantively unconscionable. Council Draft No. 3, § 5(c)(3) (December 20, 2016). Comment 3(c) explains that "waivers of aggregate-litigation processes in situations where individual suits are impractical" might fall under this rule. The Reporters' Note explains the relationship to recent Supreme Court jurisprudence:

> Subsection (c)(3) states a principle of consumer-contract law. It does not attempt to adjudicate the relationship between this principle and federal arbitration law. In particular, subsection (c)(3) does not address the possible preemption of contract-law claims under the Federal Arbitration Act. See AT&T Mobility v. Concepcion, 563 U.S. 321 (2011). We also note that the contract-law principle requiring minimum adequate redress is in tension with the reasoning underlying recent Supreme Court decisions that diminish the "effective vindication" principle with respect to federal statutory rights. See, in particular, American Express Co. v. Italian Colors Restaurant, 133 S. Ct. 2304 (2013). Although statutory rights and contractual rights could be distinguished.

Id. at 66. In May 2016 The Consumer Financial Protection Bureau (pursuant to section 1028 of the Dodd-Frank Wall Street Reform and Consumer Protection Act) proposed rules prohibiting providers of certain consumer financial products from using an arbitration agreement that "bars the consumer from filing or participating in a class action." Fed. Reg. 2016–10961.

(4)   Justice Thomas concurred in *Concepcion*, but suggested a separate ground for the outcome: "As I would read it, the FAA requires that an agreement to arbitrate be enforced unless a party successfully challenges the formation of the arbitration agreement, such as by proving fraud or duress." 563 U.S. at 353.

CHAPTER SIX

REMEDIES

1. RIGHT TO SUSPEND PERFORMANCE OR CANCEL

Recall the following passage from *Jacob & Youngs v. Kent*, reprinted in Chapter Five, Section 4(B):

> Some promises are so plainly independent that they can never by fair construction be conditions of one another. . . . Others are so plainly dependent that they must always be conditions. Others, though dependent and thus conditions when there is departure in point of substance, will be viewed as independent and collateral when the departure is insignificant.

230 N.Y. 239, 241 (1921). Contractual obligations are independent of one another when the performance of one is not a condition of the duty to perform the other. They are dependent when the performance of one is a condition of the performance of another. The modern common law default is that each party's contractual duties are dependent on the other's substantial performance of its obligations due. Or more precisely, in the words of the Second Restatement, "it is a condition of each party's remaining duties to render performances to be exchanged under an exchange of promises that there be no uncured material failure by the other party to render any such performance due at an earlier time." Restatement (Second) § 347. These *constructive conditions of exchange* provide the bases for the nonbreaching party's defensive remedies. In describing those remedies, it helps to distinguish two situations: breach by nonperformance and anticipatory breach.

A party commits *breach by nonperformance* when he or she fails without justification to perform when a promised performance is due. A breach can be either a complete failure to perform or a performance that fails to comply with contractual requirements in one or more respects.

If the nonbreaching party has already fully performed, his or her options are limited to the *affirmative remedy* of an action for damages or specific performance. Affirmative remedies require the involvement of a third-party enforcer—a court or arbitrator. If, however, the nonbreaching party still has duties to perform under the agreed exchange, a material breach is likely also to discharge those duties. In that case, the nonbreaching party might also have the *defensive remedy* of suspending his or her own performance and canceling the contract.

An *anticipatory breach*, as distinguished from a breach by nonperformance, occurs when a party, by words or conduct, repudiates a performance not yet due. A party repudiates either by expressing her intention not to perform or by voluntary acts that prevent her from performing. If (a) both parties still have obligations under the contract,

(b) the repudiation is of a material part of the agreed exchange, and (c) the repudiation has not been effectively nullified by a retraction or otherwise, the nonrepudiating party again has at their disposal both affirmative and defensive remedies. Either or both might be invoked before the time set for performance.

When the circumstances or a party's words or conduct create doubt whether their performance will be forthcoming but do not amount to a repudiation, the insecure party might still have some protection. In the proper circumstances, the insecure party may suspend performance after demanding *adequate assurance* of performance. If that assurance is not forthcoming, the insecure party may treat the failure to assure as a repudiation and resort to the usual affirmative and defensive remedies.

This section explores the nonbreaching party's defensive remedies in these various scenarios. The advantage of the defensive remedies is that they can be invoked without involving a third-party adjudicator. But exercising your defensive rights can be fraught with uncertainty. If a promisee suspends her performance and a court subsequently determines that the other side did not materially breach the contract, the promisee's suspension of performance would itself be deemed to be a breach—subjecting the promisee to liability for monetary damages.

Albert Hochster v. Edgar De La Tour

Queen's Bench, 1853.
118 Eng.Rep. 922.

* * * On the trial, before Erle, J., at the London sittings in last Easter Term, it appeared that plaintiff was a courier, who, in April, 1852, was engaged by defendant to accompany him on a tour, to commence on June 1st, 1852, on the terms mentioned in the declaration. On May 11th, 1852, defendant wrote to plaintiff that he had changed his mind, and declined his services. He refused to make him any compensation. The action was commenced on May 22d. The plaintiff, between the commencement of the action and June 1st, obtained an engagement with Lord Ashburton, on equally good terms, but not commencing till July 4th. The defendant's counsel objected that there could be no breach of the contract before June 1st. The learned judge was of a contrary opinion, but reserved leave to enter a non-suit on this objection. The other questions were left to the jury, who found for plaintiff.

* * *

■ LORD CAMPBELL, C.J. On this motion in arrest of judgment, the question arises, whether if there be an agreement between A and B whereby B engages to employ A on and from a future day for a given period of time, to travel with him into a foreign country as a courier, and to start with him in that capacity on that day, A being to receive a monthly salary during the continuance of such service, B may, before the day, refuse to perform the agreement and break and renounce it, so as to entitle A before the day to commence an action against B to recover damages for breach of the agreement; A having been ready and willing to perform it, till it was broken and renounced by B. The defendant's counsel very powerfully contended that, if the plaintiff was not contented to dissolve the contract, and to abandon all remedy upon it, he was bound to remain ready and willing to perform it till the day when the actual employment as courier in the service of the defendant was to begin; and that there could be no breach of the agreement, before that day, to give a right of action. But it cannot be laid down as a universal rule that, where by agreement an act is to be done on a future day, no action can be brought for a breach of the agreement till the day for doing the act has arrived. If a man promises to marry a woman on a future day, and before that day marries another woman, he is instantly liable to an action for breach of promise of marriage; Short v. Stone, 8 Q.B. 358. If a man contracts to execute a lease on and from a future day for a certain term, and, before that day, executes a lease to another for the same term, he may be immediately sued for breaking the contract. Ford v. Tiley, 6 B. & C. 325. So, if a man contracts to sell and deliver specific goods on a future day, and before the day he sells and delivers them to another, he is immediately liable to an action at the suit of the person with whom he first contracted to sell and deliver them. Bowdell v. Parsons, 10 East, 359. One reason alleged in support of such an action is, that the defendant has, before the day, rendered it impossible for him to perform the contract at the day; but this does not necessarily follow; for, prior to the day fixed for doing the act, the first wife may have died, a surrender of the lease executed might be obtained, and the defendant might have repurchased the goods so as to be in a situation to sell and deliver them to the plaintiff. Another reason may be that, where there is a contract to do an act on a future day, there is a relation constituted between the parties in the meantime by the contract, and that they impliedly promise that in the meantime neither will do anything to the prejudice of the other inconsistent with that relation. As an example, a man and woman engaged to marry are affianced to one another during the period between the time of the engagement and the celebration of the marriage. In this very case, of traveller and courier, from the day of the hiring till the day when the employment was to begin, they were engaged to each other; and it seems to be a breach of an implied contract if either of them renounces the engagement. This reasoning seems in accordance with the unanimous decisions of the Exchequer Chamber in Elderton v. Emmens, 6 C.B. 160, which we have followed in subsequent cases in this court. The declaration in the present case, in alleging a breach, states a great deal more than a passing intention on the part of the defendant which he may repent of, and could only be proved by evidence that he had utterly renounced the contract, or done some act which rendered it impossible for him to perform it. If the plaintiff has no remedy for breach of contract unless he treats the contract as in force, and acts upon it down to the 1st June, 1852, it follows that, till then, he must enter into no employment which will interfere with his promise "to start with the defendant on such travels on the day and year," and that he must then be properly equipped in all respects as a courier for a three months' tour on the continent of Europe. But it is surely much more rational, and more for the benefit of both parties, that, after the renunciation of the agreement by the defendant, the plaintiff should be at liberty to consider himself absolved from any future performance of it, retaining his right to sue for any damage he has suffered from the breach of it. Thus, instead of remaining idle and laying out money in preparations which must be useless, he is at liberty to seek service under another employer, which would go in mitigation of the damages to which he would otherwise be entitled for a breach of the contract. It seems strange that the defendant, after renouncing the contract, and absolutely declaring that he will never act under it, should be permitted to object that faith is given to his assertion, and that an opportunity is not left to him of changing his mind. If the plaintiff is barred of any remedy by entering into an engagement inconsistent with starting as a courier with the defendant on the 1st June, he is prejudiced by putting faith in the defendant's assertion: and it would be more consistent with principle, if the defendant were precluded from saying that he had not broken the contract when he declared that he entirely renounced it. Suppose that the defendant, at the time of his renunciation, had embarked on a voyage for Australia, so as to render it physically impossible for him to employ the plaintiff as a courier on the continent of Europe in the months of June, July and August 1852: according to decided cases, the action might have been brought before the 1st June; but the renunciation may have been founded on other facts, to be given in evidence, which would equally have rendered the defendant's performance of the contract impossible. The man who wrongfully renounces a contract into which he has deliberately entered cannot justly complain if he is immediately sued for a compensation in damages by the man whom he has injured: and it seems reasonable to allow an option to the injured party, either to sue immediately, or to wait till the time when the act was to be done, still holding it as prospectively binding for the exercise of this option, which may be advantageous to the innocent party, and cannot be prejudicial to the wrongdoer. An argument against the action before the 1st of June is urged from the difficulty of calculating the damages: but this argument is equally strong against an action before the 1st of September, when the three months would expire. In either case, the jury in assessing the damages would be justified in looking to all that had happened, or was likely to happen, to increase or mitigate the loss of the plaintiff down to the day of trial. We do not find any decision contrary to the view we are taking of this case. * * *

If it should be held that, upon a contract to do an act on a future day, a renunciation of the contract by one party dispenses with a condition to be performed in the meantime by the other, there seems no reason for requiring that other to wait till the day arrives before seeking his remedy by action: and the only ground on which the condition can be dispensed with seems to be, that the renunciation may be treated as a breach of the contract.

Upon the whole, we think that the declaration in this case is sufficient. It gives us great satisfaction to reflect that, the question being on the record, our opinion may be reviewed in a Court of Error. In the meantime we must give judgment for the plaintiff.

Judgment for plaintiff.

NOTES

(1)   What was the underlying theory of the court in *Hochster v. De La Tour?* Accepting that theory, was it necessary to give the plaintiff both an excuse for non-performance and an immediate cause of action for damages? Samuel Williston, writing over a century ago, thought not. See Samuel Williston, *Repudiation of Contracts,* 14 Harv. L. Rev. 421, 432–441 (1901).

Contemporary courts, however, follow the foundational reasoning in *Hochster v. De la Tour.* For example:

> The principle of anticipatory breach of contract is supported by sound policy considerations. Once a party has indicated an unequivocal intent to forego performance of his obligations under a contract, there is little to be gained by requiring a party who will be injured to await the actual breach before commencing suit, with the attendant risk of faded memories and unavailable witnesses. However, it is clear that there must be a definite and final communication of the intention to forego performance before the anticipated breach may be the subject of legal action.... Mere expression of difficulty in tendering the required performance, for example, is not tantamount to renunciation of the contract.

Rachmani Corp. v. 9 East 96th Street Apartment Corp., 629 N.Y.S.2d 382, 385 (N.Y.A.D. 1995). See Keith A. Rowley, *A Brief History of Anticipatory Repudiation in American Common Law,* 69 U. Cin. L. Rev. 505 (2001).

(2)   *Repudiation in the Uniform Commercial Code.* Article 2 of the UCC contains no comprehensive definition of repudiation. But it does carefully set out the options available to the aggrieved party when the other "repudiates the contract with respect to a performance not yet due the loss of which will substantially impair the value of the contract to the other. . . ." UCC § 2–610. One option is to "suspend his own performance" and "for a commercially reasonable time await performance by the repudiating party." UCC § 2–610(a) & (c). This has the advantage of preserving the contract for a possible settlement. And it allows the repudiating party to retract the repudiation before "the aggrieved party has * * * canceled or materially changed his position or otherwise indicated that he considers the repudiation final." UCC § 2–611(1). Another option, consistent with *Hochster v. De La Tour,* is to suspend performance and "resort to any remedy for breach" under UCC § 2–703 or § 2–711.

To illustrate how the second option works, suppose on November 18 the seller repudiates a promise to deliver goods on December 1. Suppose further that the buyer has already paid one-half of the contract price, with the remainder due upon delivery. Under UCC § 2–711, the buyer may "where the seller * * * repudiates * * * with respect to any goods involved * * * cancel and whether or not he has done so may in addition to recovering so much of the price as has been paid" seek damages under UCC § 2–712 or § 2–713. Under UCC § 2–106(4), cancellation occurs "when either party puts an end to the contract for breach by the other." The effect of cancellation is to discharge "all obligations which are still executory on both sides" except that the cancelling party retains "any right based on prior breach or performance" and "any remedy for breach of the whole contract or any unperformed balance." UCC § 2–106(3) & (4). See UCC §§ 1–306 and 2–720. The decision to cancel might be manifested either by notice to the breaching party or by conduct inconsistent with continuing the contract. See National Cash Register Co. v. UNARCO Industries, Inc., 490 F.2d 285 (7th Cir. 1974) (written notice); Goldstein v. Stainless Processing Co., 465 F.2d 392 (7th Cir. 1972).

(3) *Retraction of Repudiation.* In *Kentucky Natural Gas Corp. v. Indiana Gas & Chemical Corp.*, 129 F.2d 17 (7th Cir. 1942), the court considered a contract in which the Defendant agreed to purchase from the Plaintiff its requirements for natural gas and a specified minimum amount at $0.30 per unit. Plaintiff repudiated the contract, but Defendant insisted the contract was in effect and demanded performance. Thereafter, Plaintiff offered to supply some gas at $0.35 per unit. Defendant, still insisting that the original contract was in effect, accepted gas but refused to pay more than $0.30 per unit. Finally, Plaintiff stopped all deliveries of gas. At this time, Defendant was 181,982 units short on the minimum amount of gas to be purchased under the original agreement. Plaintiff dropped its claim for $0.05 per unit for gas supplied after the repudiation and sued for damages for breach of the agreement to purchase a minimum amount of gas. Defendant, for the first time, asserted that the contract was cancelled when Plaintiff repudiated.

The Seventh Circuit affirmed the district court's judgment for Plaintiff. It reasoned that at all times subsequent to the repudiation and before the trial, Defendant took the position that the contract was in effect and insisted that the Plaintiff perform under it. Thus, the parties agreed neither to rescind nor to modify the repudiated contract. Even though Plaintiff did not, in light of Defendant's election to treat the contract in force, alter its position in reliance, the court held that Defendant's election to preserve the contract was final and that "the party who has made such declaration can not alter his position even though the party who was in default has not acted in reliance thereon." Id. at 20. Neither party was misled and Plaintiff, in effect, retracted the repudiation when at the trial it withdrew its demand for the higher price and limited the claim to damages for breach of the minimum obligation. "Inasmuch as defendant had not prior to that time brought action for nonperformance but had insisted upon performance and had not materially changed its position in reliance on the attempted cancellation, the act of plaintiff in attempting to repudiate was 'nullified.'" Id. at 20. See also

Lowe v. Beaty, 145 Vt. 215 (1984) (retraction effective); UCC § 2–611 (2003); Restatement (Second) § 256 (effect of retraction).

H.B. Taylor v. Elizabeth Johnston

Supreme Court of California, 1975.
15 Cal.3d 130.

■ SULLIVAN, JUSTICE. In this action for damages for breach of contract defendants Elizabeth and Ellwood Johnston, individually and as copartners doing business as Old English Rancho, appeal from a judgment entered after a non-jury trial in favor of plaintiff H.B. Taylor and against them in the amount of $132,778.05 and costs.

Plaintiff was engaged in the business of owning, breeding, raising and racing thoroughbred horses in Los Angeles County. Defendants were engaged in a similar business, and operated a horse farm in Ontario, California, where they furnished stallion stud services. In January 1965 plaintiff sought to breed his two thoroughbred mares, Sunday Slippers and Sandy Fork to defendants' stallion Fleet Nasrullah. To that end, on January 19 plaintiff and defendants entered into two separate written contracts—one pertaining to Sunday Slippers and the other to Sandy Fork. Except for the mare involved the contracts were identical. We set forth in the margin the contract covering Sunday Slippers.[1]

---

[1]

IMPORTANT
PLEASE SIGN ORIGINAL AND RETURN AS QUICKLY AS POSSIBLE
RETAINING DUPLICATE FOR YOUR OWN FILE.

OLD ENGLISH RANCHO   January 8, 1965
Route 1, Box 224–A
Ontario, California 91761

Gentlemen:

I hereby confirm my reservation for one services to the stallion FLEET NASRULLAH for the year 1966. TERMS: $3,500.00—GUARANTEE LIVE FOAL. FEE is due and payable on or before Sept. 1, 1966.

IF stud fee is paid in full, and mare fails to produce a live foal (one that stands and nurses without assistance) from this breeding, a return breeding the following year to said mare will be granted at no additional stallion fee.

FEE is due and payable prior to sale of mare or prior to her departure from the state. If mare is sold or leaves the state, no return breeding will be granted.

STUD CERTIFICATE to be given in exchange for fees paid.

VETERINARIAN CERTIFICATE due in lieu of payment if mare is barren.

I hereby agree that OLD ENGLISH RANCHO shall in no way be held responsible for accident of any kind or disease.

Mare: SUNDAY SLIPPERS
Roan filly 1959
(Veterinary certificate must accompany all barren mares.)
Stakes winner of $64,000.00
last raced in 1962   Mr. H.B. Taylor 112 North Evergreen Street
                                       /s/Mr. H.B. Taylor

The contract provided that Fleet Nasrullah was to perform breeding services upon the respective mares in the year 1966 for a fee of $3,500, payable on or before September 1, 1966. If the stud fee was paid in full and the mares failed to produce a live foal (one that stands and nurses without assistance) from the breeding a return breeding would be provided the following year without additional fee.

On October 4, 1965, defendants sold Fleet Nasrullah to Dr. A.G. Pessin and Leslie Combs II for $1,000,000 cash and shipped the stallion to Kentucky. Subsequently Combs and Pessin syndicated the sire by selling various individuals 36 or 38 shares, each share entitling the holder to breed one mare each season to Fleet Nasrullah. Combs and Pessin each reserved three shares.

On the same day defendants wrote to plaintiff advising the latter of the sale and that he was "released" from his "reservations" for Fleet Nasrullah. Unable to reach defendants by telephone, plaintiff had his attorney write to them on October 8, 1965, insisting on performance of the contracts. Receiving no answer, plaintiff's attorney on October 19 wrote a second letter threatening suit. On October 27, defendants advised plaintiff by letter that arrangements had been made to breed the two mares to Fleet Nasrullah in Kentucky. However, plaintiff later learned that the mares could not be boarded at Spendthrift Farm where Fleet Nasrullah was standing stud and accordingly arranged with Clinton Frazier of Elmhurst Farm to board the mares and take care of the breeding.

In January 1966 plaintiff shipped Sunday Slippers and Sandy Fork to Elmhurst Farm. At that time, however, both mares were in foal and could not be bred, since this can occur only during the five-day period in which they are in heat. The first heat period normally occurs nine days, and the second heat period thirty days, after foaling. Succeeding heat periods occur every 21 days.

On April 17, 1966, Sunday Slippers foaled and Frazier immediately notified Dr. Pessin. The latter assured Frazier that he would make the necessary arrangements to breed the mare to Fleet Nasrullah. On April 26, the ninth day after the foaling, Frazier, upon further inquiry, was told by Dr. Pessin to contact Mrs. Judy who had charge of booking the breedings and had handled these matters with Frazier in the past. Mrs. Judy, however, informed Frazier that the stallion was booked for that day but would be available on any day not booked by a shareholder. She indicated that she was acting under instructions but suggested that he keep in touch with her while the mare was in heat.

Sunday Slippers came into heat on May 13, 1966. Frazier telephoned Mrs. Judy and attempted to book the breeding for May 16. She informed him that Fleet Nasrullah had been reserved by one of the shareholders for that day, but that Frazier should keep in touch with her in the event the reservation was cancelled. On May 14 and May 15 Frazier tried again but without success; on the latter date, Sunday Slippers went out of heat.

On June 4, the mare went into heat again. Frazier again tried to book a reservation with Fleet Nasrullah but was told that all dates during the heat period had been already booked. He made no further efforts but on June 7, on plaintiff's instructions, bred Sunday Slippers to a Kentucky Derby winner named Chateaugay for a stud fee of $10,000.

Sandy Fork, plaintiff's other mare awaiting the stud services of Fleet Nasrullah, foaled on June 5, 1966. Frazier telephoned Mrs. Judy the next day and received a booking to breed the mare on June 14, the ninth day after foaling. On June 13, 1966, however, she cancelled the reservation because of the prior claim of a shareholder. Frazier made no further attempts and on June 14 bred Sandy Fork to Chateaugay.

Shortly after their breeding, it was discovered that both mares were pregnant with twins. In thoroughbred racing twins are considered undesirable since they endanger the mare and are themselves seldom valuable for racing. Both mares were therefore aborted. However, plaintiff was not required to pay the $20,000 stud fees for Chateaugay's services because neither mare delivered a live foal.

The instant action for breach of contract proceeded to trial on plaintiff's fourth amended complaint, which alleged two causes of action, the first for breach of the two written contracts, the second for breach of an oral agreement. Defendants cross-complained for the stud fees. The court found the facts to be substantially as stated above and further found and concluded that by selling Fleet Nasrullah defendants had "put it out of their power to perform properly their contracts," that the conduct of defendants and their agents Dr. Pessin and Mrs. Judy up to and including June 13, 1966, constituted a breach and plaintiff "was then justified in treating it as a breach and repudiation of their contractual obligations to him," and that defendants unjustifiably breached the contracts but plaintiff did not. The court awarded plaintiff damages for defendants' breach in the sum of $103,122.50 ($99,800 net damage directly sustained plus $3,322.50 for reasonable costs and expenses for mitigation of damages). "Because of defendants' wholly unwarranted, high-handed, and oppressive breach of their contractual obligation to plaintiff, the plaintiff is entitled to recover from the defendants pre-judgment interest at the rate of 7% per annum on the sum of $99,800.00 from August 1, 1968. . . ." It was concluded that defendants should take nothing on their cross-complaint. Judgment was entered accordingly. This appeal followed.

Defendants' main attack on the judgment is two-pronged. They contend: First, that they did not at any time repudiate the contracts; and second, that they did not otherwise breach the contracts because performance was made impossible by plaintiff's own actions. To put it another way, defendants argue in effect that the finding that they breached the contracts is without any support in the evidence. Essentially they take the position that on the uncontradicted evidence in the record, as a matter of law there was neither anticipatory nor actual breach. As will appear, we conclude that the trial court's decision was based solely on findings of anticipatory breach and that we must determine whether such decision is supported by the evidence.

Nevertheless both aspects of defendants' argument require us at the outset to examine the specifications for performance contained in the contracts. (See fn. 1, ante). We note that the reservation for "one services" for Fleet Nasrullah was "for the year 1966." As the evidence showed, a breeding is biologically possible throughout the calendar year, since mares regularly come into heat every 21 days, unless they are pregnant. The contracts therefore appear to contemplate breeding with Fleet Nasrullah at any time during the calendar year 1966. The trial court made no finding as to the time of performance called for by the contracts. There was testimony to the effect that by custom in the thoroughbred racing business the breeding is consummated in a "breeding season" which normally extends from January until early July, although some breeding continues through August. It is possible that the parties intended that the mares be bred to Fleet Nasrullah during the 1966 breeding season rather than the calendar year 1966.

However, in our view, it is immaterial whether the contract phrase "for the year 1966" is taken to mean the above breeding season or the full calendar year since in either event the contract period had not expired by June 7 and June 14, 1966, the dates on which Sunday Slippers and Sandy Fork respectively were bred to Chateaugay and by which time, according to the findings . . . defendants had repudiated the contracts. There can be no *actual* breach of a contract until the time specified therein for performance has arrived. . . . Although there may be a *breach by anticipatory repudiation*; "[b]y its very name an essential element of a true anticipatory breach of a contract is that the repudiation by the promisor occur before his performance is due under the contract." . . . In the instant case, because under either of the above interpretations the time for performance had not yet arrived, defendants' breach as found by the trial court was of necessity an anticipatory breach and must be analyzed in accordance with the principles governing such type of breach. To these principles we now direct our attention.

Anticipatory breach occurs when one of the parties to a bilateral contract repudiates the contract. The repudiation may be express or implied. An express repudiation is a clear, positive, unequivocal refusal to perform . . .; an implied repudiation results from conduct where the promisor puts it out of his power to perform so as to make substantial performance of his promise impossible. . . .

When a promisor repudiates a contract, the injured party faces an election of remedies: he can treat the repudiation as an anticipatory breach and immediately seek damages for breach of contract, thereby terminating the contractual relation between the parties, or he can treat the repudiation as an empty threat, wait until the time for performance arrives and exercise his remedies for actual breach if a breach does in fact occur at such time. . . . However, if the injured party disregards the repudiation and treats the contract as still in force, and the repudiation is retracted prior to the time of performance, then the repudiation is nullified and the injured party is left with his remedies, if any, invocable at the time of performance. . . .

As we have pointed out, the trial court found that the whole course of conduct of defendants and their agents Dr. Pessin and Mrs. Judy from the time of the sale of Fleet Nasrullah up to and including June 13, 1966, amounted to a repudiation which plaintiff was justified in treating as an anticipatory breach. . . . However, when the principles of law governing repudiation just described are applied to the facts constituting this course of conduct as found by the trial court, it is manifest that such conduct cannot be treated as an undifferentiated continuum amounting to a single repudiation but must be divided into two separate repudiations.

First, defendants clearly repudiated the contracts when, after selling Fleet Nasrullah and shipping him to Kentucky, they informed plaintiff "[y]ou are, therefore, released from your reservations made to the stallion." However, the trial court additionally found that "[p]laintiff did not wish to be 'released' from his 'reservations' . . . insist[ed] on performance of the stud service agreements . . . [and] threaten[ed] litigation if the contracts were not honored by defendants. . . ." Accordingly defendants arranged for performance of the contracts by making Fleet Nasrullah available for stud service to plaintiff in Kentucky through their agents Dr. Pessin and Mrs. Judy. Plaintiff elected to treat the contracts as in force and shipped the mares to Kentucky to effect the desired performance. The foregoing facts lead us to conclude that the subsequent arrangements by defendants to make Fleet Nasrullah available to service plaintiff's mares in Kentucky constituted a retraction of the repudiation. Since at this time plaintiff had not elected to treat the repudiation as an anticipatory breach and in fact had shipped the mares to Kentucky in reliance on defendants' arrangements, this retraction nullified the repudiation. Thus, plaintiff was then left with his remedies that might arise at the time of performance.

The trial court found that after the mares had arrived in Kentucky, had delivered the foals they were then carrying and were ready for servicing by Fleet Nasrullah, plaintiff was justified in concluding from the conduct of defendants, their agent Dr. Pessin, and their subagent Mrs. Judy, that "defendants were just giving him the runaround and had no intention of performing their contract in the manner required by its terms" and in treating such conduct "as a breach and repudiation of their contractual obligation to him." . . . Since, as we have explained, defendants retracted their original repudiation, this subsequent conduct amounts to a finding of a second repudiation.

There is no evidence in the record that defendants or their agents Dr. Pessin and Mrs. Judy ever stated that Sunday Slippers and Sandy

Fork would not be serviced by Fleet Nasrullah during the 1966 breeding season or that they ever refused to perform. Frazier, plaintiff's agent who made arrangements for the breeding of the mares admitted that they had never made such a statement to him. Accordingly, there was no *express* repudiation or unequivocal refusal to perform. . . .

The trial court's finding of repudiation, expressly based on the "conduct of the defendants" and their agents suggests that the court found an implied repudiation. However, there is no implied repudiation, i.e., by conduct equivalent to an unequivocal refusal to perform, unless "the promisor *puts it out of his power to perform*." . . . Once the mares arrived in Kentucky, defendants had the power to perform the contracts; Fleet Nasrullah could breed with the mares. No subsequent conduct occurred to render this performance impossible. Although plaintiff was subordinated to the shareholders with respect to the priority of reserving a breeding time with Fleet Nasrullah, there is no evidence in the record that this subordination of reservation rights rendered performance impossible. Rather it acted to postpone the time of performance, which still remained within the limits prescribed by the contracts. It rendered performance more difficult to achieve; it may even have cast doubt upon the eventual accomplishment of performance; it did not render performance impossible.[12]

Because there was no repudiation, express or implied, there was no anticipatory breach. Plaintiff contends that defendants' conduct, as found by the trial court, indicated that "defendants were just giving him the runaround and had no intention of performing their contract" and therefore that this conduct was the equivalent of an express and unequivocal refusal to perform. Plaintiff has not presented to the court any authority in California in support of his proposition that conduct which has not met the test for an implied repudiation, i.e. conduct which removed the power to perform, may nonetheless be held to amount to the equivalent of an express repudiation and thus constitute an anticipatory breach. Without addressing ourselves to the question whether some conduct could ever be found equal to an express repudiation, we hold that defendants' conduct in this case as a matter of law did not constitute an anticipatory breach.

To constitute an express repudiation, the promisor's statement, or in this case conduct, must amount to an unequivocal refusal to perform: "A

---

[12]   Plaintiff suggests that this conduct, namely delaying plaintiff's breeding until a day not reserved by a shareholder, amounted to an anticipatory breach because Mrs. Judy inserted a condition to defendants' performance, which as the trial court found was not contemplated by the contracts. Assuming arguendo that this conduct might have amounted to a breach of contract by improperly delaying performance, at most it would have constituted only a partial breach—insufficiently material to terminate the contracts (see Rest.2d Contracts (Tent. Draft No. 8, 1973) §§ 262, 266, 268, 274). It did not constitute a repudiation of the contracts which was the sole basis of the trial court's decision since "[t]o justify the adverse party in treating the renunciation as a breach, the refusal to perform must be of the whole contract or of a covenant going to the whole consideration. . . ." (Atkinson v. District Bond Co., supra, 5 Cal.App.2d 738, 743.)

mere declaration, however, of a party of an intention not to be bound will not of itself amount to a breach, so as to create an effectual renunciation of the contract; for one party cannot by any act or declaration destroy the binding force and efficacy of the contract. To justify the adverse party in treating the renunciation as a breach, the refusal to perform must be of the whole contract . . . and must be distinct, unequivocal, and absolute." (Atkinson v. District Bond Co., supra, 5 Cal.App.2d 738, 743.)

* * *

In sum, we hold that there is no evidence in the record supportive of the trial court's finding and conclusion that defendants repudiated and therefore committed an anticipatory breach of the contracts.

In view of the foregoing conclusion we need not consider defendants' remaining contentions.

The judgment is reversed.

NOTES

(1) *When a Statement or an Act is a Repudiation.* Section 250 of Restatement (Second) provides:

> A repudiation is (a) a statement by the obligor to the obligee indicating that the obligor will commit a breach that would of itself give the obligee a claim for damages for total breach under § 243, or (b) a voluntary affirmative act which renders the obligor unable or apparently unable to perform without such a breach.

The court in *Taylor* held that at one point the defendants clearly repudiated the contract. What happened to that repudiation? If there was no effective express repudiation, was there a repudiation by conduct? If not, why not?

(2) *Adequate Assurances.* Restatement (Second) § 251(1) provides that "where reasonable grounds arise to believe that the obligor will commit" a material breach, the "obligee may demand adequate assurance of due performance and may, if reasonable, suspend any performance for which he has not already received the agreed exchange until he receives such assurance." Section 251(2) then provides that the "obligee may treat as a repudiation the obligor's failure to provide within a reasonable time such assurance of due performance as is adequate in the circumstances of the particular case." Should the plaintiff have pursued this strategy in *Taylor*?

Suppose the plaintiff had demanded adequate assurance and the defendant had replied: "There is a chance that the stud will be available before the contract expires, but if a member claims that time, you will not be entitled to those services." Would that be sufficient?

Suppose, upon a demand of adequate assurance, Ms. Taylor had said: "OK, we agree to breed Sandy Slippers the next time she is in heat regardless of claims by syndicated members, but we cannot breed Sandy Forks." What should the plaintiff do then?

(3) *Use of Declaratory Judgment.* What options are available to parties who have honest but substantial disagreements about the meaning of their

contract? Between the extremes of a negotiated settlement and a unilateral termination with all of its risks, lies the possibility of a declaratory judgment. The Federal Declaratory Judgment Act, 28 U.S.C.A. § 2201 provides:

> In a case of actual controversy within its jurisdiction * * * any court of the United States, upon the filing of an appropriate pleading, may declare the rights and other legal relations of any interested party seeking such declaration, whether or not further relief is or could be sought. Any such declaration shall have the force and effect of a final judgment or decree and shall be reviewable as such.

If there is a genuine controversy, and if time permits, declaratory relief is available to clarify and stabilize and to eliminate uncertainty as to the scope and content of existing or prospective rights. This includes the interpretation of contract rights so that a party need not risk liability for breach if he or she is wrong. The court has discretion to deny this remedy where, for example, the decree "would not terminate the uncertainty or controversy giving rise to the proceeding," Uniform Declaratory Judgment Act § 6, or where relief depends upon future hypothetical events.

PROBLEM: THE "SAFE HARBOR" DEFENSE

In the *Kaiser-Francis Oil* case, reprinted in Chapter Five, after deregulation and the market collapse, the pipeline (PGC) claimed that its performance was excused (1) under the *force majeure* clause and (2) because the gas produced did not meet the quality specification provision concerning allowable water vapor in the gas. The pipeline also proposed a contract amendment that would replace the take-or-pay arrangement with a system of flexible well-head prices that responded to changing market conditions. 870 F.2d at 567. Consider the following questions:

(1) Suppose that after some discussion, Kaiser rejected PGC's offer to modify the contract and insisted upon performance under the take-or-pay provision. PGC came back with a counterproposal, more favorable to Kaiser, and stated: "We will not make the next payment unless you negotiate with us in good faith over this proposal." What is Kaiser's legal position? What would you advise Kaiser to do? See Kaiser-Francis Oil Co. v. Producer's Gas Co., 870 F.2d 563, 566–69 (10th Cir. 1989).

(2) Suppose, instead, that PGC filed a declaratory judgment action to have the court determine whether PGC was excused under either the *force majeure* clause or because the gas had too much water. Kaiser demanded that PGC continue to make payments during the course of the litigation, estimated to take twelve months. PGC responded that there was a "good faith" dispute over the interpretation of the contract, and that PGC would not make another payment until the dispute was finally resolved by the court. At that time, PGC would perform the contract under the court's interpretation. What is Kaiser's legal position? What would you advise Kaiser to do?

Alaska Pacific Trading Co. v. Eagon
Forest Products, Inc.

Court of Appeals of Washington,1997.
85 Wash.App. 354.

■ AGID, JUDGE. [Alaska Pacific Trading Company (ALPAC) and Eagon Forest Products, Inc. (Eagon)] are both corporations engaged in importing and exporting raw logs. In April 1993, Setsuo Kimura, ALPAC's president, and C.K. Ahn, Eagon's vice president, entered into a contract under which ALPAC would ship about 15,000 cubic meters of logs from Argentina to Korea between the end of July and the end of August 1993. Eagon agreed to purchase the logs. In the next few months, the market for logs began to soften, making the contract less attractive to Eagon. ALPAC became concerned that Eagon would try to cancel the contract. Kimura and Ahn began a series of meetings and letters, apparently in an effort to assure ALPAC that Eagon would purchase the logs.

At Eagon, the home office was troubled by the drop in timber prices and initially withheld approval of the shipment. Ahn sent numerous internal memoranda to the home office to the effect that the corporation may not wish to go through with the deal, given the drop in timber prices, but that accepting the logs was "inevitable" under the contract. On August 30, Ahn sent a letter to the home office stating that he would attempt to avoid acceptance of the logs, but that it would be difficult and suggesting that they hold ALPAC responsible for shipment delay.

On August 23, Eagon received a faxed latter from ALPAC suggesting that the price and volume of the contract be reduced. Eagon did not respond to the fax. During a business meeting soon after, Kimura asked Ahn whether he intended to accept the logs. Ahn admitted that he was having trouble getting approval. Kimura thereafter believed that Eagon would not accept the shipment.

ALPAC eventually canceled the vessel that it had reserved for the logs because it believed that Eagon was canceling the contract. The logs were not loaded or shipped by August 31, 1993, but Ahn and Kimura continued to discuss the contract into September. On September 7, Ahn told Kimura that he would continue to try to convince headquarters to accept the delivery. Ahn also indicated that he did not want Kimura to sell the logs to another buyer. The same day, Ahn sent a letter to Eagon's head office indicating that "the situation of our supplier is extremely grave" and that Eagon should consider accepting the shipment in September or October.

By September 27, ALPAC had not shipped the logs. It sent a final letter to Eagon stating that Eagon had breached the contract because it failed to take delivery of the logs. Eagon's president, L.R. Haan, responded to the letter, stating that there was "no contract" because ALPAC's breach excused Eagon's performance. ALPAC filed a complaint for breach of contract in King County Superior Court. Eagon brought a motion for summary judgment, arguing that it did not breach, but that ALPAC breached by failing to deliver the logs. The trial court granted the motion and dismissed ALPAC's claims. ALPAC's motion for reconsideration was denied.

* * *

ALPAC Breached by Failing to Timely Deliver Logs

ALPAC's first contention is that it did not breach the contract by failing to timely deliver the logs because time of delivery was not a material term of the contract. ALPAC relies on common law contract cases to support its position that, when the parties have not indicated that time is of the essence, late delivery is not a material breach which excuses the buyer's duty to accept the goods. *See Cartozian & Sons, Inc. v, Ostruske-Murphy, Inc.,* 64 Wash.2d 1 (1964); *Scott Paper Co. v. City of Anacortes,* 90 Wash.2d 19 (1978). However, as a contract for the sale of goods, this contract is governed by the Uniform Commercial Code, Article II (UCC II) which replaced the common law doctrine of material breach, on which ALPAC relies, with the "perfect tender" rule. Under this rule, "if the goods or the tender of delivery fail in any respect to conform to the contract, the buyer may . . . reject the whole." RCW 62A.2–601(a). * * * ALPAC does not dispute that the contract specified a date for shipment or that the logs were not shipped by that date. Thus, under the applicable "perfect tender" rule, ALPAC breached its duty under the contract and released Eagon from its duty to accept the logs.

Parties Did Not Waive or Modify Delivery Date

ALPAC next contends that, even if failure to timely deliver is a breach, the parties modified the delivery date or Eagon waived timely delivery. The UCC II changed the common law of contracts to eliminate the need for consideration in contract modifications but did not otherwise alter the common law. RCW 62A.2–209(1). Mutual assent is still required and one party may not unilaterally modify a contract. *In re Relationship of Eggers,* 30 Wash.App. 867 (1982) . . . ALPAC argues that Eagon agreed to modify the delivery date because it did not object to ALPAC's proposed changes in the amount and delivery time. It asserts that, if Eagon had not been silent during the discussions about the contract, the logs would have been shipped. Because the law requires mutual assent, Eagon's mere silence is not sufficient to establish a material issue of fact about modification.[3]

---

[3] ALPAC also argues that Eagon induced the breach by bad faith and refusing to cooperate. It cites to several places in the record where Eagon did in fact indicate that it wished it could get out of the deal. However, it provides no valid authority for the proposition that a desire on the part of one party to avoid the deal, absent any active attempt to foil it, is sufficient to constitute frustration excusing breach. ALPAC cites to several inapplicable provisions of the UCC II and to *I–5 Truck Sales & Serv. Co. v. Underwood,* 32 Wash.App. 4 (1982), for the proposition that deceptive conduct intended to induce breach violates the requirement of good faith. *I–5 Truck Sales* interprets the automotive repair statute and makes only a passing reference to the requirement of good faith in equity cases. ALPAC also fails to explain how

ALPAC also argues that Eagon waived the shipping date because it failed to comment on its passage and continued to discuss the contract after the shipping date had passed. Waiver is a factual question. . . . Like all factual questions, a waiver issue may be resolved on summary judgment if, given the evidence in the record, a court could reach only one reasonable result. . . .

If both parties to a contract allow the reasonable time for delivery to pass without complaint, a court may infer that the parties have extended the time for performance. *Davis v. Suggs,* 10 Ohio App.3d 50, 51 (1983). Ahn and Kimura continued to negotiate until September 7, at least a week after the shipment date. Thus, Eagon may initially have waived the original shipment date as negotiations continued. However, by the end of September, when they exchanged their final correspondence, ALPAC still had not shipped the logs. Thus, even if the parties did waive the original date, ALPAC still had a duty to deliver the logs within a reasonable time. Its failure to ship the logs for an additional 20 days, while the price of logs continued to drop, was unreasonable and a breach.

ALPAC Did Not Request Assurances

ALPAC's third contention is that summary judgment was inappropriate because a material factual issue exists about whether it requested assurances from Eagon and Eagon failed to respond. The UCC II provides that:

> A contract for sale imposes an obligation on each party that the other's expectation of receiving due performance will not be impaired. When reasonable grounds for insecurity arise with respect to the performance of either party the other may in writing demand adequate assurance of due performance and until he receives such assurance may if commercially reasonable suspend any performance for which he has not already received the agreed return.

RCW 62A.2–609(1). ALPAC argues both that written requests are not necessary and that it provided a written request for assurance.

Washington courts have not directly determined whether a 2–609 demand for assurances must be in writing, or whether an oral request is sufficient. . . . Other courts have recognized that the demand for assurances must be made in writing, absent "a pattern of interaction which demonstrat[es] a clear understanding between the parties that suspension of the demanding party's performance was the alternative, if its concerns were not adequately addressed by the other party." *Scott v. Crown,* 765 P.2d 1043, 1046 (Colo.App.1988). For example, in *AMF, Inc. v. McDonald's Corp.,* 536 F.2d 1167 (7th Cir.1976), and *ARB, Inc. v. E-Systems, Inc.,* 663 F.2d 189 (D.C.Cir.1980), the courts found that the pattern of interaction between the parties made the demand for

---

Eagon's outward desire to avoid the contract rises to the level of fraud and violates the good faith requirement.

assurances sufficiently clear that no writing was necessary. In both cases, the seller supplied a prototype to the buyer which the buyer found unacceptable. The buyers clearly told the sellers they would not accept tender unless the problems with the prototypes were addressed. The courts held that these communications were sufficient even if not written. ALPAC relies on these cases to support its proposition that no written demand was needed in this case. It points out that Ahn had trouble getting approval from the Eagon home office and that Eagon knew it would lose money if the deal was completed.

Here, while Ahn had some idea that Kimura and ALPAC were concerned about the status of the contract, he did not understand that ALPAC would withhold performance as a result. This case is unlike *AMF, Inc.* and *ARB, Inc.,* in which the buyer clearly would not accept the product as it was represented in the prototype. ALPAC's concerns were not sufficiently clear to instruct Eagon that ALPAC would be withholding performance. Eagon and ALPAC each made assumptions about the other's performance under the contract, but neither clearly expressed a need for assurance. If we were to hold that, in every case where a contract becomes less favorable for one party, general discussions between the parties can be considered requests for assurances, we would defeat the purpose of 2–609. That section requires a clear demand so that all parties are aware that, absent assurances, the demanding party will withhold performance. An ambiguous communication is not sufficient. . . .

In the alternative, ALPAC argues that it did provide written request for assurances in the fax from Kimura to Eagon dated August 23, 1993 which stated:

> As we discussed, we would send a vessel to ship approx. 24–45,000 M3 of Argentina logs around mid part of Sept., 93.

> I understand, and recognize your troubles to sell, and concerns about Korean market at this time. Therefore, as a seller, I (ALPAC) will offer you to reduce volume and price . . .

> We have approx. 21,000 M3 of logs around port of Campana, Argentina, now. Therefore, I hope you can find times to check logs with me toward end of August to early Sept., 93.

> Pls let me know by return fax when is the best time to go over there. Tks, Kimura.

* * * The written demand for assurances under RCW 62A.2–609 must generally be clear and unequivocal. *Scott,* 765 P.2d at 1046. Like the oral demand, a less clear statement will be considered sufficient only when the interaction between the parties is such that they understand that the demanding party will withhold performance unless assurances are tendered. In *Smyers v. Quartz Works Corp.,* 880 F.Supp. 1425, 1433 (D.Kan.1995), the court found adequate a letter stating that a shipment of goods was ready to go out, but that the seller had not received a previously-owed check. Given the parties' prior relationship and the

context in which the letter was received, they knew that payment must precede the new shipment. Similarly, in *USX Corp. v. Union Pac. Resources Co.,* 753 S.W.2d 845, 852–53 (Tex.App.1988), the court found that repeated letters requesting information on when and how the shipments would take place were sufficient written demands for assurances. While the parties here both knew that the contract was no longer favorable to Eagon, there is no showing that Eagon would not perform, or that ALPAC expressed its belief that Eagon would not perform. The letter Kimura sent to Ahn stated only that ALPAC was willing to negotiate new terms for the contract, not that it believed Eagon would not perform. Therefore, neither the parties' interactions nor their correspondence rose to the level of a demand for assurances.

Eagon Did Not Repudiate

ALPAC's final contention is that Eagon repudiated the contract prior to the delivery date. It argues that Eagon's concern about the drop in log prices and its difficulty in getting final approval from its head office were sufficient to present a material factual issue about whether Eagon intended to accept the logs. ALPAC correctly argues that the question of anticipatory repudiation is one of fact. *CKP, Inc. v. GRS Constr. Co.,* 63 Wash.App. 601, 620 (1991). * * *

"An intent to repudiate may be expressly asserted or circumstantially manifested by conduct." *CKP, Inc.,* 63 Wash.App. at 620. However communicated, a court will not infer repudiation from "doubtful and indefinite statements that performance may or may not take place." *Wallace Real Estate Inv. Inc. v. Groves,* 124 Wash.2d 881, 898 (1994). Rather, the anticipatory breach must be a clear and positive statement or action that expresses an intention not to perform the contract. *Id.*

ALPAC argues that Kimura's refusal to go to Argentina to see the logs and Ahn's statements that Eagon would be losing money if it accepted delivery of the logs support its position that Eagon repudiated the contract. However, Kimura testified that Ahn never stated that he would not accept the cargo. Rather, Kimura assumed that the problems with approval from the home office were the equivalent of an inability or unwillingness to accept the cargo. Washington courts have refused to hold that a communication between contracting parties that raises doubt as to the ability or willingness of one party to perform, but is not an outward denial, is a repudiation of the contract. *Lovric v. Dunatov,* 18 Wash.App. 274, 282 (1977) (letter indicating that one party "may" not be able to perform was not direct and positive enough to be a repudiation). Therefore, as a matter of law, neither Eagon's expressed unhappiness about the drop in timber prices nor its problems completing the contract rise to the level of repudiation.

NOTES

(1) *Adequate Assurance Under the Code.* In addition to touching on important issues we have already covered (the perfect tender rule, modification, waiver, good faith), *Alaska Pacific Trading* illustrates important fact questions that arise in the application of UCC 2–609.

First, there is the question whether Ahn's communications created a "reasonable ground for insecurity" "according to commercial standards." Sections 2–609(1) & (2). The court in *Alaska Pacific Trading* found it unnecessary to address the issue. How do you think it would have ruled if it had? Were Ahn's communications enough to give ALPAC reason to doubt whether it would accept the logs? Would a request for modifications be enough? What about a request for modification together with a sharp downturn in the market? Note that "there must be an objective factual basis for the insecurity, rather than a purely subjective fear that the party will not perform." Top of Iowa Co-op v. Sime Farms, Inc., 608 N.W.2d 454, 466 (Iowa 2000).

Second, what suffices as a demand for adequate assurances? As Judge Agid observed, courts are sometimes willing to waive section 2–609(1)'s writing requirement. But as the court also held, the request must be unambiguous.

Third, what counts as an adequate assurance of performance? This can be a vexing question. It is clear that the insecure party can demand more than the contract originally required. But how much more? Again this is a factual question that will vary depending on the parties' relationship, the reason for the demand, and between merchants, "commercial standards." UCC 2–609(2).

(2) Larry Garvin has expressed concern that section § 2–609 gives the insecure party an opportunity to demand a forced modification. To meet the demand, the other party may be compelled to "grant ex post rights which the bargain ex ante had not provided" and thus give the insecure party a windfall. Drawing upon cognitive psychology, however, he suggests that cognitive limitations on the assessment of risk at the time of contracting may support efforts to adjust risk after the contract is made and that, in the final analysis, the resulting modification is less troubling. Larry T. Garvin, *Adequate Assurance of Due Performance: Of Risk, Duress, and Cognition,* 69 U. Colo. L. Rev. 71 (1998).

(3) *Right to Demand Adequate Assurance at Common Law.* Section 251 of the Restatement (Second) purports to state the common law rule on adequate assurance. The matter is a bit more complicated, however, in New York. *In Norcon Power Partners, L.P. v. Niagara Mohawk Power Corp.*, 92 N.Y.2d 458 (1998), the following question was certified to the New York Court of Appeals by the United States Court of Appeals for the Second Circuit:

> Does a party have the right to demand adequate assurance of future performance when reasonable grounds arise to believe that the other party will commit a breach by non-performance of a

contract governed by New York law, where the other party is solvent and the contract is not governed by the UCC?

The court answered the question in the affirmative, but hedged its bets. It agreed that the contract (a long-term contract for the sale of electricity) was not a contract for the sale of goods to which Article 2 applied. It also noted that New York had not embraced the adequate assurance doctrine outside of the statutory framework of Article 2. What to do? The court extended UCC § 2–609 to the contract by analogy, concluding that the sale of electricity was similar to a sale of goods and that parties to a "long-term commercial contract" which is "complex and not reasonably susceptible of all security features being anticipated, bargained for, and incorporated in the original contract" should have the protection of UCC § 2–609. 705 N.E.2d at 662. See also O'Connor v. Sleasman, 14 A.D.3d 986 (N.Y. App. Div. 2005) (applying *Norcon*).

The court, in a self-congratulatory opinion, refused to overrule cases rejecting the adequate assurance doctrine in other contracts. This restraint was both consistent with its "customary incremental common-law development process" and with the trail-blazing work of Holmes and Cardozo in "making interstitial law, filling gaps in the statutory and decisional rules, and at a snail-like pace giving some forward movement to the developing law." Id. at 668.

(4) *A Risky Strategy.* Although an insecure party's right to demand adequate assurance at first glance appears to enhance that party's defensive powers, the use of the tool carries considerable risk. The insecure party who wants to suspend under UCC § 2–609 must (i) have "reasonable grounds for insecurity"; (ii) demand adequate assurance; and (iii) have not received "adequate assurance" from the other side. If a party suspends and a court subsequently finds that one of these requirements was not met, the attempted defensive action will constitute a breach. What starts off as a legitimate concern about whether the other side will perform can ultimately become a finding that you yourself breached in exercising your defensive rights.

(5) *Can Parties Alter 2–609?* In *Plastic Suppliers, Inc. v. Cenveo, Inc.*, 2011 WL 4527450 (N.D.N.Y. 2011), the court found that the delivery of nonconforming goods did give rise to a reasonable ground for insecurity. But it suggested that under the contract the buyer was not permitted to suspend its performance while it awaited adequate assurances or cancel the contract if it failed to receive them "within a reasonable time not exceeding thirty days." UCC 2–609(4).

U.C.C. § 1–102 states that "the effect of provisions of this Act may be varied by agreement, except as otherwise provided in this Act. . . ." U.C.C. § 1–102(3). Section 6 of the parties' Agreement acts to vary the provisions of § 2–609. . . . That section limits the ability of an aggrieved party to terminate the Agreement by providing that, upon the occurrence of a material breach, the aggrieved party could cancel the Agreement only by "giving written notice of termination to the other" and allowing the breaching party 90 days thereafter to effectuate a cure.

Id. at *7.

Comment: The Elusive Concept of Substantial Impairment

Under UCC § 2–610(1) repudiation of a performance not yet due must "substantially impair the value of the contract to the other" before the other may take defensive action. The "substantial impairment" test in Article 2 replaced a "material breach" test in Section 45 of the Uniform Sales Act. See Plotnick v. Pennsylvania Smelting & Refining Co., 194 F.2d 859 (3d Cir. 1952) (holding that buyer's failure to pay for one installment was not a material breach).

Under Section 2–612(1), the buyer's agreement to pay the price in installments for goods delivered is not an installment contract. Nevertheless, under UCC § 2–703, the seller may cancel the contract under UCC § 2–703(f) if the buyer fails to make a payment when due or repudiates and if "the breach is of the whole contract." To constitute a "breach of the whole," the breach must "substantially impair the value of that installment" to the other party. UCC § 2–612.

An installment contract under section 2–612(2) is one that requires goods to be delivered in "separate lots to be separately accepted." In this setting, the buyer can reject a single installment "if the nonconformity substantially impairs the value of that installment" to the buyer, UCC § 2–612(2), and the buyer may cancel the contract if a "default with respect to one or more installments substantially impairs the value of the whole contract." UCC § 2–612(3).

Working without a definition, the district court in *Midwest Mobile Diagnostic Imaging v. Dynamics Corp. of America*, 965 F.Supp. 1003 (W.D.Mich. 1997), attempted to explain "substantial impairment" of the "whole" contract:

> Whether a breach constitutes "substantial impairment" of the entire contract is a question of fact. * * * To make such a determination, the Court should consider the cumulative effect of [the breaching party's] performance under the contract, based upon the totality of the circumstances. * * * Ultimately, whether the non-conformity in any given installment justifies cancellation as to the future depends not on whether such non-conformity indicates an intent or likelihood that future deliveries will also be defective, but whether the non-conformity substantially impairs the value of the whole contract. [quoting Section 2–616, comment 6]. Thus, the question is one of present breach which focuses on the importance of the nonconforming installment relative to the contracts as a whole. If the nonconformity only impairs the aggrieved party's security with regard to future installments, s/he has the right to demand

adequate assurances but . . . not an immediate right to cancel the entire contract. . . . The right to cancel will be triggered only if material inconvenience or injustice will result if the aggrieved party is forced to wait and receive an ultimate tender minus the part or aspect repudiated. [Internal quotation marks omitted.]

The same questions arise under the Convention on Contracts for the International Sale of Goods, which applies to contracts of sale between private parties whose places of business are in different countries and both countries have ratified CISG. Art. 1(1)(a). Like UCC Article 2, CISG has articles on adequate assurance, Art. 71, repudiation, Art. 72, and installment contracts, Art. 73. In an installment contract, for example, the question would be whether the buyer's failure to pay one installment gave the seller "good grounds to conclude that a fundamental breach of contract will occur with respect to future installments." If so, the seller may avoid the contract for the future. "Fundamental breach" is defined in Article 25 as: "A breach . . . [which] results in such detriment to the other party as substantially to deprive him of what he is entitled to expect under the contract, unless the party in breach did not foresee and a reasonable person of the same kind in the same circumstances would not have foreseen such a result."

Comment: Post-Breach Conduct Affecting the Cancellation Remedy

In Chapter Five, Section 4(A)(2), we saw that a promisor could "waive" a condition included in the bargain for his or her benefit. In this Section, we have assumed that a promisor's duty to render a performance was expressly or "constructively" conditioned upon performance by the other party. See Chapter Five, Section 4(B). Thus, if the other party repudiated or failed to perform a material part of the agreed exchange, the promisor's duty to perform is, at a minimum, suspended and, at a maximum, discharged. In short, the promisee can *cancel* the contract because of the other party's material breach. Under what circumstances can the promisor, by action or inaction, *waive* or alter the effect of the other's breach and thereby lose the cancellation remedy?

First, it is important to distinguish a claim for damages arising from breach from the cancellation remedy. In point of law, it is harder to waive the former than the latter. The damage claim can be discharged in whole or in part without consideration by agreement of the aggrieved party in an authenticated record. UCC § 1–306. See also Restatement (Second) §§ 273 & 277. A renunciation can also be effective without consideration or a formality if it has "induced such action or forbearance as would make a promise enforceable." Restatement (Second) § 273(c). In the absence of consideration, reliance or a formality, therefore, one would expect the damage claim to survive even though the aggrieved party has lost the cancellation remedy through inaction or election.

Second, there are a number of situations, difficult to classify, where the aggrieved party's action or inaction will foreclose a subsequent cancellation. In each case, assume that the cancellation remedy would have been available but for the aggrieved party's conduct.

1.   A repudiates the whole contract on October 1. B decides to wait a reasonable time before cancelling the contract. A then retracts the repudiation before B has canceled or "materially changed its position or otherwise indicated that it considers the repudiation final." The retraction nullifies the breach and, of course, forecloses any remedy for breach of contract. UCC § 2–611(1); Restatement (Second) § 256.

2.   S tenders goods to B on October 1. B inspects them on that date and finds a non-conformity. On November 1, B notifies S that it is rejecting the goods, UCC § 2–601, and canceling the contract. UCC § 2–711(1). On these facts, B has almost certainly lost the cancellation remedy by failing to reject the goods within a reasonable time. UCC § 2–602(1). Cancellation is available for a "rightful" rejection. Under the UCC, B has accepted the goods by failing to make an "effective rejection," UCC § 2–606(1)(b), but still could cancel if it justifiably revokes acceptance under UCC § 2–608. See UCC § 2–711(1). Revocation of acceptance, however, requires action within a reasonable time, and it is probable that this remedy is also foreclosed. Thus, B is left with a claim for damages to accepted goods. UCC § 2–714. See UCC § 2–607(3)(a). Has B, through inaction, lost its damages claim as well?

3.   C completes a construction project and O finds two breaches, one material and one not. O rejects the work and gives only the non-material breach as a reason. C "cures" the defect and O then attempts to avoid payment by citing the material breach. If C has relied to its detriment on the stated objection without reason to know about the unstated objection, O may not assert the material breach as a basis for cancellation. See New England Structures, Inc. v. Loranger, 354 Mass. 62 (1968); UCC § 2–605(1); Restatement (Second) § 248.

4.   S agrees to deliver goods to B in installments over a two-year period. At the end of the first year, S is substantially behind in deliveries and this substantially impairs the value of the whole contract. UCC § 2–612(3). Although B could cancel the contract for breach, that remedy would be lost in the following situations: (a) B sues S "with respect only to past installments or demands performance as to future installments," UCC § 2–612(3); (b) B continues to perform its part of the exchange without objecting to S's breach, see Dangerfield v. Markel, 252 N.W.2d 184 (N.D. 1977); or (c) B "accepts a non-conforming installment without seasonably notifying of cancellation." UCC § 2–612(3); Restatement (Second) §§ 246 & 247. This conduct "reinstates" the contract.

As one court put it:

Waiver of strict performance may be inferred from the circumstances or course of dealings between the parties. . . . A waiver may result from one party's express or implied assent to the continued performance of the other party without objection to the delay. . . . In addition, express representations by one party that strict compliance with a deadline will not be required, or other actions that reasonably lead the other party to believe such, will also cause an effective waiver of a time provision in a contract. Finally, a party may effectively waive a breach of agreement by the other party by continuing to insist on performance by the other party even after the breach. . . . In our case, Seismic waived the contract provision as to time of performance through its failure to object to the delay, its failure to reject the software programs when delivered, and its subsequent conduct in both assenting to the delay and requesting additional word from Digital on the completed programs.

Seismic & Digital Concepts, Inc. v. Digital Resources Corp., 590 S.W.2d 718, 721 (Tex. Civ. App. 1979).

For a systematic treatment of situations where claims, defenses and other rights can be lost by relinquishment or preclusion, see E. Allan Farnsworth, Changing Your Mind: The Law of Regretted Decisions 127–202 (1998).

2. INTRODUCTION TO AFFIRMATIVE REMEDIES

If a party proves breach, what affirmative remedy should the court provide? One can imagine all sorts of possible answers, from requiring a simple apology to tossing the breaching party in jail. In practice, U.S. courts generally find themselves choosing between two options: compensatory damages and specific performance.

How should lawmakers choose between these two remedies? In some cases, practical considerations weigh in favor of one or another. If performance is no longer possible or valuable to the nonbreaching party, the obvious choice is a damage award. If performance is still possible and a money award will not make the plaintiff whole—say because a substitute performance is not available on the market or the defendant is damage proof—specific performance might be in order. Section 4 of this chapter considers the rules governing these and other situations.

This section considers the remedial choice more generally, focusing on economic considerations. The choice can be broken into two distinct questions. First, if the remedy is money damages, what should the measure of damages be? In the last half of the twentieth century, economically oriented scholars argued for the expectation measure based on the theory of efficient breach. Second, how should courts choose between damages and specific performance? From an economic perspective, the answer to this question turns on relative transaction costs.

The efficiency theory has clearly influenced judicial understanding of contract remedies. And as discussed below, the efficient breach theory has expressly been adopted by some courts. But remember that the theory of efficient breach is not the rule, but an explanation of the rule. And though it has been enormously influential, it is neither the only possible explanation of the remedial rules we have nor immune from criticism.

<h1 style="text-align:center">Northern Indiana Public Service Co.
v. Carbon County Coal Co.</h1>

United States Court of Appeals, Seventh Circuit, 1986.
799 F.2d 265.

■ POSNER, CIRCUIT JUDGE. [In 1978, NIPSCO and Carbon County entered a 20-year contract under which Carbon County, the owner and operator of a coal mine in Wyoming, agreed to sell and NIPSCO agreed to buy approximately 1.5 million tons of coal every year for 20 years, at a price of $24 a ton, subject to upward escalation. By 1985, the contract price had escalated to $44 per ton, but, because of changed economic circumstances, NIPSCO was able to buy electricity at prices below the cost of generation. Under pressure from the Indiana Public Service Commission, NIPSCO sought a declaratory judgment that it was excused from the contract. Carbon County counterclaimed for breach of contract and moved for a preliminary injunction and specific performance. The district court granted the preliminary injunction but, after a jury verdict for Carbon County in the amount of $181 million, the court denied specific performance. NIPSCO, inter alia, appealed from the verdict and Carbon County appealed from the denial of specific performance. The court, speaking through Judge Posner, first affirmed the verdict against NIPSCO.]

* * *

This completes our consideration of NIPSCO's attack on the damages judgment and we turn to Carbon County's cross-appeal, which seeks specific performance in lieu of the damages it got. Carbon County's counsel virtually abandoned the cross-appeal at oral argument, noting that the mine was closed and could not be reopened immediately—so that if specific performance (i.e., NIPSCO's resuming taking the coal) was ordered, Carbon County would not be able to resume its obligations under the contract without some grace period. In any event the request for specific performance has no merit. Like other equitable remedies, specific performance is available only if damages are not an adequate remedy, Farnsworth, supra, § 12.6, and there is no reason to suppose them inadequate here. The loss to Carbon County from the breach of contract is simply the difference between (1) the contract price (as escalated over the life of the contract in accordance with the contract's escalator provisions) times quantity, and (2) the cost of mining the coal over the life of the contract. Carbon County does not even argue that $181 million is not a reasonable estimate of the present value of the difference. Its complaint is that although the money will make the owners of Carbon County whole it will do nothing for the miners who have lost their jobs because the mine is closed and the satellite businesses that have closed for the same reason. Only specific performance will help them.

But since they are not parties to the contract their losses are irrelevant. Indeed, specific performance would be improper as well as unnecessary here, because it would force the continuation of production that has become uneconomical. Cf. Farnsworth, supra, at 817–18. No one wants coal from Carbon County's mine. With the collapse of oil prices, which has depressed the price of substitute fuels as well, this coal costs far more to get out of the ground than it is worth in the market. Continuing to produce it, under compulsion of an order for specific performance, would impose costs on society greater than the benefits. NIPSCO's breach, though it gave Carbon County a right to damages, was an efficient breach in the sense that it brought to a halt a production process that was no longer cost-justified. . . . The reason why NIPSCO must pay Carbon County's loss is not that it should have continued buying coal it didn't need but that the contract assigned to NIPSCO the risk of market changes that made continued deliveries uneconomical. The judgment for damages is the method by which that risk is being fixed on NIPSCO in accordance with its undertakings.

With continued production uneconomical, it is unlikely that an order of specific performance, if made, would ever actually be implemented. If, as a finding that the breach was efficient implies, the cost of a substitute supply (whether of coal, or of electricity) to NIPSCO is less than the cost of producing coal from Carbon County's mine, NIPSCO and Carbon County can both be made better off by negotiating a cancellation of the contract and with it a dissolution of the order of specific performance. Suppose, by way of example, that Carbon County's coal costs $20 a ton to produce, that the contract price is $40, and that NIPSCO can buy coal elsewhere for $10. Then Carbon County would be making a profit of only $20 on each ton it sold to NIPSCO ($40–$20), while NIPSCO would be losing $30 on each ton it bought from Carbon County ($40–$10). Hence by offering Carbon County more than contract damages (i.e., more than Carbon County's lost profits), NIPSCO could induce Carbon County to discharge the contract and release NIPSCO to buy cheaper coal. For example, at $25, both parties would be better off than under specific performance, where Carbon County gains only $20 but NIPSCO loses $30. Probably, therefore, Carbon County is seeking specific performance in order to have bargaining leverage with NIPSCO, and we can think of no reason why the law should give it such leverage. We add that if Carbon County obtained and enforced an order for specific performance this would mean that society was spending $20 (in our hypothetical example) to produce coal that could be gotten elsewhere for $10—a waste of scarce resources.

As for possible hardships to workers and merchants in Hanna, Wyoming, where Carbon County's coal mine is located, we point out that none of these people were parties to the contract with NIPSCO or third-party beneficiaries. They have no legal interest in the contract. Cf. Local 1330, United Steel Workers of America v. United States Steel Corp., 631 F.2d 1264, 1279–82 (6th Cir. 1980); Serrano v. Jones & Laughlin Steel Co., 790 F.2d 1279, 1289 (6th Cir. 1986). Of course the consequences to third parties of granting an injunctive remedy, such as specific performance, must be considered, and in some cases may require that the remedy be withheld. . . . The frequent references to "public interest" as a factor in the grant or denial of a preliminary injunction invariably are references to third-party effects. . . . But even though the formal statement of the judicial obligation to consider such effects extends to orders denying as well as granting injunctive relief, . . . the actuality is somewhat different: when the question is whether third parties would be injured by an order denying an injunction, always they are persons having a legally recognized interest in the lawsuit, so that the issue really is the adequacy of relief if the injunction is denied. In Mississippi Power & Light Co. v. United Gas Pipe Line Co., 760 F.2d 618 (5th Cir. 1985), for example, a public utility sought a preliminary injunction against alleged overcharges by a supplier. If the injunction was denied and later the utility got damages, its customers would be entitled to refunds; but for a variety of reasons explained in the opinion, refunds would not fully protect the customers' interests. The customers were the real parties in interest on the plaintiff side of the case, and their interests had therefore to be taken into account in deciding whether there would be irreparable harm (and how much) if the preliminary injunction was denied. See id. at 623–26. Carbon County does not stand in a representative relation to the workers and businesses of Hanna, Wyoming. Treating them as real parties in interest would evade the limitations on the concept of a third-party beneficiary and would place the promisor under obligations potentially far heavier than it had thought it was accepting when it signed the contract. Indeed, if we are right that an order of specific performance would probably not be carried out—that instead NIPSCO would pay an additional sum of money to Carbon County for an agreement not to enforce the order—it becomes transparent that granting specific performance would make NIPSCO liable in money damages for harms to nonparties to the contract, and it did not assume such liability by signing the contract. . . .

Moreover, the workers and merchants in Hanna assumed the risk that the coal mine would have to close down if it turned out to be uneconomical. The contract with NIPSCO did not guarantee that the mine would operate throughout the life of the contract but only protected the owners of Carbon County against the financial consequences to them of a breach. As Carbon County itself emphasizes in its brief, the contract was a product of the international oil cartel, which by forcing up the price of substitute fuels such as coal made costly coal-mining operations economically attractive. The OPEC cartel is not a source of vested rights to produce substitute fuels at inflated prices.

* * *

NOTES

Is Judge Posner right that Carbon County might have sought specific performance only as a means to secure a payment from NIPSCO that is larger than contract damages would be? Is it equitable to allow a nonbreaching plaintiff to use specific performance as a threat to extract supra-compensatory payment? Is it efficient? See Ian Ayres and Kristin Madison, *Threatening Inefficient Performance of Injunctions and Contracts*, 148 U. Pa. L. Rev. 45 (1999).

Comment: The Efficient Breach Theory

In *NIPSCO v. Carbon County Coal*, Judge Posner suggests that awarding the nonbreaching party expectation damages would ensure an efficient outcome. The idea of efficient breach was first proposed in 1970 by Robert Birmingham:

> Repudiation of the obligations should be encouraged where the promisor is able to profit from his default after placing his promisee in as good a position as he would have occupied had performance been rendered. Failure to honor an agreement under these circumstances is a movement toward Pareto optimality. "Once the costs of carrying out market transactions are taken into account it is clear that such a rearrangement of rights will only be undertaken when the increase in the value of production consequent upon the rearrangement is greater than the costs which would be involved in bringing it about." [Coase, *The Problem of Social Costs*, 2 J. Law & Econ. 15–16 (1960).] To penalize such adjustments through overcompensation of the innocent party is to discourage efficient allocation of resources.

Robert L. Birmingham, *Breach of Contract, Damage Measures, and Economic Efficiency*, 24 Rutgers L. Rev. 273, 284 (1970).

One of us has described the core idea of the theory as follows:

> The simple theory [of efficient breach] purports to solve a puzzle posed by Lon Fuller and William Perdue in their 1936 article, *e Reliance Interest in Contract Damages: 1*.[1] Fuller and Perdue famously distinguish three "interests" of the nonbreaching party in obtaining relief, each corresponding to a

---

[1] L.L. Fuller & William M. Perdue, Jr., *The Reliance Interest in Contract Damages: 1*, 46 Yale L.J. 52 (1936).

damage measure. In a contract between A and B that A breaches, protecting B's restitution interest requires the return of any benefit that B directly provided A. Protecting B's reliance interest requires compensating B for any change in B's position based on the expectation of A's performance, thereby putting B in the place B would have occupied had B not entered the contract. Protecting B's expectation interest requires providing B its expected gains from the transaction, putting B in the position B would have occupied had A performed the contract. The expectation measure typically exceeds the reliance measure, which is often greater than the restitution measure. Fuller and Perdue argue that the reasons for providing restitution and reliance-based damages are easy enough to intuit. The reasons for expectation damages not so much. "[T]he promisee who has actually relied on the promise, even though he may not thereby have enriched the promisor, certainly presents a more pressing case for relief than the promisee who merely demands satisfaction for his disappointment in not getting what was promised him."[2] The puzzle is why the law should " 'compensate' the plaintiff by giving him something he never had."[3]

The simple theory of efficient breach has an answer: the expectation remedy maximizes social welfare. * * * Of the three measures, only expectation damages provide an incentive to perform if and only if performance is efficient. The reason can be explained with an example.

Suppose on January 1, Seller enters into a contract to sell goods to Buyer. Seller is to provide Buyer 100 units on or before July 1. Buyer is to pay $10 per unit, or $1,000 total, due 30 days after delivery. Seller is going to manufacture the goods in question, and expects to spend $8 per unit on production, shipment, and overhead. Buyer is going to use the units to manufacture other goods. On top of its $10 per unit payment to Seller, Buyer's costs of production, resale, and overhead are $6 per unit, and it will sell its product for $18 per unit. For each unit, therefore, the transaction generates $4 in new value: Buyer and Seller together invest a net $14 to produce a product worth $18 to willing purchasers. Out of this $4 surplus, Buyer takes $2 and Seller takes $2. If their relative bargaining strength were different, Seller and Buyer might divide that surplus differently. At a price of $9 per unit, Seller would take $1 and buyer $3; at a price of $11, the division would go the other way. The limiting factors are that Seller is unwilling to sell for

---

[2]   *Id.* at 56.

[3]   *Id.* at 52–3.

less than $8, and buyer to buy for more than $12. Neither will agree to a losing deal.

Although the transaction looks like it will create value when the parties agree to it, things could change before the time of performance. A good deal in January might look much less attractive in April. The efficient breach theory considers two types of changes: good news and bad news.

The more common scenario in the literature involves good news. Suppose on April 1, Third Party contacts Seller and offers to purchase 100 units for $1,300, or $13 per unit. Third Party is a competitor of Buyer and is willing to pay more for the goods because it has a new, less expensive production method. Whereas Buyer's production costs are $6 per unit, Third Party's costs are $3. Seller does not have the capacity to produce more than 100 units and so can sell to Third Party only if it breaches with Buyer. To keep things simple, suppose on April 1, Buyer has not yet invested any resources in the transaction and if Seller breaches, Buyer will not be able to get replacement goods elsewhere.

Sale to Third Party is more efficient than sale to Buyer. The transaction between Seller and Buyer creates $4 of value for each unit sold ($18 market price − $8 Seller costs − $6 Buyer costs). Sale to Third Party, on the contrary, will produce $7 per unit ($18 market price − $8 Seller costs − $3 Third Party costs). If we want to maximize social welfare (as measured in dollars), we want Seller to breach the contract with Buyer and sell to Third Party.

If Seller is a purely self-interested rational utility maximizer and has no other reason to perform or breach, expectation damages produce that result. The expectation measure requires Seller to pay Buyer for the profits Buyer would have earned from the transaction plus any costs Buyer has already incurred. On the facts, this means a transfer from Seller to Buyer of $2 per unit. If Seller sells to Third Party, Seller earns $5 per unit ($13 price − $8 production costs). Seller will therefore choose to breach, pay Buyer the $2 per unit in damages, and emerge with $3 per unit net profit, one dollar more than Seller would have made by performing.

Observe that if Third Party had offered Seller only $11 per unit, Seller would have chosen to perform, even though Third Party's offer is higher than the contract price. At $11, Seller initially earns $3 per unit. But after paying Buyer $2 per unit in damages, Seller emerges with only $1 net profit, making performance the preferred option. This too is the right result. Third Party's $11 offer does not indicate that Third Party values the goods more than Buyer does. Third Party might, for example, have the same production costs as Buyer's, but be willing to take $1 pro t rather than Buyer's $2. Only if Third Party offers more than $12 per unit do we know that Third Party is the more efficient recipient of the goods. More generally, in a contract between A and B, the expectation measure gives A a reason to breach in favor of C's offer only if C's price indicates that C values A's performance more than B values that performance.

* * *

Expectation damages give efficient incentives in all the scenarios for the same reason: In a contract between A and B, the social gain from A's performance is the sum of A and B's expected profits. If there is no legal remedy, when A decides between performance and breach A considers only its own expected profits. Expectation damages force A to internalize the effect of breach on B's expected profits. The measure thereby forces A to weigh all the welfare effects of performance against all the welfare effects of breach. A will perform when performance creates more value and will breach when breach creates more value. As Robert Cooter and Melvin Eisenberg put the point, "expectation damages place on the promisor the promisee's loss of his share of the contract's value in the event of breach, and thereby sweep that loss into the promisor's calculus of self-interest."[4]

We now have an answer to Fuller and Perdue's puzzle. Only expectation dam- ages give parties efficient incentives. Because neither the reliance nor the restitution measure incorporates the gains of trade, both are typically lower than the expectation measure. Under either, therefore, a self-interested rational party will sometimes breach when performance would be more efficient. Supercompensatory remedies, such as disgorgement or punitive damages, are similarly inefficient. They give a party too much reason to perform and will sometimes result in performance when breach would be more efficient. Only the expectation remedy gives parties an incentive to perform if and only if performance maximizes social welfare.

Gregory Klass, *Efficient Breach, in* Philosophical Foundations of Contract Law 362, 363–66 (G. Klass, G. Letsas & P. Saprai, eds., 2014).

In the decades since it was introduced, the theory of efficient breach has worked its way into judicial thinking about contract remedies. The Second Restatement gives the theory a nod. *Chapter 16: Introductory Note, in* Restatement (Second) of Contracts 99–100 (1983). And several state high courts have expressed their approval. See, e.g., Bhole, Inc. v.

---

[4] Robert Cooter & Melvin Aron Eisenberg, *Damages for Breach of Contract*, 73 Calif. L. Rev. 1432, 1463 (1985).

Shore Investments, Inc., 67 A.3d 444, 453 n.39. (Del. 2013) ("Delaware recognizes this principle of efficient breach."); Grynberg v. Citation Oil & Gas Corp., 573 N.W.2d 493, 500 (S.D. 1997) ("[O]ur free market system allows economically efficient breaches of contract."); Story v. City of Bozeman, 242 Mont. 436, 448 (1990) ("Parties have traditionally been free to breach their contract and pay contract damages whenever performance was not economically efficient."); L.L. Cole & Son, Inc. v. Hickman, 282 Ark. 6, 8 (1984) ("The law has long recognized the view that a contracting party has the option to breach a contract and pay damages if it is more efficient to do so.").

That said, the efficient breach theory has also been subject to significant moral and economic criticism. Moral criticisms are generally based on the thought that breach, whether efficient or not, is morally wrong, and the law should not be in the business of encouraging moral wrongs. Thus Seana Shiffrin argues:

> A virtuous agent cannot believe both that a promise be binding even if a better opportunity comes along that competes with fulfilling the promise *and* that breach of contract, involving breach of promise, is, all things considered, morally justified merely because it leads to (even only marginally) greater economic welfare.

The Divergence of Contract and Promise, 120 Harv. L. Rev. 708, 731 (2007). See also Gregory Klass, *The Rules of the Game and the Morality of Efficient Breach*, 29 Yale J. L. & Hum. 71 (2017) (considering these and other moral criticisms of the theory). Economic criticisms include the following:

> [The theory] fails to recognize that some breaches are not only inefficient, but opportunistic. It does not provide a defense of expectation damages as against other possibly equally efficient remedies. It focuses on the single perform-or-breach decision, when in fact remedial rules provide incentives to act more or less efficiently across the whole of a transaction. And it ignores other functions remedies serve, such as risk allocation and signaling.

Klass, *Efficient Breach* at 370.

Walgreen Co. v. Sara Creek Property Co.

United States Court of Appeals, Seventh Circuit, 1992.
966 F.2d 273.

■ POSNER, CIRCUIT JUDGE. This appeal from the grant of a permanent injunction raises fundamental issues concerning the propriety of injunctive relief. . . . The essential facts are simple. Walgreen has operated a pharmacy in the Southgate Mall in Milwaukee since its opening in 1951. Its current lease, signed in 1971 and carrying a 30-year, 6-month term, contains, as had the only previous lease, a clause in which the landlord, Sara Creek, promises not to lease space in the mall to anyone else who wants to operate a pharmacy or a store containing a pharmacy. . . .

In 1990, fearful that its largest tenant—what in real estate parlance is called the "anchor tenant"—having gone broke was about to close its store, Sara Creek informed Walgreen that it intended to buy out the anchor tenant and install in its place a discount store operated by Phar-Mor Corporation, a "deep discount" chain, rather than, like Walgreen, just a "discount" chain. Phar-Mor's store would occupy 100,000 square feet, of which 12,000 would be occupied by a pharmacy the same size as Walgreen's. The entrances to the two stores would be within a couple of hundred feet of each other.

Walgreen filed this diversity suit for breach of contract against Sara Creek and Phar-Mor and asked for an injunction against Sara Creek's letting the anchor premises to Phar-Mor. After an evidentiary hearing, the judge found a breach of Walgreen's lease and entered a permanent injunction against Sara Creek's letting the anchor tenant premises to Phar-Mor until the expiration of Walgreen's lease. He did this over the defendants' objection that Walgreen had failed to show that its remedy at law—damages—for the breach of the exclusivity clause was inadequate. Sara Creek had put on an expert witness who testified that Walgreen's damages could be readily estimated, and Walgreen had countered with evidence from its employees that its damages would be very difficult to compute, among other reasons because they included intangibles such as loss of goodwill.

Sara Creek reminds us that damages are the norm in breach of contract as in other cases. Many breaches, it points out, are "efficient" in the sense that they allow resources to be moved into a more valuable use. . . . Perhaps this is one—the value of Phar-Mor's occupancy of the anchor premises may exceed the cost to Walgreen of facing increased competition. If so, society will be better off if Walgreen is paid its damages, equal to that cost, and Phar-Mor is allowed to move in rather than being kept out by an injunction. That is why injunctions are not granted as a matter of course, but only when the plaintiff's damages remedy is inadequate. Northern Indiana Public Service Co. v. Carbon County Coal Co., 799 F.2d 265, 279 (7th Cir. 1986). Walgreen's is not, Sara Creek argues; the projection of business losses due to increased competition is a routine exercise in calculation. Damages representing either the present value of lost future profits or (what should be the equivalent, Carusos v. Briarcliff, Inc., 76 Ga.App. 346, 351–52 (1947)) the diminution in the value of the leasehold have either been awarded or deemed the proper remedy in a number of reported cases for breach of an exclusivity clause in a shopping-center lease. . . . Why, Sara Creek asks, should they not be adequate here?

Sara Creek makes a beguiling argument that contains much truth, but we do not think it should carry the day. For if, as just noted, damages have been awarded in some cases of breach of an exclusivity clause in a shopping-center lease, injunctions have been issued in others. . . . The choice between remedies requires a balancing of the costs and benefits of the alternatives. . . . The task of striking the balance is for the trial judge, subject to deferential appellate review in recognition of its particularistic, judgmental, fact-bound character. . . .

The plaintiff who seeks an injunction has the burden of persuasion—damages are the norm, so the plaintiff must show why his case is abnormal. But when, as in this case, the issue is whether to grant a permanent injunction, not whether to grant a temporary one, the burden is to show that damages are inadequate, not that the denial of the injunction will work irreparable harm. "Irreparable" in the injunction context means not rectifiable by the entry of a final judgment. . . .

The benefits of substituting an injunction for damages are twofold. First, it shifts the burden of determining the cost of the defendant's conduct from the court to the parties. If it is true that Walgreen's damages are smaller than the gain to Sara Creek from allowing a second pharmacy into the shopping mall, then there must be a price for dissolving the injunction that will make both parties better off. Thus, the effect of upholding the injunction would be to substitute for the costly processes of forensic fact determination the less costly processes of private negotiation. Second, a premise of our free-market system, and the lesson of experience here and abroad as well, is that prices and costs are more accurately determined by the market than by government. A battle of experts is a less reliable method of determining the actual cost to Walgreen of facing new competition than negotiations between Walgreen and Sara Creek over the price at which Walgreen would feel adequately compensated for having to face that competition.

That is the benefit side of injunctive relief but there is a cost side as well. Many injunctions require continuing supervision by the court, and that is costly. . . . A more subtle cost of injunctive relief arises from the situation that economists call "bilateral monopoly," in which two parties can deal only with each other: the situation that an injunction creates. . . . The sole seller of widgets selling to the sole buyer of that product would be an example. But so will be the situation confronting Walgreen and Sara Creek if the injunction is upheld. Walgreen can "sell" its injunctive right only to Sara Creek, and Sara Creek can "buy" Walgreen's surrender of its right to enjoin the leasing of the anchor tenant's space to Phar-Mor only from Walgreen. The lack of alternatives in bilateral monopoly creates a bargaining range, and the costs of negotiating to a point within that range may be high. Suppose the cost to Walgreen of facing the competition of Phar-Mor at the Southgate Mall would be $1 million, and the benefit to Sara Creek of leasing to Phar-Mor would be $2 million. Then at any price between those figures for a waiver of Walgreen's injunctive right both parties would be better off, and we expect parties to bargain around a judicial assignment of legal rights if the assignment is inefficient. R.H. Coase, *The Problem of Social Cost*, 3 J. Law & Econ. 1 (1960). But each of the parties would like to engross as much of the bargaining range as possible—Walgreen to press the price toward $2 million, Sara Creek to depress it toward $1 million. With so much at stake, both parties will have an incentive to devote substantial resources of time and money to the negotiation process. The process may even break down, if one or both parties want to create for future use a reputation as a hard bargainer; and if it does break down, the injunction will have brought about an inefficient result. All these are in one form or another costs of the injunctive process that can be avoided by substituting damages.

The costs and benefits of the damages remedy are the mirror of those of the injunctive remedy. The damages remedy avoids the cost of continuing supervision and third-party effects, and the cost of bilateral monopoly as well. It imposes costs of its own, however, in the form of diminished accuracy in the determination of value, on the one hand, and of the parties' expenditures on preparing and presenting evidence of damages, and the time of the court in evaluating the evidence, on the other.

The weighing up of all these costs and benefits is the analytical procedure that is or at least should be employed by a judge asked to enter a permanent injunction, with the understanding that if the balance is even the injunction should be withheld. The judge is not required to explicate every detail of the analysis and he did not do so here, but as long we are satisfied that his approach is broadly consistent with a proper analysis we shall affirm; and we are satisfied here. The determination of Walgreen's damages would have been costly in forensic resources and inescapably inaccurate. . . . The lease had ten years to run. So Walgreen would have had to project its sales revenues and costs over the next ten years, and then project the impact on those figures of Phar-Mor's competition, and then discount that impact to present value. All but the last step would have been fraught with uncertainty.

* * *

Damages are not always costly to compute, or difficult to compute accurately. In the standard case of a seller's breach of a contract for the sale of goods where the buyer covers by purchasing the same product in the market, damages are readily calculable by subtracting the contract price from the market price and multiplying by the quantity specified in the contract. But this is not such a case and here damages would be a costly and inaccurate remedy; and on the other side of the balance some of the costs of an injunction are absent and the cost that is present seems low. The injunction here, like one enforcing a covenant not to compete . . . is a simple negative injunction—Sara Creek is not to lease space in the Southgate Mall to Phar-Mor during the term of Walgreen's lease—and the costs of judicial supervision and enforcement should be negligible. There is no contention that the injunction will harm an unrepresented third party. It may harm Phar-Mor but that harm will be reflected in Sara Creek's offer to Walgreen to dissolve the injunction. (Anyway Phar-Mor is a party.) The injunction may also, it is true, harm potential customers of Phar-Mor—people who would prefer to shop at a deep-discount store than an ordinary discount store—but their preferences, too, are registered indirectly. The more business Phar-Mor would have, the more rent it will be willing to pay Sara Creek, and therefore the more Sara Creek will be willing to pay Walgreen to dissolve the injunction.

The only substantial cost of the injunction in this case is that it may set off a round of negotiations between the parties. In some cases, illustrated by Boomer v. Atlantic Cement Co., 26 N.Y.2d 219 (1970), this consideration alone would be enough to warrant the denial of injunctive relief. The defendant's factory was emitting cement dust that caused the plaintiffs harm monetized at less than $200,000, and the only way to abate the harm would have been to close down the factory, which had cost $45 million to build. An injunction against the nuisance could therefore have created a huge bargaining range (could, not would, because it is unclear what the current value of the factory was), and the costs of negotiating to a point within it might have been immense. If the market value of the factory was actually $45 million, the plaintiffs would be tempted to hold out for a price to dissolve the injunction in the tens of millions and the factory would be tempted to refuse to pay anything more than a few hundred thousand dollars. Negotiations would be unlikely to break down completely, given such a bargaining range, but they might well be protracted and costly. There is nothing so dramatic here. Sara Creek does not argue that it will have to close the mall if enjoined from leasing to Phar-Mor. Phar-Mor is not the only potential anchor tenant. Liza Danielle, Inc. v. Jamko, Inc., 408 So.2d 735, 740 (Fla.App. 1982), on which Sara Creek relies, presented the converse case where the grant of the injunction would have forced an existing tenant to close its store. The size of the bargaining range was also a factor in the denial of injunctive relief in Gitlitz v. Plankinton Building Properties, Inc., 228 Wis. 334, 339–40 (1938).

To summarize, the judge did not exceed the bounds of reasonable judgment in concluding that the costs (including forgone benefits) of the damages remedy would exceed the costs (including forgone benefits) of an injunction. We need not consider whether, as intimated by Walgreen, exclusivity clauses in shopping-center leases should be considered presumptively enforceable by injunctions. Although we have described the choice between legal and equitable remedies as one for case-by-case determination, the courts have sometimes picked out categories of case in which injunctive relief is made the norm. The best-known example is specific performance of contracts for the sale of real property. . . . The rule that specific performance will be ordered in such cases as a matter of course is a generalization of the considerations discussed above. Because of the absence of a fully liquid market in real property and the frequent presence of subjective values (many a homeowner, for example, would not sell his house for its market value), the calculation of damages is difficult; and since an order of specific performance to convey a piece of property does not create a continuing relation between the parties, the costs of supervision and enforcement if specific performance is ordered are slight. The exclusivity clause in Walgreen's lease relates to real estate, but we hesitate to suggest that every contract involving real estate should be enforceable as a matter of course by injunctions. Suppose Sara Creek had covenanted to keep the entrance to Walgreen's store free of ice and snow, and breached the covenant. An injunction would require continuing supervision, and it would be easy enough if the injunction were denied for Walgreen to hire its own ice and snow remover and charge the cost to Sara Creek. . . . On the other hand, injunctions to enforce exclusivity clauses are quite likely to be justifiable by just the considerations present here—damages are difficult to estimate with any accuracy and the injunction is a one-shot remedy requiring no continuing judicial involvement. So there is an argument for making injunctive relief presumptively appropriate in such cases, but we need not decide in this case how strong an argument.

AFFIRMED.

NOTES

(1) The theory of efficient breach is an explanation of the law's preference for expectation damages. What does Posner's opinion above say about the success of that theory? Might specific performance be equally efficient? See Alan Schwartz, *The Case for Specific Performance*, 89 Yale L.J. 271 (1979) (arguing on efficiency grounds for greater availability of specific performance).

(2) In *City Stores Co. v. Ammerman*, 266 F.Supp. 766 (D.D.C. 1967), the plaintiff obtained specific performance of defendant's agreement to grant a lease as a major tenant in a shopping center under construction despite the fact that numerous complex details were still to be agreed upon and that a great deal of supervision by the court would be required. The district court concluded that since "money damages would in no way compensate the plaintiff for loss of the right to participate in the shopping center enterprise and for the almost incalculable future advantages that might accrue to it as a result of extending its operations into the suburbs," equity required specific performance even though some supervision of both future construction and the terms of the lease would be required. In a *per curiam* affirmance, the Court of Appeals for the District of Columbia narrowed somewhat the district court's grounds for decision. The court stressed that specific performance was available because the obligation involved a commitment to lease in addition to construction and that the work was to be done on the defendant's land, making it impossible for the plaintiff to have the job done.

(3) "We do not imply that in all cases where a landlord has contracted to construct a building on its property, the landlord will be required to perform on the ground that interests in land are always specifically

enforceable. If the record shows that at the time the landlord breached its contract, other properties were available to the tenant that offered business advantages comparable to those offered by the landlord's property—except for differences in rent and overhead costs for which an adequate remedy at law exists—a Chancellor might properly deny the tenant's prayer for specific performance. Such a denial might be particularly appropriate in a case where the tenant has failed to lease comparable property that he knew or should have known was available, and where the costs arising from the delay in construction are such that the landlord will no longer get his part of the bargain if the lease is specifically enforced. A plaintiff seeking equitable relief must have acted in good faith; and if the court of equity finds that a tenant could have reasonably protected his interests but failed to do so, relief may be withheld. In the present case, however, the Chancellor made no such findings, and on appeal, Wells Fargo has not raised the issue of Easton's good faith." Easton Theatres v. Wells Fargo Land & Mortg., 265 Pa.Super. 334, 356 (1979).

Comment: Calabresi and Melamed's Cathedral

In an immensely important article, Guido Calabresi (now a Senior Judge on the Second Circuit of the United States Court of Appeals) and Doug Melamed (former head of the Justice Department's antitrust division) pointed out that legal entitlements tend to be protected in one of two distinctive ways. Guido Calabresi and A. Douglas Melamed, *Property Rules, Liability Rules, and Inalienability: One View of the Cathedral*, 85 Harv. L. Rev. 1089 (1972). Some entitlements are protected by strong "property rules" which attempt to deter third parties from non-consensually taking the entitlement. Property rule protections are punitive in nature—often involving the threat of jail or supra-compensatory, punitive fines. By contrast, other entitlements are protected by weaker "liability rules" which attempt to compensate an entitlement holder for the loss of an entitlement that is non-consensually taken. Property rules are designed for deterrence (of potential takers); liability rules are designed for compensation (of potential takees). Intentionally take my car and the criminal law sends you to jail, but if you negligently destroy my car, the law of torts says you merely have to compensate me.

Calabresi and Melamed went on to suggest that property rule protections were likely to be more efficient when "transaction costs" were low and that liability rules were more likely to be efficient when transaction costs were high. If parties can easily contract (agree to consensually transfer an entitlement), we should protect the entitlement with a strong property rule to induce them to expressly contract. But liability rules make more sense when the parties don't have an opportunity to contract—for example, in the tort setting where it would be infeasible to contract with the myriad people who might hit your car.

Curiously, Calabresi and Melamed, who surveyed vast portions of law, did not analyze how *contractual* entitlements should be protected. If

Calabresi contracts to sing at Melamed's wedding, Melamed has a contractual entitlement to Calabresi's performance. How should Melamed's entitlement be protected?

Calabresi and Melamed's theory might suggest that contractual entitlements should be protected by property rules—such as court orders of specific performance (perform or go to jail). After all, the parties were able to contract initially. Calabresi should be able to *renegotiate* if he doesn't want to perform. The singing Calabresi could buy back Melamed's contractual entitlement to hear Calabresi sing. But as emphasized above, contract law normally does not protect contractual entitlements with specific performance. Instead, the normal remedy is a liability-rule protection: expectation damages.[5]

Still, there are several instances where contractual entitlements are protected by property rules. The exceptional cases where breach gives rise to punitive damages are an obvious example. But also stiffer monetary damages that might deter a promisor from breaching in the first place have a property-rule quality. For example, in *Jacob & Youngs v. Kent,* the cost-of-replacement measure would have given future sellers strong incentives to perform. More generally, the "cost of performance" measure which measures expectation damages by how much the promisor would have to pay to perform the promise will tend to deter the promisor from breaching. Why breach if it doesn't save you any money?

Comment: Coase

The second central contribution of law and economics to contractual analysis is Ronald Coase's *The Problem of Social Cost*, 3 J. Law & Econ. 1 (1960) (the most cited article in legal academics!). The "Coase Theorem" says that in a world without transaction costs, the choice of legal rules would not affect efficiency—because private parties would always bargain their way to optimal behavior.[6] This suggests that if renegotiation were costless, property rules and liability rule protections would be equally efficient.

Oliver Wendell Holmes famously reoriented contract law toward a dyadic conception of contractual duties. For Holmes, a contractual promise was not a sacred duty that simply had to be performed. Rather, a contractual promise was merely the duty to perform or to pay (compensatory) damages. (Or in Calabresian terminology, the promisee's entitlement is protected only by a liability rule.)

---

[5]   Maybe this is because it is easier to contract initially (when there are many potential singers and weddings) than it is to renegotiate (when there is only one potential buyer and seller).

[6]   The Coase theorem has generated a huge literature—showing inter alia that the predicted effect will only hold true if the potential bargainers have sufficient information and wealth to bargain their way to the optimum.

But the Coase theorem invites a "triadic" conception of promise. For Coase a promise is a duty to (i) perform; (ii) pay damages; or (iii) renegotiate your way out of performance.

Imagine, for example, that Ayres and Klass contract in a bizarre jurisdiction that imposes "property rule" damages that are twenty times the contract price. If Ayres has promised to paint Klass's picture by the end of the year for $1,000, and Speidel comes along and offers Ayres $10,000 to paint Speidel's picture instead, the prospect of huge damages would normally deter Ayres from breaching the initial contract. But the Coase Theorem suggests that Ayres will have an incentive to approach Klass and try to buy his way out of the contract. The Coase theorem suggests that we don't have to worry about too few breaches when damages are high, because promisors will "bribe" their way out of having to perform.[7] Does efficient breach theory survive if the Coase theorem holds?

3. DAMAGES

We now turn to the rules governing the recovery of money damages. After reviewing some basic principles, we address special issues that arise in measuring damages for breach by the seller, issues that arise in measuring damages for breach by the buyer, the sometimes thorny problem of divisibility, and finally, limitations on recovery for mental distress and the rule that punitive damages are generally not recoverable. In reading through these principles, think about how they might interact with the theory of efficient breach.

(A) BASIC PRINCIPLES

A nonbreaching party's losses can generally be divided into three categories: direct, consequential, and incidental. Suppose Smirgo has agreed to sell Bisko two ovens for $30,000, but delivers only one. If the market value of each oven is $15,000, Bisko's *direct loss* is $15,000—the difference in value between the performance promised and the performance received. (If Bisko has not yet paid the price, Bisko might recover for this loss simply by withholding payment.) Suppose also that Bisko is a commercial baker, and was planning to use the ovens to expand its business. With the one oven it can net an extra $500/week; with two it would have increased its profits by $1,000/week. Bisko's inability to make the additional $500 in profits is a *consequential loss*—it is a downstream consequence of Smirgo's breach. Finally, suppose in the exercise of reasonable business judgment, Bisko sends its manager to purchase a replacement oven from Smirgo's competitor. The travel and other costs of dealing with the breach qualify as *incidental* losses.

---

[7]   Similarly, we don't have to worry about too much breach when damages are low because promisees will bribe promisors not to breach.

In order to make Bisko whole, a damage award will need to cover Bisko's direct, consequential and incidental losses. But as we shall see, the law sets several limits on such recovery. Bisko's ability to recover depends on five questions: (1) Were the losses a foreseeable consequence of the breach at the time of contracting? (2) Could Bisko have reasonably mitigated, or avoided, the losses? (3) Can Bisko prove its losses, such as lost profits, with reasonable certainty? (4) If losses are too speculative, can Bisko recover the reliance expenditures as an alternative? (5) Can Bisko recover both lost profits and reliance expenditures?

(1) BASELINES

Alice Sullivan v. James O'Connor

Supreme Judicial Court of Massachusetts, 1973.
Supra at 29.

Comment: Reliance Damages or Restitution in Losing Contracts

As we have already observed, because parties generally enter into contracts with the expectation that they will come out ahead, the expectation measure of damages is typically greater than the reliance measure. Because restitution measures only one form of reliance—the provision of a benefit pursuant to the contract—the full reliance measure often exceeds the restitution measure. Why, then, would the successful plaintiff want anything other than the expectation remedy?

One possible reason is that it can be easier to prove the reliance amount, which might involve only out-of-pocket costs, than it is to prove the expectation amount, which turns on a counterfactual hypothetical: what the nonbreaching party *would* have earned, *had* the breaching party performed. See, e.g., United States v. Behan, 110 U.S. 338 (1884); Lon L. Fuller & William Perdue, *The Reliance Interest in Contract Damages*, 46 Yale L.J. 52, 76–80 (1936).

Losing Contracts. But what if the defendant can prove that if it had completed performance the plaintiff would have suffered a loss? Suppose Owner enters into a contract with Contractor to build a house for a payment of $3,075, which owner repudiates after Contractor has incurred $2,500 of costs. Suppose also that Owner can prove that Contractor's total costs would have been $4,500. That is, Owner's breach has saved Contractor $2,000 in costs ($4,500 total − $2,500 expected) and a loss of $1,425 ($3,075 price − $4,500 cost). The contract turned out to be a losing one for Contractor. In these circumstances, Contractor is foreclosed from recovering any profit, and the reliance expenditures should be adjusted downward in proportion to the projected loss. Consider *Bausch & Lomb Inc. v. Bressler*, 977 F.2d 720, 729 (2d Cir. 1992), where the court stated: "If the breaching party establishes that the plaintiff's losses upon full performance would have equaled or exceeded its reliance expenditures, the plaintiff will recover nothing under a reliance theory." See also L. Albert & Son v. Armstrong Rubber Co., 178 F.2d 182 (2d Cir. 1949) (buyer can recover reliance expenditures subject to seller proof that buyer would have lost money on full performance). Could allowing reliance damages to be reduced by the amount of projected loss be a way of implementing expectation damages?

Restitution Alternative. It is at this point that the "quantum meruit" or restitution alternative becomes relevant. If the plaintiff can cancel the contract for material breach and prove that the defendant has been benefited by part performance, can the plaintiff recover the value of that part performance without limitation by the contract price?

The plaintiff, as part of its election of remedies under Section 373 of the Restatement (Second), is "entitled to restitution for any benefit he has conferred" on a party who commits a "total" breach "by way of part performance or reliance." This principle was embraced by the U.S. Supreme Court in *Mobil Oil Exploration v. United States*, 530 U.S. 604, 607–639 (2000). In *Mobil Oil*, the plaintiff had paid the United States $156 million in return for leases giving them the right to explore for and develop oil on public lands off the North Carolina coast. When the United States repudiated those leases (the main issue in the case), the plaintiff was entitled to recover the money paid as restitution. The Court concluded that the United States as a contracting party is "governed generally by the law applicable to contracts between private individuals" and endorsed the Restatement as a reflection "of the principles of contract law that are applicable to this case."

In awarding restitution damages, a court might enter a judgment or order "requiring restoration of a specific thing to prevent unjust enrichment" or "awarding a sum of money to prevent unjust enrichment." Restatement (Second) § 345(c) & (d). But the plaintiff is entitled to restitution "only to the extent that he has conferred a benefit on the other party by way of part performance or reliance." Section 370. This is in sharp contrast to the expectation measure, or the "loss in the value to him of the other party's performance caused by its failure or deficiency." Section 347(a). When, then, is a contractor or seller of goods and services entitled to restitution as a remedy for breach by the other? Section 373(1) provides that "on a breach by nonperformance that gives rise to a claim for damages for total breach or on a repudiation, the injured party is entitled to restitution for any benefit that he has conferred on the other party by way of part performance or reliance."

Are there any limitations? Here is one: "The injured party has no right to restitution if he has performed all of his duties under the contract and no performance by the other party remains due other than payment of a definite sum of money for that performance." See John T. Brady & Co. v. City of Stamford, 220 Conn. 432, 443–451 (1991). The contract price is not otherwise a limitation, however, and, in theory at least, the plaintiff can recover the full amount of the benefit conferred even though it would have been a losing contract had there been no breach. See Section 373, Comment d. Another possible limitation, however, lies in the measure of the restitution interest. Section 371 provides:

> If a sum of money is awarded to protect a party's restitution interest, it may as justice requires be measured by either (a) the reasonable value to the other party of what he received in terms of what it would have cost him to obtain it from a person in the claimant's position, or (b) the extent to which the other party's property has been increased in value or his other interests advanced.

How is a court to exercise this choice when, say, the market price to have similar work done is $2,000 and the increase in value to the property is $1,500? One suggestion is that the court should award the smaller amount when the plaintiff is in breach. See Section 374 and Illustration 1 to Section 371. Another suggestion is that in making the choice in a losing contract, the court should "take account of standards of good faith and fair dealing during any negotiations leading up to the rupture of contractual relations." Restatement (Second) § 373, Comment d. The question is whether the plaintiff provoked a breach in a losing contract "in order to avoid having to perform." For a concise summary, see Joseph Perillo, *Restitution in the Second Restatement of Contracts,* 81 Colum. L. Rev. 37 (1982).

Sidney Bernstein v. Ronald Nemeyer

Supreme Court of Connecticut, 1990.
213 Conn. 665.

[Plaintiffs invested $1,050,000 as limited partners in a partnership formed to purchase and renovate two apartment complexes in Houston, Texas. The plaintiffs' objectives were capital growth and a tax shelter for assets previously acquired. As an inducement to invest, the defendants made a negative cash flow guaranty: They promised to lend to the partnership the amount by which defined operating and financing expenses exceeded the cash receipts from normal business operations. The guaranty was limited in time and provisions were made for the defendants to recover loans made from income or the proceeds of any sale of the complexes. The plaintiffs were informed of the risk of foreclosure in a weak real estate market.

Despite good faith efforts and after loans to the partnership of $3,000,000 under the guaranty, the defendants defaulted on their obligations to the financiers of the project. No further loans to the partnership were made. The mortgages on the property were ultimately foreclosed and both the plaintiffs and defendants lost their entire investment.

The plaintiffs sued for rescission of the contract and restitution of their investment. The trial court denied relief, concluding inter alia that the defendant's breach of the negative cash flow guaranty was not material. The trial court also found that the plaintiffs' losses resulted from a bad market rather than the defendant's breach and that, despite the breach, the plaintiffs had fully realized their tax advantages.

On appeal, the decision was affirmed. The court, speaking through Chief Justice Peters, first held that the defendant's breach was material. In short, the trial court had not given sufficient consideration to the fact that the plaintiffs had lost the substantial benefit of the bargain and that the defendant's breach was not curable.]

II

The conclusion that the defendants' nonperformance of the negative cash flow guaranty was a material breach of the partnership agreement does not, however, end our inquiry. It follows from an uncured material failure of performance that the other party to the contract is discharged from any further duty to render performances yet to be exchanged. . . . It does not follow that the party so discharged is automatically entitled to restitution rather than to a claim for damages. We must still determine whether, in the circumstances of this case, the trial court correctly rendered judgment in favor of the defendants because the plaintiffs have failed to prove a right to restitution of the payments that they made to the partnership. We conclude that the record sustains the judgment of the trial court on this alternate ground.

"When a court grants [the remedy of restitution] for breach, the party in breach is required to account for a benefit that has been conferred on him by the injured party. . . . In contrast to cases in which the court grants specific performance or awards damages as a remedy for breach, the effort is not to enforce the promise by protecting the injured party's expectation or reliance interest, but to prevent unjust enrichment of the party in breach by protecting the injured party's restitution interest. The objective is not to put the *injured* party in as good a position as he would have been in if the contract had been performed, nor even to put the injured party back in the position he would have been in if the contract had not been made; it is, rather, to put the party in breach back in the position he would have been in if the contract had not been made." (Emphasis in original.) E.A. Farnsworth, Contracts (1982) § 12.19, p. 905; 1 G. Palmer, The Law of Restitution (1978) § 4.1, p. 369; 3 Restatement (Second), Contracts §§ 344(c) and 370 (1981); . . .[11] When an injured party seeks an award of money to protect his restitutionary interest, any award "may as justice requires be measured by either

---

[11] Section 344 of the Restatement (Second) of Contracts provides in relevant part: "Judicial remedies under the rules stated in this Restatement serve to protect one or more of the following interests of a promisee. . . .

"(c) his 'restitution interest,' which is his interest in having restored to him any benefit that he has conferred on the other party."

Section 370 provides: "A party is entitled to restitution under the rules stated in this Restatement only to the extent that he has conferred a benefit on the other party by way of part performance or reliance."

(a) the reasonable value to the other party of what he received . . . or (b) the extent to which the other party's property has been increased in value or his other interests advanced." 3 Restatement (Second), Contracts § 371 (1981).

The principles of the law of restitution demonstrate that the defendants' non-performance of the negative cash loan guaranty, although a material breach of the partnership agreement, does not automatically and unconditionally entitle the plaintiffs to recover their investment in the partnership. The award of a restitutionary remedy for breach of contract depends upon a showing of what justice requires in the particular circumstances. . . . The decision to award a particular restitutionary remedy thus necessarily rests in the discretion of the court.

In the present litigation, the trial court could reasonably have concluded that the plaintiffs had failed to establish their right to the return of their investments. We have regularly held that it is a condition of rescission and restitution that the plaintiff offer, as nearly as possible, to place the other party in the same situation that existed prior to the execution of the contract. . . . The record in this case is entirely unclear about what efforts the plaintiffs made to tender back their partnership interests to the defendants before bringing this law suit. The record likewise contains no finding that the financial condition of the partnership, at the time the plaintiffs learned of the defendants' breach, was already so impoverished that a restitutionary tender would have been pointless.

Even more damaging to the plaintiffs' claim for restitution is the trial court's affirmative finding that the defendants "suffered a great loss of their own, about three million dollars, in attempting to satisfy their obligations under the contract and, specifically, the guaranty provision." This unchallenged finding of fact supports the conclusion that the plaintiffs could not have restored the defendants to their position prior to their execution of the partnership agreement. Further, it demonstrates that, despite the defendants' material breach of the partnership agreement, the defendants' property interests have not been "increased in value or [their] other interests advanced." 3 Restatement (Second), Contracts § 371(b) (1981). In short, the plaintiffs have not proven that the defendants have been unjustly enriched.

There is no error.

Glendale Federal Bank, FSB v. United States

United States Court of Appeals, Federal Circuit, 2004.
378 F.3d 1308, cert. denied, 544 U.S. 904 (2005).

■ PLAGER, SENIOR CIRCUIT JUDGE. [In response to a crisis in the savings and loan industry in the late 1980s, the United States, acting through the Federal Home Loan Bank Board (FHLBB) induced Glendale Federal

Bank and other healthy savings and loan associations (S&Ls) to take over and operate failed S&Ls. The benefit to the United States from these so-called "supervisory mergers" was to reduce the potential liability of the now insolvent Federal Savings and Loan Insurance Corporation (FSLIC). In exchange, the United States promised to treat the excess of the purchase price over the fair market value of the S&L (good will) as capital to meet reserve requirements and to amortize the capital over a 40-year period. In short, the FHLBB promised to give Glendale and other thrifts favorable regulatory treatment until the good will was amortized.

Subsequently, the United States repudiated the favorable accounting treatment given in the supervisory mergers and, in a totally revamped regulatory scheme, required Glendale and others to contribute new capital to maintain their reserve requirements. Some thrifts, including Glendale, were able to obtain the necessary capital. Other thrifts were liquidated. Many of the thrifts sued the United States claiming breach of contract. In *United States v. Winstar*, 518 U.S. 839 (1996), the Supreme Court held that the United States had breached the supervisory merger contracts and, without providing any guidance, remanded the cases to the Federal Court of Claims for the determination of damages.]

In this *Winstar*-series case, the United States appeals the award by the Court of Federal Claims, Senior Judge Loren Smith, to Glendale Federal Bank, FSB ("Glendale") of $381 million in "wounded bank" damages; Glendale cross-appeals the trial court's denial of another $527.5 million in reliance damages.

This is the second appeal on the damages question. The first appeal arose after a lengthy trial, which resulted in an award to Glendale of $909 million in restitution and "non-overlapping reliance damages." That trial itself was the result of a remand from an earlier consolidated appeal to this court in which the United States challenged the trial court's determinations regarding liability * * * [The liability determination was upheld in *United States v. Winstar*, supra.].

Liability in favor of the plaintiff thrifts having been established, the case was returned to the trial court for determination of damages owed to plaintiffs. The trial court found for the plaintiff Glendale in the amount of $909 million. The Government again appealed. The appeal was viewed as a test of the difficult issues of measuring damages in what became known as the *Winstar* cases, of which there were some 120 in the queue. On appeal and after a thorough review of the record and the various damage theories propounded by the parties and employed by the trial court, we concluded that the award of $909 million was not supportable, and vacated the judgment. Glendale Fed. Bank, FSB v. United States, 239 F.3d 1374 (Fed.Cir. 2001).

In the course of that first damages trial Glendale had sought "expectancy damages," the kind of damages often associated with lost profits. The trial court rejected that theory, concluding that Glendale's model for expectancy damages in the form of lost profits was implausible. We agreed. The theory did not fit comfortably with the history of these cases in the years following the breach; the problems of proof suggested that any award premised on expectancy damages would be too speculative to uphold.

Faced with a situation in which as a general proposition expectancy damages were ruled out, but with a legitimate claim by the thrift for a remedy, the trial court fashioned a restitution remedy based on the assumed risk that Glendale undertook when it acquired the salvaged bank (Broward Savings and Loan, a Florida thrift). The crux of the restitution component was the market value of the liabilities assumed by Glendale at the time of the transaction, which the trial court viewed as the value of the benefit conferred on the Government by Glendale. Glendale placed the proper amount of restitution damages at $798 million; the Government argued the proper amount was zero. The trial court sided with Glendale, and after adjusting the amount for the net gains it calculated Glendale had received from the transaction, awarded $510 million.

In our review we concluded that the restitution theory was basically flawed, because it was based on an assumption that the non-breaching party was entitled to the supposed gains received by the breaching party, when those gains in the context of these cases were both speculative and indeterminate. Accordingly we vacated the trial court's award of $510 million.

Recognizing that any damages award in these cases was necessarily a matter of post hoc reconstruction of a set of facts that may have never actually transpired, we did agree with the trial court that a viable theory on which damages could be based was a reliance theory. The trial court had considered reliance theory as a basis for an award, and had added specific reliance damages of $381 million to the total award granted plaintiff; these were denominated non-overlapping reliance damages, and identified as damages for post-breach events.

We noted that in reliance damages, the critical event is the breach itself. Consequently, damages resulting from that event may be the result of actions before or after the breach. But these damages had to be real, and reasonably ascertainable. We concluded that using reliance theory as the damages measure for the losses sustained by thrifts as a result of the Government's breach in FIRREA would provide a firmer and more rational basis than the alternative theories argued by the parties. We ended our opinion noting the enormous effort and dedication to these cases by Judge Smith, and suggested that much of the extensive record before the court—compiled over 150 days in trial and constituting some 20,000 pages—might lend itself to re-evaluation consistent with the guidance provided. Which leads to the second appeal, now before us.

2.

Following the first appeal on damages and our remand to the trial court for further consideration of the issues, Glendale moved in the trial court for entry of judgment, asking the court to reinstate the post-breach "wounded bank" portion of its earlier opinion and judgment, based on the prior findings of the court. This was the $381 million. Glendale claimed an additional $527 million, which it alleged to be the actual out-of-pocket loss suffered by Glendale in its Florida division. The total, with certain adjustments, was something over $862 million. In response to Glendale's motion, the Government did its numbers, and, surprise, came up with zero.

As noted at the beginning, Judge Smith awarded Glendale the $381 million, representing the previously-determined amount of Glendale's "wounded bank" damages, and other incidental reliance damages. The trial court rejected Glendale's claim for the additional $527 million, ruling that Glendale was not entitled to recover on the remainder of its claim because its reliance model failed to measure the actual losses sustained by it as a result of the Government's breach. The Government appeals the $381 million award; Glendale cross-appeals the denial of its claim for the additional $527 million.

In response to the trial court's award of $381 million in reliance damages, the Government notes that the Glendale-invented notion of "wounded bank" damages is basically ($335 million of the $381 million) the increase in the cost of funds Glendale allegedly incurred as a result of its having been wounded by the Government's breach. These losses were said to have occurred because three years after, and as a result of, the breach, Glendale fell out of capital compliance; depositors and others became nervous about placing funds with it; the bank was required to pay more interest to attract depositors; and it was required to pay higher fees for deposit insurance.

But, argues the Government, in proving that it would not have fallen out of capital compliance but for the breach, Glendale relied upon the same model it presented in support of its earlier claim for lost profits under the now-discredited expectancy damages theory. According to the Government, since Glendale did not offer any other evidence, it failed to prove that it would have remained in capital compliance in the absence of the breach. * * *

The trial court was unimpressed with the Government's arguments. With regard to the reinstatement of the "wounded bank" damages, the trial court was of the view that there was nothing in our remand instructions that required the court to revisit its prior findings and award of post-breach reliance damages. The trial court is correct; indeed, we invited the court to proceed on the basis of the record before it. However denominated, the focus of a recovery based on the reliance interest is the real costs incurred for capital and services that the thrift would not have incurred but for the contract and its subsequent breach. Whether in a given case this properly includes the higher costs to a thrift of conducting its general business after FIRREA—the "wounded bank" claim—is a matter of proof; if too speculative, it can and should be denied as the burden lies with the plaintiff to establish its damages. In the case before us, we are unpersuaded that the trial court's factual findings and conclusions regarding reliance damages, based on the earlier record, are clearly erroneous; the judgment in that regard is fully consistent with the law as we enunciated it. The award of reliance damages in the amount of $381 million is affirmed.

[The court affirmed the trial court's determination that Glendale had not suffered any compensable operating losses in its Florida venture. The court also rejected the Government's claim that it was entitled to an offset for alleged gains made by Glendale when it sold another division.]

In sum. A large part of the problem with which the trial court has had to wrestle has been finding a viable damages theory that fits the complex fact patterns of these cases, one that is fair to the damaged thrifts, but is based on real losses sustained so as not to overcompensate for the breach. The overall liability context of contract and breach in these cases is well established by the earlier litigation and appeals in this court and in the Supreme Court. Regarding the damages to be awarded, it was anticipated—and has proved to be the case—that the specific documentary and evidentiary bases on which damages would be based would vary from case to case.

Expectancy damages theory, based on lost profits, has proven itself impractical for these cases, and generally not susceptible to reasonable proof. We have not, however, barred as a matter of law the use of expectancy/lost profits theory, see Cal. Fed. Bank, FSB v. United States, 245 F.3d 1342, 1350 (Fed.Cir. 2001), but, given the speculative nature of such a damages claim, one that has yet to be successfully established in any *Winstar* case, . . . experience suggests that it is largely a waste of time and effort to attempt to prove such damages.[3]

Restitution as a generalized theory for recovery of assumed benefits to the Government, based on non-provable paper costs, has been rejected as explained above. . . . On the other hand, we have allowed restitution for the limited purpose of returning the acquiring thrift to the *status quo ante* when specific initial contributions to an acquired thrift have been established. * * * [We] recognized that when restitution damages are based on recovery of the expenditures of the non-breaching party in performance of the contract, the award can be viewed as a form of reliance damages.

Reliance damages, however, are supportable when based on actual losses that are fully proven. "Reliance is an ideal recovery in *Winstar* cases. Despite the landscape where alternative forms of recovery are

---

[3]   See Jon W. Burd, *Where The Rabbit Hole Ends: A Working Model For Measuring Winstar-Type Damages In The Federal Circuit,* 13 Fed. Cir. B.J. 657 (2004).

speculative and loss models inherently unreliable, reliance damages can be ascertainable and fixed." Proof of reliance damages are factual determinations to be made by the trial court on the basis of the evidence presented by the plaintiff thrifts. Given the complexities of reconstructing the transactions and their consequences, absent a compelling showing of clear error, that should be the end of the matter.

* * *

The judgment of the trial court is *AFFIRMED*.

NOTES

State as clearly as you can the content of the so-called "wounded bank" damage theory. Does it include reliance expenditures made before and after the breach? What controls did the court impose on the reliance damage theory to avoid the speculative nature of theories based upon lost profits and restitution? For a more complete discussion of the so-called *Winstar* liability and damage issues, see Richard E. Speidel, Contracts in Crises: Excuse Doctrine and Retrospective Government Acts, Chapter 10 (2007).

PROBLEM: RESTITUTION AS A REMEDY FOR BREACH

C contracted with O to construct a three-foot stone wall around three sides of O's residential lot for $30,000. It is stipulated that the contract was "entire" rather than divisible and that C was to be paid the full amount upon completion. When the wall was completed on one side of the lot, O, without warning, repudiated the contract. O claimed that C's work had increased the value of the lot by $5,000 and offered C that amount to discharge the contract. C, who had encountered unexpected problems in construction, the risk of which he assumed, had incurred costs of $25,000 up to the breach. Given the unexpected difficulties, these costs to build one wall were reasonable. Experts will testify, however, that O would have had to pay $20,000 to obtain the same work from a contractor who was aware of the difficulties. C estimates that it will cost at least $25,000 to complete the project. On these facts, C should:

(a) Take the $5,000 and run;

(b) Sue "on the contract" for $25,000, his "reliance" interest;

(c) Sue in "restitution" for $20,000, the value to O of the work done in market terms;

(d) None of the above.

Comment: Disgorgement?

Andrew Kull, the ALI Reporter for the Restatement (Third) of Restitution, had this to say about restitution as a remedy for breach of contract.

The confusing role played by restitution among the remedies for breach of contract can be clarified if we distinguish remedies that serve the plaintiff's restoration interest from remedies that address the defendant's unjust enrichment. The latter are more easily recognized if we call them "disgorgement," but the term is overbroad, because the significant instances of disgorgement are limited to cases in which the plaintiff recovers more than he lost. If the law requires the maker of a promissory note to pay the holder on default, there has been a breach of contract. Absent a remedy, the defendant would be unjustly enriched at the plaintiff's expense. A judgment for the amount of the debt achieves a kind of restitution and a kind of disgorgement. But it would be a complete waste of time to classify this liability within the law of restitution, or to observe that the holder of the note was seeking disgorgement for breach.

Disgorgement awarding the plaintiff more than he lost is justified in a narrow class of cases in which the defendant's election to breach imposes harms that a potential liability for provable damages will not adequately deter. It is much easier to see the analogy between the restitutionary liability in such cases and the standard instances of restitution for wrongs than it is to identify the kind of breach that justifies disgorgement. I propose, by way of hypothesis, that the necessary breach of contract be both profitable and opportunistic. The requirement that the breach be profitable immediately excludes the vast majority of contractual defaults (including . . . the "losing contract" cases). Where breach is unprofitable, a liability for damages will adequately deter, and there is no profit to disgorge in any event. The further requirement that the breach be opportunistic limits this set of cases still further, because it excludes a breach in which the defendant renders a substitute performance that fulfills the plaintiff's expectation interest.

The propriety of a disgorgement remedy along more or less these lines has been a familiar topic of academic speculation. Some notable recent decisions apply a purported rule of contract law that is altogether different. [Kull discusses and disapproves some *Winstar*-related cases decided before *Glendale Federal Bank*.]

There are good reasons why breach has always had different consequences from fraudulent inducement, but they are among the elementary propositions of private law that receive less professional attention than formerly. The less confidence a court feels in its independent analysis of such a question, the more likely it is to look for the answer in a source like the Restatement. Read carefully, the Restatement (Second) of Contracts authorizes a form of disgorgement for breach only in circumstances where the remedy is well established, and never in an amount that exceeds the plaintiff's restoration interest. As the *Winstar* cases show, however, the second Restatement is subject to misinterpretation on this point.

Twenty years after the publication of the Restatement (Second) of Contracts, we must try once more to sort out the role of restitution in a contractual context. More than any other single factor, it is the existing vocabulary of the topic that has made this task so difficult. Ideally, we should henceforth exclude the word "restitution" from any account of the remedies for breach of an enforceable contract. We would be left with remedies that protect the plaintiff's expectation interest; remedies that protect the plaintiff's restoration interest; and the "limited extension of the disgorgement principle," whatever its ultimate contours, that Farnsworth has long recommended.

Andrew Kull, *Disgorgement for Breach, The "Restitution Interest," and The Restatement of Contracts*, 79 Tex. L. Rev. 2021 (2001).

As we noted in Chapter Three, Section 3, with little authority from US caselaw, the Restatement (Third) of Restitution, which the ALI voted to approve in 2011, recommends disgorgement for some breaches of contract.

> (1) If a deliberate breach of contract results in profit to the defaulting promisor and the available damage remedy affords inadequate protection to the promisee's contractual entitlement, the promisee has a claim to restitution of the profit realized by the promisor as a result of the breach. Restitution by the rule of this section is an alternative to a remedy in damages.

Rest. (3d) Restitution § 39(1). Does this proposed rule square with the theory of efficient breach?

(2) GENERAL LIMITS ON RECOVERY

Should the nonbreaching party be able to recover for all of its losses, no matter what their cause, how they were incurred, or the certainty of their proof? The law's answer is clearly "No." This section considers three general limits on the recovery of money damages: the mitigation rule, the foreseeability rule (a.k.a. the *Hadley* rule), and the certainty rule. As the cases illustrate, courts often deploy these rules in ways that reduce recovery below a plaintiff's actual losses. The subsequent sections on seller and buyer remedies illustrate how these rules figure into the formulas courts use to calculate damage awards.

Clark v. Marsiglia

Supreme Court, New York, 1845.
1 Denio 317.

ERROR from the N.Y.C.P. Marsiglia sued Clark in the court below in *assumpsit*, for work, labor and materials, in cleaning, repairing and improving sundry paintings belonging to the defendant. The defendant pleaded *non assumpsit*.

The plaintiff proved that a number of paintings were delivered to him by the defendant to clean and repair, at certain prices for each. They were delivered upon two occasions. As to the first parcel, for the repairing of which the price was $75, no defense was offered. In respect to the other, for which the plaintiff charged $156, the defendant gave evidence tending to show that after the plaintiff had commenced work upon them, he desired him not to go on, as he had concluded not to have the work done. The plaintiff, notwithstanding, finished the cleaning and repairing of the pictures, and claimed to recover for doing the whole, and for the materials furnished, insisting that the defendant had no right to countermand the order which he had given. The defendant's counsel requested the court to charge that he had the right to countermand his instructions for the work, and that the plaintiff could not recover for any work done after such countermand.

The court declined to charge as requested, but, on the contrary, instructed the jury that inasmuch as the plaintiff had commenced the work before the order was revoked, he had a right to finish it, and to recover the whole value of his labor and for the materials furnished. The jury found their verdict accordingly, and the defendant's counsel excepted. Judgment was rendered upon the verdict.

* * *

■ PER CURIAM.

The question does not arise as to the right of the defendant below to take away these pictures, upon which the plaintiff had performed some labor, without payment for what he had done, and his damages for the violation of the contract, and upon that point we express no opinion. The plaintiff was allowed to recover as though there had been no countermand of the order; and in this the court erred. The defendant, by requiring the plaintiff to stop work upon the paintings, violated his contract, and thereby incurred a liability to pay such damages as the plaintiff should sustain. Such damages would include a recompense for the labor done and materials used, and such further sum in damages as might, upon legal principles, be assessed for the breach of the contract; but the plaintiff had no right, by obstinately persisting in the work, to make the penalty upon the defendant greater than it would otherwise have been.

To hold that one who employs another to do a piece of work is bound to suffer it to be done at all events, would sometimes lead to great injustice. A man may hire another to labor for a year, and within the year his situation may be such as to render the work entirely useless to him. The party employed cannot persist in working, though he is entitled to the damages consequent upon his disappointment. So if one hires another to build a house, and subsequent events put it out of his power to pay for it, it is commendable in him to stop the work, and pay for what has been done and the damages sustained by the contractor. He may be under a necessity to change his residence, but upon the rule contended for, he would be obliged to have a house which he did not need and could not use. In all such cases the just claims of the party employed are satisfied when he is fully recompensed for his part performance and indemnified for his loss in respect to the part left unexecuted; and to persist in accumulating a larger demand is not consistent with good faith towards the employer. The judgment must be reversed, and a *venire de novo* awarded.

> *Judgment reversed.*

NOTES

(1) *The Mitigation Rule. Clark v. Marsiglia* presents arguably the easiest sort of case for the mitigation rule. After the defendant repudiated the contract, the plaintiff could have avoided the costs of finishing the job simply by stopping work. But should a nonbreaching party also be expected to take affirmative steps to avoid losses? The answer is "Yes." Thus Restatement (Second) § 351(1) provides that "damages are not recoverable for loss that the injured party could have avoided without undue risk, burden or humiliation." Subsection (2) provides a further qualification: "The injured party is not precluded from recovery . . . to the extent that he has made reasonable but unsuccessful efforts to avoid loss."

(2) *Does Mitigation Require Dealing With Breaching Promisor?* Suppose seller Smirgo repudiates its contract with buyer Bisko, but then offers to sell the goods to Bisko at a higher price. Delay in receiving the goods will cause Bisko significant consequential losses. Does Bisko have any "duty"[8] to deal with Smirgo if doing so is the only way avoid a six month delay in repurchasing from a third party? The Restatement says, "Yes," unless the breaching party's offer was conditioned on the nonbreaching party waiving any right to damages for breach. Restatement (Second) § 350(1) generally ordains that "damages are not recoverable for loss that the injured party could have avoided without undue risk, burden or humiliation." The associated Comment explains:

> If the party in breach offers to perform the contract for a different price, this may amount to a suitable alternative. . . . But this is not the case if the offer is conditioned on surrender by the injured party of his claim for breach.

As one court put it, the mitigation rule "has never been regarded as requiring one to yield to a wrongful demand that he may thereby save the wrongdoer from the legal consequences of his own error." Lurton, J. in Hirsch v. Georgia Iron & Coal Co., 169 Fed. 578, 581 (6th Cir. 1909). See Gunn Infiniti, Inc. v. O'Byrne, 996 S.W.2d 854, 858–59 (Tex. 1999); Schatz Distributing Co., Inc.

---

[8] "It is sometimes said that it is the 'duty' of the aggrieved party to mitigate damages, but this is misleading because he incurs no liability for his failure to act." Restatement (Second) § 350, Cmt.

v. Olivetti Corp. of America, 7 Kan.App.2d 676 (1982) (buyer of defective computer did not fail to mitigate by refusing seller's offer to resell the goods on buyer's behalf and to substitute new goods).

Hadley v. Baxendale

Court of Exchequer, 1854.
Supra at 41.

Spang Industries, Inc., Fort Pitt Bridge Division v. Aetna Casualty & Surety Co.

United States Court of Appeals, Second Circuit, 1975.
512 F.2d 365.

■ MULLIGAN, CIRCUIT JUDGE: Torrington Construction Co., Inc. (Torrington), a Connecticut corporation, was the successful bidder with the New York State Department of Transportation for a highway reconstruction contract covering 4.47 miles of road in Washington County, New York. Before submitting its bid Torrington received an oral quotation from Spang Industries, Inc., Fort Pitt Bridge Division (Fort Pitt), a Pennsylvania corporation, for the fabrication, furnishing and erection of some 240 tons of structural steel at a unit price of 27.5 cents per pound; the steel was to be utilized to construct a 270 foot long, double span bridge over the Battenkill River as part of the highway reconstruction. The quotation was confirmed in a letter from Fort Pitt to Torrington dated September 5, 1969, which stated in part: "Delivery to be mutually agreed upon." On November 3, 1969, Torrington, in response to a request from Fort Pitt, advised that its requirements for delivery and erection of the steel would be late June, 1970. On November 12, 1969, Fort Pitt notified Torrington that it was tentatively scheduling delivery in accordance with these requirements. On January 7, 1970, Fort Pitt wrote to Torrington asking if the June, 1970 erection date was still valid; Torrington responded affirmatively on January 13, 1970. However, on January 29, 1970, Fort Pitt advised that it was engaged in an extensive expansion program and that "[d]ue to unforeseen delays caused by weather, deliveries from suppliers, etc., it is our opinion that the June date cannot be met." On February 2, 1970, Torrington sent a letter requesting that Fort Pitt give a delivery date and, receiving no response, wrote again on May 12, 1970 requesting a written confirmation of the date of delivery and threatening to cancel out if the date was not reasonably close to the originally scheduled date. On May 20, 1970, Fort Pitt responded and promised that the structural steel would be shipped early in August, 1970.

Although some 25 tons of small steel parts were shipped on August 21, 1970, the first girders and other heavy structural steel were not shipped until August 24, 26, 27, 31 and September 2 and 4, 1970. Fort Pitt had subcontracted the unloading and erection of the steel to Syracuse Rigging Co. but neglected to advise it of the August 21st shipment. The steel began to arrive at the railhead in Shushan, New York about September 1st and the railroad demanded immediate unloading. Torrington was therefore compelled to do the unloading itself until Syracuse Rigging arrived on September 8, 1970. Not until September 16 was there enough steel delivered to the job site to permit Syracuse to commence erection. The work was completed on October 8, 1970 and the bridge was ready to receive its concrete deck on October 28, 1970. Because of contract specifications set by the State requiring that concrete be poured at temperatures of 40° Fahrenheit and above, Torrington had to get special permission from the State's supervising engineer to pour the concrete on October 28, 1970, when the temperature was at 32°.

Since the job site was in northern New York near the Vermont border and danger of freezing temperatures was imminent, the pouring of the concrete was performed on a crash basis in one day, until 1 a.m. the following morning, which entailed extra costs for Torrington in the form of overtime pay, extra equipment and the protection of the concrete during the pouring process.

[In July, 1971, Fort Pitt sued Torrington and its surety for the balance due on the subcontract, $72,247.37 with interest. Thereafter in 1972 Torrington made two further payments totaling $48,983.92 and sued Fort Pitt in another court for damages in the sum of $23,290.81 alleged to be caused by Fort Pitt's delay in furnishing the steel. The cases were removed to and consolidated for trial in the United States District Court for the Northern District of New York and were tried without a jury. On September 12, 1973, the court filed findings of fact and conclusions of law holding that Fort Pitt had breached its contract by its delayed delivery and that Torrington was entitled to damages in the amount of $7,653.57 but that Fort Pitt was entitled to recover $23,290.12, which was the balance due on its contract price plus interest, less the $7,653.57 damages sustained by Torrington. The Court directed that judgment be entered for Fort Pitt against Torrington and it's surety on their joint and several liability for $15,636.55 with interest from November 12, 1970.]

Fort Pitt on this appeal does not take issue with any of the findings of fact of the court below but contends that the recovery by Torrington of its increased expenses constitutes special damages which were not reasonably within the contemplation of the parties when they entered into the contract.

I

While the damages awarded Torrington are relatively modest ($7,653.57) in comparison with the subcontract price ($132,274.37), Fort Pitt urges that an affirmance of the award will do violence to the rule of Hadley v. Baxendale, 156 Eng.Rep. 145 (Ex.1854), and create a precedent which will have a severe impact on the business of all subcontractors and suppliers.

While it is evident that the function of the award of damages for a breach of contract is to put the plaintiff in the same position he would have been in had there been no breach, *Hadley v. Baxendale* limits the recovery to those injuries which the parties could reasonably have anticipated at the time the contract was entered into. If the damages suffered do not usually flow from the breach, then it must be established that the special circumstances giving rise to them should reasonably have been anticipated at the time the contract was made.

There can be no question but that *Hadley v. Baxendale* represents the law in New York and in the United States generally. . . . There is no dispute between the parties on this appeal as to the continuing viability of *Hadley v. Baxendale* and its formulation of the rule respecting special damages, and this court has no intention of challenging or questioning its principles, which Chief Judge Cardozo characterized to be, at least in some applications, "tantamount to a rule of property," Kerr S.S. Co. v. Radio Corporation of America, 245 N.Y. 284, 291 (1927).

The gist of Fort Pitt's argument is that, when it entered into the subcontract to fabricate, furnish and erect the steel in September, 1969, it had received a copy of the specifications which indicated that the total work was to be completed by December 15, 1971. It could not reasonably have anticipated that Torrington would so expedite the work (which was accepted by the State on January 21, 1971) that steel delivery would be called for in 1970 rather than in 1971. Whatever knowledge Fort Pitt received after the contract was entered into, it argues, cannot expand its liability, since it is essential under *Hadley v. Baxendale* and its Yankee progeny that the notice of the facts which would give rise to special damages in case of breach be given at or before the time the contract was made. The principle urged cannot be disputed. . . . We do not, however, agree that any violence to the doctrine was done here.

Fort Pitt also knew from the same specifications that Torrington was to commence the work on October 1, 1969. The Fort Pitt letter of September 5, 1969, which constitutes the agreement between the parties, specifically provides: "Delivery to be mutually agreed upon." On November 3, 1969, Torrington, responding to Fort Pitt's inquiry, gave "late June 1970" as its required delivery date and, on November 12, 1969, Fort Pitt stated that it was tentatively scheduling delivery for that time. Thus, at the time when the parties, pursuant to their initial agreement, fixed the date for performance which is crucial here, Fort Pitt knew that a June, 1970 delivery was required. It would be a strained and unpalatable interpretation of *Hadley v. Baxendale* to now hold that, although the parties left to further agreement the time for delivery, the supplier could reasonably rely upon a 1971 delivery date rather than one the parties later fixed. The behavior of Fort Pitt was totally inconsistent with the posture it now assumes. In November, 1969, it did not quarrel with the date set or seek to avoid the contract. It was not until late January, 1970 that Fort Pitt advised Torrington that, due to unforeseen delays and its expansion program, it could not meet the June date. None of its reasons for late delivery was deemed excusable according to the findings below, and this conclusion is not challenged here. It was not until five months later, on May 20, 1970, after Torrington had threatened to cancel, that Fort Pitt set another date for delivery (early August, 1970) which it again failed to meet, as was found below and not disputed on this appeal.

We conclude that, when the parties enter into a contract which, by its terms, provides that the time of performance is to be fixed at a later date, the knowledge of the consequences of a failure to perform is to be imputed to the defaulting party as of the time the parties agreed upon the date of performance. This comports, in our view, with both the logic and the spirit of *Hadley v. Baxendale*. Whether the agreement was initially valid despite its indefiniteness or only became valid when a material term was agreed upon is not relevant. At the time Fort Pitt did become committed to a delivery date, it was aware that a June, 1970 performance was required by virtue of its own acceptance. There was no unilateral distortion of the agreement rendering Fort Pitt liable to an extent not theretofore contemplated.

Having proceeded thus far, we do not think it follows automatically that Torrington is entitled to recover the damages it seeks here; further consideration of the facts before us is warranted. Fort Pitt maintains that, under the *Hadley v. Baxendale* rubric, the damages flowing from its conceded breach are "special" or "consequential" and were not reasonably to be contemplated by the parties. Since Torrington has not proved any "general" or "direct" damages, Fort Pitt urges that the contractor is entitled to nothing. We cannot agree. It is common place that parties to a contract normally address themselves to its performance and not to its breach or the consequences that will ensue if there is a default. . . . As the New York Court of Appeals long ago stated:

> [A] more precise statement of this rule is, that a party is liable for all the direct damages which both parties to the contract would have contemplated as flowing from its breach, if at the time they entered into it they had bestowed proper attention upon the subject, and had been fully informed of the facts. [This] may properly be called the fiction of law . . .

Leonard v. New York, Albany & Buffalo Electro-Magnetic Telegraph Co., 41 N.Y. 544, 567 (1870).[3]

It is also pertinent to note that the rule does not require that the direct damages must necessarily follow, but only that they are likely to

---

[3] A second fiction, added as an embellishment to *Hadley v. Baxendale* by Mr. Justice Holmes as federal common law in Globe Ref. Co. v. Landa Cotton Oil Co., 190 U.S. 540 (1903), would require not only knowledge of the special circumstances but a tacit agreement on the part of the party sought to be charged to accept the liability imposed by the notice. This second test has generally been rejected by the courts and commentators. Krauss v. Greenbarg, 137 F.2d 569, 571 (3d Cir. 1943), cert. denied 320 U.S. 791 (1943).

follow; as Lord Justice Asquith commented in Victoria Laundry, Ltd. v. Newman Industries, Ltd., [1949] 2 K.B. 528, 540, are they "on the cards"? We believe here that the damages sought to be recovered were also "in the cards."

It must be taken as a reasonable assumption that, when the delivery date of June 1970 was set, Torrington planned the bridge erection within a reasonable time thereafter. It is normal construction procedure that the erection of the steel girders would be followed by the installation of a poured concrete platform and whatever railings of superstructure the platform would require. Fort Pitt was an experienced bridge fabricator supplying contractors and the sequence of the work is hardly arcane. Moreover, any delay beyond June or August would assuredly have jeopardized the pouring of the concrete and have forced the postponement of the work until the spring. The work here, as was well known to Fort Pitt, was to be performed in northern New York near the Vermont border. The court below found that continuing freezing weather would have forced the pouring to be delayed until June, 1971. Had Torrington refused delivery or had it been compelled to delay the completion of the work until the spring of 1971, the potential damage claim would have been substantial. Instead, in a good faith effort to mitigate damages, Torrington embarked upon the crash program we have described. It appears to us that this eventuality should have reasonably been anticipated by Fort Pitt as it was experienced in the trade and was supplying bridge steel in northern climes on a project requiring a concrete roadway.

Torrington's recovery under the circumstances is not substantial or cataclysmic from Fort Pitt's point of view. It represents the expenses of unloading steel from the gondola due to Fort Pitt's admitted failure to notify its erection subcontractor, Syracuse Rigging, that the steel had been shipped, plus the costs of premium time, extra equipment and the cost of protecting the work, all occasioned by the realities Torrington faced in the wake of Fort Pitt's breach. In fact, Torrington's original claim of $23,290.81 was whittled down by the court below because of Torrington's failure to establish that its supervisory costs, overhead and certain equipment costs were directly attributable to the delay in delivery of the steel.

Williston has commented:

> The true reason why notice to the defendant of the plaintiff's special circumstances is important is because, just as a court of equity under circumstances of hardship arising after the formation of a contract may deny specific performance, so a court of law may deny damages for unusual consequences where the defendant was not aware when he entered into the contract *how serious an injury would result from its breach.*

11 S. Williston, supra, at 295 (emphasis added).

In this case, serious or catastrophic injury was avoided by prompt, effective and reasonable mitigation at modest cost.[7] Had Torrington not acted, had it been forced to wait until the following spring to complete the entire job and then sued to recover the profits it would have made had there been performance by Fort Pitt according to the terms of its agreement, then we might well have an appropriate setting for a classical *Hadley v. Baxendale* controversy.[8] As this case comes to us, it hardly presents that situation. We therefore affirm the judgment below permitting Torrington to offset its damages against the contract price.

* * *

NOTES

(1) To what extent is the *Spang Industries* case consistent with the "logic and spirit" of *Hadley v. Baxendale*? Are the policy bases for this limitation upon damages any clearer in the "Yankee progeny?"

(2) *Hadley v. Baxendale and the Code.* UCC § 2–715(2)(a) provides that "consequential damages resulting from the seller's breach include any loss resulting from general or particular requirements and needs of which the seller at the time of contracting had reason to know and which could not reasonably be prevented by cover or otherwise." Comment 2 states that the "liberality" of the foreseeable consequences rule is "modified by refusing to permit recovery unless the buyer could not reasonably have prevented the loss by cover or otherwise."

(3) *Judicial Discretion to Limit Recovery for Consequential Losses.* Restatement (Second) Section 351 suggests courts have discretion to further limit the recovery of otherwise proven consequential losses. In *Alaska Tae Woong Venture, Inc. v. Westward Seafoods*, 963 P.2d 1055 (Alaska 1998), the defendant breached a contract to take and process defined quantities of seafood over a several year period when it was unable to complete and open the processing plant on time. After suffering severe financial losses in the

---

[7] It is well understood that expenses incurred in a reasonable effort, whether successful or not, to avoid harm that the defendant had reason to foresee as a probable result of the breach when the contract was made may be recovered as an item of damage flowing from the breach. Elias v. Wright, 276 F. 908, 910 (2d Cir. 1921); C. McCormick, supra, § 42; Restatement, supra, § 336(2).

[8] In *Hadley v. Baxendale* a miller sought to recover the profits lost from the closing of the mill as a result of a carrier's failure to make timely delivery of a broken crankshaft to an engineering firm where it was to be used as a model for a replacement. A recovery of those profits was disallowed on the ground that it was not reasonably foreseeable that profits would be lost as a result of the breach of the contract of carriage. Lord Justice Asquith pointed out in *Victoria Laundry, Ltd. v. Newman Indus., Ltd.*, supra, that the headnote in *Hadley v. Baxendale* is misleading in stating that the clerk of the defendant carrier knew that the mill was stopped and that the broken shaft had to be delivered immediately. The *Victoria* court stated that the Court of Exchequer must have rejected this statement and decided to deny the loss of profits from the closing of the mill because the only knowledge possessed by the defendant was that the mill shaft was broken and that the plaintiffs were the millers. Otherwise, "the court must, one would suppose, have decided the case the other way round. . . ." [1949] 2 K.B. at 537. The misleading headnote, however, was considered to reflect the actual facts by at least two scholarly articles on the famous case. Bauer, *Consequential Damages in Contract*, 80 U. Pa. L. Rev. 687, 689 (1932); McCormick, *Damages for Breach of Contract*, 19 Minn. L. Rev. 497, 500 (1935).

1991 fishing season, the plaintiff sold the fishing boat to a third party and did not try to fish again. The plaintiff sued for lost profits during the 1991 season and for subsequent years. The court upheld the jury's determination of lost profits for 1991 and affirmed the decision not to award lost profits beyond 1993 even though it was foreseeable to the defendant that the breach would cause the plaintiff serious financial losses that would probably cause it to sell the vessel and, thus, lose profit opportunities for the balance of the contract. After brushing aside various distinctions and arguments, the court said:

> But these distinctions are not determinative. We have previously adopted section 351 of the Restatement (Second) of Contracts. . . . The Restatement empowers trial courts to limit damages for foreseeable loss when "justice so requires in order to avoid disproportionate compensation." Restatement (Second) of Contracts § 351(3) (1981). The comment to Section 351 notes that "[t]ypical examples of limitations imposed on damages under this discretionary power involve the denial of recovery for loss of profits." Id. at Cmt. f; . . .

> Our review of the record convinces us that Section 351 authorized the trial court to impose a reasonable legal limit on ATWV's claim of lost future profits. ATWV did not assert that Westward's breach of contract destroyed AJVS; selling the Allegiance did not put AJVS out of business. Soon after the sale, Phillips wound down the company's business. But his action appears to have been voluntary, not dictated by AJVS's economic failure; the company evidently was not insolvent at the time. And, to the extent that Phillips acted for financial reasons, the record indicates that his actions stemmed in part from problems unrelated to Westward's breach.

> By electing to stop actively engaging in business, AJVS effectively chose to make no further effort to earn *any* profits—including profits it might have earned through reinvestment of the consideration it received for selling the Allegiance. Had the company continued in business and reinvested the proceeds from the Allegiance's sale, its profits on that investment would presumably have reduced losses it suffered as a result of the vessel's absence. In light of this election, it seems anomalous for ATWV now to claim entitlement to seemingly endless years of profits that AJVS might have earned.

> ATWV does not explain how such compensation would be just. AJVS's inability to replace the Allegiance cannot alone support a finding of long-term losses. . . . Moreover, because ATWV does not claim that Westward caused AJVS's destruction, the causal nexus between Westward's breach and AJVS's loss of future earnings is necessarily uncertain. . . . Finally, no matter how predictable it was that Westward's breach would cause AJVS to lose the Allegiance, it strains credulity to think that Westward could reasonably have

anticipated perpetual liability for profits AJVS might lose in future years.

Given these circumstances, we conclude that an extended award of lost profits would be disproportionate to Westward's breach; justice does not require such compensation. See Restatement § 351(3). Accordingly, we hold that the trial court did not err in its alternative decision to preclude ATWV from claiming lost profits beyond June 30, 1993.

(4) *Foreseeability in Tort.* The foreseeable consequences test has been used to limit the scope of liability in tort as well as contract. There are, however, crucial differences. First, in tort what matters is foreseeability at the time of the alleged negligent conduct or other wrong, whereas in contract the question is foreseeability at the time of formation. Second, foreseeability in contract is about the scope of recovery—the damage calculation. In tort, foreseeability goes to the scope of the duty. If, given the nature of the conduct and the circumstances, the defendant could not reasonably foresee the risk of any harm to the plaintiff or a class of persons similarly situated, there is no duty of care owed to the plaintiff. Palsgraf v. Long Island Railroad, 248 N.Y. 339 (1928); Semler v. Psychiatric Institute of Washington, D.C., 538 F.2d 121 (4th Cir. 1976). But if the defendant has breached a tort duty owed to the plaintiff, the unforeseeability of the plaintiff's losses does not necessarily insulate the defendant from liability for them. The test, according to Judge Friendly, is whether the "very risks" that made the conduct negligent produced "other and more serious consequences to such persons that were fairly foreseeable when he fell short of what the law demanded." If so, there is full liability. If, however, the "injury sprang from a hazard different from that which was improperly risked" the defendant might not be liable for the full consequences caused. Petition of Kinsman Transit Co., 338 F.2d 708, 724 (2d Cir. 1964).

For a decision applying both foreseeability and mitigation ideas borrowed from contracts to protect a bank from economic loss caused by the negligent failure to transfer funds, consider *Evra Corp. v. Swiss Bank Corp.,* 673 F.2d 951 (7th Cir. 1982). In *Evra,* Judge Posner stated that the "rule" in *Hadley v. Baxendale* is that "consequential damages will not be awarded unless the defendant was put on notice of the special circumstances giving rise to them" and that its "animating principle" is that the "costs of the untoward consequence of a course of dealings should be borne by that party who was able to avert the consequence at least cost and failed to do so." 673 F.2d 951 at 955–56, 957. In *Evra,* which was litigated on a negligence theory, the "animating principle" borrowed from contracts required conduct in avoidance by the injured party both before and after the tort. See also Rardin v. T & D Mach. Handling, Inc., 890 F.2d 24, 26–27 (7th Cir. 1989) (Posner, J.).

(5) *Can Seller's Damages be Unforeseeable?* Orkin Pest Control once told Ayres that they would only enter into year-long contracts to provide pesticide treatments for his home. Ayres was worried that he might have to breach because he was thinking about moving to another city in six months. So like a good Holmesian, he asked "What would be the consequences if I

breach? What are you going to claim as lost profits?" Orkin steadfastly refused to tell Ayres what the damages would be. If Ayres subsequently breaches and the damages are unforeseeably high, should Ayres as a buyer be liable for only the foreseeable amount? Ayres at least can foresee that his lost-profit damages will never be higher than the contract price. See Ian Ayres, *Three Proposals to Harness Private Information in Contract*, 21 Harv. J.L. & Pub. Pol'y 135 (1997).

Hydraform Products Corp. v. American Steel & Aluminum Corp.

Supreme Court of New Hampshire, 1985.
127 N.H. 187.

■ SOUTER, JUSTICE. The defendant, American Steel & Aluminum Corporation, appeals from the judgment entered on a jury verdict against it. The plaintiff, Hydraform Products Corporation, brought this action for direct and consequential damages based on claims of negligent misrepresentation and breach of a contract to supply steel to be used in manufacturing woodstoves. American claims that prior to trial, the Superior Court (Nadeau, J.) erroneously held that a limitation of damages clause was ineffective to bar the claim for consequential damages. American further claims, inter alia, that the Trial Court (Dalianis, J.) erred (a) in allowing the jury to calculate lost profits on the basis of a volume of business in excess of what the contract disclosed and for a period beyond the year in which the steel was to be supplied; (b) in allowing the jury to award damages for the diminished value of the woodstove division of Hydraform's business; (c) in failing to direct a verdict for the defendant on the misrepresentation claim; and (d) in allowing Hydraform's president to testify as an expert witness. We hold that the trial court properly refused to enforce the limitation of damages clause, but we sustain the other claims of error and reverse the judgment.
* * *

Hydraform was incorporated in 1975 and began manufacturing and Selling woodstoves in 1976. During the sales season of 1977–78 it sold 640 stoves. It purchased steel from a number of suppliers until July 1978, when it entered into a "trial run" contract with American for enough steel to manufacture 40 stoves. Upon delivery of the steel, certain of Hydraform's agents and employees signed a delivery receipt prepared by American, containing the following language:

> "Seller will replace or refund the purchase price for any goods which at the time of delivery to buyer were damaged, defective or not in conformance with the buyer's written purchase order, provided that the buyer gives seller written notice by mail of such damage, defect or deviation within 10 days following its receipt of the goods. In no event shall seller be liable for labor costs expended on such goods or other consequential damages."

When some of the deliveries under this contract were late, Hydraform's president, J.R. Choate, explained to an agent of American that late deliveries of steel during the peak season for manufacturing and selling stoves could ruin Hydraform's business for a year. In response, American's agent stated that if Hydraform placed a further order, American would sheer and stockpile in advance, at its own plant, enough steel for 400 stoves, and would supply further steel on demand. Thereafter Hydraform did submit a purchase order for steel sufficient to manufacture 400 stoves, to be delivered in four equal installments on the first days of September, October, November and December of 1978.

American's acceptance of this offer took the form of deliveries accompanied by receipt forms. The forms included the same language limiting American's liability for damages that had appeared on the receipts used during the trial run agreement. Hydraform's employees signed these receipts as the steel was delivered from time to time, and no one representing Hydraform ever objected to that language.

Other aspects of American's performance under the trial run contract reoccurred as well. Deliveries were late, some of the steel delivered was defective, and replacements of defective steel were tardy. Throughout the fall of 1978 Mr. Choate protested the slow and defective shipments, while American's agent continually reassured him that the deficient performance would be corrected. Late in the fall, Mr. Choate finally concluded that American would never perform as agreed, and attempted to obtain steel from other suppliers. He found, however, that none could supply the steel he required in time to manufacture stoves for the 1978–79 sales season. In the meantime, the delays in manufacturing had led to cancelled orders, and by the end of the season Hydraform had manufactured and sold only 250 stoves. In September, 1979, Hydraform sold its woodstove manufacturing division for $150,000 plus royalties.

In December, 1979, Hydraform brought an action for breach of contract, which provoked a countersuit by American. In January, 1983, American moved to dismiss Hydraform's claims for consequential damages to compensate for lost profits and for loss on the sale of the business. American based the motion on the limitation of damages clause and upon its defense that Hydraform had failed to mitigate its damages by cover or otherwise. In February, 1983, Hydraform's pretrial statement filed under Superior Court Rule 62 disclosed that it claimed $100,000 as damages for lost profits generally and $220,000 as a loss on the sale of the business. Later in February, 1983, the superior court permitted Hydraform to amend its writ by adding further counts, which included claims for fraudulent and negligent misrepresentation. Hydraform did not, however, proceed to trial on the claim of fraud.

In April, 1983, Nadeau, J., denied American's motion to dismiss the claims for consequential damages. He relied on the Uniform Commercial Code as adopted in New Hampshire, RSA chapter 382–A, in ruling that the limitation of damages clause was unenforceable on the alternative grounds that the clause would have been a material alteration of the contract, see RSA 382–A:2207(2)(b), or was unconscionable or was a term that had failed of its essential purpose, see RSA 382–A:2–719(2) and (3). He further concluded that, under the circumstances of the case, the failure to cover, if proven, would not bar consequential damages.

The case was tried to a jury before Dalianis, J. American's exceptions at trial are discussed in detail below. At the close of the evidence, American objected to the use of a verdict form with provision for special findings, and the case was submitted for a general verdict, which the jury returned for Hydraform in the amount of $80,245.12.

American's first assignment of error for our consideration challenges the trial court's refusal to recognize the provision insulating American from liability for consequential damages caused by defective goods. We hold that the trial court was correct.

* * *

Since the clause was not enforceable, the trial court allowed the jury to consider Hydraform's claims for lost profits in the year of the contract, 1978, and for the two years thereafter, as well as its claim for loss in the value of the stove manufacturing business resulting in a lower sales price for the business in 1979. American argues that the court erred in submitting such claims to the jury, and rests its position on three requirements governing the recovery of consequential damages.

First, under RSA 382–A:2–715(2)(a) consequential damages are limited to compensation for "loss resulting from general or particular requirements and needs of which the seller at the time of contracting had reason to know. . . ." This reflection of Hadley v. Baxendale, 156 Eng.Rep. 145 (1854) thus limits damages to those reasonably foreseeable at the time of the contract. . . . To satisfy the foreseeability requirement, the injury for which damages are sought "must follow the breach in the natural course of events, or the evidence must specifically show that the breaching party had reason to foresee the injury." Salem Engineering & Const. Corp. v. Londonderry School Dist., 122 N.H. 379, 384 (1982). Thus, peculiar circumstances and particular needs must be made known to the seller if they are to be considered in determining the foreseeability of damages. . . .

Second, the damages sought must be limited to recompense for the reasonably ascertainable consequences of the breach. See RSA 382–A:2–715, comment 4. While proof of damages to the degree of mathematical certainty is not necessary, . . . a claim for lost profits must rest on evidence demonstrating that the profits claimed were "reasonably certain" in the absence of the breach. . . . Speculative losses are not recoverable.

Third, consequential damages such as lost profits are recoverable only if the loss "could not reasonably be prevented by cover or otherwise." § 2–715(2)(a). See § 2–712(1) (i.e., by purchase or contract to purchase goods in substitution for those due from seller). In summary, consequential damages must be reasonably foreseeable, ascertainable and unavoidable.

Applying these standards, we look first at the claim for lost profits for the manufacturing season beginning in September, 1978. There is no serious question that loss of profit on sales was foreseeable up to the number of 400 stoves referred to in the contract, and there is a clear evidentiary basis for a finding that Hydraform would have sold at least that number. There was also an evidentiary basis for the trial court's ruling that Hydraform acted reasonably even though it did not attempt to cover until the season was underway and it turned out to be too late. American had led Hydraform on by repeatedly promising to take steps to remedy its failures, and the court could find that Hydraform's reliance on these promises was reasonable up to the time when it finally and unsuccessfully tried to cover.

Lost profits on sales beyond the 400 stoves presents a foreseeability issue, however. Although American's agent had stated that American would supply steel beyond the 400 stove level on demand, there is no evidence that Hydraform indicated that it would be likely to make such a demand to the extent of any reasonably foreseeable amount. Rather, the evidence was that Mr. Choate had told American's agent that the business was seasonal with a busy period of about four months. The contract referred to delivery dates on the first of four separate months and spoke of only 400 stoves. Thus, there appears to be no basis on which American should have foreseen a volume in excess of 400 for the season beginning in 1978. Lost profits for sales beyond that amount therefore were not recoverable, and it was error to allow the jury to consider them.

Nor should the claims for profits lost on sales projected for the two subsequent years have been submitted to the jury. The impediment to recovery of these profits was not total unforeseeability that the breach could have effects in a subsequent year or years, but the inability to calculate any such loss with reasonable certainty. In arguing that a reasonably certain calculation was possible, Hydraform relies heavily on Van Hooijdonk v. Langley, 111 N.H. 32 (1971), a case that arose from a landlord's cancellation of a business lease. The court held that the jury could award damages for profits that a seasonal restaurant anticipated for the three years that lease should have run. It reasoned that the experience of one two-month season provided sufficient data for a reasonably certain opinion about the extent of future profits. The court thus found sufficient certainty where damages were estimated on the basis of one year of operation and profit, as compared with no operation and hence no profit in the later years.

Hydraform's situation, however, presents a variable that distinguishes it from *Van Hooijdonk*. In our case the evidence did not indicate that American's breach had forced Hydraform's stove manufacturing enterprise out of business, and therefore the jury could not assume that there would be no profits in later years. Without that assumption the jury could not come to any reasonably certain conclusion about the anticipated level of sales absent a breach by American. The jury could predict that Hydraform would obtain steel from another source and would be able to manufacture stoves; but it did not have the evidence from which to infer the future volume of manufacturing and sales. Thus, it could not calculate anticipated lost profits with a reasonable degree of certainty.

* * *

We consider next the claim for loss in the value of the business as realized at the time of its sale in 1979. As a general rule, loss in the value of a business as a going concern, or loss in the value of its good will, may be recovered as an element of consequential damages. . . .

In this case, however, it was error to submit the claim for diminished value to the jury, for three reasons. First, to the extent that diminished value was thought to reflect anticipated loss of profits in future years, as a capitalization of the loss, it could not be calculated with reasonable certainty for the reasons we have just discussed. Second, even if such profits could have been calculated in this case, allowing the jury to consider both a claim for diminished value resting on lost profits and a claim for the lost profits themselves would have allowed a double recovery. . . . Third, to the extent that diminished value was thought to rest on any other theory, there was no evidence on which it could have been calculated. There was nothing more than Mr. Choate's testimony that he had sold the business in September of 1979 for $150,000 plus minimum royalties, together with his opinion that the sales price was less than the business was worth. This testimony provided the jury with no basis for determining what the business was worth or for calculating the claimed loss, and any award on this theory rested on sheer speculation.

In summary, we hold that the jury should not have been allowed to consider any contract claim for consequential damages for lost profits beyond those lost on the sale of 150 stoves, the difference between the 400 mentioned in the contract and the 250 actually sold. Nor should the trial court have allowed the jury to consider the claim for loss in the value of the business.

* * *

Reversed.

NOTES

(1) *Reasonable Certainty.* The comments to Restatement (Second) § 352 explain the certainty requirement as follows:

> A party cannot recover damages for breach of a contract for loss beyond the amount that the evidence permits to be established with reasonable certainty. . . . Courts have traditionally required

greater certainty in the proof of damages for breach of a contract than in the proof of damages for a tort. The requirement does not mean, however, that the injured party is barred from recovery unless he establishes the total amount of his loss. It merely excludes those elements of loss that cannot be proved with reasonable certainty. The main impact of the requirement of certainty comes in connection with recovery for lost profits.

Why require a higher standard of proof of loss for recovery in contract than for recovery in tort? Why a higher standard of proof for proof of loss than for proof of breach?

(2) *Lost Profits Under CISG.* In *Delchi Carrier SpA v. Rotorex Corp.*, 71 F.3d 1024 (2d Cir. 1995), an American seller agreed to supply an Italian buyer 10,800 compressors in three installments for use in portable room air conditioners. The compressors did not conform to the contract and the seller was unable to cure the defect. The buyer properly avoided the contract for fundamental breach under CISG Articles 25 and 49 and bought compressors in replacement from a third party. See Article 75. The buyer, relying on Article 74, then sued for, among other things, (1) profits lost between the time of the breach and the replacement contract, (2) expense incurred before the breach in preparing for delivery and use of the compressors, and (3) expenses incurred after the breach in effecting a repurchase contract and storing the seller's goods. Article 74 provides:

> Damages for breach of contract by one party consist of a sum equal to the loss, including loss of profit, suffered by other party as a consequence of the breach. Such damages may not exceed the loss which the party in breach foresaw or ought to have foreseen, at the time of the conclusion of the contract, in the light of the facts and matters of which he then knew or ought to have known, as a possible consequence of the breach of contract.

The court concluded that the foreseeability requirement had been satisfied and that there was no failure to mitigate damages under Article 77. Thus, the buyer was entitled to the following recovery.

First, the buyer could recover the profits lost in being unable to sell air conditioners during the period between breach and the replacement contract. Assuming that the number of units that could have been sold was proven and that the buyer could have sold all of them, these profits were measured by subtracting the total variable costs, actual and hypothetical, that would have been expended from the estimated gross proceeds of the units sold. The variable costs do not include fixed costs or overhead. Thus, the so-called profit figure would include overhead if those fixed costs had been allocated to the contracts.

Second, the buyer could recover pre-breach reliance costs (those incurred to prepare for performance) even though they were not counted as variable costs in computing lost profits. There is no double recovery if the buyer recovers net profits (plus overhead) and reasonable reliance on the contract.

Third, the buyer could also recover reasonable costs incurred after the breach in an effort to effect a cure or to obtain a replacement contract. The court called them incidental costs, a phrase not used in CISG.

The court found that Article 74 did not directly support all of this, but took consolation in that fact that although the UCC did not apply *per se*, it could be applied by analogy. Do you agree? See UCC § 2–715.

(3)   *"New Business" Rule.* The ease with which lost profits can be proved may depend upon whether the plaintiff is a new or an established business. Where did the plaintiff fit in *Hydraform*? What limitations did the court impose upon recovery of the claim of lost profit?

Here is a traditional statement of the so-called "new business" or *per se* rule:

> When the business that is interfered with as a result of a breach of contract is a new business or venture, or one merely in contemplation, the anticipated profits from such business cannot be recovered as an item of damages because it cannot be rendered reasonably certain that there would have been any profits at all from the conduct of the business.

Coastland Corporation v. Third National Mortgage Co., 611 F.2d 969, 978 (4th Cir. 1979). For a collection of the authorities and arguments for and against the *per se* rule, see Note, 67 Va. L. Rev. 431 (1981) (for); Comment, 56 N.C. L. Rev. 693 (1978) (against). See generally Schaefer, *Uncertainty and the Law of Damages,* 19 Wm. & Mary L. Rev. 719 (1979). Most decisions under the UCC have rejected the *per se* rule. The crucial issue is not whether the plaintiff is a new business but whether the lost profits are proven with reasonable certainty. See, e.g., Hawthorne Industries, Inc. v. Balfour Maclaine International, Limited, 676 F.2d 1385 (11th Cir. 1982); Deaton, Inc. v. Aeroglide Corp., 99 N.M. 253 (1982) (plaintiff fails to prove damages with reasonable certainty in new business).

(4)   *Causation.* Proof issues are frequently mixed with the question of whether the breach "caused" the lost consequential profits. Thus, a buyer was denied lost profits when a delay was attributable to a tactical business decision by the buyer rather than to a defect in the seller's product. Duracote Corp. v. Goodyear Tire & Rubber Co., 2 Ohio St.3d 160 (1983). Similarly, reduced profits attributable to the plaintiff's capital structure rather than to defendant's breach of warranty were also denied. Lewis v. Mobil Oil Corp., 438 F.2d 500 (8th Cir. 1971). See also Dura-Wood Treating Co. v. Century Forest Industries, Inc., 675 F.2d 745 (5th Cir. 1982) (P ties up production facilities by decision to manufacture product which D had failed to deliver rather than by covering); Overstreet v. Norden Laboratories, Inc., 669 F.2d 1286 (6th Cir. 1982) (breach of warranty regarding vaccine did not cause brood mares to abort foals). As one court has put it, the "rule preventing recovery of 'speculative' damages referred more especially to the uncertainty as to the cause rather than uncertainty as to the measure or extent of damages." Hawthorne Industries, Inc. v. Balfour Maclaine International, Limited, 676 F.2d 1385, 1387 (11th Cir. 1982). See also Redgrave v. Boston

Symphony Orchestra, Inc., 855 F.2d 888, 891–94 (1st Cir. 1988) (claim that reputation damaged by breach is unduly speculative and too remote).

(5) *Consequential Reliance Losses*. Suppose B agrees to buy machinery from S to be delivered and installed in B's factory. The machinery will replace existing factory equipment. In anticipation of delivery, B spends $5,000 in preparing a platform for the machinery. S, however, fails to deliver the machinery and B makes no effort to replace it. The platform is not usable and must be removed. B sues S for $5,000 only, the amount invested in preparation and which was wasted by the breach. Can B recover?

In *L. Albert & Son v. Armstrong Rubber Co.*, 178 F.2d 182 (2d Cir. 1949), a pre-Code case, the court had a similar question. Speaking through Chief Judge Learned Hand, the court concluded that the plaintiff buyer could choose to recover costs expended in reliance on the defendant seller's performance rather than profits lost, but if the defendant proved that the contract would have lost money if performed, the reliance costs should have been reduced accordingly.

As the *Delchi* case, supra, suggests, however, there may be a foreseeability problem if the reliance was necessary for the buyer to use the goods rather than necessary for the buyer to perform the contract with the seller. Put differently, if the reliance is not necessary to performing the contract, it is more likely to be an expense that the seller at the time of contracting could not reasonably foresee.

(B) SELLER REMEDIES FOR BUYER'S BREACH

In many bargains, one party has agreed to render a performance—to transfer and sell goods or land, to construct a home, to perform professional services—in exchange for an agreed price, usually the payment of money. For simplicity's sake, we will call parties who promise a performance other than the payment of money "sellers" and parties whose performance consists of a money payment "buyers." Although not all contracts are between a buyer and a seller, the categories are useful for thinking about the different remedial rules that apply to breach of a duty to pay money (buyer breach, seller remedies), and breach of a duty other than the payment of money (seller breach, buyer remedies). We begin with seller remedies for buyer breach—the remedies available when a party fails to pay money due.

Unless the parties have agreed otherwise, the buyer's duty to pay, whether in a lump sum or in installments, does not arise until the performer has tendered or completed all or part of its portion of the exchange. If the seller fully performs, the seller, with one exception noted in the next case, is entitled to enforce the contract for the full amount promised plus interest. This remedy offers full protection to the nonbreaching seller's expectation interest. See, e.g., UCC §§ 1–305(a), 2–709(1)(a).

If, however, a non-breaching seller has not completed its part of the exchange before the buyer repudiates the contract or fails to make a payment due, the remedial problems become more complex. If the seller cannot recover the agreed price (arguably the best remedy), what are the alternatives?

We examined in Section 1 the seller's defensive remedies in this situation. We now explore the distinct problems confronting the seller in achieving affirmative protection upon breach or repudiation by the buyer. Look carefully for the interaction between remedial objectives and policy and the position of the performer. In the next subsection, we will reverse the coin to consider the remedial posture of the buyer upon breach or repudiation by the seller.

PROBLEM: THE OVEN CASES—SELLER'S REMEDIES

Review our introduction of the Oven Cases in Chapter One, supra at 38, and especially the questions in section (1) about Smirgo's remedies against Bisko.

Suppose Smirgo also entered into a contract with Brent's Outlet Store for the sale of 200 electric toaster ovens. The ovens were popular because of a new computer chip that monitored performance. The agreed price was $60 per oven, a total of $12,000.

Under the contract, Smirgo was to ship the goods to Brent "F.O.B. destination" (which meant that Smirgo was to pay the transportation costs— "free on board") as follows: 100 ovens in three months, June 1, and the balance on September 1. Brent agreed to pay the full price for each installment within 30 days after delivery. In establishing a price of $60 per oven, Smirgo took the following costs into account:

1.	coils, stainless steel, computer chips, and other materials for manufacturing	$30.00
2.	labor	$10.00
3.	fixed costs, e.g., overhead, etc.	$10.00
4.	transportation to buyer	$4.00
	Total variable and fixed costs	$54.00
	Expected net profit per oven	$6.00
		$60.00

Smirgo shipped and Brent accepted the first installment of ovens. On June 15, Brent telephoned and repudiated the contract. Apparently a new toaster oven with an even better chip had come on the market at $50 per oven. At the time of the repudiation, Smirgo had completed goods for the second installment and had identified them as intended for Brent. Also, it is stipulated that at all relevant times the market price for the "contract" ovens was $30.00 per oven at the point of shipment and $25.00 per oven at the place of delivery. Brent refused to retract the repudiation. Smirgo then canceled the contract and consulted an attorney. The questions posed are as follows (please consult your UCC):

(1) Will there be any problems because I (Smirgo) canceled the contract before consulting with you? See UCC §§ 2–610, 2–703 & 2–612.

(2) If I sue *before* July 1, can I recover the full price for those goods delivered? See UCC §§ 2–607(1), 2–709 & 2–723. In any event, can I recover the full price for the completed ovens sitting in my warehouse?

(3) If I can't recover the price on the second installment, I have found a local "second hand" retail outlet which is willing to buy them for $28 per oven. Nobody else in this area is interested. If I sell them now for $28, how much can I recover from Brent? The buyer says that he will pick them up at my plant. See UCC § 2–706. Suppose I can resell for $30 per oven?

(4) It will cost me $100 to arrange this resale. Can I recover this from Brent? See UCC § 2–710.

(5) Suppose I decide to hold rather than to resell the second installment of ovens. What can I recover from Brent? See UCC § 2–708. If I recover damages under § 2–708, and later the market for these ovens improves and I sell them for $70 each, do I have any duty to account to Brent?

American Mechanical Corp. v. Union Machine Co. of Lynn, Inc.

Appeals Court of Massachusetts, 1985.
21 Mass.App.Ct. 97.

■ FINE, JUSTICE. [On October 16, 1976, American contracted with Union to sell its real estate and business equipment for $135,000. Union knew that American was in financial difficulty, that it was in arrears on mortgage payments to Saugus Bank and that Saugus was pressing American to sell. Union issued a $5,000 check as a down payment, to be held in escrow until closing. On November 1, 1976, Union repudiated the contract. Saugus bank took possession of the property and, after American was unable to find another purchaser, the equipment was sold by Saugus for $35,000. On June 1, 1977, Saugus conducted a foreclosure sale and purchased the real estate for $55,000. American sued Union for breach of contract. After trial, the superior court concluded that although there was a breach of contract, American had not proved the "right to recover damages, beyond nominal damages." Upon appeal, the judgment was vacated and a final judgment was entered in favor of American in the amount of $46,000 with interest.]

* * *

Damages for Breach of Contract.

The judge ruled that the contract was one for the sale of the real estate for $100,000 and for the sale of the personal property for $35,000. Since $35,000 was obtained by the Saugus Bank & Trust Company when it sold the equipment and machinery, and that amount presumably was credited to American's account with the bank, the judge ruled that American had sustained no loss unless it did so with respect to the real estate. We need not decide whether a breakdown of the contract price between the real estate and the personalty was called for, or whether the price should be viewed as a lump sum for the entire sale. In our view, the result is not affected by any such determination. The judge ruled that the measure of damages for the breach of the agreement to purchase the real estate was the difference between the contract price and the fair market value on the date of the breach. Because he did not believe that the price obtained at the foreclosure sale, seven months after the breach, represented the fair market value of the property on the date of the breach, and because the plaintiff had produced no other evidence of the market value of the real estate on the date of the breach, the judge ruled that American had failed to prove actual damages.

The judge correctly stated the traditional rule generally applicable in measuring damages for breach of an agreement to purchase real estate. . . . He was also correct in his conclusion that the foreclosure sale price, even if some evidence of the market value, was not binding on him as establishing the market value of the property on the date of the breach. The actual sale of a piece of property normally provides strong evidence of market value, although the "evidentiary value of such sales in less than arms-length transactions is diminished." New Boston Garden Corp. v. Assessors of Boston, 383 Mass. 456, 469 (1981). . . . We assume that the bank in conducting the sale complied with its duty of due diligence, observing the procedural requirements of both the mortgage and the statute (G.L. c. 244, § 14), and acted in good faith. . . . It does not follow, however, that a sale so conducted will necessarily yield a price reflecting the full market value. . . .

Based upon his view of the applicable rule for measuring damages, and his disbelief of American's evidence of market value, the judge awarded American nominal damages only. The rule relied upon by the judge for measuring damages for breach of an agreement to purchase real estate, however, does not apply in all cases.

Consistent with general principles of contract law, the aim in measuring damages in the event of a breach is to place the injured party in as good a position as he would have been in had the contract been performed. . . . An important aspect of this principle is that if a party suing for breach of contract has sustained a loss as a result of a breach, and the loss is of such a nature that it was reasonably foreseeable by the parties or actually within their contemplation at the time the contract was entered into, then that loss may be recovered in an action for damages. . . .

There is no logical basis for treating real estate purchase and sale agreements differently from other purchase and sale agreements, or from contracts generally, for purposes of measuring damages. See 11 Williston, Contracts § 1399 (3d ed. 1968). The usual formula for measuring damages for breach of a real estate purchase and sale agreement—the difference between the contract price and the market value on the date of the breach—is merely a different formulation of the general rule for measuring contract damages. In the usual case, the contract price less the market value represents the seller's actual loss, and the formula, therefore, affords the injured seller an adequate remedy. In some cases, however, the actual loss suffered as a result of a breach exceeds the amount yielded by that formula. The question is whether, because the contract involves the sale of real estate, we may not, in such cases, refer to that aspect of the general rule of contract damages which gives recognition to actual losses sustained as a result of a breach when the losses are reasonably foreseeable or within the contemplation of the parties. That principle has been applied to contracts which are exclusively for the sale of real estate when the particular circumstances are such that the usual rule produces an inadequate remedy. . . .

American proved that it sustained a loss in the amount of $45,000, the difference between the contract price of $135,000 and the $90,000 received from the mortgagee bank's sale of the real estate, machinery, and equipment. The judge's findings make it clear that at the time the contract was entered into, Union knew that, if the sale of the property did not go through, the result would be that the bank would enforce its rights under the mortgage and that a foreclosure sale was likely. On almost identical facts, an Ohio court recently ruled that the correct measure of damages, on traditional contract principles, was the full amount of the actual loss, the contract price less the amount received for the property at the foreclosure sale. . . . We do not hesitate to reach the same result on the facts of this case. It does not seem to us to be a departure from established principles.

Union would, of course, be entitled to have American's damages reduced to the extent that American could reasonably have avoided the loss. Restatement (Second) of Contracts § 350 (1979). Thus, if, once it knew of the breach, American could reasonably have sold the property to someone else, it would be entitled to damages in an amount no greater than the difference between the contract price and the price for which it could have sold the property. Union established through cross-examination of Beckett that, following notification of the breach, no attempt was made by American to put the property back on the market. The judge found as a fact, however, that "American was unable to secure another purchaser for the realty and equipment." There is evidence in the record to support that finding. The evidentiary support consists principally of Beckett's recitation of what transpired between him and the Saugus Bank & Trust Company during the period immediately following notice of the breach. The bank moved relatively quickly to take possession, and the property was not of the kind for which one could assume there would be a ready market. Thus, it is not clear, as a practical matter, that American could have done anything to avoid the foreclosure. In any event, the burden of proving that losses could have been avoided by reasonable effort rests with the party in breach. . . . Farnsworth,

Contracts § 12.12 (1982); Restatement (Second) of Contracts § 350, Comment c (1979). Union's showing on this point was insufficient to establish that American failed to act reasonably to avoid the loss. Accordingly, there is no basis for reducing the damages to which American would otherwise be entitled because of any failure on its part to act reasonably to avoid the loss.

* * *

NOTES

(1) At what time was the market value of the real estate relevant? Suppose there was evidence that the market value was $75,000 at the date of breach and $70,000 at the date set for closing. What result under the court's reasoning? Do you think that the price produced in a foreclosure sale some seven months later at which the mortgagee, Saugus, was the purchaser reflects a "fair" market value?

Problems of proof aside, the contract price/market price standard used by the court is common in contracts for the sale of improved real estate, e.g., Frank v. Jansen, 303 Minn. 86 (1975), and contracts for the lease of realty, improved or unimproved. See F. Enterprises, Inc. v. Kentucky Fried Chicken Corp., 47 Ohio St.2d 154 (1976) (measure of damages for breach by lessee is difference between the fair market rental of the property proposed to be leased and the agreed rental to be paid in the proposed lease, such sum discounted to present value, together with any special damages arising from the breach).

A similar approach is taken under UCC § 2–708(1), especially where the seller has completed goods on hand. See Kenco Homes, Inc. v. Williams, 94 Wash.App. 219 (1999) (UCC § 2–708(1) inadequate where seller does not have completed goods on hand).

(2) *Foreclosures.* Note that the real estate in the *American Mechanical* case was sold at a foreclosure sale by the mortgagee, Saugus Bank, rather than by the vendor, American. From the proceeds, Saugus is entitled to satisfy its claim against American, including expenses incurred in enforcement. If there is a surplus, it must be paid to American. If there is a deficit, American still owes that amount to Saugus, who becomes an unsecured creditor. Similar principles are employed where a creditor with a security interest in goods repossesses them and conducts a public or private resale. See UCC §§ 9–610, 615 (1998).

(3) *Consequential Damages for Breach of Contract to Pay or Lend Money.* Increasingly, banks and other financial institutions have been sued for breach of a contract to lend money or to finance a particular venture. What is the lender's liability in these cases? The courts, relying upon Restatement (Second) § 351, Comment e, agree that the presumptive measure is the difference between the interest rate plaintiffs contracted to pay and the actual rate plaintiffs were compelled to pay to secure substitute financing. Thus, if the bank agreed to finance at 9% and the substitute rate was 10%, the 1% spread would be the base rate for damages.

But suppose the borrower is unable to obtain substitute financing and suffers other consequential damages. For example, the venture to be financed may fall through. Again, most courts agree that where it is foreseeable to the lender that substitute financing will be unavailable, the lender may be liable for the foreseeable consequential damages resulting from the breach. Whether the foreseeability requirement is satisfied and the amount of loss resulting from the breach are questions of fact to be resolved in each case. See, e.g., Hill v. Ben Franklin Sav. & Loan Ass'n, 177 Ill.App.3d 51 (1988) (foreseeability is for the jury to decide); Doyle v. Oregon Bank, 94 Or.App. 230 (1988) (failure to allege that damages were foreseeable precludes recovery).

Some courts have denied consequential damage recovery to sellers under the UCC. See e.g. Afram Export Corp. v. Metallurgiki Halyps, S.A., 772 F.2d 1358 (7th Cir. 1985). The reasoning was that since UCC § 1–106(1) prohibits the recovery of consequential damages "except as specifically provided in this Act or by other rule of law" and there is no specific provision for the seller, as there is for a buyer, see UCC § 2–715(2), the drafters must have intended to deny that remedy to sellers. This result has been sharply criticized. The withdrawn 2003 amendments to UCC § 2–710(2) would have given the seller the same claim to consequential damages as is given to the buyer.

Should the seller's damages in *American Mechanical* be recoverable as consequential damages?

Comment: Seller Mitigation

Mitigation and Leases. If an estate in land has "vested" in the lessee by a lease, the lessor's remedy upon breach by the lessee is no different than that of a vendor of land after title has passed to the vendee or a seller of goods after the buyer has accepted them: an action for the agreed rent is proper. See *Kentucky Fried Chicken Corp.*, supra. But suppose the lessee has vacated the premises. Does the lessor have any "duty" to mitigate damages by reletting the premises to another? At common law the answer was no, on the theory that an interest in land had been sold. If the lessor in fact relet the premises, the lessee's obligation would be credited by the amount obtained, but the lessor had no duty to make a reasonable effort to relet. More recently, some cases have treated the problem as if it were a contract to lease and required the lessor to make reasonable efforts to relet. The effect is that if the lessor fails to make these efforts, the lessee's obligation will be credited with the amount of rent that the lessor reasonably could have obtained. Restatement (Second) § 350, Comment b. See also Farmers and Bankers Life Insurance Co. v. St. Regis Paper Co., 456 F.2d 347 (5th Cir. 1972), holding that the lessor may elect to treat failure to pay rent under a lease as a contract to lease and seek damages based upon the difference between the lease price and the market price.

Article 2A of the UCC, dealing with leases of goods, gives the lessor some choices where the lessee fails to pay rent on accepted goods. See UCC § 2A–523. The lessor can recover the agreed rent for the balance of the lease and leave the goods with the lessee until the end of the lease term, UCC § 2A–529(1)(a), or the lessor can take possession of the leased goods, UCC § 2A–525, and either re-lease them to a third party, UCC § 2A–527, or claim damages under UCC § 2A–528. Although the lessor is not required to take possession of the goods or re-lease them, if possession is retaken, mitigation features are built into the damage remedies. See, e.g., UCC § 2A–527(2) and UCC § 2A–528(1).

Mitigation and Sale of Goods. In contracts for the sale of goods, the seller who delivers goods to the buyer in exchange for a promise to pay the price cannot (normally) recover the goods if the buyer fails to pay. The buyer, however, is liable for the price of the goods accepted. UCC § 2–709(1)(a). If the seller has possession of the goods at the time when the buyer breaches, the seller may either resell the goods to a third party, UCC § 2–706(1), or sue for damages, UCC § 2–708(1). If the seller unreasonably fails to resell goods still in its possession and identified to the contract, the buyer has some protection in the "market" damage formula in UCC § 2–708(1). The seller gets no more than the difference between the contract price and the market price at the time and place for tender. See Restatement (Second) § 350, Comment c. Thus, a mitigation principle is built into the damage formula for both leases and contracts for sale of goods.

Article 77 of CISG provides:

> A party who relies on a breach of contract must take such measures as are reasonable in the circumstances to mitigate the loss, including loss of profit, resulting from the breach. If he fails to take such measures, the party in breach may claim a reduction in the damages by which the loss should have been mitigated.

Would this be a good provision for Amended Article 2?

PROBLEM: THE OVEN CASES—UCC §§ 2–704 & 2–708(2)

Return with us now to the controversy between Smirgo, those "oven guys" and Brent's Outlet. Suppose that Brent repudiated the whole contract for 200 toaster ovens before any of the ovens had been manufactured. Recall that the total contract price was $12,000, which included the cost of shipment to Brent. You, Smirgo's attorney, have ascertained that the following situation existed at the time Smirgo learned of the repudiation:

　　a.　Smirgo operated in a highly competitive market. Smirgo manufactured several "lines" of ovens and possessed an expandable and highly flexible production capacity. Even though the ovens for Brent were a relatively new "line," Smirgo's production capacity could easily respond to increased demand. On the other hand, if demand slacked off, Smirgo could, with minimum disruption, discontinue a particular "line" and reallocate production resources to other contracts.

　　b.　Of the total fixed costs or overhead of operating the plant, Smirgo had, using generally accepted accounting principles, allocated $2,000 to Brent's contract, or, $10 per oven. These costs would have been incurred regardless of whether a contract had been entered into with Brent.

    c.   The coil, steel, chips and other materials needed for production had been purchased for $6,000 and were being processed. Using reasonable efforts to reallocate the materials to other jobs or to sell for scrap, it appears that the materials could be salvaged for $3,500.

    d.   If work is stopped, Smirgo will "save" $8.00 per oven in variable costs, mostly direct labor, or $1,600, and $4.00 per oven, or $800, in not having to incur any costs in shipping the goods to Brent.

    e.   If Smirgo completed performance under the repudiated contract, the ovens could be sold to a local buyer for $35.00 per oven, excluding transportation costs and costs incurred in arranging a resale. At no time will the general market price for these goods exceed $30 per oven.

    f.   There will be no costs of "arranging" either the salvage sale (for $3,500) or the completion sale (for $7,000).

Based upon these facts, consider the following questions:

(1) Suppose Smirgo wanted to complete the manufacturing process and resell the ovens to the local buyer for $35.00 per oven. Would this action be a failure to mitigate damages? Could Smirgo recover under UCC § 2–706? See UCC § 2–704.

(2) Suppose that Smirgo completed the manufacturing and, due to a shift in demand, the ovens were now worth $60 per oven on the market. Smirgo then resold them for $60 and sued Brent for $16.00 per oven, the "profit (including reasonable overhead) which the seller would have made from full performance by the buyer." UCC § 2–708(2). Brent argues that since Smirgo had already sold the 200 ovens for $12,000, the claimed $3,200 would amount to a double recovery. On these facts, how would you counter this argument? The question is whether a court would treat Smirgo as a "lost volume" seller.

Jerry Locks v. Gerald Wade

Superior Court of New Jersey, Appellate Division, 1955.
36 N.J.Super. 128.

■ CLAPP, S.J.A.D. Defendant appeals from a county district court judgment taken against him for breach of contract. Contract and breach are admitted or assumed on appeal; the only issue is damages.

Under the contract plaintiff leased to defendant an automatic phonograph, a juke box, for two years and agreed to supply records and replace parts wearing out. Proceeds of the operation were to be shared on a specified basis, but with a minimum of $20 per week to be paid plaintiff by defendant. Defendant, it is claimed, repudiated the contract; and plaintiff never installed the machine.

The court gave plaintiff judgment for $836—that is, the sum of $20 per week for two years, less apparently the costs plaintiff would have been put to, had he performed the contract, less also depreciation on the machine.

Defendant makes two points. The first rests on plaintiff's testimony that the component parts of the very machine he had intended to lease defendant were, after the breach, rented to others. Defendant argues that the amount plaintiff thus realized should have been credited on the claim sued upon.

Defendant would have us apply here the rule obtaining on the breach of an agreement to lease realty; that is, he claims the measure of the lessor's damages here is the difference between the agreed rental and the rental value of the property. His contention further is that even though under the agreement before us, the lessor is obliged to perform some personal services, he, in order to establish the rental value, has the burden of proving what he received on a reletting. . . .

Plaintiff, passing the questions (or most of them), meets the argument by referring to his testimony, not contradicted, that:

"The equipment called for by this agreement was readily available in the market. But locations were very hard to get."

We think the position plaintiff takes on the matter is sound. Where, as here, a plaintiff lessor agrees to lease an article of which the supply in the market is for practical purposes not limited, then the law would be depriving him of the benefit of his bargain if on the breach of the agreement, it required his claim against the lessee to be reduced by the amount he actually did or reasonably could realize on a reletting of the article. For if there had been no breach and another customer had appeared, the lessor could as well have secured another such article and entered into a second lease. In case of the breach of the first lease, he should have the benefit of both bargains and not—in a situation where the profit on both would be the same—be limited to the profit on the second of them.

An illustration with figures may make this more graphic. If the agreed rental under the lease amounts to $2,040, the cost of installation and of furnishing records and parts to $500, and the depreciation on the juke box over the period of the lease to $700, the lessor stands to make $840 on the deal. If another customer presents himself, the lessor will buy another juke box, which he is entitled to enter on his books at cost and depreciate in the same way as he does with the first. Thus, if he makes the same agreement with the second customer, he will make another $840 on the second lease. If the first lessee repudiates his agreement, the purchase of an additional machine will, of course, be unnecessary, because the first machine can be leased to the second customer. In such a situation, under defendant's theory, the lessor would receive as damages for this repudiation only the $2,040 rental agreed on under the first lease, less the $2,040 rental for the same machine under the second lease, or nothing. This would leave the lessee only the $840 profit he will make under the second lease; whereas had the first lessee lived up to his bargain, the lessor's profits would have been $840 on each of two leases, or $1,680.

We conclude that the proper measure of damages here is the difference between the contract price and the cost of performing the first contract, as the court apparently held below. In the case of realty which (unlike the juke box) is specific and not to be duplicated on the market, the lessor could not properly lease it to another for the same period unless the first lease were broken or terminated. In such a case the lessor should not be awarded two profits merely because of the first lessee's default.

So in general we may say that gains made by a lessor on a lease entered into after the breach are not to be deducted from his damages unless the breach enabled him to make the gains. The recoverable damages in the case of a contract are such as may reasonably be within the contemplation of the parties at the time of the contract . . .; and with that in view, we should not in the present case deny lessor the benefit of his bargain. * * *

Restatement of Contracts § 336(c) and Illustrations 6 and 7, and 5 Corbin, Contracts, § 1041 (1951) support these propositions. . . . The principles, however, seem not to be widely recognized, but there are cases dealing with various sorts of contracts, which can be said to sustain them. . . .

These principles lead us logically into questions with which we have no concern here—in particular, the question as to a seller's remedy on a sale of goods where he (like the plaintiff here) has for practical purposes the capacity to supply all probable customers—a matter as to which the law may perhaps be governed by statute. . . . Note, too, the change in the Sales Act proposed by the Uniform Commercial Code—Sales § 2–708 (1952), also Comment 2 thereon—a matter apparently overlooked in the 1955 amendment to the section. We limit our opinion to the situation at hand.

* * *

NOTES

(1) UCC Article 2A, covering leases of goods, has been enacted in every state except Louisiana. Section 2A–528(2), which purports to deal with the problem in *Locks v. Wade*, provides that if the measure of damages provided in subsection (1) of § 2A–528 is "inadequate to put a lessor in as good a position as performance would have, the measure of damages is the present value of the profit, including reasonable overhead, the lessor would have made from full performance by the lessee, together with incidental damages . . ., due allowance for costs reasonably incurred and due credit for payment or proceeds of disposition." Comment 5 provides in part: "Because this

subsection is intended to give the lessor the benefit of the bargain, a court should consider any reasonable benefit or profit expected by the lessor from the performance of the lease agreement. See . . . *Locks v. Wade.* . . ."

(2) In *Neri v. Retail Marine Corp.*, 30 N.Y.2d 393 (1972), the seller, a retailer, and the buyer, a consumer, entered into a contract for the sale of a pleasure boat at an agreed price of $12,587.40. After the seller had ordered the boat from the manufacturer, the buyer repudiated the contract. Shortly after, the seller, upon taking delivery of the boat from the manufacturer, resold it to a third party for $12,587.40. In the meantime, the buyer sued to recover the initial deposit of $4,250. The seller counterclaimed to recover the profit that would have been made on the sale to the buyer, some $2,579, and incidental damages in the amount of $674. The lower courts, among other things, rejected the lost profits claim as "untenable" since the boat was later sold for the same price that the buyer had contracted to pay. On appeal, this part of the decision was reversed by the New York Court of Appeals. The retail dealer had an unlimited supply of "fixed-price" goods, i.e., goods where the price is essentially fixed by the manufacturer. In this setting, the buyer's breach "costs the dealer a sale" even though the same goods are resold to a third party without any apparent loss. Had the buyer performed the contract, the seller would have made two sales instead of one. Since the breach depletes the dealer's sales to the extent of one, he should recover the lost profit from the buyer under UCC § 2–708(2).

Comment: The Lost Volume Seller Under UCC Article 2

Who is a Lost Volume Seller? Suppose that Seller contracts to manufacture and sell a specified piece of medical diagnosis equipment to Buyer for $500,000. After the goods were finished and identified to the contract, Buyer breached by refusing to accept delivery. What are Seller's remedial options under the Official Text of Article 2?

First, since Buyer did not accept the goods, Seller cannot recover the price unless a reasonable resale is not available. Seller must prove that it is "unable after reasonable effort to resell them at a reasonable price or the circumstances reasonably indicate that such effort will be unavailing." UCC § 2–709(1)(b).

Second, Seller could resell the goods under UCC § 2–706. Assuming that the resale conditions are satisfied, Seller "may recover the difference between the resale price and the contract price together with any incidental damages . . . but less expenses saved in consequence of the buyer's breach."

Third, whether or not the goods are resold, Seller can claim damages under UCC § 2–708(1) measured by the "difference between the market price at the time and place for tender and the unpaid contract price, together with any incidental damages . . . but less expenses saved in consequence of the buyer's breach."

Fourth, Seller can claim that damages under UCC § 2–708(1) are "inadequate" to put it "in as good a position as performance would have done" and that it is entitled to damages measured by the "profit (including reasonable overhead) which the seller would have made from full performance by the buyer, together with any incidental damages . . . , due allowance for costs reasonably incurred and due credit for payments or proceeds of resale" under UCC § 2–708(2).

As suggested by the *Neri* case, described in the notes to *Locks v. Wade*, the lost volume problem arises when Seller resells the goods for roughly the contract price. There is, in fact, no difference between the resale price or its surrogate, the relevant market price. Invoking the lost volume principle, Seller claims that neither the resale nor the market price measure is adequate to protect the expectation interest and that damages for Buyer's breach should be measured under UCC § 2–708(2). Under this rule, the seller can keep the proceeds of the resale *and* recover the profit that would have been made on the first sale.

This argument has been accepted by courts. A leading case is *R.E. Davis Chemical Corp. v. Diasonics, Inc.*, 826 F.2d 678 (7th Cir. 1987). *Davis,* however, is less strict than some in determining when there is a lost volume seller. For example, Robert Harris argued that a "[r]esale results in loss of volume only if three conditions are met: (1) the person who bought the resold entity would have been solicited by plaintiff had there been no breach and resale; (2) the solicitation would have been successful; and (3) the plaintiff could have performed that additional contract." Robert Harris, *A Radical Restatement of the Laws of Seller's Damages: Sales Act and Commercial Code Results Compared,* 18 Stan. L. Rev. 66, 80–83 (1965). The *Davis* court, however, stated: "[A] lost volume seller . . . has a predictable and finite number of customers and . . . has the capacity either to sell to all new buyers or to make the one additional sale represented by the resale" of the breached unit. If the seller "would have made the sale represented by the resale whether or not the breach occurred, damages measured by the difference between the contract price and the market price cannot put the lost volume seller in as good a position as it would have been in had the buyer performed." 826 F.2d at 683.

At the same time, *Davis* adds a restriction found in the law and economics literature but not in the other cases. In addition to whether Seller could have produced the additional item is the question "whether it would have been profitable for the seller to produce both units." Thus, the case was remanded for Seller to establish "not only that it had the capacity to produce the breached unit in addition to the unit resold, but also that it would have been profitable for it to have produced and sold both." 826 F.2d at 684. See also R.E. Davis Chemical Corp. v. Diasonics, Inc., 924 F.2d 709 (7th Cir. 1991).

One court attempted to restate the lost volume principle as follows:

> In passing, we observe that this lost volume situation can be described in several ways. Focusing on the breached unit, one can say that due to a market in which supply exceeds demand,

the lost volume seller cannot resell the breached unit without sacrificing the additional sale. Focusing on the additional unit, one can say that but for the buyer's breach, the lost volume seller would have made an additional sale. Focusing on both units, one can say that but for the buyer's breach, the lost volume seller would have sold both units. Each statement is equivalent to the others.

Kenco Homes, Inc. v. Williams, 94 Wash.App. 219, 225 (1999). Does this help?

Measuring Lost Profits under UCC § 2–708(2). How does one measure the profit on the breached contract under UCC § 2–708(2) and whether it would have been profitable to produce and sell both units? Here is a suggestion. First, determine the profit from the breached contract by subtracting the total variable costs of performance (TCI) from the contract price. The resulting "profit (including reasonable overhead) from full performance" is not adjusted by deducting any "proceeds of resale." As the cases, including *Davis*, have held, the "proceeds of resale" language in UCC § 2–708(2) does not apply to the lost volume calculation. Next, subtract the total variable costs that would have been incurred in producing the next unit from the contract price of that unit. This measures the profit including overhead from the second sale. Finally, if the profit on the second sale is less than the profit on the first, make an appropriate adjustment in the first sale profit. For example, an appropriate adjustment is made if the contract prices for both sales are added together and the total variable costs from producing two units are subtracted. If variable costs for the second unit are higher, they will reduce the profit figure.

Against this backdrop, the now withdrawn 2003 amendments to UCC § 2–708(2) would have provided:

> If the measure of damages provided in subsection (1) or in Section 2–706 is inadequate to put the seller in as good a position as performance would have done then the measure of damages is the profit (including reasonable overhead) which the seller would have made from full performance by the buyer, together with any incidental or consequential damages provided in this Article (Section 2–710).

Would this have been a change for the better?

For some commentators, the interpretation of Article 2 by the courts is flawed and the award of lost volume profits overcompensates the seller. See John M. Breen, *The Lost Volume Seller and Lost Profits Under UCC 2–708(2): A Conceptual, Linguistic Critique*, 50 U. Miami L. Rev. 779 (1996).

PROBLEM: THE OVEN CASES—MORE ON UCC § 2–708(2)

In the case involving Brent's Outlet, suppose Brent repudiated while Smirgo was in the middle of performing the $12,000 contract to manufacture ovens. The resale market was very bad and Smirgo, in the exercise of commercial judgment under UCC § 2–704, stopped work. At this point, the following facts can be established:

   1.   Smirgo's accountant had allocated $2,000 in fixed costs or overhead ($10 per oven) to the contract.

   2.   Smirgo will save $800 in not having to ship the goods to Brent.

   3.   Smirgo had incurred $6,000 in expenses at the time of the breach, all in steel, chips and materials needed for production. Smirgo can sell most of the materials on hand to a third party for $3,500, but the chips are now obsolete and have to be junked.

   4.   Smirgo estimated that he would have spent $600 more to perform the contract, most of it on labor.

   5.   The market price for the ovens, if completed, at the time and place for tender was $6,000.

(1)   Would Brent be successful in a claim that Smirgo's damages were determined by UCC § 2–708(1)?

(2)   How much should Smirgo recover under UCC § 2–708(2)? John Sebert argued that the formula in this case (no lost volume) should be: "Unpaid contract price less total variable costs, plus incidental damages, plus costs reasonably incurred, less proceeds of resale, and less the market value of goods retained." John A. Sebert, Jr., *Remedies Under Article Two of the Uniform Commercial Code: An Agenda for Review*, 130 U. Pa. L. Rev. 360, 412 (1981). Doesn't this make sense? Did Amended UCC § 2–708(2) follow Sebert's advice?

PROBLEM: THE SCOPE OF UCC § 2–708(1)

Seller, a middleman or jobber, agrees on January 2, 2001 to supply 9,000 units of goods to Buyer in six semi-annual installments over a three-year period. The parties agree on a fixed price of $100 per unit with the first delivery scheduled for July 1, 2001. At the time of contracting, Seller had neither units on hand nor forward contracts to purchase them from manufacturers. Seller delivered and Buyer paid for 1,500 units on July 1, 2001. At that time, the retail market price at the place of tender was $95 per unit. Shortly thereafter, the market started a steep decline and, by December 1, 2001, the retail price per unit was $45. On that date, Buyer repudiated the contract. At that time, Seller had a forward contract with a manufacturer to purchase 1,500 units for the next installment at $75 per unit. Seller had no other goods on hand or forward contracts. On January 2, 2002, when the retail market price per unit was $40, Seller tendered but Buyer rejected the second installment. Buyer reiterated that it would take no more deliveries under the contract. Seller sued Buyer for damages in March, 2002. On July 1, 2002, the relevant retail market price per unit was $50, but economists were hopeful that it would gradually recover over the next two years. The case came to trial in September 2002. Seller's attorney insisted that it was entitled to use UCC § 2–708(1) as a basis for recovery.

(1) You are Buyer's attorney and are persuaded that UCC § 2–708(1) will overcompensate Seller. Prepare a memo for the court that defends that position and presents an alternative approach. See UCC §§ 1–106(1), 2–711 through 2–723. See also Kenco Homes, Inc. v. Williams, 94 Wash.App. 219 (1999), holding that UCC § 2–708(1) is not adequate to put the seller in the same position as full performance would have when the seller does not have completed goods on hand.

(2) If UCC § 2–708(1) applies, how are damages for the buyer's repudiation measured?

Comment: Employee's Remedies for Employer Breach

If, in a contract for personal services, the employee has done the work and the employer fails to pay, the remedy is clear: the employee may sue for the agreed price. But suppose the employer repudiates the contract before work commences or terminates employment while work is underway. In the absence of a divisible contract, what damages may be recovered here? In all probability, the employee will stop work after the termination and consider or make some effort to find substitute employment. Does this mean that the employee's claim for damages will be treated like that in a construction contract or a contract for the sale of goods?

The answer is "not quite." Most courts have rejected the "constructive service" doctrine, which stated that a wrongfully discharged employee who remained ready and able to perform could recover the full amount of the agreed wage while making no effort mitigate. See Howard v. Daly, 61 N.Y. 362 (1875); Murray § 12.12. But a vestige of the rule remains.

> The general rule is that the measure of recovery by a wrongfully discharged employee is the amount of salary agreed upon for the period of service, less the amount which the employer affirmatively proves the employee has earned or with reasonable effort might have earned from other employment.

Parker v. Twentieth Century-Fox Film Corp., 89 Cal.Rptr. 737, 740 (1970). This varies from the usual rule, which allows damages based upon the "loss in the value to him of the other party's performance . . . less . . . any cost or other loss that he has avoided by not having to perform." Restatement (Second) § 347. In short, the discharged employee is not required to prove what savings were realized by the breach in order to establish damages. The employer, on the other hand, has the burden of proving that the employee failed to mitigate losses. Assuming that the employee will be paid for any work done, the amount that he or she reasonably could have obtained from other employment will be the measure of any savings realized over the balance of the contract.

There are a number of interesting problems around the fringes of this rule.

First, under what circumstances will the employee's failure to look for or refusal to take substitute employment constitute a failure to mitigate? For example, in the famous case of *Shirley MacLaine Parker v. Twentieth Century-Fox Film Corp.*, 474 P.2d 689 (Cal. 1970), Twentieth Century-Fox contracted to pay film star Shirley MacLaine $750,000 to star in its musical motion picture, *Bloomer Girl.* The studio decided not to make that movie and instead offered MacLaine a starring role in a Western, *Big Country, Big Man*, for the same amount of money. MacLaine declined the second movie and sued for the amount she had not been paid for the first. According to the *Parker* case:

> [B]efore projected earnings from other employment opportunities not sought or accepted by the discharged employee can be applied in mitigation, the employer must show that the other employment was comparable, or substantially similar, to that of which the employee has been deprived; the employee's rejection of or failure to seek other available employment of a different or inferior kind may not be resorted to in order to mitigate damages. 474 P.2d at 692.

The Supreme Court of California concluded that *Big Country* was "different or inferior" to *Bloomer Girl*, and rejected the studio's mitigation defense. Mary Jo Frug emphasized the feminist politics of Amelia Bloomer in her rereading of the case. See Mary Jo Frug, *Re-Reading Contracts: A Feminist Analysis of a Contracts Casebook*, 34 Am. U. L. Rev. 1065, 1114–22 (1985). Victor Goldberg emphasizes that the original agreement was merely a form of "option" agreement:

> The contract had a "pay-or-play" provision, common in the motion picture industry. The studio had, in effect, purchased an option on her time; they would pay her to be ready to make a particular film, but they made no promise to actually use her in making the film. When Fox canceled the project, they did not breach; they merely chose not to exercise their option. There was no breach and, therefore, there was no need to mitigate.

Victor P. Goldberg, *Bloomer Girl Revisited or How to Frame an Unmade Picture*, 1998 Wis. L. Rev. 1051. Whether the possible substitute employment was "different or inferior" or the employee's efforts to find it were reasonable are, in the main, questions of fact for each case. See, e.g., Ryan v. Superintendent of Schools of Quincy, 374 Mass. 670 (1978) (failure of discharged art teacher to find work justified on the facts).

Second, suppose after discharge the employee actually finds and takes another job. Is the employer automatically entitled to deduct that income from the damages? Although the answers are not entirely clear, if but for the breach the employee would not have had the time, capacity or energy to take the second job, the answer is "yes." This will turn on the nature and demands of the job from which the employee was discharged and whether the second job could have been undertaken without interfering with the employment promised by the defaulting employer. It goes without saying that if the employee is already moonlighting or engaged in some business at the time of discharge, the income from those existing activities should not be deducted.

Third, suppose the employee is not able to find suitable employment and is paid unemployment or similar benefits. Should those payments, which are a form of employment substitute, be deducted from damages? Restatement (Second) § 347, Comment e properly identifies this as a problem of collateral source, suggests that deducting the benefits from "collateral sources is less compelling in the case of a breach of contract than in the case of tort," and concludes that the answer "will turn on the court's perception of legislative policy rather than on the rule stated" in Section 347. John Fleming has argued that legislative policy will invariably be inconclusive and that tort policies argue against deduction even for breach of contract:

> Wrongful dismissal is simply not a breach of contract which courts will view with the detachment advocated by apologists of the "efficient" breach; its potentially devastating effect on the employee is attested by the pejorative use of the term "wrongful" from the tort vocabulary; and the collateral source rule is justified both by the need for deterrence and by the feeling that mere indemnity for his net economic loss does not compensate the employee for all his injury, emotional as well as pecuniary.

John Fleming, *The Collateral Source Rule and Contract Damages,* 71 Calif. L. Rev. 56, 81 (1983). For a well-reasoned case refusing to deduct from damages the disability payments made to a wrongfully discharged employee, see Seibel v. Liberty Homes, Inc., 305 Or. 362 (1988).

Rosario Inchaustegui v. 666 5th Avenue Limited Partnership

Supreme Court of New York, Appellate Division, 2000.
706 N.Y.S.2d 396, *aff'd*, 725 N.Y.S.2d 627 (2001).

■ SAXE, J. [In a commercial lease, the sub-tenant was required to "maintain comprehensive general public liability insurance in respect to the subleased premises and the conduct and operation of business therein, with sublessor and the landlord as additional insureds as set forth in the underlying lease." The sub-tenant obtained comprehensive general liability insurance for the subleased space, but failed to comply with the insurance procurement provisions of the sublease agreement by naming the landlord as the additional insured under the purchased policy. The plaintiff suffered personal injuries on the premises and sued the landlord for those injuries. The landlord, in turn, brought a third-party claim against the sub-tenant, Petrofin, alleging a violation of the lease's insurance procurement provision. The landlord moved for summary judgment, contending that Petrofin's failure to procure the requisite insurance coverage constituted a breach of the sublease agreement, entitling them to indemnity as well as money damages, including the costs incurred in the defense of the action. The lower court granted the motion but limited damages to the cost of maintaining and securing an independent policy of insurance. The appellate court affirmed, with certain modifications.]

Generally, when a tenant breaches a contract with a landlord with respect to the procurement of insurance to cover the risk of liability to third parties, "[t]he usual penalty . . . is to be liable for all the resulting damages. . . . However, case law limits the extent of damages available to a landlord when it procures its own insurance upon learning that the tenant has violated the lease by failing to procure insurance. These cases hold that under such circumstances the landlord's damages 'are limited to the cost of such insurance. . . .' "

The landlord contends that these cases are contrary to settled law, [and] that they are not controlling because they apply only where the contract requires or gives the landlord the option to procure its own insurance should the tenant fail to do so. [The court reviewed evolving New York cases and "fundamental" principles of contract damages.]

Applying these fundamental contract law principles to a tenant's breach of the insurance procurement provision of a lease reflects two possible categories of damages. First, if the tenant fails to obtain the contemplated insurance coverage on behalf of the landlord (whether because it procured no coverage at all, or because it neglected to have the landlord included as a named insured) in the absence of the contemplated insurance coverage, any ultimate liability judgment against the landlord would fall within the category of consequential damages, and the landlord would be entitled to recoup that amount, as well as any litigation expenses, from the tenant, since the tenant's failure to purchase insurance on behalf of the landlord could reasonably be expected to result in such economic injury to the landlord.

However, if the landlord itself purchased insurance equivalent to that which the tenant was contractually obligated to procure, regardless of whether or not its purchase was motivated by the knowledge that the tenant had breached the insurance procurement provision of the lease, the landlord's only damages arising from the tenant's breach of the lease are contract damages, equivalent to the costs of procuring the insurance policy.

The dissent takes the position that our conclusion contravenes the collateral source rule. We disagree. The purpose of that rule, which evolved in the context of tort law, is to ensure that the wrongdoer is required to pay for all damages his conduct caused to the injured party, without setoff from payments the injured party receives from other, collateral sources. . . . While the collateral source rule has been applied in some contract cases, as the dissent notes . . . we should keep in mind that the nature of contract damages is quite distinct from that of tort damages (see generally, Fleming, *The Collateral Source Rule and Contract Damages,* 71 Calif. L. Rev. 56, 60). While tort damages are expansive, focusing on the full spectrum of the harm caused by the tortfeasor, damages for a breach of contract are restrictive, limited to the economic injury actually caused to the claimant as a consequence of the other party's breach (id.).

An analysis of the application of the collateral source rule begins by determining the total extent of the damages to the injured party (here, the landlord) caused by the wrongdoer (here, the tenant). It then determines if the defendant is entitled to claim that this sum must be reduced by the amount available to the injured party from another source. Because the claim at issue here arises out of a breach of contract, the first step requires determination of the consequential economic damage caused to the landlord by the tenant's breach of the insurance procurement provision. As we discussed previously, because of the landlord's procurement of substitute insurance, the extent of damages to which it is entitled for this breach of contract is limited to the cost of its purchase of substitute coverage, and potentially, any other expenses not covered by the policy it procured. The collateral source rule is inapplicable. We are not setting off the damages to which the landlord is entitled from the tenant by the amount covered by the insurance; any insurance company's payment to the injured plaintiff is simply irrelevant to the analysis.

If this holding leaves the landlord's insurer without the right to recoup its expenses from the tenant by means of a subrogation claim, we perceive no prejudice. The premium was paid for the risk to be underwritten. Had it been the tenant, rather than the landlord, who applied to the same insurer for the coverage, the same premium would presumably have been paid and the same risk underwritten, and no subrogation claim would have been available to the insurer against the tenant.

Moreover, as the dissent recognizes, the concept of subrogation focuses on permitting the insurer to recoup its payment from "the party who has caused the damage". . . . A tenant who failed to procure insurance has breached a lease provision, but did not cause the damage underlying the liability determination. This situation is distinguishable from one where a right of subrogation is clearly appropriate, for instance, where a tenant negligently causes a fire that ultimately destroys other tenants' property. In such circumstances there is a wrongdoer against whom the landlord's insurer must have a subrogation right to seek to recoup payments it made to others, such as other building occupants.

Lastly, because we recognize that despite the coverage it obtained, there is a possibility the landlord may ultimately suffer certain other economic consequential damages as a result of the tenant's breach, besides the cost of the premiums, we modify the order of the IAS court in one relatively minor respect. Although the * * * cases seem to strictly limit the landlord's damages to the cost of the premiums, we believe the proper extent of damage recovery is slightly broader. In the cases limiting the landlord's damages to the cost of the premiums, the courts have drawn a distinction between two categories of damages. On one hand, there is the "cost of insurance", generally thought of as the premiums paid, which falls under the category of expenses the landlord has had to pay as a direct result of the breach, and for which it has no source of reimbursement; these costs are therefore recoverable by the landlord in an action against the tenant. On the other hand, the amount of any eventual liability determination against the landlord, and the costs of the defense, are not recoverable damages, inasmuch as both would be covered by the insurance procured by the landlord. . . .

The same reasoning that authorizes a damages award for premiums paid by the landlord in these circumstances would also permit recovery for certain other out-of-pocket costs suffered by the landlord and not covered by the procured insurance. For instance, if the policy procured by the landlord required some sort of co-payment, deductible, or other out-of-pocket payment by the landlord, such payments should, like the premiums, be recoverable as against the tenant who breached the procurement provision. Similarly, should the landlord's insurance rate be increased as a result of the liability claim, the increase in its future insurance premiums would be recoverable as breach of contract damages.

Accordingly, the order of the Supreme Court, New York County * * * should be modified, on the law, to the extent of adding the right of third-party plaintiffs to seek damages for any other expense arising out of the liability claim and not covered by the substitute insurance procured by the landlord, and as so modified, affirmed, without costs, and the matter remanded for determination of third-party plaintiffs' damages. * * *

(C) BUYER REMEDIES FOR SELLER'S BREACH

In cases of seller breach the remedial policies remain constant, but their applications can vary. For example, the plaintiff might have a greater opportunity to obtain specific performance of the defendant's promise to perform. See Section 4, infra. And as we shall see in this section, the recovery of consequential losses becomes more important, as the failure to deliver goods or to perform services can prevent or disrupt a planned profitable use. Thus, if a seller has failed to deliver goods that the buyer had planned to use in an operating business, the damages may include both the extra costs incurred in obtaining substitute goods from a third party (direct damages) and any profits lost because of the delay in obtaining the substitute (consequential damages).

PROBLEM: THE OVEN CASES—BUYER REMEDIES

Review again the Chapter One iteration of The Oven Cases, supra at 38. This time pay special attention to the questions about Bisko's possible recovery in section (2) of the problem.

Reliance Cooperage Corp. v. Treat

United States Court of Appeals, Eighth Circuit, 1952.
195 F.2d 977.

■ SANBORN, CIRCUIT JUDGE. [On July 12, 1950, Reliance and Treat entered a written contract under which Treat agreed to produce and deliver 300,000 "white oak bourbon staves" not later than December 31, 1950. The price was $450 per thousand, f.o.b. freight cars "nearest millsite where staves were produced." Between the middle and the end of August, 1950, Treat, by letter[9] and over the telephone, apparently repudiated the contract. On October 6, 1950, Reliance informed Treat by letter that they were not "confident" that Treat would perform and that they would hold him to "strict compliance" with the contract. Treat never replied and, in fact, delivered no staves to Reliance under the contract.

Reliance sued Treat for damages. At the trial, Treat, over Reliance's objection, testified that the price of bourbon staves began to advance beyond $450 per thousand around the end of August. On cross-examination, however, Treat conceded that a more accurate August price for staves was $525 per thousand. Treat also testified that he got $625 per thousand for staves toward the end of December. The evidence, however, would sustain a finding that the market price for staves on December 31, 1950 was "more than the contract price but not in excess of $750 a thousand."]

At the close of the evidence, the court was requested by the plaintiff to instruct the jury that the plaintiff was entitled to recover the difference between the contract price of the staves the defendant had promised to

---

[9]   It was admitted that the defendant had on August 12, 1950, sent to Ralph Ettlinger, an officer of the plaintiff, the following letter:

"Marshall, Arkansas

August 12, 1950

"Dear Mr. Ralph Ettlinger:

"I have been trying to get a letter to you for some time but they return to me. I went to Harrison yesterday and got Tom Burns Co. address trying to get in touch with you. We got a mill at Hallaster, Mo. trying to get started. Have a few Bolts will have a time getting any more. I can't make these staves up there or any where else at the price I haft to pay for Bolts. Every one else are paying $475.00 to $500.00 per M. You see I can't compete with them so if you want those staves I will haft to get around what ever the market is from time to time. You can see you seff that I can get bolts say 70a price when others paying $100.00 per foot. I think the boys can make a lot of staves fast up there if they can pay as much as others are paying if not they will haft to quit. Now you can see where I am at. The other to co. that I am making for with my other 3 mills have raised from $75.00 to $100.00 on the 1000 4½" staves and said they would cancel out as the market raises. So you do just what you want to. I can't make them unless I can buy the timber so let me hear at once. I will have a car before long.

"Yours as ever,
A.R. Treat."

deliver on or before December 31, 1950, and the market price of similar staves on that date. The court denied the request.

The jury was instructed substantially as follows: That the undisputed facts made a prima facie case of liability against the defendant for damages based upon the difference, if any, between the contract price of $450.00 per thousand staves and the market price as of December 31, 1950. That the defendant contended that he had repudiated the contract prior to that date and that it was the plaintiff's duty to mitigate its damages by purchasing the staves elsewhere. That the burden of proving his contentions was upon the defendant. That the jury was to determine whether the defendant did in fact repudiate his contract prior to December 31, 1950, and, if so, when the repudiation occurred, and whether, after such repudiation, the plaintiff by a reasonable effort could have mitigated its damages by the purchase of the staves on the open market, and whether the damages could have been completely or partially mitigated. That if, on a date prior to December 31, 1950, the defendant definitely and unequivocally advised the plaintiff that he would not deliver any staves under the contract, this would be a breach of the contract by him as of that date; and that if, after the repudiation, the plaintiff, by a reasonable effort and without undue risk or expense, could have purchased the staves on the open market at a price equal to the contract price, it was the plaintiff's duty to do so, and that the plaintiff would, in that event, be entitled to nominal damages only. That if the plaintiff by a reasonable effort and without undue risk or expense, after the repudiation, if any, by the defendant of the contract prior to December 31, 1950, could have purchased the staves on the open market at a price in excess of the contract price, then it was the plaintiff's duty to do that and mitigate its damages so far as possible, and the plaintiff would then be entitled to damages only for the difference between the market price of the staves at that time and the contract price. That if the jury failed to find that there was a breach of the contract by the defendant prior to December 31, 1950, the plaintiff was entitled to the difference between the market price of the staves on that date and the contract price.

The plaintiff objected to the instructions relating to the duty of the plaintiff to mitigate damages, and to the right of the defendant to repudiate the contract prior to December 31, 1950.

The jury returned a verdict for the plaintiff and assessed its damages at $500.00. The plaintiff appealed from the judgment entered on the verdict.

We gather from the court's instructions that its opinion was that if the defendant had definitely notified the plaintiff prior to December 31, 1950, that he would not produce and deliver staves under the contract, and that if the plaintiff, notwithstanding its insistence that the contract be fulfilled, by a reasonable effort and without undue risk or expense could then have bought similar staves on the market, the measure of its damages would be the difference between what the plaintiff would have had to pay for staves at the time the defendant announced his refusal of performance and the contract price of such staves.

* * *

There is no doubt that a party to an executory contract such as that in suit may refuse to accede to an anticipatory repudiation of it and insist upon performance, and, if he does so, the contract remains in existence and is binding on both parties, and no actionable claim for damages arises until the time for performance expires. . . .

It is our opinion that, under the undisputed facts in this case, the unaccepted anticipatory renunciation by the defendant of his obligation to produce and deliver staves under the contract did not impair that obligation or affect his liability for damages for the nonperformance of the contract, and that the measure of those damages was no different than it would have been had no notice of renunciation been given by the defendant to the plaintiff. If there had been no anticipatory repudiation of the contract, the measure of damages for nonperformance by the seller would have been the difference between the contract price and the market price of the staves on the date when delivery was due, and that is the measure which should have been applied in assessing damages in this case.

Moreover, the measure of damages would have been the same had the plaintiff accepted the anticipatory repudiation as an actionable breach of the contract. The plaintiff would still have been entitled to recover what it had lost by reason of the defendant's failure to produce and deliver by December 31, 1950, the staves contracted for, namely, the difference between the market price and the contract price of the staves on that date. The Comment in Restatement of the Law of Contracts, § 338, Measure of Damages for Anticipatory Breach, contains the following statement (page 549): "The fact that an anticipatory repudiation is a breach of contract (see § 318) does not cause the repudiated promise to be treated as if it were a promise to render performance at the date of the repudiation. Repudiation does not accelerate the time fixed for performance; nor does it change the damages to be awarded as the equivalent of the promised performance." See, also, Williston on Contracts, Rev.Ed. Vol. 5, § 1397; 46 Am.Jur., Sales, § 688.

It seems safe to say that ordinarily no obligation to mitigate damages arises until there are damages to mitigate. No damages for the nonperformance of the contract in suit accrued before December 31, 1950. Until that time the defendant, notwithstanding his anticipatory repudiation of the contract, was obligated and was at liberty to produce and deliver the staves, and had he done so the plaintiff would have been required to take and to pay for them. There is no justification for ruling that, after the plaintiff was advised that the defendant did not intend to perform, it must hold itself in readiness to accept performance from him and at the same time, at its own risk and expense, buy the staves contracted for upon the open market in the hope of reducing the defendant's liability for damages in case he persisted in his refusal to fulfill his obligations. The plaintiff did nothing to enhance its damages and seeks no special damages.

This same question as to mitigation of damages by a purchaser who insisted upon performance of a contract after a seller's anticipatory repudiation, arose in Continental Grain Co. v. Simpson Feed Co., D.C.E.D.Ark., 102 F.Supp. 354 (tried in the Eastern District of Arkansas). In that case Judge Lemley, we think, correctly decided that the purchaser was not required to attempt to mitigate his damages by buying the commodity contracted for upon the open market. Judge Lemley said, page 363 of 102 F.Supp.:

* * *

"There are two reasons for this rule. First, to require the innocent party to make an immediate purchase or sale upon receipt of notice of the other's repudiation would encourage such repudiation on the part of the seller or of the buyer as the market rose or fell. . . . Second, the immediate action of the innocent party might not have the effect of mitigating his damages, but might, on the other hand, enhance them. . . ."

The doctrine of anticipatory breach by repudiation is intended to aid a party injured as a result of the other party's refusal to perform his contractual obligations, by giving to the injured party an election to accept or to reject the refusal of performance without impairing his rights or increasing his burdens. Any effort to convert the doctrine into one for the benefit of the party who, without legal excuse, has renounced his agreement should be resisted.

The plaintiff is entitled to recover as damages the amount by which on December 31, 1950, the market price of the staves contracted for exceeded their contract price. What the market price of such staves was on that date is a question of fact which has not as yet been determined.

The judgment is reversed and the case is remanded with directions to grant a new trial limited to the issue of the amount of damages.

NOTES

(1) *Market-price damages.* (a) Suppose Reliance, on September 1, 1950, had canceled the contract for breach and purchased 300,000 barrel staves at $525 per thousand from another producer. On December 31, 1950, the market price had dropped back to $450 per thousand. What damages? See UCC § 2–712. Note that the cost of "cover" rather than the relevant market price determines the damages. If the buyer does not cover in fact, should damages be limited to the market price when the buyer should have covered? See UCC § 2–712(3). What policies support this result?

(b) Suppose Reliance had covered at $525 per thousand as above, but that the market price then rose to $750 per thousand on December 31, 1950.

Should Reliance be able to recover market-price damages a la UCC § 2–713(1). What result? What is the strongest argument for Treat? Is it persuasive that Reliance, by electing to cover should be precluded from recovering the market-price measure?

(2) *More on timing.* Evaluate the following analysis of the *Treat* case, which was decided under pre-Code law, from the standpoint of Article 2 of the UCC:

(a)   The UCC does not define what a repudiation is. This is presumably left to other principles of contract law in the state. UCC § 1–103. But see UCC § 2–609(4). The UCC does, however, prescribe the remedial alternatives available to the buyer upon a repudiation by the seller. UCC §§ 2–610 & 2–711(1).

(b)   The seller did not retract his repudiation before the time for performance arrived. Cf. UCC § 2–611(1). Since the buyer is seeking direct rather than consequential damages, there is no affirmative UCC requirement that it seek to mitigate damages by covering on the open market. Even so, covering in an unstable market might not be a reasonable responsibility to impose because of the risk involved. Cf. UCC § 2–715(2)(a). However, after repudiation by the seller, the buyer is privileged to await performance by the seller for only "a commercially reasonable time." UCC § 2–610(a). What does this mean?

(c)   The answer to this question depends upon how you read UCC § 2–713, dealing with buyer's damages for repudiation. First, the special rule for measuring repudiation damages set out in UCC § 2–723(1) does not apply here. The action did not come to trial before the time for performance arose. Thus, the measure must be determined from UCC § 2–713(1). Second, the measure for repudiation by the seller is "the difference between the market price at the time when the buyer learned of the breach and the contract price * * *." The use of the phrase "learned of the breach" rather than "learned of the repudiation" is critical. Given the policy of UCC § 2–610(a) and the language of UCC § 2–723(1), choice of the word "breach" suggests a time for measurement *later* than the time when the buyer first heard of the repudiation. Third, without more, since the buyer elected not to treat the repudiation as a breach, it first "learned of the breach" when the seller failed to deliver the goods in December. Market price, therefore, should be measured as of the December delivery date at the "place for tender." UCC § 2–713(2). This result is consistent with the *Treat* case.

(d)   This analysis, however, flies in the face of the language in UCC § 2–610(a). Permitting a buyer to wait a commercially reasonable time affords time to assess the seriousness of the seller's repudiation and legitimate business needs of the aggrieved party. Once that time has expired, the buyer's losses should be measured at the time when it *should* have covered on the open market. While not required actually to risk covering, the buyer should not be permitted to profit or to lose on a shifting market between the time that the commercially reasonable time expired and the agreed time for performance. Otherwise, speculation and unrealistic measurement of loss would be encouraged and the objective of efficient loss avoidance would be undercut. Accord Cosden Oil v. Karl O. Helm Aktiengesellschaft, 736 F.2d 1064 (5th Cir. 1984).

(e)   On the other hand, if the buyer decides to "cover" before a commercially reasonable time expires, damages will be measured under UCC § 2–712(1).

(f)   The now withdrawn 2003 amendments to UCC § 2–713(1)(b) would have provided:

> The measure of damages for repudiation by the seller is the difference between the market price at the expiration of a commercially reasonable time after the buyer learned of the repudiation, but not later than the time stated in paragraph (a) ["time for tender under the contract"] and the contract price together with any incidental or consequential damages provided in this Article . . . but less expenses saved in consequences of the seller's breach.

(g)   Section 2–708(1) provides that when the buyer breaches and the seller requests market-price damages, the figure should be based on "the market price at the time and place for tender"? Is there any justification for a different rule for seller remedies?

PROBLEM: RECOVERY OF LOST RESALE PROFITS

(1)   Bob, a retailer, entered into a contract with Sam, a manufacturer, for the purchase of goods at $100 per unit. Before the goods were delivered, Bob contracted to sell the goods to Carl, located 1,000 miles away, for $125 a unit. Sam knew at the time of contracting that Bob resold goods of this kind in the ordinary course of business but knew nothing about the prospective contract with Carl. Sam failed to deliver the goods. Bob, after considerable effort, was unable to cover on the open market and so informed Carl. Carl released Bob from any liability on the resale contract. Bob, however, sued Sam for lost profits, to be measured by the difference between the contract price and the resale price, some $25 per unit. Sam denied liability on the ground that he had no reason to foresee the particular resale contract with Carl or that Bob would be unable to cover on the open market. Therefore, there was no liability for consequential damages. What result?

(2)   Suppose that Bob could have covered at $110 per unit but failed to do so. What are Bob's damages here? Do you have enough information? Consider UCC §§ 2–711, 2–712, 2–713 & 2–715.

Jacob & Youngs v. George Kent

Court of Appeals of New York, 1921.
Supra at 850.

John and Catherine Rivers v. Barry Deane

Supreme Court of New York, Appellate Division, 1994.
619 N.Y.S.2d 419.

Defendant appeals from a judgment of Supreme Court awarding plaintiffs damages for defendant's breach of contract for the construction of an addition to plaintiffs' home. Defendant in his brief challenges only that aspect of the judgment that awarded damages to plaintiffs for the difference between the market value of the structure had it been completed pursuant to the terms of the contract and the market value of the structure as actually completed. We agree with defendant's assertion that the record does not support the court's award for diminution in value, because no such proof was presented.

At trial plaintiffs produced two experts who testified that defendant failed to construct the addition in a good and workmanlike manner. They further testified that the inadequate structural support of the addition rendered unusable the third floor of the addition, which plaintiffs had intended to use as a master bedroom and bathroom. The appeal by defendant, as limited by his brief . . . , does not contest those findings of fact.

The general rule in cases of faulty construction is that the measure of damages is the market value of the cost to repair the faulty construction. . . . The court erred in applying the "difference in value rule," as initially set forth by Justice Cardozo in Jacob & Youngs v. Kent, 230 N.Y. 239, 241, which is limited to instances where the builder's failure to perform under a construction contract is "both trivial and innocent", such that damages may be measured by the diminution in value of the building rather than the cost of tearing apart the structure and properly completing the project. Where, as here, the defect arising from the breach of the contract "is so substantial as to render the finished building partially unusable and unsafe, the measure of damage is 'the market price of completing or correcting the performance'" (Bellizzi v. Huntley Estates, 3 N.Y.2d 112, 115, quoting 5 Williston, Contracts § 1363, at 3825 [rev. ed.]). Thus, on the facts found by the court, plaintiffs are entitled to the market value of the cost of correcting the deficiencies in the addition arising from defendant's breach.

The trier of fact is in the best position to evaluate the credibility of the witnesses, who gave conflicting testimony concerning the cost of repair to the addition. Therefore, we modify the judgment appealed from by vacating the court's award of $10,000 for diminution in value due to inadequate structural support, and we remit the matter to Supreme Court for further findings of fact on the actual cost of repair for inadequate structural support and direct that judgment be entered accordingly.

Judgment unanimously modified on the law and as modified affirmed without costs and matter remitted to Supreme Court for further proceedings.

NOTES

(1) Restatement (Second) adopts a partially subjective test for the measurement of damages based upon the expectation interest. Section 347 provides, in part, that the damages are the "loss in the value to him of the other party's performance caused by the failure or deficiency" plus incidental and consequential damages less "any cost or other loss that he has avoided by not having to perform." This approach contrasts with the more objective "market" price or "cover" price formulas used in UCC §§ 2–712 & 2–713.

Section 348 provides an alternative measure where the breach "results in defective or unfinished construction and the loss in value to the injured party is not proved with sufficient certainty." Here the plaintiff "may recover damages based on (a) the diminution in the market price of the property caused by the breach, or (b) the reasonable cost of completing performance or of remedying the defects if that cost is not clearly disproportionate to the probable loss in the value to him." Section 348(2). How should *Jacob & Youngs v. Kent* and the *Rivers* case be decided under this test?

(2) In affirming a jury verdict for cost-to-complete damages in the defective construction of a home, the court in *Douglass v. Licciardi Const. Co., Inc.*, 386 Pa.Super. 292, 296–97 (1989), stated:

Sometimes, especially if the performance is defective as distinguished from incomplete, it may not be possible to prove the loss in value to the injured party with reasonable certainty. In that case he can usually recover damages based on the cost to remedy the defect. . . . Sometimes, however, such a large part of the cost to remedy the defects consists of the cost to undo what has been improperly done that the cost to remedy the defects will be clearly disproportionate to the probable loss in value to the injured party. Damages based on the cost to remedy the defects would then give the injured party a recovery greatly in excess of the loss in value to him and result in a substantial windfall. Such an award will not be made. It is sometimes said that the award would involve "economic waste," but this is a misleading expression since the injured party will not, even if awarded an excessive amount of damages, usually pay to have the defects remedied if to do so will cost him more than the resulting increase in value to him. If an award based on the cost to remedy the defects would clearly be excessive and the injured party does not prove the actual loss in value to him, damages will be based instead on the difference between the market price that the property would have had without the defects and the market price of the property with the defects. This diminution in market price is the least possible loss in value to the injured party, since he could always sell the property on the market even if it had no special value to him. . . . It is only where the cost of completing performance or of remedying the defects is clearly disproportionate to the probable loss in value to the injured party that damages will be measured by the difference between the market price that the property would have had without the defects and the market price of the property with the defects.

Also relevant is *Anuszewski v. Jurevic*, 566 A.2d 742 (Me. 1989), where the court approved an award that included both the cost to complete defective construction and a reasonable markup or profit for the general contractor. Otherwise, the plaintiff's expectation interest would not have been fully protected.

Willie Peevyhouse v. Garland Coal & Mining Company

Supreme Court of Oklahoma, 1962.
1962 OK 267.

■ JACKSON, JUSTICE. In the trial court, plaintiffs Willie and Lucille Peevyhouse sued the defendant, Garland Coal and Mining Company, for damages for breach of contract. Judgment was for plaintiffs in an amount considerably less than was sued for. Plaintiffs appeal and defendant cross-appeals. * * *

Briefly stated, the facts are as follows: plaintiffs owned a farm containing coal deposits, and in November, 1954, leased the premises to defendant for a period of five years for coal mining purposes. A "stripmining" operation was contemplated in which the coal would be taken from pits on the surface of the ground, instead of from underground mine shafts. In addition to the usual covenants found in a coal mining lease, defendant specifically agreed to perform certain restorative and remedial work at the end of the lease period. It is unnecessary to set out the details of the work to be done, other than to say that it would involve the moving of many thousands of cubic yards of dirt, at a cost estimated by expert witnesses at about $29,000.00. However, plaintiffs sued for only $25,000.00.

During the trial, it was stipulated that all covenants and agreements in the lease contract had been fully carried out by both parties, except the remedial work mentioned above; defendant conceded that this work had not been done.

Plaintiffs introduced expert testimony as to the amount and nature of the work to be done, and its estimated cost. Over plaintiffs' objections, defendant thereafter introduced expert testimony as to the "diminution in value" of plaintiffs' farm resulting from the failure of defendant to render performance as agreed in the contract—that is, the difference between the present value of the farm, and what its value would have been if defendant had done what it agreed to do.

At the conclusion of the trial, the court instructed the jury that it must return a verdict for plaintiffs, and left the amount of damages for jury determination. On the measure of damages, the court instructed the jury that it might consider the cost of performance of the work defendant agreed to do, "together with all of the evidence offered on behalf of either party".

It thus appears that the jury was at liberty to consider the "diminution in value" of plaintiffs' farm as well as the cost of "repair work" in determining the amount of damages.

It returned a verdict for plaintiffs for $5000.00—only a fraction of the "cost of performance", *but more than the total value of the farm even after the remedial work is done.*

On appeal, the issue is sharply drawn. Plaintiffs contend that the true measure of damages in this case is what it will cost plaintiffs to obtain performance of the work that was not done because of defendant's default. Defendant argues that the measure of damages is the cost of performance "limited, however, to the total difference in the market value before and after the work was performed".

It appears that this precise question has not heretofore been presented to this court. In Ardizonne v. Archer, 72 Okl. 70, this court held that the measure of damages for breach of a contract to drill an oil well was the reasonable cost of drilling the well, but here a slightly different factual situation exists. The drilling of an oil well will yield valuable geological information, even if no oil or gas is found, and of course if the well is a producer, the value of the premises increases. In the case before us, it is argued by defendant with some force that the performance of the remedial work defendant agreed to do will add at the most only a few hundred dollars to the value of plaintiffs' farm, and that the damages should be limited to that amount because that is all plaintiffs have lost. * * *

[The court found that if the remedial work were done, the market value of the Peevyhouses' farm would increase by only $300.]

It is highly unlikely that the ordinary property owner would agree to pay $29,000 (or its equivalent) for the construction of "improvements" upon his property that would increase its value only about ($300) three hundred dollars. The result is that we are called upon to apply principles of law theoretically based upon reason and reality to a situation which is basically unreasonable and unrealistic.

* * * Even in the case of contracts that are unquestionably building and construction contracts, the authorities are not in agreement as to the factors to be considered in determining whether the cost of performance rule or the value rule should be applied. The American Law Institute's Restatement of the Law, Contracts, Volume 1, Sections 346(1)(a)(i) and (ii) submits the proposition that the cost of performance is the proper measure of damages "if this is possible and does not involve *unreasonable economic waste";* and that the diminution in value caused by the breach is the proper measure "if construction and completion in accordance with

the contract would involve *unreasonable economic waste*". (Emphasis supplied.) In an explanatory comment immediately following the text, the Restatement makes it clear that the "economic waste" referred to consists of the destruction of a substantially completed building or other structure. Of course no such destruction is involved in the case now before us.

On the other hand, in McCormick, Damages, Section 168, it is said with regard to building and construction contracts that " * * * in cases where the defect is one that can be repaired or cured without *undue expense*" the cost of performance is the proper measure of damages, but where " * * * the defect in material or construction is one that cannot be remedied without *an expenditure for reconstruction disproportionate to the end to be attained*" (emphasis supplied) the value rule should be followed. The same idea was expressed in Jacob & Youngs, Inc. v. Kent, 230 N.Y. 239, as follows:

> "The owner is entitled to the money which will permit him to complete, unless the cost of completion is grossly and unfairly out of proportion to the good to be attained. When that is true, the measure is the difference in value."

It thus appears that the prime consideration in the Restatement was "economic waste"; and that the prime consideration in McCormick, Damages, and in *Jacob & Youngs, Inc. v. Kent*, supra, was the relationship between the expense involved and the "end to be attained"— in other words, the "relative economic benefit". * * *

23 O.S.1961 §§ 96 and 97 provide as follows:

> "§ 96. * * * Notwithstanding the provisions of this chapter, no person can recover a greater amount in damages for the breach of an obligation, than he would have gained by the full performance thereof on both sides * * *.

> "§ 97. * * * Damages must, in all cases, be reasonable, and where an obligation of any kind appears to create a right to unconscionable and grossly oppressive damages, contrary to substantial justice no more than reasonable damages can be recovered."

* * * *In spite of the agreement of the parties*, these sections limit the damages recoverable to a reasonable amount not "contrary to substantial justice"; they prevent plaintiffs from recovering a "greater amount in damages for the breach of an obligation" than they would have "gained by the full performance thereof".

We therefore hold that where, in a coal mining lease, lessee agrees to perform certain remedial work on the premises concerned at the end of the lease period, and thereafter the contract is fully performed by both parties except that the remedial work is not done, the measure of damages in an action by lessor against lessee for damages for breach of contract is ordinarily the reasonable cost of performance of the work;

however, where the contract provision breached was merely incidental to the main purpose in view, and where the economic benefit which would result to lessor by full performance of the work is grossly disproportionate to the cost of performance, the damages which lessor may recover are limited to the diminution in value resulting to the premises because of the non-performance.

* * * Under the most liberal view of the evidence herein, the diminution in value resulting to the premises because of non-performance of the remedial work was $300.00. After a careful search of the record, we have found no evidence of a higher figure, and plaintiffs do not argue in their briefs that a greater diminution in value was sustained. It thus appears that the judgment was clearly excessive, and that the amount for which judgment should have been rendered is definitely and satisfactorily shown by the record.

■ IRWIN, JUSTICE (dissenting).

* * * Although the contract speaks for itself, there were several negotiations between the plaintiffs and defendant before the contract was executed. Defendant admitted in the trial of the action, that plaintiffs insisted that the above provisions be included in the contract and that they would not agree to the coal mining lease unless the above provisions were included.

* * * The cost for performing the contract in question could have been reasonably approximated when the contract was negotiated and executed and there are no conditions now existing which could not have been reasonably anticipated by the parties. Therefore, defendant had knowledge, when it prevailed upon the plaintiffs to execute the lease, that the cost of performance might be disproportionate to the value or benefits received by plaintiff for the performance.

* * * In the instant action defendant has made no attempt to even substantially perform. The contract in question is not immoral, is not tainted with fraud, and was not entered into through mistake or accident and is not contrary to public policy. It is clear and unambiguous and the parties understood the terms thereof, and the approximate cost of fulfilling the obligations could have been approximately ascertained. There are no conditions existing now which could not have been reasonably anticipated when the contract was negotiated and executed. The defendant could have performed the contract if it desired. It has accepted and reaped the benefits of its contract and now urges that plaintiffs' benefits under the contract be denied. If plaintiffs' benefits are denied, such benefits would inure to the direct benefit of the defendant.

Therefore, in my opinion, the plaintiffs were entitled to specific performance of the contract and since defendant has failed to perform, the proper measure of damages should be the cost of performance. Any other measure of damage would be holding for naught the express provisions of the contract; would be taking from the plaintiffs the benefits of the contract and placing those benefits in defendant which has failed to perform its obligations; would be granting benefits to defendant without a resulting obligation; and would be completely rescinding the solemn obligation of the contract for the benefit of the defendant to the detriment of the plaintiffs by making an entirely new contract for the parties.

I therefore respectfully dissent to the opinion promulgated by a majority of my associates.

NOTES

(1)   The *Peevyhouse* case has been criticized on the ground that the diminished value award undercut both the landowner's subjective value in having his land reclaimed and a broader public interest in achieving the same results. See, e.g., Note, 49 Iowa L. Rev. 597 (1964). In 1967, the Oklahoma legislature imposed a duty upon mine operators to reclaim the land after work was done and authorized the State to contract for the work to be done if the operator defaulted. The operator must, at the start of work, post a bond covering the estimated cost of reclamation and there is no exception for cases where the cost of reclamation is disproportionate to any resulting increase in the value of the land. See 45 Okl. Stat. Ann. §§ 721–92. Section 722 provides in part:

> It is hereby declared to be the policy of this State to provide, after mining operations are completed, for the reclamation and conservation of land subjected to surface disturbance by open cut mining and thereby to preserve natural resources, to aid in the protection of wildlife and aquatic resources, to establish recreational, home and industrial sites, to protect and perpetuate the taxable value of property, and to protect and promote the health, safety, and general welfare of the people of this State.

The United States Court of Appeals for the Tenth Circuit has concluded that, in light of subsequent legislative changes, the Oklahoma Supreme Court would probably no longer follow *Peevyhouse*. Rock Island Improvement Co. v. Helmerich & Payne, Inc., 698 F.2d 1075 (10th Cir. 1983). Not so, at least where the breach results in damages to real property. The plaintiffs may recover the reasonable costs of repairing the damage to property so long as the recovery does not "exceed the depreciated value of the land itself." Schneberger v. Apache Corp., 890 P.2d 847, 849 (Okla. 1994) (breach of settlement agreement requiring reduction in level of water pollution caused by oil and gas drilling).

(2)   *"We Picked A Fine Time to Strip Mine, Lucille."* Judith Maute unearthed a wealth of information about the *Peevyhouse* dispute:

> To obtain Garland's promises of remediation, the Peevyhouses waived the right to receive $3000 cash upon executing the lease. This amount equals $50 per acre and represents the amount coal operators customarily paid landowners for any surface damages caused by the mining. Upon executing the contract, the Peevyhouses received $2000 for advance royalties, and they later

received an additional $500 royalty calculated on the total quantity of coal removed. Within days, Garland diverted a bothersome creek onto the Peevyhouse land so that it could continue mining elsewhere, unimpeded by water flow. Eventually Garland mined a small portion of the leased Peevyhouse land, but left the property earlier than expected, claiming the coal ran too deep. Heavy spring rains saturated the low-lying worksite, making it dangerously unstable. Garland made little effort to complete the promised remedial work. A bulldozer spent one day knocking off sharp peaks from the highwall and constructing a makeshift dirt fill to prevent the diverted creek from running into the pit, causing further damage.

Judith L. Maute, *Peevyhouse v. Garland Coal & Mining Co. Revisited: The Ballad of Willie and Lucille*, 89 Nw. U. L. Rev. 1341 (1995). For additional analysis, see Judith Maute's article, *The Unearthed Facts of Peevyhouse v. Garland Coal & Mining Co.*, in Douglas G. Baird, Editor, Contracts Stories (2007).

American Standard, Inc. v. Harold Schectman

Supreme Court of New York, Appellate Division, 1981.
439 N.Y.S.2d 529.

■ HANCOCK, JUSTICE. Plaintiffs have recovered a judgment on a jury verdict of $90,000 against defendant for his failure to complete grading and to take down certain foundations and other subsurface structures to one foot below the grade line as promised. Whether the court should have charged the jury, as defendant Schectman requested, that the difference in value of plaintiffs' property with and without the promised performance was the measure of the damage is the main point in his appeal. We hold that the request was properly denied and that the cost of completion—not the difference in value—was the proper measure. Finding no other basis for reversal, we affirm.

Until 1972, plaintiffs operated a pig iron manufacturing plant on land abutting the Niagara River in Tonawanda. On the 26-acre parcel were, in addition to various industrial and office buildings, a 60-ton blast furnace, large lifts, hoists and other equipment for transporting and storing ore, railroad tracks, cranes, diesel locomotives and sundry implements and devices used in the business. Since the 1870's plaintiffs' property, under several different owners, had been the site of various industrial operations. Having decided to close the plant, plaintiffs on August 3, 1973 made a contract in which they agreed to convey the buildings and other structures and most of the equipment to defendant, a demolition and excavating contractor, in return for defendant's payment of $275,000 and his promise to remove the equipment, demolish the structures and grade the property as specified.

We agree with Trial Term's interpretation of the contract as requiring defendant to remove all foundations, piers, headwalls, and other structures, including those under the surface and not visible and whether or not shown on the map attached to the contract, to a depth of approximately one foot below the specified grade lines.[2] The proof from plaintiffs' witnesses and the exhibits, showing a substantial deviation from the required grade lines and the existence above grade of walls, foundations and other structures, support the finding, implicit in the jury's verdict, that defendant failed to perform as agreed. Indeed, the testimony of defendant's witnesses and the position he has taken during his performance of the contract and throughout this litigation (which the trial court properly rejected), viz., that the contract did not require him to remove all subsurface foundations, allow no other conclusion.

We turn to defendant's argument that the court erred in rejecting his proof that plaintiffs suffered no loss by reason of the breach because it makes no difference in the value of the property whether the old foundations are at grade or one foot below grade and in denying his offer to show that plaintiffs succeeded in selling the property for $183,000— only $3,000 less than its full fair market value. By refusing this testimony and charging the jury that the cost of completion (estimated at $110,500 by plaintiffs' expert), not diminution in value of the property, was the measure of damage the court, defendant contends, has unjustly permitted plaintiffs to reap a windfall at his expense. Citing the definitive opinions of Chief Judge Cardozo in Jacob & Youngs, Inc. v. Kent, 230 N.Y. 239, he maintains that the facts present a case "of substantial performance" of the contract with omissions of "trivial or inappreciable importance" (p. 245), and that because the cost of completion was "grossly and unfairly out of proportion to the good to be attained", (p. 244), the proper measure of damage is diminution in value.

The general rule of damages for breach of a construction contract is that the injured party may recover those damages which are the direct, natural and immediate consequence of the breach and which can reasonably be said to have been in the contemplation of the parties when the contract was made. . . . In the usual case where the contractor's performance has been defective or incomplete, the reasonable cost of replacement or completion is the measure. . . . When, however, there has been a substantial performance of the contract made in good faith but defects exist, the correction of which would result in economic waste,

---

[2]   Paragraph 7 of the Agreement states in pertinent part:

After the Closing Date, Purchaser shall demolish all of the Improvements on the North Tonawanda Property included in the sale to Purchaser, cap the water intake at the pumphouse end, and grade and level the property, all in accordance with the provisions of Exhibit "C" and "C1" attached hereto.

Exhibit "C" (Notes on demolition and grading) contains specifications for the grade levels for four separate areas shown on Map "C1" and the following instruction:

Except as otherwise excepted all structures and equipment including foundations, piers, headwalls, etc. shall be removed to a depth approximately one foot below grade lines as set forth above. Area common to more than one area will be faired to provide reasonable transitions, it being intended to provide a reasonably attractive vacant plot for resale.

courts have measured the damages as the difference between the value of the property as constructed and the value if performance had been properly completed. . . . *Jacob & Youngs* is illustrative. There, plaintiff, a contractor, had constructed a house for the defendant which was satisfactory in all respects save one: the wrought iron pipe installed for the plumbing was not of Reading manufacture, as specified in the contract, but of other brands of the same quality. Noting that the breach was unintentional and the consequences of the omission trivial, and that the cost of replacing the pipe would be "grievously out of proportion" (Jacob & Youngs, Inc. v. Kent, supra, 230 N.Y. p. 244) to the significance of the default, the court held the breach to be immaterial and the proper measure of damage to the owner to be not the cost of replacing the pipe but the nominal difference in value of the house with and without the Reading pipe.

Not in all cases of claimed "economic waste" where the cost of completing performance of the contract would be large and out of proportion to the resultant benefit to the property have the courts adopted diminution in value as the measure of damage. Under the Restatement rule, the completion of the contract must involve "unreasonable economic waste" and the illustrative example given is that of a house built with pipe different in name from but equal in quality to the brand stipulated in the contract as in *Jacob & Youngs, Inc. v. Kent* (supra) (Restatement, Contracts, § 346, subd. [1], par. [a], cl. [ii], p. 573; Illustration 2, p. 576). In Groves v. John Wunder Co., 205 Minn. 163, plaintiff had leased property and conveyed a gravel plant to defendant in exchange for a sum of money and for defendant's commitment to return the property to plaintiff at the end of the term at a specified grade—a promise defendant failed to perform. Although the cost of the fill to complete the grading was $60,000 and the total value of the property, graded as specified in the contract, only $12,160 the court rejected the "diminution in value" rule, stating:

> The owner's right to improve his property is not trammeled by its small value. It is his right to erect thereon structures which will reduce its value. If that be the result, it can be of no aid to any contractor who declines performance. As said long ago in Chamberlain v. Parker, 45 N.Y. 569, 572: "A man may do what he will with his own, * * * and if he chooses to erect a monument to his caprice or folly on his premises, and employs and pays another to do it, it does not lie with a defendant who has been so employed and paid for building it, to say that his own performance would not be beneficial to the plaintiff."

(Groves v. John Wunder Co., supra, 205 Minn., p. 168).

The "economic waste" of the type which calls for application of the "diminution in value" rule generally entails defects in construction which are irremediable or which may not be repaired without a substantial tearing down of the structure as in *Jacob & Youngs*. . . .

Where, however, the breach is of a covenant which is only incidental to the main purpose of the contract and completion would be disproportionately costly, courts have applied the diminution in value measure even where no destruction of the work is entailed (see, e.g., Peevyhouse v. Garland Coal & Min. Co., 382 P.2d 109 [Okla.], cert. den. 375 U.S. 906, holding [contrary to *Groves v. John Wunder Co.*, supra] that diminution in value is the proper measure where defendant, the lessee of plaintiff's lands under a coal mining lease, failed to perform costly remedial and restorative work on the land at the termination of the lease). The court distinguished the "building and construction" cases and noted that the breach was of a covenant incidental to the main purpose of the contract which was the recovery of coal from the premises to the benefit of both parties; . . .

It is also a general rule in building and construction cases, at least under *Jacob & Youngs* in New York (see *Groves v. John Wunder Co.*, supra); . . . , that a contractor who would ask the court to apply the diminution of value measure "as an instrument of justice" must not have breached the contract intentionally and must show substantial performance made in good faith (Jacob & Youngs, Inc. v. Kent, supra, 230 N.Y. pp. 244, 245).

In the case before us, plaintiffs chose to accept as part of the consideration for the promised conveyance of their valuable plant and machines to defendant his agreement to grade the property as specified and to remove the foundations, piers and other structures to a depth of one foot below grade to prepare the property for sale. It cannot be said that the grading and the removal of the structures were incidental to plaintiffs' purpose of "achieving a reasonably attractive vacant plot for resale" (compare *Peevyhouse v. Garland Coal & Min. Co.*, supra). Nor can defendant maintain that the damages which would naturally flow from his failure to do the grading and removal work and which could reasonably be said to have been in the contemplation of the parties when the contract was made would not be the reasonable cost of completion. . . . That the fulfillment of defendant's promise would (contrary to plaintiffs' apparent expectations) add little or nothing to the sale value of the property does not excuse the default. As in the hypothetical case posed in Chamberlain v. Parker, 45 N.Y. 569, supra (cited in *Groves v. John Wunder Co.*, supra), of the man who "chooses to erect a monument to his caprice or folly on his premises, and employs and pays another to do it", it does not lie with defendant here who has received consideration for his promise to do the work "to say that his own performance would not be beneficial to the plaintiff[s]" (*Chamberlain v. Parker,* supra, p. 572).

Defendant's completed performance would not have involved undoing what in good faith was done improperly but only doing what was promised and left undone (compare *Jacob & Youngs, Inc. v. Kent,* supra; Restatement, Contracts, § 346, Illustration 2, p. 576). That the burdens of performance were heavier than anticipated and the cost of completion disproportionate to the end to be obtained does not, without more, alter the rule that the measure of plaintiffs' damage is the cost of completion. Disparity in relative economic benefits is not the equivalent of "economic waste" which will invoke the rule in *Jacob & Youngs, Inc. v. Kent* (supra) (see *Groves v. John Wunder Co.*, supra). Moreover, faced with the jury's finding that the reasonable cost of removing the large concrete and stone walls and other structures extending above grade was $90,000, defendant can hardly assert that he has rendered substantial performance of the contract or that what he left unfinished was "of trivial or inappreciable importance" (Jacob & Youngs, Inc. v. Kent, supra, 230 N.Y. p. 245). Finally, defendant, instead of attempting in good faith to complete the removal of the underground structures, contended that he was not obliged by the contract to do so and, thus, cannot claim to be a "transgressor whose default is unintentional and trivial [and who] may hope for mercy if he will offer atonement for his wrong" (Jacob & Youngs, Inc. v. Kent, supra, p. 244). We conclude, then, that the proof pertaining to the value of plaintiffs' property was properly rejected and the jury correctly charged on damages.

The judgment and order should be affirmed.

NOTES

In *American Standard*, the plaintiff's purpose was to obtain a clear, graded industrial lot for resale, and the plaintiff actually sold the lot as cleared and graded by the defendant for $183,000, "only $3,000 less than its full market value." The outcome of the case was that the plaintiff had a judgment for $90,000 *after* the property had been sold and that the difference in market value of the property in the condition at the time of sale and the property if defendant had fully performed the contract was only $3,000. How does the court justify this result? Has the plaintiff been awarded a windfall in a case where the value of the bargain to it can easily be measured in market terms? Or, would the award of diminished value rather than the cost of completion improperly reallocate a performance risk assumed by the defendant, especially since defendant intentionally refused to conform to the contract requirements?

These and other problems are well discussed in Timothy Muris, *Cost of Completion or Diminution in Market Value: The Relevance of Subjective Value*, 12 J. Legal Stud. 379 (1983). Muris suggests that an award of "cost to complete" damages protects the plaintiff's subjective value and should be made in cases where diminution is too difficult or costly to calculate and where subjective value is relevant and the cost to complete does not grossly exceed the subjective value. These conditions are most likely to be met when the plaintiff is a government agency or a consumer and the property is retained for use after the breach. See also Patricia Marschall, *Willfulness: A Crucial Factor in Choosing Remedies for Breach of Contract*, 24 Ariz. L. Rev. 733 (1982), who argues that the key factor is whether the breach was willful or non-willful. If the breach was willful and not excused, the objective of deterring breaches justifies granting the plaintiff either specific performance or the "highest possible measure of expectation damages." 24 Ariz. L. Rev. at 760. For a more general study, see Polinsky, *Risk Sharing Through Breach of Contract Remedies,* 12 J. Legal Stud. 427 (1983).

For evidence that the contractor's willful breach tipped the balance in favor of a cost-to-complete remedy protecting the plaintiff's subjective value, see Laurin v. DeCarolis Const. Co., Inc., 372 Mass. 688, 691–693 (1977) (plaintiff entitled to reasonable value of gravel taken from land rather than diminished value of land); Kaiser v. Fishman, 525 N.Y.S.2d 870 (1988) (cost-to-complete in defective construction of residence); Kangas v. Trust, 110 Ill.App.3d 876 (1982) (nonconforming construction of residence).

Comment: Buyer's Remedies for Seller's Breach of Warranty Under Article 2

A frequent source of disputes in contracts for the sale of goods is whether the seller has met the obligation of quality under the contract. The buyer may claim, either before or after the goods have been accepted, that the goods do not conform to the contract description, or that they do not conform to expectations about basic attributes or that they are not suitable for general or particular purposes that the buyer had in mind. Recall that the UCC provides for the enforcement of express warranties and, where they have not been disclaimed, of the default warranties of title, merchantability and, in appropriate cases, fitness. See Chapter Five, Section 3(A).

Suppose the seller has described the goods as a RXB 450 Disc Computer System and stated in the agreement that the system will perform six basic functions. This description and the affirmations are express warranties under UCC § 2–313. When the goods are tendered, the buyer has a right to inspect them to determine whether they conform to the express warranty. UCC § 2–513(1). A certain amount of testing may be required. If a non-conformity is discovered, the buyer may reject the goods under UCC §§ 2–601 and 2–602(2). After a "rightful" rejection, the seller has a limited "right" to cure the defects, see UCC § 2–508, and, beyond this, the buyer may encourage the cure effort. If the defects are not remedied, the buyer may pursue remedies for "rightful" rejection, which include cancellation, "cover" or damages, including consequential damages. See UCC §§ 2–711 and 2–715(2).

Suppose, however, that the buyer has accepted the goods before the defects are discovered. See UCC § 2–606 for what constitutes an acceptance. Acceptance of the goods precludes the remedy of rejection, makes the buyer liable for the price and puts the burden of proving a breach of warranty on the buyer. See UCC § 2–607. But UCC § 2–608 provides a special remedy called "revocation" of acceptance which, if properly exercised, gives the buyer the same remedial options as if the goods had been rejected. UCC § 2–608(3). "Revocation" of acceptance, however, is a complicated remedy and will be denied if the defect was insubstantial, or the buyer should have discovered it before acceptance or notice is given after an unreasonable time has elapsed since the defect was or should have been discovered. Again, if the revocation is "justifiable," the buyer can cancel the contract, obtain a substitute system through "cover" and seek any consequential damages resulting from the breach.

Finally, suppose the buyer, for one reason or another, can neither "rightfully" reject the goods nor "justifiably" revoke acceptance. Is that the end of the remedial road? The answer is "no." If timely notice of the breach has been given, see UCC § 2–607(3)(a), the buyer may recover damages for "breach in regard to accepted goods" under UCC § 2–714 and, where appropriate, for incidental and consequential damages under UCC § 2–715. Section 2–714(2) provides that, unless circumstances show other losses, the measure for breach of warranty is "the difference at the time and place of acceptance between the value of the goods accepted and the value they would have had if they had been as warranted." In this situation, the buyer must keep the goods and pay the agreed price, but the price will be adjusted downward to reflect the loss of bargain from the breach. UCC § 2–717.

One last note. All of this may change if the parties have agreed to remedies that are in addition to or differ from the usual Code scheme. For example, the buyer may give up the right to reject in exchange for the seller's promise to "cure" certain defects after acceptance. Or, the seller may attempt to "disclaim" certain warranties or exclude liability for consequential damages. See, e.g., UCC §§ 2–316 and 2–719.

PROBLEM: THE OVEN CASES—NON-CONFORMING GOODS

(1)   Suppose, in the transaction between Smirgo and Bisko, that Smirgo tendered delivery of the ovens on November 1 and that Bisko, after a reasonable inspection, accepted and put them into operation. Bisko paid the full contract price 90 days later. Thereafter, Bisko discovered a defect in the ovens which impaired their overall capacity to bake bread. This defect constituted a breach of warranty by Smirgo. Smirgo, however, refused either to correct the defect or to replace the ovens. Assume that at the time of delivery the value of the ovens as warranted was $29,500 and the value of the ovens as actually delivered was $25,000. Assume, also, that the reasonable cost to correct the defect would have been $8,000. Bisko has rejected the option of "revoking" the acceptance under UCC § 2–608 and pursuing remedies under UCC § 2–711 in favor of correcting the defect and keeping the goods. If Bisko does so, how much may Bisko recover from Smirgo for breach of warranty? See UCC §§ 2–714, 2–717, 2–715.

    a. $5,000

    b. $8,000

    c. $4,500

    d.   None of the above.

(2)   Suppose that Smirgo had expressly warranted that the ovens were fit for Bisko's particular needs and purposes. In fact, the ovens were fine for ordinary baking but did not satisfy Bisko's particular needs. It is clear that an oven of that design could not conform to the express warranty and that a different type of oven which cost $75,000 would be required. Bisko would like to recover $50,000, the difference in value between the oven that would have conformed to the warranty and the oven actually delivered. Smirgo argues that this recovery is not permitted under UCC § 2–714(2), which limits recovery to the "value of the goods accepted" not some hypothetical oven. Otherwise, Bisko would be put in a better position than promised by Smirgo. What argument should Bisko make? Should it be accepted?

Comment: Restitution of Buyer's Down Payment as Remedy for Seller's Breach

Under what circumstances can a buyer choose restitution of a down payment as a remedy for the seller's breach?

Contracts for Sale of Goods. Under UCC § 2–711(1), a buyer who cancels after a seller's breach may recover "so much of the price as has been paid. . . ." More importantly, the non-breaching buyer can have restitution of the price paid in addition to damages measured by the expectation interest. To illustrate, suppose that the buyer paid $50 down on a contract to purchase goods for $100. If the seller failed to deliver and the buyer "covered" for $120, the total recovery would be $50 (restitution under UCC § 2–711(1)) plus $20 (expectation under UCC § 2–712(2), adjusted for savings realized and incidental damages).

On the other hand, UCC § 2–711(1) does not say that the price recovery should be adjusted for a losing contract. Thus, if the market price at the time and place of delivery was $80, the buyer could recover $50 in restitution without any downward adjustment for the losing contract. See Bausch & Lomb Inc. v. Bressler, 977 F.2d 720, 729–730 (2d Cir. 1992) (down payment to seller adjusted for value of benefit to buyer from part performance). Other than this, Article 2 is relatively silent on the restitution interest. But see UCC § 2–718(2) (permitting a breaching buyer to recover in restitution the amount that payments made exceed the seller's damages); Barco Auto Leasing Corp. v. House, 202 Conn. 106 (1987) (dictum that the formula in UCC § 2–718(3)(b) should be extended to cover restitution by a breaching seller as well).

Contracts for Sale of Realty. The scope of restitution by a buyer of realty upon breach by the seller is illustrated by *Potter v. Oster*, 426 N.W.2d 148 (Iowa 1988). After the buyer was in possession of a farm for six years under a contract to sell, the seller, who had financial reverses, was unable to convey good title. The land involved, along with related tracts, had been mortgaged and, because of declining land values, the seller had defaulted and lost his equitable title to all of the land. The buyer, who had paid a total of $65,169 in principal, interest, improvements, taxes, insurance and other reliance, was unable to pay the $27,900 still due under the contract to save his property from foreclosure. The buyer then brought a suit against the seller to rescind the contract and to recover $65,169 in restitution. The trial court endorsed the restitution theory and, after deducting $10,800 for the value of six years' rental, awarded the buyer $54,369.

On appeal, the judgment was affirmed. The court first stated that in order to obtain rescission and restitution, the buyer must establish that (1) he was not in default, (2) the breach was material, and (3) legal remedies were inadequate. There was little dispute that the first two conditions were satisfied. The seller, however, argued that the buyer should be limited in damages to the difference between the market value of the land at the time of forfeiture, $35,000, and the contract balance of $27,900. The seller claimed that the risk of declining land values should be shared by the buyer and that restitution would give the buyer a windfall.

The court rejected this argument, stating that the seller had tried to limit damages by an "expectation" theory even though the buyer sued only for restitution. Even if declining land values motivated the buyer's selection of remedies, restitution was still proper where the first two conditions were satisfied and the legal remedies were inadequate.

> [L]egal remedies are considered inadequate when the damages cannot be measured with sufficient certainty. . . . [E]xpectation damages are correctly calculated as the difference between the contract price and market value at the time for performance. . . . Since the time of performance in this case would have been March 1990, the market value of the homestead and acreage cannot be predicted with any certainty, thus rendering such a formulation inadequate. More importantly, the fair market value of the homestead at the time of forfeiture is an incorrect measure of the benefit Potters lost. It fails to account for the special value Potters placed on the property's location and residential features that uniquely suited their family. For precisely this reason, remedies at law are presumed inadequate for breach of a real estate contract. . . . His characterization of the transaction as a mere market loss for Potters, compensable by a sum which would enable them to make a nominal down payment on an equivalent homestead, has no legal or factual support in this record.

426 N.W.2d at 152. Accord Kim v. Conway & Forty, Inc., 772 S.W.2d 723 (Mo. Ct. App. 1989) (buyers get restitution of earnest money when sellers fail to convey good title to condominium).

(D) DIVISIBLE AND INDIVISIBLE CONTRACTS

Many contracts are structured so that performance by one or both sides takes place in stages. In these transactions, a breach along the way can generate questions about its effect on the whole—with respect to both defensive and affirmative remedies, and regardless of whether it was a breach by the seller or the buyer. This section considers such questions.

Marcus Lowy v. United Pacific Insurance Co.

Supreme Court of California, 1967.
67 Cal.2d 87.

■ McComb, Associate Justice. Plaintiffs appeal from a judgment in favor of defendant Arnold Wolpin (hereinafter referred to as "defendant") on a cross-complaint for damages for breach of an excavation and grading contract.

Facts: Plaintiffs, owners and subdividers, entered into a contract with defendant, a licensed contractor, for certain excavation and grading work on lots and streets, together with street improvement work consisting of paving the streets and installing curbs and gutters, in a subdivision containing 89 residential lots.

After defendant had performed 98 percent of the contracted excavation and grading work, a dispute arose between the parties regarding payment of $7,200 for additional work, consisting of importing dirt for fills, necessitated by changes made by plaintiffs in the plans.

Defendant ceased performance. Plaintiffs immediately employed others to do street improvement work called for by the contract and thereafter sued defendant and his bonding company for breach of contract. Defendant answered and cross-complained for damages for breach of contract and reasonable services rendered. The trial court determined that plaintiffs were entitled to nothing against defendant and his bonding company and allowed defendant recovery on his cross-complaint.

Questions: First. *Was the contract between the parties divisible and the doctrine of substantial performance applicable?*

Yes.

The contract provided, in part, as follows: "[Defendant] agrees to provide and pay for all materials, labor, tools, equipment, light, transportation and other facilities necessary for the execution, in a good and workmanlike manner, of all the following described work: Excavation, Grading and Street Improvements in Tracts No. 26589 and 19517 in accordance with plans and specifications * * * and Exhibit 'A' attached hereto. * * * "

"The price which [plaintiffs] shall pay [defendant] for performing his obligations, as aforesaid or as hereunder set forth, is at the following prices indicated: * * *

"See Exhibits 'A' and 'B' attached hereto." (Italics added.)

Exhibit "A" states in part: "[Defendant] agrees to furnish all equipment, labor and material necessary for street improvements, onsite and offsite grading, grade and excavation and erosion control on Tracts 26589 and 19517 * * * for the lump sum price of Seventy-Three Thousand, Five Hundred Dollars ($73,500.00) including, without limitation, *all grading, compaction, cleaning, grade and erosion control and dumping,* all of which are to be performed to satisfaction of [plaintiffs]. * * * "(Italics added.)

The construction of pavement, curbs and gutters is not included in the list of specific items for which the sum of $73,500 is to be paid.

Exhibit "B" lists 45 unit prices ranging from $.04 to $4.50 per unit for use in the computation of the amount to be charged for the performance of that part of the street improvement work consisting of paving the streets and installing curbs and gutters. The unit prices are entirely unrelated to excavation and grading.

The contract further provides: "In invoicing [plaintiffs], multiply all the final quantities by the unit prices set forth in Exhibit 'B.' All quantities will be determined by Delta Engineering & Surveying Co. and approved by [defendant] and [plaintiffs], *with the exception of grading, etc., mentioned in Exhibit 'A' of this Agreement, which is a lump sum price for a complete job without any limitations.*" (Italics added.)

The latter paragraph of the contract shows clearly that the lump sum of $73,500 was not intended to include payment for paving the streets and installing curbs and gutters.

The trial court found that under the contract there were two phases of work to be performed, (1) grading and (2) street improvements; that defendant performed all the terms and conditions thereof relating to grading, except work which could be completed for $1,470, being 2 percent of the total grading cost contracted for; that defendant performed additional grading work, reasonably worth $7,200, necessitated by changes in plans on the part of plaintiffs and not attributable to defendant, which additional work was also authorized by plaintiffs through their superintendent; that plaintiffs breached the contract by employing others to do street improvement work and by not making payments to defendant for grading work done by him when due, thereby excusing further performance by defendant; and that defendant was entitled to recover on his cross-complaint for damages, as follows:

Contract price for grading	$73,500.00
Additional work	7,200.00
	80,700.00
Less amount paid defendant	— 60,227.50
	20,472.50
Less credit for uncompleted work	— 1,470.00
	19,002.50
Less credit for items paid for defendant's account	— 1,166.00
Balance owing defendant	$17,836.50

The trial court also found that defendant was entitled to reasonable attorney's fees in the sum of $4,000, the contract providing for reasonable attorney's fees to be awarded to the prevailing party in any action brought to enforce the terms and conditions thereof.

The trial court further found that defendant had breached that portion of the contract relating to street improvement work and was not entitled to recover damages for loss of profits in connection therewith.

As indicated above, the contract required the performance of two kinds of work. First, certain excavation and grading work was to be done on lots and streets. Thereafter, street improvement work, consisting of paving the streets and installing curbs and gutters, was required.

Plaintiffs agreed to pay defendant for the excavation and grading work (including street grading work) the sum of $73,500, as set forth in Exhibit "A" of the contract and they agreed to pay defendant for the paving of the streets and the installation of curbs and gutters (all commonly called "street improvement work") pursuant to the unit prices set forth in Exhibit "B" of the contract.

Accordingly, since the consideration was apportioned, the contract was a severable or divisible one. . . .[1]

Before defendant commenced the excavation and grading work, for which a lump sum price of $73,500 was set by the contract, he gave a surety bond for $73,500. When the excavation and grading work was nearing completion, and it was almost time for work under the second phase to begin, plaintiffs requested that defendant provide a surety bond

---

[1] Williston defines a divisible contract, as follows: "A contract under which the whole performance is divided into two sets of partial performance, each part of each set being the agreed exchange for a corresponding part of the set of performances to be rendered by the other promisor, is called a divisible contract. Or, as expressed in the cases:

"'A contract is divisible where by its terms, 1, performance of each party is divided into two or more parts, and 2, the number of parts due from each party is the same, and 3, the performance of each part by one party is the agreed exchange for a corresponding part by the other party.'" (6 Williston, Contracts (3d ed. 1962) § 860, pp. 252–254.)

for "street improvements" in the sum of $125,000, stating that "no work should be performed on any portion of the street improvement portion of the contract until such bond is furnished." Thus, it is clear that the parties treated the contract as a divisible one.

Under the circumstances, the fact that defendant did not perform the second phase of the contract does not prevent his recovering for work done under the first phase.

Defendant did not entirely perform under the first phase of the contract. However, the doctrine of substantial performance, ordinarily applied to building contracts, is here applicable, since the evidence shows that defendant completed 98 percent of the work under the first phase and was prevented from completing the balance through the fault of plaintiffs.

Where a person agrees to do a thing for another for a specified sum of money, to be paid on full performance, he is not entitled to any part of the sum until he has himself done the thing he agreed to do, unless full performance has been excused, prevented, or delayed by the act of the other party. (Thomas Haverty Co. v. Jones, 185 Cal. 285, 288–289.)

In Thomas Haverty Co. v. Jones, supra, we held that in the case of a building contract where the owner has taken possession of the building and is enjoying the fruits of the contractor's work in the performance of the contract, if there has been a substantial performance thereof by the contractor in good faith, if the failure to make full performance can be compensated in damages to be deducted from the price or allowed as a counterclaim, and if the omissions and deviations were not wilful or fraudulent and do not substantially affect the usefulness of the building or the purpose for which it was intended, the contractor may, in an action upon the contract, recover the amount of the contract price remaining unpaid, less the amount allowed as damages for the failure of strict performance.

Reference to the computation of items, both debit and credit, set forth in the findings in the present case, reveals an almost literal compliance with the formula approved in the *Haverty* case, supra; and there is substantial evidence to support the trial court's finding that plaintiffs themselves breached the contract and thus made impossible full performance on defendant's part.

* * *

The judgment is affirmed.

Plaintiffs are ordered to pay to defendant Wolpin additional attorney's fees on this appeal in an amount to be determined by the trial court.

NOTES

(1) *Divisibility and Substantial Performance.* Did the contractor in *Lowy* substantially perform the entire contract? If not, how did he recover the adjusted contract price for the excavation and grading work on the lots and streets? As one court put it: a divisible contract "is not two (or more) separate contracts; if it's broken it is broken entirely. The only significance of its divisibility is that the contract price will be used to determine the value of any partial performance of the contract." Fidelity and Deposit Co. of Maryland v. Rotec Indus., Inc., 392 F.3d 944, 945 (7th Cir. 2004).

(2) It is commonly stated that whether a contract is divisible depends upon the intention of the parties, and the intent to have a divisible contract may be inferred from such factors as the ease with which the agreed consideration can be apportioned to separate performances, the fungibility of those performances and the lack of evidence that the parties would have refused to deal for less than the whole. See Management Serv. Corp. v. Development Assoc., 617 P.2d 406, 408 (Utah 1980) (contract to purchase eight lots divisible). Section 240 of Restatement (Second), however, states that the question is whether the "performances to be exchanged under an exchange of promises can be apportioned into corresponding pairs of part performances so that the parts of each pair are properly regarded as agreed equivalents." According to Comment d, the "process of apportionment is essentially one of calculation and the rule can only be applied where calculation is feasible." Even so, the contract is not divisible unless it is "proper to regard the parts of each pair as agreed equivalents" and, in many cases, the "parties * * * cannot even be said to have had any actual intention on the point." Restatement (Second) § 240 cmt. e. Motivated by a desire to avoid forfeiture, the court's decision will "usually depend on considerations of fairness," such as the receipt by the aggrieved party of a part performance "worth to him roughly the same fraction of what full performance would have been worth. * * * " Put another way, the "injured party will not be required to pay for a part of the performance that he has received if he cannot make full use of that part without the remainder of the performance" and, in making this determination, a court "must * * * take account of the possibility that the remainder of the performance can be easily obtained from some other source."

(3) UCC § 2–307 provides: "Unless otherwise agreed all goods called for by a contract for sale must be tendered in a single delivery and payment is due only on such tender but where the circumstances give either party the right to make or demand delivery in lots the price if it can be apportioned may be demanded for each lot." Thus, where the circumstances indicate that a party has a right to delivery in lots, the price may be demanded for each lot if it is apportionable. UCC § 2–307 cmt. 4.

New Era Homes Corp. v. Engelbert Forster

Court of Appeals of New York, 1949.
299 N.Y. 303.

■ DESMOND, JUDGE. Plaintiff entered into a written agreement with defendants, to make extensive alterations to defendants' home, the reference therein to price and payment being as follows:

"All above material, and labor to erect and install same to be supplied for $3,075.00 to be paid as follows:

$150.00 on signing of contract,

$1,000.00 upon delivery of materials and starting of work,

$1,500.00 on completion of rough carpentry and rough plumbing,

$425.00 upon job being completed."

The work was commenced and partly finished, and the first two stipulated payments were made. Then, when the "rough work" was done, plaintiff asked for the third installment of $1,500 but defendants would not pay it, so plaintiff stopped work and brought suit for the whole of the balance, that is, for the two last payments of $1,500 and $425. On the trial plaintiff stipulated to reduce its demand to $1,500, its theory being that, since all the necessary "rough carpentry and rough plumbing" had been done, the time had arrived for it to collect $1,500. It offered no other proof as to its damages. Defendants conceded their default but argued at the trial, and argue here, that plaintiff was entitled not to the $1,500 third payment, but to such amount as it could establish by way of actual loss sustained from defendants' breach. In other words, defendants say the correct measure of damage was the value of the work actually done, less payments made, plus lost profits. The jury, however, by its verdict gave plaintiff its $1,500. The Appellate Division, Second Department, affirmed the judgment, and we granted defendants leave to appeal to this court.

The whole question is as to the meaning of so much of the agreement as we have quoted above. Did that language make it an entire contract, with one consideration for the doing of the whole work, and payments on account at fixed points in the progress of the job, or was the bargain a severable or divisible one in the sense that, of the total consideration, $1,150 was to be the full and fixed payment for "delivery of materials and starting of work", $1,500 the full and fixed payment for work done up to and including "completion of rough carpentry and rough plumbing", and $425 for the rest. We hold that the total price of $3,075 was the single consideration for the whole of the work, and that the separately listed payments were not allocated absolutely to certain parts of the undertaking, but were scheduled part payments, mutually convenient to the builder and the owner. That conclusion, we think, is a necessary one from the very words of the writing, since the arrangement there stated was not that separate items of work be done for separate amounts of money, but that the whole alteration project, including material and labor, was "to be supplied for $3,075". There is nothing in the record to suggest that the parties had intended to group, in this contract, several separate engagements, each with its own separate consideration. They did not say, for instance, that the price for all the work up to the completion of rough carpentry and plumbing was to be $1,500. They did agree that at that point $1,500 would be due, but as a part payment on the whole price. To illustrate: it is hardly conceivable that the amount of $150, payable "on signing of contract" was a reward to plaintiff for the act of affixing its corporate name and seal.

We would, in short, be writing a new contract for these people if we broke this single promise up into separate deals; and the new contract so written by us might be, for all we know, most unjust to one or the other party.

We find no controlling New York case, but the trend of authority in this State, and elsewhere, is that such agreements express an intent that payment be conditioned and dependent upon completion of all the agreed work. . . . We think that is the reasonable rule—after all, a householder who remodels his home is, usually, committing himself to one plan and one result, not a series of unrelated projects. The parties to a construction or alteration contract may, of course, make it divisible and stipulate the value of each divisible part. But there is no sign that these people so intended, see Integrity Flooring v. Zandon, supra. It follows that plaintiff, on defendants' default, could collect either in *quantum meruit* for what had been finished, . . . or in contract for the value of what plaintiff had lost—that is, the contract price, less payments made and less the cost of completion. . . .

The judgments should be reversed, and a new trial granted, with costs to abide the event.

■ LEWIS, JUDGE (dissenting).

A contract is entire or divisible depending upon the intention of the parties to be gathered from the agreement itself and the circumstances surrounding its execution. . . .

The parties to the written agreement here in suit were careful to provide that the contract price was to be paid in specified installments which, after the initial payment, were in varying amounts payable upon completion of designated stages of the work. The contracting parties thus indicated their intent to be that the part to be performed by the plaintiff was to consist of several distinct and separate items and that the price to be paid by the defendants was to be apportioned accordingly to fall due when each specified stage of the work should be completed. . . .

Concluding, as I do, that such a contract is divisible in character, . . . I would affirm the judgment.

NOTES

(1) Suppose, in *New Era Homes,* the owner had agreed to pay 80% of the contractor's total cost at each stage of completion rather than a fixed amount. Would the contract have been divisible? Should the contractor be satisfied by an action "on the contract" to recover just 80% of his cost incurred?

(2) *Progress Payments in Government Contracts.* In government supply and construction contracts, there is often a long "lead time" between the beginning of work and final delivery or completion where the contractor is uncompensated for partial performance expenditures. To alleviate the impact of this on the contractor's financial position, the government will make progress payments based upon costs incurred. In construction contracts the contractor will be paid 80% of its costs incurred at various stages of performance (compare *New Era Homes*), and in supply contracts the payments are made "as work progresses, from time to time upon request." The payments are liquidated from amounts due as construction is completed or the supplies are delivered.

PROBLEMS: DIVISIBLE OR ENTIRE CONTRACT?

(1) *The Case of the Defaulting Thresher.* Plaintiffs (P), owners of a threshing outfit, agreed with the defendant (D), a farmer, to thresh his grain at the following rates: wheat, $1.00 per bushel; oats, $.60 per bushel; flax, $1.50 per bushel. After threshing about 50% of the crop, P moved its equipment to another location because they were losing money on the job with D. D was obliged to complete the threshing of its grain at a higher price through other parties. Is P entitled to recover for the work done at the agreed price per bushel on the ground that the contract was "divisible"? See Johnson v. Fehsefeldt, 106 Minn. 202 (1908). If not, is there another basis upon which they might seek relief? See the cases that follow.

(2) *The Case of the Failed Resort Bid.* Young and Tate agreed to invest in a proposed resort project. The first stage involved putting together a bid to be made to the State. Among other things, the agreement provided that Young, because of her better credit, was to provide $50,000 for this first stage, $25,000 on January 2, 1985, and the next $25,000 "as needed." The agreement also provided that Tate "will assume liability for the first $25,000." The first payment was made, but when Tate's agent requested the second payment, Young, without justification, refused to pay. Tate then spent $32,000 in furtherance of the bid, which was ultimately rejected by the State. Young sued Tate to recover the $25,000 paid and Tate counterclaimed to recover $25,000 of the expenses incurred after Young refused to make the second payment. Assuming that Young's refusal was a breach of contract, what result? See Young v. Tate, 232 Neb. 915 (1989).

(3) *The Case of the Option to Purchase.* Pauley leased agricultural land to Simonson, who agreed to pay $36,000 for the first year in installments [$6,000 at signing and $10,000 at specified times during the balance of the first year.] After the first year the rent was $40,000 to be paid in four equal installments. The lease was to expire ninety days after the last to die of Ezra

and Elizabeth Pauley unless terminated under the lease. The lease also gave Simonson an option to purchase the land upon the last to die of the Pauleys, and Simonson was to make a $4,000 nonrefundable payment for the option at the time the lease was executed. This $4,000 payment was made. Simonson, however, failed to make a $10,000 payment in the second year of the lease leading Pauley to terminate the lease. Simonson claimed that the option to purchase the land survived the termination of the lease and could be exercised under the terms of the terminated lease. The trial court held that the option to purchase was not severable from the lease and did not survive termination of the lease. Simonson appealed, arguing that he had paid $4,000 for the option. What result? Pauley v. Simonson, 720 N.W.2d 665 (S.D. 2006).

Comment: Breach of Construction Contract and the Components Approach

New Era Homes presents a classic case of breach by the Owner while a Contractor is in the midst of performing a construction contract. Unless the contract is divisible or Contractor has "substantially" performed, an action for the agreed price for the job will not lie. Furthermore, any performance by Contractor after the breach is normally out of the question (the work is being done on Owner's land) and, in any event, would probably run afoul of the mitigation rule. See, e.g., Rockingham County v. Luten Bridge Co., 35 F.2d 301 (4th Cir. 1929) (unreasonable expenditures in performance incurred after the breach not recoverable). Put another way, Contractor would probably be ousted from the project and unable to recover for any work done after the breach. What damages can Contractor recover?

A Useful Formula. New Era Homes stated that the plaintiff "could collect either in *quantum meruit* for what had been finished . . . or in contract for what plaintiff had lost—that is, the contract price, less payments made and less the cost of completion." Leaving *quantum meruit*, or restitution, recovery aside, the calculation of compensatory damages can be illustrated as follows. If the contract price was $3,075 and, at the time of the breach, the estimated cost to complete the project was $425 (savings realized by breach, SR), and Contractor had been paid $2,000 in progress payments (PP), the damages for breach would be $3,075 (KP) less $425 (SR) less $2,000 (PP) = $650. This figure will be enhanced if Contractor can prove other losses, including incidental or consequential damages, and, of course, Owner can always attack Contractor's attempt to prove the savings realized by the breach, here $425. See generally, Edwin W. Patterson, *Builder's Measure of Recovery for Breach of Contract*, 31 Colum. L. Rev. 1286 (1931).

Note that the remainder above, $650, covers both the gain prevented by the breach and performance expenditures incurred up to the breach not covered by the progress payments. Assume, in our example, that Owner had made no payments under the contract and that the cost to complete (SR) was $425. The remainder, after subtracting $425 from $3,075, $2,650, should be broken down into components for a more thorough analysis, i.e., what part of the $2,650 represents net profit prevented, what part represents costs incurred up to the breach and, of those costs incurred, what part is variable and what part is fixed (overhead) costs? Suppose, then, that the value of the total costs incurred (TCI) at the time of breach was $2,500. The net profit prevented should be determined by subtracting from $3,075 (KP) the sum of $425 (SR) and $2,500 (TCI) for a profit figure of $150. When this is added to the TCI figure of $2,500, the total recovery for breach of contract is still $2,650. A more thorough breakdown might try to distinguish between fixed and variable costs in the $2,500 TCI figure, especially since Owner may claim that Contractor did not exercise reasonable efforts to salvage materials purchased or to reallocate labor after the breach. If Owner is correct, the TCI figure might be reduced in the amount that would have been realized if a reasonable salvage had been effected. For a fuller exploration of these complexities, see *Colorado Environments, Inc. v. Valley Grading Corp.*, 105 Nev. 464 (1989).

In the example above, the damages, whether expressed in a lump sum or components, protect both the expectation and the reliance interests. Put more directly, Contractor cannot be put in the place Owner's full performance would have put it unless it recovers both net gains prevented and unreimbursed expenses in part performance. In addition, Contractor should have the opportunity to plead and prove consequential damages resulting from the breach that were foreseeable by the defendant at the time of contracting. See Independent Mechanical Contractors, Inc. v. Gordon T. Burke & Sons, Inc., 138 N.H. 110 (1993) (profits lost in other ventures).

Burden of Proof. Who has the burden of proving what the cost of completion would have been, the plaintiff or the defendant? In a case where the plaintiff was a terminated contractor who left a construction job that was later completed by others, it was held that the initial burden of coming forward with evidence (and, perhaps, the ultimate risk of non-persuasion) was on the defendant. United States v. Merritt-Meridian Constr. Corp., 2000 WL 272177 (S.D.N.Y. 2000). The court analogized the cost to complete to a set-off, which is traditionally treated as an affirmative defense. In addition, the court concluded that the burden should be on the party with superior access to information about completion costs and who seeks to take advantage of them. In both cases, that was the defendant.

Britton v. Turner
Supreme Court of Judicature of New Hampshire, 1834.
6 N.H. 481.

Assumpsit for work and labour, performed by the plaintiff, in the service of the defendant, from March 9th, 1831, to December 27, 1831.

The declaration contained the common counts, and among them a count in *quantum meruit,* for the labor, averring it to be worth one hundred dollars.

At the trial in the C.C. Pleas, the plaintiff proved the performance of the labor as set forth in the declaration.

The defence was that it was performed under a special contract— that the plaintiff agreed to work one year, from some time in March, 1831, to March 1832, and that the defendant was to pay him for said year's labor the sum of one hundred and twenty dollars; and the defendant offered evidence tending to show that such was the contract under which the work was done.

Evidence was also offered to show that the plaintiff left the defendant's service without his consent, and it was contended by the defendant that the plaintiff had no good cause for not continuing in his employment.

There was no evidence offered of any damage arising from the plaintiff's departure, farther than was to be inferred from his non fulfillment of the entire contract.

The court instructed the jury, that if they were satisfied from the evidence that the labor was performed, under a contract to labor a year, for the sum of one hundred and twenty dollars, and if they were satisfied that the plaintiff labored only the time specified in the declaration, and then left the defendant's service, against his consent, and without any good cause, yet the plaintiff was entitled to recover, under his *quantum meruit* count, as much as the labor he performed was reasonably worth, and under this direction the jury gave a verdict for the plaintiff for the sum of $95.

The defendant excepted to the instructions thus given to the jury.

■ PARKER, J. delivered the opinion of the court. It may be assumed, that the labor performed by the plaintiff, and for which he seeks to recover a compensation in this action, was commenced under a special contract to labor for the defendant the term of one year, for the sum of one hundred and twenty dollars, and that the plaintiff has labored but a portion of that time, and has voluntarily failed to complete the entire contract.

It is clear, then, that he is not entitled to recover upon the contract itself, because the service, which was to entitle him to the sum agreed upon, has never been performed.

But the question arises, can the plaintiff, under these circumstances, recover a reasonable sum for the service he has actually performed, under the count in *quantum meruit.*

Upon this, and questions of a similar nature, the decisions to be found in the books are not easily reconciled.

It has been held, upon contracts of this kind for labor to be performed at a specified price, that the party who voluntarily fails to fulfil the contract by performing the whole labor contracted for, is not entitled to recover any thing for the labor actually performed, however much he may have done towards the performance, and this has been considered the settled rule of law upon this subject. . . .

That such rule in its operation may be very unequal, not to say unjust, is apparent.

A party who contracts to perform certain specified labor, and who breaks his contract in the first instance, without any attempt to perform it, can only be made liable to pay the damages which the other party has sustained by reason of such non performance, which in many instances may be trifling—whereas a party who in good faith has entered upon the performance of his contract, and nearly completed it, and then abandoned the further performance—although the other party has had the full benefit of all that has been done, and has perhaps sustained no actual damage—is in fact subjected to a loss of all which has been performed, in the nature of damages for the nonfulfillment of the remainder, upon the technical rule, that the contract must be fully performed in order to [justify] a recovery of any part of the compensation.

By the operation of this rule, then, the party who attempts performance may be placed in a much worse situation than he who wholly disregards his contract, and the other party may receive much more, by the breach of the contract, than the injury which he has sustained by such breach, and more than he could be entitled to were he seeking to recover damages by an action.

The case before us presents an illustration. Had the plaintiff in this case never entered upon the performance of his contract, the damage could not probably have been greater than some small expense and trouble incurred in procuring another to do the labor which he had contracted to perform. But having entered upon the performance, and labored nine and a half months, the value of which labor to the defendant as found by the jury is $95, if the defendant can succeed in this defence, he in fact receives nearly five sixths of the value of a whole year's labor, by reason of the breach of contract by the plaintiff, a sum not only utterly disproportionate to any probable, not to say possible damage which could have resulted from the neglect of the plaintiff to continue the remaining two and a half months, but altogether beyond any damage which could have been recovered by the defendant, had the plaintiff done nothing towards the fulfillment of his contract.

* * *

It is said, that where a party contracts to perform certain work, and to furnish materials, as for instance, to build a house, and the work is done, but with some variations from the mode prescribed by the contract, yet if the other party has the benefit of the labor and materials he should be bound to pay so much as they are reasonably worth. . . .

Those cases are not to be distinguished, in principle, from the present, unless it be in the circumstance, that where the party has contracted to furnish materials, and do certain labor, as to build a house in a specified manner, if it is not done according to the contract, the party for whom it is built may refuse to receive it—elect to take no benefit from what has been performed—and therefore if he does receive, he shall be bound to pay the value—whereas in a contract for labor, merely, from day to day, the party is continually receiving the benefit of the contract under an expectation that it will be fulfilled, and cannot, upon the breach of it, have an election to refuse to receive what has been done, and thus discharge himself from payment.

But we think this difference in the nature of the contracts does not justify the application of a different rule in relation to them.

The party who contracts for labor merely, for a certain period, does so with full knowledge that he must, from the nature of the case, be accepting part performance from day to day, if the other party commences the performance, and with knowledge also that the other may eventually fail of completing the entire term.

If under such circumstances he actually receives a benefit from the labor performed, over and above the damage occasioned by the failure to complete, there is as much reason why he should pay the reasonable worth of what has thus been done for his benefit, as there is when he enters and occupies the house which has been built for him, but not according to the stipulations of the contract, and which he perhaps enters, not because he is satisfied with what has been done, but because circumstances compel him to accept it such as it is, that he should pay for the value of the house.

* * *

In fact we think the technical reasoning, that the performance of the whole labor is a condition precedent, and the right to recover any thing dependent upon it—that the contract being entire there can be no apportionment—and that there being an express contract no other can be implied, even upon the subsequent performance of service—is not properly applicable to this species of contract, where a beneficial service has been actually performed; for we have abundant reason to believe, that the general understanding of the community is, that the hired laborer shall be entitled to compensation for the service actually performed, though he do not continue the entire term contracted for, and such contracts must be presumed to be made with reference to that understanding, unless an express stipulation shows the contrary.

* * *

It is easy, if parties so choose, to provide by an express agreement that nothing shall be earned, if the laborer leaves his employer without having performed the whole service contemplated, and then there can be no pretence for a recovery if he voluntarily deserts the service before the expiration of the time.

The amount, however, for which the employer ought to be charged, where the laborer abandons his contract, is only the reasonable worth, or the amount of advantage he receives upon the whole transaction, . . . and, in estimating the value of the labor, the contract price for the service cannot be exceeded.

* * *

The benefit and advantage which the party takes by the labor, therefore, is the amount of value which he receives, if any, after deducting the amount of damage. . . .

* * *

This rule, by binding the employer to pay the value of the service he actually receives, and the laborer to answer in damages where he does not complete the entire contract, will leave no temptation to the former to drive the laborer from his service, near the close of his term, by ill treatment, in order to escape from payment; nor to the latter to desert his service before the stipulated time, without a sufficient reason; and it will in most instances settle the whole controversy in one action, and prevent a multiplicity of suits and cross actions.

* * *

Applying the principles thus laid down, to this case, the plaintiff is entitled to judgment on the verdict.

The defendant sets up a mere breach of the contract in defence of the action, but this cannot avail him. He does not appear to have offered evidence to show that he was damnified by such breach, or to have asked that a deduction should be made upon that account. The direction to the jury was therefore correct, that the plaintiff was entitled to recover as much as the labor performed was reasonably worth, and the jury appear to have allowed a *pro rata* compensation, for the time which the plaintiff labored in the defendant's service. * * *

Judgment on the verdict.

NOTES

(1)   As one court put it:

Because the application of the [divisibility] doctrine depends on evidence of 'agreed equivalents,' the use of the contract price to determine entitlements when the contract has not been fully performed is defensible only when the contract itself can be said to specify the price for partial performance. . . . That condition will rarely be satisfied. If an employment contract is for a year and the employee quits after his first week on the job, it is artificial to suppose that the contract entitles him to one week's wages, for had he insisted in the contract that he be free to leave after a week the employer would probably have refused to hire him at all, or at least at the agreed wage. . . . The fact that many courts nevertheless treat employment contracts as divisible probably has less to do with the logic of the doctrine than with a policy, embodied in state wage-payment laws.

Fidelity and Deposit Co. of Maryland v. Rotec Indus., Inc., 392 F.3d 944, 947 (7th Cir. 2004) (Posner, J).

(2) The "constructive" condition dilemma facing Judge Parker in *Britton v. Turner* has been resolved in many states by legislation: the employer must pay the employee's wages at regular intervals regardless of "substantial" performance. See, e.g., 820 Ill. Comp. Stat. 115/3 (all wage earners other than executives, administrators, professionals and commission agents must be paid on a semi-monthly basis.) The employer's failure to pay as required may be a crime. See Holmes v. Tradigrain, Inc., 411 So.2d 1132 (La. Ct. App.1982); Putnam v. Oregon Dep't of Justice, 58 Or.App. 111 (1982). For an illustration of the type of question that can arise under these statutes, see *Suastez v. Plastic Dress-Up Co.*, 31 Cal.3d 774 (1982), where the California Supreme Court held that a proportionate right to a paid vacation vested in the employee as labor was rendered and, once vested, was protected from forfeiture by the applicable legislation.

(3) When you have time you must read Robert W. Gordon, *Britton v. Turner: A Signpost on the Crooked Road to "Freedom"*, in the Employment Contract, Contracts Stories 186 (Foundation Press, 2007).

Comment: Recovery in Restitution by a Plaintiff in Default

Britton v. Turner permitted a plaintiff who had arguably committed a material breach to recover the reasonable value of work done up to the breach, "less whatever damages the other party has suffered." See also Kulseth v. Rotenberger, 320 N.W.2d 920 (N.D. 1982); Kirkland v. Archbold, 113 N.E.2d 496 (Ohio Ct. App. 1953); Pinches v. Swedish Evangelical Lutheran Church, 55 Conn. 183 (1887). Put another way, although a plaintiff cannot recover "on the contract," he or she can recover in restitution the net benefit retained by the defendant after full compensation for plaintiff's breach of contract. That benefit, however, is limited by the contract price. Section 357 of the first Restatement adopted the "net benefit" test, stating that the "measure of the defendant's benefit from the plaintiff's part performance is the amount by which he has been enriched as a result of such performance * * *." Restatement § 357(3).

The first Restatement provided that restitution was not available if the plaintiff's breach was "wilful and deliberate." Restatement § 357(1). The apparent purpose of this limitation was to direct attention to the moral justification for the breach: an intentional breach is not regarded as willful and deliberate if it was "due to hardship, insolvency, or circumstances that tend appreciably toward moral justification." Restatement § 357 cmt. e. See G. Palmer, Law of Restitution § 5.1 (1978).

Section 374(1) of Restatement (Second) does not make restitution turn upon the reason for the plaintiff's breach. If the defendant is justified in refusing to perform because of the plaintiff's material breach, the "party in breach is entitled to restitution for any benefit that he has conferred by way of part performance or reliance in excess of the loss that he has caused by his own breach." See section 370 for the general requirement that a benefit be conferred for restitution. Section 371 provides the "measure" of the restitution interest. If money rather than specific restitution is sought,

> it may as justice requires be measured by either (a) the reasonable value to the other party of what he received in terms of what it would have cost him to obtain it from a person in the claimant's position, or (b) the extent to which the other party's property has been increased in value or his other interests advanced.

In no case, however, "will the party in breach be allowed to recover more than a ratable portion of the total contract price where such a portion can be determined." Restatement (Second) § 374 cmt. b. Does this approach rule out consideration of the moral justification for the breach? The answer is probably "no" when judicial discretion in measuring the restitution interest is taken into account. The measurement is made "as justice requires," and when the "party seeking restitution has himself committed a material breach * * * uncertainties as to the amount of the benefit may properly be resolved against him." Restatement (Second) § 371 cmt. a. See Illustration 1. This open-endedness is consistent with Palmer's conclusion that although restitution should not always be denied when the breach is in bad faith, it "does mean that it should be allowed less readily." In short, "the retention of some enrichment may well be just when it is brought about by plaintiff's willful and deliberate breach." Palmer at § 5.15, p. 685.

This, apparently, is still the law in New York, at least in real estate contracts, where the vendor is permitted to keep the down payment in a contract to purchase where the vendee commits a willful breach. In *Maxton Builders, Inc. v. Lo Galbo*, 68 N.Y.2d 373 (1986), the court recognized the "modern rule" that permitted restitution of the excess retained over damages but refused to overrule earlier authority to the contrary. "For more than a century it has been well settled in this State that a vendee who defaults on a real estate contract without lawful excuse, cannot recover the down payment." Id. at 378.

PROBLEMS: RESTITUTIONARY RELIEF AND THE WRONGDOER

(1) A contracted with B to construct a swimming pool on B's land for $15,000. The specifications required a designated system for the walls and floor that was guaranteed for 20 years. A, in order to shave costs on the fixed-price contract, deliberately installed a different and somewhat inferior system, which was guaranteed for 10 years. B refused to pay the contract

price and A sued for either the price or restitution. The trial court determined that although B had a functional pool for at least 10 years, A had committed a material breach. The trial court also determined that the cost to replace the system would be $20,000 and that the difference in value of the land with a pool as promised by A and the pool actually constructed was $5,000. In order to avoid "economic waste," the trial court then awarded B $5,000 damages for breach of contract. In considering A's claim for restitution, the trial court determined that: (a) the reasonable value to B of the pool constructed in terms of what it would have cost to obtain it from another pool contractor was $12,000; and (b) the difference in value of B's land with the pool actually constructed and without a pool was $5,000. What, if anything, should A recover in restitution from B?

(2) B ordered complex medical diagnostic equipment from S for $500,000 and paid $300,000 down at the time of contracting. S completed manufacturing the machine, but B, because its needs had changed, refused to accept delivery. S sued for damages and, as a lost volume seller, proved that the profit plus reasonable overhead it would have made on the contract was $80,000. B sought to recover the down payment. Assuming that S's damages are $80,000, what if anything, can B recover? See UCC § 2–718(2–4).

(E) MENTAL ANGUISH AND PUNITIVE DAMAGES

In *Sullivan v. O'Connor*, reprinted in Chapter One, the plaintiff recovered for mental anguish resulting from the defendant's breach of contract. Under what circumstances are these damages proper in an action for breach? When, if ever, might breach support an award of punitive damages? These are the two topics of this section. The ideas of mental anguish and punitive damages are in some ways very different. One is a form of compensation for nonpecuniary losses; the other is more about deterrence or retribution than making whole. But as we shall see, judicial reasoning about two often appear together in contract cases. One reason: both raise questions about where to draw the line between contract and tort.

Elliot Kaplan and Jeanne Kaplan v. Mayo Clinic
United States District Court for the District of Minnesota, 2013.
947 F.Supp.2d 1001.

■ JOHN R. TUNHEIM, DISTRICT JUDGE. This case arises out of a surgery performed on Elliot Kaplan ("Kaplan") by a surgeon at Mayo Clinic to treat pancreatic cancer, a condition which post-surgery testing revealed that Kaplan never had. Kaplan and has wife Jeanne Kaplan (collectively, "the Kaplans") filed lawsuit against Mayo Clinic and its affiliated entities (collectively, "Mayo"), as well as Dr. David Nagorney ("Dr. Nagorney"), the doctor who performed Kaplan's surgery, and Dr. Lawrence J. Burgart ("Dr. Burgart"), the doctor who erroneously diagnosed Kaplan with pancreatic cancer. The Court granted summary judgment in favor of Dr.

Nagorney. The case proceeded to trial against the other defendants on the Kaplans' claims of breach of contract and negligent failure to diagnose. At the close of the Kaplans' case, the Court granted judgment as a matter of law against them on their breach of contract claim. The jury returned a verdict for Mayo and Burgart on the Kaplans' claim for negligent failure to diagnose, and the Court entered judgment on that verdict.

On appeal, the Eighth Circuit reversed as to the breach of contract claim concluding that a reasonable jury could find that Nagorney, on behalf of Mayo, formed a contract with Kaplan when Nagorney told Kaplan that he would perform an intraoperative biopsy to confirm the cancer diagnosis before proceeding with the surgery. The Eighth Circuit found that Nagorney breached this contract when he failed to perform the promised biopsy. The Eighth Circuit remanded for further proceedings on the breach of contract claim.

The case is now before the Court on Mayo's motions in limine regarding the presentation of damages evidence at the remand trial on the Kaplans' breach of contract claim. Mayo requests that the Court . . . preclude the Kaplans from presenting evidence of pain and suffering and emotional damages in support of their breach of contract claim. . . . For the reasons explained below, the Court will grant Mayo's motion to exclude evidence of pain and suffering. . . .

* * *

The Court begins by determining whether the Kaplans may present evidence of pain and suffering and emotional distress to prove damages in relation to their breach of contract claim.

A damage award in a breach of contract action is intended to place the nonbreaching party "in the position in which he would be if the contract were performed." *Lesmeister v. Dilly*, 330 N.W.2d 95, 102 (Minn.1983). . . . Therefore, a plaintiff may recover those "damages sustained by reason of the breach which arose naturally from the breach or could reasonably be supposed to have been contemplated by the parties when making the contract as the probable result of the breach." *Lesmeister*, 330 N.W.2d at 103; *see also Franklin Mfg. Co. v. Union Pac. R.R. Co.*, 248 N.W.2d 324, 325 (Minn. 1976) ("When the damages are assessed as those which it is reasonable to suppose that the parties had in mind, what is really meant is that the law, aiming at compensation, considers it fair to hold a defendant for damages which as a reasonable man he ought to have foreseen as likely to follow from a breach. What he in fact foresaw or contemplated is immaterial." (internal quotation marks and alterations omitted)). Whether damages were reasonably foreseeable at the time of contracting is a question of fact. *See Franklin Mfg. Co.*, 248 N.W.2d at 326.

"Liability for breach of contract requires proof that damages resulted from or were caused by the breach." *Border State Bank of Greenbush v.*

Bagley Livestock Exch., Inc., 690 N.W.2d 326, 336 (Minn.Ct.App. 2004). Whether a particular damage resulted from or was caused by a breach of contract is a question for the jury. *See id.* . . .

Extra-contractual damages, on the other hand, are those which do not flow naturally from the breach and are not reasonably anticipated by the parties to the contract. *See Wild v. Rarig,* 234 N.W.2d 775, 789 (Minn. 1975). In Minnesota, extracontractual damages "are not recoverable for breach of contract except in exceptional cases where the breach is accompanied by an independent tort." *Haagenson v. Nat'l Farmers Union Prop. & Cas. Co.,* 277 N.W.2d 648, 652 (Minn. 1979). "The accompanying independent tort must be willful." *Lickteig v. Alderson, Ondov, Leonard & Sween, P.A.,* 556 N.W.2d 557, 561 (Minn. 1996). The rule disallowing extra-contractual damages is designed "to insure that contract law is not swallowed by tort law." *Deli v. Univ. of Minn.,* 578 N.W.2d 779, 782 (Minn.Ct.App. 1998).

A jury found in favor of the defendants on all of the Kaplans' tort claims and the Eighth Circuit affirmed the verdict. Therefore, there is no independent tort in the present case and the Kaplans cannot recover any extra-contractual damages. The difficulty, however, is determining whether pain and suffering and emotional distress damages constitute extra-contractual damages in the context of the alleged contract between Mayo and the Kaplans.

Although pain and suffering and emotional distress damages might seem to be the natural proximate cause of a breach in certain types of contracts, Minnesota courts have expanded the prohibition on recovering such damages in a breach of contract action, even where those damages could be reasonably within the contemplation of the parties based on the nature of the contract. *See Lickteig,* 556 N.W.2d at 561 (categorically defining emotional distress damages as "extra-contractual"); *Francis v. W. Union Tel. Co.,* 58 Minn. 252, 59 N.W. 1078, 1081 (1894) (denying recovery of emotional distress damages even after recognizing that a contract to send a sensitive telegram relates "wholly to matters of sentiment or feeling" and therefore breach of such a contract could reasonably be expected to result in mental anxiety); *Deli,* 578 N.W.2d at 781–82 (finding emotional distress damages could not be awarded on a claim for an athletic director's breach of an oral promise not to view a videotape that contained footage of the plaintiff's sexual encounter with her husband, despite the "inherently personal nature" of the contract); *Born v. Medico Life Ins. Co.,* 428 N.W.2d 585, 587, 590 (Minn.Ct.App. 1988) (stating that pain and suffering were extra-contractual damages even though the breach alleged was for a contract to provide medical insurance).

Instead of examining solely the foreseeability of certain damages to determine whether such damages may be extra-contractual, Minnesota law appears to restrict recoverable contractual damages more generally to those that are pecuniary in nature. The Minnesota Supreme Court has long held that regardless of the "nature of the contract . . . [t]he law looks only to the pecuniary value of the contract, and for its breach awards only pecuniary damages." *Francis,* 59 N.W. at 1081; *see also Beaulieu v. Great N. Ry. Co.,* 114 N.W. 353, 356 (Minn. 1907) (explaining that in the absence of an independent tort, damages for breach of contract "must be limited to the actual pecuniary loss naturally and necessarily flowing from the breach"). Therefore, in addition to requiring that contractual damages be those which flow directly from the breach and were within the contemplation of the parties, the Minnesota Supreme Court has held that contractual damages are those which "may be measured and determined by some definite rule or standard of compensation." *Beaulieu,* 114 N.W. at 355. Thus damages that are "incapable of definite calculation" and "must necessarily rest in the discretion of the jury" are extra-contractual and are recoverable only in tort actions. *Id.*

It does not appear that the Minnesota Supreme Court has ever precisely addressed whether pain and suffering and emotional distress damages are recoverable for breach of a contract between a physician and his patient. Where the Court is faced with an undecided question of Minnesota law, its role is to predict how the Minnesota Supreme Court would resolve the question. *See Spine Imaging MRI, L.L.C. v. Country Cas. Ins. Co.,* Civ. No. 10–480, 2011 WL 379100, at *6 (D.Minn. Feb. 1, 2011) (citing *Midwest Oilseeds, Inc. v. Limagrain Genetics Corp.,* 387 F.3d 705, 715 (8th Cir. 2004)).

Although many courts have recognized that "a surviving patient can maintain a cause of action for breach of an express or implied promise against a physician," *Zostautas v. St. Anthony De Padua Hosp.,* 178 N.E.2d 303, 307 (Ill. 1961), courts have disagreed about whether those surviving patients can recover damages for pain and suffering or emotional distress. Some courts have held that where "liability is predicated on the failure to perform an agreed undertaking rather than upon negligence . . . the damages are restricted to the payments made, the expenditure for nurses and medicines, or other damages that flow naturally from the breach (thereof), and do not include the patient's pain and suffering as in malpractice actions." *Id.* at 305 (citations and internal quotation marks omitted).[2] Courts limiting recoverable damages for breach of a contract by a physician have done so in part to maintain a clear distinction between tort and contract claims, emphasizing that "[a]lthough . . . actions of malpractice and breach of contract may arise

---

[2] *See also Sangdahl v. Litton,* 69 F.R.D. 641, 645 (S.D.N.Y.1976) ("If the physician fails to perform the original operation which he undertook, it would also seem that an action for breach of contract ought to lie. If such an action does lie, however, contract damages, as opposed to tort damages, will be recovered. This would exclude recovery for pain and suffering." (internal quotation marks omitted)); *Carpenter v. Moore,* 322 P.2d 125, 126–27 (Wash. 1958) ("The amount paid, or promised to be paid, is the consideration for the promise of a professional man that the patient or client will be satisfied with his work. . . . However, damages for pain and suffering, ordinarily predicated on negligence or malpractice, are not within the contemplation of the parties for the breach of a promise to do work to the satisfaction of a patient or client in the absence of some negligence or fault.").

out of the same transaction, they are distinct as to theory, proof and damages." *Id.* at 304.

Other courts, however, when faced with a contract between a physician and patient have applied the general rule of contract law that a plaintiff may recover damages that were within the contemplation of the contracting parties. In *Stewart v. Rudner,* for example, the court allowed the plaintiff to recover mental anguish and pain and suffering damages in a contract in which a physician had agreed, but failed to perform a Caesarean section, causing the death of the plaintiff's unborn child. 84 N.W.2d 816, 821, 824 (Mich. 1957). The court focused on the underlying subject matter of the parties' agreement, reasoning that this particular contract was "concerned not with trade and commerce but with life and death," a breach of which would "inevitably and necessarily result in mental anguish, pain and suffering." *Id.* at 824. Therefore, the court held that "[i]n such cases the parties may reasonably be said to have contracted with reference to the payment of damages [for mental anguish and pain and suffering] in the event of breach. Far from being outside the contemplation of the parties they are an integral and inseparable part of it." *Id.; see also Sullivan v. O'Connor,* 296 N.E.2d 183, 188–89 (Mass. 1973) ("It is all a question of the subject matter and background of the contract, and when the contract calls for an operation on the person of the plaintiff, psychological as well as physical injury may be expected to figure somewhere in the recovery, depending on the particular circumstances.").

Based upon Minnesota's general law governing contractual damages, the Court concludes that the Minnesota Supreme Court would likely follow the *Zostautas* court's approach, and preclude the Kaplans from recovering pain and suffering and emotional distress damages based upon the breach of any contract formed with Mayo. Although it is possible that pain and suffering and emotional distress could have reasonably been within the contemplation of Mayo and the Kaplans based upon the nature of the contract at issue, the Minnesota Supreme Court has expressly rejected the approach used in *Stewart* and *Sullivan* of examining the underlying nature of the contract to determine whether damages such as those for mental anguish and pain and suffering are recoverable. *See Francis,* 59 N.W. at 1081 (refusing to "allow damages for injury to the feelings resulting from a breach of contract—even one [relating wholly to matters of sentiment or feeling]"). Instead Minnesota law appears to limit damages in a contract action to those capable of measurement by "some definite rule or standard of compensation," and "to the actual pecuniary loss naturally and necessarily flowing from the breach." *Beaulieu,* 114 N.W. at 356. The Kaplans' pain and suffering as well as any emotional distress they may have suffered are damages that, although recoverable in tort, do not appear to be recoverable in a breach of contract action under Minnesota law. Therefore, the Court will preclude the Kaplans from presenting evidence of pain and suffering or emotional distress at trial to support their breach of contract action.[5]

The Court's conclusion that the Kaplans may not recover damages for pain and suffering or emotional distress is further supported by the Eighth Circuit's opinion in this case. The Eighth Circuit specifically determined that the Kaplans had "provided sufficient evidence of **economic damages** resulting from [the Whipple] to meet the final requirement for making out their contract claim." *Kaplan,* 653 F.3d at 728 (emphasis added). Furthermore, the Court notes that its conclusion is in keeping with the purpose of limiting extracontractual damages, to wit: preserving the boundary between contract and tort law. *See Deli,* 578 N.W.2d at 782. The Kaplans already brought tort claims against the defendants in this case. The jury rejected those claims, and the Eighth Circuit affirmed. The Kaplans cannot use their remaining breach of contract claim to attempt to recover all of the damages that may have been recoverable in those tort claims. Although allegedly based on some of the same conduct, the Kaplans' breach of contract action is distinct "as to theory, proof and damages," *Zostautas,* 178 N.E.2d at 304, and therefore the Kaplans may not recover damages for pain and suffering and emotional distress.

* * *

David Plotnik et al. v. John Meihaus et al.

California Court of Appeal, Fourth District, 2012.
208 Cal.App.4th 1590.

■ RYLAARSDAM, ACTING P. J.

* * *

FACTS AND PROCEDURAL BACKGROUND

Plaintiffs and their two children moved into a home in Laguna Niguel in 2003. The rear portion of the property slopes upward, abutting

---

[5] Mayo makes two additional arguments in support of its position that Kaplan cannot recover pain and suffering or emotional distress damages in this case. First, Mayo argues that Dr. Nagorney would have proceeded with the Whipple procedure even if an intraoperative biopsy had been performed and returned a negative result. Second, Mayo argues that Kaplan's alleged post-surgery symptoms are not post-Whipple symptoms or complications but are instead the product of some other medical condition. Neither of Mayo's arguments is directly relevant to the instant motion, because both merely go to causation, not to whether the damages Kaplan seeks are contractual or extra-contractual. As explained above "[l]iability for breach of contract **requires proof that damages resulted from or were caused by the breach**," and whether particular damages resulted from a breach is a question for the jury. *Border State Bank of Greenbush v. Bagley Livestock Exchange, Inc.,* 690 N.W.2d 326, 336 (Minn.Ct.App.2004) (emphasis added). Additionally, the Eighth Circuit specifically identified Mayo's first contention as a question for the jury. *Kaplan,* 653 F.3d at 728. Therefore, the parties are clearly allowed to present evidence at trial regarding whether Dr. Nagorney's breach (failing to do a biopsy) caused any of the Kaplans' claimed damages. But this conclusion does not answer the question of whether the Kaplans may seek damages for pain and suffering and emotional distress as a matter of law.

the Meihauses' lot. At the time, a three-foot high fence on the property line separated the two parcels.

Plaintiffs claimed that, shortly after moving into their home, they began to have problems with the Meihaus family. Plaintiffs built a six-foot-high fence along the parcels' common boundary. In response, Meihaus and his wife sued plaintiffs and the community association. That lawsuit was resolved in 2007 by a written settlement. In it, plaintiffs agreed to relocate the rear fence, moving it three feet back from the common boundary. The new fence has a gate that allows plaintiffs access to the portion of their property on the opposite side of the fence.

The settlement agreement contained clauses whereby each party "release[d] and discharge[d]" the other "from any and all claims, demands, or causes of action, known or unknown, which [they] now own or hold, or have at any time . . . heretofore owned. . . ." It also included a mutual restraint provision, stating "[t]he [p]arties . . . agree not to harass, vex or annoy[ ] each other either personally or by employing or encouragement of another for such purpose. Further neither party shall either verbally or in writing communicate to any other person or entity, whether in the form of purported statement of fact or opinion, any slanderous or disparaging matter concerning the personal or professional character or reputation of any other [p]arty. . . ." The settlement authorized the prevailing party's recovery of its legal expenses "in the event any action, suit or other proceeding . . . is instituted to remedy, prevent or obtain relief from a breach of this Agreement/Release [or] arising out of a breach of this Agreement/Release. . . ."

[The court summarized a litany of unpleasant encounters between the two families after the settlement agreement, including an incident in which Meihaus intentionally injured the Plotnick's dog, Romeo.]

Plaintiffs filed this lawsuit. Meihaus responded with a cross-complaint for breach of contract against plaintiffs.

The parties submitted a 33-page verdict form to the jury that sought rulings on 32 issues. The first and second special verdicts concerned whether Meihaus breached the 2007 settlement agreements as to each plaintiff. The jury found he did and awarded emotional distress damages of $35,000 to David Plotnik and $70,000 to Joyce Plotnik.

* * *

2. Breach of Contract

Plaintiffs' first cause of action alleged Meihaus breached the 2007 settlement agreement's mutual restraint clause by engaging in conduct of "harass[ing], vexing, and annoying . . . plaintiffs . . . and causing damage to [their] personal and real property. . . ." In response, Meihaus sued plaintiffs for breach of the settlement's mutual restraint clause. During cross-examination, Joyce Plotnik acknowledged telling several friends about the lawsuit and that Meihaus hit Romeo with a baseball bat. The jury found Meihaus breached the settlement agreement and awarded damages to each plaintiff. Although it also found Joyce Plotnik breached the settlement agreement, no damages were awarded to Meihaus.

Meihaus argues the evidence fails to support a finding he breached the settlement agreement, the damages awarded to plaintiffs were excessive, and, in any event, Joyce Plotnik's breach of the same agreement precludes her recovery on the contract. These contentions lack merit.

The settlement's mutual restraint clause prohibited the parties from "harass[ing], vex[ing] or annoy[ing] each other." It is true that some of the evidence plaintiffs presented about the parties' encounters would not support recovery of damages. Public interaction with people, even unfriendly neighbors, is a part of everyday life in an urban environment. Thus, testimony by Joyce Plotnik and her friends about passing Meihaus family members on public streets or seeing them driving through the neighborhood was irrelevant. The same is true for Meihaus's one-time comment to Joyce Plotnik to curb her dog's urination on neighbors' lawns.

However, other evidence does support the jury's breach of contract verdicts. Plaintiffs testified that shortly after entering into the settlement, they began to find yard clippings and debris on their property along the rear fence. David Plotnik described the clippings as similar to the foliage he saw in the Meihauses' yard. This conduct continued throughout the 18-month period between the fence settlement and the April 4, 2009 incidents. In addition, plaintiffs testified to Meihaus repeatedly making a vulgar gesture when they and their children passed him on the street. Viewing the evidence in the light most favorable to plaintiffs, as we are required to do, we also conclude the jury could find Meihaus engaged in further annoying behavior by intentionally staring at Joyce Plotnik for an extended time at the community pool. These actions supported the jury's conclusion Meihaus breached the settlement agreement.

We also reject Meihaus's attack on the damage awards for his breach of the settlement agreement. Civil Code section 3300 declares, "For the breach of an obligation arising from contract, the measure of damages . . . is the amount which will compensate the party aggrieved for all the detriment proximately caused thereby, or which, in the ordinary course of things, would be likely to result therefrom." Generally, "damages for mental suffering and emotional distress are . . . not compensable in contract actions. [Citation.]" (*Applied Equipment Corp. v. Litton Saudi Arabia Ltd.* (1994) 7 Cal.4th 503, 516.) But exceptions exist. One is where "'the breach is of such a kind that serious emotional disturbance was a particularly likely result.' [Citation.]" (*Erlich v. Menezes* (1999) 21 Cal.4th 543, 558.) "Thus, when the express object of the contract is the mental and emotional well-being of one of the contracting parties, the breach of the contract may give rise to damages for mental suffering or emotional distress. [Citations.]" (*Id.* at p. 559; see also *Westervelt v. McCullough* (1924) 68 Cal.App. 198, 208–209.)

This case is a good example of where the exception applies. It involves a dispute between neighbors sharing a common boundary. The prior lawsuit arose after plaintiffs removed the original fence and built a larger one in its place. The settlement of that action contained a mutual restraint provision to protect against the kind of activity that subsequently occurred.

Of course, the amount of damages must be reasonable. (Civ.Code, § 3359.) But " '[t]here is no fixed or absolute standard by which to compute the monetary value of emotional distress,' and a 'jury is entrusted with vast discretion in determining the amount of damages to be awarded. . . .' [Citation.]" (*Hope v. California Youth Authority* (2005) 134 Cal.App.4th 577, 595.) Consequently, as defendants acknowledge, "[o]ur power over excessive damages exists only when the facts are such that the excess appears as a matter of law, or is such as to suggest at first blush, passion, prejudice, or corruption on the part of the jury. [Citations.]" (*Rattray v. Albert* (1956) 146 Cal.App.2d 354, 356; accord *Hope v. California Youth Authority, supra,* 134 Cal.App.4th at p. 595.) Given the repeated and continuous nature of Meihaus's harassing, vexing, and annoying actions, we cannot conclude the jury's contractual damage awards are excessive as a matter of law.

Finally, Meihaus argues the contract damages awarded to Joyce Plotnik must be reversed because the jury found she also breached the settlement agreement's mutual restraint clause. "It is elementary a plaintiff suing for breach of contract must prove it has performed all conditions on its part or that it was excused from performance. [Citation.]" (*Consolidated World Investments, Inc. v. Lido Preferred Ltd.* (1992) 9 Cal.App.4th 373, 380.) Thus, "[o]ne who himself breaches a contract cannot recover for a subsequent breach by the other party." (*Silver v. Bank of America, N.T. & S.A.* (1941) 47 Cal.App.2d 639, 645.)

But "in contract law a material breach excuses further performance by the innocent party. [Citations.]" (*De Burgh v. De Burgh* (1952) 39 Cal.2d 858, 863; see also *Brown v. Grimes* (2011) 192 Cal.App.4th 265, 277.) "Normally the question of whether a breach of an obligation is a material breach, so as to excuse performance by the other party, is a question of fact. [Citations.]" (*Brown v. Grimes, supra,* 192 Cal.App.4th at p. 277.) Viewing the evidence in the light most favorable to plaintiffs, Meihaus's repeated acts of harassment supported a finding he materially breached the settlement agreement, thereby excusing Joyce Plotnik's noncompliance with the mutual restraint clause's prohibition by making disparaging statements about him to others.

* * *

We conclude Meihaus's attacks on the portion of the judgment awarding damages for breach of the settlement agreement lack merit.

* * *

NOTES

(1) Claims for mental anguish or emotional distress damages are on the borderline between contract and tort. The emotional disturbance results from a breach of contract (a wrongful termination), but the injury is to what might be called a "tort" rather than a "contract" interest. In addition to losing the value of the bargain, the plaintiff is worse off physically or emotionally than before the contract. See W. Prosser and P. Keeton, The Law of Torts § 12 (5th ed. 1984).

How did the courts in *Kaplan v. Mayo Clinic* and *Plotick v. Meihaus* draw the line between contract and tort? Can the two cases be reconciled? Can *Kaplan v. Mayo Clinic* be reconciled with *Sullivan v. O'Connor*'s holding on pain and suffering? Restatement (Second) Section 353 suggest the following rule:

> Recovery for emotional disturbance will be excluded unless the breach also caused bodily harm or the contract or the breach is of such a kind that serious emotional disturbance was a particularly likely result.

Which if any of the three cases—*Sullivan*, *Kaplan* and *Plotnick*—conforms to the Second Restatement approach?

In the comments to Section 353, the drafters identify several categories that have traditionally supported recovery for emotional disturbance: "contracts of carriers and innkeepers with passengers and guests, contracts for the carriage or proper disposition of dead bodies, and contracts for the delivery of messages concerning death." *Id.* cmt. a.

(2) In *Deli v. University of Minnesota*, 578 N.W.2d 779 (Minn.Ct.App. 1998), the claim was not for breach of contract but for promissory estoppel—which some commentators have analogized to recovery in tort. The Minnesota court, however, found that "a promissory estoppel claim sounds in contract," and therefore did not permit recovery for emotional distress. *Id.* at 782 (citing Cohen v. Cowles Media Co., 479 N.W.2d 387 (Minn. 1992), a successor to *Cohen v. Cowles Media*, reprinted in Chapter Three). Compare Hoffman v. Red Owl Stores, Inc., 26 Wis. 2d 683, 698 (1965) ("it would be a mistake to regard an action grounded on promissory estoppel as the equivalent of a breach of contract action").

(3) *Employment Contracts.* In *Gaglidari v. Denny's Restaurants, Inc.*, 117 Wash.2d 426 (1991), the court concluded that emotional distress damages were not available for breach of an employment contract. The court emphasized that an employment contract did not have "elements of personality" and that the parties had not agreed to protect those losses. According to the court, the type of contract involved rather than the nature of the breach or whether the loss was foreseeable was the critical issue.

This appears to be the prevailing view. For example, in *Francis v. Lee Enterprises, Inc.*, 89 Haw. 234, 235 (1999), the court rejected prior cases awarding damages for "tortious breach of contract" because "such a rule unnecessarily blurs the distinction between—and undermines the discrete theories of recovery relevant to—tort and contract."

> We now hold that Hawai'i law will not allow tort recovery in the absence of conduct that (1) violates a duty that is independently recognized by principles of tort law and (2) transcends the breach of the contract. Consistent with this rule, emotional distress damages will only be recoverable where the parties specifically provide for them in the contract or where the nature of the contract or where the nature of the breach clearly indicates that such damages were within the contemplation of the parties.

See generally Douglas Whaley, *Paying for the Agony: The Recovery of Emotional Distress Damages in Contract Actions,* 26 Suffolk U. L. Rev. 935 (1992). See also Erlich v. Menezes, 21 Cal.4th 543 (1999) (damages for emotional distress not available for negligent breach of contract to construct a home).

(4) The ruling from *Kaplan v. Mayo Clinic* was on a motion *in limine* asking that certain evidence be excluded. That motion did not dispose of the case, as the plaintiffs alleged damages beyond pain and suffering and emotional distress. After a trial on the breach of contract claim trial Judge Kaplan concluded:

> Because the Court concludes that Dr. Nagorney did not promise to perform an intraoperative biopsy to confirm the presence of cancer and would have performed the Whipple surgery even if he had taken an intraoperative biopsy that proved to be negative, the Court concludes that the Kaplans are not entitled to damages in this case. The Court recognizes that this is a truly unfortunate situation, as Elliot Kaplan underwent a surgery that ultimately was not necessary, and his quality of life has been diminished in the wake of that surgery. Despite the unfortunate nature of these circumstances, he may not recover damages from Mayo Clinic on his breach of contract claim.

Kaplan v. Mayo Clinic, 2015 WL 4877559, at *13 (D. Minn. 2015). Is it possible that the weakness of the plaintiff's contract claim influenced the court's earlier decision on mental suffering?

In addition to finding breach of contract, the jury in *Plotnick v. Maihaus* found for the plaintiffs on separate allegations of assault, trespass, negligence and negligent infliction of emotional distress, and awarded separate economic and emotional damages for each. Is it possible that the plaintiffs' success on these distinct tort claims made it easier for them to recover in contract for mental suffering? Should it?

PROBLEM: THE CASE OF THE DISTRESSED NEWLYWEDS

Jan and Pat were engaged in January and set the wedding date for June 21. Among other things, the couple entered a written agreement, dated

February 21, with a local band, the High Flyers, to play at the wedding reception. The couple paid $300 down and agreed to pay $700 more after the reception. The agreement said nothing about the consequences of a breach. Since the High Flyers were in great demand, Pat called on June 1 to confirm the engagement and was told by the leader, "Hey, no problem." The High Flyers, however, did not show up at the reception. On June 14, they took another job for the big evening (the fee was $2,000) and neglected to notify either Jan or Pat. After an hour of no music, Jan induced Pat's younger brother, Bob, to rig up a stereo system and play disc jockey for the rest of the evening. Jan paid Bob $75 for the job.

The couple consulted their attorney, claiming that the quality of the substitute music was inferior to that promised by the High Flyers and that they both suffered extreme anxiety and distress resulting from the deliberate breach of the type of contract where mental distress was foreseeable.

(1)   How much, if anything, should Jan and Pat recover from the High Flyers? If the High Flyers offered $375 to settle the case, would you recommend that the newlyweds accept?

(2)   Can Jan and Pat recover punitive damages? See the next cases.

Angelo Acquista v. New York Life Insurance Company

Appellate Division of New York, 2001.
730 N.Y.S.2d 272.

■ SAXE, J. This appeal considers plaintiff's entitlement to insurance benefits under three disability insurance policies purchased through defendant insurance agents Jenny Kho and Helen Kho, and issued by defendant New York Life Insurance Company.

In November 1995, plaintiff, a physician with specialties in internal and pulmonary medicine, initially became ill. While an exact diagnosis turned out to be difficult, he underwent numerous bone marrow aspirates, biopsies, and cytogenetic examinations, including blood tests, which revealed abnormalities and the presence of a blood disorder. Dr. Acquista was ultimately informed of a possible diagnosis of myelodysplasia, a disease that might convert into leukemia. His treating physicians have instructed him to avoid exposure to radiation. Presently, he suffers generally from easy fatigue, headaches, and diffuse muscle and joint pain.

However, his application for disability benefits under the three disability insurance policies was rejected by the defendant insurer, on the ground that he can still perform some of "the substantial and material duties" of his regular job or jobs and therefore is not "totally disabled." This lawsuit followed, in which plaintiff brought claims for breach of contract, bad faith and unfair practices, fraud and fraudulent misrepresentation, and negligent infliction of emotional distress.

Upon defendants' motion under CPLR 3211, the Supreme Court granted dismissal of all plaintiff's causes of action except the one based upon the policy provision for residual and partial disability benefits. We now modify the order so as to reinstate a number of the dismissed causes of action.

The Breach of Contract Claims

[The court held that the question whether the plaintiff could perform "the substantial and material duties" was factual and the trial court's determination that he could was, on the record, unwarranted. The dismissal of the breach of contract claims, therefore, was error.]

The question therefore becomes whether those tasks that plaintiff is still demonstrably able to handle, such as seeing a limited number of patients who can make office visits, are substantial enough to amount to the ability to perform "the substantial and material duties" of his regular job or jobs as they existed prior to the onset of his illness. We consider this question to involve a factual determination, precluding dismissal of plaintiff's first, second and third causes of action at this juncture.

Bad Faith Conduct

Plaintiff's fifth and sixth causes of action allege a pattern of bad faith conduct and unfair practices on the part of defendant insurer, and claim resulting emotional distress as well as economic and non-economic injury. The claim that defendant insurance company acted in bad faith is founded upon allegations that it undertook a conscious campaign calculated to delay and avoid payment on his claims, while having determined at the outset that it would deny coverage. He sets forth defendant's ongoing pattern of avoiding the claim, by which it would make multiple requests for additional documentation, upon receipt of which further documents would be demanded, after which plaintiff's claims file would then be transferred to a new examiner, who in turn would make more requests. Plaintiff adds that defendant waited more than two years to request or schedule an independent medical examination.

In seeking dismissal of the bad faith claim, defendant asserts that New York law does not recognize an independent tort cause of action for an insurer's alleged failure to perform its contractual obligations under an insurance policy. . . .

It is correct that, to date, this State has maintained the traditional view that an insurer's failure to make payments or provide benefits in accordance with a policy of insurance constitutes merely a breach of contract, which is remedied by contract damages. Yet, for some time, courts and commentators around the country have increasingly acknowledged that a fundamental injustice may result when a traditional contract analysis is applied to circumstances where insurance claims were denied despite the insurers' lack of a reasonable basis to deny them (see generally . . . , Note, *First Party Bad Faith: The Search for a Uniform Standard of Culpability,* 52 Hastings L.J. 181, 187–189 [2000]).

Under the traditional analysis, because insurance policies are viewed as contracts for the payment of money only, the damages available for an insurer's failure to pay or provide benefits has been limited to the amount of the policy plus interest. . . . Yet, an award, at the conclusion of litigation, of money damages equal to what the insurer should have paid in the first place, may not actually achieve the goal of contract damages, which is to place the plaintiff in the position he would have been in had the contract been performed. . . .

Among other things, this concept of damages presumes that a plaintiff has access to an alternative source of funds from which to pay that which the insurer refuses to pay. This is frequently an inaccurate assumption. Additionally, an insured's inability to pay that which the insurer should be covering may result in further damages to the insured. Of course, limiting the potential damages to the policy amount also fails to address the potential for emotional distress or even further physical injury that may result where a plaintiff under the strain of serious medical problems is forced to also undertake the stress of extended litigation. What is more, if statutory interest is lower than that which the insurer can earn on the sums payable, the insurer has a financial incentive to decline to cover or pay on a claim. . . .

In view of the inadequacy of contract remedies where an insurer purposefully declines or avoids a claim without a reasonable basis for doing so, a majority of states have responded to this need for a more suitable remedy by adopting a tort cause of action applicable to circumstances where an insurer has used bad faith in handling a policyholder's claim. . . .

This cause of action is generally stated as a breach of the insurer's duty of good faith. Under this approach, where an insured demonstrates more than merely a denial of benefits promised under a policy of insurance, but instead, that the insurer's denial of the claim was deliberately made in bad faith, with knowledge of the lack of a reasonable basis for the denial, the insured may be entitled to compensatory tort damages.

Other states, troubled by imposing upon insurance companies a tort duty in such circumstances, have instead expanded the scope of contract remedies to encompass more than just the policy limits. These courts have instead held that the contract damages available, where an insurer fails to pay benefits to which the insured was entitled, may include foreseeable money damages beyond the policy limit. . . . While some states would exclude compensation for mental or emotional distress unrelated to physical injury, caused by the denial of a payment others include the possibility of consequential damages for mental distress or aggravation. . . . Of course, such non-economic losses would be compensable only in circumstances where they were a foreseeable result of a breach at the time the policy was entered into.

We are unwilling to adopt the widely-accepted tort cause of action for "bad faith" in the context of a first-party claim, because we recognize that to do so would constitute an extreme change in the law of this State. Essentially, we accept the more conservative approach adopted by the minority of jurisdictions that "the duties and obligations of the parties [to an insurance policy] are contractual rather than fiduciary. . . ." However, as this Court has recently acknowledged, "an insured should have an adequate remedy to redress an insurer's bad faith refusal of benefits under its policy. . . ." Providing such a remedy cannot be accomplished where a policyholder who makes out a claim of bad faith avoidance of a valid insurance claim may only obtain a judgment for the face amount of the policy.

Therefore, in order to ensure the availability of an appropriate and sufficient remedy, we [conclude] that there is no reason to limit damages recoverable for breach of a duty to investigate, bargain, and settle claims in good faith to the amount specified in the insurance policy. Nothing inherent in the contract law approach mandates this narrow definition of recoverable damages. Although the policy limits define the amount for which the insurer may be held responsible in performing the contract, they do not define the amount for which it may be liable upon a breach.

We consider the need for this form of damages to be apparent. The problem of dilatory tactics by insurance companies seeking to delay and avoid payment of proper claims has apparently become widespread enough to prompt most states to respond with some sort of remedy for aggrieved policyholders. To term such a claim "unique to these parties" as the dissent does, and therefore not warranting a remedy beyond that traditionally available for an insurer's failure to pay on a claim, is to utterly ignore this fact.

As to the dissent's suggestion that the claim of bad faith is undermined by our finding that an issue of fact exists as to whether plaintiff is entitled to coverage at all, we must recall that we have before us a dismissal motion under CPLR 3211. Just as it may ultimately be found that plaintiff was entitled to coverage, it may also be found, as he alleges, that the insurer's delay, avoidance and ultimate rejection of the claim was based not upon a reasonable assessment of the situation but rather, solely upon its own financial self-interest. For this Court to say, in the context of a motion under CPLR 3211, that the denial of benefits was reasonable as a matter of law, is to reject out of hand plaintiff's factual assertions and to accept the facts as defendant insurer alleges them to be.

* * *

■ ANDRIAS, J. (dissenting in part). [Judge Andrias agreed that on the breach of contract claims "there are questions of fact presented, which cannot be determined as a matter of law on this dismissal motion, as to whether plaintiff was 'totally disabled' within the meaning of the three subject insurance policies. . . ." The dissent was that the remaining claims sounding in tort, including bad faith, should have been dismissed.]

Plaintiff's tort claims are based upon his allegations that, even though he provided all requested documentation, New York Life continued to delay in determining his claim; that he made a reasonable settlement demand, which New York Life wrongfully and unjustifiably refused to accept; and, that New York Life's dilatory tactics in delaying processing of his claim included shuffling plaintiff from employee to employee. Such allegations, however, describe what is essentially a "private" contract dispute over policy coverage and the processing of a claim which is unique to these parties, not conduct which affects the consuming public at large. . . . Militating against any causes of action based upon New York Life's alleged bad faith in processing and denying plaintiff's claim is our finding that there are issues of fact as to whether plaintiff's ailments qualify him for coverage under the subject policies. The majority questions the validity of the foregoing statement in the context of a motion to dismiss. However, such finding is significant in that it undermines his claim of bad faith denial of benefits by demonstrating that despite defendant's thorough investigation and evaluation of plaintiff's claim there is still uncertainty as to its merits. As noted . . . encouraging premature settlement of claims would contravene an insurer's "contractual right and obligation of thorough investigation." * * *

[The dissent relied upon New York precedents that a "claim based on an alleged breach of the implied covenant of good faith and fair dealing should be dismissed as duplicative of a cause of action for breach of contract." Moreover, allegations of a conscious campaign to delay a decision on claims are insufficient to establish that the insurer's conduct "constituted a 'gross disregard' of the insured's interest—that is, a deliberate or reckless failure to place on equal footing the interests of its insured with its own interests when considering a settlement offer. . . . In other words, a bad-faith plaintiff must establish that the defendant insurer engaged in a pattern of behavior evincing a conscious or knowing indifference to the probability that an insured would be held personally accountable for a large judgment if a settlement offer within the policy limits were not accepted. . . ." In order to meet this standard, a plaintiff would have to allege and ultimately prove that the insurer unreasonably "failed to carry out an investigation," failed to "evaluate" the feasibility of settlement (in this case, plaintiff's claim) or, failed to offer the policy limits (in this case, pay plaintiff's claim), after the merits of the claim were "clearly and fully assessed." Here, on the other hand, plaintiff's complaint is really the opposite: that defendant took too much time in investigating and evaluating his claim before denying it, after its merits were "clearly and fully assessed."]

NOTES

(1) In *Harris v. Provident Life & Accident Ins. Co.*, 310 F.3d 73 (2d Cir. 2002), the court ruled that New York does not recognize a "separate cause of action for breach of the implied covenant of good faith and fair dealing when a breach of contract claim based on the same facts is also pled." 310 F.3d at 81. The court also noted that there is a disagreement over whether the *Acquista* case, supra, was correct in holding that the plaintiff was entitled to consequential damages for an alleged bad faith breach of an insurance contract. 310 F.3d at 80, n. 3. For a summary of New York law on the question, see Alan J. Pierce, *Insurance Law*, 59 Syracuse L. Rev. 887, 901–09 (2009).

(2) John Grisham's novel, *The Rainmaker*, concerns a medical insurance company that had a corporate policy of not paying claims. If such a case occurred in real life, should punitive damages lie for promissory fraud? Should emotional harm and other consequential damages potentially exceeding the policy limit be awarded for breach of duty of good faith?

Boise Dodge, Inc. v. Robert E. Clark

Supreme Court of Idaho, 1969.
92 Idaho 902.

■ McQUADE, JUSTICE. [Clark purchased an automobile from Boise Dodge with 165 miles showing on the odometer and described by a salesman as "new." In fact, the car was a "demonstrator" and the general manager knew that the odometer had been set back from 6,968 miles. Clark traded in a car valued at $1,100 and issued checks for $500 and $1,562 for the balance of the purchase price. Payment was stopped when Clark discovered that the car was "used." Boise sued on the checks and Clark counterclaimed for damages for breach of contract and deceit as well as punitive damages. The court, after trial, instructed the jury that it might find damages for breach of contract (the difference between the car's value as represented and its actual value) or for deceit (the difference between the price paid for the car and its actual value). On the theory that the contract had been affirmed rather than rescinded, the jury found for Boise in the amount of the checks, some $2,062, and for Clark in the amount of $350, the difference between the value of the car as represented, $2,400, and its actual value, $2,050. This award was not contested on appeal. The court also instructed the jury that it could award punitive damages if it found Boise's actions to have been willful, wanton, gross or outrageous but that the punitive damages must bear a reasonable relation to any actual damages found. The jury awarded punitive damages to Clark in the amount of $12,500. On appeal, respondent Boise presented a single ultimate issue: whether or not the award of punitive damages was proper. The Court affirmed the judgment, holding first that the plaintiff was entitled to an award of some punitive damages.]

Appellant complains mainly about the amount of punitive damages awarded. The court gave its Instruction No. 18 as follows:

"There is no fixed or mathematical proportion, ratio, or relation between amount of actual damages and amount of exemplary or punitive damages, which in a proper case may be awarded, but such an award must not be so disproportionate to actual damages sustained as to be result of passion or prejudice rather than reason, and such an award must bear some reasonable relation or proportion to actual damages, and exemplary damages must bear some relation to damages complained of and cause thereof." (Tr. 104).

This instruction also correctly stated the law relevant to the determination of an amount of punitive damages in an action at law. The question thus becomes whether the jury can be said as a matter of law to have exceeded the bounds of its discretion in making the award of damages.

We note preliminarily that, under the instructions of the court on the measure of actual damages sustained by respondent Clark, the jury apparently applied the standard for breach of contract rather than that for the tort of deceit. We do not view that course of action by the jury as indicating a negation of the elements of misrepresentation, fraud or deceit present in the case. In any event, from the legal point of view of the imposition of punitive damages in this case, it does not matter whether respondent's counterclaim technically sounded in contract or tort. The rule established in Idaho is that punitive damages may be assessed in contract actions where there is fraud, malice, oppression or other sufficient reason for doing so. This rule recognizes that in certain cases elements of tort, for which punitive damages have always been recoverable upon a showing of malice, may be inextricably mixed with elements of contract, in which punitive damages generally are not recoverable. In such cases, punitive damages are allowed according to the substance of a showing of willful fraud.

The assessment of punitive damages, like the assessment of all damages, is in the first instance for the discretion of the jury. Though the existence of punitive damages has been denounced as anomalous in the law, "[d]espite such denunciations the great majority of states retain the doctrine of exemplary damages in full force." The criticism that punitive damages are superfluous in view of the criminal law fallaciously assumes complete identity of criminal and civil punishment. The existence of such a remedy serves useful, if limited, functions in the law as a means of punishing conduct which consciously disregards the rights of others and as a means of deterring tortious conduct generally.

Various jurisdictions, including Idaho, have limited the discretion of juries in imposing punitive damages by declaring that the amount of punitive damages must bear a "reasonable relation" to the amount of actual damages. It is never made clear precisely upon what basis an amount of punitive damages will be declared "reasonable" or "unreasonable" in relation to the amount of actual damages, especially in view of the often-repeated statement that no strict mathematical ratio is to be applied. Of course, the ratios of punitive to actual damages which may be gleaned from the cases have little precedential value when excised from their respective factual settings. This is true because the culpability of a defendant's conduct and the sociological significance of damages as a deterrent vary from case to case. Thus, the true basis for an award of one amount of punitive damages as opposed to another amount lies in an overall appraisal of the circumstances of the case.

The amount of actual damages sustained by a plaintiff is one indication of the culpability of the defendant's acts, but it cannot be the sole criterion for the assessment of punitive damages. Also relevant is the prospective deterrent effect of such an award upon persons situated similarly to the defendant, the motives actuating the defendant's conduct, the degree of calculation involved in the defendant's conduct, and the extent of the defendant's disregard of the rights of others. These are legitimate concerns of the law, and the application of any fixed arithmetic ratio to all cases in which punitive damages are assessed would be arbitrary. It therefore must be recognized that the requirement of a "reasonable relation" between actual and punitive damages serves as a rough device available to trial and appellate courts for the purpose of paring down plainly extreme awards of punitive damages.

Applying these principles to the case at bar, we are satisfied that the jury's award of $12,500 punitive damages against Boise Dodge, Inc., was justified, and [the] court below did not commit error in refusing to set aside that verdict. This is a case of calculated commercial fraud in broad disregard of the rights not only of respondent Clark but the consuming public generally. It occurs in an area of sales in which consumers are unable to gain accurate information about the product. On this basis we find particularly appropriate the reasoning used in the case of Walker v. Sheldon, [179 N.E.2d 497 (1961),] in which the New York Court of Appeals determined that punitive damages would be allowed in fraud and deceit actions. That case involved the fraudulent commercial activities of Comet Press which were characterized as a "virtually larcenous scheme to trap generally the unwary." That court, in a thoughtful opinion by Judge Fuld, stated:

> "Exemplary damages are more likely to serve their desired purpose of deterring similar conduct in a fraud case, such as that before us, than in any other area of tort. One who acts out of anger or hate, for instance, in committing assault or libel, is not likely to be deterred by the fear of punitive damages. On the other hand, those who deliberately and coolly engage in a far-flung fraudulent scheme, systematically conducted for profit, are very much more likely to pause and consider the consequences if they have to pay more than the actual loss

suffered by an individual plaintiff. An occasional award of compensatory damages against such parties would have little deterrent effect. A judgment simply for compensatory damages would require the offender to do no more than return the money which he had taken from the plaintiff. In the calculation of his expected profits, the wrongdoer is likely to allow for a certain amount of money which will have to be returned to those victims who object too vigorously, and he will be perfectly content to bear the additional cost of litigation as the price for continuing his illicit business. It stands to reason that the chances of deterring him are materially increased by subjecting him to the payment of punitive damages."

Those considerations are fully applicable to the case at bar.

* * *

The judgment of the court below is affirmed. Costs to respondent.

NOTES

(1) *Punitive Damages for Breach of Contract?* The traditional rule was that "punitive damages are not recoverable for breach of contract." Restatement (First) § 342. Section 355 of Restatement (Second) opened the door just a crack: "Punitive damages are not recoverable for a breach of contract unless the conduct constituting the breach is also a tort for which punitive damages are recoverable." A common statement of the rule is that the breach must constitute an "independent and willful tort accompanied by fraud, malice, wantonness or oppression." McIntosh v. Magna Systems, Inc., 539 F.Supp. 1185, 1190 (N.D.Ill. 1982). See Miller Brewing Co. v. Best Beers of Bloomington, Inc., 608 N.E.2d 975, 982 (Ind. 1993) (punitive damages not available in contract actions unless plaintiff establishes "each element of a recognized tort for which Indiana law would permit the recovery of punitive damages"). See also William S. Dodge, *The Case for Punitive Damages in Contracts*, 48 Duke L.J. 629, 636–51 (1999) (describing developments in state courts). As *Aquista v. New York Life Insurance* illustrates, however, not all states recognize the tort.

(2) The purposes of punitive damages may involve punishment, deterrence and, to a lesser extent, compensation.

Often, the function of punitive damages * * * is to legitimate the jury's giving vent to a sense of outrage at the conduct of the defendant and to relieve it of the sometimes difficult task of quantifying the degree to which the plaintiff has literally been harmed. Further, punitive damages are assessed to deter conduct of a serious antisocial or irresponsible nature.

Madisons Chevrolet, Inc. v. Donald, 109 Ariz. 100, 103–04 (1973). In commercial transactions, however, the courts have resisted imposing punitive damages even though the breach was "knowing and willful." As one court put it, compensatory damages are sufficient for the plaintiff "without the necessity of assuaging his feelings or allaying community outrage" and that the award of punitive damages for a "pure" breach of contract would "seriously jeopardize the stability and predictability of commercial transactions, so vital to the smooth and efficient operation of the modern American economy." General Motors Corp. v. Piskor, 281 Md. 627, 634–639 (1977).

(3)   The reluctance of courts to award punitive damages for breach of contract parallels recent attacks upon the power of courts to award punitive damages in tort law. In *BMW of North America, Inc. v. Gore*, 517 U.S. 559 (1996), the Supreme Court held that the 14th Amendment prohibits a state protecting its legitimate interests from imposing "grossly excessive" punitive damages on a tortfeasor. The discretion of state courts to award punitive damages is limited by the state interest to be protected and the reprehensibility of the defendant's conduct. Assuming a legitimate state interest, the award of punitive damages must not be grossly out of proportion to the severity of the offense.

Comment: *Seaman's* and Obstructive Breach

California, like many states, recognizes that every contract is subject to an implied covenant of good faith and fair dealing. The question is when, if ever, a breach of the implied covenant may constitute a tort for which punitive damages may be awarded. California courts have long held that in contracts for insurance, the insurer's refusal to settle within the terms of an insurance policy or to pay an undisputed claim of an insured may be a bad faith tort, for which the insured can recover damages for mental anguish and punitive damages.

In *Seaman's Direct Buying Service, Inc. v. Standard Oil Company of California*, 36 Cal.3d 752 (1984), the California Supreme Court considered whether tort liability for a "bad faith breach" should be extended beyond insurance or other contracts where "special circumstances" exist. Its answer was a qualified "yes."

> For the purposes of this case it is * * * sufficient to recognize that a party to a contract may incur tort remedies when, in addition to breaching the contract, it seeks to shield itself from liability by denying, in bad faith and without probable cause, that the contract exists.
>
> It has been held that a party to a contract may be subject to tort liability, including punitive damages, if he coerces the other party to pay more than is due under the contract terms through the threat of a lawsuit, made "without probable cause and with no belief in the existence of the cause of action." (Adams v. Crater Well Drilling, Inc., 276 Or. 789, 793 (1976).) There is little difference, in principle, between a contracting party obtaining excess payment in such manner, and a contracting party seeking to avoid all liability on a meritorious contract claim by adopting a "stonewall" position ("see you in court") without probable cause and with no belief in the existence of a

defense. Such conduct goes beyond the mere breach of contract. It offends accepted notions of business ethics. . . . Acceptance of tort remedies in such a situation is not likely to intrude upon the bargaining relationship or upset reasonable expectations of the contracting parties.

206 Cal.Rptr. at 363.

Concurring in a 1989 case, Judge Alexander Kozinski sharply criticized the *Seaman's* rule:

> Nowhere but in the Cloud Cuckooland of modern tort theory could a case like this have been concocted. One large corporation is complaining that another obstinately refused to acknowledge they had a contract. For this shocking misconduct it is demanding millions of dollars in punitive damages. I suppose we will next be seeing lawsuits seeking punitive damages for maliciously refusing to return telephone calls or adopting a condescending tone in interoffice memos. Not every slight, nor even every wrong, ought to have a tort remedy. The intrusion of courts into every aspect of life, and particularly into every type of business relationship, generates serious costs and uncertainties, trivializes the law, and denies individuals and businesses the autonomy of adjusting mutual rights and responsibilities through voluntary contractual agreement.

* * *

> Perhaps most troubling, the willingness of courts to subordinate voluntary contractual arrangements to their own sense of public policy and proper business decorum deprives individuals of an important measure of freedom. The right to enter into contracts—to adjust one's legal relationships by mutual agreement with other free individuals—was unknown through much of history and is unknown even today in many parts of the world. Like other aspects of personal autonomy, it is too easily smothered by government officials eager to tell us what's best for us. The recent tendency of judges to insinuate tort causes of action into relationships traditionally governed by contract is just such overreaching. It must be viewed with no less suspicion because the government officials in question happen to wear robes.

Oki America, Inc. v. Microtech Intern., Inc., 872 F.2d 312, 314–317 (9th Cir. 1989) (Kozinski, J., concurring).

More recently, Gregory Klass has defended the *Seaman's* rule. Klass observes that the bad acts in *Seaman's* involved not a breach of a first-order duty to perform, but the defendant's attempt to avoid liability for what it knew was a first-order breach. Punitive or other extracompensatory remedies are warranted in these situations because of a catch-22.

> [T]o recover compensatory damages for the breach of a duty to cooperate [in recovery of damages for a first-order breach], a plaintiff must be able to demonstrate harm. The primary harm of an obstructive breach is that it prevents the promisee from recovering for breach of the underlying, or first-order, duty. Showing that harm requires independent proof of first-order breach—that the plaintiff was entitled to the damages she did not recover. But if the plaintiff can prove first-order breach, she can recover on that basis—which means that the obstructive breach has not harmed her. The upshot is a catch-22: a plaintiff can show obstructive harm only if she has not suffered it.

Gregory Klass, *Contracting for Cooperation in Recovery*, 117 Yale L.J. 2, 5 (2007). Kozinski's critique therefore misses the mark.

> [W]hether or not *Seaman's* was part of a larger trend, what it said was relatively narrow: tort damages are appropriate where "a contracting party seek[s] to avoid all liability on a meritorious contract claim by adopting a 'stonewall' position ('see you in court') without probable cause and with no belief in the existence of a defense." [686 P.2d at 1167.] Stonewalling of this sort is, in my terms, obstruction of recovery. Read narrowly, the *Seaman's* rule does not impose a Cloud Cuckooland generic duty of good manners, but is supported by many of the above arguments for permitting the parties to adopt extracompensatory remedies for obstructive breach. Thus court-assessed compensatory damages alone neither insure against nor deter the sort of stonewalling at issue in *Seaman's*. Punitive damages or other extracompensatory remedies are necessary. Moreover, where there is a measure of distrust and uncertainty at the outset of a deal, the parties themselves might rationally prefer *Seaman's* protection. A promisee who knows that the promisor faces a significant deterrent against unreasonably denying the existence of the contract knows she is more likely to recover in the case of nonperformance, and will therefore be more willing to enter into the transaction. Finally, Kozinski is simply wrong when he writes that *Seaman's* "denies individuals and businesses the autonomy of adjusting mutual rights and responsibilities through voluntary contractual agreement." [T]he rules against penalties and punitive damages already deny parties the ability to contract for meaningful duties to cooperate in recovery. *Seaman's* simply flipped the rule. Where before there was never meaningful legal liability for postbreach obstruction, *Seaman's* held that such behavior should always be subject to punitive liability in tort.

Id. at 39–40.

In 1995, the California Supreme Court appeared to abandon the *Seaman's* rule "in favor of a general rule precluding tort recovery for noninsurance contract breach, at least in the absence of violation of 'an independent duty arising from principles of tort law' . . . other than the bad faith denial of the existence of, or liability under, the breached contract." Freeman & Mills, Inc. v. Belcher Oil Co., 11 Cal.4th 85 (1995).

White Plains Coat & Apron Co. v. Cintas Corp.

Court of Appeals of New York, 2007.
867 N.E.2d 381 (N.Y. 2007).

■ KAYE, CHIEF JUDGE. Plaintiff, White Plains Coat & Apron Co., Inc., is a New York-based linen rental business. Its competitor, defendant Cintas Corp., is a nationwide business that rents similar products to commercial customers. White Plains alleges that it had five-year exclusive service contracts with customers and that, knowing of these arrangements, Cintas nonetheless induced dozens of White Plains' customers to breach their contracts and enter into rental agreements with Cintas. White Plains by letter demanded that Cintas desist solicitation and discontinue servicing White Plains' contract customers, enclosing a list of customers allegedly solicited improperly. Cintas denied knowledge of any contracts and continued its solicitation.

White Plains sued Cintas in United States District Court for the Southern District of New York for tortious interference with existing customer contracts. After discovery, Cintas sought summary judgment, arguing that it had no knowledge of contracts with White Plains and had not induced any breach. While noting "a small element of doubt" in New York law (and itself suggesting a need for certification to this Court), the District Court granted summary judgment and dismissed the complaint, ruling orally that Cintas' legitimate interest as a competitor to solicit business and make a profit alone triggered the defense of economic justification. Given Cintas' economic interest, the court concluded, to survive summary judgment White Plains had to show that Cintas acted with malice or illegality, and failed to do so. The court later denied White Plains' motion for reconsideration, finding that defendant did not need an ownership interest in the breaching party's business in order to assert the economic interest defense.

On White Plains' appeal, the Court of Appeals for the Second Circuit reviewed New York's law on tortious interference with contract, noting that procuring "the breach of a contract in the exercise of equal or superior right is acting with just cause or excuse and is justification for what would other- wise be an actionable wrong."[1] The court observed, however, that there was an important open state law question regarding the economic interest defense. While satisfied that the defense applies when the tortfeasor has a preexisting legal or financial relationship with the breaching party—not present in the case before us—the Second

---

[1] *White Plains Coat & Apron Co., Inc. v. Cintas Corp.*, 460 F.3d 281, 283 (2d Cir.2006), *quoting Foster v. Churchill*, 87 N.Y.2d 744, 750 (1996) (internal quotation marks omitted).

Circuit sought clarification as to the broader reach of the defense and therefore certified the following potentially dispositive question to us: "Does a generalized economic interest in soliciting business for profit constitute a defense to a claim of tortious interference with an existing contract for an alleged tortfeasor with no previous economic relationship with the breaching party?" We answer that question in the negative.

Analysis

It is a familiar proposition that one "who intentionally and improperly interferes with the performance of a contract (except a contract to marry) between another and a third person by inducing or otherwise causing the third person not to perform the contract, is subject to liability to the other for the pecuniary loss resulting to the other from the failure of the third person to perform the contract."[4] Though long a part of our law, this commonly asserted tort continues to generate a spate of decisions, with sometimes varying views. At bottom, as a matter of policy, courts are called upon to strike a balance between two valued interests: protection of enforceable contracts, which lends stability and predictability to parties' dealings, and promotion of free and robust competition in the marketplace.

While New York law recognizes the tort of interference with both *prospective* and *existing* contracts, "greater protection is accorded an interest in an existing contract (as to which respect for individual contract rights outweighs the public benefit to be derived from unfettered competition) than to the less substantive, more speculative interest in a prospective relationship (as to which liability will be imposed only on proof of more culpable conduct on the part of the interferer)."[5]

In a contract interference case—as here—the plaintiff must show the existence of its valid contract with a third party, defendant's knowledge of that contract, defendant's intentional and improper procuring of a breach, and damages. In response to such a claim, a defendant may raise the economic interest defense—that it acted to protect its own legal or financial stake in the breaching party's business. The defense has been applied, for example, where defendants were significant stockholders in the breaching party's business; where defendant and the breaching party had a parent—subsidiary relationship; where defendant was the breaching party's creditor; and where the defendant had a managerial contract with the breaching party at the time defendant induced the breach of contract with plaintiff.

A defendant who is simply plaintiff's competitor and knowingly solicits its contract customers is not economically justified in procuring the breach of contract.[11] In other words, mere status as plaintiff's competitor is not a legal or financial stake in the breaching party's

---

4   Restatement (Second) of Torts § 766.

5   *Guard-Life Corp. v. Parker Hardware Mfg. Corp.*, 50 N.Y.2d 183, 191 (1980).

11   *See* Restatement (Second) of Torts § 768(2).

business that permits defendant's inducement of a breach of contract. We do not subscribe to the District Court's view that "the only answer . . . is to go out and do it also to the other guy." Rather, the answer is succinctly articulated in the New York Pattern Jury Instructions: "When the defendant is simply a competitor of the plaintiff seeking prospective customers and plaintiff has a customer under contract for a definite period, defendant's interest is not equal to that of plaintiff and would not justify defendant's inducing the customer to breach the existing contract."[12] To conclude otherwise—to answer the certified question in the affirmative—would blur the distinction between tortious interference with existing, enforceable contracts and tortious interference with prospective contractual relations, where, as a matter of policy, the balance of interests is different.

Finally, we note that protecting existing contractual relationships does not negate a competitor's right to solicit business, where liability is limited to improper inducement of a third party to breach its contract. Sending regular advertising and soliciting business in the normal course does not constitute inducement of breach of contract. A competitor's ultimate liability will depend on a showing that the inducement exceeded "a minimum level of ethical behavior in the marketplace."[14]

Accordingly, the certified question should be answered in the negative.

NOTES

(1) *The Torts of Intentional Interference.* As the court in White Plains quotes, Section 766 of the Restatement (Second) of Torts provides:

> One who intentionally and improperly interferes with the performance of a contract (except a contract to marry) between another and a third person by inducing or otherwise causing the third person not to perform the contract, is subject to liability to the other for the pecuniary loss resulting to the other from the failure of the third person to perform the contract.

In addition to intentional interference with existing contracts, courts have found tort liability for a third party's intentional interference with prospective contracts and for a third party's negligent interference. See Restatement (Second) Torts §§ 766A–766C. Section 767 identifies seven factors courts should consider in determining whether interference was improper: "(a) the nature of the actor's conduct, (b) the actor's motive, (c) the interests of the other with which the actor's conduct interferes, (d) the interests sought to be advanced by the actor, (e) the social interests in protecting the freedom of action of the actor and the contractual interests of

---

[12] 2 N.Y. PJI2d 3:56, at 507–508 (2007).

[14] *Guard-Life*, 50 N.Y.2d at 200 (Cooke, Ch. J., dissenting in part); *see also V. Marangi Carting Corp. v. Judex Enters.*, 171 Misc.2d 820 (Sup.Ct., N.Y. County 1997).

the other, (f) the proximity or remoteness of the actor's conduct to the interference and (g) the relations between the parties."

(2) *Some History.* The tort of intentional interference originates in *Lumley v. Gye*, which established the rule of tort liability for "a person who wrongfully and maliciously, or, which is the same thing, with notice, interrupts the relation subsisting between master and servant by procuring the servant to depart from the master's service, or by harbouring and keeping him as servant after he has quitted it and during the time stipulated for as the period of service, whereby the master is injured." 118 E.R. 749, 752–53 (Q.B. 1852). *Lumley v. Gye* was a companion case to *Lumley v. Wagner*, which appears later in this Chapter.

(3) *Remedies for Intentional Interference.* Most states follow the Second Restatement (Second) of Torts ¶ 774A, which provides that a successful intentional interference plaintiff may recover, in the appropriate cases, "(a) the pecuniary loss of the benefits of the contract or the prospective relation; (b) consequential losses for which the interference is a legal cause; and (c) emotional distress or actual harm to reputation, if they are reasonably to be expected to result from the interference." Comment a further explains that "Since the tort is an intentional one, punitive damages are recovered in these actions under appropriate circumstances." In *White Plains Coat & Apron*, the New York Court of Appeals did not address the remedy question. But other courts have assumed that New York law would allow punitive damages in a sufficiently egregious case of intentional interference. *See, e.g.,* Unijax, Inc. v. Champion Int'l, Inc., 683 F.2d 678, 687 (2d Cir. 1982) ("Proof of malice or motivation to harm is indispensable to sustain a finding of tortious interference with prospective business advantage and to support an award of punitive damages," applying New York law).

(4) *Efficient Breach.* How does the availability of punitive damages for the tort of intentional interference square with the law's strong preference for compensatory damages only in actions for breach? Can it be reconciled with the theory of efficient breach? Harvey Perlman argues:

> If allocational efficiency is the objective of contract law, legal rules should encourage persons to search for and to take advantage of more highly valued uses for resources under their command. In efficiency terms, there is no reason why formation of one contract should bring the process to a halt or prevent third parties from inducing nonperformance of inefficient contracts. Contract rules seem designed to facilitate breach where efficiency gains result; the inducer liability rule, in contrast, seems designed to reduce the number of such breaches and thus runs counter to a plausible objective of contract doctrine.

Harvey S. Perlman, *Interference with Contract and Other Economic Expectancies: A Clash of Tort and Contract Doctrine*, 49 U. Chi. L. Rev. 61, 82–83 (1982).

One response is that courts' willingness to award punitive damages in intentional interference claims is evidence against the picture that supports the theory of efficient breach.

Like promissory estoppel cases, good-faith cases, and other "problem" cases that "classical" contract has had to embrace in becoming "neoclassic," interference-with-contract cases reflect, I believe, the notions of community that we bring to solving transactional problems. These cases at times recognize relationships that contract doctrine would not and often restrict individuals in situations where the logic of individualist contract reasoning suggests they should be free. These tort cases thus give occasion to reflect on policies that foster community and trust within our broader law governing relationships and to consider the implications of those usually quiet policies for our formal law of contracts.

William J. Woodward, Jr., *Contractarians, Community, and the Tort of Interference with Contract*, 80 Minn. L. Rev. 1103, 1108–09 (1993).

(5) *The Reach of Intentional Interference.* New technologies have provided new questions about the tort's reach. Can web advertisers claim that distributors of ad-blocking software are intentionally interfering with their advertising contracts? See Andrew Saluke, *Ad-Blocking Software as Third-Party Tortious Interference with Advertising Contracts*, 7 Fla. St. U. Bus. Rev. 87 (2008). What about a programmer who freely distributes software that users can install to modify a computer game in way that violates the game's end user license agreement? See MDY Indus., LLC v. Blizzard Entm't, Inc., 616 F. Supp. 2d 958 (D. Ariz. 2009); Jessica Gallegos, Note, *A New Role for Tortious Interference in the Digital Age: A Model to Enforce End User License Agreements*, 38 Fla. St. U. L. Rev. 411 (2011).

4. Injunctive Relief

In the materials just considered, a primary objective has been to determine the amount of money damages due to the successful contract plaintiff. If the court decides that the defendant is liable for damages and enters a money judgment against the defendant, that judgment is enforced against the defendant's property, that is, *in rem*. If the property is insufficient, the enforcement process may be renewed until the judgment is satisfied or the obligation is discharged. See the comment on The Enforcement of Money Judgments in Chapter One.

The defendant, however, will not be imprisoned for failure to pay the obligation represented by the judgment. See Note, *Imprisonment for Debt: In the Military Tradition,* 80 Yale L.J. 1679 (1971).[10] Under the

---

[10] Most state constitutions prohibit imprisonment for at least certain types of debt. See, e.g., S.D. Const. art. VI, § 15 ("[n]o person shall be imprisoned for debt arising out of or founded upon a contract."). But there has been a growing tendency for courts to uphold the constitutionality for non-payment of judgments in certain contexts (such as child support) where the debtor is found to have the means to pay or surprisingly even if the court finds that the defendant had an ability to earn income but willfully chose not to work. See, e.g., Moss v. Superior Ct., 17 Cal.4th 396 (1998). In fact the United States Supreme Court even held that there is no right to counsel before being jailed for contempt under these statutes. Turner v. Rogers, 564 U.S. 431, 436–437 (2011) ("Each month the family court clerk reviews outstanding child support orders, identifies those in which the supporting parent has fallen more than five days behind, and sends that parent an order to 'show cause' why he should not be held in

current regime for contract breach money judgments, the Holmesian choice is not to perform or pay damages, but to perform the contract or run the risk that the plaintiff will sue, secure a judgment, and ultimately recover some amount by levying on the defendant's personal assets. This is the plaintiff's remedy *at law* for breach of contract.

Equitable remedies make it possible for the plaintiff to obtain the performance promised by the defendant rather than damages. The court has power to issue a personal order to the defendant, directing conduct of a specified sort, and to punish noncompliance by either a fine or imprisonment for contempt. An injunction is the main form of this personal, coercive order. In a breach of contract action, the injunction may prohibit the defendant from taking a specified course of action or compel specific performance of the contract or both. See Kaiser Trading Co. v. Associated Metals & Minerals Corp., 321 F.Supp. 923 (N.D.Cal. 1970) (seller ordered to deliver goods sold and enjoined from selling them to others). Here, then, the order is directed to the person—it is *in personam*—and denies the defendant the choice to perform or pay damages. Although the contempt power appears to punish the defendant's refusal to comply, the real purpose is to coerce performance. In the words of some immortal bard, the defendant has "the keys to the jailhouse in his own pocket."

When is the plaintiff entitled to an equitable remedy for breach of contract? A.W.B. Simpson reports that although the origin of the principle "equity treats as done that which ought to be done" remains unclear, specific performance was granted by the English Court of Chancery in land cases by the mid-fifteenth century. A.W.B. Simpson, A History of the Common Law of Contract 595–598 (1975). Since that time, specific enforcement of contracts for the sale of land has been the rule rather than the exception, the reason being "that land is assumed to have a peculiar value, so as to give an equity for a specific performance, without reference to its quality or quantity." Simpson also states that before the development of the writ of assumpsit in the seventeenth century, the Chancery Court regularly issued *in personam* orders in a wide range of contract disputes. What happened next is too long and complicated to relate here in full. But as the adequacy and availability of money damages improved, the scope of the common law expanded and England's market system developed and diversified, it became more difficult for plaintiffs to demonstrate that contract remedies in the law courts were so inadequate that invocation of the power of the Chancery Court was justified. So in matters other than land contracts, it became

---

contempt. . . . At the [show cause] hearing that parent may demonstrate that he is not in contempt, say, by showing that he is not able to make the required payments. If he fails to make the required showing, the court may hold him in civil contempt. And it may require that he be imprisoned unless and until he purges himself of contempt by making the required child support payments (but not for more than one year regardless)."). The U.S. Constitution might not prevent a legislature from criminalizing failure to pay civil judgments when defendants have the wherewithal to pay.

customary to say that specific performance was the exception rather than the rule or that equitable remedies were "extraordinary." See John P. Dawson, *Specific Performance in France and Germany,* 57 Mich. L. Rev. 495 (1959), where a preference for specific performance is noted in the civil law tradition. As an American court put the traditional principle, specific performance is "largely a discretionary remedy to prevent substantial injury where no adequate remedy at law obtains. . . ." Stokes v. Moore, 262 Ala. 59 (1955).

We have already seen the rules for injunctive relief at work in Judge Posner's opinions in *NIPSCO v. Carbon County Coal* and *Walgreen v. Sara Creek Property*, both reprinted earlier in this chapter. In *eBay Inc. v. MercExchange, L.L.C.*, Justice Thomas described the generalized requirements for obtaining an injunction as follows:

> According to well-established principles of equity, a plaintiff seeking a permanent injunction must satisfy a four-factor test before a court may grant such relief. A plaintiff must demonstrate: (1) that it has suffered an irreparable injury; (2) that remedies available at law, such as monetary damages, are inadequate to compensate for that injury; (3) that, considering the balance of hardships between the plaintiff and defendant, a remedy in equity is warranted; and (4) that the public interest would not be disserved by a permanent injunction.

547 U.S. 388 (2006). What, more specifically, must the plaintiff show to persuade the court to exercise that discretion and grant equitable relief?

The following materials are designed to provide the answer. As you read them, keep the following questions in mind:

1. What was the inadequacy in the legal remedy asserted by the plaintiff to justify equitable relief? The focus here should be upon the ease with which the plaintiff can obtain a substitute performance from the available market and the impact upon the plaintiff if that substitute is costly or not readily available.

2. What, if any, are the practical problems involved in enforcing an *in personam* order in the particular case? Can and should the court order an artist to paint, a singer to sing or a builder to build? How is the court to supervise the mandated performance when the standards are aesthetic or, perhaps, the agreement is indefinite? As you will see, courts have found it easier to order the defendant in a personal service contract to refrain from doing rather than to perform.

3. Are there any questions of fairness associated with enforcing the contract or problems of morality associated with the plaintiff's conduct? For example, would specific enforcement of the contract be unconscionable because of disproportion in the exchange? Or, to quote some choice maxims, must the plaintiff

"do equity to receive equity" or "come into equity with clean hands"?

4. Can the plaintiff recover damages in addition to equitable relief? Suppose the requested equitable remedy is not available—can the court award damages in lieu of specific performance or must it remand the case for further consideration?

Curtice Brothers Co. v. Catts
Court of Chancery of New Jersey, 1907.
72 N.J.Eq. 831.

Complainant is engaged in the business of canning tomatoes and seeks the specific performance of a contract wherein defendant agreed to sell to complainant the entire product of certain land planted with tomatoes. Defendant contests the power of this court to grant equitable relief.

■ LEAMING, V.C. The fundamental principles which guide a court of equity in decreeing the specific performance of contracts are essentially the same whether the contracts relate to realty or to personalty. By reason of the fact that damages for the breach of contract for the sale of personalty are, in most cases, easily ascertainable and recoverable at law, courts of equity, in such cases withhold equitable relief. Touching contracts for the sale of land the reverse is the case. But no inherent difference between real estate and personal property controls the exercise of the jurisdiction. Where no adequate remedy at law exists specific performance of a contract touching the sale of personal property will be decreed with the same freedom as in the case of a contract for the sale of land. Professor Pomeroy, in referring to the distinction, says:

"In applying these principles, taking into account the discretionary nature of the jurisdiction, an agreement for the sale of land is *prima facie* presumed to come within their operation so as to be subject to specific performance, but a contrary presumption exists in regard to agreements concerning chattels." Pom. on Const. § 11.

Judge Story urges that there is no reasonable objection to allowing the party who is injured by the breach of any contract for the sale of chattels to have an election either to take damages at law or to have a specific performance in equity. 2 Story Eq.Jur. (13th Ed.) § 717a. While it is probable that the development of this branch of equitable remedies is decidedly toward the logical solution suggested by Judge Story, it is entirely clear that his view can not at this time be freely adopted without violence to what has long been regarded as accepted principles controlling the discretion of a court of equity in this class of cases. The United States Supreme Court has probably most nearly approached the view suggested by Judge Story. In Mechanics Bank of Alexandria v. Seton, 1 Pet. (U.S.) 299, 305, Mr. Justice Thompson, delivering the opinion of that court, says: "But notwithstanding this distinction between personal contracts for goods and contracts for lands is to be found laid down in the books as a general rule, yet there are many cases to be found where specific performance of contracts relating to personalty have been enforced in chancery, and courts will only view with greater nicety contracts of this description than such as relate to land." See also Barr v. Lapsley, 1 Wheat. (U.S.) 151. In our own state contracts for the sale of chattels have been frequently enforced and the inadequacy of the remedy at law, based on the characteristic features of the contract or peculiar situation and needs of the parties, have been the principal grounds of relief. . . .

I think it clear that the present case falls well within the principles defined by the cases already cited from our own state. Complainant's factory has a capacity of about one million cans of tomatoes. The season for packing lasts about six weeks. The preparations made for this six weeks of active work must be carried out in all features to enable the business to succeed. These preparations are primarily based upon the capacity of the plant. Cans and other necessary equipments, including labor, must be provided and secured in advance with reference to the capacity of the plant during the packing period. With this known capacity and an estimated average yield of tomatoes per acre the acreage of land necessary to supply the plant is calculated. To that end the contract now in question was made, with other like contracts, covering a sufficient acreage to insure the essential pack. It seems immaterial whether the entire acreage is contracted for to insure the full pack, or whether a more limited acreage is contracted for and an estimated available open market depended upon for the balance of the pack; in either case a refusal of the parties who contract to supply a given acreage to comply with their contracts leaves the factory helpless except to whatever extent an uncertain market may perchance supply the deficiency. The condition which arises from the breach of the contracts is not merely a question of the factory being compelled to pay a higher price for the product; losses sustained in that manner could, with some degree of accuracy, be estimated. The condition which occasions the irreparable injury by reason of the breaches of the contracts is the inability to procure at any price at the time needed and of the quality needed the necessary tomatoes to insure the successful operation of the plant. If it should be assumed as a fact that upon the breach of contracts of this nature other tomatoes of like quality and quantity could be procured in the open market without serious interference with the economic arrangements of the plant, a court of equity would hesitate to assume to interfere, but the very existence of such contracts proclaims their necessity to the economic management of the factory. The aspect of the situation bears no resemblance to that of an ordinary contract for the sale of merchandise in the course of an ordinary business. The business and its needs are extraordinary in that the maintenance of all of the conditions prearranged to secure the pack are a necessity to insure the successful operation of the plant. The breach of the contract by one planter differs but in degree from a breach by all.

The objection that to specifically perform the contract personal services are required will not divest the court of its powers to preserve the benefits of the contract. Defendant may be restrained from selling the crop to others, and if necessary, a receiver can be appointed to harvest the crop.

A decree may be devised pursuant to the prayer of the bill. By reason of the manner in which the facts on which the opinion is based were stipulated, no costs will be taxed.

NOTES

(1)   This case, decided in 1907, involved a contract for the sale of goods. UCC § 2–716(1) provides:

> (1)   Specific performance may be decreed where the goods are unique or in other proper circumstances.
>
> (2)   The decree for specific performance may include such terms and conditions as to payment of the price, damages, or other relief as the court may deem just.
>
> (3)   The buyer has a right of replevin for goods identified to the contract if after reasonable effort he is unable to effect cover for such goods or the circumstances reasonably indicate that such effort will be unavailing * * *.

The Comments state that UCC § 2–716 furthers a "more liberal attitude than some courts have shown in connection with the specific performance of contracts of sale" through emphasis upon the "commercial feasibility of replacement." Specific performance is "no longer limited to goods which are already specific or ascertained at the time of contracting." Further:

> The test of uniqueness under this section must be made in terms of the total situation which characterizes the contract. Output and requirements contracts involving a particular or peculiarly available source or market present today the typical commercial specific performance situation, as contrasted with contracts for the sale of heirlooms or priceless works of art which were usually involved in the older cases. However, uniqueness is not the sole basis of the remedy under this section for the relief may also be granted "in other proper circumstances" and inability to cover is strong evidence of "other proper circumstances."

How would *Curtice Brothers v. Catts* be decided under the UCC?

(2)   *Enjoining a Buyer to Pay*. Can a seller get specific performance under Article 2? UCC § 2–716 appears to be limited to buyers and there is no section authorizing specific performance for sellers. The now withdrawn 2003 amendments to § 2–703(2) would have clarified this omission to provide that a seller can "obtain specific performance under Section 2–716." But when would such a remedy be appropriate? Suppose the buyer has accepted

the goods and refused to pay the price. Can the seller get an *in personam* order directing the buyer to pay (or go to jail for contempt) or must the seller try to recover the price *in rem* under UCC § 2–709(1)?

(3) *"Unique" or in "Other Proper Circumstances."* When are goods "unique" within the meaning of UCC § 2–716(1)? In the cotton fiasco of 1973, growers of cotton made contracts to sell cotton to be planted on their land to middlemen for roughly $0.30 per pound. Delivery was to be made after the cotton was harvested, ginned and bailed. Between the time of contracting and the time of delivery, the price of cotton rose to roughly $0.90 per pound. Cotton was available on the market, but in uncertain quantities. When the growers refused to deliver, the buyers brought suit for specific performance. In *R.L. Kimsey Cotton Co., Inc. v. Ferguson*, 233 Ga. 962 (1975), the parties stipulated in the contract that the cotton was "unique." The court, without extended discussion, granted specific performance. But in *Duval & Co. v. Malcom*, 233 Ga. 784 (1975), the same court held that, in the absence of a stipulation of uniqueness, a dramatic price rise not accompanied by an inability to cover in the open market did not constitute "other proper circumstances" under UCC § 2–716(1). The court stated that "other proper circumstances" was not a "license to afford specific performance for all commercial goods and turn the courts into referees in commerce." Presumably the court was swayed by the fungibility of cotton. But if a blight had ruined the cotton to be grown by the seller, perhaps he would have been excused under UCC § 2–613, because the cotton involved was "required" by the contract. If the cotton was "required" by the contract, should not that mean that the goods were unique? What about replevin in the cotton cases?

(4) *Irreparable Harm?* The uniqueness requirement is related to the more principle that equitable remedies are unavailable if legal remedies will adequately repair the harm. But Douglas Laycock, after reviewing how courts actually apply the irreparable harm rule, found:

> Courts have escaped the rule by defining adequacy in such a way that damages are never an adequate substitute for plaintiff's loss. Thus, our law embodies a preference for specific relief if plaintiff wants it. The principal doctrinal expression of this preference is the rule that damages are inadequate unless they can be used to replace the specific thing that plaintiff lost. Damages can be used in this way for only one category of losses: to replace fungible goods or routine services in an orderly market. In that context, damages and specific relief are substantially equivalent. Either way, plaintiff winds up with the very thing he wanted, and the preference for specific relief becomes irrelevant. In all other contexts, there is ample basis in precedent and principle for holding that damages are inadequate.

Douglas Laycock, The Death of the Irreparable Injury Rule 12–13 (1991).

(5) *Injunction Against Breach.* In an action for specific performance, when may the plaintiff, in order to preserve the status quo, obtain a temporary or permanent injunction restraining the defendant from breaching the contract? Traditionally courts have considered four flexible

and interdependent factors: 1) Without such relief, will the plaintiff suffer irreparable harm; 2) Is there a substantial probability of success on the merits; 3) Will others be injured by the injunction; and 4) Will the injunction be inconsistent with or further the public interest? In addition, the injunction may be denied unless the facts as stated justify a specific performance decree. In *Brady v. National Football League*, 640 F.3d 785, 796 (8th Cir. 2011), the Eight Circuit vacated a district court order temporarily enjoining a management lock-out of professional football players in a collective bargaining dispute. Applying a similar four-factor test, the court reasoned, *inter alia*:

> [T]his is a case in which one party or the other likely will suffer some degree of irreparable harm no matter how this court resolves the motion for a stay pending appeal. We do not agree, however, with the district court's apparent view that the balance of the equities tilts heavily in favor of the Players. The district court gave little or no weight to the harm caused to the League by an injunction issued in the midst of an ongoing dispute over terms and conditions of employment. The court found irreparable harm to the Players because the lockout prevents free agents from negotiating contracts with any team, but gave no weight to harm that would be caused to the League by player transactions that would occur only with an injunction against the lockout.

(6) *Mutuality of Remedy.* Should the buyer have specific performance against the seller even if the seller would not have been able to have specific performance against the buyer? Courts have held that mutuality of remedy is not required. Pallas v. Black, 226 Neb. 728 (1987). But see City of Wichita Falls v. Republic Ins. Co., 2002 WL 31111768 (Tex. App. Dallas 2002) (stating, in dicta, that "[m]utuality of remedy is the right of both parties to a contract to obtain specific performance"); Hilton v. Nelsen, 283 N.W.2d 877 (Minn. 1979) (mutuality of remedy is one element which may be considered in determining whether to award specific performance of a real estate contract). The alleged remedial inequality is balanced by the court's power in equity to condition the decree to insure that the defendant receives the agreed exchange. The issue is both illuminated and resolved in Section 3386 of the California Civil Code:

> Notwithstanding that the agreed counter performance is not or would not have been specifically enforceable, specific performance may be compelled if:
>
> (a) Specific performance would otherwise be an appropriate remedy, and
>
> (b) The agreed counter performance has been substantially performed or its concurrent or future performance is assured or, if the court deems necessary, can be secured to the satisfaction of the court.

Accord Restatement (Second) § 363.

(7) *Specific Performance in Restatement (Second).* Under Restatement (Second), specific performance of a contract or an order enjoining its

nonperformance are remedies available for breach. See §§ 345(b), 357. The relief may be granted at the discretion of the court, the order "will be drawn as best to effectuate the purposes for which the contract was made and on such terms as justice requires," § 358(1), and "damages or other relief may be awarded in the same proceeding" in addition to specific performance or an injunction. § 358(3). But "specific performance or an injunction will not be ordered if damages would be adequate to protect the expectation interest of the injured party," § 359(1). Section 360 provides the "factors" affecting the adequacy of damages, viz., "(a) the difficulty of proving damages with reasonable certainty, (b) the difficulty of procuring a suitable substitute performance by means of money awarded as damages, and (c) the likelihood that an award of damages could not be collected." Comment a to Section 359, however, notes the "tendency to liberalize the granting of equitable relief by enlarging the classes of cases in which damages are not regarded as an adequate remedy" and concludes:

> Adequacy is to some extent relative, and the modern approach is to compare remedies to determine which is more effective in serving the ends of justice. Such a comparison will often lead to the granting of equitable relief. Doubts should be resolved in favor of the granting of specific performance or injunction.

Peter Linzer has stated that this comment is "vague" and that Restatement (Second) adopts an "equivocal approach to the availability of specific performance." *On the Amorality of Contract Remedies—Efficiency, Equity and the Second Restatement,* 81 Colum. L. Rev. 111, 120 (1981). Linzer argues for the general use of specific performance on grounds of both efficiency and fairness. Id. at 138–39.

(8) *Unconscionable Bargains.* Specific performance may be denied for reasons other than the adequacy of the legal remedy. See, e.g., Da Silva v. Musso, 53 N.Y.2d 543 (1981) (mutual mistake). One such control is that the plaintiff must come into equity with "clean hands." But the conduct that sullies the hands must relate to the subject matter of the litigation and affect the "equitable" relations between the litigants. See, e.g., New York Football Giants, Inc. v. Los Angeles Chargers Football Club, Inc., 291 F.2d 471 (5th Cir. 1961).

Another general limitation is that equity will not specifically enforce an inequitable or unconscionable bargain, see Campbell Soup Co. v. Wentz, 172 F.2d 80 (3d Cir. 1948), and that a "shockingly" inadequate consideration may be sufficient to deny relief. But whether the consideration is inadequate or the bargain otherwise unfair "must be viewed prospectively, not retrospectively." Tuckwiller v. Tuckwiller, 413 S.W.2d 274, 278 (Mo. 1967). See Arthur Leff, *Unconscionability and the Code: The Emperor's New Clause,* 115 U. Pa. L. Rev. 485, 528–41 (1967). Thus, where agreed prices for the purchase of cotton were fair at the time of contracting, a subsequent and dramatic price increase the risk of which the seller was held to assume did not foreclose specific performance. R.L. Kimsey Cotton Co., Inc. v. Ferguson, 233 Ga. 962 (1975). See also Restatement (Second) § 364(1)(c) (specific performance or an injunction "will be refused if such relief would be unfair because * * * the exchange is grossly inadequate or the terms of the contract are otherwise unfair").

Comment: Specific Performance Under the United Nations Convention on Contracts for the International Sale of Goods

CISG gives the buyer and the seller a right to require the breaching party to perform its obligations without regard to the adequacy of alternative remedies. Thus, if the seller fails to deliver the buyer may "require performance by the seller of his obligation," CISG Arts. 45(1)(a), 46(1), and if the buyer fails to pay the price or take delivery as agreed the seller "may require the buyer to pay the price, take delivery, or perform his other obligations." CISG Arts. 61(1)(a), 62. See also Article 46(2) & (3), where the buyer has a limited right to require the seller to deliver substitute goods or to "remedy the lack of conformity by repair."

CISG, however, does not state how the order requiring performance is to be enforced. This is left to procedures at the place where enforcement is sought. Moreover, Article 28 provides:

> If, in accordance with the provisions of this Convention, one party is entitled to require performance of any obligation by the other party, a court is not bound to enter a judgment for specific performance unless the court would do so under its own law in respect of similar contracts of sale not governed by this Convention.

This Article seems to tell a judge in a state or federal court in the United States that he or she need not order specific performance under the Convention unless the seller or buyer could get such a remedy under the UCC. For an overview, see Steven Walt, *For Specific Performance Under The United Nations Sales Convention*, 26 Texas Int'l L.J. 211 (1991).

Lumley v. Wagner
Court of Chancery, 1852.
1 De GM & G 604.

■ LORD ST LEONARDS LC.

* * *

The question which I have to decide in the present case arises out of a very simple contract, the effect of which is, that the defendant Johanna Wagner should sing at Her Majesty's Theatre for a certain number of nights, and that she should not sing elsewhere (for that is the true construction) during that period.

* * *

[I]n all sound construction, and according to the true spirit of the agreement, the engagement to perform for three months at one theatre must necessarily exclude the right to perform at the same time at another theatre. It was clearly intended that J Wagner was to exert her vocal abilities to the utmost to aid the theatre to which she agreed to attach herself. I am of opinion that if she had attempted, even in the absence of any negative stipulation, to perform at another theatre, she would have broken the spirit and true meaning of the contract as much as she would now do with reference to the contract into which she has actually entered.

Wherever this court has not proper jurisdiction to enforce specific performance, it operates to bind men's consciences, as far as they can be bound, to a true and literal performance of their agreements; and it will not suffer them to depart from their contracts at their pleasure, leaving the party with whom they have contracted to the mere chance of any damages which a jury may give.

The exercise of this jurisdiction has, I believe, had a wholesome tendency towards the maintenance of the good faith which exists in this country to a much greater degree perhaps than in any other; and although the jurisdiction is not to be extended, yet a judge would desert his duty who did not act up to what his predecessors have handed down as the rule for his guidance in the administration of such an equity.

It was objected that the operation of the injunction in the present case was mischievous, excluding the defendant J Wagner from performing at any other theatre while this court has no power to compel her to perform at Her Majesty's Theatre. It is true that I have not the means of compelling her to sing, but she has no cause of complaint if I compel her to abstain from the commission of an act which she has bound herself not to do, and thus possibly cause her to fulfil her engagement.

The jurisdiction which I now exercise is wholly within the power of the court, and being of opinion that it is a proper case for interfering, I shall leave nothing unsatisfied by the judgment I pronounce. The effect, too, of the injunction in restraining J Wagner from singing elsewhere may, in the event of an action being brought against her by the plaintiff, prevent any such amount of vindictive damages being given against her as a jury might probably be inclined to give if she had carried her talents and exercised them at the rival theatre: the injunction may also, as I have said, tend to the fulfilment of her engagement; though, in continuing the injunction, I disclaim doing indirectly what I cannot do directly.

Curb Records, Inc. v. Samuel T. McGraw

Court of Appeals of Tennessee, 2012.
2012 WL 4377817.

■ ANDY D. BENNETT, J.

* * *

In March 1997, Tim McGraw and Curb entered into a recording agreement under which McGraw would render his services as a recording artist exclusively for Curb during the term of the agreement. The agreement provides for an initial period during which McGraw was required to deliver three albums. After the initial period, McGraw granted Curb six options, "each to extend the term of this agreement for one option period commencing immediately upon the expiration of the then current period . . . and continuing until nine (9) months after your Delivery to Curb of all Masters required during such option period." During each option period, McGraw was required to record and deliver to Curb "a number of Masters sufficient for one (1) album of then customary playing time." The agreement contains the following key provisions concerning the duration of each option period:

> The individual producer of the Masters, and the selections to be recorded, are subject to the mutual approval of you and Curb. . . . [Y]ou hereby agree to record and Deliver (and Curb hereby acknowledges that you shall be permitted to Deliver) to Curb all Masters in fulfillment of each album of your recording commitment hereunder (excluding Greatest Hits, Live albums etc.) subsequent to the "First LP" (as defined below) no earlier than twelve (12) months nor later than eighteen (18) months following Delivery to Curb of the immediately preceding album in fulfillment of your recording commitment hereunder (excluding Greatest Hits, Live albums, etc.). At such time, if any, that Curb elects to release any Greatest Hits album embodying Masters under this agreement and/or the Prior McGraw Agreement, Curb may in Curb's sole discretion, further extend the time frame for Delivery set forth in the previous sentences of the next such album of your recording commitment by up to a maximum of six (6) additional months in any single instance.

The agreement further provides that Curb is the "perpetual owner of all Masters (and all other recordings . . . embodying your performances made during the term hereof)."

McGraw recorded and delivered three albums during the initial period and one album during each of the first four option periods. On October 22, 2010, McGraw gave to Curb a group of masters for an album entitled *Emotional Traffic*. The current dispute arose when Curb refused to accept these masters in satisfaction of McGraw's contractual obligations for the fifth option period.

On May 13, 2011, Curb filed a complaint for a declaratory judgment against McGraw in which Curb alleged that McGraw was in breach of the agreement because he refused to record and deliver the fifth option period album in accordance with the terms of the agreement. Among Curb's assertions is that McGraw recorded the masters for *Emotional Traffic* prior to the fifth option period. The complaint includes a prayer for the following relief:

> 1.   That the Court declare that Tim McGraw is in breach of the Recording Agreement because, among other things, he has failed and refused to record and Deliver the fifth Option Period

Album during the six (6) month period ending April 20, 2011 pursuant to the terms of the Recording Agreement; and

2. That the Court declare that the Emotional Traffic Masters do not and cannot constitute the fifth Option Period Album; and

* * *

7. That the Court enjoin Tim McGraw from providing personal services as a recording artist, or agreeing to do so, other than to Curb Records for so long as he, among other things, fails and refuses to record and Deliver to Curb Records the fifth Option Period Album and the sixth Option Period Album under the Recording Agreement;. . . .

McGraw counterclaimed for breach of contract, breach of implied covenant of good faith and fair dealing, and intentional interference with business relationships.

On September 29, 2011, the trial court entered an agreed scheduling order providing for "bifurcated proceeding that will first make a final determination whether or not Curb is entitled to prevent Mr. McGraw, by injunction or otherwise, from recording for entities other than Curb, followed by the progression of a trial on the merits." * * *

After the . . . hearing in November 2011, the court denied Curb's request for injunctive relief and, on December 8, 2011, entered a memorandum and order. In denying Curb's request for injunctive relief, the trial court expressly reserved for adjudication at trial "the question of whether *Emotional Traffic* constitutes the Fifth Option Album and whether Mr. McGraw deprived Curb Records of its pre-approval rights, in breach of the parties' contract." * * *

On appeal, Curb argues that the trial court erred in concluding that Curb failed to demonstrate irreparable harm from McGraw's breach; and that the trial court erred in adjudicating the ownership of the recordings at issue.

STANDARD OF REVIEW

A trial court's decision to grant or deny a request for a temporary injunction is reviewed under an abuse of discretion standard. . . . Similarly, the decision to grant or deny permanent injunctive relief rests within the discretion of the trial court and is reviewed for an abuse of that discretion. *Vintage Health Res., Inc. v. Guiangan*, 309 S.W.3d 448, 466 (Tenn.Ct.App.2009). Under the abuse of discretion standard, a reviewing court cannot substitute its judgment for the trial court's judgment. . . . Rather, a reviewing court will find an abuse of discretion only if the trial court "applied incorrect legal standards, reached an illogical conclusion, based its decision on a clearly erroneous assessment of the evidence, or employ[ed] reasoning that causes an injustice to the complaining party." *Konvalinka v. Chattanooga-Hamilton Cnty. Hosp. Auth.*, 249 S.W.3d 346, 358 (Tenn.2008). . . .

ANALYSIS

Before addressing Curb's arguments, we will seek to clarify the appropriate analytical framework. * * * Pursuant to caselaw, there are four factors to be considered by a trial court in deciding whether to issue a temporary injunction: the threat of irreparable harm, the balance between the harm to be prevented and the injury to be inflicted if the injunction issues, the probability that the applicant will succeed on the merits, and the public interest. *Moody v. Hutchison,* 247 S.W.3d 187, 199–200 (Tenn.Ct.App.2007). With respect to permanent injunctive relief, the analysis differs somewhat as, in the typical situation, the court has ruled in favor of the applicant on the merits and must determine whether permanent injunctive relief is an appropriate remedy. See *Vintage Health,* 309 S.W.3d at 467. Because, in the present case, the parties agreed to submit the issue of permanent injunctive relief for resolution prior to a trial on the merits, the trial court stated that it had "essentially merged the consideration of Plaintiff's request for a temporary injunction with Plaintiff's request for a permanent injunction."

Curb's . . . argument is that the trial court "incorrectly applied the law to the facts in concluding that Curb Records has suffered no irreparable harm." Thus, Curb disagrees with the trial court's conclusion of law concerning irreparable harm. We note that, even if we examine the propriety of this particular decision de novo, the trial court's ultimate determination not to grant injunctive relief must be reviewed for an abuse of discretion.

In its conclusions of law, the trial court stated that "Curb Records has arguably shown some likelihood of success on its breach of contract claim with respect to the timing issue and, to a lesser extent, on the pre-approval issue." The court went on to make the following findings regarding irreparable harm and the appropriateness of injunctive relief:

> The Court concludes that Curb Records has not made a showing of irreparable harm sufficient to warrant the Court's grant of a temporary injunction preventing Mr. McGraw from continuing his recording career. Additionally, the Court concludes that Curb Records is, in part seeking specific performance against Mr. McGraw and that this relief is disfavored under Tennessee law. Curb Records' contention that Mr. McGraw can, in essence, cure the alleged breach by recording additional songs or an additional album while affording Curb Records pre-approval rights amounts to request for specific performance in a personal services contract where the parties have differences that would make this process exceedingly difficult.

> Curb Records is seeking permanent injunctive relief prohibiting Mr. McGraw from continuing his recording career as a musician for any other recording company. This requested relief appears heavy-handed and legally impermissible under the

circumstances, given: 1) the limited nature and extent of the alleged breach of contract upon which Curb Records has shown some likelihood of success; 2) the fact that Mr. McGraw's alleged breach occurred near the end (rather than at the beginning) of a multiple-year contractual relationship with Curb Records; 3) Mr. McGraw provides unique services as a recording artist that the public has an interest in being made available while this dispute proceeds through the courts, subject to any monetary judgment this Court may award after the trial on the merits; 4) Mr. McGraw's conduct in recording *Emotional Traffic* and delivering it to Curb Records afforded Curb Records the benefit of Mr. McGraw's unique and extraordinary talent; and 5) an injunction would likely have an adverse and disproportionate effect on the body of musical recording work Mr. McGraw would be permitted to produce during this important period in Mr. McGraw's musical career.

The trial court ultimately reached the following conclusion: "Under all of the unique circumstances described in this Memorandum and Order, the Court concludes that Curb Records will not suffer irreparable harm if Mr. McGraw records for himself or for another record company. Curb Records has an adequate remedy at law."

On appeal, Curb asserts that the factual findings made by the trial court necessitate the legal conclusion that Curb suffered irreparable harm. Curb argues that "breach of an exclusive personal services contract by a unique and exceptional performer constitutes irreparable harm." It is undisputed that McGraw is a unique and exceptional artist. For purposes of ruling on injunctive relief, the trial court essentially accepted Curb's allegations that McGraw breached the contract. These two facts do not, however, necessitate a conclusion of irreparable harm.

A court is to use its equitable power to grant injunctive relief sparingly. *Vintage Health,* 309 S.W.3d at 467. The following principles are instructive:

> The general rule in respect of contracts for personal services is that for breach thereof a party must avail himself of the remedy afforded at law. It is a familiar and well established doctrine that courts of equity will not exercise jurisdiction to grant a decree for specific performance of a contract for personal services except perhaps in very exceptional cases or under very exceptional circumstances. *Neither, as a general rule, will equity indirectly enforce a contract for personal services by an injunction restraining the employee from leaving the services of the employer, except to prevent breach of contract by one who possesses some special, unique, or extraordinary qualifications, where it would be difficult, if not impossible, to replace his services, and damages obviously would be inadequate to remedy the loss.*

Bunns v. Walkem Dev. Co., Inc., 385 S.W.2d 917, 923 (Tenn.Ct.App. 1964) (quoting 49 Am.Jur.2D *Specific Performance* § 134) (emphasis added). While Tennessee cases have recognized a special exception for contracts involving unique and extraordinary services, unique and extraordinary services do not make injunctive relief appropriate in all cases. *See Cagle v. Hybner,* 2008 WL 2649643, at *20 (Tenn.Ct.App. July 3, 2008).

In *Cagle v. Hybner,* the court considered the propriety of specific performance or an injunction preventing a songwriter from composing any songs for others until the songwriter fulfilled his obligations to a publisher under a songwriter agreement. *Id.* at * 18–21. After acknowledging the general rule against specific performance to enforce a personal service contract and the limited exception regarding services for unique and extraordinary skills, the court stated that "such extraordinary relief is not appropriate unless *the court* can determine that the contract is 'clear, definite, complete and free from any suspicion of fraud and unfairness.' " *Id.* at *18–19 (quoting *Johnson v. Browder,* 207 S.W.2d 1, 3 (Tenn.1947)). Because the only basis to determine the sufficiency of the songwriter's future performance was the subjective opinion of the publisher, the court concluded that the contract did not provide the required clear and definite criteria. *Id.* at *19, 207 S.W.2d 1. The court went on to conclude that specific performance also was not appropriate because of the "undesirability of compelling the continuance of personal association after disputes have arisen and confidence and loyalty are gone." *Id.* at *20, 207 S.W.2d 1 (quoting Restatement (First) Of Contracts § 379 cmt. d (1932)).

While much of the court's analysis in *Cagle* focused on specific performance, the court also considered injunctive relief. *Id.* In concluding that injunctive relief was not appropriate, the court stated:

> A promise to render personal service exclusively for another will not be enforced by injunction against serving another person if its probable result will be to compel a performance involving personal relations the enforced continuance of which is undesirable. *Restatement (Second) of Contracts* § 367 (1981). In the present matter, if Cagle is enjoined from writing songs for anyone other than Hybner until Cagle has composed and delivered 76.52 songs Hybner determines, in his sole discretion, to be of commercially marketable quality, then Cagle may forever be enjoined from songwriting or may be forced into involuntary servitude to Hybner for years. Such a circumstance places Hybner in a position of overwhelming power, which we find to be unfair, and thus, inequitable.

Id. Thus, although injunctive relief may be appropriate in cases involving contracts for unique and extraordinary services, such relief may not be appropriate where the contract does not provide sufficiently definite terms and/or where an injunction would amount to an involuntary servitude. *See also News Mart, Inc. v. State ex rel. Webster,* 561 S.W.2d

752, 753 (Tenn.1978) (injunction must describe enjoined activities with specificity); *Cooper Mgmt., LLC v. Performa Entm't, Inc.,* 2002 WL 1905318, at *3 (Tenn.Ct.App. Aug.15, 2002) (length of injunction to be based on objective, not subjective, standard).

Curb cites a multitude of cases from other jurisdictions in support of its position that the trial court should have found irreparable harm. . . . We agree with McGraw, however, that these cases are all distinguishable from the present case because they involved contracts for a specific length of time. In this case, the contract lacks a specific durational limit; rather, as in *Cagle,* the contract would continue until Curb determined that McGraw had met his contractual obligations. In *Ichiban Records, Inc. v. Rap-A-Lot Records, Inc.,* 933 S.W.2d 546, 552 (Tex.App. 1996), the court declined to enforce by injunction a contract without a specific time limit.

Thus, even though McGraw is undisputedly an entertainer offering unique and extraordinary services, the trial court did not err in finding that there was no irreparable harm or in exercising its discretion to conclude that injunctive relief was not appropriate. As in *Cagle,* this case involves a contract whose duration depends upon the exercise of discretion by the party seeking the injunction. The requested injunction would essentially place McGraw in a position of choosing between the end of his recording career or the indefinite continuation of a relationship with Curb that has become contentious.

NOTES

(1) *No Specific Performance of Personal Service Contracts.* The rule against specific performance of personal service contracts is widely recognized. Restatement (Second) Section 367(1): "A promise to render personal services will not be specifically enforced."

Why not? According to Comment a, the reasons fall into three overlapping categories: (1) It is undesirable to compel the continuation of a personal relationship after a dispute has undercut confidence and loyalty; (2) The difficulties inherent in passing judgment on the quality of what frequently is a subjective performance are too great; and (3) An award requiring performance may impose a form of involuntary servitude that is prohibited by the 13th Amendment to the Constitution. See In re A.P. Johnson, 178 B.R. 216, 221–222 (BAP 9th Cir. 1995); Read v. Wilmington Senior Center, Inc., 1992 WL 296870 (Del.Ch. 1992). See also Restatement (Second) §§ 365, 366.

(2) *Negative Injunctions.* The *Lumley* doctrine was adopted in the United States in the late nineteenth century, see McCaull v. Braham, 16 Fed. 37 (S.D.N.Y. 1883), and expanded equity jurisdiction in two ways: first, by enforcing the negative covenant where the direct promise was not specifically enforceable, and second, by granting the plaintiff an injunction where comparable relief was not available to the defendant. See, e.g., Philadelphia Ball Club v. Lajoie, 202 Pa. 210 (1902) (absence of mutual remedy not fatal to injunction).

Moreover, the injunction, whose primary purpose is to protect the plaintiff from unfair competition from a contract breacher whose unique services cannot easily be replaced, is available whether or not an express negative covenant has been made. As Corbin put it, an injunction against competition is proper if the competition "will do additional irreparable injury to the plaintiff, and if the injunction may induce proper performance of the entire contract by economic pressure without at the same time creating harmful personal relations." 5A Corbin § 1206, p. 412.

That said, as *Curb Records v. McGraw* illustrates, the contemporary rule does not sanction Lord St. Leonard's statement that the defendant "has no cause of complaint if I compel her to abstain from the commission of an act which she has bound herself not to do, and thus possibly cause her to fulfil her engagement." Restatement (Second) Section 367(2) provides:

> A promise to render personal service exclusively for one employer will not be enforced by an injunction against serving another if its probable result will be to compel a performance involving personal relations the enforced continuance of which is undesirable or will be to leave the employee without other reasonable means of making a living.

English courts similarly will enforce an express covenant not to work elsewhere, but only if the breaching party has some other reasonable means of earning a living. G. Treitel, The Law of Contract 970–974 (10th ed. 1999). The defendant must not be given a choice between starving and working for the plaintiff.

(3) Why did the court affirm the denial of a negative injunction against Tim McGraw in *Curb Records*? Suppose Curb Records asks you to restructure their standard recording contract in a way that is more likely to support a negative injunction. What would you suggest?

(4) Courts regularly include the public interest among the factors relevant to the decision whether or not to grant an injunction. What do you think about the trial court's suggestion in *Curb Records* that "Mr. McGraw provides unique services as a recording artist that the public has an interest in being made available"?

Comment: The Gendered Origins of the *Lumley* Doctrine

This comment is excerpted from a generative article on gender by Lea S. VanderVelde:

> In the familiar case of *Lumley v. Wagner*, [42 Eng. Rep. 687, 693 (Ch. 1852)] the English Court of Equity held that although opera singer Johanna Wagner could not be ordered to perform her contract, she would be enjoined from singing at any competing music hall for the term of the contract. *Lumley* is usually lauded in first year contracts courses as a just and fair decision, one that illustrates the proper distinction between equitable orders that force performance (unworkable and unjust) and equitable orders that prevent performance (sometimes workable, usually

practical, and not necessarily unjust). * * * How did the rule of *Lumley v. Wagner* come to be incorporated into the canon of rules pertaining to equitable intervention in cases of departing employees?

* * *

[I] offer a tentative explanation of this phenomenon: that the *Lumley* rule's reception in the United States was facilitated by the fact that the majority of cases that employers won were cases involving women. I have chosen the term "gendered" to describe this phenomenon because the term covers a broad range of gender-specific elements that recur in this line of cases. . . . The phenomenon was not a simple one of misogyny or sexism, and it did not appear uniformly in every case involving a woman employee. Deeper cultural constructions of the role of women in the public workplace, particularly the very public workplace of the stage, explain the phenomenon better than would attributions of sexism to the few key individuals involved. A woman appearing in public on the stage posed a particular challenge to the dominant norm of the Victorian Era that women were supposed to remain in the privacy of the home.

I maintain that, unlike male actors, nineteenth-century women performers were less likely to be viewed as free and independent employees. Nineteenth-century women were generally perceived as relationally bound to men. In this line of cases, that perception of women manifested itself in the need to bind actresses to their male theater managers. Moreover, in the view of the dominant culture, women performers were more likely to be perceived as subordinate than were their male counterparts. The decisions in this line of cases reflect larger "belief systems out of which knowledge is constructed, [belief systems that] place constraints on thought [and] that have real consequences for the behavior of individuals who live within them." [Alice Kessler-Harris, A Woman's Wage: Historical Meanings and Social Consequences 1 (1990).] This conceptualization of women in the nineteenth century paved the way for the adoption of the *Lumley* rule in America.

The story that emerges is one of reversal of a legal rule due in large part to the increasing presence of women in the acting profession. When *Lumley* first appeared in the United States, the cultural repulsion to anything that even hinted of slavery led to its unequivocal rejection. But later in the century, the cultural aversion to mastery had lessened and no longer seemed to apply to men's domination of women in particular. In the later cases, courts were harsher upon women defendants who attempted to leave their employment than they were in the few parallel cases involving men. And, in the later cases, courts were harsher upon women than they had been earlier in the century. By the end of the century, the courts' subjugation of actresses to the control of theater managers surpassed even the language of their contracts and became an incident of a status classification constructed largely by the courts, rather than the consequence of any voluntary agreement between the parties.

Although no court articulated gender as a factor influencing its decision, the tone of the opinions as well as the pattern of results demonstrates that the courts of New York, where the core cases were litigated, were unable to ignore differential cultural constructions of women's proper behavior as reflected in the larger society and in other legal rules. Women's attempts to control their work lives and to assert their agency and independence by terminating employment that they no longer found desirable was no more to be tolerated than the emerging trend of women's attempts to divorce their husbands. Although courts deciding employment cases spoke of "binding men's consciences," they rarely did so when presented with male defendants. The courts appeared more willing and even eager to sanction what they perceived as women's infidelity to their male employers.

Lea S. VanderVelde, *The Gendered Origins of the Lumley Doctrine: Binding Men's Consciences and Women's Fidelity*, 101 Yale L.J. 775, 775–780 (1992). Does gender, race or class explain the development of other contractual doctrines or other patterns of contract enforcement?

Although there are many variables to consider, the *Lumley* principle has survived in the United States and found its home in the domain of professional sports and entertainment, where it is now applied to men as well as women. At times the papers have been full of reports about players and coaches of exceptional and not so exceptional talent who have joined other teams in violation of contracts or "reserve" clauses and have been enjoined from competing until the period of commitment to the plaintiff team has expired. For a typical example, see Nassau Sports v. Peters, 352 F.Supp. 870 (E.D.N.Y. 1972) (hockey). In recent years, however, many professional leagues have adopted rules that effectively prevent the issue from arising. But see Star Boxing, Inc. v. Tarver, 2002 WL 31867729 (S.D.N.Y.) (boxing).

5. AGREED-UPON REMEDIES

So far we have been considering remedial rules developed by courts or legislators. But just as parties have the power to contract for the obligations they want, why not give them the power to contract for the remedies for the breach of those obligations? In fact, the law gives parties the ability to alter the default remedies for breach. But as we shall see, it also places several important limits on that power.

(A) LIQUIDATED DAMAGES

As we have seen, punitive damages are not recoverable in the ordinary action for breach of contract. This is generally true even if the defendant's breach is willful. Courts insist that the remedial objective is to compensate the plaintiff, not to punish the defendant.

But what if the parties provide in their contract what the damages are to be in the event of breach, and they set a figure which is greatly in excess of probable harm? Is such a provision objectionable from the standpoint of fairness or justice? Would it be upheld in court? Consider the following judicial and scholarly statements:

> More than three centuries ago, in *The Merchant of Venice,* Shakespeare tellingly illustrated the evil of agreements which exact a "pound of flesh." Since that time, courts have grappled with the problem of oppressive contracts through the doctrine of unconscionability. Originating in Equity as a form of relief against the harshness of penal bonds, this doctrine has been employed by courts to deny enforcement to harsh and unreasonable contract terms. Today we are asked to determine whether the liquidated damages provisions of several commercial leasing agreements are unconscionable as a matter of law. In reaching our decision, we must resolve a significant tension between two important goals served by rules governing the enforceability of liquidated damages clauses: rejecting clauses which operate as a penalty or forfeiture while upholding provisions which are reasonable attempts by parties to estimate the probable damages which would flow from a breach. This tension is an example of a more general conflict between contract law as a system of private ordering and contract law as an expression of the public interest. * * *

> On the one hand, courts will not enforce such a provision if it operates as a penalty or forfeiture clause. . . . The law is clear that contractual terms providing for the payment of a sum disproportionate to the amount of actual damages exact a penalty and are unenforceable. . . . The rationale for this principle is that contractual terms fixing damages in an amount clearly disproportionate to actual loss seek to deter breach through compulsion and have an *in terrorem* effect: fearing severe economic loss, the promisor is compelled to continue performance, while the promisee may reap a windfall well in excess of his just compensation. . . .

> On the other hand, courts uphold contractual provisions fixing damages for breach when the terms constitute a reasonable mechanism for estimating the compensation which should be paid to satisfy any loss flowing from the breach. . . . These provisions have value in situations where it is difficult to

1128   Remedies   Chapter 6

estimate the amount of actual damages. From these principles, the standards for evaluating appellants' claim that the challenged lease terms are unconscionable are easily discernible. Contractual provisions fixing liquidated damages in the event of breach will not be voided as unconscionable or contrary to public policy if the amount liquidated bears a reasonable proportion to the probable loss and the amount of actual loss is incapable or difficult of precise estimation. . . . If the amount fixed by contract is plainly or grossly disproportionate to the probable loss, the contractual provisions exact a penalty and will not be enforced. . . .

Leasing Service Corp. v. Justice, 673 F.2d 70, 73 (2d Cir. 1982) (Kaufman, J.).

The judicial attitude towards contract clauses that specify the amount to be paid in the event of breach is one of the few areas of contract law that has received generally adverse criticism from economic analysts. The traditional rule against the enforcement of "penalty" clauses runs strongly counter to the elaboration of the efficiency criterion, particularly in commercial contexts.

Several reasons account for the economists' antagonism. First, the assumption of rationality entails that a party will not accept a clause for which he is inadequately compensated. When the promisee demands a "penalty clause," the promisor will agree only if the price is increased sufficiently to cover any increase in the cost of performance. Thus, if parties are "rational", no contract should require performance when the (expected) costs to party A of performing exceed the (expected) benefits to party B of receiving it. Of course, the parties may have different expectations as to the likelihood of some contingency occurring, and one may be more accurate than the other. Moreover, the occurrence of the contingency may impose some inequality of costs and benefits between the parties. But, since it seems plausible that commercial contractors act largely in their "rational" self-interest, it is likely that both parties initially saw a benefit even in a clause which a court later terms a penalty. This benefit might simply be to trade a risk that one party perceives as high to a second party who perceives it as low. Such trades may be "efficient" because trading the risk may be cheaper for the first party than correcting or improving his estimate of the risk to which he was exposed. In that event, judicial intervention after the fact would only serve to induce excessively costly gathering of information. Alternatively, the benefits to the parties may be more "substantial" than those arising from different perceptions. For instance, a new entrant into a market may be willing to accept a clause imposing a penalty in the event his product fails to meet some quality standard precisely because he has no other means of credibly assuring quality and thereby successfully entering the market.

A second reason economists criticize limitations on liquidated damage clauses lies in the informational advantage that the parties themselves are presumed to have; at the time of contracting the parties are likely to have better information about any idiosyncratic damages that might be incurred than a court will have at or after the time of breach. Particularly in markets where substitute performance is difficult to obtain, this informational advantage argues strongly for liberal enforcement of liquidated damage clauses. An analogous argument derives from the widespread belief that expectation damages are in fact undercompensatory. If the law seeks to promote efficient decisions to perform or not, then allowing parties to estimate damages in advance will induce more appropriate decisions in this respect than court-imposed rules.

A third problem with the current proscription of "penalty" clauses lies in its implicit distributional bias; it forces the parties to allocate some risks in a particular way. Suppose the breach is caused by the appearance of a third party willing to pay more for the good than the first buyer agreed to pay. The ban on penalties (together with a rule of expectation damages) effectively allocates the entire gain from the appearance of the third party to the seller, while the parties might rationally have wished to divide this risk differently. On the other hand, if the breach is prompted by an uneconomic increase in costs, expectation damages allocates all of the loss to the breaching party, while contractors, negotiating before the breach, might knowingly have chosen to share this risk differently.

These arguments suggest that the current rules governing liquidated damage clauses are too restrictive. They do not necessarily contend that every liquidation clause, whether it appears to be a "penalty" or not, should be permitted. Most commentators would make exceptions for clauses that resulted from defective bargaining procedures (akin to those covered by unconscionability). These defects, however, seem unlikely to occur in commercial contexts, where one can presume that the parties are sophisticated and rational in their negotiations. Other commentators suggest that liquidated damage clauses be policed for more than fraud or oppression in bargaining. In some circumstances, a clause which unduly benefitted one party might stimulate it to induce a breach by the other; in that case, these commentators suggest the clause should not be enforced.

Lewis Kornhauser, *An Introduction to the Economic Analysis of Contract Remedies*, 57 U. Colo. L. Rev. 683, 720–21 (1986) [Reprinted with permission].

To begin with, bounded rationality and rational ignorance have a special bearing on liquidated damages provisions. Contracting parties will normally find it relatively easy to evaluate proposed performance terms, such as subject matter, quantity, and price. In contrast, at the time the contract is made it is often impracticable, if not impossible, to imagine all the scenarios of breach. Similarly, the inherent complexity of determining the application of a liquidated damages provision to every possible breach scenario is often likely to exceed actors' calculating capabilities.

Even on the doubtful assumption that a party could imagine all breach scenarios and calculate the application of a liquidated damages provision to every possible breach, the benefits of extensive search and information processing on these issues will often seem to be very low as compared to the costs. A party who contracts to buy or sell a commodity normally expects to perform. Accordingly, the benefits of deliberating very carefully on performance terms are compelling, and the costs of such deliberation are usually not undue in relation to the benefits. In contrast, the same party will not normally expect that a liquidated damages provision will ever come into play against him—partly because he intends to perform, and partly because experience will tell him that in general there is a high rate of performance of contracts. For example, if contracts are performed at least 95 percent of the time (which observation suggests is likely), all the costs of processing the more remote applications of a liquidated damages provision would have to be taken into account, but the benefits of such processing would have to be discounted by 95 percent. The resulting cost-benefit ratio will often provide a substantial disincentive for processing every possible application of a liquidated damages provision, even if it were in fact possible to imagine every such scenario. As a result, contracting parties are likely often to not even try to think liquidated damages provisions through, and are therefore unlikely to fully understand the implications of such provisions.

The problem of disposition also bears significantly on liquidated damages provisions. Because actors tend to be unrealistically optimistic, a contracting party will probably believe that his performance is more likely, and his breach less likely, than is actually the case. Accordingly, unrealistic optimism will reduce even further the deliberation that actors give to liquidated damages provisions.

Finally, defective capabilities have particular relevance to liquidated damages provisions. The availability heuristic may lead a contracting party to give undue weight to his present intention to perform, which is vivid and concrete, as compared with the abstract possibility that future circumstances may compel him to breach. Because a contracting party is likely to take the sample of present evidence as representative of the future, he is apt to overestimate the extent to which his present intention to perform is a reliable predictor of his future intentions. Because actors have faulty telescopic faculties, a contracting party is likely to overvalue the benefit of the prospect of performance, which will normally begin to occur in the short term, as against the cost of the prospect of a breach, which will typically occur, if at all, only down the road. Because actors tend to underestimate risks, a contracting party is likely to underestimate the risk that a liquidated damages provision will take effect.

Melvin Aron Eisenberg, *The Limits of Cognition and the Limits of Contract*, 47 Stan. L. Rev. 211, 227–28 (1995).

Southwest Engineering Co. v. United States

United States Court of Appeals, Eighth Circuit, 1965.
341 F.2d 998, cert. denied, 382 U.S. 819.

■ VAN OOSTERHOUT, CIRCUIT JUDGE. Plaintiff Southwest Engineering Company, hereinafter called Southwest, has appealed from summary judgment dismissing its complaint against the United States for recovery of $8,300 withheld as liquidated damages for delay in performance on four construction contracts entered into between Southwest and the United States.

This appeal is before us upon an agreed statement of the record. Four contracts entered into between Southwest and the Government called for the construction by Southwest of three V.O.R. radio facilities at Readsville, Blackwater, and Maryland Heights, Missouri, and for a high intensity approach light lane at Lambert Field, Missouri. Each of the contracts fixed a completion date and provided for liquidated damages on a per diem basis for each day's delay beyond the agreed completion date. The agreed liquidated damage on the Lambert Field project was $100 per day, and $50 per day on each of the other projects. Each contract contained the general provisions set forth in Standard Form 23–A (March 1953) prescribed by the General Services Administration, including, among others, a provision that plaintiff was not to be charged with delays "due to unforeseeable causes beyond the control and without the fault or negligence of the Contractor, including, but not restricted to, acts of God or of the public enemy, acts of the Government, in either its sovereign or contractual capacity, acts of another contractor in the performance of a contract with the Government, fires, floods, epidemics, quarantine restrictions, strikes, freight embargoes, and unusually severe weather, or delays of subcontractors or suppliers due to such causes." Within ten days from the beginning of any such delay, plaintiff was to notify the contracting officer in writing of the causes of delay. The contracting officer was to ascertain the facts and extent of the delay, and extend the time for completing the work when "in his judgment the findings of fact justify such an extension." His findings of fact were to be final, subject only to appeal to the "head of the department."

The Blackwater project was completed 97 days late. Plaintiff requested time extensions, alleging the delay resulted from causes for which it was not responsible, including acts and omissions of defendant. Administrative appeals resulted in extensions by the C.A.A. because of delays by the Government, and, later on, a remission of an additional $4,200 liquidated damages by the Comptroller General under the authority of 41 U.S.C. § 256a, because of late delivery of Government-furnished material. This left $550 (11 days) withheld as liquidated damages on the Blackwater project.

The Readsville project was completed 84 days late. Administrative appeals resulted in a three-days extension, leaving liquidated damages for 81 days totalling $4,050.

The Maryland Heights project was completed 48 days late. On administrative appeal, a fourteen-days extension was allowed resulting in liquidated damages of $1,700 for 34 days delay.

The Lambert Field project was completed 54 days late, 34 days extension was granted, leaving $2,000 as liquidated damages for 20 days delay.

The parties stipulated "although each project was not completed until after the date prescribed in its contract, defendant suffered no actual damage on any project." The Government withheld the liquidated damages for delays provided in the contracts after giving credit for the extensions of time administratively allowed. This suit by Southwest is for recovery of the $8,300 so withheld as liquidated damages. The Government counterclaimed for the liquidated damages here involved. Plaintiff by reply admitted the projects were not completed within the time limits as administratively extended but denied the Government was entitled to liquidated damages because the Government caused and contributed to the delays and because the Government suffered no actual damages.

The trial court determined that the Government was entitled to liquidated damages in the amount claimed, offset such damages which equaled the amount of payments withheld, sustained the motion for summary judgment, and dismissed the complaint.

Southwest as a basis for reversal urges the trial court's decision was induced by two erroneous views of the law, either of which requires reversal. The points relied upon for reversal are thus stated:

* * *

2. "The court erred in awarding the Government liquidated damages because a contract provision for liquidated damages is clearly a penalty and not enforceable where the party seeking to enforce it formally admits he sustained no actual damage."

At the outset, we observe that the contracts here involved were entered into pursuant to federal law by an authorized federal agency. Federal law controls in the construction and determination of rights under federal contracts. Priebe & Sons, Inc. v. United States, 332 U.S. 407, 411. . . .

In the Priebe case, the Supreme Court states:

"It is customary, where Congress has not adopted a different standard, to apply to the construction of government contracts the principles of general contract law. United States v. Standard Rice Co., 323 U.S. 106, 111, and cases cited. That has been done in other cases where the Court has considered the enforceability of 'liquidated damages' provisions in government contracts." 332 U.S. 407.

* * *

Southwest's second point in substance is that the parties' stipulation that the Government suffered no actual damage bars any recovery of liquidated damages. Such stipulation was made. It relates to the situation as it existed at the time of the completion of the work. The stipulation does not go to the extent of agreeing that the parties at the time of contracting did not reasonably contemplate that damages would flow from a delay in performance.

The contracts prescribe the payments to be made for delays as liquidated damages. Southwest urges that such provision is a penalty provision. The agreed record is highly condensed and does not show the contract price for the various projects, but such projects appear to be substantial. There is no showing that the liquidated damages for delay provided for are beyond damages reasonably contemplated by the parties at the time of the contract.

Two requirements must be considered to determine whether the provision included in the contract fixing the amount of damages payable on breach will be interpreted as an enforceable liquidated damage clause rather than an unenforceable penalty clause: First, the amount so fixed must be a reasonable forecast of just compensation for the harm that is caused by the breach, and second, the harm that is caused by the breach must be one that is incapable or very difficult of accurate estimation. . . .

Whether these requirements have been complied with must be viewed as of the time the contract was executed rather than when the contract was breached or at some other subsequent time. Courts presently look with candor upon provisions that are deliberately entered into between parties and therefore do not look with disfavor upon liquidated damage stipulations. . . .

In the Bethlehem Steel case, the Court sets out the standard to be applied for determining whether a liquidated damage provision can be upheld as follows: "The question always is, What did the parties intend by the language used? When such intention is ascertained it is ordinarily the duty of the court to carry it out." 205 U.S. 105, 119.

Here Southwest has failed to establish that the intention of the parties was to do anything other than execute a valid liquidated damage provision.

Priebe & Sons, Inc. v. United States, supra, * * * speaks of standards applicable to allowance of liquidated damages, stating:

"Today the law does not look with disfavor upon 'liquidated damages' provisions in contracts. When they are fair and reasonable attempts to fix just compensation for anticipated loss caused by breach of contract, they are enforced. * * * They serve a particularly useful function when damages are uncertain in nature or amount or are unmeasurable, as is the case in many government contracts. * * * And the fact that the damages suffered are shown to be less than the damages contracted for is not fatal. These provisions are to be judged as of the time of making the contract." 332 U.S. 407, 411–412.

* * *

We recognize that there are cases . . . which reach a contrary result.

We believe that the cases holding that the situation existing at the time of the contract is controlling in determining the reasonableness of liquidated damages are based upon sound reasoning and represent the weight of authority. Where parties have by their contract agreed upon a liquidated damage provision as a reasonable forecast of just compensation for breach of contract and damages are difficult to estimate accurately, such provision should be enforced. If in the course of subsequent developments, damages prove to be greater than those stipulated, the party entitled to damages is bound by the liquidated damage agreement. It is not unfair to hold the contractor performing the work to such agreement if by reason of later developments damages prove to be less or nonexistent. Each party by entering into such contractual provision took a calculated risk and is bound by reasonable contractual provisions pertaining to liquidated damages.

Southwest has completely failed to demonstrate that the court committed an error of law in determining that absence of actual damages at the time of breach of the contract or thereafter does not bar recovery of liquidated damages. The court at least impliedly found that the liquidated damage provisions of the contracts here involved were reasonable when viewed in the light of circumstances existing at the time the contract was entered into. We find nothing in the record which would compel a contrary conclusion. The court committed no error in allowing liquidated damages.

The judgment appealed from is affirmed.

NOTES

(1) *Liquidated Damages Under the UCC and Restatement (Second).* UCC § 2–718(1) provides:

> Damages for breach by either party may be liquidated in the agreement but only at an amount which is reasonable in the light of the anticipated or actual harm caused by the breach, the difficulties of proof of loss, and the inconvenience or nonfeasibility of otherwise obtaining an adequate remedy. A term fixing unreasonably large liquidated damages is void as a penalty.

How does this approach differ from that adopted in *Southwest Engineering*? Does the Code appear to be more supportive or less supportive of the power of contracting parties to fix the amount of damage in advance of breach?

Restatement (Second) § 356(1), drafted so as to harmonize with UCC § 2–718, reads: "Damages for breach by either party may be liquidated in the agreement but only at an amount that is reasonable in the light of the anticipated or actual loss caused by the breach and the difficulties of proof of loss. A term fixing unreasonably large liquidated damages is unenforceable on grounds of public policy as a penalty."

The mention of the time of breach as well as the time of contracting raises a number of questions. For example, what if the agreed upon figure is unreasonable in the light of anticipated loss but reasonable in the light of actual loss? Or what if it is reasonable in the light of anticipated harm, but not reasonable in terms of actual harm caused by the breach?

(2) *"Time of Contracting" Test.* Most jurisdictions follow the "time of contracting" test. See Watson v. Ingram, 124 Wash.2d 845 (1994). This approach makes the most sense when both parties, in negotiations, have addressed themselves to the inability of standard damages to provide adequate compensation under the peculiar facts of their case. On the other hand, liquidated damage clauses often serve the interest of one party more than the other and can be the product of superior bargaining power. Put another way, the ability of one party—the plaintiff—to overstate remedies may raise the same problems posed when a defendant has attempted to limit liability through disclaimer clauses or other "agreed" remedies. See Melodee Lane Lingerie Co. v. American District Telephone Co., 18 N.Y.2d 57 (1966); Fritz, *"Underliquidated" Damages as a Limitation of Liability,* 33 Tex. L. Rev. 196 (1954).

But not all jurisdictions follow this approach. In *Irving Tire Co., Inc. v. Stage II Apparel Corp.,* 646 N.Y.S.2d 528, 530 (N.Y.A.D. 1996), for example, the court refused to enforce a purported liquidated damage clause where the damages actually arising from the breach were readily ascertainable and the "sum fixed is disproportionate to the landlord's loss." Arguably, the hindsight rule, i.e., the power of a court to assess the liquidation in light of actual damage caused by the breach, becomes more appealing when the plaintiff has been able to impose the clause on the defendant with little or no actual bargaining. In view of this, how well does *Southwest Engineering* fit the realities of most government contracting? Do you suppose the contractor had any say about inclusion of the liquidated damage clause or its amount? Did the contractor fail to satisfy its burden of proof in attacking the clause? See, generally, Gantt & Breslauer, *Liquidated Damages in Federal Government Contracts*, 47 B.U. L. Rev. 71 (1967).

(3) Might one be able to disguise an impermissible penalty by phrasing it in terms of an "alternative performance" or as a "premium" for timely performance? See Blank v. Borden, 11 Cal.3d 963 (1974). For example, how would you classify a "take-or-pay" commitment, as an alternative performance or a liquidated damage clause? See Universal Resources Corp. v. Panhandle Eastern Pipe Line Co., 813 F.2d 77 (5th Cir. 1987) (alternative performance). Comment c to Restatement (Second) § 356 provides:

> Sometimes parties attempt to disguise a provision for a penalty by using language that purports to make payment of the amount an alternative performance under the contract, that purports to offer a discount for prompt performance, or that purports to place a valuation on property to be delivered. Although the parties may in good faith contract for alternative performances and fix discounts or valuations, a court will look to the substance of the agreement to determine whether this is the case or whether the parties have attempted to disguise a provision for a penalty that is unenforceable under this Section. In determining whether a contract is one for alternative performances, the relative value of the alternatives may be decisive.

(4) Eric Talley has suggested that the limitation on liquidated damages may reduce "both parties' incentives and abilities to engage in deceptive behavior during renegotiation, and it thereby mitigates the inefficiencies that usually accompany bilateral monopoly." Eric L. Talley, Note, *Contract Renegotiation, Mechanism Design, and the Liquidated Damages Rule*, 46 Stan. L. Rev. 1195, 1218–42 (1994); but see Lars A. Stole, *The Economics of Liquidated Damage Clauses in Contractual Environments with Private Information*, 8 J. L. Econ. & Org. 582 (1992).

(5) Where, at the time of the breach, the plaintiff has fully performed and the defendant has failed to pay money due, efforts to liquidate damages are more difficult to sustain. As one court put it: "In this context [breach by lessee of a covenant to pay rent] it is a relevant general rule that a failure to pay a sum of money due will rarely, if ever, justify a further sum, in excess of interest, to be paid by way of liquidated damages. On the contrary, such a requirement is likely to be condemned as a penal forfeiture which the law will not recognize." Breitel, J. in Manhattan Syndicate, Inc. v. Ryan, 220 N.Y.S.2d 337, 340–41 (1961). But see United Merchants and Manufacturers,

Inc. v. Equitable Life Assurance Society, 674 F.2d 134 (2d Cir. 1982) (applying New York law, court upheld provision in loan agreement that upon default the principal of the note plus interest would be due, together with an amount equal to the pre-payment charges that would be payable if the borrower were pre-paying the note). See also Garrett v. Coast & Southern Federal Savings & Loan Association, 9 Cal.3d 731 (1973) (holding late charge assessed at 2% of unpaid balance of due notes is void because parties "failed to make a reasonable endeavor to estimate a fair compensation which would be sustained on the default").

PROBLEM: THE CASE OF THE DISAPPOINTED FANS

A fervent group of Chicago Bears football fans, living in Chicago, decided to charter a bus to an NFL game between the Bears and the Packers, played that year at Champaign–Urbana, Illinois while Soldier Field was under renovation. "Rabid" Ron was authorized by the group to negotiate the charter. In negotiating the matter with Mr. Smith, president of the Reliable Transit Co. (and a "Cheese Head"), Ron stressed how important it was to his group that they arrive in plenty of time for the game, that it would not be televised this year, this group was exceptionally interested in the rivalry and would be terribly disappointed if anything went wrong. In short, Ron stated that his group would want damages if a charter were arranged and the bus did not go. Mr. Smith stated that he would be glad to arrange the charter (there were six weeks to go) for a flat fee of $750, round trip, but that the usual practice was to expressly limit liability of the Company for failure "to go" to a return of any amount paid on the charter. This was unsatisfactory to Ron. After more negotiations and consultation with the other "fans," Ron made the following proposition to Smith: "Look, I've talked with my group and here's the way it is. We will pay you $1,500 for the charter if you will agree to pay us $15,000 as liquidated damages if, for any reason, the bus fails to go and we miss the game. We are willing to pay $750 extra to know that our disappointment will be well compensated if we don't go. Take it or leave it." Smith agreed and an appropriate written contract was prepared which included the "liquidated damage" clause. The "group" paid $750 on the charter and were told to assemble at a specified point in Davis no later than 7:30 AM on game day. As by now you have suspected, the bus did not show at 7:30 AM or at anytime on game day. In fact, Smith chartered the bus to a group of Packers fans in the Chicago suburbs who paid $3,000 for the charter. By the time it was clear what had happened, it was not possible for Ron to arrange another method of transportation and none of the Bears fans saw the game (which turned out to be a blessing in disguise).

Ron has demanded $15,000 from Smith and been politely refused. Smith, however, did tender back to Ron the $750, which Ron, so far, has refused. Ron and a few of his fans are in your law office and have asked your assessment of their chances. What would you advise? See Charles Goetz and Robert Scott, *Liquidated Damages: Penalties and the Just Compensation Principle: Some Notes on an Enforcement Model and a Theory of Efficient Breach*, 77 Colum. L. Rev. 554 (1977).

PROBLEM: THE CASE OF THE "BIG SHIP" DEAL

Big Sugar Company, owner of a sugar plantation in Hawaii, was in need of a ship to transport raw sugar—the crushed cane in the form of coarse brown crystal—from the islands to the mainland. Sugar is a seasonal crop, and Big Sugar had storage capacity in Hawaii for no more than a quarter of the crop. It was, therefore, imperative to have assured transportation. To this end, Big Sugar entered into extensive negotiations with Tall Ships, Inc. for the construction and sale of a ship specially designed for this purpose. Eventually, the parties executed a written contract for a sale of such a ship for $24,000,000. The agreed delivery date was April 30, with a provision for payment by Tall Ships of $17,000 for each day's unexcused delay in delivery.

The ship was not delivered until October 30, some 150 days late. Fortunately for Big Sugar, it was able to avoid catastrophic losses by utilizing older equipment and renting from others. A fair estimate of the loss actually caused by Tall Ship's breach is $250,000.

(1)   What, if anything, should Big Sugar recover from Tall Ships? Cf. California and Hawaiian Sugar Co. v. Sun Ship, Inc., 794 F.2d 1433 (9th Cir. 1986).

(2)   Suppose that Big Sugar's actual losses, after reasonable efforts to mitigate damages, were $7,500,000. What, if anything, should Big Sugar recover from Tall Ships?

(3)   Suppose that at the time of contracting, Tall Ships had stated, "We don't care about estimating actual damages if we breach. We won't pay more than $5,000 per day under any circumstances." Big Sugar agreed to a clause limiting the per diem liability to $5,000. If Big Sugar's actual loss was $17,000, what if anything can be recovered?

Cellphone Termination Fee Cases

California Court of Appeal, First District, 2011.
193 Cal.App.4th 298.

■ BRUINIERS, JUDGE. These consolidated appeals are from a judgment after trial in a consumer class action against wireless telephone carrier Sprint Spectrum, L.P. (Sprint), challenging its policy of charging early termination fees (ETF's) to customers terminating service prior to expiration of defined contract periods. The trial court found the ETF's to be unlawful penalties under Civil Code section 1671, subdivision (d), enjoined enforcement, and granted restitution/damages to the plaintiff class in the amount of ETF's collected by Sprint during the class period, $73,775,975. A jury found that class members who had been charged ETF's had violated the terms of their contracts with Sprint, and that Sprint's actual damages exceeded the ETF charges Sprint had collected. The resulting setoff negated any monetary recovery to the class. The trial court, reasoning that the jury had failed to follow its instructions on Sprint's actual damages, granted the plaintiffs' motion for a partial new trial . . . on that issue.

Sprint appeals the decision invalidating the ETF's and enjoining their enforcement, and the court's grant of the motion for partial new trial on damages. Plaintiffs cross-appeal, alleging that the trial court erred in permitting Sprint to assert damage claims as setoffs to class claims for recovery of ETF's paid. In the published portions of this opinion we address the issues of federal preemption and the application of section 1671, subdivision (d). We affirm in all respects.

I.   BACKGROUND

Sprint is a national cellular service carrier, providing cellular telephone service in California. In 2003, lawsuits were filed in Alameda County and in Orange County against Sprint and other cellular service providers alleging that the ETF's violated California consumer protection laws and constituted unauthorized penalties under section 1671. This action and others were coordinated under Judicial Council order before Judge Ronald Sabraw in the Alameda County Superior Court. . . .

Plaintiffs contended that the ETF's were adopted and utilized by Sprint to stop erosion of its customer base by penalizing early termination of customer contracts, and as a revenue opportunity. . . . In 1999, Sprint began to study the concept of term contracts with ETF's as a means to reduce its "churn" rates, and tested use of ETF's in selected markets. Sprint reported monthly wireless churn rates in 1998 of 3.3 percent, and in 1999 of 3.4 percent. Sprint adopted term contracts incorporating the $150 ETF nationwide in May 2000. Sprint reduced its churn rate to 2.8 percent in 2000. * * *

After Sprint's August 2005 merger with Nextel, Sprint increased the amount of the early termination fee to $200. Sprint's postmerger $200 ETF was based on Nextel's premerger ETF. There was no evidence of any cost study made in connection with Nextel's initial adoption of its $200 ETF (also in 2000), and Nextel did not prepare any written analysis of its decision to implement ETF's.

It was undisputed that Sprint assessed ETF's totaling $299,473,408 during the class period, and collected $73,775,975. Dr. Selwyn opined that, as a result of early contract terminations, Sprint avoided capital expenditures and variable costs which were equal to about 98.6 percent of its monthly recurring charges. He calculated Sprint's total lost profits from early terminations over the entire class period at $17,619,322.

* * * Sprint's experts contended that an ETF is a part of the price the consumer pays for the "bundle" of the handset and cellular service, and is part of the quid pro quo for the rate reductions included in long-term plans. * * *

To contest Plaintiffs' claims that the ETF's were unlawful liquidated damage provisions, and in support of its cross-complaint, Sprint sought to prove that its actual damages were substantially greater than the fees charged. * * * Sprint calculated that: the Payer Class had 1,986,537 members; early terminations, on average, occurred with 13.25 months left on the term of the contract; and early terminations caused Sprint to lose $49.16 per month in monthly recurring charges. Baliban testified that costs avoided when a class member terminated early equaled about 18 percent of Sprint's monthly recurring charges. Dr. Taylor opined that Sprint suffered damages of $987 million from early terminations, consisting of Sprint's net revenue loss (monthly recurring charges lost minus costs avoided), less the amount of ETF's actually collected.

On June 12, 2008, the jury returned a verdict with special findings as follows: "1. What is the total dollar amount of early termination fees that plaintiffs and the class members paid to Sprint? $73,775,975. [¶] 2. Did plaintiffs and the class members breach their contracts with Sprint? Yes. [¶] 3. State the total dollar amount of Sprint's actual damages, if any, caused by early terminations of plaintiffs' and class members' contracts: $225,697,433." The damages found by the jury were the exact amount of ETF's charged to class members, but which were unpaid.

The Trial Court's Statement of Decision

On December 4, 2008, after considering objections to its proposed statement of decision, the trial court issued its statement of decision. The court first reviewed the trial evidence presented and made its findings of fact. It initially accepted the jury's determination of Sprint's damages from early termination of consumer contracts in the amount of $225,697,433.

* * * The court determined that Sprint could not justify the ETF's as a negotiated "alternative means of performance" under the contract, since they were invoked as liquidated damages upon a breach of the contract.

As a consequence of its determination that the ETF's were unlawful under section 1671, subdivision (d), the court found that Plaintiffs had prevailed on their claims for violations of the [Consumer Legal Remedies Act] CLRA (§ 1770, subds. (a)(14), (19)), UCL (§ 17200, et seq.), unjust enrichment, and for money had and received. The court ordered restitution to the class in the amount of collected ETF's ($73,775,975); enjoined Sprint from further efforts to collect ETF's assessed during the class period; and ordered Sprint to advise third party assignees of uncollected claims of the court's order. The court then, while questioning the validity of the jury's verdict on damages, applied the setoff in favor of Sprint resulting from the jury's verdict and determined that neither the class nor Sprint would be entitled to any monetary recovery. The setoff did not affect the injunctive relief granted.

* * * On January 27, 2009, the trial court granted plaintiffs' motion for new trial on the issue of actual damages (Question 3) and on the setoff calculation. In granting the motion for new trial on the issue of Sprint's actual damages (Question 3), the court observed that it was "inconceivable that the jury considered the days of comprehensive and complex testimony . . . regarding Sprint's lost revenue and avoidable

costs and determined that Sprint's actual total economic damages from all class members were exactly equal to the amount of unpaid ETF's due from those class members who had not paid the ETF" and that the "finding that Sprint's actual damages were $225,697,433 compels the conclusion that the jury did not follow the instructions to determine Sprint's actual total economic damages." * * *

II. DISCUSSION

* * *

B.   Section 1671

The trial court found that an ETF operated primarily as a liquidated damage clause. Because Sprint failed to prove that, in adopting ETF's, it made any effort "to determine what losses it would sustain from breach by the early termination of its contracts" or "to estimate a fair average compensation for such losses," it failed to satisfy the reasonable endeavor test and the ETF's were consequently unlawful penalties under section 1671, subdivision (d).

A provision in a consumer contract "liquidating damages for the breach of the contract is void except that the parties to such a contract may agree therein upon an amount which shall be presumed to be the amount of damage sustained by a breach thereof, when, from the nature of the case, it would be impracticable or extremely difficult to fix the actual damage." (§ 1671, subds. (c)(1), (d).) Because liquidated damage clauses in consumer contracts are presumed void, the burden is on the proponent of the clause to rebut that presumption.

Decisions interpreting this statute have created a two-part test for determining whether a liquidated damages provision is valid: (1) fixing the amount of actual damages must be impracticable or extremely difficult, and (2) the amount selected must represent a reasonable endeavor to estimate fair compensation for the loss sustained. "Absent either of these elements, a liquidated damages provision is void. . . ." (Hitz, 38 Cal.App.4th at 288, italics added.) A liquidated damages provision need not, however, be expressly negotiated by both parties to a form contract in order to be valid.

Impracticability may be established by showing "that the measure of actual damages would be a comparatively small amount and that it would be economically impracticable in each instance of a default to require a [seller] to prove to the satisfaction of the [consumer] the actual damages by accounting procedures." (Garrett, 9 Cal.3d at 742.) The trial court found that, although Sprint could readily calculate its lost monthly revenue per customer in the event of a default, it would have been impracticable to determine Sprint's avoidable costs, and therefore impracticable to determine actual damages at the inception of the contracts. Plaintiffs do not challenge this finding.

"Determining whether a reasonable endeavor was made depends upon both (1) the motivation and purpose in imposing the charges, and

(2) their effect." (Utility Consumers, 135 Cal.App.4th at 1029.) "[T]he focus is not . . . on whether liquidated damages are disproportionate to the loss from breach, but on whether they were intended to exceed loss substantially—a result of which is to generate a profit." (Hitz, 38 Cal.App.4th at 289.) A liquidated damages provision that "bears no reasonable relationship to the range of actual damages that the parties could have anticipated would flow from a breach" is an unlawful penalty that compels a forfeiture upon a breach of contract. Such penalties are " 'ineffective, and the wronged party can collect only the actual damages sustained.' "

In order to establish the reasonable endeavor required, evidence must exist that the party seeking to impose liquidated damages " 'actually engaged in some form of analysis to determine what losses it would sustain from [a] breach, and that it made a genuine and non-pretextual effort to estimate a fair average compensation for the losses to be sustained.' " (Hitz, 38 Cal.App.4th at 291.) The trial court made a finding that "when Sprint implemented the ETF in 2000, and increased it in 2005, it made no endeavor—reasonable or otherwise—to determine what losses it would sustain from breach or to estimate a fair average compensation for such losses." Sprint "did no analysis that considered the lost revenue from contracts, the avoidable costs, and Sprint's expected lost profits from contract terminations." The ETF amounts were set not based on the basis of any actual or estimated loss, but "from a competitive standpoint." Sprint's purpose in adopting the ETF was to control churn and was implemented, "primarily as a means to prevent customers from leaving." After adoption of ETF's, Sprint succeeded in reducing its churn rate to 2.8 percent in 2000. * * *

Sprint counters that "undisputed evidence" at trial showed that the ETF's were not intended to exceed losses, and that Sprint officials were "aware that their ETFs would recover only a fraction of the revenue lost as a result of early terminations." Sprint asserts that any charge that "does not overstate actual damages cannot be a penalty." Sprint cites testimony that early terminations occurred on average with 13.25 months left on a contract, depriving Sprint of average revenues of $49.16 per month in monthly recurring charges per customer and that it lost over $650 in revenue for each early termination. Sprint points out that the ETF's do not even cover their costs of adding new customers, which averaged $388 dollars during the class period. It contends that the evidence showed that it "well understood that due to competitive forces, the ETF could not be set anywhere near a level that would compensate it for a customer's breach through early termination." * * *

We note first that, as to Sprint's motive and purpose, whatever information as to costs and revenues Sprint may have been "aware" of, it cites to no evidence in the trial record that any of this information was part of the calculus in deciding to impose ETF's, or in determining the amount of an ETF. Further, we do not second-guess the trial court's factual determinations as to Sprint's motivation and purpose. While Sprint contends that it satisfied both prongs of the reasonable endeavor test in adopting ETF's, the real focus of its argument is on the effect of the ETF's. The thrust of that argument is that so long as the ETF amount is shown in practice to be less than Sprint's actual damages, the effect is not to generate a profit, whatever Sprint's motive and purpose, and nothing more is required to meet the test. * * *

Sprint was required to show that it actually engaged in some form of analysis to determine what losses it would sustain from breach,[25] and that it made a genuine effort to estimate a fair average compensation for the losses to be sustained. Sprint may be correct that in retrospect its ETF's were reasonable in amount in light of its actual loss, and that they may have actually have been beneficial in practice to at least some of its customers. However, institutional intuition is not a substitute for analytical evaluation and retrospective rationalization does not excuse the objective assessment required at the inception of the contract.

C.   Alternative Performance

Sprint also sought to defend use of ETF's as "alternative performance," permitting subscribers to terminate contracts before the end of the agreement by paying a fee. "[T]o constitute a liquidated damage clause the conduct triggering the payment must in some manner breach the contract." (Morris v. Redwood Empire Bancorp 128 Cal.App.4th 1305, 1315 (2005)) A contractual provision that merely provides an option of alternative performance of an obligation does not impose damages and is not subject to section 1671 limitations.

In evaluating the legality of a provision, a court must first determine its true function and operation. "[W]hen it is manifest that a contract expressed to be performed in the alternative is in fact a contract contemplating but a single, definite performance with an additional charge contingent on the breach of that performance, the provision cannot escape examination in light of pertinent rules relative to the liquidation of damages." To hold otherwise "would be to condone a result which, although directly prohibited by the Legislature, may nevertheless be indirectly accomplished through the imagination of inventive minds." (108 Cal.Rptr. 845.) * * *

The court found that the ETF provisions "did not give customers a rational choice of paying the ETF or completing the contract," because the language of the ETF provision permitted Sprint to impose the fee on customers involuntarily. The court noted that "[o]f those customers who were charged an ETF, 80% were terminated by Sprint and experienced

---

[25] Sprint complains that the trial court improperly required that it engage in a "formal study" in order to justify imposition of an ETF. It did not, and we also decline to specify as a matter of law what particular type of analysis is required to establish reasonable endeavor. We observe that Sprint was readily able to calculate its monthly recurring charges and lost revenues at the time of trial. Here, at least as is reflected in the trial record, there was an absence of any analysis at the time the decisions to impose ETF's were made.

the ETF as the imposition of liquidated damages. . . ." As the trial court stated, "If this case concerned a Sprint clause that stated customers could terminate term contracts early by paying a fee, then that fee might well be an alternative means of performance." Instead, "Sprint declared contracts breached, terminated service, and imposed ETFs as liquidated damages resulting from the asserted breaches." * * *

The court found that "Sprint has not met its burden of establishing that the predominant effect of the ETF provisions was to provide consumers with an alternate means of performing their contracts." Substantial evidence supports the findings.

III. DISPOSITION

The judgment of the trial court is affirmed. The matter is remanded for retrial on the issue Sprint's damages, and the calculation of any offset to which Sprint may be entitled. Neither party shall recover costs on this appeal.

NOTES

(1) *One Size Fits All.* The ETFs in *Sprint* were not pro-rated. But today, partly in response to liability concerns most cellphone contracts have pro-rated liquidated damages. For example, Sprint currently subtracts $10 from $200 for every month before breach but with a $50 minimum. See Chang, Analysis of Various Provisions in Cell-Phone Contracts (2011) available at www.faircontracts.org. In *United Air Lines, Inc. v. Austin Travel Corp.*, 867 F.2d 737 (2d Cir. 1989), the court upheld enforcement of a relatively untailored liquidated damages provision finding that the liquidated amounts "were at the time of execution a reasonable forecast of damages in case of breach." The court responded to the lack of tailoring concern by emphasizing that "liquidated damages can only be owed to United in the event of a material breach by Austin."

(2) *Profiting from a Penalty.* In 2001, Acme Rental Car started charging a $150 penalty for driving more than 80 miles per hour (in their GPS equipped cars). The state of Connecticut challenged the policy on consumer protection grounds—arguing that it was an unfair and deceptive practice to profit from a liquidated damages provision. American Car Rental, Inc. v. Commissioner of Consumer Prot., 273 Conn. 296 (2005). The opinion suggests that the penalty would be unenforceable regardless of how well it was disclosed to consumers. Is it ever reasonable to profit from a liquidated damage provision? The same contracts also charged renters $5/gallon (when the market price for gas was less than $2.40) if the car was returned without a full tank of gas. Would a contingent speeding fee have been legit? Could Acme have succeeded if they had characterized the provision as "alternative performance" as was tried in the *Sprint* decision? Would Connecticut attack a provision that was reframed as discount—$200 to rent the car; $150 cash back if you don't speed. See Ian Ayres and Barry Nalebuff, Connecticut's Speeder-Friendly Crackdown, N.Y. Times, Aug. 31, 2001, at A19.

(3) *A Rationale for Treating Seemingly Equivalent Frames Differently.* The *Sprint* decision suggests at least a partially substantive test for deciding whether a provision constitutes alternative performance or a penalty. But a purely formal test—turning merely on whether the early termination fee is framed as back-end damages or front-end prices might have some cognitive justification. It might be argued that prices are highly salient, and consumers know that they have to be on guard to try to get a good deal. The law, by prohibiting profits on anything characterized as "liquidated damages," might help economize on consumers' limited attention. Under such a rule, consumers would need not focus as much on liquidated damage provisions, which must be provided at cost, and instead could concentrate on the prices which sellers are free to mark up.

(4) In *Lake Ridge Academy v. Carney*, 66 Ohio St.3d 376 (1993), the court, in upholding a clause in a school "reservation agreement" that imposed liability for full tuition if the reservation were not canceled before a stated date, used a three step test to determine whether the parties had agreed upon liquidated damages or a penalty: "Where the parties have agreed on the amount of damages, ascertained by estimation and adjustment, and have expressed this agreement in clear and unambiguous terms, the amount so fixed should be treated as liquidated damages and not as a penalty, if the damages would be (1) uncertain as to amount and difficult of proof, and if (2) the contract as a whole is not so manifestly unconscionable, unreasonable, and disproportionate in amount as to justify the conclusion that it does not express the true intention of the parties, and if (3) the contract is consistent with the conclusion that it was the intention of the parties that damages in the amount stated should follow the breach thereof." 613 N.E.2d at 188. Is this helpful?

Comment: Disclaimer, Exculpation and Under-Liquidated Damage Clauses

A careful distinction must be drawn between clauses that disclaim or exculpate liability from specified conduct, such as an alleged breach of warranty or negligence, and clauses that vary or limit remedies for that conduct.

A good example of the former are clauses in contracts for the sale of goods where the seller attempts to disclaim liability if the goods are not merchantable, see UCC § 2–314, or are unfit for the buyer's particular purposes, see UCC § 2–315. These implied warranty disclaimers are enforceable if one of the altering rules found in UCC § 2–316 (e.g., conspicuous language) is satisfied and, in effect, put the risk of product quality on the buyer. Another example is contract clauses purporting to exculpate one party from the consequences of negligence.

An example of the latter are clauses that provide an exclusive, limited remedy upon breach or attempt to exclude or limit liability for consequential damages resulting from a breach. See UCC § 2–719. A subtle form of exculpation or exclusion takes the form of a liquidated damage clause which, in effect, sets a limit almost always under the amount of actual damage caused by negligence or breach of contract. A classic example is the case where one party agrees to install and maintain a telephone system designed promptly to detect and report fires or burglary. These contracts invariably contain a clause providing some limitation, such as if the contractor "should be found liable for loss or damage due to a failure of service in any respect, its liability shall be limited to a sum equal to ten percent of the annual service charge or $250, whichever is the greater." If the contractor is negligent and this negligence causes losses of, say, $50,000, will the limitation clause be enforced?

The answer appears to be "yes." In California, the issue has been treated as involving liquidated damages and the limitation has been enforced under Cal. Civ. Code §§ 1670 & 1671. In New York, the clause is treated as an effort to limit liability rather than to liquidate damages and is enforced where the limitation is conspicuous and the other party could have obtained "more coverage . . . for a negotiable fee." See Melodee Lane Lingerie Co. v. American District Telephone Co., 18 N.Y.2d 57 (1966). If the other party has a choice to pay more for greater protection and selects less, it would be "unfair to hold the defendant liable for the grossly disproportionate losses sustained by the plaintiff." Rinaldi & Sons v. Wells Fargo Alarm Service, 367 N.Y.S.2d 518, 522 (1975). Does it matter whether insurance against the risk is available at a reasonable cost?

(B) DAMAGES LIMITATIONS

FIxing a sum certain in a liquidated damages clause is not the only way parties might attempt to settle in advance the remedy for breach. They might, for example, provide that in the event of breach the seller's obligation is only to repair or replace the goods. The applicable Code provision is Section 2–719, which provides as follows:

(1)   Subject to the provisions of subsection (2) and (3) of this section and of the preceding section on liquidation and limitation of damages,

(a)   the agreement may provide for remedies in addition to or in substitution for those provided in this Article and may limit or alter the measure of damages recoverable under this Article, as by limiting the buyer's remedies to return of the goods and repayment of the price or to repair and replacement of non-conforming goods or parts; and

(b)   resort to a remedy as provided is optional unless the remedy is expressly agreed to be exclusive, in which case it is the sole remedy.

(2)   Where circumstances cause an exclusive or limited remedy to fail of its essential purpose, remedy may be had as provided in this Act.

(3) Consequential damages may be limited or excluded unless the limitation or exclusion is unconscionable. Limitation of consequential damages for injury to the person in the case of consumer goods is prima facie unconscionable but limitation of damages where the loss is commercial is not.

The materials which follow deal with aspects of this "agreed remedy" problem. See also Chapter Five, Section 3(A)(3). As we'll see in the next case, § 2–719(2) limits a seller's attempts to substitute monetary damages with "repair and replace" provisions.

Lewis Refrigeration Co. v. Sawyer Fruit, Vegetable and Cold Storage Co.

United States Court of Appeals, Sixth Circuit, 1983.
709 F.2d 427.

■ NEWBLATT, DISTRICT JUDGE.

I.   FACTS

This is an appeal in a diversity action originally brought on March 18, 1974 by Lewis Refrigeration Co. (hereinafter Lewis) against Sawyer Fruit, Vegetable and Cold Storage Cooperative Co. (hereinafter Sawyer). Lewis sued Sawyer to collect a balance allegedly due under an agreement in which Lewis sold Sawyer a freezer. Sawyer counterclaimed against Lewis asserting counts of breach of contract, breach of warranty and misrepresentation.

The case arose out of a 1970 contract between Sawyer and Lewis. The contract provided for Lewis to sell Sawyer an individually quick-frozen freezer. The typed portion of the contract covered contract pages 2–7; the printed portion covered contract pages 7–12.

The typed portion of the contract contained warranties that the freezer was capable of processing six thousand pounds of various fruits per hour and that the freezer would use no more than 1.8 liquid pounds of Freon per one hundred pounds of frozen products. Paragraph 6A of the typewritten portion of the contract contained a clause setting out a guarantee obligating Lewis to supply, for a given period of time, the Freon that the freezer consumed over the warranted rate. Paragraph B3 of the printed portion of the agreement provided that, in the event the machine failed to perform at the warranted rates, Lewis would have the right to repair or replace promptly the malfunctioning part of the machine. Paragraph B3 provided that rescission was the only other available remedy.

In addition to paragraph B3, the contract contained another remedy limitation. This limitation, found at paragraph B4 of the handwritten portion of the contract, excluded consequential damages.

A consent judgment eventually was entered in favor of Lewis for the claim for the balance due on the contract. Trial on Sawyer's counterclaim began on April 4, 1978. After denying Lewis's motions for a directed verdict and for judgment notwithstanding the verdict, the district court instructed and then sent the case to the jury. A verdict was returned for Sawyer in the amount of $25,823 in lost profits and $27,080 in excess Freon costs.

In this appeal, Lewis advances four arguments: (1) the district court erroneously allowed the jury to consider whether, under the state of Washington version of UCC § 2–719(2), the paragraph B3 repair and rescission limitation failed its essential purpose; (2) the district court erred by not generally disallowing consequential damages in favor of benefit of the bargain damages under Washington's version of UCC § 2–714(2); (3) the district court should have granted a new trial on the ground that Sawyer failed to amend and supplement discovery responses as required by Rule 26(e)(2) of the Federal Rules of Civil Procedure; (4) the district court erroneously omitted making a judicial determination of whether the B3 consequential damages exclusion was unconscionable— in the absence of such a determination the consequential damages exclusion should have blocked the jury from awarding consequential damages.

We shall now consider each of the four arguments advanced by Lewis. For the reasons to follow, we affirm the district court as to the first three arguments and vacate and remand as to the fourth argument.

II.   LEGAL ANALYSIS

A.   Failure of Repair and Rescission Remedy to Achieve its Essential Purpose.

The first argument raised by Lewis involves the district court's treatment of RCW § 62A.2–719(2), the state of Washington's statutory version of UCC § 2–719(2). The statute provides:

> "Where circumstances cause an exclusive or limited remedy to fail of its essential purpose, remedy may be had as provided in this Title."

Lewis argues that the district court erroneously allowed the jury to reach the issue of whether the paragraph B3 repair and rescission exclusive remedy failed its essential purpose as described in Section 2–719(2). Lewis contends that its motions for directed verdict and judgment notwithstanding the verdict should have been granted as to the issue of the repair and rescission remedy barring the award of any other damages. Lewis thus urges us to vacate the jury's verdict to the extent that it includes $25,823 in lost profit consequential damages.

In opposing this argument, Sawyer contends that it presented enough evidence to permit a reasonable fact finder to determine that the exclusive remedy contractual provision failed its essential purpose. In deciding this issue, we shall separately consider the repair and rescission portions of the exclusive remedy.

Lewis appears to concede that the repair remedy failed its essential purpose. . . . We agree. In any event, there can be no doubt but that the record contains trial evidence adequate to support the conclusion that Lewis was unable to repair promptly the freezer to meet performance warranties. . . .

Furthermore, we note that Washington appellate decisions clearly hold that a seller's inability to repair fully a product causes the repair and rescission remedy to fail of its essential purpose under RCW 62A.2–719(2). . . . We thus conclude that a jury could reasonably have determined that the repair remedy failed its essential purpose under Section 2–719(2).

A much closer question obtains with respect to the rescission remedy. Sawyer contends that the jury could reasonably have determined that the rescission remedy failed its essential purpose because of either of the following two reasons: (1) Lewis would have been extremely reluctant to rescind the transaction or (2) Sawyer would have experienced severe financial loss in the event the contract was rescinded.

Sawyer's first contention must be rejected outright. The Section 2–719(2) "essential purpose" language refers to circumstances that make it exceedingly impractical to carry out the essence of an agreed-upon remedy. Given that Lewis had categorically refused to rescind the transaction, the rescission provision could have been enforced in a court action, and thus the essence of the remedy could have been carried out.

As to the rescission remedy, Sawyer contends that there was enough evidence in the record to permit a reasonable jury to conclude that Lewis deliberately concealed the machine's inability to meet cherry processing warranties until sometime in 1972. By this time, Sawyer contends, it had made significant commitments with respect to frozen products. Sawyer further asserts that rescission and the concomitant removal of the freezer in 1972 would have been financially destructive in that it would have caused Sawyer to lose revenues and breach important commitments.

Having studied the record below, we believe that there was adequate evidence to support Sawyer's version as set out above. Letters and trial testimony indicate that Lewis was either unable or reluctant to promptly and effectively administer performance tests on the cherries. This well could have prevented Sawyer from making an intelligent decision on rescission until 1972, by which time Sawyer had made numerous frozen product commitments. . . .

We believe it was appropriate for the jury to consider these circumstances in connection with the issue of whether the rescission remedy failed of its essential purpose. Washington cases hold that an exclusive remedy fails its essential purpose where a conceded defect is not detectable until it is impractical to effectuate the exclusive remedy. While the latent defect theory is most often applied in cases involving the repair remedy, and while the facts of this case are not nearly as strong as Sawyer seems to believe, we find that it was not erroneous for the district court to allow the jury to consider whether Lewis concealed the facts until such time as a rescission would have caused severe financial damages to Sawyer. And given that this factual version was true, it was within the ambit of Section 2–719(2) for the jury to find that the rescission remedy failed of its essential purpose. Thus, we reject appellant's contention that the district court erred by allowing the jury to consider the evidence in this case as applied to the issue of whether the repair and rescission remedy failed its essential purpose under RCW 62A.2–719(2).

B.   Lewis's General Argument Against Consequential Damages.

Lewis next contends that, assuming arguendo that the repair and rescission remedy failed of its essential purpose, the district court should generally have prohibited the jury from awarding consequential damages. This argument is bottomed on Lewis's apparent belief that damages in breach of warranty actions are confined to the benefit of the bargain measure of damages set out in RCW 62A.2–714(2).

This contention is patently incorrect. RCW 62A.2–714(3) authorizes consequential damages in appropriate cases. RCW 62A.2–715(2) then provides that consequential damages from a seller's breach include losses reasonably foreseeable that cannot be mitigated by cover.

Cover is not an issue in this appeal. And since there is a good deal of evidence in the record indicating that the freezer was to be an important part of Lewis's production, we conclude that a reasonable jury easily could have determined that Lewis should have foreseen that its breach of warranty would cause consequential damages. . . . Thus, it certainly was not erroneous for the district court to not generally preclude damages for lost profits.

C.   Sawyer's Failure to Supplement Discovery Responses.

[The Court rejected Lewis' argument for a new trial based on alleged discovery abuses of Sawyer.]

D.   District Court's Failure to Make a Separate Determination of Unconscionability Under RCW § 62A.2–719(3).

Lewis's final argument centers on the district court's treatment of the paragraph B4 exclusion of consequential damages. This paragraph excludes consequential damages apparently under the authority of RCW 62A.2–719(3), the Washington version of UCC § 2–719(3). RCW 62A.2–719(3) provides in pertinent part:

> Limitation of consequential damages for injury to the person in the case of goods purchased primarily for personal, family or household use or of any services related thereto is invalid unless it is proved that the limitation is not unconscionable . . . Limitation of other consequential damages is valid unless it is established that the limitation is unconscionable.

The district court did not give a separate instruction on the paragraph B4 consequential damages exclusion. Instead, the district court merely instructed that lost profits could be awarded:

> "if you find that circumstances not caused by Sawyer Fruit . . . caused the exclusion of lost profits to deprive Sawyer Fruit of the substantial value of its bargain under the Agreement." . . .

Apparently, the district court believed that if the jury determined that the exclusive repair and rescission remedy failed of its essential purpose, the exclusion of consequential damages provision automatically became unconscionable under Section 2–719(3). Alternatively, the district court may have believed that the "remedy may be had as provided in the act" phrase of RCW 62A.2–719(2) authorizes all UCC damages—including consequential damages—upon a finding of unconscionability.

While a number of courts have taken the general approach of the district court, a larger number of courts—including the Courts of Appeals of the Third and Ninth Circuits—have construed subsection (3) of UCC § 2–719 as the governing provision on the issue of consequential damages. We believe that this is the correct approach.

In arriving at this conclusion, we are mindful that Washington law governs this case. And while the Washington appellate courts have not squarely decided this issue, it is notable that in 1955 the Washington Supreme Court indicated that analogous provisions in the Uniform Sales Act should be dealt with separately and distinctly. See Ketel v. Hovick, 47 Wash.2d 368 (1955). Furthermore, for several reasons, we believe that sound statutory construction leads to the conclusion that subsection (3) of RCW 62A.2–719 must be viewed as the governing provision on the issue of consequential damages exclusion.

In this respect it should first be noted that, absent the specific language of subsection (3), the general language of subsection (2) would seem to cover the issue of consequential damages. Since it is a basic principle of statutory construction that the particular governs over the general, we believe that the Section 2–719 drafters intended subsection (3) to deal with the issue of consequential damages.

Second, the distinctly different substantive content of subsections (2) and (3) must be considered. Subsection (2) turns on the failure of essential purpose; subsection (3) turns on a judicial determination of unconscionability. Unconscionability deals with grossly unequal bargaining power at the time of the contracts formation. As numerous decisions have pointed out, unconscionability rarely exists unless the buyer is a consumer. Indeed, the consumer orientation of subsection (3) is reflected in the subsection's different allocations of proof. Where the transaction involves a consumer buyer, the limitation is prima facie unconscionable. Where the transaction does not involve a consumer, however, the exclusion of consequential damages is not prima facie unconscionable.

Thus, subsection (3) is a powerful provision designed to protect against abuse of consumers in contract formation. The Official UCC comment to UCC § 2–719(3) indicates, however, that another basic purpose of subsection (3) is to allow merchants to allocate business risks. This purpose is consonant with the general UCC philosophy of freedom in commercial transactions. Taking these two statutory policies together, we believe that Section 2–719(3) is meant to allow freedom in excluding consequential damages unless a consumer is involved in the contract. This freedom would be abridged by the sweeping interpretation of subsection (2) applied by the district court.

We thus hold that the district court had an obligation to take evidence and then determine whether the consequential damages exclusion clause was unconscionable. In the absence of an unconscionability determination, the district court should have allowed the paragraph B2 consequential damages exclusion to stand. Accordingly, we must vacate the portion of the judgment reflecting the jury's award of $25,283 in lost profits and remand this case to the district court for a judicial determination of whether the consequential damages exclusion clause was unconscionable. In the event the district court determines that the consequential damages clause was not unconscionable, the jury's award of $25,823 in lost profits must be voided.[19]

III. CONCLUSION AND ORDER

We hereby affirm the district court as to the issues discussed in Parts IIA–IIC of the foregoing Opinion. We hereby Vacate the jury's award of $25,823 in lost profits and Remand to the district court for the reasons stated in Part IID of this Opinion. On remand, the district court is to conduct the proceedings specified in part IID of this Opinion.

NOTES

(1) *Integral Part of Commercial Warranty Package.* A clause attempting to exclude liability for consequential damages is an common part of a commercial warranty package that (1) *gives* the buyer an express warranty that the goods are free from defects in material and workmanship, (2) *disclaims* all other warranties, express or implied, (3) *limits* the remedy for breach of the express warranty to repair or replacement of the defective part or workmanship, and (4) *excludes* consequential damages from the scope of liability. This "package" is supported by the UCC, see UCC §§ 2–313(1), 2–316, 2–719(1) & 2–719(3).

The recurring question (dozens of cases have tried to resolve it) is the fate of the excluder clause in the package when the limited remedy fails of its essential purpose. Unless the contract clearly states that the excluder

---

[19] The jury's award of $27,080 in Freon costs should not be disturbed even if the consequential damages limitation is upheld. This is because the Freon costs are incidental damages rather than consequential damages. See Lewis v. Mobil Oil Corp., 438 F.2d 500 (C.A.8, 1971). See generally White and Summers, *Uniform Commercial Code,* pp. 312–314.

depends upon the availability of the limited remedy (i.e., you don't get your excluder unless I get my limited remedy), most courts have interpreted UCC § 2–719 to separate the excluder from the package. Thus, the buyer might get damages from the seller under UCC § 2–714 but not consequential damages unless the excluder was unconscionable under UCC § 2–719(3). This is rare in commercial cases. See, e.g., Rheem Mfg. Co. v. Phelps Heating & Air Conditioning, Inc., 746 N.E.2d 941 (Ind. 2001).

(2) Here is an example of a carefully drafted limited remedy package with an exclusion of consequential damages:

WARRANTY/LIMITATION OF LIABILITY

1. WARRANTY—The Corporation warrants that the equipment to be delivered will be of the kind and quality described in the order or contract [and] will be free of defects in workmanship or material. Should any failure to conform to this warranty appear within one year after the initial date of synchronization, the Corporation shall, upon notification thereof and substantiation that the equipment has been stored, installed, maintained and operated in accordance with the Corporation's recommendations and standard industry practice, correct such nonconformities, including nonconformance with the specifications, at its option, by suitable repair or replacement at the Corporation's expense. This warranty is in lieu of all warranties of merchantability, fitness for purpose, or other warranties, express or implied, except of title and against patent infringement. Correction of nonconformities, in the manner and for the period of time provided above, shall constitute fulfillment of all liabilities of the Corporation to the Purchaser, whether based on contract, negligence or otherwise with respect to, or arising out of such equipment.

2. LIMITATION OF LIABILITY—The Corporation shall not be liable for special, or consequential damages, such as, but not limited to, damage or loss of other property or equipment, loss of profits or revenue, loss of use of power system, cost of capital, cost of purchased or replacement power, or claims of customers of Purchaser for service interruption. The remedies of the Purchaser set forth herein are exclusive, and the liability of the Corporation with respect to any contract, or anything done in connection therewith such as the performance or breach thereof, or from the manufacture, sale, delivery, resale, installation or use of any equipment covered by or furnished under this contract whether in contract, in tort, under any warranty, or otherwise, shall not, except as expressly provided herein, exceed the price of the equipment or part on which such liability is based.

Comment: Consumers, Article 2, The Magnuson-Moss Warranty Act and State Lemon Laws

Consumer buyers and lessees frequently encounter the so-called warranty package, which disclaims implied warranties of merchantability or fitness, excludes consequential damages, and establishes the seller's option to repair or replace defective products as the exclusive remedy. In 1975 Congress passed the Magnuson-Moss Warranty Act, 15 U.S.C. sec. 2301 et seq. to address the potential for abuse. Section (a) of the Act provides in part that "No supplier may disclaim . . . any implied warranty to a consumer . . . [if] such supplier makes any written warranty. . . ." 15 U.S.C. § 2308(a). Section (b), however, provides that "implied warranties may be limited in duration to the duration of a written [express] warranty of reasonable duration, if such limitation is conscionable and is set forth in clear and unmistakable language and prominently displayed on the face of the warranty." These limitations apply regardless of whether the written warranty is a full or limited warranty and preempt state law.

Magnusson-Moss also requires sellers to disclose whether their warranties are "full" or "limited." A *full* warranty does not limit the duration of implied warranties; requires the warrantor to remedy defects within a reasonable time at no extra charge to the consumer; permits consumers to rescind or obtain a new product if the item sold cannot be conveniently repaired; and requires any exclusion of consequential damages to be stated in conspicuous language. All other warranties are *limited*. 15 U.S.C. §§ 2303–2304. The legislative goals and effects have been summarized as follows:

> This disclosure requirement seeks to increase the warranty coverage available to consumers in two ways. First, Congress hoped that firms would be embarrassed to describe their warranties as "limited" and so would make "full" warranties. Almost all firms, however, offer only "limited" warranties, apparently interpreting "full" to mean "too much." Second, if the concise labels "full" and "limited" would succinctly communicate to consumers the scope of warranty coverage, consumers could compare the coverage of different firms at greatly reduced cost. . . . But because almost all firms use limited warranties, . . . no more information exists now than existed before passage of the Act.

Alan Schwartz and Robert E. Scott, Commercial Transactions: Principles and Policies 226 (2d ed. 1991). The result is that consumers get greater protection against disclaimers under limited warranties but, as a practical matter, do not get that new car or trailer or washing machine from the seller. Such a remedy might be available under state lemon laws, which typically require the dealer to supply a replacement new car if efforts to repair or replace defects are not accomplished within a reasonable time.

(C) SPECIFYING INJUNCTIVE RELIEF

Ed Bertholet & Associates, Inc. v. Ed Stefanko

Court of Appeals of Indiana, 1998.
690 N.E.2d 361.

■ GARRARD, JUDGE. Ed Bertholet & Associates, Inc. ("Bertholet") appeals the trial court's denial of its petition for a preliminary injunction, claiming that the trial court erred by not enforcing a contractually agreed upon injunction. . . .

On December 2, 1994, Ed Stefanko ("Stefanko") entered into an employment contract with Bertholet to work as a bail bondsman. This contract included a covenant not to compete that provided for an injunction in the event of a breach of the covenant. On April 17, 1997, Stefanko voluntarily quit working for Bertholet and soon began working as a bail bondsman for a local competitor. Bertholet filed suit to enforce the covenant not to compete and sought a restraining order and injunction. . . . After holding a hearing on the preliminary injunction, the trial court denied Bertholet's petition on July 2, 1997. The trial court based its denial on Bertholet's failure to demonstrate irreparable harm. Bertholet appeals this decision. . . .

Bertholet first claims that the trial court was bound by Bertholet's contract with Stefanko to grant the injunction even if its petition did not satisfy the requirements of Indiana Trial Rule 65. Alternatively, Bertholet argues that if the trial court was not bound by the contract, the trial court erred by determining that Bertholet failed to demonstrate irreparable harm. We first turn to Bertholet's claim that the trial court was bound to issue the injunction by the contract with Stefanko.

The determination to grant or deny a preliminary injunction rests within the trial court's equitable discretion and that determination will be reversed only upon an abuse of that discretion. Northern Indiana Pub. Service v. Dozier (Ind.Ct.App. 1996). An injunction is an extraordinary equitable remedy that should be granted with great caution and only used sparingly.

> Discretion to grant or deny an injunction is measured by several factors: (1) whether the plaintiff's remedies at law are inadequate, causing irreparable harm pending resolution of the substantive action; (2) whether the plaintiff has at least a reasonable likelihood of success at trial; (3) whether the plaintiff's threatened injury outweighs the potential harm to the defendant resulting from the granting of the injunction; and (4) whether the public interest will be disserved.

Fumo v. Medical Group of Michigan City, [590 N.E.2d 1103] (Ind.Ct.App. 1992).

Bertholet argues that it does not have to satisfy the four requirements set forth in *Fumo* because its contract with Stefanko entitled it to injunctive relief. In support of this argument, Bertholet relies on *Hacienda Restaurant v. Hacienda Franchise,* [569 N.E.2d 661] (Ind.Ct.App. 1991). Much like the present case, in *Hacienda Restaurant* we dealt with a covenant not to compete that provided for an injunction as a remedy for any breach. Bertholet contends that because we upheld the grant of the injunction in *Hacienda Restaurant,* the trial court was required to give effect to the contract provision at issue here. We initially observe that upholding the trial court's exercise of its discretion to grant an injunction does not establish that it would have been error for the court to have refused an injunction. Furthermore, we affirmed the grant of an injunction in *Hacienda Restaurant* because the plaintiff had met all four of the requirements for an injunction, not because of the contract's provision for an injunction. In fact, noting that this question had not been addressed in Indiana, we stated, "[w]e express doubt that a court *must* give effect to such a provision in exercising its equitable jurisdiction." Id. (emphasis in original). Despite Bertholet's claim, *Hacienda Restaurant* does not stand for the proposition that a trial court must grant an injunction based upon a contractual agreement for that remedy.

In *Stokes v. Moore,* 262 Ala. 59 (1955), the Alabama Supreme Court discussed whether a contractual provision of the sort involved here was binding on a trial court. The *Stokes* court stated:

> We do not wish to express the view that an agreement for the issuance of an injunction, if and when a stipulated state of facts arise in the future, is binding on the court to that extent. Such an agreement would serve to oust the inherent jurisdiction of the court to determine whether an injunction is appropriate when applied for and to require its issuance even though to do so would be contrary to the opinion of the court.

In Indiana, parties may not contractually oust the jurisdiction of the courts. The contract provision for an issuance of an injunction would impermissibly remove the determination of whether to grant or deny an injunction from the discretion of the trial court and oust that court's inherent jurisdiction. We agree with *Stokes* and hold that contract provisions requiring the issuance of an injunction are *not* binding upon the trial court.

Having determined that the trial court was not contractually required to issue the injunction, we now must determine whether the trial court properly denied Bertholet's petition. We initially note that in order to qualify for an injunction, Bertholet must satisfy the four elements discussed in *Fumo,* supra. In this challenge to the trial court's determination, it is Bertholet's burden to demonstrate irreparable harm.

Bertholet claims that Stefanko could have used copies of its bond forms and its list of former clients to take clients away from Bertholet. Aside from its bald assertion of irreparable harm, Bertholet does not explain how the harm was irreparable. Bertholet has not shown any irreparable harm. Moreover, Bertholet has failed to show that its remedies at law would be inadequate. The contract with Stefanko contains a liquidated damages provision which requires Stefanko to pay Bertholet 15% of any bonds he writes while in violation of the covenant not to compete. By its own agreement with Stefanko, Bertholet set an adequate monetary remedy in the liquidated damages provision. Because Bertholet has failed to carry its burden of demonstrating irreparable harm and an adequate remedy at law exists, we hold that the trial court did not err by denying Bertholet's petition for a preliminary injunction.

Affirmed.

NOTES

(1) *Contracting for Injunctions.* The now withdrawn 2003 proposed revision to UCC § 2–716(1) would have provided: "In a contract other than a consumer contract, specific performance may be decreed if the parties have agreed to that remedy. However, even if the parties agree to specific performance, specific performance may not be decreed if the breaching party's sole remaining contractual obligation is the payment of money." Do you think passage of this provision overcome courts' reluctance, evinced in the *Stefanko* decision, to enforce specific performance provisions? Are there any good reasons why sophisticated parties shouldn't be able to contract for an equitable remedy?

(2) *Contracting Against Injunctions.* As noted in Chapter Four, Section 7, courts will not enforce covenants not to compete unless they are "reasonable," which in turn depends upon such factors as whether the employee's services are "special, unique or extraordinary," or there is a risk that the employee will disclose trade secrets or solicit the employer's customers. The duration and scope of the restraint with regard to both the geographic and product market are also relevant to the inquiry. See Data Management v. Greene, supra at 630. If the restriction passes the test of reasonableness, in whole or in part, the probabilities are that normal damage remedies will be inadequate. There is a risk of irreparable harm that cannot be measured with reasonable certainty. Without more, a court should enforce the employee's promise not to compete through an injunction. In some contracts, however, there may be a clause attempting to liquidate the probable damages in the event of breach. For example, the contract may provide that in the event of breach the employee will pay the employer $100,000 as "liquidated damages and not a penalty" for the breach. If the liquidated damage provision is valid and the contract provides that is the *exclusive* remedy, the employer is not entitled to injunctive relief. It must take the money and run. In the absence of an exclusive remedy clause, however, the employer has a choice: Enforce the liquidated damage clause or seek an injunction. The employer cannot have both (do you see why?). If the employer obtains an injunction, however, the employer may recover any actual damages caused between the time of the breach and the date the injunction issues. See Karpinski v. Ingrasci, 28 N.Y.2d 45 (1971);

Restatement (Second) § 361 (provision for liquidated damages will not bar injunctive relief).

CHAPTER SEVEN

THIRD-PARTY INTERESTS

We turn now to two issues often given short shrift in first-year courses: (i) a party's ability subsequent to an initial contract to assign the entitlement to or delegate the duties of performance to third persons (who are not in privity with the parties); and (ii) a party's ability as part of the initial contract to confer on third-party beneficiaries (who do not provide any consideration for those benefits) an entitlement to performance.

1. ASSIGNMENT OF RIGHTS

Once contractual rights and duties exist, can they be sold or given to another? More specifically, can one assign rights to or delegate duties of performance to someone else? This section discusses the assignment of rights, then next the delegation of duties.

Basic Assignment Transactions. There are two common transaction types that produce assignments. In the first, A sells and delivers goods to or performs services for B who promises to pay the price at some future time. A's right against B is commonly called an account receivable. In the second, C agrees to provide D some future performance, and D promises to pay as work progresses. Since C, unlike A, has not yet earned payment by performance under the contract, the right against D is commonly called a contract right, although under the UCC it is swept under a broad definition of "account." UCC § 9–102(a)(2). Note that both A and C have extended credit. If they need cash before B's and D's duties mature, they may try to assign or sell the account or contract right to a third party for an immediate but discounted cash payment. If there is a willing third party, and if the law permits enforcement of A's and C's contract rights against B and D, A and C can convert a promise of future payment into present cash. This ability is the hallmark of a credit economy. It permits a third party to immediately finance A and C on the strength of B's and D's promises.

Occasionally, a contractor in the position of C will attempt to transfer the contract as a whole to the third party, i.e., assign the rights and delegate the duties. More frequently a construction contractor will assign rights to a bank for immediate financing and delegate some performance duties to subcontractors. As you might imagine, the risks involved to the third party who pays value for rights or assumes the responsibility for performance are considerable, and those risks can vary from transaction to transaction. See Grant Gilmore, *The Assignee of Contract Rights and His Precarious Security*, 74 Yale L.J. 216 (1964). For example, the rights of an assignee are, in general, subject to all the terms of the contract between the assignor and the account debtor and to any claim or defense arising therefrom. See UCC § 9–404(a); Restatement (Second) §§ 334–339.

Since assignments are commonplace today—indeed one cannot imagine our complex credit economy existing without them—it may come as a surprise to learn that at one time common law courts refused to recognize the assignability of a "chose in action," including a right arising *ex contractu*.[1] The emphasis on the personal relationship of the contracting parties, discernible also in the development of third-party beneficiary contracts, tended to make the lack of privity an insurmountable obstacle to the third party's right of action. But when common law courts steadfastly refused to recognize assignments, the law merchant, presumably in response to commercial demand, developed a considerable body of assignment doctrine. As the economy expanded, the common law courts, spurred on by courts of equity, came to fashion legal doctrine that in effect permitted the assignment of a contract right.[2]

Effect of UCC Article 9. The widespread adoption of UCC Article 9, the secured transactions article, has supplanted much of the common law of assignment. Article 9 applies to "a transaction, regardless of form, that creates a security interest in personal property or fixtures by contract" as well as the "sale of accounts, chattel paper, payment intangibles, or promissory notes." UCC § 9–109(a)(1) & (3). Expressly excluded from its scope are the "assignment of accounts, chattel paper, payment intangibles, or promissory notes which is for the purpose of collection only," as well as the "assignment of a right to payment under a contract to an assignee that is also obligated to perform under the contract." UCC § 9–109(d)(5) & (6).

With one exception, the emphasis in this section is on assignment law that is not preempted by Article 9.

Assignment of "Future Accounts" under Article 9. Owning an asset—a tract of land, an automobile, a chose in action—generates several legal and practical advantages. One can, for example, obtain money, either by

---

[1] The severe proscription of maintenance and champerty, the unlawful interference in or purchase of an interest in another's lawsuit, helped create a climate of judicial disfavor to the notion of one suing to enforce a right arising out of a transaction to which one was not privy.

[2] This was accomplished ostensibly within the framework of settled law, but actually amounted to a sharp departure from precedent. The "owner" of the right could appoint another as agent for collection and agree that the latter would keep the proceeds. As time went on, even if the transaction was formally denominated an assignment, courts would say the effect was to create a power of attorney, enabling the "assignee" to sue in the name of the "assignor." There were serious drawbacks to this agency evasion, however. The "assignor" could revoke the agency, and revocation was effected automatically by death or bankruptcy. To overcome this defect in the process, litigants appealed, characteristically, to the Chancery court. And, again characteristically, equity responded. If the "assignee" gave value, he or she would be treated as "owner" of the claim, which ownership could not be divested by the "assignor's" attempted revocation or by death or bankruptcy. At this point the future of assignment doctrine was assured. While there persisted for years language that described choses in action as assignable in equity but not at law, the subsequent merger of law and equity caused even this terminology to all but disappear. The result is that the power of assignment is firmly embedded in the law, and judicial attention has been given to the implications and ramifications of this power. See Lon L. Fuller, Basic Contract Law 585–92 (1947).

transferring ownership (as in a sale) or by using the asset as security for a loan (as in a mortgage or pledge). But what if the asset has no present existence in the ordinary sense, such as fish to be caught, gears to be manufactured, crops to be grown, or accounts receivable from future sales? Can there be a present sale or assignment of this expectancy? Why should not one be able to sell anything that another is willing to buy, provided the transaction does not violate public policy?

In a modern economy, it is particularly useful for sellers to assign their expected accounts receivable for future sales as security to help the seller receive credit. The financing of accounts receivable has developed into a major industry. Indeed, the transfer of these rights may be the most notable contemporary implementation of the power of assignment. Early in the twentieth century, however, courts were hostile to the assignment of *future* accounts—accounts not yet generated. See, e.g., Taylor v. Barton-Child Co., 228 Mass. 126 (1917). To circumvent such precedents, it was deemed necessary for the debtor/seller to execute supplementary assignments as the accounts came into existence.

This changed in the middle of the twentieth century, as reflected in Restatement (Second) § 321:

> (1) Except as otherwise provided by statute, an assignment of a right to payment expected to arise out of an existing employment or other continuing business relationship is effective in the same way as an assignment of an existing right.
> (2) Except as otherwise provided by statute and as stated in Subsection (1), a purported assignment of a right expected to arise under a contract not in existence operates only as a promise to assign the right when it arises and as a power to enforce it.

Article 9 of the UCC goes even further in facilitating the sale or assignment of future accounts. UCC § 9–204(1) provides that, except for transactions involving consumer goods and commercial tort claims, "a security agreement may create or provide for a security interest in after-acquired collateral." The effect is to generally permit between businesses the assignment of accounts not yet in existence. The secured party can include in the security agreement an "after-acquired property" clause, file a financing statement with the proper officer, give value to the debtor, and thereby be assured of a perfected security interest at the time when the debtor obtains rights in the described collateral—including any "accounts receivable" subsequently acquired. No further agreement or filing is required.

Sale of Goods. For the sale of goods, the assignment of contractual rights is presumptively valid "unless otherwise agreed" or unless "the assignment would materially change the duty of the other party, or increase materially the burden or risk imposed on him by his contract." UCC § 2–210(2); accord Restatement (Second) § 317(2).

There are relatively few cases where the assignment of a contract right alone has been held to materially increase the obligor's risk, especially where the right is to the payment of money. See Collins Co., Ltd. v. Carboline Co., 125 Ill.2d 498 (1988) (assignment by buyer of right to express warranty does not materially increase seller's risk); Evening News Association v. Peterson, 477 F.Supp. 77 (D.D.C.1979) (assignment of right to services of newscaster does not materially increase risk); Tennell v. Esteve Cotton Co., 546 S.W.2d 346 (Tex. Civ. App. 1976) (buyer's assignment of cotton contract does not materially increase seller's risk). For an example of a holding that an assignment would materially increase the obligor's risk, see Kingston v. Markward & Karafilis, Inc., 134 Mich.App. 164 (1984) (assignment of right to indemnification materially increases risk).

Once a right to payment is due, the UCC also allows promisees to assign their rights even if the initial contract prohibits assignment—thus giving promisees an immutable option to assign rights no longer executory, including a right to damages for breach or a right to payment of an "account." See UCC § 2–210(2) and UCC § 9–406(d).

Future Wages. Modern legislation has limited the assignability of "future wages." A few states prohibit all such assignments; most regulate the practice, as by restricting the amount of wages subject to assignment, etc. See Statutory Note, Restatement (Second) Ch. 15.

Irrevocable Gratuitous Assignments. Restatement (Second) § 332(1) provides: "(1) Unless a contrary intention is manifested, a gratuitous assignment is irrevocable if (a) the assignment is in a writing either signed or under seal that is delivered by the assignor; or (b) the assignment is accompanied by delivery of a writing of a type customarily accepted as a symbol or as evidence of the right assigned." In both parts, one expressly and the other impliedly, the pattern adopted is consistent with the requirement respecting gifts of chattels that a symbolic or constructive "delivery" is required.

Herman Allhusen v. Caristo Construction Corp.

Court of Appeals of New York, 1952.
303 N.Y. 446.

■ FROESSEL, J. Defendant, a general contractor, subcontracted with the Kroo Painting Company (hereinafter called Kroo) for the performance by the latter of certain painting work in New York City public schools. Their contracts contained the following prohibitory provision: "The assignment by the second party [Kroo] of this contract or any interest therein, or of any money due or to become due by reason of the terms hereof without the written consent of the first party [defendant] shall be void." Kroo subsequently assigned certain rights under the contracts to Marine Midland Trust Company of New York, which in turn assigned said rights to plaintiff. These rights included the "moneys due and to become due" to

Kroo. The *contracts* were not assigned, and no question of improper delegation of contractual duties is involved. No written consent to the assignments was procured from defendant.

Plaintiff as assignee seeks to recover, in six causes of action, $11,650 allegedly due and owing for work done by Kroo. Defendant answered with denials, and by way of defense set up the afore-mentioned prohibitory clause, in addition to certain setoffs and counterclaims, alleged to have existed at the time of the assignments. It thereupon moved for summary judgment under rule 113 of the Rules of Civil Practice, and demanded dismissal of plaintiff's several causes of action on the sole ground that the prohibitory clause constituted a defense sufficient as a matter of law to defeat each cause of action. Special Term dismissed the complaint, holding that the prohibition against assignments "must be given effect." The Appellate Division affirmed, one Justice dissenting on the ground that the "account receivable was assignable by nature, and could not be rendered otherwise without imposing an unlawful restraint upon the power of alienation of property." . . .

Whether an anti-assignment clause is effective is a question that has troubled the courts not only of this State but in other jurisdictions as well. . . .

Our courts have not construed a contractual provision against assignments framed in the language of the clause now before us. Such kindred clauses as have been subject to interpretation usually have been held to be either (1) personal covenants limiting the covenantee to a claim for damages in the event of a breach . . . , or (2) ineffectual because of the use of uncertain language. . . . But these decisions are not to be read as meaning that there can be no enforcible contractual prohibition against the assignment of a claim; indeed, they are authority only for the proposition that, in the absence of language clearly indicating that a contractual right thereunder shall be nonassignable, a prohibitory clause will be interpreted as a personal covenant not to assign.

* * *

[The court reviewed relevant New York cases.]

In the light of the foregoing, we think it is reasonably clear that, while the courts have striven to uphold freedom of assignability, they have not failed to recognize the concept of freedom to contract. In large measure they agree that, where appropriate language is used, assignments of money due under contracts may be prohibited. When "clear language" is used, and the "plainest words . . . have been chosen", parties may "limit the freedom of alienation of rights and prohibit the assignment." . . . We have now before us a clause embodying clear, definite and appropriate language, which may be construed in no other way but that any attempted assignment of either the contract or any rights created thereunder shall be "void" as against the obligor. One would have to do violence to the language here employed to hold that it is merely an agreement by the subcontractor not to assign. The objectivity of the language precludes such a construction. We are therefore compelled to conclude that this prohibitory clause is a valid and effective restriction of the right to assign.

Such a holding is not violative of public policy. . . . Plaintiff's claimed rights arise out of the very contract embodying the provision now sought to be invalidated. The right to moneys under the contracts is but a companion to other jural relations forming an aggregation of actual and potential interrelated rights and obligations. No sound reason appears why an assignee should remain unaffected by a provision in the very contract which gave life to the claim he asserts.

Nor is there any merit in plaintiff's contention that section 41 of the Personal Property Law, Consol. Laws, c. 41, requires that the prohibitory clause be denied effect. Because the statute provides that a person may transfer a claim, it does not follow that he may not contract otherwise. Countless rights granted by statutes are voluntarily surrendered in the everyday affairs of individuals. In Rosenthal Paper Co. v. National Folding Box & Paper Co., 226 N.Y. 313, 325–326, we noted: "The general rule now prevailing * * * that any property right, not necessarily personal, is assignable, *is overcome only by agreement of the contracting parties* or a principal of law or public policy. In this jurisdiction the statute, in effect, so provides [referring to the predecessor of section 41 of the Personal Property Law]."

The judgment should be affirmed, with costs.

NOTES

(1) In terms of legal consequence, what is the difference between saying the prohibition deprived Kroo of the power to assign, rather than merely created a duty on his part not to do so? What policy conflicts are discernible in a case of this type?

(2) *Assignment of Claims Against the United States.* There has been legislation prohibiting the assignment of executory contract claims against the United States since 1792. See 41 U.S.C.A. § 15 and 31 U.S.C.A. § 203. As a noted practitioner of government contract law put it, the basic purposes of this prohibition are to "protect the government against harassment caused by a multiplication of the firms with which it has to deal; prevent collusive bidding; prevent persons of influence from buying up claims against the government which then might be used against government officials; preserve for the government any defense it might have against the assignor by way of set-off or counterclaim; and secure for the government the performance of the firm with which it contracts." Gilbert Cuneo, Government Contracts Handbook 7 (1962). In 1940, however, an amendment was approved by Congress permitting contractors to assign money due or to become due from the United States under a contract providing for payments aggregating $1,000 or more to a "bank, trust company, or other financing institution." The purpose was to assist government contractors in obtaining private

financing on the security of the government's promise to pay for work done or to be done.

Carol Owen v. CNA Insurance/Continental Casualty Company

Supreme Court of New Jersey, 2001.
167 N.J. 450.

■ STEIN, J. This appeal involves a tort victim who brought an action against a liability insurer for a declaratory judgment that the non-assignment clause in a structured settlement agreement was unenforceable. The trial court granted summary judgment in favor of the tort victim, holding that under current law the non-assignment clause was unenforceable. The Appellate Division reversed, concluding that the enforceability of the non-assignment clause depended on its materiality to the primary purposes of the settlement agreement and remanding the matter for further fact finding on that question. One member of the appellate panel dissented, stating that "a holding that the assignment in this case was ineffective has no current legitimate provenance in law." The tort victim appealed as of right based on the dissent below. . . . The specific issue is whether the non-assignment clause in the structured settlement agreement at issue is enforceable.

I

In September 1983, plaintiff Carol Owen (Owen) signed a release in favor of parties she had sued in a personal-injury action arising out of a slip-and-fall accident at a Bamberger's Store in East Brunswick, New Jersey. . . . In connection with that release, Owen entered into a settlement agreement with the tortfeasor's insurer, Continental Casualty Corporation (Continental). . . . Under the terms of the settlement agreement, Owen was entitled to receive an initial lump sum payment of $10,000, attorney's fees of $15,000, and five deferred periodic payments totaling $81,067.24. The periodic payments were scheduled as follows: December 21, 1986—$6,505.48; December 21, 1991—$9,558.68; December 21, 1996—$14,044.84; December 21, 2001—$20,636.48; December 21, 2006—$30,321.76. The non-assignment provision of the settlement agreement stated:

> The claimant shall have the right to change the Contingent Payee at any time during the term of this Agreement by filing written notice with the Company, such change to be effective when accepted by the Company in writing as of the date such notice was signed, except as to any payments made by the Company before such change was accepted. To the extent provided by law, the aforesaid deferred lump sum payments shall not be subject to assignment, transfer, commutation, or encumbrance, except as provided herein.

Because of mounting medical bills due to illness unrelated to her lawsuit, in December 1997 Owen entered into a "Purchase and Sale Agreement" with Metropolitan Mortgage and Securities Company (Metropolitan) pursuant to which she agreed to " 'sell, convey, transfer and assign' to Metropolitan all her 'rights and benefits' under the settlement agreement with [Continental] for $8,520.20." . . . At the time of the assignment to Metropolitan, Owen was entitled to receive the 2001 ($20,636.48) and 2006 ($30,321.76) payments under the structured settlements. . . . However, the parties dispute whether Owen sold both remaining payments or only the 2001 payment to Metropolitan. . . . Under the assignment agreement, Owen also agreed (1) to defend, indemnify, and hold Metropolitan harmless for any claim that her periodic payments were not assignable and (2) to "order and conduct [her] affairs [so] as to prevent the assertion of any claim that the Benefits were not assignable." . . .

In January 1998, in furtherance of the assignment, Owen sent Continental a notarized letter directing it to send "all future payments and other mail" to a new address in Syracuse, New York. Continental responded by sending Owen a copy of the settlement agreement and noting that the deferred periodic payments were not subject to assignment. After Owen's attorney wrote three letters to Continental seeking confirmation that Continental had changed the address, Continental in turn requested confirmation that Owen resided at the Syracuse address. Owen's counsel responded by enclosing a draft letter of complaint to the New Jersey Department of Banking and Insurance (Department of Insurance) and indicated that she would file the complaint in the absence of immediate written acknowledgment that Continental had changed Owen's address. In another letter, Owen's counsel indicated that Owen's place of residence was "irrelevant" and demanded again that Continental change the address to which future payments were to be sent. In response, Continental then advised Owen's counsel that

> Continental Casualty Company is required to make payments to the claimant. The payments are not assignable by the claimant. Accordingly, the payments are always sent to the claimant's actual address. The Company does not send payments to a street address at which the claimant does not reside.

Subsequently, Owen filed a complaint with the Department of Insurance, but the Department took no action.

* * *

II

Although our statutes do not contain specific provisions regulating the transfer of structured settlement rights,[3] effective January 1, 1963, the Uniform Commercial Code (U.C.C.) became the governing statutory law in New Jersey regulating commercial transactions throughout the State. *N.J.S.A.* 12A:10–106. A threshold issue is whether Article 9 of the U.C.C. affects the validity of Continental's non-assignment clause. *N.J.S.A.* 12A:9–318(4) provides:

> A term in any contract between an account debtor and an assignor is ineffective if it prohibits assignment of an account or prohibits creation of a security interest in chattel paper or a security interest in a general intangible for money due or to become due or requires the account debtor's consent to the assignment or security interest.

Although that provision invalidates contractual non-assignment provisions, *N.J.S.A.* 12A:9–104(k) provides that Article 9 does not apply "[t]o a transfer in whole or in part of any claim arising out of tort." Because the meaning of "any claim arising out of tort" is not explicitly defined in the statute, whether or not section 9–104(k)'s exclusion applies to the proceeds of tort claims has become a highly controversial issue. The Appellate Division determined that the exclusion in *N.J.S.A.* 12A:9–104(k) also applied to the proceeds of tort claims. . . . However, no clear majority rule exists concerning the application of Article 9 to tort claim proceeds. *Barclays Bus. Credit, Inc. v. Four Winds Plaza Partnership,* 938 F.Supp. 304, 308 (D.Vi.1996).

[The court reviewed the arguments for and against applying Article 9 to assignments of proceeds of tort claims.]

Putting to one side the Article 9 debate and focusing instead on New Jersey assignment law, we note that *N.J.S.A.* 2A:25–1 provides that "all judgments and decrees recoverable in any of the courts" in New Jersey are assignable. Thus, New Jersey law generally permits the assignment of settlement proceeds unless the parties have expressly agreed otherwise. *Chelsea-Wheeler Coal Co. v. Marvin,* 134 N.J. Eq. 432 (E. & A. 1944), established the common-law doctrine that a contractual provision that prohibits the assignment of rights under a contract may be disregarded when it is not the main purpose of the contract. [The court discussed the case, which held that the main purpose of the assignment of proceeds under a life insurance contract was to provide a modest, regular income to the assignee and that, therefore, the clause prohibiting the assignment was not effective.]

Since the 1944 decision in *Chelsea-Wheeler,* we have not again considered the effect of contractual provisions limiting or prohibiting

---

[3] [However, on December 4, 2000, the New Jersey Senate adopted a bill which would prohibit transfer of structured settlement rights "unless the transfer has been approved in advance in a final court order or order of a responsible administrative authority."—Eds.]

assignments. However, in *Garden State Buildings L.P. v. First Fidelity Bank, N.A.*, 305 N.J.Super. 510 (App. Div. 1997), the Appellate Division addressed the issue, relying primarily on Section 322 of the Restatement of Contracts, which states in pertinent part:

> (2) A contract term prohibiting assignment of rights under the contract, unless a different intention is manifested, (a) does not forbid assignment of a right to damages for breach of the whole contract or a right arising out of the assignor's due performance of his entire obligation; (b) gives the obligor a right to damages for breach of the terms forbidding assignment but does not render the assignment ineffective; (c) is for the benefit of the obligor, and does not prevent the assignee from acquiring rights against the assignor or the obligor from discharging his duty as if there were no such prohibition.

[Restatement (Second) of Contracts § 322 (1981).]

The crucial phrase in section 322 is "unless a different intention is manifested." Courts diverge, however, regarding the standard for determining when parties to a contract have sufficiently manifested an intention to prohibit the power of assignment.

* * *

To resolve the issue, the Appellate Division looked to Restatement section 322(2) as well as to out-of-state case law. . . . The court adopted the following test as the standard for determining whether non-assignment language in a contract invalidates an assignment made in violation of the contractual provisions:

> [T]o reveal the intent necessary to preclude the power to assign, or cause an assignment violative of contractual provisions to be wholly void, such clause must contain express provisions that any assignment shall be void or invalid if not made in a certain specified way. . . .

The Appellate Division held that, absent such express provisions, the assignment is valid, and that the obligor simply has the right to damages.

In adopting the standard advocated by Restatement section 322, the Appellate Division joined other jurisdictions that follow the general rule that contractual provisions limiting or prohibiting assignments operate only to limit a party's *right* to assign the contract, but not their *power* to do so, unless the parties manifest an intent to the contrary with specificity. *Bel-Ray Co. v. Chemrite (Pty) Ltd.*, 181 F.3d 435, 442 (3d Cir. 1999). * * *

In other jurisdictions, courts generally uphold non-assignment provisions of structured-settlement agreements when they include language stating that a plaintiff or payee shall not "have the power to sell, mortgage, encumber, or anticipate the Periodic Payments." *Liberty*

Life Assurance Co. v. Stone Street Capital, Inc., 93 F. Supp. 2d 630, 637 (D. Md. 2000). . . .

In another relevant section, the Restatement of Contracts recognizes the validity of assignments of contractual rights, but with three important exceptions:

> (2) A contractual right can be assigned unless
>
>> (a) the substitution of a right of the assignee for the right of the assignor would materially change the duty of the obligor, or materially increase the burden or risk imposed on him by his contract, or materially impair his chance of obtaining return performance, or materially reduce its value to him, or
>>
>> (b) the assignment is forbidden by statute or is otherwise inoperative on grounds of public policy, or
>>
>> (c) assignment is validly precluded by contract.
>
> [*Restatement (Second) of Contracts* § 317 (1981).]

Comment d to section 317 indicates that exception (a) involves a fact-sensitive inquiry in which "[w]hat is a material variation, an increase in burden or risk, or an impairment of the obligor's expectation of counter-performance . . . depends on the nature of the contract and on the circumstances."

In [*Grieve v. General Am. Life Ins. Co.,* 58 F.Supp.2d 319 (D.Vt.1999)] the court found that all three exceptions to the general assignability of rights under a contract recognized by section 317(2) applied to a structured settlement. After setting out the tax treatment of structured settlements in sections 104(a) and 130 of the Internal Revenue Code, that court determined that an assignment might cause the company funding the structured settlement to lose its eligibility for favorable tax treatment. *Id.* at 323. The court also was satisfied, however, that the assignment of settlement proceeds materially increased the risks to the company funding the structured settlement, which resulted in a material reduction of the value of the contract for that company. *Ibid.* * * *

[The court reviewed other cases to the same effect and the treatment of structured settlements under the Internal Revenue Code.]

Based on those Code provisions, the typical personal-injury structured settlement operates in the following manner. The tortfeasor's insurance company assigns to another company, a structured-settlement company (typically a subsidiary of the insurance company), its liability to make the periodic payments to the plaintiff. In exchange for assuming its liability, the insurance company pays the structured-settlement company a lump sum that the insurance company immediately can deduct from its gross income. The structured settlement company then uses the lump sum to purchase an annuity to fund the periodic payments to the plaintiff. If the transaction meets the requirements of section 130, the structured-settlement company would not have to report the lump sum as income until it received the annuity payments, at which time it would be entitled to an offsetting deduction for periodic payments made to the plaintiff. And if the plaintiff meets the requirements of section 104(a)(2), he or she could exclude the periodic payments from his or her gross income, including only any portion of the periodic payment that represents interest income generated by the annuity.

III

A preliminary issue before us is whether the application of Article 9 of the U.C.C. is controlling. The Appellate Division concluded that Article 9 did not prohibit the non-assignment provision of the structured-settlement agreement because the express exclusion of tort claims from Article 9 includes tort-settlement proceeds. . . . Specifically, the Appellate Division concluded that "Article 9's express exclusion of tort claims includes the proceeds of a tort claim, and therefore . . . Article 9 does not prohibit the non-assignment provision of plaintiff's contract with defendant." However, because we reach the same conclusion regarding the enforceability of the non-assignment clause irrespective of whether Article 9 applies to the proceeds of tort claims, and in view of the likely enactment of a statute specifically regulating assignments of structured settlements, we focus on whether the non-assignment provision is otherwise enforceable under New Jersey law and decline to decide whether tort-settlement proceeds are included in the express exclusion of tort claims of Article 9. * * *

Sections 322 and 317 are the relevant sections in the Restatement of Contracts dealing with assignments of contractual rights. Section 322 addresses the effect of contract terms that prohibit assignment of rights under a contract. Section 317 recognizes the validity of assignments, but specifically identifies important exceptions that limit the assignability of contractual rights. We are persuaded that the combined application of those two sections provides the best analytical framework to assess the validity of non-assignment provisions in a contract.

With regard to whether the non-assignment provision in Owen's structured-settlement agreement contains the explicit language necessary to void the assignment, we analyze the non-assignment provision under Restatement section 322, which embodies the general, now-majority rule that contractual provisions prohibiting or limiting assignments operate only to limit the parties' right to assign the contract, but not their power to assign, unless the parties manifest with specificity an intent to the contrary. In the absence of such a manifestation, a non-assignment provision is interpreted merely as a covenant not to assign, the breach of which renders the assigning party liable in damages. The assignment, however, remains valid and enforceable.

The non-assignment provision contained in Owen's structured settlement agreement stated: "To the extent provided by law, the aforesaid deferred lump sum payments shall not be subject to assignment, transfer, commutation, or encumbrance, except as provided herein." In our view, that language merely constitutes a covenant not to assign. It contains no specific prohibition on the power to make an assignment, and it does not specifically state that the assignments are "void," "invalid" or "that the assignee shall acquire no rights or the nonassigning party shall not recognize any such assignment." . . . Therefore, the non-assignment provision does not "reveal the intent necessary to preclude the power to assign, or cause an assignment violative of contractual provisions to be wholly void." . . . Thus, because the language does not specifically restrict Owen's power of assignment, the assignment is not void under section 322(2) of the Restatement.

With regard to section 317 of the Restatement, we address Continental's argument that the assignment of Owen's rights under the settlement agreement could cause it to face tax-reporting issues it allegedly bargained to avoid. We note that Owen's structured settlement agreement with Continental is not the typical personal-injury structured settlement in which a tortfeasor's insurance company assigns to a structured-settlement company its liability to make the periodic payments to the plaintiff. This record reveals that there is no structured-settlement company to which Continental paid a lump sum to purchase an annuity with the purpose of making periodic payments to Owen. As we understand the transaction, Continental itself undertook to make periodic payments to Owen. Because there is no structured-settlement company involved, section 130 of the Internal Revenue Code does not appear to entitle Continental to an offsetting deduction for periodic payments made to Owen.

Moreover, because Owen's structured settlement agreement was signed in 1983, the same year that Congress established the tax-incentive scheme favoring structured settlements, this settlement agreement apparently was not designed to take advantage of that favorable tax treatment. Accordingly, we reject Continental's contention that the assignment would cause it to lose tax benefits that it never anticipated receiving. . . . [T]he assignment would not cause Continental to "lose its eligibility for favorable tax treatment."

* * *

Accordingly, because the language in the non-assignment provision in Owen's structured settlement agreement does not specifically restrict Owen's power of assignment, and because the assignment would not "materially increase the burden or risk" imposed on Continental, we hold that in the context of this record Continental's non-assignment clause is unenforceable. We emphasize that because our holding is based on the record before us, it should not be understood to indicate that non-assignment provisions in structured settlement agreements generally are unenforceable.

We express our concern about the exceptionally high interest charge imposed by Metropolitan as compensation for its lump sum payment to Owen, and we anticipate that the Legislature will take cognizance of such interest charges in its statutory regulation of structured settlement assignments.

IV

We acknowledge that the terms of the original assignment agreement between Owen and Metropolitan may not be possible to implement because of the time that has elapsed between the agreement and our determination that the assignment is enforceable. We reverse the judgment of the Appellate Division and remand the matter to the Law Division to resolve any open issues relating to the terms and scope of the assignment that are susceptible to resolution by the court.

NOTES

(1) The *Owen* case is one of several decisions dealing with the enforceability of assignments of the right to payment created by structured settlements of tort and other claims. See, e.g., In re Kaufman, 37 P.3d 845 (Okl. 2001); Liberty Life Assur. Co. of Boston v. Stone Street Capital, Inc., 93 F.Supp.2d 630 (D.Md.2000) (anti-assignment clause valid and enforceable). Frequently, the stream of payments is created by an annuity established to implement the structured settlement. As the court notes, New Jersey, N.J.S.A. § 2A:16–63 et seq. (and now 26 other states, including California and New York), has enacted legislation regulating these transactions. Review the statute, mentioned in the decision's footnote, supra. Would it change the result in this case? What is the purpose of this statute? See In re Transfer of Structured Settlement Rights by Spinelli, 353 N.J.Super. 459 (2002) (interpreting New Jersey's new legislation). See also Henry E. Smith, *Structured Settlements as Structures of Rights*, 88 Va. L. Rev. 1953 (2002); Gregory Scott Crespi, *Selling Structured Settlements: The Uncertain Effect of Anti-Assignment Clauses*, 28 Pepp. L. Rev. 787 (2001).

(2) In the absence of regulatory legislation, the assignee's strategy is to claim that the assignment of the right to payment is a secured transaction subject to Article 9 of the UCC. Why? The quick answer is that clauses prohibiting such assignments are, with some limitations, not effective. UCC § 9–406(d). The problem is that Article 9 does not apply to the assignment of a claim "arising in tort," UCC § 9–109(c)(12), or the transfer of a claim "under a policy of insurance." UCC § 9–109(c)(8). See Espinosa v. United of Omaha, 139 N.M. 691 (App. 2006) (anti-assignment clause in annuity-paying tort claims is excluded from Article 9). What is not clear is whether the assignment of rights under an annuity set up to implement the structured settlement of a tort claim is a claim arising in tort or under a policy of insurance. Courts have disagreed. Compare West Loop Sav. Ass'n v. Knostman, 1992 WL 511854 (S.D. Tex. 1992), aff'd, 993 F.2d 90 (5th Cir. 1993) (claims under annuities not excluded) with Wonsey v. Life Ins. Co. of North America, 32 F. Supp. 2d 939, 942 (E.D. Mich. 1998) (annuity is a policy of insurance).

(3) The *Owen* court ducks the Article 9 issue because it could achieve the same result, enforcement of the assignment, under the common law and the Restatement. Do you agree? If you were the company promising to pay, how would you redraft the contract to ensure that assignments were prohibited?

(4) *The Feds Step In.* The service of paying money today in exchange for the assignment of future structured-settlement payments is referred to as "factoring." Congress in 2002 imposed a tax equal to 40 percent of the amount paid by the factoring company "on any person who acquires directly or indirectly structured settlement-payment rights" unless approval is first obtained from a state court that has determined the transaction is in the best interests of the person who wants to sell. See 26 U.S.C. § 5891 (2002).

(5) For another example of public policy limiting the power to assign rights, see Gurski v. Rosenblum & Filan, LLC, 276 Conn. 257 (2005) (holding that the assignment of a legal malpractice claim or its proceeds to a judgment creditor in a medical malpractice action violated public policy and was not enforceable).

Continental Purchasing Co. v. Van Raalte Co.

Supreme Court of New York, Appellate Division, 1937.
295 N.Y.S. 867.

■ EDGCOMB, J. This action is brought by the plaintiff, as assignee of Ethel L. Potter, to recover from the Van Raalte Company, Inc., the employer of Mrs. Potter, the sum of $19.20, wages earned by her while employed by the company. The defendant claims exoneration from liability by reason of having paid the amount involved direct to the assignor.

It is conceded that on April 21, 1934, Mrs. Potter assigned to the plaintiff all wages, or claims for wages, salary, or commission earned, or to be earned, and all claims or demands due her from any person, firm, or corporation by whom she was employed, or who might owe her money, as security for the payment of an account which the Steckler Sporting Goods Store had against her, and which account had been purchased by and assigned to the plaintiff.

This assignment, having been made prior to July 1, 1934, when section 46 was added to the Personal Property Law by chapter 738 of the Laws of that year (section 1), is not void by reason of any statutory prohibition relating to wage assignments. Neither is such transfer contrary to public policy . . . .

While the assignee of a chose in action succeeds to all the rights of the assignor, a debtor is not affected by the assignment until he has notice thereof. If he pays his indebtedness to the assignor in ignorance of the assignment, he is relieved from all liability to the assignee. He may set up against the claim of the assignee any defense acquired prior to notice which would have been available against the assignor had there been no assignment. . . .

After notice of the transfer, however, the debtor is put on his guard, and if he pays the assignor any money which, under the assignment, belongs to the assignee, or if he does anything prejudicial to the rights of the latter, he is liable for the resulting damage. . . .

No set form of notice is required. It is sufficient if such information is given the debtor as will fully inform him that the alleged assignee is the owner of the chose in action, or as will serve to put him on inquiry. . . .

Here the plaintiff protected itself against any bona fide payments made by the debtor to its employee by giving the defendant a written notice of this assignment on September 12, 1934. Seven days later defendant acknowledged receipt of the notice, and suggested that, inasmuch as Mrs. Potter had no other income except her weekly earnings, it would be a great accommodation if a deduction of $2 per week could be made until the total amount of plaintiff's claim was paid. Plaintiff consented to this adjustment, and withdrew its formal notice. But defendant still knew of the assignment, and on six occasions during the following two months deducted $1.50 from Mrs. Potter's wages, and forwarded the same to the plaintiff. This arrangement was discontinued after November 20th. Plaintiff then gave defendant another formal notice of the assignment, and demanded payment direct to it of the wages due Mrs. Potter, and called attention to the fact that any sums paid to the employee would not relieve the defendant from its obligation to the plaintiff. With full knowledge that the plaintiff was entitled to receive Mrs. Potter's wages, defendant has chosen to pay them to Mrs. Potter. In so doing, defendant acted at its peril.

Defendant claims immunity from liability in this action because of the fact that neither the original assignment, nor a copy thereof, was ever filed with or exhibited to it. This defense has found favor in the courts below. Such a requirement is not necessary to render a debtor liable to the assignee of a chose in action for the failure to pay him a debt owed to the assignor. Especially is that so where, as here, no such demand or request has ever been made. . . . The cases relied upon by the respondent do not lay down any different rule.

Here a full and complete notice of the assignment was given to the defendant, and a demand was made that the assignor's wages be paid to the plaintiff. Defendant never questioned the existence or validity of the transfer, nor asked for any additional proof thereof. On the contrary, it acknowledged its validity, and made six separate payments to the assignee, totaling $9, in reliance thereon. Later it utterly ignored plaintiff's rights in the premises, and paid the assignor her wages as they became due, notwithstanding the fact that it knew this money belonged to the plaintiff. Its only excuse for so doing was the fact that Mrs. Potter was receiving aid from a local charitable organization, and that the matter had been referred to that organization for a decision. Under these circumstances, defendant cannot escape its liability to the plaintiff because it paid Mrs. Potter's wages to her.

For the reasons stated, we think that the judgments of the City Court of Dunkirk, and of the County Court of Chautauqua county, should be reversed with costs, and that judgment should be ordered in favor of the plaintiff for the sum of $19.20, with interest thereon from the 21st day of November, 1934.

* * *

NOTES

(1) If, after April 21, 1934, the defendant, without notice of the assignment, had paid Ethel Potter, would the plaintiff here have been successful against the defendant? Does the answer depend upon whether the assignment was operative at that time or when notification was given to the obligor?

(2) *Modification of Contract After Notification of Assignment.* Since the obligor, after notice of the assignment, cannot secure a discharge by payment thereafter to the assignor, it would seem to follow as well that one cannot thereafter be discharged by obtaining a release from the assignor, or by executing an accord and satisfaction or a novation. One must get a discharge from the assignee. It also follows that the original parties cannot then modify the contract. The consent of the assignee is essential to a modification. It has been argued that this may be commercially inconvenient, especially where a prime contractor must make adjustments with subcontractors as the work progresses.

This policy is continued and elaborated in UCC § 9–406(a) & (b). What if an account debtor continues to make payments to the assignor after receiving a proper notice? Unless the assignee knows and does not object, the obligation is not discharged. UCC § 9–406(a).

(3) *Counterclaims and Set-Offs.* Clearly the assignee must be concerned about defenses available to the obligor, such as fraud, failure of consideration and the like. But account must also be taken of possible counterclaims and set-offs which the obligor might assert against the assignor, whether growing out of the original transaction or collateral transactions. UCC § 9–404(a) provides:

> Unless an account debtor has made an enforceable agreement not to assert defenses or claims, and subject to [certain exceptions], the rights of an assignee are subject to: (1) all terms of the agreement between the account debtor and assignor and any defense or claim in recoupment arising from the transaction that gave rise to the contract; and (2) any other defense or claim of the account debtor against the assignor which accrues before the account debtor receives a notification of the assignment authenticated by the assignor or the assignee.

See also Restatement (Second) § 336.

(4) *Assignor's Liability to Assignee.* If the assignee, when suing the obligor, is met with a valid defense, he or she must then consider the possibility of recourse against the assignor. Even absent the assignor's

promise or representation that no defense was available, thereby furnishing the basis for an express warranty, the assignee may still be successful.

> [T]he assignor of a chose in action, for a valuable consideration, impliedly warrants to the assignee that the chose assigned is a valid, subsisting obligation in his favor against the debtor to the extent to which it purports to be such, and as a general rule the assignor of a claim impliedly warrants that it is valid and that the debtor or obligator is liable to pay it, and if in fact the claim is invalid, the assignor is liable to the assignee for the amount paid for the assignment.

Friedman v. Schneider, 186 S.W.2d 204, 206 (1945). It will be noted that an assignor does not warrant that the obligor is solvent or will perform the obligation. Restatement (Second) § 333(2).

This points out a significant difference between assignments and negotiable instruments. Unless otherwise specified in the instrument, the indorser of a negotiable note dishonored by the maker is obliged to pay the amount due on the instrument to a person "entitled to enforce the instrument." UCC § 3–415(a). In addition to this liability, the indorser, if a transferor of the instrument, gives the warranties stated in UCC § 3–416.

(5) *Priority of Successive Assignees of the Same Right.* Suppose that AR assigned a contract right against D to AE#1 for value. Later, AR assigned the same contract right to AE#2, who takes for value and without notice. AE#2 notified D of the assignment but AE#1 did not. When the debt is due, both AE#1 and AE#2 demand full payment from D. Who should D pay? Put differently, which assignee should have priority?

American courts have largely rejected the English rule that priority goes to the assignee who first notified the debtor. See, e.g., *Salem Trust Co. v. Manufacturers' Finance Co.*, 264 U.S. 182 (1924). Unless modified by statute, many states follow the Restatement rule that priority goes to the assignee whose enforceable assignment is first in time unless the second assignee, in good faith and without reason to know of the prior assignment, "gives value and obtains (i) payment or satisfaction of the obligation, (ii) judgment against the obligor, (iii) a new contract with the obligor by novation, or (iv) possession of a writing of a type customarily accepted as a symbol or as evidence of the right assigned." Restatement (Second) § 342. See generally, Axelrod, *Successive Assignments—Conflicting Priorities,* 14 U. Dayton L. Rev. 295 (1989).

Under UCC Article 9, priority usually goes to the first assignee or purchaser of accounts to perfect a security interest in the accounts by filing a financing statement. See UCC § 9–322. The first to file has priority even though he or she knows that there is an assignment earlier in time.

Comment: A Comparison of the Assignment Process and the Negotiation Process

In the assignment process the assignor transfers a contract right to the assignee. The assignor's right of performance from the obligor is thereby extinguished, in whole or in part depending upon whether it is a total or partial assignment, and the assignee acquires a right to such performance. Restatement (Second) § 317(1). A corollary is that the right is not somehow transformed in the process; it is subject to the same imperfections as before. Thus, if the obligor, when sued by the assignor, could have successfully asserted a defense (e.g., lack of consideration), this defense is also available against the assignee. Restatement (Second) § 336. If, however, the obligor has entered into an enforceable agreement with the obligee not to assert defenses against an assignee, the assignee takes the assignment free of those defenses. See UCC § 9–403(b).

By contrast, a holder in due course of a negotiable instrument may obtain in the negotiation process a right superior to that of the one from whom he or she receives the instrument. One does not simply "step into the shoes" of the other. The extraordinary legal effect given to a negotiable instrument derives from the law merchant and is carefully delineated by statute. The writing must meet certain formal requirements, UCC § 3–104, and must be transferred in prescribed ways, UCC § 3–202. If the one to whom the instrument is transferred qualifies as a holder in due course, UCC § 3–304, he or she takes the instrument free of many defenses, UCC § 3–305. For example, suppose in exchange for merchandise, the maker executes and delivers to the payee a negotiable promissory note for the purchase price. The payee indorses the note and delivers it to a third person, the holder, in repayment of an outstanding loan. Even though the maker is able to assert against the payee a number of ordinary defenses, such as lack or failure of consideration, the maker is not able to so defend against one who is a holder in due course.

The emergence in our legal system of the concept of negotiability has been of inestimable value in facilitating commercial transactions. It is an important part of "the triumph of the good faith purchaser," aptly characterized as "one of the most dramatic episodes in our legal history." Grant Gilmore, *The Commercial Doctrine of Good Faith Purchase*, 63 Yale L.J. 1057 (1954). A high-energy economic system is dependent upon the free flow of commerce; accordingly, impediments to voluntary exchange should be kept to a minimum. Allowing the purchaser of a right evidenced by a negotiable note to prevail, despite the availability of so-called "personal defenses" of the maker, enhances the value of negotiable paper.

It is now, however, an "unfair or deceptive act or practice" under Section 5 of the Federal Trade Commission Act for a seller who ordinarily sells or leases goods or services to consumers to enter into a consumer credit contract which does not contain the following provision in at least ten point, bold face type:

ANY HOLDER OF THIS CONSUMER CREDIT CONTRACT IS SUBJECT TO ALL CLAIMS AND DEFENSES WHICH THE DEBTOR COULD ASSERT AGAINST THE SELLER OF

GOODS OR SERVICES OBTAINED PURSUANT HERETO OR WITH THE PROCEEDS HEREOF. RECOVERY HEREUNDER BY THE DEBTOR SHALL NOT EXCEED AMOUNTS PAID BY THE DEBTOR HEREUNDER.

16 C.F.R. § 433.2. See Michael F. Sturley, *The Legal Impact of the Federal Trade Commission's Holder in Due Course Notice on a Negotiable Instrument: How Clever Are the Rascals at the FTC?*, 68 N.C. L. Rev. 953 (1990).

2. DELEGATION OF DUTIES

To what extent can one party delegate the duty of performance created by a contract to a third party without the consent of the other party? For example, can an artist delegate a contractual duty to paint a portrait to another artist without consent of the client? If so (and this is highly dubious), suppose the other artist fails to paint. What, if anything, is the liability of the delegator?

The tests for delegation under both the Second Restatement and the UCC turn on the idea of a "substantial interest." The Second Restatement provides:

> (1) An obligor can properly delegate the performance of his duty to another unless the delegation is contrary to public policy or the terms of his promise. (2) Unless otherwise agreed, a promise requires performance by a particular person only to the extent that the obligee has a substantial interest in having that person perform or control the acts promised. (3) Unless the obligee agrees otherwise, neither delegation of performance nor a contract to assume the duty made with the obligor by the person delegated discharges any duty or liability of the delegating obligor.

Restatement (Second) § 318. And according to the UCC:

> A party may perform his duty through a delegate unless otherwise agreed or unless the other party has a substantial interest in having his original promisor perform or control the acts required by the contract. No delegation of performance relieves the party delegating of any duty to perform or any liability for breach.

UCC § 2–210(1).

Sally Beauty Co. v. Nexxus Products Co., Inc.

United States Court of Appeals, Seventh Circuit, 1986.
801 F.2d 1001.

■ CUDAHY, J. Nexxus Products Company ("Nexxus") entered into a contract with Best Barber & Beauty Supply Company, Inc. ("Best"), under which Best would be the exclusive distributor of Nexxus hair care products to barbers and hair stylists throughout most of Texas. When Best was acquired by and merged into Sally Beauty Company, Inc. ("Sally Beauty"), Nexxus cancelled the agreement. Sally Beauty is a wholly-owned subsidiary of Alberto-Culver Company ("Alberto-Culver"), a major manufacturer of hair care products and a competitor of Nexxus. Sally Beauty claims that Nexxus breached the contract by cancelling; Nexxus asserts by way of defense that the contract was not assignable or, in the alternative, not assignable to Sally Beauty. The district court granted Nexxus' motion for summary judgment, ruling that the contract was one for personal services and therefore not assignable. We affirm on a different theory—that this contract could not be assigned to the wholly-owned subsidiary of a direct competitor under section 2–210 of the Uniform Commercial Code.

* * *

The fact that this contract is considered a contract for the sale of goods and not for the provision of a service does not, as Sally Beauty suggests, mean that it is freely assignable in all circumstances. The delegation of performance under a sales contract (whether in conjunction with an assignment of rights, as here, or not) is governed by UCC section 2–210(1). . . . The UCC recognizes that in many cases an obligor will find it convenient or even necessary to relieve himself of the duty of performance under a contract, see Official Comment 1, UCC § 2–210 ("[T]his section recognizes both delegation of performance and assignability as normal and permissible incidents of a contract for the sale of goods."). The Code therefore sanctions delegation except where the delegated performance would be unsatisfactory to the obligee: "A party may perform his duty through a delegate unless otherwise agreed to or unless the other party has a substantial interest in having his original promisor perform or control the acts required by the contract." UCC § 2–210(1), Tex. Bus. & Com. Code Ann. § 2–210(a) (Vernon 1968). Consideration is given to balancing the policies of free alienability of commercial contracts and protecting the obligee from having to accept a bargain he did not contract for.

We are concerned here with the delegation of Best's duty of performance under the distribution agreement, as Nexxus terminated the agreement because it did not wish to accept Sally Beauty's substituted performance.[6] Only one Texas case has construed section 2–210 in the context of a party's delegation of performance under an executory contract. In McKinnie v. Milford, 597 S.W.2d 953 (Tex.Civ.App.1980, writ ref'd, n.r.e.), the court held that nothing in the

---

[6] If this contract is assignable, Sally Beauty would also, of course, succeed to Best's rights under the distribution agreement. But the fact situation before us must be distinguished from the assignment of contract rights that are no longer executory (e.g., the right to damages for breach or the right to payment of an account), which is considered in UCC section 2–210(2). . . . The policies underlying these two situations are different and, generally, the UCC favors assignment more strongly in the latter. See UCC § 2–210(2) (non-executory rights assignable even if agreement states otherwise).

Texas Business and Commercial Code prevented the seller of a horse from delegating to the buyer a pre-existing contractual duty to make the horse available to a third party for breeding. "[I]t is clear that Milford [the third party] had no particular interest in not allowing Stewart [the seller] to delegate the duties required by the contract. Milford was only interested in getting his two breedings per year, and such performance could only be obtained from McKinnie [the buyer] after he bought the horse from Stewart." Id. at 957. In *McKinnie,* the Texas court recognized and applied the UCC rule that bars delegation of duties if there is some reason why the non-assigning party would find performance by a delegate a substantially different thing than what he had bargained for.

In the exclusive distribution agreement before us, Nexxus had contracted for Best's "best efforts" in promoting the sale of Nexxus products in Texas. UCC § 2–306(2) . . . states that "[a] lawful agreement by either buyer or seller for exclusive dealing in the kind of goods concerned imposes unless otherwise agreed an obligation by the seller to use best efforts to supply the goods and by the buyer to use best efforts to promote their sale." This implied promise on Best's part was the consideration for Nexxus' promise to refrain from supplying any other distributors within Best's exclusive area. See Official Comment 5, UCC § 2–306. It was this contractual undertaking which Nexxus refused to see performed by Sally.

In ruling on Nexxus' motion for summary judgment, the district court noted: "Unlike Best, Sally Beauty is a subsidiary of one of Nexxus' direct competitors. This is a significant distinction and in the court's view, it raises serious questions regarding Sally Beauty's ability to perform the distribution agreement in the same manner as Best." Memorandum Opinion and Order at 7. In Berliner Foods Corp. v. Pillsbury Co., 633 F. Supp. 557 (D.Md.1986), the court stated the same reservation more strongly on similar facts. Berliner was an exclusive distributor of Haagen-Dazs ice cream when it was sold to Breyer's, manufacturer of a competing ice cream line. Pillsbury Co., manufacturer of Haagen-Dazs, terminated the distributorship and Berliner sued. The court noted, while weighing the factors for and against a preliminary injunction, that "it defies common sense to require a manufacturer to leave the distribution of its products to a distributor under the control of a competitor or potential competitor." Id. at 559–60.[7] We agree with these assessments and hold that Sally Beauty's position as a wholly-owned subsidiary of Alberto-Culver is sufficient to bar the delegation of Best's duties under the agreement.

---

[7]   The effort by the dissent to distinguish *Berliner* merely because the court there apparently assumed in passing that distributorship agreements were a species of personal service contracts must fail. The *Berliner* court emphasizes that the sale of a distributorship to a competitor of the supplier is by itself a wholly sufficient reason to terminate the distributorship.

* * * At oral argument, Sally Beauty argued that the case should go to trial to allow it to demonstrate that it could and would perform the contract as impartially as Best. It stressed that Sally Beauty is a "multi-line" distributor, which means that it distributes many brands and is not just a conduit for Alberto-Culver products. But we do not think that this creates a material question of fact in this case.[8] When performance of personal services is delegated, the trier merely determines that it is a personal services contract. If so, the duty is *per se* nondelegable. There is no inquiry into whether the delegate is as skilled or worthy of trust and confidence as the original obligor: the delegate was not bargained for and the obligee need not consent to the substitution. * * *

The judgment of the district court is AFFIRMED.

■ POSNER, J., dissenting.

* * *

My brethren find this a simple case—as simple (it seems) as if a lawyer had undertaken to represent the party opposing his client. But notions of conflict of interest are not the same in law and in business, and judges can go astray by assuming that the legal-services industry is the pattern for the entire economy. The lawyerization of America has not reached that point. Sally Beauty, though a wholly owned subsidiary of Alberto-Culver, distributes "hair care" supplies made by many different companies, which so far as appears compete with Alberto-Culver as vigorously as Nexxus does. * * *

Selling your competitor's products, or supplying inputs to your competitor, sometimes creates problems under antitrust or regulatory law—but only when the supplier or distributor has monopoly or market power and uses it to restrict a competitor's access to an essential input or to the market for the competitor's output. . . . There is no suggestion that Alberto-Culver has a monopoly of "hair care" products or Sally Beauty a monopoly of distributing such products, or that Alberto-Culver would ever have ordered Sally Beauty to stop carrying Nexxus products. Far from complaining about being squeezed out of the market by the acquisition, Nexxus is complaining in effect about Sally Beauty's refusal to boycott it!

How likely is it that the acquisition of Best could hurt Nexxus? Not very. Suppose Alberto-Culver had ordered Sally Beauty to go slow in pushing Nexxus products, in the hope that sales of Alberto-Culver "hair care" products would rise. Even if they did, since the market is competitive Alberto-Culver would not reap monopoly profits. Moreover, what guarantee has Alberto-Culver that consumers would be diverted from Nexxus to it, rather than to products closer in price and quality to

---

[8]   We do not address here the situation in which the assignee is not completely under the control of a competitor. If the assignee were only a partially-owned subsidiary, there presumably would have to be fact-finding about the degree of control the competitor-parent had over the subsidiary's business decisions.

Nexxus products? In any event, any trivial gain in profits to Alberto-Culver would be offset by the loss of goodwill to Sally Beauty; and a cost to Sally Beauty is a cost to Alberto-Culver, its parent. Remember that Sally Beauty carries beauty supplies made by other competitors of Alberto-Culver; Best alone carries "hair care" products manufactured by Revlon, Clairol, Bristol-Myers, and L'Oreal, as well as Alberto-Culver. Will these powerful competitors continue to distribute their products through Sally Beauty if Sally Beauty displays favoritism for Alberto-Culver products? Would not such a display be a commercial disaster for Sally Beauty, and hence for its parent, Alberto-Culver? * * *

Another relevant consideration is that the contract between Nexxus and Best was for a short term. Could Alberto-Culver destroy Nexxus by failing to push its products with maximum vigor in Texas for a year? In the unlikely event that it could and did, it would be liable in damages to Nexxus for breach of the implied best-efforts term of the distribution contract. Finally, it is obvious that Sally Beauty does not have a bottleneck position in the distribution of "hair care" products, such that by refusing to promote Nexxus products vigorously it could stifle the distribution of those products in Texas; for Nexxus has found alternative distribution that it prefers—otherwise it wouldn't have repudiated the contract with Best when Best was acquired by Sally Beauty.

Not all businessmen are consistent and successful profit maximizers, so the probability that Alberto-Culver would instruct Sally Beauty to cease to push Nexxus products vigorously in Texas cannot be reckoned at zero. On this record, however, it is slight. And there is no principle of law that if something happens that trivially reduces the probability that a dealer will use his best efforts, the supplier can cancel the contract. * * * At most, so far as the record shows, Nexxus may have had grounds for "insecurity" regarding the performance by Sally Beauty of its obligation to use its best efforts to promote Nexxus products, but if so its remedy was not to cancel the contract but to demand assurances of due performance. See UCC § 2–609; Official Comment 5 to § 2–306. No such demand was made.

NOTES

(1) In the assignment of an executory bilateral contract, is the "probable intention of the assignee" to assume duties as well as rights?

(2) UCC § 2–210(4): "An assignment of 'the contract' or of 'all my rights under the contract' or an assignment in similar general terms is an assignment of rights and unless the language or the circumstances (as in an assignment for security) indicate the contrary, it is a delegation of performance of the duties of the assignor and its acceptance by the assignee constitutes a promise by him to perform those duties. This promise is enforceable by either the assignor or the other party to the original contract." See Continental Can Co. v. Poultry Processing, Inc., 649 F.Supp. 570, 573 (D. Me. 1986) (phrase is "term of art"); Restatement (Second) § 328(1).

(3) *The Case of "All in the Family."* Tandem Productions, Inc., producer of "All in the Family," and Columbia Broadcasting System, Inc. entered into a contract covering the distribution and syndication of the series. In a "Memorandum of Agreement," it was provided that "CBS may assign its rights hereunder in full or in part to any person, firm or corporation provided, however, that no such assignment shall relieve CBS of its obligations hereunder." Later CBS purported to assign to Viacom International, Inc. the rights it possessed to distribute and syndicate television programs, including "All in the Family." Tandem maintained that this transcended the power of assignment granted by the written agreement, insisting that CBS could only assign the right to receive distribution and syndication fees called for by the contract but not relinquish or delegate obligations. Do you agree? See Viacom International, Inc. v. Tandem Productions, Inc., 526 F.2d 593 (2d Cir.1975).

3. THIRD-PARTY BENEFICIARIES

For a consideration furnished by B (e.g., delivery of merchandise), A promises to render a performance (e.g., payment of $1,000) to T. If A refuses to abide by the commitment, may T successfully sue A for breach of contract? Have A and B conferred a contractual right upon T, who was not privy to the transaction? Stated another way, is T a protected third-party beneficiary of the A-B contract?

It might first be wondered why A and B would ever so agree. A's apparent purpose is the receipt of the merchandise, but what of B's? B might in this way pay a debt owed to T or might simply wish to give T the $1,000. In either situation, what objections would you expect to be asserted as a bar to recovery? That T did not pay for A's promise; i.e., did not furnish the consideration? That T was a stranger to the transaction; i.e., was not the promisee? Are these sound objections? In short, ought A and B be recognized as having the power to confer a contractual right upon T?

Assuming a general willingness to recognize such third-party beneficiary contracts, how is a court in a particular case to determine when the third party acquires a right against the promisor? Surely one ought not be able to sue in every case where performance of the contract would somehow inure to his or her benefit. But where is the line to be drawn? What are properly to be regarded as elements of judgment?

Granted the right of a beneficiary to sue in a particular case, what is the nature of that right? What defenses can A assert against T? Moreover, after execution of the contract, may A and B so act as to deprive T of any rights in the transaction?

(A) CREATION OF RIGHTS

KMART Corp. v. Balfour Beatty, Inc.

District Court of the Virgin Islands, 1998.
994 F.Supp. 634.

■ MOORE, C.J. This matter is before the Court on motion of defendant Balfour Beatty Incorporated ["BBI"] to dismiss on the basis that plaintiff, KMART Corporation ["KMART"] is not an intended third-party beneficiary of a construction contract ["contract"] between BBI and the plaintiff's landlord, Tutu Park Ltd. ["TPL"]. In the event this Court denies the motion and holds that plaintiff is a third-party beneficiary of the contract, BBI has requested that the action be stayed pending enforcement of the contract's arbitration clause. The Court has diversity jurisdiction in this case. . . .

I.   FACTS

In January of 1992, BBI entered into a contract with TPL for the design and construction of a shopping center in St. Thomas. In September of 1995, the roof of the shopping center was damaged by the winds accompanying Hurricane Marilyn.

KMART Corporation was one of the tenants of the shopping center. Contending that it is a third-party beneficiary of the construction contract, plaintiff instituted this action in August, 1997, alleging breach of contract and negligence.

For its part, KMART points out that a number of provisions in the relevant documents indicate that the parties intended to convey a benefit to KMART. The specifications for the construction as described in defendant Bentley Engineers & Architects documentation ["Bentley Specifications"] call for the construction schedules to comply with KMART's requirements. The drawings made in the design phase of performance were to be submitted to KMART. Warranties of work performed by defendant and its subcontractors were to be executed in KMART's favor and submitted directly to KMART.

II.   APPLICATION OF LAW AND FACT

BBI asserts that, because it is not a party to the construction contract, KMART may not claim relief under the agreement and moves to dismiss for failure to state a claim under Fed.R.Civ.P. 12(b)(6). In considering such a motion, the Court is constrained to view all factual allegations in KMART's amended complaint as true and to give it the benefit of every reasonable inference. . . . BBI further prays that, if the Court should find KMART to be a party to the contract, the instant litigation should be stayed pending arbitration as mandated in the contract. The Court will address each of defendant's motions in turn.

In sum, the Court finds that KMART is indeed a third-party beneficiary to the contract and that, as such, KMART is bound by the contract's terms to submit its claims to arbitration.

A.   KMART's Standing As A Third-Party Beneficiary

Section 302 of the Restatement (Second) of Contracts ["Restatement"] provides a blueprint for determining whether or not a party is an intended third-party beneficiary.[1]

> (1)   Unless otherwise agreed between promisor and promisee, a beneficiary of a promise is an intended beneficiary if recognition of a right to performance in the beneficiary is appropriate to effectuate the intention of the parties[2] and either:
>
> > (a)   the performance of the promise will satisfy an obligation of the promisee to pay money to the beneficiary; or
> >
> > (b)   the circumstances indicate that the promisee intends to give the ⸱beneficiary the benefit of the promised performance.
>
> (2)   An incidental beneficiary is a beneficiary who is not an intended beneficiary.

An intended beneficiary acquires a right under the contract. *Id.* § 304 ("A promise in a contract creates a duty in the promisor to any intended beneficiary to perform the promise, and the intended beneficiary may enforce the duty."). An incidental beneficiary does not. *Id.* § 315 ("An incidental beneficiary acquires by virtue of the promise no right against the promisor or the promisee."). Promises to render performances other than the payment of money require some expression of an intent by the parties to give the benefit of performance to the beneficiary. *Id.* § 304 cmt. c.[3]

In a 1985 case construing the Restatement (First) of Contracts, a Maryland court found that "one is a[n] [intended] beneficiary when 'performance of the promise will satisfy an actual or supposed or asserted duty of the promisee to the beneficiary.'" *District Moving & Storage Co., Inc. v. Gardiner & Gardiner, Inc.,* 63 Md.App. 96 (1985). In *District*

---

[1]   Absent local law to the contrary, the Restatements of Law will control. V.I.Code Ann. tit. 1 § 4 (1994).

[2]   The Restatement (Second) abandons the familiar dichotomy of donee and creditor beneficiary used in the earlier Restatement because, according to the commentary the terms, "carry overtones of obsolete doctrinal difficulties." *Restatement (Second) of Contracts,* ch. 14 Introductory Note (1981). Any beneficiary that acquires rights under a contract, whether a donee or creditor beneficiary according to the first Restatement, is an intended beneficiary according to the Restatement (Second).

[3]   In the older cases involving construction contracts, courts generally denied recovery. *See,* E. Allen Farnsworth, *Contracts* § 10.4 at 756–57 (2d ed.1990). However, the modern trend seems to countenance expanded recognition of third-party beneficiary status. *Id.* Such appears to be the case in this circuit. *See, e.g., Pierce Assoc. v. Nemours Foundation,* 865 F.2d 530 (3d Cir.1988) (applying Delaware law).

Moving, the landlord owed a contractual duty under a lease to provide the putative third-party beneficiary with a building.

Just as the Maryland court had no difficulty finding the tenant was a third-party beneficiary to the construction contract, so does this Court find that KMART was a third-party beneficiary of the construction contract between BBI and TPL. The contractual duty of performance owed by BBI to its promisee, TPL, would satisfy TPL's duty to its beneficiary, KMART. KMART, then, is a third party beneficiary to the construction contract between BBI and TPL.

Continuing to bear in mind the requirement to construe factual issues in favor of the non-movant, the language of the contract at issue here also conveys an intent among the contracting parties to bestow a benefit upon KMART. The contract's specifications call for construction schedules to comport with KMART's requirements. The drawings to be used were to be submitted to KMART and all warranties were to be executed in KMART's favor. All of these facts support a conclusion that BBI and TPL entered into the construction contract to erect a building for the benefit of KMART.

BBI asserts that the following contract provision specifically excludes KMART as a third-party beneficiary:

> 2.2.9 The Design/Builder warrants **to the Owner** . . . that the Work will be of good quality, free from faults and defects, and in conformance with the Contract Documents. (emphasis added).

The contract defines "owner" as TPL. Even if this paragraph could be read as BBI urges, the inclusion of provisions in the contract specifications contemplating KMART's active participation in design and construction of the building creates an ambiguity which, at this stage of the litigation, must be resolved in the plaintiff's favor.

Other common law courts have applied different standards, principally two, to determine whether or not the parties to a contract intended to benefit one claiming third-party beneficiary status. Some attempt to determine if the performance of the contract runs to the putative third-party beneficiary. . . . Others, and the increasingly more modern view, hold that it is enough that the promisor (here, BBI) understood that the promisee had an intent to benefit the third party (here, KMART).

Under either formulation, the result is the same. Given the lease plaintiff had with TPL, and the extensive involvement of KMART in the specifications for the construction of the space, there is little question but that the performance in this case, construction of the building, ran directly to the benefit of the plaintiff. The promisor, BBI, clearly had notice that its promisee, TPL, had an intent to benefit KMART.

For all these reasons the Court concludes that KMART is an intended third-party beneficiary to the BBI-TPL contract. KMART can enforce such rights as it may have under that contract per Restatement § 304.

B.   BBI's Motion For Stay To Enforce Arbitration

The Court can quickly dispense with the defendant's motion for stay to enforce arbitration. Here, BBI is on solid ground.

As BBI points out in its reply memorandum, the very case KMART, and ultimately, this Court, relies upon as authority that it is entitled to third party beneficiary status held that the third-party beneficiary was bound by the contract's arbitration clause. Then too, defendant reminds the Court of its dictum that a "third-party beneficiary cannot accept the benefits and avoid the burdens or limitations of a contract; the third-party beneficiary assumes the legal obligations as well as the rights of its promisee." American Fidelity Fire Insurance Co. v. Construcciones Werl, Inc., 407 F. Supp. 164, 182 (D.Vi.1975). * * *

The Court holds that the contract at issue in this motion contains an arbitration clause sufficient to require the submission of the plaintiff's dispute to arbitration.

NOTES

(1) *Restatement Categories.* The First Restatement defined contract beneficiaries as follows in § 133(1):

> Where performance of a promise in a contract will benefit a person other than the promisee that person is . . . : (a) a donee beneficiary if it appears from the terms of the promise in view of the accompanying circumstances that the purpose of the promisee in obtaining the promise of all or part of the performance thereof is to make a gift to the beneficiary or to confer upon him a right against the promisor to some performance neither due nor supposed or asserted to be due from the promisee to the beneficiary; (b) a creditor beneficiary if no purpose to make a gift appears from the terms of the promise in view of the accompanying circumstances and performance of the promise will satisfy an actual or supposed or asserted duty of the promisee to the beneficiary . . .; (c) an incidental beneficiary if neither the facts stated in Clause (a) nor those stated in Clause (b) exist.

The First Restatement's distinction between creditor and donee beneficiaries is not preserved in the revised Restatement. Defining "donees" as recipients of a "gift promise," and "creditors" as recipients of "a promise to discharge the promisee's duty," arguably compels courts to restrict recovery to cases in which a gift or debt moving from promisee to third party exists in a legal or quasi-legal sense. The creditor category is on its face limited, since it includes only third parties who either possess a legal "right . . . against the promisee" presently barred by technicalities or to whom the promisee owes an "actual or supposed or asserted duty." Although the donee category is more open-ended, use of the terms "donee" and "gift" at least provides opportunities for courts to restrict recovery to cases where a traditional donative intent is clear. See, e.g., United States v. Inorganics, Inc., 109 F.Supp. 576, 579–80 (E.D. Tenn. 1952), where the court denied relief because no "beneficial impulse" existed.

Restatement (Second) § 302 provides:

> (1) Unless otherwise agreed between promisor and promisee, a beneficiary of a promise is an intended beneficiary if recognition of a right to performance in the beneficiary is appropriate to effectuate the intention of the parties and either (a) the performance of the promise will satisfy an obligation of the promisee to pay money to the beneficiary; or (b) the circumstances indicate that the promisee intends to give the beneficiary the benefit of the promised performance. (2) An incidental beneficiary is a beneficiary who is not an intended beneficiary.

See generally, David M. Summers, Note, *Third Party Beneficiaries and the Restatement (Second) of Contracts*, 67 Cornell L. Rev. 880 (1982).

Was the desired avoidance of the old categories complete? It seems the drafters did not come up with an entirely "new" test; many courts have long employed variations on the intent theme to resolve third-party beneficiary problems.

(2) *The Concept of Privity and the Third-Party Beneficiary Contract.* The third-party beneficiary contract involves judicial recognition of the power of contracting parties to vest rights in others. The recognition of the power to assign a contract right both paves the way for validation of third-party beneficiary contracts and enables one to properly analyze the so-called lack of privity objection.

> Privity, in the law of contracts, is merely the name for a legal relation arising from right and obligation. For example, A, by contract, secures a promise from B. A may transfer his right of enforcement to C. C thereby succeeds to A's right of action, and, in consequence, comes into the relationship with A and B which we call privity of contract. Instead of waiting to do it by assignment, A may, at the outset, extract from B the same promise in favor of C.

La Mourea v. Rhude, 209 Minn. 53, 56 (1940).

(3) *Weakening Resistance.* For over a century Massachusetts resisted the movement in this country recognizing third-party beneficiary contracts. In 1979, however, the Supreme Judicial Court of Massachusetts joined ranks with the other jurisdictions in a forthright opinion that acknowledged "the handwriting has long been on the wall." Choate, Hall & Stewart v. SCA Services, Inc., 378 Mass. 535, 546 (1979). Third-party claimants continue to fare poorly in other common law jurisdictions. For example, despite the initiative in some early cases, the English courts, since at least the middle of the nineteenth century, have rejected third-party recovery. Tweddle v. Atkinson, 1 B. & S. 393 (1861). The courts have, however, managed to fashion various "exceptions," so as to allow recovery in certain situations. See G. H. Treitel, The Law of Contract 594–618 (10th ed. 1999) (discussing inter alia the Contracts (Rights of Third Parties) Bill of 1998). For a discussion of Canadian resistance, see Comment, 59 Can. B. Rev. 549 (1981).

Constance Hale v. Robert Groce

Supreme Court of Oregon, 1987.
304 Or. 281.

■ LINDE, J. Defendant, who is an attorney, was directed by a client to prepare testamentary instruments and to include a bequest of a specified sum to plaintiff. After the client's death, it was discovered that the gift was not included either in the will or in a related trust instrument. After an unsuccessful attempt to obtain judicial reformation of the will and trust, plaintiff brought the present action for damages against the attorney.

The complaint alleged as two separate claims, first, that defendant was negligent in a number of particulars and, second, that he failed to carry out a contractual promise to his client, the decedent, which the decedent had intended specifically for the benefit of plaintiff. In other states plaintiffs in such cases have sometimes been allowed to recover on one or both of these theories, as negligently injured parties or as third-party beneficiaries under a contract. It is a new question in this court.

* * *

We agree that the beneficiary in [this type of case] is not only a plausible but a classic "intended" third-party beneficiary of the lawyer's promise to his client within the rule of Restatement section 302(1)(b) and may enforce the duty so created, as stated id. section 304. See, e.g., Johnson v. Doughty, 236 Or. 78, 83 (1963), Parker v. Jeffery, 26 Or. 186, 189 (1894) (stating rule that a contract may be enforced by one for whose benefit it was intended). The promise, of course, was not that the lawyer would pay plaintiff the stipulated sum, and it is too late for the lawyer to perform the promise that he did make, but this does not preclude an action for damages for the nonperformance. In principle, such an action is available to one in plaintiff's position.

* * *

[W]e reverse so much of the decision of the Court of Appeals as affirmed the dismissal of the contract claim.

NOTES

(1) *The Case of Alleged Referee Malpractice.* In a basketball game between Purdue and Iowa on March 6, 1982, James C. Bain, a referee, called a foul on an Iowa player, which resulted in free throws that gave Purdue a last-minute victory. John and Karen Gillispie operated a store, known as Hawkeye John's Trading Post, that specialized in University of Iowa sports memorabilia. Alleging that Bain's performance was below the standard of competence required of a professional referee, they sought damages for malpractice (asserting that the Iowa loss eliminated it from the Big Ten championship and destroyed a potential market for Gillispies' memorabilia touting Iowa as a Big Ten champion) and as beneficiaries of a contract between Bain and the Big 10. In rejecting both tort and contract claims, the

trial judge observed: "Heaven knows what uncharted morass a court would find itself in if it were to hold that an athletic official subjects himself to liability every time he might make a questionable call. The possibilities are mind boggling." The Court of Appeals affirmed. Bain v. Gillispie, 357 N.W.2d 47 (Iowa App. 1984).

(2) *The Privity Barrier and Economic Loss.* In *J'Aire Corp. v. Gregory*, 157 Cal.Rptr. 407 (1979), Contractor agreed with Owner to renovate a building. Tenant, operator of a restaurant in the building, sued Contractor, based upon alleged negligence of Contractor in delaying completion of the work and resulting in loss of business by Tenant. The court concluded: "Where the risk of harm is foreseeable, as it was in the present case, an injury to the plaintiff's economic interests should not go uncompensated merely because it was unaccompanied by any injury to his person or property." 157 Cal.Rptr. 407. Tenant chose to sue Contractor rather than Owner, because it "did not wish to upset its friendly relations with the building owner and thereby jeopardize the continuation of the lease arrangement." Gary T. Schwartz, *Economic Loss in American Tort Law: The Examples of J'Aire and of Products Liability*, 23 San Diego L. Rev. 37, 41 (1986).

The privity barrier has been lowered for tort actions, whether negligence or strict liability, where the plaintiff seeks compensation for personal injury or property damage, but, by and large, the citadel still stands where the plaintiff seeks recovery of economic loss. See, e.g., East River S.S. Corp. v. Transamerica Delaval, Inc., 476 U.S. 858 (1986). For an argument that the privity defenses should be abolished in economic loss cases, see Richard E. Speidel, *Warranty Theory, Economic Loss, and the Privity Requirement: Once More Into the Void*, 67 B.U. L. Rev. 9 (1987).

Irma Zigas v. Superior Court

California Court of Appeal, 1981.
120 Cal.App.3d 827.

■ FEINBERG, J. * * * Petitioners are tenants of an apartment building at 2000 Broadway in San Francisco, which was financed with a federally insured mortgage in excess of $5 million, pursuant to the National Housing Act (12 U.S.C. § 1701 et seq.) (the Act) and the regulations promulgated thereunder (24 C.F.R. § 207 et seq.). They seek in a class action, inter alia, damages for the landlords' (real parties in interest) violation of a provision of the financing agreement which requires that the landlords charge no more than the Department of Housing and Urban Development (HUD) approved schedule of rents. The trial court has sustained demurrers without leave to amend to 5 causes of action of 15 alleged, apparently on the ground that there is no right in the tenants to enforce the provisions of an agreement between their landlords and the federal government.

Petitioners allege that their landlords were required under their contract with HUD to file a maximum rental schedule with HUD and to refrain from charging more than those rents without the prior approval of the Secretary of HUD. Petitioners further allege that real parties are, and have been, charging rent in excess of the maximums set out in the rental schedule; the complaint avers that real parties have collected excessive rents and fees in an amount exceeding $2 million.

In addition to sustaining demurrers as to the third-party causes of action, the trial court granted real parties' motion to strike all references to the Act, the regulations promulgated thereunder, and the terms of the agreement between HUD and real parties. It is these orders sustaining the demurrers and granting the motion to strike that petitioners seek to have set aside.

* * *

At this juncture, we conclude as follows: Granted that the National Housing Act does not create a *federal* statutory right of action in petitioners, nevertheless, they may have standing to sue based on a cause of action under applicable state law.

We turn now to the question of whether petitioners have a cause of action under California law. . . .

California law clearly allows third-party suits for breaches of contract where no government agency is a party to the contract. (Civ. Code, § 1559.) Whether such suits are allowed when the government contracts with a private party depends upon analysis of the decisions in Shell v. Schmidt (1954) 126 Cal. App. 2d 279, and Martinez v. Socoma Companies, Inc., supra, 11 Cal. 3d 394.

In *Shell,* plaintiffs sued as third-party beneficiaries to defendant's contract with the Federal Housing Authority (FHA). The contract entailed an agreement by the defendant to build homes for sale to veterans according to plans and specifications submitted by the defendant to FHA in return for which FHA gave priorities to the defendant to secure the materials necessary for the building.

In deciding that plaintiffs had standing to enforce the terms of the contract between the defendant and the FHA, the *Shell* court relied on common law principles as embodied in Civil Code section 1559, which states: "A contract, made expressly for the benefit of a third person, may be enforced by him at any time before the parties thereto rescind it." Applying this provision to the facts before it, the *Shell* court observed: "Once it is established that the relationship between the contractor and the government is contractual, it follows that veterans purchasing homes, that is, the class intended to be protected by that contract, are third party beneficiaries of that contract. As already pointed out, the statute and the regulations passed thereunder resulting in the contract were passed to aid and assist veterans and for their benefit. Purchasing veterans constitute the class intended to be benefitted, and the contract must therefore be for their benefit." (Id., 126 Cal. App. 2d at p. 290.)

It is evident that petitioners are entitled to maintain a third-party cause of action under the *Shell* rationale. Real parties do not dispute the contractual nature of their relationship with HUD. And it is clear that a requirement of HUD approval of rent increases could *only* benefit the tenants.

Furthermore, even the most cursory review of the statutes and regulations which resulted in the contract in the present case leads to the conclusion that the tenants constitute the class which Congress intended to benefit. As stated in 12 United States Code section 1701t: "The Congress affirms the national goal, as set forth in section 1441 of Title 42, of 'a decent home under a suitable living environment for every American family.'" (Section 1713(b) of Title 12, United States Code, also provides, in part: "*The insurance of mortgages under this section is intended to facilitate particularly the production of rental accommodations, at reasonable rents,* . . . The Secretary is, therefore, authorized . . . to take action, by regulation or otherwise, which will direct the benefits of mortgage insurance hereunder primarily to those projects which make adequate provision for families with children, and *in which every effort has been made to achieve moderate rental charges.*" (Emphasis added, see also 24 C.F.R. § 207.19(e).)

* * *

In the subsequent case of Martinez v. Socoma Companies, Inc., *supra*, 11 Cal. 3d 394, the court approved of the result in *Shell* but, at the same time, applied a different standard.[2] Plaintiffs in *Martinez* sought to enforce the terms of a contract between Socoma Companies, Inc. and the Secretary of Labor. Under this agreement, defendants received government funds in exchange for a promise to hire and train "hard core unemployed" residents of a "Special Impact Area" in East Los Angeles. Defendants failed to perform, and plaintiffs, who were residents of East Los Angeles and members of the class which the government intended to benefit, sought to recover under the contract.

In holding that the plaintiffs had no standing to sue as third-party beneficiaries, the *Martinez* court adopted a more restrictive standard than that embodied in Civil Code section 1559, choosing instead to be guided by the principles set forth in section 145 of the Restatement of Contracts: "'A promisor bound to the United States or to a State or municipality by contract to do an act or render a service to some or all of the members of the public, is subject to no duty under the contract to such members to give compensation for the injurious consequences of performing or attempting to perform it, or of failing to do so, unless, . . .

---

[2]   The *Martinez* court approved of the result in *Shell,* based upon a finding that the legislation under which the homes in *Shell* were built included a provision empowering the government to obtain payment by the contractor to the veteran purchasers for deficiencies resulting from failure to comply with specifications. (*Martinez, supra,* at p. 403, 113 Cal. Rptr. 585, 521 P.2d 841.) Thus, the intent to compensate which Restatement, Contracts, section 145 requires was present. However, the *Shell* court made no mention of section 145.

an intention is manifested in the contract, as interpreted in the light of the circumstances surrounding its formation, *that the promisor shall compensate members of the public for such injurious consequences . . .'"* (Martinez v. Socoma Companies, Inc., *supra,* at pp. 401–402, 113 Cal. Rptr. 585; Contracts, *supra,* § 145.)[3]

Thus, under *Martinez,* standing to sue as a third-party beneficiary to a government contract depends on the intent of the parties as manifested by the contract and the circumstances surrounding its formation. "Insofar as intent to benefit a third person is important in determining his right to bring an action under a contract, it is sufficient that the promisor must have understood that the promisee had such intent. No specific manifestation by the promisor of an intent to benefit the third person is required." (Lucas v. Hamm (1961) 56 Cal. 2d 583, 591.) We therefore must determine, from the terms of the contract between HUD and real parties and the attendant circumstances, whether there was manifested an intention that petitioners be compensated in the event of real parties' nonperformance. Mindful of the rule that "[w]hen a complaint is based on a written contract which it sets out in full, a general demurrer to the complaint admits not only the contents of the instrument but also any pleaded meaning to which the instrument is reasonably susceptible." (Martinez v. Socoma Companies, Inc., supra, 11 Cal. 3d at p. 400) and focusing upon the precepts of *Martinez* as to standing, we are of the view that the case falls within *Shell;* that is to say, appellants were direct beneficiaries of the contract and have standing, and not, as in *Martinez,* incidental beneficiaries without standing.

We explicate:

1.   In *Martinez,* the contract between the government and Socoma provided that if Socoma breached the agreement, Socoma would refund to the government that which the government had paid Socoma pursuant to the contract between them. Thus, it is clear in *Martinez* that it was the government that was out of pocket as a consequence of the breach and should be reimbursed therefor, not the people to be trained and given jobs. In the case at bench, as in *Shell,* the government suffered no loss as a consequence of the breach, it was the renter here and the veteran purchaser in *Shell* that suffered the direct pecuniary loss.

2.   Unlike *Martinez,* too, in the case at bench, no governmental administrative procedure was provided for the resolution of disputes arising under the agreement. Thus, to permit this litigation would in no way affect the "efficiency and uniformity of interpretation fostered by these administrative procedures." (Martinez v. Socoma Companies, Inc.,

---

[3]   It has been suggested that section 145 was meant only to preclude lawsuits for *consequential* damages arising out of government contracts, because the resulting potential liability may be disproportionately burdensome in relation to the value of the promised performance. (See Rest., Contracts, *supra,* § 145, illus. 1 and 2. . . .) Thus, the underlying rationale of section 145 is inapplicable where, as here, the money sought is not a *consequence* of the breach, it is the breach. In such a situation, standard third-party beneficiary doctrines should apply. . . .

supra, 11 Cal. 3d at p. 402.) On the contrary, as we earlier noted, lawsuits such as this promote the federal interest by inducing compliance with HUD agreements.

3.   In *Martinez,* the court held that "To allow plaintiffs' claim would nullify the limited liability for which defendants bargained and which the Government may well have held out as an inducement in negotiating the contracts." (At p. 403.) Here, there is no "limited liability." As we shall point out, real parties are liable under the agreement, *without limitation,* for breach of the agreement.

4.   Further, in *Martinez,* the contracts "were designed not to benefit individuals as such but to utilize the training and employment of disadvantaged persons as a means of improving the East Los Angeles neighborhood." (At p. 406.) Moreover, the training and employment programs were but one aspect of a "broad, long-range objective" (*id.*) contemplated by the agreement and designed to benefit not only those to be trained and employed but also "other local enterprises and the government itself through reduction of law enforcement and welfare costs." (*Ibid.*) . . .

5.   Finally, we believe the agreement itself manifests an intent to make tenants direct beneficiaries, *not* incidental beneficiaries, of real parties' promise to charge no more than the HUD approved rent schedule.

Section 4(a) and 4(c) of the agreement, providing that there can be no increase in rental fees, over the approved rent schedule, without the prior approval in writing of HUD, were obviously designed to protect the tenant against arbitrary increases in rents, precisely that which is alleged to have occurred here. Certainly, it was not intended to benefit the Government as a guarantor of the mortgage.

Furthermore, the provision in section 11(d) of the agreement, authorizing the Secretary of HUD to "[a]pply to any court . . . for specific performance . . . , for an injunction against any violation . . . or *for such other relief as may be appropriate*" (emphasis added) would entitle the secretary to seek restitution on behalf of the tenants overcharged, for such relief would surely be "appropriate." (See Porter v. Warner Co. (1946) 328 U.S. 395 . . .) Thus, there was an intent upon the part of the government in executing the agreement with real parties, to secure the return of any rents exacted in excess of the rent schedule.

We are supported in our view by section 17 of the Agreement which specifically provides that real parties are personally liable, "(a) for funds . . . of the project coming into their hands which, by the provisions [of the Agreement] *they are not entitled to retain*; and (b) for their own acts and deeds or acts and deeds of other [sic] which they have authorized in violation of the provisions [of the Agreement]." (Emphasis added.)

By the allegations of the complaint, real parties have "retained" in excess of two million ($2,000,000) dollars in violation of the Agreement.

Therefore, they are liable for that sum. To whom should they be liable? To ask the question is to answer it. It is not the government from whom the money was exacted; it was taken from the tenants. Therefore, it should be returned to the tenants.

In the face of this evidence of intent to direct the benefits of mortgage insurance to the tenants of the facilities involved, real parties argue that petitioners have no standing to sue because enforcement of the agreement is vested solely in the Secretary. They point to 12 United States Code section 1731a, which empowers the Secretary to refuse the benefits of participation to any mortgagor who violates the terms of the agreement. However, section 1731a's authorization does not constitute the exclusive remedy for enforcement of the agreement by the Secretary or by third parties. As stated by the court in *Shell v. Schmidt*, supra, 126 Cal. App. 2d at p. 287: "This fundamental purpose would, in many cases, be defeated if the statute were interpreted so as to deprive the veterans of their normal remedies to the benefit of defaulting contractors—the very class it was the purpose of the statute to protect the veterans against. It must be held, therefore, that the enumeration of remedies in the statute merely created new enumerated remedies and was not intended to and did not deprive the veterans of any action for fraud or breach of contract that they might have under general contract principles."

* * *

Thus, for reasons we have set forth, appellants are entitled to maintain a third-party beneficiary action against real parties.

NOTES

(1) One writer, in commenting upon *Martinez,* underscores a particular difficulty in utilizing the "intention to benefit" standard when the Federal government is one of the contracting parties: "The relevant intent to be divined is no longer that of a single individual or entity, but rather that of an amalgam of legislative bodies, administrative agencies, and government officials—each of whom may have differing expectations and objectives with regard to the contract." Recent Cases, 88 Harv. L. Rev. 646, 651–52 (1975). Since the government's decision to benefit a certain group through a contract is usually based on broad policy objectives, it is urged that these objectives be taken into account in determining the rights of the various beneficiaries. The author draws an analogy to the question of whether a court should imply a private right of action from a statute:

> When implying a private right of action, courts have carefully considered the impact of an additional remedy in the hands of private parties on the legislative policy underlying the statute. Courts tend to imply a right of action when there is evidence that existing remedies are inadequate and that additional remedies would increase the likelihood of compliance and afford direct relief to a class which the legislature wished to protect. Strong arguments

against allowing such a right arise when it would interfere with the policy goals of the legislature by imposing disproportionate liability or impinging excessively on administrative discretion.

Id. at 653.

(2) *Problems: Varieties of Third-Party Beneficiary Controversy.* (a) *The Case of the Ingested Birds.* A jet crashed because of the ingestion of a large number of birds swarming over the airport and an adjacent garbage dump. Are injured passengers entitled to sue as third-party beneficiaries of a contract between the Federal Aviation Administration and the County under which the latter agreed "to restrict the use of land adjacent to or in the vicinity of the airport to activities and purposes compatible with normal airport operations including landing and take-off of aircraft"? See Miree v. United States, 538 F.2d 643 (5th Cir. 1976).

(b) *The Case of the Striking Ferry Workers.* Union ferry workers went out on strike in violation of a collective bargaining agreement with a State agency, thereby causing a cessation of normal ferry service during a holiday weekend. Could a resort owner, who lost bookings, sue as third-party beneficiary of this contract? See Burke & Thomas, Inc. v. International Organization of Masters, Mates & Pilots, 92 Wash.2d 762 (1979).

(c) *The Case of the Unimproved Roads.* Developer, in order to obtain approval of a subdivision plot, agreed with County to construct certain road improvements. Developer failed to keep its commitment. Can lot owners in the subdivision sue as third-party beneficiaries of the Developer/County contract? See Vale Dean Canyon Homeowners Association v. Dean, 100 Or.App. 158 (1990).

(d) *The Case of the Parking Meter Contract.* City entered into a contract with Company for the maintenance of parking meters, the contract specifying certain minimum wages and working conditions. Employees of Company seek to persuade the court that they are third-party beneficiaries of this contract. Will they succeed? See Alicea v. City of New York, 145 A.D.2d 315 (1988).

(e) *The Case of the Ungrateful Medical Student.* A scholarship fund agreed to pay a medical student $200 monthly during his time in medical school, in exchange for his promise to practice upon graduation in a specified area. Are the residents of the area third-party beneficiaries of this contract? See Suthers v. Booker Hospital District, 543 S.W.2d 723 (Tex. Civ. App. 1976).

(f) *The Case of the Cable Television Subscribers.* City granted franchise to television cable company, prescribing a rate schedule. Could subscribers bring an action as third-party beneficiaries to recover damages for violation of the schedule? See Bush v. Upper Valley Telecable Co., 96 Idaho 83 (1973).

(g) *The Case of the Bank's Loan Commitment.* Vendor contracts to sell land to Purchaser, conditional upon Purchaser securing loan. Bank makes the loan commitment to Purchaser and then reneges. Is Vendor an intended beneficiary of the Bank-Purchaser contract? See Khabbaz v. Swartz, 319 N.W.2d 279 (Iowa 1982).

(h) *The Case of the Undelivered Machine.* Company A, in need of a particular type of machine, contacts Company B. B learns that yet another company, Company C, owns such a machine. B asks A to examine the machine on C's premises. A does so and thereafter enters into a contract with B to buy the machine. B then contracts with C for the purchase of the machine, the contract providing that shipment is to be direct to A and the latter is to pay the freight. Later A, B and C enter into negotiations whereby the delivery date specified in the contracts is extended. Thereafter, A and B get into a dispute (on an unrelated matter) and B directs C to ship the machine to yet another party. C does so. Is A a protected beneficiary of the B/C contract? See Corrugated Paper Products, Inc. v. Longview Fibre Co., 868 F.2d 908 (7th Cir. 1989).

(i) *The Case of the Federal Tax Lien.* Taxpayer underpaid federal income taxes, and the United States secured a tax lien. Thereafter, Taxpayer and his wife executed a property settlement in contemplation of their impending divorce. The agreement required the taxpayer to convey certain property to his wife, who was required, in turn, to sell the property and was authorized to retain any proceeds of sale after existing liens and mortgages were paid off. Was the United States a third-party beneficiary of this agreement? See United States v. Wood, 877 F.2d 453 (6th Cir. 1989).

(j) *The Case of the Pre-Paid Legal Plan.* The Fraternal Order of Police made available to "a member and his eligible dependents" a pre-paid legal plan. One of the services under the plan was described as "[d]omestic problems—including divorce, legal separation, adoption of children, change of name." A law firm servicing the plan represented a member in a divorce action. His wife also requested representation by the firm, but was refused on grounds of conflict of interest. She then retained other counsel and later claimed reimbursement from the plan for her lawyer's fees as a third-party beneficiary of the contract. What result? See Baltimore City Lodge No. 3 of Fraternal Order of Police, Inc. v. Mantegna, 61 Md.App. 694 (1985).

(k) *The Case of the Injured Tenant.* Was a tenant, who was injured during an electrical blackout, an intended beneficiary of a contract between electric company and landlord? See Shubitz v. Consolidated Edison Co., 301 N.Y.S.2d 926 (1969). Cf. Koch v. Consolidated Edison Co., 62 N.Y.2d 548 (1984) (suit by city and public benefit corporations to recover damages allegedly sustained from utility's gross negligence that caused citywide blackout).

(l) *The Case of the Stranded Motorist.* An oil company had a contract with the New York State Thruway Authority, under which it had the exclusive right to service cars on the thruway. The company promised to provide roadside automobile service to disabled vehicles within thirty minutes from the time called. The decedent's car had a flat tire at about 3:00 P.M. About an hour later a state trooper stopped by and radioed a request for assistance to the oil company. Not having received any assistance by 6:00 P.M., the decedent attempted to change the tire himself. In doing so he experienced difficulty and complained of chest pains. He was taken to a hospital and died 28 days later. Was the decedent, as user of the thruway, a third-party beneficiary of the contract between the oil company and the thruway authority? See Kornblut v. Chevron Oil Co., 407 N.Y.S.2d 498 (1978).

(m) *The Case of the Housing Project Tenants.* The owners of a housing project entered into a contract with the Secretary of Housing and Urban Development. One of the provisions of this "Regulatory Agreement" obligated the owners to maintain the premises in good repair and condition. Citing numerous failures to properly maintain the premises, tenants asserted rights as third-party beneficiaries. What result? See Little v. Union Trust Co. of Maryland, 45 Md.App. 178 (1980). Cf. Ayala v. Boston Housing Authority, 404 Mass. 689 (1989) (tenants sue city housing authority for failing to inspect for lead paint hazards and for failing to enforce elimination of those hazards).

(n) *The Case of the Defective Appraisal.* Purchaser signed a contract to purchase certain property, conditional upon his obtaining a loan. Upon applying for a loan, a bank officer informed him that there would have to be an appraisal of the property before the loan could be approved. The purchaser paid the bank $100 for the appraisal, and the bank arranged for the defendant to do the appraisal. If the defendant-appraiser negligently failed to discover, and to disclose in his report, serious structural defects in the property, what are the purchaser's prospects of recovery? Upon what theory? See Alva v. Cloninger, 51 N.C.App. 602 (1981).

(o) *The Case of the Undelivered Body.* The children of Rozena Neal, deceased, arranged with Inman Nationwide Shipping to transport their mother's body to Alabama for burial. Inman contracted in turn with Republic Airlines, which, through some error, delayed the shipment. Could the children claim as third-party beneficiaries of the Inman/Republic contract? See Neal v. Republic Airlines, Inc., 605 F.Supp. 1145 (N.D. Ill. 1985).

(p) *The Case of the Fake Diamond Ring.* Fiancé buys "diamond" ring from Jeweler and gives it to his prospective bride as an engagement ring. The ring turns out to be nothing more than "cut glass or cubic zirconia." Can she maintain a suit for breach of contract as a third-party beneficiary? See Warren v. Monahan Beaches Jewelry Center, Inc., 548 So.2d 870 (Fla. App. 1989).

(q) *The Case of the Infringed Trademark.* Suppose that S develops a website for Fantasy Baseball enthusiasts and registers the domain name "Speiderman" with a domain name registrar licensed by the Internet Corporation for Assigned Names and Numbers (ICANN). As a condition to registration, S must agree to "arbitrate" any claims that the domain name is "identical or confusingly similar" to a registered trademark of a third person. Sure enough, the holder of the Spiderman trademark files a claim and seeks to have the domain name Speiderman canceled. S objects, arguing that since the trademark holder did not sign a written agreement to arbitrate, it cannot compel S to arbitrate. Does the trademark holder qualify as an intended beneficiary of the contract between S and ICANN? See Collins v. International Dairy Queen, 2 F. Supp. 2d 1465 (M.D. Ga.1998) (non-signatory of arbitration clause is an intended beneficiary). But see E. I. DuPont de Nemours v. Rhone Poulenc Fiber, 269 F.3d 187, 195–99 (3d Cir.

2001) (no intended beneficiary on facts). For an overview, see Richard E. Speidel, *ICANN Domain Name Dispute Resolution, the Revised Uniform Arbitration Act, and the Limitations of Modern Arbitration Law,* 6 J. Small & Emerging Bus. L. 167 (2002).

(r)   *The Case of the Civil Rights Claim.* MacDonald, a shareholder and officer of JWM Investments, sued for civil rights violations under 42 U.S.C. § 1981, based upon a claim that JWM had entered into contracts with Domino's, which Domino's had breached because of racial animus toward MacDonald. The Court held that under Section 1981, a plaintiff cannot state a claim unless he has rights under an existing contract that he wishes "to make and enforce" and that have been impaired. McDonald was, as a shareholder, not a party to the JWM/Domino's contracts and, according to the Court, was not an intended beneficiary of the contracts. Thus, there was no right to claim damages under Section 1981. Domino's Pizza, Inc. v. McDonald, 546 U.S. 470 (2006). See also Jou v. Dai-Tokyo Royal State Insurance Co., 116 Hawai'i 159 (2007) (neither regulatory statute nor third-party beneficiary law created right in plaintiff to enforce insurance contract entered by other parties).

(B) NATURE OF RIGHTS

Edward Tweeddale v. Daniel Tweeddale

Supreme Court of Wisconsin, 1903.
116 Wis. 517.

[In exchange for consideration received from his mother, the defendant, Daniel Tweeddale, gave his mother a bond for support secured by a mortgage on certain land. The bond indebtedness was $1,350, with the condition (among others) that in case the defendant should sell the land, $1,200 should immediately become due from him to his mother, $50 should likewise become due to his sister, and $100 to his brother, the plaintiff Edward Tweeddale. Subsequently, the defendant did sell the land, making operative the foregoing promises. The defendant made a settlement with his mother, fully discharging him of all obligation to her, and she released the mortgage. The plaintiff brought a foreclosure action, insisting that such release did not bar him from recovery. Neither the plaintiff nor his sister knew that the bond and mortgage made any provision for them until after the mortgage was discharged. The trial court held that plaintiff had no cause of action, and ordered the complaint dismissed.]

■ MARSHALL, J. * * * [T]he turning point in the case, in the mind of the circuit judge, we apprehend, was that the beneficiaries did not know of the agreement and did not accept the same or in any way become parties thereto till their mother, with the consent of Daniel Tweeddale, rescinded the transaction. . . . Whether the benefit secured to the third person is a gift, strictly so called, or one intended, when realized, to discharge some liability of such promisee to the third person does not change the situation. It is the exchange of promises between the immediate parties, and the operation of law thereon, that binds the promisor to the third person. The idea which ruled this case,—that where a person for a consideration paid to him by another agrees to pay a sum of money to a third person, a stranger to the transaction, the latter does not thereby become possessed of the absolute right to the benefit of the promise, nor until he accepts the same in some way; and that while he is ignorant of the promise, or thereafter, at any time before he assents to the transaction, it may be rescinded,—we must admit is well supported in the books. The authorities so holding, in the main, go upon the ground that privity between parties is absolutely essential to a liability of one to another of a contractual nature, and that until the third person brings himself into privity with the one who has promised to be his debtor by at least assenting thereto, he has at least no legal right to the benefit of the promise; and that, till then, the parties to the transaction may rescind it or change it as they see fit. There is also much authority to the effect that, while the element of privity between the promisor and the third person is essential to render the promise absolutely binding upon the former, no act of the latter is necessary thereto; that the law, operating upon the acts of the parties to the transaction, creates the privity immediately upon its being consummated between them, and that neither one nor both of them can thereafter, without the third person's consent, enforce the promise. * * *

It is useless to endeavor to review the authorities touching the subject before us with a view of harmonizing them upon any one single theory as to the principle upon which the liability to the third person is based or as to what are the essential elements to effect it.

* * *

Without further discussion of the matter we adhere to the doctrine that where one person, for a consideration moving to him from another, promises to pay to a third person a sum of money, the law immediately operates upon the acts of the parties, establishing the essential of privity between the promisor and the third person requisite to binding contractual relations between them, resulting in the immediate establishment of a new relation of debtor and creditor, regardless of the relations of the third person to the immediate promisee in the transaction; that the liability is, as binding between the promisor and the third person as it would be if the consideration for the promise moved from the latter to the former and such promisor made the promise directly to such third person, regardless of whether the latter has any knowledge of the transaction at the time of its occurrence; that the liability being once created by the acts of the immediate parties to the transaction and the operation of the law thereon, neither one nor both of such parties can thereafter change the situation as regards the third person without his consent. It is plainly illogical to hold that immediately upon the completion of the transaction between the immediate parties thereto, the law operates upon their acts and creates the element of privity between the promisor and the third person, and at the same time to hold that such third person's status as regards the promise may be changed thereafter without his consent. The idea that privity between the promisor and the third person is necessary to render the transaction between the original parties thereto beyond the reach of either of them to revoke it, or both acting together to rescind it, springs from the supposed necessity of contractual relations between the promisor and the third person, binding upon the promisor at law. The moment such essential is established, it seems clear that such third person's right accrues and becomes absolute.

NOTES

(1) *When Should the Third Party's Right Vest?*

Suppose A and B enter into a contract for the benefit of C. Suppose further that C never knew of the agreement between A and B, and therefore had placed no reliance on such contract, and in nowise had changed his position. Is the contract between A and B, the moment executed, like the laws of the Medes and Persians—no longer subject to change? * * * Is the contractual status of the parties immutably fixed? Before A and B are permitted to change or abrogate their agreement must they of necessity secure consent of the third party C, who, until then, is a stranger to the contract, and at all times a mere windfall volunteer? To hold that the moment A and B enter into an agreement for the benefit of C, that such third party C has at that moment and under all circumstances acquired an interest in the contract which is indefeasibly vested, is an affront to common sense.

Stanfield v. W.C. McBride, Inc., 88 P.2d 1002, 1005–06 (Kan. 1939).

(2) *Vesting and the Restatement.* The First Restatement § 142 recognized the right of a donee beneficiary as vesting immediately upon execution of the contract, but the Restatement did not accord the creditor beneficiary such favorable treatment. Is there a sound basis for the differentiation? Cf. Restatement (Second) § 311:

(1) Discharge or modification of a duty to an intended beneficiary by conduct of the promisee or by a subsequent agreement between promisor and promisee is ineffective if a term of the promise creating the duty so provides. (2) In the absence of such a term, the promisor and promisee retain power to discharge or modify the duty by subsequent agreement. (3) Such a power terminates when the beneficiary, before he receives notification of the discharge or modification, materially changes his position in justifiable reliance on the promise or brings suit on it or manifests assent to it at the request of the promisor or promisee.

The Supreme Court of Pennsylvania has refused to abandon its long-held adherence to Restatement § 142, which makes a contractual gift to a donee beneficiary irrevocable upon execution of the contract, in contrast with Restatement (Second) § 311, which postpones vesting until a beneficiary "materially changes his position in justifiable reliance on the promise or brings suit on it or manifests assent to it at the request of the promisor or promisee." Biggins v. Shore, 523 Pa. 148 (1989).

(3) *"Acceptance" by Beneficiary.* The Indiana Supreme Court has affirmed that the right to rescind or modify a third-party beneficiary contract, without the assent of the beneficiary, ceases once the contract is *accepted, adopted or acted upon* by the third party. In re Estate of Fanning, 263 Ind. 414 (1975). This has been characterized as the "majority view." Detroit Bank & Trust Co. v. Chicago Flame Hardening Co., Inc., 541 F.Supp. 1278, 1283 (N.D. Ind. 1982). But what is meant by "acceptance"? Is a beneficiary's knowledge of the contract, coupled with a failure to object, sufficient to "vest" the right? *Detroit Bank*, applying Indiana law, said it was not. The court did indicate that there would be such a "presumption of acceptance" in the case of an infant beneficiary, a view not supported by the drafters of the revised Restatement. See Restatement (Second) § 311, cmt. d.

Comment: The Donative Anti-Discrimination Promise

Ian Ayres and Jennifer Brown have offered to license the use of a certification mark called the "Fair Employment Mark" if an employer abides by the substantive terms of the "Employment Non-Discrimination Act," or "ENDA" (a not-yet-enacted bill which prohibits disparate treatment on the basis of sexual orientation). In essence, in return for a license to use the mark an employer must promise not to discriminate on the basis of sexual orientation. The license agreement includes the provision:

> THIRD-PARTY BENEFICIARIES. Licensee and Licensor agree to designate as express third-party beneficiaries of this agreement all persons and entities that would be entitled to sue if ENDA were in effect (including governmental civil rights enforcement agencies). In particular, Licensee and Licensor designate as express third-party beneficiaries all persons who are or have been employed by the Licensee or applied for employment with the Licensee during the term of the license. The Licensee and Licensor intend that these third-party beneficiaries will have the right to sue the Licensee for any breach of this agreement and have a legal right to the same remedies (including damages and injunctive relief) to which they would be entitled if ENDA were in effect.

See Fair Employment Mark, http://www.fairemploymentmark.org. If a licensee employer discriminated against an employee on the basis of the employee's sexual orientation, could the employee sue the licensee for breaching its promise not to discriminate? Ian Ayres & Jennifer Gerarda Brown, *Mark(et)ing Nondiscrimination: Privatizing ENDA with a Certification Mark*, 104 Mich. L. Rev. 1639 (2006).

What are the outer bounds of creating open-ended donative classes? Imagine that a newspaper entered into an agreement with a source which said in part:

> In return for the participation of the source as an interviewee, the publication promises to compensate anyone who is damaged by a factual misrepresentation printed in an article that expressly quotes the source. . . . Any one explicitly named in the article is an express third party beneficiary of this contract and thereby has a right to directly sue the publication if it breaches its promise to compensate. The publication and the source intend for this to be a legally binding agreement. The reporter in agreeing to this contract on behalf of the publication represents that the reporter has actual and apparent authority to enter into this contract on behalf of the publication.

Ian Ayres, Compensating for Reckless Reporting, Balkinization (Feb. 21, 2005), http://www.balkin.blogspot.com/2005/02/compensating-for-reckless-reporting.html. Would anyone who is named in the article have a right to sue for damage from factual misrepresentations? Could the contract have covered anyone named in the other articles as well?

INDEX

References are to Pages